February 25–29, 2012
New Orleans, LA, USA

Association for
Computing Machinery

Advancing Computing as a Science & Profession

PPoPP'12

Proceedings of the 2012 ACM SIGPLAN Symposium on
Principles and Practice of Parallel Programming

Sponsored by:

ACM SIGPLAN

Advancing Computing as a Science & Profession

The Association for Computing Machinery
2 Penn Plaza, Suite 701
New York, New York 10121-0701

Notice to Past Authors of ACM-Published Articles
ACM intends to create a complete electronic archive of all articles and/or other material previously published by ACM. If you have written a work that has been previously published by ACM in any journal or conference proceedings prior to 1978, or any SIG Newsletter at any time, and you do NOT want this work to appear in the ACM Digital Library, please inform permissions@acm.org, stating the title of the work, the author(s), and where and when published.

ISBN: 978-1-4503-1160-1 (Digital)

ISBN: 978-1-4503-1371-1 (Print)

Additional copies may be ordered prepaid from:

ACM Order Department
PO Box 30777
New York, NY 10087-0777, USA

Phone: 1-800-342-6626 (USA and Canada)
+1-212-626-0500 (Global)
Fax: +1-212-944-1318
E-mail: acmhelp@acm.org
Hours of Operation: 8:30 am – 4:30 pm ET

Printed in the USA

Chairs' Welcome

It is our great pleasure to welcome you to the 17th ACM SIGPLAN Symposium on Principles and Practice of Parallel Programming (PPoPP'12). PPoPP continues its tradition of serving as a leading forum for research in all aspects of parallel software, including theoretical foundations, programming models, algorithms, applications, and systems software. With the ubiquity of parallelism in commodity processors and the increasing use of GPUs for high-performance computing, the effective use of parallel systems is being recognized as one of the most challenging problems faced today.

PPoPP'12 received 173 complete paper submissions. In addition to the 25 program committee members, 75 members of the external review committee provided reviews for the papers. Two rounds of reviewing were conducted, with at least three reviews being obtained in the first round, with additional reviews being obtained in the second round for papers where needed. After extensive discussions at an in-person two-day program committee meeting in November 2011, 26 full papers were selected for presentation at the conference. PPoPP'12 continues the tradition of poster presentations of high quality submissions that could not be accepted as full papers. This year's conference features 32 poster presentations over two sessions.

PPoPP'12 is again co-located this year with the International Symposium on High-Performance Computer Architecture (HPCA), allowing attendees of one conference the option of attending talks at the other. We feature two joint HPCA/PPOPP keynote presentations. Sanjeev Kumar from Facebook will present a keynote on "Social Networking at Scale," and Keshav Pingali from the University of Texas at Austin will present a keynote entitled "Parallel Programming Needs Data-Centric Foundations."

PPoPP'12 is a result of the efforts of a large number of people. Our thanks, first and foremost, to the authors of all the submissions, the keynote speakers, and workshop and tutorial presenters, for providing the intellectual content of the program. We are grateful for the tireless efforts of the program committee and external review committee, and the program subchairs: Xiaoming Li, publicity and web; Xipeng Shen, workshops and tutorials; Sriram Krishnamoorthy, publications; David Koppelman, local arrangements; Gerald Baumgartner, finance; John Cavazos, registration. We are grateful for the support provided by Carrie Stein, Karen Jones and a number of volunteers. We thank Luis Ceze for making arrangements for the program committee meeting on the campus of the University of Washington, and Rich Gerber for exceptional assistance with the START conference management software. We are grateful to Lisa Tolles and the team at Sheridan Printing for an efficient and streamlined publication process. Finally, our thanks to ACM SIGPLAN for its ongoing sponsorship; to the steering committee (Keshav Pingali, Calin Cascaval, Mary Hall, David Padua, and Pen Yew) for their guidance; and to our partners for their financial support.

P. (Saday) Sadayappan	**J. (Ram) Ramanujam**
PPoPP'12 Program Chair	*PPoPP'12 General Chair*
The Ohio State University, USA	*Louisiana State University, USA*

Table of Contents

PPoPP 2012 Conference Organization ix

Session 1: GPU Tools

- **Scalable Framework for Mapping Streaming Applications Onto Multi-GPU Systems** 1
  Huynh Phung Huynh *(A*STAR Institute of High Performance Computing)*,
  Andrei Hagiescu, Weng-Fai Wong *(National University of Singapore)*,
  Rick Siow Mong Goh *(A*STAR Institute of High Performance Computing)*
- **A Performance Analysis Framework for Identifying Potential Benefits in GPGPU Applications** 11
  Jaewoong Sim, Aniruddha Dasgupta, Hyesoon Kim, Richard Vuduc *(Georgia Institute of Technology)*
- **Efficient Performance Evaluation of Memory Hierarchy for Highly Multithreaded Graphics Processors** 23
  Sara S. Baghsorkhi, Isaac Gelado, Matthieu Delahaye, Wen-mei W. Hwu
  (University of Illinois at Urbana-Champaign)

Session 2: Communication & SIMD Optimization

- **Communication Avoiding Symmetric Band Reduction** 35
  Grey Ballard, James Demmel, Nicholas Knight *(University of California, Berkeley)*
- **Faster Topology-Aware Collective Algorithms Through Non-minimal Communication** 45
  Paul Sack, William Gropp *(University of Illinois at Urbana-Champaign)*
- **Efficient SIMD Code Generation for Irregular Kernels** 55
  Seonggun Kim *(Samsung Advanced Institute of Technology)*, Hwansoo Han *(Sungkyunkwan University)*
- **Extending a C-like Language for Portable SIMD Programming** 65
  Roland Leißa, Sebastian Hack *(Saarland University)*, Ingo Wald *(Intel Corporation)*

Session 3: Programming Models

- **A Hybrid Approach of OpenMP for Clusters** 75
  Okwan Kwon, Fahed Jubair, Rudolf Eigenmann, Samuel Midkiff *(Purdue University)*
- **DOJ: Dynamically Parallelizing Object-Oriented Programs** 85
  Yong hun Eom, Stephen Yang, James C. Jenista, Brian Demsky *(University of California, Irvine)*
- **S: A Scripting Language for High-Performance RESTful Web Services** 97
  Daniele Bonetta, Achille Peternier, Cesare Pautasso, Walter Binder *(University of Lugano)*

Session 4: GPU Algorithms

- **A GPU Implementation of Inclusion-Based Points-to Analysis** 107
  Mario Méndez-Lojo *(University of Texas)*, Martin Burtscher *(Texas State University)*,
  Keshav Pingali *(University of Texas)*
- **Scalable GPU Graph Traversal** 117
  Duane Merrill *(University of Virginia)*, Michael Garland *(NVIDIA Corporation)*,
  Andrew Grimshaw *(University of Virginia)*
- **GPU-based NFA Implementation for Memory Efficient High Speed Regular Expression Matching** 129
  Yuan Zu, Ming Yang, Zhonghu Xu, Lin Wang, Xin Tian, Kunyang Peng, Qunfeng Dong
  (University of Science and Technology of China)

Session 5: Concurrent Data Structures

- **A Methodology for Creating Fast Wait-Free Data Structures** 141
  Alex Kogan, Erez Petrank *(Technion, Israel Institute of Technology)*

- **Concurrent Tries with Efficient Non-Blocking Snapshots** 151
  Aleksandar Prokopec *(École Polytechnique Fédérale de Lausanne)*, Nathan G. Bronson *(Stanford University)*, Phil Bagwell *(Typesafe)*, Martin Odersky *(École Polytechnique Fédérale de Lausanne)*
- **A Speculation-Friendly Binary Search Tree** 161
  Tyler Crain *(IRISA)*, Vincent Gramoli *(École Polytechnique Fédérale de Lausanne)*, Michel Raynal *(IRISA)*
- **PARRAY: A Unifying Array Representation for Heterogeneous Parallelism** 171
  Yifeng Chen, Xiang Cui, Hong Mei *(Peking University)*

Session 6: Parallel Algorithms

- **Internally Deterministic Parallel Algorithms Can Be Fast** 181
  Guy E. Blelloch *(Carnegie Mellon University)*, Jeremy T. Fineman *(Georgetown University)*, Phillip B. Gibbons *(Intel Labs)*, Julian Shun *(Carnegie Mellon University)*
- **Deterministic Parallel Random-Number Generation for Dynamic-Multithreading Platforms** 193
  Charles E. Leiserson, Tao B. Schardl, Jim Sukha *(Massachusetts Institute of Technology)*,
- **Scalable Parallel Minimum Spanning Forest Computation** 205
  Sadegh Nobari, Thanh-Tung Cao *(National University of Singapore)*, Panagiotis Karras *(Rutgers University)*, Stéphane Bressan *(National University of Singapore)*

Session 7: Correctness and Fault Tolerance

- **GKLEE: Concolic Verification and Test Generation for GPUs** 215
  Guodong Li *(Fujitsu Laboratories of America)*, Peng Li, Geof Sawaya, Ganesh Gopalakrishnan *(University of Utah)*, Indradeep Ghosh, Sreeranga P. Rajan *(Fujitsu Labs of America)*
- **Algorithm-based Fault Tolerance for Dense Matrix Factorizations** 225
  Peng Du, Aurelien Bouteiller, George Bosilca, Thomas Herault, Jack Dongarra *(University of Tennessee, Knoxville)*
- **Efficient Deadlock Avoidance for Streaming Computation with Filtering** 235
  Jeremy D. Buhler, Kunal Agrawal, Peng Li, Roger D. Chamberlain *(Washington University in St. Louis)*

Session 8: Scheduling and Synchronization

- **Lock Cohorting: A General Technique for Designing NUMA Locks** 247
  David Dice, Virendra J. Marathe *(Oracle Labs)*, Nir Shavit *(Massachusetts Institute of Technology & Tel-Aviv University)*
- **Revisiting the Combining Synchronization Technique** 257
  Panagiota Fatourou *(University of Crete & FORTH ICS)*, Nikolaos D. Kallimanis *(University of Ioannina)*
- **A Work-Stealing Scheduler for X10's Task Parallelism with Suspension** 267
  Olivier Tardieu *(IBM T.J. Watson Research Center)*, Haichuan Wang *(University of Illinois at Urbana-Champaign)*, Haibo Lin *(IBM Research - China)*

Poster Session 1 (Monday)

- **Automatic Communication Optimizations Through Memory Reuse Strategies** 277
  Muthu Baskaran, Nicolas Vasilache, Benoit Meister, Richard Lethin *(Reservoir Labs Inc.)*
- **FlexBFS: A Parallelism-Aware Implementation of Breadth-First Search on GPU** 279
  Gu Liu, Hong An, Wenting Han, Xiaoqiang Li, Tao Sun, Wei Zhou, Xuechao Wei, Xulong Tang *(University of Science and Technology of China)*
- **Programming Parallel Embedded and Consumer Applications in OpenMP Superscalar** 281
  Michael Andersch, Chi Ching Chi, Ben Juurlink *(Technische Universität Berlin)*
- **An Overview of Medusa: Simplified Graph Processing on GPUs** 283
  Jianlong Zhong, Bingsheng He *(Nanyang Technological University)*
- **Optimizing Remote Accesses for Offloaded Kernels: Application to High-Level Synthesis for FPGA** 285
  Christophe Alias, Alain Darte, Alexandru Plesco *(UCB-Lyon)*

- **Using GPU's to Accelerate Stencil-based Computation Kernels for the Development of Large Scale Scientific Applications on Heterogeneous Systems** 287
  Jian Tao *(Louisiana State University)*, Marek Blazewicz *(Poznań Supercomputing and Networking Center)*, Steven R. Brandt *(Louisiana State University)*
- **Mechanizing the Expert Dense Linear Algebra Developer** 289
  Bryan Marker, Robert van de Geijn, Don Batory *(The University of Texas at Austin)*, Andy Terrel *(Texas Advanced Computing Center)*, Jack Poulson *(The University of Texas at Austin)*
- **The Boat Hull Model: Adapting the Roofline Model to Enable Performance Prediction for Parallel Computing** 291
  Cedric Nugteren, Henk Corporaal *(Eindhoven University of Technology)*
- **Speculative Parallelization on GPGPUs** 293
  Min Feng, Rajiv Gupta, Laxmi N. Bhuyan *(University of California, Riverside)*
- **Adapting the Polyhedral Model as a Framework for Efficient Speculative Parallelization** 295
  Alexandra Jimborean, Philippe Clauss, Benoît Pradelle, Luis Mastrangelo, Vincent Loechner *(INRIA & LSIIT & University of Strasbourg)*
- **An Overview of CMPI: Network Performance Aware MPI in the Cloud** 297
  Yifan Gong, Bingsheng He, Jianlong Zhong *(Nanyang Technological University)*
- **OpenCL as a Unified Programming Model for Heterogeneous CPU/GPU Clusters** 299
  Jungwon Kim, Sangmin Seo, Jun Lee, Jeongho Nah, Gangwon Jo, Jaejin Lee *(Seoul National University)*
- **BDDT: Block-Level Dynamic Dependence Analysis for Deterministic Task-Based Parallelism** 301
  George Tzenakis, Angelos Papatriantafyllou, John Kesapides, Polyvios Pratikakis *(FORTH)*, Hans Vandierendonck *(FORTH & Ghent University)*, Dimitrios S. Nikolopoulos *(FORTH)*
- **Portable Parallel Performance from Sequential, Productive, Embedded Domain-Specific Languages** 303
  Shoaib Kamil, Derrick Coetzee, Scott Beamer, Henry Cook, Ekaterina Gonina *(University of California, Berkeley)*, Jonathan Harper *(Mississippi State University)*, Jeffrey Morlan, Armando Fox *(University of California, Berkeley)*
- **Communication-Centric Optimizations by Dynamically Detecting Collective Operations** 305
  Torsten Hoefler *(University of Illinois at Urbana-Champaign)*, Timo Schneider *(Chemnitz University of Technology)*

Poster Session 2 (Tuesday)

- **LHlf: Lock-free Linear Hashing (poster paper)** 307
  Donghui Zhang *(Microsoft Jim Gray Systems Lab)*, Per-Åke Larson *(Microsoft Research)*
- **Wait-Free Linked-Lists** 309
  Shahar Timnat, Anastasia Braginsky, Alex Kogan, Erez Petrank *(Technion, Israel Institute of Technology)*
- **Scalable Parallel Debugging with Statistical Assertions** 311
  Minh Ngoc Dinh, David Abramson, Chao Jin *(Monash University)*, Andrew Gontarek, Bob Moench, Luiz DeRose *(Cray Inc.)*
- **Verification of Software Barriers** 313
  Alexander Malkis, Anindya Banerjee *(IMDEA Software Institute)*,
- **Collective Algorithms for Sub-communicators** 315
  Anshul Mittal, Thomas George, Yogish Sabharwal *(IBM Research India)*, Nikhil Jain *(University of Illinois at Urbana Champaign)*, Sameer Kumar *(IBM T.J. Watson Research Center)*
- **Synchronization Views for Event-loop Actors** 317
  Joeri De Koster, Stefan Marr, Theo D'Hondt *(Vrije Universiteit Brussel)*
- **CPHASH: A Cache-Partitioned Hash Table** 319
  Zviad Metreveli, Nickolai Zeldovich, M. Frans Kaashoek *(Massachusetts Institute of Technology)*
- **RACECAR: A Heuristic for Automatic Function Specialization on Multi-core Heterogeneous Systems** 321
  John R. Wernsing, Greg Stitt *(University of Florida)*

- **A Lock-Free, Array-Based Priority Queue** 323
  Yujie Liu, Michael Spear *(Lehigh University)*
- **An Infrastructure for Dynamic Optimization of Parallel Programs** 325
  Albert Noll, Thomas R. Gross *(ETH Zurich)*
- **Automatic Datatype Generation and Optimization** 327
  Fredrik Kjolstad *(Massachusetts Institute of Technology)*,
  Torsten Hoefler, Marc Snir *(University of Illinois at Urbana-Champaign)*
- **NDetermin: Inferring Nondeterministic Sequential Specifications for Parallelism Correctness** 329
  Jacob Burnim, Tayfun Elmas, George Necula, Koushik Sen *(University of California, Berkeley)*
- **Concurrent Breakpoints** 331
  Chang-Seo Park, Koushik Sen *(University of California, Berkeley)*
- **Establishing a Miniapp as a Programmability Proxy** 333
  Andrew I. Stone *(Colorado State University)*, John M. Dennis *(National Center for Atmospheric Science)*,
  Michelle Mills Strout *(Colorado State University)*
- **OpenMP-Style Parallelism in Data-Centered Multicore Computing with R** 335
  Lei Jiang *(Louisiana State University)*, Pragneshkumar B. Patel *(University of Tennessee)*,
  George Ostrouchov *(Oak Ridge National Laboratory)*, Ferdinand Jamitzky *(Leibniz Supercomputing Centre)*
- **Performance Analysis of Parallel Constraint-Based Local Search** 337
  Yves Caniou *(JFLI, CNRS / NII)*, Daniel Diaz *(University of Paris 1-Sorbonne)*,
  Florian Richoux, Philippe Codognet *(JFLI, CNRS / UPMC / University of Tokyo)*,
  Salvador Abreu *(Universidade de Évora & CENTRIA FCT/UNL)*

Author Index 339

PPOPP 2012 Conference Organization

General Chair: J. Ramanujam *(Louisiana State University, USA)*

Program Chair: P. Sadayappan *(The Ohio State University, USA)*

Workshops and Tutorials Chair: Xipeng Shen *(College of William and Mary, USA)*

Proceedings Chair: Sriram Krishnamoorthy *(Pacific Northwest National Laboratory, USA)*

Local Arrangements Chair: David Koppelman *(Louisiana State University, USA)*

Web and Publicity Chair: Xiaoming Li *(University of Delaware, USA)*

Registration Chair: John Cavazos *(University of Delaware, USA)*

Finance Chair: Gerald Baumgartner *(Louisiana State University, USA)*

Steering Committee Chair: Keshav Pingali *(University of Texas at Austin, USA)*

Steering Committee:
Calin Cascaval *(Qualcomm, USA)*
Mary Hall *(University of Utah, USA)*
David Padua *(University of Illinois, USA)*
Pen-Chung Yew *(Academica Sinica, Taiwan & University of Minnesota, USA)*

Program Committee:
Emery Berger *(University of Massachusetts at Amherst, USA)*
Uday Bondhugula *(Indian Institute of Science, India)*
Greg Bronevetsky *(Lawrence Livermore National Laboratory, USA)*
Luis Ceze *(University of Washington, USA)*
Brad Chamberlain *(Cray, USA)*
Sandhya Dwarkadas *(University of Rochester, USA)*
Rudi Eigenmann *(Purdue University, USA)*
Michael Garland *(Nvidia, USA)*
Rajiv Gupta *(University of California at Riverside, USA)*
Francois Irigoin *(MINES ParisTech, France)*
Sriram Krishnamoorthy *(Pacific Northwest National Laboratory, USA)*
Andrew Lumsdaine *(Indiana University, USA)*
John Mellor-Crummey *(Rice University, USA)*
Mario Mendez-Lojo *(Advanced Micro Devices, USA)*
Frank Mueller *(North Carolina State University, USA)*
Michael O'Boyle *(University of Edinburgh, UK)*
John Owens *(University of California at Davis, USA)*
Padma Raghavan *(Pennsylvania State University, USA)*
Vijay Saraswat *(IBM Research, USA)*
Martin Schulz *(Lawrence Livermore National Laboratory, USA)*
Xipeng Shen *(College of William and Mary, USA)*

Program Committee (continued): Michelle Strout *(Colorado State University, USA)*
Jeff Vetter *(Oak Ridge National Laboratory and Georgia Tech., USA)*
Sam Williams *(Lawrence Berkeley National Laboratory, USA)*
Jingling Xue *(University of New South Wales, Australia)*

External Review Committee:

Gul Agha
Kunal Agrawal
Gagan Agrawal
Alex Aiken
George Almasi
Srinivas Aluru
Nancy Amato
Scott Baden
Martin Burtscher
Dhruva Chakrabarti
Barbara Chapman
Arun Chauhan
Albert Cohen
Bronis R. de Supinski
Steven Derrien
Jim Dinan
Thomas Fahringer
Cormac Flanagan
Guang Gao
Maria Garzaran
Ganesh Gopalakrishnan
Ramasamy Govindarajan
Naga Govindaraju
Ananth Grama
Paul Hargrove
Tim Harris
Yuxiong He
Torsten Hoefler
Wei-Chung Hsu
Costin Iancu
Roy Ju
Laxmikant Kale
Mahmut Kandemir
Jens Knoop
Milind Kulkarni
Jaejin Lee
Zhiyuan Li
Kamesh Madduri
Allen Malony
Virendra Marathe
Maged Michael
Sam Midkiff
Eliot Moss
Madanlal Musuvathi
Dimitrios Nikolopoulos
Vijay Pai
Scott Pakin
Santosh Pande
Srinivasan Parthasarathy
Erez Petrank
Rodric Rabbah
Sanjay Rajopadhye
Thomas Rauber
Lawrence Rauchwerger
Juan Carlos Saez
Marc Shapiro
Tatiana Shpeisman
Arrvindh Shriraman
Allan Snavely
Marc Snir
Michael Spear
Nathan Tallent
Kenjiro Taura
Michael Taylor
Philippas Tsigas
Christoph von Praun
Richard Vuduc
Peng Wu
Ayal Zaks
Binyu Zang
Antonia Zhai
Xiaodong Zhang
Huiyang Zhou

Additional Reviewers (continued):

Andreas Prell
Gil Rapaport
Kaushik Ravichandran
Eugene Ressler
Olivier Rojo
Adrian Sampson
William Scherer III
Carsten Scholtes
Sangmin Seo
Shishir Sharma
Subodh Sharma
Reza Shiftehfar
Sunil Shrestha
Yingchong Situ
Timmie Smith
Moulik Soni
Abhishek Sreenivasa
Tom St. John
Jeff Stuart
Hakan Sundell
Peter Thoman
Nathan Thomas
Chen Tian
Kai Tian
Daniel Tomkins
Sean Treichler
Antonino Tumeo
Ioannis Venetis
Kaibo Wang
Zheng Wang
Jeremiah Willcock
Benjamin P. Wood
Alec Wu
Xing Wu
Xintian Yang
Yi Yang
Tomofumi Yuki
Mani Zandifar
Xiao Zhang
Yongpeng Zhang
Zheng Zhang
Yili Zheng
Christopher Zimmer
Stephane Zuckerman

Sponsor:

Supporters:

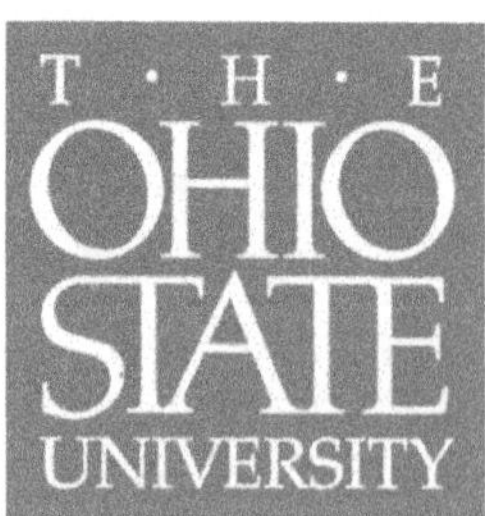

Scalable Framework for Mapping Streaming Applications onto Multi-GPU Systems

Huynh Phung Huynh
A*STAR Institute of High Performance Computing
Singapore
huynhph@ihpc.a-star.edu.sg

Andrei Hagiescu[1] Weng-Fai Wong
School of Computing
National University of Singapore
Singapore
{hagiescu,wongwf}@comp.nus.edu.sg

Rick Siow Mong Goh
A*STAR Institute of High Performance Computing
Singapore
gohsm@ihpc.a-star.edu.sg

Abstract

Graphics processing units leverage on a large array of parallel processing cores to boost the performance of a specific streaming computation pattern frequently found in graphics applications. Unfortunately, while many other general purpose applications do exhibit the required streaming behavior, they also possess unfavorable data layout and poor computation-to-communication ratios that penalize any straight-forward execution on the GPU. In this paper we describe an efficient and scalable code generation framework that can map general purpose streaming applications onto a multi-GPU system. This framework spans the entire core and memory hierarchy exposed by the multi-GPU system. Several key features in our framework ensure the scalability required by complex streaming applications. First, we propose an efficient stream graph partitioning algorithm that partitions the complex application to achieve the best performance under a given shared memory constraint. Next, the resulting partitions are mapped to multiple GPUs using an efficient architecture-driven strategy. The mapping balances the workload while considering the communication overhead. Finally, a highly effective pipeline execution is employed for the execution of the partitions on the multi-GPU system. The framework has been implemented as a back-end of the StreamIt programming language compiler. Our comprehensive experiments show its scalability and significant performance speedup compared with a previous state-of-the-art solution.

Categories and Subject Descriptors D.3.4 [*Programming languages*]: Processors—Code generation

General Terms Algorithms, Performance, Design

1. Introduction

The interest in using Graphics Processing Units (GPUs) for general purpose computation has expanded beyond the high performance computing community [19, 20] into mainstream computing. GPUs are parallel processors that consist of a number of *streaming multiprocessors* (SM), which in turn are made up of a number of processing cores running in lockstep. They support the execution of computational *kernels* – blocks of threads executed together on each of the available SMs. Massive parallelism is achieved as a large number of threads is interleaved onto the smaller number of processing cores. In order to ease the task of GPU developers, several GPU programming models have been proposed, such as OpenCL [16] and CUDA [1].

General purpose streaming applications are suitable for GPU processing as they expose significant task and data-level parallelism. Hence, several stream programming languages were proposed to ease the expression of parallelism in such applications [4, 8]. These languages capture computation in the form of a stream graph, where the graph nodes can consist of self-contained tasks, or finer-grained compute elements. StreamIt [8] is a platform-independent stream programming language that distinguishes among the alternative options. It is suitable for compilation onto a large number of platforms due to the fine-grained parallelism it exposes. It has also proved to be a suitable candidate for GPU compilation [11, 12, 23].

Usually, stream graphs are compiled and the code from the resulting nodes is mapped individually as GPU *kernels*. The code in each kernel expresses how a number of consecutive node executions are processed by the architecture. Multiple executions are handled in parallel, in distinct GPU threads. The adjacent nodes in the stream graph communicate through *channels*, currently implemented as FIFO queues in memory. At the beginning of a node execution, input data is read from a channel, and at the end of the execution, the output data is written to a different channel, all in a phased manner. Conventional GPU mapping may place these channels in either the GPU global memory, or the faster but size-limited SM memory [2].

One straightforward implementation strategy is to place channels in the global memory. As GPU code tend to instantiate a large number of threads, the hardware scheduler is relied upon to interleave these threads so as to hide potential stalls caused by global memory accesses [1]. Unfortunately, increasing the number of threads will decrease the number of registers allocated to each of them, potentially causing additional spills to global memory. In addition, more threads will require more input, output and local data stored in the global memory, increasing further memory traffic, and saturating the available memory bandwidth rapidly. For streaming applications, in particular, the intensive memory access at the beginning and end of each node execution that accesses the channels can exacerbate these problems.

[1] The first and second authors contributed equally to this paper

[2] The nVidia way of referring to this as *shared memory* is potentially confusing.

PPoPP'12, February 25–29, 2012, New Orleans, Louisiana, USA.

On the other hand, if the channels are placed in the fast SM memory, the number of parallel executions is limited by the small size of this memory. The resulting thread pool may underutilize the GPU processing cores. If the computation-communication ratio is low, this also undermines the utilization of any prefetching techniques.

To overcome the issues mentioned above, an automated GPU mapping framework for StreamIt applications [11] has been proposed. That framework instantiated a mixed pool of compute and memory access threads that maximized the utilization of the SM memory available. The resulting computation structure also maximized the utilization of the GPU cores given the memory constraint. However, this implementation is limited to a single partition. Hence, the application performance was severely limited if the working set size grew large enough such that insufficient parallel threads could be instantiated in the SM memory.

In this paper we present a mapping strategy that can handle complex streaming applications where the overall memory requirement for efficient implementations is larger than the available SM memory. This is achieved through an efficient graph partitioning algorithm that splits the application into several smaller partitions that satisfy the SM memory constraint, hence achieve good performance individually.

Scalability of our method is demonstrated by the ability to distribute the resulting partitions on a multi-GPU system. In addition, one or more partitions can be mapped to each GPU, resulting in a combined spatial and temporal distribution. The strategy also identifies graph nodes that are not suitable for GPU implementation, and map these nodes to CPU cores. Furthermore, the communication overhead between partitions is considered during the mapping step. This is necessary because a high volume of data streamed between partitions has to pass through one or more of the slower levels of the memory hierarchy, as determined by the locality of the partitions.

The following are the key contributions of this work:

- a scalable code generation framework that handles complex StreamIt applications (Section 4)
- an algorithm that divides large applications onto several partitions valid under SM memory constraints (Section 5).
- a multi-GPU mapping and orchestration scheme for these partitions (Section 6).

To the best of our knowledge, this is the first work on mapping StreamIt onto a single compute node that has multiple GPUs. The comprehensive set of experiments shows that, despite the fact that the application is not trivially parallel, our method was able to significantly improve performance by utilizing multiple GPUs.

2. Related Work

The StreamIt programming language [8] is based on synchronous data flow graphs [18]. It has been compiled on a myriad of architectures including multi-cores [9], Cell [17], Raw [8] and even FPGAs [10]. Moreover, there is previous research in coarse-grained mapping of StreamIt to GPU platforms [23].

The GPU mapping usually involves kernels that communicate to each other through global memory. Therefore, the overall performance is limited by the high latency of accessing this memory [24]. Recently proposed methods [11, 12] improved the memory access scheme by using two classes of dedicated threads for: (1) loading / storing data from global memory to SM memory and (2) computing using data preloaded in SM memory. The two methods contrast in how computation is organized. One exploits the coarse-grained task parallelism exposed by StreamIt graph nodes [12], leaving behind significant data-parallel optimizations opportunities available in each stream graph schedule execution. The other took advantage of finer-grained data level parallelism opportunities, where a single execution of the stream graph schedule spans several computing threads [11]. However, the latter method does not scale well with large applications because it attempts to map the entire stream graph schedule to a single partition.

Besides utilizing multiple partitions, a promising solution to deal with the scalability issue is the utilization of multi-GPU systems. Such systems are well-suited to process large data set applications [22]. Execution on multi-GPU systems has been improved through various run-time schemes, such as load balancing [5] and speculative execution [6]. Many of these schemes can be complemented by static methods that estimate the performance of an application running on the multi-GPU system, based on characterizing computation and different communication costs [21]. Performance modeling for GPU architectures was comprehensively investigated by analytic and quantitative approaches [3, 25] which highlighted the important balance between computation and memory access, as well as the utilization of SM memory. However, none of those works has attempted to map applications automatically, nor to provide an execution model for streaming languages onto multiple GPUs in an integrated approach.

Given the above challenges, this multi-GPU mapping work will also tackle the scalability of the solution [11], by partitioning the StreamIt application before mapping it. This is the first mapping attempt that integrates optimal GPU kernel generation, load-balanced mapping, communication reduction, and pipelined orchestration for multi-GPUs systems.

3. Background

3.1 StreamIt programming language

StreamIt was designed to expose the parallel and pipelined nature of the streaming applications. The high-level structure of a StreamIt program is a graph whose basic nodes are *filters* which communicate through channels. Filters can be combined to execute in *pipelines*. The data flow of the filters can also be distributed using *splitters* and *joiners* that describe parallel execution paths in the application. These two constructs expose the coarse-grained task parallelism in the application.

Filters are written in C-like code with special constructs to access their input and output channels. A filter consumes data from an input channel using *pop* constructs, and produces data on the output channel using *push* constructs. The input (output) rates between two filters may be different but they are statically defined. Therefore, multiple filter executions may be required to match the rates between filters. This exposes fine-grained data parallelism in the streaming application. The StreamIt compiler takes into account the non-matching rate of input (output), as well as dependencies among filters in the stream graph, to generate a static schedule for the entire graph. The static schedule contains *operators* (filters, splitters, joiners), which can be iteratively executed to process all the incoming data. Note that multiple copies of the schedule can be executed in parallel to process different data segments, as long as the filters in the schedule do not maintain internal state. The filters also have the capability to *peek* data beyond what they are going to consume through *peek* constructs. This feature allows structured data dependencies between consecutive filter executions and do not restrict parallel execution.

3.2 Mapping onto GPUs

The number of processing cores in streaming multiprocessors (SM) continues to increase with each new generation of GPUs (up to 48 cores per SM in the most recent nVidia GPUs, compared to S2050's 32 cores and S1070's 16 cores). Therefore, the number of threads supported in each SM also increases proportionally. The threads of each SM are divided into groups of 32 threads, called *warps*. Warp executions are interleaved by a hardware scheduler on the small number of processing cores. All threads in the same warp execute the same instruction at each time step (lockstep execution, a variant of SIMD) and divergent flow is serialized. However, threads that belong to different warps are independent of any divergent flow penalty. The hardware scheduler selects a warp for execution and dispatches the instruction from the selected warp to the processing cores. While the instruction is propagated through the execution pipeline, or while it waits for memory operands, the scheduler switches to execute a different warp with zero-overhead. As a result, though a large number of parallel threads can be spawned, their executions are actually interleaved on the processing cores.

Another reason behind instantiating a large number of threads is to hide the long delay of GPU global memory access through the interleaving mechanism described above. When mapping StreamIt applications onto GPUs, global memory access becomes more frequent because fine-grained operators have to communicate to each other through memory channels. Even if SM memory is used to prefetch the data from global memory, the bottleneck is still visible because operators seldom reuse the data they read from the channels. Previous work [11] describes a scheme that reduces the pressure on global memory access for streaming applications. First, several operators can be executed in the same GPU kernel, where they communicate through SM memory. Then, two distinct classes of threads are instantiated: memory access ($\mathcal{M}$) threads and compute ($\mathcal{C}$) threads. $\mathcal{M}$ threads are only responsible to prefetch data from global memory to SM memory while $\mathcal{C}$ threads only perform computations on the data prefetched by $\mathcal{M}$ threads. An efficient heuristic is used to determine the number of $\mathcal{C}$ and $\mathcal{M}$ threads as well as the execution schedule for those threads. The data-level parallelism available inside the stream graph is analyzed, such that entire executions of the stream graph are mapped onto multiple $\mathcal{C}$ threads inside an SM. This scheme is replicated on all the other SMs to fully utilize the GPU.

Such a mapping flow is feasible if the memory requirement for the parallel stream graph executions is less than or equal to the capacity of SM memory. Increasing memory requirement from large data-set and complex streaming applications, would result in a reduction of the number of supported parallel executions. The alternative investigated by this paper is to split the stream graphs of those applications into smaller partitions whose memory requirements match the SM memory constraint. To enable further scalability, we investigate the mapping of those partitions onto a multi-GPU platform. Altogether, we propose a scalable mapping framework for mapping streaming applications onto GPUs. The overview of the framework is presented in the next section.

4. Scalable Mapping Framework

The scalable mapping framework proposed in this paper is based on a recent work on automated GPU mapping for StreamIt applications [11]. The input to the framework are the applications written in the StreamIt language. The StreamIt compiler [8] analyzes the input program to generate a schedule of operators, as well as perform some common optimizations. It is the stream graph expressed in the schedule that is the input for our framework.

The components that form this framework, shown in shadows in Figure 4, provide the following:

- A stream graph partitioning algorithm that breaks complex StreamIt applications into smaller partitions that utilize the SMs efficiently.
- A global mapping step that balances the partitions among the available GPUs.

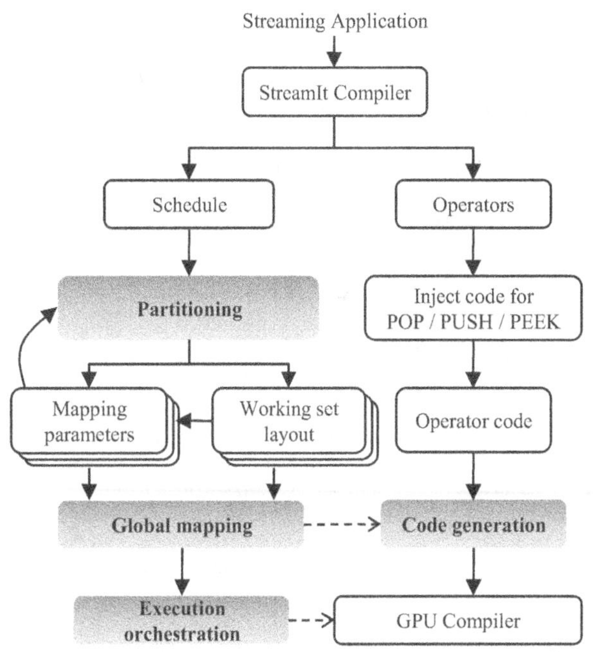

Figure 1. Scalable Mapping Framework.

- A code generator that provides C code for the partitions, as well as code coordinating the communication between them, based on the mapping result.
- A pipelined execution orchestration for the partitions.

The stream graph partitioning component prunes the design space by analysing the validity and estimated performance of the possible partitions (details in Section 5). The performance estimation considers the specification of the target GPU. The result of this partitioning is a set of convex and disjoint sub-graphs which are ready for mapping to GPU. Operators that maintain internal state are included in separate partitions that are executed on the CPU cores. For each GPU partition, we compute a compact memory layout [11] that can be realized in the fast SM memory. Given the memory layout for each partition, the other parallel code mapping parameters are determined by heuristics [11]. These heuristics depend on the specifications of the target GPU.

The push, pop and peek primitives of each operator in the schedule are annotated with information about how the channels in the SM memory are to be accessed correctly. These annotation will be used during the automatic code generation process.

Finally, the resulting set of partitions is passed to a global mapping step which assigns each partition to a specific GPU or CPU core. At this stage, communication channels between partitions are also instantiated (details in Section 6). The generated code is orchestrated by an execution environment which contains: (1) a multi-threaded controller which will run on the host CPU, and (2) the inter-partition memory communication scheme for pipelined execution. The controller consists of threads that coordinate the kernels loaded on each GPU, as well as threads that execute the CPU partitions.

5. Stream Graph Partitioning

Given a stream graph, the objective of partitioning is to maximize the overall performance of the stream graph, while ensuring that the partitions satisfy resource constraints, and yet effectively utilize the GPU.

5.1 Definitions

A stream graph $G(V, C)$ represents the data flow within the stream application. The nodes V represent the *operators*, and the edges C represent the channels (dependencies) between the operators. A *channel* connects the output of a producer operator to the input of a consumer operator. As advanced features of StreamIt such as feedback loops and portals are not supported, $G(V, C)$ is always a directed acyclic graph.

A partition P must be a convex subgraph, as non-convex subgraphs cause heavy communication to the adjacent subgraphs. Even worse, they may lead to deadlocks. P is convex if there does not exist a path in $G(V, C)$ from an operator $V_m \in P$ to another operator $V_n \in P$, which contains an operator $V_p \notin P$.

5.2 Partitioning Algorithm

The method employed to identify suitable partitions relies on the well-known k-way graph partitioning algorithm [14]. In this algorithm, the nodes of a graph are partitioned into k roughly equal partitions so that the weight of the edges between nodes in different partitions (edge-cut) is minimized. Intuitively, this results in load balanced partitions that have minimum communication. However, our partitioning differs from the standard algorithm in several aspects: (1) the number of partitions k is not an input to the problem – the value of k will be determined during the run-time of the algorithm such that it maximizes the overall performance, (2) there are convexity and memory constraints on each partition – these constraints affect the performance of combined partitions, and (3) the objective of the algorithm is to maximize the performance of the application. The performance objective is estimated as $\sum_{i=1...k} T(P_i)$ where T is an estimation of the execution time of P_i. Even if multiple GPUs are utilized, a balanced distribution of the partitions to the multiple GPUs ensures that this objective continues to reflect the overall stream graph execution performance.

Nevertheless, the *multi-level graph partitioning* (MLGP) algorithm used to solve the k-way problem can be effectively employed to solve our problem. In MLGP, the nodes in the original graph are grouped to create coarser nodes (the *coarsening phase*). The original graph is iteratively coarsened down to k partitions, over a number of levels, in order to create the initial partitioning solution (the *partitioning phase*). Then, the initial solution is *uncoarsened* back to the original graph by using the same number of levels as in the coarsening phase. While uncoarsening, the partitioning solution is refined by the movement of nodes to adjacent partitions so as to improve the overall performance.

We adapt an efficient multi-level algorithm [14] to our graph partitioning problem. This approach has also been effectively used in other contexts [13]. In our approach we continue to decrease the number of partitions as long as overall performance of the entire stream graph is still increasing. Because we do not have a particular k value as the input to our graph partitioning, we eliminate the k-partitioning limit from the MLGP algorithm. Alternatively, the number of partitions of the solution is the number of nodes in the coarsest graph obtained. The details of the coarsening and uncoarsening phases are described below.

5.3 Coarsening phase

From the original directed stream graph, we create a sequence of coarser graphs $G_i = (V_i, C_i)$ by clustering together pairs of nodes. A node $u \in V_{i+1}$ in a coarsened graph G_{i+1} at level $i + 1$ is the result of merging two *matching* nodes $v, w \in V_i$ of the finer graph G_i at level i such that u is convex and can be implemented on the GPU. Otherwise, if we can not find a convex combination, node u is simply set to vertex $v \in V_i$ of G_i. Note that each node u in a coarse graph is a sub-graph of G_0 when projected from the constituent nodes of u in the finer graph. In G_2 of Figure 2, the subgraph corresponding to coarse vertices $\{0,1\}$ consists of vertices $\{0,3,5,6,7,9\}$ of G_0. After constructing coarser nodes, we build the edges C_{i+1} of the coarse graph. There is a directed edge between two nodes in coarser graph G_{i+1} if there exists a directed edge between the constituent nodes in the finer graph G_i.

In our matching heuristics, the nodes of G_i are visited in random order. We select an unmatched node $v \in V_i$, and then iterate through the unmatched nodes adjacent to v to find a possible match w under the convexity constraint. We consider only adjacent nodes because there will be significant communication overhead among coarse nodes if we merge non-adjacent nodes. Two nodes are merged if their matching yields the best performance gain. The performance gain here is defined as: $\Delta T = T(w) + T(v) - T(u)$.

The estimation of T is based on the amount of SM memory required by the subgraph executions, because this determines the number of subgraph executions that can be run in parallel. The SM memory requirement is derived through channel layout analysis. While previous work employs an algorithm which considers the influence of fragmentation on the channel layout [11], the complexity of the partitioning algorithm can be reduced by using an estimation which does not consider the effect of fragmentation.

In case a feasible matching for v can not be found, u inherits only a single node v. In Figure 2, nodes 1 and 4 of G_1 are matched to form node 1 of G_2 while node 2 of G_1 is assigned to node 0 of G_2. Note that the filters that maintain state are more suited for CPU execution (i.e. node 1 in G_0), because they can not be parallelized. Therefore, we prevent these filters from being matched as they will be included in special partitions to be mapped to CPU cores.

If the graph cannot be coarsened any further, i.e., $G_{i+1} = G_i$, the coarsening phase ends. Let $G_m = (V_m, C_m)$ be the coarsest graph achieved. The initial partitioning solution utilizes this configuration, and each node $v \in V_m$ is selected as a partition. The number of partitions, k, is just $|V_m|$. This value is not an input as is the case in the standard k-way problem, but it is only determined when the coarsest graph is reached. These initial partitions will be refined as we go through the uncoarsening phase back to G_0. In Figure 2, the coarsening phase goes through a sequence of coarse graphs $\{G_0, G_1, G_2, G_3\}$ and the initial coarsening leads to three partitions P_0, P_1 and P_2.

5.4 Uncoarsening Phase

From the coarsest graph G_m, the initial partitions are projected back to the original graph by traversing a sequence of finer graphs $G'_{m-1}, \ldots, G'_0$, where G'_i is a refinement of G_i. During this uncoarsening process, we need to trace the partition to which the finer nodes belong. Let $P(v)$ be the partition assignment for a node v. Each node of the coarsest graph G_m represents a partition, so, utilizing this notation, $P(v_i) = P_i$ ($v_i \in V_m$). Because nodes in a level $i + 1$ graph include one or two nodes from the level i graph, the partitioning information can easily be propagated through all the levels.

Moving nodes from one partition to another may yield improvements. G_j is less coarse than G_{j+1}. Therefore, there is more freedom to move the nodes in G_j. The movement may reduce the communication or increase the combined performance of the partitions after the move. There are local movement heuristics based on the Kernighan-Lin (KL) [15] or Fiduccia-Mattheyses (FM) [7] partitioning algorithms which can yield good results for bi-partitioned graphs. However, using the KL or FM methods in a k-way problem leads to significant complexity, because a node from a partition can move to several other partitions. Instead, for our problem, we developed a simple and efficient movement algorithm inspired from a greedy refinement method [14].

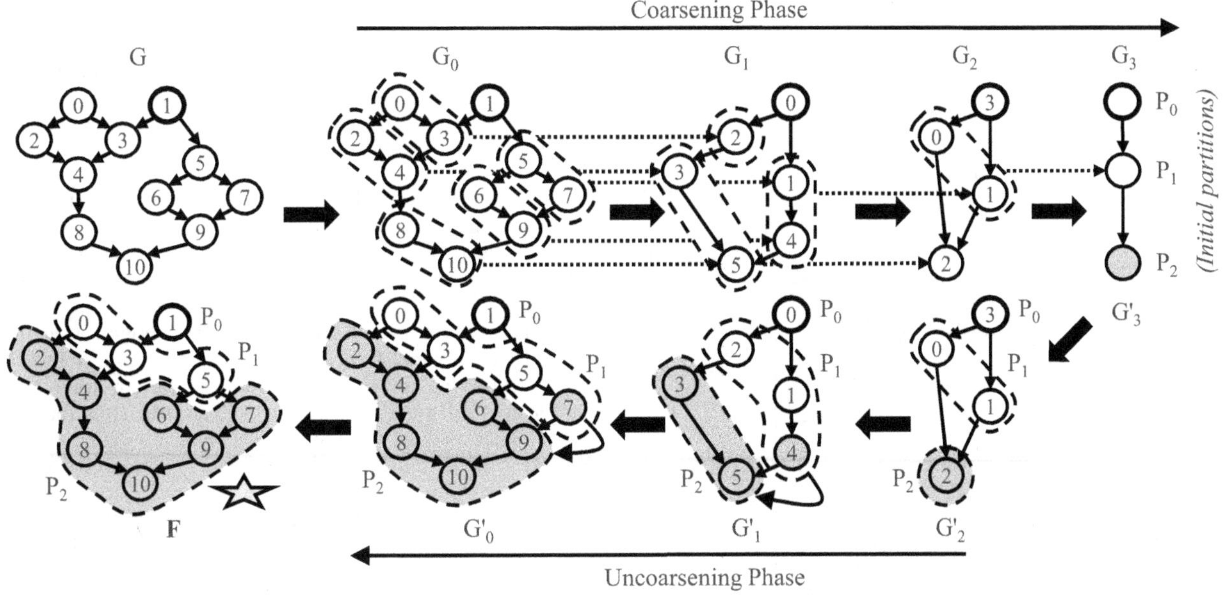

Figure 2. Illustration of Multi-Level Graph Partitioning. The dashed lines show the projection of a vertex from a coarser graph to a finer graph.

Our movement algorithm tries to move the boundary nodes of a partition to the adjacent partitions. A boundary node of partition P_i in coarse graph $G_j = (V_j, E_j)$ is a node $v \in V_j$ that has at least one adjacent node $u \in V_j$ that belongs to a different partition ($P(v) \neq P(u)$). In Figure 2, nodes {2,4,6,9} in G'_0 are the boundary nodes of partition P_2, while {8,10} are the internal ones. We randomly select a boundary node v to move from partition $P(v)$ (the *source partition*) to the neighborhood partitions $P(u)$ (the *destination partition*). For G'_0 in Figure 2, a neighborhood partition of node 7 is P_2. After moving node v from source partition $P(v)$ to the destination partition $P(u)$, if the source and the destination partitions still satisfy the convexity and SM memory constraints, the movement is deemed valid and would transform the two original partitions $P(v)$ and $P(u)$ into the new partitions $P(v)'$ and $P(u)'$. Among the valid movements of the boundary node v to the neighborhood partitions, the movement which has the highest $\Delta T = T(P(v)) + T(P(u)) - T(P(v)') - T(P(u)')$ is selected and node v is moved to that particular destination partition. The source and destination partitions are updated respectively. The moved nodes will not be considered again for analysis during the current coarsening level. The movement algorithm for the current level stops if there are no more boundary nodes to move. Once the movement algorithm for G_i finishes, the uncoarsening phase continues by projecting back to G_{i-1}. Finally, after G'_0 is analysed, we obtain the final assignment of the nodes to partitions. In Figure 2, node 4 is moved from P_1 to P_2 when G'_1 is analysed, and node 7 is moved when G'_0 is analysed. The result is the partitioned graph F, which captures the refinements to the partitioning solution.

6. Execution on a multi-GPU platform

After the original stream graph is partitioned, we need to map the partitions onto the multiple GPUs and CPU cores such that the workload is balanced. In this section, we first describe how such a balanced mapping is achieved. We will also describe the execution model that ensures the efficient utilization of the mapped partitions.

6.1 Partition Mapping

Each partition that belongs to the solution F obtained in Section 5 forms a single node in the coarsest graph G_m. An edge between any two level $i+1$ nodes exists if there is an edge connecting constituent nodes of those two coarse nodes in G_i. The edge is assigned a *weight* which is the sum of the communication overhead of the level i edges. The communication overhead is the ratio between the data amount exchanged by two level $i+1$ nodes, and the memory transfer bandwidth between CPU and GPU. In order to map G_m onto a system with x GPUs, we need to distribute the partitions in G_m onto x processing elements with the objectives: (1) the load should be balanced, and (2) the overhead of the communication edges should be minimized. The k-way partitioning algorithm is a good match for this problem because it splits the nodes of a graph into x roughly equal partitions such that the communication between the different partitions is minimized.

An exception are the partitions that maintain internal states. They correspond to individual filters due to the coarsening restrictions from Section 5. These partitions are pre-mapped to CPU threads and are not included in this second k-way partitioning pass. The remaining partitions are analysed, and divided among the x GPUs.

6.2 Communication channels

After mapping, each GPU has to multiplex the execution of the several partitions assigned to it. The code for a GPU kernel corresponding to each partition is generated as described in Section 3.2, with additional code inserted to assist with the pipelined execution of the partitions. The execution schedule on each GPU is coordinated by a dedicated CPU thread. Additional CPU threads are launched to support the CPU partitions.

The entire execution schedule utilizes memory-based FIFO (First In First Out) channels for data transfer. The FIFO length ensures that there will be no stall during the execution. Each FIFO element contains data corresponding to a large number of stream executions. This coarse data granularity takes advantage of the exposed data parallelism, and hides the unnecessary overhead of handling data separately for independent iterations within a partition. Overall, three levels of data transfer are employed between: (1) the different partitions, (2) the asynchronous launches of the partition kernel using GPU streams, and (3) the compute $\mathcal{C}$ and memory access $\mathcal{M}$ threads inside each GPU partition.

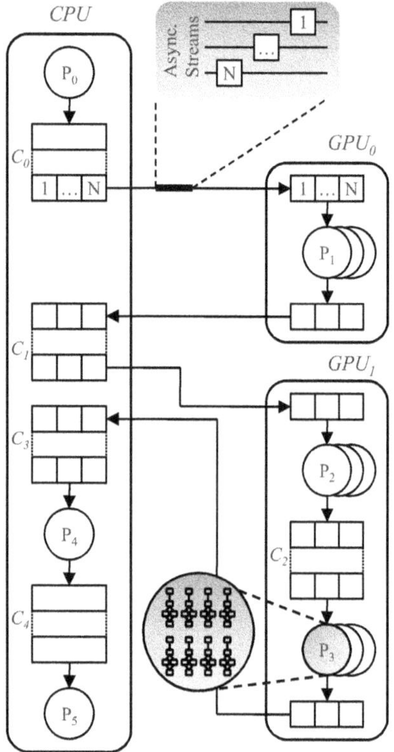

Figure 3. Execution and data transfer among partitions on multiple GPUs

Level 1 data transfer We spawn $x+y$ CPU threads to manage the parallel execution on the x GPUs and the y additional threads supporting CPU partitions. CPU synchronization primitives ensure uncorrupted access to the channels between the partitions. The FIFO channels between two CPU partitions or two partitions executed on the same GPU employ a standard circular buffer where memory pointers are passed directly between the threads.

However, when data needs to be transferred between CPU and GPU partitions, an additional buffering scheme that copies the channel data from CPU/GPU memory to GPU/CPU memory is used. For example, in Figure 3, the data in channel C_3 between partition P_3 (on GPU_1) and partition P_4 (on CPU) requires this buffering scheme.

Finally, in order to transfer data between partitions on different GPUs, the data is always copied first to the CPU, where the FIFO channel is implemented. Afterwards, data is copied from CPU memory to the other GPU using the buffering scheme described above. In Figure 3, the output buffer of partition P_1 (in GPU_0) is copied to the channel C_1 in CPU memory and data from this channel is copied to the input buffer of partition P_2 (in GPU_1).

Our communication scheme between partitions on different GPUs can be easily adapted to the recent peer-to-peer memory access in CUDA 4.0 [1]. Note that peer-to-peer memory access is specific to nVidia GPUs. Moreover, in order to use peer-to-peer memory access in our pipeline execution, we still need to perform synchronization among different CPU threads to ensure that memory accesses are uncorrupted. More importantly, peer-to-peer memory copy between two GPUs can not be initiated until all commands previously issued to either GPU have completed, and has to complete before any asynchronous commands issued after the copy to either GPU can start. This may downgrade the benefit of peer-to-peer communication in comparison with communication through CPU, which can benefit from the support of asynchronous GPU streams.

Level 2 data transfer The asynchronous streaming support for the GPUs is utilized to hide the CPU/GPU memory copy overhead. The coarse data elements from the FIFO channels are divided into smaller fragments. We generate an asynchronous stream of memory copy and partition kernel launch requests to process the GPU copy and execution. As the operations on these fragments are independent, memory transfers and kernel executions of different fragments can overlap. N fragments are created, as shown in Figure 3. Each stream will coordinate data transfer and execution for its corresponding fragment. While Stream 1 is performing computation of fragment 1 in GPU_0, Stream 2 can transfer fragment 2 from *CPU* to GPU_0.

If several partitions are mapped to a single GPU, these partitions are time multiplexed. In Figure 3, the execution of partition P_3 and P_2 are interleaved.

Level 3 data transfer Each GPU kernel executes multiple iterations over the group of parallel executions of the stream graph partition it includes [11]. Using a mix of $\mathcal{C}$ and $\mathcal{M}$ threads, data can be prefetched and computed without stalls inside each SM. This heterogeneous scheme can be executed efficiently on the GPU architecture as long as $\mathcal{C}$ and $\mathcal{M}$ threads are allocated into different *warps*. In such an implementation, $\mathcal{C}$ threads never access slow GPU memory and can compute a larger number of stream graph executions using exclusively a small workset *WS* stored in SM memory. Concurrently, $\mathcal{M}$ threads fetch the next input data from GPU memory to a double buffer *DB* in SM memory and store back the previous output data. A single synchronization point is required, when prefetched data from *DB* is swapped in *WS* and the previously computed results are swapped out from *WS* to *DB*.

The stream graph partitions supported by our implementation are connected through multiple input and output channels. Their corresponding data should be swapped between *WS* and *DB*. This is trivial only when a single input and output channel is involved [11]. In this case, the input channel corresponds to a contiguous range of memory locations, which overlaps with the output channel in *DB* and may also overlap in *WS*. Simply iterating through the data stored in *DB* in the correct direction ensures that no data is corrupted, and it is possible to swap data in parallel using multiple GPU threads. However, special care is required to support multiple channels.

The *WS* memory range corresponding to the channels of each graph operator is determined by a static memory allocator, based on liveness analysis. This allocator ensures that the channels receive a contiguous memory range (as a result, gaps may occur between channels). The input and output channels of a stream graph partition are also stored in *WS*, and the allocator may place them arbitrarily. If multiple channels need to be swapped from *WS* to *DB* and no additional constraints are in place, the actual location of the channels can lead to long dependency chains which may prevent swapping pairs of elements.

A possible scenario is shown in Figure 4a. The shaded boxes are the current channels in *WS* and *DB*. In this example the elements from input I_0 can not be swapped into their designated location in *WS* as long as the contents of the output channel O_1 has not been swapped out. However, this output channel can not be moved as it will corrupt I_1 which has not been processed yet. Also, I_1 can not be processed as it will corrupt O_0, etc. Utilizing temporary

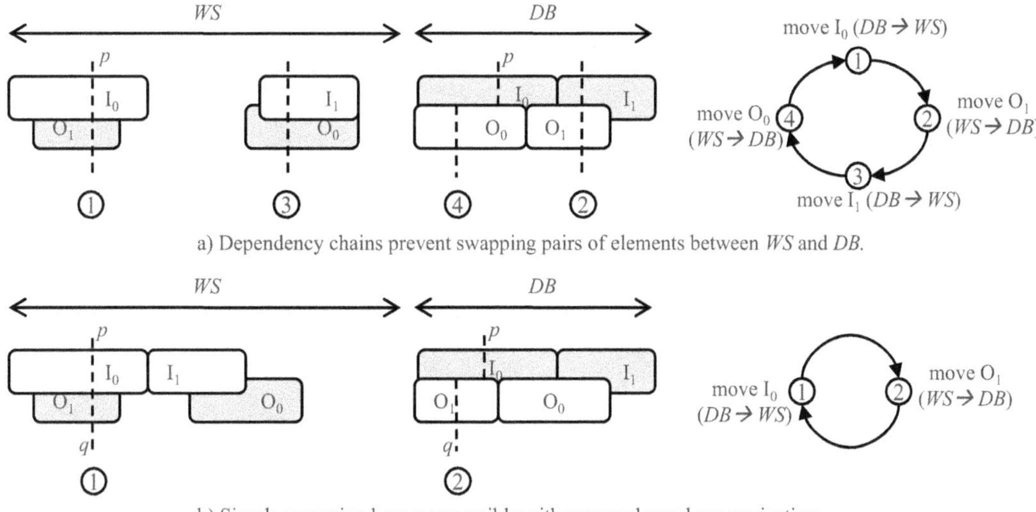

Figure 4. Execution snapshot showing the challenges of partition I/O handling. The inputs for the next iteration have to swap with the outputs of the previous iteration.

memory storage is not feasible because the SM memory is limited and any extension degrades performance. Therefore, we propose an extension of the single channel swapping scheme that ensures that single element swaps can proceed without data corruption.

We direct the static allocator to layout the input channels without fragmentation from the first location in *WS*. This is possible as there are no previous data in *WS*. However, for outputs, we can not ensure that they are allocated in a contiguous fashion, but we can record the order in which they are allocated. The same order is replicated in the *DB*, where both input and output channels can be allocated contiguously. Such a layout is illustrated in Figure 4b.

Using this layout guarantees corruption free swapping, and we can prove this through induction on the index in *DB*. The basis case is for the first location in *DB*. The input stored at location 0 in *DB* can be moved to *WS*, and any output value it overwrites in *WS* can be moved to *DB* at the same location, because the outputs are compacted, in order, in *DB*. This can be implemented by storing the output first in a temporary register, and saving it afterwards to *DB*. If no output element exists in *WS* at location 0, there still obviously is no data corruption.

Assuming there is no data corruption until index $p-1$ in *DB*, when the input element at index p in *DB* is moved to location p in *WS* it may overwrite an unmoved output. In this case, the overwritten output element has to be moved to index $q \leq p$ in the contiguous sequence of outputs in *DB*. This inequality is ensured by the contiguous allocation of input buffers in *WS* and *DB*, and the possible fragmentation of the outputs in *WS*. Therefore, the movement of the output to the index q in *DB* does not corrupt any input not yet transferred. This concludes the induction case if the number of inputs is larger than the number of outputs. Otherwise, the remaining outputs can be transferred to *DB* safely, as there is no remaining input in *DB*.

The automatically generated code relies on the above channel allocation. We infer a set of intervals where the swap indices for both input and output increase linearly. For each such interval, swaps can be applied to pairs of elements at consecutive locations.

6.3 Mapping Parameters Selection

Code generation for each GPU partition requires a few parameters, such as the number of $\mathcal{C}$ and $\mathcal{M}$ threads, or the number of parallel $\mathcal{C}$ threads, S, supporting each stream graph partition execution. We first determine the number of concurrent executions of the partition that can be handled by each SM, based on the SM memory size and the memory requirement of each stream graph partition execution. Then, we allocate S threads for each partition execution, exploiting the data parallelism of the partition extracted through the stream graph structure. Finally, we need to match the data transfer requirements of the $\mathcal{C}$ threads with a corresponding number of $\mathcal{M}$ threads to minimize the stalls [11]. The same parameters are replicated for all SMs, as the SMs process parallel fragments of the input data. These parameters were estimated once during the performance evaluation of each partition in Section 5. However, during the final code generation step, we compute the exact SM memory layout, and the resulting footprint may increase due to fragmentation.

The number of N concurrent GPU streams utilized for the level 2 data transfer can influence how much of the CPU to GPU data transfer overhead is hidden. However, there is some penalty associated with each GPU partition kernel launch, and this surfaces if too many concurrent streams are utilized. In our implementation, we utilized 4 parallel streams to provide a good coverage of the memory transfer delays.

7. Experimental Results

In order to show the scalability and efficiency of our automated framework, we present the performance achieved on mapping several StreamIt benchmarks. These benchmarks (described in Table 1) are a representative set of the StreamIt benchmarks suite [2]. They were processed automatically by the framework, and code was generated for multiple partitions. The benchmarks were altered to create larger stream graphs by utilising a parameter N (i.e. the graph of DES for N = 40 reached 1047 filters). The stream graphs are mapped onto one to four GPUs connected to the same CPU host. The benchmarks were augmented with source and sink filters that include code to verify the results of the computations. Because these filters maintain internal state, this also validated the support we provide for such filters. Our framework was implemented as a back-end to the StreamIt 2.1.1 compiler. The baseline CPU timing was obtained on an Intel Xeon CPU E5405 running at 2 GHz, with the executable generated through the uniprocessor back-end

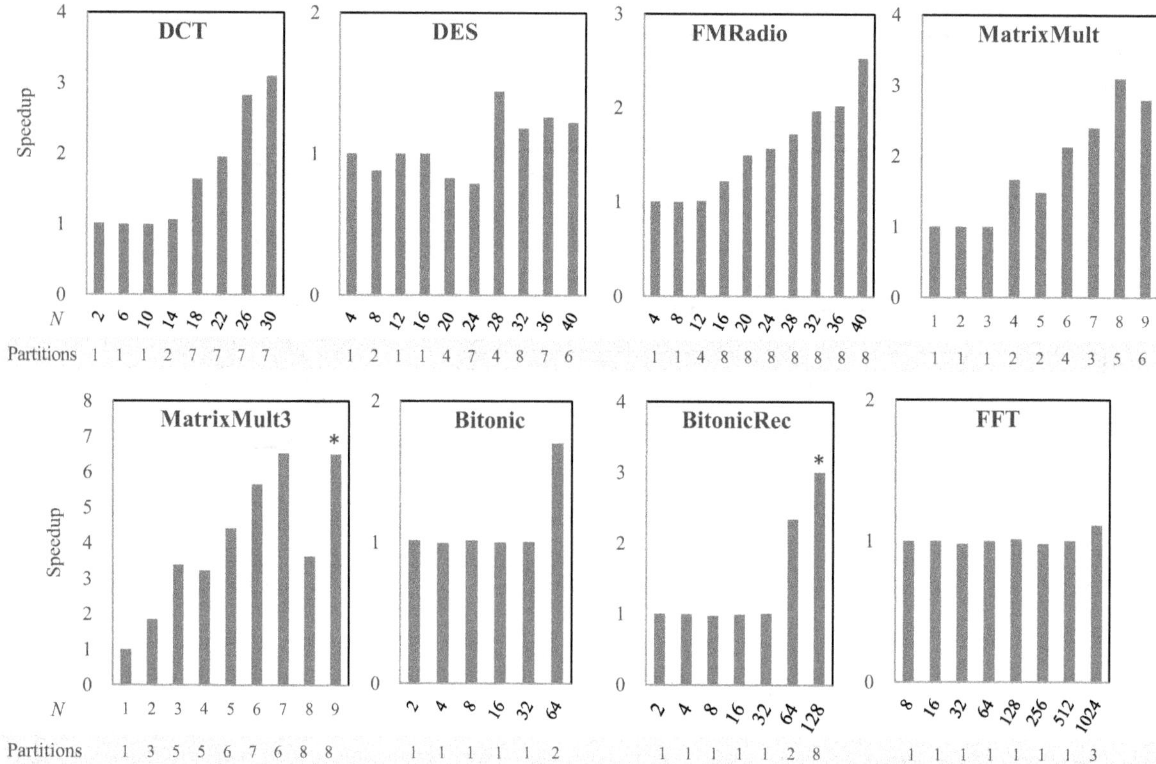

Figure 5. Mapping to a single partition and to multiple partitions (the number of partitions is listed under the graphs) on a single GPU. The speedup is the execution time ratio between the two. Design points marked with (*) were not supported by a single partition implementation.

of StreamIt, and compiled using the '-O3' option of GCC 4.1.2. The experiments target the newer C2070 "Fermi" GPU platforms.

Comparison with the single partition mapping Figure 5 shows the speedup achieved on a single GPU by our multiple partition mapping compared to the previous single partition mapping [11]. It also shows the number of partitions generated for each benchmark instance (the shadowed row under the values of N). Most benchmarks benefit from multiple partitions when N increases. Using our proposed algorithm, multiple partitions yielded better performance than a single partition, because each partition requires a much smaller memory footprint. If only a single partition is used, the large working set resulted in poorer performance. To capture the CPU to GPU transfer overhead, the benchmarks maintain stateful source / sink filters. The additional speedup can be as high as $6.53\times$. In addition, there are a few cases where a single partition mapping could not return a solution (such as MatrixMult3 for size 9). However, for some benchmarks, such as Bitonic, DES or FFT, the working set size does not change significantly, and both single and multiple partitions mappings had similar performance.

Multiple partitions on a single GPU Figure 6 shows the speedup of the proposed partitioning approach relative to the CPU baseline. While the speedup may diminish for large values of N, this approach proves capable of sustaining good throughput for most benchmarks. If the size of the benchmark is too large to fit the SM memory, the benchmark is split into multiple partitions. In some cases, the overhead of data communication among the partitions severely impacted performance.

Multi-GPU mapping We tested large benchmarks running on multiple GPUs using the orchestration described in Section 6. The speedup obtained by running the benchmarks on 2 to 4 GPUs compared to a single GPU mapping is shown in Figure 7. In general, when the size of the benchmark is not large enough, multiple GPUs do not provide any benefit. In these cases, a single GPU mapping is the best solution. The single GPU implementation corresponds to the white bars in the figure. This is mainly due to the communication overhead of transferring the data between the GPU and the CPU that could not be completely masked by computation.

However, the multi-GPU implementation proves profitable if N increases. As shown in Figure 6, the speedup of the single GPU mapping diminishes for large benchmarks. However, in this case, mapping to multiple GPUs starts to show its advantages. The speedup reaches $2.97\times$ compared to a single GPU mapping. This is evidence that for applications that have large working sets, our multi-GPU solution can effectively speed up their execution.

Mapping to multiple GPUs (Figure 7) shows some divergent performance results for different values of N. The divergence can be explained because the nature of the stream graph itself may lead to solutions that are easily balanced on a specific number of GPUs, and adding additional GPUs may affect the balancing. Moreover, if significant communication exists between fine-grained filters, the performance will hardly increase if we put those filters across multiple GPUs.

Moreover, Figure 7 offers an indirect insight that the communication overhead can be effectively masked. The performance boost of a 2 GPU solution, compared to that achieved on a single GPU, is affected by several factors (such as how the workload is balanced between the 2 GPUs) in addition to the overhead of the complex communication mechanism. However, some design points of DES and MatrixMult3 mapped to 2 GPUs reach 1.93x and 1.83x speedup respectively, compared to a single GPU solution that does not have inter-GPU communication.

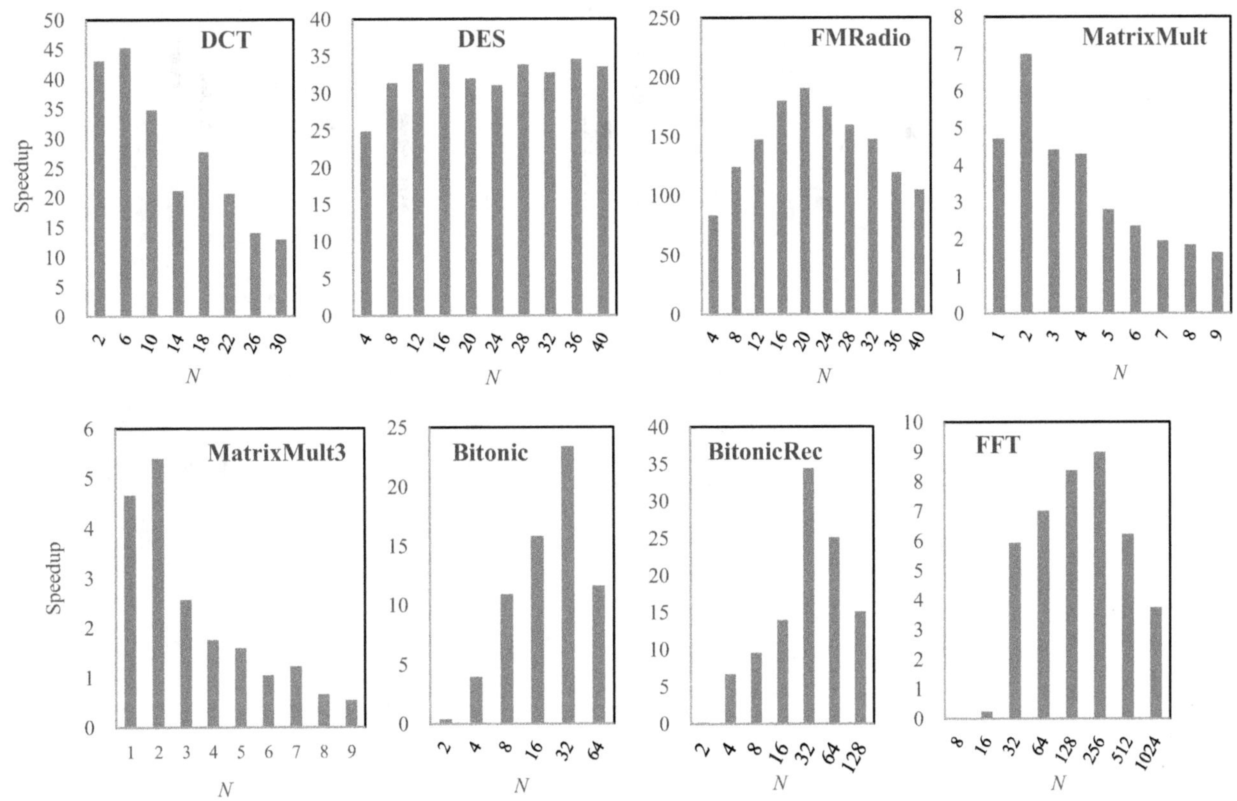

Figure 6. Mapping to a single GPU. The speedup is reported relative to a CPU implementation.

8. Conclusion

We proposed a scalable framework that automatically maps most stream processing applications onto GPUs. We developed an efficient graph partitioning algorithm that splits the complex application into several partitions, each of which can utilize the small on-chip SM memory effectively, and hence achieve good performance. Our proposed strategy obtained performance that augments that of a previous single partition solution. In addition, our proposed strategy is able to scale the performance to up to four GPUs. We also support stateful filters by running them on the CPU cores. The code generation scheme proposed is able to orchestrate the exchange of data within the individual GPUs, between the multiple GPUs, as well as the GPUs and the CPU cores. The results indicate the scalability and improvement when several GPUs are targeted.

It is conceivable that certain embarrassingly parallel applications can be mapped successfully to large scale multi-node, multi-GPU systems. However, on a single node, it is unlikely that the number of GPUs per node will increase significantly beyond the current four due to power, interconnect, and form-factor issues. Our work is the first to show that complex and often tightly coupled streaming applications can be successfully partitioned and mapped automatically onto multiple GPUs. As future work, we would like to investigate how even larger and more complex applications can be specified in StreamIt (or its derivative) so as to run on a large cluster of multi-GPU nodes.

Benchmark	Description	Original N [11]
Bitonic	Sorting algorithm for N float elements applying the bitonic algorithm	8
BitonicRec	Same as above, recursive method	8
DCT	Discrete Cosine Transform for a matrix of $N \times N$ floats	8
DES	DES encryption algorithm with N rounds, input 8 bytes, output as 16 hex digits	16
FFT	Fine grained FFT transform on N elements	32
FMRadio	$(N+3)$-band equalizer radio	8
MatrixMult	Blocked matrix multiplication algorithm for $2N \times 2N$ matrices, split into blocks of 2×2	2
MatrixMult3	Same as above for $(3N+3) \times (3N+3)) \times ((3N+3) \times 3N)$ matrices, with blocks of 3×3	–

Table 1. Benchmark characterization.

References

[1] NVIDIA CUDA 4.0. http://developer.nvidia.com/cuda-toolkit-40.

[2] Streamit benchmarks. http://groups.csail.mit.edu/cag/streamit/shtml/benchmarks.shtml.

[3] S. S. Baghsorkhi, M. Delahaye, S. J. Patel, W. D. Gropp, and W.-m. W. Hwu. An adaptive performance modeling tool for GPU architectures. In *The 15th ACM SIGPLAN Symposium on Principles and Practice of Parallel Programming (PPoPP '10)*, 2010.

[4] I. Buck, T. Foley, D. Horn, J. Sugerman, K. Fatahalian, M. Houston, and P. Hanrahan. Brook for GPUs: stream computing on graphics hardware. In *ACM SIGGRAPH '04*, 2004.

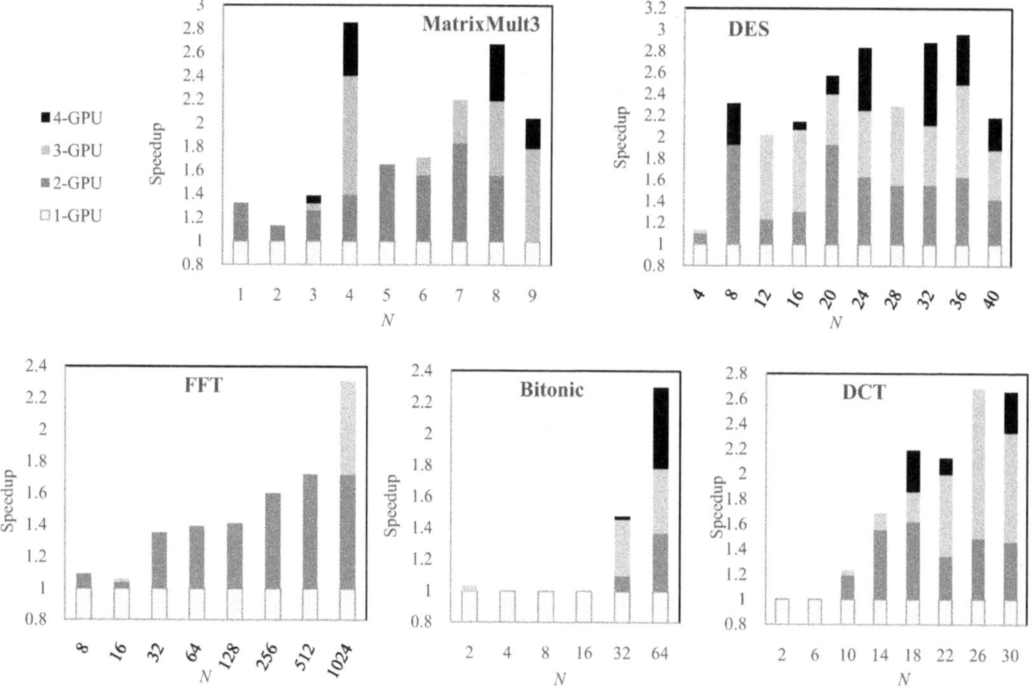

Figure 7. Additional speedup resulted from the mapping to multiple GPUs compared to a single GPU.

[5] L. Chen, O. Villa, S. Krishnamoorthy, and G. R. Gao. Dynamic load balancing on single- and multi-GPU systems. In *2010 IEEE International Parallel and Distributed Processing Symposium (IPDPS'10)*, 2010.

[6] G. Diamos and S. Yalamanchili. Speculative execution on multi-GPU systems. In *2010 IEEE International Parallel and Distributed Processing Symposium (IPDPS '10)*, 2010.

[7] C. M. Fiduccia and R. M. Mattheyses. A linear-time heuristic for improving network partitions. In *The 19th Design Automation Conference (DAC '82)*, 1982.

[8] M. I. Gordon, W. Thies, M. Karczmarek, J. Lin, A. S. Meli, A. A. Lamb, C. Leger, J. Wong, H. Hoffmann, D. Maze, and S. Amarasinghe. A stream compiler for communication-exposed architectures. In *The 10th international conference on Architectural support for programming languages and operating systems (ASPLOS '02)*, Oct 2002.

[9] M. I. Gordon, W. Thies, and S. Amarasinghe. Exploiting coarse-grained task, data, and pipeline parallelism in stream programs. In *The 12th international conference on Architectural support for programming languages and operating systems (ASPLOS '06)*, 2006.

[10] A. Hagiescu, W.-F. Wong, D. F. Bacon, and R. Rabbah. A computing origami: folding streams in FPGAs. In *The 46th Annual Design Automation Conference (DAC '09)*, 2009.

[11] A. Hagiescu, H. P. Huynh, W. F. Wong, and R. S. M. Goh. Automated architecture-aware mapping of streaming applications onto GPUs. In *2011 IEEE International Parallel and Distributed Processing Symposium (IPDPS '11)*, 2011.

[12] A. H. Hormati, M. Samadi, M. Woh, T. Mudge, and S. Mahlke. Sponge: portable stream programming on graphics engines. In *The 16th international conference on Architectural support for programming languages and operating systems (ASPLOS '11)*, 2011.

[13] H. P. Huynh, Y. Liang, and T. Mitra. Efficient custom instructions generation for system-level design. In *2010 International Conference on Field-Programmable Technology (FPT '10)*, 2010.

[14] G. Karypis and V. Kumar. Multilevel k-way partitioning scheme for irregular graphs. *Journal of Parallel and Distributed Computing*, 1998.

[15] B. W. Kernighan and S. Lin. An efficient heuristic procedure for partitioning graphs. *The Bell System Technical Journal*, 1970.

[16] Khronos OpenCL Working Group. *The OpenCL Specification, version 1.0.29*, 8 December 2008.

[17] M. Kudlur and S. Mahlke. Orchestrating the execution of stream programs on multicore platforms. In *The 2008 ACM SIGPLAN conference on Programming language design and implementation (PLDI '08)*, 2008.

[18] E. A. Lee and D. G. Messerschmitt. Static scheduling of synchronous data flow programs for digital signal processing. *IEEE Transactions on Computers*, 36(1), 1987.

[19] J. Nickolls and W. J. Dally. The GPU computing era. *IEEE Micro*, 30, 2010. ISSN 0272-1732.

[20] J. D. Owens, D. Luebke, N. Govindaraju, M. Harris, J. Krger, A. E. Lefohn, and T. J. Purcell. A survey of general-purpose computation on graphics hardware. *Computer Graphics Forum*, 26(1), 2007.

[21] D. Schaa and D. Kaeli. Exploring the multiple-GPU design space. In *2011 IEEE International Parallel and Distributed Processing Symposium (IPDPS'11)*, 2009.

[22] J. A. Stuart and J. D. Owens. Multi-GPU MapReduce on GPU clusters. In *2011 IEEE International Parallel and Distributed Processing Symposium (IPDPS '11)*, 2011.

[23] A. Udupa, R. Govindarajan, and M. J. Thazhuthaveetil. Software pipelined execution of stream programs on GPUs. In *The 7th annual IEEE/ACM International Symposium on Code Generation and Optimization (CGO '09)*, 2009.

[24] H. Wong, M.-M. Papadopoulou, M. Sadooghi-Alvandi, and A. Moshovos. Demystifying GPU microarchitecture through microbenchmarking. In *2010 IEEE International Symposium on Performance Analysis of Systems & Software (ISPASS '10)*, 2010.

[25] Y. Zhang and J. D. Owens. A quantitative performance analysis model for GPU architectures. In *(The 17th International Symposium on High Performance Computer Architecture (HPCA '11))*, 2011.

A Performance Analysis Framework for Identifying Potential Benefits in GPGPU Applications

Jaewoong Sim   Aniruddha Dasgupta† *   Hyesoon Kim   Richard Vuduc

Georgia Institute of Technology   Power and Performance Optimization Labs, AMD†

{jaewoong.sim, hyesoon.kim, riche}@gatech.edu   aniruddha.dasgupta@amd.com

Abstract

Tuning code for GPGPU and other emerging many-core platforms is a challenge because few models or tools can precisely pinpoint the root cause of performance bottlenecks. In this paper, we present a performance analysis framework that can help shed light on such bottlenecks for GPGPU applications. Although a handful of GPGPU profiling tools exist, most of the traditional tools, unfortunately, simply provide programmers with a variety of measurements and metrics obtained by running applications, and it is often difficult to map these metrics to understand the root causes of slowdowns, much less decide what next optimization step to take to alleviate the bottleneck. In our approach, we first develop an analytical performance model that can precisely predict performance and aims to provide programmer-interpretable metrics. Then, we apply static and dynamic profiling to instantiate our performance model for a particular input code and show how the model can predict the potential performance benefits. We demonstrate our framework on a suite of micro-benchmarks as well as a variety of computations extracted from real codes.

Categories and Subject Descriptors C.1.4 [*Processor Architectures*]: Parallel Architectures; C.4 [*Performance of Systems*]: Modeling techniques; C.5.3 [*Computer System Implementation*]: Microcomputers

General Terms Measurement, Performance

Keywords CUDA, GPGPU architecture, Analytical model, Performance benefit prediction, Performance prediction

1. Introduction

We consider the general problem of how to guide programmers or high-level performance analysis and transformation tools with performance information that is precise enough to identify, understand, and ultimately fix performance bottlenecks. This paper proposes a performance analysis framework that consists of an analytical model, suitable for intra-node analysis of platforms based on graphics co-processors (GPUs), and static and dynamic profiling tools. We argue that our framework is suitable for performance diagnostics through examples and case studies on real codes and systems.

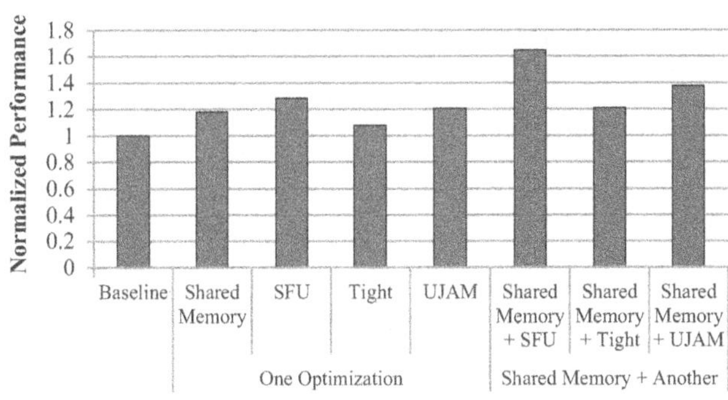

Figure 1. Performance speedup when some combinations of four independent optimization techniques are applied to a baseline kernel.

Consider an experiment in which we have a computational kernel implemented on a GPU and a set of n independent candidate optimizations that we can apply. Figure 1 shows the normalized performance when some combinations of four independent optimization techniques are applied to such a kernel, as detailed in Section 6.2.1. The leftmost bar is the parallelized baseline. The next four bars show the performance of the kernel with exactly one of four optimizations applied. The remaining bars show the speedup when one more optimization is applied on top of $Shared\ Memory$, one of the optimizations.

The figure shows that each of four optimizations improves performance over the baseline, thereby making them worth applying to the baseline kernel. However, most of programmers cannot estimate the degree of benefit of each optimization. Thus, a programmer is generally left to use intuition and heuristics. Here, $Shared\ Memory$ optimization is a reasonable heuristic starting point, as it addresses the memory hierarchy.

Now imagine a programmer who, having applied $Shared\ Memory$, wants to try one more optimization. If each optimization is designed to address a particular bottleneck or resource constraint, then the key to selecting the next optimization is to understand to what extent each bottleneck or resource constraint affects the current code. In our view, few, if any, current metrics and tools for GPUs provide this kind of guidance. For instance, the widely used occupancy metric on GPUs indicates only the degree of thread-level parallelism (TLP), but not the degree of memory-level or instruction-level parallelism (MLP or ILP).

In our example, the kernel would not be improved much if the programmer tries the occupancy-enhancing $Tight$ since $Shared\ Memory$ has already removed the same bottleneck that

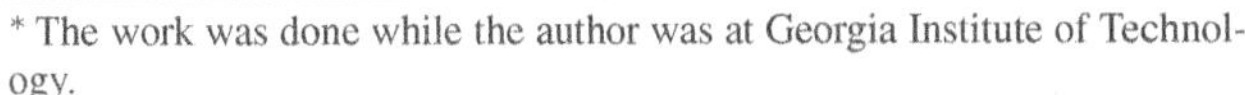

* The work was done while the author was at Georgia Institute of Technology.

PPoPP'12, February 25–29, 2012, New Orleans, Louisiana, USA.

Tight would have. On the other hand, if the programmer decides to apply *SFU*, which makes use of special function units (SFUs) in the GPU, the kernel would be significantly improved since *Shared Memory* cannot obtain the benefit that can be achieved by *SFU*.

Our proposed framework, *GPUPerf*, tries to provide such understanding. GPUPerf *quantitatively* estimates potential performance benefits along four dimensions: inter-thread instruction-level parallelism (B_{itilp}), memory-level parallelism (B_{memlp}), computing efficiency (B_{fp}), and serialization effects (B_{serial}). These four metrics suggest what types of optimizations programmers (or even compilers) should try first.

GPUPerf has three components: *a frontend data collector, an analytical model, and a performance advisor*. Figure 2 summarizes the framework. GPUPerf takes a CUDA kernel as an input and passes the input to the frontend data collector. The frontend data collector performs static and dynamic profiling to obtain a variety of information that is fed into our GPGPU analytical model. The analytical model greatly extends an existing model, the MWP-CWP model [9], with support for a new GPGPU architecture ("Fermi") and addresses other limitations. The performance advisor digests the model information and provides *interpretable* metrics to understand potential performance bottlenecks. That is, by inspecting particular terms or factors in the model, a programmer or an automated tool could, at least in principle, use the information directly to diagnose a bottleneck and perhaps prescribe a solution.

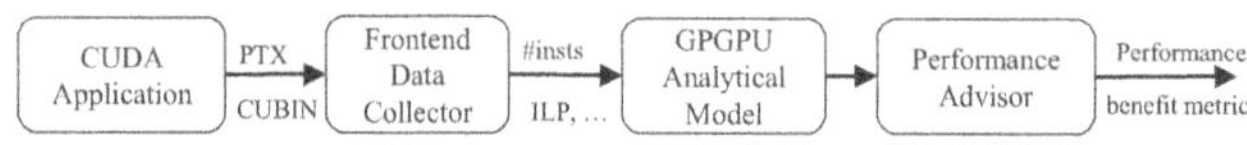

Figure 2. An overview of GPUPerf.

For clarity, this paper presents the framework in a "reverse order." It first describes the key potential benefit metrics output by the performance advisor to motivate the model, then explains the GPGPU analytical model, and lastly explains the detailed mechanisms of the frontend data collector. After that, to evaluate the framework, we apply it to six different computational kernels and 44 different optimizations for a particular computation. Furthermore, we carry out these evaluations on actual GPGPU hardware, based on the newest NVIDIA C2050 ("Fermi") system. The results show that our framework successfully differentiates the effects of various optimizations while providing interpretable metrics for potential bottlenecks.

In summary, our key contributions are as follows:

1. We present a comprehensive performance analysis framework, GPUPerf, that can be used to predict performance and understand bottlenecks for GPGPU applications.
2. We propose a simple yet powerful analytical model that is an enhanced version of the MWP-CWP model [9]. Specifically, we focus on improving the *differentiability* across distinct optimization techniques. In addition, by following the work-depth-graph formalism, our model provides a way to interpret model components and relates them directly to performance bottlenecks.
3. We propose several new metrics to *predict* potential performance benefits.

2. MWP-CWP Model

The analytical model developed for GPUPerf is based on the one that uses MWP and CWP [9]. We refer to this model as the MWP-CWP model in this paper. The MWP-CWP model takes the following inputs: the number of instructions, the number of memory requests, and memory access patterns, along with GPGPU architecture parameters such as DRAM latency and bandwidth. The total execution time for a given kernel is predicted based on the inputs. Although the model predicts execution cost fairly well, the understanding of performance bottlenecks from the model is not so straightforward. This is one of the major motivations of GPUPerf.

2.1 Background on the MWP-CWP Model

Figure 3 shows the MWP-CWP model. The detailed descriptions of the model can be found in [9]. Here, we breifly describe the key concepts of the model. The equations of MWP and CWP calculations are also presented in Appendix A.[1]

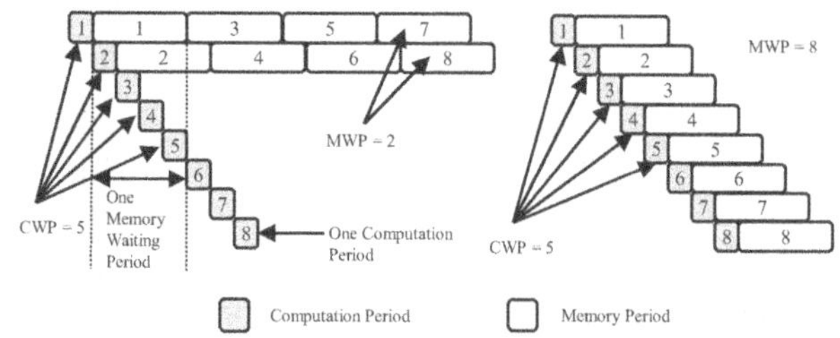

Figure 3. MWP-CWP model. (left: MWP < CWP, right: MWP > CWP)

Memory Warp Parallelism (MWP): MWP represents the maximum number of warps[2] per streaming multiprocessor (SM) [3] that can access the memory simultaneously. MWP is an indicator of memory-level parallelism that can be exploited but augmented to reflect GPGPU SIMD execution characteristics. MWP is a function of the memory bandwidth, certain parameters of memory operations such as latency, and the number of active warps in an SM. Roughly, the cost of memory operations is modeled to be the number of memory requests over MWP. Hence, modeling MWP correctly is very critical.

Computation Warp Parallelism (CWP): CWP represents the number of warps that can finish their one computation period during one memory waiting period plus *one*. For example, in Figure 3, CWP is 5 in both cases. One computation period is simply the average computation cycles per one memory instruction. CWP is mainly used to classify three cases, which are explained below.

Three Cases: The key component of the MWP-CWP model is identifying how much (and/or which) cost can be hidden by multi-threading in GPGPUs. Depending on the relationship between MWP and CWP, the MWP-CWP model classifies the three cases described below.

1. *MWP < CWP:* The cost of computation is hidden by memory operations, as shown in the left figure. The total execution cost is determined by memory operations.
2. *MWP >= CWP:* The cost of memory operations is hidden by computation, as shown in the right figure. The total execution cost is the sum of computation cost and one memory period.
3. *Not enough warps:* Due to the lack of parallelism, both computation and memory operation costs are only partially hidden.

2.2 Improvements over the MWP-CWP Model

Although the baseline model provides good prediction results for most GPGPU applications, some limitations make the model oblivious to certain optimization techniques. For instance, it assumes

[1] MWP and CWP calculations are updated for the analytical model in GPUPerf.

[2] Warp, a group of 32 threads, is a unit of execution in a GPGPU.

[3] SM and core are used interchangeably in this paper.

that a memory instruction is always followed by consecutive dependent instructions; hence, MLP is always one. Also, it ideally assumes that there is enough instruction-level parallelism. Thus, it is difficult to predict the effect of prefetching or other optimizations that increase instruction/memory-level parallelism.

Cache Effect: Recent GPGPU architectures such as NVIDIA's Fermi GPGPUs have a hardware-managed cache memory hierarchy. Since the baseline model does not model cache effects, the total memory cycles are determined by multiplying memory requests and the average global memory latency. We simply model the cache effect by calculating average memory access latency (AMAT); the total memory cycles are calculated by multiplying memory requests and AMAT.

SFU Instruction: In GPGPUs, expensive math operations such as transcendentals and square roots can be handled with dedicated execution units called *special function units* (SFUs). Since the execution of SFU instructions can be overlapped with other floating point (FP) instructions, with a good ratio between SFU and FP instructions, the cost of SFU instructions can almost be hidden. Otherwise, SFU contention can hurt performance. We model these characteristics of special function units.

Parallelism: The baseline model assumes that ILP and TLP are enough to hide instruction latency, thereby using the *peak* instruction throughput when calculating computation cycles. However, when ILP and TLP are not high enough to hide the pipeline latency, the effective instruction throughput is less than the peak value. In addition, we incorporate the MLP effect into the new model. MLP can reduce total memory cycles.

Binary-level Analysis: The MWP-CWP model only uses information at the PTX level.[4] Since there are code optimization phases *after* the PTX code generation, using only the PTX-level information prevents precise modeling. We develop static analysis tools to extract the binary-level information and also utilize hardware performance counters to address this issue.

3. Performance Advisor

The goal of the performance advisor is to convey performance bottleneck information and estimate the potential gains from reducing or eliminating these bottlenecks. It does so through four potential benefit metrics, whose impact can be visualized using a chart as illustrated by Figure 4. The x-axis shows the cost of memory operations and the y-axis shows the cost of computation. An application code is a point on this chart (here, point A). The sum of the x-axis and y-axis values is the execution cost, but because computation and memory costs can be overlapped, the final execution cost of T_{exec} (e.g., wallclock time) is a different point, A', shifted relative to A. The shift amount is denoted as $T_{overlap}$. A diagonal line through $y = x$ divides the chart into *compute bound* and *memory bound* zones, indicating whether an application is limited by computation or memory operations, respectively. From point A', the benefit chart shows how each of the four different potential benefit metrics moves the application execution time in this space.

A given algorithm may be further characterized by two additional values. The first is the ideal computation cost, which is generally the minimum time to execute all of the essential computational work (e.g., floating point operations), denoted T_{fp} in Figure 4. The second is the minimum time to move all data from the DRAM to the cores, denoted by T_{mem_min}. When memory requests are prefetched or all memory service is hidden by other computation, we might hope to hide or perhaps eliminate all of the memory operation costs. Ideally, an algorithm designer or programmer could provide estimates or bounds on T_{fp} and T_{mem_min}. However,

[4] PTX is an intermediate representation used before register allocation and instruction scheduling.

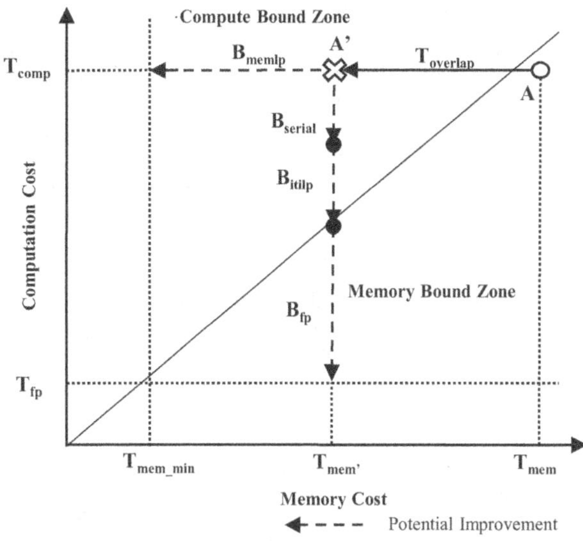

Figure 4. Potential performance benefits, illustrated.

when the information is not available, we could try to estimate T_{fp} from, say, the number of executed FP instructions in the kernel.[5]

Suppose that we have a kernel, at point A', having different kinds of inefficiencies. Our computed benefit factors aim to quantify the degree of improvement possible through the elimination of these inefficiencies. We use four potential benefit metrics, summarized as follows.

- B_{itilp} indicates the potential benefit by increasing inter-thread instruction-level parallelism.
- B_{memlp} indicates the potential benefit by increasing memory-level parallelism.
- B_{fp} represents the potential benefit when we ideally remove the cost of inefficient computation. Unlike other benefits, we cannot achieve the 100% of B_{fp} because a kernel must have some operations such as data movements.
- B_{serial} shows the amount of savings when we get rid of the overhead due to serialization effects such as synchronization and resource contention.

B_{itilp}, B_{fp}, and B_{serial} are related to the computation cost, while B_{memlp} is associated with the memory cost. These metrics are summarized in Table 1.

Name	Description	Unit
T_{exec}	Final predicted execution time	cost
T_{comp}	Computation cost	cost
T_{mem}	Memory cost	cost
$T_{overlap}$	Overlapped cost due to multi-threading	cost
T'_{mem}	$T_{mem} - T_{overlap}$	cost
T_{fp}	Ideal T_{comp}	ideal cost
T_{mem_min}	Ideal T_{mem}	ideal cost
B_{serial}	Benefits of removing serialization effects	benefit
B_{itilp}	Benefits of increasing inter-thread ILP	benefit
B_{memlp}	Benefits of increasing MLP	benefit
B_{fp}	Benefits of improving computing efficiency	benefit

Table 1. Summary of performance guidance metrics.

[5] In our evaluation we also use the number of FP operations to calculate T_{fp}.

4. GPGPU Analytical Model

In this section we present an analytical model to generate the performance metrics described in Section 3. The input parameters to the analytical model are summarized in Table 2.

4.1 Performance Prediction

First, we define T_{exec} as the overall execution time, which is a function of T_{comp}, T_{mem}, and $T_{overlap}$, as shown in Equation (1).

$$T_{exec} = T_{comp} + T_{mem} - T_{overlap} \tag{1}$$

As illustrated in Figure 4, the execution time is calculated by adding computation and memory costs while subtracting the overlapped cost due to the multi-threading feature in GPGPUs. Each of the three inputs of Equation (1) is described in the following.

4.1.1 Calculating the Computation Cost, T_{comp}

T_{comp} is the amount of time to execute compute instructions (excluding memory operation waiting time, but including the cost of executing memory instructions) and is evaluated using Equations (2) through (10).

We consider the computation cost as two components, a parallelizable base execution time plus overhead costs due to serialization effects:

$$T_{comp} = \underbrace{W_{parallel}}_{\text{Base}} + \underbrace{W_{serial}}_{\text{Overhead}} . \tag{2}$$

The base time, $W_{parallel}$, accounts for the number of operations and degree of parallelism, and is computed from basic instruction and hardware values as shown in Equation (3):

$$W_{parallel} = \underbrace{\frac{\#\text{insts} \times \#\text{total\_warps}}{\#\text{active\_SMs}}}_{\text{Total instructions per SM}} \times \underbrace{\frac{\text{avg\_inst\_lat}}{\text{ITILP}}}_{\text{Effective throughput}} . \tag{3}$$

The first factor in Equation (3) is the total number of instructions that an SM executes, and the second factor indicates the *effective* instruction throughput. Regarding the latter, the average instruction latency, avg_inst_lat, can be approximated by the latency of FP operations in GPGPUs. When necessary, it can also be precisely calculated by taking into account the instruction mix and the latency of individual instructions on the underlying hardware. The value, ITILP, models the possibility of inter-thread instruction-level parallelism in GPGPUs. In particular, instructions may issue from multiple warps on a GPGPU; thus, we consider global ILP (i.e., ILP among warps) rather than warp-local ILP (i.e., ILP of one warp). That is, ITILP represents how much ILP is available among all executing to hide the pipeline latency.

ITILP can be obtained as follows:

$$\text{ITILP} = \min\left(\text{ILP} \times N, \text{ITILP}_{max}\right) \tag{4}$$

$$\text{ITILP}_{max} = \frac{\text{avg\_inst\_lat}}{\text{warp\_size}/\text{SIMD\_width}}, \tag{5}$$

where N is the number of active warps on one SM, and SIMD_width and warp_size represent the number of vector units and the number of threads per warp, respectively. On the Fermi architecture, SIMD_width $=$ warp_size $= 32$. ITILP cannot be greater than ITILP_{max}, which is the ITILP required to fully hide pipeline latency.

We model serialization overheads, W_{serial} from Equation (2), as

$$W_{serial} = O_{sync} + O_{SFU} + O_{CFdiv} + O_{bank}, \tag{6}$$

where each of the four terms represents a source of overhead—synchronization, SFU resource contention, control-flow divergence, and shared memory bank conflicts. We describe each overhead below.

Synchronization Overhead, O_{sync}: When there is a synchronization point, the instructions after the synchronization point cannot be executed until all the threads reach the point. If all threads are making the same progress, there would be little overhead for the waiting time. Unfortunately, each thread (warp) makes its own progress based on the availability of source operands; a range of progress exists and sometimes it could be wide. The causes of this range are mainly different DRAM access latencies (delaying in queues, DRAM row buffer hit/miss etc.) and control-flow divergences. As a result, when a high number of memory instructions and synchronization instructions exist, the overhead increases as shown in Equations (7) and (8):

$$O_{sync} = \frac{\#\text{sync\_insts} \times \#\text{total\_warps}}{\#\text{active\_SMs}} \times F_{sync} \tag{7}$$

$$F_{sync} = \Gamma \times \text{avg\_DRAM\_lat} \times \underbrace{\frac{\#\text{mem\_insts}}{\#\text{insts}}}_{\text{Mem. ratio}}, \tag{8}$$

where Γ is a machine-dependent parameter. We chose 64 for the modeled architecture based on microarchitecture simulations.

SFU Resource Contention Overhead, O_{SFU}: This cost is mainly caused by the characteristics of special function units (SFUs) and is computed using Equations (9) and (10) below. As described in Section 2.2, the visible execution cost of SFU instructions depends on the ratio of SFU instructions to others and the number of execution units for each instruction type. In Equation (9), the *visibility* is modeled by F_{SFU}, which is in $[0, 1]$. A value of $F_{SFU} = 0$ means none of the SFU execution costs is added to the total execution time. This occurs when the SFU instruction ratio is less than the ratio of special function to SIMD units as shown in Equation (10).

$$O_{SFU} = \frac{\#\text{SFU\_insts} \times \#\text{total\_warps}}{\#\text{active\_SMs}} \times \underbrace{\frac{\text{warp\_size}}{\text{SFU\_width}}}_{\text{SFU throughput}} \times F_{SFU} \tag{9}$$

$$F_{SFU} = \min\left\{\max\left\{\underbrace{\frac{\#\text{SFU\_insts}}{\#\text{insts}}}_{\text{SFU inst. ratio}} - \underbrace{\frac{\text{SFU\_width}}{\text{SIMD\_width}}}_{\text{SFU exec. unit ratio}}, 0\right\}, 1\right\}. \tag{10}$$

Control-Flow Divergence and Bank Conflict Overheads, O_{CFdiv} and O_{bank}: The overhead of control-flow divergence (O_{CFdiv}) is the cost of executing additional instructions due, for instance, to divergent branches [9]. This cost is modeled by counting all the instructions in both paths. The cost of bank conflicts (O_{bank}) can be calculated by measuring the number of shared memory bank conflicts. Both O_{CFdiv} and O_{bank} can be measured using hardware counters. However, for control-flow divergence, we use our instruction analyzer (Section 5.2), which provides more detailed statistics.

4.1.2 Calculating the Memory Access Cost, T_{mem}

T_{mem} represents the amount of time spent on memory requests and transfers. This cost is a function of the number of memory requests, memory latency per each request, and the degree of memory-level parallelism. We model T_{mem} using Equation (11),

$$T_{mem} = \underbrace{\frac{\#\text{mem\_insts} \times \#\text{total\_warps}}{\#\text{active\_SMs} \times \text{ITMLP}}}_{\text{Effective memory requests per SM}} \times \text{AMAT}, \tag{11}$$

where AMAT models the average memory access time, accounting for cache effects. We compute AMAT using Equations (12) and (13):

$$\text{AMAT} = \text{avg\_DRAM\_lat} \times \text{miss\_ratio} + \text{hit\_lat} \quad (12)$$

$$\text{avg\_DRAM\_lat} = \text{DRAM\_lat} + (\text{avg\_trans\_warp} - 1) \times \Delta. \quad (13)$$

avg_DRAM_lat represents the average DRAM access latency and is a function of the baseline DRAM access latency, DRAM_lat, and transaction departure delay, Δ. In GPGPUs, memory requests can split into multiple transactions. In our model, avg_trans_warp represents the average number of transactions per memory request in a warp. Note that it is possible to expand Equation (12) for multiple levels of cache, which we omit for brevity.

We model the degree of memory-level parallelism through a notion of inter-thread MLP, denoted ITMLP, which we define as the number of memory requests per SM that is concurrently serviced. Similar to ITILP, memory requests from different warps can be overlapped. Since MLP is an indicator of intra-warp memory-level parallelism, we need to consider the overlap factor of multiple warps. ITMLP can be calculated using Equations (14) and (15).

$$\text{ITMLP} = \min\left(\text{MLP} \times \text{MWP}_{\text{cp}}, \text{MWP}_{\text{peak\_bw}}\right) \quad (14)$$

$$\text{MWP}_{\text{cp}} = \min\left(\max\left(1, \text{CWP} - 1\right), \text{MWP}\right) \quad (15)$$

In Equation (14), MWP_{cp} represents the number of warps whose memory requests are overlapped during one computation period. As described in Section 2.1, MWP represents the *maximum* number of warps that can simultaneously access memory. However, depending on CWP, the number of warps that can concurrently issue memory requests is limited.

$\text{MWP}_{\text{peak\_bw}}$ represents the number of memory warps per SM under peak memory bandwidth. Since the value is equivalent to the maximum number of memory requests attainable per SM, ITMLP cannot be greater than $\text{MWP}_{\text{peak\_bw}}$.

4.1.3 Calculating the Overlapped Cost, T_{overlap}

T_{overlap} represents how much the memory access cost can be hidden by multi-threading. In the GPGPU execution, when a warp issues a memory request and waits for the requested data, the execution is switched to another warp. Hence, T_{comp} and T_{mem} can be overlapped to some extent. For instance, if multi-threading hides all memory access costs, T_{overlap} will equal T_{mem}. That is, in this case the overall execution time, T_{exec}, is solely determined by the computation cost, T_{comp}. By contrast, if none of the memory accesses can be hidden in the worst case, then T_{overlap} is 0.

We compute T_{overlap} using Equations (16) and (17). In these equations, F_{overlap} approximates how much T_{comp} and T_{mem} overlap and N represents the number of active warps per SM as in Equation (4). Note that F_{overlap} varies with both MWP and CWP. When CWP is greater than MWP (e.g., an application limited by memory operations), then F_{overlap} becomes 1, which means all of T_{comp} can be overlapped with T_{mem}. On the other hand, when MWP is greater than CWP (e.g., an application limited by computation), only part of computation costs can be overlapped.

$$T_{\text{overlap}} = \min(T_{\text{comp}} \times F_{\text{overlap}}, T_{\text{mem}}) \quad (16)$$

$$F_{\text{overlap}} = \frac{N - \zeta}{N}, \quad \zeta = \begin{cases} 1 \ (\text{CWP} \leq \text{MWP}) \\ 0 \ (\text{CWP} > \text{MWP}) \end{cases} \quad (17)$$

4.2 Potential Benefit Prediction

As discussed in Section 3, the potential benefit metrics indicate performance improvements when it is possible to eliminate the delta between the ideal performance and the current performance. Equations (18) and (19) are used to estimate the ideal compute and memory performance (time). Alternatively, an algorithm developer might provide these estimates.

Model Parameter	Definition	Source
#insts	# of total insts. per warp (excluding SFU insts.)	Sec. 5.1
#mem_insts	# of memory insts. per warp	Sec. 5.1
#sync_insts	# of synchronization insts. per warp	Sec. 5.2
#SFU_insts	# of SFU insts. per warp	Sec. 5.2
#FP_insts	# of floating point insts. per warp	Sec. 5.2
#total_warps	Total number warps in a kernel	Sec. 5.1
#active_SMs	# of active SMs	Sec. 5.1
N	# of concurrently running warps on one SM	Sec. 5.1
AMAT	Average memory access latency	Sec. 5.1
avg_trans_warp	Average memory transactions per memory request	Sec. 5.2
avg_inst_lat	Average instruction latency	Sec. 5.2
miss_ratio	Cache miss ratio	Sec. 5.1
size_of_data	The size of input data	source code
ILP	Inst.-level parallelism in one warp	Sec. 5.3
MLP	Memory-level parallelism in one warp	Sec. 5.3
MWP (Per SM)	Max #warps that can concurrently access memory	Appx.A
CWP (Per SM)	# of warps executed during one mem. period plus one	Appx.A
$\text{MWP}_{\text{peak\_bw}}$ (Per SM)	MWP under peak memory BW	Appx.A
warp_size	# of threads per warp	32
Γ	Machine parameter for sync cost	64
Δ	Transaction departure delay	Table 3
DRAM_lat	Baseline DRAM access latency	Table 3
FP_lat	FP instruction latency	Table 3
hit_lat	Cache hit latency	Table 3
SIMD_width	# of scalar processors (SPs) per SM	Table 3
SFU_width	# of special function units (SFUs) per SM	Table 3

Table 2. Summary of input parameters used in equations.

$$T_{\text{fp}} = \frac{\#\text{FP\_insts} \times \#\text{total\_warps} \times \text{FP\_lat}}{\#\text{active\_SMs} \times \text{ITILP}} \quad (18)$$

$$T_{\text{mem\_min}} = \frac{\text{size\_of\_data} \times \text{avg\_DRAM\_lat}}{\text{MWP}_{\text{peak\_bw}}} \quad (19)$$

Then, the benefit metrics are obtained using Equations (20)-(23), where $\text{ITILP}_{\text{max}}$ is defined in Equation (5):

$$B_{\text{itilp}} = W_{\text{parallel}} - \frac{\#\text{insts} \times \#\text{total\_warps} \times \text{avg\_inst\_lat}}{\#\text{active\_SMs} \times \text{ITILP}_{\text{max}}} \quad (20)$$

$$B_{\text{serial}} = W_{\text{serial}} \quad (21)$$

$$B_{\text{fp}} = T_{\text{comp}} - T_{\text{fp}} - B_{\text{itilp}} - B_{\text{serial}} \quad (22)$$

$$B_{\text{memlp}} = \max\left(T'_{\text{mem}} - T_{\text{mem\_min}}, 0\right). \quad (23)$$

5. Frontend Data Collector

As described in Section 4, the GPGPU analytical model requires a variety of information on the actual binary execution. In our framework, the frontend data collector does the best in accurately obtaining various types of information that instantiates the analytical model. For this purpose, the frontend data collector uses three different tools/ways to extract the information: compute visual profiler, instruction analyzer (IA), and static analysis tools, as shown in Figure 5.

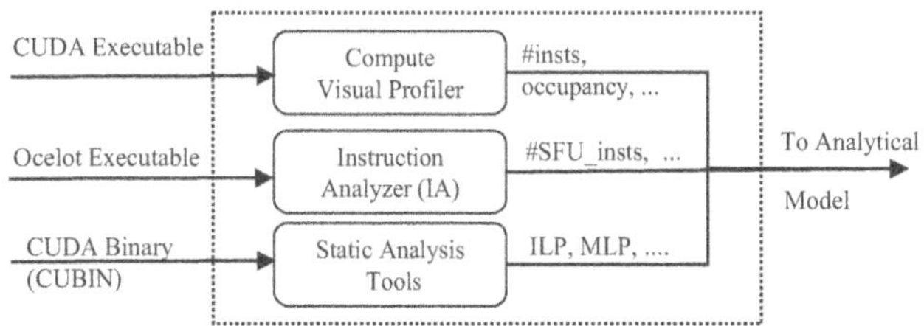

Figure 5. Frontend data collector.

5.1 Compute Visual Profiler

We use Compute Visual Profiler [14] to access GPU hardware performance counters. It provides accurate architecture-related information: occupancy, total number of global load/store requests, the number of registers used in a thread, the number of DRAM reads/writes and cache hits/misses.

5.2 Instruction Analyzer

Although the hardware performance counters provide accurate runtime information, we still cannot obtain some crucial information. For example, instruction category information, which is essential for considering the effects of synchronization and the overhead of SFU utilization, is not available.

Our instruction analyzer module is based on Ocelot [6], a dynamic compilation framework that emulates PTX execution. The instruction analyzer collects instruction mixture (SFU, Sync, and FP instructions) and loop information such as loop trip counts. The loop information is used to combine static analysis from CUDA binary (CUBIN) files and run-time execution information. Although there is code optimization from PTX to CUBIN, we observe that most loop information still remains the same.

5.3 Static Analysis Tools

Our static analysis tools work on PTX, CUBIN and the information from IA. The main motivation for using static analysis is to obtain ILP and MLP information in binaries rather than in PTX code. Due to instruction scheduling and register allocation, which are performed during target code generation, the degree of parallelism between PTX and CUBIN can be significantly different. Hence, it is crucial to calculate ILP/MLP on binaries.

First, we disassemble a target CUBIN file with cuobjdump [13]. We then build a control flow graph (CFG) and def-use chains with the disassembled instructions. The number of memory requests between a load request (def) and the first instruction that sources the memory request (use) is a local MLP. The average of local MLPs in a basic block is the basic block MLP. For ILP, we group the instructions that can be scheduled together within a basic block. (If an instruction has true dependencies to any of other instructions, they cannot be issued at the same cycle.) Then, the basic block ILP is the number of instructions in the basic block over the number of groups in the block.

Second, we combine this static ILP/MLP information with the dynamic information from IA.[6] Basically, we give high weights to ILP/MLP based on basic block execution frequency. The following equation shows the exact formula. In the equation, ILP/MLP for basic block (BB) K is denoted as ILP(MLP)_K. $\text{ILP(MLP)}_\text{AVG}$ is the same as ILP/MLP in Equations (4) and (14).

$$\text{ILP(MLP)}_\text{AVG} = \sum_{\text{K}=1}^{\#\text{BBs}} \frac{\text{ILP(MLP)}_\text{K} \times \#\text{accesses\_to\_BB}_\text{K}}{\#\text{basic\_blocks}}$$

6. Results

Evaluation: Our evaluation consists of two major parts.

- We show that our GPGPU analytical model improves over the prior state-of-the-art for current generation Fermi-based GPUs (Section 6.1). Since this model is the basis for our benefit analysis, validating is critical.
- We show how the benefit metrics can be applied to a variety of GPGPU codes (Sections 6.2–6.4). Our goal is to see to what extent our benefit metrics can help assess potential performance bottlenecks and candidate optimizations.

[6] We match loop information from IA and basic block information from static analysis to estimate the basic block execution counts.

Processor Model: For all of our experiments, we use NVIDIA's Tesla C2050, whose hardware specifications appear in Table 3. Memory model parameters used in this study (DRAM_lat and Δ) are measured using known techniques [9], while cache latencies and FP latency are obtained using micro-benchmarks which we design for this study. We use the default L1/shared configuration where the cache sizes are 16KB and 48KB, respectively. We use the CUDA 3.2 Toolkit.

Workloads: For Section 6.1, we use micro-benchmarks that are designed to have different ILP values and FMA (fused multiply-add) instructions. For real code, we select the workloads using the following criteria: kernels from a full application (Section 6.2), CUDA SDK (Section 6.3), and a public benchmark suite (Section 6.4).

Model	Tesla C2050
Processor clock	1.15 GHz
Memory bandwidth	144.0 GB/s
Compute capability	2.0
The number of SMs	14
The number of SPs (per SM)	32
The number of SFUs (per SM)	4
Shared memory (per SM)	48 KB
L1 cache (per SM)	16 KB
L2 cache	768 KB
FP latency, FP_lat	18
DRAM latency, DRAM_lat	440
Departure delay, Δ	20
L1 cache latency	18
L2 cache latency	130

Table 3. The specifications of the GPGPU and model parameters used in this study.

6.1 Improvements of the Analytical Model

Inter-Thread ILP, ITILP in Eq. (4): Figure 6 shows the performance measured on Tesla C2050 when we have different ILP and TLP for the same kernel. For instance, ILP=2 indicates that all warps have the same ILP value of two. The x-axis represents TLP as the number of active warps per SM, and the y-axis is normalized to the performance when both ILP and TLP are one. The result shows that increasing ITILP leads to a performance improvement up to some points by providing more parallelism, but after the points, it does not help improve performance by merely increasing ILP or TLP. In the graph, the performance becomes stable at the points where ITILP is around 18-24. (The number of warps is 18 for ILP=1, 10 for ILP=2, and eight for ILP=3.) As shown in Figure 7, our analytical model captures this effect and provides better analysis by modeling ITILP, which is not considered in the MWP-CWP model. Figure 7 also shows that B_itilp adequately estimates the possible performance gains by providing inter-thread ILP.

Awareness of SFU Contentions, O_SFU in Eq. (9): Figure 8 shows the execution time and B_serial when we vary the number of SFU instructions per eight FMA instructions. The line graphs represent the actual execution and the predicted time of MWP-CWP and new models, while the bar graph shows B_serial normalized to the predicted time of each variation. The result shows that the cost of SFU instructions is almost hidden when there is one SFU instruction per eight FMAs. As the number of SFU instructions increases, however, the execution of SFU instructions significantly contributes to the total execution time, and our model adequately reflects the overhead cost while the MWP-CWP model fails to predict the overhead. In addition, B_serial indicates that the serialization

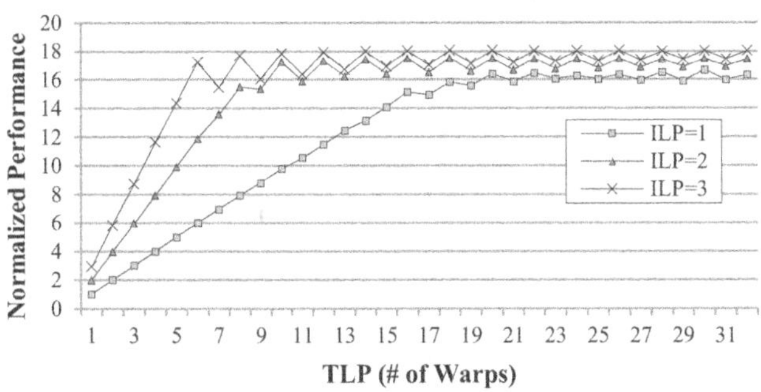

Figure 6. ITILP micro-benchmark on Tesla C2050.

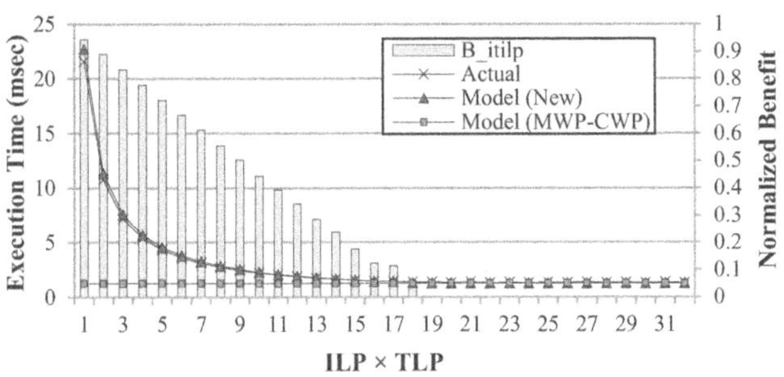

Figure 7. ITILP: Comparison between MWP-CWP and new models.

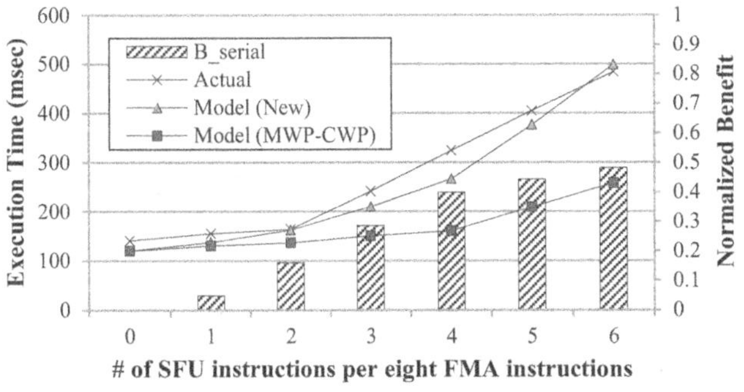

Figure 8. The execution time and B_{serial} when increasing the number of SFU instructions per eight FMA instructions.

effects might be the performance bottleneck, which implies that the ratio of SFU and FMA instructions is not optimal.

Code optimization effects: As we have discussed in Section 2.2, our model improves on the previously proposed the MWP-CWP model in a way that can differentiate distinct optimizations. Figure 9 shows the comparisons between the two models for real code of FMM_U (Section 6.2). The y-axis shows the performance improvements when different optimization techniques are applied to the baseline in FMM_U. The result shows that our model successfully predicts the performance impact resulting from code optimizations, but the MWP-CWP model often estimates the benefit as less than the actual one, or even the opposite. For instance, although prefetching improves performance in real hardware, the MWP-CWP model predicts that the optimization leads to a performance degradation. In general, as shown in Figure 9, our model can estimate the performance delta resulting from several code optimizations more accurately than the MWP-CWP model.

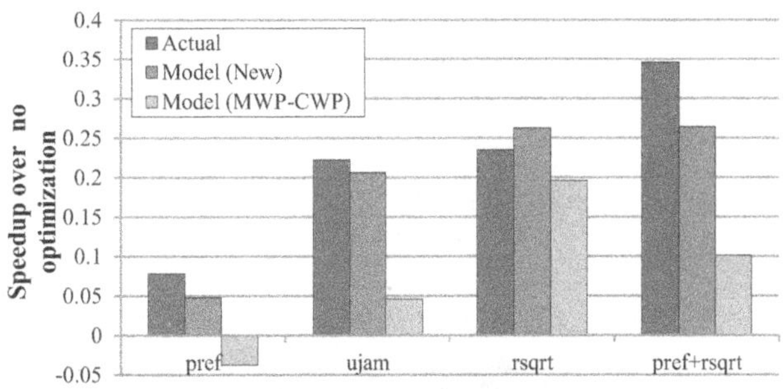

Figure 9. The performance improvement prediction over the baseline FMM_U of the MWP-CWP and our models.

6.2 Case Study of Using the Model: FMM_U

We apply our model to an implementation of the *fast multipole method* (FMM), an $O(n)$ approximation method for n-body computations, which normally scale as $O(n^2)$ [8]. We specifically consider the most expensive phase of the FMM, called the *U-list* phase (FMM_U), which is a good target for GPU acceleration. The FMM_U phase appears as pseudocode in Algorithm 1.

Algorithm 1 FMM_U algorithm

1: **for** each *target* leaf node, B **do**
2:     **for** each *target* point $t \in B$ **do**
3:         **for** each neighboring *source* node, $S \in U(B)$ **do**
4:             **for** each *source* point $s \in S$ **do**
5:                 ϕ_t += $F(s, t)$ /* E.g., force evaluation */

The parallelism and dependency structure are straightforward. The loop iterations at line 1 are completely independent, as are those at line 2. Using an owner-computes assignment of threads to targets is natural. The loop in lines 4–5 implements a reduction. There is considerable data reuse; the sizes of B and S in Algorithm 1 are always bounded by some constant q, and there are $O(q^2)$ operations on $O(q)$ data, where q is typically $O(1,000)$. The FMM_U is typically compute bound.

6.2.1 FMM Optimizations

Prefetching (pref): Prefetching generates memory requests in advance of their use to avoid stalls. For FMM_U, the data access patterns are fairly predictable. We consider prefetching $s \in S$ into registers. On current GPUs, explicit software prefetching can help since there are no hardware prefetchers. Prefetching can increase memory- and instruction-level parallelism.

Use Shared Memory (shmem): To limit register pressure, we can use shared memory (scratchpad space) instead. In FMM_U, it is natural to use this space to store large blocks of S. This approach yields two benefits. First, we increase memory-level parallelism. Second, we increase the reuse of source points for all targets.

Unroll-and-Jam (ujam): To increase register-level reuse of the target points, we can unroll the loop at line 2 and then fuse (or "jam") the replicated loop bodies. The net effects are to reduce branches, thereby increasing ILP, as well as to increase reuse of each source point s. The trade-off is that this technique can also increase register live time, thereby increasing the register pressure.

Data Layout (trans): When we load points data into GPU shared memory, we can store these points using an array-of-structures (AoS) or structure-of-arrays (SoA) format. By default, we use SoA; the "trans" optimization uses AoS.

Vector Packing (vecpack): Vector packing "packs" multiple memory requests with short data size into a larger request, such as

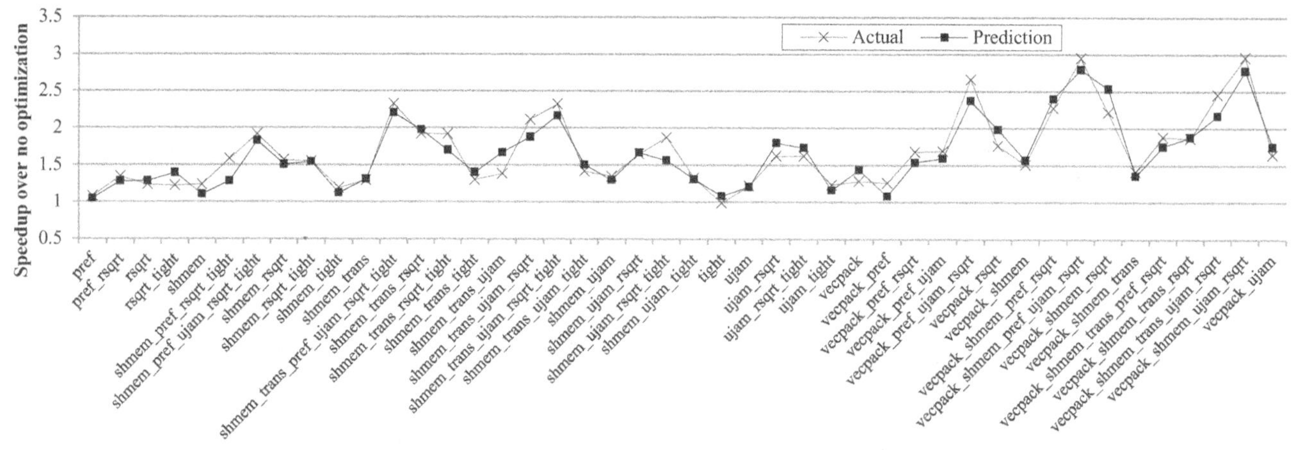

Figure 10. Speedup over the baseline of actual execution and model prediction on 44 different optimizations.

replacing four separate 32-bit requests into a single 128-bit request, which can be cheaper. This technique increases MLP as well as reduces the number of instructions. Vector packing is also essentially a structure-of-arrays to array-of-structures transformation.

Tight (tight): The "tight" optimization utilizes the 'float4' datatype to pack data elements. However, this technique is different from vecpack above since it still issues four of the 32-bit memory requests.

Reciprocal Square Root - SFU (rsqrt): Our FMM_U can replace separate divide and square root operations with a single reciprocal square-root. This exploits the dedicated special function unit (SFU) hardware available for single-precision transcendental and multiplication instructions on NVIDIA GPUs.

6.2.2 Performance Prediction

Figure 10 shows the speedup over the baseline kernel of actual execution and its prediction using the proposed model. The x-axis shows the code optimization space, where 44 optimization combinations are presented. The results show that, overall, the model closely estimates the speedup of different optimizations. More importantly, the proposed model follows the trend and finds the best optimization combinations, which makes our model suitable for identifying potential performance benefits.

6.2.3 Potential Benefit Prediction

To understand the performance optimization guide metrics, we first compute potential benefit metrics for the baseline, which are as follows: $B_{\text{serial}} = 0$, $B_{\text{memlp}} = 0$, $B_{\text{itilp}} = 6068$, and $B_{\text{fp}} = 9691$. Even from the baseline, it is already limited by computation. Hence, techniques to reduce the cost of computation are critical.

Figure 11 shows actual performance benefits and B_{itilp} when the shared memory optimization (*shmem*) is applied on top of different combinations of optimizations. For example, *ujam* indicates the performance delta between *ujam* and *ujam* + *shmem* optimizations. In the graph, both *Actual* and B_{itilp} are normalized to the execution time before *shmem* is applied. Using the shared memory improves both MLP and ILP. It increases the reuse of source points, which also increases ILP. Hence, the benefit of using the shared memory can be predicted using B_{itilp}, because $B_{\text{memlp}} = 0$. As shown in the figure, B_{itilp} predicts the actual performance benefit closely for most of the optimization combinations except *tight* optimizations. The interaction between *shmem* and *tight* optimizations should be analyzed further.

Figure 12 represents the performance speedup and potential benefits normalized to the baseline execution time when optimizations are applied one by one. For the baseline, a high B_{fp} value indicates that the kernel might have the potential to be improved. Hence, it is a reasonable decision to try to optimize the baseline kernel. As we apply adequate optimization techniques that improve the kernel, the potential benefit decreases. When *vecpack*, *rsqrt*, *shmem* and *ujam* have been applied, the potential benefit metric indicates that the kernel may have very small amount of inefficient

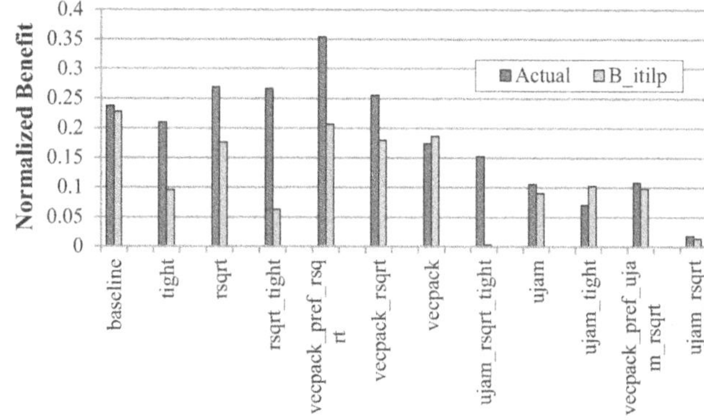

Figure 11. Actual performance benefit and B_{itilp} when *shmem* is applied to each optimization in the x-axis.

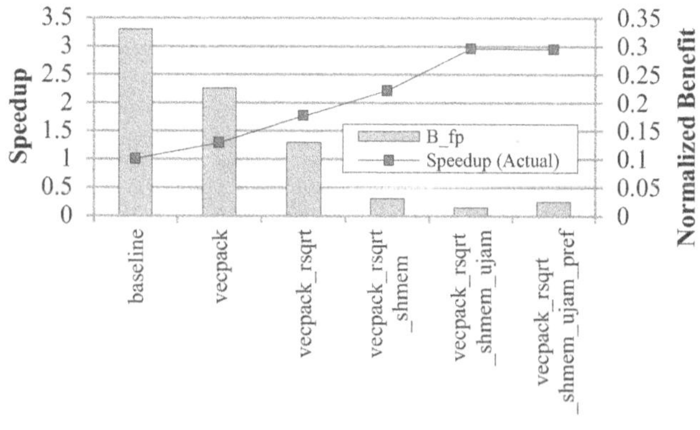

Figure 12. Performance speedup and potential benefits when applying optimizations to the baseline one by one.

computation and the potential performance gain through further optimizations might be limited. As shown in the last bar, $pref$ does not lead to a performance improvement. Rather, B_{fp} slightly increases due to the inefficient computation for prefetching code.

6.3 Reduction

6.3.1 Optimization Techniques

Reduction has seven different kernels (K0–K6) to which different optimization techniques are applied. Table 4 shows the optimization techniques applied to each kernel.

Eliminating Divergent Branches: Branch divergence occurs if threads in a warp take different paths due to conditional branches. When a warp executes divergent branches, it serially executes both branch paths while disabling threads that are not on the current path. By eliminating divergent branches, we can increase the utilization of the execution units.

Eliminating Shared Memory Bank Conflicts: Eliminating bank conflicts causes shared memory banks to be serviced simultaneously to any shared memory read or write requests.

Reducing Idle Threads: As reduction proceeds, the number of threads that work on data reduces. Thus, this technique packs more computations into threads, thereby reducing the number of idle threads.

Loop Unrolling: As described in Section 6.2, loop unrolling alleviates the loop overhead while eliminating branch-related instructions. Thus, reducing the number of instructions will improve performance for compute-bound kernels.

	K0	K1	K2	K3	K4	K5	K6
Eliminating Divergent Branches		O	O	O	O	O	O
Eliminating Bank Conflicts			O	O	O	O	O
Reducing Idle Threads (Single)				O	O	O	
Loop Unrolling (Last Warp)					O		
Loop Unrolling (Completed)						O	O
Reducing Idle Threads (Multiple)							O

Table 4. Optimization techniques on reduction kernels.

6.3.2 Results

Figure 13 shows the actual execution time and the outcome of the analytical model. The model closely estimates the execution time over optimizations. Figure 14 shows the benefit X-Y chart of the reduction kernels. From K0 to K5, the kernels are in the compute-bounded zone. All the memory operation cost is hidden because the cost of computation is higher than that of memory operations; thus, B_{memlp} is zero because of $T'_{mem} = 0$. In addition, even from the K0 kernel, the ITILP value is already the peak value, so B_{itilp} is also zero.

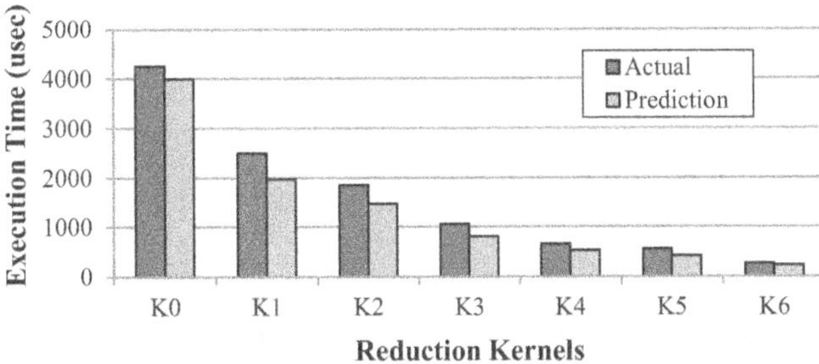

Figure 13. Actual and model execution time of the reduction kernels.

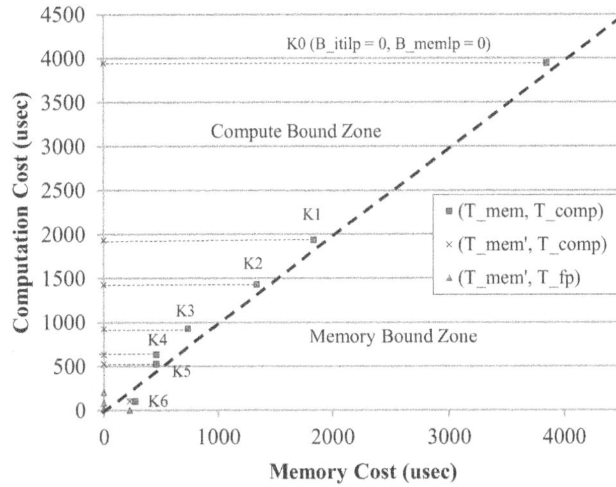

Figure 14. Benefit X-Y chart of the reduction kernels.

From the chart, we can observe that there are huge gaps between the (T'_{mem}, T_{comp}) and (T'_{mem}, T_{fp}) of each kernel, which implies that the kernels suffer from computing inefficiency. Once we eliminate most of the inefficiency of computation, kernel (K6) becomes memory bounded.

The benefit X-Y chart also indicates that, although some optimization techniques attempt to reduce the overhead of serialization, the actual benefits mainly come from improving the efficiency of computation. In particular, the number of instructions was significantly reduced by each optimization, which proves our findings.

6.4 Parboil Benchmark

6.4.1 Optimization Techniques

Parboil [17] has algorithm-specific optimization techniques. In this section we explain each of them briefly. Table 5 shows the techniques applied to the evaluated applications.

Regularization: This optimization is a preprocessing step that converts irregular workloads into regular ones. In order to do so, the workloads can be spread over multiple kernels or even to CPUs.

Binning: This optimization pre-sorts input elements into multiple bins based on location in space. For each grid point, only bins within a certain distance are used for computation, thereby preventing each thread from reading the entire input.

Coarsening: Thread coarsening is a technique in which each thread works on several elements instead of one to amortize redundant computation overhead.

Tiling/Data Reuse: This optimization moves data, which can be shared by multiple threads, into the shared memory to reduce global memory accesses. To maximize the advantage of the shared memory, computation is distributed among threads.

Privatization: Privatization allows each thread to have its own copy of output data. The results from all threads are later combined when all the writings from all threads are finished. This technique alleviates the contention of write accesses to the same output data by multiple threads.

6.4.2 Results

Figure 15 shows the actual and predicted time for the applications in the parboil benchmarks. The results show that the optimization techniques for `cutcp` are effective, while the techniques for `tpacf` fail to effectively optimize the kernel. Our model also predicts the same.

	cutcp	tpacf	Potential Benefit Metrics
Regularization	O		B_{fp}
Binning	O		B_{fp}
Coarsening	O		B_{fp}
Tiling/Data Reuse		O	B_{memlp}, B_{fp}
Privatization		O	B_{memlp}, B_{serial}, B_{itilp}

Table 5. Optimization techniques on the evaluated applications and relevant potential benefit metrics.

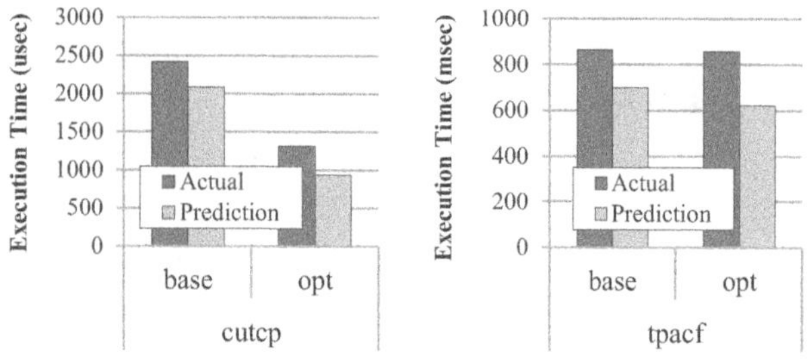

Figure 15. Actual and predicted time of cutcp and tpacf in the parboil benchmarks.

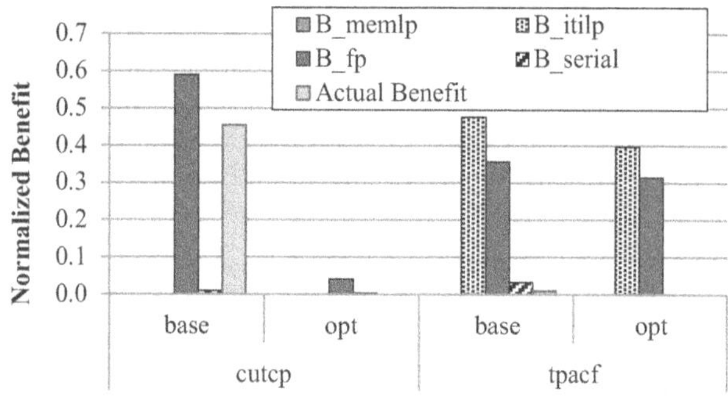

Figure 16. Benefit metrics in the parboil benchmarks.

The results can be further analyzed with the potential benefit metrics in Figure 16, where benefit metrics are normalized to the baseline execution time. The benefit metrics lead to two conclusions. First, `cutcp` achieves most of the potential performance benefits in the optimized version. Hence, trying to further optimize the kernel might not be a good idea. Second, the baseline of `tpacf` also had high performance benefit potential, but the applied optimizations failed to achieve some of the benefits.

Surprisingly, although `tpacf` has the high potential benefits of B_{itilp}, the optimization techniques are not designed for that. This explains why there is almost no performance improvement from the baseline. Tiling, data reuse, and privatization mostly target improving memory operations. In fact, the optimized kernel significantly reduces the number of memory requests, which can lead to a performance improvement in GPGPUs where there are no caches. In the Fermi GPGPUs, unfortunately, most of the memory requests hit the caches, thereby resulting in no B_{memlp}. Hence, programmers or compilers should focus more on other optimizations to increase instruction-level or thread-level parallelism.

7. Related Work

7.1 GPU Performance Modeling

In the past few years, many studies on GPU performance modeling have been proposed. Hong and Kim [9] proposed the MWP-CWP based GPU analytical model. Concurrently, Baghsorkhi et al. [2] proposed a work flow graph (WFG)-based analytical model to predict the performance of GPU applications. The WFG is an extension of a control flow graph (CFG), where nodes represent instructions and arcs represent latencies. Zhang and Owens [20] proposed a performance model where they measured the execution time spent on the instruction pipeline, shared memory, and global memory to find the bottlenecks. Although Zhang and Owens also target identifying the bottlenecks, their method does not provide estimated performance benefits. Furthermore, our analytical model addresses more detailed performance bottlenecks, such as SFU resource contention.

Williams et al. [18] proposed the Roofline model, which is useful for visualizing compute-bounded or memory-bounded multicore architectures. Our X-Y benefit chart not only shows these limitations but also estimates ideal performance benefits.

Our work is also related to a rich body of work on optimizations and tuning of GPGPU applications [4, 7, 12, 15, 16, 19]. Ryoo et al. [16] introduced two metrics to prune optimization space by calculating the utilization and efficiency of GPU applications. Choi et al. [4] proposed a performance model for a sparse matrix-vector multiply (SpMV) kernel for the purpose of autotuning. A GPGPU compiler framework proposed by Yang et al. [19] performs GPGPU-specific optimizations, which can improve naive GPGPU kernels.

7.2 Performance Analysis Tools for CUDA

A handful of tools are available for the performance analysis of CUDA applications. However, most of the tools simply provide the performance metrics of the current running application. On the contrary, GPUPerf estimates potential performance benefit, thereby providing guidelines for how to optimize applications. As we discussed in Section 5, GPUPerf utilizes several tools such as visual profiler [14], Ocelot [6], and cuobjdump [13] to obtain accurate and detailed basic program analysis information.

Kim and Shrivastava [10] presented a tool that can be used for analyzing memory access patterns of a CUDA program. They model major memory effects such as memory coalescing and bank conflict. However, they do not deal with run-time information as their approach is a compile-time analysis, which often leads to inaccurate results for cases such as insufficient parallelism.

Meng et al. [11] proposed a GPU performance projection framework. Given CPU code skeletons, the framework predicts the cost and benefit of GPU acceleration. Their predictions are also built on the MWP-CWP model, but our work greatly improves on the MWP-CWP model.

There are also GPU simulators that can be used for program analysis. A G80 functional simulator called *Barra* by Collange et al. [5] can execute NVIDIA CUBIN files while collecting statistics. Bakhoda et al. [3] analyzed CUDA applications by implementing a GPU simulator that runs PTX instruction set. A heterogeneous simulator called MacSim [1] can also be used for obtaining detailed statistics on CUDA workloads.

8. Conclusions

The GPUPerf framework determines what bottlenecks are present in code and also estimates potential performance benefits from removing these bottlenecks. The framework combines an accurate analytical model for modern GPGPUs (e.g., Fermi-class) as well as a set of interpretable metrics that directly estimate potential improvements in performance for different classes of performance optimization techniques. We demonstrate these performance benefit predictions on FMM_U with 44 optimization combinations and several other benchmarks. The results show that the predicted potential benefit estimates are both informative and attainable.

Based on our case studies, we found that among four metrics, B_{itilp} and B_{fp} are easy to exploit through a variety of optimizations. The B_{memlp} metric is often zero indicating that most evaluated CUDA applications are in fact limited only by computation in Fermi-class GPGPUs. The B_{fp} metric generally has a relatively high value, which implies that removing compute inefficiencies is the key to achieving ideal performance. For example, coarsening and binning reduce such compute inefficiencies greatly in the parboil benchmarks.

Our future work will integrate this framework into compiler tools that can be directly used to improve parallel program efficiency on GPGPUs and other many-core platforms.

Acknowledgments

Many thanks to Sunpyo Hong, Jiayuan Meng, HPArch members, and the anonymous reviewers for their suggestions and feedback on improving the paper. We gratefully acknowledge the support of the National Science Foundation (NSF) CCF-0903447, NSF/SRC task 1981, NSF CAREER award 0953100, NSF CAREER award 1139083; the U.S. Department of Energy grant DE-SC0004915; Sandia National Laboratories; the Defense Advanced Research Projects Agency; Intel Corporation; Microsoft Research; and NVIDIA. Any opinions, findings and conclusions or recommendations expressed in this material are those of the authors and do not necessarily reflect those of NSF, SRC, DOE, DARPA, Microsoft, Intel, or NVIDIA.

References

[1] MacSim. http://code.google.com/p/macsim/.

[2] S. S. Baghsorkhi, M. Delahaye, S. J. Patel, W. D. Gropp, and W. W. Hwu. An adaptive performance modeling tool for gpu architectures. In *PPoPP*, 2010.

[3] A. Bakhoda, G. Yuan, W. W. L. Fung, H. Wong, and T. M. Aamodt. Analyzing cuda workloads using a detailed GPU simulator. In *IEEE ISPASS*, April 2009.

[4] J. W. Choi, A. Singh, and R. W. Vuduc. Model-driven autotuning of sparse matrix-vector multiply on gpus. In *PPoPP*, 2010.

[5] S. Collange, M. Daumas, D. Defour, and D. Parello. Barra: A parallel functional simulator for gpgpu. *Modeling, Analysis, and Simulation of Computer Systems, International Symposium on*, 0:351–360, 2010.

[6] G. Diamos, A. Kerr, S. Yalamanchili, and N. Clark. Ocelot: A dynamic compiler for bulk-synchronous applications in heterogeneous systems. In *PACT-19*, 2010.

[7] Y. Dotsenko, S. S. Baghsorkhi, B. Lloyd, and N. K. Govindaraju. Auto-tuning of fast fourier transform on graphics processors. In *Proceedings of the 16th ACM symposium on Principles and practice of parallel programming*, PPoPP '11, 2011.

[8] L. Greengard and V. Rokhlin. A fast algorithm for particle simulations. *Journal of Computational Physics*, 73(2):325–348, Dec. 1987.

[9] S. Hong and H. Kim. An analytical model for a gpu architecture with memory-level and thread-level parallelism awareness. In *ISCA*, 2009.

[10] Y. Kim and A. Shrivastava. Cumapz: A tool to analyze memory access patterns in cuda. In *DAC '11: Proc. of the 48th conference on Design automation*, June 2011.

[11] J. Meng, V. Morozov, K. Kumaran, V. Vishwanath, and T. Uram. Grophecy: Gpu performance projection from cpu code skeletons. In *SC'11*, November 2011.

[12] J. Meng and K. Skadron. Performance modeling and automatic ghost zone optimization for iterative stencil loops on gpus. In *ICS*, 2009.

[13] NVIDIA. CUDA OBJDUMP. http://developer.nvidia.com.

[14] NVIDIA Corporation. NVIDIA Visual Profiler. http://developer.nvidia.com/content/nvidia-visual-profiler.

[15] L.-N. Pouchet, U. Bondhugula, C. Bastoul, A. Cohen, J. Ramanujam, and P. Sadayappan. Combined iterative and model-driven optimization in an automatic parallelization framework. In *SC '10*, 2010.

[16] S. Ryoo, C. I. Rodrigues, S. S. Stone, S. S. Baghsorkhi, S.-Z. Ueng, J. A. Stratton, and W. mei W. Hwu. Program optimization space pruning for a multithreaded gpu. In *CGO-6*, pages 195–204, 2008.

[17] The IMPACT Research Group, UIUC. Parboil benchmark suite. http://impact.crhc.illinois.edu/parboil.php.

[18] S. Williams, A. Waterman, and D. Patterson. Roofline: an insightful visual performance model for multicore architectures. *Commun. ACM*, 52(4):65–76, 2009.

[19] Y. Yang, P. Xiang, J. Kong, and H. Zhou. A gpgpu compiler for memory optimization and parallelism management. In *Proc. of the ACM SIGPLAN 2010 Conf. on Programming Language Design and Implementation*, 2010.

[20] Y. Zhang and J. D. Owens. A quantitative performance analysis model for GPU architectures. In *HPCA*, 2011.

A. Calculating CWP and MWP

A.1 CWP

$$\mathrm{CWP} = \min(\mathrm{CWP\_full}, N) \quad \text{(A.1)}$$

$$\mathrm{CWP\_full} = \frac{\mathrm{mem\_cycles} + \mathrm{comp\_cycles}}{\mathrm{comp\_cycles}} \quad \text{(A.2)}$$

$$\mathrm{comp\_cycles} = \frac{\#\mathrm{insts} \times \mathrm{avg\_inst\_lat}}{\mathrm{ITILP}} \quad \text{(A.3)}$$

$$\mathrm{mem\_cycles} = \frac{\#\mathrm{mem\_insts} \times \mathrm{AMAT}}{\mathrm{MLP}} \quad \text{(A.4)}$$

mem_cycles: memory waiting cycles per warp
comp_cycles: computation cycles per warp
#insts: number of instructions per warp (excluding SFU insts.)
#mem_insts: number of memory instructions per warp

A.2 MWP

$$\mathrm{MWP} = \min\left(\frac{\mathrm{avg\_DRAM\_lat}}{\Delta}, \mathrm{MWP}_{\mathrm{peak\_bw}}, N\right) \quad \text{(A.5)}$$

$$\mathrm{MWP}_{\mathrm{peak\_bw}} = \frac{\mathrm{mem\_peak\_bandwidth}}{\mathrm{BW\_per\_warp} \times \#\mathrm{active\_SMs}} \quad \text{(A.6)}$$

$$\mathrm{BW\_per\_warp} = \frac{\mathrm{freq} \times \mathrm{transaction\_size}}{\mathrm{avg\_DRAM\_lat}} \quad \text{(A.7)}$$

mem_peak_bandwidth: bandwidth between the DRAM and GPU cores (e.g., 144.0 GB/s in Tesla C2050)
freq: clock frequency of the SM processor
(e.g., 1.15 GHZ in Tesla C2050)
transaction_size: transaction size for a DRAM request
(e.g., 128B in Tesla C2050)
BW_per_warp: bandwidth requirement per warp

Efficient Performance Evaluation of Memory Hierarchy for Highly Multithreaded Graphics Processors

Sara S. Baghsorkhi Isaac Gelado Matthieu Delahaye Wen-mei W. Hwu
University of Illinois at Urbana-Champaign
Urbana, IL 61801
{bsadeghi, igelado, matthieu, hwu} @illinois.edu

Abstract

With the emergence of highly multithreaded architectures, performance monitoring techniques face new challenges in efficiently locating sources of performance discrepancies in the program source code. For example, the state-of-the-art performance counters in highly multithreaded graphics processing units (GPUs) report only the overall occurrences of microarchitecture events at the end of program execution. Furthermore, even if supported, any fine-grained sampling of performance counters will distort the actual program behavior and will make the sampled values inaccurate. On the other hand, it is difficult to achieve high resolution performance information at low sampling rates in the presence of thousands of concurrently running threads. In this paper, we present a novel software-based approach for monitoring the memory hierarchy performance in highly multithreaded general-purpose graphics processors. The proposed analysis is based on memory traces collected for snapshots of an application execution. A trace-based memory hierarchy model with a Monte Carlo experimental methodology generates statistical bounds of performance measures without being concerned about the exact inter-thread ordering of individual events but rather studying the behavior of the overall system. The statistical approach overcomes the classical problem of disturbed execution timing due to fine-grained instrumentation. The approach scales well as we deploy an efficient parallel trace collection technique to reduce the trace generation overhead and a simple memory hierarchy model to reduce the simulation time. The proposed scheme also keeps track of individual memory operations in the source code and can quantify their efficiency with respect to the memory system. A cross-validation of our results shows close agreement with the values read from the hardware performance counters on an NVIDIA Tesla C2050 GPU. Based on the high resolution profile data produced by our model we optimized memory accesses in the sparse matrix vector multiply kernel and achieved speedups ranging from 2.4 to 14.8 depending on the characteristics of the input matrices.

Categories and Subject Descriptors C.1.2 [*Processor Architecture*]: Multiple Data Stream Architectures; C.4 [*Performance of Systems*] – Modeling Techniques

General Terms Design, Measurement, Performance

Keywords GPU, Memory hierarchy, Performance evaluation

PPoPP'12, February 25–29, 2012, New Orleans, Louisiana, USA.

1. Introduction

Graphics processors are optimized for throughput oriented workloads, which allowed early GPUs to not include traditional data caches. More recent GPUs have added small per-core L1 caches to capture inter-thread reuse, and larger unified L2 caches to exploit inter-core sharing. This is a significant step forward to better support a more diverse set of workloads and reduce some of the performance discrepancies that previously existed. Yet, support for application developers and compiler designers to investigate the behavior of the source code regions that cause performance bottlenecks has been limited. While current GPUs provide a set of performance counters that collect raw statistics for microarchitecture events such as the overall number of misses for the L1 and the L2 caches, the counter values cannot be monitored or sampled during a program execution. Likewise, support for time-based sampling is provided through application programming interfaces [13] that can be inserted in the source code at the user level. While a time-based sampling built on top of these interfaces can help identify hotspots in a program, a fine-grained sampling approach is not feasible as the high sampling rate will likely distort the accuracy of the profile data. On the other hand, infrequent sampling will increase the number of blind spots and reduce the precision of the measurements.

Profiling the performance of highly multithreaded applications is not confined to recently introduced high performance accelerators. Salapura et al. [16] discuss the significance of the feedback derived from the performance statistics in high performance computing systems such as Blue Gene and propose a new performance counter architecture that scales better with the number of concurrent events in a highly multithreaded system. We propose an alternative software-level approach to capture performance statistics with respect to a highly parallel interleaved memory system and in the presence of a large number of concurrent threads. Our approach does not require the instrumented application to have the same execution timing as the uninstrumented version. The relative ordering of events, e.g., memory loads and stores from concurrently running threads, is reconstructed following a Monte Carlo technique after traces are collected. The Monte Carlo approach allows us to systematically analyze the sensitivity of the predictions with respect to the reconstructed orderings of memory events.

We also propagate the source code locations of memory loads and stores. As a result, we are capable of producing precise and high resolution profile statistics. Most highly multithreaded applications are memory bound and their performance is strongly dependent on efficient use of the memory subsystem. Therefore, in this work we focus on performance modeling the GPU memory hierarchy.

1.1 Related Work

Performance analysis and profiling tools designed for massively parallel systems traditionally targeted coarse-grained instrumentation of multi-threaded environments that use MPI, OpenMP, or a mix of both. Examples of such tools are Vampir [10], TAU [17], and Paraver [14]. Similar to our trace collection mechanism, they usually use a library which when linked and called by an application, collects traces of events. Nevertheless, our trace collection mechanism is completely transparent and requires minimal effort on the developer's part. Furthermore, these tools collect both events information and the time stamps when those events were collected and use the collected time stamps to combine traces from different processes. While this approach introduces little distortion for coarse-grained tracing of events such as entering a shared region, acquiring a lock, or beginning of an MPI data transfer, it cannot be applied to the fine-grained event sampling used in this work for tracking individual memory operations in thousands of concurrently running threads. Our goal is not to construct the exact ordering of the events, rather to set up an execution context similar and close to the actual one; and if we have enough statistical evidence that the reconstructed orderings are close enough to the the actual one, we rely on them to model the inter-thread interactions and interferences.

Previous work in the area of performance tuning and modeling of graphics processors [15, 3, 7, 22] did not consider data caches and the inter-thread interaction of memory operations; they either assumed the memory system is not a bottleneck [15] or modeled a flat simple memory system for the previous GPU generations [3, 7, 22]. These models either combine static analysis and dynamic trace collection via manually inserted probes in the source code [3], or use functional simulators such as GPUOcelot [5] that emulate the GPU execution on a CPU to collect traces. Our parallel trace collection, on the other hand, is transparently integrated into the GPU kernel and incurs much less overhead. The previous work did not provide source-level performance feedback either.

Detailed GPU simulators such as GPUSim [4] and Mult2Sim [21] perform cycle accurate microarchitectural simulations that requires accounting for the timing of microarchitectural events and results in long running simulations. Our approach does not require to keep track of accurate timing of microarchitecture events and therefore incurs less simulation overhead. In addition, our simulation runs (the Monte Carlo random trials) can be executed in parallel. We also provide high resolution source-level performance feedback, which can better guide optimizations.

1.2 Contributions

The main contributions of this paper are:

- We propose a stochastic model of memory hierarchy for highly multithreaded execution environments: While major configuration parameters for the underlying hardware are extracted through microbenchmarking as discussed in Section 2, we use a Monte Carlo approach (randomized trials) to capture the sources of non-determinisim in the simulation model, e.g., the relative arrival ordering of the memory requests at each level of the memory hierarchy. This stochastic approach is presented in Section 3. Experiments presented in Section 5 confirms that the proposed approach yields fast convergence with respect to randomized trials and high accuracy when compared against values read from the hardware performance counters.
- We devise a parallel trace collection mechanism that runs on a GPU and gathers memory traces to capture the intra-thread, inter-thread and inter-core interactions of the memory accesses issued from a set of concurrently running threads. Generated traces are later combined together through the stochastic memory hierarchy modeling framework to predict hit rates for the L1 and L2 caches and measure the expected latency of the main memory. The trace collection is implemented as a source to source compiler transformation module that seamlessly inserts probes inside the GPU kernel (device code) and required routines to handle trace buffers in the surrounding code (host code). The trace collection mechanism, which is discussed in Section 4 incurs modest execution overhead and results in minimal user intervention.
- We keep track of the source code location of memory operations and quantify the efficiency of each individual one with respect to the GPU memory hierarchy. In Section 6, we show how based on the resultant profiling data we estimate the latency of each static load in a program. This information can be used later to target memory optimizations such as tiling and data layout.

2. A Highly Multithreaded Architecture Model

In this section, we define a machine model for a highly parallel graphics processor targeting general purpose and compute oriented workloads. The model must be simple enough to facilitate study and efficient evaluation of the graphics processors. On the other hand, it need to enclose enough details so that it can reflect a realistic behavior of the hardware. In what follows, we highlight a few fundamental differences reflected in this model that separates graphics processors from their peer multi-core processors:

Throughput-oriented Computing: GPUs emphasize high throughput and Single Instruction Multiple Thread (SIMT) performance by having streaming processors running neighboring threads in lock-step and executing the same instruction on different data. This microarchitectural grouping of threads which can affect both control flow and memory access efficiency introduces the concept of *warp* – a group of threads that composes a hardware vector unit.

Hardware Thread Scheduling: Preemptive thread scheduling by the operating system cannot efficiently support a throughput oriented environment. Therefore, GPUs implement thread scheduling through a dedicated hardware. A global thread block scheduler assigns blocks of threads to *streaming multiprocessors*, which are arrays of streaming processors that implement the SIMT execution model. In this work, we will consider a fine-grained round robin scheduling paradigm with respect to the relative order of thread blocks assigned to each streaming multiprocessor. This mapping is the closest model to the dynamic scheduling scheme that the hardware implements. Within a multiprocessor, a warp scheduler alternates between different warps following a weighted round robin scheme.

Bulk Instruction Scheduling: To make the model tractable and avoid fine-grained scheduling of instructions within a GPU kernel, which would result in a full system simulation, we propose a bulk scheduling scheme. The computation within a kernel is divided into a sequence of memory loads followed by a sequence of compute or store instructions. When static memory loads are repeated within a dynamic instruction stream, in the presence of enclosing loop constructs, they end up in separate sequences that are sequentially executed. Therefore, a back-edge in the control flow will terminate a sequence. Another delimitating factor is the existence of data-dependance between static memory operations. For example, if the index expression of a memory load is computed based on the value that is being read by a previous load, the second load will start a new sequence. Explicit synchronization instructions will also mark the end of the current sequence. Above simplifications preserve enough information about the instruction stream so that the model can reflect a reasonable representation of the kernel computation. Meanwhile, it is general enough that can approximate different instruction scheduling schemes adopted by different GPU vendors. For example, AMD's GPUs are designed based on a Very Long Instruction Word (VLIW) instruction set architecture; multiples of instructions that can execute in parallel are packed into statically scheduled VLIW bundles. These bundles then compose relatively short *clauses*; clauses are initiated by control flow instructions and may only contain a single type of instruction, e.g., memory loads or ALU instructions. In contrast, NVIDIAs GPUs require more sophisticated scheduling logic for fine-grained scoreboarding and resolving dependencies within the dynamic stream of instructions. With the bulk instruction scheduling scheme these level of details are abstracted.

Throughput-oriented Memory System: GPUs conserve memory bandwidth by grouping together, if possible, loads and stores issued within the same warp. Each *coalesced* memory access then uses a single memory request while moving multiple elements of data. Traditionally, highly multithreaded architectures such as HEP [18], M-Machine [6], Tera MTA [19] and more recently multithreaded graphics processors employ hardware multi-threading for fast context switches to tolerate memory latency. Following this approach to tolerate memory latency, the early multithreaded architectures did not include data caches. More recent GPUs such as those based on NVIDIA's Fermi architecture [11] added caches as means to conserve memory bandwidth. Private L1 caches expoit interthread data sharing to reduce the memory bandwidth consumption by each core. A shared unified L2 further reduces offchip bandwidth requirements by exploiting data re-use between cores. The throughput oriented environment also influences the design and functionality of the memory hierarchy. For example, data caches are no longer optimized for exploiting long term locality as their effective size shrinks with the high number of concurrently running threads. These caches are rather designed to exploit short-term spatial and temporal data locaity across the concurrently executing threads.

2.1 Microbenchmarks

We use a set of microbenchmarks to determine memory hierarchy configurations and management policies; in this work we adapt our model to the profile of the Tesla C2050 GPU. Our microbenchmark suite is built around a GPU kernel that traverses elements of one or more linked-lists in a circular (wrap-around) fashion, invoked with a single GPU thread unless stated otherwise.

Cache Parameters: We first measure the cache block size by varying the strides accessing the elements of a linked-list. The experiment initially implies only a cache block size of 128 bytes. This leads one to the conclusion that either there is no higher level caches or the cache block size of the higher level caches are at most 128 bytes. Next, we determine the size of the cache(s) using a fixed stride of 128 bytes (the L1 cache block size) accessing elements of a linked-list. Results from running this microbenchmark on the Tesla C2050 suggest a 16KB first-level cache and a 768KB second-level cache. The Fermi L1 cache can be deactivated though a compiler switch. With that option available, we further investigate the cache block size of the second level cache, which yields an L2 cache block size of 32 bytes. Based on this outcome, we assume that on an L1 miss four consecutive L2 cache blocks are accessed. We also measure that both L1 and L2 caches are 64-way set associative. A 64-way set associative L1 may at first glance look unreasonable, but it is justified with an average measured L1 access latency of 52 cycles; we measured average L1 and L2 access times of 90 and 250 nanoseconds. We later show, in Section 3.2.3, how we customize the measurement of the global memory access time for each application.

Inclusive, Exclusive or Victim: We also need to determine whether the second-level cache is inclusive or exclusive. Therefore, we run a microbenchmark using a linked-list of size equal to the L1 cache capacity for as many thread blocks as the number of available streaming multiprocessors plus one, i.e., 15 thread blocks for the Tesla C2050 GPU. To ensure that different thread blocks are not scheduled at the same time on the same streaming multiprocessor, we enforce each thread block to have the maximum number of in flight warps that can be simultaneously scheduled on each streaming multiprocessor. However, only one thread is performing memory accesses in each thread block. Each of the first 14 thread blocks access elements of 14 completely distinct linked-lists. The last thread block, which is roughly executed after the first 14 finish their execution, randomly chooses one of the previously accessed linked-lists to start its memory accesses. Memory accesses from the first 14 thread blocks will miss in both L1 and L2 caches. However, memory accesses of the last thread block will hit in the L2, if the cache is inclusive and in the L1 if the last thread block is scheduled on the same core as the thread block that has previously accessed the list. We run this microbenchmark 1024 times, and discard the results that indicate the accesses from the last thread block hit in the L1 cache. Next, We run a new experiment: this time all 15 thread blocks access distinct linked-lists. We compare the average memory latency for these two set of experiments. The results indicate a lower memory latency for the case that the last thread block reads from a previously accessed linked-list, which leads us to the conclusion that the second-level cache is inclusive.

Write Policy and Prefetching: Since the L1 caches are relatively small considering the number of inflight threads for each core, it makes sense to forward stores directly to the shared L2 cache. We verified this scenario through microbenchmarking. By closely investigating the numbers reported by the hardware counters, we also verified that stores hit in the L2 only if the corresponding cache block has been activated via a write request, and that the L2 follows a write back, write allocate policy for stores. So for the memory hierarchy model we assume that when a store request reaches the L2, if the cache block is valid it writes to the cache while setting the dirty bit for that block. If the block is not valid, it updates the memory and brings the cache block to the cache and set its valid bit. We also ruled out hardware prefetching by inspecting the number of memory requests reported by the performance counters for microbenchmarks that could potentially trigger hardware prefetching.

3. The Stochastic Memory Hierarchy Model

In this section we describe how a stochastic model of the GPU memory hierarchy is built on top of the deterministic memory model discussed earlier in Section 2. In our stochastic model, the order of memory requests being issued is partially determined by random variables. Memory traces are collected by instrumenting the GPU kernel at the source code level to record the memory addresses accessed during the kernel execution. The instrumentation framework, which is discussed in more detail in Section 4 is designed as a source-to-source transformation module. Static probes are inserted within the GPU kernel source code to record the memory addresses read from and written to by active threads for a subset of thread blocks as the GPU kernel is executed. This subset of thread blocks represents a snapshot of the kernel execution whose dimensions are determined heuristically based on the number of concurrently executing threads, the average number of dynamic memory operations per warp, and the size of the last level cache.

3.1 Spatial and Temporal Locality – Intra-thread and Inter-thread Interactions

To understand the performance of a GPU kernel with respect to the memory hierarchy, it is necessary to collect enough traces to capture:

- the intra-thread locality and interaction of memory operations
- the inter-thread and inter-thread-block locality and interactions

To capture spatial locality and inter-thread interferences the execution snapshot for trace collection is extended horizontally. We collect traces for thread blocks that are potentially scheduled close together on different cores (streaming multiprocessors), i.e., thread blocks with consecutive logical IDs. To account for the temporal locality and intra-thread interactions the execution snapshot is extended such that enough traces are collected within a single thread. The threshold is determined by the capacity of the last level cache and the total number of inflight threads. If required, the execution snapshot is extended across the boundaries of multiple thread blocks that are scheduled back-to-back on a single core. With this approach, a subset of the memory traces is collected, but the subset is detailed enough to reflect locality and interactions within the group of concurrently running threads.

If required, traces can be collected for multiple snapshots of the kernel execution. However, our initial experiments confirm that applying the model to traces collected from a single snapshot produces precise and accurate enough estimations. This is quite expected as the computation in a typical GPU kernel is structured around a Single Program Multiple Data (SPMD) programming model.

The above approach, is to some extent similar to the time sampling technique introduced by Laha et al. [8]. They used contiguous segments of memory accesses over certain time intervals for trace driven simulation of single-thread workloads. For large caches and in a single-thread execution model, the cold-start error caused due to unknown status of the cache at the start of each trace simulation is a major source of inaccuracy. In a highly multithreaded execution model, the effect of the cold-start error is fairly insignificant; the execution environment setup for throughput oriented caches limits their ability in exploiting long-term temporal locality. We expect that the same limitation will hold in future GPUs as parallelism scales with at least the same rate as the size of the caches increases.

3.2 The Monte Carlo Approach

Collected traces exhibit precise intra-warp (intra-thread) ordering of memory references. But they do not maintain any information on the relative order of memory references issued from different warps or thread blocks. Note that our approach does not rely on the execution order of memory loads and stores when collecting traces. The rationale for not relying on the ordering during the execution of the instrumented GPU kernel is that adding static probes to the kernel source code:

- changes the kernel resource usage (number of registers), which may consequently alter the streaming multiprocessors occupancy, i.e., the number of concurrently active thread blocks.
- increases the number of inflight memory operations, which will distort the state of caches and the level of congestion in the memory hierarchy.
- changes the instruction mix of the GPU kernel and introduces spurious synchronization or stall points.

As a result, instrumenting the kernel will introduce considerable timing distortions in the execution order of the memory references. To account for this effect, the order of memory requests arriving at each level of the memory hierarchy is reconstructed via a Monte Carlo method, which is an efficient sampling approach for systems with individual behaviors highly coupled together. Traces are then driven into each level of the memory hierarchy in our simulator according to the randomly sampled ordering in each run based on the following steps:

1. Given a pool of memory requests waiting to be serviced at each level of the memory hierarchy:
   (a) Generate a valid random ordering from the pool of available memory requests.
   (b) Drive traces to the current memory hierarchy module following the ordering derived in step (a).
   (c) Obtain performance estimations for the current level and prepare the pool of memory request to be serviced by the next memory hierarchy level.
2. Repeat step 1 for a sufficiently large number of times.
3. Determine the probability distribution of results using histograms and summarize the confidence of the predictions.

The output of the model is a probabilistic performance behavior of the memory system such as hit ratios for the first and second level caches. If certain performance behaviors are most frequently observed – even with limited knowledge about the exact relative ordering of inter-thread memory requests – they are statistically sound representatives of the system performance. In other words, if different random orderings result in noticeably different performance statistics (a wide spread histogram) then the predictions are not reliable. Otherwise, though we have not followed the actual inter-thread ordering when driving traces into the simulator, we have set up an execution context similar and close enough to the actual one. In such a case, we evaluate the performance of memory operations within the execution contexts reconstructed following the above steps.

3.2.1 Schedule Deviation

As independent thread blocks are scheduled to run on streaming multiprocessors, their executions start to fall out of sync with each other due to non-uniform memory access latencies, different number of memory operations and computation loads as individual threads or warps may follow different control flow paths, etc. To account for these schedule deviations, when scheduling loads and stores from inflight warps, random start (alignment) points are chosen for thread blocks scheduled simultaneously across different streaming multiprocessors. The horizontal dashed lines in Figure 1 highlight the execution snapshots devised based on random start

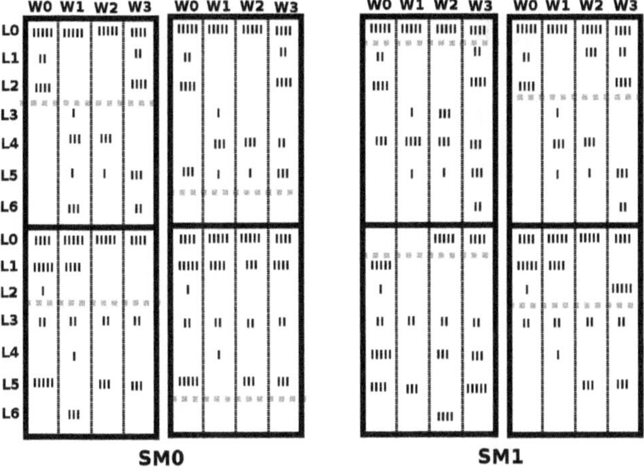

Figure 1. Random points mimic schedule deviation for simultaneously scheduled thread blocks

points for two multiprocessors. In this example, snapshots are expanded across two back-to-back scheduled thread blocks – each composed of four warps: W0, W1, W2 and W3. Each multiprocessor executes two thread blocks simultaneously. Tiny bars in front of dynamic memory operations L0,..., L6 represent individual memory transactions being issued for the corresponding memory vector instructions. The entry is empty if none of the threads within the warp have executed the corresponding load or store.

3.2.2 Scheduling Traces

Following the alignment of simultaneously scheduled thread blocks, we start picking traces from warps within these thread blocks and drive them into the L1 caches. The scheduling scheme used preserves the vector nature of the memory references issued by threads within a warp. Memory references are coalesced based on the size of the data being accessed and the cache block size. Coalesced accesses (memory transactions) for each warp are bound together to ensure that they are all scheduled at the same time. Each warp of a thread block has a queue of ready-to-issue memory transactions. Attached to each memory transaction is a unique ID that corresponds to the source code location of the memory load or store that has triggered the transaction.

Figure 2 illustrates the layout of the stochastic memory hierarchy simulator. The intra-core trace schedulers pick traces from the warp queues following a weighted round robin fashion. Traces are sent to the L1 caches in the order that they have been picked. Loads update the status and counters of the L1 caches. All stores and the loads that miss in the L1 are forwarded to the L2 cache. When scheduling traces from a warp queue, the scheduler continues picking transactions from the same warp if the corresponding cache lines are triggered by static memory operations within the same scheduling sequence, provided that no data-dependence has been recorded between back to back scheduled accesses. This scheduling policy follows the concept of bulk instruction scheduling discussed earlier in Section 2.

The inter-core trace scheduler picks traces from the L1 queues based on a weighted random scheduling algorithm. Loads and stores that miss in the L2 cache along with store evictions are placed into the main memory request queue shown in Figure 2.

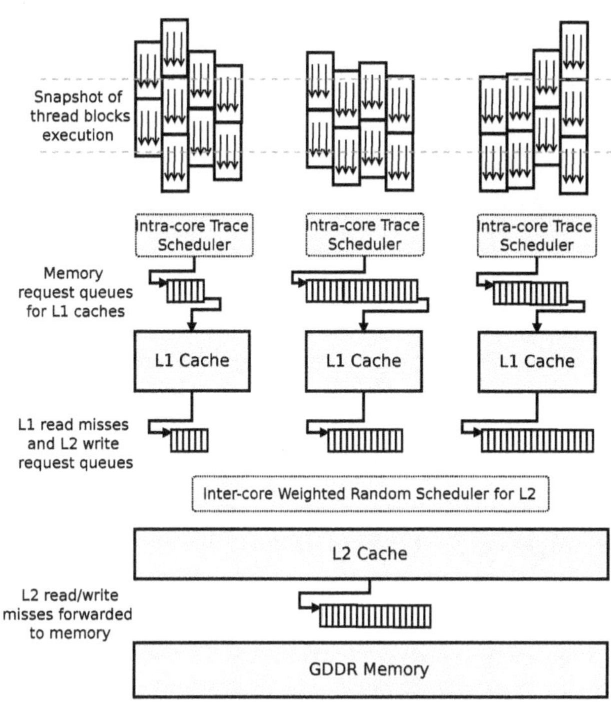

Figure 2. The stochastic memory hierarchy model

3.2.3 Main Memory

In the context of a highly multithreaded environment, memory latency observed from a single-thread execution is not necessarily a meaningful measure of performance. Congestions in the memory system may add to the memory latency. Congestion pattern is characterized based on how efficiently the shared resource is utilized by the memory requests that arrive close in time. The main memory in a GPU is organized into a number of interleaved channels. Depending on how memory accesses are spread across these channels the effective memory bandwidth and latency will change. To estimate the effective memory latency observed by memory operations issued close to each other, memory accesses that reach the main memory are grouped together following a uniform random distribution.

To form groups of simultaneously issued memory loads or stores, random number of memory requests are picked from the queue of misses arrived from the L2 cache. Each group can contain up to 32 memory requests which is the maximum number of distinct memory transactions a core can issue simultaneously, i.e., the memory vector size. Then up to 14 groups are picked, i.e., one per each streaming multiprocessor, to form a set of memory requests that reach the main memory relatively at the same time.

The addresses in these aggregated groups of memory transactions are then normalized and translated into indices of an array whose elements are the size of a single main memory transaction (32 bytes). The indices are then loaded into a microbenchmark and the main memory access latency for each batch of concurrently scheduled accesses is measured via the internal clock register. Figure 3 shows the probability density function of the observed latencies collected by the above approach for the sparse matrix vector multiplication benchmark. The general rule is that more frequent random accesses and higher number of memory bank conflicts will degrade the main memory efficiency and increase the expected latency. If a

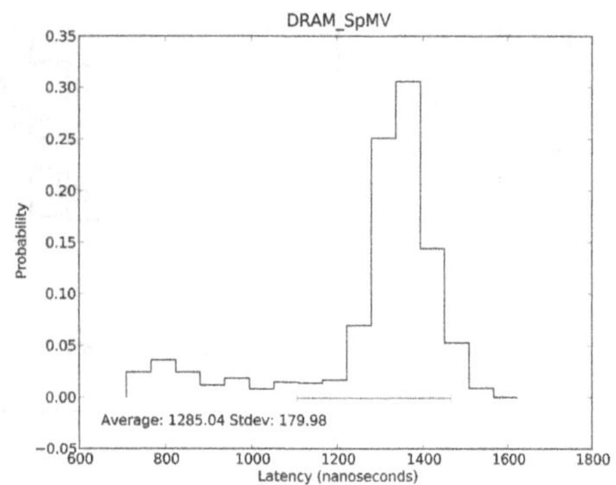

Figure 3. Probability distribution for the main memory latency – SpMV kernel

dominant measured latency exists, we use it as a proper statistical representative latency for the memory accesses that miss in the L2 cache.

4. Software Framework

This section discusses the framework that collects dynamic memory traces for the stochastic memory hierarchy simulator discussed in Section 3.

4.1 Instrumenting the Kernel

To collect and analyze the memory addresses accessed by a given kernel, additional instructions are inserted inside the kernel (the GPU device code) and the CPU host code. This is performed automatically by a source-to-source transformation module that is run before the actual compilation of the program. This module and the actual compiler are wrapped together into a new compiler driver that can replace the original compiler in a project build system. This minimal level of intervention simplifies the use of the framework significantly.

The source-to-source transformation module performs the following source code modifications:

- Inserts *memory address probes* into the kernel source code at locations where the kernel is performing a read or a write operation. A probe as shown in Listing 1 is a call to a function that will be in charge of storing the memory address accessed as well as a unique ID that identifies the source code location of the memory operation.
- Stores for each memory address probe, its exact source code location and the size of the element being accessed into a static array.
- Adds allocation and deallocation routines for the trace collection buffer before and after the launch of the GPU kernel. A pointer to the buffer is added as an extra argument to the kernel invocation code. The organization of the trace buffer is explained later in Section 4.2.
- Adds an additional parameter to the kernel that communicates to the probes the location within the buffer that they need to store the corresponding trace information.
- Adds routines to compute the original kernel occupancy.
- Adds routines that collect traced memory addresses and post-process them for the memory hierarchy simulation model.

```
__global__ void SpMV(_sampling_device_buffer *
    _samples, float *x, const float *val, ...)
{
  _sampling_status  _this_thrd_status;
  _init_sampling_status(samples, &this_thrd_status);

  tid = threadIdx.y;
  bid = blockIdx.y;
  t=0;
  myi = bid * BLOCKSIZE + tid;

  if ( myi < (numRows) ){

    _sample_mem_index(samples, &this_thrd_status, 0,
       &(rowInd[myi]));
    lb = rowInd[myi];

    _sample_mem_index(samples, &this_thrd_status, 2,
       &(rowInd[myi + 1]));
    ub = rowInd[myi+1];

    for (j=lb; j<ub; j++) {

      _sample_mem_index(samples, &this_thrd_status, 4,
         &(indices[j]));
      ind = indices[j];

      _sample_mem_index(samples, &this_thrd_status, 6,
         &(y[ind]));
      yval = y[ind];

      _sample_mem_index(samples, &this_thrd_status, 8,
         &(val[j]));
      t += val[j] * yval;

    }
    _sample_mem_index(samples, &this_thrd_status, 1,
       &(x[myi]));
    x[myi] = t;

  }

  _release_buffer(&_this_thrd_status);
}
```

Listing 1. Instrumented SpMV – device code

To initiate trace collection for a subset of simultaneously executing thread blocks, one need to know the thread block occupancy for a streaming multiprocessor and the number of available streaming multiprocessors; the latter is obtained via a call to the NVIDIA's programming APIs. The former is computed as follows: The occupancy of a GPU kernel is the ratio of the number of active warps to the maximum number warps supported on a streaming multiprocessor [12]. The occupancy is determined by the amount of resources that the kernel consumes. Resources can be allocated either statically or at the kernel invocation time. Occupancy is also dependent on the GPU device that the kernel will be executed on. Before starting the source-to-source transformation, the driver calls NVIDIA's `nvcc` compiler to collect kernel-specific information required to compute the occupancy, which includes the number of registers and the size of shared memory used. The instrumentation module also inserts calls to NVIDIA's programming interfaces to identify the GPU device that the kernel will be executed on. It then computes the occupancy of the kernel just before its invocation, where it also collects the kernel invocation parameters whose values are required for the occupancy computation, i.e., the thread block dimensions and the amount of shared memory dynamically allocated.

The source to source transformation module is built on top of Clang [1], the C language family frontend for LLVM [9]. Clang has been modified so that it can correctly parse a subset of CUDA [13] source code and build the abstract syntax tree of both the host and device code. Each node of the tree precisely records its exact location within the source code, even when the node is the result of one or more macro instantiations. This property is essential for the transformation module to provide accurate source level feedback.

The output of the transformation cannot be generated directly from a modified abstract syntax tree: To build the abstract syntax tree, a header containing the declaration of CUDA types and runtime functions must be preincluded. The serialization of the abstract syntax tree would contains these additional declarations. But `nvcc` preincludes a header file as well. So, if `nvcc` is run to compile the source code generated from the abstract syntax tree, it will result in duplicated declaration errors. Therefore, the output of the transformation is a patch file that is applied to the user source code. The modifications that need to be applied to the original source code are recorded as a list of source code insertion operations that are later used to generate the patch file. This mechanism leverages the Rewriter API that Clang provides.

Redundant loads and stores that are likely to be eliminated by the back-end compiler are not instrumented. To achieve this, a global value numbering analysis is implemented to identify the redundant memory accesses and a basic pointer alias analysis is used to determine if a memory operation will be removed through redundant load elimination.

The instrumentation of the source code must be done with an unmodified abstract syntax tree to ensure that the source locations are correct. However, the abstract syntax tree must be modified to increase the quality of the global value numbering analysis: Expression trees are canonicalized to increase the chance that two arithmetically equivalent expressions have the same tree representation. This means that the source code must be instrumented before the analysis is performed. As a result, the source code is over-instrumented. After the analysis is performed, the results are forwarded to the patch file generation module to skip the unnecessary instrumented memory operations.

A significant challenge in instrumenting the memory operations is identifying the correct type of the address space being accessed by a pointer, e.g., global memory, shared memory, etc. The type of a pointer cannot be used to infer which address space it points to as it can change during the lifetime of the pointer. A dataflow-based algorithm is used to disambiguate the address space that a pointer refers to for each segment of the source code. When incapable of resolving the actual pointer type, it conservatively associates the pointer to the global memory, similar to the `nvcc` compiler.

4.2 Recording Traces

The memory address probes inserted within the kernel store the addresses accessed by each thread into a trace buffer. The implementation of these probes and the design of the buffer are inherent to the execution model within the GPU: The threads within a warp are executed in lock-step and the warps within a thread block are executed concurrently. Therefore, the probes are designed to store per-warp rather than per-thread memory accesses. In addition, the buffer is designed so that its size does not limit the acquisition of an unbounded amount of memory addresses.

A trace buffer is composed of a number of block buffers. Each block buffer itself contains a set of warp buffers – one for each warp in the thread block – as illustrated in Figure 4. The number of block buffers is equal to the number of simultaneously active thread blocks in the GPU. We use a per-block-buffer locking mechanism to prevent concurrent accesses to the same buffer from multiple thread blocks. Each block buffer has a counter that holds the number of active threads using the buffer. When zero, the buffer is free to be acquired. A thread block acquires exclusive rights to the buffer when it successfully exchanges, via an atomic operation, the value zero in the counter with the number of threads that it contains. Each thread will atomically decrement this counter just before terminating. A warp buffer is a ring buffer with fixed-sized lines that are wide enough to hold for each thread within a warp, an address value and a static ID associated with the source code location of the corresponding memory operation. When an active thread executes a probe, the next available line in the warp buffer is updated and a line counter is incremented. The buffer is originally initialized with invalid addresses (odd values). So when an inactive thread does not store any address it can be easily captured.

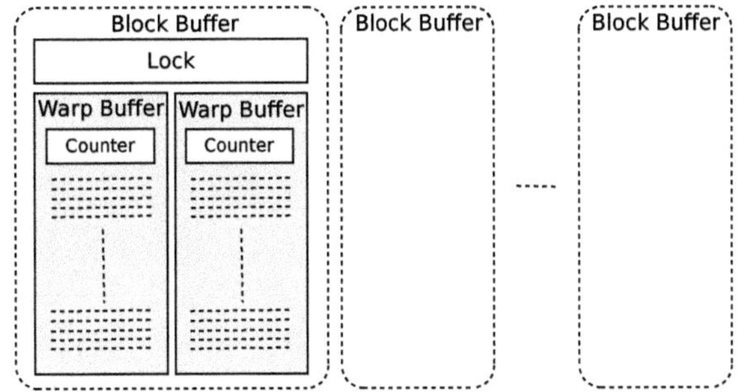

Figure 4. Organization of the trace buffer

Probes will spin on the warp buffer counter when the buffer is full. During the kernel execution, the host program constantly snoops at individual warp-buffer counters. When a warp buffer is full, the host program reads the content of the warp buffer (traces) and resets the warp buffer counter. Now, threads that were spinning on the counter will resume to record traces. When enough traces are gathered, the host program sets the counters to a predefined value to disable probes inside the kernel. The exact layout of the buffer is computed based on thread block dimensions, number of concurrently active thread blocks and the overall size of the buffer itself.

To allow both the host and the device code access the buffer concurrently, the buffer is allocated using pinned-memory. Pinned-memory is the host memory that is removed from the virtual memory, so it is not paged out by the operating system. Since the atomic operations operating on a pinned-memory are not atomic from the point of view of the host [13], the communication between host and device is implemented via un-cached load and store operations by inlining NVIDIA's PTX assembly to treat cached memory lines stale and bypass the GPU L2 cache via write-through stores.

5. Experimental Evaluation

In this section, we present the result of application of the stochastic memory hierarchy model discussed in Section 3 to several GPU applications. The results, which are presented in terms of the L1 hit ratios for loads and the L2 hit ratios for loads and stores are cross validated against the overall hit ratios reported by the hardware performance counters.

5.1 Experiments Setup

The proposed memory hierarchy modeling approach is validated on an NVIDIA Tesla C2050 general-purpose graphics processor. The benchmarks suite chosen covers GPU kernels commonly used in scientific computing and signal processing applications: dense

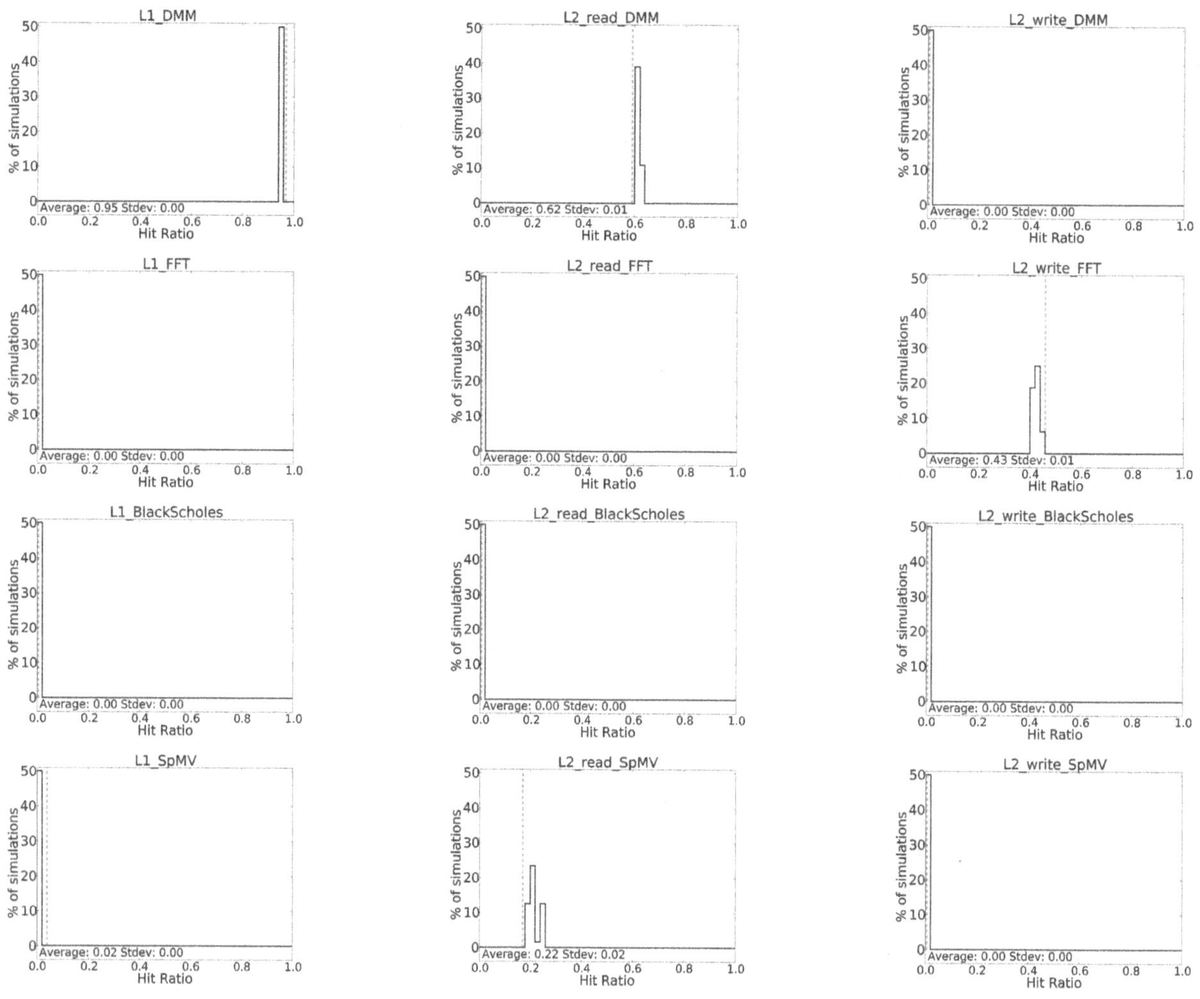

Figure 5. Probability distribution for the L1 read, L2 read and L2 write predicted hit ratios – Part 1

matrix multiplication (DMM), sparse matrix vector multiplication (SpMV), fast Fourier transform (FFT), Black Scholes, the 3D lattice-Boltzmann method (LBM), merge sort (global and shared memory versions), and a 3D stencil computation. These benchmark also exhibit diverse behavior with respect to memory access patterns, data-dependent control flow and memory references, mix of load and store operations, and the locality level available.

The overall probability distributions for the L1 and the L2 cache hit rates are generated by the proposed stochastic model for the discussed GPU benchmarks and results are displayed in Figures 5 and 6. Each histogram shows the probability of a specific predicted hit ratio on the y-axis based on results obtained from 64 simulations. The dashed vertical red line marks the hit ratios reported by the hardware counters.

5.2 Sampling Error – Precision

We report the average and the standard deviation for the predicted hit ratios in Figures 5 and 6. The standard deviation describes the spread of the predicted hit ratios and determines how random variations affects the sensitivity and reliability of the proposed memory model. A small standard deviation – 0.01 on average for the outputs of the model – indicates that the predictions from the model are robust with respect to the randomly sampled ordering of memory requests. Based on the central limit theorem [20] the probability of the expected predicted hit ratios being within the confidence interval of $[\widehat{E}_n - 2\widehat{\sigma}_n, \widehat{E}_n + 2\widehat{\sigma}_n]$ is 95%, where $\widehat{E}_n$ and $\widehat{\sigma}_n$ are the average hit ratios and standard deviations shown in Figures 5 and 6.

5.3 Sampling Overhead

Figure 7 shows changes in the standard deviation of the predictions for the L2 reads in the SpMV kernel as the number of random samples increases; the L2 predictions for loads in the SpMV kernel have the highest standard deviation within our experiments. Nevertheless, a small standard deviation of 0.02 or 2% miss prediction indicates that predictions exhibit a low tendency to be spread out. Based on Figure 7, a relatively fast convergence for the standard deviation (starting after 20 simulations) suggests that larger sample sizes will produce barely noticeable increase in the precision of the predictions specially after 60 simulation runs. For this kernel when run with an input matrix of randomly distributed non-zero elements (51 on average per row), it takes 17.7 seconds to collect traces for an execution snapshot that is 4 times the size of the concurrently running threads on all 14 streaming multiprocessors. It then takes 3.16 minutes on an Intel Core-i7 processor running at 2.8 GHz to finish one simulation and propagate and collect performance statistics. Most of the overhead is in driving traces from the private L1

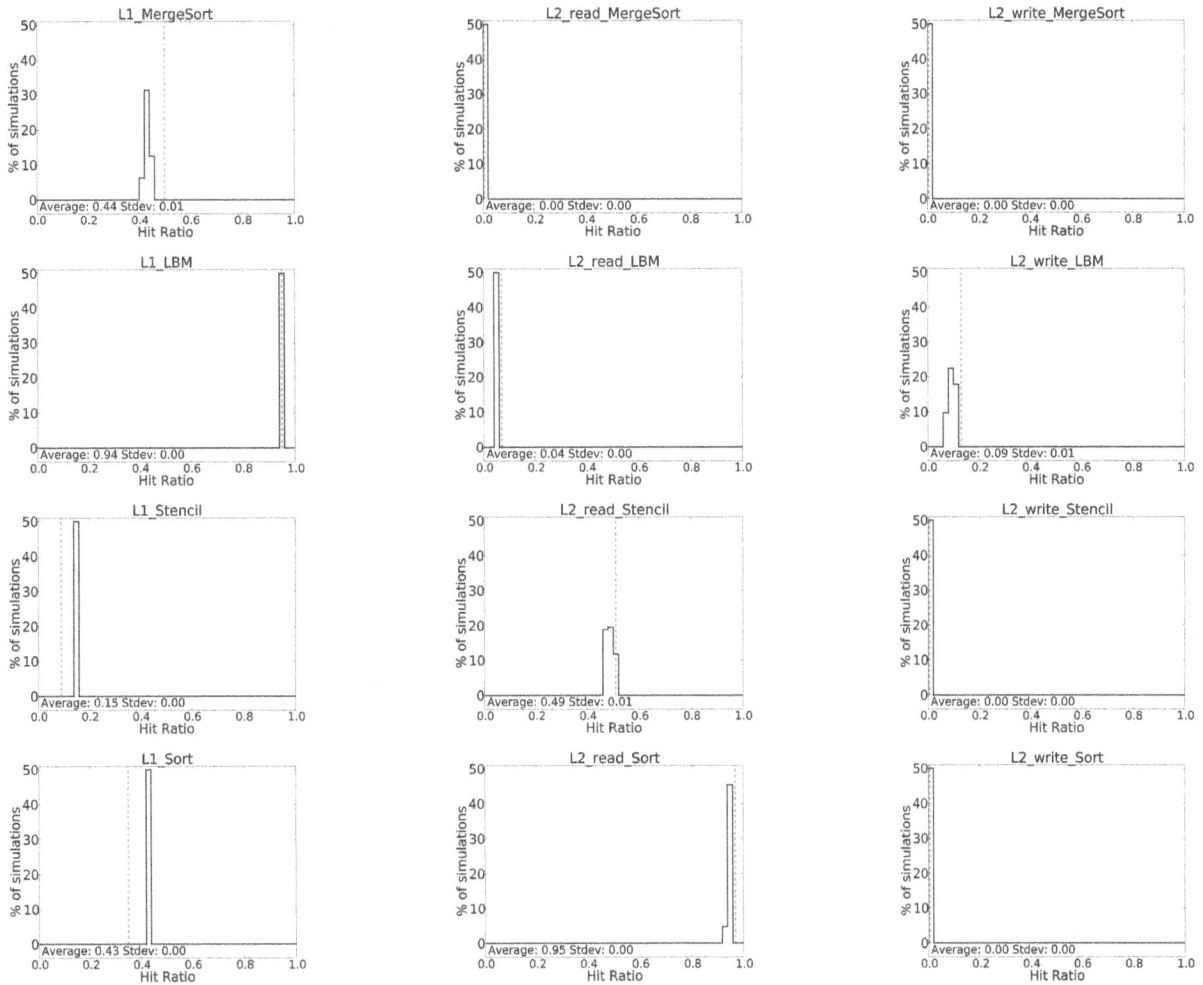

Figure 6. Probability distribution for the L1 read, L2 read and L2 write predicted hit ratios – Part 2

caches to the unified L2 cache. The SpMV benchmark represents the end of the spectrum with slower convergence rates (after 20 simulation runs) for the L1 and L2 hit ratio predictions, at least within the benchmark suite used for our study. In general, a handful of simulation runs converge very quickly or the simulations can stop after the results converge within the desired threshold. In addition, multiple simulation runs can be executed in parallel to reduce the overall simulation overhead.

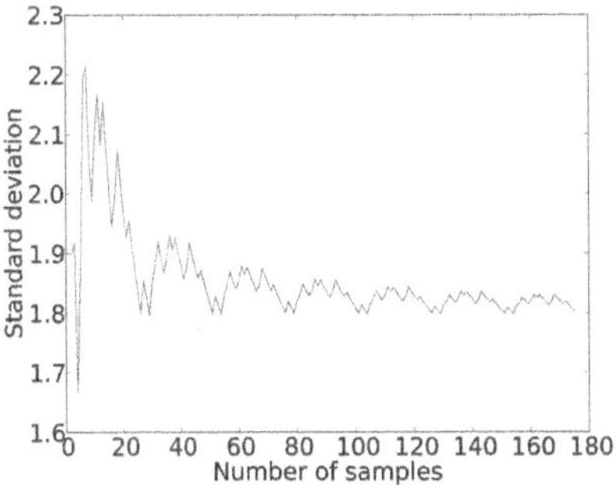

Figure 7. Fast convergence of the standard deviation for the L2 read hit ratio predictions – SpMV kernel

5.4 Systematic Error – Accuracy

We use absolute error to measure the accuracy of our predictions. Relative error is a more meaningful measure of accuracy than the absolute error when the predicted values are large and unbounded. For the predicted hit ratios, relative error does not relate closely to the performance associated with the difference in the predictions. For example, when using the relative error one gets the same value of error for the following pairs of predicted and actual hit ratios: $(0.02, 0.04)$, $(0.2, 0.4)$ and $(0.4, 0.8)$. The fact that the above errors would be judged to have equal importance is not correct from microarchitecture point of view.

We cross-validated the results predicted by the memory hierarchy model with those read from the hardware performance counters provided by the NVIDIA. The performance counters cannot be read or sampled during the kernel execution. Before running the kernel, an environment variable is set to activate the counters. After the kernel execution is finished, the values of the counters that reflect the overall performance statistics with respect to all memory references are written into a log file. The vertical dashed lines in Figures 5 and 6 highlight the hit ratios computed based on values read from the hardware counters. When compared against hardware counters, the proposed approach have an average absolute error of

```
1   float t = 0;
2   unsigned int myi = bid * BLOCKSIZE + tid;
3
4   if ( myi < numRows ){
5       unsigned int lb = rowIndices[myi];
6       unsigned int ub = rowIndices[myi+1];
7       for (j = lb; j < ub; j++) {
8         unsigned int ind = indices[j];
9         yval = y[ind];
10        t += val[j] * yval;
11      }
12      x[myi] = t;
13  }
```

Listing 2. SpMV kernel

3.4% for the L1 read hit ratios, 1.9% for the L2 read hit ratios and 0.8% for the L2 write hit ratios.

6. High Resolution Performance Statistics

In this section, we discuss how high resolution performance statistics are generated by coupling source code level information and the profile data produced by the memory hierarchy model. This comprehensive view of the level of memory efficiency exploited by individual data structures or memory operations within a particular code segment is a crucial step for targeted memory optimizations. We later illustrate though a simple example how this low level information can highlight inefficient memory accesses and play up the data structures that are ideal candidates for optimization.

6.1 The Average Latency per each Static Load

In Section 3.2.3, we presented a microbenchmarking approach to measure the main memory access time, T_m, specific to each application. We also measured the L1 and the L2 cache latencies, denoted by t_1 and t_2, with a simple microbenchmark. We later predicted hit ratios by the proposed memory hierarchy model for the L1 and L2 caches, denoted by H_1 and H_2. In this section, we combine all these results using the following simple access latency equation:

$$X = H_1 \cdot t_1 + (1 - H_1) \cdot [H_2 \cdot t_2 + (1 - H_2) \cdot T_m]$$

In the above equation values of T_m, H_1 and H_2 can change from one simulation run to the other. Furthermore, H_1 and H_2 are the L1 and the L2 hit ratios for a specific static load; since we propagate down the source code location of each memory operation, we can also estimate the hit ratios for individual loads in the program. After substituting the corresponding values from multiple simulation runs, X becomes a random variable. Based on the expected value of X we estimate the expected memory latency of each static load in the kernel source code. For example, Figure 8 shows the the expected memory latency for each of the 5 static loads in the SpMV kernels. This information can be used to target memory optimizations such as tiling and data layout transformation for specific data structures in the program.

6.2 Case Study: Sparse Matrix Vector Multiplication Kernel

In this section we show through an example how the discussed high resolution performance information can be used to apply targeted optimizations. Initial examination of the sparse matrix vector multiplication kernel source code shown in Listing 2 implies that loads from lines 8 and 10 each exhibits a high level of intra-thread temporal locality as they are executed within a tight loop using consecutive indices. Therefore, the latencies for these loads are expected to be low. On the other hand, memory references from the load in line 9 are not analyzable statically and are expected to follow an irregular pattern resulting in poor data locality. Nevertheless, results reported by our memory hierarchy model are different from the speculations derived based on manual examination of the source code. Based on this new information when considering the interactions among the concurrently running threads, loading the vector value y in line 9 is more efficient compared to the other two static loads that were expected to exploit a high degree of locality. The very low performance of these loads makes them the most promising candidates for memory optimization in spite of the of the potential overhead that will be introduced.

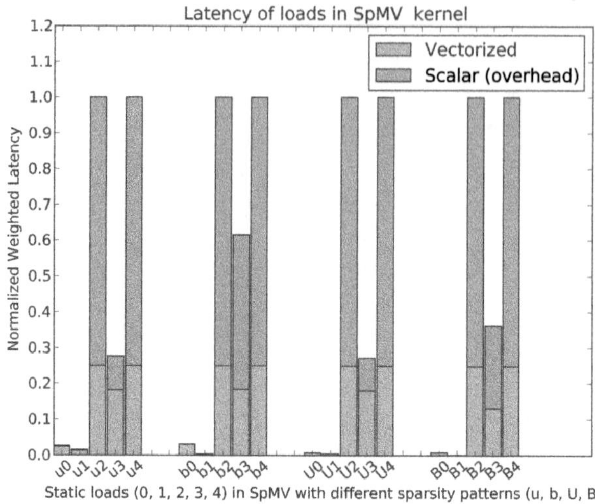

Figure 8. Breakdown of memory latency for static loads in scalar and vectorized SpMV kernels for 4 input matrices: u = an average of 32 non-zero elements per row randomly distributed, b = an average of 32 non-zeros per row with a block diagonal distribution, U = an average of 128 non-zeros randomly distributed, B = an average of 128 non-zeros with a block diagonal distribution.

We applied intra-thread vectorization, a well-known technique to capture temporal locality, to loads from lines 8 and 10. Intra-thread vectorization exploits the data reuse that cannot be efficiently captured by the data caches (the loaded cache lines are evicted before being reused) by packing multiple low performing loads into a single vector load. Listing 3 shows the optimized version of the SpMV kernel, which uses just enough extra registers to maintain the initial occupancy level of the streaming multiprocessors.

We studied the performance improvements of the optimized SpMV kernel with 4 input matrices (u, b, U, and B) differing in the average number of non-zeros per row and the sparsity pattern. Input matrices for u and b configurations have on average 32 none-zero elements while U and B matrices have 128 non-zeros. Non-zeros are randomly distributed in u and U matrices while b and B are block diagonal sparse matrices. Figure 8 shows the predicted load latency for each static load in the scalar and the vectorized SpMV kernels in a stacked format – generated by our stochastic memory hierarchy model – for the 4 resultant configurations. The latencies were normalized with respect to the latency of the least performing load in the scalar kernel for each of the 4 configurations. Based on the profile data shown in Figure 8, reducing the number of inefficient loads in the vectorized configuration will also mitigate the cache trashing effect for vector y, specially in case of block diagonal matrices where y benefits from a higher degree of locality. The execution times measured for different SpMV configurations

```
float t = 0;
unsigned int myi = bid * BLOCKSIZE + tid;
if ( myi < numRows ){
 unsigned int lb = rowIndices[myi];
 unsigned int ub = rowIndices[myi+1];

    //prologue code — alignment adjustment
                .
                .
    for (j = newlb; j < newub; j+=4) {
       uint4 ind = indices[j/4];
       float4 value = val[j/4];
       float yval = y[ind.x];
         t += value.x * yval;
       yval = y[ind.y];
         t += value.y * yval;
       yval = y[ind.z];
         t += value.z * yval;
       yval = y[ind.w];
         t += value.w * yval;
    }
    //epilogue code — alignment adjustment
                .
                .
    x[myi] = t;
}
```

Listing 3. Vectorized SpMV kernel

discussed above comply with the profile data shown in Figure 8; vectorized kernels show major performance improvements with speedups of 2.4 (u), 3.63 (b), 2.5 (U), and 14.8 (B).

7. Conclusions and Future Work

This paper presents a novel solution to the problem of providing meaningful performance feedback to developers for highly multithreaded graphics processors. Our stochastic modeling technique allows us to use a simple tracing approach without concerns for distorted execution timing. It further provides error bounds and confidence level information in the presence of scheduling uncertainties and allows us to minimize the cost of tracing and simulation. The close match between the generated predictions and the measured hardware performance counter values provides good validation for our model. The high resolution performance statistics generated through coupling source code level instrumentation and the memory hierarchy simulation provides a comprehensible view of the level of memory efficiency being exploited by individual data structures in the program. This information, though still far from specific optimization hints to a developer or a compiler, is a crucial and fundamental step forward towards that goal. While our model is demonstrated and validated based on CUDA applications and the Tesla C2050 hardware, it is applicable to other highly multithreaded processors. We plan to extend the system to OpenCL [2] applications and the AMD GPUs in the near future.

Acknowledgments

We would like to acknowledge the support of the Gigascale Systems Research Center, funded under the Focus Center Research Program. In addition, we wish to thank Sam Williams and anonymous reviewers for providing helpful comments.

References

[1] http://clang.llvm.org/.

[2] *The OpenCL Specification*, 2009.

[3] S. S. Baghsorkhi, M. Delahaye, S. J. Patel, W. D. Gropp, and W.-m. W. Hwu. An adaptive performance modeling tool for GPU architectures. In *Proceedings of the 15th ACM SIGPLAN symposium on Principles and practice of parallel programming*, pages 105–114, 2010.

[4] A. Bakhoda, G. Yuan, W. Fung, H. Wong, and T. Aamodt. Analyzing CUDA workloads using a detailed GPU simulator. In *Performance Analysis of Systems and Software, 2009. ISPASS 2009. IEEE International Symposium on*, pages 163 –174, 2009.

[5] G. Diamos, A. Kerr, and M. Kesavan. A dynamic compilation framework for ptx. http://code.google.com/p/gpuocelot.

[6] M. Fillo, S. W. Keckler, W. J. Dally, N. P. Carter, A. Chang, Y. Gurevich, and W. S. Lee. The M-Machine multicomputer. In *Proceedings of the 28th annual international symposium on Microarchitecture*, pages 146–156, 1995.

[7] S. Hong and H. Kim. An analytical model for a GPU architecture with memory-level and thread-level parallelism awareness. In *Proceedings of the 36th annual international symposium on Computer architecture*, pages 152–163, 2009.

[8] S. Laha, J. H. Patel, and R. K. Iyer. Accurate low-cost methods for performance evaluation of cache memory systems. *IEEE Trans. Comput.*, 37:1325–1336.

[9] C. Lattner and V. Adve. LLVM: A compilation framework for lifelong program analysis & transformation. In *Proceedings of the international symposium on Code generation and optimization: feedback-directed and runtime optimization*, pages 75–86, 2004.

[10] W. Nagel, A. Arnold, M. Weber, H. Hoppe, and K. Solchenbach. *VAMPIR: Visualization and analysis of MPI resources*. KFA, ZAM, 1996.

[11] J. Nickolls and W. J. Dally. The GPU computing era. *IEEE Micro*, 30:56–69, March 2010.

[12] NVIDIA. CUDA occupancy calculator.

[13] NVIDIA Staff. *NVIDIA CUDA Programming Guide 4.0*, 2011.

[14] V. Pillet, J. Labarta, T. Cortes, and S. Girona. PARAVER: A tool to visualise and analyze parallel code. In *Proceedings of WoTUG-18: Transputer and occam Developments*, volume 44, pages 17–31, 1995.

[15] S. Ryoo, C. I. Rodrigues, S. S. Stone, S. S. Baghsorkhi, S.-Z. Ueng, J. A. Stratton, and W.-m. W. Hwu. Program optimization space pruning for a multithreaded GPU. In *Proceedings of the 6th annual IEEE/ACM international symposium on Code generation and optimization*, pages 195–204, 2008.

[16] V. Salapura, K. Ganesan, A. Gara, M. Gschwind, J. C. Sexton, and R. E. Walkup. Next-generation performance counters: Towards monitoring over thousand concurrent events. In *Proceedings of the ISPASS 2008 - IEEE International Symposium on Performance Analysis of Systems and software*, pages 139–146, 2008.

[17] S. Shende and A. Malony. The TAU parallel performance system. *International Journal of High Performance Computing Applications*, 20(2):287, 2006.

[18] B. J. Smith. Readings in computer architecture. chapter Architecture and applications of the HEP mulitprocessor computer system, pages 342–349. Morgan Kaufmann Publishers Inc., 2000.

[19] A. Snavely, L. Carter, J. Boisseau, A. Majumdar, K. S. Gatlin, N. Mitchell, J. Feo, and B. Koblenz. Multi-processor performance on the tera MTA. In *Proceedings of the 1998 ACM/IEEE conference on Supercomputing*, pages 1–8, 1998.

[20] H. Stark and J. Woods. *Probability, random processes, and estimation theory for engineers*. Prentice-Hall, Inc. Upper Saddle River, NJ, USA, 1986.

[21] R. Ubal, J. Sahuquillo, S. Petit, and P. López. Multi2Sim: A Simulation Framework to Evaluate Multicore-Multithreaded Processors. Oct. 2007.

[22] Y. Zhang and J. D. Owens. A quantitative performance analysis model for GPU architectures. In *Proceedings of the 17th IEEE International Symposium on High-Performance Computer Architecture*, 2011.

Communication Avoiding Symmetric Band Reduction

Grey Ballard James Demmel Nicholas Knight
UC Berkeley
{ballard,demmel,knight}@cs.berkeley.edu

Abstract

The running time of an algorithm depends on both arithmetic and communication (i.e., data movement) costs, and the relative costs of communication are growing over time. In this work, we present both theoretical and practical results for tridiagonalizing a symmetric band matrix: we present an algorithm that asymptotically reduces communication, and we show that it indeed performs well in practice.

The tridiagonalization of a symmetric band matrix is a key kernel in solving the symmetric eigenvalue problem for both full and band matrices. In order to preserve sparsity, tridiagonalization routines use annihilate-and-chase procedures that previously have suffered from poor data locality. We improve data locality by reorganizing the computation, asymptotically reducing communication costs compared to existing algorithms. Our sequential implementation demonstrates that avoiding communication improves runtime even at the expense of extra arithmetic: we observe a 2× speedup over Intel MKL while doing 43% more floating point operations.

Our parallel implementation targets shared-memory multicore platforms. It uses pipelined parallelism and a static scheduler while retaining the locality properties of the sequential algorithm. Due to lightweight synchronization and effective data reuse, we see 9.5× scaling over our serial code and up to 6× speedup over the PLASMA library, comparing parallel performance on a ten-core processor.

Categories and Subject Descriptors G.1.3 [*Numerical Analysis*]: Numerical Linear Algebra - Eigenvalues and eigenvectors (direct and iterative methods); F.2.1 [*Analysis of Algorithms and Problem Complexity*]: Numerical Algorithms and Problems - Computations on matrices

General Terms Algorithms, Performance, Theory

Keywords Symmetric eigenvalue problem, Communication avoiding algorithms, Band reduction

1. Introduction

The running time of an algorithm depends on both the number of floating point operations performed (*arithmetic*) and the amount of data moved (*communication*) through the memory hierarchy of a single processor and, in the parallel case, across a network between processors. The cost of moving data on today's machines already greatly exceeds the cost of performing floating point operations on it, and architectural trends indicate that this processor-memory gap is growing exponentially over time [8]. Thus, we are interested in new algorithms which reduce the communication costs of existing ones, even at the expense of doing more arithmetic.

In this work, we present a new algorithm for the tridiagonalization of a symmetric band matrix in order to compute its eigenvalues. While the symmetric band problem is interesting in its own right, this work was motivated by the high communication costs of the standard algorithms for solving the dense symmetric eigenproblem via tridiagonalization. Greater efficiency can be obtained if the tridiagonalization procedure is split into two stages: reducing the full matrix to band form and then reducing the band matrix to tridiagonal form. While high performance has been obtained for the computations in the first stage [14, 16], the efficiency of computations during the second stage has been limited by high communication costs. Thus, by reducing the communication and improving the algorithm for tridiagonalizing a band matrix, we can also improve the fastest algorithm for tridiagonalizing a full matrix.

While we focus on tridiagonalizing symmetric matrices in this work, the ideas here can be readily applied to bidiagonalization procedures used in computing the singular values of a general band matrix. Band reduction is a subroutine within the fastest algorithm for bidiagonalizing a general matrix [15] as well as within algorithms for computing the SVD of a sparse matrix [18].

Our new algorithm, Communication Avoiding Symmetric Band Reduction (CA-SBR), asymptotically reduces communication costs (as specified by our communication model) compared to previous approaches, and our implementation achieves higher sequential performance than vendor libraries such as Intel's Math Kernel Library (MKL). We also parallelize our algorithm for shared memory machines, and we show that our implementation achieves higher performance than the state-of-the-art Parallel Linear Algebra for Scalable Multi-core Architectures (PLASMA) library [2]. Our algorithm (both sequential and parallel) includes a large set of parameters which allows for tuning the implementation to a particular hardware. Because the design space is so large, an automatic performance tuning scheme would be helpful to optimize the implementation for a given machine.

Communication Model In order to measure the communication costs of an algorithm, we model a sequential machine with two levels of memory hierarchy (fast and slow) and count the number of words moved between these two levels during the execution of the algorithm; this we call the *bandwidth cost*. This model is sometimes referred to as the two-level I/O or disk access model (see, e.g., [1]) and the number of words moved is also known as the I/O-complexity of the algorithm. We use M to denote the size of the fast memory in words. If words are stored contiguously in slow memory, then they can be read or written together as a *message*. We are also interested in the number of messages transferred between

PPoPP'12, February 25–29, 2012, New Orleans, Louisiana, USA.

Algorithm	Flops	Words Moved	Data Re-use
Schwarz [20]	$4n^2b$	$O(n^2b)$	$O(1)$
M-H [17]	$6n^2b$	$O(n^2b)$	$O(1)$
Kaufman [12]	$4n^2b$	$O(n^2b)$	$O(1)$
SBR [4]	$5n^2b$	$O(n^2 \log b)$	$O\left(\frac{b}{\log b}\right)$
Raj. [18]	$4n^2b$	$O(n^2 \log b)$	$O\left(\frac{b}{\log b}\right)$
CA-SBR	$5n^2b$	$O\left(\frac{n^2b^2}{M}\right)$	$O\left(\frac{M}{b}\right)$

Table 1. We compare the arithmetic and communication costs of previous sequential algorithms with our communication avoiding approach for symmetric band matrices of n columns and b subdiagonals on a sequential machine with fast memory of size M. The table assumes that $nb > M$ and that $2 \leq b \leq \sqrt{M}/3$. The third column (data re-use, also referred to as computational intensity) is given by the ratio of flops performed to words read from slow memory. The communication cost of SBR and Raj. assumes optimal parameter choices, and analysis for all algorithms is given in Sec. 3.

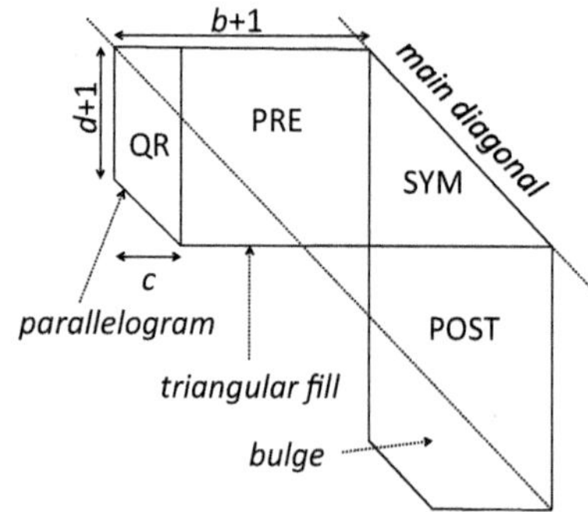

Figure 1. Following the notation of [4], the bulge chasing operation based on an orthogonal similarity transformation can be decomposed into four parts. There are d diagonals in each bulge and c is the number of columns annihilated during a bulge chase which leaves behind triangular fill.

fast and slow memory, which we call the *latency cost*. In our model, messages may range in size from one word to M words.

Theoretical Improvements Table 1 shows the arithmetic and bandwidth costs of several existing algorithms compared with our CA-SBR algorithm. The arithmetic costs differ by small constant ratios, while the differences in communication cost can be asymptotic. The last column shows the data reuse (i.e., the number of flops performed for each word read from slow memory) which is given by the ratio of the previous two columns. There exist communication lower bounds for many linear algebra algorithms including Cholesky, LU, and QR decompositions [3], and in many cases there are algorithms which provide matching upper bounds. Interestingly, CA-SBR is not subject to these bounds and in fact beats them, as described in Sec. 3.6.

The use of CA-SBR also improves the asymptotic complexity of computing the eigenvalues of a full symmetric matrix. In the two-stage tridiagonalization approach, the reduction of the matrix to band form can be done in a communication-optimal way with the use of the TSQR algorithm [6]. Using our new algorithm, the communication costs of the band reduction stage are lower order terms for all n and M. This is an asymptotic improvement over any existing direct tridiagonalization approach (see Sec. 3.7).

Practical Improvements As shown in Sec. 6, we obtain significant speedups over state-of-the-art libraries. On a 10-core Intel Westmere-EX processor, we achieved a 2× speedup over MKL's `dsbtrd` routine running with one thread and a 6× speedup over PLASMA's `pdsbrdt` routine with using 10 threads, on a problem of dimension $n = 24000$ and bandwidth $b = 300$ (the largest problem size in our test set).

2. Preliminaries

2.1 Notation

We will borrow notation from [4] and the authors' related papers to describe the terminology associated with successive band reduction (SBR). While we do not give a complete description of SBR here, Fig. 2 in [4] is particularly helpful for visualizing the framework.

Let $B \in \mathbb{R}^{n \times n}$ be symmetric and banded with bandwidth b (i.e., having $2b + 1$ nonzero diagonals). Because we will preserve symmetry, it is sufficient to store and operate on only the lower $b+1$ diagonals of B. The SBR approach reduces this matrix to a symmetric tridiagonal matrix T via orthogonal similarity transformations which comprise an orthogonal matrix Q such that $QBQ^T = T$. In this work, we are concerned with finding only eigenvalues, so we do not need to construct or store Q.

In a given *sweep*, SBR eliminates d subdiagonals in sets of c columns,[1] using an annihilate-and-chase approach. We assume Householder transformations are used; each set of transformations eliminates a $d \times c$ *parallelogram* of nonzeros while the symmetric update creates trapezoidal-shaped fill (a *bulge*). Using analogous orthogonal similarities, SBR chases each bulge off the end of the band, translating the bulge b columns to the right with each chase. Fig. 1 shows the data access pattern of a single bulge chase. A QR decomposition computes the orthogonal matrix that annihilates the parallelogram; the corresponding rows are updated with a PRE-multiplication of the orthogonal matrix; the lower half of the symmetric submatrix is updated from the left and right with a SYM operation; and the corresponding columns are updated with a POST-multiplication by the transpose of the orthogonal matrix, creating the next bulge.

We define the *working bandwidth* to be the number of subdiagonals necessary to store the $b + 1$ diagonals of the matrix as well as the d diagonals that store temporary fill-in during the course of a sweep. As observed in [17], we note that an entire bulge need not be eliminated; only the first c columns of the bulge must be annihilated to prevent subsequent bulges introducing nonzeros beyond the working bandwidth. This results in temporary *triangular fill*.

We index sweeps with an integer i, where $i = 1$ is the first sweep. We let $b_1 = b$ be the initial bandwidth. We index the parallelograms which initiate each bulge chase by j and the sequence of following bulges by the ordered pairs (j, k). We will refer to j as the parallelogram number and k as the bulge number.

2.2 Related Work

Sequential Algorithms The two papers of Bischof, Lang, and Sun [4, 5] provide a general framework of sequential band reduction algorithms. Their approach (described in Sec. 2.1) generalizes most of the previous work.

The annihilate-and-chase strategy began with Rutishauser and Schwarz in 1963. Rutishauser [19] identifies two extreme points in the SBR algorithm design space: (1) a Givens based approach with b sweeps and $c_i = d_i = 1$ for each i and (2) a column-based approach with one sweep where $c_1 = 1$ and $d_1 = b - 1$. Rutishauser's first approach only considered pentadiagonal matrices; Schwarz [20] generalized the algorithm to arbitrary bandwidths. Later, Schwarz [21] proposed a different algorithm based

[1] We depart from the LAPACK-style notation `nb` of [4].

on Givens rotations which does not fit in the SBR framework. This algorithm eliminates entries by column rather than by diagonal and does not generalize to parallelograms.

Muraka and Horikoshi [17] improved on Rutishauser's column-based algorithm by noting that computation can be saved by eliminating only the first column of the triangular bulge rather than the entire triangle.

Kaufman [11] implemented the Rutishauser/Schwarz algorithm [19, 20], but chased multiple element-size bulges in one vector operation. Her motivation for chasing multiple bulges was not locality but rather to increase the length of the vector operation beyond the bandwidth b. Several years later, Kaufman [12] took the approach of [21] in order to maximize the vector operation length (especially in the case of large b) and make use of a BLAS subroutine when appropriate. The current LAPACK reference code for band reduction (`dsbtrd`) is based on [12].

More recently, Rajamanickam [18] proposed and implemented a different way of eliminating a parallelogram and chasing its fill. Their algorithm uses Givens rotations to eliminate the individual entries of a parallelogram, and instead of creating a large bulge, the update rotations are pipelined such that as soon as an element is filled in outside the band, it is immediately annihilated. The rotations are carefully ordered to obtain temporal locality as well as stride-one access. By avoiding the large fill-in, their algorithm does up to 50% fewer flops than the Householder-based elimination of parallelograms within SBR.

Parallel Algorithms Lang [13] implemented a distributed-memory parallel version of the band reduction algorithm in [17]. Later, Lang [14] considered shared-memory parallel machines in the context of the dense symmetric eigenproblem but found that parallelizing the full-to-banded reduction (using multithreaded BLAS routines) was more important than improving performance in the band reduction.

Luszczek et al. [16] implemented the band reduction algorithm from [17] in PLASMA [2], using dynamic DAG-scheduling of tile-based tasks. Their pipelining of bulge-chases across multiple threads is much more efficient than multithreaded BLAS, avoiding synchronization costs from fork-join parallelism. They distinguish between "right-looking" and "left-looking" variants: right-looking algorithms chase a bulge entirely off the band before eliminating the next parallelogram, left-looking algorithms chase bulges only far enough to allow for the next bulge to be created (see Constraint 3.2). For example, the SBR framework [4] is right-looking while Kaufman's algorithm [12] is left-looking. In [16], they found improved performance with a left-looking variant.

Later, Haidar et al. [9] reduced the runtime of [16] with a modified scheduler and band reduction algorithm. The modified algorithm also eliminates entries by column, but avoided fill-in and reduced computation with pipelined Givens rotations as in [18].

2.3 Our Contributions

Analysis of Communication Complexity By applying our two-level memory model, we compare the asymptotic communication costs of the different existing band reduction approaches. In Sec. 3.7, we explain theoretically that the poor performance achieved by previous implementations is due to a lack of data locality.

New Sequential Algorithm By parameterizing the algorithm design space more generally than in previous works and identifying means of achieving data locality, we propose a new algorithm in Sec. 3.2 that asymptotically reduces communication costs. We exploit the flexibility of the SBR framework [4] to take multiple sweeps for the purposes of achieving locality within a single bulge chase, and we reorder (interleave) independent bulge chases to achieve locality across multiple bulge chases.

Parallelization of Sequential Algorithm While avoiding communication reduces the theoretical runtime on a sequential computer, we also show in Sec. 4 that our sequential algorithm can be parallelized efficiently for a shared-memory machine. We describe our static scheduling of work which uses lightweight synchronization between neighbors. We also discuss the tradeoffs between data locality and parallelism.

High Performance Implementation Finally, we illustrate our implementations of both sequential and parallel algorithms. In Sec. 5 we describe the large tuning parameter space and the tradeoffs it represents. While neither exhaustive nor automatic tuning are within the scope of this work, we report performance results in Sec. 6 for heuristically tuned parameter values and compare to state-of-the-art libraries. In the sequential case, we obtain up to a $2\times$ speedup over MKL, and in the parallel case, we obtain a $6\times$ speedup over PLASMA running with 10 threads.

3. Sequential Algorithm

The goal of our sequential algorithm is to reorganize computation within the SBR framework in order to avoid communication. We consider taking multiple sweeps and chasing multiple bulges to reduce the number of words and messages that must be moved between fast and slow memory during the execution of the algorithm.

In this work, we will assume the initial bandwidth b is bounded above by $\sqrt{M}/3$. This is a reasonable assumption if the band reduction is used as the second stage of a two-stage reduction of a full symmetric matrix to tridiagonal form. For larger bandwidths, another approach must be taken to avoid communication. We will also assume that $nb > M$; otherwise, the problem is trivial with respect to communication as the original band can be read entirely into the fast memory and the problem solved without any further communication.

3.1 Achieving Data Locality

We achieve data locality (i.e., avoid communication) by maximizing two important parameters in our algorithmic space subject to the constraints described below.

Blocking Householder transformations The first means of achieving data locality is within a single bulge chase. Since c Householder vectors are computed to eliminate the first c columns of the bulge, every entry in the PRE, SYM, and POST regions is updated by c left and/or right Householder transformations, which can be blocked. Assuming all the data involved in a bulge chase (see Fig. 1) reside in fast memory, $O(c)$ flops are performed for every entry read from slow memory.

We identify the following algorithmic constraint. If it is violated, then the parallelogram annihilated after performing the QR and left-sided update will be partially filled back in by the right-sided update (this implies wasted computation).

Constraint 3.1. *To annihilate a parallelogram within the SBR framework, the dimensions of the parallelogram must satisfy*

$$c + d \leq b.$$

While increasing c improves data locality, because of Constraint 3.1, it limits the size of d. Because d is the number of diagonals eliminated in a sweep, this constraint creates a tradeoff between locality and progress towards tridiagonalization. We will navigate this tradeoff by setting $c_i = d_i = b_i/2$ at each sweep, reducing to tridiagonal after $\log b$ sweeps.

Chasing multiple bulges The second means of achieving data locality is across bulge chases. If ω bulges can be chased through the same set of columns without moving data to or from slow memory, then we have achieved $O(\omega)$ reuse of those columns. We first establish the following constraint.

Constraint 3.2. *No bulge may be chased into a set of columns still occupied by a previously created bulge.*

If this constraint is violated, then the fill will expand beyond the working bandwidth of the sweep. While it is possible to eliminate this extra fill, we wish to avoid the extra computation and storage necessary to do so. Chasing the first c columns of a bulge and leaving behind the triangular fill is the least amount of work required to prevent the fill from exceeding the working bandwidth.

To help ensure satisfaction of Constraint 3.2, we state the following facts regarding parallelograms, bulges, and sets of bulges.

Fact 3.3. *Given a sweep of SBR with parameters b, c, and d,*

(a) the jth parallelogram occupies columns $1 + (j-1)c : jc$,
(b) bulge (j, k) occupies columns $1 + (j-1)c + kb - d : jc + kb$,
(c) bulges (j, k) and $(j+1, k-2)$ do not overlap.[2]

Because of Constraint 3.2, we need many columns to contain multiple bulges. Specifically, from Fact 3.3, we see that the ω bulges

$$\{(j,k), (j+1, k-2), \ldots, (j+\omega-1, k-2(\omega-1))\}$$

occupy mutually disjoint column sets, and together this set occupies $(\omega-1)(2b-c)+c+d$ columns (recall that we only store the lower half of the matrix).

Our goal is to determine a working set of columns that fits in fast memory and maximizes the number of bulges (ω) that can be chased as a set, where each bulge is chased ℓ times in turn. The following fact specifies the size of a particular working set (in columns) based on the bandwidth of the matrix and the number of bulges in the set.

Fact 3.4. *Suppose b and ω are even and let $c = d = b/2$ and $\ell = \frac{3}{2}\omega$. The set of ω bulges*

$$\{(j,k), (j+1, k-2), \ldots, (j+\omega-1, k-2(\omega-1))\}$$

spans $\frac{3}{2}\omega b - \frac{1}{2}b$ columns. If the bulges are chased in turn ℓ times each, starting with the right-most bulge (j, k) and ending with the left-most bulge $(j+\omega-1, k-2(\omega-1))$, then there is no violation of Constraint 3.2, and the entire operation requires a working set of $3\omega b - \frac{1}{2}b$ columns.

Fig. 2 demonstrates the working set with $\omega = 2$ bulges $\ell = 3$ times each on a matrix with bandwidth $b = 8$ where $c = d = 4$. Letting $c = d = b/2$, since the working bandwidth includes $b + d + 1 \approx \frac{3}{2}b$ diagonals, the total number of words in the working set is $\frac{9}{2}\omega b^2$, ignoring lower-order terms. Thus, to ensure that the working set fits in the fast memory of size M words, we must satisfy the following constraint (which is specific to the case $c = d = b/2$ and $\ell = \frac{3}{2}\omega$).

Constraint 3.5. *The number of bulges chased at a time must not exceed the following upper bound: $\omega \leq \frac{2}{9}\frac{M}{b^2}$.*

3.2 Sequential CA-SBR

The communication avoiding sequential algorithm, shown in Alg. 1, is based on the framework given in [4]. At each sweep i, we cut the remaining bandwidth b_i in half by setting $d_i = b_i/2$. We also set $c_i = b_i/2$ which satisfies Constraint 3.1. To make the analysis simpler for this successive halving approach, we assume that the initial bandwidth b is a power of two. We include explicit memory operations within the algorithm in order to determine the communication costs: *writes* imply moving data from fast memory to slow memory and *reads* imply moving data from slow memory to fast memory.

[2] Note that if $2c+d \leq b$, bulges (j, k) and $(j+1, k-1)$ also do not overlap.

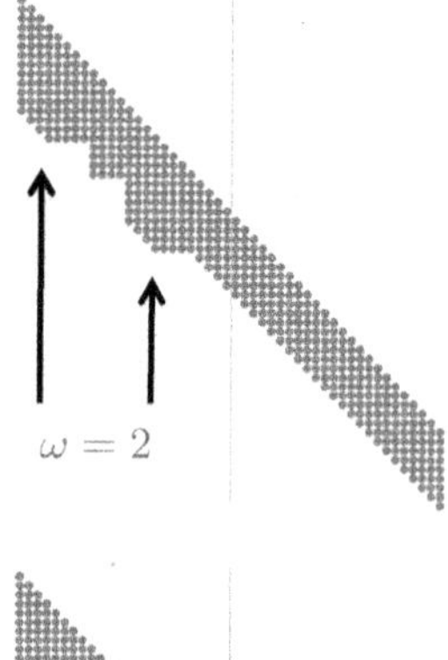

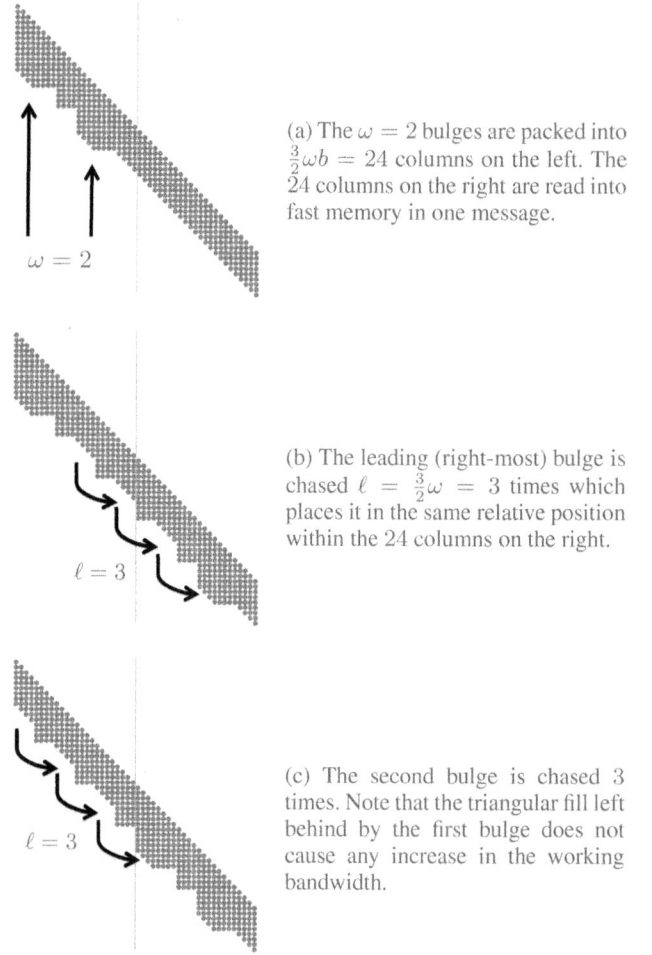

(a) The $\omega = 2$ bulges are packed into $\frac{3}{2}\omega b = 24$ columns on the left. The 24 columns on the right are read into fast memory in one message.

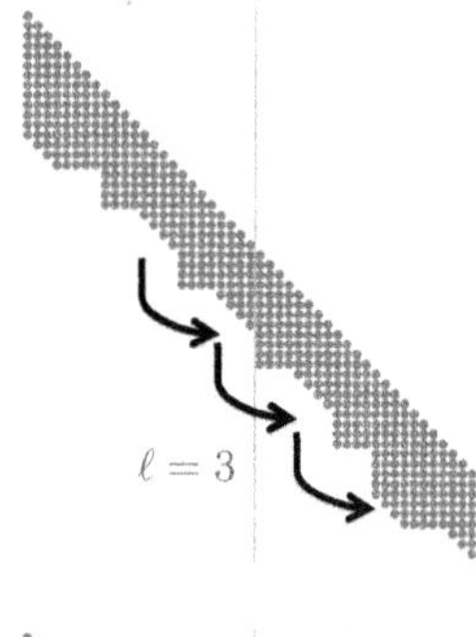

(b) The leading (right-most) bulge is chased $\ell = \frac{3}{2}\omega = 3$ times which places it in the same relative position within the 24 columns on the right.

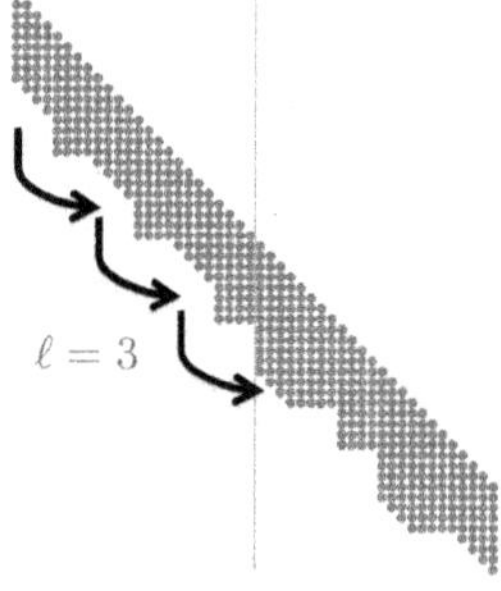

(c) The second bulge is chased 3 times. Note that the triangular fill left behind by the first bulge does not cause any increase in the working bandwidth.

Figure 2. This figure demonstrates line 9 of Alg. 1. The parameters shown are $b = 8$, $c = 4$, and $d = 4$; $\omega = 2$ bulges are chased $\ell = 3$ times each. Only $2\ell b$ columns of the band are shown, corresponding to a working set assumed to fit in fast memory. The working bandwidth includes the diagonals which contain bulges.

Our main deviation from the original SBR framework is reordering the individual bulge-chasing operations. Instead of chasing one parallelogram's bulge off the end of the band before annihilating the next parallelogram (i.e., the right-looking variant), we chase multiple bulges at a time. We let ω_i denote the number of bulges chased at a time (during sweep i). When chasing a set of bulges, we work right-to-left, chasing each bulge ℓ_i times in turn. In this way, no bulges overlap and after all bulges are chased, the relative positions of the bulges are maintained. This process is shown in Fig. 2 and corresponds to line 9 in Alg. 1. By satisfying Constraint 3.5, we ensure that the entire operation can be performed on columns which all fit in fast memory simultaneously. We note that while this theoretical algorithm defines a constant ratio between ω_i and ℓ_i in order to simplify analysis, these parameters can be tuned independently in practice.

We omit the details of creating a set of bulges (line 5) and of chasing bulges at the end of the band (line 11). Both the arithmetic and communication costs of creating ω_i bulges or chasing ω_i bulges off the end of the band are dominated by that of chasing

Algorithm 1 Sequential Communication Avoiding SBR

Require: initial bandwidth $b \leq \sqrt{M}/3$ is a power of 2

1: $t = \min\{\log b, \lceil \log \frac{nb}{M} \rceil\}$
2: **for** $i = 1$ to t **do**
3: $\quad b_i = \frac{b}{2^{i-1}},\ c_i = \frac{b_i}{2},\ d_i = \frac{b_i}{2},\ \omega_i = 2\left\lfloor \frac{M}{9b_i^2} \right\rfloor,\ \ell_i = \frac{3}{2}\omega_i$
4: $\quad$ **while** not reached end of band **do**
5: $\quad\quad$ create next set of ω_i bulges
6: $\quad\quad$ **while** not reached end of band **do**
7: $\quad\quad\quad$ write previous $\ell_i b_i$ columns of band
8: $\quad\quad\quad$ read next $\ell_i b_i$ columns of band
9: $\quad\quad\quad$ chase ω_i bulges ℓ_i times each
10: $\quad\quad$ **end while**
11: $\quad\quad$ chase ω_i bulges off the end of the band
12: $\quad$ **end while**
13: $\quad$ copy band into data structure with column height $\frac{3}{2}b_{i+1}$
14: **end for**
15: **if** $t < \log b$ **then**
16: $\quad$ read remaining band into fast memory
17: $\quad$ reduce band to tridiagonal
18: $\quad$ write output to slow memory
19: **end if**

the ω_i bulges ℓ_i times each. Also, since neither operation occurs in the inner loop of the algorithm, they contribute only lower order terms to the costs of the entire algorithm.

The computation of t in line 1 determines the sweep (if any) after which the remaining band fits entirely in fast memory. Note that if $n > M$, then the band will never fit in fast memory and $t = \log b$. If the band becomes small enough to fit in fast memory, then the algorithm will stop the main loop (lines 2–14) and fall to the clean-up code in lines 15–19 which simply reads the band into fast memory, reduces all the way to tridiagonal form (using any algorithm), and writes the result back to slow memory.

3.3 Arithmetic cost

Consider one sweep of SBR with the parameters b, c, and d. Assuming none of the orthogonal updates are blocked, the arithmetic cost of chasing a bulge using Householder transformations (Fig. 1) is $8bcd + 4cd^2 + O(cd)$ flops. For each parallelogram eliminated, the bulge must be chased the length of the trailing band, in increments of b columns. Thus, the total number of bulge chases during a sweep is

$$\sum_{j=1}^{n/c} \left(8bcd + 4cd^2\right) \frac{n - jc}{b},$$

ignoring lower order terms. This expression can be simplified to yield the following fact (which agrees with equation (3) in [4]).

Fact 3.6. *The arithmetic cost of eliminating d diagonals from a matrix with bandwidth b using SBR is* $\left(4d + 2\frac{d^2}{b}\right) n^2 + O(n^2)$.

The order of operations specified by the algorithm does not affect the arithmetic count. Given the cost of the ith sweep specified by Fact 3.6, since $d_i = b_i/2$ and $\sum d_i = b - 1$, the arithmetic cost of Alg. 1 (ignoring lower order terms) is

$$\sum_{i=1}^{\log b} \left(4d_i + 2\frac{d_i^2}{b_i}\right) n^2 = 5n^2 b.$$

See Sec. 5.3 for a discussion of different approaches to chasing individual bulges and implications on performance.

3.4 Bandwidth cost

In determining the communication costs of Alg. 1, we must consider two cases. If $n > M$, then $\log b < \lceil \log \frac{nb}{M} \rceil$ and the main loop (lines 2–14) will be executed $\log b$ times, reducing the band all the way to tridiagonal. However, if $n < M$, then at some point the bandwidth will become small enough such that the entire band fits in fast memory. At this point, the algorithm reduces to lines 15–19 and the only communication required to finish the reduction is that of reading the band into fast memory and writing the tridiagonal output back to slow memory for a cost of $O(nb_{t+1})$ words.

We now consider the ith sweep, where we assume the band is too large to fit in fast memory. The dominant communication cost is in the innermost loop (lines 6–10). The number of words in each column is $\frac{3}{2}b_i$, so the bandwidth cost of one iteration of the inner loop is $3\ell_i b_i^2 = O(M)$ words. The inner loop is executed $O(\frac{n}{\ell_i b_i})$ times for each set of bulges, and there are $O(\frac{n}{c_i \omega_i})$ sets of bulges during the sweep. Thus, the bandwidth cost of one sweep is $O(n^2 b_i^2 / M)$ words.

The bandwidth cost (i.e., number of words moved) of Alg. 1 is

$$\sum_{i=1}^{t} O\left(\frac{n^2 (b/2^i)^2}{M}\right) + O(nb_{t+1}) = O\left(\frac{n^2 b^2}{M} + nb\right).$$

3.5 Latency cost

We will assume the band matrix is stored in LAPACK band storage format (column-major with column height equal to the working bandwidth) so that any block of columns of the band will be stored contiguously in slow memory. After each set of subdiagonals is annihilated from a column block, the algorithm packs the remaining diagonals into a smaller data structure (see line 13) to maintain a packed column-major layout for all successive sweeps. This increases the memory footprint by no more than a factor of two (it can also be done in place).

As in the previous section, if the band becomes small enough to fit in fast memory, then the communication costs of completing the algorithm are reduced to reading the band and writing the tridiagonal output. In this case, the latency cost is 2 messages. When the band is too large to fit in fast memory, the dominant latency cost is that of the innermost loop. Since consecutive columns are stored contiguously, the latency cost per iteration of the innermost loop is 2 messages. As argued above, the inner loop is executed $O(\frac{n}{\ell_i b_i})$ times for each set of bulges, and there are $O(\frac{n}{c_i \omega_i})$ sets of bulges during the sweep. Thus, the latency cost of one sweep is $O(n^2 b_i^2 / M^2)$ messages.

The latency cost (i.e., number of messages moved) of Alg. 1 is

$$\sum_{i=1}^{t} O\left(\frac{n^2 (b/2^i)^2}{M^2}\right) + O(1) = O\left(\frac{n^2 b^2}{M^2} + 1\right).$$

3.6 Related Lower Bounds

No communication lower bound has been established for annihilate-and-chase band reduction algorithms, so we cannot conclude that Alg. 1 is communication–optimal in an asymptotic sense. In fact, the general communication lower bound result of [3], which applies to many algorithms in numerical linear algebra including matrix multiplication and many QR-decomposition algorithms, does not apply to SBR or its variants because they fail to satisfy "forward progress" (Definition 4.3 in [3]). That is, the lower bound proof requires that an orthogonal transformation algorithm not fill in a previously created zero–this occurs frequently in SBR.

The main result of [3] states that the lower bound for the number of words moved by an applicable algorithm which performs G flops is $\Omega(G/\sqrt{M})$ for sufficiently large problems. Since Alg. 1 performs $O(n^2 b)$ flops and moves $O(n^2 b^2 / M)$ words (for large bands), its communication complexity drops below the lower bound by a factor of $O(\sqrt{M}/b)$ for $2 \leq b \leq \sqrt{M}/3$. For small b and large n (such that the band does not fit entirely in fast memory), this discrepancy is as much as $O(\sqrt{M})$. Thus, our algorithm shows that not only does the lower bound proof technique not apply to annihilate-and-chase algorithms, the bound itself must not apply.

3.7 Communication Complexity of Related Work

In this section we assume that $nb > M$ (the matrix does not fit in fast memory) as before. Otherwise, the communication costs are the same for all algorithms. In the case that $n < M$ (i.e., one or more diagonals fit in fast memory), the analysis becomes more complicated when the bandwidth is reduced such that the remaining band matrix fits in fast memory; however, the asymptotic costs do not change except where noted.

We first consider the sequential algorithm that does not fit into the SBR framework. While Kaufman's algorithm [12] (third row of Table 1) chases multiple bulges, it is left-looking in order to maximize the vector operation length, so it does not limit the size of the working set to fit in fast memory. As a result, the algorithm has to read at least one of each pair of entries to be updated by a Givens rotation from slow memory. Thus, the data reuse is $O(1)$ and the total number of words transferred between fast and slow memory is proportional to the number of flops: $O(n^2b)$.

Consider an algorithm within the SBR framework with parameters $\{b_i, c_i, d_i\}$ which does not chase multiple bulges at a time ($\omega_i = 1$). Since the SBR framework is right-looking, the remaining band must be read for each parallelogram eliminated. During the ith sweep, there are $O(n/c_i)$ parallelograms and each parallelogram is chased $O(n/b_i)$ times on average. The amount of data accessed during one bulge chase is at least $O(b_i(c_i + d_i))$ words –for example, b_i columns are accessed during the left-sided update and each bulge occupies $c_i + d_i$ rows. Thus, the number of words read during the ith sweep is $O(n^2(1 + d_i/c_i))$.

Given this cost per sweep, consider using b sweeps with $c_i = d_i = 1$ at each sweep as in [19, 20] (first row of Table 1), and consider using one sweep with $c_1 = 1$ and $d_1 = b - 1$ as in [17, 19] (second row of Table 1). In both cases the total number of words read is $O(n^2b)$. However, if an SBR scheme uses the successive halving approach as in Alg. 1 (without chasing multiple bulges), setting $c_i = d_i = b_i/2$ over $\log b$ sweeps, then the bandwidth cost can be reduced to $O(n^2 \log b)$ (or $O\left(n^2 \log \frac{nb}{M}\right)$ in the case that $n < M$). Note that the approach of [18] yields the same communication costs as the SBR framework, so using successive halving will also allow the Raj. algorithm to move $O(n^2 \log b)$ words while performing fewer flops than SBR (see the fourth and fifth rows of Table 1).

For all band reduction algorithms, data locality improves near the end of a sweep due to the shrinking trailing band. This is related to the observation in [16], that left-looking variants of SBR can achieve better data locality than right-looking variants. At the beginning of a left-looking sweep, the working set grows more slowly than the right-looking variant. However, because left-looking variants continue to add bulges to the band, the working set will eventually exceed the fast memory size, and the cost of work done while the working set is large will dominate the communication costs of the entire algorithm. Thus, while the left-looking approach does reduce communication, it does not do so asymptotically.

Considering the band reduction within the context of tridiagonalizing a full symmetric matrix, there are other optimizations for reducing communication such as blocking trailing matrix updates [7] and *fusing* multiple BLAS-2 operations with common operands (applied in [10] to the related problem of bidiagonalization). However, these approaches can only reduce the $O(n^3)$ words moved by a constant factor. As mentioned in the introduction, a two-stage tridiagonalization approach can reduce data movement asymptotically, by a factor that depends on the size of the fast memory.

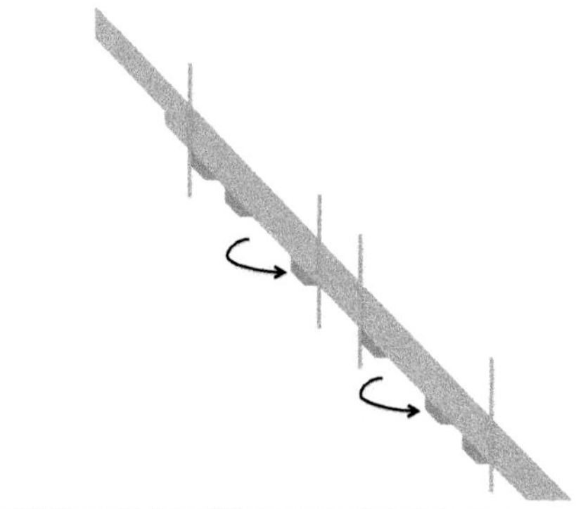

Figure 3. This figure demonstrates the pipelined parallelism available in successive band reduction. The vertical bars denote the width of a task–chasing ω bulges ℓ times each–and synchronization prevents any two tasks from overlapping. In this figure, $\omega = 3$ and $\ell = 1$.

4. Parallel Shared-Memory Algorithm

We extend the communication–efficient sequential algorithm to a shared–memory parallel computer by pipelining the computation. As shown in Fig. 3, if a set of bulges is being chased near the end of the band, the next set of bulges can be created and chased near the beginning of the band in parallel. We consider chasing ω bulges ℓ times each (line 9 in Alg. 1 and Fig. 2) to be the main unit of computation (a task), and we ensure that no tasks overlap.

4.1 Static Assignment

We assign tasks to threads round-robin: each thread creates a set of bulges, chases that set of bulges off the band, and then is ready for another task. Assuming ω and ℓ are chosen such that the size of the data associated with one task fits in the thread's local fast memory, then each thread must read the entire band exactly once in order to create and chase a set of bulges off the band.

We have also considered another strategy: assigning threads to columns rather than bulges. That is, each thread chases bulges through its columns and then waits for the next bulges to arrive from its neighbor. This way, each of the p threads accesses only $O(nb/p)$ of the data rather than streaming through the entire band. However, dependencies prevent two neighbors from computing simultaneously, and load balancing becomes more difficult since more computation occurs at the end of the band. In distributed memory, Lang [13] hid this extra latency by overlapping communication with computation. We plan to address this strategy in future work.

Equating tasks and bulge chases will also work well with dynamic assignment, e.g. in PLASMA [2]. A task can be made coarse-grained (large ω and ℓ) for small bandwidths which will improve locality and help alleviate the high scheduling overhead mentioned in [9, 16].

4.2 Synchronization

Before executing a task, each thread determines which columns will be updated by the task (using Fact 3.3). By maintaining a global array of first columns and last columns and assuming the round-robin static scheduling, each thread need check only that its last column does not exceed the previous thread's first column. If the task does overlap the previous thread's task, then the thread spin-waits until it is safe to proceed. In this way, the synchronization occurs only between nearest neighbors. With a slight modification, this strategy additionally permits interleaving across sweeps–however, we did not explore this further.

4.3 Data Locality

When a thread's working set fits in its fast memory, that thread achieves the same data locality as in the sequential case. By maximizing ω_i and ℓ_i at each sweep subject to Constraint 3.5), each thread need only communicate b/M words and b/M^2 messages per flop. However, the cost of each word or message read is not captured by our model: words may be read from main memory, a shared cache, or another thread's private cache; our model also ignores data traffic due to synchronization.

4.4 Parallelism

The amount of available parallelism is proportional to the ratio of the size of the (remaining) band to the size of a task, where size is measured in number of columns. The size of a task on the ith sweep is a function of b_i, c_i, d_i, ω_i, and ℓ_i. Fact 3.4 considers the case $c_i = d_i = b_i/2$ and $\ell_i = \frac{3}{2}\omega_i$; for general ℓ_i, the number of columns is $\left(\frac{3}{2}\omega_i + \ell_i - \frac{1}{2}\right) b_i$. Therefore, the width of a task increases with both ω_i and ℓ_i, and the amount of available parallelism decreases with those parameters. We showed in Sec. 4.3 that increasing ω_i and ℓ_i reduces communication costs. Thus, these parameters expose a tradeoff between data locality and parallelism.

Since the size of the working set is also proportional to the current bandwidth b_i, the amount of available parallelism increases as the bandwidth decreases. Thus, it may be more beneficial for large bandwidths to eliminate fewer diagonals than in the sequential case, in order to perform fewer flops when less parallelism is available. By decreasing d_i we may increase c_i, so in this case we can achieve greater parallelism (in the overall reduction) and better data locality (in the current sweep). We observe this in Sec. 6.

5. Tuning Parameters

5.1 Reduction Sequence

The original SBR algorithm and our communication–avoiding version are both based on successively reducing the bandwidth over multiple sweeps. Thus, the highest level tuning parameter is the number of sweeps and the number of diagonals eliminated during each sweep $\{d_i\}$. These parameters can be identified by dynamic programming: [4] finds a sweep sequence that minimizes flops. If $d_1 = b - 1$, then SBR performs $6n^2b$ flops (assuming Householder vectors are used). If $d_i = 1$ for $1 \le i \le b$, then it performs $4n^2b$ flops. All other choices of reduction sequences fall between these two extremes–our theoretical approach of successive halving performs $5n^2b$ flops.

We extended the approach in [4]: we first benchmarked single-sweep performance and then used dynamic programming to minimize runtime, thus taking both computation and communication costs into account.

5.2 Sweep Parameters

For a given sweep ((b, d) pair), there are three main tuning parameters to determine. By Constraint 3.1, the width (c) of the parallelograms to eliminate can be chosen between 1 and $b - d$. This choice of c does not affect the flop count of the sweep to leading order, but it does affect the communication costs. Theory suggests that maximizing c improves performance without tradeoff, for a given sweep. Also, we must determine the number of bulges in a set (ω) and the number of times to chase each individual bulge (ℓ). Algorithmically, ω and ℓ are not constrained; theory suggests that they should be maximized subject to the working set size constraint to reduce communication and minimized to increase parallelism.

5.3 Bulge-Chasing Parameters

Given a sweep with parameters b, d, and c, the next level of tuning chooses how to chase an individual bulge. As shown in Fig. 1, there are four main operations in a bulge chase, but their implementations are not specified. Since all the data involved in a single bulge chase resides in fast memory, the tuning parameters at this level do not affect the theoretical communication costs. We identify three methods of chasing a bulge, which vary in the number of flops performed and in the expected performance of those flops.

Unblocked Householder transformations (BLAS 2 approach) With BLAS 2 subroutines, we work left to right through the parallelogram (QR operation), computing each Householder vector and applying the entire two-sided update, updating all four regions from Fig. 1, before moving to the next Householder vector. These updates can be reordered in many ways.

This approach performs $8bcd + 4cd^2 + O(cd)$ flops, as in Sec. 3.3. This approach is performance-portable since it uses the BLAS, but only BLAS 2 performance can be expected.

Blocked Householder transformations (BLAS 3 approach) We can also apply the Householder vectors in a blocked fashion using the (compact) WY representation, which uses BLAS 3 kernels. The width of this (inner) blocking factor is another tunable parameter which can range from 1, yielding the unblocked approach, to c. Again, the blocked updates can be reordered in many ways. Although the arithmetic costs increase when blocking Householder transformations, the BLAS 3 kernels often outperform BLAS 2 kernels by attaining reuse in smaller caches.

Since LAPACK band storage is column-major, we can call any BLAS routine by adjusting the leading dimension parameter. However, there is a slight difficulty calling LAPACK drivers like `dlarfg/b`, which do not perform parallelogram-shaped QRs. This can be solved by padding with an additional c diagonals of explicit zeros, or by performing the QR and part of the POST operation with BLAS 2 subroutines. We implemented the latter approach.

Pipelined-Givens approach We can also chase a bulge using Givens rotations. In [18], each entry of a parallelogram is annihilated by a single Givens rotation, and the rotations are pipelined to avoid bulges and triangular fill. This approach is also used in [9] for the case $c_1 = 1$ and $d_1 = b - 1$. In both cases, this approach reduces the flop count for an individual bulge chase and achieves a total arithmetic cost of $4n^2b$ for any reduction sequence and choice of c_i. However, it prevents the use of tuned BLAS subroutines and requires processor-specific code to utilize the hardware efficiently.

5.4 Parallel tuning

The sweep parameters also depend on the number of threads available because of the tradeoffs between locality and parallelism. This suggests it may be better to assign tasks to a smaller number of threads, and perhaps to call multithreaded BLAS and LAPACK routines for each bulge chase. We did not explore this possibility.

6. Results

Experimental Setup We benchmark all implementations on an Intel multicore server with four 10-core Westmere-EX processors on distinct sockets. Each socket has a 24MB shared L3 cache, and each core has a private 256KB L2 and 32KB L1. The peak double-precision floating point rate of each core is 9.04 GFLOPS – all experiments are double-precision). To avoid NUMA issues, we confine all parallel experiments to one socket and 10 threads.

We consider problems of dimension 4000 to 24000 in increments of 4000 and bandwidth 50 to 300 in increments of 50. This range of problems matches previous work [16]; about half the problems fit in any processor's L3 cache and half do not. In the context of full symmetric tridiagonalization, the bandwidth of the band matrix is given by the block size used in the full-to-banded stage, which is tuned for performance. In PLASMA, the optimal value is

n / b	50	100	150	200	250	300
24000	1.84	1.58	1.40	1.39	1.41	1.47
20000	1.87	1.75	1.46	1.43	1.45	1.49
16000	1.87	1.98	1.61	1.50	1.52	1.53
12000	1.85	2.14	1.88	1.68	1.63	1.60
8000	1.86	2.18	2.14	2.04	1.98	1.87
4000	1.88	2.19	2.15	2.20	2.31	2.36

Table 2. Performance of MKL `dsbtrd` in GFLOPS ($p=1$)

n / b	50	100	150	200	250	300
24000	3.87	4.68	4.59	5.02	4.51	4.17
20000	3.88	4.52	4.67	5.31	4.61	4.14
16000	3.58	3.79	4.67	5.41	4.64	4.17
12000	3.43	3.62	4.25	5.71	4.72	3.98
8000	2.35	3.02	3.37	4.43	4.36	3.58
4000	2.14	2.22	3.50	3.40	3.42	2.77

Table 3. Performance of PLASMA `pdsbrdt` in GFLOPS ($p=10$)

in the range of 100 to 200. In the context of a sparse eigenvalue or SVD problem which is reduced to a band problem, the bandwidth may be in a wider range.

Implementations We compare CA-SBR to the band reduction routines in MKL and PLASMA, as well as our own implementation of a non-communication-avoiding approach. Our code is written in C using pthreads, compiled with ICC v.11.1.073 with flags `-O3 -fast`, and linked with sequential MKL v.10.3. We also implemented an OpenMP version and saw similar performance.

MKL implements the band-to-tridiagonal reduction with the LAPACK routine `dsbtrd`. The reference LAPACK version of `dsbtrd` implements Kaufman's algorithm [12], and performance suggests that MKL does the same. Table 2 shows the performance for MKL's `dsbtrd`. This routine has not been parallelized in MKL. We note that MKL implements SBR as part of a full-to-tridiagonal reduction in their computational routine `dsyrdb`; unfortunately, the MKL interface does not expose the band reduction subroutine in isolation, so we cannot make comparisons with MKL's SBR.

PLASMA implements the algorithm in [9] which includes the band reduction routine `pdsbrdt`. We built PLASMA v.2.4.1 with the same version of ICC and (sequential) MKL, as well as the `hwloc` package. Because their code is open source, we were able to instrument it to benchmark `pdsbrdt` in isolation. Table 3 shows the performance for PLASMA's `pdsbrdt`.

To determine how strongly CA-SBR performance depends on avoiding communication and on parallelism, we also compare CA-SBR against our parallel implementation of the Murata-Horikoshi algorithm [17] (i.e., taking one sweep with $c = 1$, $d = b - 1$, and $\omega = \ell = 1$), which we will refer to as "par-MH". Since this algorithm uses $c = 1$ and $\omega = 1$, we say that it does not avoid communication.

Heuristic Tuning of CA-SBR As described in Sec. 5.1, we use dynamic programming to find an optimal reduction sequence for each n and b and for sequential and parallel cases separately. In the sequential case, the dynamic program suggests when $b_1 = 50$ or $b_1 = 100$, we should pick $b_2 = 1$, (one sweep), while when $b_1 > 100$, it suggests two sweeps: $b_2 = 50$ and $b_3 = 1$. In parallel, the dynamic program again suggests when $b_1 = 50$ to pick $b_2 = 1$, but suggests more complicated sequences of two and three sweeps for larger problems. For a simpler parallel scheme, we choose to reduce $b_1 = 300$ with $b_2 = 200$, $b_3 = 50$, $b_4 = 1$; when $100 < b_1 < 300$, we choose $b_2 = 50$, $b_3 = 1$; when $b_1 \leq 100$, we choose $b_2 = 1$.

We fix $c_i = b_i - d_i$ for each sweep as suggested in Sec. 5.2, and set $\omega_i = \ell_i = 1$. Contrary to our predictions, choosing $\omega_i > 1$

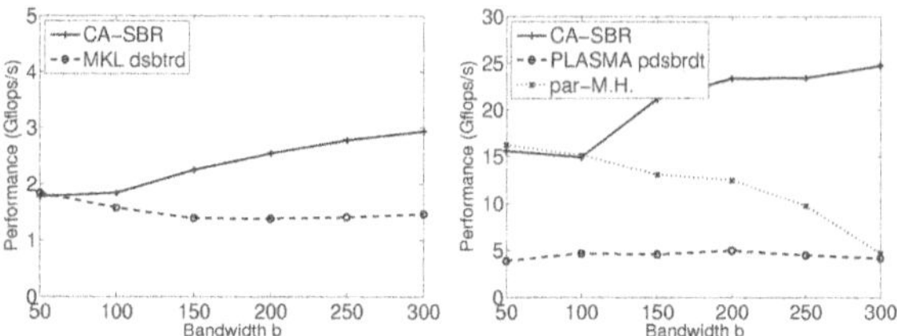

(a) Performance plot varying bandwidth for fixed $n = 24000$, $p = 1$ (left) and $p = 10$ (right)

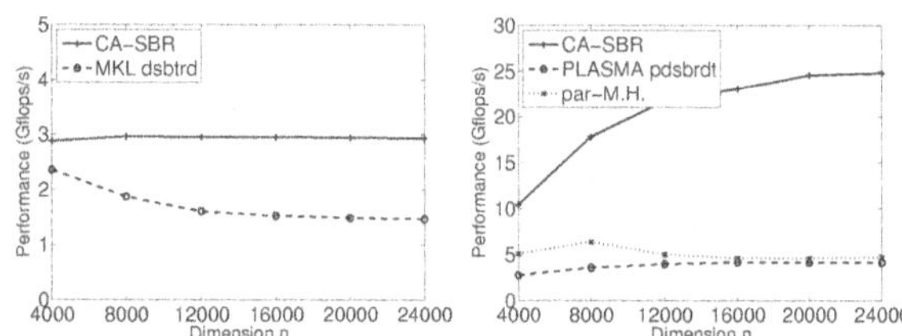

(b) Performance plot varying dimension for fixed $b = 300$, $p = 1$ (left) and $p = 10$ (right)

Figure 4. Performance comparison of all implementations. Effective flop rates shown for comparison–the actual CA-SBR flop rate may be up to 50% higher.

had less than a 20% improvement over $\omega_i = 1$ for the problem sizes mentioned above. We saw up to 40% improvements on much larger problems ($n = 80000$, $b = 50$), and suspect the benefits will continue to become more pronounced for still larger problems.

We believe $\omega > 1$ demonstrates a modest impact because, while it achieves locality in the two-level memory model, it is not necessarily optimal between all pairs of levels in a memory hierarchy. With $c > 1$, we can achieve reuse throughout the memory hierarchy by using tuned BLAS 3 kernels. When $c > 1$, we used the BLAS 3 bulge-chasing approach with an inner blocking factor of 32, otherwise we used the BLAS 2 approach (see Sec. 5.3).

General Results To compare multiple implementations on one plot, we take two one-dimensional slices of the two-dimensional problem size space. Fig. 4 includes two performance plots: (a) presents performance for fixed $n = 24000$ (the largest dimension) and varying bandwidths and (b) shows performance for fixed $b = 300$ (the largest bandwidth) and varying dimension. The plots on the left represent sequential algorithms and those on the right represent parallel algorithms ($p = 10$). Note that we plot *effective* flop rates, that is, in terms of the $4n^2b$ flops required by a Givens-based approach. Our *actual* flop rates are higher due to additional computation (up to 50%) in the SBR approach.

Sequential Results Table 4 gives the performance of sequential CA-SBR in GFLOPS. The peak floating point rate of one core is 9.04 GFLOPS and we benchmarked sequential MKL `dgemm` at 8.3 GFLOPS, so our best sequential performance achieves 33% of peak and 36% of `dgemm`, counting effective flops. The actual flop rates were 46% of peak and 50% of `dgemm`.

Fig. 5 shows a heat map of the speedup of sequential CA-SBR over MKL `dsbtrd`. Because the performance of MKL degrades as the problems become too large for the L3 whereas CA-SBR improves with larger dimension and bandwidth, the largest speedups occur in the upper right quadrant of the heat map. However, since MKL performs fewer flops, it outperforms CA-SBR for some small problems which fit in L3. The largest speedup observed was 2× for $n = 24000$ and $b = 300$.

24000	1.78	1.85	2.25	2.55	2.78	2.93
20000	1.77	1.86	2.27	2.56	2.80	2.94
16000	1.77	1.87	2.27	2.57	2.80	2.95
12000	1.78	1.87	2.27	2.58	2.81	2.95
8000	1.80	1.85	2.27	2.59	2.80	2.96
4000	1.63	1.87	2.28	2.58	2.82	2.88
n/b	**50**	**100**	**150**	**200**	**250**	**300**

Table 4. Performance of sequential CA-SBR in GFLOPS. Each row corresponds to a matrix dimension, and each column corresponds to a matrix bandwidth. Effective flop rates are shown–actual performance may be up to 50% higher.

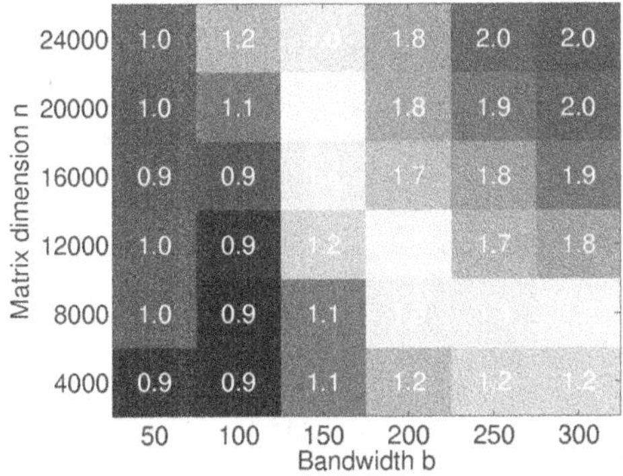

Figure 5. Speedups of sequential CA-SBR over MKL

24000	15.59	14.92	21.17	23.43	23.48	24.79
20000	16.29	16.47	20.81	22.78	22.89	24.56
16000	15.80	17.32	20.81	22.02	22.34	23.08
12000	16.06	18.29	20.19	20.28	20.76	21.74
8000	15.64	17.14	18.39	17.62	16.56	17.80
4000	13.36	12.56	12.82	11.48	10.26	10.44
n/b	**50**	**100**	**150**	**200**	**250**	**300**

Table 5. Performance of parallel CA-SBR in GFLOPS. Each row corresponds to a matrix dimension, and each column corresponds to a matrix bandwidth. As in Table 4, we count only effective flops.

Parallel Results Table 5 gives the performance of parallel CA-SBR in GFLOPS. The peak floating point rate of one socket is 90.4 GFLOPS and we benchmarked parallel MKL `dgemm` at 83 GFLOPS, so our best parallel performance achieves 27% of peak and 30% of `dgemm`, counting effective flops. The actual flop rates were 36% of peak and 40% of `dgemm` peak.

Fig. 6 shows three heat maps of the speedup of parallel CA-SBR over (a) the best sequential CA-SBR, (b) PLASMA's `pdsbrdt`, and (c) par-MH (our parallel implementation of [17]) . Note that sequential and parallel versions of CA-SBR are tuned individually.

Because the available parallelism increases with the ratio of n to b (as noted in Sec. 4.4), we see better parallel speedups over the sequential code in the upper left quadrant of Fig. 6(a). The largest parallel speedup ($p = 10$) was just under $10\times$ for a problem of size $n = 12000$ and $b = 100$, which fits in L3 and permits high parallelism.

In Fig. 6(b), we see that CA-SBR outperforms PLASMA for all problem sizes benchmarked, with speedup numbers ranging from $3\times$ to $6\times$. We observe two areas of greatest improvements: small dimension and small bandwidth (lower left) and large dimension and large bandwidth (upper right). We believe that in the first case, CA-SBR outperforms PLASMA because while there is parallelism available in both approaches, our static schedule and lightweight synchronization have less overhead than the more general–purpose dynamic scheduler within PLASMA. CA-SBR does not avoid communication for these problem sizes, since $c_i = 1$ here, and $\omega_i = 1$ throughout. In the second case, CA-SBR outperforms PLASMA because communication costs become dominant and CA-SBR benefits from greater locality–by taking multiple sweeps, CA-SBR avoids communication by maximizing c_i. For the largest problem size ($n = 24000$ and $b = 300$) we observed a $6\times$ speedup.

We confine the parallel benchmark to one of four sockets because neither our code nor PLASMA are optimized for NUMA architectures. To test scalability across sockets, we benchmark the largest problem size over all 40 cores on the machine and found that the $6\times$ speedup over PLASMA dropped to a $4\times$ speedup across all four sockets. Our best flop rate improves to 29 GFLOPS (effective). Neither code scales well from 10 cores to 40, but PLASMA has slightly higher relative improvement.

By comparing CA-SBR to par-MH (see Fig. 6(c)), we can see exactly when communication avoidance pays off. Because parallel CA-SBR takes only one sweep for the smallest two bandwidths (i.e., $c = 1$) and we chose $\omega = 1$, the two algorithms are equivalent for these bandwidths. For the mid-range bandwidths, CA-SBR takes two sweeps and we see about a $2\times$ speedup over par-MH. For the largest bandwidth $b = 300$, and especially as n increases, we observe speedups of up to $5\times$. Because these matrices do not fit in L3, we conclude that the communication cost differences in the two algorithms explains the difference in performance.

7. Conclusions

In theory, both band reduction and dense matrix-matrix multiplication (`dgemm`) have $O(n)$ possible data reuse. When the problem does not fit in fast memory (of size M words), `dgemm` can attain $\Theta(\sqrt{M})$ data reuse, while our CA-SBR algorithm achieves $\Theta(M/b)$ reuse, provided $b = O(\sqrt{M})$. This constraint on b also ensures that the reuse is always asymptotically at least as large as `dgemm`, and when $b \ll \sqrt{M}$, we can actually attain better reuse than `dgemm`. Whereas previous work suggested that band reduction is memory-bound [9], we have shown that this is not true: CA-SBR is at least as computationally intense as `dgemm`.

When the starting bandwidth $b > \sqrt{M}/3$, we must use a different approach to avoid communication. We conjecture that we can attain $O(\sqrt{M})$ reuse on every sweep, provided we incorporate the CA-QR algorithm [6] into each bulge chase. Once we have reduced the bandwidth to $O(\sqrt{M})$, we may use the CA-SBR approach.

We only considered the problem of finding eigenvalues, which permitted us to discard the Householder transformations generated in the QR phase of each bulge chase. In order to compute eigenvectors, these transformations must be accumulated to form the $n \times n$ orthogonal matrix Q. While the choice of reduction sequence does not increase the number of flops in the band reduction beyond 50% of the cost of any other approach, the arithmetic cost of the orthogonal updates will increase by a factor proportional to the number of sweeps taken. Whether the reduction in communication outweighs the increase in arithmetic cost in practice remains to be seen.

The SBR framework generalizes to the problem of bidiagonalization [18], which is used to solve the singular value decomposition. Our CA-SBR approach also generalizes, and we plan to describe this approach in future work.

We have also developed a distributed memory parallel algorithm that uses the second static schedule described in Sec. 4.1. This algorithm communicates asymptotically less than previous parallel algorithms mentioned in Sec. 2.2; due to our positive results here, we expect that our algorithm will perform better in practice.

We are aware that the PLASMA researchers have been working to improve their `pdsbrdt` performance since the v.2.4.1 release,

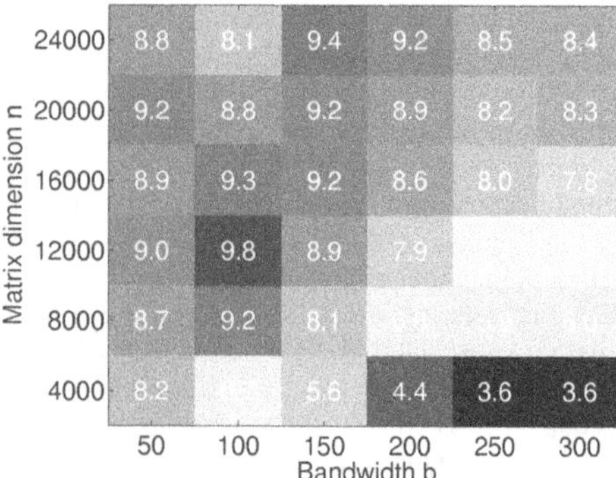

(a) Speedups of par. CA-SBR over seq. CA-SBR

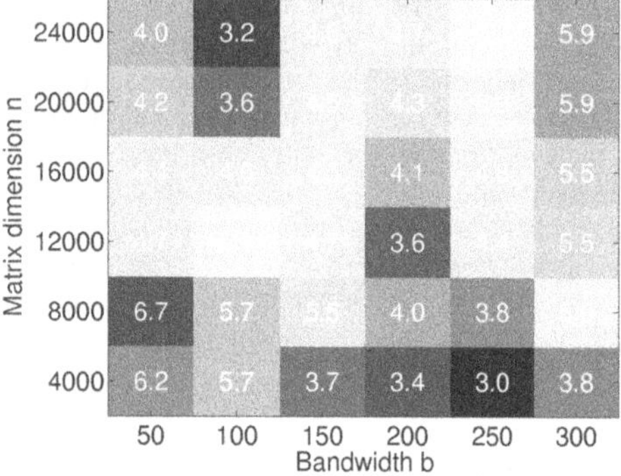

(b) Speedups of parallel CA-SBR over PLASMA

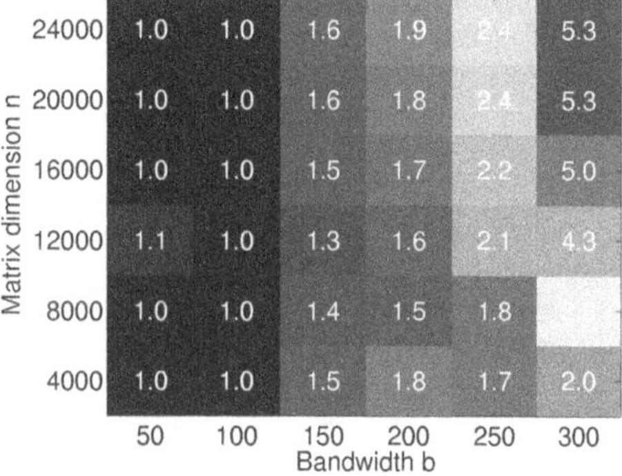

(c) Speedups of parallel CA-SBR over par-MH

Figure 6. Speedups of parallel CA-SBR ($p = 10$)

especially on NUMA architectures. We hope to collaborate and merge our sets of optimizations.

Acknowledgments

Research supported by Microsoft (Award #024263) and Intel (Award #024894) funding and by matching funding by U.C. Discovery (Award #DIG07-10227). Additional support comes from Par Lab affiliates National Instruments, Nokia, NVIDIA, Oracle, and Samsung. Also supported by U.S. DOE grants DE-SC0003959, DE-AC02-05-CH11231, and by NSF SDCI under Grant Number OCI-1032639.

References

[1] AGGARWAL, A., AND VITTER, J. S. The input/output complexity of sorting and related problems. *Comm. ACM 31*, 9 (1988), 1116–1127.

[2] AGULLO, E., DONGARRA, J., HADRI, B., KURZAK, J., LANGOU, J., LANGOU, J., LTAIEF, H., LUSZCZEK, P., AND YARKHAN, A. PLASMA users' guide, 2009. http://icl.cs.utk.edu/plasma/.

[3] BALLARD, G., DEMMEL, J., HOLTZ, O., AND SCHWARTZ, O. Minimizing communication in linear algebra. *SIAM Journal on Matrix Analysis and Applications 32*, 3 (2011), 866-901.

[4] BISCHOF, C., LANG, B., AND SUN, X. A framework for symmetric band reduction. *ACM Trans. Math. Soft. 26*, 4 (2000), 581–601.

[5] BISCHOF, C. H., LANG, B., AND SUN, X. Algorithm 807: The SBR Toolbox—software for successive band reduction. *ACM Trans. Math. Soft. 26*, 4 (2000), 602–616.

[6] DEMMEL, J., GRIGORI, L., HOEMMEN, M., AND LANGOU, J. Communication-optimal parallel and sequential QR and LU factorizations. *SIAM J. Sci. Comput.* (2011). To appear.

[7] DONGARRA, J., HAMMARLING, S., AND SORENSEN, D. Block reduction of matrices to condensed forms for eigenvalue computations. *Journal of Computational and Applied Mathematics 27* (1989).

[8] FULLER, S. H., AND MILLETT, L. I., Eds. *The Future of Computing Performance: Game Over or Next Level?* The National Academies Press, Washington, D.C., 2011.

[9] HAIDAR, A., LTAIEF, H., AND DONGARRA, J. Parallel reduction to condensed forms for symmetric eigenvalue problems using aggregated fine-grained and memory-aware kernels. *Proceedings of the ACM/IEEE Conference on Supercomputing* (2011).

[10] HOWELL, G., DEMMEL, J., FULTON, C., HAMMARLING, S., AND MARMOL, K. Cache efficient bidiagonalization using BLAS 2.5 operators. *ACM Trans. Math. Softw. 34*, 3 (2008), 14:1-14:33.

[11] KAUFMAN, L. Banded eigenvalue solvers on vector machines. *ACM Trans. Math. Softw. 10* (1984), 73–86.

[12] KAUFMAN, L. Band reduction algorithms revisited. *ACM Trans. Math. Softw. 26* (December 2000), 551–567.

[13] LANG, B. A parallel algorithm for reducing symmetric banded matrices to tridiagonal form. *SIAM J. Sci. Comput. 14*, 6 (1993), 1320–1338.

[14] LANG, B. Efficient eigenvalue and singular value computations on shared memory machines. *Par. Comp. 25*, 7 (1999), 845 – 860.

[15] LTAIEF, H., LUSZCZEK, P., AND DONGARRA, J. High performance bidiagonal reduction using tile algorithms on homogeneous multicore architectures. Tech. Rep. 247, LAPACK Working Note, May 2011. Submitted to ACM TOMS.

[16] LUSZCZEK, P., LTAIEF, H., AND DONGARRA, J. Two-stage tridiagonal reduction for dense symmetric matrices using tile algorithms on multicore architectures. In *Proceedings of the IEEE International Parallel and Distributed Processing Symposium* (2011).

[17] MURATA, K., AND HORIKOSHI, K. A new method for the tridiagonalization of the symmetric band matrix. *Information Processing in Japan 15* (1975), 108–112.

[18] RAJAMANICKAM, S. *Efficient Algorithms for Sparse Singular Value Decomposition*. PhD thesis, University of Florida, 2009.

[19] RUTISHAUSER, H. On Jacobi rotation patterns. In *Proceedings of Symposia in Applied Mathematics* (1963), vol. 15, pp. 219–239.

[20] SCHWARZ, H. Algorithm 183: Reduction of a symmetric bandmatrix to triple diagonal form. *Comm. ACM 6*, 6 (June 1963), 315–316.

[21] SCHWARZ, H. Tridiagonalization of a symmetric band matrix. *Numerische Mathematik 12* (1968), 231–241.

Faster Topology-aware Collective Algorithms Through Non-minimal Communication *

Paul Sack William Gropp

Department of Computer Science
University of Illinois at Urbana-Champaign
paulsack@illinois.edu wgropp@illinois.edu

Abstract

Known algorithms for two important collective communication operations, allgather and reduce-scatter, are minimal-communication algorithms; no process sends or receives more than the minimum amount of data. This, combined with the data-ordering semantics of the operations, limits the flexibility and performance of these algorithms. Our novel non-minimal, topology-aware algorithms deliver far better performance with the addition of a very small amount of redundant communication. We develop novel algorithms for Clos networks and single or multi-ported torus networks. Tests on a 32k-node BlueGene/P result in allgather speedups of up to 6x and reduce-scatter speedups of over 11x compared to the native IBM algorithm. Broadcast, reduce, and allreduce can be composed of allgather or reduce-scatter and other collective operations; our techniques also improve the performance of these algorithms.

Categories and Subject Descriptors D.1.3 [*Concurrent Programming*]: Parallel Programming

General Terms Algorithms, Performance

Keywords Collective-communication algorithms

1. Introduction

Known algorithms for collective communication in MPI have been designed to minimize data movement, across the network and in memory. The output of any collective operation must be in a certain order. These requirements together severely curtail the options for collective algorithms. In this work, we show that a small increase in the amount of data communicated can have an enormous effect on performance by reducing congestion and allowing for multi-port algorithms.

* This research used resources of the Argonne Leadership Computing Facility at Argonne National Laboratory, which is supported by the Office of Science of the U.S. Department of Energy under contract DE-AC02-06CH11357. This work was supported in part by the U.S. Department of Energy under contract DE-FG02-08ER25835 and by the National Science Foundation under grant 0837719. We thank the anonymous reviewers, Brian Greskamp, and Jeff Hammond for their helpful comments.

PPoPP'12, February 25–29, 2012, New Orleans, Louisiana, USA.

Many supercomputers with Clos ("fat-tree") networks have less bisection bandwidth than injection bandwidth. The Roadrunner system, currently at number 7 on the Top 500 list [12], has a two-level tree, where the top level provides for just over 25% of the injection bandwidth from the processor cores into the lower level. All supercomputers with torus networks have less bisection bandwidth than injection bandwidth. In other words, under certain bisect communication patterns, congestion will limit performance.

Unfortunately, many widely-used collective communication algorithms make use of bisect patterns that cause the worst congestion. Also, multi-ported switches on torus networks allow for nodes to exchange messages on multiple links simultaneously, but collective algorithms do not take advantage of this.

The essence of our approach is that we temporarily relax the requirement that the output of an operation must be in a particular order as specified in the MPI standard. Instead, we require only that the output be in the same order on every process. We then add a small extra stage of communication either before or after the operation that restores the correct ordering. On an n-node system, this increases the amount of communication by a factor of only $1/n$ to $2/n$. On the other hand, it eliminates or sharply reduces congestion and allows the use of multi-port algorithms.

Specifically, for all networks, we reorder the communication stages in the recursive-doubling allgather and recursive-halving reduce-scatter algorithms, and, for mesh or torus networks, we execute three or six three-dimensional bucket operations in parallel. This produces the correct result in the wrong order; one extra stage of communication restores the correct order.

These algorithms deliver better performance on any network that can suffer from congestion or allows multi-ported communication. In tests on an IBM Blue Gene/P, our best algorithm delivers up to 6x better performance for allgather, and up to 11x better performance for reduce-scatter over the native algorithm. For larger problems, broadcast, reduce, and allreduce are usually decomposed into a scatter and allgather, reduce-scatter and gather, or reduce-scatter and allgather, respectively. Our methods improve the performance of these operations as well.

In Section 2, we discuss known algorithms and related work and show why the performance of minimal-communication algorithms is limited by network congestion and the use of one port at a time in multiport networks. In Section 3, we present our new algorithms. In Section 4, we evaluate the performance of our algorithms on a large supercomputer and compare predicted and measured performance. We discuss future work and conclude in Section 5.

2. Background

In the allgather operation, each process i of P processes has an input vector X_i of length n. After the operation is complete, each process has the same copy of output vector Y of length nP. Vector Y consists of each X_i concatenated in rank order. *I.e.*, $Y = X_0X_1X_2 \cdots X_{P-1}$. Essentially, every process broadcasts its input vector X to all the other processes.

In the reduce-scatter operation, each process has an input vector X_i of length nP. Afterwards, each process has an output vector Y_i of length n. In the operation, blocks of n input elements from each X_i are combined using the reduction operator, and the result from block i is stored on the process with rank i. E.g., Y_0 will be formed from the first n elements of each X_i; Y_1 will be formed from the second n elements of each X_i and so on. Formally, $Y_i = \oplus_{p=0}^{P-1} X_p[in : (i+1)n)$, where $\oplus$ is the reduction operator (*e.g.*, sum, maximum, product, etc.).

Allgather can be easily implemented as P broadcast calls; similarly, reduce-scatter can be implemented as P reduce calls, but more sophisticated algorithms deliver better performance.

These two algorithms are particularly important, because several other MPI operations can be efficiently implemented as combinations of allgather or reduce-scatter and other operations. In this work, we focus on allgather; the inverse of the communication pattern in each allgather algorithm is the same as the communication pattern in the corresponding reduce-scatter algorithm.

2.1 Network model

Of the many network performance models that one can use in analyzing collective operations, we base ours on a simple, frequently-used model that incorporates two parameters: α, the startup cost per message, and β, the bandwidth cost per byte. A third parameter, γ, is used in other work to represent the cost of applying the reduction operator. We ignore the cost of applying reduction operators in our model; our algorithms do not affect this cost. We use two models; one, the common α/β model which does not consider congestion or topology, and another that extends the α/β model to consider congestion and topology.

We charge α once for each pair of send and receive messages. We explore *single-port* networks, in which each process can send and receive one message at a time, and *multi-port* networks, where each process can send and receive as many messages as each node has links. We assume there is only one MPI process on each node. Multiple processes on a node are best handled using a hierarchical MPI library, such as [15].

No-congestion model: The first model ignores topology and congestion. β represents the bandwidth with which each processor is connected to the network. Each process can only send and receive one message in each stage in this model. The α term for an algorithm is simply the number of stages, since each process can exchange up to one message per stage. The β term is found by summing the maximum message size per stage over all the stages. This model can also be seen as one in which each processor is connected by one link to a full crossbar interconnect.

Equations derived using this model will be labeled as plain C. This was the model used in developing algorithms for MPICH [16, 17] and other work that ignores congestion or topology.

Congestion-aware model: The second model incorporates topology and congestion. δ replaces β and represents the link speed. We add a penalty factor in the δ term to represent congestion. Topology and congestion-aware equations we will label as C_{Clos} or C_{torus}. In this model, processors on torus networks can send and receive messages on every link simultaneously.

For simplicity, each processor can send and receive up to one message on each link per stage. The α term is derived by summing the maximum number of messages exchanged in each stage by any one process over all the stages. The δ term is derived by summing the amount of data transferred over the busiest link in each stage over all the stages.

On a Clos network, each process has one link, so $\delta = \beta$, and $C_{Clos} = C$ for algorithms that do not suffer from congestion.

On a 3-d torus network, each process has six links, but can only use one at a time in the simple model. Thus, $\delta = \beta$ and $C_{torus} = C$ for single-ported algorithms that do not suffer from congestion.

Our congestion-aware model cannot model multi-port algorithms where the message activity on different ports is unsynchronized. In [14], we propose a more detailed model that can. This is only necessary for modeling our multi-port allgather algorithm on non-cubic 3-d torus networks.

Clos model: For the Clos network, we consider networks parameterized by R, the radix of the switches, and μ, the ratio of the minimum bisection bandwidth to injection bandwidth, which is subject to the constraint: $0 < \mu \leq 1$. In an optimal Clos network, the number of up links and down links for any non-root, non-terminal switch will each be $R/2$. The root switches will each have R down links. Each bottom-level switch will be connected to T nodes and $R - T$ level-two switches, where $\frac{R-T}{T} \geq \mu$. This is the same idealized model of a Clos network as is used in [1] to minimize the number of switches on a system of a given size subject to constraints on μ and R. Switches with a radix of 128 or 256 will likely be used in supercomputers in the near future [4].

Our model for Clos networks underestimates the congestion seen in real-world Clos networks. Hoefler studied the bandwidth delivered by Infiniband Clos networks, which use static routing tables in the switches [9]. The delivered bandwidth was found to be 55-60% of that which could be delivered with ideal routing, due to hot spots. Zahavi inspected the communication patterns of all common collective algorithms on a Clos network and presented an algorithm for generating routing tables that prevent congestion in Clos networks where the bisection bandwidth matches the injection bandwidth [19]. This accelerates collective algorithms by 40% when an application uses the whole system.

In our model, we assume that Clos networks have perfect oracular routing. Our algorithms will improve the performance of collective algorithms on real Clos networks more than our model predicts.

2.2 Non-topology-aware algorithms

One simple allgather algorithm is the ring algorithm, composed of $P - 1$ stages. In every stage, process i sends data to process $i - 1 \mod P$ and receives data from process $i + 1 \mod P$. In the first stage, process i sends its input vector X_i and receives vector $X_{i+1 \mod P}$. In the subsequent $P - 2$ stages, each process sends the vector it received in the previous step. In stage s, where the stages are numbered from 0 to $P - 2$, each process sends $X_{i+s \mod P}$ and receives $X_{i+s+1 \mod P}$.[1]

After P steps, each process has the full output vector $Y = X_0X_1X_2 \cdots X_{P-1}$.

The ring algorithm is easy to analyze: there are $P - 1$ stages, so the message-startup cost is $P - 1$. In a 3-d torus or Clos network, the ring algorithm will not cause any congestion, and the bandwidth term will be $n \cdot (P - 1)$. The ring algorithm is optimal with respect to the bandwidth term on single-port networks.

Therefore, the cost is:

$$C = (P - 1)\alpha + n(P - 1)\beta.$$

A similar ring algorithm exists for the reduce-scatter operation. In the first stage, each process i sends process $i - 1$ the elements from its input vector corresponding to process $i + 1$, *i.e.*, $X_i[(i + 1)n : (i + 2)n)$. It receives from process $i + 1$ the data corresponding to process $i+2$ and combines this data (using the re-

[1] Hereafter, arithmetic on process ranks is assumed to be circular on the number of processes P.

duction operator) with the elements in X_i corresponding to process $i+2$. This proceeds similarly for the $s-2$ remaining stages.

The ring algorithms can also be run in the opposite direction.

An important algorithm for allgather is known as the recursive-doubling algorithm. It is composed of $\log_2 P$ stages. In the first stage, process i exchanges its input vector X_i of n elements with the process whose rank only differs in the last bit. In the second stage, process i exchanges $2n$ elements with the process whose rank only differs in the second-last bit. In stage s (from 0 to $\log_2 P - 1$), process i exchanges $2^s n$ elements with process i XOR 2^s. It is named the recursive-doubling algorithm because the amount of data exchanged and the portion of the output vector Y that is filled doubles in each stage.

The corresponding algorithm for reduce-scatter is known as the recursive-halving algorithm. In the first stage, processes whose high bits differ exchange half of the input vector, in the second stage, processes whose second-highest bits differ exchange one fourth of the input vector, and so on.

If there is no congestion, the bandwidth term is given by the summation: $\sum_{s=0}^{\log_2 P-1} 2^s n = n(P-1)$, and the cost is:

$$C = \log_2 P\alpha + n(P-1)\beta.$$

This algorithm is optimal with respect to the startup cost; data cannot be broadcast from one process to $P-1$ other processes in under $\log_2 P$ stages. However, on a $\mu < 1$ Clos network or a torus, there will be congestion.

Clos network: Let us consider first a Clos network where each terminal switch is connected to T nodes, where T is a power-of-two. In the first few stages, where 2^s is less than T, all communication will be between nodes connected to the same switch and there will be no congestion. In the remaining stages, all communication will be between nodes connected to different switches, and the performance will suffer by a factor of $1/\mu$. Thus,

$$\begin{aligned} C_{Clos} &= \log_2 P\alpha + n\delta\{(1+2+4+\cdots+T/2) \\ &+ (1/\mu)(T+2T+4T+\cdots+P/2)\} \\ &= \log_2 P\alpha + n\delta\{(T-1)+(1/\mu)(P-T)\} \\ &\approx \log_2 P\alpha + (nP/\mu)\delta, \end{aligned}$$

where the approximation holds for $P \gg T$.

Thus, the effect of congestion reduces the performance of this algorithm by a factor of $1/\mu$ on the bandwidth term.

3-d torus: Let us consider the performance of the algorithm on a system composed of P nodes arranged in a $p \times p \times p$ 3-d torus, where p is a power-of-two. We assume that the nodes are numbered in increasing order in the X dimension, then the Y dimension, then the Z dimension.

In the first stage, nodes at a rank distance of one apart exchange input vectors. These nodes will be neighbors in the X dimension, so there will be no congestion. In the second stage, nodes at a rank distance of two apart exchange twice as much data as in the first step. If $X \geq 4$, these nodes will be two hops away in the X dimension, and there will be a congestion factor of two. In the third step, messages four times as large will travel four hops in the X dimension, with 4-fold congestion, and so on. In the second-last stage in each dimension, stage $\log_2 p - 1$, messages will travel $p/4$ hops and suffer $p/4$-way congestion. Since this is a torus, in the final stage in each dimension, stage $\log_2 p$, messages will travel $p/2$ hops, but will suffer only $p/4$-way congestion because in this stage only, the extra wrap-around link provided by the torus can be used to relieve congestion.

Once we reach the stage where the rank distance between nodes equals X, neighbors in the Y dimension exchange data, and so on.

If we revisit our model, we get a bandwidth term of:

$$\begin{aligned} & n\delta(1+p+p^2)\{1\cdot 1+2\cdot 2+4\cdot 4+\cdots+ \\ & (p/4)\cdot(p/4)+(p/2)\cdot(p/4)\} \\ = \; & n\delta(1+p+p^2)\{\sum_{i=0}^{\log_2 p-1} 4^i - p^2/8\} \\ = \; & n\delta(1+p+p^2)\{(1/3)(p^2-1)-p^2/8\} \\ = \; & n\delta(1+p+p^2)((5/24)p^2-1/3) \\ \approx \; & (5/24)nP^{4/3}\delta \end{aligned}$$

and a total cost:

$$C_{torus} \approx \log_2 P\alpha + (5/24)nP^{4/3}\delta.$$

Each factor 1, p, or p^2 represents the size of the first message exchanged in dimension X, Y, and Z, respectively. The first factor in each term in the summation represents the message size in the $\log_2 p$ stages in that dimension and the second term represents the congestion factor; note that the last two stages in each dimension have the same congestion factor: $p/4$.

The recursive-doubling algorithm is used for shorter messages in MPICH due to its lower startup cost term, and the ring algorithm is used for longer messages [7, 8].

2.3 Topology-aware algorithms

The 3-d bucket allgather algorithm is formed by executing the ring algorithm in each dimension in turn. *E.g.*, on a $P = p \times p \times p$ network, messages of size n circulate in the X dimension, then messages of size np circulate in the Y dimension, then messages of size np^2 circulate in the Z dimension.

This reduces the number of messages substantially and incurs a total cost:

$$C_{torus} = 3(\sqrt[3]{P}-1)\alpha + n(P-1)\delta$$

Similarly, the 3-d bucket reduce-scatter algorithm is formed by executing three ring reduce-scatter algorithms, starting with np^2 elements per message in the Z dimension, then np elements per message in the Y dimension, then n elements per message in the X dimension.

3. Design

In this section, we present several non-minimal recursive-doubling and bucket algorithms.

We add a stage of communication before the allgather operation and after the reduce-scatter operation that enables us to reorder the stages of the algorithms while preserving correctness. It also enables the use of multiple ports in a multi-port torus network.

3.1 Recursive-doubling algorithm

The recursive-doubling allgather algorithm presented above can be described as a *distance-doubling*, recursive-doubling algorithm, because the numerical distance between communicating processes doubles in every stage $(1, 2, 4, \ldots, P/2)$. Thus, the stages with the largest messages suffer from the worst congestion.

3.1.1 Solution for Clos networks

To resolve this, we propose a recursive-doubling, *distance-halving* allgather algorithm for Clos networks and a reordered recursive-doubling allgather algorithm for mesh or torus networks.

In the distance-halving algorithm, in each stage s, processes exchange $n2^s$ elements, as in all recursive-doubling algorithms. Process i exchanges data with process i XOR $P2^{-(s+1)}$. *I.e.*, in the first stage, processes whose ranks differ only in the highest bit exchange data, in the second stage, processes whose ranks differ only in the next-highest bit exchange data, and so on.

The cost is then:

$$\begin{aligned} C_{Clos} &= \log_2 P\alpha + n\delta\{(1/\mu)(1+2+4+\cdots+P/(2T)) \\ &+ (P/T + 2P/T + 4P/T + \cdots + P/2)\} \\ &= \log_2 P\alpha + n\delta\{(1/\mu)(P/T-1) + (P - P/T)\} \\ &\approx log_2 P\alpha + nP\{1 + 1/(\mu T)\}\delta \end{aligned}$$

From the first stage until the last stage where $P2^{-s+1} \geq T$, all messages must travel through multiple switches and incur congestion determined by the parameter μ. The largest messages in the final stages travel through only one switch with no congestion.

This analysis assumes P and T are powers-of-two. It is a close approximation for other values of T. If 2^a is the largest power of two that evenly divides T, then in the last a stages all the messages will travel through only one switch. For the next handful of stages, some pairs of processes will exchange messages through only one switch and others through several switches. Whether or not congestion occurs in the intermediate stages depends on the value of μ and T, but it is sharply curtailed in any case. There is no concise equation for the exact value when T is not a power-of-two.

This algorithm reduces the bandwidth term in the cost from $(nP/\mu)\delta$ to $nP\{1 + 1/(\mu T)\}\delta$, and is close to the optimal bandwidth term, $nP\delta$, for typical values of μT, however, the data is no longer in the correct order.

In the usual distance-doubling, recursive-doubling algorithm, each process receives a message in each stage containing elements in the output vector adjacent to elements that the process already has. *E.g.*, process 0 starts with element 0, receives element 1 in stage 1, receives elements 2 and 3 in stage 2, 4-7 in stage 3, and so on. In each stage, each process simply concatenates the data it receives with the data it already has.

In the distance-halving, recursive-doubling algorithm, each process still concatenates the data it has with the data it receives in each stage, but the output ends up in the wrong order. The input vector X_i should start at offset ni in the output vector Y, but instead will end up at offset $n\tilde{i}$, where $\tilde{i}$ is the bit-reverse of i.

To rectify this, we simply have processes i and $\tilde{i}$ exchange input vectors before the algorithm begins. Then each input vector ends up at the correct offset in the output vector.

We add this stage to the algorithm's cost:

$$\begin{aligned} C_{Clos} &= \log_2 P\alpha + nP\{1 + 1/(\mu T)\}\delta + \\ &\quad \alpha + (n/\mu)\delta \\ &\approx (\log_2 P + 1)\alpha + nP\{1 + 1/(\mu T)\}\delta. \end{aligned}$$

Each process sends and receives nP bytes instead of $n(P-1)$, a negligible difference.

For typical Clos networks, $1/(\mu T)$ is a small number and:

$$C_{Clos} \approx (\log_2 P)\alpha + nP\delta.$$

For the corresponding recursive-halving, distance-doubling reduce-scatter algorithm, processes i and $\tilde{i}$ exchange output vectors.

3.1.2 Solution for torus networks

For mesh or torus networks, we *could* use the distance-halving allgather algorithm and expect an improvement, since the largest message in the last stage will not be delayed by congestion and the next largest message will have a congestion factor of 2 instead of $\sqrt[3]{P}/4$. The distance-halving algorithm is really a quasi-topology-aware algorithm, since it will perform well for any network in which nodes are numbered rationally.

We can do better if we further reorder the stages. As before, let us assume that the network has $P = p \times p \times p$ nodes, where p is a power-of-two. In stages one through three, nodes $p/2$ hops apart in the X, Y, and Z dimensions, respectively, exchange data, suffering $p/4$-fold congestion. In the next three stages, processes $p/4$ hops apart exchange data, suffering $p/4$-fold congestion again. In the next group of three stages, congestion will be reduced to a factor of $p/8$, and will continue to halve for each subsequent group of three stages. In the last three stages, immediate neighbors exchange data with no congestion.

The bandwidth term is then:

$$\begin{aligned} & (1+2+4)n\{\sum 1 \cdot p/4 + 8 \cdot p/4 + \cdots + P/8 \cdot 1\}\delta \\ \approx\; & 7n(p/2)\{\sum_{i=0}^{\log_2 p - 1} 4^i\}\delta \\ \approx\; & (7/6)np^3\delta \\ =\; & (7/6)nP\delta. \end{aligned}$$

The first message exchanged in each dimensions is of size n times 1, 2, or 4. The first term in the summation reflects the size of the message; the first message exchanged in dimension X will be of size $1n$, the second message exchanged in dimension X will be of size $8n$, etc. The second term in the summation represents the congestion in that stage of the algorithm.

The data exchange to preserve the correct ordering is more complex. Let us define a schedule, S, which dictates the distance between pairs of communicating processes in each stage. More precisely, S is a vector that specifies which bit differs between communicating pairs of processes in each stage.

For the distance-doubling, recursive-doubling algorithm, $S[s] = s$, since in stage s, process i and process i XOR 2^s exchange data. For the distance-halving algorithm, $S[s] = \log_2 P - 1 - s$. For the torus-reordered algorithm with XYZ process numbering:

$$\begin{aligned} S[s] = \{&3\log_2 p - 1, 2\log_2 p - 1, \log_2 p - 1, \\ &3\log_2 p - 2, 2\log_2 p - 2, \log_2 p - 2, \\ &\ldots, \\ &2\log_2 p, \log_2 p, 0\}. \end{aligned}$$

For example, for a 512-node system arranged as an 8x8x8 3-d torus, $S[s]$ can range from 0 to 8 (since $\log_2 512 = 8 + 1$). For distance-doubling, $S = \{0, 1, 2, 3, 4, 5, 6, 7, 8\}$. For distance-halving, $S = \{8, 7, 6, 5, 4, 3, 2, 1, 0\}$. For the remapped algorithm, one optimal schedule is $S = \{8, 5, 2, 7, 4, 1, 6, 3, 0\}$. (The entries in S for each group of three consecutive stages can be permuted.)

This table shows the full schedule:

Stage	S[s]	Distance	Hops	Congestion	Size $\times n$
0	8	256	4 (Z)	2	1
1	5	32	4 (Y)	2	2
2	2	4	4 (X)	2	4
3	7	128	2 (Z)	2	8
4	4	16	2 (Y)	2	16
5	1	2	2 (X)	2	32
6	6	64	1 (Z)	1	64
7	3	8	1 (Y)	1	128
8	0	1	1(X)	1	256

Note that the communication in the three stages with the largest messages occurs without congestion.

We define a mapping function R, where $R(S, i)$ is the process which sends its input vector to process i before the allgather operation (or to which process i sends its output vector after the reduce-scatter operation). $R(S, i)$ permutes the bits in i according to S.

The process with rank i can be expressed using bit vector b_i, where $i = \sum_{r=1}^{\lceil \log_2 P \rceil} 2^{r-1} b_i[r]$. *E.g.*, if $P = 16$, $b_{11} = \{1, 1, 0, 1\}$. In the data-swapping stage, rank i then receives its data from rank $R(S, i) = \sum_{r=1}^{\lceil \log_2 P \rceil} 2^{r-1} b_i[S[r]]$.

We have investigated the exact traffic patterns in the data swapping phase for several different network sizes and found that none cause any congestion, but we cannot prove this. However, a 3-d $p \times p \times p$ torus has $2p^2$ bisection bandwidth, therefore the bandwidth cost for this phase cannot exceed $n(P/2)/(2p^2)\delta = (n/4)\sqrt[3]{P}\delta$. The bandwidth cost of the extra stage is marginal compared to the bandwidth cost of the main algorithm.

Thus, the total cost is:

$$\begin{aligned} C_{torus} &\leq (\log_2 P + 1)\alpha + ((7/6)nP + (n/4)\sqrt[3]{P})\delta \\ &\approx (\log_2 P)\alpha + (7/6)nP\delta. \end{aligned}$$

3.2 Bucket algorithm

The bandwidth term in the bucket algorithm is optimal for the single-port model on a 3-d torus. The number of stages, $3\sqrt[3]{P} - 1$, is more than the $\log_2 P$ stages of the recursive-doubling algorithm but much less than the $P - 1$ stages of the 1-d ring algorithm.

However, on a multi-port 3-d torus network, each process can exchange messages with all six of its neighbors simultaneously. The bucket algorithm does not take advantage of this. Our approach extends the bucket algorithm to use all six ports.

In our algorithm, we run six bucket operations simultaneously in a way that avoids congestion. We label the six buckets XYZ^+, XYZ^-, YZX^+, YZX^-, ZXY^+, and ZXY^-. The + buckets run clockwise in each dimension and the - buckets run counter-clockwise in each dimension. XYZ^+ and XYZ^- both circulate in the X dimension, then the Y dimension, then the Z dimension. Similarly, both YZX buckets circulate in the Y dimension, then the Z dimension, then the X dimension. We divide the input and output vectors into six sections, one for each bucket. Buckets 0 and 1 refer to the XYZ buckets, 2 and 3 to the YZX buckets, and 4 and 5 to the ZXY buckets.

The cost is then:

$$\begin{aligned} C_{torus} &= 6 \cdot (3\sqrt[3]{P} - 1)\alpha + (n/6)(P - 1)\delta \\ &\approx 18\sqrt[3]{P}\alpha + (n/6)(P - 1)\delta \end{aligned}$$

For large problems, the performance loss from the 6-fold increase in the number of messages is more than offset by the 6-fold decrease in the bandwidth term.

However, we face a familiar problem: out-of-order data.

Let us show how the the 6-way bucket algorithm reorders the data. Suppose that each process i has 6 elements in its input vector $X_i = \{A_i, B_i, C_i, D_i, E_i, F_i\}$. The correct output would be $Y = \{A_0 - F_0, A_1 - F_1, \ldots A_{P-1} - F_{P-1}\}$. However, instead, in the first part of Y, we will get $Y[0 : n/6) = \{A_0, A_1, \ldots, A_{P-1}\}$. In the second part, we will get $Y[n/6 : n/3) = \{B_0, B_1, \ldots, B_{P-1}\}$. In the third part (from YZX^+), we will get $Y[n/3 : n/2) = \{C_0, C_p, C_{2p}, \ldots, C_{P-1}\}$, since the output will be in YZX order. The data in the remaining three sections will be similarly perturbed.

To solve this, we number each of the six sections in each input vector X_i. Section j in input X_i is assigned *section identifier* $6i+j$. In the correct output vector, all the input sections are arranged in section id order. In total, we have $6P$ sections. Sections whose id is between 0 and $P - 1$ must be placed in the first bucket, XYZ^+; sections whose id is between P and $2P - 1$ must be placed in the second bucket, XYZ^-, and so on.

Next is the question of *where* to place each section in the correct bucket. Section s must be at offset $s \mod P$ in the output of the corresponding bucket. For the two XYZ buckets, this is achieved by placing section s in the corresponding input bucket on process $s \mod P$.

For the YZX buckets, section s must be placed in one of the YZX buckets on the process whose rank *would be* $s \mod P$ if the processes were numbered in YZX order. Since they are not, we rotate the bits in $s \mod P$ to find the rank of the process which have section s in its input buffer.

Consider an $8 \times 8 \times 8$ torus again. The segment id of the third segment from process 200 is $s = 200 \cdot 6 + 3 = 1203$. $\lfloor 1203/P \rfloor = 2$, therefore this segment will be in bucket 2: YZX^+. Its offset within YZX^+ is $1203 \mod P = 179$. This segment must start from the input vector of the process whose YZX order is 179. We then take the 9-bit quantity 179 and rotate it clockwise 3 bits to put it in XYZ order. The rotated offset is 410. Therefore the segment whose id is 1203 should be placed in $X_{410}[YZX^+]$.

For segments in the ZXY buckets, we rotate $s \mod P$ 6-bits clockwise (or 3-bits counter-clockwise).

To summarize, for each of the 6 sections in each input vector X_i, we assign a section id: $s = 6i + j$, where j is a value from 0 to 5. This section should be placed in bucket $\lfloor s/P \rfloor$. We then find the quantity $s \mod P$. If the section maps to either XYZ bucket, then this section should be sent to process $s \mod P$. If the section is in either YZX bucket, we rotate $s \mod P$ by $\log_2 p$ bits clockwise and send the data to process $(s \mod P) >> \log_2 p$.[2] If the section is in either ZXY bucket, we rotate $s \mod P$ by $\log_2 p$ bits counter-clockwise and send the data to $(s \mod P) << \log_2 p$.

The correct data remapping for this algorithm or the remapped recursive-doubling algorithm can also be determined empirically quite easily by observing the order of the output.

Including the data-shuffling stage, the cost is:

$$\begin{aligned} C_{torus} &= (18\sqrt[3]{P} + 6)\alpha + ((n/6)(P - 1) + n)\delta \\ &\approx 18\sqrt[3]{P}\alpha + (n/6)(P - 1)\delta. \end{aligned}$$

The additional data movement adds negligible overhead.

Non-cube torus networks are easily handled. Each of the six bucket operations waits until all the others have finished circulating in each dimension before moving on to circulate in the next dimension. We found that performance suffered greatly if we allowed multiple bucket operations to compete for the same links.

Performance in the first two stages will be limited by the pair of buckets circulating on the largest dimension. In the last stage, in which the messages are much larger than in the first two stages, the buckets will have more equal performance. The buckets circulating along the longest dimension will have the smallest messages, and the buckets circulating along the shortest dimension will have the largest messages.

Consider a network where $X < Y < Z$. In the last stage, the slowest bucket will be the XYZ buckets and the quickest the YZX buckets. XYZ buckets will circulate $Z-1$ messages of XYn bytes, for a total of $XY(Z - 1)n$ bytes. The YZX buckets will circulate $X - 1$ messages of YZ bytes, for a total of $(X - 1)YZ$ bytes. On large systems, the difference is not important.

Messages whose size is not a multiple of six are also simple to handle. We use a similar technique to that used in [18] for the irregular `MPI_Allgatherv` problem. We round-up the input size to the next multiple of six bytes and shift the data from higher processes to lower processes. Processes whose rank assignment is near P may have empty input buffers. This will involve each process sending at most two messages or receiving up to six messages, but typically no

[2] $>>$ and $<<$ are the cyclical clockwise and counter-clockwise bit rotation operators.

process will receive more than three messages. The amount of data exchanged in this stage will be no more than n bytes per process.

For 3-d meshes, or partitions of 3-d tori, the 6-way bucket algorithm will cause a congestion load of 2 on each link (since there is no wrap-around link). The 3-way bucket algorithm would then be preferred for its lower startup cost.

A variation of this algorithm was presented in [11]. Instead of adding an extra stage of communication to restore the correct data ordering, they reorder the data after the allgather operation or before the reduce-scatter operation. We also considered three alternatives to the extra stage: using MPI types to send and receive messages with non-contiguous memory addresses, packing the data into temporary buffers before sending messages and unpacking the data from temporary buffers after receiving messages, and reordering the data in-memory at the end. We found all three to have poor performance. The presentation in [11] is difficult to follow, since they extend the bucket algorithm but present the ring algorithm instead in their description of the base bucket algorithm. They explored multiple methods of multithreading the operation of the 6-way bucket algorithm; we do not. We will compare our performance results with theirs in the following section.

3.3 Other algorithms

Long broadcast operations in MPICH use the Van de Geijn algorithm, in which the operation is composed of a scatter operation followed by an allgather operation [3]. Similarly, the long reduce operation can be composed of an reduce-scatter, followed by an gather, and the long allreduce can be broken into an reduce-scatter call followed by allgather. Our algorithms can accelerate all of these operations. Further, the data reordering stages can often be made to cancel out; this happens naturally for allreduce. With simple changes, the data reordering can be folded into the gather or scatter operation. In fact, MPICH already uses a recursive-halving, distance-doubling reduce-scatter as the basis for the long reduce and allreduce operations, with no explanation.

3.4 Other related work

The algorithms used in OpenMPI [6] and MPICH, broadly-speaking, are chosen as those that are best under our two-parameter model, but they ignore network congestion, since these are generic libraries. The specific algorithms used in MPICH are described in [17]. Notably, the algorithm for the big allgather and big reduce-scatter problems uses an embedded one-dimensional ring. In [16], the same authors provide more detail but cover fewer algorithms. In particular, the often-encountered recursive-doubling and recursive-halving patterns are well-explained.

In [2], a clever broadcast algorithm is developed for two-dimensional mesh topologies, which achieves $\log_2 P$ scaling. Their algorithm is based on the common binary-tree algorithm. For an $p \times p$ network, in step s, each node that has a copy of the message sends it to a node that does not at a distance of $p2^{-s}$ hops away. This avoids the congestion inherent in running generic binary-tree algorithms on meshes.

In [13], several reduction algorithms are analyzed and implemented on a two-dimensional mesh, including binomial tree-based algorithms, recursive halving algorithms, a two-phase bucket-based algorithm, and several hybrids. The optimal choice, analytically and empirically, depended upon the size of the reduction.

4. Evaluation

All experiments were performed on a 40k-node Blue Gene/P system. Partitions of 512 nodes or more form 3-d tori. Smaller partitions form 3-d meshes. The Blue Gene/P has a torus network for point-to-point messages and some collective-communication operations and a tree network for other collective-communication operations. Both networks have special features to accelerate collective communication. The torus network has a "deposit bit" feature in which a message can be put on the network once and every node along a line in the torus can receive it. This is particularly helpful for broadcast operations. The switches in the tree network support in-place integer reduction operations.

The 512-node allocation forms an 8x8x8-node cube. The 32k-node allocations forms a 32x32x32-node cube. The allocations in between are non-cubic. The Z dimension doubles until it reaches 32 nodes, then the Y dimension doubles until 32, then the X dimension doubles. We run one MPI process per node. The system provides a simple interface for finding the size of each dimension in an allocation and the coordinates of each process in the allocation. By default, processes are numbered in XYZ order.

Each node is comprised of four PowerPC 450 microprocessors and a switch. Each switch has 3 bidirectional links on the tree network of 850 MB/s per direction and 6 bidirectional links on the torus network of 425 MB/s per switch per direction. The minimum packet size is 32 bytes, with 16 bytes of payload data and 16 bytes of header data. The maximum size is 256 bytes with 240 bytes of payload data. After accounting for the overhead in the packet headers and the acknowledgement packets, the maximum bandwidth per link is 88% of the raw bandwidth. According to IBM, with 6-way bidirectional communication, 93% of that is the peak that can be delivered, *i.e.*, 425 MB/s$\times 6 \times 2 \times .88 \times .93 = 4.18$ GB/s [10]. In our data, we report the one-way bandwidth into or out of a node. The bandwidth calculations count the time but not the data exchanged in the extra stage for the reordered recursive-doubling algorithms. *I.e.*, we report $n(P-1)/t$, where n is the input message size on each process, P is the number of processes, and t is the amount of time each operation takes.

The output of each combination of algorithm, size, and number of processes was verified for correctness.

In each figure, the message size refers to the size of the input vector for the allgather operation or the output vector for the reduce-scatter operation, *i.e.*, the value of n from Section 3. The size of the output allgather vector or input reduce-scatter vector is this value times the number of processes, *i.e.*, nP.

4.1 Allgather performance

The left plot in Figure 1 shows the performance of the one-port allgather algorithms on an 8x8x8 512-node 3-d torus. The recursive-doubling, distance-doubling algorithm (*rd doubling*) is the better of the two non-topology-aware algorithms for smaller messages, due to the lower message count of the recursive-doubling algorithms, and the ring algorithm is better for larger messages, due to the absence of congestion in the ring algorithm. The quasi-topology-aware recursive-doubling, distance-halving algorithm (*rd halving*), with one more stage of communication, beats the recursive-doubling, distance-halving algorithm for all message sizes.

For the topology-aware algorithms, the optimally-scheduled recursive-doubling algorithm (*rd optimal*) is better for smaller messages and the bucket algorithm is better for larger messages. This is expected, since the recursive-doubling algorithm has fewer stages but a larger bandwidth term. The bucket algorithm does reach the upper bound of 375 MB/s. The native algorithm is generally better than all the single-port algorithms for small messages on small partitions. We plot data from the native algorithm on the default `MPI_COMM_WORLD` communicator.

Figure 2 shows the performance of the multi-port algorithms. We include the native BlueGene/P allgather algorithm in this figure. For small messages, the native algorithm running on a copy of `MPI_COMM_WORLD` performs far worse than the native algorithm on `MPI_COMM_WORLD`. The 3-bucket algorithm delivers up to 1120

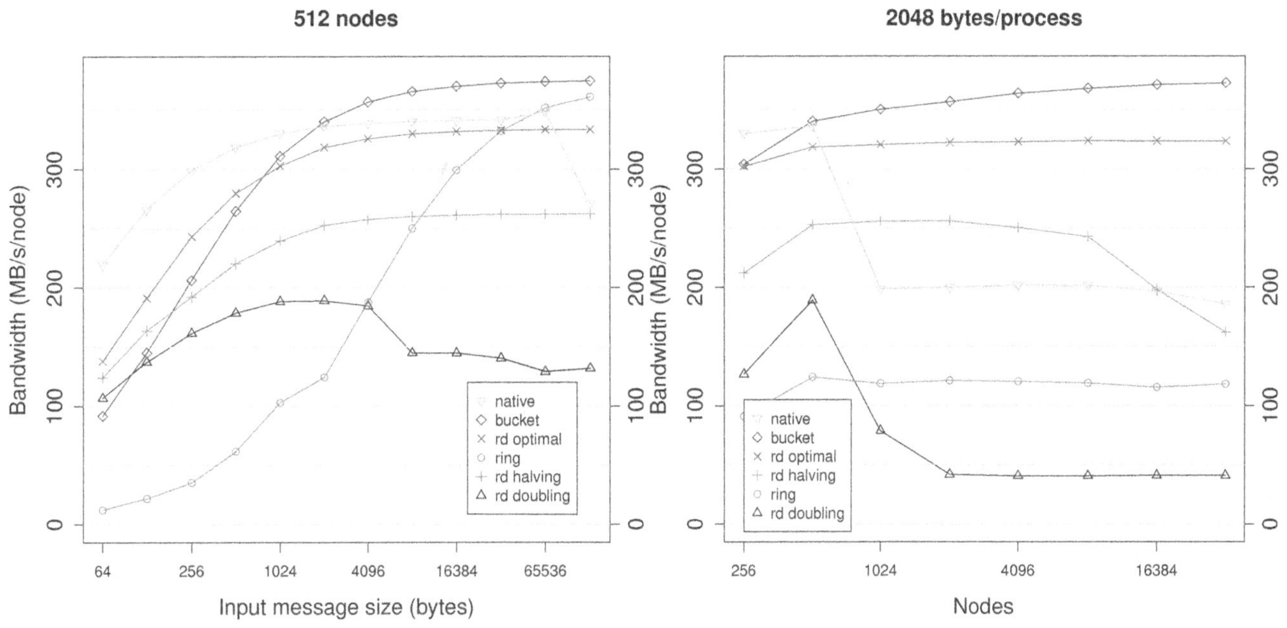

Figure 1. Performance of single-port allgather algorithms.

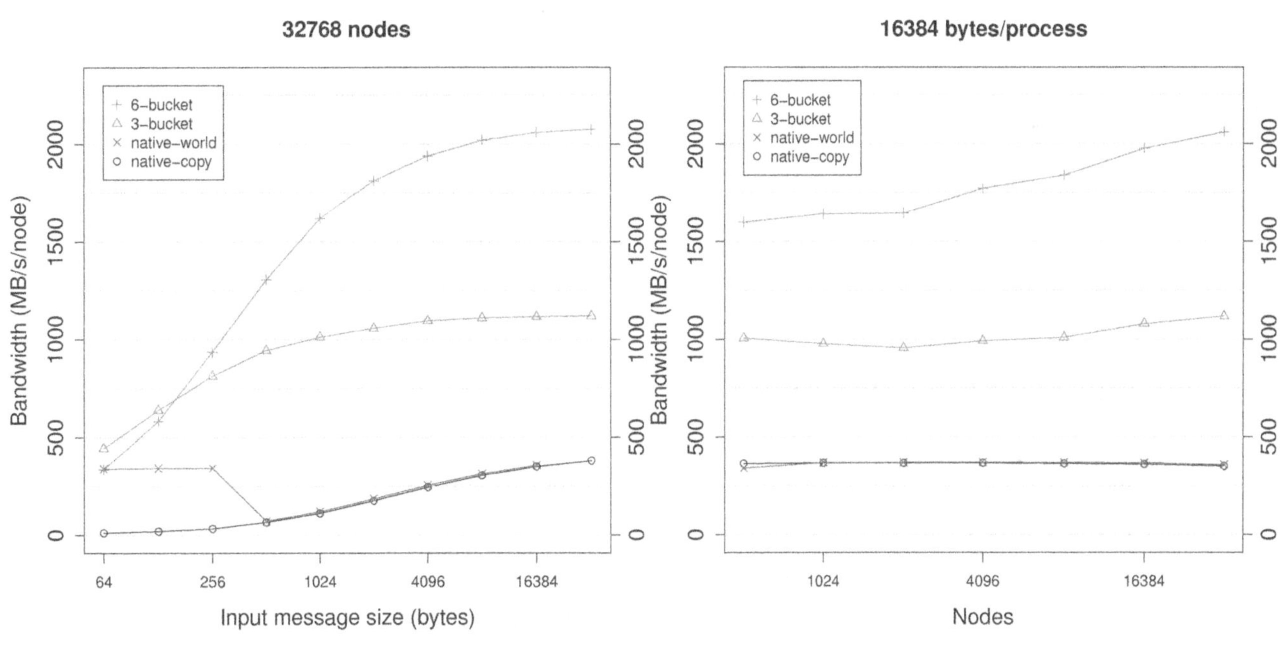

Figure 2. Performance of multi-port allgather algorithms.

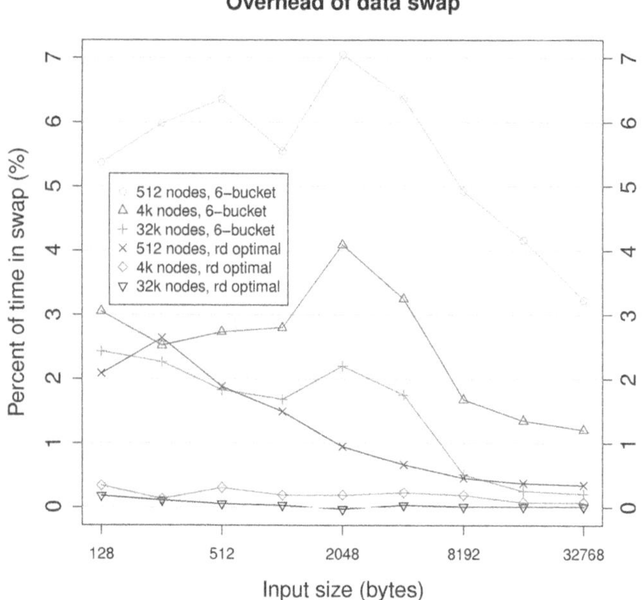

Figure 3. Overhead of input data shuffle stage

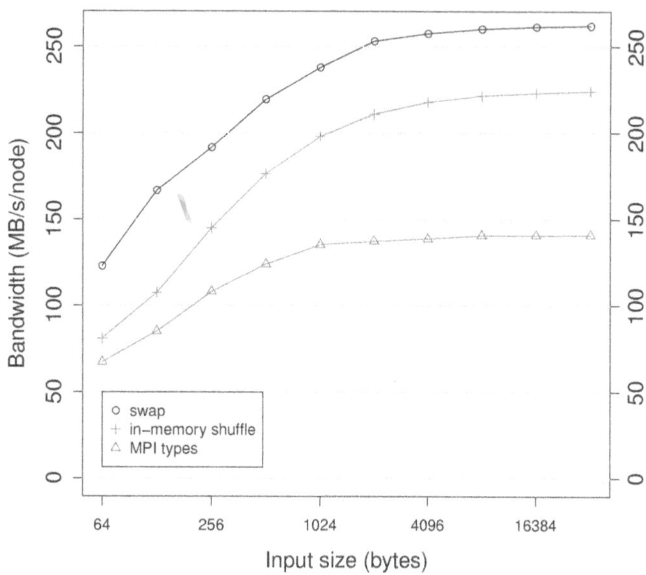

Figure 4. Alternatives to input data shuffle

MB/s, or 99.5% of the achievable link bandwidth of three ports. The 6-bucket algorithm delivers up to 2075 MB/s, which is 99% of the achievable link bandwidth of 6 ports. This is 5.5x better than the native algorithm.

Figure 3 shows the amount of time spent in the additional data-exchange steps for the optimally-remapped recursive-doubling algorithm (*rd optimal*) and the 6-way bucket algorithm. Restoring the correct order and handling arbitrary message sizes involves many more messages for the multi-port bucket algorithm. Moreover, the bulk of the bucket algorithm is about six times quicker than the recursive-doubling algorithm. This is why we observe more overhead for the bucket algorithms. In any case, the overhead is quite small and decreases as we scale the number of processes.

In Figure 4, we show the performance of two alternatives to the additional stage of communication for the recursive-doubling, distance-halving allgather operation running on 512 nodes (*swap*). We could reorder the data in memory after the recursive-doubling operation is complete (*in-memory shuffle*). We load data from bit-reversed offsets in a temporary output buffer and store the data in sequential order in the proper output buffer; this was quicker than the reverse. As we explained in the previous section, the extra stage in our non-minimal algorithms involves exchanging n to $2n$ bytes per process across the network, whereas the in-memory shuffle requires shuffling nP bytes of data in memory. We also tried using MPI types to read and write strided, non-contiguous data. Both proved slower than our method with an extra stage of communication. We chose to use the distance-halving algorithm for this experiment, since the system is likely to deliver better performance exchanging strided, non-contiguous messages than non-contiguous messages with a more complex memory layout.

4.2 Reduce-scatter performance

Figure 5 shows the performance of the reduce-scatter variations. As mentioned above, the communication pattern of reduce-scatter is the reverse of that of the allgather operation. The input vector on each process is arranged as 32-bit integer values and we sum them to form the output vector.

The native algorithm is slowest for small messages. During development, we observed that our algorithms were spending much time in memory-allocation routines. We rearranged the code to use preallocated temporary buffers; the native algorithm must allocate temporary storage. Further, our implementation only supports the case where each process receives an equal portion of the output vector; the native algorithm also supports unequal distributions of the output vector. Supporting irregular distribution of the output vector could be easily folded into the extra order-restoring stage of communication. The native algorithm could also check whether the distribution is regular with a short reduce operation.

We again see that the native algorithm is much slower on a copy of `MPI_COMM_WORLD`. The performance is equally poor for a subpartition of `MPI_COMM_WORLD`. It seems likely that the hardware-supported reduction on the tree network is only available on `MPI_COMM_WORLD`.

The non-topology-aware recursive-halving, distance-halving algorithm (*rh halving*), performs the worst. The semi-topology-aware distance-doubling algorithm (*rh doubling*) performs better, followed by the optimally-remapped recursive-halving algorithm (*rh optimal*). The bucket and 6-bucket algorithms perform best, except for smaller messages with smaller allocations. The 6-bucket algorithm performs much better than the others, except for small messages with the smaller 512-node allocation.

4.3 Measured versus predicted performance

We now compare the measured performance for several allgather algorithms with the performance predicted by our model from Section 2.1. The δ term is simply the reciprocal of the link speed (375 MB/s) for one or three-port algorithms, and 7% less for six-port algorithms. The ring algorithm on the 32k-node partition consists of 32767 stages comprised of one message per stage per process and has a latency of 206 ms with a zero-byte input message. Thus, $\alpha = 206\ \text{ms}/32767 = 6.29\mu\text{s}$.

In Section 3, we developed approximate equations for the performance of different allgather algorithms; we ignored minor terms, such as the extra messages our algorithms introduce. On

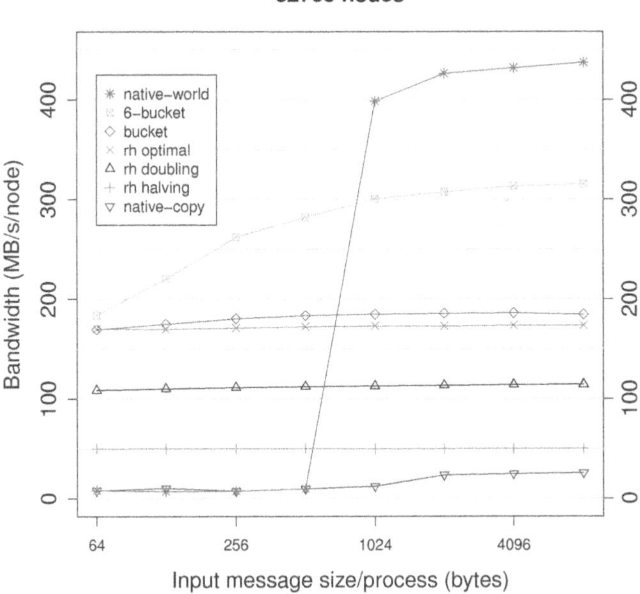

Figure 5. Performance of reduce-scatter algorithms.

large systems, these terms are negligible. In this analysis, we do not throw out any terms. Further, our equations assumed cubic torus networks. Here, we directly apply our congestion-aware performance model by counting messages and bytes; we do not use any equations. Our model here assumes that the messages sent on different ports in multi-port algorithms are synchronized; they all begin and end at the same time and have the same size. This model cannot model multi-port bucket algorithms on non-cubic torus networks. In [14], we present a more detailed model that handles this case. Essentially, the α term is still charged for every message on every port, and the β term is determined by the slowest of the 3 or 6 buckets in each phase of the algorithm. On cubic torus networks, the two models are equivalent.

In Figure 6, we compare the predicted versus measured performance of the optimally-remapped and distance-doubling recursive-doubling, and the single-port, three-port, and six-port bucket allgather algorithms with 64-byte or 32-kilobyte input messages per process. For clarity, we exclude the 64-byte 6-bucket algorithm from the plot. We introduce a factor of 0.93 into the predicted performance for the 6-port bucket algorithm, since the system penalizes the per-port bandwidth under 6-port communication by 7%. We see the least agreement between the model and the data for small messages on small partitions. This indicates that message start-up costs are optimistically modeled by our model; for larger messages or large partitions, the more accurate bandwidth term in our model dominates. This is not surprising: our model implicitly assumes zero-latency global synchronization between stages of communication and the absence of system noise or operating system effects. For small messages, this inaccuracy is magnified.

4.4 Comparison with related work

As mentioned above in Section 3.2, Jain and Sabharwal also implemented 6-way bucket algorithms [11]. Their evaluation was also on a Blue Gene/P system. Their multi-threaded allgather algorithm delivers about the same performance as our single-threaded implementation with an extra stage. Their single-threaded algorithm performs about 30% worse. On the other hand, their multi-threaded reduce-scatter algorithm performs much better than ours, since they can spread the application of the reduction operator over multiple threads. Their single-threaded reduce-scatter algorithm has similar performance to ours. Instead of an extra stage of communication, they reorder the data in memory after the allgather algorithm and before the reduce-scatter algorithm, as we do in the experiment whose results are shown in 4. It is unclear to us how they can do this reordering so efficiently, since we tried this and performance suffered greatly, as Figure 4 shows.

5. Conclusion and future work

5.1 Future work

The 6-way bucket algorithms perform very well, but have the drawback of a larger number of messages compared to the recursive-doubling or recursive-halving algorithms. We plan to investigate the performance of a hybrid algorithm. In the hybrid algorithm, we would replace the first two phases of the 6-bucket algorithm with a 3-way reordered recursive-doubling operation. The recursive-doubling portion of the algorithm would only operate in two dimension. Overall, we would have three simultaneous recursive-doubling operations followed by six simultaneous bucket operations. This is in the same vein as the work on hybrid reduction algorithms for 2-d meshes explored in [13].

The recursive-doubling algorithms only work when the number of processes is a power-of-two. We would like to use our technique to improve the efficiency of Bruck's algorithm [5], where, in each stage, process i sends data to process $i + 2^s$ and receives data from process $i - 2^s$.

We would also like to validate our algorithms on a Clos network; we chose to use a Blue Gene/P system for our first experiments since topology information is so accessible. Further, the Blue Gene/P job scheduler schedules contiguous blocks of nodes. Many job schedulers on Clos networks do not, since Clos networks generally have a larger bisection bandwidth to injection bandwidth ratio, and fewer problems naturally map to a Clos network, so topology information is less useful.

Finally, we plan to develop multi-port versions of other MPI operations, such as scatter. We do not think a multi-port recursive-doubling algorithm would be useful, since it has only a small advantage over the bucket algorithm for small messages due to its low message count. We evaluated the Van de Geijn broadcast algorithm (scatter followed by allgather) using our allgather algorithms. We found the native scatter to limit our performance; with an efficient scatter algorithm, our Van de Geijn broadcast algorithm should deliver good performance.

5.2 Conclusion

Many widely-used allgather and reduce-scatter algorithms do not reach their full potential for several reasons. They are single-ported or not topology-aware. In all of them, processes send and receive the minimal amount of data. In contrast, our algorithms are non-minimal because we add an extra stage of communication to restore the correct data order. This flexibility enables us to reorder the stages of communication or run multiple operations in parallel on a multi-port network. The overhead of the extra stage is small and this leads to substantially better performance compared to minimal-communication algorithms.

To summarize: we show that non-minimal collective algorithms deliver far better performance than minimal collective algorithms. We show that collective algorithms need not preserve the correct ordering as long as the misordering is universal, as a simple extra stage can restore the correct ordering. We present a novel semi-topology-aware algorithm that works well on a variety of networks and is optimal on Clos networks, a novel topology-aware recursive-

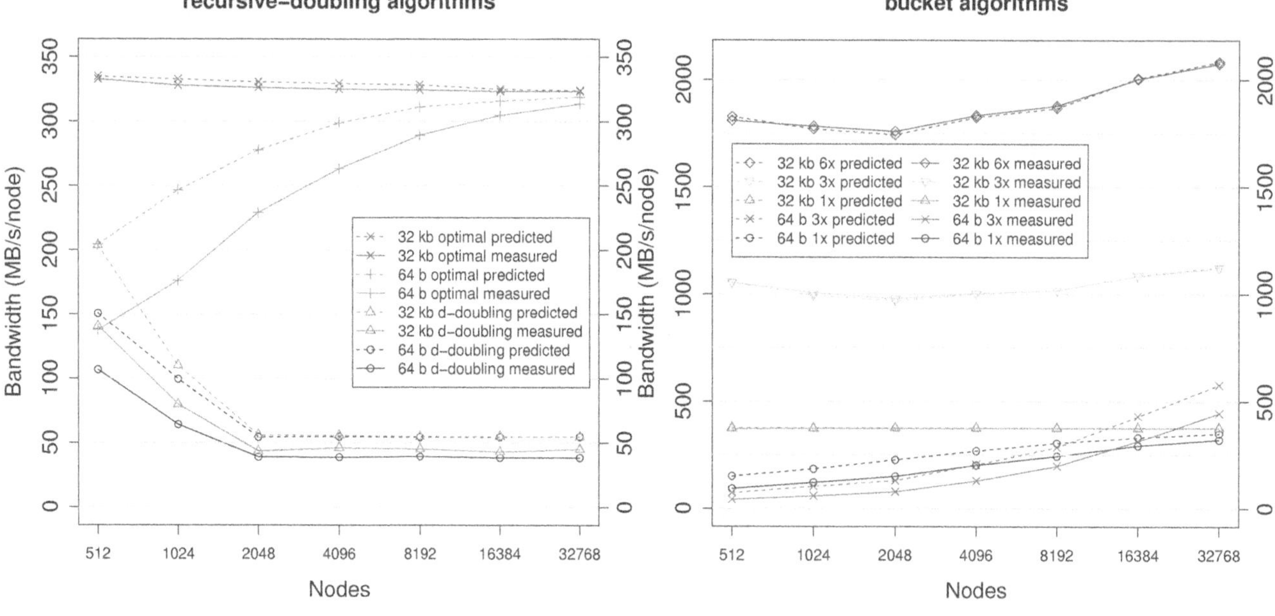

Figure 6. Measured versus predicted performance.

doubling allgather and recursive-halving reduce-scatter algorithm for mesh or torus networks, and a novel multi-port bucket algorithm for multi-port mesh or torus networks. Our allgather algorithm delivers within 1% of the maximum deliverable multi-port bandwidth of a Blue Gene/P system, which is 5.5x better than the native algorithm, and our analytical model matches measured results.

References

[1] J. H. Ahn, N. Binkert, A. Davis, M. McLaren, and R. S. Schreiber. HyperX: Topology, routing, and packaging of efficient large-scale networks. In *Proc of the Conf. on High Performance Computing Networking, Storage and Analysis*, SC '09, pages 41:1–41:11, New York, NY, USA, 2009. ACM.

[2] M. Barnett, D. G. Payne, and R. A. van de Geijn. Optimal broadcasting in mesh-connected architectures. Technical report, Austin, TX, USA, 1991.

[3] M. Barnett, S. Gupta, D. G. Payne, L. Shuler, R. van de Geijn, and J. Watts. Interprocessor collective communication library (intercom). In *Proc. of the Scalable High Performance Computing Conf.*, pages 357–364. IEEE Computer Society Press, 1994.

[4] K. Bergman, S. Borkar, D. Campbell, W. Carlson, W. Dally, M. Denneau, P. Franzon, W. Harrod, J. Hiller, S. Karp, S. Keckler, D. Klein, R. Lucas, M. Richards, A. Scarpelli, S. Scott, A. Snavely, T. Sterling, R. S. Williams, and K. Yelick. Exascale computing study: Technology challenges in achieving exascale systems, 2008.

[5] J. Bruck, , C.-T. Ho, S. Kipnis, E. Upfal, and D. Weathersby. Efficient algorithms for all-to-all communications in multi-port message-passing systems. In *IEEE Transactions on Parallel and Distributed Systems*, pages 298–309, 1997.

[6] E. Gabriel, G. E. Fagg, G. Bosilca, T. Angskun, J. J. Dongarra, J. M. Squyres, V. Sahay, P. Kambadur, B. Barrett, A. Lumsdaine, R. H. Castain, D. J. Daniel, R. L. Graham, and T. S. Woodall. Open MPI: Goals, concept, and design of a next generation MPI implementation. In *Proc. 11th European PVM/MPI Users' Group Meeting*, pages 97–104, Budapest, Hungary, September 2004.

[7] W. Gropp, E. Lusk, N. Doss, and A. Skjellum. A high-performance, portable implementation of the MPI message passing interface standard. *Parallel Computing*, 22(6):789–828, Sept. 1996.

[8] W. D. Gropp and E. Lusk. *User's Guide for* `mpich`, *a Portable Implementation of MPI*. Mathematics and Computer Science Division, Argonne National Laboratory, 1996. ANL-96/6.

[9] T. Hoefler, T. Schneider, and A. Lumsdaine. Multistage Switches are not Crossbars: Effects of Static Routing in High-Performance Networks. In *Proc. of the 2008 IEEE Int. Conf. on Cluster Computing*. IEEE Computer Society, Oct. 2008. ISBN 978-1-4244-2640.

[10] IBM-Blue-Gene-Team. Overview of the IBM Blue Gene/P project. *IBM Journal of Research and Development*, 52(1/2):199–220, 2008.

[11] N. Jain and Y. Sabharwal. Optimal bucket algorithms for large MPI collectives on torus interconnects. In *Proc. of the 24th ACM Int. Conf. on Supercomputing*, ICS '10, pages 27–36, 2010.

[12] H. Meuer, E. Strohmaier, J. Dongarra, and H. Simon. *TOP500 Supercomputing Sites*, 2011 (accessed May 13, 2011). `http://top500.org`.

[13] B. L. Payne, M. Barnett, R. Littlefield, D. G. Payne, and R. A. van De Geijn. Global combine on mesh architectures with wormhole routing. In *Proc. of 7 th Int. Parallel Proc. Symp*, 1993.

[14] P. Sack. *Scalable Collective Message-passing Algorithms*. PhD thesis, University of Illinois at Urbana-Champaign, 2011.

[15] H. Tang and T. Yang. Optimizing threaded MPI execution on SMP clusters. In *Proc. of 15th ACM int. conf. on supercomputing*, pages 381–392. ACM Press, 2001.

[16] R. Thakur and W. Gropp. Improving the performance of collective operations in MPICH. In *Recent Advances in Parallel Virtual Machine and Message Passing Interface. Number 2840 in LNCS, Springer Verlag (2003) 257-267 10th European PVM/MPI User's Group Meeting*, pages 257–267. Springer Verlag, 2003.

[17] R. Thakur and R. Rabenseifner. Optimization of collective communication operations in MPICH. *Int. Journal of High Performance Computing Applications*, 19:49–66, 2005.

[18] J. L. Träff, A. Ripke, C. Siebert, P. Balaji, R. Thakur, and W. Gropp. A pipelined algorithm for large, irregular all-gather problems. *Int. Journal High Performance Computing Applications*, 24:58–68, February 2010.

[19] E. Zahavi. Fat-trees routing and node ordering providing contention free traffic for MPI global collectives. *Parallel and Distributed Processing Workshops and PhD Forum*, 0:761–770, 2011.

Efficient SIMD Code Generation for Irregular Kernels

Seonggun Kim
RP Core Group, Samsung Advanced Institute of Technology, Yongin 446-712, Korea
seonggun.kim@gmail.com

Hwansoo Han
School of Information and Communication Engineering, Sungkyunkwan University, Suwon 440-746, Korea
hhan@skku.edu

Abstract

Array indirection causes several challenges for compilers to utilize single instruction, multiple data (SIMD) instructions. Disjoint memory references, arbitrarily misaligned memory references, and dependence cycles in loops are main challenges to handle for SIMD compilers. Due to those challenges, existing SIMD compilers have excluded loops with array indirection from their candidate loops for SIMD vectorization. However, addressing those challenges is inevitable, since many important compute-intensive applications extensively use array indirection to reduce memory and computation requirements. In this work, we propose a method to generate efficient SIMD code for loops containing indirected memory references. We extract both inter- and intra-iteration parallelism, taking data reorganization overhead into consideration. We also optimally place data reorganization code in order to amortize the reorganization overhead through the performance gain of SIMD vectorization. Experiments on four array indirection kernels, which are extracted from real-world scientific applications, show that our proposed method effectively generates SIMD code for irregular kernels with array indirection. Compared to the existing SIMD vectorization methods, our proposed method significantly improves the performance of irregular kernels by 91%, on average.

Categories and Subject Descriptors D.3.4 [*Programming Languages*]: Processors—Code generation; C.1.2 [*Processor Architectures*]: Multiple Data Stream Architectures—Single-instruction-stream, multiple-data-stream processors (SIMD)

General Terms Performance, Experimentation, Algorithms

Keywords DFG-based vectorization, Irregular kernels, SIMD processors

1. Introduction

Most modern processor architectures employ single instruction, multiple data (SIMD) units. Using SIMD instructions, processors can simultaneously execute the same operation on multiple data packed into a register. For programmers, SIMD capabilities are one of most important leverages to exploit the data level parallelism inherent in their applications with a low power and low complexity processor design. As power efficiency becomes a significant issue in various computing environments, utilizing SIMD capabilities becomes much more desirable than depending solely on out-of-order execution units to improve system performance [22].

In order to provide a transparent performance improvement as in out-of-order execution, optimizing compilers are expected to automatically transform programs written in high-level languages into corresponding machine code that efficiently utilizes the underlying SIMD architecture. Various techniques have been proposed to automatically generate SIMD code [10, 11, 15, 23] and to address the difficulties in SIMD code generation such as memory alignment [6], data permutations [20], interleaved data [17], etc. Those techniques are now well-established and even incorporated into several production compilers. Algorithms handling regular structures such as multimedia processing have quite well benefitted from those SIMD compilers.

Still, there are several types of important computations for which existing compilers cannot achieve any evident performance improvement. A notable type of such computations is code with array indirections, which usually arise from sparse data manipulation. Sparse data structures are extensively used to reduce the memory and computation requirements in many application domains including scientific applications such as computational fluid dynamics and molecular dynamics. Since the compute-intensive kernels of those applications involve array indirections, it is important to make the kernels to efficiently utilize SIMD units. Existing SIMD compilation techniques, however, cannot handle array indirections very well.

The difficulties in handling array indirections mainly come from the irregularity of their access patterns. Consider an array reference `x[idx[i]]`, where the accesses to the array `x` are dictated by the contents of the array `idx`. The actual element of `x` that each loop iteration accesses with an index variable `i` is unknown at compile-time. As a consequence, compilers are hardly able to infer any useful properties of the access pattern such as alignment, adjacency, and dependence among indirected references.

The lack of knowledge on access pattern incurs several challenges in SIMD compilation, which have not been effectively addressed by the existing techniques. The access pattern irregularity from array indirections makes the indirected references be treated as disjoint (or non-contiguous) from each other in compiler analysis. As a result, they cannot be aggregated into a single vector memory reference. This prevents many widely-used compiler techniques from exploiting SIMD capabilities. Since SIMD compilers often use adjacent memory references as initial seeds to explore SIMD opportunities, code with array indirections are excluded from their SIMD targets due to disjoint references [11, 26]. In addition, the alignment of each reference inside a loop varies from one iteration to another. To cover all the possible alignment

PPoPP'12, February 25–29, 2012, New Orleans, Louisiana, USA.

cases, compilers have to conservatively generate packing and unpacking code with inefficient instruction sequences. Recent works take account of data organization optimization to handle disjoint accesses, but they are limited to fixed stride accesses and static alignments [6, 17, 20], or require special hardware support [3, 16]. Thus, those works still cannot be adopted to handle irregular access patterns from array indirection on today's commodity hardware.

In this work, we propose a compilation method to generate efficient SIMD code for loops containing indirected memory references. In order to effectively address the aforementioned challenges, this work pursues the following objectives:

- **Exploit both intra- and inter-iteration parallelism.** Data-level parallelism often simultaneously resides both within a body of loop and across loop iterations. This fact encourages compilers to extract parallelism from various scopes. Although some existing approaches [11, 26] pursue intra- and inter-iteration parallelism simultaneously, they are not adequate for the cases with indirected memory references. Our work provides a compilation method feasible for disjoint memory references from array indirections.
- **Generate mixed scalar and SIMD operations.** The traditional way of handling dependence cycles (loop-carried dependences) is to distribute such parts into separate loops. This often causes the increased reuse distance of memory accesses and shorter loop body that may hurt the instruction level parallelism. This work generates the mixed scalar and SIMD instructions within the same loop body. It is also useful for inherently sequential operations such as function calls or those are not supported by SIMD instruction set architectures.
- **Minimize data reorganization overhead.** Since most SIMD units have restrictive memory units, they can only access continuous and properly aligned data. Thus, the burden to gather, scatter, and realign data frequently lies on software. The data reorganization overhead is one of the most significant reason why existing SIMD compilers are unsuccessful on indirected memory references. This work proposes heuristics to find the optimal placement of data reorganization code so that their overheads can be amortized by the performance gains of following SIMD instructions.

Our measurements on a Cell SPU [8] show that for several scientific kernels with array indirections, our method can generate more efficient SIMD code than existing techniques. It achieves average speedup factor of 2.83, while the other existing ones achieve up to 1.48, for four kernels extracted from several real-world scientific benchmarks.

The rest of this paper is organized as follows. Section 2 discusses the existing SIMD compilation methods and introduces an example that motivates this work. Section 3 describes the proposed SIMD compilation method. Experimental evaluations are presented in Section 4. Finally, Section 5 concludes this paper.

2. Background

2.1 Existing SIMD Compilation Methods

As SIMD extensions are similar to vector processors, SIMD compilation techniques first originated from traditional vectorization techniques for vector processors [1]. Those algorithms are based on the notion of data dependence along with several classical loop transformations. Strip-mining, scalar expansion, reduction processing, and loop distribution are major loop transformation techniques used to enhance parallelism [10, 23]. In spite of similarities, there exist several differences between vector processors and SIMD extensions [19]. The most prominent differences arise from the weaker memory units of SIMD extensions. In contrast to those of vector processors, the memory units of SIMD extensions usually do not support scatter-gather style operations. They only allow to access memory locations that are aligned at vector register length boundaries. Eichenberger et al. proposed a method for vectorizing loops with misaligned stride-one memory references [6]. Ren et al. optimized a sequence of multiple data reorganization for statically misaligned data [20]. Nuzman et al. extended a loop-based vectorization technique to handle computations with non-unit stride accesses to data, where the strides are power of 2 [17]. However, there has been no loop-based vectorization for arbitrary stride memory references. This work handles non-affine memory references due to array indirections.

Another type of SIMD compilation methods is based on the extraction of instruction-level parallelism within a basic block. Leupers presented a code selection algorithm that can generate alternative covers for a given data flow graph by using SIMD instructions [15]. Larsen and Amarasinghe proposed *Superword Level Parallelism* (SLP) algorithm that packs isomorphic instructions within a basic block starting from adjacent memory references [11]. Those methods commonly perform loop unrolling beforehand in order to extract inter-iteration parallelism as well. For computations on disjoint data, they still fail to extract inter-iteration parallelism. Barik et al. presented a DAG covering algorithm using dynamic programming for vector instruction selection [2]. Their cost model considers several possibilities to pack scalar values into vector registers and is able to handle interleaved data. These basic block level approaches complement or extend the loop-level approaches. However, they lose some vectorization opportunities that require the context of the enclosing loops. Such examples include reduction recognition, loop peeling for misaligned accesses, loop versioning for runtime pointer disambiguation, etc.

To overcome this problem, methods to integrate basic block approaches with loop-based approaches are proposed. Wu et al. presents a simdization framework based on virtual vectors, which abstract contiguous data elements with no alignment and length constraints [26]. In their framework, individual data elements are aggregated into virtual vectors at multiple phases for basic-block, short-loop, and loop levels. Rosen et al. extended the loop-based vectorization originally proposed to handle interleaved accesses so that it can exploit superword level parallelism under the awareness of loop contexts [21]. Both of them successfully extracts SIMD parallelism from various sources, but only for regular accesses that are contiguous or interleaved with static power-of-2 strides. On the other hand, our method balances inter- and intra-iteration parallelism according to the data reorganization costs even in the presence of arbitrary stride memory references and dynamically decided alignments.

In real-world computations, loops can have operations that are inherently unvectorizable due to dependence cycles or the nature of operations themselves. Traditional loop-based techniques handle such operations by using loop distribution [10, 23]. Since loop distribution based approaches require several additional loop transformations such as scalar expansion and strip-mining, they often become unnecessarily complex and sometimes fail to convert loops into vectorizable forms. The SLP algorithm addresses this problem in a simplified way; it only combines packable (vectorizable) statements and leaves the rests as they are [11]. In this way, the SLP algorithm generates a mixed code of vector and scalar instructions, which, according to their experiments, achieves better performance than a loop-distributed code. The need of *mixed-mode simdization* is also discussed in [26], even though they provide little details about the implementation. We also pursue the advantage of mixed scalar-vector code, while focusing on the optimization of data reorganization among scalar, vector, and superword operations.

```
1  for (k=nj0; k<nj1; k++) {
2      j          = 3*jjnr[k];
3
4      jx         = pos[j];
5      jy         = pos[j+1];
6      jz         = pos[j+2];
7
8      dx         = ix-jx;
9      dy         = iy-jy;
10     dz         = iz-jz;
11     rsq        = dx*dx + dy*dy + dz*dz;
12
13     rinv       = 1.0/sqrt(rsq);
14
15     rinvsq     = rinv*rinv;
16     rinvsix    = rinvsq*rinvsq*rinvsq;
17     vnb6       = c6*rinvsix;
18     vnb12      = c12*rinvsix*rinvsix;
19     fs         = (vnb12-vnb6+vcoul)*rinvsq;
20
21     fac[j]    -= dx*fs;
22     fac[j+1]  -= dy*fs;
23     fac[j+2]  -= dz*fs;
24 }
```

Figure 1. The most time-consuming loop of 435.gromacs in SPEC CPU2006. This abbreviated code calculates the interaction between only one atom pair, while the original code calculates for nine atom pairs.

2.2 Motivating Example

Fig. 1 shows the inner-most loop of the irregular kernel excerpted and abbreviated from the function `inl1130` of 435.gromacs in SPEC CPU2006 benchmark suite. The loop spends about 75% of the execution time of 435.gromacs benchmark for the reference input. The example loop has several obstacles to SIMD compilation: arbitrary stride memory accesses (line 4-6 and 21-23), loop-carried dependences (line 21-23), and a function call (line 13). The array `pos` and `fac` are indirectly accessed by the value of `j`, which is actually derived from a value in the array `jjnr`. Since the actual value of the `j` is unknown at compile-time, compilers are unable to determine the access patterns of the references on `pos` and `fac`. For those unknown access patterns, compilers regard them as disjoint and arbitrarily mis-aligned across iterations. To utilize SIMD instructions, compilers generate inefficient data reorganization code, which considers all possible cases of alignments. Compilers also have to assume that the statements at line 21-23 cause loop-carried dependence, since they may read and write the same locations at different iterations. Loop-carried dependence prevents the loop from being parallelized and selected for SIMD candidates, unless compilers recognize irregular array-reduction from those statements. In addition, function calls are often unvectorizable due to side effects or no parallel implementation being available. Although the call to `sqrt` at line 13 is usually recognized by compilers as a SIMD candidate, for illustration purpose we assume that `sqrt` has no available vector counterpart in this paper.

Due to the above mentioned obstacles, existing compilers may fail to make use of SIMD instructions for the example loop in Fig. 1. Even if they partially vectorize some statements in the loop, they can achieve a limited performance improvement. First, we consider loop-based vectorization methods [1], which vectorize a data-parallel loop as a whole. To apply the loop-based vectorization, compilers have to distribute the example loop in Fig. 1 into several smaller loops and find any data-parallel loops among them. In this example, the loop is required to be divided into four loops: two data-parallel loops (each contains line 2-11 and line 15-19, respectively) and two sequential loops (each contains line 13 and line 21-23, respectively). This approach can hurt instruction-level parallelism, since those short loop bodies make it difficult to find instruction schedules that efficiently exploit instruction-level parallelism. Moreover, this approach incurs many additional memory operations to transfer data among the distributed loops. Loop distribution often requires associated scalar expansion to store intermediate values generated from the preceding loop and used in the later loops. For example, the scalar variable `rsq` has to be expanded into an array, when the loop in Fig. 1 is divided after the line 11. The intermediate data are now passed via memory variables rather than registers. This increases not only the number of instructions, but also the size of memory footprint proportional to the number of loop iterations. Additional loop transformations such as strip mining can help to alleviate the increased memory requirements, but it requires complex analysis such as polyhedral analysis to automatically configure optimal transformation sequences [7]. To make efficient SIMD compilation techniques for irregular kernels, compilers should be able to partially vectorize some portion of statements in a given loop, without distributing it.

Second, we consider basic-block-based techniques such as SLP algorithm [11]. They can effectively address the problems with loop distribution, but they still fail to find inter-iteration parallelism when each iteration accesses a disjoint memory location as in the example loop in Fig. 1. In theory, basic-block-based algorithms can examine a basic block and search for any instructions that can be executed in parallel. In practice, the search space can explode exponentially, as the number of instructions increases. Thus, brute-force searching tends to fail on large basic blocks. The SLP algorithm alleviates the problem by using adjacent memory references as initial seeds of their search process. It first finds references that are adjacent with each other so that they can be packed into a single vector reference. Then, it expands the pack set by adding more parallel instructions that are connected to the existing pack set through use-def relations. In this approach, they use loop unrolling to transform inter-iteration parallelism into intra-iteration parallelism. This method subsumes loop-based vectorization, when every reference in a loop is adjacent across iterations. For the example loop in Fig. 1, however, the SLP algorithm can only extract parallelism within line 2-11 and line 21-23. The majority of the operations (line 15-19), which can be actually executed in parallel across the iterations, still remain in scalar (unvectorized) forms. The heuristic based on the contiguity of memory references can be trapped into local optima, when the references are disjoint across iterations. In order to extract the full parallelism, we need to search for parallelism more globally but without exploding search space.

3. A SIMD Compilation Method

In this section, we propose a SIMD compilation method to address the problems discussed in the previous sections. The proposed method examines the data-flow graph (DFG) of the loop body to exploit parallelism. By introducing additional attributes on its nodes and edges, a DFG can be easily extended to retain useful information such as dependences, alignment, contiguity, etc. Using DFG's enables us to adopt graph algorithms in our SIMD compilation method. For example, we can distinguish between parallel parts and sequential parts by using a strongly-connected components discovery algorithm. In addition, graph search algorithms can be used to determine how many operations benefit from a given data reorganization operation. This can be useful to effectively estimate if the data reorganization costs are acceptable.

Fig. 2 shows the steps of our proposed SIMD compilation method. Our method is implemented in the LLVM compiler infrastructure [14]. We rely on the front-end of LLVM (`llvm-gcc`) to parse source code, perform pre-optimization, and emit the LLVM

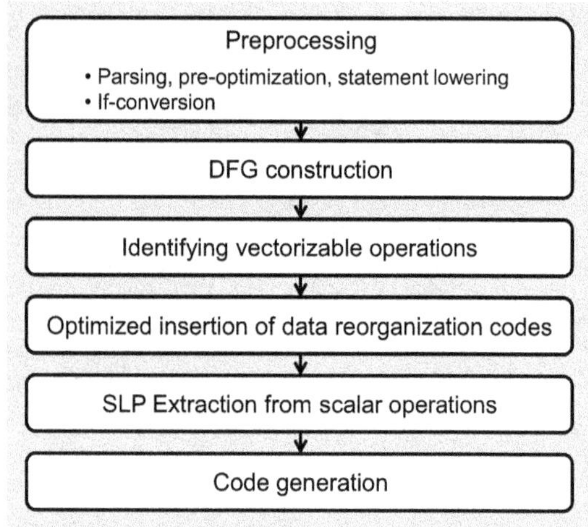

Figure 2. Steps of our SIMD compilation method

intermediate representation (IR), which is three-address static single assignment (3A-SSA) form [1]. Then, for each inner-most loop, the DFG of the loop body is constructed from the LLVM IR. To make the DFG construction step simple, we transform control dependence into data dependence with if-conversion [1]. True data dependence is represented with a directed edge on the DFG, which is actual data flow to be implemented through a register. Besides data flow among operations, the DFG includes memory dependence as a special data flow between memory operations. Unlike data dependence through registers, memory dependence is *may*-information. Compilers conservatively assume dependence between two memory operations, if there is a possibility for data to flow between them through a memory location.

To identify all the vectorizable operations in the DFG, we traverse the DFG and find any dependence cycles along the data flows. An operation cannot be vectorized if it is a part of a dependence cycle. Some operations cannot be vectorized at all, as they do not have corresponding SIMD instructions in the ISA of the target architecture. Once the vectorizable operations are discovered, the next step is to determine which vectorizable operations will be actually vectorized. Considering the data reorganization overheads, we select operations to be vectorized. At the same time, we place necessary data reorganization operations so that the overall performance is maximized. After the selection, several operations may still remain in scalar forms. We extract intra-iteration parallelism from the remaining scalar operations by using an algorithm similar to the SLP algorithm [11]. The reorganization code between a vector operation and a superword operation is also optimized with the consideration of communication patterns. Finally, a code is emitted from the DFG to have mixed scalar and SIMD instructions. The following subsections describe each of the core steps in detail.

3.1 Building the Data-flow Graph

A DFG is defined as a directed graph $G = (V, E)$, where V is a set of operations and E is a set of ordered pair (v_i, v_j) which indicates the operation v_j uses the result of the operation v_i as an operand. Fig. 3 shows the DFG for the loop body of the example code in Fig. 1. For DFGs in our work, we extend the definition of E to capture memory dependence as well. If two operations v_i and v_j may access possibly the same memory location and at least one of them is write operation, we insert edges between v_i and v_j to explicitly present the ordering constraint between them. Note that two operations can mutually precede each other on different iterations, when their subscript functions intersect. In such cases,

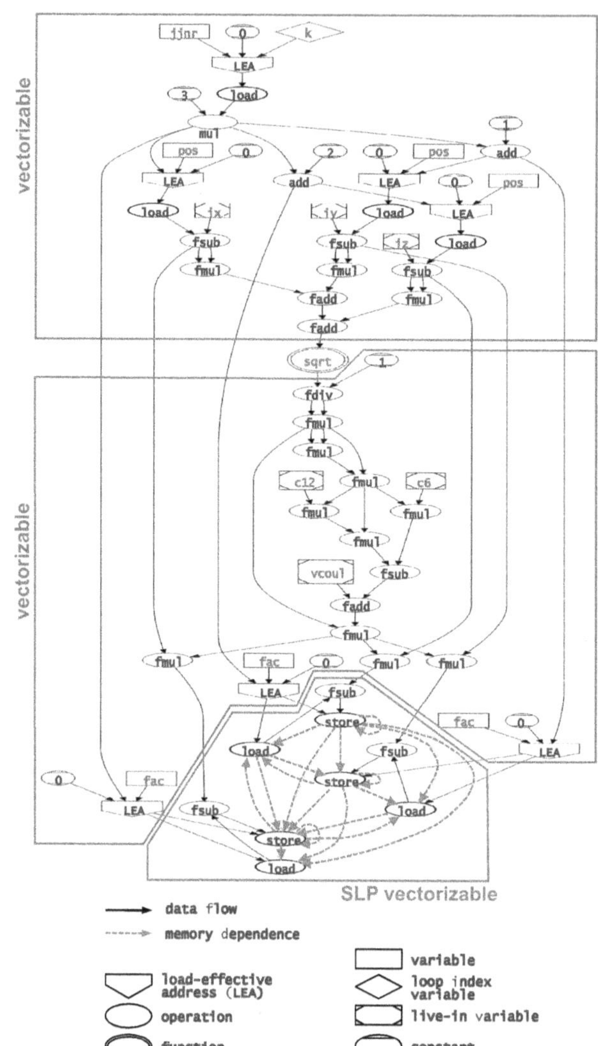

Figure 3. DFG for the body of the example loop in Fig. 1. Operations, which are not part of strongly connected components (SCCs), are vectorizable across iterations. Function `sqrt` is unvectorizable. An SCC (combination of three `load-fsub-store`'s) at the bottom is vectorizable by exploiting intra-loop parallelism

we insert two edges for both directions. We also insert two edges with opposite directions, if we cannot determine the precedence between operations. We separately maintain the edges incurring loop-carried dependence and the edges incurring loop-independent dependence, since we do not have to take loop-carried dependence into account when extracting intra-iteration parallelism.

The set of DFG nodes, V, is constructed by scanning the loop body. A statement in the loop body is one-to-one mapped to a DFG node, as every statement in 3A-SSA form has only one operation. To construct the set of edges, E, we use information of def-use relation and memory dependence. Def-use information is naturally encoded in SSA form, as there is only one operation that defines a variable. For memory dependence, we implement a dependence analysis based on the dependence testing techniques used in PFC, a parallelizing compiler at Rice university [1]. Since our work targets inner-most loops, we only require zero index variable (ZIV) and single index variable (SIV) tests. Pointer alias information for memory dependence analysis is inferred by Data Structure Analysis [13] or given by programmers with the `restrict` qualifier in C [25].

3.2 Identifying Vectorizable Operations

In this step, inter-iteration (or cross-iteration) parallelism is discovered. For each operation, we determine whether it is *vectorizable* – i.e., its multiple instances from consecutive iterations can be grouped into a corresponding vector operation and executed in parallel.

If operations do not have their vector counterparts, they cannot be vectorized inherently. For example, AltiVec [5] SIMD instruction set does not support double-precision floating point vector operations. Function calls are also unvectorizable, unless there are corresponding vector implementations. This step uses a list of available SIMD instructions and vectorized versions of libraries to find inherently unvectorizable operations. Memory operations are special cases in that unit stride memory operations are regarded as vectorizable ones, whereas non-unit stride operations are regarded as unvectorizable ones.

In addition, operations in any dependence cycles must be executed in sequence to preserve programs' behavior. Such operations can be identified from a DFG by applying Tarjan's algorithm for finding strongly connected components (SCCs) of a directed graph [24]. In Fig. 3, we identify vectorizable nodes, which are surrounded by two upper polygons (top and middle) labeled as *vectorizable*. Since the function `sqrt` does not have a proper vectorized version, it is excluded from vectorizable nodes. The nodes surrounded by the bottom polygon labeled as *SLP vectorizable* are initially determined as unvectorizable ones, as they form an SCC. Moreover, some of them are memory operations (`load` and `store`) and their access patterns are non-unit stride across iterations. Such memory operations cannot be included within the set of vectorizable nodes.

Some special kinds of SCCs, however, can be executed in parallel. First, *induction* can be vectorized. Since it increases or decreases a variable by a fixed amount on every iteration, it can be executed in parallel if we initialize the corresponding vector variable with a proper initial value for each parallel thread. Second, *reduction* can also be vectorized, even though it forms a dependence cycle. Due to its associative nature, the order of computations in reduction does not affect its result. The associativity of FP operations can decided by a compiler option and we enable vectorization of FP reductions in this work. For those two types of SCCs, we exclude the operations within them from SCCs by pattern recognition and allow them to be vectorized. The initialization and accumulation code for parallel induction and reduction are not added in this step, but will be added at the later code generation step. In Fig. 3, the variable `k` at the top diamond box is an induction variable – i.e., a loop index variable. Operations for the index variable can be vectorized at the loop header, which is not shown in Fig. 3 though. Three `load-fsub-store` patterns at the bottom are array reductions, but we do not exclude them from SCCs. Since array reductions require array privatization which in general demands a large space overhead, we only recognize scalar reductions to exclude from SCCs. Thus, the nodes surrounded by the bottom polygon remain as unvectorizable operations. Later, *superword-level-parallelism* extraction will vectorize them.

All the nodes identified as vectorizable ones in this step become candidates for vectorization. The actual vectorization will be determined at the next step according to the required data reorganization cost.

3.3 Optimized Insertion of Data Reorganization

In this step, we reduce the data reorganization overhead by optimizing the insertion of packing and unpacking code for disjoint data.

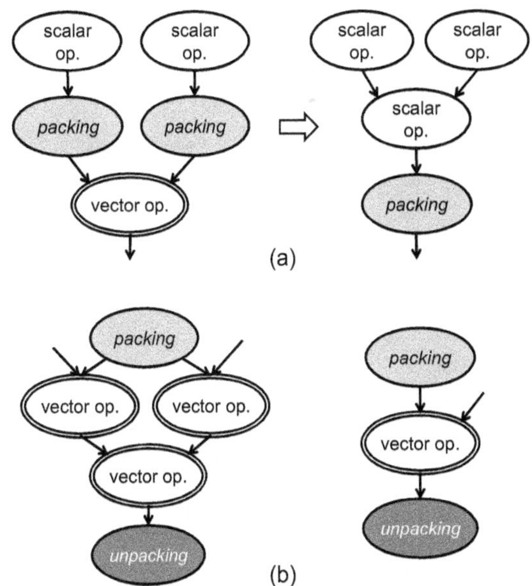

Figure 4. Heuristics for optimized insertion of packing and unpacking: (a) *lazy packing*; if a vector node uses multiple packed operands (left), it may be beneficial to pack its results instead of its operands (right), (b) *effective range of packing (ERP)*; the packing at the left enables three vector operations, while the packing at the right enables only one vector operation.

The values generated by scalar operations must be packed into a vector register in order to be used by a vector operation. Similarly, the result of a vector operation should be unpacked into several scalar values if they are later used by scalar operations. As a result, a packing node should be placed on each edge from a scalar node to a vector node, and an unpacking node on each edge from a vector node to a scalar node. The packing and unpacking nodes are later translated to a sequence of shuffle instructions and rotate instructions, respectively. Packing/unpacking n elements in a vector register generally requires $n - 1$ binary shuffle/rotate operations. For example, packing four scalar values can be implemented using two shuffle instructions and one select instruction in the Cell processor. Due to such additional data reorganization, vectorizing a certain operation may increase the number of executed instructions. We rather keep such operations in scalar forms by selectively vectorizing beneficial operations only. Finding the optimal placement of packing and unpacking is necessary to maximize the overall performance of generated SIMD code.

We use heuristic approaches to find beneficial vectorization cases. The heuristics in our approach are as follows.

- **Lazy packing.** If a vector node takes operands from multiple packing nodes, it may be beneficial to pack its result rather than its sources. An example case is shown in Fig. 4(a). The number of added instructions in two packing nodes are larger than the number of reduced instructions due to one vector operation. Packing n elements in a vector register requires $n - 1$ binary shuffle operations, which results in $2\times(n-1)$ extra instructions for two packing nodes. Since $n - 1$ instructions are saved by one vector operation, the total number of executed instructions rather increases.
- **Effective range of packing.** If the result of one packing node is used multiple times either directly or indirectly, it can be beneficial. We call those vector operations the *effective range* of packing. In Fig. 4(b), the packing node at the left figure is used

```
procedure OptimizePackUnPack(G = (V, E))
    V_V ← {v | v is vectorizable }                          ▷ vector nodes
    V_S ← V − V_V                                           ▷ scalar nodes
    E_DU ← {e | e ∈ E, e is also a def-use relation }
    repeat
        V_prv ← V_V, V_C ← ∅                 ▷ V_C: candidates to revert
        P ← {(v_i, v_j) ∈ E_DU | v_i ∈ V_S ∧ v_j ∈ V_V}
                             ▷ P: packing nodes represented with edges
        for ∀v ∈ V_V do                                     ▷ lazy packing
            if |P_v| ≥ 2, P_v = {∀(v_i, v) ∈ P} then
                if RevertDecision({v}) ≡ true then
                    V_C ← V_C ∪ {v}
                end if
            end if
        end for
        for ∀v, s.t. ∃(v, v_i) ∈ P do                      ▷ effective range
            V_ER ← EffectiveRange(v)
            if |V_ER| ≤ k then
                if RevertDecision(V_ER) ≡ true then
                    V_C ← V_C ∪ V_ER
                end if
            end if
        end for
        for ∀v, s.t. ∃(v, v_i) ∈ P do                              ▷ revert
            if ∀(v, v_i) ∈ P, v_i ∈ V_C then
                V_V ← V_V − {v_i}, V_S ← V_S ∪ {v_i}
            end if
        end for
    until V_V ≡ V_prv                      ▷ repeat until V_V not changed
    FinalizePackUnpack(V_V, V_S)
end procedure
```

Figure 5. Algorithm for optimized insertion of packing and unpacking.

by three vector operations. Meanwhile, the packing node at the right figure is used by only one vector operation. Assume the packing cost is $n - 1$. Since the packing cost at the left case is amortized by savings from three vector operations, we want to keep the current packing node. However, the packing cost at the right case is the same as the savings. If we eliminate such unprofitable packing, we may be able to improve the performance. Real benefits should be estimated by actually reverting the vector operation to the scalar one and rearranging the packing/unpacking nodes around it. Through the real estimation, we can finally decide whether we keep the packing node or not.

- **Packing first**. Unpacking is dependent on packing. If no packed data flow exists, unpacking is unnecessary. This is why elimination of packing often leads to elimination of associated unpacking. If data is already packed in memory, loading them with a vector load operation makes a packed data flow. In such a case, unpacking is needed if that packed data flow finds its way to scalar operations regardless of corresponding packing nodes. In our heuristics, we first optimize the placement of packing nodes. Unpacking nodes are then added only when necessary.

Using the above heuristics, our optimization algorithm determines which vectorizable operations will be actually vectorized. Inserting necessary packing and unpacking is done after the optimization. Fig. 5 shows how the heuristic algorithm works.

In our algorithm, we assume that all the vectorizable nodes (V_V) are vectorized and necessary packing and unpacking nodes are added. Then we iteratively revert unprofitable vector nodes to scalar nodes by considering the overhead of data reorganization and the benefit of vector execution. Using the aforementioned heuristics, we select the vector operations to investigate their benefits. Using the cost estimation function, RevertDecision, we estimate the net saving of the unvectorized version of the operations. If the cost is estimated to be beneficial, we select those vector nodes as the candidate nodes (V_C) to revert back to scalar ones. An example is shown in Fig. 6 to illustrate how the cost estimation function works. Two vector operations inside the dashed polygon may be unprofitable, as they require several packing and unpacking as shown in the left side of the figure. If they are reverted back to scalar operations as shown in the right side of the figure, they require unpacking only once. Since the data reorganization overhead is reduced, the overall performance can be improved despite the fact that the operations inside the dashed polygon are executed sequentially. In our work, we use the number of instructions as a metric to estimate the performance. We also assume that packing and unpacking are done by binary shuffle operations – i.e. the costs of packing and unpacking are $n - 1$ instructions, respectively. The cost estimation can be improved, if we take into account more low-level hardware information such as instruction latency and the number of available registers. For example, an accurate cost model used in the vectorization pass of Trimaran compiler back-end improves the benefits [12]. Most middle-end transformations, however, often adopt abstracted cost models, as the effect of such hardware constraints on performance significantly varies at the machine-specific back-ends.

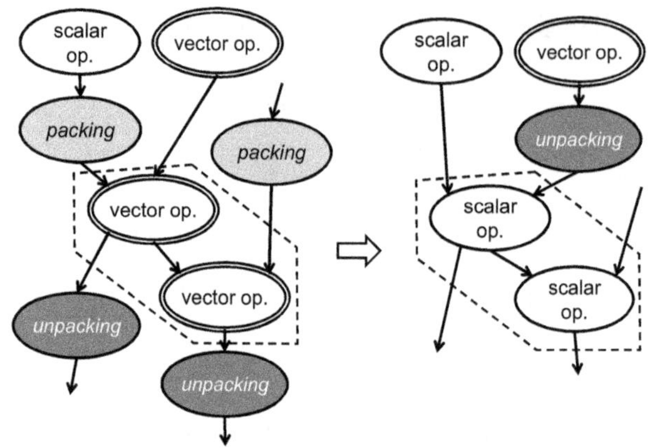

Figure 6. Revert unprofitable vector operations to scalar ones. Since the vector operations inside the dashed line require several data reorganization (left figure), they would rather be unvectorized (right figure).

The first for-loop (*lazy packing*) examines all the vectorizable nodes that use operands from multiple packing nodes. If the cost estimation decides to revert the vector operation, the corresponding node is added to the set of candidate nodes. The second for-loop (*effective range*) finds the effective range of each packing node and count the number of vector operations within the effective range. This can be easily calculated by using breadth-first search starting from a given packing node until it encounters unpacking nodes. If the number of vector operations with the effective range is less than or equal to *k*, which is two in our work, the algorithm examines the set of vector nodes within the effective range to decide whether reverting them to scalar operations is beneficial. The third for-loop (*revert*) decides which candidate nodes actually be reverted to scalar ones. It should be noted that a packing node can be completely eliminated only if its every user turns into scalar operation. On the other hand, an unpacking node can be eliminated promptly when its source node turns into a scalar operation. This is why we mark unprofitable vector operations as candidates, instead of reverting them immediately. The if-condition inside the for-loop checks if all the users of a packing are candidates for reverting. Only when the condition is true, it actually reverts all the candidate vector operations to scalar ones.

We repeat the reverting process until no new operations are reverted. Since our heuristics find and estimate candidates locally, the results still could be only locally optimal. Repeating the whole reverting process, however, can lead to a better optimization result. Since the reverting process converts only vector nodes into scalar nodes, not vice versa, the process is monotonic. In addition, the number of vector operations is finite. As a result, the repetition is guaranteed to be terminated. Once the vector operations are finally decided, necessary packing and unpacking nodes are actually added to the DFG ($FinalizePackUnpack$). After the DFG is finalized, the loop is unrolled as many times as *vector length* by replicating all nodes except vector nodes. The vector length is determined by the smallest data type used in vector operations. For example, if 8-bit values are the smallest data used in vector operations, then the vector-length is 16 for a 128-bit datapath.

3.4 Extracting Superword-level Parallelism from the Remaining Scalar Operations

After extracting inter-iteration parallelism by finalizing vector operations, we attempt to exploit intra-iteration parallelism from the remaining scalar operations. This is also called *superword-level parallelism (SLP)* [11]. The term *superword* denotes wide-length data packed for intra-iteration parallelism, whereas *vector* for inter-iteration parallelism.

Among the remaining scalar operations, some operations can be combined and executed in parallel. Ignoring loop-carried dependence, we can find multiple independent operations with identical functionalities from DFGs. The data reorganization overheads are still considered to find beneficial intra-iteration parallelism. To execute such operations in parallel, we pack them into superword operations by adopting the SLP algorithm [11]. Unlike the original SLP algorithm, we do not take the memory alignment into account during superword packing. Finding the maximally extended combination of superword operations, we pack any pair of adjacent memory references into the initial superword pack set. After collecting all superword pack sets, we divide the superword operations at alignment boundaries. For the cases of indirected references, their alignment information will be unavailable. In such cases, we can rely on data reorganization before actual superword operations begin. In superword parallelism exploration, we still estimate the benefits with the consideration of data reorganization overheads. If superword operations are not profitable, we revert them back to scalar operations.

For superword operations, data reorganization code should be placed to interoperate with vector operations and scalar operations. When superword operations take their operands from vector operations, unpacking the outputs of vector operations and repacking data for superword operations are required. Instead, we *transpose* the outputs of vector operations as shown in Fig. 7(a). In general, transpose of data can be used when superword operations take operands from vector operations and vice versa. If we unpack vectors and repack them for superwords, many individual scalar variables are needed. For the example shown in Fig. 7(a), we may need 12 scalar variables to hold all the unpacked results – $x_0, ..., x_3, y_0, ..., y_3, z_0, ..., z_3$. This type of reorganization may also incur memory accesses due to the lack of registers. Meanwhile, the transpose of data can be done with binary shuffle operations among SIMD registers, which results in much faster reorganization than unpacking and repacking with a dozen of scalar variables.

For SIMD units that have no special support for unaligned memory accesses, data reorganization must be performed in code. However, for a particular operation sequence that updates misaligned superword, we can optimize its reorganization code. We particularly recognize *load-compute-store* patterns to simplify the reorganization for misaligned data, as shown in Fig. 7(b). Existing works [6, 18] analyze alignment requirements for memory references and reduce the number of generated shift operations. Array indirections, however, hinder the effective alignment analysis, as the alignment offsets are unknown at compile time. For such cases, compilers generate reorganization code with the *zero-shift policy* [6]. This means each misaligned vector data is shifted to the zero offset in a SIMD register, immediately after the load operation. Then, it is shifted back to fit into the alignment of the store address just before the store operation. This case is depicted in the left side of Fig. 7(b). If misaligned vector data is loaded, computed and stored back to the same memory address, we know that the alignment offsets of both load and store are the same. Even though the exact alignment offset is still unknown at compile time, we can exploit the fact that the alignment offsets are the same by applying *dominant-shift policy* [6] as depicted in the right side of Fig. 7(b).

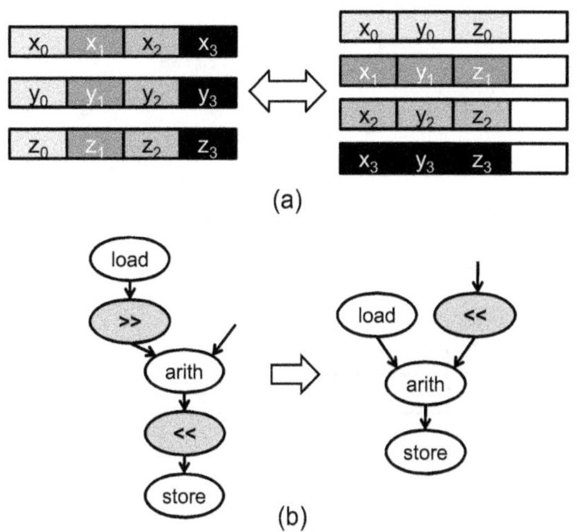

Figure 7. Data reorganization for superwords: (a) *transpose* of data between vectors and superwords, (b) in-place update of an unaligned superword for *load-compute-store*

3.5 Code Generation

In this last step, our SIMD compiler emits linear code from the transformed DFG. The code for parallelizing reduction and induction, packing live-in scalar values, and unpacking live-out vector variables should be additionally generated. Our code emission is rather straight-forward, since a node in DFGs is one-to-one mapped to a specific operation in 3A-SSA form as described in Section 3.1. In our work, we actually emit linear code in C language with SIMD intrinsics. Since the back-end of our compiler currently generates less reliable machine code for our target processor, we use a native compiler for the target processor to generate efficient binary executables. The operations in DFGs are emitted in C code by using *as-soon-as-possible (ASAP)* schedule. Since native compilers will handle instruction scheduling, a simple scheduling policy during the C code emission is enough to eventually generate efficient binary code.

Since our SIMD vectorization method retains dependence cycles within a loop body, operations in dependence cycles are replicated by unrolling as many times as vector length within the vectorized loop. Since the operations in dependence cycles have loop-carried dependence, the replicated operations tend to form long data flows among them. Thus, they are likely to fall on a critical

Kernel	Extracted From (Function/Application/Suite)			Exec. Time	General Category
CF	`ComputeForces()`	Moldyn	CHAOS	90.9%	Molecular dynamics
INL	`inl1130()`	435.gromacs	SPEC CPU2006	81.5%	Chemistry/molecular dynamics
CPEF	`calc_pair_energy_fullelect()`	444.namd	SPEC CPU2006	12.9%	Structural biology
FORMS	`FORMS()`	416.gamess	SPEC CPU2006	23.5%	Quantum chemical computations

Table 1. The Benchmark Kernels

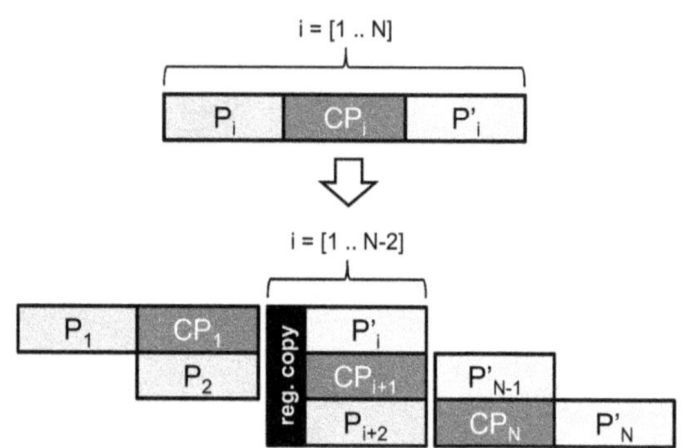

Figure 8. Software pipelining using explicit register copying. When a loop has dependence cycles, the largest cycle among them divides the loop body into three parts: operations before the cycle (P_i), ones in the cycle (CP_i), and ones after the cycle (P'_i). Each part forms a stage of pipelining. Data from the prior stage are forwarded to the next stage by explicit copy instructions at the beginning of each iteration.

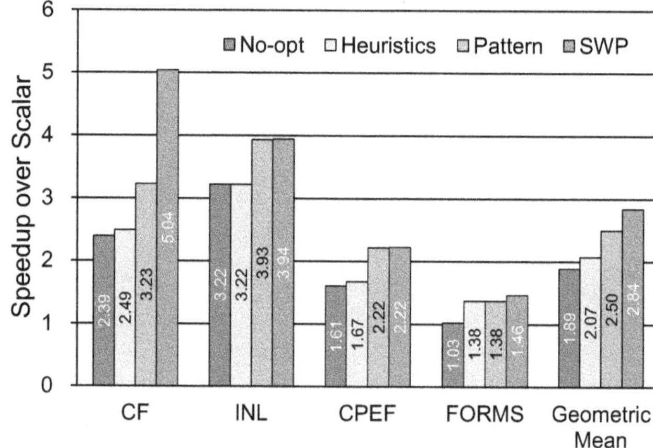

Figure 9. Speedup factors achieved by the proposed method for varying optimization configurations.

path of the schedule for the SIMD vectorized loop. To hide the latencies of those instructions on the critical path, we adopt software pipelining by splitting the loop body into three stages as shown in Fig. 8. We select the largest dependence cycle in the loop and divide the loop body into three parts: operations before the cycle (P_i), ones in the cycle (CP_i), and ones after the cycle (P'_i). Three stage software pipelining is applied with the three divided parts and data generated from the prior iteration are explicitly copied to the current iteration at the beginning of each iteration.

Software pipelining increases the chance that multiple instructions' latencies are overlapped among another. By overlapping latencies, the generated code has a better chance to enhance instruction level parallelism of the loop, which is particularly important for processors with in-order execution units. One concern in our software pipelining is that explicit register copies for forwarding data among iterations can increase the number of executed instructions and register pressure as well. Another concern is that stages may not fully overlap with each other due to memory clobbers even with software pipelining. Ultimately, these two effects can deter software pipelined loop from gaining performance boot.

4. Experimental Results

4.1 Experimental Setup

To evaluate the performance gains of the proposed method, we compile four irregular kernels from scientific applications and measure their execution times on a Synergistic Processor Unit (SPU) of the Cell processor [8]. An SPU has a SIMD processing unit and a 256KB local store. The SIMD unit has a VLIW-like two-way in-order execution pipeline with 128-bit vector data path. SPUs can execute load and store instructions only upon its local store and therefore its memory latencies are constant. We implemented the proposed method on top of the LLVM compiler infrastructure [14]. Since the LLVM compiler back-end supports the SPU only experimentally, we made the transformation to emit C codes. The generated C codes are then compiled by GCC version 4.1.1 with optimization level 3. Experiments in this section were conducted on a Sony PlayStation3 that has a Cell processor running at 3.2GHz and 256MB XDR RAM. We use the performance counter of the SPU to measure execution cycles.

Table 1 lists the benchmark kernels used in this experiments. Since this work addresses challenges due to array indirection, we only collected the inner-most loops containing array indirections, by examining the most time-consuming functions of the floating point applications from SPEC CPU2006 and CHAOS benchmark suites [4, 9]. Each kernel has several indirect references for both read and write accesses. The nature of the indirect references in the kernels are similar to the example in Fig. 1. We named the kernels after their enclosing functions. The third column of Table 1 shows the fraction of each function's execution time. Except for FORMS, each function consists only of a single loop nest that contains the extracted kernel. In case of FORMS, the function has nine loop nests in similar form. We selected the fifth one since it has the average number of instructions.

In these experiments, we converted the kernels to run with single precision floating point numbers because only single precision floating point instructions are fully-pipelined in the SPUs. We also reduced the input data of each benchmark so that it can fit in the local storage of the SPUs. The real contents of input data have actually no effect on the performance of the kernels since the SPUs are cache-less and have in-order execution units.

4.2 Performance Results

Fig. 9 shows the speedup factors achieved by the proposed SIMD compilation method accumulatively applying the optimization techniques presented in Section 3. The speedups shown in Fig. 9 are measured by cumulatively applying each optimization.

	Total Inst.	Single Issued Instructions	Dual Issued Instructions	Stall Cy.	Perf. Est.
CF (-)	313	151 (48.24%)	162 (51.76%)	80	312
(SWP)	325	71 (21.85%)	254 (78.15%)	7	205
INL (-)	907	383 (42.23%)	524 (57.77%)	15	660
(SWP)	989	315 (31.85%)	674 (68.15%)	6	658
CPEF (-)	552	116 (21.01%)	436 (78.99%)	8	342
(SWP)	570	88 (15.44%)	482 (84.56%)	1	330
FORMS (-)	444	56 (12.61%)	388 (87.39%)	37	287
(SWP)	454	28 (6.17%)	426 (93.83%)	2	243

(-) SW pipelining is not applied. (SWP) SW pipelining is applied.

Table 2. Static timing analysis of the kernels on SWP

- *No-opt*: No optimization techniques is applied. All the identified vectorizable operations in Section 3.2 are entirely vectorized and superword-level parallelism is exploited from the remaining scalar operations.
- *Heuristics*: The data reorganization optimization in Section 3.3 is applied. The identified vectorizable operations are selectively vectorized based on the benefit estimation heuristics.
- *Pattern*: The patterns in Section 3.4 are recognized and applied for superword level parallelism. This is cumulatively applied to the code from *Heuristics*.
- *SWP*: The software pipelining technique in Section 3.5 is also cumulatively applied to the code from *Pattern*.

The two techniques for optimizing data reorganization costs, *Heuristics* and *Pattern*, improve the average performance by about 10% and 20%, respectively. The result of *Pattern* shows that the data reorganization costs arisen between vector instructions and superword instructions can be effectively reduced by simple pattern-based optimizations. Since there is no extracted superword-level parallelism in FORMS, *Pattern* shows no performance improvement. The performance improvement of FORMS mainly comes from the *effective range of packing* heuristic, as the kernel accumulates the multiplication results between several pairs loaded by indirected references.

Table 2 shows the static timing analysis of the kernels before and after applying software pipelining. We count the number of instructions, single and double issued ones separately, and stall cycles in the loop body of each kernel. The results are obtained by using the timing analysis tool `spu-timing` in the CellSDK 3.0. The performance estimation shown in the column 6 (*Perf. Est.*) is calculated by summing the number of single issued instructions, a half of the number of dual issued instructions, and the number of stall cycles. As shown in Table 2, the software pipelining technique effectively increases the fraction of dual issued instructions and reduces the number of stall cycles for all cases. However, it also increases the number of total instructions since it introduces the additional copy instructions for passing intermediate values across the stages. In CF, which originally had the highest fraction of single issued instructions and the biggest number of stall cycles, software pipelining improves its performance by 34%. On the other hand, software pipelining hardly improves or even degrades the performance of CPEF and INL in Fig. 9, as it requires too many additional copy instructions (for INL) and the original code was already tightly scheduled (for CPEF). In FORMS, the performance improvement mainly comes from the reduced stall cycles.

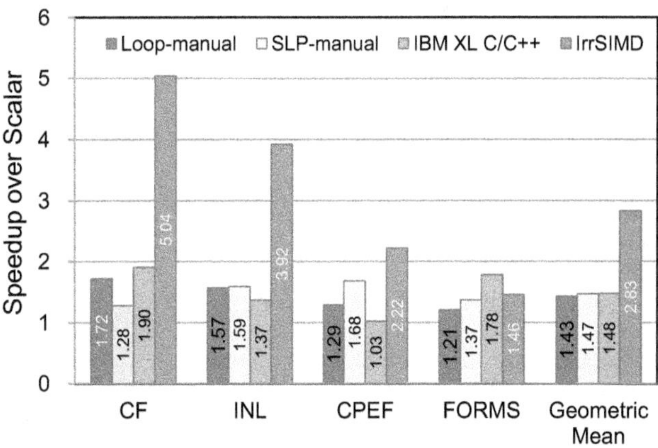

Figure 10. Comparison of speedup for the loop-based vectorization, the SLP algorithm, IBM XL C/C++, and our proposed method (*IrrSIMD*).

4.3 Comparison with Traditional SIMD Compilation Methods

We compare the performance benefit of the proposed method with two widely-used SIMD compilation methods, the loop-based vectorization and the superword-level parallelism, and a commercial compiler IBM XL C/C++ V10.1 whose auto-vectorization is based on [6, 26]. To perform comparison studies, we manually transformed the kernels based on the algorithms described in the work of Sreraman et al. [23] and Larsen et al. [11]. When applying the SLP algorithm, we impose a slight modification to handle array indirection within iterations. The SLP algorithm requires alignment information for each memory reference, but this is unavailable for indirected references. To remedy the SLP, for any pair of adjacent references whose alignment information is unavailable, we deliberately pack them expecting to find better performance gain. If such pair is proved to be unprofitable, we revert them back to scalar operations and find another extended combinations. This modified algorithm is the same as our heuristics presented in Section 3.4. For IBM XL C/C++, we compiled the benchmark codes with various optimization level (O2-O5) and reported the best results. The auto-vectorization option of IBM XL C/C++ is enabled at O3 and higher.

Fig. 10 shows the speedup of the loop-based vectorization using loop distribution (Loop-manual), the SLP algorithm (SLP-manual), the IBM XL C/C++ compiler (IBM XL C/C++), and our proposed method (IRRSIMD). Our method achieves the speedup factor of 2.83 on average, while the loop-based vectorization and the SLP algorithm achieve 1.43 and 1.47 on average, respectively. Since the loop-based vectorization and the SLP algorithm can only extract either intra- or inter-iteration parallelism for the benchmarks, they obtained lower performance than ours which was able to extract both intra- and inter-iteration parallelism. IBM XL C/C++ achieved the average speedup of 1.48. However, the transformation reports from `-qreport` option showed that no innermost loops are SIMD vectorized. The performance gain of XL C/C++ is mainly based on better extraction of instruction-level parallelism, such as code hoisting and modulo scheduling, rather than SIMD parallelism.

5. Conclusion and Future Work

Array indirection causes several important challenges for SIMD compilation including disjoint memory references, unknown alignment, dependence cycles, etc. Due to those challenges, automatic vectorization has been hardly able to achieve a certain performance improvement in the presence of array indirection. There have been only hardware approaches to address the challenges arisen from array indirection [3, 16].

In our work, we proposed a SIMD compilation method to vectorize loops that have indirected array references. The proposed method directly manipulates a data flow graph of a loop body to explicitly expose data reorganization and capture as much data-level parallelism contained in the loop as possible. Our method extracts both inter- and inter-iteration parallelism while balancing them with the consideration of data reorganization cost. It generates mixed scalar and SIMD instructions without loop distribution; the unvectorizable operations and unprofitable parallel operations also remain in the original loop body along with the SIMD operations. It optimizes the data transfer between vector and scalar operations as well as between vector and superword operations by recognizing communication patterns. Our experiments conducted on a Cell SPU show that our proposed method improves performance of several kernels drawn from a class of real-world scientific applications with the average speedup of 2.83, which almost doubles the speedup achieved by the previous automatic vectorization techniques.

The proposed scheme can further be improved by integrating the techniques for alignment optimization [6] and data permutation optimization [20]. Since those techniques use expression tree or use-def chain, they can be seamlessly integrated to a DFG-based approach. It may also be useful to include the reorganization pattern used to vectorize power-of-2 stride memory references [17]. It would provide more solid evaluation of the proposed scheme to measure the performance on various architectures including highly-optimized superscalar processors.

Acknowledgments

This research was supported by the Ministry of Education, Science and Technology, Korea under the NRF grant (NRF-2009-0084870), and the Ministry of Knowledge Economy, Korea under the NIPA ITRC support program (NIPA-2011-C1090-1100-0010). We gratefully acknowledge Center for Manycore Programming in Seoul National University for providing computing resources.

References

[1] R. Allen and K. Kennedy. *Optimizing Compilers for Modern Architectures: A Dependence-Based Approach*. Morgan Kaufmann, 2002.

[2] R. Barik, J. Zhao, and V. Sarkar. Efficient selection of vector instructions using dynamic programming. In *Proceedings of the 2010 43rd Annual IEEE/ACM International Symposium on Microarchitecture*, MICRO '43, pages 201–212, 2010.

[3] H. Chang and W. Sung. Efficient vectorization of SIMD programs with non-aligned and irregular data access hardware. In *Proceedings of the 2008 International Conference on Compilers, Architectures and Synthesis for Embedded Systems*, CASES '08, pages 167–176, 2008.

[4] R. Das, M. Uysal, J. Saltz, and Y.-S. Hwang. Communication optimizations for irregular scientific computations on distributed memory architectures. *J. Parallel Distrib. Comput.*, 22:462–478, Sep. 1994.

[5] K. Diefendorff, P. K. Dubey, R. Hochsprung, and H. Scales. AltiVec extension to PowerPC accelerates media processing. *IEEE Micro*, 20: 85–95, Mar./Apr. 2000.

[6] A. E. Eichenberger, P. Wu, and K. O'Brien. Vectorization for SIMD architectures with alignment constraints. In *Proceedings of the ACM SIGPLAN 2004 Conference on Programming Language Design and Implementation*, PLDI '04, pages 82–93, 2004.

[7] T. Grosser, H. Zheng, R. A, A. Simburger, A. Grosslinger, and L.-N. Pouchet. Polly - polyhedral optimization in llvm. In *First International Workshop on Polyhedral Compilation Techniques (IMPACT'11)*, 2011.

[8] M. Gschwind, H. P. Hofstee, B. Flachs, M. Hopkins, Y. Watanabe, and T. Yamazaki. Synergistic processing in Cell's multicore architecture. *IEEE Micro*, 26:10–24, Mar. 2006.

[9] J. L. Henning. SPEC CPU2006 benchmark descriptions. *SIGARCH Comput. Archit. News*, 34:1–17, Sep. 2006.

[10] A. Krall and S. Lelait. Compilation techniques for multimedia processors. *Int. J. Parallel Program.*, 28:347–361, Aug. 2000.

[11] S. Larsen and S. Amarasinghe. Exploiting superword level parallelism with multimedia instruction sets. In *Proceedings of the ACM SIGPLAN 2000 Conference on Programming Language Design and Implementation*, PLDI '00, pages 145–156, 2000.

[12] S. Larsen, R. Rabbah, and S. Amarasinghe. Exploiting vector parallelism in software pipelined loops. In *Proceedings of the 38th annual IEEE/ACM International Symposium on Microarchitecture*, MICRO 38, pages 119–129, 2005.

[13] C. Lattner. *Macroscopic Data Structure Analysis and Optimization*. PhD thesis, Computer Science Dept., University of Illinois at Urbana-Champaign, Urbana, IL, May 2005. [online] `http://llvm.cs.uiuc.edu`.

[14] C. Lattner and V. Adve. LLVM: A compilation framework for lifelong program analysis & transformation. In *Proceedings of the 2004 International Symposium on Code Generation and Optimization (CGO'04)*, Palo Alto, California, Mar 2004.

[15] R. Leupers. Code selection for media processors with SIMD instructions. In *Proceedings of the conference on Design, Automation and Test in Europe*, DATE '00, pages 4–8, 2000.

[16] D. Naishlos, M. Biberstein, S. Ben-David, and A. Zaks. Vectorizing for a SIMdD DSP architecture. In *Proceedings of the 2003 International Conference on Compilers, Architecture and Synthesis for Embedded Systems*, CASES '03, pages 2–11, 2003.

[17] D. Nuzman, I. Rosen, and A. Zaks. Auto-vectorization of interleaved data for SIMD. In *Proceedings of the 2006 ACM SIGPLAN Conference on Programming Language Design and Implementation*, PLDI '06, pages 132–143, 2006.

[18] I. Pryanishnikov, A. Krall, T. U. Wien, and N. Horspool. Pointer alignment analysis for processors with SIMD instructions. In *Proceedings of the 5th Workshop on Media and Streaming Processors*, pages 50–57, 2003.

[19] G. Ren, P. Wu, and D. Padua. A preliminary study on the vectorization of multimedia applications for multimedia extensions. In *Languages and Compilers for Parallel Computing*, volume 2958 of *Lecture Notes in Computer Science*, pages 420–435. 2004.

[20] G. Ren, P. Wu, and D. Padua. Optimizing data permutations for SIMD devices. In *Proceedings of the 2006 ACM SIGPLAN Conference on Programming Language Design and Implementation*, PLDI '06, pages 118–131, 2006.

[21] I. Rosen, D. Nuzman, and A. Zaks. Loop-aware SLP in GCC. In *Proceedings of GCC Developers' Summit*, pages 131–142, 2007.

[22] J. Shalf, S. Dosanjh, and J. Morrison. Exascale computing technology challenges. In *Proc. International Meeting on High Performance Computing for Computational Science*, volume 6449 of *Lecture Notes in Computer Science*, pages 1–25, 2011.

[23] N. Sreraman and R. Govindarajan. A vectorizing compiler for multimedia extensions. *Int. J. Parallel Program.*, 28:363–400, Aug. 2000.

[24] R. Tarjan. Depth-first search and linear graph algorithms. *SIAM Journal on Computing*, 1(2):146–160, 1972.

[25] D. Walls. How to use the `restrict` qualifier in C. Sun Microsystems, Sun Developer Network (SDN), March 2006. [online] `http://developers.sun.com/`.

[26] P. Wu, A. E. Eichenberger, A. Wang, and P. Zhao. An integrated simdization framework using virtual vectors. In *Proceedings of the 19th annual International Conference on Supercomputing*, ICS '05, pages 169–178, 2005.

Extending a C-like Language for Portable SIMD Programming

Roland Leißa Sebastian Hack
Compiler Design Lab, Saarland University
{leissa, hack}@cs.uni-saarland.de

Ingo Wald
Visual Applications Research, Intel Corporation
ingo.wald@intel.com

Abstract

SIMD instructions are common in CPUs for years now. Using these instructions effectively requires not only vectorization of *code*, but also modifications to the *data layout*. However, automatic vectorization techniques are often not powerful enough and suffer from restricted scope of applicability; hence, programmers often vectorize their programs manually by using intrinsics: compiler-known functions that directly expand to machine instructions. They significantly decrease programmer productivity by enforcing a very error-prone and hard-to-read assembly-like programming style. Furthermore, intrinsics are not portable because they are tied to a specific instruction set.

In this paper, we show how a C-like language can be extended to allow for portable and efficient SIMD programming. Our extension puts the programmer in total control over where and how control-flow vectorization is triggered. We present a type system and a formal semantics of our extension and prove the soundness of the type system. Using our prototype implementation IVL that targets Intel's MIC architecture and SSE instruction set, we show that the generated code is roughly on par with handwritten intrinsic code.

Categories and Subject Descriptors D.1.3 [*Concurrent Programming*]: Parallel programming; D.3.1 [*Formal Definitions and Theory*]: Semantics, Syntax

General Terms Languages, Performance, Theory

Keywords language theory, parallel programming, polymorphism, semantics, SIMD, SIMT, type system, vectorization

1. Introduction

SIMD instructions are available on commodity processors for more than a decade now. Many developers from various domains (for example, high-performance graphics [7], databases [37], or bioinformatics [6]) use SIMD instructions to speed up their applications. Many of those algorithms are not massively data-parallel but contain data-parallel and scalar parts intermixed at a fine granularity. To illustrate this, let us run through the fundamental techniques which are necessary in order to port traditional code to SIMD architectures by considering the small example in Figure 1. It is taken (and slightly modified) from a paper by Zhou and Ross about the use of SIMD instructions to speed up data base operations [37]. The program scans data records for a certain criterion and returns the value of the first record for which the criterion holds. In this particular example, we assume that at most one element in the array fulfills the criterion.[1]

```
struct data_t {
  int key;
  int other;
};

int search(data_t* data, int N) {
  for (int i = 0; i < N; i++) {
    int x = data[i].key;
    if (4 < x & x <= 8) return x;
  }
  return -1;
}
```

Figure 1. Example program (by Zhou and Ross [37])

```
struct simd_data_t {
  simd_int key;
  simd_int other;
};

int search(simd_data_t* data, int N) {
  for (int i = 0; i < N/L; ++i) {
    simd_int x   = load(data[i].key);
    simd_int cmp = simd_and(simd_lt(4, x),
                            simd_le(x, 8));
    int mask     = simd_to_mask(cmp);
    if (mask != 0) {
      simd_int result = simd_and(mask, x);
      for (int j = 0; j < log2(L); j++)
        result = simd_or(result,
                 whole_reg_shr(result, 1 << j));
      return simd_extract(result, 0);
    }
  }
  return -1;
}
```

Figure 2. Manually vectorized example program

The hand-vectorized version of the program is shown in Figure 2. We assume that `L` is the native vector length of the target machine, i.e., there are `L` slots in one SIMD register and each slot can hold exactly one `int`. When performing vector computations we refer to the computations applied to a certain slot index as *SIMD* or *vector lane*. The program takes `L` data items from the array at once and processes them in parallel. It features the three most common techniques used to adapt a program for SIMD instructions:

Adapting the data layout. Fetching `L` values in parallel from memory is tremendously faster, if they lie consecutively in memory. Thus, the traditional *array of structures* layout (AoS, see Figure 3a) is not suitable for SIMD programming, as it requires non-contiguous memory access—called *scatter* and *gather* (S/G)—that severely degrades performance. A *structure of arrays* (SoA, see Figure 3b) provides a better solution. However, a loop over an SoA must maintain one pointer for each

PPoPP'12, February 25–29, 2012, New Orleans, Louisiana, USA.

[1] Zhou and Ross mention searching in B^+ trees with unique keys as an application.

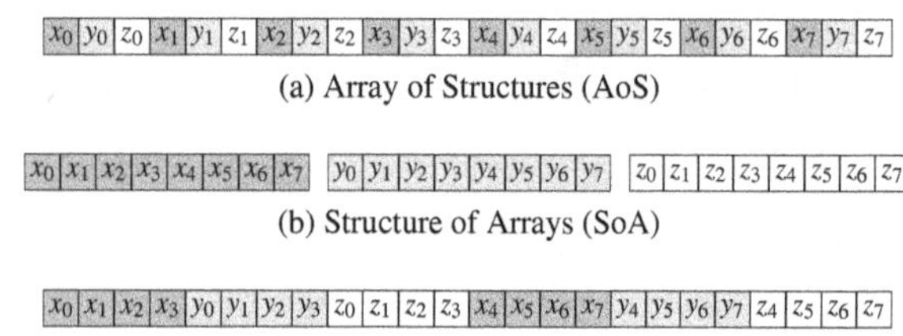

(a) Array of Structures (AoS)

(b) Structure of Arrays (SoA)

(c) Hybrid Structure of Arrays (Hybrid SoA)

Figure 3. Different array layouts with vector length 4 for a struct with three members: `x`, `y` and `z`

member. For this reason and due to data locality problems, the *hybrid SoA* (see Figure 3c) is superior, as this layout does not suffer from these problems. It emerges by first inflating the original struct to the vector length (we call this unit a *block* and the process of doing so *type vectorization*) and then grouping this block in an array. This data layout is regarded best practice in SIMD programming and is recommended by various application notes of all major CPU manufacturers, e.g. [13]. These blocks can be used to build other vectorized data structures like linked lists or trees just as well.

Control-flow to data-flow conversion. In line 9, the comparison is evaluated on all `L` loaded items in parallel. The result is a vector of booleans being *true* for those vector lanes for which the comparison was *true*. That mask has then to be converted into an ordinary **`int`** in order to use it in the conditional branch in line 12. In line 13, the mask is used to discard all values for which the comparison was *false*.

Seamless integration of scalar and vectorized code. While several statements of our example program perform data-parallel computations, the inner loop (lines 14–16) is *not* vectorized. It performs a scan-like operation: by successively shifting and OR-ing the *whole* SIMD variable, the first non-zero element of the vector is propagated to element 0 of the vector. It is typical for manually vectorized code to have a strong interaction between scalar and vector code.

This example illustrates the current state of the art in hand-tuning programs for SIMD instruction sets and clearly shows its limitations. First, vector code has to be written using assembly-like intrinsics: compiler-known functions that directly correspond to an assembly instruction. While operator overloading can improve the readability of expressions, control structures can usually not be overloaded. Hence, the control to data-flow conversion has to be performed manually by explicit handling of masks. This severely degrades the readability of the code because control statements are replaced by clumsy mask handling code. Furthermore, intrinsics directly expose a concrete instruction set architecture (ISA) to the programmer. Accordingly, intrinsics code is not only inherently unportable between different processor architectures but also within different revisions of the ISA *within* the same processor family.

Second, the definition of data structures is no longer compositional: To vectorize a struct, the programmer has to create a new type where the members of the struct are vectorized (see Figure 2). Often she is interested in the scalar *and* the vectorized type because she often refers to a single component of a vector. Hence, all types would have to be written twice. However, it is reasonable for the programmer to assume that she can obtain the vectorized version of a data type `T` by applying a type constructor, say `T` **`block`**`[N]`, which yields the desired block type. Furthermore, the compiler *knows* that `T` **`block`**`[N]` is the `N` times vectorized version of `T`. This is important for parametric polymorphism (see below) and correct handling of S/G in the type system.

Third, the hand-vectorized function of Figure 2 works *only* in a vector context. Many functions however should work in a scalar *and* in a vector context. Hence, functions should be polymorphic with respect to vectorization where possible.

We believe it to be clear that the code transformations presented above cannot be carried out automatically. Current optimizing compilers vectorize loop nests which have to satisfy strong prerequisites. Automatic interprocedural data-structure rewriting or automatic scalar/vectorial code switching are out of the scope of what an optimizing compiler for a traditional C-like language can do. Furthermore, porting an algorithm to SIMD instructions does not only change the mapping of a *given* implementation to another hardware but often requires adapting the implementation of the algorithm itself. For example, note lines 13–17 in Figure 2 differ from the corresponding code in Figure 1.

On GPUs, which internally also make extensive use of SIMD, this issue is addressed by not using a traditional scalar programming paradigm like in C, but rather using the SIMT paradigm (single instruction, multiple threads) as employed in CUDA [30] or OpenCL [17]: In the SIMT paradigm each program—called *kernel*—is always instantiated *n* times to *n* logical *threads*. These threads all execute this same program at the same time but on different data; SIMD is then employed by always processing *k* such threads together where *k* is the SIMD width. A group of *k* threads is also called *warp*. Each of a warp's *k* threads run one SIMD lane. In this programming paradigm, the user writes scalar-looking, C-like code, and the control-flow to data-flow conversion along with the necessary predication is mostly handled by the hardware.

While SIMT is a very powerful paradigm that allows to express parallelism in a scalar-looking way, it also has its disadvantages. In particular, in a SIMT language *everything* is always vectorized, which closely matches the execution model of such GPUs, but does not easily allow to express scalar parts of a program. Executing truly scalar code then requires explicitly masking off all but one thread of a block and costly explicit synchronization between the warps in a block, since the hardware usually needs to run multiple such warps in parallel. Furthermore, by explicitly *hiding* the effects of vectorization, these languages have no means of allowing the programmer to define vectorized data layouts, thus leaving her with the choice between inefficient AoS data layouts (and costly AoS to (hybrid) SoA conversions on access), or manual vectorization of data structures. Above all, writing all the glue code in order to merge the host code with the kernels is very inconvenient.

1.1 Contributions

In this paper, we propose a different programming model for data-parallel programming that combines the advantages of both scalar and SIMT programming, and is especially suited for machines with explicit SIMD instructions. We do this by defining a small core language called VecImp (see Sections 2 and 4), which extends the type system and formal semantics of an existing formalization of a substantial subset of C, called Imp (see Section 3).

- In contrast to the SIMT model, we do not require the strict separation in host code and kernels but integrate vectorization seamlessly into the language. Moreover, we allow to mix scalar and SIMT programming (and scalar and vectorized data structures) in the same basic blocks.
- We provide a type qualifier **`block`**`[N]` to obtain a block of vector length `N`. The example code

  ```
  struct vec3 { float x, y, z; };
  vec3 block[4] v;
  ```

  produces the following memory layout for `v`:

x_0	x_1	x_2	x_3	y_0	y_1	y_2	y_3	z_0	z_1	z_2	z_3

- In contrast to the vectorize-everything paradigm of SIMT, a VecImp program starts in a *scalar* context. We use the type system of VecImp to trigger vectorization: An if-statement with a vector-type condition is vectorized.

```
int block[4] v, w;
if (v < w) /* vectorized */ else /* vectorized */
```

- We implemented several features of VecImp in our research language IVL and evaluated the performance of the vectorized code experimentally on several benchmarks. Our target machine was a 16-wide Intel® Many Integrated Core (MIC) processor [14, 32]. We are within 4% to 15% of the performance of hand-written intrinsic code. Writing the IVL code was almost as easy as writing traditional scalar code. Besides that, IVL code is fully portable because it does not contain any architecture-dependent details (see Section 5). The programs can just be re-compiled for the SSE back-end.

2. VecImp at a Glance

As outlined in the introduction, a programmer often wants to perform SIMD operations only on certain lanes and not on the whole vector. We call these lanes *active lanes*. In hardware, this is either accomplished by *predicated execution* [32] or *blending* (SSE, AVX). In the first case, each vector instruction is equipped with a mask, which indicates active lanes, and a vector instruction performs the operation only for active lanes. In the latter case, vector instructions always perform operations for all lanes. Unwanted effects must be later on masked out by so-called blend operations. The programming model of VecImp exposes predicated execution to the programmer, although blending can be used by the compiler in order to emulate this execution model. For this reason, every statement in VecImp is executed in a *scalar* or *vector context*. For typing, the context corresponds the vector length of the current predication mask—also called *current mask*. The programmer has read access to this variable by the `current_mask` keyword. A context of length one is called *scalar context*. In VecImp, evaluation begins in a scalar context and control-flow statements like `if` or `while` spawn different vector contexts:

```
// vector length of context = 1; current_mask = T
int  block[4] v = <0,3,4,1>;
int  block[4] w = 3;      // <3,3,3,3> via broadcast
bool block[4] m = v < w; // <T,F,F,T>
++v;                      // <1,4,5,2>
if (m) {
  // vector length of context = 4; current_mask =  m
  v += 2; // <3,4,5,4>
} else {
  // vector length of context = 4; current_mask = ~m
  v += 3; // <3,7,8,4>
}
// vector length of context = 1; current_mask = T
```

As can be seen in this example, a type modifier `block[N]` is available. This qualifier recursively inflates the data type to be of vector length `N`. If a qualifier is elided, the variable is *unbound*. This means that the vector length is inferred by the vector length of the right-hand side. If a right-hand side does not exist, the vector length of the current context is used:

```
struct vec3 { float x, y, z; };
// scalar context
vec3 block[4] v;
vec3          w = v; // vec3 block[4];
vec3          x;     // vec3 block[1];
```

Let us now implement a dot product:

```
float dot(vec3 a, vec3 b) {
    return a.x*b.x + a.y*b.y + a.z*b.z;
}
```

All *unbound* parameters of functions in VecImp are polymorphic in their vector length and so are `a` and `b`. The vector length of an *unbound* return type is automatically inferred. Thus, a call-site in a scalar context

```
1  struct data_t {
2    int key;
3    int other;
4  };
5
6  int search(data_t *scalar data, int scalar N) {
7    int L = lengthof(*data);
8    for (int i = 0; i < N/L; ++i) {
9      int x = data[i].key;
10     if (4 < x & x <= 8)
11       int block[L] result = [x, 0];
12       scalar {
13         for (int j = 0; j < log2(L); ++j)
14           result |= whole_reg_shr(result, 1 << j);
15         return get(x, 0);
16       }
17   }
18   return -1;
19 }
```

Figure 4. Example program in VecImp

```
vec3 block[4]  a = /*...*/;
vec3 scalar    b = /*...*/;
float block[4] r = dot(a, b);
```

instantiates a version of `dot` with this signature:

```
float block[4] dot(vec3 block[4] a, vec3 scalar b);
```

If a scalar and a vectorial value are mixed in an operation, the scalar value is broadcast. Thus, the uses of `b.x`, `b.y` and `b.z` get implicitly broadcast in this version. But what happens, if we call the same function from a vectorial context?

```
if (a.x < b.x) { // enter context of length 4
    float block[4] r = dot(a, b); /*...*/
}
```

This time `dot` must know of the current mask. For this reason, we pass the current mask as hidden parameter to `dot`. In VecImp, functions are also polymorphic in the context they are called in. Thus, the signature of this `dot` instance is:

```
float block[4] dot(bool block[4] current_mask,
                   vec3 block[4] a, vec3 scalar b);
```

As a more sophisticated example, let us reconsider the introductory example in VecImp (Figure 4). The function `search` can be invoked with a pointer to an ordinary array of `data_t` or a hybrid SoA of `data_t`. However, the pointer itself is scalar, denoted by the `scalar` modifier which is just shorthand for `block[1]`. Hence, one cannot pass a vector of pointers to `search`. Similarly, `N` stays scalar in all possible instances of `search`. Consider the call-site in a scalar context:

```
data_t block[4] *data; /*...*/
int x = search(data, N);
```

The type of `data` is an unbound pointer to a hybrid SoA of length 4 of `data_t`. Since `data` is declared in a scalar context, `data` itself is instantiated as scalar while the referenced type remains vectorial. Since `search` is invoked from a scalar context, the context of this particular `search` instance created for this call-site is scalar, too. As `L` and `i` in line 7 and 8, respectively, inherit the vector length from the right-hand side, these variables are scalar. Now consider line 9: Since the type of the right-hand side is `int block[4]` and `x` is unbound, `x` is also of vector type `int block[4]`. As `x` is now of vector type, the if statement in line 10 is vectorized. Thus, reading from `x` just obtains the (by precondition unique) found key which is—via the assignment in line 11—written into the vector `result`. However, the inactive lanes of `result` would stay undefined and we therefore set them explicitly to `0`. This is important because subsequently, the vector `result` is processed as a whole and not in a vectorized mode: The algorithm propagates the found key to position 0. For this reason, we want to enter a scalar context again. The `scalar` keyword in front of a statement stores the current mask on a stack and resets it to the scalar mask. Hence, the for loop beginning in line 13 is executed in a scalar context. After the for loop finishes execution, the scalar element at position 0 of the vector is returned.

In the case that `search` is invoked on scalar data, the whole procedure degenerates to a scalar program whose semantics is equivalent to the program in Figure 1. Although we cannot gain an optimized vectorial program from a scalar one, we can still extract the scalar version from a program written in a polymorphic way.

3. Formalization

In this section, we first introduce the notation used throughout this paper and then the imperative language IMP.

The set which holds all powers of two is referred to as $\mathbb{P} := \{2^i \mid i \in \mathbb{N}\}$. We use $\overline{a}$ as shorthand for a sequence $a_0, \ldots, a_{|\overline{a}|-1}$ with zero or more elements, while $|\overline{a}|$ denotes the number of items in a sequence. The term $\overline{a}^+$ represents a sequence with one or more elements. Sequences are propagated into more complex expressions while global values and constants remain untouched. Thus, $\overline{(a, 3)}$ expands to $(a_0, 3, \ldots, a_{|\overline{a}|-1}, 3)$.

3.1 Types

We use calligraphic letters to indicate sets of types and use small Greek letters for types. The size of a type τ given in bytes is referred to as $|\tau|$. Furthermore, we make use of the following conventions:

We use standard C-like primitive integer and floating point types whose sizes (in bytes) must be a power of two. Booleans are denoted by `bool` := {T, F}. The size of a `bool` is implementation-dependent and not transparent to the programmer. We pool these types into a set of *atomic types* $\mathcal{A}$.

A pointer τ^* points to a location which is interpreted to be of type τ; the size of a pointer is also implementation-dependent.

A record $\rho := \{\overline{\tau}^+\}$ is compounded of other element types $\overline{\tau}^+$. A record may not (in)directly contain an element of its own type, but cycles induced by pointers are allowed (as in C). A projection $\rho.i$, where $i \in \mathbb{N} \wedge 0 \leq i < |\overline{\tau}^+|$, grabs τ_i. An implementation is free to add additional padding space between the elements of a record. This implies that the size of a record is machine dependent, too. The set of all types which can be built with atomic types, records and pointers is denoted by $\mathcal{T}$.

A *vector type* ν with element type $\tau \in \mathcal{A} \cup \{\pi^* \mid \pi \in \mathcal{V}\}$ and $l \in \mathbb{P}$ elements is written as $\langle \tau \mid l \rangle$. An instance of such a type ν is written as $\langle \overline{e} \rangle$. The set of all types which can be built with scalar types and vector types is denoted by $\mathcal{V}$.

3.2 IMP

Before describing the vector extensions, we briefly review the imperative language IMP we extend. IMP is a substantial subset of C. Its formalization is closely related to Norrish [27].

The syntax is given in Figure 5. To simplify matters, we assume that each function has exactly one return statement and function calls are used instead of typical in- and prefix operators (although we silently make use of operators in later VECIMP examples, for the sake of readability; moreover, we use named structs instead of tuples and other syntactic sugar for the same reason). A representative set of type inference and evaluation rules is given in Figure 7. The complete set of rules is contained in the full version of the paper [20, appx. A].

Typing rules. Static semantics maintains a type map Γ, which maps identifiers to types, and has read-access to a function map Φ, which maps identifiers to a function's signature and body. The type map is altered in a declaration (see T-DECL). On the other hand the occurrence of a variable is resolved by a lookup of the given identifier in this map (see T-VAR). Type inference rules must differentiate between statements and expressions. Statements yield the dummy type ϵ. Since expressions can return lvalues, type inference rules acknowledge this fact by an internal lvalue type ${}^{l}\tau$ (read *lvalue of type* τ). If we want to state that a type must not be an lvalue, we write ${}_{r}\tau$. In many typing rules both lvalue and value types are allowed in a given premise. We annotate such a type as ${}^{l}_{r}\tau$ as shorthand (see T-ASSIGN).

e	::=		*Expressions:*
		$\mathtt{c}_\alpha$	constant of type $\alpha \in \mathcal{A}$
	|	`id`	variable
	|	e.`i`	projection
	|	&e	address
	|	*e	dereferencing
	|	e_1`[`e_2`]`	indexing
	|	`id(`$\overline{e}$`)`	invoke
s	::=		*Statements:*
		`;`	skip
	|	{ $\hat{s}$ }	scope
	|	e`;`	expression-statement
	|	t `id;`	declaration
	|	$e_2 = e_1$`;`	assignment
	|	t `id` = e`;`	initialization
	|	`if (`e`)` s_1 `else` s_2	if-else
	|	`while (`e`)` s	while
$\hat{s}$	::=		*Scoped statements:*
		s	statement
	|	$\hat{s}\ s$	sequence
t	::=		*Type:*
		$\alpha \in \mathcal{A}$	base
	|	t^*	pointer
	|	$\{\overline{t}^+\}$	record
f	::=		*Function:*
		ϵ	empty
	|	$f_1\ f_2$	sequence
	|	t `id(`$\overline{t\ \mathtt{id}}$`)` { s `return` e`;` }	function

Figure 5. Syntax of IMP

Evaluation rules. Dynamic semantics uses small step semantics evaluating a program a in scope σ and state M in one step to a program a' in scope σ' in a new state M' with the help of the function map Φ. The state M is a memory map, mapping an address to an `i8`. We assume M to be infinite and initialized with random values. A scope σ consists of an address map A which maps an identifier of a variable to the starting address in memory and a type map T which maps an identifier to a type. In order to extract a subsequence of n bytes starting at address/offset a of a memory map M or a byte sequence m, we use $M\langle a, n\rangle$ or $m\langle a, n\rangle$ as shorthand, respectively.

As already outlined, expressions can evaluate to values and lvalues. A value consists of a sequence of bytes m and a type τ and is written as $\mathscr{V}(m, \tau)$. An lvalue $\mathscr{L}(a, \tau)$ consists of an address a and a type τ and represents a reference to a memory location. Both constructs are added to the syntax (but are not directly usable by the programmer and hence do not appear in Figure 5). For instance, E-VAR looks up the identifier of a variable in the address and type map to build an lvalue. Statements can evaluate to the final configuration "`;`" (read *skip*).

A declaration (see E-DECL) allocates memory and updates the type and address maps accordingly. The function alloc(σ, τ) is used for this task. It returns an address pointing to $|\tau|$ bytes of usable memory. An assignment (see E-ASSIGN) updates the memory map at the position pointed to by the given left-hand side lvalue with the given right-hand side value.

In order to memorize an old scope σ when entering a new one we use the special construct "$\{\ s\ \}^\sigma$" which is also added to the "internal" syntax (see E-INSCOPE and E-OUTSCOPE).

e	::=	...	*Expressions:*
	|	`current_mask`	current mask
s	::=	...	*Statements:*
	|	`scalar` s	scalar
t	::=		*Type:*
		$\alpha \in \mathcal{A}\ q$	base
	|	$t^*\ q$	pointer
	|	$\{\overline{t}^+\}\ q$	record
q	::=		*Qualifiers:*
		ϵ	unbound
	|	`block`	auto block
	|	`block[i]`	block

Figure 6. Syntax changes of IMP in order to obtain VECIMP: The current-mask expression and the scalar statement are added. Types follow a different grammar along with the new qualifier rule.

Theorem 1 (Soundness of IMP). *Each well-typed* IMP *program is either in its final configuration or*

1. *there exists an evaluation rule which progresses evaluation and*
2. *the resulting program after application of an evaluation rule preserves well-typedness.*

See the full version of the paper for details and the complete proof of this theorem [20, appx. A].

4. Extending IMP

In the following sections, we show how to extend IMP to its vector counterpart VECIMP. The needed modifications of IMP's syntax in order to obtain VECIMP are given in Figure 6. During discussion it is important to understand that VECIMP is just a substantial intentionally small calculus. Practical languages may add as much syntactic sugar as needed. Furthermore, languages with powerful abstraction mechanisms can build higher-level vector programming constructs (see Section 7).

An excerpt of the typing and evaluation rules, which are referred to in this section, is shown in Figure 8. We have already seen in the introductory example that we must keep track of the current mask while doing SIMD computations. This has several implications. First, all typing rules need a new variable $\Lambda \in \mathbb{P}$ called *current vector length* or *context*. Likewise, all evaluation rules need a new scope variable $P_\sigma \in \langle \texttt{bool} \mid l \rangle$ $(l \in \mathbb{P})$, which reflects predication. We extend our notation of extracting a byte sequence to a predicated extraction $M\langle P, a, n\rangle$ or $m\langle P, a, n\rangle$, respectively, where P is a mask. This *current mask* or *predication variable* can be queried via the **`current_mask`** keyword, which is added as expression to the syntax. Generally, a statement is only executed if the current mask is not entirely false. In the special case that $\Lambda = 1$ and accordingly $P_\sigma = \langle \mathrm{T} \rangle$, we are in a scalar context.

4.1 Types

The context influences the generation of types while the programmer retains tight control over this process with the help of few qualifiers (see T-, E-DECLL). Type vectorization is a recursive process:

- A **`block`** type adopts the vector length of the current context, i.e., in a scalar context the type stays scalar.
- A **`block[i]`** type always receives vector length `i` where `i` is a compile time constant. The special case `i` = 1 means a scalar type and we write **`scalar`** as syntactic sugar for **`block[1]`**. In the case that `i` > 1 does not match the current vector length, a type error occurs.
- Types without explicit qualifier are qualified as *unbound.* These types adopt the vector length of the current recursion. Top level unbound types either infer the vector length from the right-hand side (in an initialization, see T- and E-INIT) or adopt the current vector length (in a declaration statement, see T- and E-DECL).
- Records are never vectorized. Instead the qualifier of a record controls recursively vectorization for *unbound* element types.

The type constructor of a qualified type t in context Λ is defined as follows:[2]

$$\mathrm{vec}_\Lambda : t \times \mathbb{P} \to \mathcal{V} \cup \{\bot\}$$

$$(v, n) \mapsto \begin{cases} \bot & \text{if } v = \tau \in \mathcal{T}\ \texttt{block}[i]\ \wedge\ \Lambda \neq i > 1, \\ \langle \alpha \mid n \rangle & \text{if } v = \alpha \in \mathcal{A}, \\ \langle \alpha \mid \Lambda \rangle & \text{if } v = \alpha \in \mathcal{A}\ \texttt{block}, \\ \langle \alpha \mid i \rangle & \text{if } v = \alpha \in \mathcal{A}\ \texttt{block}[i], \\ \langle \mathrm{vec}_\Lambda(\tau, n)^* \mid n \rangle & \text{if } v = \tau^*, \\ \langle \mathrm{vec}_\Lambda(\tau, n)^* \mid \Lambda \rangle & \text{if } v = \tau^*\ \texttt{block}, \\ \langle \mathrm{vec}_\Lambda(\tau, n)^* \mid i \rangle & \text{if } v = \tau^*\ \texttt{block}[i], \\ \{\overline{\mathrm{vec}_\Lambda(\tau, n)}^+\} & \text{if } v = \{\overline{\tau}^+\}, \\ \{\overline{\mathrm{vec}_\Lambda(\tau, \Lambda)}^+\} & \text{if } v = \{\overline{\tau}^+\}\ \texttt{block}, \\ \{\overline{\mathrm{vec}_\Lambda(\tau, i)}^+\} & \text{if } v = \{\overline{\tau}^+\}\ \texttt{block}[i]. \end{cases}$$

Consider the following example:

```
struct Bar { int c; int block d; };
struct Foo { int a; int block b; Bar scalar bar; };
// current vector length = 4
Foo foo;
int i = 0;
```

Upon the declaration of `foo` $\mathrm{vec}_4(\texttt{Foo}, 4)$ is applied in order to vectorize the type. Member `a` gets vectorized as it sees 4 as parameter; `b` gets vectorized, because it sees 4 as current vector length; however, `c` stays scalar, because it sees length 1 passed to vec_4 via **`Bar scalar bar`**; finally, `d` gets vectorized for the same reason as `b`. The variable `i` stays scalar as the right-hand side is also scalar.

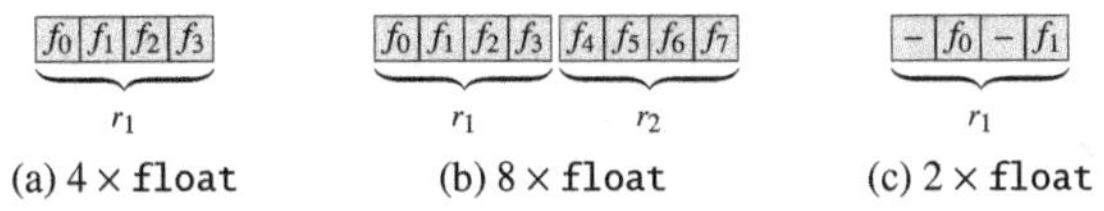

Figure 9. Different packagings of `floats` into hardware SIMD registers of 16 byte width

In order to exploit SIMD hardware efficiently, it is very important to organize data in a way that maximum coherence is achieved, i.e., optimally all SIMD lanes are occupied and none lie idle. If the desired vector length is equal to the one which is available in hardware, all elements can be put seamlessly into one register (Figure 9a). If the desired vector length exceeds the native one, several registers must be allocated (Figure 9b). In the case that the requested length is smaller than the native one, padding space must be inserted. One possible solution is depicted in Figure 9c, albeit other possibilities may be more advantageous for the underlying hardware. As case b) usually increases register pressure and case c) decreases throughput, it is important to choose the vector length wisely. A compiler can provide a built-in mechanism for querying the preferred vector length of a type for the given target machine:

```
struct T { double d; float f; }
T block[preferred_lengthof(T)] t;
```

See Section 7 for additional suggestions in order to abstract away other low-level details.

The current vector length also restricts types that may occur. *Access* of type τ in context Λ is only granted in a scalar context, *or* if the type is scalar, *or* if the current vector length and the one of

[2] Note that cyclic dependencies in types induced by pointers can be resolved by first defining an opaque type and not to follow that pointer and later on refining that field.

$$\boxed{\Phi,\Gamma \vdash e : \tau,\Gamma} \qquad\qquad \boxed{\Phi, a, \sigma, M \to a', \sigma', M'}$$

$$\frac{\mathtt{id} \in dom(\Gamma)}{\Phi,\Gamma \vdash \mathtt{id} : {}^{l}\Gamma(\mathtt{id}), \Gamma}\ \text{T-VAR} \qquad \frac{\mathtt{id} \in dom(T_\sigma)}{\Phi, \mathtt{id}, \sigma, M \to \mathscr{L}(A_\sigma(\mathtt{id}), T_\sigma(\mathtt{id})), \sigma, M}\ \text{E-VAR}$$

$$\frac{\Phi,\Gamma \vdash s : \epsilon,\Gamma'}{\Phi,\Gamma \vdash \{\ s\ \} : \epsilon,\Gamma}\ \text{T-SCOPE} \qquad \frac{}{\Phi, \{\ s\ \}, \sigma, M \to \{\ s\ \}^{\sigma}, \sigma, M}\ \text{E-INSCOPE}$$

$$\frac{}{\Phi, \{\ ;\ \}^{\sigma'}, \sigma, M \to\ ;, \sigma', M}\ \text{E-OUTSCOPE}$$

$$\frac{\tau = t \quad \mathtt{id} \notin dom(\Gamma)}{\Phi,\Gamma \vdash t\ \mathtt{id;} : \epsilon, \Gamma[\mathtt{id} := \tau]}\ \text{T-DECL} \qquad \frac{\tau = t \quad \mathrm{alloc}(\sigma,\tau) = a}{\Phi, t\ \mathtt{id;}, \sigma, M \to\ ;, \sigma\begin{bmatrix} T := T[\mathtt{id} := \tau], \\ A := A[\mathtt{id} := a] \end{bmatrix}, M}\ \text{E-DECL}$$

$$\frac{\Phi,\Gamma \vdash e_1 : {}^{l}_{r}\tau,\Gamma \quad \Phi,\Gamma \vdash e_2 : {}^{l}\tau,\Gamma}{\Phi,\Gamma \vdash e_2 = e_1\mathtt{;} : \epsilon,\Gamma}\ \text{T-ASSIGN} \qquad \frac{}{\Phi, \mathscr{L}(a,\tau) = \mathscr{V}(m,\tau);, \sigma, M \to\ ;, \sigma, M := M[\langle a, |\tau|\rangle := m]}\ \text{E-ASSIGN}$$

$$\frac{\Phi,\Gamma \vdash e : {}^{l}_{r}\mathtt{bool},\Gamma \quad \Phi,\Gamma \vdash s_1 : \epsilon,\Gamma_1 \quad \Phi,\Gamma \vdash s_2 : \epsilon,\Gamma_2}{\Phi,\Gamma \vdash \mathtt{if}\ (e)\ s_1\ \mathtt{else}\ s_2 : \epsilon,\Gamma}\ \text{T-IF}$$

$$\frac{}{\Phi, \mathtt{if}\ (\mathscr{V}(\mathsf{T},\mathtt{bool}))\ s_1\ \mathtt{else}\ s_2, \sigma, M \to \{\ s_1\ \}^{\sigma}, \sigma, M}\ \text{E-IFT}$$

$$\frac{}{\Phi, \mathtt{if}\ (\mathscr{V}(\mathsf{F},\mathtt{bool}))\ s_1\ \mathtt{else}\ s_2, \sigma, M \to \{\ s_2\ \}^{\sigma}, \sigma, M}\ \text{E-IFF}$$

$$\frac{\Phi,\Gamma \vdash e : {}^{l}_{r}\mathtt{bool},\Gamma \quad \Phi,\Gamma \vdash s : \epsilon,\Gamma'}{\Phi,\Gamma \vdash \mathtt{while}\ (e)\ s : \epsilon,\Gamma}\ \text{T-WHILE} \qquad \frac{}{\Phi, \mathtt{while}\ (e)\ s, \sigma, M \to \mathtt{if}\ (e)\ \{\ s\ \mathtt{while}\ (e)\ s\ \}, \sigma, M}\ \text{E-WHILE}$$

Figure 7. Static (left) and dynamic (right) semantics of IMP (excerpt)

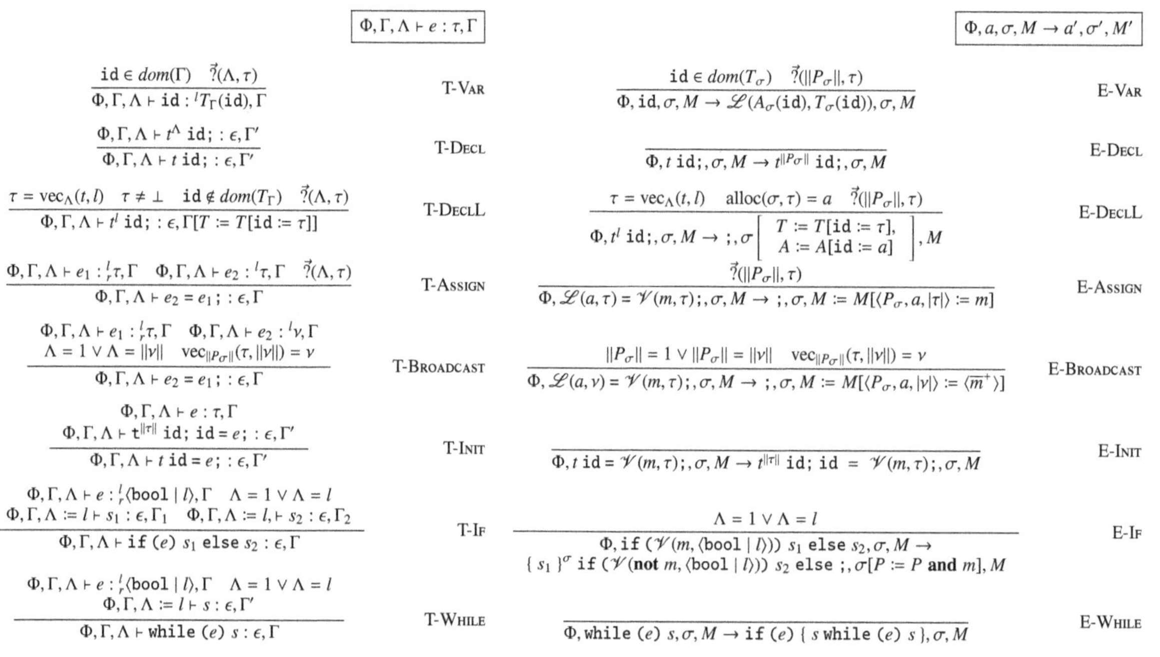

Figure 8. Static (left) and dynamic (right) semantics of VECIMP (excerpt)

the type match:

$$\vec{?} : \mathbb{P} \times \mathcal{V} \to \mathtt{bool}$$
$$(\Lambda, \tau) \mapsto \Lambda = 1 \ \lor\ \|\tau\| = 1 \ \lor\ \Lambda = \|\tau\|$$

where $\|\tau\|$ denotes the vector length of type τ. Moreover, a scalar variable on the right-hand side of an assignment can be *broadcast* to a vector variable on the left-hand side. This is accomplished by replicating the given value to all lanes (see T- and E-BROADCAST).

4.2 Triggering Control-Flow Vectorization

Conditionally executing code is usually achieved by testing a boolean and either running one or another code path. IMP supports typical if- and while-statements. In VECIMP we enhance these constructs by allowing boolean vectors as conditional expressions as well. Generally, the vector length of the header must either match the one of the current mask, or a scalar conditional occurs in a vectorial context, or the conditional is in a scalar context. The latter case triggers vectorization. This means that control-flow is converted to data-flow which gives the programmer the illusion that different SIMD lanes are executed on different control-flow branches. Care must be taken when different branches have side-effects like I/O-accesses. These side-effects may happen in an unexpected order. For this reason, it is important that the programmer at least roughly understands, how the control-flow vectorization is accomplished. For the sake of simplicity, we concentrate on simple structural control-flow in this paper. For vectorization of arbitrary control-flow we refer to Karrenberg and Hack [16].

If/Else. In VECIMP, both the then-block and the else-block are evaluated (see T-IF and E-IF). In the then-block the current mask and the test mask are combined with an AND operation whereas

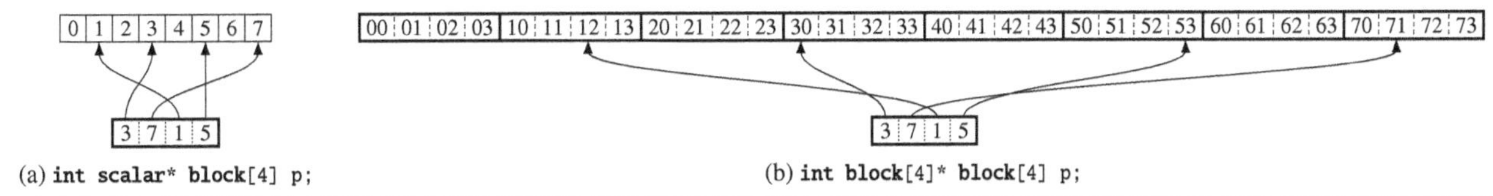

(a) `int scalar* block[4] p;` (b) `int block[4]* block[4] p;`

Figure 10. Involved address calculation when indexing a vectorial pointer `p` with an index vector `int block[4] x = <3,7,1,5>`. A read `p[x]` obtains in case a) `<3,7,1,5>` and in case b) `<30,71,12,53>`. Note that both variants yield an `int block[4]`.

the else-block uses the complementary test mask. Note that an if statement degenerates to standard IMP semantics if an ordinary boolean is used in the header, since statements are not executed if the predication variable is completely false.

While. We define the semantics of the while-construct as a recursive program transformation to an if-statement containing a while-statement (see T-WHILE and E-WHILE). If every element of this mask evaluates to false, the body is not executed at all. Otherwise, the body must be entered while adjusting the current mask. Analogously to the if-statement, a while-statement degenerates to an ordinary while-statement when testing a scalar boolean.

4.2.1 The Scalar Statement

Sometimes it is desirable to deactivate vectorization within a kernel and proceed with scalar computations (see the introductory example in Section 1). This can be realized by adding a *scalar statement* to the syntax. This statement saves the current mask, sets the current mask to the scalar *true* value, executes the inner statement in a scalar context, and restores the saved mask afterwards. Using the scalar statement, several sequential patterns of algorithms using SIMD instructions can be implemented.

Reactivating the old mask. Although the old mask is reset after termination of the scalar statement, it may be nevertheless useful to temporarily reactivate the mask within this statement. This can be achieved by manually saving the current mask before executing the scalar statement and using the saved mask in an if-statement. Since a store just sets the active lanes, it is also important to set the inactive lanes manually to *false*. The example in Figure 4 makes use of some syntactic sugar in order to initialize elements in both active and inactive lanes. This syntactic sugar

```
T var = [true_values, false_values};
```

translates to:

```
bool mask;       // a mask; we are in a vector context
scalar { mask = false; } // set all lanes to false
mask = current_mask;     // set all active lanes to true
T var;
scalar {
   if (mask) var = true_values;  // set active lanes
   else      var = false_values; // set inactive lanes
}
```

Scalarize each active lane. Using a consecutive bit scan over the old mask can yield the index of each prior active lane. In the following example each active component of `v` of type `T block[N]` is extracted:

```
bool mask = [current_mask, current_mask];
scalar
  for(int i=bitscan(mask,0); i>=0; i=bitscan(mask,i+1)) {
    T s = get(v, i);
    //...
  }
```

A **bitscan** scans a given mask, beginning at the given index, from left to right for the next entry set to *true*. In order to indicate the case that no further *true* follows, a negative value is returned.

The loop body can now do scalar computations with `v`, broadcast this value in order to vectorize another computation, or collect such values in another data structure which can be later on used for further vectorizations, for instance.

Uniquely scalarize each active lane. A more sophisticated technique only extracts unique values from active lanes. In the example above the following adjustment of the mask in each iteration before the next **bitscan** blends out duplicates:

```
mask &= s != v;
```

4.3 Address Calculation

Since both a pointer itself and its referenced type may be scalar or vectorial, four possibilities emerge: Scalar pointers to scalar data are ordinary pointers as known from C. Scalar pointers to vectorial data integrate seamlessly into IMP as the layout of the referenced type is irrelevant for typing and semantics. However, when dealing with vectorial pointers, the programmer must use an index vector. Vectorial indexing to scalar data effectively performs a S/G (see Figure 10a) and obtains a vector. Vectorial indexing to vectorial data is more involved as depicted in Figure 10b: Each lane i "sees" the ith component of a vector located at address `get(p, i) + get(x, i)` and hence read/write access with this vectorial indexing gathers/scatters an `int block[4]`.

4.4 Parametric Polymorphism

An important feature of VECIMP is that all functions are parametric towards vectorization. This means that all unbound types which appear in the signature and the vector context itself are parametric. Upon invocation a new version of the function is instantiated (like templates in C++). This has several consequences:

- Type checking and evaluation is done with the current context/mask. This changes the vector length of all **block** variables and unbound variables in declaration statements.
- All unbound function arguments try to adopt the vector length of the parameter (like an initialization).
- If the return type is unbound the type checker infers its vector length from the return expression.
- As the semantics of all syntactical constructs depends on the instantiated types, the behaviour of the function is also dependent on these parameters.

4.5 Soundness

All these additions and changes to IMP do not harm the type system and using the same definition of soundness as in Theorem 1 (see the full version of the paper for details [20, appx. B]) we can state:

Theorem 2 (Soundness of VECIMP). *VECIMP's type system is* sound.

5. The IVL Vectorizing Language

IVL is a prototypical R&D compiler that applies many of the proposed concepts to generate vectorized code for the Intel® MIC architecture and SSE instruction set.

5.1 IVL's Back-Ends

MIC is a many-core x86 architecture in which each x86 core is augmented with a 16-wide vector unit accessed through a rich vector instruction set. MIC supports both S/G as well as efficient masking/predication via a separate set of 16-bit mask registers.

In a vectorized context IVL emits MIC code that runs on L lanes in parallel, while all *scalar* constructs are executed in the core's scalar pipe, and scalar data is held in scalar registers. Rather than allowing arbitrary vector lengths, IVL currently only supports a small set of vectorization lengths per compilation unit. In particular, on MIC we currently support 16-wide and ("double-pumped") 32-wide vectorization for MIC (with 16 being the default). The SSE back-end supports 4 wide, and a future Intel® AVX back-end will also support 8 wide vectorization.

Note that MIC and SSE instruction sets fundamentally differ in many aspects: SSE and MIC have different native vector lengths, SSE does not support hardware accelerated S/G and uses blending in order to emulate predicated execution. Given our experience in implementing the SSE and MIC back-ends, we think implementing additional back-ends supporting other SIMD CPU types and ISAs is straightforward.

IVL acts as source-to-source compiler in the sense that it translates IVL code to a special "C++ with intrinsics" code that is then passed to the official Intel® C/C++ compiler [11] (icc) for MIC. This allows the programmer to visually inspect (and possibly modify) the emitted code, and to use this code with tools like debuggers, performance analyzers, etc.

5.2 Supported Types and Language Constructs

IVL currently supports a significant subset of C and a small set of additional keywords to guide vectorization. In terms of types, IVL fully supports bools as well as (32-bit) ints, uints, and floats, but currently only partially supports 8-bit, 16-bit, and 64-bit data types. IVL also fully supports structs, arrays, and references (including vector references to vectorized types), but only partially supports pointers.

As IVL currently only supports one global vector length N per compilation unit, VecImp's `block[N]` is called `varying`, and `block[1]` is called `uniform`. Like VecImp, IVL supports *unbound* variables, and full polymorphism in parameter type length. In terms of control-flow IVL supports all of `if/else`, `do`, `while`, `for`, `break`, `continue`, and `return`, with the sole exception of `goto`. In addition, IVL also supports some simple reduction operations like "`varying bool any(varying bool)`" or "`varying bool none(varying bool)`" in order to determine whether at least one or no element in a boolean vector is *true*.

5.3 On-demand Vectorization

Vectorization in IVL is done *on demand*: Similar to the behavior of templates in C++, IVL parses struct and function definitions but does not emit anything until *instances* of those types and functions are required. For example, when IVL encounters a global variable of a vectorized type, it emits a vectorized form of this type (in C++ code). Vectorization of code is triggered when IVL encounters a function with the `kernel` keyword; it will then emit a C function for this kernel (plus some additional helper functions to allow calling this function from the host machine if required), and will vectorize this kernel's body, which in turn will on-demand emit all functions called by this body, etc.

Statements and expressions operating on varying types will emit vector intrinsics, while purely uniform expressions/statements *will* emit only scalar code even when inside a vectorized function (like proposed by VecImp). This is highly desirable in that it uses precious vector registers and costly vector instructions only where required, and enables a mix of scalar and vector expressions that MICs superscalar architecture (with parallel scalar U and vector V pipes) is particularly good at. For example, if a for-loop in a (vectorized) function uses a loop condition that only depends on a uniform function parameter that respective loop control code will use only scalar x86 instructions.

Polymorphism in vector length. Polymorphism also works like proposed in VecImp: Unbound function arguments are bound when IVL encounters its call site, and are then bound to the vector length of the respective argument. This means that the same *logical* function can end up being emitted in multiple incarnations (depending on which of its parameters are uniform or varying). This, too, is highly desirable in that information about which data are uniform is *preserved* across function calls—usually leading to significantly more efficient code and storage than if all scalar data had been broadcast to vector form upon the first function call (as would happen in a pure SIMT paradigm). In particular, a given control-flow statement in an input function can get emitted in scalar form in one function instance, and vectorized in another.

Like polymorphism in C++, this mechanism requires the function to be known at compile-time; to use a function across different compilation units one either has to explicitly specify all parameters' vector lengths, or explicitly instantiate this function in one compilation unit.

5.4 IVL Examples

Though a full performance analysis is beyond the scope of this paper, we give a brief overview over some examples realized with our current IVL compiler, all running on a 32-core 900MHz Knights Ferry prototype board. Since IVL also has an SSE back-end, the exactly same examples will also run on any SSE-enabled architecture, but for the sake of brevity we restrict ourselves to only the Knights-Ferry results.

Proof-of-concept examples. We ported `Mandelbrot`, `nbody`, and `VolumeRender` from the CUDA SDK. These examples ran more or less "out of the box". Since IVL does not currently support any native hardware-texturing, the `VolumeRender` example has to resort to "manual" tri-linear interpolation to sample the volume, but nevertheless already reaches roughly 30 frames per second. For all other examples, both ease of porting and resulting performance matched or exceeded expectations. As just one example, the publicly available `aobench` benchmark [3] required only trivial modification to port to IVL,[3] while rendering a 1024^2 frame (with 16 samples per pixel and 16 rays per sample) in an impressive 402ms.

Ray tracer examples. As a somewhat more challenging example, we also implemented an IVL ray tracer with various shaders *into* an existing Knight's Ferry ray tracing system [36]. The IVL-based traversal, intersection, and shading code was linked together with manual intrinsics code for data structure construction and other renderers. In this setting, IVL and manual C code were actually sharing the same data structures! First, we integrated an intentionally simple *eyelight* shader into the framework. As a next step, we included an *ambient occlusion* (AO) renderer requiring random number generation, quasi-Monte Carlo sampling, CDF inversions and recursion, involving both incoherent data access patterns and significant SIMD divergence.

Comparison to hand-written code. To better quantify the performance of IVL's code we also ran some experiments where we compared IVL-generated code to manually-written reference intrinsics code (in all cases, the reference code was written *before* the IVL code). For the `eyelight` ray tracer, IVL renders a 1600×1024 frame in 13.8 million cycles, vs 13.28m cycles in reference intrinsics code, a difference of only 4% (an exact reference version for the AO renderer is not available, due to that code's complexity).

Finally, we also ran an artificial *k-nearest neighbor* benchmark for which we had reference code for a variety of architectures. This benchmark is highly non-trivial in both control-flow and data access patterns. In this workload, IVL requires 755 million cycles (for 1 million 50-neighbor queries in a 1 million point dataset), as compared to 656m cycles for the hand-coded version—a difference of 15%.

[3] For example, IVL does not support doubles, yet, so both the IVL *and* the reference implementation have been modified to use floats.

The performance gap is mostly encumbered by that fact that IVL is a source-to-source compiler emitting vectorized code and relies on `icc` for optimizations. This compiler does not yet recognize some patterns which are suitable for optimizations but would have been applied by a human intrinsics programmer. `ispc` (see Section 6) on the other hand generates LLVM assembly code and ships its own set of specific optimizations for such patterns.

6. Related Work

While some efforts exist to integrate short vector types into languages, over the past years several data parallel languages have been developed in order to tackle programming for SIMD hardware. These languages can be basically subdivided into *data-parallel languages* and *vector* (or *array*) *programming languages*. Independent from that, several automatic vectorization techniques exist.

Short vector data types. With the help of C++ operator overloading or built-in support for short vector types in C [9, sec. 6.49], standard operator syntax can be used instead of writing intrinsics. This does not only increase readability but also portability of the source code as each back-end can resort to its specific SIMD ISA. However, type and control-flow vectorization must still be handled manually by the programmer. Especially, manual conversion of control-flow to data dependence is problematic as this—besides being very error-prone—again introduces architectural dependent low-level details to the source code: This approach has no means of abstracting blending/predicated execution.

Data-parallel languages. OpenCL and CUDA have already been discussed in Section 1. These languages are strongly influenced from shading languages whose programming model is similar but more limited than the former ones. One of the first shading languages implemented is RenderMan [10] which originally targeted a virtual SIMD array machine. Programs for this language are also written for a single scalar thread, while the compiler and the runtime system assured to instantiate this thread for all available SIMD lanes. RenderMan pioneered the concept of *uniform* and *varying* variables. *Uniform* variables are only set once for each set of properties. *Varying* variables on the other hand are allowed to change as a function of position. For instance, vertex normals in a Phong shader must be interpolated and must therefore be declared as *varying*.

Our work is close to the Intel® SPMD Program Compiler (`ispc`) [12]. This LLVM based compiler, where a program is instantiated n times to run on n SIMD lanes, currently supports several SSE revisions and AVX. Although IVL and `ispc` are two independent projects, we fostered an ongoing discussion with the `ispc` authors, which influenced each other's work. Thus, `ispc` and IVL/VecImp share many concepts: implicit handling of blending, automatic control-flow vectorization and **`uniform`** and **`varying`** variables among other features. There are also some differences: `ispc` does not support parametric polymorphism while `ispc`'s pointer support is more mature than IVL's one, for instance.

Another data-parallel language is C^n [22] which is in contrast to many other languages a real extension to C. C^n targets a special kind of SIMD machine, similar to IBM's Cell processor. There, a main processor controls n processing elements (PEs) that all have their own local memory. C^n extends the type system by two modifiers `mono` and `poly`. `poly` values sit in the memory of the PEs. The type system is used to trigger DMA transfers from the main CPU to the PEs. However, due to this different hardware model, C^n does not support `poly` values in compound data structures. More precisely, `mono` and `poly` are *storage-class specifiers* and not *type qualifiers*.

Vector programming languages. These languages are very powerful when dealing with mathematical vectors and matrices, i.e., arrays of atomic types. But this is also the main problem: Since arrays are a too high-level abstraction for short vector SIMD processors, it is very difficult to write efficient code for these machines when dealing with higher data structures. There does not exist any built-in way in order to deal efficiently with compound data, as this would contradict the array programming philosophy.

In some languages of this category like APL [15] or MatLab [23], the programmer has to manually vectorize control-flow. Others like Vector C [21], Vector Pascal [25], Intel's Array Building Blocks (ArBB [24], formerly known as Ct [8]) or Nesl [4] provide special constructs and/or enhance scalar constructs to work with vectors for this task.

Nesl integrates nested vectors as first class citizens in a pure functional language similar to ML. However, Nesl does not integrate imperative control structures and low-level constructs like pointers as we do.

ArBB/Ct is inspired by Nesl and can be seen as a Nesl library for C/C++. ArBB is a functional array language with an interface to C++. At first glance, it looks like a language extension to C++ for vector processing. However, ArBB uses operator overloading to construct an intermediate representation of the vector program which is compiled and executed *lazily* by a just-in-time compiler in the ArBB library. While this has several advantages, like adaption of vectorization to the system the program is currently running on, it has the disadvantage of having a second language within another language: ArBB requires own types (`i32` instead of `int`, etc.), own control structures (`_for ... _end_for` instead of the common `for` loop), and sometimes own operators (`(call)(f)(a, b)` instead of `f(a, b)`). Furthermore, the user has to understand the execution model precisely: ArBB expressions are used to *construct* a program. Putting `a+=b` in an *ordinary* loop will create as many expressions in the IR as the loop iterates. VecImp however combines both, scalar and vector computing in the same language.

Automatic vectorization. Vectorizing compilers go back to the early 1980s [1, 2]. Basic predication techniques have been introduced in this line of work [1]. Many different automatic vectorization techniques have been developed since then. The majority of approaches target vectorization of straight-line code loop bodies [28, 35]. There, instruction-level parallelism (ILP) is created by loop unrolling, or more sophisticated transformations (e.g. polyhedral techniques [5]) are applied. Other approaches exploit ILP in code that can contain control structures (like conditionals and loops) [18, 19, 33] for vectorization or vectorize a whole function [16]. Often, those approaches rely on preceding transformations that create this ILP. Outer-loop vectorization [26, 29, 31] goes beyond a loop body by integrating inner loops into vectorization. Another idea is to use the SIMD register file as fast cache [34].

As stated in the introduction, automatic vectorization is not applicable in our setting. The modifications to the data structure layout and the resulting changes in the code are not local to some code part. They often affect the whole program. Furthermore, algorithms substantially change, when they are programmed with SIMD instructions in mind. Current static analyses and code transformations are not able to perform such transformations automatically in a satisfactory way. Our work focuses on the programmer who explicitly wants to program for a CPU equipped with a SIMD instruction set without exposing her to assembly-level programming. This clientele is not satisfied with automatic techniques that only work on small code parts and depend on a preceding analysis that is not transparent to the programmer.

7. Conclusions and Future Work

The first practical experiences show that code emitted by IVL is comparable to hand-written intrinsic code. Smarter compiler transformations and back-ends would even produce higher quality code.

A hybrid SoA container class. As a next step, we would like to integrate this model into a C/C++ compiler. VecImp only changes

IMP where necessary and the added features are only minimum requirements in order to describe low-level SIMD programming in an abstract way. Often used programming patterns can be further abstracted with standard higher-level language features in order to reduce boilerplate code and increase portability. In particular, the C++ template mechanism would allow to define a hybrid SoA container class: Similar to `std::vector` which abstracts a traditional C array, one could implement a wrapper around a `T block[N]*`:

```
// scalar context throughout this example
struct vec3 { float x, y, z; };
// vec3 block[N]* pointing to ceil(n/N) elements
hsoa<vec3> vecs(n);
// preferred vector length of vec3 automatically derived
static const int N = hsoa<vec3>::vector_length;
int i = /*...*/
hsoa<vec3>::block_index ii = /*...*/
vec3 v = vecs[i];              // gather
vecs[i] = v;                   // scatter
vec3 block[N] w = vecs[ii];    // fetch whole block
hsoa<vec3>::ref r = vecs[i];   // get proxy to a scalar
r = v;                         // pipe through proxy
// for each element
vecs.foreach([](vec3& scalar v) { /*...*/ });
```

The inner type `hsoa<vec3>::ref` consists of a pointer pointing to the block in question and a lane index. Furthermore, this class is equipped with some conversion operators in order to automatically convert this proxy to the scalar base type (`vec3` in this case).

The `foreach` method is particularly interesting: Most of the time, i.e., while not processing one of the two border areas, each iteration can fetch a whole `vec3 block[N]& scalar`. The border areas must be handled specially—either by setting up an appropriate mask, or by scalarizing the border sections. This special setup is factored out in the `foreach` method which invokes different versions of the polymorphic lambda function and the user of `foreach` does not have to care about border areas anymore.

Block hierarchy. One could also imagine having a hierarchy of blocks. This information would also be annotated at the type and could be used in order to abstract blocks/work groups in CUDA/OpenCL or the layers of the cache hierarchy like cache lines and page sizes. A long term goal would be a language which emits SIMD CPU code and PTX/CUDA code dependent on the types which trigger the invocation of a kernel. Additional setup code would also be automatically generated.

Acknowledgments

The authors would like to thank Sigurd Schneider and Jan Schwinghammer who helped with the formalization of the type system. Furthermore, Ralf Karrenberg, Christoph Mallon and Phillip Slusallek were involved in the discussion of our work. William M. Mark, Matt Pharr and Sven Woop from Intel also gave a lot of valuable feedback and in particular the aforementioned collaboration regarding Matt's `ispc` project was crucial to the realization of IVL. Much of this work has been funded by the Intel Visual Computing Institute and the German ministry for education and research via the ECOUSS project.

References

[1] J. R. Allen, K. Kennedy, C. Porterfield, and J. Warren. Conversion of Control Dependence to Data Dependence. In *POPL*, 1983.

[2] R. Allen and K. Kennedy. Automatic Translation of FORTRAN Programs to Vector Form. *ACM Trans. Program. Lang. Syst.*, 1987.

[3] aobench. URL http://code.google.com/p/aobench/.

[4] G. E. Blelloch et al. Implementation of a Portable Nested Data-Parallel Language. In *PPOPP*, 1993.

[5] A. Darte, Y. Robert, and F. Vivien. *Scheduling and Automatic Parallelization*. Birkhauser Boston, 2000.

[6] M. Farrar. Striped Smith–Waterman speeds database searches six times over other SIMD implementations. *Bioinformatics*, 23:156–161, January 2007.

[7] I. Georgiev and P. Slusallek. RTfact: Generic Concepts for Flexible and High Performance Ray Tracing. In *IEEE/Eurographics Symposium on Interactive Ray Tracing*, 2008.

[8] A. Ghuloum et al. Future-Proof Data Parallel Algorithms and Software on Intel Multi-Core Architecture. *Intel Technology Journal*, 11(04), November 2007.

[9] GNU Press. Using the GNU Compiler Collection. For GCC version 4.6.2.

[10] P. Hanrahan and J. Lawson. A Language for Shading and Lighting Calculations. In *SIGGRAPH*, 1990.

[11] Intel Corp. Intel® Compilers and Libraries. URL http://software.intel.com/en-us/articles/intel-compilers.

[12] Intel Corp. Intel SPMD Program Compiler. URL http://ispc.github.com.

[13] Intel Corp. Intel® 64 and IA-32 Architectures Optimization Reference Manual, 2009.

[14] Intel Corp. The Intel Many Integrated Core (MIC) Architecture, 2010.

[15] K. E. Iverson. *A Programming Language*. John Wiley & Sons, Inc., 1962.

[16] R. Karrenberg and S. Hack. Whole Function Vectorization. In *CGO*, 2011.

[17] Khronos Group. *OpenCL 1.0 Specification*, 2009.

[18] A. Krall and S. Lelait. Compilation Techniques for Multimedia Processors. *Int. J. Parallel Program.*, 28(4):347–361, 2000.

[19] S. Larsen and S. Amarasinghe. Exploiting Superword Level Parallelism with Multimedia Instruction Sets. *PLDI*, 35(5):145–156, 2000.

[20] R. Leißa, S. Hack, and I. Wald. Extending a C-like Language for Portable SIMD Programming. The full version of our PPoPP'12 paper available online at http://www.cdl.uni-saarland.de/projects/vecimp.

[21] K.-C. Li and H. Schwetman. Vector C—A Vector Processing Language. *Journal of Parallel and Distributed Computing*, 2(2):132 – 169, 1985.

[22] A. Lokhmotov, B. R. Gaster, A. Mycroft, N. Hickey, and D. Stuttard. Revisiting SIMD Programming. In *LCPC*, pages 32–46, 2007.

[23] MatLab. URL http://www.mathworks.com/products/matlab.

[24] M. McCool. A Retargetable, Dynamic Compiler and Embedded language. In *CGO*, 2011.

[25] G. Michaelson and P. Cockshott. Vector Pascal, an array language, 2002.

[26] V. Ngo. *Parallel Loop Transformation Techniques For Vector-Based Multiprocessor Systems*. PhD thesis, University of Minnesota, 1994.

[27] M. Norrish. *C formalised in HOL*. PhD thesis, University of Cambridge, 1998.

[28] D. Nuzman and R. Henderson. Multi-platform Auto-vectorization. In *CGO*, 2006.

[29] D. Nuzman and A. Zaks. Outer-Loop Vectorization: Revisited for Short SIMD Architectures. In *PACT*, 2008.

[30] NVIDIA. *CUDA Programming Guide*, 2009.

[31] R. G. Scarborough and H. G. Kolsky. A vectorizing Fortran compiler. *IBM J. Res. Dev.*, 30(2):163–171, 1986.

[32] L. Seiler et al. Larrabee: A Many-Core x86 Architecture for Visual Computing. In *SIGGRAPH*, 2008.

[33] J. Shin. Introducing Control Flow into Vectorized Code. In *PACT '07*, 2007.

[34] J. Shin, C. Jacqueline, and M. W. Hall. Compiler-Controlled Caching in Superword Register Files for Multimedia Extension Architectures. In *PACT*, 2002.

[35] N. Sreraman and R. Govindarajan. A Vectorizing Compiler for Multimedia Extensions. *Int. J. Parallel Program.*, 28(4):363–400, 2000.

[36] I. Wald. Fast Construction of SAH BVHs on the Intel® Many Integrated Core (MIC) Architecture. *IEEE Transactions on Visualization and Computer Graphics*, 99, 2010.

[37] J. Zhou and K. A. Ross. Implementing Database Operations Using SIMD Instructions. In *SIGMOD*, 2002.

A Hybrid Approach of OpenMP for Clusters

Okwan Kwon Fahed Jubair Rudolf Eigenmann Samuel Midkiff

School of Electrical and Computer Engineering, Purdue University
West Lafayette, IN, 47907, USA
{kwon7, fjubair, eigenman, smidkiff}@purdue.edu

Abstract

We present the first fully automated compiler-runtime system that successfully translates and executes OpenMP shared-address-space programs on laboratory-size clusters, for the complete set of regular, repetitive applications in the NAS Parallel Benchmarks. We introduce a hybrid compiler-runtime translation scheme. Compared to previous work, this scheme features a new runtime data flow analysis and new compiler techniques for improving data affinity and reducing communication costs. We present and discuss the performance of our translated programs, and compare them with the performance of the MPI, HPF and UPC versions of the benchmarks. The results show that our translated programs achieve 75% of the hand-coded MPI programs, on average.

Categories and Subject Descriptors D.3.4 [*Programming Languages*]: Processors—Code generation, Compilers, Optimization

General Terms Languages, Algorithms, Performance

Keywords OpenMP, MPI, Translator, Optimization, Hybrid, Runtime Data Flow Analysis, Runtime Environment

1. Introduction

The fundamental goal of the system described in this paper is to enable improved programming models for clusters, with a focus on laboratory-scale clusters of ten to one hundred nodes. At the same time, we aim to increase the portability of existing parallel codes written in OpenMP to cost-effective, larger machines.

The state of the art in programming cluster platforms is MPI – the "assembly language of parallel processing". Message passing programs reflect the underlying architectures' distributed address spaces. In MPI, programmers must explicitly partition the programs' data and insert messages to communicate between processors that own data and those that reference the data, which is a tedious and error prone process.

Several attempts have been made in the past to provide a higher-level programming abstraction for clusters. Shared, or global, address spaces promise higher productivity, as software engineers do not need to deal with data partitioning and communication. The challenge in providing such abstractions is two-fold. The underlying compilers or runtime systems need to translate the shared address space program to target the distributed hardware. This is difficult because the problem of finding the best distribution of computation and data for parallel processors/memories and orchestrating communication into a program that runs efficiently is extremely complex. Furthermore, any implementation scheme faces the classic difficulty of the compiler having overly conservative static knowledge of the full program execution (values of many variables are unknown until runtime) and runtime systems not knowing what will happen later in the program's execution. In addition, it has been pointed out that shared address space models, while promising higher productivity, also hide the complexity and costs of the underlying communication from the programmer and thus are vulnerable to "performance errors". We will comment on the difficulty of the translation from a shared to a distributed address space in Section 3, which leads to our OpenMP-to-MPI compiler-runtime scheme; we will discuss performance errors in Section 4 on performance evaluation.

Our paper is related to previous efforts that also proposed shared address space programming models for cluster architectures. One of the largest efforts was the development of High Performance Fortran (HPF) [11]. There are significant differences between the OpenMP-to-MPI translation approach presented here and that of HPF. Like OpenMP, HPF provides directives to specify parallel loops; however, HPF's focus is on data distribution directives as well as parallelization and scheduling of loop execution based on those directives. Data partitioning is explicitly given by these directives and computation partitioning is guided by them [10]. Data typically has a single owner and computation is performed by the owner of the written data, i.e., the *owner computes* rule. In contrast to HPF, OpenMP has no user-defined data distribution input. Our scheme does not derive computation partitioning from data distribution information. Instead, computation is distributed among processors based on OpenMP directives and data may move between different *dynamic owners* at different times during the program's execution. We compare the performance of our translator with an available HPF compiler.

PGAS (Partitioned Global Address Space) languages, such as UPC [19], Co-array Fortran [15], Titanium [21], and X10 [7], are programming paradigms that have been proposed to ease programming effort by providing a global address space that is logically partitioned between threads. For most cases, the programmer needs to specify the affinity between threads and data. In our work, the programmer writes a standard OpenMP shared memory program and the hybrid compiler/runtime translator converts this program into a message-passing executable. We will compare the performance of our translated OpenMP with available UPC programs.

Another approach to extending the ease of shared memory programming to clusters is the use of a Software Distributed Shared Memory (SDSM) system [8]. SDSM is a runtime system that provides a shared address space abstraction on distributed memory architectures. Researchers have proposed numerous optimization techniques to reduce remote memory access latency on SDSM.

PPoPP'12, February 25–29, 2012, New Orleans, Louisiana, USA.

Many of these optimization techniques aim to perform pro-active data movement by analyzing data access patterns either at compile-time or at runtime. The model has also been used in a commercial system (Intel's Cluster OpenMP [12]), but is no longer supported. Previous work has shown SDSMs to be substantially inferior to MPI programs, primarily due to the page granularity at which they operate. We will show that our translator comes close to MPI performance for the applications considered in this paper.

The hybrid compiler-runtime scheme applied in this paper also relates to many approaches that attempt to move optimization decisions into runtime [5, 6, 17]. A notable representative of hybrid analysis is Parasol [17]. Parasol's goal is runtime detection of parallelism; it is based on the LMAD array access representation [16], whose complex expressions are being evaluated at runtime. While this scheme and ours both use a hybrid approach, the aims and underlying algorithms are substantially different.

In this paper, we present a compiler-runtime scheme and a fully automated implementation that is able to translate the entire class of *regular and repetitive* applications of the NAS Parallel Benchmarks from their shared-address-space source (written in OpenMP) to message passing programs (using MPI), delivering performance close to hand-coded MPI programs. This paper builds on techniques introduced in [14], which presented a translator for a subset of the applications considered here. We also introduce a new compiler technique that improves data affinity by considering the dynamic owner of the data. Furthermore, this paper presents a novel *runtime data flow analysis technique* to optimize communication. The corresponding analysis is done at compile time in [14]. We will discuss and quantify the intrinsic limitations of the compile-time scheme as well as the overheads of the runtime scheme. In this paper, we call the previous approach [14] and our translation system OMPD-CT (Compile-time) and OMPD-RT (Runtime) respectively.

In this paper we make the following contributions:

- We present a fully automated translator and a runtime system that is able to successfully execute the OpenMP versions of all regular, repetitive applications of the NAS benchmarks on clusters.
- We introduce a hybrid compiler-runtime translation scheme. The scheme features a new runtime data flow analysis technique and a compiler technique for improving data affinity.
- We present and discuss the performance results of our scheme, as well as those obtained with HPF and UPC versions of our benchmarks, using available translators.
- We quantitatively compare compile-time and runtime communication generation schemes. We discuss intrinsic limitations of compile-time techniques as well as overheads of runtime techniques.

The remainder of the paper is organized as follows. Section 2 describes the system on which we build and identifies opportunities for improvement. Section 3 describes our hybrid compiler-runtime system. Performance of seven translated programs and other metrics of interest are evaluated in Section 4, followed by conclusions and future work in Section 5.

2. Foundation and Opportunities

Our translator builds on related work [14] that presented early results for a system that extended OpenMP beyond shared-memory architectures. Our novel contributions improve on this foundation in terms of both performance and application range.

The previous approach (OMPD-CT) translated OpenMP programs to message passing programs in two steps: (1) Translation

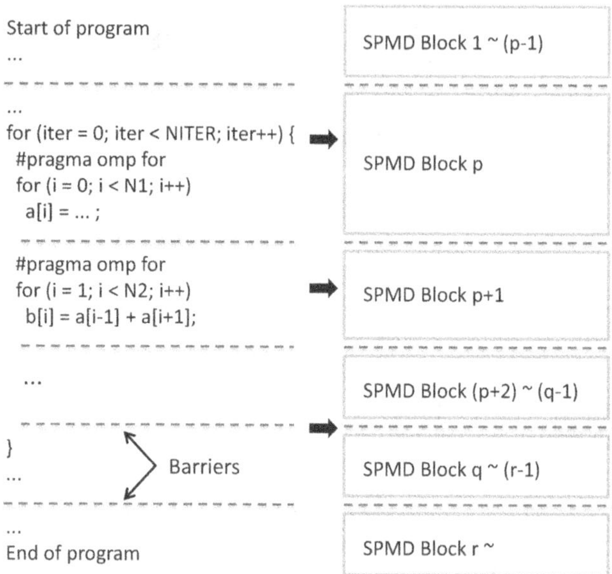

Figure 1: The translation system captures the structure of a regular-loop based OpenMP program as a series of SPMD blocks and barriers between them.

of OpenMP to SPMD form and (2) communication analysis and generation. A key feature of the first step is the partitioning of work onto the distributed MPI processes of the resulting SPMD program. In contrast to related approaches that are guided by data-distribution information, such as HPF, the *iterations of parallel loops* are partitioned and distributed. As a result, data may be written or read by different processes in different parts of a program. Data ownership thus is dynamic. The compiler analyzes the written and read data for each process; communication is generated from this access information, such that data written (defined) is sent to all future readers (uses).

Figure 1 shows the structure of a program for this approach. The unit of compiler analysis in the translated program is an *SPMD block*. Typically, programs contain a series of parallel and serial loops, enclosed by an outer serial loop (often a time-stepping loop). Parallel loops usually generate SPMD blocks that are work-shared, i.e., the iterations are partitioned, while a serial code section generates a replicated block [14]. The compiler analyzes local uses and definitions for each SPMD block. The sets of the local uses and local definitions of process i are denoted by $LUSE_i$ and $LDEF_i$, respectively. LUSE represents a set of all $LUSE_i$, and LDEF the set of all $LDEF_i$, for $0 \leq i \leq nprocs - 1$.

LDEF and LUSE are the results of the array data flow analyses [14] based on the Cetus array section analysis. For each dimension of an array, the accessed region with lower bound (LB) and upper bound (UB) are summarized as [LB:UB]. LDEF and LUSE are analyzed by *Reaching-All Definitions* analysis and *Live-Any* analysis respectively.

In this paper, we consider applications that are *repetitive and regular*. This means that the communication pattern is the same in all iterations of the outer serial loop enclosing the SPMD blocks. The runtime system will evaluate this pattern in the first iteration and reuse it from then on. The programs are regular in that loop bound and array subscript expressions are affine. This requirement is not strict for the analysis of read accesses; the compiler overestimates array ranges (LUSEs) in the presence of non-affine expressions, at the cost of increased communication.

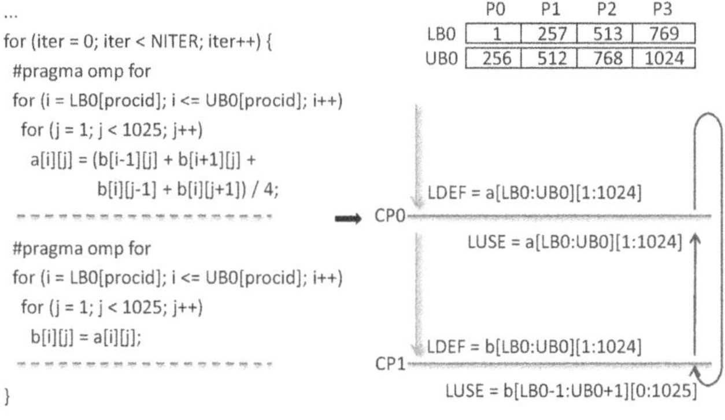

...
for (iter = 0; iter < NITER; iter++) {
#pragma omp for
for (i = LB0[procid]; i <= UB0[procid]; i++)
for (j = 1; j < 1025; j++)
a[i][j] = (b[i-1][j] + b[i+1][j] +
b[i][j-1] + b[i][j+1]) / 4;
#pragma omp for
for (i = LB0[procid]; i <= UB0[procid]; i++)
for (j = 1; j < 1025; j++)
b[i][j] = a[i][j];
}
...
P0 P1 P2 P3
LB0 1 257 513 769
UB0 256 512 768 1024
LDEF = a[LB0:UB0][1:1024]
CP0
LUSE = a[LB0:UB0][1:1024]
LDEF = b[LB0:UB0][1:1024]
CP1
LUSE = b[LB0-1:UB0+1][0:1025]

Figure 2: The compiler analyzes producer and consumer information from each SPMD block and puts the results in communication points around the SPMD block.

Communication is generated at the end of each SPMD block, i.e., at a *communication point* (CP). This is done by intersecting the LDEF with the *global use* (GUSE) which is all future LUSEs exposed to this CP. This algorithm is the centerpiece of the communication generation step; it was performed by the compiler in OMPD-CT [14]. The compiler passes the LDEF and GUSE information to the runtime system, which in turn computes their intersection and generates the communication.

Opportunities: The precision of the communication analysis is performance critical. Precise array section analysis allows the communication to be kept to a minimum, as illustrated in Figure 2. If the compiler has insufficient knowledge, it conservatively overestimates the GUSE sets. Even when program expressions do not depend on program input data, overestimation may result from operations on array sections during data flow analysis. In particular, subtractions of symbolic section representations tend to produce expressions of undesirable complexity, warranting approximation. Furthermore, cycles in the control flow graph may necessitate approximations in the computed GUSE sets. Such overestimation was one reason for the limited performance in the previous work [14] for large applications. The key opportunity being exploited in the present paper is to put more responsibility on the runtime, when symbolic expressions have become known values. In Section 4.9, we will show that the needed analysis can be done at runtime with low overhead.

A second opportunity being exploited is the data affinity resulting from the iteration distribution. The previous approach chose a fixed iteration-to-process assignment for all loops, resulting in data unnecessarily changing the dynamic owner, as for example in the FT benchmark. In the present paper, the compiler considers the dynamic data ownership and adjusts data affinity between the data producer and consumer, so as to reduce communication.

3. Hybrid Communication Analysis and Generation System

Our translation system includes a hybrid, compiler-runtime scheme for communication analysis that exploits the opportunities mentioned in the previous section. This section describes the novel elements:

- In addition to the basic OpenMP-to-SPMD translation described above, the compiler performs *Dynamic Owner Alignment*, which adjusts data affinity to reduce communication. This is described in Section 3.1.

Algorithm 1 Dynamic Owner Alignment Optimization

for each cp **in** {all communication points} **do**
  LUSESET ← collect INF LUSEs
  ensure:
    1) Each *LUSE* is from a single read access
    2) The last producer's *LDEF* defines its entire array
  for each *LUSE* **in** *LUSESET* **do**
    dim ← Get the partitioned dimension of the *LDEF*
    lb[], ub[] ← Get the partitioned bounds from the *LDEF*
    stmt ← statement containing the read access of interest
    expr ← array index expression of *stmt*
    Enclose *stmt* by if statement of the form
      if (*lb*[procid] ≤ *expr* ≤ *ub*[procid]) {
        stmt;
      }
    Update the *LUSE* to reflect the new bounds
  end for

  Restore the original loop bounds
end for

- The compiler interacts with the runtime system through a new interface, described in Section 3.2.
- The runtime system performs dynamic array section data flow analysis and generates communication, described in Section 3.3.

3.1 Compiler: Dynamic Owner Alignment

Dynamic Owner Alignment (DOA) is a compiler technique that improves data affinity. DOA adjusts the computation such that data uses happen on the process that previously produced them (i.e., by the dynamic owner). This optimization is able to transform a local USE set from its conservative form ([-INF:+INF]) into a narrow range([LB:UB]), with the effect that communication is eliminated.

Algorithm 1 describes the necessary steps for the transformation. For each LUSE candidate, it ensures the validity of the transformation by checking two conditions. If they are met then the transformation proceeds and the compiler finds the partitioned dimension of the last producer LDEF of the array by searching through the predecessor CPs. Next, it finds the bounds ([LB:UB]) of the partitioned dimension from the LDEF, and inserts an "if statement". The loop reverts to its original bounds and all processes execute all statements. The if-condition selects the execution of those statement instances that use data already present in the current process. Finally, the compiler updates the [-INF:+INF] LUSE by [LB:UB]. With this transformation, the communication between the LDEF and the transformed LUSE is completely removed.

A representative code example before and after the optimization is given in Figure 3. The code shows a reduction operation, where each process computes a partial reduction on a local private copy of the reduction variable *sum* and then performs the global update from the local values. The 1024 elements are summed up via indirection arrays. The initial SPMD transformation block-partitions the iterations. Because of the indirection, the compiler is unable to determine the accessed array ranges, which would result in extensive communication. The DOA optimization causes all processes to revert to their original iteration space, but each operates on the data it currently owns. As a result, no communication is needed. (Note that this transformation resembles but differs from the "owner computes" rules applied by HPF compilers. Owner-computes states that

```
...
LDEF = a[LB1:UB1][0:511]
...
// will expose LUSE =
// a[-INF:+INF][-INF:+INF]
// original code:
// #pragma omp for
// for (i = 0; i < 1024; i++)
for (i = LB2[procid];
       i <= UB2[procid]; i++) {
    s = expr1(i) % 512;
    t = expr2(i) % 512;
    sum += a[s][t];
}

// reduction for 'sum'
```

→

```
...
LDEF = a[LB1:UB1][0:511]
...
// compiler replaces LUSE by
// a[LB1:UB1][-INF:+INF]
for (i = 0; i < 1024; i++) {
    s = expr1(i) % 512;
    t = expr2(i) % 512;
    if (s >= LB1[procid] &&
        s <= UB1[procid]) {
        sum += a[s][t];
    }
}

// reduction for 'sum'
```

Figure 3: DOA transforms a conservative [-INF:+INF] LUSE expression into a form of [LB:UB] to improve data affinity.

a computation is performed by the process owning (as per the data distribution directives) the data *written* by the computation.)

Section 4.6 discusses the resulting performance improvements of the DOA optimization.

3.2 Compiler-Runtime Interface

The compiler-runtime interface facilitates the interoperation of the two system components. The compiler analyzes the data writes (LDEF) and reads (LUSE) by each SPMD block and informs the runtime system (RTS) thereof. Based on this information, the RTS computes the global uses (GUSEs) exposed at each communication point by performing a runtime data flow analysis. For this purpose, the compiler also passes information about the control flow graph to the RTS. Furthermore, at each communication point, the compiler calls the RTS to activate the requisite part of the data flow computation and schedule needed communication.

The interface is designed to compute the GUSEs efficiently at runtime. Note that LDEFs and LUSEs are already summarized to facilitate efficient GUSE computation at runtime. Since each LDEF/LUSE section is mapped to a communication point, the total number of sections passed to the RTS is proportional to the number of communication points. Furthermore, not all of the communication points are related to an array symbol. Thus, each array symbol maintains a reduced CFG by pruning out unrelated communication points to make the runtime evaluation fast.

The interface functions include `update_def(...)` and `update_use(...)` for informing the RTS of data accesses, `cfg_node(...)` for passing control flow graph information, and `rts_communicate(...)` for actions needed at each communication point. Each function has a communication point identifier as a parameter. Additional parameters include the data range descriptors, CFG connectivity information, and the data type.

The placement of these functions in the translated program is as follows. `cfg_node()` functions are called during program initialization, allowing the RTS to setup a basic CFG structure. The functions `update_def(...)` and `update_use(...)` are usually placed (hoisted) before the outermost serial loop, taking advantage of the fact that communication patterns are repetitive with respect to this loop and, thus, the access ranges are loop invariant. In the absence of such an outer loop, the functions are placed at the corresponding communication points. This information allows the RTS to annotate the control flow graph with local DEF and USE sets. The RTS initializes these annotations to the unknown range [-INF:+INF]. In effect, if the control flow algorithm needs a range before it has become known, it uses a conservative value. The `rts_communicate(...)` function is inserted at each communication point.

3.3 Runtime System: Dynamic Array Section Data Flow Analysis

The role of the RTS is to evaluate global use (GUSE) sections, schedule and execute communications. It has five stages:

1. Construction of Runtime Control Flow Graphs (RCFGs);
2. Update of nodes of an RCFG;
3. Evaluation of the GUSEs of a RCFG;
4. Scheduling communication;
5. Invoking scheduled communications.

3.3.1 Constructing and updating RCFG

A runtime control flow graph needs to be constructed for every array that is involved in communication. The compiler passes necessary information about CFGs collected at compile-time through the `cfg_node(...)` functions. The information includes various identifiers, the shape of the CFGs, and other necessary values. Each RCFG is identified by a unique number, RCFGID. The created RCFG records information about its symbol, such as the base address, the symbol's name string, the element type, dimension, and rank of each dimension. Each node in an RCFG also has its unique number (NODEID) and a corresponding CP number (CPID). With the combination of RCFGID and NODEID a node in a RCFG can be identified and used.

The `update_def()` and `update_use()` functions receive one or more sections and update them in the node of the corresponding RCFG. They check whether the sections are different from the old sections, if they exist, and update only when the new sections are different. They then mark the RCFG as dirty so that GUSEs will be newly evaluated later.

Algorithm 2 shows how `rts_communicate()` does the third, fourth, and fifth stages. When a program execution arrives at a CP, the `rts_communicate()` function examines if there is a RCFG that is associated with the CP and was marked as dirty by any update function call. If there is an RCFG and it is marked dirty, then the RTS performs the evaluation of GUSEs, scheduling and invoking communications. If it is not marked as dirty, then GUSEs of the RCFG are up-to-date and the RTS already has all information to invoke communication functions.

3.3.2 Evaluation of Global Use Sections (GUSE)

The GUSE evaluation uses an any-path backward data flow analysis. The analysis is performed by function `cfg_evaluate()` whenever the corresponding RCFG becomes dirty, as shown in Algorithm 2. The goal is to determine all future use sections seen by a given communication point. This information (GUSEOUT) is then intersected with the local definitions LDEF of the preceding SPMD block to generate communication messages.

Let p be the index of an SPMD block and CP(p) the communication point terminating block p. LDEF(p) represents the local definitions of block p and LUSE(p) are the local uses at CP($p-1$). For process i, GUSEIN$_i$(p) is the set of sections that is live upon entrance to the SPMD block p. Similarly, GUSEOUT$_i$(p) is the set of sections of process i that is live upon exiting the SPMD block p. Let Succ(p) be the set of all successors of the SPMD block p in the RCFG. GUSEOUT and GUSEIN for process i can be calculated as follows.

$$GUSEOUT_i(p) = \bigcup_{k \in Succ(p)} GUSEIN_i(k)$$

Algorithm 2 Pseudo code of rts_communicate() and cfg_evaluate().

```
rts_communicate(int cpid) {
  cfg_set ← control flow graphs of arrays involved in cpid
  for all cfg in cfg_set do
    if cfg is marked as dirty then
      call cfg_evaluate(cfg)
    endif
  end for

  schedule communication(cpid)
  invoke communication(cpid)
}

cfg_evaluate(cfg) {
  worklist ← build a work list from cfg in reverse topological order
  while work ← get_work(worklist) exists do
    node ← work's node
    calculate node's GUSEOUT from cfg
    if node's GUSEOUT is changed then
      mark node's GUSEOUT as dirty to reschedule communication
    endif
    calculate GUSEIN from cfg and node
    if node's GUSEIN is changed then
      put predecessors of node in worklist
    endif
    free work
  end while
  mark cfg as clean
}
```

$$GUSEIN_i(p) = \Big(GUSEOUT_i(p) - KILL(p)\Big) \bigcup GEN_i(p)$$

The upward exposed GUSEIN$_i(p)$ should not contain the sections that will be communicated in the CP after the SPMD block p, or redundant communication will happen; KILL(p) is defined as LDEF(p), which includes all LDEF$_i(p)$ for $0 \leq i \leq nprocs - 1$, while GEN$_i(p)$ is the same as LUSE$_i(p)$. Thus, even though the formulas resemble the conventional live variable analysis, our analysis is different in that GEN$_i(p)$, GUSEIN$_i(p)$, and GUSEOUT$_i(p)$ are localized for process i, while KILL spans all processes.

Algorithm 2 uses a work list; it starts from the terminal nodes in reverse topological order. The terminal nodes have empty GUSEOUTs because they do not have successors. The evaluation finishes when the work list becomes empty, which means none of the evaluated sections changed. GUSEOUTs are evaluated for and by all processes.

During the GUSE calculation, we use a precise subtraction method as shown in Fig. 4 to prevent loss of accuracy. It depicts a worst-case fragmentation scenario, where an n-dimensional array incurs the maximum number of fragmented sections, $2n$. The case of merging multiple sections into one is explained in the next section, and the performance of evaluating GUSEs will be discussed in Section 4.10.

3.3.3 Scheduling and invoking communication messages

Recall that the global use sets (GUSEs) express all future uses exposed at a communication point (CP), and local def sets (LDEF) express the data defined in the block terminated by the CP. The above algorithm has computed GUSEs at a given CP. To generate actual communication messages, we now intersects LDEF and GUSE for each pair of processes and for each array symbol. We have implemented efficient intersection functions for the given array range representations.

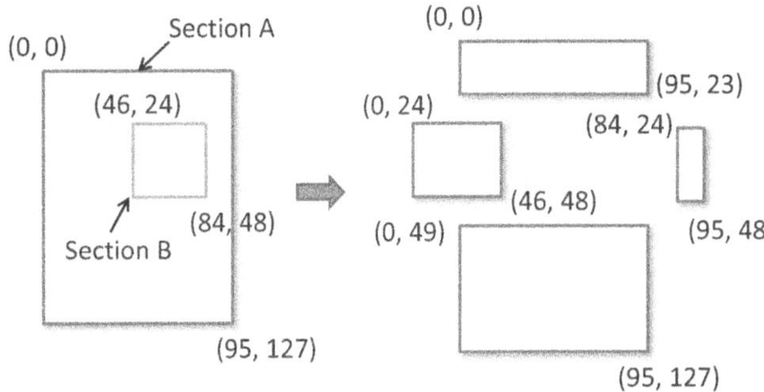

Figure 4: The RTS uses a precise subtraction method to maintain accurate intermediate USE sections. It slices Section A by excluding Section B from the highest to the lowest dimension.

GUSEs, even for a single array, may consist of a number of section fragments. To reduce the number of fragments after doing the intersections, at the cost of increased communication volume, the RTS makes a conservative approximation of them. This approximation extends at most to the boundaries of the intersecting LDEF range, as it would be incorrect to communicate data that has not been defined. Multiple LDEF ranges (e.g., stemming from multiple array access expressions) typically lead to multiple ranges that need to be communicated.

After intersecting, the RTS calls MPI messages to communicate the resulting data ranges. To deal with multiple, non-contiguous array ranges, we make use of the MPI library's ability to accept derived data types for subarrays. Using this rich feature, the MPI communication functions pack and unpack non-contiguous ranges into efficient messages.

The RTS uses different different communication operations. At each CP, the RTS creates a *communication schedule*, expressing the selected message type for each involved array symbol. For example, if the RTS determines that only neighbor communication happens, it chooses point-to-point communication. Determining the communication schedule is the role of the fourth stage of Section 3.3. Our RTS currently chooses between point-to-point with the left and right neighbors, allgather (or scatter), all-to-all, and reduction. The need for the communication type to agree on the sender and receiver side makes this selection non-trivial. We are currently using a simple, but effective heuristic.

`MPI_Alltoallw()` has proven to be an especially useful communication function. It supports generalized all-to-all communication that allows different data types, numbers of elements and displacement of sent and received data. Since it is able to control how many elements to send and receive, and displacement information for each process, it can be configured to be used as point-to-point, gather/scatter for one or all processes, all-to-all or any combination of them. However, its performance is dependent on the performance of the communication library. In our evaluation environment, it is slower than the explicit allgather communication and a point-to-point communication for a process (procid) with its direct left (procid-1) and right (procid+1) processes. Thus, the RTS detects these two types of communication patterns with the given intersection results to use explicit communication functions instead of `MPI_Alltoallw()`. Section 4.8 compares the use of `MPI_Alltoallw()` with `MPI_Allgather()` and `MPI_Isend`/`MPI_Irecv` followed by `MPI_Waitall()`. (Note, that only the synchronous version of `MPI_Alltoallw()` is available in the common MPICH2 and MVAPICH2 implementations. Improved support is planned in the coming MPICH3 release.)

Finally, the RTS uses the communication schedule just built to generate communication. It calls communication functions according to the communication type stored in the schedule data structure. For example, if the communication type is all-to-all, then the data structure will contain all information for the parameters of `MPI_Alltoallw()`. All communication schedules in a CP will be ordered and executed sequentially because the function is synchronous.

4. Evaluation

In this section, we evaluate the OMPD-RT system with seven publicly available benchmarks ranging from micro-kernels to applications. We provide short descriptions of each benchmark, the number of communication points, and the communication patterns. We compare the overall performance of OMPD-RT applications with their corresponding MPI program. Total execution time and speedup versus serial version is presented, followed by a discussion of the overhead of the runtime GUSE evaluation. In addition, performance comparisons among HPF, OMPD-RT, UPC and MPI are provided.

4.1 Experimental setup

We evaluate the performance on 32 nodes of a community cluster with two MPI processes per node, for a total of 64 MPI processes. The nodes are connected by an InfiniBand network, which provides 10 Gbps of bandwidth. Each node has two quad-core Intel Xeon E5410 processors running at 2.33Ghz with 6MB L2 caches per processor and 16GB of memory. The system is running a 64-bit Linux kernel, version 2.6.18, and MVAPICH2 version 1.5 MPI. We compiled all programs with gcc64 4.4.0 at optimization level 3. For the results in Section 4.11, we used MPICH2 version 1.4 MPI to use 1Gbps Ethernet and MVAPICH2 version 1.5 MPI to use the InfiniBand network. The PGI compiler suite version 11 is used for Fortran, C, and HPF. For the results in section 4.12, we used two available compilers to compile UPC codes: GCC UPC 4.5.1.2 compiler [2] and Berkeley UPC 2.12.2 compiler[1] [1]. UPC executables are always run with Berkeley UPC runtime 2.12.2 [1].

We timed each benchmark several times and recorded the minimum execution time, to eliminate network fluctuation due to foreign processes. We also ran the OMPD-RT and MPI programs ran in turn to further reduce these effects. Each graph has an axis labeled "Speedup" – this is the ratio of the execution time of the serial version of the benchmark running on one processor to the execution time of the translated benchmark running on the number of processors indicated on the x-axis.

We show results for seven benchmarks: JACOBI and SPMUL are micro-kernels available online and the other five are from the NAS Parallel Benchmark suites (NPB) [4], which provide serial, OpenMP and MPI versions in a package. We used the NPB2.3-omp-C suite [13] for the EP, CG, and FT benchmarks, and made C versions for BT and SP from the NPB3.3-OMP suite by translating their Fortran version to C version with the only significant non-syntactic change being to convert from a column-major to row-major array layout[2]. These programs include all NAS Parallel Benchmark that have regular, loop-based computations, and the communication pattern is repetitive, which means the producer and consumer relationship is static during their execution; the hoisting process in Section 3.2 plays an important role in reducing runtime overhead. The Class C input is used for all NPB programs.

The translation process from an OpenMP input to an OMPD-RT output code is fully automated. FT has manual modifications to the OpenMP code and their performance results after this modification are discussed in Section 4.6.

4.2 JACOBI Micro Kernel

JACOBI is a micro-kernel that solves Laplace equations using Jacobi iteration. It uses two $1{,}024 \times 1{,}024$ matrices with 100,000 iterations. It represents a basic point-to-point communication patterns because each process communicates only with its direct left and right neighbors[3]. Thus, JACOBI can be used to measure a system's point-to-point communication performance.

Figure 5a shows that the translated OMPD-RT program performs as fast as the MPI version because our RTS chooses the best communication type, i.e., point-to-point.

4.3 SPMUL Micro Kernel

SPMUL is a micro-kernel that performs matrix-vector multiplications. It uses a $100{,}000 \times 100{,}000$ sparse matrix as input. Both the OMPD-RT and the MPI programs partition the input matrix in one dimension[4]. Due to an indirection vector used for reading accesses, the communication pattern is all-gather. Thus, SPMUL can be used to measure a system's all-gather communication performance.

Figure 5b shows that the translated OMPD-RT program performs as fast as the MPI version. As the case of JACOBI, the RTS chooses `MPI_Allgatherv()` instead of `MPI_Alltoallw()`, and it makes OMPD-RT performance match with the hand-coded MPI version.

4.4 EP Benchmark

EP is a highly parallel kernel, often used to explore the upper limit of the floating point performance of a parallel system. The MPI version communicates by using only a reduction function, while the OpenMP version uses a critical section to perform the reduction operation on shared array variables. This critical section is detected at compile-time, above the abstraction interface, and is transformed into `ompd_allreduce()` function calls.

Figure 5d shows that the performance of both the OMPD-RT and the MPI versions is identical.

4.5 CG Benchmark

CG implements a conjugate gradient method, with a sparse matrix-vector multiplication taking most of the time. The benchmark has irregular read accesses on arrays via an indirection vector because of its unstructured grid computations.

The translated and the MPI programs have different data partitioning schemes. The MPI version partitions the sparse input matrix using a 2-D block distribution, which requires a smaller number of processes for reduction communication. By contrast, our translation scheme partitions the input matrix using a simple 1-D block distribution; this is because only the outer-most loop of the matrix-vector multiply computation is parallelized in the OpenMP version.

Our analysis of CG shows that performance could be improved further by developing compiler techniques that analyze array expressions in the presence of indirect accesses, hence reducing or eliminating the conservative [-INF:+INF] expression. Doing so is beyond the scope of this paper, however.

---

[1] Berkeley UPC-to-C translator translates UPC to C which then is compiled using the GCC compiler

[2] The code of BT and SP in NPB2.3-omp-C suite is not as clean as the NPB3.3 BT and SP. SP in NPB2.3-omp-C was translated to C without considering the conversion of the column to row major mode, so we translated them from NPB3.3-OMP.

[3] The leftmost process communicates only with its right process and the rightmost process with its left process.

[4] The NPB CG benchmark partitions its input matrix along two dimensions.

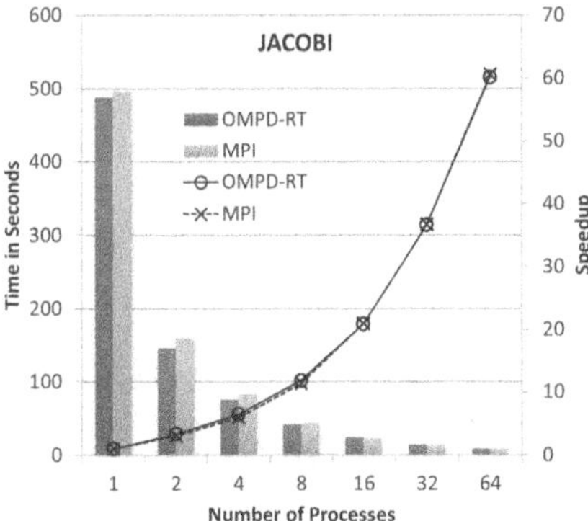

(a) The OMPD-RT JACOBI performance matches its MPI counterpart.

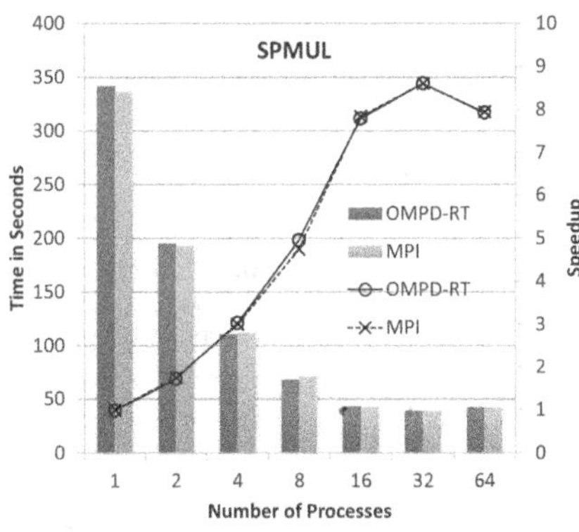

(b) The OMPD-RT SPMUL performance matches its MPI counterpart.

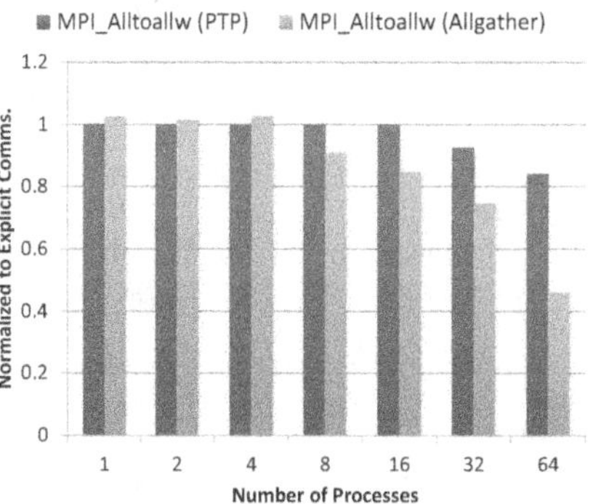

(c) The performance of MPI_Alltoallw() used for point-to-point and allgather communications is compared with its explicit communication functions. MPI_Alltoallw() performs 84% and 46% of explicit point-to-point explicit point-to-point and allgather communication schemes, respectively.

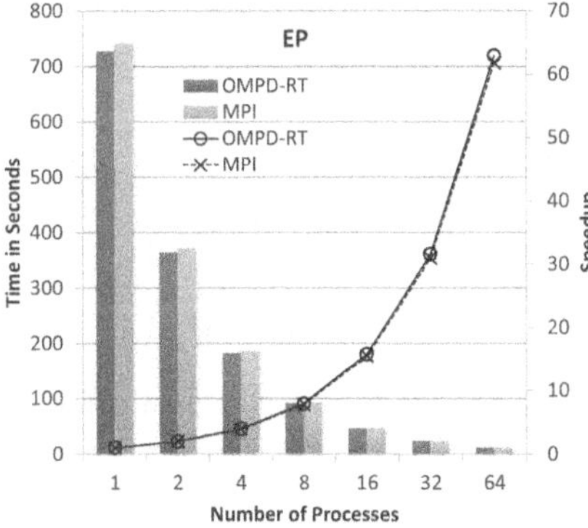

(d) The OMPD-RT EP performance matches its MPI counterpart. The transformation from a critical section to array reductions makes the communication pattern identical as well as their performance.

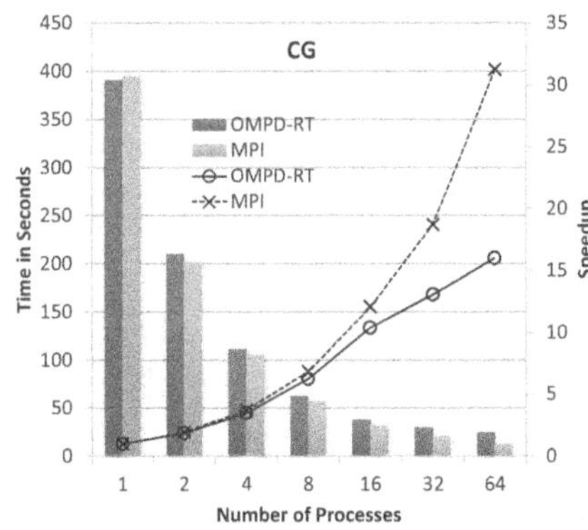

(e) The OMPD-RT CG performance scales according to the number of processes, but is behind the MPI performance. OMPD-RT is approximately 50% slower than MPI on 64 processes.

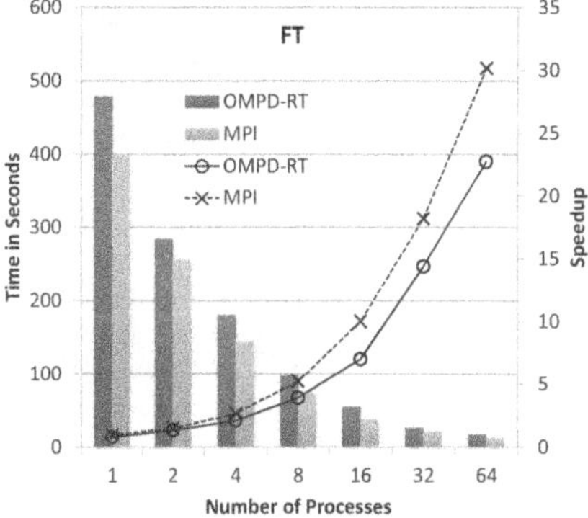

(f) The OMPD-RT FT performance scales according to the number of processes, achieving 75% of the performance of its MPI counterpart.

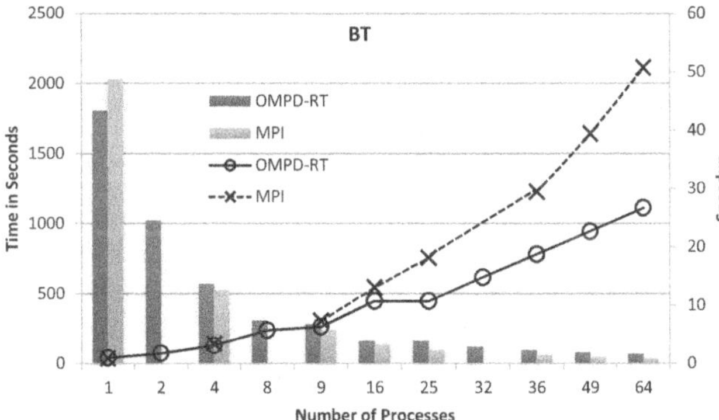

(g) The OMPD-RT BT achieves 52% of the performance of its MPI counterpart. Even though the OMPD-RT versions are slower than the MPI versions, their performance is scalable up to 64 processes.

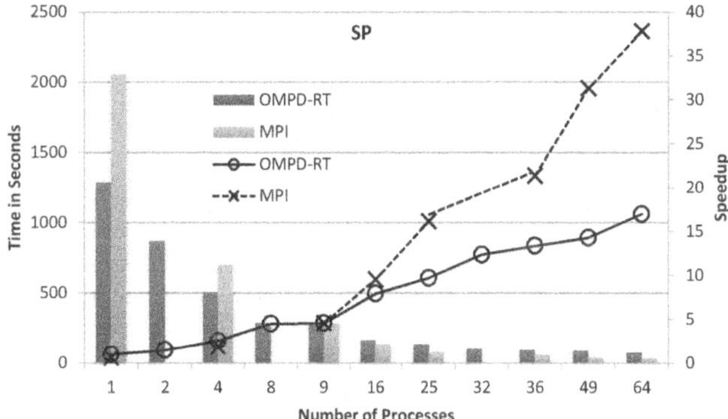

(h) The OMPD-RT SP achieves 45% of the performance of its MPI counterpart. Even though the OMPD-RT versions are slower than the MPI versions, their performance is scalable up to 64 processes.

Figure 5: For the seven benchmarks, OMPD-RT achieves 75% of the hand-coded MPI programs, on average.

4.6 FT Benchmark

FT solves a 3-D partial differential equation using Fast Fourier Transforms. It can be used to test the communication performance of a system because it is very message intensive.

The OMPD-RT version has a manual change to the original OpenMP code that splits a `dcomplex` data structure into real and imaginary `double` parts. This is done because the current translator only supports native C data types, but not structured data types. The performance difference shown on one process in Fig. 5f is from the split, which affects cache performance. However, the effect diminishes as the number of processes increases resulting in smaller problem size per process and less impact from the CPU caches.

The major communication pattern of the MPI version is all-to-all, and the OpenMP version implements the computation by parallelizing loops along the z-axis and y-axis alternatively. This OpenMP computation pattern produces LDEF and LUSE sections partitioned in different dimensions and the RTS identifies their intersection as an all-to-all communication pattern. Thus, the translated version and the MPI version have identical communication patterns.

FT shows the most pronounced performance difference compared to related work [14] (other than BT and SP, which were not included). Figure 6 compares the results. The key techniques in our system are Dynamic Owner Alignment and Runtime GUSE Evaluation. The figure also shows the effect of manually applied advanced affinity analysis, showing the potential for improvements beyond the techniques presented here.

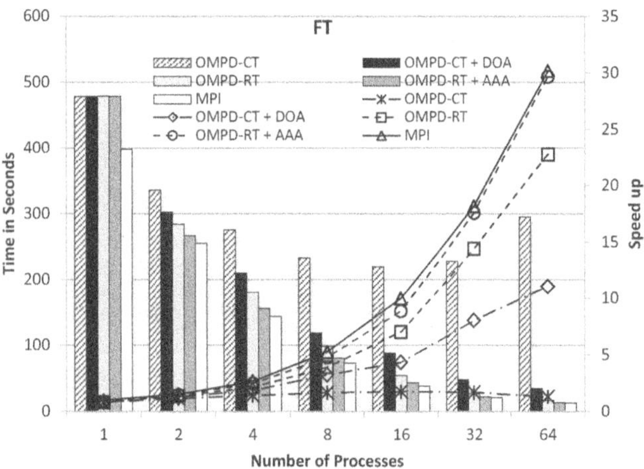

Figure 6: With the advanced affinity analysis (AAA), FT performs as fast as the MPI version on 64 processes.

OpenMP FT has a checksum function that does reduction operations with 1,024 selected elements in a shared array. Since the elements are picked from the entire data space of the shared array using the modulus operator (%), the USE section becomes [-INF:+INF][-INF:+INF][-INF:+INF]. The dynamic owner-computes compiler optimization in Section 3.1 transforms this infinite section into an affine [LB:UB][-INF:+INF][-INF:+INF] section and it completely removes the communication at the CP.

The fourth bar (OMPD-RT + AAA) is obtained by applying advanced affinity analysis (AAA) to the OpenMP source code manually. Sometimes it is beneficial for communication to partition a different dimension than the one specified by the users to increase affinity between LDEF and LUSE. The transformation removes communication from a CP in the `evolve()` function, gaining additional 30% performance. Implementing AAA would require new compiler techniques, such as detecting parallelizable indices from loops and deciding which loop to parallelize within a program's global scope.

In summary, with 64 processes, OMPD-RT's performance is 75% of MPI's, and with the help of AAA it could match the performance of the hand-coded MPI program.

4.7 BT and SP Benchmarks

BT solves a synthetic system of nonlinear partial differential equations using block tri-diagonal solver, while SP solves it using a penta-diagonal solver. Since the BT and SP algorithms have a similar structure and expose the same problems in OMPD-RT, we will discuss them together.

The algorithms of the OpenMP and MPI versions of the benchmarks are different; The OpenMP versions have parallel loops partitioned along the z-axis and y-axis alternatively as the OpenMP FT does, while the MPI versions solves the problem by using multi-partition scheme [20] which requires a square number of processes; a process in the multi-partition scheme communicates only with its neighbors in the 3-D space. Thus, unlike FT, the translated OMPD-RT versions and MPI versions have a different communication scheme. Because of this difference, the OMPD-RT version can use an arbitrary number of processes, including 2, 8, and 32, while the MPI version is limited to the square numbers of processes shown in Fig. 5g and 5h. The OMPD-RT BT and SP reach 52% and 45% of the performance of their MPI counterpart, respectively.

Even though we attribute the major performance difference to the different communication scheme, we identified some possible improvements that can be made to our system. For example, the compiler partitions parallel loops based on the iteration space, but for BT and SP it generates communications at the boundaries of processes' accessed data. Those boundary communications can be avoided when using a partitioning method based on the data space instead of the iteration space. These changes are beyond the scope of this paper, and are future work.

OMPD-RT BT and SP have mixed communication patterns. They have point-to-point, allreduce, all-to-all, and a combination of point-to-point and all-to-all communications. The combination of the point-to-point and all-to-all communication results from the union of USE sections just before the LDEF and GUSE intersection operation; A process sends and receives its full LDEF section with its direct neighbors, but with the other processes it sends and receives data in the all-to-all pattern. The communication scheme using `MPI_Alltoallw()` works well with this mixed pattern and provides reasonable performance.

4.8 MPI_Alltoallw() vs. Explicit communication calls.

Section 3.3.3 explained why the RTS uses `MPI_Alltoallw()` as well as two additional communication types. Here we compare the performance of `MPI_Alltoallw()` with explicit communication functions, such as allgather and point-to-point with a process' direct neighbor processes.

Using the JACOBI and SPMUL benchmarks which are the representative cases for the above patterns, Fig. 5c shows the performance of `MPI_Alltoallw()` normalized to the explicit point-to-point and the allgather performance. The efficiency of `MPI_Alltoallw()` is 84% and 46% of the explicit point-to-point and the allgather communication on 64 processes, respectively. Thus, it motivates the RTS to integrate the communication type detection step in the scheduling communication message step 3.3.3, and the RTS chooses the best scheme dynamically.

4.9 Performance Comparison of Compile-time and Runtime GUSE Evaluations

The runtime GUSE computation aims to improve accuracy of GUSE relative to the compile time method. Figure 7 shows how much speedup is made for each benchmark on 64 processes. For JACOBI, SPMUL and EP, the runtime scheme does not improve the GUSE accuracy because of the small number of communication points. CG also shows little improvement, even though it has 52 communication points, because it has one dimensional data space and its data partition is simple and static. However, for large applications, such as FT, BT, and SP, the runtime evaluation improves performance substantially, making it an essential technique for realistic and large size applications.

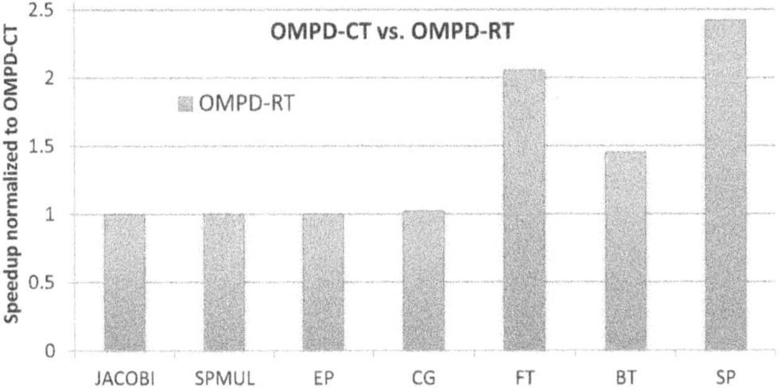

Figure 7: Comparison of speedup from the compile time and the runtime GUSE evaluation.

4.10 Runtime Overhead

The number of communication points affects the runtime overhead of evaluating GUSEs and is typically proportional to the size of the program. Table 1 shows the number of communication points in each benchmark.

Table 1: Numbers of communication points

Benchmark	JA	SPMUL	EP	CG	FT	BT	SP
# of CPs	2	2	2	52	22	71	79

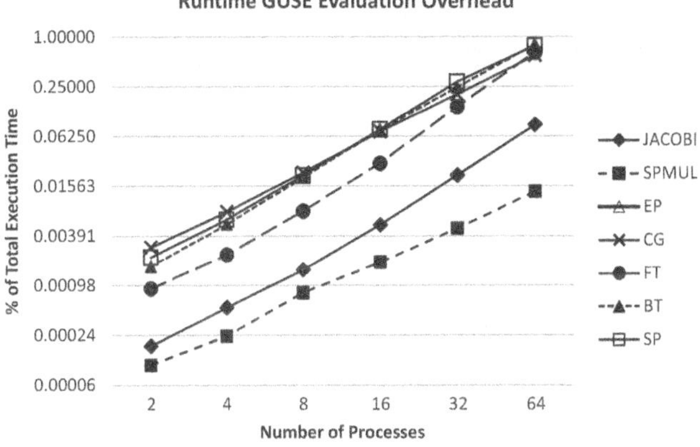

Figure 8: Evaluation of GUSEs incurs the largest overhead of our system. The runtime system shows acceptable overhead up to 64 processes. Additional optimizations will be needed for larger clusters.

Figure 8 shows the runtime GUSE evaluation overhead. All of the seven benchmarks have less than 1% overhead on up to 64 processes. EP does not incur runtime overhead because there are no LDEF and LUSE sections used to evaluate GUSEs. The overhead looks proportional to the number of communication points. The sum of the other runtime overheads, such as updating sections and creating RCFG and intersections, is not shown because it is much less than the GUSE evaluation.

Improving the scalability of our runtime techniques is part of our ongoing work. One opportunity is to parallelize the runtime algorithm. Each process has full information about the sections of the other processes, making it possible to perform localized evaluations with global exchange of the results.

4.11 Performance comparison with HPF

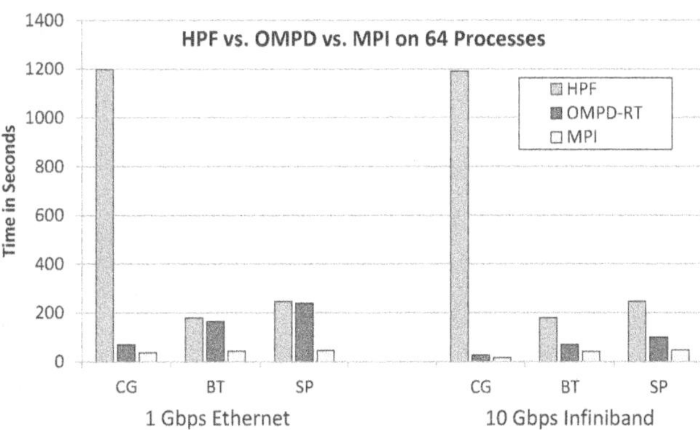

Figure 9: The translated OMPD-RT programs perform better than the hand-coded HPF programs on 64 processes.

Figure 9 shows performance comparisons among available HPF, OMPD-RT, and MPI programs on 64 processes. NPB3.0-HPF is used and FT is not shown because there are compilation errors from the FT HPF code. The HPF results show that the HPF programs used here do not take advantage of InfiniBand (IB), even though they are linked with the IB library, so we show 1Gbps Ethernet (1GE) results as well. The HPF CG suffers from the huge communication overhead of redistributing the p array, so it shows poor performance [9]. The OMPD-RT BT and SP with 1GE perform less than those with IB because the programs use a global data exchange using all-to-all communication, while the MPI BT and SP are optimized to communicate among neighbor processes in the 3-D space as discussed in Section 4.7. The translated OMPD-RT programs are still faster than the hand-coded HPF programs.

4.12 Performance comparison with UPC

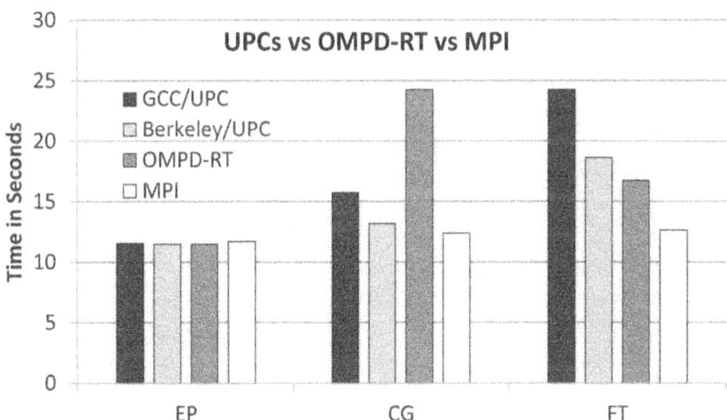

Figure 10: Execution times of UPC, OMPD-RT and MPI on 64 processes. UPC programs are compiled with two available compilers.

Unified Parallel C (UPC) has been proposed to ease programming effort by providing a global shared address space. It gives programmers more control than OpenMP; programmers can specify the affinity between thread and data with additional efforts. There are publicly available NPB programs written in UPC.

We obtained UPC versions of the EP, CG and FT benchmarks from GWU NPB suite version 2.4 [3]. BT and SP benchmarks are not available. There are multiple versions of CG and FT with progressively advanced hand optimizations. Figure 10 shows the performance of the fastest ones, together with the OMPD-RT and MPI benchmark versions on 64 processes. In EP, all benchmarks achieved almost the same performance. In CG, both UPC versions outperform OMPD-RT, Berkeley UPC by 1.83 and GCC UPC by 1.54. In FT, OMPD-RT outperforms both UPC versions, Berkeley UPC by 1.11 and GCC UPC by 1.49. For more detailed study about Berkeley UPC performance on clusters, see [18].

5. Conclusions

We have presented a hybrid, compiler-runtime system for translating and executing OpenMP programs on clusters. The system features a novel runtime data flow analysis and communication generation scheme as well as a compiler technique for improving data affinity.

Our system shows that it is feasible to use OpenMP as a programming model for clusters of up to one hundred processes, which are important platforms for research laboratories and small enterprises. This holds for an important class of applications, which are regular and exhibit repetitive communication behavior. Our system derives the distribution of data automatically from the source program, unlike approaches such as HPF and UPC, which involve the user in this task. Our results show that it is possible to hide this task from the user.

The presented hybrid approach puts significant responsibility on the runtime system. We have shown that, for the considered class of applications, this approach is feasible, the system is able to overcome limitations of static compiler techniques and the runtime overhead can be kept small.

Our system achieves, on average, 75% of the performance of hand-tuned MPI applications. Hand-tuned applications will always achieve better performance; however, we have also identified several optimizations that may bring the performance even closer to MPI and improve the scalability beyond the platform size that this paper focused on. Developing these optimizations is a topic of our ongoing work.

Acknowledgments

This work was supported, in part, by the National Science Foundation under grants No. 0720471-CNS, 0707931-CNS, 0833115-CCF, and 0916817-CCF.

References

[1] Berkeley UPC - Unified Parallel C. Available at: upc.lbl.gov.

[2] GCC Unified Parallel C. Available at: www.gccupc.org.

[3] UPC NAS Parallel Benchmarks from The George Washington University High Performance Computing Laboratory. Available at: threads.hpcl.gwu.edu/sites/npb-upc.

[4] D. H. Bailey, E. Barszcz, J. T. Barton, D. S. Browning, R. L. Carter, R. A. Fatoohi, P. O. Frederickson, T. A. Lasinski, H. D. Simon, V. Venkatakrishnan, and S. K. Weeratunga. The NAS Parallel Benchmarks. 1991.

[5] M. M. Baskaran, N. Vydyanathan, U. K. R. Bondhugula, J. Ramanujam, A. Rountev, and P. Sadayappan. Compiler-assisted dynamic scheduling for effective parallelization of loop nests on multicore processors. In *Proceedings of the 14th ACM SIGPLAN symposium on Principles and Practice of Parallel Programming*, PPoPP '09, pages 219–228, New York, NY, USA, 2009. ACM.

[6] D. Baxter, R. Mirchandaney, and J. H. Saltz. Run-time parallelization and scheduling of loops. In *Proceedings of the first annual ACM symposium on Parallel Algorithms and Architectures*, SPAA '89, pages 303–312, New York, NY, USA, 1989. ACM.

[7] P. Charles, C. Grothoff, V. Saraswat, C. Donawa, A. Kielstra, K. Ebcioglu, C. von Praun, and V. Sarkar. X10: An Object-oriented Approach to Non-uniform Cluster Computing. In *Proceedings of the 20th annual ACM SIGPLAN conference on Object-oriented Programming, Systems, Languages, and Applications. (OOPSLA '05)*, pages 519–538, New York, NY, USA, 2005. ACM.

[8] S. Dwarkadas, A. L. Cox, and W. Zwaenepoel. An Integrated Compile-Time/Run-Time Software Distributed Shared Memory System. In *Proc. of the 7th Symposium on Architectural Support for Programming Languages and Operating Systems (ASPLOS VII)*, pages 186–197, 1996.

[9] M. Frumkin, H. Jin, and J. Yan. Implementation of NAS Parallel Benchmarks in High Performance Fortran. In *Symposium on Parallel and Distributed Processing*, 2000.

[10] M. Gupta, S. Midkiff, E. Schonberg, V. Seshadri, D. Shields, K.-Y. Wang, W.-M. Ching, and T. Ngo. An HPF compiler for the IBM SP2. In *Supercomputing '95: Proceedings of the 1995 ACM/IEEE conference on Supercomputing (CDROM)*, page 71, New York, NY, USA, 1995. ACM.

[11] High Performance Fortran Forum. High Performance Fortran language specification, version 1.0. Technical Report CRPC-TR92225, Houston, Tex., 1993.

[12] J. P. Hoeflinger. Extending OpenMP to Clusters. White Paper, 2006.

[13] K. Kusano, M. Sato, T. Hosomi, and Y. Seo. The Omni OpenMP Compiler on the Distributed Shared Memory of Cenju-4. In *OpenMP Shared Memory Parallel Programming*, volume 2104 of *Lecture Notes in Computer Science*, pages 20–30. Springer Berlin / Heidelberg, 2001.

[14] O. Kwon, F. Jubair, S.-J. Min, H. Bae, R. Eigenmann, and S. Midkiff. Automatic Scaling of OpenMP Beyond Shared Memory. In *LCPC 2011: Proceedings of the 24th International Workshop on Languages and Compilers for Parallel Computing*, Sept. 2011.

[15] R. W. Numrich and J. Reid. Co-array Fortran for Parallel Programming. *SIGPLAN Fortran Forum*, 17(2):1–31, 1998.

[16] Y. Paek, J. Hoeflinger, and D. Padua. Efficient and precise array access analysis. *ACM Trans. Program. Lang. Syst.*, 24:65–109, January 2002.

[17] S. Rus, L. Rauchwerger, and J. Hoeflinger. Hybrid analysis: static & dynamic memory reference analysis. In *Proceedings of the 16th International Conference on Supercomputing*, ICS '02, pages 274–284, New York, NY, USA, 2002. ACM.

[18] H. Shan, F. Blagojević, S.-J. Min, P. Hargrove, H. Jin, K. Fuerlinger, A. Koniges, and N. J. Wright. A programming model performance study using the NAS parallel benchmarks. *Scientific Programming*, 18:153–167, August 2010.

[19] UPC Consortium. UPC Language Specifications, v1.2. Technical Report LBNL-59208, Lawrence Berkeley National Laboratory, 2005.

[20] R. F. V. D. Wijngaart. Efficient Implementation of a 3-Dimensional ADI Method on the iPSC/860. In *In Supercomputing '93*, pages 102–111, 1993.

[21] K. A. Yelick, L. Semenzato, G. Pike, C. Miyamoto, B. Liblit, A. Krishnamurthy, P. N. Hilfinger, S. L. Graham, D. Gay, P. Colella, and A. Aiken. Titanium: A high-performance java dialect. *Concurrency - Practice and Experience*, 10(11-13):825–836, 1998.

DOJ: Dynamically Parallelizing Object-Oriented Programs

Yong hun Eom Stephen Yang James C. Jenista Brian Demsky
University of California, Irvine
{yeom, stephey, jjenista, bdemsky}@uci.edu

Abstract

We present Dynamic Out-of-Order Java (DOJ), a dynamic parallelization approach. In DOJ, a developer annotates code blocks as tasks to decouple these blocks from the parent execution thread. The DOJ compiler then analyzes the code to generate heap examiners that ensure the parallel execution preserves the behavior of the original sequential program. Heap examiners dynamically extract heap dependences between code blocks and determine when it is safe to execute a code block.

We have implemented DOJ and evaluated it on twelve benchmarks. We achieved an average compilation speedup of 31.15× over OoOJava and an average execution speedup of 12.73× over sequential versions of the benchmarks.

Categories and Subject Descriptors D.1.3 [*Programming Techniques*]: Concurrent Programming—Parallel Programming

General Terms Algorithms, Performance

Keywords Parallel Programming, Dynamic Analysis, Object-Oriented Analysis, Heap Analysis, Parallelization

1. Introduction

With the wide-scale deployment of multi-core processors and the impending arrival of many-core processors, software developers must write parallel software to realize the benefits of continued improvements in microprocessors. Developing parallel software using today's development tools can be challenging. Experience has shown that applications written in today's thread and lock-based model are prone to both data races and deadlocks.

Hardware has long benefited from extracting unstructured parallelism from sequential instruction streams through out-of-order execution [28]. Processors dynamically extract dependences between sequential instructions and then execute the instructions in parallel while preserving dependences. This paper leverages the same proven techniques at a coarser granularity to parallelize software.

Task-based dataflow programming models such as StarSs[11], OoOJava[17], and Sequoia[12] have recently emerged as a new parallel programming approach. These approaches implement the well-known out-of-order execution approach from hardware in software using tasks as the basic work unit. The approach can be viewed as a hybrid that executes a task-based von Neumann program using a dataflow execution model. In this model, tasks are *dispatched* by a sequential thread and begin executing when their dependences are resolved. When a task finishes execution, it *retires*. If a thread attempts to access data produced by one of its child tasks, the thread must stall until the child retires. Previous work on task-based dataflow programming models either required the developer to explicitly state dependences between tasks (StarSs) or used heavyweight static heap analysis (OoOJava).

The goal of this paper is to make the programming model from OoOJava practical by addressing the two primary technical challenges for deploying OoOJava in the real world. Scaling the reachability analysis used by OoOJava to large programs remains an open research problem. A major advantage of the DOJ approach is that it can achieve nearly the same runtime performance while relying only on standard pointer analysis. This enables DOJ to potentially leverage recent work on pointer analysis (flow-sensitive pointer analysis has been scaled to over a million lines of code [13]). A second limitation of the static analysis approach taken in OoOJava is that it is hard for the developer to know when the analysis will extract sufficiently strong reachability properties to enable parallelization. The hybrid approach taken in this paper depends less on the precision of the static heap analysis; in DOJ, heap analysis imprecision typically results only in less optimized runtime checks.

In this paper we introduce a new approach to dynamically extract heap dependences between tasks. Our approach uses a static effects analysis to conservatively determine the possible heap effects of a task. While the results of the static effects analysis are not precise enough by themselves to parallelize many applications, they are sufficiently precise to build efficient, dynamic analyses that can precisely compute heap effects. A major advantage of this new approach is that the dynamic analyses can identify conflicts between tasks more precisely than a fully static analysis.

1.1 Basic Approach

DOJ respects all of the program dependences of the original sequential program. Dependences are either control dependences or data dependences. DOJ respects control dependences trivially by requiring all tasks to have exactly one exit. DOJ further divides data dependences into two categories: variable dependences and heap dependences. Variable dependences occur when one task writes to a variable and another task reads from that variable. DOJ uses the same value forwarding approach as OoOJava to eliminate write-after-write and write-after-read hazards on variables to enable parallelization. Heap dependences occur when one task writes to an object field and another task accesses that same field.

DOJ abstracts heap reads and writes using static *heap effects* expressed in terms of *heap roots*. We call heap effects that may introduce a heap dependence between two tasks *potentially conflicting effects*. A heap root is a variable that is live into a task and through which deeper heap references are obtained.

Heap roots occur in two contexts: a heap root is either a variable that is accessed by a task, or a variable that references the first object along a heap path accessed by the code following the exit

PPoPP'12, February 25–29, 2012, New Orleans, Louisiana, USA.

of a task. In the latter case, we refer to the statement that accesses the variable as a potential *stall site* because the execution of that statement may have to stall until a previous task completes. DOJ uses static effects analysis to characterize the heap effects of a code block in order to produce a heap path and allocation site sensitive abstraction called an *effects finite state machine* (EFSM).

DOJ uses EFSMs to build *heap examiners* for each heap root. Heap examiners only traverse the fields that are necessary to compute the target objects for all potentially conflicting effects; this information is sufficient to dynamically detect the absence of heap dependences between tasks and enable parallelization. A heap root may potentially reference a very large data structure; traversing such data structures can incur large overheads. DOJ addresses this with lightweight but less precise dynamic checks based only on static heap effects to extract dependences between tasks. The less precise approach executes concurrently with heap examiners and limits the worst case overhead of traversing large data structures by ensuring that tasks never run significantly slower than the sequential code. Once a task is dispatched, the task is guaranteed to have no conflicts and runs to completion without any extra overhead.

DOJ has four primary advantages over the static approach taken by OoOJava: (1) its dynamic analysis is, in general, more precise than the previous static analysis, (2) its dynamic analysis is sensitive to the actual fields traversed by tasks and not just reachability through any path, (3) the dynamic analysis can more easily scale to large code bases, and (4) DOJ can determine that non-conflicting updates to the same data structure can run in parallel.

1.2 Contributions

This paper makes the following contributions:

- **Heap Examiners:** It presents heap examiners, a heap path-sensitive, statically-directed dynamic analysis for predicting the heap effects of a code block before it runs. Heap examiners improve the precision of the static effects analysis to enable DOJ to effectively parallelize our benchmarks.
- **Optimizations:** It presents a set of pruning optimizations that reduce the overhead of heap examiners.
- **Hierarchical Approach to Heap Dependences:** It presents a hierarchy of approaches for detecting heap dependences. The hierarchy includes both (1) a precise approach to determine heap dependences to extract parallelism and (2) a fast and imprecise approach to limit the worst case dynamic overheads.
- **An Implementation and Evaluation:** We have implemented DOJ and evaluated its performance on twelve benchmarks.

2. Example

Figure 1 presents an example DOJ program. The loop in Line 9 of the example creates one hundred Foo data structures and inserts them into a set. The loop in Line 16 iterates over Foo data structures in the set, calls the `compute` method on each `Foo` data structure, and then sums the return values from the calls to `compute`.

DOJ extends the sequential Java programming model in the same way as OoOJava — it adds the *task* annotation to the sequential Java programming model, which tells the compiler that the code block enclosed in the task should be decoupled from the parent thread's execution and be executed when its dependences are resolved. Tasks may be nested and may contain arbitrary code, with the exception that tasks have a single exit. We call a task dynamically nested within another task a child and parent task, respectively. If the parent thread performs an operation that may conflict with or use data from one of its child tasks, it must stall until that task retires. It is important to note that task annotations never affect the semantics of the program; DOJ guarantees that the execution always preserves the sequential semantics of the unannotated program.

Calls to the `compute` method in Line 20 from the same iteration of the outer loop in Line 15 operate on disjoint data and therefore can execute in parallel. However, calls from different iterations of the outer loop may have data conflicts. We added the task declaration in Line 19 to allow calls to the `compute` method to execute (possibly out-of-order) when their data dependences are resolved. Tasks have names for pedagogical convenience; task names have no semantic meaning. The summation in Line 23 has both a dependence on the `compute` method from the same loop iteration as well as the `sum` variable's value from the previous loop iteration. We added the task declaration in Line 22 to allow the loop to execute past the summation to dispatch additional `par` task instances.

We note that programming models like Cilk [22] have an explicit reduction construct for code like Line 23. Reductions should be commutative operations and may commit out of order, which breaks sequential semantics but may expose additional parallelism. DOJ trades this parallelism opportunity for a stronger guarantee: task annotations never change the sequential semantics, which lets developers reason using a single-threaded model.

We also note that the iteration over a set in Line 16 defeats most static approaches to automatic parallelization. Automatic static parallelization of this loop is difficult because it requires extracting complex properties about the behavior of the set implementation. The approach for identifying task dependences in DOJ handles any single-threaded control structure: counted loops, data-dependent loops, recursive tasks, etc.

```
1  public class Foo {
2    Bar cntr;
3    Bar inc;
4    public Foo(Bar cntr, Bar inc) {
5      this.cntr=cntr; this.inc=inc;
6    }
7    public static void main(String x[]) {
8      HashSet set=new HashSet();
9      for(int i=0; i<100; i++) {
10       Bar cntr=new Bar(i);              //Allocation site 1
11       Bar inc=new Bar(1);               //Allocation site 2
12       set.add(new Foo(cntr, inc)); //Allocation site 3
13     }
14     int sum=0;
15     for(int j=0; j<10; j++) {
16       for(Iterator it=set.iterator(); it.hasNext(); ) {
17         Foo f=(Foo) it.next();
18         int val;
19         task par {                    //Parallelizable task
20           val=f.compute();
21         }
22         task seq {                    //Sequential task
23           sum+=val;
24         }
25       }
26     }
27     System.out.println("Total:"+sum);
28   }
29   public int compute() {
30     return cntr.value+=inc.value;
31   }
32 }
33
34 public class Bar {
35   public Bar(int value) {
36     this.value=value;
37   }
38   public int value;
39 }
```

Figure 1. DOJ Example

2.1 Data Dependences

Recall that DOJ splits data dependences into two categories: variable dependences and heap dependences. A variable dependence occurs when one task writes to a variable and another task reads from that variable. The tasks in the example contain several variable dependences. The `par` task in Line 19 has a read dependence on the parent thread for the reference stored in the variable `f` and writes a value to the variable `val`. A `seq` task instance from Line 22 has a read dependence on the value written to the variable `val` by the `par` task instance from the same loop iteration. A `seq` task instance has a read dependence on the value written to the variable `sum` by the previous instance of the `seq` task. The parent thread has a dependence in Line 27 on the value of the `sum` variable written by the last instance of the `seq` task. DOJ's variable dependence analysis automatically discovers these variable dependences.

Heap dependences occur when one task instance writes to the field of an object and another task instance accesses the same object field. There are heap dependences between instances of the `par` task in the example. Each instance of the `par` task reads and updates the `value` field of a `Bar` object and then obtains a reference to this `Bar` object by following the `cntr` field of the `Foo` object referenced by the variable `f`. Most static heap analyses would determine that instances of the `par` task update the `value` field of objects allocated at allocation site 1, and therefore may conflict with each other and cannot be safely parallelized.

2.2 Abstracting Heap Effects

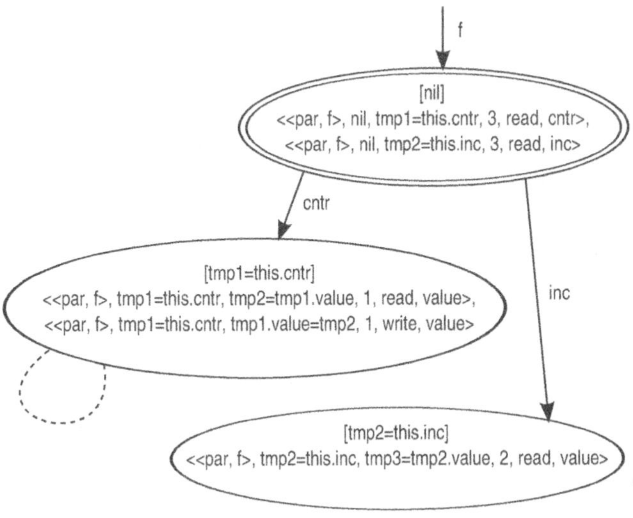

Figure 2. Initial EFSM for Task `par`

DOJ uses effects finite state machines (EFSMs) to abstract the heap effects of tasks and code blocks between tasks. EFSMs are both heap path and allocation site sensitive; for each heap effect, the EFSM captures the heap path that the application code uses to reach the affected object and the allocation site of the affected object. Intuitively, an EFSM abstracts the code of a task with respect to heap accesses.

EFSMs are compiled into heap examiners; heap examiners perform the heap traversal abstracted by the EFSM to compute the set of affected objects for each static heap effect.

The initial state in an EFSM corresponds to an object referenced from a variable at the task entrance or stall site, and the other states correspond to objects referenced from dereference statements in the code an EFSM abstracts. States are annotated with *effects tuples* that abstract the heap effects the task performs on objects abstracted by the state. An edge abstracts the action of dereferencing an object to obtain references to further objects — the edge begins at the statement that obtained a reference to the object to be dereferenced and ends at the dereference statement that reads the reference from that object's fields. The edge is labeled with the field or variable that was read to obtain the new object reference. Edges therefore capture the heap paths that tasks can potentially traverse through the heap.

Figure 2 presents the initial EFSM for the `par` task. The edge labeled `f` directed into the initial state indicates that the initial object reference is obtained by reading the variable `f`. The annotation `[nil]` indicates that this state abstracts object references at the task entrance. The effect annotation on the initial state, ⟨⟨`par`, `f`⟩, `nil`, `tmp1` = `this.cntr`, 3, `read`, `cntr`⟩, indicates that object references abstracted by this state that were allocated at allocation site 3 may flow to the statement `tmp1=this.cntr`, and that statement may then read the `cntr` field of those objects. The outgoing edge labeled `cntr` shows that this effect takes an object reference obtained at the task entrance, reads its `cntr` field, and makes the object referenced by the `cntr` field available at the exit of the dereference statement `tmp1=this.cntr`. This edge abstracts the effect of the `cntr` dereference that appears in the `compute` method that is called by the `par` task. The two effects on the edge's destination state abstract the read and write of the `value` field in Line 30.

The presence of a dashed line between two states indicates a potential conflict between those states. For example, the dashed line on the state `[tmp1=this.cntr]` indicates that effects represented by that state can conflict with themselves.

2.3 Optimizing EFSMs

DOJ compiles EFSMs into heap examiners that dynamically compute the heap effects of a task by performing the traversal abstracted by the EFSM. Therefore, edges in an EFSM have a runtime cost — the heap examiner must traverse these edges[1] to compute the set of objects that a task may affect. In many cases, the compiler can statically determine that some of the heap effects in an EFSM can never introduce runtime heap dependences between tasks. Our compiler uses a set of rules to prune irrelevant heap effects from EFSMs. The compiler uses the type of effect (read or write), the allocation site of the affected object, and the affected field to compute whether a given heap effect can conflict (i.e., introduce heap dependences between tasks) with any other heap effect. If a heap effect can never conflict, we can safely prune that heap effect from the EFSM. If an edge in an EFSM does not lead to any conflicting heap effects, there is no reason to traverse that edge and it can be safely pruned from the EFSM, as described in Section 4.4.3. We describe in Section 4.4.4 how our compiler can merge redundant EFSM states to further optimize the heap examiners.

Figure 3 presents the result of pruning the EFSM in Figure 2. The examiner corresponding to this effects graph no longer inspects the `Bar` object referenced by the `inc` field because the compiler has determined that the `Bar` object is only read, so the `inc` reference does not lead to a potentially conflicting heap effect.

2.4 Runtime Checks

DOJ compiles the optimized EFSMs into C code that computes the set of affected objects for each potentially conflicting heap effect. For the example, the heap examiner for the current `par` task instance would first find the `Foo` object referenced by variable `f`, then follow that object's `cntr` field to a `Bar` object. This `Bar` object is compared to the `Bar` objects of all previous instances

[1] More precisely, a heap examiner traverses concrete references that are abstracted by edges in an EFSM.

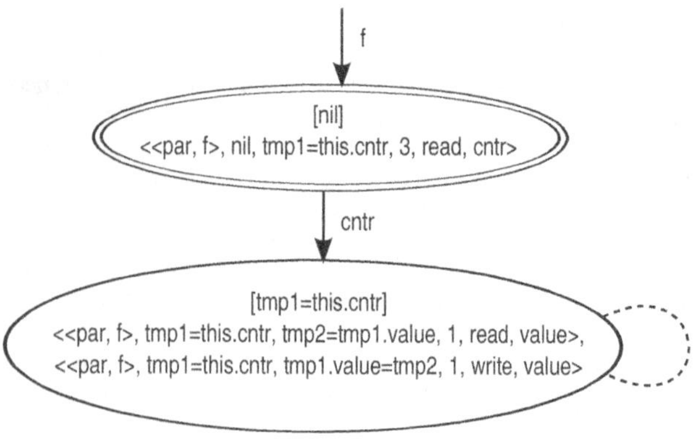

Figure 3. Pruned EFSM

of the `par` task that have not retired. If the `Bar` object for the current `par` task is unique in this collection, the current task can be executed immediately in parallel with all other outstanding `par` task instances.

DOJ combines the precise dynamic check that traverses the heap with a lightweight, coarse-grained conflict detection approach that detects whether two task instances can conflict based only on the static task effects. Both approaches execute concurrently and either approach can detect the absence of heap conflicts.

3. Variable Dependence Analysis

DOJ handles variable dependences using the same approach as OoOJava. In this section, we briefly outline this approach for completeness. A detailed explanation can be found in the OoOJava paper [17]. The basic approach forwards variable values to eliminate variable anti-dependences to enable multiple instances of the same task to execute in parallel.

Recall that a task has a variable dependence on an earlier task if it reads a variable that was last written to by the earlier task. The variable dependence analysis extracts the variable dependences between tasks. Variable dependence analysis abstracts the source of a variable's current value with a variable source tuple. A variable source tuple contains three parts: (1) the name of the task that produced the value, (2) which instance of that task—relative to the most recent dynamic instance—produced the value and (3) the variable to which the task wrote the value. Variable source tuples statically characterize how the program's execution propagates values in variables between tasks. An intra-procedural, data-flow analysis computes the variable source tuples for every live variable at every program point. Variable source tuples provide the necessary information to route the values of variables between tasks.

We next describe how the compiler uses the results of the variable dependence analysis to generate code. We divide code generation for accessing a variable `x` within task t_{curr} into three categories based on the analysis results at the relevant program point:

Immediate Access: When all of the source tuples are from the current task instance t_{curr}, its ancestors, or their siblings, the variable currently stores the actual value. Therefore, the compiler simply generates normal code to access the variable `x` immediately.

Optimized Stall: When all of the source tuples are from a single instance of a child t_{child}, then the compiler knows which dynamic task instance will provide the value for variable `x`. In this case the generated code will stall the current task until t_{child} retires and copy the value of `x`. If the same task can be determined to be the source of other variables, the compiler generates code to also read those values. This optimization avoids extra dynamic checks for future accesses to those variables.

Dynamic Tracking: Otherwise, the variable dependence analysis cannot track the source statically. In this case, the compiler identifies the program points at which the statically known variable sources became unknown. The compiler inserts code at these points to dynamically track which task generates the variable's value.

4. Heap Examiners

Heap dependences pose a challenge for automatically parallelizing code that manipulates data structures. DOJ reasons about a heap access in terms of (1) the heap root used to reach the accessed heap object and (2) the path taken through the heap from the heap root to the affected object. Two tasks can have a heap dependence only when both of the following two conditions are true: (1) one task writes to a field f of an object allocated at site a and a second task either reads or writes to the field f of an object allocated at site a and (2) there must exist a *potentially conflicting object*. A potentially conflicting object is reachable from both tasks by starting from a heap root and following only heap references allowed by statements in the task. We call such a pair of accesses *potentially conflicting accesses*.

4.1 Overview of Approach

Heap examiners inspect the heap prior to executing a task to compute the task's heap dependences. A heap examiner walks the same heap that the task would walk to identify potentially conflicting objects. One challenge is that a task may mutate the heap and then walk across newly created references. The heap examiner cannot mutate the heap, therefore the compiler analysis must convert the task's traversal of the heap into a traversal of the heap as it existed at the beginning of the task.

DOJ calculates heap dependences of a task by checking the set of affected objects against objects that may be accessed by any previously dispatched tasks that have not yet retired. A task may be dispatched as soon as the affected objects identified by its heap examiner will no longer be accessed by any previous task.

To construct a heap examiner, it is possible to simply use a points-to graph to compute all paths to the affected objects, but this approach would result in an overly conservative set of affected objects and unnecessarily incur extra runtime overheads for traversing irrelevant paths. Moreover, consider a relatively common pattern in which multiple tasks update disjoint, localized sections of a data structure (e.g., BarnesHut). Computing affected objects without considering access paths would result in heap examiners that cannot determine that the tasks' updates are disjoint.

DOJ uses static effects to build EFSMs that in turn are compiled into heap examiners. Section 4.2 presents the static heap effects analysis, Section 4.3 presents a method for checking conflicts statically, and Section 4.4 describes how our implementation translates static heap effects into EFSMs that conservatively approximate a task's heap effects dynamically.

4.2 Heap Effects Analysis

While the effects analysis is similar in some aspects to the effects analysis used in OoOJava, the effects analysis for DOJ must extract much more fine-grained information that captures the heap path used to obtain an object reference in order to build an EFSM from a program's heap accesses.

4.2.1 Analysis Domains

DOJ represents an effect as a 6-tuple $\langle h, \mathtt{st}^{\text{from}}, \mathtt{st}^{\text{curr}}, a^{\text{aff}}, o, f\rangle \in U \subseteq H \times ST \times ST \times A \times O \times F$, where h is the heap root used to access the affected object, $\mathtt{st}^{\text{from}}$ is the field or array dereference statement that provided a reference to the affected object, $\mathtt{st}^{curr}$ is the program statement that produced the effect, $a^{aff} \in A$ is the allocation site of the affected object, $o \in O = \{\mathtt{read}, \mathtt{write}\}$ is the operation, and $f \in F$ is the affected field.

Recall that the analysis uses two types of heap roots. The first type of heap root abstracts the objects referenced by a task's input variables (variables live into the task that are accessed by the task). The second type abstracts objects referenced by live variables in sections of a task following the exit of a child task. Formally, a heap root h is given by the tuple $\langle \mathtt{st}, v\rangle \in H \subseteq ST \times V$, where $\mathtt{st}$ is either a stall site or a task entrance, V is the set of variables in the program, and v is the stall site variable or input variable.

The analysis assumes the presence of a pointer analysis. Our implementation uses a flow-sensitive, field-sensitive pointer analysis. We believe that field-sensitivity is important for most Java applications. However, flow-insensitive pointer analysis should be sufficient for the general techniques from DOJ. We assume the pointer analysis abstracts objects with a set of heap nodes $n \in N$ and heap references with a set of edges (points-to set) $e \in E \subseteq V \times N \cup N \times F \times N$. We define helper functions $E(\mathtt{x}) = \{\langle \mathtt{x}, n\rangle \in E\}$ and $E(\mathtt{x}, \mathtt{f}) = \{\langle n, \mathtt{f}, n'\rangle \in E \mid \langle \mathtt{x}, n\rangle \in E\}$. We assume that the pointer analysis provides a function $\mathcal{A}$ that maps heap nodes to allocation sites. Though we assume a heap node abstracts objects allocated at only one site, modifications to support pointer analyses in which heap nodes abstract objects allocated at multiple sites are straightforward. The analysis computes at each program point the mapping $R \subseteq E \times H \times ST$ from an edge to both (1) the heap root and (2) the last dereference statement in the sequence of dereferences that were used to reach the edge's target. At each program point, the analysis also computes a set of variables $\mathcal{L}$ for which the application may have to stall before accessing the object they reference. The set $\mathcal{L}$ only includes variables if they reference data structures with conflicts.

The mapping R and set $\mathcal{L}$ both form lattices. The partial order ($\sqsubseteq$) is defined by the subset relation ($\subseteq$); join ($\sqcup$) is set union ($\cup$); bottom ($\bot$) is the empty set ($\emptyset$); and top ($\top$) is the maximally full set. The lattices have finite heights because their domains are finite.

The analysis generates a set of effects U for the program. Note that there is only one set of effects for the entire program.

4.2.2 Transfer Functions

For pedagogical purposes, we decompose the effects analysis into two passes. The first pass computes the mapping R from edges in the points-to graph to the heap roots used to access the edges' target objects. The second pass then uses the mapping R to compute the application's set of effects U. Our actual implementation integrates both analyses into the pointer analysis implementation. Figure 4 presents the transfer functions for computing the mapping R from edges to heap roots. The analysis introduces new heap roots into points-to graphs at two classes of statements: (1) task enter statements and (2) statements of a parent task that may have to stall to avoid heap conflicts with a child task. These statements create new heap roots for the corresponding variable's edges. Heap roots are then subsequently propagated to newly created references because we are interested in determining which heap root was used to access an affected object.

The heap roots analysis uses a simple supporting analysis to pre-compute which variable accesses may require stalls. This supporting analysis is relevant for sections of code following the exit of a task. The goal of this analysis is to compute the set of variables $\mathcal{L}$ for which accesses to the objects referenced by these variables may require a stall to wait for heap dependences on child tasks to resolve. Figure 4 presents the transfer functions for computing the set $\mathcal{L}$. At the exit of a child task, the set $\mathcal{L}$ contains all live variables that reference objects. At the entrance of a task, the set $\mathcal{L}$ is empty

st	$R' = (R_a - \text{KILL}) \cup \text{GEN}$
`x = ...`	$\text{KILL} = \{\forall\langle e, h, \mathtt{st}^{\text{from}}\rangle \in R \mid e \in E(\mathtt{x})\}$
`x = new`	$R_a = R$ $\text{GEN} = \emptyset$ $\mathcal{L}' = \mathcal{L} \backslash \{\mathtt{x}\}$
`x = y`	$R_a = R$ $\text{GEN} = \{\langle\langle \mathtt{x}, n\rangle, h, \mathtt{st}^{\text{from}}\rangle \mid \forall\langle \mathtt{y}, n\rangle \in E,$ $\langle\langle \mathtt{y}, n\rangle, h, \mathtt{st}^{\text{from}}\rangle \in R\}$ $\mathcal{L}' = \{v \in V \mid (v \in \mathcal{L} \wedge v \neq \mathtt{x}) \vee (\mathtt{y} \in \mathcal{L} \wedge v = \mathtt{x})\}$
`x = y.f`	$R_a = R \cup \{\langle\langle \mathtt{y}, n\rangle, \langle \mathtt{st}, \mathtt{y}\rangle, nil\rangle \mid \forall\langle \mathtt{y}, n\rangle \in E, \mathtt{y} \in \mathcal{L}\}$ $\text{GEN} = \{\langle\langle \mathtt{x}, n'\rangle, h, \mathtt{st}^{\text{from}}\rangle \mid \forall\langle n, \mathtt{f}, n'\rangle \in E(\mathtt{y}, \mathtt{f}),$ $(\langle\langle n, \mathtt{f}, n'\rangle, h, \mathtt{st}^{\text{from}}\rangle \in R_a\}$ $\cup \{\langle\langle \mathtt{x}, n'\rangle, h, \mathtt{st}^{\mathtt{x=y.f}}\rangle \mid \forall\langle n, \mathtt{f}, n'\rangle \in E(\mathtt{y}, \mathtt{f}),$ $\langle\langle \mathtt{y}, n\rangle, h, \mathtt{st}^{\text{from}}\rangle \in R_a)\}$ $\mathcal{L}' = \mathcal{L} \backslash \{\mathtt{x}, \mathtt{y}\}$
`x.f = y`	$R_a = R \cup \{\langle\langle \mathtt{x}, n\rangle, \langle \mathtt{st}, \mathtt{x}\rangle, nil\rangle \mid \forall\langle \mathtt{x}, n\rangle \in E, \mathtt{x} \in \mathcal{L}\}$ $\cup \{\langle\langle \mathtt{y}, n\rangle, \langle \mathtt{st}, \mathtt{y}\rangle, nil\rangle \mid \forall\langle \mathtt{y}, n\rangle \in E, \mathtt{y} \in \mathcal{L}\}$ $\text{KILL} = \emptyset$ $\text{GEN} = \{\langle\langle n, \mathtt{f}, n'\rangle, h, \mathtt{st}^{\text{from}}\rangle \mid \forall\langle \mathtt{x}, n\rangle \in E, \forall\langle \mathtt{y}, n'\rangle \in E,$ $\langle\langle \mathtt{y}, n'\rangle, h, \mathtt{st}^{\text{from}}\rangle \in R_a\}$ $\mathcal{L}' = \mathcal{L} \backslash \{\mathtt{x}, \mathtt{y}\}$
$\mathtt{enter}(t_{\text{curr}})$	$R_a = R$ $\text{KILL} = \{\langle e, \langle \mathtt{st}, v\rangle, \mathtt{st}^{\text{from}}\rangle \mid \mathtt{st} \text{ is a stall site}\}$ $\text{GEN} = \{\langle\langle v, n\rangle, \langle t_{\text{curr}}, v\rangle, nil\rangle \mid v \text{ is an input variable for}$ $t_{\text{curr}} \wedge \langle v, n\rangle \in E\}$ $\mathcal{L}' = \emptyset$
$\mathtt{exit}(t_{\text{curr}})$	$R_a = R$ $\text{KILL} = \{\langle e, \langle \mathtt{st}, v\rangle, \mathtt{st}^{\text{from}}\rangle \mid \mathtt{st} \text{ is a stall site} \vee v \text{ is an input}$ $\text{variable for the current instance of } t_{\text{curr}}\}$ $\text{GEN} = \emptyset$ $\mathcal{L}' = V$

Figure 4. Transfer Functions for Computing Heap Roots

st	$U' = U \cup GEN$
`x=y.f`	$\text{GEN} = \{\langle h, \mathtt{st}^{\text{from}}, \mathtt{st}^{\mathtt{x=y.f}}, \mathcal{A}(n), \mathtt{read}, \mathtt{f}\rangle \mid \forall\langle \mathtt{y}, n\rangle \in E,$ $\langle\langle \mathtt{y}, n\rangle, h, \mathtt{st}^{\text{from}}\rangle \in R_a\}$
`x.f=y`	$\text{GEN} = \{\langle h, \mathtt{st}^{\text{from}}, \mathtt{st}^{\mathtt{x.f=y}}, \mathcal{A}(n), \mathtt{write}, \mathtt{f}\rangle \mid \forall\langle \mathtt{x}, n\rangle \in E,$ $\langle\langle \mathtt{x}, n\rangle, h, \mathtt{st}^{\text{from}}\rangle \in R_a\}$

Figure 5. Transfer Functions for Generating Effects

because all data structures can be accessed without needing to stall for child tasks. The transfer functions for $\mathcal{L}$ remove a variable at a statement that reads the variable and therefore serves as a potential stall site for the data structure referenced by the variable.

Figure 5 presents the transfer functions for computing heap effects. Load statements and store statements are the only statements that operate on object fields in the heap and therefore are relevant for collecting effects. These transfer functions record for each field access: the heap root that was used to reach the object, the allocation site of the object, the operation, and the field that the statement accessed. The analysis simply accumulates effects into a global set U. Note that the effects analysis treats array operations as normal field accesses on a special array field.

4.2.3 Interprocedural Extension

Our implementation contains an interprocedural extension to the heap roots and effects analyses. This interprocedural analysis propagates the heap root annotations from the caller to the callee. Then it merges heap root annotations from all callers to a method and analyzes a single context. When mapping analysis results from a callee back to the caller context, the interprocedural analysis uses a call graph to identify and remove heap root annotations that are impossible in the given caller context. This process preserves analysis precision by preventing the erroneous propagation of heap roots from one caller to another, while avoiding the cost of analyzing multiple caller contexts.

4.3 Static Conflict Detection

DOJ considers a task to have a heap dependence on an earlier task when both of the following two conditions are true: (1) the two tasks are siblings or a parent stall site/child task pair and (2) the effects of the two tasks conflict. Note that we attribute all of a child task's effects to its parent, which confines the possible dependence relations to those identified in (1). This simplifies static conflict detection and dynamic dependence tracking.

Consider a task t_0 with the effect $\langle h_0, \mathtt{st}_0^{\mathrm{from}}, \mathtt{st}_0^{\mathrm{curr}}, a_0^{\mathrm{aff}}, o_0, f_0\rangle$ and a task t_1 with the effect $\langle h_1, \mathtt{st}_1^{\mathrm{from}}, \mathtt{st}_1^{\mathrm{curr}}, a_1^{\mathrm{aff}}, o_1, f_1\rangle$. DOJ conservatively assumes all such effects conflict with the following exceptions:

1. If $a_0^{\mathrm{aff}} \neq a_1^{\mathrm{aff}}$, then there is no conflict because the objects must be different if they were allocated at different sites.
2. If $o_0 = o_1 = \mathtt{read}$, then there is no conflict because reads do not conflict.
3. If $f_0 \neq f_1$, then there is no conflict because the two effects access different fields.

4.4 Dynamic Conflict Detection

Imprecision in static effects analyses often makes them insufficient to parallelize programs. This imprecision arises because their abstractions collapse many objects into a single static heap node. Consider two instances of the same task that update disjoint objects. The updated objects are likely to be represented by the same static heap node, and therefore the static analysis results do not contain enough information to determine that the two task instances do not conflict. In addition to directly using the static analysis results to detect possible conflicts, DOJ uses the results of the effects analysis to generate heap examiners. Heap examiners traverse the heap reachable from a task's heap roots to compute at runtime the set of concrete objects that are the target of statically identified effects. The runtime is able to resolve conflicts with better precision than static analysis by computing the concrete targets of the effects.

4.4.1 Generating the Effects Finite State Machine

DOJ generates a heap examiner for each heap root in the program. This process begins by generating an EFSM. The EFSM captures all of the effects of the task on the part of the heap reachable from the given heap root. The compiler begins to generate an EFSM for a heap root by first collecting all of the effects for the given heap root. We formalize the EFSM as a collection of states $\phi \in \Phi$, and a collection of transitions between the states $\langle \phi^{\mathrm{from}}, f, \phi^{\mathrm{to}}\rangle \in T \subseteq \Phi \times F \times \Phi$. The effects map $\mathcal{M} \subseteq \Phi \times U$ maps states in the EFSM to the set of effects associated with that state.

The compiler initially generates a state in the EFSM for each program statement that appears in an effect in the heap root's effect set and a special initial state, *nil*. We formalize the initial mapping of program statements to states with the function $\mathcal{S} : ST \rightarrow \Phi$.

For each effect $\langle h, \mathtt{x = y.f}, \mathtt{st}^{\mathrm{curr}}, a^{\mathrm{aff}}, o, f\rangle$, if the field f references an object, the compiler adds the transition $\langle \mathcal{S}(\mathtt{x = y.f}), f, \mathcal{S}(\mathtt{st}^{\mathrm{curr}})\rangle$ to the EFSM. Note that if the field f stores a primitive, the compiler does not add a transition to the EFSM. In either case, the compiler then adds the effects mapping pair $\langle \mathcal{S}(\mathtt{x = y.f}), \langle h, \mathtt{x = y.f}, \mathtt{st}^{\mathrm{curr}}, a^{\mathrm{aff}}, o, f\rangle\rangle$ to the map $\mathcal{M}$.

4.4.2 Computing Static Conflicts

The compiler next computes the set of potentially conflicting effects C for each EFSM. The computation begins by identifying all potentially concurrently executing EFSMs (including other instances of itself). Potentially concurrently executing EFSMs are those that share a parent task; the parent task of a stall site EFSM is the task in which the stall site appears. An exception is that two stall site EFSMs with the same parent can never execute simultaneously and therefore can never conflict.

For each effect e in the EFSM, the analysis looks for a potentially conflicting effect in a potentially concurrently executing EFSM. If such an effect is found, the effect e is added to the EFSM's set of conflicting effects C.

4.4.3 Pruning the EFSM

The EFSM will be used to generate a heap examiner that computes at runtime the exact concrete objects that a given effect could apply to. An EFSM may contain effects that the analysis determines can never cause a conflict. In this case, the heap examiner does not need to compute which objects such an effect could apply to. Pruning such effects from the EFSM is beneficial as it optimizes the corresponding examiner by removing extraneous work.

DOJ applies the following rules to prune EFSMs until no rule applies:

1. **Irrelevant Transitions:** If there is no path from a given transition to some state with a potentially conflicting effect, then the code block will never conflict on an object that is reached through this transition. The compiler prunes such transitions.
2. **Irrelevant Effects:** If an effect has no conflicts and no corresponding transition, the effect is irrelevant and therefore the compiler prunes it.

4.4.4 Merging States in the EFSM

The algorithm as described can generate EFSMs with multiple transitions that each read the same field of an object in the same state. While it is possible that such transitions can improve the precision of heap examiners, we expect that they typically serve only to add additional runtime overhead. The compiler therefore includes a merging phase that merges extraneous states with the goal of reducing runtime overhead.

When the analysis identifies pairs of transitions that originate from the same state and read the same field of objects from the same allocation state, it merges the destination states of those transitions.

4.4.5 Compiling EFSMs

DOJ compiles the pruned EFSMs into heap examiners. We begin our presentation with the basic compilation approach and will later discuss optimizations. Examiners are structured as a graph traversal with a `tovisit` queue that stores objects to be visited and a `discovered` set that stores which objects have been discovered. The body of the loop is a `switch` statement on the state of the object, with a case for each state in the pruned EFSM. Each case contains a nested `switch` statement on the allocation site of the object, with a case for each allocation site in the given state of the EFSM. The case for an allocation site examines each field for which the state has an outgoing edge for the given allocation site.

Figure 6 presents a heap examiner for the pruned effects graph from Figure 3. The case statement in Line 10 examines the `cntr` field of objects in the initial state from allocation site 3. The case

```
1  void parExaminer(Object f) {
2    Pair pinit=new Pair(f, INITSTATE);
3    tovisit.push(pinit);
4    discovered.add(pinit);
5    while(!tovisit.isEmpty()) {
6      Pair p=tovisit.pop();
7      switch(p->state) {
8        case INITSTATE:
9          switch(p->obj->allocSite) {
10           case 3:
11             Object cntr=p->obj->cntr;
12             Pair pcntr=new Pair(cntr, CNTRSTATE);
13             if (cntr!=NULL &&
14                 !discovered.contains(pcntr)) {
15               discovered.add(pcntr);
16               tovisit.push(pcntr);
17             }
18             break;
19         }
20         break;
21       case CNTRSTATE:
22         switch(p->obj->allocSite) {
23           case 1:
24             addWriteEffect(p->obj);
25             break;
26         }
27         break;
28     }
29   }
30 }
```

Figure 6. Examiner for the Heap Root `f`

statement in Line 23 processes the write effect for objects from allocation site 1.

Tree Structure Optimization While the heap examiner compilation strategy must support data structures with arbitrary possibly-cyclic structures, many data structures contain components with tree-like structures. DOJ optimizes traversals of these tree-like components. We note that all cycles in an EFSM must contain at least one state with two or more incoming edges. The traversal loop only contains case statements for heap nodes that are either (1) referenced directly by the heap root variable or (2) have two or more incoming edges. From each such heap node, the compiler inlines the traversal code for the part of the EFSM that is transitively reachable from that node through nodes with at most one incoming reference. One side effect of this optimization is that an object can potentially be traversed more than once, for example when every element of an array references a single object, however such duplication is safe and the traversal is guaranteed to terminate.

Figure 7 presents the tree-optimized EFSM for the example. The traversal of objects allocated at site 1 has been inlined into the case statement for objects allocated at site 3.

Heap Examiner Conflicts Heap conflicts can cause naïve heap examining strategies to traverse the wrong set of objects. Figure 8 illustrates the potential issue. Consider three tasks given in execution order: the first with the heap root `f`, the second with the heap root `g`, and the third with the heap root `h`. The heap examiner for the second task could potentially read the wrong reference from the `x` field of the `Baz` object if it started before the first task finished. Reading the wrong reference could cause the heap examiner to wrongly conclude that the second and third task do not have a conflict even if they access the same instance of class `Foz`.

If a heap examiner traverses a reference for which it has a potential read conflict on the specific object, the examiner must stall until the conflicting task instance retires. When necessary, the compiler generates code to implement a heap examiner stall.

A heap examiner can also conflict with its own task instance if that instance begins executing before its heap examiner terminates

```
void parExaminer(Object f) {
  Pair pinit=new Pair(f, INITSTATE);
  tovisit.push(pinit);
  discovered.add(pinit);
  while(!tovisit.isEmpty()) {
    Pair p=tovisit.pop();
    switch(p->state) {
      case INITSTATE:
        switch(p->obj->allocSite) {
          case 3:
            Object cntr=o->cntr;
            if (cntr!=NULL && cntr->allocSite==1)
              addWriteEffect(o);
            break;
        }
        break;
    }
  }
}
```

Figure 7. Tree Optimization of the Examiner for the Heap Root `f`

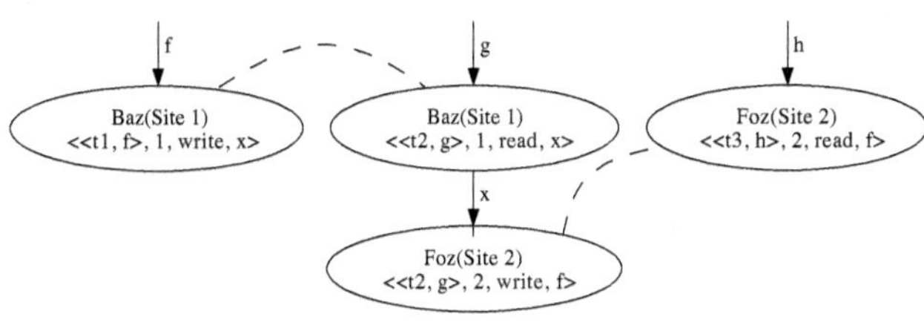

Figure 8. Heap Examiner Conflicts

(this can occur if the static check clears the task instance to execute). Specifically, if a task instance (1) reads from a reference field and uses the reference to perform potentially conflicting accesses (so the heap examiner will traverse the field) and (2) later overwrites the reference field, then the task instance can conflict with its own heap examiner. Our compiler statically identifies such dereferences in the EFSM and then generates a check after the dereference to verify that the task instance has not started executing. If the task has already started, the heap examiner stops traversing the heap and stalls to wait for the task to retire.

Weakly-Connected Components Extension The traversal of heap roots can be parallelized by separating the pruned EFSMs into weakly-connected components. This enables two optimizations: turning off individual heap examiners in favor of static resolution and parallelizing the heap examiners.

5. Runtime System

DOJ is architected as a set of *worker threads* that each contain a local work queue and implement a work stealing scheduling strategy. The DOJ compiler converts the entire program into tasks, with a wrapper task for the program's `main` method. DOJ supports hierarchical composition of tasks — tasks can dispatch other tasks. We refer to a worker thread that is currently executing a task that dispatches child tasks as a *parent thread*.

DOJ uses two approaches in parallel to determine whether a task may perform heap accesses that conflict with previously dispatched but not retired tasks. The first approach performs a dynamic object traversal to precisely determine conflicts, but can potentially take a long time. There is a companion *heap examiner thread* that implements this approach for each parent thread. The heap examiner thread examines the actual heap to determine whether the current task conflicts with previous dispatched, but not retired tasks. The heap examiner thread uses a *heap scoreboard* to detect potential conflicts between tasks. The second approach is based on static analysis results and is imprecise, but extremely fast. Each parent thread implements this approach with a *static effects queue* that uses static heap effects as determined by the compiler to detect conflicts between tasks. A task no longer has a conflict when its static effects queue reports all previously dispatched tasks with potential conflicts have retired. If either approach shows the absence of a potential conflict, DOJ dispatches the task. Intuitively, the combination of these two approaches works well because when the heap examiner resolves conflicts quickly the system can expose the parallelism, while static effects queues limit the worst case overheads for dynamically checking very large data structures.

5.1 Task Records

Each task instance has a *task record*. Each task record has a `NumUnresolvedDependences` count of the task's unresolved dependences; when this count reaches zero all of the task's dependences have resolved and the task can be safely executed. This count is updated by an atomic subtract instruction; updates to the count never need to obtain a lock. There is a structure in the task record for each heap root. This structure contains a `QueueDependences` count that tracks how many static queues the task record must clear to show the absence of a conflict for the given heap root. The structure also contains the `ObjDependences` count that tracks how many objects must clear the heap scoreboard to show the absence of a conflict for this heap root. The `ObjectList` contains a list of heap scoreboard bins that contain objects for this heap root that must be removed when the task retires. If the heap scoreboard clears the heap root, it zeros the `QueueDependences` count. Whichever approach zeros the `QueueDependences` count first for a heap root decrements the task's `NumUnresolvedDependences` count. Locks are never acquired to update these counters as the compiler generates atomic instructions to perform the updates.

If the static effects queue determines the absence of a conflict, it is possible for a task to retire before the task's heap examiners finish. When the task retires, its `DoneExecuting` flag is set. When this flag is set, the heap examiner stops and clears the traversal flag to indicate that it has halted. The task retire procedure then removes the traversed objects for the task from the heap scoreboard. If the heap examiner has not started, the task retire procedure uses an atomic operation on the traversal status flag to prevent the heap examiners for the given task record from traversing its heap roots.

5.2 Heap Scoreboards

DOJ uses a heap scoreboard to track at the object granularity the potentially conflicting heap effects between tasks. Figure 9 illustrates the heap scoreboard data structure. The heap scoreboard is implemented as an array of *access queues*. The array is indexed by the hash of the affected object's object identifier.[2]

Each access queue keeps track of potential conflicts between tasks that access objects whose object identifiers hash to that queue. Access queues are implemented as a singly linked list. The heap effects of newly dispatched tasks are enqueued at the tail. Once a heap effect for a task t reaches the head of an access queue, the given effect does not conflict with any task that was dispatched before task t. We say that such effects are *resolved*. When a task retires, its heap effects are removed from the access queues.

Access queues contain two types of nodes: *read nodes* and *write nodes*. Read nodes track read effects; read effects do not conflict with each other. Therefore all consecutive read effects resolve when as a group they are at the head of the access queue. Write nodes track write effects; write effects conflict with each other and read effects. Therefore a write effect can resolve only when it reaches the head of its access queue. Each node stores both the task and a mask bitmap of the task heap roots for which that item tracks conflicts. It is important to note that a heap examiner inserts only objects with potentially conflicting effects into the heap scoreboard.

While only one heap examiner thread inserts objects into a given heap scoreboard, multiple threads can remove objects or resolve heap roots. The heap scoreboard uses atomic exchange operations on the `head` fields on the bins to lock a bin.

We typically size heap scoreboards to have a hundred thousand or more bins. False conflicts can occur if two objects hash to the same bin and in theory reduce the available parallelism. In practice, our heap scoreboards contain enough bins to prevent such conflicts from limiting parallelism in most applications.

We note that a task can retire before it clears either the heap scoreboard or static effects queues. Both data structures have been designed to allow entries to retire before they reach the head.

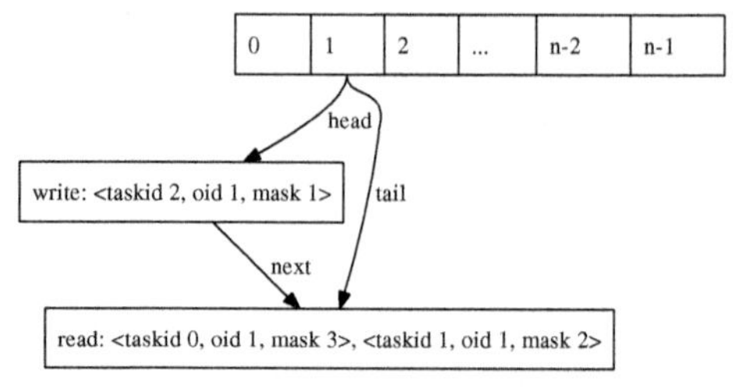

Figure 9. Heap Scoreboard

5.3 Static Effects Queue

DOJ uses a static effects queue to quickly track potentially conflicting accesses between tasks. DOJ generates a *conflict graph* from the results of the static analysis described in Section 4.2. A conflict graph has a node for each heap root of each task; there is an edge between two nodes if the corresponding code blocks may have a conflicting access through the corresponding heap roots. DOJ compiles the conflict graph into static effects queues that dynamically track the conflicts. The mapping problem can be viewed as a graph covering problem; to enforce the data dependence constraints, all edges in a conflict graph must be covered. The algorithm uses a greedy algorithm to try to minimize the number of queues used to cover the edges in the conflict graph.

A static effects queue has two types of queue items: a sequential item and a parallel item. A sequential item holds one task and that task must wait until the previous queue item retires and must retire before the next queue item begins. A parallel item holds multiple tasks that can execute in parallel. Each item stores both the task and a bitmap of the heap roots for which the item tracks conflicts.

6. Evaluation

We have implemented DOJ and evaluated it on a 1.9 GHz 24-core AMD Magny-Cour Opteron with 16 GB of memory. Our compiler generates C code which is then compiled by GCC. We enabled the highest optimization level in GCC and classic optimizations in our compiler. Our implementation and benchmarks are available at `http://demsky.eecs.uci.edu/compiler.php`.

We selected a diverse set of benchmarks to provide an interesting cross-section of application behaviors and a variety of algorithmic structures and ported them to DOJ. We included all of the large benchmarks from the Java Grande Benchmark suite [27], namely RayTracer, MolDyn, MonteCarlo, SOR, and Crypt. We selected Power and Voronoi from the JOlden benchmark suite [5],

[2] We use object identifiers instead of object pointers to support garbage collection without having to rebuild the heap scoreboard.

Benchmark	Lines	Compilation Times Sequential	OoOJava	DOJ	Speedup OoOJava	DOJ
Voronoi	4,007	3.41s	>1hr†	13.26s	N/A†	10.27×
BarnesHut	3,771	2.98s	N/A†	3.67s	N/A†	11.26×
RayTracer	3,683	1.99s	52.69s	4.18s	18.52×	18.07×
Tracking	5,419	4.31s	851.45s	6.83s	19.83×	20.05×
Crypt	2,765	1.91s	4.57s	2.63s	18.88×	19.47×
MonteCarlo	6,281	1.85s	14.45s	2.90s	22.08×	21.16×
KMeans	3,868	2.05s	13.53s	3.29s	12.60×	11.46×
MolDyn	2,565	2.04s	20.42s	4.09s	14.10×	13.91×
Power	2,565	1.94s	15.47s	2.58s	19.99×	5.58×
Labyrinth (a)	4,923	2.35s	171.52s	5.09s	11.31×	0.70×
Labyrinth (b)	4,923	2.35s	171.52s	5.09s	10.43×	9.99×
SOR	3,028	1.78s	4.65s	3.25s	9.88×	12.90×
MergeSort	2,610	1.67s	3.02s	2.14s	12.50×	10.65×

Figure 10. Compilation Times (Smaller is Better) and Speedups(Higher is Better)‡

MergeSort from DPJ suite [4], Tracking from SD-VBS [30], and BarnesHut from Lonestar [19]. We selected both KMeans and Labyrinth from the STAMP benchmark suite [6] to explore benchmarks with irregular parallelism. STAMP categorizes benchmarks by metrics; KMeans and Labyrinth were categorized at opposite points on all metrics. We compiled and executed three versions of the benchmarks: *sequential* is the original sequential version, *DOJ* is the DOJ version, and *OoOJava* is the OoOJava version.

6.1 Compilation Times

A major advantage of DOJ over previous work on OoOJava is compilation time. We compiled each benchmark on a 2.27GHz 8-core Intel Nehalem Xeon with 12GB of memory. Figure 10 presents the time taken to compile each benchmark into C code. DOJ took on average 4.49 seconds to compile the benchmarks and at most 13.26 seconds. This is on average 31.15× faster than OoOJava and at most 124.69× faster than OoOJava.

6.2 Performance

We next present performance data derived from execution times averaged over 10 runs. For each experiment we computed the standard error as a percentage of the benchmark's average total execution time. The average standard error across our benchmark suite was 1.8% with a 6.1% maximum error.

Figures 10 and 11 present speedups of the benchmark implementations generated by OoOJava and DOJ over the original sequential versions (without tasks) compiled with the same compiler. DOJ dedicates one or more cores to execute heap examiners while the other cores execute tasks, placing an upper bound of 23× on the observed speedups ignoring improvements due to cache effects. OoOJava does not dedicate any cores to a runtime component, so the upper bound for OoOJava speedups is 24×. With that in mind, the speedups observed for DOJ implementations are almost as good as—and in some cases better than—the OoOJava implementations.

Figure 12 presents the speedup curves as a function of the number of cores for the DOJ versions. We have omitted results for benchmarks that use a divide and conquer structure as they do naturally run on arbitrary numbers of cores. We observe that most benchmarks scale well to the number of cores in our test system. Note that these benchmarks use a flat task structure; restructuring the benchmarks to use hierarchically structured tasks would of course enable them to scale to much larger core counts.

†OoOJava is overly conservative for BarnesHut and cannot generate a meaningful parallel implementation. For Voronoi, OoOJava did not complete its heap analysis within the hour we allocated.

‡All speedups are reported relative to sequential, statically compiled Java code with no tasks.

Voronoi has a divide-and-conquer algorithm with a sequential merge that limits parallelism. OoOJava's compilation of Voronoi did not terminate within an hour. However, DOJ generated a parallel Voronoi implementation that achieved a significant speedup.

OoOJava cannot generate a meaningful parallel implementation of BarnesHut because all bodies are reachable from each other and limitations of the approach prevent it from determining that updates to bodies are localized. In contrast, DOJ can generate heap examiners from static effects that allow many non-conflicting updates to proceed in parallel on the single oct-tree that models the computation, which achieved a significant speedup.

DOJ achieved nearly identical performance to OoOJava for the RayTracer, Tracking, and Crypt benchmarks.

MonteCarlo has a highly parallel workload of independent simulations and a sequential task that aggregates the results.

Parallelism in KMeans is limited by a non-trivial serial computation following each parallel iteration of the clustering algorithm. The serial computation is executed in a separate task which, by virtue of having three heap roots leading to possible effects, requires three heap examiners. In this case, the conflicts are between consecutive instances of the sequential task and with heap accesses made by the parent thread following the last iteration. The heap examiner efficiency is sufficient to extract the parallelism in KMeans.

Parallelism in MolDyn is similar to KMeans; however, the parallel task instances in MolDyn read from many particle objects that conflict with the particle updates in the sequential task. In this case the dynamic analysis visits many objects yet still is able to extract much parallelism.

We parallelized Power by partitioning each sub-tree of the power simulation into a task. Power is a challenging benchmark for DOJ because it performs a lightweight computation that modifies a very large number of objects. The heap examiners generated by DOJ traverses 49,140 objects per parallel phase, 26,040 of which are updated and therefore potentially conflicting. Even with such a large set of potentially conflicting updates and a relatively lightweight computation, DOJ still achieved a significant speedup.

Labyrinth is an interesting case of a speculative algorithm that can be successfully parallelized with a deterministic system. Our first experiment resulted in an execution time worse than the sequential version, shown as Labyrinth (a) in Figure 10. Each parallel task is assigned a copy of the three-dimensional array that represents the maze and calculates routes that may conflict with other routes proposed in parallel. The grid dimensions were originally specified in the order 512×512×7. A set of scratch grids is recycled among parallel tasks and in order to check that components of the scratch grid are not shared with another parallel task, a heap examiner must traverse all of the 262,144 (512×512) one dimension component array objects. In the worst case DOJ is designed to run only marginally slower than a sequential execution, because static effect queues will resolve conflicts ahead of heap examiners and allow execution of all tasks in the original sequential order. The slowdown from Labyrinth is not caused by DOJ but from Labyrinth's speculative approach to parallelism that discards conflicting routes. We verified this hypothesis by reducing the parallel batch size to one, which results in an execution that takes approximately the same time as the sequential version because no solutions are discarded. When we transformed the input to an equivalent problem with reordered dimensions, namely 7×512×512, the heap examiners must still visit 3,584 objects but are able to resolve conflicts quickly enough to achieve a significant speedup, reported as Labyrinth (b). While it is straightforward to handle multidimensional arrays as a special case, Labyrinth provided an interesting example of the limits of DOJ.

The speedup for SOR is limited because the benchmark is memory bandwidth-limited. Tasks access a large amount of data relative

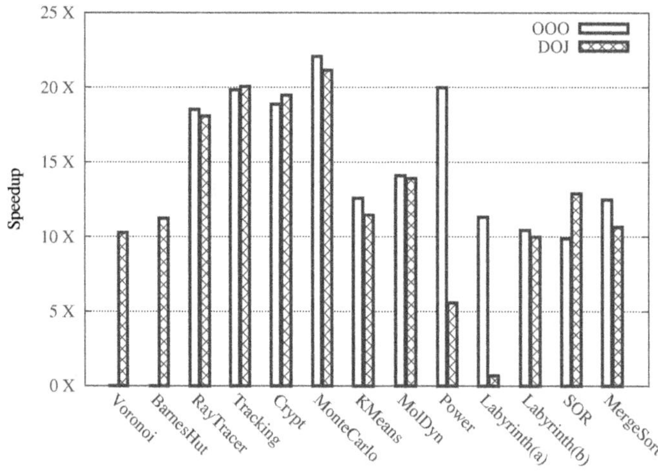

Figure 11. Benchmark Speedups Plot (Higher is Better)‡

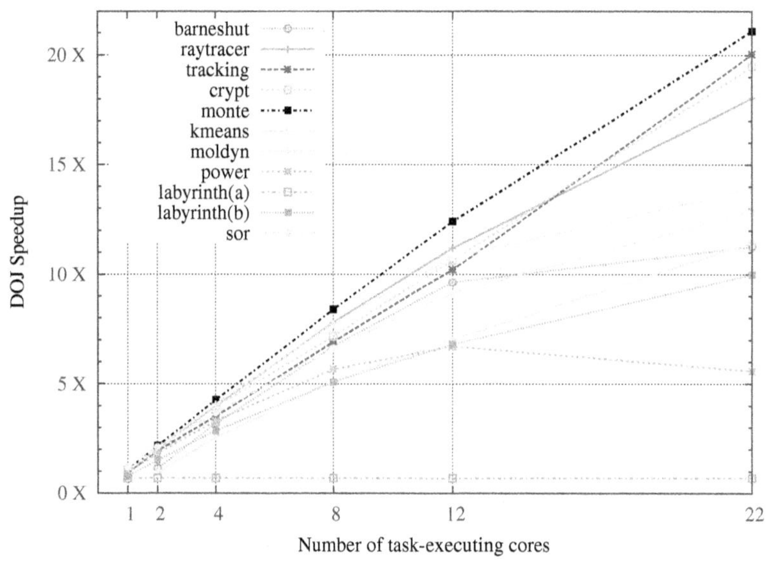

Figure 12. DOJ Speedups Scaling (Higher is Better)‡

to the computation requiring significant memory bandwidth. We confirmed this by measuring the average execution of the parallel tasks for a 23-worker implementation and a 2-worker implementation of SOR. The body of parallel tasks for this benchmark performs no synchronization or system calls, so differences in execution time can only be attributed to the memory system. For 23-workers the average execution of the parallel task is 329,189 processor cycles and for 2 workers, 222,429 processor cycles.

DOJ achieved a better speedup for SOR than OoOJava because of differences in the runtime components. The generated heap examiners in the DOJ version perform traversals with no depth, and so perform a simple dynamic check similar to the check in OoOJava. However, OoOJava's runtime conflict queues must support a wider variety of ordering constraints than DOJ. As a result, DOJ can be more heavily optimized and for SOR outperforms OoOJava.

MergeSort from DPJ has a sequential merge phase that limits parallelism at all levels of recursion. However, DOJ still achieved a significant speedup.

6.3 Implementation Overheads

We measured task dispatch overhead for a microbenchmark that issues 500,000 lightweight tasks. The average time over ten executions to dispatch a task was 1886 processor cycles on the AMD Magny-Cour Opteron. For comparison, we conducted this experiment on an 8-core Intel Nehalem Xeon and measured the average of ten executions to be 982 processor cycles.

To quantify the overhead of our compiler, we compared the generated code against the OpenJDK JVM 14.0-b16 and GCC. The sequential version of Crypt compiled with our compiler ran 4.6% faster than on the JVM. We also developed a C++ version compiled with GCC and found our compiler's version ran 25% slower than the C++ version. Our compiler implements array bounds checking; with array bounds checking disabled, the binary from our compiler runs only 5.4% slower than the C++ binary. We used the optimization flag -O3 for the C++ version as well as for the underlying C code generated by our compiler. This is in close agreement with more extensive experiments on six benchmarks that we performed in earlier publications. Those experiments measured an average overhead for our compiler with array bounds checks disabled of 4.9% relative to GCC.

6.4 Parallelization Discussion

Our parallelization efforts typically began by profiling a benchmark and selecting computationally expensive blocks to enclose in tasks. We found task annotations easy to use; an inexperienced undergraduate ported the first version of Labyrinth. On average we changed only 20 lines of each benchmark.

Several of the benchmarks had a top-level loop to distribute work, making the placement of tasks easy. For other benchmarks our typical process for inserting tasks started with identifying a sequence of computationally intensive code that we expected (1) would be often repeated and (2) had no dependences between instances; we wrapped such a block in a task. Next we looked for statements dependent on the output of the parallel task along the execution path back to the definition of the parallel task. Many loops in our benchmarks worth parallelizing had parallel work at the beginning of the loop body followed by a sequence of iteration-interdependent statements in the rest of the body. Our goal was to enclose in a task any statements that would stall the parent thread from issuing new parallel task instances. Benchmarks like RayTracer and Monte had partially parallel loops that were easily partitioned into one parallel task and one sequential task.

7. Related Work

Several approaches to parallelism rely on correct developer annotations including OpenMP [7], Cilk [22], and JCilk [9]. Annotation errors in such systems can cause data races. A major advantage of DOJ is that annotation errors never cause correctness concerns.

Functional languages [20] provide strong correctness guarantees for parallel programs by prohibiting state mutation. Macro-dataflow languages [8, 14, 33] leverage the dataflow approach on larger granularity code segments. DOJ can be viewed as a system for executing sequential code using a dataflow execution model.

Speculative programming models [2, 10, 31, 32] offer a similar programming model as DOJ but can incur significant overheads to support rollback—possibly even repeated rollbacks—in the case of mis-speculation. DOJ avoids the rollback overhead by verifying that a task can safely run to completion before starting the task.

OoOJava [16, 17] uses the same programming model as DOJ. OoOJava uses sophisticated static disjoint reachability analysis [18, 21] to parallelize programs. DOJ borrows variable dependence analysis from OoOJava and significantly extends OoOJava's effects analysis to extract sufficient information to implement heap examiners. DOJ removes the need for a static reachability analysis and therefore can scale to larger code bases. DOJ's dynamic strategy relies less on the precision of static analysis and can determine the absence of conflicts even when paths exist between the conflicting objects. Moreover, DOJ can determine that tasks affect only a localized part of a data structure, while OoOJava assumes that a task can affect any reachable part of the data structure.

Synchronization Via Scheduling [3] uses a similar task-based model to DOJ but dynamically computes reachability to track heap dependences. This potentially makes the creation of a heap reference an $O(n)$ operation. They introduce a new language CDML that is similar to C++ but includes task-related constructs. They use Bloom filters to detect variable conflicts. DOJ takes a significantly more sophisticated approach to variable conflicts — our approach eliminates antidependences that would otherwise limit parallelism.

Hybrid analysis [25] shares inspiration with DOJ; both use static analysis to classify code of interest as possibly or always parallelizable, and for statically possible cases a customized dynamic analysis further refines the decision. However, whereas hybrid analysis targets Fortan arrays, calculating when code segments might access common array elements, DOJ instead targets Java-like languages which commonly layer object-oriented abstractions and where parallelism is often determined by object sharing patterns. Additionally, hybrid analysis computes a slice to calculate statically unknown addresses, and runs the slice to decide parallel safety. In the object-oriented domain a slice may contain heap modifications, so a slicing strategy will almost certainly require rollback mechanisms. DOJ avoids speculation with read-only heap examiners, which are sound approximations of code segments.

Other approaches require extensive developer annotations to avoid unchecked access to data structures [4, 24] or additional code to create serialization sets [1]. DOJ requires minimal annotations, which are easy to reason about and give DOJ a low barrier to entry.

StarSs dynamically schedules function invocation when a function's operands are available [11]. StarSs does not analyze heap dependences and therefore restricts functions to pass-by-value and forbids passing data structures that contain pointers.

DOJ differs from inspector-executor approaches [23, 26] in that it supports complex object-oriented data structures, uses the results of static analysis to avoid inspecting most memory accesses, and does not require a runtime preprocessing phase. Van der Spek, Holm, and Wijshoff describe an approach to transform pointer-traversing loops into array-traversing loops in order to apply well known array parallelization techniques [29]; the array version of a function may only be invoked when it has been previously changed and the root of its data dependencies have not changed. DOJ always attempts to execute tasks out of order and may succeed in cases where this inspector-executor approach cannot.

Decoupled software pipelining (DSWP) [15] maps memory operations in a loop that may conflict to the same thread of a software pipeline. While this approach simplifies the necessary heap analysis, it limits parallelism — at most one core can write to a statically identified heap region. In contrast, DOJ can execute instances of write instructions across many cores. DOJ also uses a sophisticated heap dependence analysis that can determine that some write statements of a loop are conflict-free where DSWP cannot. DSWP extracts very fine-grained parallelism compared to DOJ; the techniques are likely synergistic.

8. Conclusion

For parallel programming to become mainstream, parallel programming must become easier. We presented a new approach to parallel programming that uses lightweight annotations to suggest parallelization of a sequential program. DOJ generates dynamic heap dependence analyses that automatically extract heap dependences and can guarantee that the parallel execution has the same behavior as the sequential execution. We successfully parallelized twelve applications and achieved significant speedups. Moreover, we found that parallelizing applications with DOJ was straightforward and required only minor modifications to our benchmarks.

Acknowledgments

This research was supported by the National Science Foundation under grants CCF-0846195 and CCF-0725350. We would like to thank the anonymous reviewers for their helpful comments.

References

[1] M. D. Allen, S. Sridharan, and G. S. Sohi. Serialization sets: A dynamic dependence-based parallel execution model. In *Proceedings of the 14th ACM SIGPLAN Symposium on Principles and Practice of Parallel Programming*, pages 85–96, 2009.

[2] E. D. Berger, T. Yang, T. Liu, and G. Novark. Grace: Safe multithreaded programming for C/C++. In *Proceeding of the 24th ACM SIGPLAN Conference on Object-Oriented Programming, Systems, Languages, and Applications*, pages 81–96, 2009.

[3] M. J. Best, S. Mottishaw, C. Mustard, M. Roth, A. Fedorova, and A. Brownsword. Synchronization via scheduling: Techniques for efficiently managing shared state. In *Proceedings of the 2011 ACM SIGPLAN Conference on Programming Language Design and Implementation*, 2011.

[4] R. L. Bocchino, Jr., V. S. Adve, D. Dig, S. V. Adve, S. Heumann, R. Komuravelli, J. Overbey, P. Simmons, H. Sung, and M. Vakilian. A type and effect system for deterministic parallel Java. In *Proceeding of the 24th ACM SIGPLAN Conference on Object-Oriented Programming, Systems, Languages, and Applications*, 2009.

[5] B. Cahoon and K. S. McKinley. Data flow analysis for software prefetching linked data structures in Java. In *Proceedings of the 10th International Conference on Parallel Architectures and Compilation Techniques*, 2001.

[6] C. Cao Minh, J. Chung, C. Kozyrakis, and K. Olukotun. STAMP: Stanford transactional applications for multi-processing. In *Proceedings of the IEEE International Symposium on Workload Characterization*, 2008.

[7] L. Dagum and R. Menon. OpenMP: An industry-standard API for shared-memory programming. *IEEE Computing in Science and Engineering*, 5(1):46–55, 1998.

[8] K. Dai. Code parallelization for the LGDG large-grain dataflow computation. In *Proceedings of the Joint International Conference on Vector and Parallel Processing*, volume 457, pages 243–252. Springer Berlin / Heidelberg, 1990.

[9] J. S. Danaher, I.-T. A. Lee, and C. E. Leiserson. The JCilk language for multithreaded computing. In *Synchronization and Concurrency in Object-Oriented Languages*, 2005.

[10] C. Ding, X. Shen, K. Kelsey, C. Tice, R. Huang, and C. Zhang. Software behavior oriented parallelization. In *Proceedings of the 2007 ACM SIGPLAN Conference on Programming Language Design and Implementation*, pages 223–234, 2007.

[11] Y. Etsion, F. Cabarcas, A. Rico, A. Ramirez, R. M. Badia, E. Ayguade, J. Labarta, and M. Valero. Task superscalar: An out-of-order task pipeline. In *43rd Annual IEEE/ACM International Symposium on Microarchitecture*, 2010.

[12] K. Fatahalian, T. J. Knight, M. Houston, M. Erez, D. Reiter, H. Larkhoon, L. Ji, Y. Park, M. Ren, A. Aiken, W. J. Dally, and P. Hanrahan. Sequoia: Programming the memory hierarchy. In *Proceedings of the ACM/IEEE Conference on Supercomputing*, 2006.

[13] B. Hardekopf and C. Lin. Flow-sensitive pointer analysis for millions of lines of code. In *Proceedings of the 9th Annual IEEE/ACM International Symposium on Code Generation and Optimization*, 2011.

[14] C. Huang and L. V. Kale. Charisma: Orchestrating migratable parallel objects. In *Proceedings of the ACM International Symposium on High Performance Distributed Computing*, pages 75–84, 2007.

[15] J. Huang, A. Raman, T. B. Jablin, Y. Zhang, T.-H. Hung, and D. I. August. Decoupled software pipelining creates parallelization opportunities. In *Proceedings of the 8th Annual IEEE/ACM International Symposium on Code Generation and Optimization*, pages 121–130, 2010.

[16] J. C. Jenista, Y. Eom, and B. Demsky. OoOJava: An out-of-order approach to parallel programming. In *Second USENIX Workshop on Hot Topics in Parallelism*, 2010.

[17] J. C. Jenista, Y. Eom, and B. Demsky. OoOJava: Software out-of-order execution. In *Proceedings of the 16th ACM SIGPLAN Symposium on Principles and Practice of Parallel Programming*, 2011.

[18] J. C. Jenista, Y. Eom, and B. Demsky. Using disjoint reachability for parallelization. In *Proceedings of the 20th International Conference on Compiler Construction*, 2011.

[19] M. Kulkarni, M. Burtscher, C. Cascaval, and K. Pingali. Lonestar: A suite of parallel irregular programs. In *IEEE International Symposium on Performance Analysis of Systems and Software*, 2009.

[20] H.-W. Loidl, F. Rubio, N. Scaife, K. Hammond, S. Horiguchi, U. Klusik, R. Loogen, G. J. Michaelson, R. Peña, S. Priebe, A. J. Rebón, and P. W. Trinder. Comparing parallel functional languages: Programming and performance. *Higher-Order and Symbolic Computation*, 16(3):203–251, 2003.

[21] M. Naik and A. Aiken. Conditional must not aliasing for static race detection. In *Proceedings of the Symposium on Principles of Programming Languages*, 2007.

[22] K. H. Randall. *Cilk: Efficient Multithreaded Computing*. PhD thesis, Massachusetts Institute of Technology, 1998.

[23] L. Rauchwerger, N. M. Amato, and D. A. Padua. Run-time methods for parallelizing partially parallel loops. In *Proceedings of the 9th International Conference on Supercomputing*, pages 137–146, 1995.

[24] M. C. Rinard, D. J. Scales, and M. S. Lam. Jade: A high-level, machine-independent language for parallel programming. *Computer*, 26:28–38, 1993.

[25] S. Rus, L. Rauchwerger, and J. Hoeflinger. Hybrid analysis: Static & dynamic memory reference analysis. *International Journal on Parallel Programming*, 31:251–283, 2003.

[26] J. H. Saltz and R. Mirchandaney. Run-time parallelization and scheduling of loops. *IEEE Transactions on Computers*, 40(5):603–612, May 1991.

[27] L. A. Smith, J. M. Bull, and J. Obdrzálek. A parallel Java Grande benchmark suite. In *Proceedings of the SC2001*, 2001.

[28] R. M. Tomasulo. An efficient algorithm for exploiting multiple arithmetic units. *IBM Journal of Research and Development*, 11(1):25–33, 1967.

[29] H. L. A. van der Spek, C. W. M. Holm, and H. A. G. Wijshoff. How to unleash array optimizations on code using recursive data structures. In *Proceedings of the 24th International Conference on Supercomputing*, pages 275–284, 2010.

[30] S. K. Venkata, I. Ahn, D. Jeon, A. Gupta, C. Louie, S. Garcia, S. Belongie, and M. B. Taylor. SD-VBS: The San Diego Vision Benchmark Suite. In *Proceedings of the IEEE International Symposium on Workload Characterization*, 2009.

[31] C. von Praun, L. Ceze, and C. Caşcaval. Implicit parallelism with ordered transactions. In *Proceedings of the 12th ACM SIGPLAN Symposium on Principles and Practice of Parallel Programming*, pages 79–89, 2007.

[32] A. Welc, S. Jagannathan, and A. Hosking. Safe futures for Java. In *Proceeding of the 20th ACM SIGPLAN Conference on Object-Oriented Programming, Systems, Languages, and Applications*, volume 40, pages 439–453, 2005.

[33] J. Zhou and B. Demsky. Bamboo: A data-centric, object-oriented approach to multi-core software. In *Proceedings of the 2010 ACM SIGPLAN Conference on Programming Language Design and Implementation*, 2010.

S: a Scripting Language for High-Performance RESTful Web Services

Daniele Bonetta Achille Peternier Cesare Pautasso Walter Binder

Faculty of Informatics, University of Lugano – USI
Lugano, Switzerland
{name.surname}@usi.ch

Abstract

There is an urgent need for novel programming abstractions to leverage the parallelism in modern multicore machines. We introduce *S*, a new domain-specific language targeting the server-side scripting of high-performance RESTful Web services. *S* promotes an innovative programming model based on explicit (control-flow) and implicit (process-level) parallelism control, allowing the service developer to specify which portions of the control-flow should be executed in parallel. For each service, the choice of the best level of parallelism is left to the runtime system. We assess performance and scalability by implementing two non-trivial composite Web services in *S*. Experiments show that *S*-based Web services can handle thousands of concurrent client requests on a modern multicore machine.

Categories and Subject Descriptors D.1.3 [*Concurrent Programming*]: Parallel Programming

General Terms Languages, Performance

Keywords RESTful Web services, Multicores, Scalable service execution

1. Introduction

Even if modern server infrastructures for hosting Web services feature highly parallel multicore processors, most existing software and programming languages make it a challenge to fully benefit from the power of such hardware platforms. Given the intrinsically parallel nature of service-based applications, the opportunity exists to design service-oriented architectures which can take advantage of the asynchronous, message-based interactions between independent (i.e., share-nothing) services to make efficient usage of multicore hardware.

In this paper we describe the design of a new language, called *S*, which targets the domain of RESTful Web service [10] development and composition. We find that stateless interactions among RESTful Web services and the explicit management of their state is very useful to identify which parts of a service-oriented architecture can be parallelized.

Even if it is possible to design scalable systems using any language, we believe that embedding specific constraints in the design of a language can make the corresponding guidance more directly available to developers. Thus, we also discuss our novel implicit state-oriented programming model, which has been embedded in the design of the *S* language.

S features native support for architectural-level abstractions, such as services and resources, and allows developers to script service behavior in terms of request handlers associated with the uniform interface of each resource. The state of resources is explicitly marked so that the compiler can statically distinguish the functional behavior from the stateful elements and provide the runtime with enough information such that the correct parallelization strategy can be applied. Likewise, developers do not have to worry about synchronization issues due to concurrent client requests as these are dealt with by the runtime system. The *S* compiler currently includes a backend targeting the JavaScript language and makes use of a runtime based on Node.js [19]. It features automatic code de-synchronization (as Node.js is a single-process, asynchronous server) as well as out-of-order parallel execution. As we demonstrate with non-trivial case studies, the *S* runtime can transparently and efficiently parallelize the execution of RESTful Web services across multiple CPU cores while serving thousands of concurrent clients.

This paper makes the following contributions: it introduces the design and the parallel programming model of the *S* language. It describes its compiler, which detects which portions of code can be executed in parallel and automatically optimizes them for concurrent execution. It presents the main architectural patterns used at runtime to parallelize the execution of the *S* language featuring dynamic replication of services and automatic load balancing.

The rest of this paper is structured as follows: in Section 2 we provide the necessary background to understand the characteristics of the HTTP protocol that we leverage in the design of the *S* language, as described in Section 3. Section 4 presents the *S* language syntax. In Section 5 we explain how the language is compiled into server-side JavaScript to be executed on the *S* runtime, described in Section 6. Sections 7 and 8 provide an evaluation of the *S* runtime system. Section 9 presents related work, and Section 10 concludes this paper.

PPoPP'12, February 25–29, 2012, New Orleans, Louisiana, USA.

2. Background

2.1 RESTful Web Services and the HTTP Protocol

RESTful services are Web services which make full usage of the HTTP protocol [10]. HTTP is the client/server protocol at the core of the World Wide Web [1]. It is based on the notions of globally addressable *resource* (any element published by the server that the client can interact with), stateless interactions (no state should be shared between clients and the server after a request has completed so that servers can treat every request independently from the previous ones), and uniform interfaces (the fixed and well-defined set of possible "actions" that the client can perform on any resource). The uniform interface of HTTP consists of the so-called HTTP methods. The main methods are GET, PUT, DELETE, and POST, which are used to read, create/modify, delete, or access resources. A key aspect of the HTTP protocol is that any method has a precise effect on the state of the receiving resource. GET requests, for instance, are not expected to alter the state of the resource they are applied to. Therefore, multiple GET requests can be safely processed in parallel. Likewise, the value (or representation) of resources fetched using GET methods can be cached. PUT and DELETE methods, on the other hand, are *idempotent* methods: no matter how many times the same PUT/DELETE request will be issued on the same resource, the result will be identical. As a consequence, such requests can be processed by the server in a non-deterministic order and can be retried in case of failure as many times as needed. Conversely, POST methods do not have any property, thus, POST requests must be executed exactly once. Resources can also be retrieved using different representation formats (e.g., HTML, plain text, PDF, JSON, XML). We do not further discuss this aspect as it does not affect parallelism, which is the main focus of this paper.

2.2 JavaScript for Server-Side Development

JavaScript is the most widely used language for client-side development of Web applications. Its distinguishing features are its flexibility, its prototype-based object orientation, its functional nature, as well as its HTML interoperability based on the Document-Object Model (DOM). Despite of being perceived as an inefficient language (like many other dynamically typed languages), JavaScript code is nowadays executed very efficiently. In fact, its wide distribution has spawned many engineering efforts directed at the implementation of high-performance JavaScript virtual machines, such as Google's V8, Safari's Webkit, and Firefox's SpiderMonkey. Given its origins as a scripting language embedded in the Web Browser, JavaScript has not been originally designed to express process-level parallelism. It has only been recently extended to offer support for parallel computations structured according to the master/worker pattern with HTML5 WebWorkers [13].

The increasingly good performance offered by JavaScript virtual machines has motivated the adoption of JavaScript also as a server-side scripting language. Notable in this field is Node.js: a server-side JavaScript framework running on top of Google's V8 which can be used for the development of I/O-bound networking-intensive applications. Node.js features an asynchronous event-driven runtime based on a single-process event-based architecture inspired by the one of Python's Twisted [9], which enables it to handle thousands of concurrent requests on a single V8 instance. Given its single-threaded design (which helps to deal with many concurrency issues), Node.js can exploit modern multicore machines only with approaches based on the master/worker pattern. Also, its asynchronous, event-driven programming model could result to be verbose in complex service development. Conversely, having JavaScript on the server-side clearly represents a great advantage for the end-to-end development of service-oriented applications. Thus, we have chosen to base the design of the *S* language on JavaScript and add the missing features (i.e., parallelism and modularization in terms of services and resources), as described in the following sections.

3. The Design of the *S* Language

S is an extension of the JavaScript programming language targeting the design of service-oriented architectures, with particular focus on RESTful Web service development and composition. *S* extends JavaScript with new features for service scripting, such as synchronous interaction primitives, out-of-order parallel execution of I/O-bound tasks, as well as declarative support for publishing, consuming, and composing REST resources. The aim of the language is to enable the development of high-performance RESTful Web services. The main design drivers are as follows:

High Abstraction Level. The language introduces novel primitives such as *services, resources,* and *request handlers* to the JavaScript language. These abstractions address the lack of modularity constructs in JavaScript and provide scoping and lifecycle semantics specific to RESTful Web services. The goal is to let the developer declare the structural decomposition of a service-oriented architecture so that the compiler and the runtime have enough information to derive which services and which resources can be replicated for scalability and parallelization purposes.

Simple Parallel Programming Model. Defining a programming model to let the developer exploit the parallelism available in modern hardware represents a major challenge. *S* embraces a simple yet powerful programming model with the main aim of easing the parallelization of services. In this way, the developer can focus on the semantics of the interaction among different services, and delegate the parallelism management mostly to the runtime.

JavaScript Support. The language is designed to be JavaScript compatible. This has the notable advantage of bringing all the features of a client-side language (for instance, the DOM and JSON support) to a server-side language, without sacrificing performance (thanks to the Node.js-based runtime).

3.1 The Programming Model of *S*

The programming model of *S* is based on two main components: the deterministic control of any state change during the execution of the service and a simple yet powerful approach to parallelism.

Implicit State-oriented Programming. One of the major sources of complexity and performance degradation for parallel applications is the management of shared state. *S* solves this issue by forcing the developer to specify which operations will alter the state, and by decoupling the management of the state from the access to shared state. In *S*, different services do not share state by design. Resources within the same service may share state. The developer is thus forced to explicitly describe any possible interaction among services in terms of HTTP methods. In this way, the semantics of any HTTP method is enforced. Therefore, resources implementing the GET method will not be allowed to alter any private or shared state, while resources implementing the POST method will be provided with complete access to both shared and private state. This clear division of state visibility, together with a clear separation of stateless and stateful operations, enables the compiler to explicitly control how the state of a RESTful Web service is accessed and manipulated.

Parallel Programming Model. *S* approaches parallel programming with a separation between what can be parallelized by the developer within the behavior of a specific request handler and what can be parallelized by the runtime to handle multiple concurrent requests.

The goal is to let developers write the service logic assuming that all the state will be and remain consistent no matter how many concurrent clients access the service. Furthermore, the developer does not have any control over the degree of parallelism used to execute the service as the runtime autonomously decides how many parallel processes should be allocated to run each service. In more detail, the runtime makes use of the implicit state-oriented programming assumptions to infer which parallelization strategy to apply. Therefore, read-only requests can be easily parallelized, while update-requests need to be serialized. Likewise, stateless services can be replicated, while stateful services can be replicated but their state needs to be kept synchronized by the runtime. The necessary locks and synchronization mechanisms are entirely managed by the runtime.

Conversely, developers can focus their parallelization efforts on reducing the overall response time of a request handler and on speeding up the interaction with external services. Such optimizations make use of two common high-level control-flow parallelism constructs which help to overlap the execution of multiple I/O operations. As we will show, these out-of-order parallelism constructs do not require the developer to reason in terms of threads or parallel processes, since the parallel execution of the instructions of the request handler is also managed by the runtime.

4. The *S* Service Scripting Language

4.1 Syntax

The *S* language is informally introduced with the examples in this section. The syntax of *S* is an extension of the JavaScript syntax; thus, any valid JavaScript statement can be used in *S*, with some limitations introduced to comply with the implicit state-oriented programming model. The JavaScript syntax has been extended to enable explicit parallelism statements such as out-of-order execution of I/O-bound operations, and explicit interaction with external HTTP resources.

The main entity of the language is the *service*. Services have local scoping, which means that two different services cannot share any global variable. Instead, since each service entity corresponds to an independently managed Web service at runtime, two service entities can communicate via HTTP.

Each `service` statement can declare one or more *resources* with the corresponding *request handlers*. Request handlers represent the event-driven entry point for programming the Web service behavior. Any request to the resources associated with a service is processed by a specific handler, defined using the `on` statement. Request handlers can react to any of the HTTP methods (such as GET, PUT, DELETE, and POST), and are associated with a unique resource identifier, specified with the `res` keyword. Services can have multiple request handlers. Following our state-oriented programming model, the scoping of handlers is also local: variables declared within the scope of a handler cannot be accessed from another request handler.

Stateless (or purely functional) handlers can be associated with read-only GET methods. This implies that any JavaScript function invoked within GET request-handlers must be side-effects free. Since the other HTTP methods could alter the state of resources, the language supports the implementation of stateful request handlers in the following way. Request handlers sharing the same resource name (i.e., the same URL) with the need of a shared state can declare special static variables, identified by the `state` keyword. Such variables do not lose their state once the request handler has been invoked, and have their visibility limited within the scope of the declaring handlers.

State variables declared within an `on` construct are only addressable within that request handler, while state variables declared within the scope of a `service` block (or a `res` block with multiple `on` blocks) are accessible to request handlers sharing the same URL path. No state can be shared among different URL paths.

Handlers accessing the shared state do not have to implement any synchronization mechanism, and the consistency of the shared state is guaranteed by the runtime.

Finally, according to the HTTP specification, HTTP POST methods can cause the creation of new resources within the service. The language supports the creation of new resources at runtime by embedding nested resource declarations within request handlers. Such nested resources will be instantiated once the execution reaches their declaration point and will remain available to clients as long as they are not deleted.

```
// To be invoked with:
//   GET /data
//   PUT /data?value='...'

service helloWorld {
   state shared = 'World'
   res '/data' on GET { respond 'Hello ' + shared }
   res '/data' on PUT { shared = query.value }
}
```

Listing 1. Simple stateful service in *S*.

4.2 A Simple Stateful Service

A simple Web service written in *S* is shown in Listing 1. The code corresponds to a simple "Hello World" service with a shared state (`shared`) and two request handlers: `on GET` and `on PUT`. When receiving HTTP GET requests (on the `/data` URL), the corresponding handler accesses the shared state and responds with the "Hello World" string. Since the GET method is idempotent and safe, the language allows GET handlers neither to modify any shared state, nor to declare any local state variable. This enables the runtime to execute multiple GET request handlers in parallel. The runtime system (and not the developer) is responsible for managing synchronization upon access to the shared state, and no explicit locking is required.

The service also implements the HTTP PUT request handler to modify the state of a resource. When receiving a PUT request (to the full path specified through the `res` keyword, e.g., `/data?value='universe'`), the value stored in the shared state is altered. Due to the stateful nature of this request handler, which implies that the state `shared` will change for every new PUT request, the runtime system

```
// To be invoked with:
//   GET /search?q=...

service proxy {
   res '/search' on GET {
      res g = 'http://google.ch/search?q=@'
      if(query.q)
         respond g.get(query.q)
      else
         respond 'Invalid query'
   }
}
```

Listing 2. Simple proxy service.

cannot execute multiple PUT handlers in parallel, therefore, requests of this class are processed sequentially (fairness is not guaranteed). Also, concurrent GET requests cannot be processed consistently while a PUT handler is altering the shared state. The runtime system is therefore responsible for managing the parallel execution of GET handlers, that will answer with an outdated version of the shared state, and for updating the version of the state once its value will have been modified. The implicit locking runtime mechanism is aware of the actual state of the data elements that are shared. Thus, two different PUT handlers operating on two different states will be executed in parallel with no serialization.

In the previous example, the PUT handler uses a local object called `query`. This is a special object automatically created and managed by the runtime, containing all the information relative to the incoming HTTP request. The object is generated for each new request and its visibility is limited to one handler body scope. *S* provides another object with similar purpose, called `response`, managing every aspect of the response (e.g., HTTP headers, status codes, etc.).

4.3 RESTful Service Composition and Dynamic Nested Resources

Server-side applications often need to interact with external services, becoming a composition of existing services exposed as a new service. In *S*, the resources of external services are first-class entities, also defined through the `res` keyword.

The code of Listing 2 describes a proxy service receiving an input value (`q`) to be forwarded to another RESTful Web service (the Google search engine). In the code, `g` is an *external resource* managed by an external Web service. To support a complete binding between the URL addressing the external service and the corresponding entity in *S*, the resource can be declared using one or more `@` placeholders. In the example, this solution allows mapping the first argument of `g.get()` to the first parameter of the URL's query (i.e., `q`). When multiple parameters are expected, multiple `@` symbols can be used.

Having external resources as first-order entities makes the composition of external services straightforward. The example in Listing 3 presents a meta-search service which composes two popular search engines (Google and Microsoft Bing). As opposed to returning the results of the search as a response to the request (as done in the example in Listing 2), the code associates the result with a dynamically created resource (`/total/{id}`) and the client is redirected to it. To do so, the client invokes the server like in the previous examples, but instead of receiving a direct response, it receives an HTTP 302 code (redirect) pointing to the newly created resource containing the combined results from the two searches, which can be read using a GET request.

```
   // To be invoked with:
   //   POST /search?q=...
   //   GET /total/{id}

1  service composition {
2     res '/search' on POST {
3        function combine(a,b) { ... }
4        state id = 0; id++
5        res g = 'http://google.ch/search?q=@'
6        res b = 'http://bing.com/search?q=@'
7        var total =
            combine(g.get(query.q),b.get(query.q))
8        res '/total/'+id {
9           on GET { respond total }
10       }
11       respond { 302 : { Location : '/total/'+id }}
12    }
13 }
```

Listing 3. Service composition in *S*.

This example also shows other interesting aspects. First, it uses a local state variable, called `id`. As described in the previous section, state variables can be used to manage a persistent state in request handlers that do not have to be idempotent. This is the case of the POST method, which is used to create new resources according to the HTTP specification. The semantics of state variables is straightforward: when declared, they can be initialized with a given value (`id = 0`, in our example). Successive invocations of the same request handler will ignore the initialization. In this way, the first time the `on POST` handler is invoked the state variable is initialized to zero and incremented. At the second invocation, the state variable has a value of 1 that is incremented as a result of the `id++` operation, ensuring that a unique identifier for the newly created resource (line 8) is assigned.

Another relevant feature shown in the example are nested resources. A new resource is created using the `res` keyword. The resource is created within the scope of the resource handler, but with an independent URL path. The new resource is declared specifying the path it will refer to (in our example, a string composed of `/total/` plus the unique identifier managed through the state variable) and one or more request handlers for the new resource. The scoping strategy adopted for nested resources declaration is the following: the new nested resource is created with a snapshot of all the global and local variables accessible within the event handler construct at the moment of its creation. According to our example, for instance, the new nested resource `/total` is allowed to access the `total` variable. Thus, when the new resource is accessed by a client, it responds with the value of `total` at the moment of its creation.

4.4 Explicit Control-Flow Parallelism Constructs

Service composition is a key feature of *S*. However, the invocation of multiple independent services is an I/O-bound operation that usually implies non-negligible latency. *S* allows speeding up service composition by performing I/O-bound operations in parallel. To this end, the language exploits an out-of-order parallelism model through the `par` and the `pfor` constructs.

Every set of instructions included in a `par` block is evaluated with respect to its data dependencies and control-flow. Any set of instructions with no such dependencies is executed in parallel, while the others wait for their data dependencies to be satisfied. This approach preserves the data-flow semantics of the original code, while introducing a partial

```
    // To be invoked with:
    //   GET /search?q=...

1   service helloPar {
2      res '/search' on GET {
3         function combine(a,b) { ... }
4         par {
5            res g = 'http://google.ch/search?q=@'
6            res b = 'http://bing.com/search?q=@'
7            respond combine(g.get(query.q),
                             b.get(query.q))
8         }
9      }
10  }
```

Listing 4. Usage of the `par` construct in *S*.

control-flow ordering which enables the compiler to schedule independent I/O-bound operations to be processed concurrently.

In addition to this construct, the `pfor` construct enables the parallel execution of code over multiple elements of one same data collection. In this case, the compiler checks that no data dependency is present among the different iterations and, if possible, executes the body of the loop in parallel for any element of the collection. Finally, `par` constructs can be nested into `pfor` constructs to further increase the code parallelization.

Listing 4 shows an example service using the `par` construct. This service is a different version of the example already discussed in Listing 3. The example shows how easy it is to parallelize the block of instructions performing the invocation of external services. The *S* compiler automatically identifies that the statements at lines 5 and 6 can be executed in parallel, and performs the two operations concurrently, waiting for both to complete before executing the next statement at line 7. Function calls are considered as field accesses, which means that the body of the `combine` function will not be parallelized. Also, functions are assumed to be side-effects free.

5. Compile-time Support

The result of the compilation process of an *S* program is a set of JavaScript source files. Each of these source files is passed to the *S* runtime which binds the compilation output to a set of parallel processes supporting the execution of implicit and explicit parallel operations.

5.1 Synchronous to Asynchronous Event-Driven Compilation

Any resource-related operation (i.e., any valid HTTP service invocation) is coded as a synchronous operation in *S*. This helps keeping the source code readable, and does not require the developer to write every service invocation as a set of complex nested callbacks, as it would be required when done in plain JavaScript. However, to fully exploit the benefits of the event-driven V8 runtime offered by Node.js, the JavaScript executable code generated by the compiler should be event-based, thus asynchronous. To address this issue, and to support synchronous service invocations in an asynchronous event-based runtime environment, the compiler uses the following de-synchronization strategy. While traversing the *S* Abstract Syntax Tree, the compiler performs these rewriting operations:

1) Each control-flow block performing I/O operations (e.g., constructs such as `if`, `for`, etc.) is compiled to a separate JavaScript function. JavaScript has static scoping: the scoping of any variable is preserved declaring all the global variables in an external block which will include all the inner levels.

2) Blocks containing an I/O operation are subdivided into two equivalent blocks: the first contains a runtime system call to trigger the beginning of the I/O operation. The latter contains an event handler that recovers the execution of the resource invocation when the I/O operation completes. The tree rewriting is done recursively (i.e., blocks with more than one I/O operation are subdivided into as many blocks as needed). Finally, each of the rewritten blocks is compiled into an independent JavaScript function.

3) To preserve the original Control-Flow Graph (CFG) topology, all the compiled function blocks are enriched with an event notification mechanism. The runtime allows managing the asynchronous execution of any function associated with a specific event. The compiler appends an `emit()` runtime call at the end of each block. In this way, when a block completes its execution, the runtime is notified and can pass control to the next blocks.

4) The compiler computes a possible correct sequence of function calls triggered by event notifications (according to the CFG of the input code). These are mapped to invocations of another runtime component, called `scheduler`. Thanks to this component, the control-flow of the service can be driven according to specific events using a callback mechanism. By calling the runtime method `execOn(event, function)`, the runtime can tie the execution of a specific function as the consequence of a specific event. The compiler exploits this mechanism to reconstruct the correct control-flow of a request handler.

Overall, the CFG is converted to an Event-Driven Control Graph (EDCG), where every block is executed as a response to a triggered event and not as a consequence of a JavaScript control-flow construct evaluation. Whereas the final asynchronous code will be less efficient compared to its corresponding synchronous version, the advantage is that it becomes possible to use one process to overlap multiple parallel executions. This is important in our application domain, where a limited number of execution processes should scale to handle a very large number of concurrent clients.

5.2 Out-of-Order Parallel Execution

The compilation scheme adopted to transform synchronous code to its asynchronous executable version takes advantage of event-based function calling made available through Node.js. The event-based execution of different instruction blocks can be further exploited to implement the out-of-order parallel execution of I/O-bound operations. To this end, the compiler performs a static analysis of the source code identifying all the resource-related operations. For each `par`/`pfor` block, the compiler analyzes the contextual information relative to each variable access and modification, computing a per-instruction Data Dependency Graph (DDG). The graph is then compacted by clustering instructions which do not imply I/O-bound operations. At the end, the resulting DDG is traversed to reconstruct the correct calling tree and the corresponding scheduling instructions are emitted. The scheduler runtime object allows to schedule the execution of a specific block according to multiple events. At runtime, the scheduler suspends the execution until all parallel branches of the DDG are finished. In this way, the compiler guarantees that the data dependencies of the sequential execution are respected.

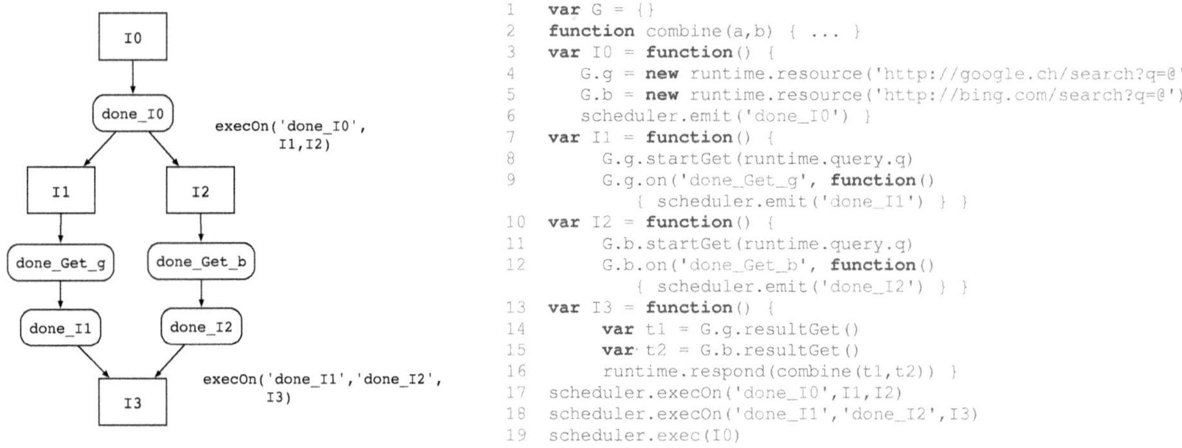


```
var G = {}
function combine(a,b) { ... }
var I0 = function() {
   G.g = new runtime.resource('http://google.ch/search?q=@')
   G.b = new runtime.resource('http://bing.com/search?q=@')
   scheduler.emit('done_I0') }
var I1 = function() {
     G.g.startGet(runtime.query.q)
     G.g.on('done_Get_g', function()
         { scheduler.emit('done_I1') } }
var I2 = function() {
     G.b.startGet(runtime.query.q)
     G.b.on('done_Get_b', function()
         { scheduler.emit('done_I2') } }
var I3 = function() {
     var t1 = G.g.resultGet()
     var t2 = G.b.resultGet()
     runtime.respond(combine(t1,t2)) }
scheduler.execOn('done_I0',I1,I2)
scheduler.execOn('done_I1','done_I2',I3)
scheduler.exec(I0)
```

Listing 5. Event-Driven Control Graph (left) corresponding to the JavaScript code (right) as produced by the *S* compiler for the source *S* code in Listing 4.

Listing 5 shows a portion of the JavaScript code as emitted by the *S* compiler. This code is the compiled version of the code snipped presented in Listing 4. The example shows how the synchronous-to-asynchronous compilation process and the `par` statement are converted into asynchronous event-based JavaScript. In the same figure, the EDCG of the *S* source is shown. Rounded boxes contain events, while square boxes describe a function call triggered by (incoming edge) or emitting (outgoing edge) a specific event. The interaction with the external resource (for instance `g.get()`) is compiled using the `runtime.resource` object, which emits an event (e.g., `done_Get_g`) when the remote invocation has completed. These events will trigger the `done_I1` and `done_I2` events asynchronously. Once both events have been triggered, the scheduling component of the runtime will resume the execution of the last block `I3` of the request handler, which can access the results fetched in parallel from the two resources.

6. The *S* Runtime

The JavaScript code generated by the compiler is executed by the *S* runtime. The runtime is running on top of the Google JavaScript V8 virtual machine and Node.js. We extended the V8+Node.js runtime with additional native modules, which provide support for load balancing, process control, and inter-process communication. Also, the runtime further extends the *S* language explicit parallelism mechanism (enabled through the `par`/`pfor` constructs) with implicit parallelism (handling multiple client requests in parallel). This implicit parallelism support is implemented in the runtime, based on a number of specialized concurrent processes, efficiently communicating through shared memory data channels or HTTP according to the context.

6.1 Resource Request Routing

By design, each *S* request handler is independent of the others in that its code can only access variables declared within its local scope or variables declared as shared state within the resource or the service. This allows the compiler to produce a separate JavaScript source file as output for each resource handler. These files are deployed for execution by the runtime, which publishes each service through its own TCP/IP address and port. To allow multiple request handlers to listen on the same port, the runtime makes use of another independent process, called *request router* (RR). The RR is responsible for opening the TCP connection port of the service, and for accepting HTTP requests from external clients. As soon as a new client request is received, the RR process accepts it and extracts the routing information by parsing the resource URL and HTTP method of the HTTP request header. With it, the RR identifies the request handler process responsible for the specific request URL.

To do so, the RR manages a routing table listing the mapping between resource URLs, methods, and process identifiers of the corresponding request handler processes. In order to deal with nested resources, the routing table is dynamically managed and updated as soon as new nested resources are added to a service.

The management of shared state relies on a similar approach. Each shared state variable is managed by an independent autonomous state manager process responsible for ensuring the consistency of the state as it is exposed to concurrent requests. All the stateful request handlers are processed by the state manager, while stateless requests are processed by external processes holding a cached version of the state. The semantics of the HTTP uniform interface enables each state manager to process multiple idempotent and safe requests in parallel.

Similarly, pure stateful request handlers (i.e., request handlers accepting only PUT, POST, and DELETE methods) also use a state manager. However, since no stateless operations are present, the state is not replicated among different processes, but it is located within the process hosting the request handlers.

Nested resources are also managed as independent processes, like any regular request handler. The only difference is that nested resources are dynamically registered and unregistered from the service routing table.

Since external RESTful services and different request handlers correspond to the same entity in *S* (managed through the `res` keyword), the runtime system is responsible for dynamically resolving each resource's address and using the appropriate communication mechanism. Therefore, communications between different resources within the same ser-

```
// To be invoked with:
//   PUT /crawl?startFrom=...&depth=...
//   GET /urlsDiscovered

service crawler {
   res '/crawl' on PUT {
      function scan(page) { ... }
      res url = query.startFrom
      var list = scan(url.get())
      if(query.depth>1)
         pfor(var i in list) {
            par {
               res crawl =
                     '/crawl?startFrom=@&depth=@'
               res discovered =
                     '/urlsDiscovered?val=@'
               crawl.put(list[i],query.depth-1)
               discovered.put(list[i])
         } }
   }
   res '/urlsDiscovered' {
      state urls = new Array()
      on PUT {
         urls.push(query.val)
      }
      on GET {
         respond urls
      }
} }
```

Listing 6. Parallel Web Crawler in *S*.

vice are carried out through shared memory communication channels, while communications with external services are carried out with standard TCP sockets and HTTP.

6.2 Parallel Runtime Architecture

As discussed in Section 2.1, the semantics of the HTTP protocol allows processing multiple requests to the same resource in parallel. In more detail, *S* concurrently processes multiple requests of some type (like GET), while others (like POST) require exclusive access. Following the design of the *S* language, also requests associated with stateless handlers can be easily parallelized. Only request handlers altering a private state cannot be executed in parallel to ensure consistency.

To identify which request handlers can be executed in parallel, in conjunction to the HTTP semantics, *S* leverages a compile-time static analysis. The analysis is based on the verification of access patterns to shared states. When (at compile-time) a stateless resource is found, it is marked with a special identifier allowing the runtime to parallelize the execution of the specific handler

Request handlers that cannot be parallelized are executed as a single process by the runtime system. Depending on the available hardware resources, other handlers are replicated among multiple processes and requests are automatically load-balanced among them by the so-called *Stateless Resource Manager* (SLR).

7. Case Studies

Complex services requiring the interaction with several external services can be easily implemented in *S*. In this section, we illustrate two common Web services developed in *S*. The scalability of the two services will be evaluated in Section 8.

The first case study demonstrates a self-parallelizing Web crawler. The service implementation shows the flexibility of the language regarding service composition. The crawler service composes services by crawling external Web pages, and by recursively calling itself. The example also shows how

```
// To be invoked with:
//   POST /start?urls=...&key=...
//   GET /red/...

service mapred {
   res '/start' on POST {
      state id = 0; id++
      res '/red/'+id {
         state s = 0
         on GET { respond s }
         on PUT { s += query.count }
      }
      respond { 302 :
         { Location : '/red/'+id } }
      pfor(var i in query.urls) {
         res scan = '/map?url=@&key=@&id=@'
         scan.put(query.urls[i], query.key, id)
      }
   }
   res '/map' on PUT {
      function scan(page,key) { ... }
      res url = query.url
      var page = url.get()
      res reduce = '/red/'+query.id+'?count=@'
      reduce.put(scan(page, query.key))
   }
}
```

Listing 7. Map-Reduce in *S*.

stateless request handlers can benefit from parallel execution without having the developer to deal with process-level parallelism.

The second example is a Map-Reduce service operating on external resources. The service features several parallel components, resulting in a complex runtime architecture.

7.1 Web Crawler Service

The source code of the Web crawler case study is presented in Listing 6. The service recursively traverses a set of linked HTML pages and collects their URLs. It is composed of two resources, one used to crawl a Web page and the other (`/urlsDiscovered`) used to collect and to publish the results of a crawl.

The service is invoked with a PUT request on the `/crawl` resource. The corresponding request handler downloads the first external resource (a Web page specified by the client in the request with the `startFrom` parameter), and calls the `scan` method. This function implements a simple HTML parser which scans the given input data (containing the downloaded Web page) and returns an array containing all the URLs found. Then, for each URL contained in the `list`

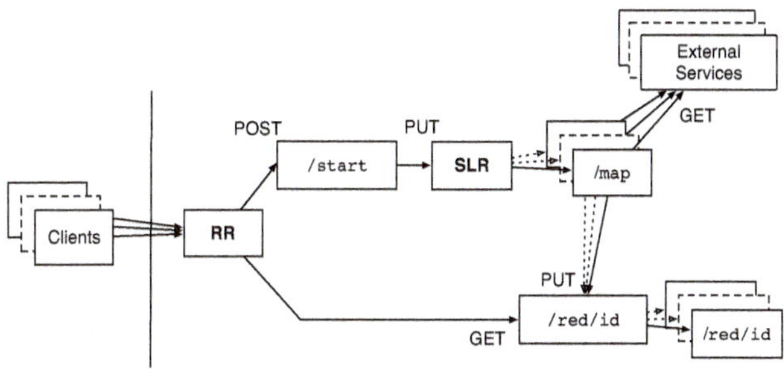

Figure 1. Runtime architecture of the Map-Reduce Web service case study as executed by the *S* runtime system.

array, the service recursively calls itself to scan for further URLs. Meanwhile, all the URLs identified by the service are saved. The `/crawl` request handler is kept stateless by sending a PUT request to the `/urlsDiscovered` resource.

Since the `/crawl` resource is stateless (that is, it is not directly changing a shared state nor maintaining a local state), the runtime can handle multiple requests in parallel. The stateless nature of the handler, coupled with the usage of the `pfor` construct, automatically parallelizes the execution of the resource handler. In fact, for each set of URLs found at any recursive invocation, the `crawl` handler receives multiple parallel requests generated by itself. Since the runtime does not make any difference between requests coming from clients or from internal request handlers, the `crawl` handler reacts as if it would have to respond to an increasing number of client requests, and will thus use an increasingly larger amount of execution resources, effectively parallelizing the Web crawling operation.

7.2 Map-Reduce Service

Map-Reduce computations are composed of a parallel computation (the "map" function) followed by a sequential gathering operation (the "reduce" function). Listing 7 shows how this can be implemented in *S*. The Map-Reduce service publishes a `/start` resource, which receives as input a keyword and a list of external URLs corresponding to a list of Web pages (for instance, the list of Web pages could be the result of the computation performed by the crawler Web service presented before). Right after a client POST request is handled, like for many common Map-Reduce applications. The service applies a function (`scan`) which is executed in parallel and counts the number of occurrences of the given keyword in all the Web pages. Finally, the result is stored in a shared state, and is made available through a new nested resource, so that each client will have a personalized result.

The example exploits the two parallelism models provided by *S* and presents a complex runtime architecture, including nested resources and shared state management.

First, at line 10, the `pfor` construct is used to parallelize the download of all the URLs received as input. In this way, the `/start` resource can invoke the `/map` resource multiple times in parallel. This is possible thanks to the static analysis performed by the *S* compiler. Since the `/map` resource is stateless (it only has a PUT request handler with no private state) the runtime can execute multiple requests to `/map` concurrently.

An overview of the runtime architecture used to run the Map-Reduce service example is shown in Figure 1. Each box in the figure represents an independent process. Arrows indicate routing paths as specified by the *S* runtime, while dotted boxes represent processes that can be dynamically parallelized by the runtime, determining the right number of parallel processes to be executed on the fly based on the available resources.

8. Performance Evaluation

S has been designed to enable the development of high performance RESTful services. In this section, we provide an evaluation of the performance of the two case studies presented in the prior section. Our results clearly demonstrate that services written in *S* can benefit from the parallel runtime architecture and scale to handle thousands of concurrent client requests when deployed on multicore machines.

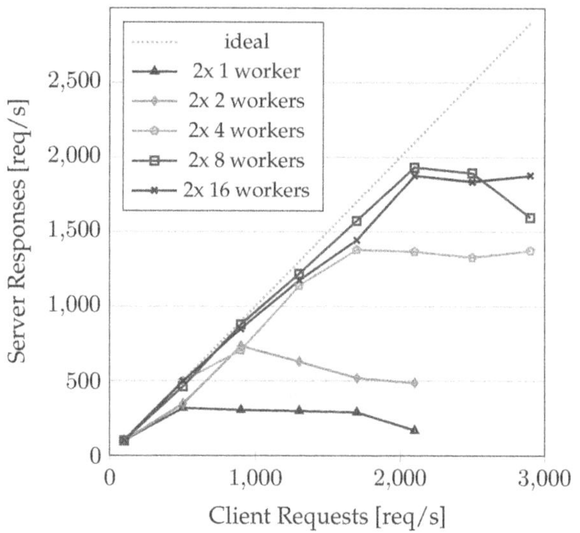

Figure 2. Map-Reduce scalability experiment.

8.1 Map-Reduce Service

The scalability of the *S* Map-Reduce service has been evaluated through the following experiment measuring how well it can use an increasing number of CPU cores to serve an increasing number of clients. The service has been deployed on a server machine with a total of 24 cores.

The experiment has been executed with the `/map` resource downloading a pool of Web pages hosted on a different machine. For each client request, the Map-Reduce service is requested to download a total of five Web pages in parallel and to count, for each page, the number of times a given keyword appears. The number of external pages to download has been set to such a low value to measure the service's scalability without any risk of network bandwidth saturation. Every incoming client request to the `/start` resource triggers five concurrent outgoing requests to the `/map` resource, which again performs an HTTP GET request to retrieve the given Web page.

Results are described in Figure 2. The experiment has been executed by configuring the service to use an increasing number of parallel workers, up to a maximum limit of 32 processes (16 parallel processes for the Map phase and 16 for the Reduce phase). The chart shows that this service scales almost linearly up to the limit of the physical resources available in the system.

8.2 Web Crawler Service

The algorithm implemented by the Web Crawler service forces the service to call itself recursively for each new URL found in the page currently being analyzed. This generates an increasing number of Web pages to be crawled for each iteration, corresponding to an increasing number of client requests for the service to be processed.

The service is started by a single request sent from the client, containing an URL from where to start the crawling process, and the level of recursion depth to halt the service at. Due to the nondeterministic nature of the Web, the performance of a Web crawler cannot be measured using real Web pages. For this reason, we have created a set of ad hoc Web pages representing a (potentially) infinite binary tree. The regular structure of the tree lets us use the number of

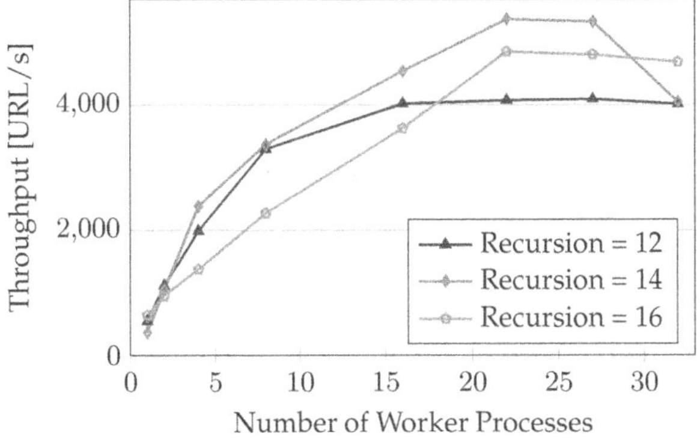

Figure 3. Crawler scalability with different recursion depths.

nodes crawled as a measure of the performance of the service. The crawler service is deployed on the same 24 cores machine of the previous experiment.

In Figure 3 the evaluation of the crawler service implemented in *S* is presented. The chart shows the average throughput of the service (number of crawled URLs per second) as obtained using different parallelism degrees. The three curves correspond to three different depth levels of the tree, namely 12, 14, and 16, corresponding to about 8.2×10^3, 3.3×10^4, and 1.3×10^5 Web pages to crawl.

Each curve has been obtained by increasing the maximum number of parallel resources allocated for the service. The chart in the figure clearly shows how the service is able to exploit the underlying parallel hardware up to the scalability limit imposed by the hardware resources available in the system.

Another evaluation of the parallel algorithm executed by the crawler service can be done considering the way the service visits the crawling tree over time. To this end, in Figure 4 the temporal evolution of the service is shown with regard to the number of requests received by the service, and the number of responses it has been able to return. The four charts present the evolution of these two metrics over time for four different upper bounds of parallel workers.

The chart with a single worker shows how the recursive tree traversal code makes the service continuously receive requests for new nodes to be crawled. Since only one worker process is processing the requests, the service can then begin to answer only when it has reached the crawling frontier (that is, it has visited all the leaf nodes of the tree). This is equivalent to the standard evolution of a sequential invocation of recursive functions: the call stack continues to grow until the recursion can be stopped.

More interesting things happen when the service is allowed to exploit parallel resources. As visualized in the remaining plots, the service is able to overlap the tree traversal with the answer reconstruction. This is mainly due to the associative nature of the crawling operation, as the result can be reconstructed independently of the order in which the tree is visited. Increasing the number of parallel workers available in the system both increases throughput and reduces the total execution time.

9. Related Work

The idea of exploiting state-related information to identify whether an application can be parallelized has been discussed in the context of the so-called Permission-Based programming [4]. Permissions are annotations on variables and objects such as "read-only" [14] which can be used to address several issues in software engineering, including concurrency [6]. A relevant approach in the direction of Permission-Based programming languages is represented by the Plaid language [3]. Plaid is a programming language where concurrency is the rule, and dependencies between operations are specified using permissions, allowing the runtime to automatically execute applications concurrently. Similarly to Plaid, *S* exploits the way state is managed to infer which operations can be executed in parallel. As opposed to Plaid's approach, *S* state-related primitives are implicitly defined using the unique semantics of the HTTP protocol.

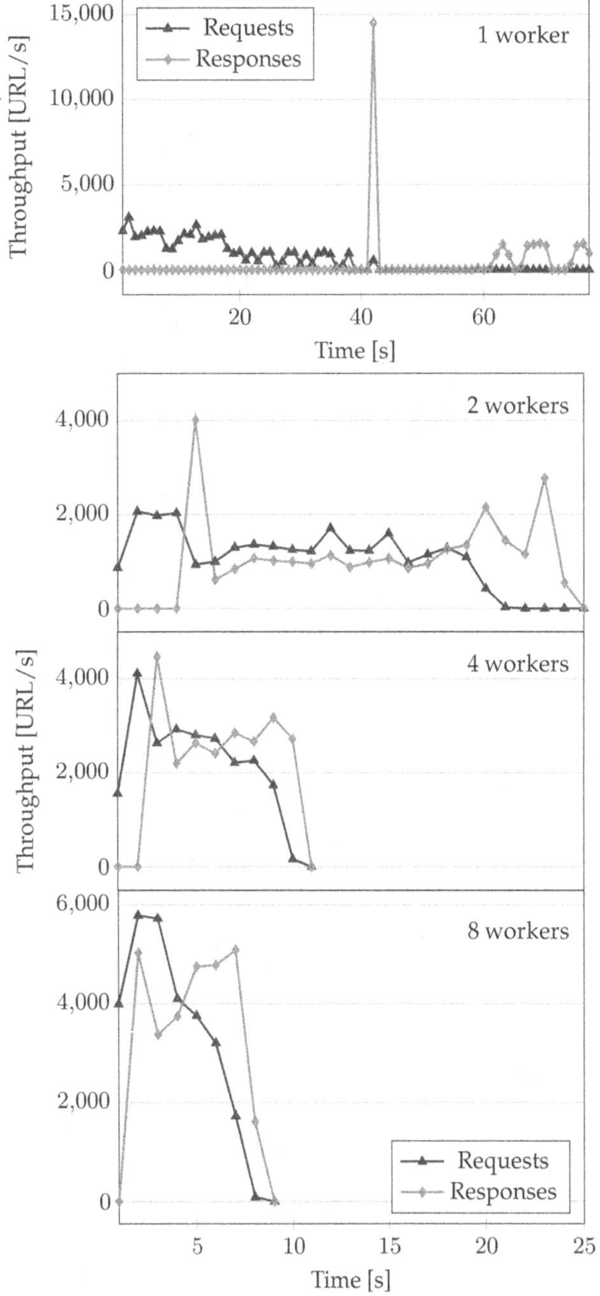

Figure 4. Crawler running with 1, 2, 4, and 8 workers.

S resources and the corresponding request handlers are influenced by Actors [2]. Unlike traditional actor-based languages (e.g., Erlang [20] or Scala [12]) the Actor-based semantics in *S* is kept implicit, and the way a handler processes messages coming from other peers (or external clients) depends on the kind of method associated with the request.

Self-parallelizing runtime system is featured in several frameworks. An approach similar to the self-parallelizing strategy implemented in *S* is represented by the Self Replicating Object (SRO) programming model presented in [17]. SRO are objects able to partition their state to permit a parallel execution. Similarly to the implicit parallelism in *S*, SRO objects can identify whether the state of a component allows parallel execution or not. One relevant difference is that the *S* runtime does not partition state.

With aims similar to the ones behind the parallelism constructs of *S*, the programming model of OoO-Java enables the automatic parallelization of Java code through the out-of-order execution of data-independent instructions [15]. Differently from the general purpose of OoO-Java, *S* supports out-of-order execution of different operations only for I/O-bound operations. Other speculative models can be seen as an alternative to *S* parallelism constructs [5, 21], as well as notation-based models [7, 18]. Due to the peculiarity of the Web services domain, the solution of parallelizing I/O-bound operations adopted in *S* aims at combining the strengths of both approaches as it enables the developer to explicitly identify which part of the code should be parallelized (as with annotations) without any risk of altering the original sequential semantics (as guaranteed by deterministic speculative approaches).

Out of the realm of server-side development technologies, JavaScript-based approaches have been proposed in several cases. Flapjax [16], for instance, is a JavaScript-compatible language based on a Functional Reactive Programming model [8]. Similarly to *S*, Flapjax adopts an event-driven approach, and similarly to the *S* compiler, Flapjax code is compiled to JavaScript. Finally, an exhaustive performance analysis of several JavaScript applications is presented in [11].

10. Conclusion and Future Work

In this paper we presented the *S* service scripting language, its compiler, and its runtime system. The initial domain targeted by the language consists of service-oriented applications, for which a parallel runtime architecture suitable for high-performance execution of RESTful Web services has been developed. The language features explicit control-flow parallelism constructs which developers can apply to speed up the execution of individual request handlers. Additionally, the language leverages its implicit state-oriented programming model to automatically parallelize the execution of stateless and stateful services by employing de-synchronization and self-parallelization techniques. The results presented in the paper show how applications developed using the *S* language can efficiently exploit parallel architectures such as multicore machines to scale in the number of clients they can serve concurrently.

A further extension of the *S* language and runtime system will deal with another class of modern Web services, namely HTTP-based streaming services. In such a context, the *S* self-parallelizing runtime will also have to deal with non regular streams, and will have to adapt to the actual frequency of incoming requests. We also have started to experiment with self-tuning mechanisms based on auto-scaling techniques which not only take into account the number of cores available on the machine but also dynamically adjust the allocation of processes to cores based on their actual workload.

Acknowledgments

The work presented in this paper has been supported by the Swiss National Science Foundation with the SOSOA project (SINERGIA grant nr. CRSI22_127386).

References

[1] HTTP protocol specification. URL `http://www.w3.org/Protocols/rfc2616/rfc2616.html`.

[2] G. Agha. *Actors: a model of concurrent computation in distributed systems*. MIT Press, Cambridge, MA, USA, 1986.

[3] J. Aldrich, J. Sunshine, D. Saini, and Z. Sparks. Typestate-oriented programming. In *Proc. of OOPSLA*, pages 1015–1022, 2009.

[4] J. Aldrich, R. Garcia, M. Hahnenberg, M. Mohr, K. Naden, D. Saini, S. Stork, J. Sunshine, E. Tanter, and R. Wolff. Permission-based programming languages: Nier track. In *Proc. of ICSE*, pages 828–831, 2011.

[5] E. D. Berger, T. Yang, T. Liu, and G. Novark. Grace: safe multi-threaded programming for C/C++. In *Proc. of OOPSLA*, pages 81–96, 2009.

[6] C. Boyapati, R. Lee, and M. Rinard. Ownership types for safe programming: preventing data races and deadlocks. In *Proc. of OOPSLA*, pages 211–230, 2002.

[7] L. Dagum and R. Menon. Openmp: An industry-standard api for shared-memory programming. *IEEE Comput. Sci. Eng.*, 5: 46–55, January 1998.

[8] C. Elliott and P. Hudak. Functional reactive animation. In *Proc. of ICFP*, pages 263–273, 1997.

[9] A. Fettig and G. Lefkowitz. *Twisted network programming essentials*. O'Reilly, 2005.

[10] R. T. Fielding. *Architectural Styles and the Design of Network-based Software Architectures*. PhD thesis, University of California, Irvine, 2000.

[11] E. Fortuna, O. Anderson, L. Ceze, and S. Eggers. A limit study of JavaScript parallelism. In *Proc. of IISWC*, pages 1–10, 2010.

[12] P. Haller and M. Odersky. Scala actors: Unifying thread-based and event-based programming. *Theor. Comput. Sci.*, 410:202–220, February 2009.

[13] I. Hickson. Web workers. World Wide Web Consortium, Working Draft WD-workers-20110310, March 2011.

[14] J. Hogg. Islands: aliasing protection in object-oriented languages. In *Proc. of OOPSLA*, pages 271–285, 1991.

[15] J. C. Jenista, Y. h. Eom, and B. C. Demsky. OoOJava: software out-of-order execution. In *Proc. of PPoPP*, pages 57–68, 2011.

[16] L. A. Meyerovich, A. Guha, J. Baskin, G. H. Cooper, M. Greenberg, A. Bromfield, and S. Krishnamurthi. Flapjax: a programming language for ajax applications. In *Proc. of OOPSLA*, pages 1–20, 2009.

[17] K. Ostrowski, C. Sakoda, and K. Birman. Self-replicating objects for multicore platforms. In *Proc. of ECOOP*, pages 452–477, 2010.

[18] K. H. Randall. *Cilk: efficient multithreaded computing*. PhD thesis, 1998.

[19] S. Tilkov and S. Vinoski. Node.js: Using JavaScript to build high-performance network programs. *IEEE Internet Computing*, 14:80–83, November 2010.

[20] R. Virding, C. Wikström, and M. Williams. *Concurrent programming in ERLANG (2nd ed.)*. Prentice Hall International (UK) Ltd., 1996.

[21] C. von Praun, L. Ceze, and C. Caşcaval. Implicit parallelism with ordered transactions. In *Proc. of PPoPP*, pages 79–89, 2007.

A GPU Implementation of Inclusion-based Points-to Analysis *

Mario Méndez-Lojo[1] Martin Burtscher[2] Keshav Pingali[1,3]

[1] Institute for Computational Engineering and Sciences, University of Texas, Austin, USA
[2] Dept. of Computer Science, Texas State University, San Marcos, USA
[3] Dept. of Computer Science, University of Texas, Austin, USA
marioml@ices.utexas.edu, burtscher@txstate.edu, pingali@cs.utexas.edu

Abstract

Graphics Processing Units (GPUs) have emerged as powerful accelerators for many *regular* algorithms that operate on dense arrays and matrices. In contrast, we know relatively little about using GPUs to accelerate highly *irregular* algorithms that operate on pointer-based data structures such as graphs. For the most part, research has focused on GPU implementations of graph analysis algorithms that do not modify the structure of the graph, such as algorithms for breadth-first search and strongly-connected components.

In this paper, we describe a high-performance GPU implementation of an important graph algorithm used in compilers such as gcc and LLVM: Andersen-style inclusion-based points-to analysis. This algorithm is challenging to parallelize effectively on GPUs because it makes extensive modifications to the structure of the underlying graph and performs relatively little computation. In spite of this, our program, when executed on a 14 Streaming Multiprocessor GPU, achieves an average speedup of 7x compared to a sequential CPU implementation and outperforms a parallel implementation of the same algorithm running on 16 CPU cores.

Our implementation provides general insights into how to produce high-performance GPU implementations of graph algorithms, and it highlights key differences between optimizing parallel programs for multicore CPUs and for GPUs.

Categories and Subject Descriptors D.1.3 [*Programming Techniques*]: Concurrent Programming—Parallel Programming

General Terms Algorithms, Languages, Performance

Keywords Inclusion-based Points-to Analysis, Irregular Programs, Graph Algorithms, GPU, CUDA

1. Introduction

GPU hardware is designed to process blocks of pixels at high speed and with wide parallelism, so it is well suited for executing regular algorithms that operate on dense vectors and matrices. We understand much less about how to use GPUs efficiently to execute *irregular* algorithms that use dynamic data structures like graphs and trees. Harish *et al.* [14] pioneered this field with their CUDA implementations of algorithms such as breadth-first search and single-source shortest paths. BFS has recently received much attention in the GPU community [19, 24, 26]. Barnat *et al.* [5] implemented a GPU algorithm for finding strongly-connected components in directed graphs and showed that it achieves significant speedup with respect to Tarjan's sequential algorithm. Other irregular algorithms that have been successfully parallelized using GPUs are n-body simulations and some dataflow analyses [9, 30].

An important characteristic of most of the irregular algorithms that have been implemented to date on GPUs is that they are graph analysis algorithms that do not modify the structure of the underlying graph [5, 14, 19, 24, 26]; when they do modify the graph structure, the modifications can be predicted statically and appropriate data structures can be pre-allocated for the program [9, 30]. However, there are many important graph algorithms in which edges or nodes are dynamically added to (or removed from) the graph at runtime in an unpredictable fashion, such as mesh refinements [11], compiler optimizations [3], and social network maintenance [7]. In TAO analysis [29], which is an algorithmic classification for irregular codes, these are called *morph* algorithms. Implementation of a morph algorithm on a GPU is challenging because it is unclear how to support dynamically changing graphs on a GPU; in particular, static graph representations such as compressed row storage (CRS), which work well on GPUs, cannot be used.

In this paper, we describe the first high-performance GPU implementation of a very important morph algorithm: Andersen's inclusion-based points-to analysis [3], which is a compiler analysis algorithm that takes a program as input and infers an over-approximation of the set of variables pointed to by each pointer in the program. Inclusion-based points-to analysis provides a good trade-off between precision of results and speed of analysis, and it has been incorporated into several production compilers including gcc and LLVM. A multi-CPU, shared memory implementation of this algorithm is presented by Méndez-Lojo *et al.* [25]; it achieves an average speedup of 6x on sixteen cores relative to a highly-tuned sequential implementation by Hardekopf [13], when analyzing a suite of 14 benchmark programs.

Although our paper focuses mainly on inclusion-based points-to analysis, many of the ideas presented here (especially the graph representation) are applicable to the implementation of other morph codes on the GPU. In addition, our work adds another data point to the ongoing debate regarding the performance of CPU and GPU architectures and their associated programming models [10, 20, 22, 34], and it confirms that modern GPUs can be used to accelerate a wide range of applications.

We summarize the contributions of this paper below.

- A GPU implementation of Andersen's analysis requires fundamental modifications with respect to the CPU code. The modifications include adapting the data structures to the GPU memory model (Section 4), distributing work to threads using novel scheduling policies and avoiding explicit worklists (Section 5), adding new algorithmic features based on primitives (sorts, pre-

* This work was supported in part by NSF grants 111176, 0923907, 0833162,0719966, and 0702353 and by grants from Qualcomm, NEC and Intel. This work was also supported in part by equipment and grants from NVIDIA Corporation.

PPoPP'12, February 25–29, 2012, New Orleans, Louisiana, USA.

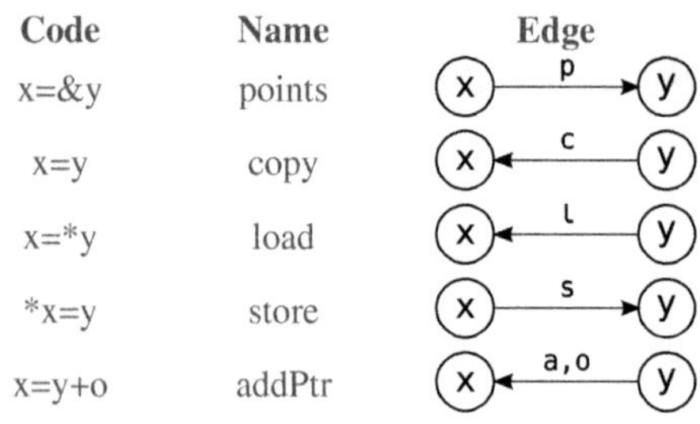

Code
Name
Edge
x=&y
points
x=y
copy
x=*y
load
*x=y
store
x=y+o
addPtr
p
c
l
s
a,o

Figure 1. Basic edge types

fix sums) that can be executed very efficiently on the GPU (Sections 5 and 6), and minimizing the overhead penalty derived from exchanging data between the CPU and the GPU (Section 6). This paper can be useful for understanding some of the differences between optimizing codes for multicores and GPUs.

- We describe a graph representation suited for the implementation of morph algorithms on GPUs (Section 4). Our graph data structure is based on 'wide' sparse bit vectors and does not impose any constraint on the structure of the graph, allowing the algorithm to add and remove edges dynamically. This is the first GPU implementation of arbitrary graphs that takes into account three relevant performance factors: global address alignment, shared memory bank conflicts and thread divergence.
- Previous work [25, 31] shows how to formulate Andersen's points-to analysis as a graph rewriting problem. In Section 5, we introduce a modified set of rewrite rules such that any number of rules can be executed simultaneously without synchronization. These new rewrite rules are useful independent of the architecture chosen for the parallelization of the algorithm.
- Our GPU code, written in CUDA, outperforms an existing multi-CPU version of the same algorithm [25], achieving an average speedup of 7x with respect to the state of the art sequential CPU implementation [13].

The rest of this paper is organized as follows. Section 2 introduces Andersen's points-to analysis, formulating it as a graph rewriting system. A brief overview of the GPU hardware and software model is given in Section 3. Sections 4 and 5 describe how to compactly represent sparse graphs for morph algorithms on the GPU and how to implement the graph rewrite rules without resorting to synchronization. Important optimizations tailored to the GPU hardware are discussed in Section 6. Section 7 presents experimental results comparing the performance of the GPU, multi-core CPU, and sequential CPU implementations. Related work is discussed in Section 8. Section 9 summarizes our findings and concludes.

2. Inclusion-based points-to analysis

Points-to analysis is a static analysis technique that determines what a pointer variable may point to during the execution of a program. The results of this analysis are useful for program optimization, program verification, debugging and whole program comprehension [17]. The literature contains many variations of points-to analysis: context-sensitive versus context-insensitive, flow-sensitive versus flow-insensitive, etc. [3, 6, 12, 13, 15, 33, 35]. These variations make different trade-offs between precision and running time, but production compilers like gcc and LLVM seem to have settled on context-insensitive, flow-insensitive points-to analysis because the more precise alternatives are currently intractable for very large programs.

2.1 Andersen-style points-to analysis

The most popular algorithm for context-insensitive, flow-insensitive points-to analysis is known as inclusion-based or Andersen-style analysis [3]. The asymptotic worst-case complexity of the algorithm is $O(n^3)$, where n is the number of variables in the program, although this worst-case behavior is rarely observed in practice: there is a plethora of heuristics (e.g., [12, 13, 32]) that dramatically speed up the analysis.

Traditionally, inclusion-based points-to analysis is formulated as a set-constraint problem. Each statement in the input program adds a new constraint to the system, which is iteratively solved until a fixpoint is reached. However, many constraint problems can also be formulated in terms of graph rewriting rules [16, 31]. We now describe a graph-based formulation [25] of Andersen's analysis.

1. *Initialization.* The input program is read, discarding any statement not related to pointer manipulations. Since we assume that we are analyzing C programs, there are five statements of interest: $x = \&y$ (points), $x = y$ (copy), $x = *y$ (load), $*x = y$ (store), and $x = y{+}o$ (pointer arithmetic, abridged as 'addPtr').
2. *Constraint graph creation.* For each pointer variable in the input program, we add a new node to a *constraint* graph, which is the only data structure required by this particular formulation of the analysis. For each pointer-related statement, we add an edge as indicated in Figure 1. Note that the resulting graph might contain multiple edges of different types between two given nodes. An example is shown in Figure 3. The program contains five variables and four statements, so the initial constraint graph in Figure 3(a) has five nodes and four edges.
3. *Solving constraints.* Most of the analysis time is spent in this phase, in which we repeatedly apply a set of four rewrite rules in any order. The rules are listed in Figure 2. Intuitively, each rewrite rule updates the graph locally to satisfy some constraint. For brevity, we will only cover the intuition behind the copy rule; a more formal explanation of each rule can be found elsewhere [25]. The copy rule states that if variable y has an outgoing points edge to z and an outgoing copy edge to x, then an edge of type points must exist between x and z. In other words, the rule augments the points-to set of x by adding one variable that is already present in the points-to set of y. Newly added edges are shown using dashed lines. The formula in the last row indicates the postcondition that will hold once we have applied all the copy rules involving x and y: the points-to set of y is a subset of that of x.

   Notice that each rewrite rule is triggered if there is a node with two outgoing edges at which the relevant invariant is not satisfied because of a missing edge between two variables in the constraint graph. Such a node is called an *active* node. In Figure 2, the active node for each rule is shaded. When an active node is processed and a new edge is added to the graph, it may cause other nodes to become active. There may be many active nodes in a given constraint graph, a fact that we exploit in the parallel algorithm described in Section 2.2.

When no more graph rewrite rules can be applied, the process terminates. Termination is ensured because the process only adds new edges to the constraint graph, and there is only a finite number of edges that can be added. The solution to the points-to problem can be read off the points-to subgraph. It can be proven that the resulting solution is equivalent to the one obtained by solving a system of constraints.

An example of this graph-based analysis is illustrated in Figure 3. In the initial state (a), there are two active nodes, x and z. We choose to apply the copy rule for z first, adding a new points edge $y \xrightarrow{p} w$. Now x is the only active node, firing a store rule that

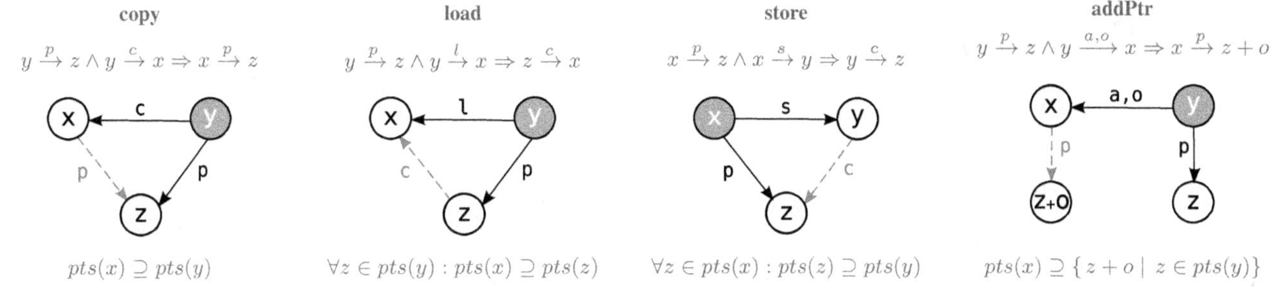

copy
$y \xrightarrow{p} z \wedge y \xrightarrow{c} x \Rightarrow x \xrightarrow{p} z$
$pts(x) \supseteq pts(y)$
load
$y \xrightarrow{p} z \wedge y \xrightarrow{l} x \Rightarrow z \xrightarrow{c} x$
$\forall z \in pts(y) : pts(x) \supseteq pts(z)$
store
$x \xrightarrow{p} z \wedge x \xrightarrow{s} y \Rightarrow y \xrightarrow{c} z$
$\forall z \in pts(x) : pts(z) \supseteq pts(y)$
addPtr
$y \xrightarrow{p} z \wedge y \xrightarrow{a,o} x \Rightarrow x \xrightarrow{p} z + o$
$pts(x) \supseteq \{ z + o \mid z \in pts(y)\}$

Figure 2. Constraint graph rewriting rules

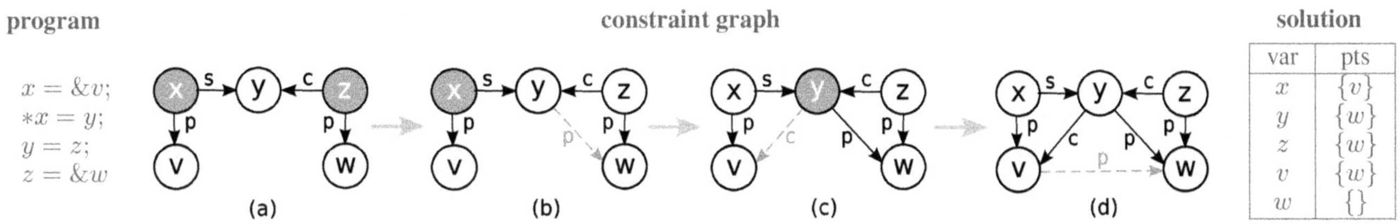

var	pts
x	$\{v\}$
y	$\{w\}$
z	$\{w\}$
v	$\{w\}$
w	$\{\}$

Figure 3. Graph rewrite example

adds $y \xrightarrow{c} v$. After applying another copy rule (transition from (c) to (d)), the preconditions of all the rewrite rules are satisfied and we reach a fixpoint. The points-to solution is shown on the right hand side of Figure 3.

2.2 Parallelism in Andersen's points-to analysis

Graph rewrite rules can be applied concurrently, provided that the graph data structure is properly synchronized such that edges can be added to it in a concurrent fashion. To understand this simple parallelization scheme, consider the possible scenarios that can happen when a rule R is adding an edge from x to y:

- Another rule reads an edge that starts at node x. This edge will not be removed by R because no edges are removed.
- Another rule adds an edge $x \rightarrow z$ such that $y \neq z$. This new edge cannot affect the update rule executed by R because it does not depend on that edge. On the other hand, the concrete representation of the edge set needs to be synchronized so it supports concurrent additions. For example, in Figure 3(a), there are two active nodes x and z, and both are trying to add a new outgoing edge to y. In a parallel setting, we allow the two rules to perform the addition concurrently.
- Another rule tries to add the *same* edge. The two rules can be interleaved in any fashion and the final state will be the same. The work performed by one of the activities is redundant, but it is irrelevant which one actually performs the edge addition.

The parallelism in inclusion-based points-to analysis is a particular example of *amorphous data-parallelism*, a generalization of data-parallelism that is ubiquitous in irregular programs [29]. Note that this parallelism is independent of the programming model or the underlying parallel hardware: it is a property of the algorithm.

3. GPU architecture and programming model

We briefly describe the micro-architecture of modern graphics processors and the CUDA programming model for using them. Although we focus on NVIDIA GPUs, the concepts discussed here also apply to other similar architectures.

The Fermi architecture [1] on which our work is based consist of up to 16 identical streaming multiprocessors (SMs), each of which contains 32 tightly coupled processing elements (PEs) that are sometimes called CUDA cores. Whereas each PE is able to run an independent thread of instructions, all 32 PEs in an SM must either execute the same instruction in the same cycle or wait. This Single Instruction Multiple Thread (SIMT) execution model is tantamount to running instructions that conditionally operate on 32 individual data items. A set of 32 threads that run together in this manner is called a *warp*.

Warps are automatically subdivided by the hardware into sets of threads that want to execute the same instruction. The sets are then serially executed until they re-converge, which degrades performance. Therefore, it is very important to avoid *thread divergence*, i.e., situations where not all threads follow the same control flow, as occur in certain if-then-else and looping statements.

Up to 48 warps can simultaneously be resident in an SM. The PEs execute the warps in multithreading style to hide latencies, that is, the PEs in an SM are time-shared among the warps. Because only one warp is actively executed in any one cycle, threads belonging to different warps can execute different instructions. The PEs do not support out-of-order execution within threads but are able to arbitrarily interleave warps. Hence, it is important to have a large number of warps running concurrently to extract the full performance of the GPU.

The memory subsystem is also optimized for warp-based execution. If the threads in a warp simultaneously access words in main memory that lie in the same aligned 128-byte segment, the hardware merges the 32 reads or writes into one *coalesced* memory transaction that is as fast as accessing a single word. But if a warp requests 32 scattered words, the hardware has to perform 32 separate memory transactions. Thus, coalesced memory accesses are crucial to achieve a high memory bandwidth.

The PEs within an SM share a pool of parallel threads called *thread block*, synchronization hardware, an L1 data cache, and a software-controlled cache called *shared memory*. The shared memory is as fast as the L1 data cache and allows threads in a thread block to quickly exchange data. A warp can simultaneously access 32 words in shared memory as long as the words reside in different banks or all accesses within a bank request the same word.

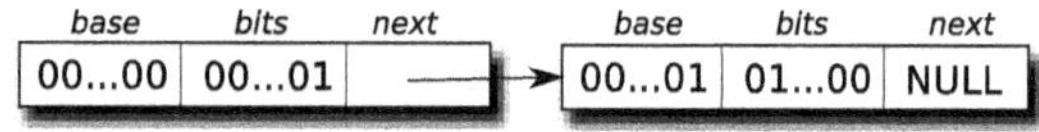

Figure 4. Sparse bit vector representing $\{0, 62\}$ (*bits* is assumed to be 32 bits wide)

Otherwise, bank conflicts occur that result in (partial) serialization of the 32 accesses.

The SMs operate largely independently. They can only communicate through global memory (DRAM). Thus, synchronization between SMs must be accomplished using atomic operations on global memory locations.

NVIDIA's CUDA programming model extends the C/C++ programming language with several parallel programming primitives to exploit the architectural capabilities of GPUs. A CUDA program consists of host code running on the CPU and device code running on the GPU. The device code includes one or more functions, called *kernels*, that can be invoked by the CPU.

4. Graph representation on the GPU

Creating an efficient data structure to represent the constraint graph under the GPU memory model is a challenging problem. The data structure has to compactly represent millions of edges (the analysis of the linux kernel results in a constraint graph with 1.498 billion edges) and allow dynamic modifications. At the same time, the memory layout of the graph has to be specifically designed for the GPU architecture to minimize memory transactions, maximize coalescing, and avoid divergence within the threads of a warp.

One feasible representation for the constraint graph is an adjacency matrix. For instance, the points-to graph can be represented by an $n \times n$ dense matrix (where n is the number of variables in the program); call this matrix P. If we assign a unique id to each variable in the program, then $P(i, j) = 1$ if the variable with id i points to the variable with id j. In a similar fashion, matrices C, S, L and A would represent the other types of edges in our problem.

The matrix representation has one major advantage: the graph rewrite rules can be expressed in terms of matrix-matrix multiplications, which can be performed quickly on a GPU (NVIDIA provides the CUBLAS library for this purpose). For example, we can apply all the available copy rules at once and update the points-to matrix P by computing $P = P + C^t * P$.

The disadvantage of this approach is that it wastes a lot of space since graphs in this application are very sparse. We computed the initial and final density of the P and C matrices using the points-to algorithm of Hardekopf [13] to analyze three inputs: the gcc compiler, the vim editor and the linux kernel. Densities are calculated as the number of non-zero entries in the corresponding matrix (i.e., the number of edges in the graph) divided by the total number of entries, which is n^2. It can be seen that both the initial and final matrices are very sparse. (The matrices for load, store and pointer arithmetic edges are also extremely sparse.)

input	P_i	P_f	C_i	C_f
gcc	$5 * 10^{-7}$	$6 * 10^{-4}$	$6 * 10^{-6}$	$4 * 10^{-5}$
vim	$2 * 10^{-7}$	$8 * 10^{-4}$	$10 * 10^{-7}$	$2 * 10^{-5}$
linux	$1 * 10^{-7}$	$2 * 10^{-3}$	$2 * 10^{-7}$	$2 * 10^{-4}$

An alternative representation tailored to sparse graphs is the Compressed Sparse Row representation. The limitation in this case is that Andersen's analysis, like other morph codes, dynamically adds new edges to the graph. Since the final number of neighbors for each node in the constraint graph cannot be statically predicted and can vary dramatically from variable to variable, adjacency list-based representations like CSR are not adequate.

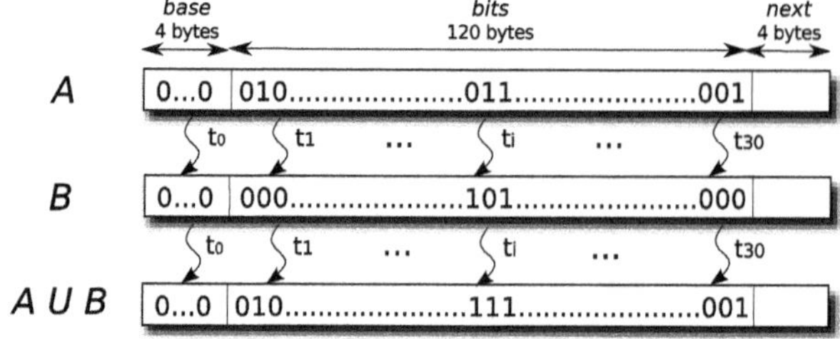

Figure 5. Union of two sparse bit vector elements on the GPU using a warp

One representation of sparse graphs that allows the addition and removal of new edges is based on sparse bit vectors. A sparse bit vector is a data structure that compactly represents sets of integers. Internally, it is a linked list in which each element contains three fields: the *base* of that element, the *bits*, and a pointer to the next element. The base indicates the range of integers possibly contained in the current element; the bits indicate whether a particular integer belongs to the set or not.

Figure 4 shows the representation of a set of integers P using a sparse bit vector. The *bits* field is 32 bits wide, so each element can store up to 32 integers. The first element of P has base 0, so it can only contain numbers between 0 and 31. Since the rightmost bit is set, 0 is in P. Since the 30th bit of the element with base 1 is also set and 32*1+30=62, we have $P = \{0, 62\}$. By assigning unique integer identifiers to each variable in the program, a sparse bit vector can be used to represent the set of neighbors of a given variable. In our example, if P represents the points-to set of variable x, then $pts(x) = \{0, 62\}$. Sparse bit vectors have been used in some CPU implementations of points-to analysis ([13, 15, 23], among others).

The sparse bit vectors used in our implementation occupy 128 bytes per element. The base and the next pointer use one word each; the rest of the space is dedicated to the *bits* field. Therefore, each element can hold up to 960 integers. The 32-word width matches the GPU memory bus. Assuming that the elements are 128-byte aligned, bringing one element from global into shared memory requires exactly one transaction: thread i ($i \in \{0..31\}$) brings in the i-th word. Once the element is in shared memory, each thread of the warp can manipulate its own word without causing any bank conflicts. Finally, many set operations can be performed concurrently by all the threads within a warp with little divergence.

Consider, for example, the union of two sparse bit vector elements with the same base, defined as the bitwise OR of their respective *bits* fields: only the thread that corresponds to the *next* word will diverge, since performing an OR of two identical bases does not change the base. Set intersection can be implemented in a similar fashion using the logical AND operation. A visual representation of the union operation is depicted in Figure 5. It takes one memory transaction (400-800 cycles [2]) to transfer each element from global to shared memory, one cycle to do the bitwise OR of the two elements, and another transaction to write the result back to global memory.

The 128-byte element representation we propose can waste large amounts of memory. For instance, if we want to represent a singleton set using a standard bit vector element (in many CPU implementations [13, 23], the *bits* field is 4 bytes-wide) we need only 12 bytes, ten times less space than what the wide representation requires. However, sets containing large sequences of contiguous integers benefit from wider elements: the set $\{0, .., 959\}$ occupies 128 bytes, while the standard representation requires 360 bytes (thirty elements) of storage.

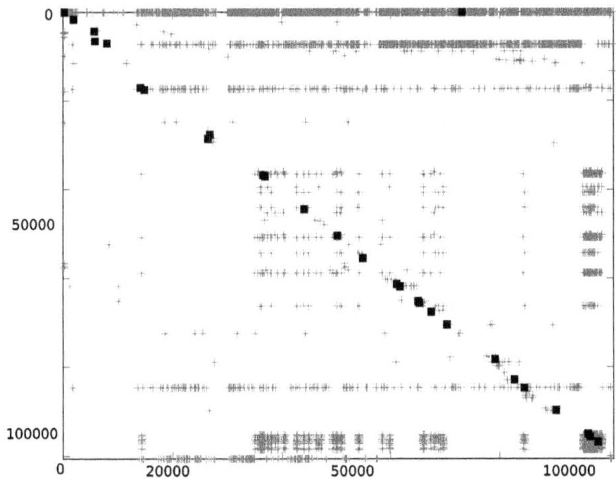

Figure 6. Adjacency matrix of the gcc points-to graph

Using wide elements can also result on a performance penalty when most of the words in the *bits* field are zero, since the amount of useful work performed by the threads within a warp diminishes. Consider the example in Figure 5: if a thread is performing bitwise operations such as union or intersection on two empty words, then it is basically working on data that is not useful to the algorithm.

We compared the storage needed by the wide and standard bit vector representations when storing the final constraint graph. We used Hardekopf's points-to analysis [13] and the same inputs as in the experiments in Section 7. On average, the GPU-tailored sparse bit vectors use 2.3x more space. The reason why using wider elements is fairly efficient is that the analyzed programs exhibit spatial locality. If a variable points at some other variable i, then there is a high probability that it also points to variables with identifiers close to i. This holds because identifiers are sequentially assigned to variables as they appear in the program, so variables in the same block/function receive similar ids.

This distribution can be observed in Figure 6, in which we plotted the adjacency matrix for the points-to edges at the beginning (solid squares) and at the end (shaded crosses) of the analysis. Since Andersen's algorithm does not removes edges, the initial edges are also part of the final graph. The input is gcc, which has 120K variables. As we can see in Figure 6, the initial points-to subgraph corresponds almost perfectly to a diagonal adjacency matrix: variables point to others that appear close together in the program. After repeatedly applying the rewrite rules, there is a clustering effect in the points-to sets: once a variable is determined to possibly point to another variable in some other block, then it probably might point to its aliases, too. In Figure 6, we also observe that some nodes have a large number of incoming points-to edges; they correspond to global variables and allocation sites.

In summary, the proposed graph representation is a good fit for the implementation of morph algorithms on a GPU. Furthermore, it is the first implementation of arbitrary graphs we are aware of that takes into account global address alignment, shared memory bank conflicts and thread divergence. Since we expect that the graph being manipulated by other algorithms (in particular, flow analyses) will also be sparse and share the same locality characteristics as in our application, we believe that irregular codes such as [30] could benefit from our representation.

5. Parallel rule application on the GPU

A parallel CPU implementation of Andersen's algorithm depends on multiple features that have been studied in depth in the context of that particular hardware model: concurrent data structures, work schedulers, dynamic memory allocators, etc. However, there is no standard GPU counterpart for many of these basic building blocks. In this section, we present solutions for some of these problems.

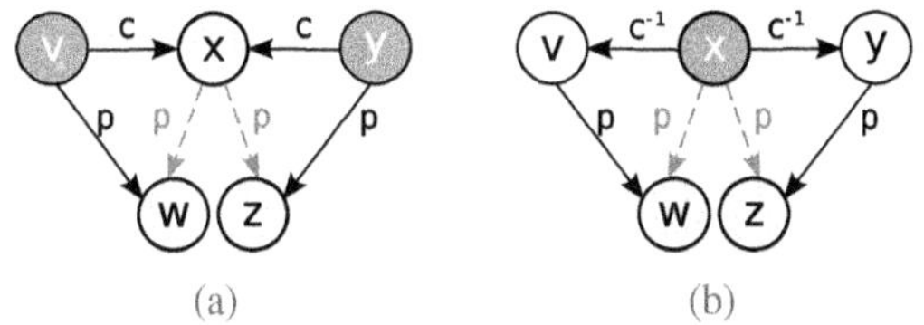

Figure 8. Simultaneous application of copy rules requires synchronization, which can be avoided by reversing the copy edges

Parallel execution of the rewrite rules in Figure 2 requires synchronization in the graph data structure. An example is shown in Figure 8(a): both copy rules simultaneously try to add an outgoing edge to node x, so synchronization is needed. Modern GPUs support atomic compare and swap operations, but overusing them may result in a substantial performance penalty. We devised a novel algorithmic solution to dramatically reduce the amount of synchronization needed to implement Andersen's analysis.

Figure 8(b) shows the intuitive idea: instead of storing an outgoing copy edge in the source variable, we store the *reversed* edge, which we denote by c^{-1}, in the destination node. The copy rule is adapted for this new type of edge, and now we add $x \xrightarrow{p} z$ if there exists a path $x \xrightarrow{c^{-1}} y \xrightarrow{p} z$. The modified rewrite rule is called a reversed copy rule, or copy^{-1} rule. Note that the only active node in Figure 8(b) is x. The benefit of the new formulation is that, as long as there are no two concurrent rules working on the same active node, we do not depend on synchronization: active nodes only add outgoing edges to themselves.

The new set of rewrite rules is shown in Figure 7. They require flipping the copy, load, and pointer arithmetic edges. The store^{-1} rule also depends on storing the incoming points-to edges. Modifications made by a 'reversed' rewrite rule are now local: the edge is added to the active node of that rule.

The distribution of work to threads is done in a warp-centric manner, in a very similar way to [18]. Each active node is assigned to a warp, which executes all the possible rules of a specific type. The selected level of granularity seems to be adequate: a) using an entire block to process and active node will result in many idle threads since there is very little work to be done for some variables, b) using one thread will result in high intra-warp divergence (poor performance) since the number of rewrite rules that need to be applied is not uniform across active nodes.

The pseudo-code of Andersen's algorithm on the GPU is shown in Figure 9. The comments indicate whether the code is being executed on the CPU, GPU or is a data transfer between the two devices. The input is read on the CPU and then transferred to the GPU, where we create the initial constraint graph (*initialize* kernel). Then, we repeatedly apply each reversed graph rewrite rule (*rule* kernel) on the GPU until the constraint graph reaches a fixpoint. The termination condition is verified on the CPU by first transferring a Boolean variable from the global memory of the GPU. When the process terminates, we copy the solution (i.e., the points-to edges) to the CPU. Note that the rest of the constraint graph is necessary for the solving phase but is not part of the output of this algorithm.

The *rule* kernel is executed entirely on the GPU. Each warp is assigned a variable x and then applies the transitive closure to the edges of the specified types. Multiple warps will never work on the same variable because variables are assigned by atomically

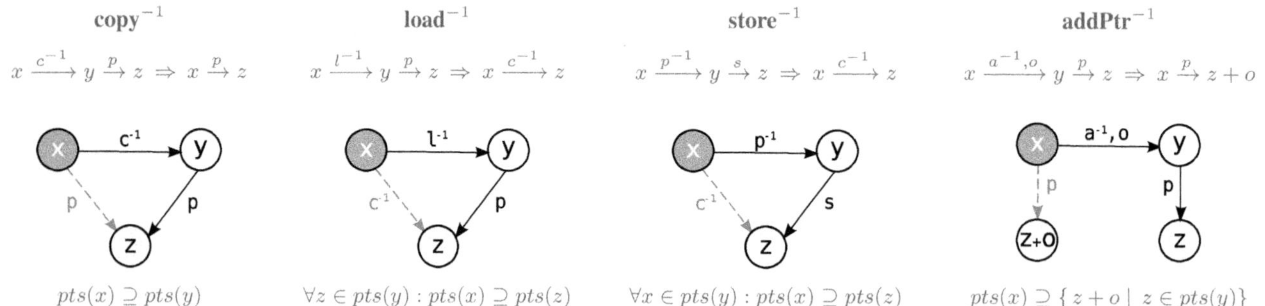

copy^{-1}
$x \xrightarrow{c^{-1}} y \xrightarrow{p} z \Rightarrow x \xrightarrow{p} z$
$pts(x) \supseteq pts(y)$
load^{-1}
$x \xrightarrow{l^{-1}} y \xrightarrow{p} z \Rightarrow x \xrightarrow{c^{-1}} z$
$\forall z \in pts(y) : pts(x) \supseteq pts(z)$
store^{-1}
$x \xrightarrow{p^{-1}} y \xrightarrow{s} z \Rightarrow x \xrightarrow{c^{-1}} z$
$\forall x \in pts(y) : pts(x) \supseteq pts(z)$
addPtr^{-1}
$x \xrightarrow{a^{-1},o} y \xrightarrow{p} z \Rightarrow x \xrightarrow{p} z+o$
$pts(x) \supseteq \{ z+o \mid z \in pts(y) \}$

Figure 7. Constraint graph rewriting rules, modified to avoid synchronization

```
andersen():
  read input                                  // CPU
  transfer initial constraints                // CPU→GPU
  initialize_kernel()                         // GPU
  do
     rule_kernel(C^-1, P, P)                  // GPU
     rule_kernel(L^-1, P, C^-1)               // GPU
     rule_kernel(P^-1, S, C^-1)               // GPU
     rule_kernel(A^-1, P, P)                  // GPU
     transfer changed                         // GPU→CPU
  while changed                               // CPU
  transfer P                                  // GPU→CPU

rule_kernel(R, S, T):                         // GPU
  foreach x in variables
    if R ≠ A^-1
      foreach x -R-> y
         union S-neighbors of y to T-neighbors of x
    else
      foreach x -a^-1,o-> y
         N ← add o to each S-neighbor of y
         union N to T-neighbors of x

    if T-neighbors of x changed
      changed ← true
```

Figure 9. Pseudo-code of Andersen's algorithm on the GPU

incrementing a global integer. Thus, our algorithm does not need an explicit worklist for the active elements (unlike most of the CPU implementations we know of); instead, we simply check if it is possible to apply a given rule to *all* variables. Since there are many warps (see Section 7) executing concurrently, the overhead of processing non-active nodes is almost negligible.

The transitive closure is implemented as follows. Given a variable x, we traverse the set of neighbors for the first relation (variable R in the pseudo code). The traversal implies decoding the sparse bit vector representing the outgoing edges of that type. For each neighbor y, we union the sparse bit vector containing all its S-neighbors with the sparse bit vector that contains the T-neighbors of x. The pointer arithmetic rule requires an extra step, since we need to add the offset to each points-to neighbor of y before performing the union. The computation of the union of two adjacency lists is explained in Section 4.

The union of two adjacency list might result in the addition of new elements to the sparse bit vector representing the adjacency list of a particular combination of variable and edge type. Although recent CUDA implementations offer dynamic memory allocation [2], we created a custom allocator. We divided a region of global memory into two *element pools*. One is dedicated to the points-to edges and the other is used for all other types of edges. Each time a warp has to allocate a new element, it simply atomically increments the pointer to the next free element in the corresponding pool. The division of the heap into two regions has two advantages: a) the more regions we have, the lower the contention on the free list pointers is and, more importantly, b) all elements containing points-to edges are stored together. When the analysis terminates, we can minimize the amount of data transferred from the GPU to the CPU by copying only the points-to region.

6. Optimizations

We now describe several GPU-based optimizations that dramatically improve the performance of our implementation.

6.1 Minimize memory consumption

The store^{-1} rewrite rule in Figure 7 introduces a performance problem since it depends on also storing the reversed (incoming) points-to edges, which can be prohibitive in terms of memory usage. In order to avoid this, we use a different, two-phase strategy to implement the store rule. In the first phase, we create a worklist containing all pairs of variables (x, y) such that y has outgoing store edges, and $y \xrightarrow{p} x$ is in the constraint graph. In the second phase, we assign all pairs with an identical first component to the same warp. Since an active node is processed by only one warp, there is no synchronization required except for removing elements from the worklist. Creating an explicit worklist to handle store edges may seem expensive, but it performs well in practice because the number of store edges is very small for most input programs (about 5% of the edges in the final graph).

6.2 Avoid redundant rule application

The graph rewrite rules in Figure 7 need to be applied only once. For instance, the copy^{-1} rule does not need to be fired in a particular iteration if the points-to sets of all the variables have not changed during the last iteration of the main loop in the pseudo-code in Figure 9.

A possible solution to avoid repeated work is to distinguish between two types of points-to edges: the ones that have been added to the constraint graph *before* the last iteration (P) and the ones added during the last and current iterations (ΔP). The distinction results in two major modifications of the algorithm: a) the graph rewrite rules are now defined in terms of edges in ΔP, not P, and b) we need an additional kernel that performs the updates $\Delta P = \Delta P - P$ and $P = P \cup \Delta P$.

The idea of working exclusively on the newly added edges is not novel [15]. However, the GPU implementation benefits from it in two distinct ways:

- At the beginning of each iteration, we transfer ΔP from the GPU to the CPU in parallel with the execution of the rewrite kernels using streams [2]. This approach completely hides the transfer latency and greatly reduces the overall runtime.

	K			V		
	$\{a,c\}$	$\{b\}$	$\{a,c\}$	x	y	z
hash(K)	38	12	38	x	y	z
sort(K,V)	12	38	38	y	x	z
diff(K)	0	1	0	y	x	z
prefix(K, max)	0	1	1	y	x	z

Figure 10. Example of detection of ΔP-equivalent variables

- Computing differences between sets of edges (i.e., differences between sparse bit vectors) can be efficiently implemented using a warp-based approach that is similar to the union operation.

6.3 Detect pointer-equivalent variables

ΔP-equivalent variables have the same outgoing ΔP edges in the current iteration. It is desirable to identify ΔP-equivalent variables, since much redundant work can be avoided. For example, assume that the $\Delta P(x) = \{a,c\}$, $\Delta P(y) = \{b\}$ and $\Delta P(z) = \{a,c\}$. If the three variables are copy^{-1} neighbors of some other node in the constraint graph, then applying the copy^{-1} rule to x (or z) and then to y produces the same result as applying it to all three variables because the new points-to sets of x and z are identical.

Detection of ΔP-equivalent variables is extremely efficient on the GPU. We illustrate the mechanism with an example. In Figure 10, we have a map containing keys (ΔP) and values (variables). The key at column i corresponds to the value at the same column (e.g., $\Delta P(x) = \{a,c\}$). We first compute a hash value for the keys and then sort both keys and values according to the hash. Then we apply a difference function between keys such that $K'(i) = i$ if $K(i-1) \neq K(i)$ or $i = 0$. The final step computes a prefix sum of the keys, using the maximum operator: $K'(i) = max(K_0, ..., K_i)$. The final map verifies that the variable at column i is ΔP-equivalent to the one at column $K(i)$. For example, variable z has the same ΔP as variable $V(K(2)) = V(1) = x$.

Detection of ΔP-equivalent variables is implemented using the Thrust library [28], which supports fast data-parallel operations such as sorting, prefix sums, and reductions. It is interesting to note that the multi-CPU implementation of [25] does not try to detect ΔP-equivalent variables, and it is not clear whether the described mechanism will perform well on a CPU.

6.4 Collapse cycles

When two or more variables belong to a cycle of copy^{-1} edges, they are pointer-equivalent (i.e., their points-to sets will be identical by the end of the analysis) and the corresponding strongly connected component can be collapsed. For example, a pair of statements of the form *a = b; b = a;* produces a cycle of constraints that imply that *pts(a) = pts(b)*. In the literature, cycle detection comes in two flavors: *offline* methods [32] look for cycles during a preprocessing phase whereas *online* methods [12] look for cycles during the solving process.

Some intermediate techniques, such as Hybrid Cycle Detection [13] (HCD), combine the two: potential cycles are identified in the offline phase, and these are collapsed during analysis. Potential cycles arise from statements of the form **a = b; b = *a;*. Without knowing *pts(a)*, we do not know the nodes that participate in cycles with *b*, so these cycles cannot be eliminated during preprocessing, but we can remove them during the constraint solving process whenever we add nodes to *pts(a)*.

Our implementation of Andersen's analysis uses only Hybrid Cycle Detection. Offline techniques greatly improve the performance of the sequential version, but they often introduce a bottleneck to scalability in the parallel codes. The offline phase of HCD is executed on the CPU. The online phase is implemented as a GPU kernel, and it implies merging variables that are pointer equivalent (i.e., variables that belong to the same strongly connected component), by selecting one *representative* node and adding to it all the outgoing edges of the non-representative variables.

Cycle collapsing seems to require implementing two extra graph operations: node and edge deletion. An alternative approach that performs well in practice is to ignore non-representative variables and their edges. A warp only processes variables identified as representative in a *representative table* in global memory.

program	vars	stmts	program	vars	stmts
ex	11	13	vim	246	108
perl	54	68	php	339	325
python	92	111	mplayer	537	377
nh	97	114	gimp	558	649
svn	107	139	pine	612	315
gcc	120	156	linux	1,503	420
gdb	232	241	tshark	1,555	1,789

Figure 11. Benchmark suite: number of variables and statements (in thousands)

7. Experimental evaluation

This section compares the performance of Andersen's analysis on the GPU with two previous CPU implementations: a sequential version by Hardekopf [13] and our multi-CPU version [25]. The source code of the multi-CPU and GPU analyses is available at `http://clip.dia.fi.upm.es/~mario/`. In the rest of this section, we refer to the multi-CPU version as the *reference* implementation.

The reference implementation is very similar to the sequential analysis, except for the necessary synchronization on the data structures and minor algorithmic modifications. However, the GPU implementation introduces major algorithmic changes, as described in the previous sections. Another important difference is the use of a Binary Decision Diagram [8] data structure. The benefits of BDDs in the context of points-to analysis have been touted by many researchers [6, 35]. The reference implementation uses a BDD to compactly represent the points-to edges, while all the other types of edges are internally represented using sparse bit vectors. In contrast, our implementation only uses 'wide' sparse bit vectors because BDDs are extremely complex and ill-suited for GPUs.

Figure 11 shows the benchmark suite used in our experiments. It consists of fourteen C programs ranging from 11K to 1555K variables (nodes in the constraint graph) and 13K to 1789K statements (initial edges). Most of the programs in our benchmark suite have been used by other researchers in this area [13, 25].

We evaluated the performance of the CUDA implementations on a 1.15 GHz NVIDIA Tesla C2070 GPU with 14 streaming multiprocessors (448 processing elements, i.e., CUDA cores) and 6 GB of main memory. This Fermi GPU has a 64 KB L1 cache per SM. We dedicate 48 KB to shared memory (user-managed cache) and 16 KB to the hardware-managed cache. All the streaming multiprocessors share an L2 cache of 768 KB. We compiled the CUDA code with nvcc v4.1 RC2 and the -arch=sm_20 flag.

To execute the CPU codes, we used a machine running Ubuntu 10 with four 4-core 2.7 GHz AMD Opteron processors. The 16 CPU cores share 24 GB of main memory. Each core has a 64 KB L1 cache and a 512 KB L2 cache. Each processor has a 6 MB L3 cache that is shared among its four cores. The sequential implementation is written in C++ and compiled with gcc and the -O3 flag. The reference implementation is written in Java on top of the Galois framework [21]. The Java Virtual Machine used is the 64-bit Sun HotSpot server version 1.6.0_24.

input	CPU-s	CPU-1	CPU-16	GPU
ex	400	3.17	1.54	**5.00**
gcc	1,000	1.20	**4.63**	3.57
nh	1,280	1.22	5.54	**6.74**
perl	1,990	1.12	6.18	**6.22**
vim	10,110	1.30	**9.39**	1.28
tshark	12,110	0.89	3.53	**5.13**
svn	14,630	0.96	5.70	**10.09**
python	17,890	0.85	3.99	**14.54**
gimp	20,500	0.92	**7.83**	3.45
gdb	31,300	0.90	6.95	**9.40**
pine	38,950	0.92	4.93	**5.21**
php	44,670	0.86	5.97	**6.54**
mplayer	66,260	0.83	6.07	**7.97**
linux	120,340	1.05	7.67	**10.39**

Figure 12. Runtimes (in ms) for the sequential online phase (CPU-s column), and speedups achieved by CPU-x and GPU

Each GPU kernel can be configured with respect to the number of blocks and the number of threads per block it uses. Having many threads per block seems to be a good choice, since communication among threads within the same block is cheaper (they can communicate through the local memory of the streaming multiprocessor). However, the hardware imposes limits on the number of threads per block (1024 in Fermi GPUs). Other factors that impose constraints on the number of threads per block are the register and the shared memory usage. The number of persistent blocks and threads per block used by the most relevant kernels in our implementation is shown in the following table.

kernel	blocks	threads
update P, ΔP	14	1024
cycle collapsing (HCD)	14	512
copy^{-1} / load^{-1} / store^{-1}	14	864
addPtr^{-1}	14	1024

Since the GPU used in our experiments has fourteen SMs, we use that many blocks. Within each block, the thread count is not always maximized since operations on sparse bit vectors heavily rely on caching of data in the fast shared memory. In our warp-based approach, a kernel with 1024 threads (32 warps) restricts the shared memory usage of each warp to just 1,536 bytes.

The first set of results, shown in Figure 12, contains the online analysis times (in milliseconds) for each program in the benchmark suite using the sequential analysis, denoted by CPU-s. We sorted the inputs according to the sequential analysis runtimes, which are not always proportional to the number of variables or statements. The other columns list the speedups achieved by the reference implementation using x threads (CPU-x) and the implementation discussed in this paper (GPU). In the case of CPU-x, we only show the results for one and sixteen threads. The best speedups are marked in bold.

In the case of CPU-s and GPU, each benchmark was run three times (there is very little variability) and the median runtime (or its speedup) is reported. In the case of CPU-x, in order to minimize the effects of JIT compilation, each benchmark was run five times, and the speedup achieved by the median runtime is reported. We also minimized the influence of garbage collection in the CPU-x results by maximizing the size of the JVM heap to the point where the measured time spent in GC is always zero. Finally, we verified that the three outputs (points-to of every variable in the original program) are identical.

The first observation about Figure 12 is that the reference implementation has better scalability than what was previously reported [25]: the average scalability when using 16 threads is 6.07x

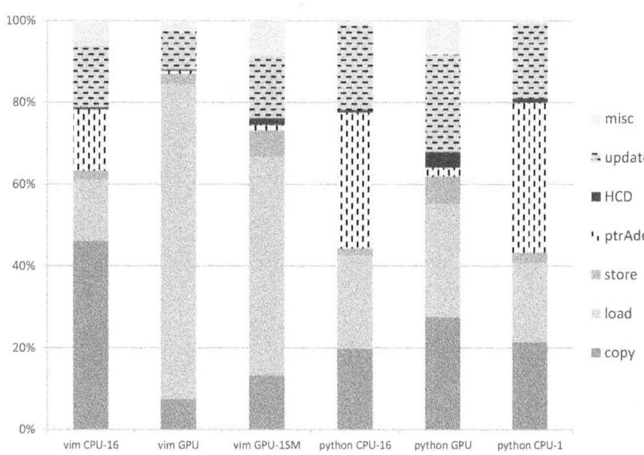

Figure 13. Breakdown of the online analysis times for the vim and python benchmarks

if we exclude the ex benchmark, which is an obvious outlier because of its small size. Another observation is that the multi-CPU implementation using one thread is faster than the sequential version for some of the inputs, which is counter-intuitive. This is due to minor algorithmic changes in the multi-core version, which reduce the memory usage and simplify the scheduling policy [27] (i.e., how elements are removed from the worklist).

The GPU implementation performs remarkably well. For all the inputs, it is significantly faster than the sequential analysis. For 11 out of 14 benchmarks, it is also faster than the best reference runtime, which always happens at the highest thread count, except for ex. Although the results indicate that GPU outperforms CPU-x, we acknowledge that establishing a completely fair comparison between the two parallel codes is difficult: there are remarkable differences at the algorithmic, language and hardware levels. For instance, the reference implementation is written in Java whereas the GPU code is written in low-level CUDA. From the hardware perspective, the two machines used in our experiments have a similar number of processing units (fourteen streaming multiprocessors and sixteen cores, respectively), but the CPU cores are significantly faster, exploit instruction-level parallelism, and contain large caches. In any case, it might come as a surprise that CUDA codes can be competitive with highly-tuned multi-core implementations for algorithms as irregular as Andersen's points-to analysis.

Our experimental data reveal the different behavior of the two parallel analyses. For instance, the CUDA code performs significantly worse for the vim input (8x slowdown with respect to CPU-16) but much better for python (3.5x speedup). We broke down the online analysis times of these two benchmarks to understand the cause of the performance differences. The results are shown in Figure 13. We divided the algorithm into seven components: the rewrite rules, updating P and ΔP, cycle collapsing (HCD), and a miscellaneous category that includes worklist accesses (CPU-x) and detection of pointer-equivalent variables (GPU).

The left hand-side of Figure 13 shows the breakdowns of the time spent analyzing vim by CPU-16, GPU and GPU-1SM, which is identical to GPU except for the fact that only one streaming multiprocessor is active. This last bit of information is useful for finding scalability issues; for instance, the breakdown of GPU looks similar to that of GPU-1SM, and both reveal that the GPU implementation spends a lot of time computing load rules. In this particular case, we found that the data representation was responsible for the slowdown. Operations involving BDDs can be cached because the operands have canonical representations. The memo-

	CPU-s		CPU-16			GPU		
input	offline	online	offline	online	speedup	offline	online	speedup
ex	20	400	73	259	1.27	73	80	**2.75**
gcc	340	1,000	210	216	**3.15**	210	280	2.73
nh	270	1,280	156	231	4.01	156	190	**4.48**
perl	160	1,990	121	322	4.85	121	320	**4.88**
vim	250	10,110	153	1,077	**8.42**	153	7,870	1.29
tshark	3,090	12,110	1,567	3,432	3.04	1,567	2,360	**3.87**
svn	210	14,630	188	2,568	5.38	188	1,450	**9.06**
python	220	17,890	167	4,488	3.89	167	1,230	**12.96**
gimp	1,110	20,500	634	2,618	**6.65**	634	5,950	3.28
gdb	490	31,300	265	4,502	6.67	265	3,330	**8.84**
pine	670	38,950	333	7,900	4.81	333	7,470	**5.08**
php	620	44,670	352	7,486	5.78	352	6,830	**6.31**
mplayer	750	66,260	375	10,921	5.93	375	8,310	**7.72**
linux	1,210	120,340	543	15,685	7.49	543	11,580	**10.03**

Figure 14. Comparison of runtimes (in ms) for the whole analysis: CPU (sequential), CPU (parallel, 16 threads), and GPU

ization is very useful when the same operation is applied over and over during analysis, as it happens in vim. In fact, disabling this cache in the reference implementation results in an average slowdown of almost two orders of magnitude.

The breakdown of python (right hand-side of Figure 13) shows that, in the reference implementation, there is no phase with major scalability issues since the CPU-16 plot is almost identical to that of CPU-1. Instead, the measured performance slowdown (with respect to GPU) is caused by the slower execution of the pointer arithmetic rules. Adding an integer ($offset$) to every element in a set is a highly data-parallel operation when its internal representation uses sparse bit vectors: a left shift of the $bits$ field by $offset$ positions. The CPU implementations cannot use the same approach because points-to sets are represented with a BDD.

Figure 14 compares the *total* analysis runtimes, which do not include the time spent in reading the inputs from disk. We show the runtimes of the sequential, the reference (using sixteen threads), and the GPU implementation. For each version, we show the time spent in the offline and online phase. As explained in Section 6, we only use the Hybrid Cycle Detection technique. Since its offline component is always executed on the CPU, the runtimes in the *offline* column are identical for GPU and CPU-16. An important observation is that the offline phase is significantly faster in the parallel implementations because it has been partially parallelized. Finally, the *speedup* column is the total runtime of the corresponding parallel implementation divided by the sequential total runtime. The best speedups are marked in bold.

The GPU total runtimes do include the time involved in exchanging information between the CPU and the GPU. Although in many GPU algorithms this transfer represents a major bottleneck for the overall performance, our implementation overlaps the transfer of the points-to subgraph with the execution of the rewrite rules, cf. Section 6. The time to transfer the initial constraint graph from the CPU to the GPU is negligible (never more than 10 ms).

The average speedup of the reference implementation is 6x; the GPU code achieves a 7x average speedup. These results are remarkable given that some phases of the offline optimizations such as the detection of Strongly Connected Components (SCC) are still sequential. It is future work to implement the offline phase in CUDA and evaluate the benefit of using GPU versions of the SCC algorithm [5].

8. Related Work

There have been numerous implementations of parallel graph algorithms using various computer architectures, including distributed memory supercomputers [36], shared memory supercomputers [4], and multi-core SMP machines [21]. In the context of points-to analyses, the only parallel implementation we know of [25] has been discussed in depth in previous sections.

Graphics Processing Units have only recently been used for the parallelization of irregular programs. Harish [14] describes CUDA implementations of important graph algorithms such as BFS, Single Source Shortest Paths, Minimum Spanning Tree, etc. In all these algorithms, the structure of the graph being manipulated remains unchanged, which significantly simplifies the GPU implementation. Hong [18] proposes a warp-centric approach for the parallelization of BFS, which is similar to the solution adopted in this paper for distributing work among threads.

Burtscher [9] describes a GPU implementation of an n-body simulation (Barnes Hut algorithm) that is based on unbalanced octrees, which is twice as fast as a multicore implementation running on 128 CPU cores. In this algorithm, the octree used to record the spatial decomposition of the bodies is populated in the initialization phase, so synchronization is required to correctly grow the tree. However, over 80% of the execution time is spent in the force calculation phase, which does not modify the octree's structure.

The closest work to this paper is the GPU implementation of a 0-CFA analysis by Prabhu *et al* [30]. As in Andersen's algorithm, the graph containing the solution for the dataflow analysis only grows over time until a fixpoint is reached. Our work improves on their solution in several ways:

- Our sparse bit vector representation allows arbitrary, dynamic addition of edges to the graph. In contrast, the size of the adjacency list used by Prabhu is statically determined: if too many outgoing edges are added to a node, the execution is aborted. Also, a substantial amount of memory is wasted for variables with few outgoing edges.
- We modified the graph rewrite rules to avoid synchronization, which is required in the implementation by Prabhu.
- The transfer of data between the GPU and the CPU does not impose any performance penalty in our implementation.

9. Conclusions and future work

Our work presents solutions for many of the challenges involved in implementing highly efficient codes on the GPU. In particular, we have shown that porting code from the CPU to the GPU demands fundamental changes in the data structures and algorithmic components being used: classical CPU solutions would result in very poor performance on the GPU. Other important aspects, such as the data transfer between devices, are absent from CPU implementations and need to be carefully included in the design of any GPU code. We expect other researchers in the area to benefit from the techniques presented in this paper, thus reducing the effort required to implement complex algorithms on GPUs.

This paper also confirms that it is possible to efficiently implement highly irregular codes such as Andersen's analysis on the GPU. Although the graphics card utilized in our experiments is cheaper than the multi-CPU machine we are comparing against, we achieve better performance on the GPU. It is interesting to note that although the programming effort involved in the GPU implementation was significantly larger (35% more person-hours) than for the SMP implementation [25], the CUDA version is quite compact in terms of source code size, requiring only 3,000 lines of code (compared to 9,000 in the CPU version). This is primarily due to the smaller set of data structures used by the GPU implementation.

In the future, we intend to implement several other irregular algorithms for which there exist highly competitive, parallel CPU implementations [29]. We expect the programming effort to become less as the GPU architecture and programming model evolve toward supporting more general-purpose features.

References

[1] NVIDIA's Next Generation CUDA Compute Architecture: Fermi. http://www.nvidia.com/content/PDF/fermi_white_papers/NVIDIA_Fermi_Compute_Architecture_Whitepaper.pdf, 2010.

[2] *CUDA C Programming Guide 4.0.* NVIDIA, 2011.

[3] L. O. Andersen. *Program Analysis and Specialization for the C Programming Language*. PhD thesis, DIKU, University of Copenhagen, May 1994. (DIKU report 94/19).

[4] David A. Bader and Kamesh Madduri. Designing multithreaded algorithms for breadth-first search and st-connectivity on the cray mta-2. In *Proceedings of the 2006 International Conference on Parallel Processing*, ICPP '06, pages 523–530, Washington, DC, USA, 2006. IEEE Computer Society.

[5] J. Barnat, P. Bauch, L. Brim, and M. Češka. Computing Strongly Connected Components in Parallel on CUDA. In *Proceedings of the 25th IEEE International Parallel & Distributed Processing Symposium (IPDPS'11)*, pages 541–552. IEEE Computer Society, 2011.

[6] Marc Berndl, Ondrej Lhoták, Feng Qian, Laurie Hendren, and Navindra Umanee. Points-to analysis using BDDs. In *Proc. Conf. on Programming Language Design and Implementation (PLDI)*, pages 103–114, New York, NY, USA, 2003. ACM.

[7] Ulrik Brandes and Thomas Erlebach, editors. *Network Analysis: Methodological Foundations*. Springer-Verlag, 2005.

[8] Randal E. Bryant. Graph-based algorithms for boolean function manipulation. *IEEE Transactions on Computers*, 35:677–691, 1986.

[9] Martin Burtscher and Keshav Pingali. An efficient CUDA implementation of the tree-based barnes hut n-body algorithm. In *GPU Computing Gems Emerald Edition*, pages 75–92. Morgan Kaufmann, 2011.

[10] Shuai Che, Michael Boyer, Jiayuan Meng, David Tarjan, Jeremy W. Sheaffer, and Kevin Skadron. A performance study of general-purpose applications on graphics processors using cuda. *J. Parallel Distrib. Comput.*, 68:1370–1380, October 2008.

[11] L. Paul Chew. Guaranteed-quality mesh generation for curved surfaces. In *Proc. Symp. on Computational Geometry (SCG)*, 1993.

[12] Manuel Fähndrich, Jeffrey S. Foster, Zhendong Su, and Alexander Aiken. Partial online cycle elimination in inclusion constraint graphs. In *Proc. Conf. on Programming Language Design and Implementation (PLDI)*, pages 85–96, New York, NY, USA, 1998. ACM.

[13] Ben Hardekopf and Calvin Lin. The ant and the grasshopper: fast and accurate pointer analysis for millions of lines of code. In *Proc. Conf. on Programming Language Design and Implementation (PLDI)*, 2007.

[14] Pawan Harish and P. J. Narayanan. Accelerating large graph algorithms on the gpu using cuda. In *HiPC'07: Proceedings of the 14th international conference on High performance computing*, pages 197–208, Berlin, Heidelberg, 2007. Springer-Verlag.

[15] Nevin Heintze and Olivier Tardieu. Ultra-fast aliasing analysis using cla: a million lines of c code in a second. *SIGPLAN Not.*, 36(5):254–263, 2001.

[16] Fritz Henglein. Type inference and semi-unification. In *Proceedings of the 1988 ACM conference on LISP and functional programming*, LFP '88, pages 184–197, New York, NY, USA, 1988. ACM.

[17] Michael Hind. Pointer analysis: haven't we solved this problem yet? In *PASTE '01: Proceedings of the 2001 ACM SIGPLAN-SIGSOFT workshop on Program analysis for software tools and engineering*, pages 54–61, New York, NY, USA, 2001. ACM.

[18] Sungpack Hong, Sang Kyun Kim, Tayo Oguntebi, and Kunle Olukotun. Accelerating cuda graph algorithms at maximum warp. In *Proceedings of the 16th ACM symposium on Principles and practice of parallel programming*, PPoPP '11, pages 267–276, New York, NY, USA, 2011. ACM.

[19] Sungpack Hong, Tayo Oguntebi, and Kunle Olukotun. Efficient parallel graph exploration on multi-core cpu and gpu. In *20th International Conference on Parallel Architectures and Compilation Techniques*, PACT'11, 2011.

[20] Song Huang, Shucai Xiao, and Wu chun Feng. On the energy efficiency of graphics processing units for scientific computing. In *IPDPS*, pages 1–8, 2009.

[21] Milind Kulkarni, Keshav Pingali, Bruce Walter, Ganesh Ramanarayanan, Kavita Bala, and L. Paul Chew. Optimistic parallelism requires abstractions. *SIGPLAN Not. (Proceedings of PLDI)*, 42(6):211–222, 2007.

[22] Victor W. Lee, Changkyu Kim, Jatin Chhugani, Michael Deisher, Daehyun Kim, Anthony D. Nguyen, Nadathur Satish, Mikhail Smelyanskiy, Srinivas Chennupaty, Per Hammarlund, Ronak Singhal, and Pradeep Dubey. Debunking the 100x gpu vs. cpu myth: an evaluation of throughput computing on cpu and gpu. In *Proceedings of the 37th annual international symposium on Computer architecture*, ISCA '10, pages 451–460, New York, NY, USA, 2010. ACM.

[23] Ondřej Lhoták and Laurie Hendren. Scaling Java points-to analysis using Spark. In G. Hedin, editor, *Compiler Construction, 12th International Conference*, volume 2622 of *LNCS*, pages 153–169, Warsaw, Poland, April 2003. Springer.

[24] Lijuan Luo, Martin Wong, and Wen-mei Hwu. An effective gpu implementation of breadth-first search. In *Proceedings of the 47th Design Automation Conference*, DAC '10, pages 52–55, New York, NY, USA, 2010. ACM.

[25] Mario Méndez-Lojo, Augustine Mathew, and Keshav Pingali. Parallel inclusion-based points-to analysis. In *Proceedings of the 24th Annual ACM SIGPLAN Conference on Object-Oriented Programming, Systems, Languages, and Applications (OOPSLA'10)*, October 2010.

[26] Duane G. Merrill, Michael Garland, and Andrew S. Grimshaw. Scalable gpu graph traversal. In *17th ACM SIGPLAN Symposium on Principles and Practice of Parallel Programming*, PPoPP'12, 2012.

[27] Donald Nguyen and Keshav Pingali. Synthesizing concurrent schedulers for irregular algorithms. In *ASPLOS '11: Proceedings of International Conference on Architectural Support for Programming Languages and Operating Systems*, 2011.

[28] NVIDIA. Thrust library version 1.4.0. http://code.google.com/p/thrust/.

[29] Keshav Pingali, Donald Nguyen, Milind Kulkarni, Martin Burtscher, M. Amber Hassaan, Rashid Kaleem, Tsung-Hsien Lee, Andrew Lenharth, Roman Manevich, Mario Méndez-Lojo, Dimitrios Prountzos, and Xin Sui. The tao of parallelism in algorithms. In *Proceedings of the 32nd ACM SIGPLAN conference on Programming language design and implementation*, PLDI '11, pages 12–25, New York, NY, USA, 2011. ACM.

[30] Tarun Prabhu, Shreyas Ramalingam, Matthew Might, and Mary Hall. Eigencfa: accelerating flow analysis with gpus. In *Proceedings of the 38th annual ACM SIGPLAN-SIGACT symposium on Principles of programming languages*, POPL '11, pages 511–522, New York, NY, USA, 2011. ACM.

[31] Thomas W. Reps. Program analysis via graph reachability. Technical Report Technical Report Number 1386, University of Wisconsin, 1998.

[32] Atanas Rountev and Satish Chandra. Off-line variable substitution for scaling points-to analysis. In *Proc. Conf. on Programming Language Design and Implementation (PLDI)*, pages 47–56, New York, NY, USA, 2000. ACM.

[33] Bjarne Steensgaard. Points-to analysis in almost linear time. In *POPL '96: Proceedings of the 23rd ACM SIGPLAN-SIGACT symposium on Principles of programming languages*, pages 32–41, New York, NY, USA, 1996. ACM.

[34] Richard Vuduc, Aparna Chandramowlishwaran, Jee Choi, Murat Guney, and Aashay Shringarpure. On the limits of gpu acceleration. In *Proceedings of the 2nd USENIX conference on Hot topics in parallelism*, HotPar'10, pages 13–13, Berkeley, CA, USA, 2010. USENIX Association.

[35] John Whaley and Monica S. Lam. Cloning-based context-sensitive pointer alias analysis using binary decision diagrams. In *Proc. Conf. on Programming Language Design and Implementation (PLDI)*, pages 131–144, New York, NY, USA, 2004. ACM.

[36] Andy Yoo, Edmond Chow, Keith Henderson, William McLendon, Bruce Hendrickson, and Umit Catalyurek. A scalable distributed parallel breadth-first search algorithm on bluegene/l. In *Proceedings of the 2005 ACM/IEEE conference on Supercomputing*, SC '05, pages 25–, Washington, DC, USA, 2005. IEEE Computer Society.

Scalable GPU Graph Traversal

Duane Merrill
University of Virginia
Charlottesville
Virginia
USA
dgm4d@virginia.edu

Michael Garland
NVIDIA Corporation
Santa Clara
California
USA
mgarland@nvidia.com

Andrew Grimshaw
University of Virginia
Charlottesville
Virginia
USA
grimshaw@virginia.edu

Abstract

Breadth-first search (BFS) is a core primitive for graph traversal and a basis for many higher-level graph analysis algorithms. It is also representative of a class of parallel computations whose memory accesses and work distribution are both irregular and data-dependent. Recent work has demonstrated the plausibility of GPU sparse graph traversal, but has tended to focus on asymptotically inefficient algorithms that perform poorly on graphs with non-trivial diameter.

We present a BFS parallelization focused on fine-grained task management constructed from efficient prefix sum that achieves an asymptotically optimal $O(|V|+|E|)$ work complexity. Our implementation delivers excellent performance on diverse graphs, achieving traversal rates in excess of 3.3 billion and 8.3 billion traversed edges per second using single and quad-GPU configurations, respectively. This level of performance is several times faster than state-of-the-art implementations both CPU and GPU platforms.

Categories and Subject Descriptors G.2.2 [**Discrete Mathematics**]: Graph Theory – Graph Algorithms; D.1.3 [**Programming Techniques**]: Concurrent programming; F.2.2 [**Analysis of Algorithms and Problem Complexity**]: Nonnumerical Algorithms and Problems – Computations on discrete structures, Geometrical problems and computations

General Terms Algorithms, performance

Keywords Breadth-first search, GPU, graph algorithms, parallel algorithms, prefix sum, graph traversal, sparse graph

1. Introduction

Algorithms for analyzing sparse relationships represented as graphs provide crucial tools in many computational fields ranging from genomics to electronic design automation to social network analysis. In this paper, we explore the parallelization of one fundamental graph algorithm on GPUs: breadth-first search (BFS). BFS is a common building block for more sophisticated graph algorithms, yet is simple enough that we can analyze its behavior in depth. It is also used as a core computational kernel in a number of benchmark suites, including Parboil [26], Rodinia [10], and the emerging Graph500 supercomputer benchmark [29].

PPoPP'12, February 25–29, 2012, New Orleans, Louisiana, USA.

Contemporary processor architecture provides increasing parallelism in order to deliver higher throughput while maintaining energy efficiency. Modern GPUs are at the leading edge of this trend, provisioning tens of thousands of data parallel threads.

Despite their high computational throughput, GPUs might appear poorly suited for sparse graph computation. In particular, BFS is representative of a class of algorithms for which it is hard to obtain significantly better performance from parallelization. Optimizing memory usage is non-trivial because memory access patterns are determined by the structure of the input graph. Parallelization further introduces concerns of contention, load imbalance, and underutilization on multithreaded architectures [3, 21, 32]. The wide data parallelism of GPUs can be particularly sensitive to these performance issues.

Prior work on parallel graph algorithms has relied on two key architectural features for performance. The first is multithreading and overlapped computation for hiding memory latency. The second is fine-grained synchronization, specifically atomic read-modify-write operations. Atomic mechanisms are convenient for coordinating the dynamic placement of data into shared data structures and for arbitrating contended status updates. [3–5]

Modern GPU architectures provide both. However, serialization from atomic synchronization is particularly expensive for GPUs in terms of efficiency and performance. In general, mutual exclusion does not scale to thousands of threads. Furthermore, the occurrence of fine-grained and dynamic serialization within the SIMD width is much costlier than between overlapped SMT threads.

For machines with wide data parallelism, we argue that software prefix sum [7, 17] is often a more suitable approach to data placement. Prefix sum is a bulk-synchronous algorithmic primitive that can be used to compute scatter offsets for concurrent threads given their dynamic allocation requirements. Efficient GPU prefix sums [24] allow us to reorganize sparse and uneven workloads into dense and uniform ones in all phases of graph traversal.

Our work as described in this paper makes contributions in the following areas:

Parallelization strategy. We present a GPU BFS parallelization that performs an asymptotically optimal linear amount of work. It is the first to incorporate fine-grained parallel adjacency list expansion. We also introduce local duplicate detection techniques for avoiding race conditions that create redundant work. We demonstrate that our approach delivers high performance on a broad spectrum of structurally diverse graphs. To our knowledge, we also describe the first design for multi-GPU graph traversal.

Empirical performance characterization. We present detailed analyses that isolate and analyze the expansion and contraction

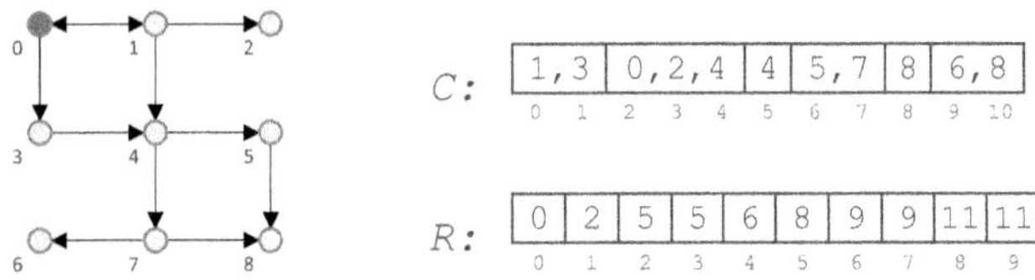

Traversal from source vertex v_0		
BFS Iteration	**Vertex frontier**	**Edge frontier**
1	{0}	{1,3}
2	{1,3}	{0,2,4,4}
3	{2,4}	{5,7}
4	{5,7}	{6,8,8}
5	{6,8}	{}

Fig. 1. Example sparse graph, corresponding CSR representation, and frontier evolution for a BFS beginning at source vertex v_0.

Algorithm 1. The simple sequential breadth-first search algorithm for marking vertex distances from the source s.

Input: Vertex set V, row-offsets array R, column-indices array C, source vertex v_s
Output: Array $dist[0..n\text{-}1]$ with $dist[v_i]$ holding the distance from v_s to v_i
Functions: *Enqueue*(*val*) inserts *val* at the end of the queue instance. *Dequeue*() returns the front element of the queue instance.

```
Q := {}
for i in 0 .. |V|-1:
  dist[i] := ∞
dist[s] := 0
Q.Enqueue(s)
while (Q != {}) :
  i = Q.Dequeue()
  for offset in R[i] .. R[i+1]-1 :
    j := C[offset]
    if (dist[j] == ∞)
      dist[j] := dist[i] + 1;
      Q.Enqueue(j)
```

aspects of BFS throughout the traversal process. We reveal that serial and warp-centric expansion techniques described by prior work significantly underutilize the GPU for important graph genres. We also show that the fusion of neighbor expansion and inspection within the same kernel often yields worse performance than performing them separately.

High performance. We demonstrate that our methods deliver excellent performance on a diverse body of real-world graphs. Our implementation achieves traversal rates in excess of 3.3 billion and 8.3 billion traversed edges per second (TE/s) for single and quad-GPU configurations, respectively. In context, recent state-of-the-art parallel implementations achieve 0.7 billion and 1.3 billion TE/s for similar datasets on single and quad-socket multicore processors [3].

2. Background

Modern NVIDIA GPU processors consist of tens of multiprocessor cores, each of which manages on the order of a thousand hardware-scheduled threads. Each multiprocessor core employs data parallel SIMD (single instruction, multiple data) techniques in which a single instruction stream is executed by a fixed-size grouping of threads called a *warp*. A *cooperative thread array* (or CTA) is a group of threads that will be co-located on the same multiprocessor and share a local scratch memory. Parallel threads are used to execute a single program, or *kernel*.

2.1 Breadth-first search

We consider graphs of the form $G = (V, E)$ with a set V of n vertices and a set E of m directed edges. Given a source vertex v_s, our goal is to traverse the vertices of G in breadth-first order starting at v_s. Each newly-discovered vertex v_i will be labeled by (a) its distance d_i from v_s and/or (b) the predecessor vertex p_i immediately preceding it on the shortest path to v_s. For simplicity, we identify the vertices v_0 .. v_{n-1} using integer indices. The pair (v_i, v_j) indicates a directed edge in the graph from $v_i \rightarrow v_j$, and the adjacency list $A_i = \{v_j \mid (v_i, v_j) \in E\}$ is the set of neighboring vertices incident on vertex v_i. We treat undirected graphs as symmetric directed graphs containing both (v_i, v_j) and (v_j, v_i) for each undirected edge. In this paper, all graph sizes and traversal rates are measured in terms of directed edge counts.

We represent the graph using an adjacency matrix **A**, whose rows are the adjacency lists A_i. The number of edges within sparse graphs is typically only a constant factor larger than n. We use the well-known compressed sparse row (CSR) sparse matrix format to store the graph in memory consisting of two arrays. Fig. 1 provides a simple example. The column-indices array C is formed from the set of the adjacency lists concatenated into a single array of m integers. The row-offsets R array contains $n + 1$ integers, and entry $R[i]$ is the index in C of the adjacency list A_i. We store graphs in the order they are defined and do not perform any preprocessing in order to improve locality or load balance.

Algorithm 1 presents the standard sequential BFS method. It operates by circulating the vertices of the graph through a FIFO queue that is initialized with v_s [11]. As vertices are dequeued, their neighbors are examined. Unvisited neighbors are labeled with their distance and/or predecessor and are enqueued for later processing. This algorithm performs linear $O(m+n)$ work since each vertex is labeled exactly once and each edge is traversed exactly once.

2.2 Parallel breadth-first search

The FIFO ordering of the sequential algorithm forces it to label vertices in increasing order of depth. Each depth level is fully explored before the next. Most parallel BFS algorithms are *level-synchronous*: each level may be processed in parallel as long as the sequential ordering of levels is preserved. An implicit race condition can exist where multiple tasks may concurrently discover a vertex v_j. This is generally considered benign since all such contending tasks would apply the same d_j and give a valid value of p_j.

Structurally different methods may be more suitable for graphs with very large diameters, e.g., algorithms based on the method of Ullman and Yannakakis [30]. Such alternatives are beyond the scope of this paper.

As illustrated in Fig. 1, each iteration of a level-synchronous method identifies both an edge and vertex *frontier*. The edge-frontier is the set of all edges to be traversed during that iteration or, equivalently, the set of all A_i where v_i was marked in the previous iteration. The vertex-frontier is the unique subset of such neighbors that are unmarked and which will be labeled and expanded for the next iteration. Each iteration logically (1) expands vertices into an edge-frontier, i.e., neighbor expansion; and then (2) contracts them to a vertex-frontier, i.e., status-lookup and filtering.

Quadratic parallelizations. The simplest parallel BFS algorithms inspect every edge or, at a minimum, every vertex during every iteration. These methods perform a quadratic amount of work. A vertex v_j is marked when a task discovers an edge $v_i \rightarrow v_j$ where v_i has been marked and v_j has not. Vertex-oriented variants must subsequently expand and mark the neighbors of v_j. Their work complexity is $O(n^2+m)$ as there may n BFS iterations in the worst case.

Quadratic parallelization strategies have been used by almost all prior GPU implementations. The static assignment of tasks to vertices (or edges) trivially maps to the data-parallel GPU machine model. Each thread's computation is completely independent from that of other threads. Harish *et al.* [16] and Hussein *et al.* [20] describe vertex-oriented versions of this method. Deng *et al.* present an edge-oriented implementation [12].

Hong *et al.* [18] describe a vectorized version of the vertex-oriented method that is similar to the CSR sparse matrix-vector (SpMV) multiplication approach by Bell and Garland [6]. Rather than threads, warps are mapped to vertices. During neighbor expansion, the SIMD lanes of an entire warp are used to strip-mine the corresponding adjacency list.

These quadratic methods are isomorphic to iterative SpMV in the algebraic semi-ring where the usual (+, ×) operations are replaced with (min, +), and thus can also be realized using generic implementations of SpMV [14].

Linear parallelizations. A work-efficient parallel BFS algorithm should perform $O(n+m)$ work. To achieve this, each iteration should examine only the edges and vertices in that iteration's logical edge and vertex-frontiers, respectively.

Frontiers may be maintained *in core* or *out of core*. An in-core frontier is processed online and never wholly realized. On the other hand, a frontier that is managed out-of-core is fully produced in off-chip memory for consumption by the next BFS iteration after a global synchronization step. Implementations typically prefer to manage the vertex-frontier out-of-core. Less global data movement is needed because the average vertex-frontier is smaller by a factor of $\bar{d}$ (average out-degree). For each iteration, tasks are mapped to unexplored vertices in the input vertex-frontier queue. Their neighbors are inspected and the unvisited ones are placed into the output vertex-frontier queue for the next iteration.

The typical approach for improving utilization is to reduce the task granularity to a homogenous size and then evenly distribute these smaller tasks among threads. This is done by expanding and inspecting neighbors in parallel. The implementation can either: (a) spawn all edge-inspection tasks before processing any, wholly realizing the edge-frontier out-of-core; or (b) carefully throttle the parallel expansion and processing of adjacency lists, producing and consuming these tasks in-core.

Leiserson and Schardl [21] designed an implementation for multi-socket systems that incorporates a novel multi-set data structure for tracking the vertex-frontier. Bader and Madduri [4] describe an implementation for the Cray MTA-2 using the hardware's full-empty bits for efficient queuing into an out-of-core vertex frontier. Both approaches perform parallel adjacency-list expansion, relying on runtimes to throttle edge-processing tasks in-core.

Luo *et al.* [22] present an implementation for GPUs that relies upon a hierarchical scheme for producing an out-of-core vertex-frontier. To our knowledge, theirs is the only prior attempt at designing a work-efficient BFS algorithm for GPUs. Threads perform serial adjacency list expansion and use an upward propagation tree of child-queue structures in an effort to mitigate the contention overhead on any given atomically-incremented queue pointer.

Distributed parallelizations. It is often desirable to partition the graph structure amongst multiple processors, particularly for very large datasets. The typical partitioning approach is to assign each processing element a disjoint subset of V and the corresponding adjacency lists in E. For a given vertex v_i, the inspection and marking of v_i as well as the expansion of v_i's adjacency list must occur on the processor that owns v_i. Distributed, out-of-core edge queues are used for communicating neighbors to remote processors. Incoming neighbors that are unvisited have their labels marked and their adjacency lists expanded. As adjacency lists are expanded, neighbors are enqueued to the processor that owns them. The synchronization between BFS levels occurs after the expansion phase.

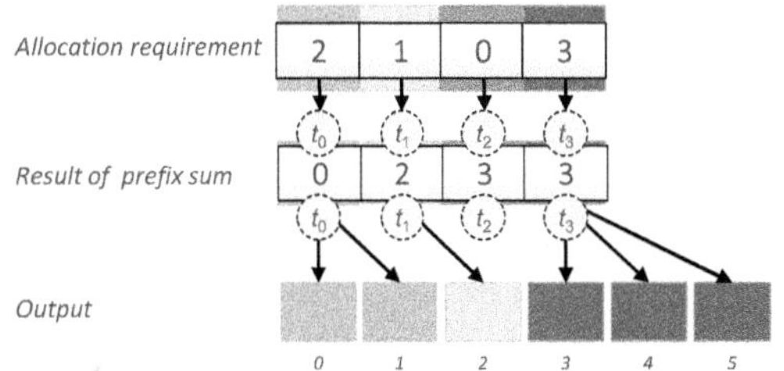

Fig. 2. Example of prefix sum for computing scatter offsets for run-length expansion. Input order is preserved.

It is important to note that distributed BFS implementations that construct predecessor trees will impose twice the queuing I/O as those that construct depth-rankings. These variants must forward the full edge pairing (v_i, v_j) to the remote processor so that it might properly label v_j's predecessor as v_i.

Yoo *et al.* [33] present a variation for BlueGene/L that implements a two-dimensional partitioning strategy for reducing the number of remote peers each processor must communicate with. Xia and Prasanna [32] propose a variant for multi-socket nodes that provisions more out-of-core edge-frontier queues than active threads, reducing the contention at any given queue and flexibly lowering barrier overhead.

Agarwal *et al.* [3] describe an implementation for multi-socket systems that implements both out-of-core vertex and edge-frontier queues for each socket. Scarpazza *et al.* [27] describe a similar hybrid variation for the Cell BE processor architecture where DMA engines are used instead of threads to perform parallel adjacency list expansion.

Our parallelization strategy. In comparison, our BFS strategy expands adjacent neighbors in parallel; implements out-of-core edge and vertex-frontiers; uses local prefix sum in place of local atomic operations for determining enqueue offsets; and uses a best-effort bitmask for efficient neighbor filtering. We further describe the details in Section 5.

2.3 Prefix sum

Given a list of input elements and a binary reduction operator, *prefix scan* produces an output list where each element is computed to be the reduction of the elements occurring earlier in the input list. *Prefix sum* connotes a prefix scan with the addition operator. Software-based scan has been popularized as an algorithmic primitive for vector and array processor architectures [7–9] and as well as for GPUs [13, 24, 28].

Prefix sum is a particularly useful mechanism for implementing cooperative allocation, i.e., when parallel threads must place dynamic data within shared data structures such as global queues. Given a list of allocation requirements for each thread, prefix sum computes the offsets for where each thread should start writing its output elements. Fig. 2 illustrates prefix sum in the context of run-length expansion. In this example, the thread t_0 wants to produce two items, t_1 one item, t_2 zero items, and so on. The prefix sum computes the scatter offset needed by each thread to write its output element. Thread t_0 writes its items at offset zero, t_1 at offset two, t_3 at offset three, etc. In the context of parallel BFS, parallel threads use prefix sum when assembling global edge frontiers from expanded neighbors and when outputting unique unvisited vertices into global vertex frontiers.

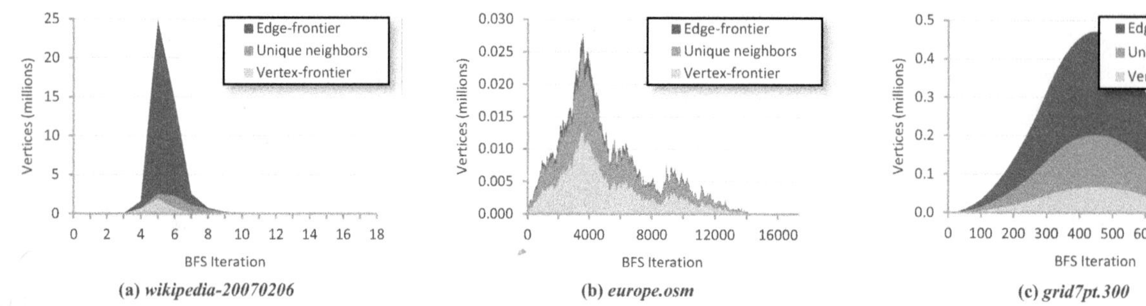

(a) *wikipedia-20070206* (b) *europe.osm* (c) *grid7pt.300*

Fig. 3. Sample frontier plots of logical vertex and edge-frontier sizes during graph traversal.

3. Benchmark Suite

3.1 Graph datasets

Our benchmark suite is composed of the thirteen graphs listed in Table 1. We generate the square and cubic Poisson lattice graph datasets ourselves. The *random.2Mv.128Me* and *rmat.2Mv.128Me* datasets are constructed using GTgraph [15]. The *wikipedia-20070206* dataset is from the University of Florida Sparse Matrix Collection [31]. The remaining datasets are from the 10th DIMACS Implementation Challenge [1].

One of our goals is to demonstrate good performance for large-diameter graphs. The largest components within these datasets have diameters spreading five orders of magnitude. Graph diameter is directly proportional to average search depth, the expected number of BFS iterations for a randomly-chosen source vertex.

3.2 Logical frontier plots

Although our sparsity plots reveal a diversity of locality, they provide little intuition as to how traversal will unfold. Fig. 3 presents sample *frontier plots* of logical edge and vertex-frontier sizes as functions of BFS iteration. Such plots help visualize workload expansion and contraction, both within and between iterations. The ideal numbers of neighbors expanded and vertices labeled per iteration are constant properties of the given dataset and starting vertex.

Frontier plots reveal the concurrency exposed by each iteration. For example, the bulk of the work for the *wikipedia-20070206* dataset is performed in only 1-2 iterations. The hardware can easily be saturated during these iterations. We observe that real-world datasets often have long sections of light work that incur heavy global synchronization overhead.

Finally, Fig. 3 also plots the duplicate-free subset of the edge-frontier. We observe that a simple duplicate-removal pass can perform much of the contraction work from edge-frontier down to vertex-frontier. This has important implications for distributed BFS. The amount of network traffic can be significantly reduced by first removing duplicates from the expansion of remote neighbors.

We note the direct application of this technique does not scale linearly with processors. As p increases, the number of available duplicates in a given partition correspondingly decreases. In the extreme where $p = m$, each processor owns only one edge and there are no duplicates to be locally culled. For large p, such decoupled duplicate-removal techniques should be pushed into the hierarchical interconnect. Yoo *et al.* demonstrate a variant of this idea for BlueGene/L using their MPI set-union collective [33].

Name	Sparsity Plot	Description	n (10^6)	m (10^6)	$\bar{d}$	Avg. Search Depth
europe.osm		European road network	50.9	108.1	2.1	19314
grid5pt.5000		5-point Poisson stencil (2D grid lattice)	25.0	125.0	5.0	7500
hugebubbles-00020		Adaptive numerical simulation mesh	21.2	63.6	3.0	6151
grid7pt.300		7-point Poisson stencil (3D grid lattice)	27.0	188.5	7.0	679
nlpkkt160		3D PDE-constrained optimization	8.3	221.2	26.5	142
audikw1		Automotive finite element analysis	0.9	76.7	81.3	62
cage15		Electrophoresis transition probabilities	5.2	94.0	18.2	37
kkt_power		Nonlinear optimization (KKT)	2.1	13.0	6.3	37
coPapersCiteseer		Citation network	0.4	32.1	73.9	26
wikipedia-20070206		Links between Wikipedia pages	3.6	45.0	12.6	20
kron_g500-logn20		Graph500 RMAT (A=0.57, B=0.19, C=0.19)	1.0	100.7	96.0	6
random.2Mv.128Me		$G(n, M)$ uniform random	2.0	128.0	64.0	6
rmat.2Mv.128Me		RMAT (A=0.45, B=0.15, C=0.15)	2.0	128.0	64.0	6

Table 1. Suite of benchmark graphs

4. Microbenchmark Analyses

A linear BFS workload is composed of two components: $O(n)$ work related to vertex-frontier processing, and $O(m)$ for edge-frontier processing. Because the edge-frontier is dominant, we focus our attention on the two fundamental aspects of its operation: *neighbor-gathering* and *status-lookup*. Although their functions are trivial, the GPU machine model provides interesting challenges for these workloads. We investigate these two activities in the following analyses using NVIDIA Tesla C2050 GPUs.

4.1 Isolated neighbor-gathering

This analysis investigates serial and parallel strategies for simply gathering neighbors from adjacency lists. The enlistment of threads for parallel gathering is a form task scheduling. We evaluate a spectrum of scheduling granularity from individual tasks (higher scheduling overhead) to blocks of tasks (higher underutilization from partial-filling).

(a) serial

(b) coarse-grained, warp-based cooperative expansion (emphasis on controlling thread)

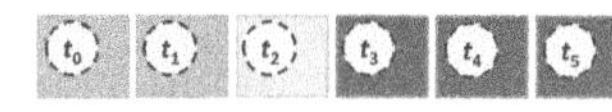

(c) fine-grained, scan-based cooperative expansion

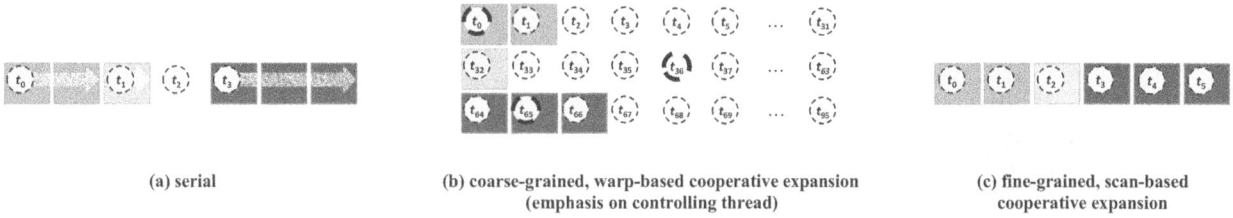

Fig. 4. Alternative strategies for gathering four unexplored adjacency lists having lengths 2, 1, 0, and 3.

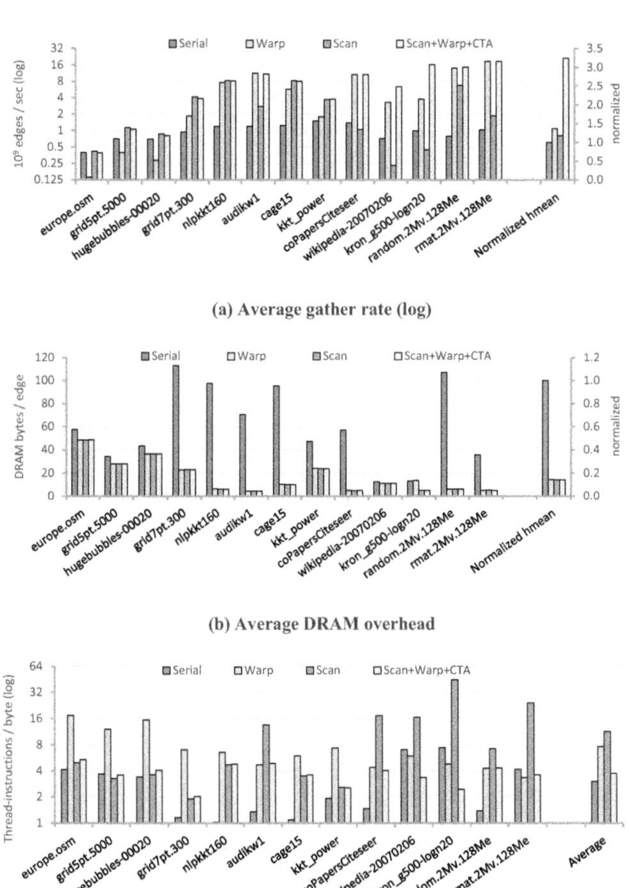

(a) Average gather rate (log)

(b) Average DRAM overhead

(c) Average computational intensity (log)

Fig. 5. Neighbor-gathering behavior. Harmonic means are normalized with respect to serial-gathering.

For a given BFS iteration, our test kernels simply read an array of preprocessed row-ranges that reference the adjacency lists to be expanded and then load the corresponding neighbors into local registers[1]. The gathered neighbors are not output into a global edge frontier (which would require extra overhead from prefix sum and scatter).

Serial gathering. Each thread obtains its preprocessed row-range bounds for the vertex it is to expand and then serially acquires the corresponding neighbors from the column-indices array *C*. Fig. 4a illustrates four threads assigned to gather four unexplored adjacency lists having lengths 2, 1, 0, and 3. Graphs having non-uniform degree distributions can impose significant load imbalance between threads within the same warp.

Coarse-grained, warp-based gathering. This approach performs a coarse-grained redistribution of gathering workloads. Instead of processing adjacency lists individually, each thread will enlist its entire warp to gather its assigned adjacency list. Consider our example adjacency lists as being assigned to threads from different warps. Fig. 4b illustrates three warps gathering the three non-empty adjacency lists in "broadside" parallel fashion, each under the control of a specific thread.

Enlistment operates by having each thread attempt to vie for control of its warp by writing its thread-identifier into a single word shared by all threads of that warp. Only one write will succeed, thus determining which is subsequently allowed to command the warp as a whole to gather its corresponding neighbors. The enlistment process repeats until all threads have all had their adjacent neighbors gathered.

Although it provides better workload balance, this approach can suffer underutilization within the warp. Many datasets have an average adjacency list size that is much smaller than the warp width, leaving warp read transactions under filled. Furthermore, there may also be load imbalance between warps when threads within one warp have significantly larger adjacency lists to expand than those in others.

Fine-grained, scan-based gathering. This approach performs a fine-grained redistribution of gathering workloads. Threads construct a shared array of column-indices offsets corresponding to a CTA-wide concatenation of their assigned adjacency lists. For our running example, the prefix sum in Fig. 2 illustrates the cooperative expansion of column-indices offsets into a shared gather vector. As illustrated in Fig. 4c, we then enlist the entire CTA to gather the referenced neighbors from the column-indices array *C* using this perfectly packed gather vector. This assignment of threads ensures that no SIMD lanes are unutilized during global reads from *C*.

Compared to the two previous strategies, the entire CTA participates in every read. Any workload imbalance between threads is not magnified by expensive global memory accesses to *C*. Instead, workload imbalance can occur in the form of underutilized cycles during offset-sharing. The worst case entails a single thread having more neighbors than the gather buffer can accommodate, resulting in the idling of all other threads while it alone shares gather offsets.

Scan+warp+CTA gathering. We can mitigate this imbalance by supplementing fine-grained scan-based expansion with coarser CTA-based and warp-based expansion. CTA-wide gathering is similar to warp-based gathering, except threads vie for control of the entire CTA for strip-mining very large adjacency lists. Then we apply warp-based gathering to acquire adjacency smaller than the CTA size, but greater than the warp width. Finally we perform scan-based gathering to efficiently acquire the remaining "loose ends".

This hybrid strategy limits all forms of load imbalance from adjacency list expansion. The fine-grained work redistribution of

[1] For full BFS, we do not perform any preprocessing

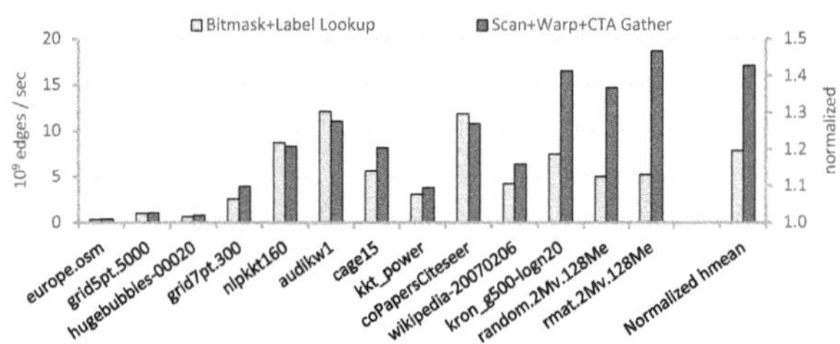

Fig. 6. Comparison of status-lookup with neighbor-gathering.

scan-based gathering limits imbalance from SIMD lane underutilization. Warp enlistment limits offset-sharing imbalance between threads. CTA enlistment limits imbalance between warps. And finally, any imbalance between CTAs can be limited by oversubscribing GPU cores with an abundance of CTAs or implementing coarse-grained tile-stealing mechanisms for CTAs to dequeue tiles at their own rate. We implement both CTA-scheduling policies, binding one or the other for each kernel as an architecture-specific tuning decision.

Analysis. We performed 100 randomly-sourced traversals of each dataset, evaluating these kernels on the logical vertex-frontier for every iteration. Fig. 5a plots the average edge-processing throughputs for each strategy in log-scale. The datasets are ordered from left-to-right by decreasing average search depth.

The serial approach performs poorly for the majority of datasets. Fig. 5b reveals it suffers from dramatic over-fetch. It plots bytes moved through DRAM per edge. The arbitrary references from each thread within the warp result in terrible coalescing for SIMD load instructions.

The warp-based approach performs poorly for the graphs on the left-hand side having average ≤ 10. Fig. 5c reveals that it is computationally inefficient for these datasets. It plots a log scale of computational intensity, the ratio of thread-instructions versus bytes moved through DRAM. The average adjacency lists for these graphs are much smaller than the number of threads per warp. As a result, a significant number of SIMD lanes go unused during any given cycle.

Fig. 5c also reveals that that scan-based gathering can suffer from extreme workload imbalance when only one thread is active within the entire CTA. This phenomenon is reflected in the datasets on the right-hand size having skewed degree distributions. The load imbalance from expanding large adjacency lists leads to increased instruction counts and corresponding performance degradation.

Combining the benefits of bulk-enlistment with fine-grained utilization, the hybrid scan+warp+CTA demonstrates good gathering rates across the board.

4.2 Isolated status-lookup and concurrent discovery

Status-lookup is the other half to neighbor-gathering; it entails checking vertex labels to determine which neighbors within the edge-frontier have already been visited. Our strategy for status-lookup incorporates a bitmask to reduce the size of status data from a 32-bit label to a single bit per vertex. CPU parallelizations have used atomically-updated bitmask structures to reduce memory traffic via improved cache coverage [3, 27].

Because we avoid atomic operations, our bitmask is only a conservative approximation of visitation status. Bits for visited vertices may appear unset or may be "clobbered" due to false-sharing within a single byte. If a status bit is unset, we must then check the corresponding label to ensure the vertex is safe for marking. This scheme relies upon capacity and conflict misses to update stale bitmask data within the read-only texture caches.

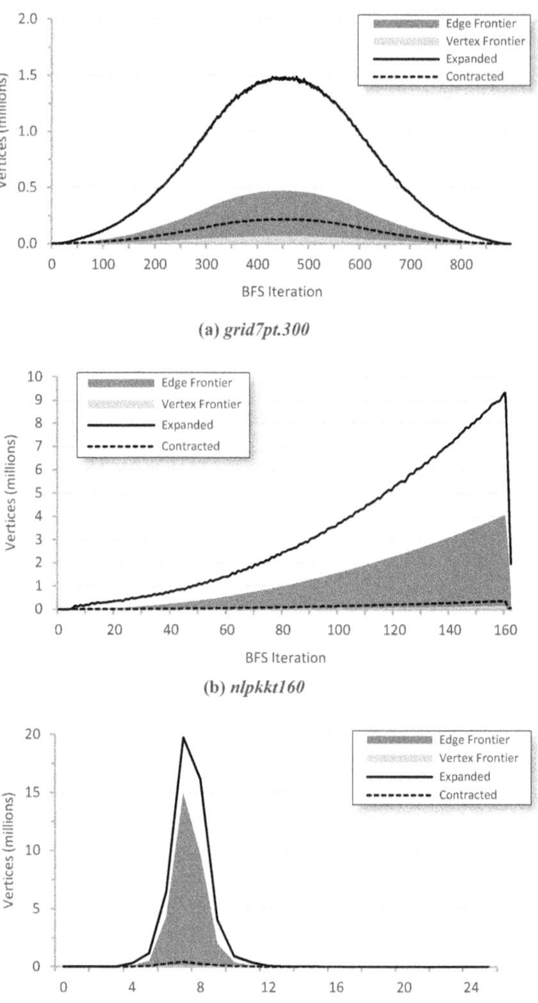

(a) *grid7pt.300*

(b) *nlpkkt160*

(c) *coPapersCiteseer*

Fig. 7. Actual expanded and contracted queue sizes without local duplicate culling, superimposed over logical frontier sizes. The redundant expansion factors are 2.6x, 1.7x, and 1.1x for the *grid7pt.300*, *nlpkkt160*, and *coPapersCiteseer* datasets, respectively.

Similar to the neighbor-gathering analysis, we isolate the status-lookup workload using a test-kernel that consumes the logical edge-frontier at each BFS iteration. The filtered neighbors are not output into a global vertex frontier (which would require extra overhead from prefix sum and scatter). Fig. 6 compares the throughputs of lookup versus gathering workloads. We observe that status-lookup is generally the more expensive of the two. This is particularly true for the datasets on the right-hand side having high average vertex out-degree. The ability for neighbor-gathering to coalesce accesses to adjacency lists increases with , whereas accesses for status-lookup have arbitrary locality.

Concurrent discovery. The effectiveness of status-lookup during frontier contraction is influenced by the presence of duplicate vertex identifiers within the edge-frontier. Duplicates are representative of different edges incident to the same vertex. This can pose a problem for implementations that allow the benign race condition. When multiple threads concurrently discover the same vertices via these duplicates, the corresponding adjacency lists will be expanded multiple times.

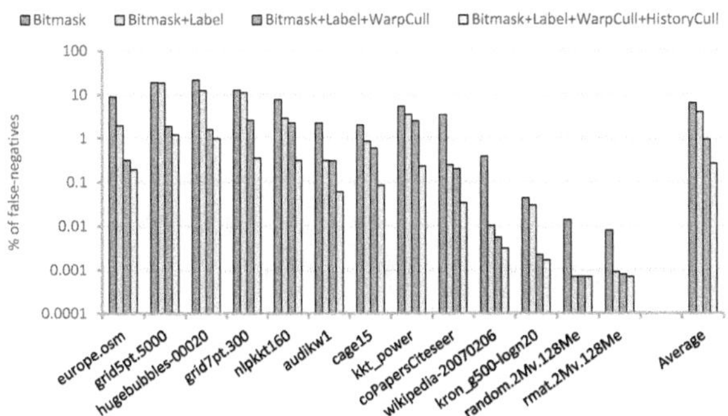

Fig. 8 Percentages of false-negatives incurred by status-lookup strategies.

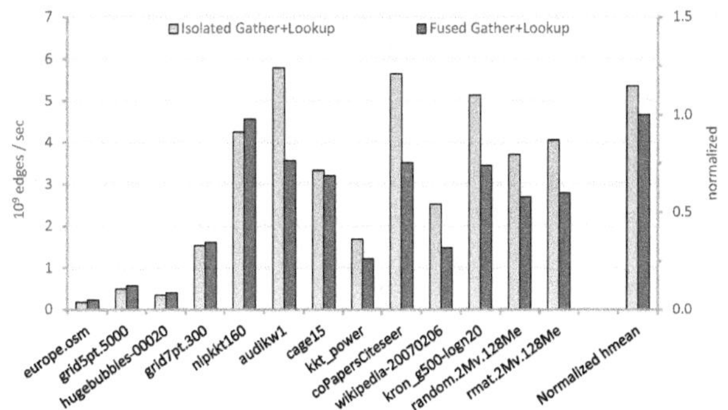

Fig. 9. Comparison of isolated versus fused neighbor-gathering and lookup.

Prior CPU parallelizations have noted the potential for redundant work, but concluded its manifestation to be negligible [21]. Concurrent discovery on CPU platforms is rare due to a combination of relatively low parallelism (~8 hardware threads) and coherent L1 caches that provide only a small window of opportunity around status-inspections that are immediately followed by status updates.

The GPU machine model, however, is much more vulnerable. If multiple threads within the same warp are simultaneously inspecting same vertex identifier, the SIMD nature of the warp-read ensures that all will obtain the same status value. If unvisited, the adjacency list for this vertex will be expanded for every thread.

We illustrate the effects of redundant expansion upon overall workload for several datasets using a simplified version of the *two-phase* BFS implementation described in Section 5.3. These expansion and contraction kernels make no special effort to curtail concurrent discovery. Fig. 7 plots the actual numbers of vertex identifiers expanded and contracted for each BFS iteration alongside the corresponding logical frontiers. The deltas between these pairs reflect the generation of unnecessary work. We define the *redundant expansion factor* as the ratio of neighbors actually enqueued versus the number of edges logically traversed.

The problem is severe for spatially-descriptive datasets. These datasets exhibit nearby duplicates within the edge-frontier due to their high frequency of convergent exploration. For example, simple two-phase traversal incurs 4.2x redundant expansion for the 2D lattice *grid5pt.5000* dataset. Even worse, the implementation altogether fails to traverse the *kron_g500-logn20* dataset which encodes sorted adjacency lists. The improved locality enables the redundant expansion of ultra-popular vertices, ultimately exhausting physical memory when filling the edge queue.

This issue of redundant expansion appears to be unique to GPU BFS implementations having two properties: (1) a work-efficient traversal algorithm; and (2) concurrent adjacency list expansion. Quadratic implementations do not suffer redundant work because vertices are never expanded by more than one thread. In our evaluation of linear-work serial-expansion, we observed negligible concurrent SIMD discovery during serial inspection due to the independent nature of thread activity.

In general, the issue of concurrent discovery is a result of false-negatives during status-lookup, i.e., failure to detect previously-visited and duplicate vertex identifiers within the edge-frontier. Atomic read-modify-write updates to visitation status yield zero false-negatives. As alternatives, we introduce two localized mechanisms for reducing false-negatives: (1) *warp culling* and (2) *history culling*.

Warp culling. This heuristic attempts to mitigate concurrent SIMD discovery by detecting the presence of duplicates within the warp's immediate working set. Using shared-memory per warp, each thread hashes in the neighbor it is currently inspecting. If a collision occurs and a different value is extracted, nothing can be determined regarding duplicate status. Otherwise threads write their thread-identifier into the same hash location. Only one write will succeed. Threads that subsequently retrieve a different thread-identifier can safely classify their neighbors as duplicates to be culled.

History culling. This heuristic complements the instantaneous coverage of warp culling by maintaining a cache of recently-inspected vertex identifiers in local shared memory. If a given thread observes its neighbor to have been previously recorded, it can classify that neighbor as safe for culling.

Analysis. We augment our isolated lookup tests to evaluate these heuristics. Kernels simply read vertex identifiers from the edge-frontier and determine which should not be allowed into the vertex-frontier. For each dataset, we record the average percentage of false negatives with respect to $m - n$, the ideal number of culled vertex identifiers.

Fig. 8 illustrates the progressive application of lookup mechanisms. The bitmask heuristic alone incurs an average false-negative rate of 6.4% across our benchmark suite. The addition of label-lookup (which makes status-lookup safe) improves this to 4.0%. Without further measure, the compounding nature of redundant expansion allows even small percentages to accrue sizeable amounts of extra work. For example, a false-negative rate of 3.5% for traversing *kkt_power* results in a 40% redundant expansion overhead.

The addition of warp-based culling induces a tenfold reduction in false-negatives for spatially descriptive graphs (left-hand side). The history-based culling heuristic further reduces culling inefficiency by a factor of five for the remainder of high-risk datasets (middle-third). The application of both heuristics allows us to reduce the overall redundant expansion factor to less than 1.05x for every graph in our benchmark suite.

4.3 Coupling of gathering and lookup

A complete BFS implementation might choose to fuse these workloads within the same kernel in order to process one of the frontiers online and in-core. We evaluate this fusion with a derivation of our scan+warp+CTA gathering kernel that immediately inspects every gathered neighbor using our bitmap-assisted lookup strategy. The coupled kernel requires $O(m)$ less overall data movement than the other two put together (which effectively read all edges twice).

Fig. 9 compares this fused kernel with the aggregate throughput of the isolated gathering and lookup workloads performed separately. Despite the additional data movement, the separate kernels outperform the fused kernel for the majority of the benchmarks. Their extra data movement results in net slowdown, however, for the latency-bound datasets on the left-hand side having limited bulk concurrency. The implication is that fused approaches are preferable for fleeting BFS iterations having edge-frontiers smaller than the number of resident threads.

The fused kernel likely suffers from TLB misses experienced by the neighbor-gathering workload. The column-indices arrays occupy substantial portions of GPU physical memory. Sparse gathers from them are apt to cause TLB misses. The fusion of these two workloads inherits the worst aspects of both: TLB turnover during uncoalesced status lookups.

5. Single-GPU Parallelizations

A complete solution must couple expansion and contraction activities. In this section, we evaluate the design space of coupling alternatives by constructing full implementations for processing BFS iterations. Further algorithmic detail can be found in our technical report [25].

5.1 Expand-contract (out-of-core vertex queue)

Our single-kernel *expand-contract* strategy is loosely based upon the fused gather-lookup benchmark kernel from Section 4.3. It consumes the vertex queue for the current BFS iteration and produces the vertex queue for the next. It performs parallel expansion and filtering of adjacency lists online and in-core using local scratch memory.

This kernel requires $2n$ global storage for input and output vertex queues. The roles of these two arrays are reversed for alternating BFS iterations. A traversal will generate $5n+2m$ explicit data movement through global memory. All m edges will be streamed into registers once. All n vertices will be streamed twice: out into global frontier queues and subsequently back in. The bitmask bits will be inspected m times and updated n times along with the labels. Each of the n row-offsets is loaded twice.

Each CTA performs three local prefix sums per block of dequeued input. One is computed during scan-based gathering. The other two are used for computing global enqueue offsets for valid neighbors during CTA-based and scan-based gathering. Although GPU cores can efficiently overlap concurrent prefix sums from different CTAs, the turnaround time for each can be relatively long. This can hurt performance for fleeting, latency-bound BFS iterations.

5.2 Contract-expand (out-of-core edge queue)

Our *contract-expand* strategy filters previously-visited and duplicate neighbors from the current edge queue. The adjacency lists of the surviving vertices are then expanded and copied out into the edge queue for the next iteration.

This kernel requires $2m$ global storage for input and output edge queues. Variants that label predecessors, however, require an additional pair of "parent" queues to track both origin and destination identifiers within the edge-frontier. A traversal will generate $3n+4m$ explicit global data movement. All m edges will be streamed through global memory three times: into registers from C, out to the edge queue, and back in again the next iteration. The bitmask, label, and row-offset traffic remain the same as for *expand-contract.*

Despite a much larger queuing workload, the *contract-expand* strategy is often better suited for processing small, fleeting BFS iterations. It incurs lower latency because CTAs only perform local two prefix sums per block: one each for computing global enqueue offsets during CTA/warp-based and scan-based gathering. We overlap these prefix sums to further reduce latency. By operating on the larger edge-frontier, the *contract-expand* kernel also enjoys better bulk concurrency in which fewer resident CTAs sit idle.

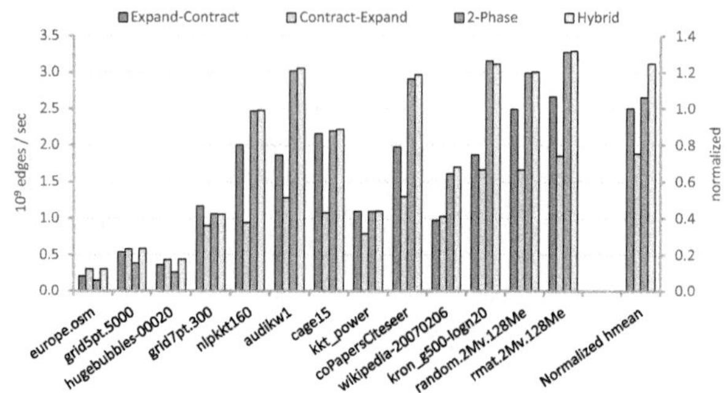

Fig. 10 BFS traversal performance. Harmonic means are normalized with respect to the *expand-contract* implementation.

5.3 Two-phase (out-of-core vertex and edge queues)

Our *two-phase* implementation isolates the expansion and contraction workloads into separate kernels. The expansion kernel employs the scan+warp+CTA gathering strategy to obtain the neighbors of vertices from the input vertex queue. As with the *contract-expand* implementation above, it performs two overlapped local prefix sums to compute scatter offsets for the expanded neighbors into the global edge queue.

The contraction kernel begins with the edge queue as input. Threads filter previously-visited and duplicate neighbors. The remaining valid neighbors are placed into the outgoing vertex queue using another local prefix sum to compute global enqueue offsets.

These kernels require $n+m$ global storage for vertex and edge queues. A *two-phase* traversal generates $5n+4m$ explicit global data movement. The memory workload builds upon that of *contract-expand*, but additionally streams n vertices into and out of the global vertex queue.

5.4 Hybrid

Our hybrid implementation combines the relative strengths of the *contract-expand* and *two-phase* approaches: low-latency turnaround for small frontiers and high-efficiency throughput for large frontiers. If the edge queue for a given BFS iteration contains more vertex identifiers than resident threads, we invoke the *two-phase* implementation for that iteration. Otherwise we invoke the *contract-expand* implementation. The hybrid approach inherits the $2m$ global storage requirement from the former and the $5n+4m$ explicit global data movement from the latter.

5.5 Strategy evaluation

In comparing these strategies, Fig. 10 plots average traversal throughput across 100 randomly-sourced traversals of each dataset using a single NVIDIA Tesla C2050. As anticipated, the *contract-expand* approach excels at traversing the latency-bound datasets on the left and the *two-phase* implementation efficiently leverages the bulk-concurrency exposed by the datasets on the right. Although the *expand-contract* approach is serviceable, the *hybrid* approach meets or exceeds its performance for every dataset.

The importance of work-compaction. With in-core edge-frontier processing, the *expand-contract* implementation is designed for one-third as much global queue traffic. The actual DRAM savings are substantially less. We only measured a 50% reduction in measured DRAM workload for datasets with large $\bar{d}$. Furthermore, the workload differences are effectively lost in excess over-fetch traffic for the graphs having small $\bar{d}$: they use large memory transactions to retrieve small adjacency lists.

Graph Dataset	CPU Parallel (linear-work)		GPU* (quadratic-work [18])	GPU* (linear-work *hybrid* strategy)	
	*Distance BFS rate*** [21]	*Predecessor BFS rate**** [3]	*Distance BFS rate*	*Distance BFS rate (sequential speedup****)*	*Predecessor BFS rate (sequential speedup****)*
europe.osm			0.00014	0.31 (11x)	0.31 (11x)
grid5pt.5000			0.00078	0.6 (7.4x)	0.57 (7.0x)
hugebubbles-00020			0.00061	0.43 (15x)	0.42 (15x)
grid7pt.300	0.12		0.012	1.1 (29x)	0.97 (26x)
nlpkkt160	0.47		0.21	2.5 (9.7x)	2.1 (8.2x)
audikw1			1.2	3.0 (4.6x)	2.5 (3.9x)
cage15	0.23		0.50	2.2 (18x)	1.9 (15x)
kkt_power	0.11		0.18	1.1 (23x)	1.0 (21x)
coPapersCiteseer			2.2	3.0 (6.0x)	2.5 (5.0x)
wikipedia-20070206	0.19		0.39	1.6 (25x)	1.4 (22x)
kron_g500-logn20			1.5	3.1 (13x)	2.5 (10x)
random.2Mv.128Me		0.50	1.2	3.0 (29x)	2.4 (23x)
rmat.2Mv.128Me		0.70	1.3	3.3 (22x)	2.6 (17x)

Table 2. Average single-socket graph traversal rates (10^9 TE/s). * NVIDIA 14-core 1.15 GHz Tesla C2050. ** Intel 4-core 2.5 GHz Core i7. *** Intel 8-core 2.7 GHz Xeon X5570. **** GPU speedup versus sequential method on Intel 3.4GHz Core i7 2600K.

The *contract-expand* implementation performs poorly for graphs having large $\bar{d}$. This behavior is related to a lack of explicit workload compaction before neighbor gathering. It executes nearly 50% more thread-instructions during BFS iterations with very large contraction workloads. This is indicative of SIMD underutilization. The majority of active threads have their neighbors invalidated by status-lookup and local duplicate removal. Cooperative neighbor-gathering becomes much less efficient as a result.

5.6 Comparative performance

Table 2 compares the distance and predecessor-labeling versions of our *hybrid* strategy with prior BFS parallelizations for both GPU and multicore CPU architectures.

Distance vs. predecessor-labeling. Our performance disparity between the two BFS problem types is largely dependent upon average vertex degree $\bar{d}$. Smaller $\bar{d}$ incurs larger DRAM over-fetch which reduces the relative significance of added parent queue traffic. For example, the performance impact of exchanging parent vertices is negligible for *europe.osm*, yet is as high as 19% for *rmat.2Mv.128Me*.

Contemporary GPU parallelizations. In comparing our approach with the recent quadratic-work method of Hong *et al.* [18], we evaluated their implementation directly on our corpus of sparse graphs. We observed a 4.2x harmonic mean slowdown across all datasets. As expected, their implementation incurs particularly large overheads for high diameter graphs, notably a 2300x slowdown for *europe.osm*. At the other end of the spectrum, we measured a 2.5x slowdown for *rmat.2Mv.128Me*, the lowest diameter dataset.

The only prior published linear-work GPU performance evaluation is from Luo et al. [22]. In the absence of their hand-tuned implementation, we compared our implementation against the specific collections of 6-pt lattice datasets[2] and DIMACS road network datasets[3] referenced by their study. Using the same model GPU (a previous-generation NVIDIA GTX280), our *hybrid* parallelization respectively achieved 4.1x and 1.7x harmonic mean speedups for these two collections.

Contemporary multicore parallelizations. It is challenging to contrast CPU and GPU traversal performance. The construction of high performance CPU parallelizations is outside the scope of this work. Table 2 cites the recent single-socket CPU traversal rates by Leiserson et al. [21] and Agarwal et al. [3] for datasets common to our experimental corpus. With an NVIDIA C2050, we achieve harmonic mean speedups of 8.1x and 4.2x versus their respective 4-core and 8-core parallelizations.

To give perspective on the datasets for which we do not have published CPU performance rates, we note these two studies report sub-linear performance scaling per core. In this vein, we compare GPU traversal performance with our own efficient sequential implementation on a state-of-the-art Intel 4-core 3.4 GHz Core i7 2600K. Despite fewer memory channels on our newer CPU, the performance of our sequential implementation exceeds their single-threaded results.

With respect to this single-threaded implementation, we consider a 4x GPU speedup as being competitive with contemporary CPU parallelizations. As listed in Table 2, our C2050 traversal rates exceed this factor for all benchmark datasets. In addition, the majority of our graph traversal rates exceed 12x speedup, the perfect scaling of three such CPUs. At the extreme, our average *wikipedia-20070206* traversal rates outperform the sequential CPU version by 25x, i.e., eight CPU-equivalents.

Relative to the sequential CPU implementation, we also note that our methods perform equally well for large and small-diameter graphs alike. Our *hybrid* strategy provides traversal speedups of an order of magnitude for both the *europe.osm* and the *kron_g500-logn20* datasets.

6. Multi-GPU Parallelization

Communication between GPUs is simplified by a unified virtual address space in which pointers can transparently reference data residing within remote GPUs. PCI-express 2.0 provides each GPU with an external bidirectional bandwidth of 6.6 GB/s. Under the assumption that GPUs send and receive equal amounts of traffic, the rate at which each GPU can be fed with remote work is conservatively bound by 825×10^6 neighbors / sec, where neighbors are 4-byte identifiers. This rate is halved for predecessor-labeling.

6.1 Design

We implement a simple partitioning of the graph into equally-sized, disjoint subsets of V. For a system of p GPUs, we initialize each processor p_i with an (m/p)-element C_i and (n/p)-element R_i and $Labels_i$ arrays. Because the system is small, we can provision each GPU with its own full-sized n-bit best-effort bitmask.

We stripe ownership of V across the domain of vertex identifiers. Striping provides good probability of an even distribution of adjacency list sizes across GPUs, an important property for maintaining load balance in small systems. However, this method of partitioning progressively loses any inherent locality as the number of GPUs increases.

[2] Regular degree-6 cubic lattice graphs of size 1M, 2M, 5M, 7M, 9M, and 10M vertices

[3] New York, Florida, USA-East, and USA-West datasets from the 9th DIMACS Challenge corpus [2].

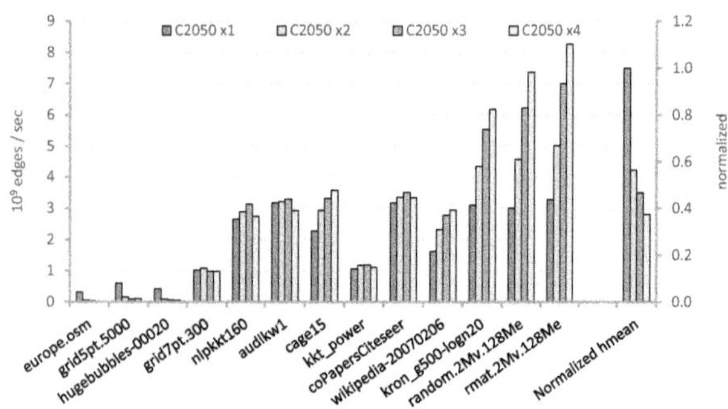

Fig. 11. Average multi-GPU traversal rates. Harmonic means are normalized with respect to the single GPU configuration.

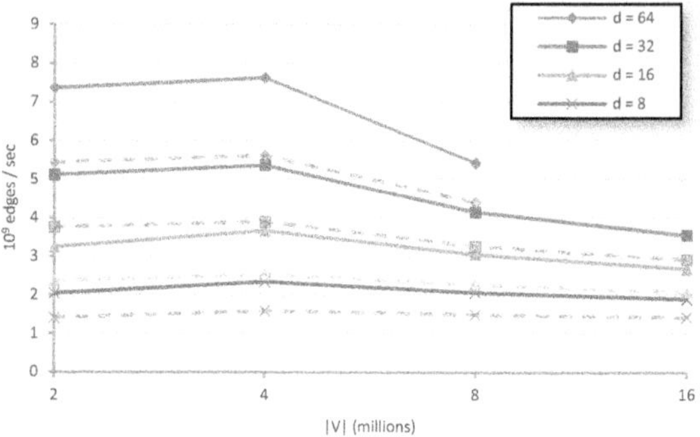

Fig. 12. Multi-GPU sensitivity to graph size and average out-degree for uniform random graphs using four C2050 processors. Dashed lines indicate predecessor labeling variants.

Graph traversal proceeds in level-synchronous fashion. The host program orchestrates BFS iterations as follows:

1. Invoke the *expansion* kernel on each GPU_i, transforming the vertex queue $Qvertex_i$ into an edge queue $Qedge_i$.
2. Invoke a fused *filter+partition* operation for each GPU_i that sorts neighbors within $Qedge_i$ by ownership into *p* bins. Vertex identifiers undergo opportunistic local duplicate culling and bitmask filtering during the partitioning process. This partitioning implementation is analogous to a three-kernel radix-sorting pass [23].
3. Barrier across all GPUs. The sorting must be completed on all GPUs before any can access their bins on remote peers. The host program uses this opportunity to terminate traversal if all bins are empty on all GPUs.
4. Invoke *p*-1 *contraction* kernels on each GPU_i to stream and filter the incoming neighbors from its peers. Kernel invocation simply uses remote pointers that reference the appropriate peer bins. This assembles each vertex queue $Qvertex_i$ for the next BFS iteration.

The implementation requires $(2m+n)/p$ storage for queue arrays per GPU: two edge queues for pre and post-sorted neighbors and a third vertex queue to avoid another global synchronization after Step 4.

6.2 Evaluation

Fig. 11 presents traversal throughput as we scale up the number of GPUs. We experience net slowdown for datasets on the left having average search depth > 100. The cost of global synchronization between BFS iterations is much higher across multiple GPUs.

We do yield notable speedups for the three rightmost datasets. These graphs have small diameters and require little global synchronization. The large average out-degrees enable plenty of opportunistic duplicate filtering during partitioning passes. This allows us to circumvent the PCI-e cap of 825×10^6 edges/sec per GPU. With four GPUs, we demonstrate traversal rates of 7.4 and 8.3 billion edges/sec for the uniform-random and RMAT datasets respectively.

As expected, this strong-scaling is not linear. For example, we observe 1.5x, 2.1x, and 2.5x speedups when traversing *rmat.2Mv.128Me* using two, three, and four GPUs, respectively. Adding more GPUs reduces the percentage of duplicates per processor and increases overall PCI-e traffic.

Fig. 12 further illustrates the impact of opportunistic duplicate culling for uniform random graphs up to 500M edges and varying out out-degree . Increasing yields significantly better performance. Other than a slight performance drop at n=8 million vertices when the bitmask exceeds the 768KB L2 cache size, graph size has little impact upon traversal throughput.

To our knowledge, these are the fastest traversal rates demonstrated by a single-node machine. The work by Agarwal et al. is representative of the state-of-the-art in CPU parallelizations, demonstrating up to 1.3 billion edges/sec for both uniform-random and RMAT datasets using four 8-core Intel Nehalem-based XEON CPUs [3]. However, we note that the host memory on such systems can further accommodate datasets having tens of billions of edges.

7. Conclusion

This paper has demonstrated that GPUs are well-suited for sparse graph traversal and can achieve very high levels of performance on a broad range of graphs. We have presented a parallelization of BFS tailored to the GPU's requirement for large amounts of fine-grained, bulk-synchronous parallelism.

Furthermore, our implementation performs an asymptotically optimal amount of work. While quadratic-work methods might be acceptable in certain very narrow regimes [18, 19], they suffer from high overhead and did not prove effective on even the lowest diameter graphs in our experimental corpus. Our linear-work method compares very favorably to state-of-the-art multicore implementations across our entire range of benchmarks, which spans five orders of magnitude in graph diameter.

Beyond graph search, our work distills several general themes for implementing sparse and dynamic problems for the GPU machine model:

- Prefix sum can serve as an effective alternative to atomic read-modify-write mechanisms for coordinating the placement of items within shared data structures by many parallel threads.
- In contrast to coarse-grained parallelism common on multicore processors, GPU kernels cannot afford to have individual threads streaming through unrelated sections of data. Groups of GPU threads should cooperatively assist each other for data movement tasks.
- Fusing heterogeneous tasks does not always produce the best results. Global redistribution and compaction of fine-grained tasks can significantly improve performance when the alternative would allow significant load imbalance or underutilization.
- The relative I/O contribution from global task redistribution can be less costly than anticipated. The data movement from reorganization may be insignificant in comparison to the

actual over-fetch traffic from existing sparse memory accesses.

- It is useful to provide separate implementations for saturating versus fleeting workloads. Hybrid approaches can leverage a shorter code-path for retiring underutilized phases as quickly as possible.

8. References

[1] 10th DIMACS Implementation Challenge: *http://www.cc.gatech.edu/dimacs10/index.shtml*. Accessed: 2011-07-11.

[2] 9th DIMACS Implementation Challenge: *http://www.dis.uniroma1.it/~challenge9/download.shtml*. Accessed: 2011-07-11.

[3] Agarwal, V. et al. 2010. Scalable Graph Exploration on Multicore Processors. *2010 ACM/IEEE International Conference for High Performance Computing, Networking, Storage and Analysis* (New Orleans, LA, USA, Nov. 2010), 1-11.

[4] Bader, D.A. and Madduri, K. Designing Multithreaded Algorithms for Breadth-First Search and st-connectivity on the Cray MTA-2. *2006 International Conference on Parallel Processing (ICPP'06)* (Columbus, OH, USA), 523-530.

[5] Bader, D.A. et al. On the Architectural Requirements for Efficient Execution of Graph Algorithms. *2005 International Conference on Parallel Processing (ICPP'05)* (Oslo, Norway), 547-556.

[6] Bell, N. and Garland, M. 2009. Implementing sparse matrix-vector multiplication on throughput-oriented processors. *Proceedings of the Conference on High Performance Computing Networking, Storage and Analysis* (New York, NY, USA, 2009), 18:1–18:11.

[7] Blelloch, G.E. 1990. *Prefix Sums and Their Applications*. Synthesis of Parallel Algorithms.

[8] Blelloch, G.E. 1989. Scans as primitive parallel operations. *IEEE Transactions on Computers*. 38, 11 (Nov. 1989), 1526-1538.

[9] Chatterjee, S. et al. 1990. Scan primitives for vector computers. *Proceedings of the 1990 ACM/IEEE conference on Supercomputing* (Los Alamitos, CA, USA, 1990), 666–675.

[10] Che, S. et al. 2009. Rodinia: A benchmark suite for heterogeneous computing. *2009 IEEE International Symposium on Workload Characterization (IISWC)* (Austin, TX, USA, Oct. 2009), 44-54.

[11] Cormen, T.H. et al. 2001. *Introduction to Algorithms*. MIT Press.

[12] Deng, Y. (Steve) et al. 2009. Taming irregular EDA applications on GPUs. *Proceedings of the 2009 International Conference on Computer-Aided Design* (New York, NY, USA, 2009), 539–546.

[13] Dotsenko, Y. et al. 2008. Fast scan algorithms on graphics processors. *Proceedings of the 22nd annual international conference on Supercomputing* (New York, NY, USA, 2008), 205–213.

[14] Garland, M. 2008. Sparse matrix computations on manycore GPU's. *Proceedings of the 45th annual Design Automation Conference* (New York, NY, USA, 2008), 2–6.

[15] GTgraph: A suite of synthetic random graph generators: *https://sdm.lbl.gov/~kamesh/software/GTgraph/*. Accessed: 2011-07-11.

[16] Harish, P. and Narayanan, P.J. 2007. Accelerating large graph algorithms on the GPU using CUDA. *Proceedings of the 14th international conference on High performance computing* (Berlin, Heidelberg, 2007), 197–208.

[17] Hillis, W.D. and Steele, G.L. 1986. Data parallel algorithms. *Communications of the ACM*. 29, 12 (Dec. 1986), 1170-1183.

[18] Hong, S. et al. 2011. Accelerating CUDA graph algorithms at maximum warp. *Proceedings of the 16th ACM symposium on Principles and practice of parallel programming* (New York, NY, USA, 2011), 267–276.

[19] Hong, S. et al. 2011. Efficient Parallel Graph Exploration for Multi-Core CPU and GPU. (New York, NY, USA, 2011), to appear.

[20] Hussein, M. et al. 2007. On Implementing Graph Cuts on CUDA. *First Workshop on General Purpose Processing on Graphics Processing Units* (Boston, MA, Oct. 2007).

[21] Leiserson, C.E. and Schardl, T.B. 2010. A work-efficient parallel breadth-first search algorithm (or how to cope with the nondeterminism of reducers). *Proceedings of the 22nd ACM symposium on Parallelism in algorithms and architectures* (New York, NY, USA, 2010), 303–314.

[22] Luo, L. et al. 2010. An effective GPU implementation of breadth-first search. *Proceedings of the 47th Design Automation Conference* (New York, NY, USA, 2010), 52–55.

[23] Merrill, D. and Grimshaw, A. 2011. High Performance and Scalable Radix Sorting: A case study of implementing dynamic parallelism for GPU computing. *Parallel Processing Letters*. 21, 02 (2011), 245-272.

[24] Merrill, D. and Grimshaw, A. 2009. *Parallel Scan for Stream Architectures*. Technical Report #CS2009-14. Department of Computer Science, University of Virginia.

[25] Merrill, D. et al. 2011. *High Performance and Scalable GPU Graph Traversal*. Technical Report #CS2011-05. Department of Computer Science, University of Virginia.

[26] Parboil Benchmark suite: *http://impact.crhc.illinois.edu/parboil.php*. Accessed: 2011-07-11.

[27] Scarpazza, D.P. et al. 2008. Efficient Breadth-First Search on the Cell/BE Processor. *IEEE Transactions on Parallel and Distributed Systems*. 19, 10 (Oct. 2008), 1381-1395.

[28] Sengupta, S. et al. 2008. *Efficient parallel scan algorithms for GPUs*. Technical Report #NVR-2008-003. NVIDIA.

[29] The Graph 500 List: *http://www.graph500.org/*. Accessed: 2011-07-11.

[30] Ullman, J. and Yannakakis, M. 1990. High-probability parallel transitive closure algorithms. *Proceedings of the second annual ACM symposium on Parallel algorithms and architectures - SPAA '90* (Island of Crete, Greece, 1990), 200-209.

[31] University of Florida Sparse Matrix Collection: *http://www.cise.ufl.edu/research/sparse/matrices/*. Accessed: 2011-07-11.

[32] Xia, Y. and Prasanna, V.K. 2009. Topologically Adaptive Parallel Breadth-first Search on Multicore Processors. *21st International Conference on Parallel and Distributed Computing and Systems (PDCS'09)* (Nov. 2009).

[33] Yoo, A. et al. A Scalable Distributed Parallel Breadth-First Search Algorithm on BlueGene/L. *ACM/IEEE SC 2005 Conference (SC'05)* (Seattle, WA, USA), 25-25.

GPU-based NFA Implementation for Memory Efficient High Speed Regular Expression Matching *

Yuan Zu Ming Yang Zhonghu Xu Lin Wang Xin Tian Kunyang Peng Qunfeng Dong †

Institute of Networked Systems (IONS) & School of Computer Science and Technology
University of Science and Technology of China
Hefei, Anhui, P. R. China

wyn@mail.ustc.edu.cn yangm@ustc.edu.cn {xzhh,xiaquhet,tianxin,pengkuny}@mail.ustc.edu.cn qunfeng@ustc.edu.cn

Abstract

Regular expression pattern matching is the foundation and core engine of many network functions, such as network intrusion detection, worm detection, traffic analysis, web applications and so on. DFA-based solutions suffer exponentially exploding state space and cannot be remedied without sacrificing matching speed. Given this scalability problem of DFA-based methods, there has been increasing interest in NFA-based methods for memory efficient regular expression matching. To achieve high matching speed using NFA, it requires potentially massive parallel processing, and hence represents an ideal programming task on Graphic Processor Unit (GPU). Based on in-depth understanding of NFA properties as well as GPU architecture, we propose effective methods for fitting NFAs into GPU architecture through proper data structure and parallel programming design, so that GPU's parallel processing power can be better utilized to achieve high speed regular expression matching. Experiment results demonstrate that, compared with the existing GPU-based NFA implementation method [9], our proposed methods can boost matching speed by 29~46 times, consistently yielding above 10Gbps matching speed on NVIDIA GTX-460 GPU. Meanwhile, our design only needs a small amount of memory space, growing exponentially more slowly than DFA size. These results make our design an effective solution for memory efficient high speed regular expression matching, and clearly demonstrate the power and potential of GPU as a platform for memory efficient high speed regular expression matching.

* This work was supported in part by the Ministry of Education (MOE) Program for New Century Excellent Talents (NCET) in University, by the Science and Technological Fund of Anhui Province for Outstanding Youth under Grant No. 10040606Y05, by the Fundamental Research Funds for the Central Universities under Grant No. WK0110000007 and Grant No. WK0110000019, by the National Natural Science Foundation of China under Grant No. 61073184, and by Jiangsu Provincial Science Foundation under Grant No. BK2011360.

† All correspondence should be directed to Prof. Qunfeng Dong (Email: qunfeng@ustc.edu.cn).

PPoPP'12, February 25–29, 2012, New Orleans, Louisiana, USA.

Categories and Subject Descriptors C.2.0 [*Computer-Communication Networks*]: General—Security and protection (e.g., firewalls); D.1.3 [*Programming Techniques*]: Concurrent Programming—Parallel programming; F.1.1 [*Computation by Abstract Devices*]: Models of Computation—Automata (e.g., finite, push-down, resource-bounded)

General Terms Algorithm, Design, Experimentation, Performance, Security

Keywords CUDA, Deep Packet Inspection, GPU, NFA, Pattern Matching, Regular Expression Matching

1. Introduction

Regular expression pattern matching is the foundation and core engine of many network functions, such as intrusion detection, worm detection, traffic analysis, web applications and so on. For instance, known worm signatures can be each formulated as a regular expression pattern; if such a regular expression pattern finds a match in network traffic, an alert of detecting the corresponding worm can be generated for taking actions accordingly. Besides, regular expression matching has also found a broad range of applications in other technological fields such as web, database, text processing, programming languages and so on.

Given the fundamental importance of regular expression matching, intensive research has been conducted in the past years, in order to obtain high speed and, no less importantly, memory efficient solutions. In spite of this long line of research, it is inherently hard to accommodate the two Genies — matching speed and storage space — into one jar. Specifically, regular expressions are matched using either deterministic finite automaton (DFA) or nondeterministic finite automaton (NFA), each having its own merits and problems.

DFA is guaranteed to process each input character with one state lookup and transition, as it has precisely one single active state at any time; this enables DFA to provide fast and stable matching speed. However, this processing efficiency is achieved at the cost of exponentially exploding storage space; just a few regular expression patterns have been sufficient to generate a gigantic DFA containing hundreds of thousand states. With this exponential explosion, practical systems can hardly scale with even moderate size pattern sets; while in practice, real life systems (such as the Snort intrusion detection system [2]) have already deployed thousands of patterns, to be matched against network traffic flowing at link speeds (e.g. 10Gbps OC-192 link speed). To remedy this problem, numerous methods have been proposed for compressing DFA storage space. Although these research efforts have achieved impressive results [4–7, 10, 11, 16, 17, 19, 23–28], none has been able to deflate the exponential explosion of storage space while preserving the matching speed of original uncompressed DFA.[1]

Given this scalability problem of DFA-based methods, there has been increasing potential interest in NFA-based solutions for memory efficient regular expression matching. Unlike DFA, each NFA state can have multiple possible transitions on an input character, and NFA can have multiple states active simultaneously. This non-deterministic nature enables NFA to represent a pattern set with a much smaller state space, growing linearly instead of exponentially with pattern set size. Hence, NFA-based solutions are inherently memory efficient. However, as each NFA state can go on activating multiple other states, the NFA can have unpredictably many active states, on all of which state transitions have to be performed for an input character. Given that, to achieve high matching speed, it requires potentially massive parallel processing, and hence represents an ideal programming task on Graphic Processor Unit (GPU) [3, 12–15, 18, 22, 29, 30].

Recently, there has been a GPU-based NFA implementation method called *iNFAnt* [9] proposed by Cascarano et al. for memory efficient regular expression matching. While it is memory efficient like all NFA-based solutions, it has not been able to understand and exploit some important properties of NFA for potentially drastic performance boost, as we shall achieve in this work. Consequently, their method has only been able to match at a few hundred megabits per second, lagging far behind high speed link rates.

In this work, we shall analyze and demonstrate some important properties of NFA, using real life pattern sets as examples. Based on this understanding of NFA properties as well as GPU architecture, we shall conduct in-depth study, both experimental and analytical, of how NFAs can be best fitted into GPU architecture through proper data structure and parallel programming design, so that GPU's parallel processing power can be fully mobilized to achieve high speed regular expression matching. In particular, our study will proceed in three stages, each stage building upon the insights and design obtained in the preceding stage. In each stage, we shall figure out through experiments and analysis some key limitations of the preceding design, and then demonstrate how should we reform our design so that matching speed can be boosted significantly.

We evaluated the performance of our GPU-based NFA implementation design using real life pattern sets collected from the Snort intrusion detection system [2], on NVIDIA GTX-460 GPU. Experiment results demonstrate that, compared with iNFAnt [9], our GPU-based solution can boost matching speed by 29$\sim$46 times, consistently yielding matching speed above 10Gbps. Meanwhile, compared with exponentially growing DFA state space, our NFA-based design only needs a very small amount of memory space, growing exponentially more slowly than DFA size. These results make our proposed design an effective solution for memory efficient high speed (e.g. 10Gbps OC-192 link speed) regular expression matching, and clearly demonstrate the power and potential of GPU as a platform for memory efficient high speed regular expression matching.

The rest of this paper is organized as follows. We start in Section 2 with an introduction of the existing GPU-based NFA implementation method [9] proposed by Cascarano et al., as well as relevant GPU architecture knowledge. Then in Section 3, the first stage of our study, we shall reveal through analysis the key drawback of that design, which motivates our basic design. We present this basic design and verify its effectiveness through experiment results. The limitation of this basic design will subsequently be analyzed and enhanced in the second stage of our study in Section 4, whose effectiveness will also be verified through experiment results. In the third stage of our study, we shall figure out the key issues of this design and culminate our study with the *Virtual NFA* design in Section 5. After evaluating our Virtual NFA design in Section 6, we conclude the paper in Section 7.

[1] In the literature, there are TCAM-based DFA deflation methods [20, 21] proposing to effectively deflate DFA state space while preserving one memory lookup per input character. However, TCAM is well known to take much more hardware expense, power consumption and chip area than RAM-based computing architectures, which is the focus of this work.

2. State of the art

The entire design of iNFAnt [9] is built upon three data structures (as shown in Figure 1): NFA transition table, current active state vector (CASV) and future active state vector (FASV). CASV is a bit vector where each bit corresponds to a distinct NFA state; if an NFA state is currently active, its corresponding bit in CASV is set, and is cleared otherwise. Similarly, FASV is such a bit vector indicating whether each NFA state will be active after performing relevant transitions on the current input character. A bit more complex is the NFA transition table, which is stored as 256 arrays for compressed storage space, each array consisting of the NFA's transitions on one of the 256 possible input characters. For example in Figure 1, the array corresponding to character a stores the NFA's transitions on character a.

As we have discussed in Section 1, NFA-based regular expression matching can be slow for each individual packet. To achieve high matching throughput, a bunch of packets are to be matched simultaneously, exploiting the massive parallel processing power of GPU. Each packet is handled by a separate matching process (consisting of a certain number of threads); the NFA transition table is to be shared by the matching processes of all packets, while the matching process of each packet has its own CASV and FASV.

Upon these data structures, the matching process of a packet is carried out by an exclusive set of threads; the number of threads is equal to the maximum number of NFA transitions in any of the 256 arrays, which is 34 in Figure 1. The entire matching process of a packet can be viewed as an iterative process; during each iteration, one input character is matched using the NFA. The process of matching an input character can be summarized as follows.

Step 1. Each thread uses the input character as an index to locate which of the 256 arrays (of transitions) to look up. The base address of the array is obtained.

Step 2. Within the set of threads for matching the same packet, each thread is assigned a unique thread ID (starting from zero), which is used by the thread as the offset plus the above obtained base address to get the corresponding NFA transition stored in that position in the array. For example in Figure 1, suppose there are 34 threads working to match a packet; the thread with thread ID 5 will obtain the sixth NFA transition stored in the transition array corresponding to input character a.

Step 3. The obtained transition is composed of a source state ID and a destination state ID, meaning if the source state is active, the destination state will be active after matching the input character. Hence, each thread will use the source state ID as an index into the CASV to find out if the source state is currently active. If yes, it uses the destination state ID as an index into the FASV to set the bit belonging to that destination state.

Step 4. After all transitions have been processed, FASV is copied into CASV, and then cleared for next input character.

In practice, the number of transitions stored in the 256 arrays can exceed the number of threads we use for each packet; multiple rounds of the above operations described in step 2 and step 3 can be conducted to process all transitions in an array. For example in Figure 1, there can be 34 transitions in an array. If we use one warp of 32 threads to process a packet, it simply takes two rounds of step

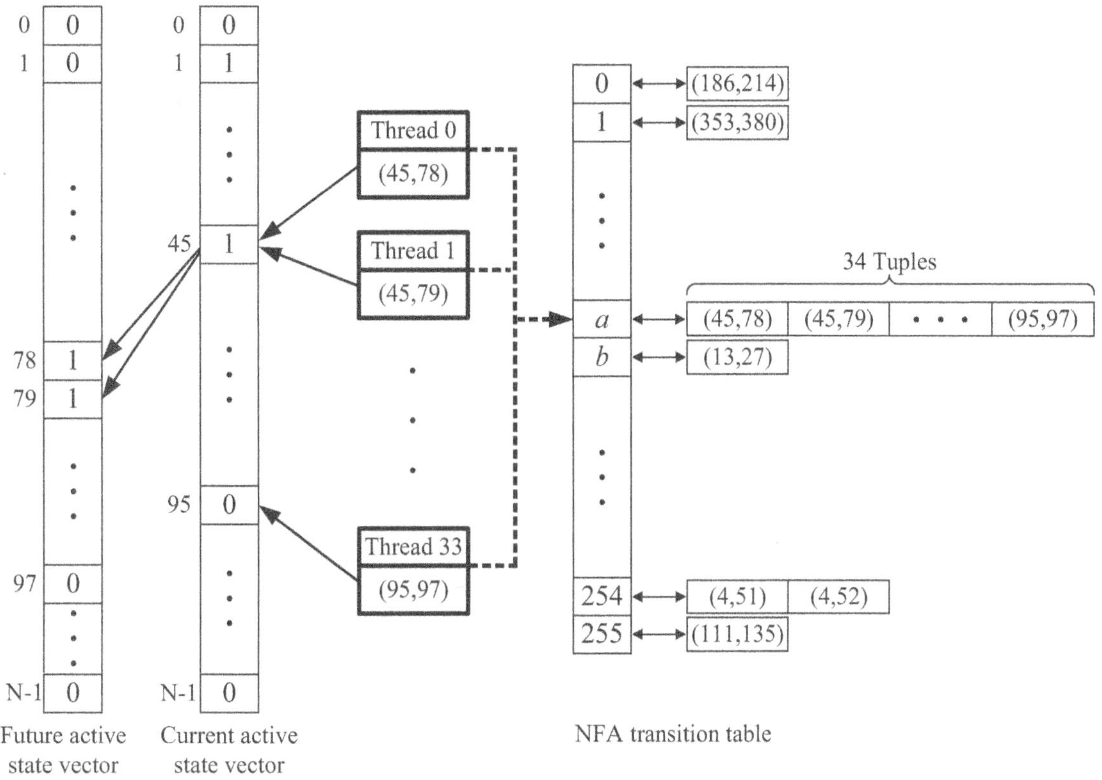

Figure 1. Data structures of iNFAnt.

2-3 operations to process these 34 transitions. In the sequel, we shall use a Snort pattern set consisting of 36 regular expression patterns (denoted by *Snort36*) as an example for illustration; its NFA can take up to five rounds of these operations to finish matching an input character.

We start our work with evaluating the performance of this GPU-based NFA implementation on NVIDIA GTX-460 GPU, using the *Snort36* pattern set. (Details about experiment setup are presented in Section 6.) The obtained matching speed is 0.26 Gbps, which is far below needed to keep up with today's high speed link rates (e.g. 10Gbps OC-192 link speed). In Section 3, we shall analyze the design drawbacks of iNFAnt, which motivate our basic design.

3. Basic design

The iNFAnt design has two major drawbacks. Firstly, the number of NFA transitions on an input character can be large, consuming a significant amount of computing resources. Especially, as GPU threads are allocated and launched in warps, each warp consisting of 32 threads, even more computing resources can be consumed. For example in Figure 1, there are 34 transitions on input character a; it will take 64 threads to process. (Actually, this is equivalent to letting one warp of 32 threads work on it for two rounds.) Secondly, notice that in step 3 of iNFAnt design, depending on whether the obtained source state is currently active or not, different threads may next execute different instructions. In current SIMD GPU architecture, such execution divergence will make the threads in one warp proceed in a sequentialized instead of parallel manner, resulting in severe performance degradation. (In Section 4.3, we shall present a systematic demonstration and analysis of how our proposed design eliminates divergence as well as potential conflict among concurrent threads.)

In light of the above insights, we now propose a different design that is immune to these problems. Our key motivating observation is that, while the number of NFA transitions on an input character can be large, the number of NFA states that can be active simultaneously is much smaller. For the NFA of pattern set *Snort36*, the number of transitions to be processed for an input character can be over five times larger than the maximum number of simultaneously active states. Therefore, while a large number of threads may be needed to process the transitions in iNFAnt design, it turns out that most of these threads will find its obtained source state inactive; their transition processing work is hence wasted. That said, if we could (somehow) accurately identify and locate those active NFA states, and make each thread responsible for performing transitions for one of the active states, the number of threads needed for matching an input character (and hence packet) can be greatly reduced, leading to significant boost in matching speed.

For that purpose, we maintain an *active state array* to record active states, as shown in Figure 2. Just for illustration purpose, let us say the array consists of 32 elements, each containing the state ID (Sid) of an active NFA state. A warp of 32 threads are dedicated for each packet, with the kth thread responsible for the kth element of the array. Upon receiving an input character, the kth thread checks the kth element for an active state ID. The state ID and the input character are combined together to form a two-dimensional index into the NFA transition table, which is essentially a two-dimensional array as shown in Figure 2, to obtain the NFA transitions to be performed.

Then, here comes the problem — into which element of the active state array should a thread write its obtained destination state as the new active state? This write operation has to be collision-free among the 32 threads. Otherwise, if two or more threads write their destination states into the same element and the destination states

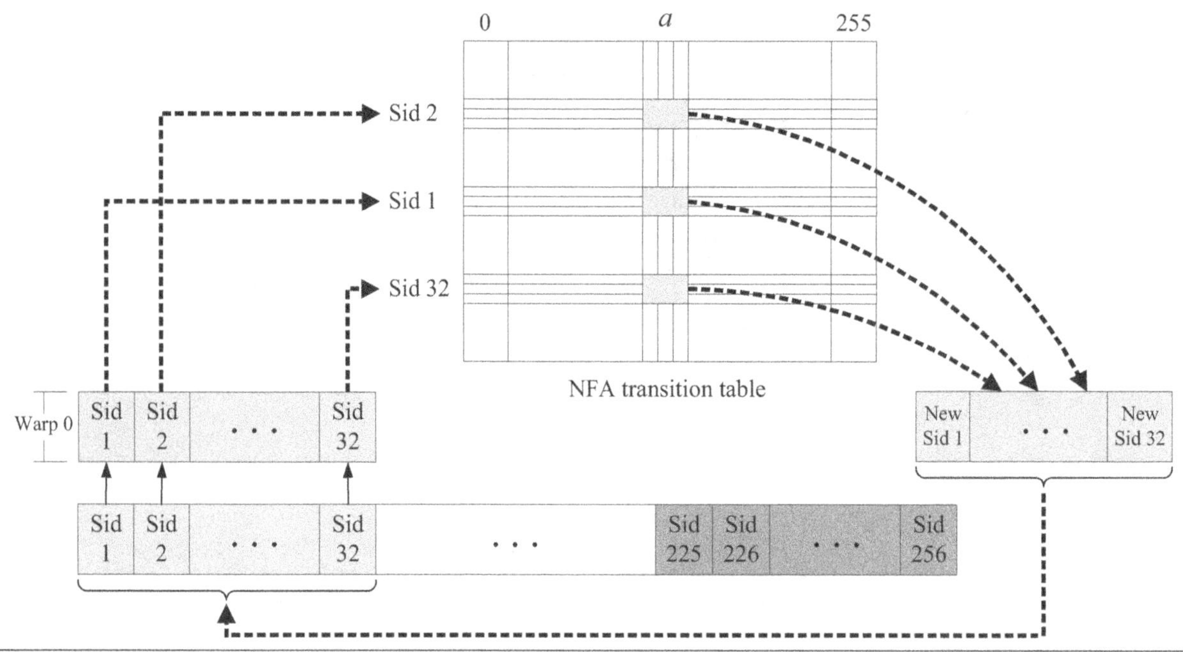

Figure 2. Data structures of our basic design.

are not the same, some of these new active states will be mistakenly overwritten by each other.

To solve this problem, we propose to partition NFA states into a number of *compatible groups*, such that states in the same compatible group can never be active simultaneously. Then, we can assign each element in the active state array to a distinct compatible group; different states in the same compatible group can safely share the same active state array element, since they cannot be active simultaneously and hence cannot be written to that element simultaneously. Every NFA state (as the destination state) can be safely written into the active state array element assigned to its compatible group, without worrying about collision. Because even if multiple threads are writing into the same active state array element, the destination state they are writing must be the same state; otherwise, such different destination states can be active simultaneously and should not have been in the same compatible group.

We mark every NFA state with its compatible group ID, which is equal to the index of the active state array element assigned to all the states in that compatible group. Each thread can simply write its obtained destination state into the active state array element indexed by the destination state's compatible group ID.

3.1 Compatibility between NFA states

For partitioning NFA states into compatible groups, we first need to figure out if two NFA states can be active simultaneously. One simple solution is to use a 2-dimensional incompatibility table. If state i and state j can be active simultaneously (which we call *incompatible*, meaning they cannot share the same active state array element), table entry (i, j) is set `true`; otherwise, we call them *compatible* and table entry (i, j) is set `false`. Using this incompatibility table, compatibility relationship between NFA states can be discovered with the following iterative breadth-first search algorithm.

Suppose the NFA states are numbered 0, 1, 2, ..., n-1. At the beginning, we have n incompatible state pairs in the form of (i, i), meaning state i is incompatible with itself; these n state pairs are stored in a queue. Then, during each iteration of the algorithm, we take out the state pair (i, j) at the head of the queue. For every possible input character c, we find out the destination state set D_i for state i and the destination state set D_j for state j, respectively. All the states in $D_i \cup D_j$ can be active simultaneously, meaning they are incompatible. For every such state pair (i', j') in $D_i \cup D_j$, if table entry (i', j') is not `true`, we set it `true` and append (i', j') to the queue. The algorithm terminates when the queue becomes empty. During each iteration, one state pair is removed from the queue, while there are n^2 distinct state pairs in total and each state pair enters the queue no more than one time. Therefore, the algorithm runs for no more than n^2 iterations.

If two NFA states i and j are marked incompatible, they are incompatible, the algorithm has actually followed a string of input character(s) which can cause the NFA to transition from one certain state to both i and j. That means i and j can be active simultaneously and hence are truly incompatible.

If two NFA states i and j are not marked incompatible, they are not incompatible. To prove by contradiction, suppose states i and j can actually be active simultaneously, which means there exists at least one shortest string w of l input character(s) that can cause the NFA to transition from the start state q_0 to both i and j. Now consider a sequence $S_i = \{q_0, i_1, i_2, \ldots, i_l{=}i\}$ of states traversed by the NFA in processing this shortest string, starting from the start state q_0 and ending in state i. In parallel, there is also such a sequence $S_i = \{q_0, j_1, j_2, \ldots, j_l{=}j\}$ for state j. Pairing the counterpart states in these two sequences gives us a sequence of state pairs, $S_i = \{(q_0, q_0), (i_1, j_1), (i_2, j_2), \ldots, (i_l{=}\mathrm{i}, j_l{=}\mathrm{j})\}$, traversed by the NFA. Obviously, no state pair can appear twice in this sequence. Because that means the input string can be further reduced into a shorter string and can still cause the NFA to transition from the start state to both i and j. Since there are n^2 distinct state pairs in total, the sequence contains at most n^2 state pairs, meaning the shortest input string contains at most n^2-1 characters. As the breadth-first search algorithm can run as many as n^2 iterations, processing one character during each iteration, the algorithm must be able to find out such a shortest string and hence mark state i and state j as incompatible. It is thus proven by contradiction that state i and state j are truly compatible.

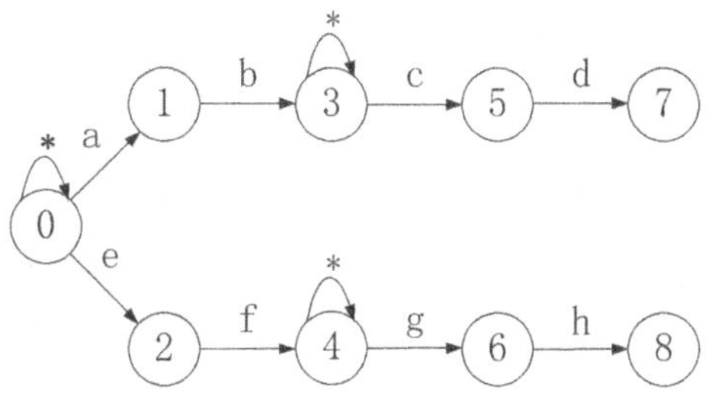

Figure 3. NFA for matching `ab.*cd` and `ef.*gh`.

For example, consider two regular expressions, `ab.*cd` and `ef.*gh`. The first expression defines a pattern where `ab` is followed by `cd`, with zero or more arbitrary characters between them. The second expression defines a similar pattern. The NFA for matching these two regular expressions is shown in Figure 3. Its incompatibility table is given in Table 1.

	0	1	2	3	4	5	6	7	8
0	√	√	√	√	√	√	√	√	√
1	√	√		√	√				
2	√		√	√	√				
3	√	√	√	√	√	√	√	√	√
4	√	√	√	√	√	√	√	√	√
5	√			√	√	√			
6	√			√	√		√		
7	√			√	√			√	
8	√			√	√				√

Table 1. Incompatibility table of the NFA in Figure 3.

3.2 Compatible group

With this compatibility relationship between NFA states available, we use a graph theoretic algorithm to partition NFA states into compatible groups. Every NFA state is represented by a distinct vertex; if two NFA states are incompatible, they are connected by an edge. Therefore, a compatible group of states form an independent set in this graph. Our algorithm proceeds in an iterative manner; in each iteration, one independent set of vertices (i.e., states) are obtained and removed from the graph, leaving a residual graph for subsequent iterations. Once all vertices have been removed from the graph, all NFA states have been partitioned into the obtained independent sets (i.e., compatible groups).

Next, we describe the algorithm for obtaining an independent set during each iteration. This algorithm is also an iterative algorithm. During each iteration of this algorithm, we pick an edge connecting two vertices u and v such that the sum of u's degree and v's degree (in the residual graph) is the largest (among all edges in the residual graph); u and v are temporarily removed from the residual graph. If the remaining graph is an independent set, it is taken as the new independent set. One possible case in this algorithm is, after temporarily removing an edge (u, v), all vertices in the residual graph have been removed and hence the obtained independent set is actually an empty set. In this case, we shall take $\{u\}$ and $\{v\}$ as two new independent sets. Finally, we check if some previously picked vertices can also be added into the new independent set(s), and do so if possible. The remaining vertices of those picked edges will form the new residual graph, from which the next independent set will be obtained.

For example, consider the NFA in Figure 3. In the constructed graph for partitioning into compatible groups, states 0, 3 and 4 are connected with each other and hence form a 3-clique; they are also connected with the other six states, while the other six states are not connected with each other. The NFA states are partitioned into compatible groups (i.e., independent sets) as follows.

- *Independent Set 1:* In this initial graph, any one of the following three edges can be picked first: (0, 3), (0, 4) and (3, 4). Without loss of generality, suppose we pick edge (0, 3) and temporarily remove it from the graph. In the remaining graph, every edge is incident to state 4. Again, we assume without loss of generality that edge (4, 1) is picked and temporarily removed. The remaining vertices — $\{2, 5, 6, 7, 8\}$ — now form an independent set. Finally, we find that among the four vertices temporarily removed, state 1 can actually be added into this obtained independent set, which we do. Thus, the residual graph will be composed of states 0, 3 and 4, forming a 3-clique.
- *Independent Set 2:* In the residual 3-clique, assume again without loss of generality that edge (0, 3) is picked; state 4 as the only remaining vertex forms an independent set. The residual graph is now edge (0, 3) alone.
- *Independent Set 3 & 4:* After we pick the only edge (0, 3), there is no other vertex left. Hence, we shall take $\{0\}$ and $\{3\}$ as two new independent sets.

The entire NFA is thus partitioned into four compatible groups: $\{1, 2, 5, 6, 7, 8\}$, $\{0\}$, $\{3\}$ and $\{4\}$.

3.3 Matching operations

Compared with iNFAnt, the entire process of matching an input character is quite simple for each thread in our design, and can be summarized as follows. (Detailed issues including data structures, memory layout, conflict and divergence will be discussed in Section 4.)

Step 1. Each thread reads in the next input character from the packet it is processing.

Step 2. Each thread obtains the current active state ID stored in its assigned active state array element, and clear that element for properly recording the new active state.

Step 3. Each thread combines the obtained active state ID with the input character to form a two-dimensional index into the NFA transition table (stored in GPU's texture memory), in order to obtain the destination state(s) it should write into the active state array as new active state(s).

Step 4. For each destination state obtained, the thread writes the destination state into the active state array element corresponding to the destination state's compatible group ID.

Step 5. Finally, each thread checks if the obtained destination state is an accepting state. If it is, a local flag is set to indicate that the packet being processed has matched the regular expression pattern represented by that accepting state. For example in Figure 3, accepting states 7 and 8 represent matching of patterns `ab.*cd` and `ef.*gh`, respectively.

If the number of compatible groups and hence the number of active state array elements exceed the number of threads in a warp dedicated to processing each packet, which is 32, the 32 threads can simply repeat step 2-5 for more rounds. The only adjustment needed is that, during the kth round, the index of the active state array element read/written by the ith thread is $(k-1) \times 32 + i$. For ease of discussion, we shall refer to the operations in step 2-5 as state transition operations.

This design is not only simpler than iNFAnt, in terms of both data structures and matching operations, but also much more efficient. On *Snort36*, the matching speed obtained by our design is

1.38 Gbps, about five times the matching speed of iNFAnt. In our experiments, we observed that for an input character, the number of NFA transitions to be processed in iNFAnt can be five times the number of compatible groups in our design.[2] This well explains the 5× speedup achieved by our design. It also verifies the validity of our analysis of iNFAnt's design drawbacks, as well as the motivating ideas underlying our design.

3.4 Discussion

In fact, the idea of splitting NFA states into compatible groups can be generalized to help boost the performance of other GPU-based parallel applications as well. In particular, every parallel application is composed of a set of concurrent tasks. In NFA-based regular expression matching, each task consists of the state transition operations to be performed for individual NFA states. At a certain moment, each task may and may not need to be performed, depending on some condition. In NFA-based regular expression matching, this task-specific condition is whether each individual NFA state is active or not. According to this condition, we can group these tasks into compatible groups, each consisting of tasks that need not be performed simultaneously. It suffices to allocate an exclusive thread for each compatible group of tasks (like in our design), instead of allocating an exclusive thread for each task (like in iNFAnt's design). As a result, the parallel application's performance can be effectively boosted.

4. Memory layout and optimizations

In this section, we shall describe the detailed data structures of our basic design, as well as their memory layout and the operations on them. Through in-depth analysis and experiments, we shall present effective optimizations that will significantly boost the performance of our design. Moreover, we shall also analyze potential conflict and divergence among threads, and demonstrate how they are eliminated from our design through optimized implementation.

4.1 NFA transition table

In our basic design, the NFA transition table is simply implemented as a two-dimensional array, stored in GPU's texture memory. Each table entry is defined as an `int4` type, composed of four internal elements named `w`, `x`, `y` and `z`, respectively. Each internal element is 32-bit `int` type, encoding a distinct destination state. In CUDA, such a 128-bit `int4` type NFA transition table entry can be fetched with one single memory access.

Within each 32-bit internal element encoding a destination state, the least significant two bytes are used to record the destination state's state ID, supporting 65,536 NFA states, which have been more than enough for practical pattern sets. Within the most significant two bytes of the internal element, the least significant five bits are used to encode the destination state's compatible group ID, giving us 32 compatible groups (corresponding to a warp of 32 threads); the most significant bit is used to indicate whether the destination state is an accepting state; the middle 10 bits are unused for now.

With this simple data structure design, we can allow every NFA state to have up to four destination states on a given input character. In our experiments, we have never found any NFA state that has more than four destination states on any given input character. Nevertheless, in our final design presented in Section 5, we shall address the theoretically possible case where an NFA state can have more than four destination states on a given input character.

To handle the realistic case where there are less than four destination states in an NFA transition table entry, we introduce a *dumb state* into the NFA. If an NFA transition table entry contains less than four destination states, we shall add some dumb states to fill up the `int4` type table entry. For example, for a table entry with two real destination states, we can record them as `w` and `x`, respectively; then, we record a dumb state into `y` and `z`, respectively. The dumb state has transitions on all possible input characters, leading back to the dumb state itself. We implement the dumb state like a real NFA state and assign it to a compatible group according to the algorithm described in Section 3.

[2] Note that the number of compatible groups can be larger than the maximum number of simultaneously active states.

4.2 Active state array

Each warp (consisting of 32 threads) maintains its own active state array (consisting of 32 elements), stored in GPU's shared memory. Each active state array element is also 32-bit `int` type, the same as the four destination states stored in each NFA transition table entry, since destination states are stored in active state array elements.

4.3 Conflict and divergence

Next, we analyze the operations involved in our design, demonstrating how potential conflict and divergence are solved through optimized implementation. As described in Section 3, the operations involved in processing an input character are as follows.

Step 1. *Obtain the next input character.* Input characters are obtained in two stages: (1) from global memory to shared memory; (2) from shared memory to each thread. During the first stage, all the 32 threads in a warp read the same 32-byte packet slice, each thread reading a different byte in the 32-byte slice; there is no conflict. All the threads execute the same read operation, except the target addresses are different; there is no divergence, either. After the first stage, a slice of 32 characters are transferred from global memory to a buffer in the shared memory, to be read and processed in the second stage. The second stage consists of 32 rounds of state transition operations, processing one character from the buffer in each round. During each round, all the 32 threads in a warp read the same next character from the buffer in shared memory. There is no divergence, and the same byte in shared memory can be read by all the threads simultaneously without conflict.

Step 2. *Obtain the current active state.* Each thread reads the current active state ID stored in its assigned active state array element, and clears that element for properly recording the new active state. There is neither divergence nor conflict.

Step 3. *Obtain the destination states.* Each thread combines the current active state ID with the input character to form a two-dimensional index into the NFA transition table, in order to obtain the destination state(s) it will write into the active state array as new active state(s). Here, notice that not all active state array elements will contain a valid active NFA state; for example, the entire NFA may have only one state active at that moment and many active state array elements simply do not contain any valid active NFA state. To avoid divergence, even if a thread does not obtain a valid NFA state ID from its active state array element, it still must index into the NFA transition table and read out some table entry, just like a thread that has obtained a valid active state ID. For that purpose, as the "clear" operation after reading from the active state array element, we can let each thread put the dumb state into its active state array element. If no new active state is subsequently written into that element, during the next round the thread will read out this dumb state as its active state. Since the dumb state is physically stored in the NFA transition table like a real state, it allows the thread to perform subsequent state transition operations as if the obtained dumb state is a real NFA state. Even if multiple threads all obtain the dumb state as their current active state and hence read the same NFA transition table entry simultaneously, there will not be conflict. Because GPU will coalesce these read requests into one

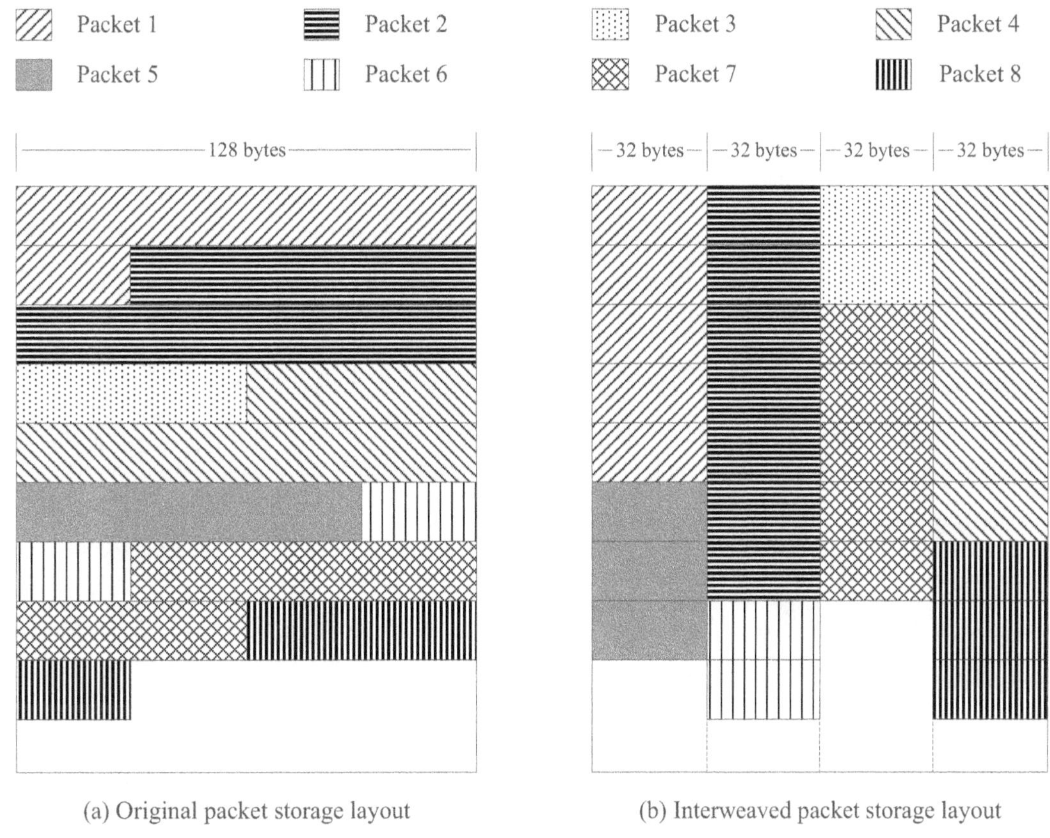

(a) Original packet storage layout

(b) Interweaved packet storage layout

Figure 4. Packet storage layout in global memory.

single read request, before issuing the read operation to the texture memory.

Step 4. *Update the active state array.* Each thread writes every obtained destination state into the active state array element assigned to that destination state's compatible group. There is no divergence, since each thread obtains precisely four destination states, possibly including dumb states, and the dumb state is physically stored in the NFA transition table as well. As to conflict, it is possible that two threads may write their destination states into the same active state array element simultaneously. On one hand, note that the two destination states being written will be active simultaneously; on the other hand, the two destination states being written into the same active state array element means they are in the same compatible group. Therefore, the only possibility is that the two destination states are the same state. The active state array is stored in GPU's shared memory. Such concurrent writes can proceed simultaneously, while only one of the concurrent writes will go through. Since the concurrent writes are writing the same destination state into the same active state array element, it does not matter which one goes through. Thus, no cost is paid for this collision.

Step 5. *Record pattern matching information.* As the last step, each thread checks if the obtained destination state is an accepting state. If it is, a local flag is set to indicate that the packet being processed has matched the pattern represented by that accepting state. As the 32-bit encoding of the destination state contains a bit indicating whether the destination state is an accepting state, we can simply let each thread write that indicator bit into a local flag. To avoid conflict, each thread is allocated a local flag of its own, stored in shared memory for fast access. Since all the threads execute the same write operation into their own flag, there is no conflict or divergence. Finally, after the entire packet has been processed, the local flags will be transferred to global memory for subsequent processing. For each packet, if any one of the threads has its flag set, it means the packet has matched some pattern and hence requires subsequent further processing.

4.4 Input packets

In our basic design, incoming packets are simply stored sequentially (in GPU's global memory), one after one in order of arrival, as shown in Figure 4(a). All the 32 threads in a warp read the same next byte simultaneously, since they are supposed to work on this same byte. GPU will coalesce their read requests for this same byte in global memory into one single request for that byte, before issuing to the global memory.

However, GPU is actually able to perform even more powerful coalescence. Specifically, GPU manages its global memory as aligned 128-byte blocks, each block having the same size as a cache line. With every single global memory read operation, GPU can fetch such a 128-byte block out of the global memory and store it into a cache line for subsequent quick access. Therefore, GPU actually combines all read requests targeting within the same 128-byte block into one request.

Given that, we modify packet storage layout in global memory to better exploit this feature of GPU architecture. In particular, we partition every packet into 32-byte slices (with padding if needed). Slices from different packets are interweaved together, so that a 128-byte block in global memory is likely (although not necessarily) composed of four slices from four different packets, as shown in Figure 4(b). Then in our program, the 32 threads within a warp each reads a different byte from the same 32-byte slice, using their thread ID as offset inside the slice. These 32 concurrent read requests are coalesced into one request for the block containing that slice, and the 32 bytes read out of global memory are then stored in the shared memory, to be processed in the next 32 rounds of state transition operations.

GPU achieves high computing performance through inherent massive parallelism, by processing a large number of packets concurrently. A large number of warps will be running concurrently inside GPU. By mixing slices from different packets into 128-byte blocks, after one of the four packet slices is fetched by the warp responsible for processing that packet, the entire 128-byte block is stored into a cache line; it increases the chance that the warps fetching the other three packet slices in the same block will find their slices already in the cache line. Consequently, computing performance can be effectively boosted. For example, the matching speed achieved by our design on *Snort36* is raised from 1.38 Gbps to 4.01 Gbps, a $3\times$ speedup.

Packet slicing and interweaving as described above are done by CPU, which transmits 32-byte slices from different packets to GPU in interweaving order. Before slicing and transmitting packets to GPU, CPU can sort packets (in order of arrival) into four queues. For example, suppose there are eight packets, which are originally stored sequentially as shown in Figure 4(a). After sorting them into four queues, CPU transmits the first 32-byte slice from each queue to GPU, then the second slice from each queue to GPU, and so on, leading to the storage layout as shown in Figure 4(b), where each row is a 128-byte block.

4.5 Discussion

The idea of interweaving slices of different packets into the same 128-byte block can also be generalized to boost performance of other GPU-based parallel applications. On one hand, parallel applications achieve high computing performance through massive parallelism; many warps run at the same time. On the other hand, GPU has a fixed number of cache lines. Thus, if we can preload data of more warps into the fixed number of cache lines, more (concurrently running) warps will benefit from higher cache hit ratio. In the example of our regular expression matching application, the data of each warp is the packet to be processed by that warp; the way to load data of more warps into cache is to make data of different warps share the same 128-byte block, by slicing and interweaving data of different warps. In other GPU-based parallel applications, data of different warps can be similarly sliced and interweaved for improved performance.

5. Virtual NFA

Thus far, we have stuck to the simplistic design principle of dedicating a whole warp of 32 threads to processing every single packet, without worrying about the following realistic issues.

- Firstly, if an NFA can never have 32 compatible groups, some of the 32 threads in a dedicated warp will be running in vain, which means wasted computing power.
- Secondly, if an NFA can have more than 32 compatible groups, the 32 threads in a dedicated warp will need two or more rounds of state transition operations to finish processing an input character. Again, this means degraded matching performance.
- Thirdly, each NFA transition table entry is assumed to contain at most four destination states, nicely fitting into the `int4` data type. However, this assumption may and may not be the case in practice. How can we handle more than four destination states residing in one table entry, or prevent such cases from happening?

In this section, we present a more elaborated design that is able to address all these issues, by transforming an original NFA into a *virtual NFA* whose states can be partitioned into a small fixed number of, say K, compatible groups ($K = 4$ in our design); each compatible group is still handled by one separate thread. After transformation into such a virtual NFA, no matter how many compatible groups are needed for the original NFA, we can always process a packet using K threads and one round of state transition operations for each input character, leading to fast and stable matching speed. This will address the first two issues discussed above. Furthermore, by using K threads for each packet, instead of using all the 32 threads in a warp for one single packet in our basic design, $\lfloor \frac{32}{K} \rfloor$ packets instead of one packet can be processed by a warp of 32 threads simultaneously. In our design where $K = 4$, eight packets can be processed by a warp of 32 threads simultaneously. As a result, further multiplied matching speed can be achieved.

Finally, if we transform into such a virtual NFA that only $K = 4$ compatible groups are needed, we will be able to ensure that at most $K = 4$ states can be active simultaneously in the virtual NFA. Since destination states residing in the same NFA transition table entry can obviously become active simultaneously, having at most four simultaneously active states directly means none of the virtual NFA's transition table entries can contain more than four destination states. Thus, the third issue discussed above will be solved as well.

The entire process of transforming an original NFA into a virtual NFA is composed of two stages: (1) grouping original NFA states into compatible groups; (2) combining compatible groups into K compatible super groups. The first stage has been described in Section 3. In the rest of this section, we shall present our detailed solution for the second stage. First of all, combining multiple compatible groups into one super group immediately raises a question: now multiple states in a super group can be active simultaneously, how can we transform the super group into a compatible one where at most one of its states can be active at any time, so that it can still be properly handled using one active state array element and one single thread? We answer this question in Section 5.1, with the notion of *virtual state*. Based on that, we shall then present in Section 5.2 an algorithm for combining compatible groups into such compatible super groups. Finally in Section 5.3, we describe relevant adjustment to the basic design for efficient implementation of the virtual NFA design.

5.1 Virtual state

Suppose multiple compatible groups are combined into one super group. Now, two different states (say X and Y) within this super group, originally from two different compatible groups, can be active simultaneously. In this case, our basic design may not be able to preserve proper operation of the NFA. Because on an input character, there can be two active states A and B that lead to destination states X and Y, respectively, while X and Y are combined into the same super group. The threads responsible for processing A and B will then try to write X and Y into the same active state array element assigned to their super group. Consequently, either X or Y will be lost due to this collision.

Therefore, we need a solution for uniquely representing the status of such a super group, in terms of which states in this super group are currently active. For that, we think of each distinct status of the super group as a distinct *virtual state* of the super group. By replacing the original NFA states in this super group with such virtual states representing all possible combinations of active states in the super group, the super group will be transformed into a compatible group where at most one of its virtual states can be active at any time.

Just for illustration purpose, let us suppose all the nine NFA states in Figure 3 are somehow allocated to the same super group. Each virtual state of this super group represents a set of active states in this super group. For instance, if states 0 and 2 are active in the NFA in Figure 3, the virtual state at that point is the active state set $\{0, 2\}$. We encode every virtual state of the super group as a bit vector that is unique within the range of this super group. The super group's bit vector is composed of smaller bit vectors, each representing the sole active state within a distinct compatible group that has been combined into that super group.

To encode a compatible group of m states, we only need a bit vector of $\lceil \log(m+1) \rceil$ bits; because at most one of the states in a compatible group can be active at any time. We assign to each state a unique internal ID within the compatible group (starting from 1). The bit vector being all zero means none of the states in this compatible group is currently active; otherwise, the bit vector records the internal ID of the sole active state in that compatible group.

Suppose the nine NFA states are grouped into four compatible groups — $\{0\}$, $\{3\}$, $\{4\}$ and $\{1,2,5,6,7,8\}$ — that are combined into one single super group. Within the compatible group $\{1,2,5,6,7,8\}$, states 1, 2, 5, 6, 7 and 8 are assigned 1, 2, 3, 4, 5 and 6 as their internal ID, respectively. Internal ID 0 is reserved for the situation that none of the states is active. (This is why the number of bits in the bit vector is $\lceil \log(6+1) \rceil$ instead of $\lceil \log 6 \rceil$, although they do not make any difference in this particular example.) If states 0 and 2 are currently active in this super group, the bit vector encoding the virtual state representing active state set $\{0, 2\}$ will be `1 0 0 010`, composed of the four smaller bit vectors encoding its four composing compatible groups. The first single-bit vector indicates state 0, the only state in compatible group $\{0\}$, is currently active; the next two single-bit vectors similarly indicate that states 3 and 4 are not active; the last 3-bit vector `010` indicates that state 2 in compatible group $\{1,2,5,6,7,8\}$ is currently active. It is clear that any virtual state of this nine-state super group can be uniquely represented by such a 6-bit vector.

In general cases, compatible groups of an NFA can be combined into up to four such super groups. To assign to each virtual state a state ID that is unique within the entire NFA, we can sort the super groups in non-increasing order of their size; within each super group, virtual states can be sorted in lexicographic order of the bit vectors encoding the virtual state. Then in this sorted list of all virtual states, the kth virtual state can be assigned state ID k-1, which is clearly unique within the entire NFA. At this point, the NFA is composed of these virtual states instead of the original NFA states, and hence is referred to as a *virtual NFA*. Each virtual state's state ID can be used as the row number of this virtual state in the virtual NFA's transition table, just like the original NFA.

In this virtual NFA, every super group is now a compatible group — at most one virtual state of each super group can be active at any time. Consequently, we can safely assign to each compatible super group one active state array element and one thread, just like we allocate to each compatible group one active state array element and one thread in our basic design. Proper operation of the virtual NFA is thus achieved with the same mechanism as our basic design.

5.2 Combining into super groups

Suppose the states of an original NFA are partitioned into n compatible groups, following the method described in Section 3. We now proceed to combine these n compatible groups into K super groups, which will then be transformed into compatible super groups of virtual states as described in Section 5.1.

In principle, the way we group these n groups into K super groups will not directly affect matching speed. However, it can have considerable impact on the total number of virtual states, and hence storage space of the virtual NFA. To minimize the virtual NFA's state space, we want to minimize the length of the bit vector encoding individual super groups. To achieve this objective, we sort the n compatible groups in decreasing order of their size. We allocate the largest compatible group to the first super group. Then, note that every time we add a compatible group into a super group, the bit vector encoding that super group is appended with the bit vector encoding the joining compatible group. Therefore, we add each remaining compatible group to the super group whose encoding bit vector is currently the shortest.

Just for illustration, suppose we are to use $K = 2$ super groups for the example NFA in Figure 3. The NFA, as described in Section 3.2, is partitioned into four compatible groups. We first allocate the largest compatible group, $\{1, 2, 5, 6, 7, 8\}$, to the first super group. Then, we keep allocating the remaining three compatible groups to the second super group, since its bit vector is always shorter than the bit vector of the first super group. Consequently, the bit vectors of both super groups are 3-bit long. In total, the virtual NFA is thus composed of $2 \times 2^3 = 16$ virtual states.

5.3 Memory layout and state transition

Unlike in the basic design, where every warp of 32 threads are dedicated to a single packet, we hereby allocate 4 threads for each packet only, having 8 packets share the 32 threads in each warp. Accordingly, we partition every packet into 4-byte slices (with padding if needed). To interweave slices from different packets together, CPU sorts packets (in order of arrival) into 32 queues; then, CPU keeps transmitting the next 4-byte slice from each queue to GPU, producing an interweaved storage layout where each 128-block of GPU's global memory is composed of 4-byte slices from the 32 queues.

Then in our program, the 32 threads in a warp each reads a different byte from the 4-byte slice of its packet; the kth thread reads the $(((k-1) \bmod 4)+1)$th byte in the 4-byte slice of the $\lceil k/4 \rceil$th packet. The 32 read requests are coalesced into one read request for the contiguous 32-byte region within a 128-byte block of GPU's global memory. The eight slices are read out with one single memory access and then stored in the shared memory. During each of the following four rounds of state transition operations, one byte from each of the eight slices will be processed by the four threads responsible for the packet where that slice is from.

To perform state transition for an input byte, the kth thread reads the virtual state stored in the kth active state array element, and clear that element for properly recording the new active virtual state. Then, each thread uses the obtained active virtual state ID and the input character as a two-dimensional index to obtain the destination virtual states from the virtual NFA's transition table. For each destination virtual state obtained by the kth thread, suppose it belongs to the lth compatible super group where $1 \le l \le 4$; corresponding to that super group is the $(4 \times \lfloor (k-1)/4 \rfloor + l)$th active state array element, into which the destination virtual state is written.

With this virtual NFA design using four compatible super groups and hence four threads for each packet, we achieved 12.50 Gbps matching speed on *Snort36*, representing a $3\times$ speedup compared with the design in Section 4.

6. Experiments

We evaluated the performance of our GPU-based NFA implementation method using real life pattern sets collected from the Snort intrusion detection system [2], packet traces generated using the workload generator introduced in [8] and NVIDIA GTX-460 GPU. We evaluated our proposed method through experiments based on six Snort pattern sets and compared with iNFAnt [9]. Characteristics of the pattern sets and packet traces are reported in Section 6.1.

	Snort16				Snort23			
	$p_M = 0.05$	$p_M = 0.35$	$p_M = 0.65$	$p_M = 0.95$	$p_M = 0.05$	$p_M = 0.35$	$p_M = 0.65$	$p_M = 0.95$
Virtual NFA (Gbps)	13.08	13.93	13.17	12.41	13.36	13.23	13.42	13.01
iNFAnt (Gbps)	0.44	0.38	0.36	0.33	0.43	0.37	0.34	0.31
Virtual NFA/iNFAnt Speedup	29.39	35.98	36.01	36.52	29.95	34.01	39.18	40.91
	Snort24				**Snort27**			
	$p_M = 0.05$	$p_M = 0.35$	$p_M = 0.65$	$p_M = 0.95$	$p_M = 0.05$	$p_M = 0.35$	$p_M = 0.65$	$p_M = 0.95$
Virtual NFA (Gbps)	13.20	12.52	12.43	12.32	13.15	12.34	10.28	10.08
iNFAnt (Gbps)	0.43	0.39	0.34	0.31	0.43	0.39	0.31	0.28
Virtual NFA/iNFAnt Speedup	30.37	31.76	36.15	38.59	30.30	31.62	32.55	35.33
	Snort34				**Snort36**			
	$p_M = 0.05$	$p_M = 0.35$	$p_M = 0.65$	$p_M = 0.95$	$p_M = 0.05$	$p_M = 0.35$	$p_M = 0.65$	$p_M = 0.95$
Virtual NFA (Gbps)	13.12	13.79	12.04	12.52	13.18	13.99	12.99	12.50
iNFAnt (Gbps)	0.42	0.36	0.32	0.29	0.41	0.33	0.30	0.26
Virtual NFA/iNFAnt Speedup	31.08	37.43	37.24	42.38	31.73	42.22	42.01	46.31

Table 2. Matching speed.

Matching speed results are reported in Section 6.2. Storage space results are reported in Section 6.3.

6.1 Experiment setup

As shown in Table 3, the six Snort pattern sets used in our experiments are diverse in nature. Some pattern sets are relatively simple, while some others are much more complex. Consequently, in terms of inflation ratio (i.e., DFA size divided by NFA size), their DFAs are larger than their NFAs by 15.51 times to 281.22 times; their DFAs consist of 13,825 states to 190,951 states.

	DFA size	NFA size	DFA/NFA inflation
Snort-16	67,682	447	151.41
Snort-23	32,518	518	62.77
Snort-24	13,886	575	24.14
Snort-27	106,452	499	213.33
Snort-34	13,825	891	15.51
Snort-36	190,951	679	281.22

Table 3. Characteristics of pattern sets.

Workloads to be used as input character stream are generated for each individual pattern set, respectively, using the workload generator proposed in [8]. Every workload is generated as a byte stream, according to a specified parameter p_M. When generating the next byte, it is chosen with probability p_M such that the byte will lead away from the start state (of the pattern set's finite automaton); with probability $1-p_M$, the next byte is chosen randomly. After a workload is generated by the workload generator, we partition the workload into 1KB segments, each segment representing the payload of a packet.

For each pattern set, we generated four types of workloads using $p_M = 0.05, p_M = 0.35, p_M = 0.65$ and $p_M = 0.95$, respectively. Each generated workload is 280KB in length. For each p_M value, we generated a number of such workloads and combine them into a single large workload, which is 256MB in size and divided into 256K packets. In total, 24 such large workloads are generated.

6.2 Matching speed

We run our virtual NFA design and iNFAnt[3] on each of the 24 workloads, and report the matching speed results in Table 2. 4,096 blocks, each consisting of 256 threads, are employed for each workload. Here, matching speed is calculated by dividing workload size with the time taken to finish matching the workload.[4] As we can see, on all pattern sets and parameter settings, our virtual NFA design consistently achieves matching speed above 10Gbps (OC-192 link rate). Compared with iNFAnt, our virtual NFA design can boost matching speed by 29~46 times.

6.3 Memory space

To compare the scalability our virtual NFA design with DFA-based methods, we conducted a series of experiments to reveal the growth trend of virtual NFA size. For a pattern set (which in this case is *Snort-36* whose DFA is the largest) consisting of n patterns, we generated a series of $\lceil n/4 \rceil$ subsets. The kth subset consists of the first MIN$(4k, n)$ patterns of the original pattern set. For each subset, we measured the number of states in the virtual NFA and the DFA, respectively. Then, we plot the results in Figure 5, where the X-axis represents the number of virtual NFA states and the Y-axis represents the number of DFA states. As we can see, the virtual NFA size tends to grow exponentially more slowly than the DFA size, demonstrating much better scalability.

We also measured the storage space needed for implementing the pattern sets. The virtual NFA transition tables of *Snort16*, *Snort23*, *Snort24*, *Snort27*, *Snort34* and *Snort36* use 3.02MB, 6.5MB, 3.06MB, 12.5MB, 6.13MB and 14MB, respectively.[5] As virtual NFA transition tables are stored in inexpensive texture memory (which has up to 1GB capacity on NVIDIA GTX-460 GPU), these memory space requirements incur very low cost.

[3] The authors of iNFAnt[9] proposed a multi-striding technique for accelerating iNFAnt, by processing multiple bytes per state transition. However, through private communication we have confirmed with the authors that their experiments reported in [9] are actually erroneous and the proposed multi-striding technique is not as practical as demonstrated by the experiment results in [9]. Therefore, we compared our design with their basic iNFAnt design, where one byte is processed per state transition.

[4] The experiment results did not include the time spent on constructing virtual NFAs. Because the goal is to boost matching speed. Virtual NFA construction is a one time cost; after the virtual NFA is constructed, we will not need to pay this cost again during the matching process, until the regular expressions change (which may not happen over days/months).

[5] For these virtual NFAs, we are able to use 64-bit `short4` type instead of 128-bit `int4` type for their transition table entry.

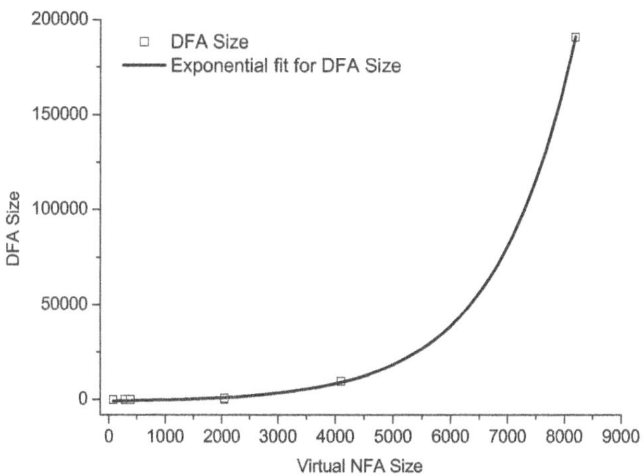

Figure 5. Growth trend of virtual NFA size.

7. Conclusions

In this work, we analyzed and demonstrated some important properties of NFA, using real life pattern sets as examples. Based on this understanding of NFA properties as well as GPU architecture, we conducted in-depth study, both experimental and analytical, of how NFAs can be best fitted into GPU architecture through proper data structure and parallel programming design, so that GPU's parallel processing power can be effectively mobilized to achieve high speed regular expression matching. The three pivot ideas of our design include compatible group, packet interweaving and transforming the original NFA into our proposed virtual NFA.

We evaluated the performance of our virtual NFA design using real life pattern sets collected from the Snort intrusion detection system [2], on NVIDIA GTX-460 GPU. Experiment results demonstrate that, virtual NFA can achieve 29$\sim$46 times speedup, consistently yielding over 10Gbps matching speed. Meanwhile, compared with DFA size, our virtual NFA design only needs a very small amount of memory space, growing exponentially more slowly than DFA size. These results make our virtual NFA design an effective solution for memory efficient high speed (e.g. 10Gbps OC-192 link speed) regular expression matching, and clearly demonstrate the power and potential of GPU as a platform for memory efficient high speed regular expression matching.

References

[1] *PCRE - Perl Compatible Regular Expressions*. http://www.pcre.org/.

[2] *Snort intrusion detection system*. http://www.snort.org/.

[3] S. S. Baghsorkhi, M. Delahaye, S. J. Patel, W. D. Gropp, and W. mei W. Hwu. An adaptive performance modeling tool for GPU architectures. In *Proceedings of ACM PPoPP*, 2010.

[4] M. Becchi and P. Crowley. A hybrid finite automaton for practical deep packet inspection. In *Proceedings of CoNext*, 2007.

[5] M. Becchi and P. Crowley. An improved algorithm to accelerate regular expression evaluation. In *Proceedings of ANCS*, 2007.

[6] M. Becchi and P. Crowley. Efficient regular expression evaluation: Theory to practice. In *Proceedings of ANCS*, 2008.

[7] M. Becchi and P. Crowley. Extending finite automata to efficient match perl-compatible regular expressions. In *Proceedings of CoNext*, 2008.

[8] M. Becchi, M. Franklin, and P. Crowley. A workload for evaluating deep packet inspection architectures. In *Proceedings of IISWC*, 2008.

[9] N. Cascarano, P. Rolando, F. Risso, and R. Sisto. iNFAnt: NFA pattern matching on GPGPU devices. *SIGCOMM CCR*, 40(5):21–26, 2010.

[10] M. Chen. TCAM-based high speed regular expression matching. Bachelor thesis, Institute of Networked Systems (IONS), University of Science and Technology of China, June 2010.

[11] M. Chen, Q. Dong, and K. Peng. TCAM-based DFA implementation: A novel approach to efficient regular expression matching. Technical report, Institute of Networked Systems (IONS), University of Science and Technology of China.

[12] J. W. Choi, A. Singh, and R. W. Vuduc. Model-driven autotuning of sparse matrix-vector multiply on GPUs. In *Proceedings of ACM PPoPP*, 2010.

[13] Y. Dotsenko, S. S. Baghsorkhi, B. Lloyd, and N. K. Govindaraju. Auto-tuning of fast fourier transform on graphics processors. In *Proceedings of PPOPP*, 2011.

[14] S. Hong, S. K. Kim, T. Oguntebi, and K. Olukotun. Accelerating CUDA graph algorithms at maximum warp. In *Proceedings of ACM PPoPP*, 2011.

[15] J. Kim, H. Kim, J. H. Lee, and J. Lee. Achieving a single compute device image in OpenCL for multiple GPUs. In *Proceedings of ACM PPoPP*, 2011.

[16] S. Kumar, B. Chandrasekaran, J. Turner, and G. Varghese. Curing regular expressions matching algorithms from insomnia, amnesia, and acalculia. In *Proceedings of ANCS*, 2007.

[17] S. Kumar, S. Dharmapurikar, F. Yu, P. Crowley, and J. Turner. Algorithms to accelerate multiple regular expressions matching for deep packet inspection. In *Proceedings of ACM SIGCOMM*, 2006.

[18] S. Lee, S.-J. Min, and R. Eigenmann. OpenMP to GPGPU: a compiler framework for automatic translation and optimization. In *Proceedings of ACM PPoPP*, 2009.

[19] C. R. Meiners, J. Patel, E. Norige, E. Torng, and A. X. Liu. Fast regular expression matching using small TCAMs for network intrusion detection and prevention systems. In *Proceedings of USENIX Security*, August 2010.

[20] K. Peng, Q. Dong, and M. Chen. TCAM-based DFA deflation: A novel approach to fast and scalable regular expression matching. In *Proceedings of ACM/IEEE IWQoS*, 2011.

[21] K. Peng, S. Tang, Q. Dong, and M. Chen. Chain-based DFA deflation for fast and scalable regular expression matching using TCAM. In *Proceedings of ANCS*, 2011.

[22] E. F. O. Sandes and A. C. M. de Melo. CUDAlign: using GPU to accelerate the comparison of megabase genomic sequences. In *Proceedings of ACM PPoPP*, 2010.

[23] R. Smith, C. Estan, and S. Jha. XFA: Faster signature matching with extended automata. In *Proceedings of IEEE Symposium on Security and Privacy*, 2008.

[24] R. Smith, C. Estan, S. Jha, and S. Kong. Deflating the big bang: fast and scalable deep packet inspection with extended finite automata. In *Proceedings of ACM SIGCOMM*, 2008.

[25] R. Smith, N. Goyal, J. Ormont, K. Sankaralingam, and C. Estan. Evaluating GPUs for network packet signature matching. In *Proceedings of ISPASS*, 2009.

[26] G. Vasiliadis, S. Antonatos, M. Polychronakis, E. P. Markatos, and S. Ioannidis. Gnort: High performance network intrusion detection using graphics processors. In *Proceedings of RAID*, 2008.

[27] G. Vasiliadis, M. Polychronakis, S. Antonatos, E. P. Markatos, and S. Ioannidis. Regular expression matching on graphics hardware for intrusion detection. In *Proceedings of RAID*, 2009.

[28] F. Yu, Z. Chen, Y. Diao, T. V. Lakshman, and R. H. Katz. Fast and memory-efficient regular expression matching for deep packet inspection. In *Proceedings of ANCS*, 2006.

[29] Y. Zhang, J. Cohen, and J. D. Owens. Fast tridiagonal solvers on the GPU. In *Proceedings of ACM PPoPP*, 2010.

[30] M. Zheng, V. T. Ravi, F. Qin, and G. Agrawal. GRace: a low-overhead mechanism for detecting data races in GPU programs. In *Proceedings of ACM PPoPP*, 2011.

A Methodology for Creating Fast Wait-Free Data Structures *

Alex Kogan
Department of Computer Science
Technion, Israel
sakogan@cs.technion.ac.il

Erez Petrank
Department of Computer Science
Technion, Israel
erez@cs.technion.ac.il

Abstract

Lock-freedom is a progress guarantee that ensures overall program progress. Wait-freedom is a stronger progress guarantee that ensures the progress of each thread in the program. While many practical lock-free algorithms exist, wait-free algorithms are typically inefficient and hardly used in practice. In this paper, we propose a methodology called *fast-path-slow-path* for creating efficient wait-free algorithms. The idea is to execute the efficient lock-free version most of the time and revert to the wait-free version only when things go wrong. The generality and effectiveness of this methodology is demonstrated by two examples. In this paper, we apply this idea to a recent construction of a wait-free queue, bringing the wait-free implementation to perform in practice as efficient as the lock-free implementation. In another work, the fast-path-slow-path methodology has been used for (dramatically) improving the performance of a wait-free linked-list.

Categories and Subject Descriptors D.3.3 [*Programming Languages*]: Language Constructs and Features – Concurrent programming structures; E.1 [*Data Structures*]: Lists, stacks, and queues

General Terms Algorithms, Performance

Keywords Concurrent data structures, non-blocking synchronization, wait-free queues, lock-free algorithms

1. Introduction

The evolution of multi-core systems necessitates the design of scalable and efficient concurrent data structures. A common approach to achieve these goals is by constructing *non-blocking* algorithms. Such algorithms ensure that no thread accessing the data structure is postponed indefinitely while waiting for other threads that operate on that data structure.

Most non-blocking data structure implementations provide a *lock-free* progress guarantee, ensuring that among all threads that try to apply an operation, at least one will succeed. While some lock-free algorithms are quite scalable and efficient [7, 20, 24], they all allow workloads in which all but one thread starve. Such workloads cannot occur with *wait-free* algorithms, which ensure that each thread applies its operation in a bounded number of steps, independently of what other threads are doing. This property is valuable in real-time systems, operating systems or systems operating under a service level agreement, with a (hard or soft) deadline on the time required to complete each operation. It is valuable as well in heterogeneous systems, in which threads may execute at different speeds and where faster threads may repeatedly delay slower ones, as might happen, for example, in systems composed of different computing units, such as CPUs and GPUs.

In practice, while having desirable properties, wait-free algorithms are rightly considered inefficient and hard to design [6, 13]. Their inefficiency is said to be largely attributable to the helping mechanism [12], which is a key mechanism employed by most wait-free algorithms. This mechanism controls the way threads help each other to complete their operations, and usually leads to complicated algorithms, as each operation must be ensured to be applied exactly once. In practice, this often results in the usage of a greater number of expensive atomic operations, such as compare-and-swap (CAS), which degrade the performance of wait-free algorithms even when contention is low.

Moreover, most helping mechanisms known to us suffer from two problematic properties. First, upon starting an operation, a thread immediately begins to help other threads, sometimes interfering with their operations and almost always creating higher contention in the system. In most cases, the helped threads could have finished their operations by themselves if only they were given some time to execute without help. Second, the helping mechanisms are designed to operate sequentially, in the sense that all concurrently running threads help other operations in exactly the same order. These two properties cause much useless work due to high redundancy.

In this work, we propose a general methodology, denoted *fast-path-slow-path*, for constructing wait-free data structures. This methodology strives to be as scalable and fast as lock-free algorithms, while guaranteeing a bound on the number of steps required to complete each operation. To accomplish these goals, each operation is built from *fast* and *slow* paths, where the former ensures good performance, while the latter serves as a fall-back to achieve wait-freedom. Normally, the fast path is a customized version of a lock-free algorithm, while the slow path is a customized version of a wait-free one. A thread makes several attempts to apply an operation on the fast path; only if it fails to complete, it switches to the slow path, where the completion is guaranteed. We stress that our design allows threads to execute operations on the fast and slow paths in parallel. In particular, a thread that fails to apply its operation on the fast path does not cause all other threads to waste time waiting for its operation to be completed. Moreover, in contrast to the common definition of a fast path as "a shortcut through a complex algorithm taken by a thread running alone"[13], our design allows several threads to run on the fast path and finish their operations concurrently.

* This work was supported by the Israeli Science Foundation grant No. 283/10. The work of A. Kogan was also supported by the Technion Hasso Plattner Center.

PPoPP'12, February 25–29, 2012, New Orleans, Louisiana, USA.

Similarly to other wait-free algorithms, our methodology employs a helping mechanism, but one that avoids the drawbacks discussed above. In particular, the helping is *delayed* and *parallel*. The first property means that threads will delay any helping attempts when concurrent operations exist. The opportunistic idea is that during that delay, the contending operation might be finished, and no further help will be required. The latter property means that threads that do decide to help will attempt to help different operations, reducing the contention and redundant work created by sequential helping.

The applicability and effectiveness of our methodology is demonstrated by two examples. First, we use it to create a fast FIFO wait-free queue. The queue design is implemented in Java[1]. It is evaluated and compared to the lock-free queue by Michael and Scott [20], which is considered one of the most efficient and scalable lock-free queue implementations [13, 16, 25]. We also compare it to the recent wait-free queue by Kogan and Petrank [15]. The evaluation shows that along with the proven wait-free progress guarantee, the queue constructed in this paper delivers in practice the same performance as the queue of Michael and Scott, while both queues perform substantially better than the recent wait-free queue of Kogan and Petrank. As a second example, the fast-path-slow-path methodology has been also used on the wait-free linked-list independently published in these proceedings [23]. There too, this methodology yields a dramatic improvement in the algorithm's performance, while maintaining the wait-free progress guarantee.

In addition to making wait-free algorithms as fast as lock-free ones, the fast-path-slow-path methodology can be used to provide different level of progress guarantees to different entities. For example, it can be used to run real-time threads side-by-side with non-real-time threads, as the real-time threads use the slow path (or both paths) to obtain a predictable maximum response time, whereas the non-real-time threads only use the fast path without operation-level progress guarantee. Another use of this methodology is in distinguishing phases in the execution. Sometimes emergent phases require predictable guaranteed progress for each thread, while at other times, the system can run only the fast path to achieve fast execution in practice with no such progress guarantee. The interoperability of the two paths may be useful in any other scenario that requires different progress guarantees according to various execution parameters.

2. Related work

The idea of designing a concurrent algorithm with a fast path intended for no contention and a slow path for a contended case has been used in various domains of computer science. For example, it appears in solutions for the mutual exclusion problem [2, 17, 26], write barrier implementations in garbage collectors [18], and in implementations of composite locks [13].

Despite (and, maybe, due to) having strong progress guarantees, very few explicitly designed wait-free data structures are known (for the few that do exist, see [15, 23] and references therein). A common generic method for constructing wait-free data structures is to apply *universal constructions*, originally proposed by Herlihy[10, 13]. (See [3] for an updated survey of various improvements proposed since then.) Such constructions provide a generic method for transforming any sequential data structure implementation into a linearizable wait-free implementation. The wait-freedom is usually achieved by using a special *announce* array, in which threads write details on the operations they intend to apply. The contending threads traverse this array in a particular order and help pending operations to complete. Threads help other threads in a way that essentially reduces concurrency and creates large redundancy, especially when the number of contending threads is high: All threads try to apply the same operations, and in exactly the same order. In our work we show that trying to apply operations before involving other threads (i.e., before using the *announce* array) is crucial to the good performance of a wait-free algorithm. Moreover, the helping mechanism proposed in this paper allows parallel and delayed helping, eliminating the drawbacks of most previous wait-free constructions.

A related idea was considered by Moir [21], who proposed to implement wait-free transactions by utilizing a lock-free version of a multi-word CAS operation, denoted MWCAS[2]. A wait-free transaction optimistically applies a MWCAS operation; if it fails, it asks help from a transaction that did succeed. Our methodology is different in many aspects. Most importantly, while Moir's transactions always go through the costly MWCAS operation, which requires, among other things, (logically) locking and unlocking all words referenced by the transaction using expensive atomic operations, our methodology lets most operations finish on the (efficient) fast path, especially in the low contention scenario. The fast path is in practice as fast as the underlying lock-free implementation (e.g., in the queue shown in Section 4, the `dequeue` operation on the fast path requires just a single CAS).

Recently, Fatourou and Kallimanis [5] suggested a wait-free universal construction, where they utilize the idea of *operation combining* [8, 27]. There, a thread accessing the data structure creates a copy of the state of the global object, applies its operation along with all other pending operations of threads accessing the data structure concurrently, and tries to update the shared pointer (to the state of the simulated object) to point to the local (modified) copy of the object's state. This technique produces efficient wait-free algorithms for data structures having a small state (in particular, the queue and the stack), but is not efficient for data structures with larger states (such as linked-lists, trees, or hash tables). Moreover, the construction in [5] builds on the availability of a Fetch&Add atomic primitive that has an additional "wait-free" guarantee in the hardware: it is required that when several Fetch&Add operations conflict, they will be served in a starvation-free manner. This Fetch&Add instruction, especially with the additional guarantee, is not universally supported. Without this primitive, the construction becomes lock-free, and the performance degrades significantly [5].

3. The fast-path-slow-path methodology

Our methodology for constructing fast wait-free data structures is shown schematically in Figure 1. In a nutshell, the idea is that: each operation is built from a *fast path* and a *slow path*, where the former is a version of a lock-free implementation of that operation, and the latter is a version of a wait-free implementation. Both implementations are customized to cooperate with each other. Each thread first tries to apply its operation using the fast path. In most lock-free algorithms known to us, a thread tries to apply its operation by performing CAS (or equivalent) primitives on shared variables until it succeeds; if it fails, the thread retries the operation from the beginning (or some other earlier stage) (e.g., [4, 7, 9] and many others). In our approach, we limit the number of such retries by a global parameter, called `MAX_FAILURES` (denoted by X in Figure 1).

If a thread succeeds in applying its operation on the data structure in less than `MAX_FAILURES` trials, it finishes (i.e., returns the execution to the caller of that operation). If a thread fails in `MAX_FAILURES` trials, it realizes there is high contention and moves to the slow path. There, it publishes its intention to apply an opera-

[1] We also implemented our design in C (cf. Section 4.4).

[2] Moir provides an implementation of MWCAS, which he calls "conditionally wait-free", i.e., a lock-free implementation that accepts a call-back for an external helping mechanism. See [21] for details.

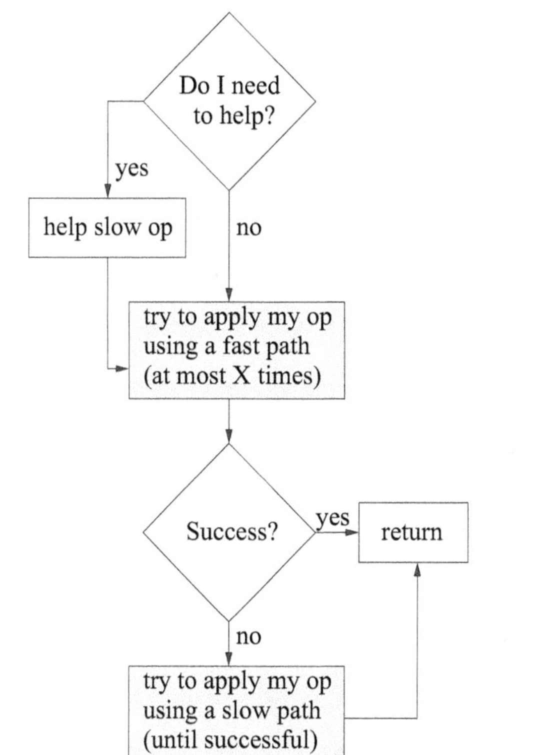

Figure 1. The fast-path-slow-path methodology.

tion in a special `state` array. This array holds one entry per thread, and contains information on the type of operation being applied and a phase number. The latter is a simple counter increased by the thread every time it enters the slow path. After the operation is published in `state`, the thread keeps trying to apply it by following the slow path until it succeeds.

To achieve wait-freedom, we need to ensure that the number of trials in the slow path is bounded. For this purpose, we employ a *delayed helping mechanism*, which is based upon an auxiliary array of helping records. Thus, in addition to an entry in the `state` array, each thread maintains a helping record rec_i. There, it stores the ID of another thread, $curTid_i$, and a phase number, $lastPhase_i$. When a thread t_i starts an operation on the data structure, and before it enters the fast path, it checks whether the thread $curTid_i$ is trying to apply an operation with the same phase number as was recorded earlier in $lastPhase_i$. If so, t_i helps $curTid_i$ first to apply the operation. In any case, t_i updates its helping record with the ID of the next thread (i.e., $curTid_i + 1$ modulo the number of threads) and with the phase number of that next thread, which is read from the `state` array. Only afterwards does t_i proceed with the fast path and, if necessary, with the slow path (cf. Figure 1).

Note that in contrast to many wait-free algorithms (e.g., [3, 5, 11, 15, 21]), this helping mechanism does not require a thread to help another concurrently running operation the moment the thread realizes there is contention. Rather, the helping is delayed to the next time the thread accesses the data structure, in the hope that the contending operation will be finished by that time and no further helping will be necessary.

In order to reduce the amortized management cost of helping records, we enhance the helping mechanism further by adding a counter, called $nextCheck_i$, to each helping record rec_i. Each time a thread t_i creates a new helping record, t_i sets the $nextCheck_i$ counter to a predefined `HELPING_DELAY` constant. On t_i's next operations on the data structure, t_i decrements the $nextCheck_i$ counter for each operation. Only when this counter reaches zero, does t_i check whether its help to $curTid_i$ is required. Thus, t_i actually checks whether its help is required only once in its `HELPING_DELAY` operations.

4. Fast wait-free queue

In this section, we show how the design methodology presented in Section 3 is applied to construct a fast wait-free queue. The design of the fast path and the slow path is based on the lock-free queue by Michael and Scott [20] (referred to hereafter as the MS-queue) and the recent wait-free queue by Kogan and Petrank [15] (referred to as the KP-queue), respectively. A brief description of the key design features of these two algorithms can be found in Appendix A.

Since the design of the MS-queue was published, several papers have proposed various optimized lock-free queues (e.g., [16, 22]). Yet, we chose to base our example on the MS-queue mainly due to its simplicity. We stress that the main purpose of this work is to create a wait-free implementation that is in practice as fast as the lock-free one, thus, obtaining wait-freedom without paying a performance cost. We do not presume to improve on the most efficient concurrent data structures available today.

4.1 Implementation details

4.1.1 Auxiliary structures

Similarly to many dynamically-allocated queues, our queue is based on an internal singly-linked list with references maintained to its head and tail, denoted, respectively, as `head` and `tail`. The auxiliary structures for list nodes, as well as for helping records and entries of the `state` array that were described in Section 3, are given in Figure 2. Notice the `enqTid` field added to the `Node` class. As described in Appendix A.2, this field is used in the KP-queue to identify threads that are in the middle of their `enqueue` operations in order to help them to complete these operation. In our case, this field serves a similar purpose and helps to synchronize between `enqueue` operations running on the slow and fast paths, as will be explained in Section 4.1.2. For the `dequeue` operation, we use a different mechanism (described below in this section) and thus do not require an additional field in the `Node` class.

The `OpDesc` class serves to hold descriptors of operations executed by threads on the slow path. Each thread maintains one instance of this class in the array called `state`. `OpDesc` contains the phase number (which counts the number of thread's operations on the slow path), the flags specifying whether the thread has a pending operation on the slow path and if so, its type, and a reference to a list node; this reference has a meaning specific to the type of operation. In addition, each thread maintains one helping record, which is an instance of the `HelpRecord` class. The structure of `HelpRecord` follows the design presented in Section 3. In particular, it contains fields for the ID of a thread that might need help, the phase number recorded for that thread, and a counter used to determine when the next check for helping should be performed.

The internal fields of the queue are given in Figure 3, and the queue constructor is in Figure 4. While the `tail` reference maintained in our queue is implemented as an `AtomicReference` object (like in the MS-queue [13]), the `head` reference is implemented as an `AtomicStampedReference` object. The latter encapsulates a reference to an object along with an integer stamp. Both reference and stamp fields can be updated atomically, either together or individually (for more information, including how this object can be implemented in C/C++ languages, refer to [13], pp. 235–236). In our case, the stamp has a role similar to the `enqTid` field in `Node`, i.e., to identify the thread that is in the middle of its `dequeue` operation on the slow path. More details are provided in Section 4.1.2.

```
1  class Node {
2    int value;
3    AtomRef<Node> next;
4    int enqTid;

5    Node (int val) {
6      value = val;
7      next = new
         AtomRef<Node>();
8      enqTid = −1;
9    }
10 }
```

```
11 class OpDesc {
12   long phase;
13   boolean pending;
14   boolean enqueue;
15   Node node;

16   OpDesc (long ph, boolean pend,
       boolean enq, Node n) {
17     phase = ph; pending = pend;
18     enqueue = enq; node = n;
19   }
20 }
```

```
21 class HelpRecord {
22   int curTid;
23   long lastPhase;
24   long nextCheck;

25   HelpRecord() { curTid = −1; reset(); }

26   void reset() {
27     curTid = (curTid + 1) %
         NUM_THRDS;
28     lastPhase = state.get(curTid).phase;
29     nextCheck = HELPING_DELAY;
30   }
31 }
```

Figure 2. Auxiliary structures.

```
32 AtomStampedRef<Node> head;
33 AtomRef<Node> tail;

34 AtomRefArray<OpDesc> state;
35 HelpRecord helpRecords[];
```

Figure 3. Queue class fields.

```
36 FastWFQueue () {
37   Node sentinel = new Node(−1);
38   head = new AtomicStampedReference<Node>(sentinel, −1);
39   tail = new AtomicReference<Node>(sentinel);

40   state = new AtomicReferenceArray<OpDesc>(NUM_THRDS);
41   helpRecords = new HelpRecord[NUM_THRDS];

42   for (int i = 0; i < state.length(); i++) {
43     state.set(i, new OpDesc(−1, false, true, null));
44     helpRecords[i] = new HelpRecord();
45   }
46 }
```

Figure 4. Queue constructor.

```
47 void help_if_needed() {
48   HelpRecord rec = helpRecords[TID];
49   if (rec.nextCheck−− == 0) {
50     OpDesc desc = state.get(rec.curTid);
51     if (desc.pending && desc.phase == rec.lastPhase) {
52       if (desc.enqueue) help_enq(rec.curTid, rec.lastPhase);
53       else help_deq(rec.curTid, rec.lastPhase);
54     }
55     rec.reset();
56   }
57 }
```

Figure 5. The method called by threads at the entrance to the fast path. It helps an operation on the slow path if this help is necessary.

4.1.2 Fast path

Do I need to help? Before attempting to apply an operation on the fast path, a thread t_i invokes the `help_if_needed()` method, where it checks whether some other thread needs its help (Figure 5). The thread t_i executing this method reads its helping record (Line 48). According to the value of the `nextCheck` counter, t_i decides whether it has to check the status of the thread whose ID is written in the record (Line 49). If so, it accesses the entry of that thread (denote it as t_j) in `state`, and checks if t_j has a pending operation with a phase number equal to `lastPhase` (from t_i's helping record) (Lines 50–51). In such a case, t_i helps to complete t_j's operation according to the type of operation written in t_j's operation descriptor (Lines 52–53). The methods `help_deq()` and `help_enq()` are part of the slow path and are explained in Section 4.1.3. Finally, t_i resets its helping record (Line 55), recording the current phase number of the next thread (in a cyclic order) and setting the `nextCheck` counter to the `HELPING_DELAY` value (cf. Figure 2).

Enqueue operation The details of the `enqueue` operation executed by threads running on the fast path are provided in Figure 6. A thread t_i starts with a call to the `help_if_needed()` method (Line 59), which was explained above. Next, t_i initializes the `trials` counter and tries to append a new node to the end of the internal linked-list. The number of such trials is limited by the `MAX_FAILURES` parameter, which controls when t_i will give up and switch to the slow path. Each trial is similar to the one performed in the MS-queue, that is, t_i identifies the last node in the list by reading `tail` (Line 63) and tries to append a new node after that last node with a CAS (Line 67). The only difference from the MS-queue is in the way `tail` is fixed when t_i identifies that some `enqueue` operation is in progress (i.e., `tail` references some node whose `next` reference is different from `null`). In the MS-queue, the fix is done by simply updating `tail` to refer to the new last node. In our case, the fix is carried out by the `fixTail()` method, which is aware of the existence of the slow path. In particular, it checks whether the `enqTid` field of the last node in the list is set to a default value -1 (Line 79). If so, it means that the last node was inserted into the list from the fast path, and thus `tail` can simply be updated to refer to it (as done in the MS-queue). Otherwise, the last node was inserted from the slow path. Thus, we need first to update the entry in the `state` array corresponding to the thread whose ID = `enqTid` (clearing its `pending` flag), and only after that can we update `tail`. (Without updating `state`, we may create a race between threads trying to help the same `enqueue` operation on the slow path). This functionality is carried out by `help_finish_enq()`, explained in Section 4.1.3.

Finally, if t_i fails to append a new node within `MAX_FAILURES` trials, it calls the `wf_enq()` method (Line 76), which transfers the execution of the `enqueue` operation to the slow path.

Dequeue operation Figure 7 provides the details of the `dequeue` operation executed by threads running on the fast path. Similarly to `enqueue`, the `dequeue` operation starts with calling `help_if_needed()` (Line 86) and initializing the `trials` counter (Line 87). In the **while** loop (Lines 88–108), a thread tries to update `head` to refer to the next element in the queue (or throw an exception if it finds the queue empty). If the thread fails to complete this in `MAX_FAILURES` trials, it switches to the slow path, calling the `wf_deq()` method (Line 109).

We use a slightly modified version of the **while** loop of the `dequeue` operation in the MS-queue [20]: as in the MS-queue, when a queue is found to be empty (Line 93) but there is an `enqueue` operation in progress (Line 97), the dequeuing thread helps to complete that `enqueue` first. In our case, however, the dequeuing thread needs to be aware of the path on which the `enqueue` operation is progressing. For this purpose, we use the `fixTail()` method described above.

We also modify the original MS-queue implementation with regard to how the removal of the first element of the queue is handled. As in the case of `enqueue`, we need to synchronize between con-

```
void enq(int value) {
  help_if_needed(); // check first if help is needed
  Node node = new Node(value);
  int trials = 0; // init the trials counter
  while (trials++ < MAX_FAILURES) {
    Node last = tail.get();
    Node next = last.next.get();
    if (last == tail.get()) {
      if (next == null) { // enqueue can be applied
        if (last.next.compareAndSet(next, node)) {
          tail.compareAndSet(last, node);
          return;
        }
      } else { // some enqueue operation is in progress
        fixTail(last, next); // fix tail, then retry
      }
    }
  }
  wf_enq(node); // switch to the slow path
}

void fixTail(Node last, Node next) {
  if (next.enqTid == -1) { // next node was appended on the fast path
    tail.compareAndSet(last, next);
  } else { // next node was appended on the slow path
    help_finish_enq();
  }
}
```

Figure 6. The enqueue operation on the fast path.

```
85  int deq() throws EmptyException {
86    help_if_needed(); // check first if help is needed
87    int trials = 0; // init the trials counter
88    while (trials++ < MAX_FAILURES) {
89      Node first = head.getReference();
90      Node last = tail.get();
91      Node next = first.next.get();
92      if (first == head.getReference()) {
93        if (first == last) { // queue might be empty
94          if (next == null) { // queue is empty
95            throw new EmptyException();
96          }
97          fixTail(last, next); // some enqueue operation is in progress
98        } else if (head.getStamp() == -1) {
99          // no dequeue was linearized on the slow path
100         int value = next.value;
101         if (head.compareAndSet(first, next, -1, -1)) {
102           return value;
103         }
104       } else { // some dequeue was linearized on the slow path
105         help_finish_deq(); // help it to complete, then retry
106       }
107     }
108   }
109   return wf_deq(); // switch to the slow path
110 }
```

Figure 7. The dequeue operation on the fast path.

current **dequeue** operations running on the fast and slow paths. For this purpose, we use the stamp of the **head** reference. As explained in Section 4.1.3, the **dequeue** operation run by a thread t_j on the slow path is linearized when t_j writes the ID of the thread for which the **dequeue** is performed (i.e., j or the ID of the thread helped by t_j) into the **head**'s stamp. Thus, in the fast path, a thread t_i checks first if the **head**'s stamp holds a default (-1) value (Line 98). If so, then as in the original MS-queue, t_i tries to update **head** to refer to the next node in the underlying list (Line 101). Otherwise, t_i realizes that the first element of the queue has been removed by a **dequeue** operation that runs on the slow path. Thus, t_i helps first to complete that **dequeue** operation (Line 105) by updating the state of the thread whose ID is written in the **head**'s stamp and swinging **head** to refer to the next node in the linked-list. This is done by the **help_finish_deq()** method, which is explained in Section 4.1.3.

4.1.3 Slow path

Enqueue operation The **enqueue** operation run by a thread t_i on the slow path is given in Figure 8. It starts from writing a new operation descriptor into the entry of t_i in the **state** array. The new descriptor is created with a phase number increased by 1 from the value that appears in the previous descriptor of t_i. Essentially, the phase number counts the number of operations run by a thread on the slow path. Also, t_i updates the **enqTid** field of the new node it tries to insert into the linked-list, with its ID (i in this example). Afterwards, t_i calls the **help_enq()** method.

The **help_enq()** method is executed either by a thread that tries to enqueue a new element on the slow path, or by a thread that starts a fast path and has decided to help another thread (this is the method called from **help_if_needed()**). Its implementation is similar to that of the KP-queue. A thread tries to append a new node to the end of the linked-list as long as the corresponding **enqueue** operation remains pending, i.e., as long as it was not completed by another concurrently running and helping thread. When the thread succeeds to append the new node (by swinging the **next** reference of the last node in the list to refer to the new node), it calls **help_finish_enq()**, where it clears the **pending** flag in the entry in **state** of the thread for which it executed **help_enq()** and updates **tail** to refer to the newly appended node.

Dequeue operation Similarly to **enqueue**, the **dequeue** operation run by threads on the slow path starts with writing a new operation descriptor into the **state** array (cf. Figure 9). Afterwards, the **help_deq()** method is called. This method is also called by threads that decide to help another **dequeue** operation in **help_if_needed()**.

In **help_deq()**, assuming the queue is not empty, a thread t_i tries to write its ID (or the ID of the thread that it helps in **help_if_needed()**) into the stamp in **head**. Once t_i succeeds in doing so, the **dequeue** operation of t_i (or the thread helped by t_i) has been linearized. This explains why we actually need **head** to be stamped. If, for instance, we used a **deqTid** field in list nodes and linearize an operation on the slow path at a successful update of this field (as done in the KP-queue), a race between **dequeue** operations run on the fast and slow paths might ensue: While the operation on the fast path is linearized at the instant the **head** reference is updated, the operation on the slow path would be linearized when the **deqTid** field of the first node in the queue is modified.

Following the write of thread's ID into the stamp, t_i calls **help_finish_deq()**, where the **pending** flag of the linearized **dequeue** operation is cleared and **head** is fixed to refer to the next node in the underlying linked-list.

4.2 Correctness

In the short version of our paper, we provide only the highlights of the proof that the given implementation of the concurrent queue is correct and wait-free, deferring the further details to the longer version. In particular, we review the computation model, define linearization points for queue operations, and explain why our algorithm guarantees wait-freedom.

4.2.1 Computation model

Our model of a concurrent multithreaded system follows the linearizability model defined in [14]. In particular, we assume that programs are run by n deterministic threads, which communicate by executing atomic operations on shared variables from some pre-

```
void wf_enq(Node node) {
  long phase = state.get(TID).phase + 1; // increase the phase counter
  node.enqTid = TID;
  // announce enqueue
  state.set(TID, new OpDesc(phase, true, true, node));
  help_enq(TID, phase); // help your own operation to complete
  help_finish_enq(); // make sure tail is properly updated[15]
}

void help_enq(int tid, long phase) {
  while (isStillPending(tid, phase)) {
    Node last = tail.get();
    Node next = last.next.get();
    if (last == tail.get()) {
      if (next == null) { // enqueue can be applied
        // avoid racing with other helping threads [15]
        if (isStillPending(tid, phase)) {
          // try to append the new node to the list
          if (last.next.compareAndSet(next,state.get(tid).node)) {
            help_finish_enq();
            return;
          }
        }
      } else { // some enqueue operation is in progress
        help_finish_enq();    // help it first, then retry
      }
    }
  }
}

void help_finish_enq() {
  Node last = tail.get();
  Node next = last.next.get();
  if (next != null) {
    // read the enqTid field of the last node in the list
    int tid = next.enqTid;
    if (tid != -1) { // last node was appended on the slow path
      OpDesc curDesc = state.get(tid);
      if (last == tail.get() && state.get(tid).node == next) {
        // switch the pending flag off
        OpDesc newDesc =
          new OpDesc(state.get(tid).phase, false, true, next);
        state.compareAndSet(tid, curDesc, newDesc);
        tail.compareAndSet(last, next); // update tail
      }
    } else { // last node was appended on the fast path
      tail.compareAndSet(last, next); // update tail
    }
  }
}
```

Figure 8. The enqueue operation on the slow path.

defined, finite set. Threads are run on computing cores, or processors, and the decision which thread will run when and on which processor is made solely by a scheduler. Normally, the number of processors is much smaller than the number of threads. Each thread is assumed to have an ID in a range between 0 and $n-1$. In fact, this assumption can be easily relaxed by means of a wait-free renaming algorithm (e.g., [1]). We also assume that each thread can access its ID and the value of n.

When scheduled to run, a thread performs a sequence of computation steps. Each step is either a local computation or an atomic operation on at most one shared variable. We assume that the shared memory supports atomic reads, writes, and compare-and-swap operations. The latter, abbreviated as CAS, is defined with the following semantics: CAS(v, *old*, *new*) changes the value of the shared variable v to *new* (and returns *true*) if and only if its value just before CAS is applied is equal to *old*. We refer to such CAS operations as *successful*. Otherwise, the value of v is unchanged, *false* is returned, and we refer to such CAS operations as *unsuccessful*. Note that we do not require any special operations to support stamped shared variables. Such variables, required by our implementation, can be implemented with atomic operations men-

```
int wf_deq() throws EmptyException {
  long phase = state.get(TID).phase + 1; // increase the phase counter
  // announce dequeue
  state.set(TID, new OpDesc(phase, true, false, null));
  help_deq(TID, phase); // help your own operation to complete
  help_finish_deq(); // make sure head is properly updated [15]

  Node node = state.get(TID).node; // check the node recorded in state
  if (node == null) { // dequeue was linearized on the empty queue
    throw new EmptyException();
  }
  // return the value of the first non-dummy node [15]
  return node.next.get().value;
}

void help_deq(int tid, long phase) {
  while (isStillPending(tid, phase)) {
    Node first = head.getReference();
    Node last = tail.get();
    Node next = first.next.get();
    if (first == head.getReference()) {
      if (first == last) { // queue might be empty
        if (next == null) { // queue is empty
          OpDesc curDesc = state.get(tid);
          if (last == tail.get() && isStillPending(tid, phase)) {
            // record null in the node field,
            // indicating that the queue is empty
            OpDesc newDesc =
              new OpDesc(state.get(tid).phase, false, false, null);
            state.compareAndSet(tid, curDesc, newDesc);
          }
        } else { // some enqueue operation is in progress}
          help_finish_enq(); // help it first, then retry
        }
      } else {
        OpDesc curDesc = state.get(tid);
        Node node = curDesc.node;
        // avoid racing with other helping threads [15]
        if (!isStillPending(tid, phase)) break;
        if (first == head.getReference() && node != first) {
          OpDesc newDesc =
            new OpDesc(state.get(tid).phase, true, false, first);
          // try to record a reference to the first node in the list
          if (!state.compareAndSet(tid, curDesc, newDesc)) {
            continue;
          }
        }
        head.compareAndSet(first, first, -1, tid); // try to stamp head
        help_finish_deq(); // help thread that won the stamp to complete
      }
    }
  }
}

void help_finish_deq() {
  Node first = head.getReference();
  Node next = first.next.get();
  int tid = head.getStamp(); // read the stamp on head
  if (tid != -1) { // last dequeue was linearized on the slow path
    OpDesc curDesc = state.get(tid);
    if (first == head.getReference() && next != null) {
      // switch the pending flag off
      OpDesc newDesc =
        new OpDesc(state.get(tid).phase, false, false, state.get(tid).node);
      state.compareAndSet(tid, curDesc, newDesc);
      head.compareAndSet(first, next, tid, -1); // update head
    }
  } // last dequeue was linearized on the fast path - nothing to do here
}

boolean isStillPending(int tid, long ph) {
  return state.get(tid).pending && state.get(tid).phase <= ph;
}
```

Figure 9. The dequeue operation on the slow path.

tioned above either by introducing a level of indirection (this is how `AtomicStampedReference` in Java is implemented) or by stealing a few bits from the value of the variable [13].

A concurrent queue is a data structure with operations linearizable [14] to those of a sequential queue. The latter supports two operations: `enqueue` and `dequeue`. The first operation accepts an element as an argument and inserts it into the queue. The second operation does not accept any argument, and removes and returns the oldest element from the queue. If the queue is empty, the `dequeue` operation returns a special value (or throws an exception).

4.2.2 Linearizability

The operations of the concurrent queue presented above are composed of the fast and slow paths. Thus, each operation has linearization points on each of the two paths, where the points on the slow path can be reached only if the points on the fast path are not reached. Given an operation executed by a thread t_i, note that the source lines corresponding to the linearization points on the fast path can be executed only by t_i, while the lines corresponding to the linearization points on the slow path can be executed either by t_i or by any other thread t_j that tries to help t_i by running `help_enq()` or `help_deq()` from `help_if_needed()`. In the definition below, we refer to a `dequeue` operation that returns a value as *successful*, while a `dequeue` that ends by throwing an exception is referred to as *unsuccessful*. An `enqueue` operation is always successful.

Definition 1. *The linearization points for operations applied on the fast path are as follows:*

- *An* `enqueue` *operation is linearized at the successful CAS in Line 67.*
- *A successful* `dequeue` *operation is linearized at the successful CAS in Line 101.*
- *An unsuccessful* `dequeue` *operation is linearized in Line 90.*

The linearization points for operations applied on the slow path are as follows:

- *An* `enqueue` *operation is linearized at the successful CAS in Line 128.*
- *A successful* `dequeue` *operation is linearized at the successful CAS in Line 201.*
- *An unsuccessful* `dequeue` *operation is linearized in Line 174.*

Note that the linearization points on the fast path correspond to the linearization points of the MS-queue [20]. Similarly, the linearization points for operations applied on the slow path correspond to the points of the KP-queue [15]. The proof of correctness of the linearization points defined above is far beyond the scope of this short paper. Our full proof is composed of two parts. First, we show that nodes corresponding to queue elements are inserted and removed to/from the queue according to the FIFO semantics. In the second part of the proof, we show that each operation executed on the slow path is linearized exactly once.

4.2.3 Wait-freedom

We provide an overview of the proof of the wait-free progress guarantee. This proof also has two parts. First, we show that the algorithm is lock-free. For this purpose, we prove that every time a thread fails to linearize an operation, either by applying an unsuccessful CAS or by failing to pass one of the verification conditions in the **if**-statements (e.g., in Lines 65, 66, 92, etc.), some other thread makes progress and does succeed in linearizing an operation. The proof is based on a straightforward inspection of code lines that modify the underlying linked-list, in a way similar to the lock-freedom proof in [20].

The second part of our proof shows that the number of steps taken by a thread before its pending operation is linearized, is limited. The following lemma is at the heart of this part. For brevity, we refer to the `HELPING_DELAY` and `MAX_FAILURES` constants by D and F, respectively.

Lemma 1. *The number of steps required for a thread to complete an operation on the queue is bounded by* $O(F + D \cdot n^2)$.

Sketch of proof: Consider a pending operation run by a thread t_i on the slow path. In the worst case, this operation will remain pending until all other threads in the system decide to help it to complete (in Line 52 or Line 53). A thread t_j will decide to help t_i after it completes at most $O(D \cdot n)$ operations. This is because t_j might complete up to D operations before it decides to help a thread whose ID is written in t_j's helping record, and t_j might help all other $n-1$ threads before it gets to t_i. However, once t_j starts helping t_i, it will not stop helping it until t_i actually makes progress. Thus, the number of operations that might linearize before *all* other threads decide to help t_i is $O(D \cdot n^2)$. Furthermore, since the algorithm is lock-free, it is guaranteed that once all threads are helping t_i, the operation of t_i will be completed in a constant number of steps.

Now consider the thread t_i when it starts its operation on the queue on the fast path. It may realize in `help_if_needed()` that it needs to help another thread t_k before attempting to execute its own operation. Following similar arguments, the number of operations that might linearize before t_i returns from `help_if_needed()` is bounded by $O(D \cdot n^2)$. Afterwards, t_i makes several attempts to linearize its operation on the fast path. Given that the algorithm is lock-free, it might fail if during its attempts other operations succeed to linearize. As the number of such attempts is limited by `MAX_FAILURES`, after at most $O(F)$ steps t_i will switch into the slow path, and by the above argument will complete its operation in at most $O(D \cdot n^2)$ steps. Thus, after at most $O(F + D \cdot n^2)$ steps in total, t_i will complete its operation. □

4.3 Performance

In our performance study, we compare our fast wait-free queue with the lock-free MS-queue and the wait-free KP-queue. For the MS-queue, we use the Java implementation given in [13]. The KP-queue has several versions presented in [15]; for our study, we use the optimized one. We employ several versions of the fast wait-free queue, each configured with different `MAX_FAILURES` and `HELPING_DELAY` parameters. We denote by WF(x,y) the version with `MAX_FAILURES` set to x and `HELPING_DELAY` set to y.

The study was carried out on a machine featuring a shared-memory NUMA server with 8 quadcore AMD 2.3GHz processors (32 physical cores in total), operating under Ubuntu 10.10 and installed with 16GB RAM attached to each processor. All tests were run in OpenJDK Runtime version 1.6.0 update 20, using the 64-Bit Server VM, with -Xmx16G -Xms16G flags. In our tests, we varied the number of threads between 1 and 64. Starting with an empty queue, we performed two common queue benchmarks [15, 16, 20]. First, we ran the `enqueue-dequeue` benchmark, where each thread performs numerous (100000, in our case) iterations of an `enqueue` operation followed by a `dequeue` operation. Second, we ran the 50%-`enqueue` benchmark, where on each iteration every thread randomly chooses which operation to perform with equal chances to `enqueue` and `dequeue` (with 100000 iterations per thread). Note that the queue in both benchmarks remains short or even empty, maximizing the contention between threads performing `enqueue` and `dequeue`. To mimic local computations performed by threads after accessing the queue, we inserted a small and random delay after each operation on the queue [16, 20]. The delay was achieved by running some simple calculation in a loop with a randomly chosen number of iterations [16]. We note that the results in tests without local computations were qualitatively the same.

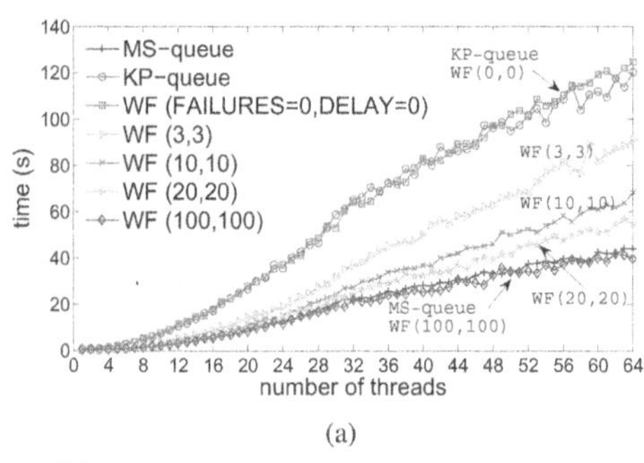

(a)

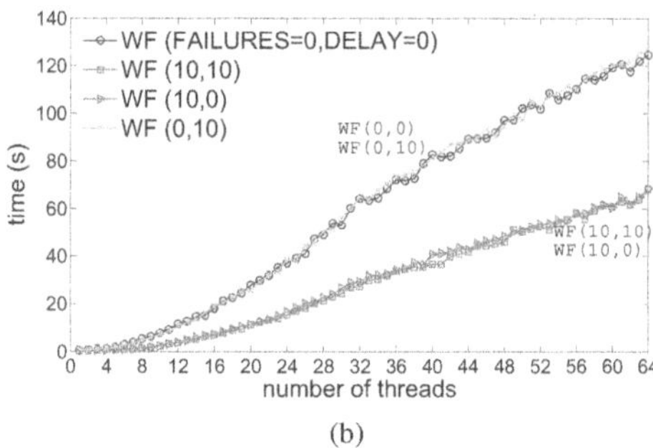

(b)

Figure 10. Total completion time for various queues and the `enqueue-dequeue` benchmark.

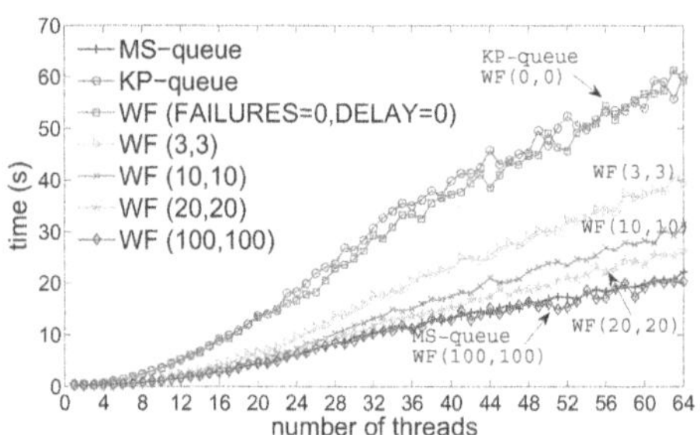

Figure 11. Total completion time for various queues and the 50%-`enqueue` benchmark.

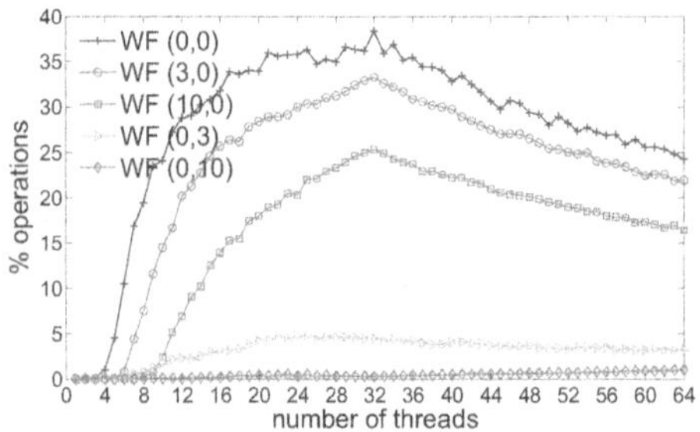

Figure 12. Percentage of operations that help other operations (`enqueue-dequeue` benchmark).

We report the total completion time for each of the tested queues, as well as some interesting statistics on the number of operations that actually use the slow path and those that actually decide to help. Each reported point is an average of ten experiments run with the same parameters. We note that the standard deviation (not shown for the sake of readability) for the total completion time figures was up to 15%, with the majority of results having deviation around 8% and below. (In our tests on other machines with fewer cores, the standard deviation was smaller than that). Other results, concerning the statistics of the executions, were much noisier, as they depended on the actual execution interleaving created by the system scheduler. Nonetheless, every reported performance phenomenon was reproduced in several repeated runs of our benchmarks.

Figure 10 summarizes the total completion time numbers for various queue implementations and the `enqueue-dequeue` benchmark. In particular, Figure 10a shows that the WF(0,0) version exhibits performance very close to that of the KP-queue, while both queues perform roughly 3 times worse than the MS-queue. This happens since all operations in WF(0,0) use only the slow path, which is far less efficient then the MS-queue. Increasing the `MAX_FAILURES` and `HELPING_DELAY` parameters reduces the number of operations that require the slow path. In fact, when both parameters are set to 100, the fast wait-free queue steadily achieves performance similar to that of the MS-queue. Consequently, these results demonstrate that our wait-free design can achieve the performance and scalability of a lock-free algorithm.

Our other experiments (as shown in Figure 10b) suggest that giving threads the chance to complete their operation on the fast path (i.e., increasing the number of trials) is highly effective (e.g., the performance of WF(10,0) is similar to WF(10,10)). On the other hand, reducing their helping work (by increasing the delay in making an attempt to help other threads) does not change the performance significantly (e.g., the performance of WF(0,10) is similar to WF(0,0)). Note that even when a thread t_i provides help on each operation (i.e., when `HELPING_DELAY=0`), it only helps another thread t_j that did not make progress since t_i's previous operation. As shown below, this small delay already ensures that the amount of work put into the helping effort is limited.

Figure 11 shows the performance results for the 50%-`enqueue` benchmark. In general, all queue implementations exhibit similar behavior as in the `enqueue-dequeue` benchmarks, but the total completion time numbers are 2 time smaller. This is because in the 50%-`enqueue` benchmark, each thread performs half of the operations of the first benchmark. We note that all measured queues produced similar relative behavior in both benchmarks. Thus, due to lack of space, we will focus only on the `enqueue-dequeue` benchmark for the rest of this section.

Figure 12 shows the percentage of queue operations that decide to help other operations in the `help_if_needed()` method. Here, increasing the `MAX_FAILURES` parameter decreases the number of times threads help other operations to complete. As we will see below, this is a side-effect of the fact that, with a higher `MAX_FAILURES` parameter, fewer operations enter the slow path and request help. At the same time, increasing the `HELPING_DELAY` parameter has a much greater effect even though all operations having `MAX_FAILURES` set to 0 enter the slow path. This shows that the delayed helping can potentially reduce the amount of redundant work created by threads helping each other. It is interesting also to note that the percentage of helping operations for all queues increases until the number of threads reaches the number of available cores (32) and then slightly, but continuously decreases. The first phenomenon is explained by increased contention, i.e., more operations are repeatedly delayed due to contention and thus helped by others. When the number of threads goes beyond the number

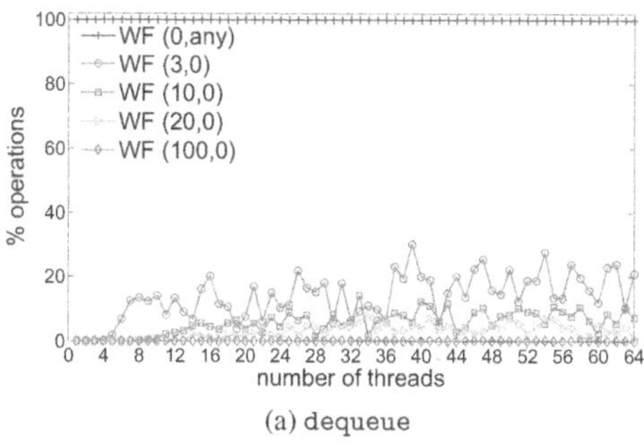

(a) dequeue

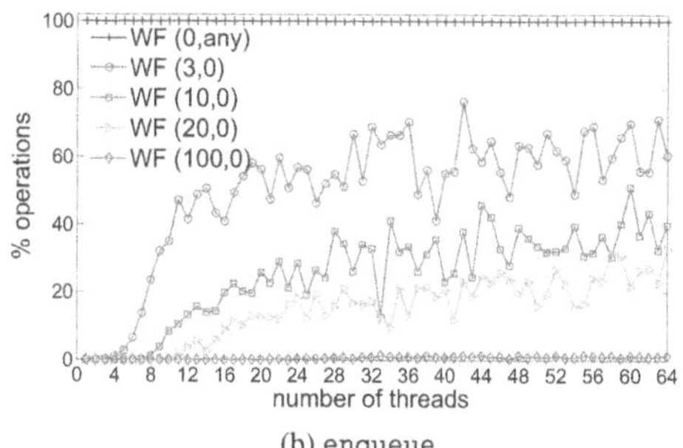

(b) enqueue

Figure 13. Percentage of **enqueue** (a) and **dequeue** (b) operations completing on the slow path (**enqueue-dequeue** benchmark).

of cores, at every moment of execution some threads are switched off. Attempts to help them either return immediately because these threads have no active pending operations, or require one help operation. Once this help is done, no further help operations are executed until the thread regains execution. Thus, a smaller percentage of the total number of operations actually help other operations.

Finally, Figures 13a and 13b show the percentage of `dequeue` and `enqueue` operations that enter the slow path, respectively. For the former, 3 trials are almost always sufficient to ensure that only 20–30% of the operations complete on the slow path. At the same time, for the latter, in order to avoid many operations from entering the slow path, a higher value of `MAX_FAILURES` is required. This might be because `dequeue` is more efficient, requiring just one CAS. Thus, the chances are greater that a `dequeue` operation running on the fast path will complete with just a few trials. Note that for both operations, setting `MAX_FAILURES` to 100 almost eliminates the use of the slow path. Essentially, this number depends on the maximal contention level in the system. (In our tests on other machines with fewer cores, not reported here due to space limits, this number was significantly lower).

Given these results, one may ask why not just always use large values for both parameters so that the slow path will not be used? The proof sketch of the wait-freedom property in Section 4.2 shows that these parameters govern the bound on the worst-case time required to complete each operation on the queue. Thus, they control the tradeoff between the practical performance and the theoretical bound on the worst-case completion time of each operation.

4.4 Memory management

The implementation of our queue is provided in Java, a garbage-collected language, which simplifies the memory management and avoids problems related to it, such as the ABA problem [13]. We have also implemented our queue in C using the Hazard Pointers technique [19] for memory management. Although only minor modifications to the algorithm are required, their precise details are beyond the scope of this short paper.

5. Summary

We presented the fast-path-slow-path methodology for creating fast and scalable wait-free data structures. The key feature in this methodology is designing each operation as a combination of the fast path and the slow path. Good performance is achieved when the fast path is extensively utilized and due to the fact that concurrent operations can proceed on both paths in parallel. Our measurements show that most operations can complete without facing too many failed attempts, even in a highly concurrent environment. Thus, operations almost always complete using the fast path only, and the execution is fast. The application of our methodology is demonstrated in this paper by constructing a new wait-free queue. The performance evaluation of the obtained queue shows that it can be as fast as the efficient lock-free queue of Michael and Scott [20]. Subsequent work [23] utilizes our methodology to improve the performance of a wait-free linked-list.

Acknowledgments

We thank Idit Keidar and Dmitri Perelman for letting us use their multi-core machine for the experiments reported above. Also, we thank the anonymous reviewers for their valuable comments.

References

[1] Y. Afek and M. Merritt. Fast, wait-free (2k-1)-renaming. In *ACM Symp. on Principles of Distr. Comp. (PODC)*, pages 105–112, 1999.

[2] J. H. Anderson and Y.-J. Kim. A new fast-path mechanism for mutual exclusion. *Distrib. Comput.*, 14:17–29, 2001.

[3] P. Chuong, F. Ellen, and V. Ramachandran. A universal construction for wait-free transaction friendly data structures. In *Proc. ACM Symposium on Parallel Algorithms (SPAA)*, pages 335–344, 2010.

[4] F. Ellen, P. Fatourou, E. Ruppert, and F. van Breugel. Non-blocking binary search trees. In *Proc. ACM PODC*, pages 131–140, 2010.

[5] P. Fatourou and N. D. Kallimanis. A highly-efficient wait-free universal construction. In *Proc. ACM Symposium on Parallel Algorithms (SPAA)*, pages 325–334, 2011.

[6] F. E. Fich, V. Luchangco, M. Moir, and N. Shavit. Obstruction-free algorithms can be practically wait-free. In *Proc. Int. Conference on Distributed Computing (DISC)*, pages 78–92, 2005.

[7] T. L. Harris. A pragmatic implementation of non-blocking linked-lists. In *Proc. Int. Conference on Distributed Computing (DISC)*, pages 300–314, 2001.

[8] D. Hendler, I. Incze, N. Shavit, and M. Tzafrir. Flat combining and the synchronization-parallelism tradeoff. In *Proc. ACM Symposium on Parallel Algorithms (SPAA)*, pages 355–364, 2010.

[9] D. Hendler, N. Shavit, and L. Yerushalmi. A scalable lock-free stack algorithm. *J. Parallel Distrib. Comput.*, 70(1):1–12, 2010.

[10] M. Herlihy. Wait-free synchronization. *ACM Trans. Program. Lang. Syst.*, 13(1):124–149, 1991.

[11] M. Herlihy. A methodology for implementing highly concurrent objects. *ACM Trans. Program. Lang. Syst.*, 15(5):745–770, 1993.

[12] M. Herlihy, V. Luchangco, and M. Moir. Obstruction-free synchronization: Double-ended queues as an example. In *Proc. Conf. on Distributed Computing Systems (ICDCS)*, pages 522–529, 2003.

[13] M. Herlihy and N. Shavit. *The Art of Multiprocessor Programming*. Morgan Kaufmann, 2008.

[14] M. Herlihy and J. M. Wing. Linearizability: A correctness condition for concurrent objects. *ACM Trans. Program. Lang. Syst.*, 12(3):463–492, 1990.

[15] A. Kogan and E. Petrank. Wait-free queues with multiple enqueuers and dequeuers. In *Proc. ACM Symposium on Principles and Practice of Parallel Programming (PPOPP)*, pages 223–234, 2011.

[16] E. Ladan-Mozes and N. Shavit. An optimistic approach to lock-free fifo queues. *Distributed Computing*, 20(5):323–341, 2008.

[17] L. Lamport. A fast mutual exclusion algorithm. *ACM Trans. Comput. Syst.*, 5:1–11, 1987.

[18] Y. Levanoni and E. Petrank. An on-the-fly reference-counting garbage collector for java. *ACM TOPLAS*, 28(1):1–69, 2006.

[19] M. M. Michael. Hazard pointers: Safe memory reclamation for lock-free objects. *IEEE Trans. Parallel Distrib. Syst.*, 15(6):491–504, 2004.

[20] M. M. Michael and M. L. Scott. Simple, fast, and practical non-blocking and blocking concurrent queue algorithms. In *Proc. ACM Symp. on Principles of Distr. Comp. (PODC)*, pages 267–275, 1996.

[21] M. Moir. Transparent support for wait-free transactions. In *Proc. Conf. on Distributed Computing (DISC)*, 1998.

[22] M. Moir, D. Nussbaum, O. Shalev, and N. Shavit. Using elimination to implement scalable and lock-free FIFO queues. In *Proc. ACM SPAA*, pages 253–262, 2005.

[23] S. Timnat, A. Braginsky, A. Kogan, and E. Petrank. Poster paper: Wait-free linked-lists. To appear in *Proc. ACM Symposium on Principles and Practice of Parallel Programming (PPOPP)*, 2012.

[24] K. R. Treiber. Systems programming: Coping with parallelism. Technical report RJ-5118, IBM Almaden Research Center, 1986.

[25] P. Tsigas and Y. Zhang. A simple, fast and scalable non-blocking concurrent FIFO queue for shared memory multiprocessor systems. In *Proc. ACM SPAA*, pages 134–143, 2001.

[26] J.-H. Yang and J. H. Anderson. A fast, scalable mutual exclusion algorithm. *Distributed Computing*, 9:1–9, 1994.

[27] P.-C. Yew, N.-F. Tzeng, and D. H. Lawrie. Distributing hot-spot addressing in large-scale multiprocessors. *IEEE Trans. Comput.*, 36:388–395, 1987.

A. Building blocks

In our work we show a design methodology, which, when applied on a lock-free and a wait-free version of a data structure, can derive a new wait-free algorithm that will be as fast and scalable as the given lock-free algorithm. In this paper, the application of this methodology is exemplified by a construction of a new and fast wait-free queue algorithm. In order to provide the required background for understanding the design of this construction, we briefly review the principle ideas behind the lock-free queue by Michael and Scott [20] and the recent wait-free queue by Kogan and Petrank [15]. These two queues are referred to in the paper as the MS-queue and the KP-queue respectively, and serve as a basis for our new wait-free queue construction.

A.1 The lock-free MS-queue

The MS-queue [20] utilizes an internal singly-linked list of nodes, which keeps elements of the queue. The algorithm maintains two references to the head and tail of the list with corresponding names: `head` and `tail`. In order to enqueue a new element, a thread creates a new node with this element and verifies that `tail` indeed refers the last node of the list (i.e., a node with the `next` reference set to null). If not, the thread fixes `tail` first. Otherwise, the thread tries to swing the `next` reference of that last node to refer to the new node (using a CAS operation). If it succeeds, the thread fixes `tail` to refer to the new node (using another CAS). Otherwise, it realizes that some concurrently running thread has changed the list, and restarts the operation.

The `dequeue` operation is even simpler. A thread reads the value of the first node in the list and tries to swing `head` to refer to the second node in the list (using CAS). If it succeeds, the thread returns the value it has read; otherwise, it restarts the operation. Special care is given to the case of an empty queue: If a thread finds both `head` and `tail` referencing the same node and there is no `enqueue` in progress (i.e., the `next` reference of that node is `null`), an exception is thrown (or some other action is taken, such as returning a special $\perp$ value). If `head` and `tail` reference the same node, but the `next` reference of that node is not `null`, the dequeuing thread realizes that there is some `enqueue` in progress. Thus, it first helps this `enqueue` to complete (by fixing `tail`) and then reattempts its `dequeue` operation.

A.2 The wait-free KP-queue

The KP-queue [15] extends the ideas of the MS-queue in two main directions. First, to guarantee wait-free progress, the KP-queue utilizes a dynamic priority-based helping mechanism where younger threads (having lower logical priority) help older threads to apply their operations. The mechanism is implemented by means of (1) an auxiliary `state` array, in which each thread writes details on its current operation, and (2) phase numbers chosen by threads in monotonically increasing order before they try to apply their operations on the queue. Thus, when a thread t_i wants to apply an operation on the queue, it chooses a phase number that is higher than phases of threads that have previously chosen phase numbers for their operations. Then t_i helps all threads with the phase number smaller than or equal to t_i's phase (including itself) to apply their pending operations. It learns about pending operations from the `state` array.

Second, to ensure correctness, and in particular, to avoid applying the same operation more than once, the authors propose a three-step scheme used to design each of the two queue operations, `enqueue` and `dequeue`. This scheme requires two new fields, `enqTid` and `deqTid`, to be added to each node in the underlying linked-list. These fields hold the ID of a thread that tries to insert (or remove) a node to (from, respectively) the list. They are used by other concurrently running threads to identify the thread that is in the middle of an operation on the queue, and help it to complete its operation in progress.

In more detail, in order to enqueue a new element, a thread t_i creates a new node with the `enqTid` field set to i. Then it writes a reference to this node along with the chosen phase number into the `state` array. Afterwards, t_i proceeds by helping all threads with a phase smaller than or equal to t_i's phase. When it reaches its own operation, and provided its own operation was not completed yet by another concurrently running and helping thread, t_i tries to put its new element at the end of the underlying list (using CAS). If it succeeds, t_i marks its operation as linearized (i.e., clears the `pending` flag) in `state` (using another CAS) and attempts to fix the `tail` reference (using a third CAS). If t_i finds a node X behind the node referred by `tail`, it reads the `enqTid` field stored in X, marks the operation of the corresponding thread as having been linearized, and only then fixes the `tail` reference and tries again to insert its own node.

In order to dequeue an element from the queue, a thread t_j passes through the following four stages (after writing a new phase in `state` and helping other threads, if necessary, and provided the queue is not empty): (1) stores a reference to the first node of the list in its entry in `state`; (2) tries to write its ID, j, into the `deqTid` field of the first node in the list; (3) if successful, marks its operation as linearized in its entry in `state`, and (4) swings the `head` reference to the next element in the list. Each of the stages corresponds to a CAS operation. Similarly to `enqueue`, if t_j fails in Stage (2), it reads the `deqTid` field stored in the first node of the list, marks the operation of the corresponding thread as linearized, fixes the `head` reference and tries again to remove another node from the list.

Concurrent Tries with Efficient Non-Blocking Snapshots

Aleksandar Prokopec
EPFL
aleksandar.prokopec@epfl.ch

Nathan G. Bronson
Stanford
ngbronson@gmail.com

Phil Bagwell
Typesafe
phil.bagwell@typesafe.com

Martin Odersky
EPFL
martin.odersky@epfl.ch

Abstract

We describe a non-blocking concurrent hash trie based on shared-memory single-word compare-and-swap instructions. The hash trie supports standard mutable lock-free operations such as insertion, removal, lookup and their conditional variants. To ensure space-efficiency, removal operations compress the trie when necessary.

We show how to implement an efficient lock-free snapshot operation for concurrent hash tries. The snapshot operation uses a single-word compare-and-swap and avoids copying the data structure eagerly. Snapshots are used to implement consistent iterators and a linearizable size retrieval. We compare concurrent hash trie performance with other concurrent data structures and evaluate the performance of the snapshot operation.

Categories and Subject Descriptors E.1 [*Data structures*]: Trees

General Terms Algorithms

Keywords hash trie, concurrent data structure, snapshot, non-blocking

1. Introduction

When designing concurrent data structures, lock-freedom is an important concern. Lock-free data structures generally guarantee better robustness than their lock-based variants [11], as they are unaffected by thread delays. A fundamental difference is that lock-free data structures can continue to work correctly in the presence of failures, whereas a failure may prevent progress indefinitely with a lock-based data structure.

While obtaining a consistent view of the contents of the data structure at a single point in time is a trivial matter for data structures accessed sequentially, it is not clear how to do this in a non-blocking concurrent setting. A consistent view of the data structure at a single point in time is called a *snapshot*. Snapshots can be used to implement operations requiring global information about the data structure – in this case, their performance is limited by the performance of the snasphot.

Our contributions are the following:

1. We describe a complete lock-free concurrent hash trie data structure implementation for a shared-memory system based on single-word compare-and-swap instructions.

PPoPP'12, February 25–29, 2012, New Orleans, Louisiana, USA.

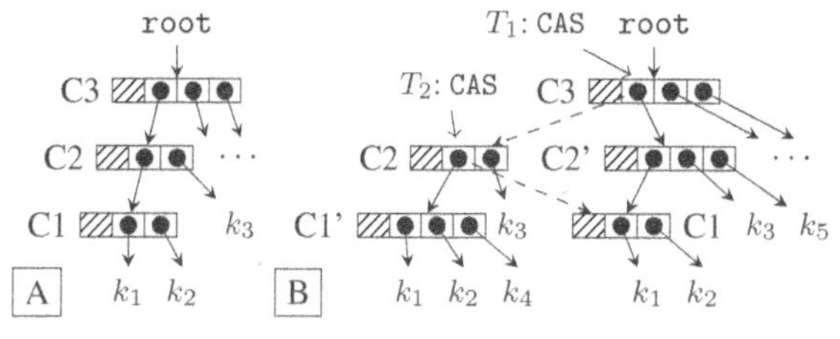

Figure 1. Hash tries

2. We introduce a non-blocking, atomic constant-time snapshot operation. We show how to use them to implement atomic size retrieval, consistent iterators and an atomic clear operation.
3. We present benchmarks that compare performance of concurrent tries against other concurrent data structures across different architectures.

Section 2 illustrates usefulness of snapshots. Section 3 describes basic operations on concurrent tries. Section 4 describes snapshots. Section 5 presents various benchmarks. Section 6 contains related work and Section 7 concludes.

2. Motivation

Most stock concurrent collection implementations include operations such as the atomic lookup, insert and remove operations. Operations that require global data structure information or induce a global change in the data structure, such as size retrieval, iterator creation or deleting all the elements are typically implemented with no atomicity guarantees (e.g. the Java `ConcurrentHashMap` and the `ConcurrentSkipListMap` [14]) or require a global lock. Ideally, these operations should have a constant running time and be nonblocking. Given an atomic snapshot, implementing these operations seems to be trivial.

Collection frameworks such as Intel TBB or STAPL parallelize bulk operations on data. They do this by relying on iterators that traverse disjunct parts of the collection. Many algorithms exhibit an interesting interplay of parallel traversal and concurrent updates. One such example is the PageRank algorithm, implemented using Scala parallel collections [21] in Figure 2. In a nutshell, this iterative algorithm updates the rank of the pages until the rank converges. The rank is updated based on the last known rank of the pages linking to the current page (line 4). Once the rank becomes smaller than some predefined constant, the page is removed from the set of pages being processed (line 5). The *for* loop that does the updates is executed in parallel. After the loop completes, the arrays containing the previous and the next rank are swapped in line 7, and the next iteration commences if there are pages left.

The main point about this algorithm is that the set of pages being iterated is updated by the remove operation during the parallel traversal. This is where most concurrent data structures prove inadequate for implementing this kind of algorithms – an iterator may or may not reflect the concurrent updates. Scala parallel collections can remedy this by removing the test in line 5 and adding another parallel operation `filter` to create a new set of pages without those that converged – this new set is traversed in the next iteration. The downside of this is that if only a few pages converge during an iteration then almost the entire set needs to be copied. If the iterators used for parallel traversal reflected only the elements present when the operation began, there would be no need for this. We show in Section 5 that avoiding the additional `filter` phase enhances performance.

```
1 while (pages.nonEmpty) {
2   for (page <- pages.par) {
3     val sum = page.incoming.sumBy(p => last(p) / p.links)
4     next(page) = (1 - damp) / N + damp * sum
5     if (next(page) - last(page) < eps) pages.remove(page)
6   }
7   swap(next, last)
8 }
```

Figure 2. Parallel PageRank implementation

3. Basic operations

Hash array mapped tries (or simply hash tries) described previously by Bagwell [2] are trees composed of internal nodes and leaves. Leaves store key-value bindings. Internal nodes have a 2^W-way branching factor. In a straightforward implementation, each internal node is a 2^W-element array. Finding a key proceeds as follows. If the internal node is at the level l, then the W bits of the hashcode starting from the position $W * l$ are used as an index to the appropriate branch in the array. This is repeated until a leaf or an empty entry is found. Insertion uses the key to find an empty entry or a leaf. It creates a new leaf with the key if an empty entry is found. Otherwise, the key in the leaf is compared against the key being inserted. If they are equal, the existing leaf is replaced with a new one. If they are not equal (meaning their hashcode prefixes are the same) then the hash trie is extended with a new level.

Bagwell describes an implementation that is more space-efficient [2]. Each internal node contains a bitmap of length 2^W. If a bit is set, then the corresponding array entry contains either a branch or a leaf. The array length is equal to the number of bits in the bitmap. The corresponding array index for a bit on position i in the bitmap *bmp* is calculated as $\#((i-1) \odot bmp)$, where $\#(\cdot)$ is the bitcount and $\odot$ is a bitwise AND operation. The W bits of the hashcode relevant at some level l are used to compute the bit position i as before. At all times an invariant is preserved that the bitmap bitcount is equal to the array length. Typically, W is 5 since that ensures that 32-bit integers can be used as bitmaps. Figure 1A shows a hash trie example.

The goal is to create a concurrent data structure that preserves the space-efficiency of hash tries and the expected depth of $O(log_{2^W}(n))$. Lookup, insert and remove will be based solely on CAS instructions and have the lock-freedom property. Remove operations must ensure that the trie is kept as compact as possible. Finally, to support linearizable lock-free iteration and size retrievals, the data structure must support an efficient snapshot operation. We will call this data structure a *Ctrie*.

Intuitively, a concurrent insertion operation could start by locating the internal node it needs to modify and then create a copy of that node with both the bitmap and the array updated with a reference to the key being inserted. A reference to the newly created node could then be written into the array of the parent node using the CAS instruction. Unfortunately, this approach does not work. The fundamental problem here is due to races between an insertion of a key into some node $C1$ and an insertion of another key into its parent node $C2$. One scenario where such a race happens is shown in Figure 1. Assume we have a hash trie from the Figure 1A and that a thread T_1 decides to insert a key k_5 into the node $C2$ and creates an updated version of $C2$ called $C2'$. It must then do a CAS on the first entry in the internal node $C3$ with the expected value $C2$ and the new value $C2'$. Assume that another thread T_2 decides to insert a key k_4 into the node $C1$ before this CAS. It will create an updated version of $C1$ called $C1'$ and then do a CAS on the first entry of the array of $C2$ – the updated node $C1'$ will not be reachable from the updated node $C2'$. After both threads complete their CAS operations, the trie will correspond to the one shown in Figure 1B, where the dashed arrows represent the state of the branches before the CASes. The key k_4 inserted by the thread T_2 is lost.

We solve this problem by introducing indirection nodes, or I-nodes, which remain present in the Ctrie even as nodes above and below change. The CAS instruction is performed on the I-node instead of on the internal node array. We show that this eliminates the race between insertions on different levels.

The second fundamental problem has to do with the remove operations. Insert operations extend the Ctrie with additional levels. A sequence of remove operations may eliminate the need for the additional levels – ideally, we would like to keep the trie as compact as possible so that the subsequent lookup operations are faster. In Section 3.2 we show that removing an I-node that appears to be no longer needed may result in lost updates. We describe how to remove the keys while ensuring compression and no lost updates.

The Ctrie data structure is described in Figure 3. Each Ctrie contains a root reference to a so-called indirection node (I-node). An I-node contains a reference to a single node called a *main node*. There are several types of main nodes. A tomb node (T-node) is a special node used to ensure proper ordering during removals. A list node (L-node) is a leaf node used to handle hash code collisions by keeping such keys in a list. These are not immediately important, so we postpone discussion about T-nodes and L-nodes until Sections 3.2 and 3.3, respectively. A Ctrie node (C-node) is an internal main node containing a bitmap and the array with references to *branch nodes*. A branch node is either another I-node or a singleton node (S-node), which contains a single key and a value. S-nodes are leaves in the Ctrie (shown as key-value pairs in the figures).

The pseudocode in Figures 4, 6, 8, 9, 11, 13, 15 and 16 assumes short-circuiting semantics of the conditions in the *if* statements. We use logical symbols in boolean expressions. Pattern matching constructs match a node against its type and can be replaced with a sequence of *if-then-else* statements – we use pattern matching for conciseness. The colon (`:`) in the pattern matching cases should be read as *has type*. The keyword `def` denotes a procedure definition. Reads, writes and compare-and-set instructions written in capitals are atomic. This high level pseudocode might not be optimal in all cases – the source code contains a more efficient implementation.

The rest of the section describes the basic update operations.

3.1 Lookup and insert operations

A lookup starts by reading the root and then calls the recursive procedure `ilookup`, which traverses the Ctrie. This procedure either returns a result or a special value `RESTART`, which indicates that the lookup must be repeated.

The `ilookup` procedure reads the main node from the current I-node. If the main node is a C-node, then (as described in Section 3) the relevant bit `flag` of the bitmap and the index `pos` in the array are computed by the `flagpos` function. If the bitmap does not contain the relevant bit (line 10), then a key with the required

```
structure Ctrie {
  root: INode
  readonly: boolean
}

structure Gen

structure INode {
  main: MainNode
  gen: Gen
}

MainNode:
  CNode | TNode | LNode

Branch:
  INode | SNode

structure CNode {
  bmp: integer
  array: Branch[2^W]
}

structure SNode {
  k: KeyType
  v: ValueType
}

structure TNode {
  sn: SNode
}

structure LNode {
  sn: SNode
  next: LNode
}
```

Figure 3. Types and data structures

hashcode prefix is not present in the trie, so a NOTFOUND value is returned. Otherwise, the relevant branch at index pos is read from the array. If the branch is an I-node (line 12), the `ilookup` procedure is called recursively at the next level. If the branch is an S-node (line 14), then the key within the S-node is compared with the key being searched – these two keys have the same hashcode prefixes, but they need not be equal. If they are equal, the corresponding value from the S-node is returned and a NOTFOUND value otherwise. In all cases, the linearization point is the read in the line 7. This is because no nodes other than I-nodes change the value of their fields after they are created and we know that the main node was reachable in the trie at the time it was read in the line 7 [20].

If the main node within an I-node is a T-node (line 17), we try to remove it and convert it to a regular node before restarting the operation. This is described in more detail in Section 3.2. The L-node case is described in Section 3.3.

```
1 def lookup(k)
2   r = READ(root)
3   res = ilookup(r, k, 0, null)
4   if res ≠ RESTART return res else return lookup(k)
5
6 def ilookup(i, k, lev, parent)
7   READ(i.main) match {
8     case cn: CNode =>
9       flag, pos = flagpos(k.hash, lev, cn.bmp)
10      if cn.bmp ⊙ flag = 0 return NOTFOUND
11      cn.array(pos) match {
12        case sin: INode =>
13          return ilookup(sin, k, lev + W, i)
14        case sn: SNode =>
15          if sn.k = k return sn.v else return NOTFOUND
16      }
17    case tn: TNode =>
18      clean(parent, lev - W)
19      return RESTART
20    case ln: LNode =>
21      return ln.lookup(k)
22  }
```

Figure 4. Lookup operation

When a new Ctrie is created, it contains a root I-node with the main node set to an empty C-node, which contains an empty bitmap and a zero-length array (Figure 5A). We maintain the invariant that only the root I-node can contain an empty C-node – all other C-nodes in the Ctrie contain at least one entry in their array. Inserting a key k_1 first reads the root and calling the procedure `iinsert`.

The procedure `iinsert` is invoked on the root I-node. This procedure works in a similar way as `ilookup`. If it reads a C-node within the I-node, it computes the relevant bit and the index in the array using the `flagpos` function. If the relevant bit is not in the bitmap (line 31) then a copy of the C-node with the new entry is created using the `inserted` function. The linearization point is a successful CAS in the line 33, which replaces the current C-node with a C-node containing the new key (see Figures 5A,B,C where two new keys k_1 and k_2 are inserted in that order starting from an empty Ctrie). An unsuccessful CAS means that some other operation already wrote to this I-node since its main node was read in the line 28, so the insert must be repeated.

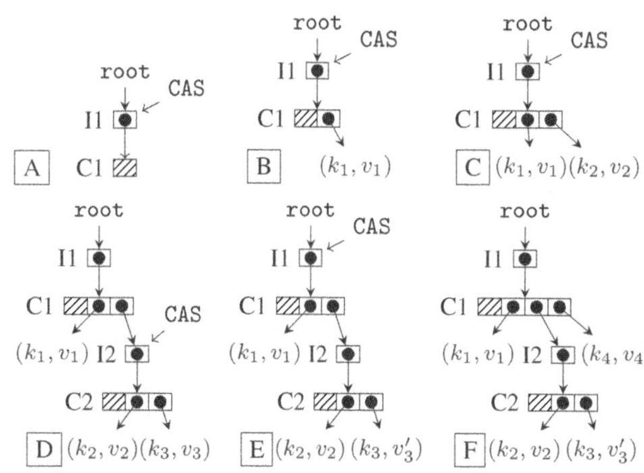

Figure 5. Ctrie insert

```
23 def insert(k, v)
24   r = READ(root)
25   if iinsert(r, k, v, 0, null) = RESTART insert(k, v)
26
27 def iinsert(i, k, v, lev, parent)
28   READ(i.main) match {
29     case cn: CNode =>
30       flag, pos = flagpos(k.hash, lev, cn.bmp)
31       if cn.bmp ⊙ flag = 0 {
32         ncn = cn.inserted(pos, flag, SNode(k, v))
33         if CAS(i.main, cn, ncn) return OK
34         else return RESTART
35       }
36       cn.array(pos) match {
37         case sin: INode =>
38           return iinsert(sin, k, v, lev + W, i)
39         case sn: SNode =>
40           if sn.k ≠ k {
41             nsn = SNode(k, v)
42             nin = INode(CNode(sn, nsn, lev + W))
43             ncn = cn.updated(pos, nin)
44             if CAS(i.main, cn, ncn) return OK
45             else return RESTART
46           } else {
47             ncn = cn.updated(pos, SNode(k, v))
48             if CAS(i.main, cn, ncn) return OK
49             else return RESTART
50           }
51       }
52     case tn: TNode =>
53       clean(parent, lev - W)
54       return RESTART
55     case ln: LNode =>
56       if CAS(i.main, ln, ln.inserted(k, v)) return OK
57       else return RESTART
58   }
```

Figure 6. Insert operation

If the relevant bit is present in the bitmap, then its corresponding branch is read from the array. If the branch is an I-node, then `iinsert` is called recursively. If the branch is an S-node and its key is not equal to the key being inserted (line 40), then the Ctrie has to be extended with an additional level. The C-node is replaced with its updated version (line 44), created using the `updated` function that adds a new I-node at the respective position. The new I-node has its main node pointing to a C-node with both keys. This scenario is shown in Figures 5C,D where a new key k_3 with the same hashcode prefix as k_2 is inserted. If the key in the S-node is equal to the key being inserted, then the C-node is replaced with its updated version with a new S-node. An example is given in the Figure 5E where a new S-node (k_3, v_3') replaces the S-node (k_3, v_3) from the Figure 5D. In both cases, the successful CAS instructions in the lines 44 and 48 are the linearization point.

Note that insertions to I-nodes at different levels may proceed concurrently, as shown in Figures 5E,F where a new key k_4 is added at the level 0, below the I-node $I1$. No race can occur, since the I-nodes at the lower levels remain referenced by the I-nodes at the upper levels even when new keys are added to the higher levels. This will not be the case after introducing the remove operation.

3.2 Remove operation

The remove operation has a similar control flow as the lookup and the insert operation. After examining the root, a recursive procedure `iremove` reads the main node of the I-node and proceeds casewise, removing the S-node from the trie by updating the C-node above it, similar to the insert operation.

The described approach has certain pitfalls. A remove operation may at one point create a C-node that has a single S-node below it. This is shown in Figure 7A, where the key k_2 is removed from the Ctrie. The resulting Ctrie in Figure 7B is still valid in the sense that the subsequent insert and lookup operations will work. However, these operations could be faster if (k_3, v_3) were moved into the C-node below $I1$. After having removed the S-node (k_2, v_2), the remove operation could create an updated version of $C1$ with a reference to the S-node (k_3, v_3) instead of $I2$ and write that into $I1$ to compress the Ctrie. But, if a concurrent insert operation were to write to $I2$ just before $I1$ was updated with the compressed version of $C1$, the insertion would be lost.

To solve this problem, we introduce a new type of a main node called a tomb node (T-node). We introduce the following invariant to Ctries – if an I-node points to a T-node at some time t_0 then for all times greater than t_0, the I-node points to the same T-node. In other words, a T-node is the last value assigned to an I-node. This ensures that no inserts occur at an I-node if it is being compressed. An I-node pointing to a T-node is called a *tombed I-node*.

The remove operation starts by reading the root I-node and calling the recursive procedure `iremove`. If the main node is a C-node, the `flagpos` function is used to compute the relevant bit and the branch position. If the bit is not present in the bitmap (line 69), then a `NOTFOUND` value is returned. In this case, the linearization point is the read in the line 66. Otherwise, the branch node is read from the array. If the branch is another I-node, the procedure is called recursively. If the branch is an S-node, its key is compared against the key being removed. If the keys are not equal (line 75), the `NOTFOUND` value is returned and the linearization point is the read in the line 66. If the keys are equal, a copy of the current node without the S-node is created. The *contraction* of the copy is then created using the `toContracted` procedure. A successful CAS in the line 79 will substitute the old C-node with the copied C-node, thus removing the S-node with the given key from the trie – this is the linearization point.

If a given C-node has only a single S-node below and is not at the root level (line 101) then the `toContracted` procedure

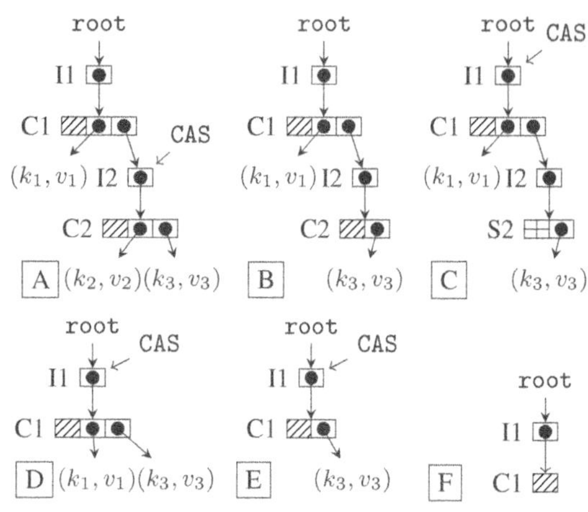

Figure 7. Ctrie remove

```
59 def remove(k)
60   r = READ(root)
61   res = iremove(r, k, 0, null)
62   if res ≠ RESTART return res
63   else return remove(k)
64
65 def iremove(i, k, lev, parent)
66   READ(i.main) match {
67     case cn: CNode =>
68       flag, pos = flagpos(k.hash, lev, cn.bmp)
69       if cn.bmp ⊙ flag = 0 return NOTFOUND
70       res = cn.array(pos) match {
71         case sin: INode =>
72           iremove(sin, k, lev + W, i)
73         case sn: SNode =>
74           if sn.k ≠ k
75             NOTFOUND
76           else {
77             ncn = cn.removed(pos, flag)
78             cntr = toContracted(ncn, lev)
79             if CAS(i.main, cn, cntr) sn.v else RESTART
80           }
81       }
82       if res = NOTFOUND ∨ res = RESTART return res
83       if READ(i.main): TNode
84         cleanParent(parent, in, k.hash, lev - W)
85       return res
86     case tn: TNode =>
87       clean(parent, lev - W)
88       return RESTART
89     case ln: LNode =>
90       nln = ln.removed(k)
91       if length(nln) = 1 nln = entomb(nln.sn)
92       if CAS(i.main, ln, nln) return ln.lookup(k)
93       else return RESTART
94   }
```

Figure 8. Remove operation

returns a T-node that wraps the S-node. Otherwise, it just returns the given C-node. This ensures that every I-node except the root points to a C-node with at least one branch. Furthermore, if it points to exactly one branch, then that branch is not an S-node (this scenario is possible if two keys with the same hashcode prefixes are inserted). Calling this procedure ensures that the CAS in the line 79 replaces the C-node $C2$ from the Figure 7A with the T-node in Figure 7C instead of the C-node $C2$ in Figure 7B. This CAS is the linearization point since the S-node (k_2, v_2) is no longer in the trie. However, it does not solve the problem of compressing the Ctrie (we ultimately want to obtain a Ctrie in Figure 7D). In fact, given a Ctrie containing two keys with long matching hashcode prefixes, removing one of these keys will create a arbitrarily long chain of C-nodes with a single T-node at the end. We introduced the invariant that no tombed I-node changes its main node. To remove the tombed I-node, the reference to it in the C-node above must be changed with a reference to its *resurrection*. A resurrection of a tombed I-node is the S-node wrapped in its T-node. For all other branch nodes, the resurrection is the node itself.

To ensure compression, the remove operation checks if the current main node is a T-node after removing the key from the Ctrie (line 83). If it is, it calls the `cleanParent` procedure, which reads the main node of the parent I-node `p` and the current I-node `i` in the line 113. It then checks if the T-node below `i` is reachable from `p`. If `i` is no longer reachable, then it returns – some other thread must have already completed the contraction. If it is reachable then it replaces the C-node below `p`, which contains the tombed I-node `i` with a copy updated with the resurrection of `i` (CAS in the line 122). This copy is possibly once more contracted into a T-node at a higher level by the `toContracted` procedure.

```
95  def toCompressed(cn, lev)
96    num = bit#(cn.bmp)
97    ncn = cn.mapped(resurrect(_))
98    return toContracted(ncn, lev)
99
100 def toContracted(cn, lev)
101   if lev > 0 ∧ cn.array.length = 1
102     cn.array(0) match {
103       case sn: SNode => return entomb(sn)
104       case _ => return cn
105     }
106   else return cn
107
108 def clean(i, lev)
109   m = READ(i.main)
110   if m: CNode CAS(i.main, m, toCompressed(m, lev))
111
112 def cleanParent(p, i, hc, lev)
113   m, pm = READ(i.main), READ(p.main)
114   pm match {
115     case cn: CNode =>
116       flag, pos = flagpos(k.hash, lev, cn.bmp)
117       if bmp ⊙ flag = 0 return
118       sub = cn.array(pos)
119       if sub ≠ i return
120       if m: TNode {
121         ncn = cn.updated(pos, resurrect(m))
122         if ¬CAS(p.main, cn, toContracted(ncn, lev))
123           cleanParent(p, i, hc, lev)
124       }
125     case _ => return
126   }
```

Figure 9. Compression operations

To preserve the lock-freedom property, all operations that read a T-node must help compress it instead of waiting for the removing thread to complete the compression. For example, after finding a T-node lookups call the `clean` procedure on the parent node in the line 17. This procedure creates the *compression* of the given C-node – a new C-node with all the tombed I-nodes below resurrected. This new C-node is contracted if possible. The old C-node is then replaced with its compression with the CAS in the line 110. Note that neither `clean` nor `cleanParent` are ever called for the parent of the root, since the root never contains a T-node. For example, removing the S-node (k_3, v_3) from the Ctrie in Figure 7D produces a Ctrie in Figure 7E. A subsequent remove produces an empty trie in Figure 7F.

Both insert and lookup are tail-recursive and may be rewritten to loop-based variants, but this is not so trivial with the remove operation. Since remove operations must be able to compress arbitrary long chains of C-nodes, the call stack is used to store information about the path in the Ctrie being traversed.

3.3 Hash collisions

In this implementation, hash tries use a 32-bit hashcode space. Although hash collisions are rare, it is still possible that two unequal keys with the same hashcodes are inserted. To preserve correctness, we introduce a new type of nodes called list nodes (L-nodes), which are basically persistent linked lists. If two keys with the same hashcodes collide, we place them inside an L-node.

We add another case to the basic operations from Section 3. Persistent linked list operations `lookup`, `inserted`, `removed` and `length` are trivial and not included in the pseudocode. We additionally check if the updated L-node in the `iremove` procedure has length 1 and replace the old node with a T-node in this case.

Another important change is in the `CNode` constructor in line 42. This constructor was a recursive procedure that creates additional C-nodes as long as the hashcode chunks of the two keys are equal at the given level. We modify it to create an L-node if the level is greater than the length of the hashcode – in our case 32.

3.4 Additional operations

Collection classes in various frameworks typically need to implement additional operations. For example, the `ConcurrentMap` interface in Java defines four additional methods: `putIfAbsent`, `replace` any value a key is mapped to with a new value, `replace` a specific value a key is mapped to with a new value and `remove` a key mapped to a specific value. All of these operations can be implemented with trivial modifications to the operations introduced in Section 3. For example, removing a key mapped to a specific value can be implemented by adding an additional check `sn.v = v` to the line 74. We invite the reader to try to inspect the source code of our implementation.

Methods such as `size`, `iterator` or `clear` commonly seen in collection frameworks cannot be implemented in a lock-free, linearizable manner so easily. The reason for this is that they require global information about the data structure at one specific instance in time – at first glance, this requires locking or weakening the contract so that these methods can only be called during a quiescent state.

It turns out that for Ctries these methods can be computed efficiently and correctly by relying on a constant time lock-free, atomic snapshot.

4. Snapshot

While creating a consistent snapshot often seems to require copying all of the elements of a data structure, this is not generally the case. Persistent data structures present in functional languages have operations that return their updated versions and avoid copying all the elements, typically achieving logarithmic or sometimes even constant complexity [19].

A persistent hash trie data structure seen in standard libraries of languages like Scala or Clojure is updated by rewriting the path from the root of the hash trie to the leaf the key belongs to, leaving the rest of the trie intact. This idea can be applied to implement the snapshot. A generation count can be assigned to each I-node. A snapshot is created by copying the root I-node and setting it to the new generation. When some update operation detects that an I-node being read has a generation older than the generation of the root, it can create a copy of that I-node initialized with the latest generation and update the parent accordingly – the effect of this is that after the snapshot is taken, a path from the root to some leaf is updated only the first time it is accessed, analogous to persistent data structures. The snapshot is thus an $O(1)$ operation, while all other operations preserve an $O(\log n)$ complexity, albeit with a larger constant factor.

Still, the snapshot operation will not work as described above, due to the races between the thread creating the snapshot and threads that have already read the root I-node with the old generation and are traversing the Ctrie in order to update it. The problem is that a CAS that is a linearization point for an insert (e.g. in the line 48) can be preceeded by the snapshot creation – ideally, we want such a CAS instruction to fail, since the generation of the Ctrie root has changed. If we used a DCAS instruction instead, we could ensure that the write occurs only if the Ctrie root generation remained the same. However, most platforms do not support an efficient implementation of this instruction yet. On closer inspection, we find that an RDCSS instruction described by Harris et al. [10] that does a double compare and a single swap is enough to implement safe updates. The downside of RDCSS is that its software implementation creates an intermediate descriptor object. While such a construction is general, due to the overhead of allocating and later garbage collecting the descriptor, it is not optimal in our case.

We will instead describe a new procedure called generation-compare-and-swap, or GCAS. This procedure has semantics similar to that of the RDCSS, but it does not create the intermediate object except in the case of failures that occur due to the snapshot being taken – in this case the number of intermediate objects created per snapshot is $O(t)$ where t is the number of threads invoking some Ctrie operation at the time.

4.1 GCAS procedure

The `GCAS` procedure has the following preconditions. It takes 3 parameters – an I-node `in`, and two main nodes `old` and `n`. Only the thread invoking the `GCAS` procedure may have a reference to the main node `n`[1]. Each main node must contain an additional field `prev` that is not accessed by the clients. Each I-node must contain an additional immutable field `gen`. The `in.main` field is only read using the `GCAS_READ` procedure.

```
def GCAS(in, old, n)
  r = READ(in.main)
  if r = old ∧ in.gen = READ(root).gen {
    WRITE(in.main, n)
    return ⊤
  } else return ⊥
```

Figure 10. GCAS semantics

Its semantics are equivalent to an atomic block shown in Figure 10. The `GCAS` is similar to a CAS instruction with the difference that it also compares if I-node `gen` field is equal to the `gen` field of the Ctrie root. The `GCAS` instruction is also lock-free. We show the implementation in Figure 11, based on single-word CAS instructions. The idea is to communicate the intent of replacing the value in the I-node and check the generation field in the root before committing to the new value.

The `GCAS` procedure starts by setting the `prev` field in the new main node `n` to point at main node `old`, which will be the expected value for the first CAS. Since the preconditions state that no other thread sees `n` at this point, this write is safe. The thread proceeds by proposing the new value `n` with a CAS instruction in line 129. If the CAS fails then `GCAS` returns ⊥ and the CAS is the linearization point. If the CAS succeeds (shown in Figure 12B), the new main node is not yet committed – the generation of the root has to be

[1] This is easy to ensure in environments with automatic memory management and garbage collection. Otherwise, a technique similar to the one proposed by Herlihy [11] can be used to ensure that a thread does not reuse objects that have already been recycled.

```
127 def GCAS(in, old, n)
128   WRITE(n.prev, old)
129   if CAS(in.main, old, n) {
130     GCAS_Commit(in, n)
131     return READ(n.prev) = null
132   } else return ⊥
133
134 def GCAS_Commit(in, m)
135   p = READ(m.prev)
136   r = ABORTABLE_READ(root)
137   p match {
138     case n: MainNode =>
139       if (r.gen = in.gen ∧ ¬readonly) {
140         if CAS(m.prev, p, null) return m
141         else return GCAS_Commit(in, m)
142       } else {
143         CAS(m.prev, p, new Failed(p))
144         return GCAS_Commit(in, READ(in.main))
145       }
146     case fn: Failed =>
147       if CAS(in.main, m, fn.prev) return fn.prev
148       else return GCAS_Commit(in, READ(in.main))
149     case null => return m
150   }
151
152 def GCAS_READ(in)
153   m = READ(in.main)
154   if (READ(m.prev) = null) return m
155   else return GCAS_Commit(in, m)
```

Figure 11. GCAS operations

compared against the generation of the I-node before committing the value, so the tail-recursive procedure `GCAS_Commit` is called with the parameter `m` set to the proposed value `n`. This procedure reads the previous value of the proposed node and the Ctrie root. We postpone the explanation of the `ABORTABLE_READ` procedure until Section 4.2 – for now it can be considered an ordinary atomic `READ`. It then inspects the previous value.

If the previous value is a main node different than `null`, the root generation is compared to the I-node generation. If the generations are equal, the `prev` field in `m` must be set to `null` to complete the GCAS (Figure 12C). If the CAS in the line 140 fails, the procedure is repeated. If the generations are not equal, the `prev` field is set to a special `Failed` node whose previous value is set to `m.prev` (Figure 12D), and the `GCAS_Commit` procedure is repeated. This special node signals that the `GCAS` has failed and that the I-node main node must be set back to the previous value.

If the previous value is a failed node, then the main node of the I-node is set back to the previous value from the failed node by the CAS in the line 147 (Figure 12D,E). If the CAS is not successful, the procedure must be repeated after rereading the main node.

If the previous value is `null`, then some other thread already checked the generation of the root and committed the node, so the method just returns the current node.

Once the `GCAS_Commit` procedure returns, `GCAS` checks if the `prev` field of the proposed node is `null`, meaning that the value had been successfully committed at some point.

If the proposed value is rejected, the linearization point is the CAS in line 147, which sets the main node of an I-node back to the previous value (this need not necessarily be done by the current thread). If the proposed value is accepted, the linearization point is the successful CAS in the line 140 – independent of that CAS was done by the current thread or some other thread. If the linearization point is external, we know it happened after `GCAS` was invoked. We know that the `gen` field does not change during the lifetime of an I-node, so it remains the same until a successful CAS in the line 140. If some other thread replaces the root with a new I-node with a different `gen` field after the read in the line 136, then no other thread

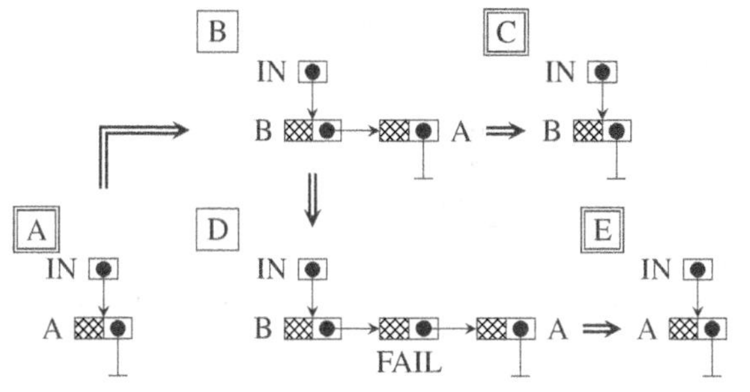

Figure 12. GCAS states

```
...
  case sin: INode =>
    if (startgen eq in.gen)
      return iinsert(sin, k, v, lev + W, i, startgen)
    else
      if (GCAS(cn, atGen(cn, startgen)))
        iinsert(i, k, v, lev, parent, startgen)
      else return RESTART
...
def atGen(n, ngen)
  n match {
    case cn: CNode => cn.mapped(atGen(_, ngen))
    case in: INode => new INode(GCAS_READ(in), ngen)
    case sn: SNode => sn
  }
```

Figure 13. I-node renewal

that observed the root change will succeed in writing a failed node, since we assumed that the CAS in the line 140 succeeded.

To ensure lock-freedom, the `GCAS_READ` procedure must help commit if it finds a proposed value. After reading the main node, it checks if its `prev` field is set to `null`. If it is, it can safely return the node read in line 153 (which is the linearization point) since the algorithm never changes the `prev` field of a committed node and comitting a node sets the `prev` field to `null`. If `prev` is different than `null`, the node hasn't been committed yet, so `GCAS_Commit` is called to complete the read. In this case, the value returned by `GCAS_Commit` is the result and the linearization points are the same as with `GCAS` invoking the `GCAS_Commit`.

Both `GCAS` and `GCAS_READ` are designed to add a non-significant amount of overhead compared a single CAS instruction and a read, respectively. In particular, if there are no concurrent modifications, a `GCAS_READ` amounts to an atomic read of the node, an atomic read of its `prev` field, a comparison and a branch.

4.2 Implementation

We now show how to augment the existing algorithm with snapshots using the `GCAS` and `GCAS_READ` procedures. We add a `prev` field to each type of a main node and a `gen` field to I-nodes. The `gen` field points to generation objects allocated on the heap. We do not use integers to avoid overflows and we do not use pointers to the root as generation objects, since that could cause memory leaks – if we did, the Ctrie could potentially transitively point to all of its previous snapshot versions. We add an additional parameter `startgen` to procedures `ilookup`, `iinsert` and `iremove`. This parameter contains the generation count of the Ctrie root, which was read when the operation began.

Next, we replace every occurence of a CAS instruction with a call to the `GCAS` procedure. We replace every atomic read with a call to the `GCAS_READ` procedure. Whenever we read an I-node while traversing the trie (lines 12, 37 and 71) we check if the I-node generation corresponds to `startgen`. If it does, we proceed as before. Otherwise, we create a copy of the current C-node such that all of its I-nodes are copied to the newest generation and use `GCAS` to update the main node before revisiting the current I-node again. This is shown in Figure 13, where the `cn` refers to the C-node currently in scope (see Figures 4, 6 and 8). In line 43 we copy the C-node so that all I-nodes directly below it are at the latest generation before updating it. The `readonly` field is used to check if the Ctrie is read-only - we explain this shortly. Finally, we add a check to the `cleanParent` procedure, which aborts if `startgen` is different than the `gen` field of the I-node.

All `GCAS` invocations fail if the generation of the Ctrie root changes and these failures cause the basic operations to be restarted. Since the root is read once again after restarting, we are guaranteed to restart the basic operation with the updated value of the `startgen` parameter.

One might be tempted to implement the snapshot operation by simply using a CAS instruction to change the `root` reference of a Ctrie to point to an I-node with a new generation. However, the snapshot operation can copy and replace the root I-node only if its main node does not change between the copy and the replacement.

We use the `RDCSS` procedure described by Harris et al. [10], which works in a similar way as `GCAS`, but proposes the new value by creating an intermediate descriptor object, which points to the previous and the proposed value. We do not see the cost of allocating it as critical since we expect a snapshot to occur much less often than the other update operations. We specialize `RDCSS` – the first compare is on the root and the second compare is always on the main node of the old value of the root. `GCAS_READ` is used to read the main node of the old value of the root. The semantics correspond to the atomic block shown in Figure 14.

```
def RDCSS(ov, ovmain, nv)
  r = READ(root)
  if r = ov ∧ GCAS_READ(ov.main) = ovmain {
    WRITE(root, nv)
    return ⊤
  } else return ⊥
```

Figure 14. Modified RDCSS semantics

To create a snapshot of the Ctrie the root I-node is read. Its main node is read next. The `RDCSS` procedure is called, which replaces the old root I-node with its new generation copy. If the `RDCSS` is successful, a new Ctrie is returned with the copy of the root I-node set to yet another new generation. Otherwise, the snapshot operation is restarted.

```
def snapshot()
  r = RDCSS_READ()
  expmain = GCAS_READ(r)
  if RDCSS(r, expmain, new INode(expmain, new Gen))
    return new Ctrie {
      root = new INode(expmain, new Gen)
      readonly = ⊥
    }
  else return snapshot()
```

Figure 15. Snapshot operation

An observant reader will notice that if two threads simultaneously start a `GCAS` on the root I-node and an `RDCSS` on the root field of the Ctrie, the algorithm will deadlock[2] since both locations contain the proposed value and read the other location before committing. To avoid this, one of the operations has to have a higher

[2] Actually, it will cause a stack overflow in the current implementation.

priority. This is the reason for the ABORTABLE_READ in line 136 in Figure 11 – it is a modification of the RDCSS_READ that writes back the old value to the root field if it finds the proposal descriptor there, causing the snapshot to be restarted. The algorithm remains lock-free, since the snapshot reads the main node in the root I-node before restarting, thus having to commit the proposed main node.

Since both the original Ctrie and the snapshot have a root with a new generation, both Ctries will have to rebuild paths from the root to the leaf being updated. When computing the size of the Ctrie or iterating the elements, we know that the snapshot will not be modified, so updating paths from the root to the leaf induces an unnecessary overhead. To accomodate this we implement the readOnlySnapshot procedure that returns a read only snapshot. The only difference with respect to the snapshot procedure in Figure 15 is that the returned Ctrie has the old root r (line 167) and the readonly field is set to $\top$. The readonly field mentioned earlier in Figures 3, 11 and 13 guarantees that no writes to I-nodes occur if it is set to $\top$. This means that paths from the root to the leaf being read are not rewritten in read-only Ctries. The rule also applies to T-nodes – instead of trying to clean the Ctrie by resurrecting the I-node above the T-node, the lookup in a read-only Ctrie treats the T-node as if it were an S-node. Furthermore, if the GCAS_READ procedure tries to read from an I-node in which a value is proposed, it will abort the write by creating a failed node and then writing the old value back (line 139).

```
def iterator()
  if readonly return new Iterator(RDCSS_READ(root))
  else return readOnlySnapshot().iterator()

def size()
  sz, it = 0, iterator()
  while it.hasNext sz += 1
  return sz

def clear()
  r = RDCSS_READ()
  expmain = GCAS_READ(r)
  if ¬RDCSS(r, expmain, new INode(new Gen)) clear()
```

Figure 16. Snapshot-based operations

Finally, we show how to implement snapshot-based operations in Figure 16. The size operation can be optimized further by caching the size information in main nodes of a read-only Ctrie – this reduces the amortized complexity of the size operation to $O(1)$ because the size computation is amortized across the update operations that occurred since the last snapshot. For reasons of space, we do not go into details nor do we show the entire iterator implementation, which is trivial once a snapshot is obtained.

5. Evaluation

We performed experimental measurements on a JDK6 configuration with a quad-core 2.67 GHz Intel i7 processor with 8 hyperthreads, a JDK6 configuration with an 8-core 1.165 GHz Sun UltraSPARC-T2 processor with 64 hyperthreads and a JDK7 configuration with four 8-core Intel Xeon 2.27 GHz processors with a total of 64 hyperthreads. The first configuration has a single multicore processor, the second has a single multicore processor, but a different architecture and the third has several multicore processors on one motherboard. We followed established performance measurement methodologies [9]. We compared the performance of the Ctrie data structure against the ConcurrentHashMap and the ConcurrentSkipListMap from the Java standard library, as well as the Cliff Click's non-blocking concurrent hash map implementation [5]. All of the benchmarks show the number of threads used on the x-axis and the throughput on the y-axis. In all experiments, the Ctrie supports the snapshot operation.

The first benchmark called $insert$ starts with an empty data structure and inserts $N = 1000000$ entries into the data structure. The work of inserting the elements is divided equally between P threads, where P varies between 1 and the maximum number of hyperthreads on the configuration (x-axis). The y-axis shows throughput – the number of times the benchmark is repeated per second. This benchmark is designed to test the scalability of the resizing, since the data structure is initially empty. Data structures like hash tables, which have a resize phase, do no seem to be very scalable for this particular use-case, as shown in Figure 17. On the Sun UltraSPARC-T2 (Figure 18), the Java concurrent hash map scales for up to 4 threads. Cliff Click's nonblocking hash table scales, but the cost of the resize is so high that this is not visible on the graph. Concurrent skip lists scale well in this test, but Ctries are a clear winner here since they achieve an almost linear speedup for up to 32 threads and an additional speedup as the number of threads reaches 64.

The benchmark $lookup$ does $N = 1000000$ lookups on a previously created data structure with N elements. The work of looking up all the elements is divided between P threads, where P varies as before. Concurrent hash tables perform especially well in this benchmark on all three configurations – the lookup operation mostly amounts to an array read, so the hash tables are $2 - 3$ times faster than Ctries. Ctries, in turn, are faster than skip lists due to a lower number of indirections, resulting in fewer cache misses.

The $remove$ benchmark starts with a previously created data structure with $N = 1000000$ elements. It removes all of the elements from the data structure. The work of removing all the elements is divided between P threads, where P varies. On the quad-core processor (Figure 17) both the Java concurrent skip list and the concurrent hash table scale, but not as fast as Ctries or the Cliff Click's nonblocking hash table. On the UltraSPARC-T2 configuration (Figure 18), the nonblocking hash table is even up to 2.5 times faster than Ctries. However, we should point out that the nonblocking hash table does not perform compression – once the underlying table is resized to a certain size, the memory is used regardless of whether the elements are removed. This can be a problem for long running applications and applications using a greater number of concurrent data structures.

The next three benchmarks called $90 - 9 - 1$, $80 - 15 - 5$ and $60 - 30 - 10$ show the performance of the data structures when the operations are invoked in the respective ratio. Starting from an empty data structure, a total of $N = 1000000$ invocations are done. The work is divided equally among P threads. For the $90 - 9 - 1$ ratio the Java concurrent hash table works very well on both the quad-core configuration and the UltraSPARC-T2. For the $60 - 30 - 10$ ratio Ctries seem to do as well as the nonblocking hash table. Interestingly, Ctries seem to outperform the other data structures in all three tests on the 4x 8-core i7 (Figure 19).

The $preallocated - 5 - 4 - 1$ benchmark in Figure 18 proceeds exactly as the previous three benchmarks with the difference that it starts with a data structure that contains all the elements. The consequence is that the hash tables do not have to be resized – this is why the Java concurrent hash table performs better for P up to 16, but suffers a performance degradation for bigger P. For $P > 32$ Ctries seem to do better. In this benchmarks, the nonblocking hash table was 3 times faster than the other data structures, so it was excluded from the graph. For applications where the data structure size is known in advance this may be an ideal solution – for others, preallocating may result in a waste of memory.

To evaluate snapshot performance, we do 2 kinds of benchmarks. The $snapshot - remove$ benchmark in Figure 20 is similar to the $remove$ benchmark – it measures the performance of removing all the elements from a snapshot of a Ctrie and compares that time to removing all the elements from an ordinary Ctrie. On both i7 configurations (Figures 17 and 19), removing from a snapshot is up to 50% slower, but scales in the same way as removing from an ordinary Ctrie. On the UltraSPARC-T2 configuration (Figure 18), this gap is much smaller. The benchmark $snapshot - lookup$ in Figure 21 is similar to the last one, with the difference that all the elements are looked up once instead of being removed. Looking up elements in the snapshot is slower, since the Ctrie needs to be fully reevaluated. Here, the gap is somewhat greater on the UltraSPARC-T2 configuration and smaller on the i7 configurations.

Finally, the $PageRank$ benchmark in Figure 22 compares the performance of iterating parts of the snapshot in parallel against the performance of filtering out the page set in each iteration as explained in Section 2. The snapshot-based implementation is much faster on the i7 configurations, whereas the difference is not that much pronounced on the UltraSPARC-T2.

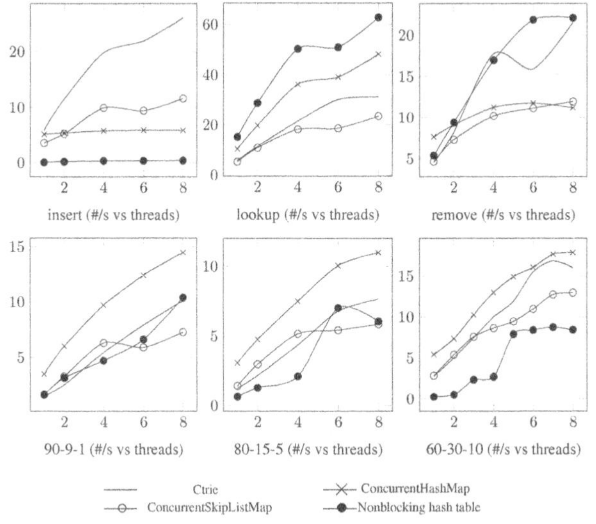

Figure 17. Basic operations, quad-core i7

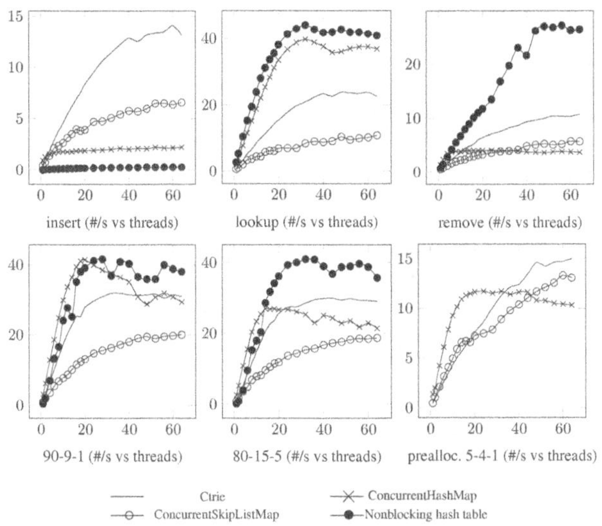

Figure 18. Basic operations, 64 hyperthread UltraSPARC-T2

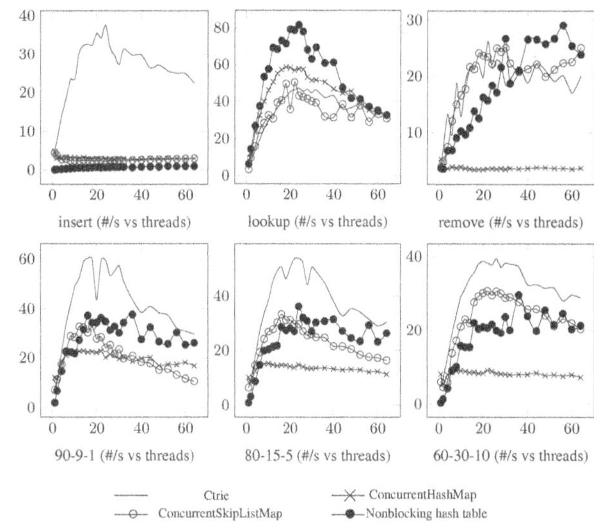

Figure 19. Basic operations, 4x 8-core i7

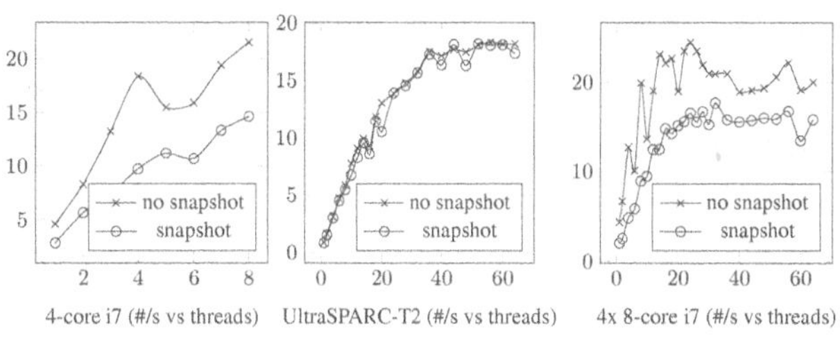

Figure 20. Remove vs. snapshot remove

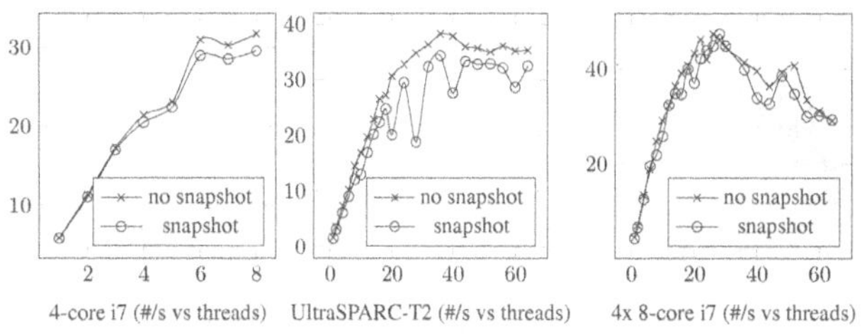

Figure 21. Lookup vs. snapshot lookup

6. Related work

Moir and Shavit give an overview of concurrent data structures [18]. A lot of research was done on concurrent lists, queues and concurrent priority queues. Linked lists are an inefficient implementation of a map abstraction because they do not scale well and the latter two do not support the basic map operations.

Hash tables are resizeable arrays of buckets. Each bucket holds some number of elements that is expected to be constant. The constant number of elements per bucket requires resizing the data structure as more elements are added – sequential hash tables amortize the resizing cost the table over other operations [6]. While the individual concurrent hash table operations such as insertion or removal can be performed in a lock-free manner as shown by Maged [17], resizing is typically implemented with a global lock. Although the cost of resizing is amortized against operations by

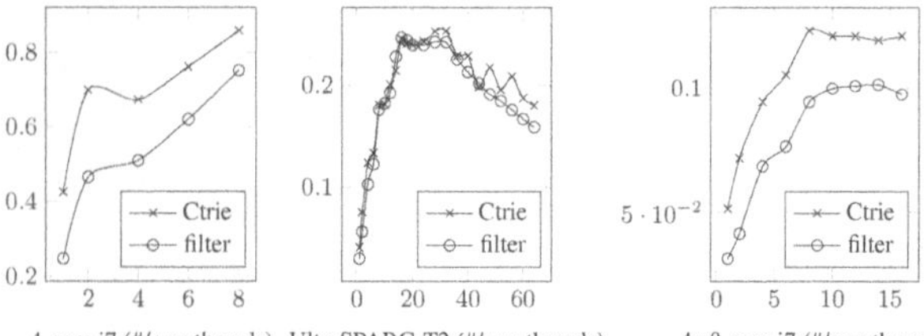

Figure 22. Pagerank

one thread, this approach does not guarantee horizontal scalability. Lea developed an extensible hash algorithm that allows concurrent searches during the resizing phase, but not concurrent insertions and removals [14]. Shalev and Shavit give an innovative approach to resizing – split-ordered lists keep a table of hints into a single linked list in a way that does not require rearranging the elements of the linked list when resizing the table [25].

Skip lists store elements in a linked list. There are multiple levels of linked lists that allow logarithmic time insertions, removals and lookups. Skip lists were originally invented by Pugh [23]. Pugh proposed concurrent skip lists that achieve synchronization using locks [22]. Concurrent non-blocking skip lists were later implemented by Lev, Herlihy, Luchangco and Shavit [12] and Lea [14].

Concurrent binary search trees were proposed by Kung and Lehman [13] – their implementation uses a constant number of locks at a time that exclude other insertion and removal operations, while lookups can proceed concurrently. Bronson et al. presented a scalable concurrent implementation of an AVL tree based on transactional memory mechanisms that require a fixed number of locks to perform deletions [4]. Recently, the first non-blocking implementation of a binary search tree was proposed [7].

Tries were originally proposed by Brandais [3] and Fredkin [8]. Trie hashing was applied to accessing files stored on the disk by Litwin [15]. Litwin, Sagiv and Vidyasankar implemented trie hashing in a concurrent setting [16], however, they did so by using mutual exclusion locks. Hash array mapped trees, or hash tries, are tries for shared-memory described by Bagwell [2]. To our knowledge, there is no nonblocking concurrent implementation of hash tries prior to our work. A correctness proof for the basic operations is presented as part of our tech report on the version of concurrent hash tries that do not support lock-free snapshots [20].

A persistent data structure is a data structure that preserves its previous version when being modified. Efficient persistent data structures are in use today that re-evaluate only a small part of the data structure on modification, thus typically achieving logarithmic, amortized constant and even constant time bounds for their operations. Okasaki presents an overview of persistent data structures [19]. Persistent hash tries have been introduced in standard libraries of languages like Scala [24] and Clojure.

`RDCSS` and `DCAS` software implementations have been described by Harris [10]. In the past, `DCAS` has been used to implement lock-free concurrent deques [1].

7. Conclusion

We described a concurrent implementation of the hash trie data structure with lock-free update operations. We described an $O(1)$ lock-free, atomic snapshot operation that allows efficient traversal, amortized $O(1)$ size retrieval and an $O(1)$ clear operation. It is apparent that a hardware supported DCAS instruction would simplify the design of both update and the snapshot operations.

As a future work direction, we postulate that the GCAS approach can be applied to other data structures – given a CAS-based concurrent data structure and its persistent sequential version, a lock-free, atomic snapshot operation can be implemented by adding a generation counter fields to nodes in the data structure and replacing the CAS instructions that are linearization points with GCAS instructions. This approach appears to be particularly applicable to tree-based data structures.

Acknowledgments

We would like to express our thanks to prof. Doug Lea at the State University of New York at Oswego for his help. We would also like to thank Eva Darulova and Tihomir Gvero at the EPFL for the useful discussions we've lead.

References

[1] O. Agesen, D. L. Detlefs, C. H. Flood, A. Garthwaite, P. A. Martin , N. Shavit , G. L. Steele Jr.: DCAS-Based Concurrent Deques. SPAA, 2000.

[2] P. Bagwell: Ideal Hash Trees. EPFL Technical Report, 2001.

[3] R. Brandais: File searching using variable length keys. Proceedings of Western Joint Computer Conference, 1959.

[4] N. G. Bronson, J. Casper, H. Chafi, K. Olukotun: A Practical Concurrent Binary Search Tree. Proceedings of the 15th ACM SIGPLAN Symposium on Principles and Practice of Parallel Programming, 2009.

[5] C. Click: Towards a Scalable Non-Blocking Coding Style. http://www.azulsystems.com/events/javaone_2007/2007_LockFreeHash.pdf

[6] T. H. Cormen, C. E. Leiserson, R. L. Rivest, C. Stein: Introduction to Algorithms, 2nd Edition. The MIT Press, 2001.

[7] F. Ellen, P. Fatourou, E. Ruppert, F. van Breugel: Non-blocking binary search trees. PODC, 2010.

[8] E. Fredkin: Trie memory. Communications of the ACM, 1960.

[9] A. Georges, D. Buytaert, L. Eeckhout: Statistically Rigorous Java Performance Evaluation. OOPSLA, 2007.

[10] T. L. Harris, K. Fraser, I. A. Pratt: A Practical Multi-word Compare-and-Swap Operation. DISC, 2002.

[11] M. Herlihy: A Methodology for Implementing Highly Concurrent Data Structures. PPOPP, 1990.

[12] M. Herlihy, Y. Lev, V. Luchangco, N. Shavit: A Provably Correct Scalable Concurrent Skip List. OPODIS, 2006.

[13] H. Kung, P. Lehman: Concurrent manipulation of binary search trees. ACM Transactions on Database Systems (TODS), vol. 5, issue 3, 1980.

[14] Doug Lea's Home Page: http://gee.cs.oswego.edu/

[15] W. Litwin: Trie Hashing. Proceedings of the 1981 ACM SIGMOD international conference on Management of data, 1981.

[16] W. Litwin, Y. Sagiv, K. Vidyasankar: Concurrency and Trie Hashing. Acta Informatica archive, vol. 26, issue 7, 1989.

[17] Maged M. Michael: High Performance Dynamic Lock-Free Hash Tables and List-Based Sets. SPAA, 2002.

[18] M. Moir, N. Shavit: Concurrent data structures. Handbook of Data Structures and Applications, Chapman and Hall, 2004.

[19] C. Okasaki: Purely Functional Data Structures. Cambridge University Press, 1999.

[20] A. Prokopec, P. Bagwell, M. Odersky: Cache-Aware Lock-Free Concurrent Hash Tries. EPFL Technical Report, 2011.

[21] A. Prokopec, P. Bagwell, T. Rompf, M. Odersky, A Generic Parallel Collection Framework. Euro-Par 2011 Parallel Processing, 2011.

[22] William Pugh: Concurrent Maintenance of Skip Lists. UM Technical Report, 1990.

[23] William Pugh: Skip Lists: A Probabilistic Alternative to Balanced Trees. Communications ACM, volume 33, 1990.

[24] The Scala Programming Language Homepage. http://www.scala-lang.org/

[25] O. Shalev, N. Shavit: Split-Ordered Lists: Lock-Free Extensible Hash Tables. Journal of the ACM, vol. 53., no. 3., 2006.

A Speculation-Friendly Binary Search Tree

Tyler Crain
IRISA
France
tyler.crain@irisa.fr

Vincent Gramoli
EPFL
Switzerland
vincent.gramoli@epfl.ch

Michel Raynal
IRISA, Institut Universitaire de France
France
raynal@irisa.fr

Abstract

We introduce the first binary search tree algorithm designed for speculative executions. Prior to this work, tree structures were mainly designed for their pessimistic (non-speculative) accesses to have a bounded complexity. Researchers tried to evaluate transactional memory using such tree structures whose prominent example is the red-black tree library developed by Oracle Labs that is part of multiple benchmark distributions. Although well-engineered, such structures remain badly suited for speculative accesses, whose step complexity might raise dramatically with contention.

We show that our *speculation-friendly tree* outperforms the existing transaction-based version of the AVL and the red-black trees. Its key novelty stems from the *decoupling* of update operations: they are split into one transaction that modifies the abstraction state and multiple ones that restructure its tree implementation in the background. In particular, the speculation-friendly tree is shown correct, reusable and it speeds up a transaction-based travel reservation application by up to 3.5×.

Categories and Subject Descriptors D.3.3 [*Programming Languages*]: Language Constructs and Features—Concurrent programming structures; E.1 [*Data Structures*]: Trees; D.2.13 [*Software Engineering*]: Reusable Software—Reusable libraries

General Terms Algorithms, Languages, Performance

Keywords Background Rebalancing, Optimistic Concurrency, Transactional Memory

1. Introduction

The multicore era is changing the way we write concurrent programs. In such context, concurrent data structures are becoming a bottleneck building block of a wide variety of concurrent applications. Generally, they rely on invariants [32] which prevent them from scaling with multiple cores: a tree must typically remain sufficiently balanced at any point of the concurrent execution.

New programming constructs like transactions [20, 33] promise to exploit the concurrency inherent to multicore architectures. Most transactions build upon *optimistic synchronization*, where a sequence of shared accesses is executed speculatively and might abort. They simplify concurrent programming for two reasons. First, the programmer only needs to delimit regions of sequential code into transactions or to replace critical sections by transactions to obtain a safe concurrent program. Second, the resulting transactional program is reusable by any programmer, hence a programmer composing operations from a transactional library into another transaction is guaranteed to obtain new deadlock-free operations that execute atomically. By contrast, *pessimistic synchronization*, where each access to some location x blocks further accesses to x, is harder to program with [30, 31] and hampers reusability [16, 18].

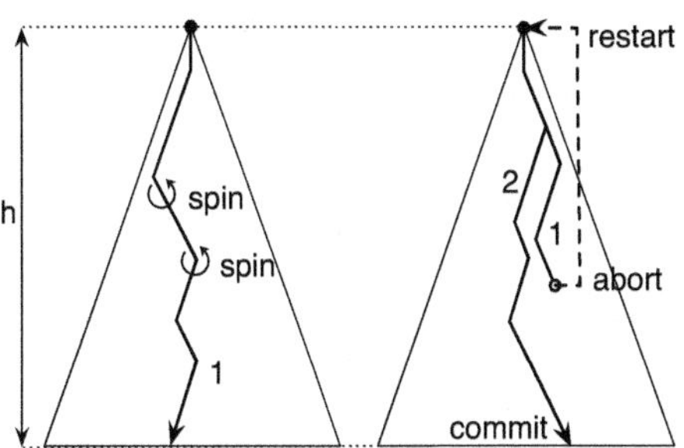

Figure 1. A balanced search tree whose complexity, in terms of the amount of accessed elements, is **(left)** proportional to h in a pessimistic execution and **(right)** proportional to the number of restarts in an optimistic execution

Yet it is unclear how one can adapt a data structure to access it efficiently through transactions. As a drawback of the simplicity of using transactions, the existing transactional programs spanning from low level libraries to topmost applications directly derive from sequential or pessimistically synchronized programs. The impacts of optimistic synchronization on the execution is simply ignored.

To illustrate the difference between optimistic and pessimistic synchronizations consider the example of Figure 1 depicting their step complexity when traversing a tree of height h from its root to a leaf node. On the left, steps are executed pessimistically, potentially spinning before being able to acquire a lock, on the path converging towards the leaf node. On the right, steps are executed optimistically and some of them may abort and restart, depending on concurrent thread steps. The pessimistic execution of each thread is guaranteed to execute $O(h)$ steps, yet the optimistic one may need to execute $\Omega(hr)$ steps, where r is the number of restarts. Note that r depends on the probability of conflicts with concurrent transactions that depends, in turn, on the transaction length and h. Although it is clear that a transaction must be aborted before violating the abstraction implemented by this tree, e.g., inserting k successfully in a set where k already exists, it is unclear whether a transaction must be aborted before slightly unbalancing the tree implementation to strictly preserve the balance invariant.

PPoPP'12, February 25–29, 2012, New Orleans, Louisiana, USA.

We introduce a *speculation-friendly* tree as a tree that transiently breaks its balance structural invariant without hampering the abstraction consistency in order to speed up transaction-based accesses. Here are our contributions.

- We propose a speculation-friendly binary search tree data structure implementing an associative array and a set abstractions and decoupling the operations that modify the abstraction (we call these *abstract transactions*) from operations that modify the tree structure itself but not the abstraction (we call these *structural transactions*). An abstract transaction either inserts or deletes an element from the abstraction and in certain cases the insertion might also modify the tree structure. Some structural transactions rebalance the tree by executing a distributed rotation mechanism: each of these transactions executes a local rotation involving only a constant number of neighboring nodes. Some other structural transactions unlink and free a node that was logically deleted by a former abstract transaction.
- We prove the correctness (i.e., linearizability) of our tree and we compare its performance against existing transaction-based versions of an AVL tree and a red-black tree, widely used to evaluate transactions [7, 11, 13, 14, 19, 21, 34]. The speculation-friendly tree improves by up to 1.6× the performance of the AVL tree on the micro-benchmark and by up to 3.5× the performance of the built-in red-black tree on a travel reservation application, already well-engineered for transactions. Finally, our speculation-friendly tree performs similarly to a non-rotating tree but remains robust in face of non-uniform workloads.
- We illustrate (i) the portability of our speculation-friendly tree by evaluating it on two different Transactional Memories (TMs), TinySTM [14] and $\mathscr{E}$-STM [15] and with different configuration settings, hence outlining that our performance benefit is independent from the transactional algorithm it uses; and (ii) its reusability by composing straightforwardly the remove and insert into a new move operation. In addition, we compare the benefit of relaxing data structures into speculation-friendly ones against the benefit of only relaxing transactions, by evaluating elastic transactions. It shows that, for a particular data structure, refactoring its algorithm is preferable to refactoring the underlying transaction algorithm.

The paper is organized as follows. In Section 2 we describe the problem related to the use of transactions in existing balanced trees. In Section 3 we present our speculation-friendly binary search tree. In Section 4 we evaluate our tree experimentally and illustrate its portability and reusability. In Section 5 we describe the related work and Section 6 concludes.

2. The Problem with Balanced Trees

In this section, we focus our attention on the structural invariant of existing tree libraries, namely the *balance*, and enlighten the impact of their restructuring, namely the *rebalancing*, on contention.

Trees provide logarithmic access time complexity given that they are balanced, meaning that among all downward paths from the root to a leaf, the length of the shortest path is not far apart the length of the longest path. Upon tree update, if their difference exceeds a given threshold, the structural invariant is broken and a rebalancing is triggered to restructure accordingly. This threshold depends on the considered algorithm: AVL trees [1] do not tolerate the longest length to exceed the shortest by 2 whereas red-black trees [4] tolerate the longest to be twice the shortest, thus restructuring less frequently. Yet in both cases the restructuring is triggered immediately when the threshold is reached to hide the imbalance from further operations.

Generally, one takes an existing tree algorithm and encapsulates all its accesses within transactions to obtain a concurrent tree whose accesses are guaranteed atomic (i.e., linearizable), however, the obtained concurrent transactions likely *conflict* (i.e., one accesses the same location another is modifying), resulting in the need to abort one of these transactions which leads to a significant waste of efforts. This is in part due to the fact that encapsulating an *update* operation (i.e., an insert or a remove operation) into a transaction boils down to encapsulating four phases in the same transaction:

1. the modification of the abstraction,
2. the corresponding structural adaptation,
3. a check to detect whether the threshold is reached and
4. the potential rebalancing.

A transaction-based red-black tree An example is the transaction-based binary search tree developed by Oracle Labs (formerly Sun Microsystems) and other researchers to extensively evaluate transactional memories [7, 11, 13, 14, 19, 21, 34] . This library relies on the classical red-black tree algorithm that bounds the step complexity of pessimistic insert/delete/contains. It has been slightly optimized for transactions by removing sentinel nodes to reduce false-conflicts, and we are aware of two benchmark-suite distributions that integrate it, STAMP [7] and synchrobench[1].

Each of its update transactions encapsulate all the four phases given above even though phase (1) could be decoupled from phases (3) and (4) if transient violations of the balance invariant were tolerated. Such a decoupling is appealing given that phase (4) is subject to conflicts. In fact, the algorithm balances the tree by executing rotations starting from the position where a node is inserted or deleted and possibly going all the way up to the root. As depicted in Figure 2(a) and (b), a rotation consists of replacing the node where the rotation occurs by the child and adding this replaced node to one of its subtrees. A node cannot be accessed concurrently by an abstract transaction and a rotation, otherwise the abstract transaction might miss the node it targets while being rotated downward. Similarly, rotations cannot access common nodes as one rotation may unbalance the others.

Moreover, the red-black tree does not allow any abstract transaction to access a node that is concurrently being deleted from the abstraction because phases (1) and (2) are tightly coupled within the same transaction. If this was allowed the abstract transaction might end up on the node that is no longer part of the tree. Fortunately, if the modification operation is a deletion then phase (1) can be decoupled from the structural modification of phase (2) by marking the targeted node as logically deleted in phase (1) effectively removing it from the set abstraction prior to unlinking it physically in phase (2). This improvement is important as it lets a concurrent abstract transaction travel through the node concurrently being logically deleted in phase (1) without conflicting. Making things worse, without decoupling these four phases, having to abort within phase (4) would typically require the three previous phases to restart as well. Finally without decoupling only contains operations are guaranteed not to conflict with each other. With decoupling, insert/delete/contains do not conflict with each other unless they terminate on the same node as described in Section 3.

To conclude, for the transactions to preserve the atomicity and invariants of such a tree algorithm, they typically have to keep track of a large *read set* and *write set*, i.e., the sets of accessed memory locations that are protected by a transaction. Possessing large read/write sets increases the probability of conflicts and thus reduces concurrency. This is especially problematic in trees because the distribution of nodes in the read/write set is skewed so that the

[1] http://lpd.epfl.ch/gramoli/php/synchrobench.php

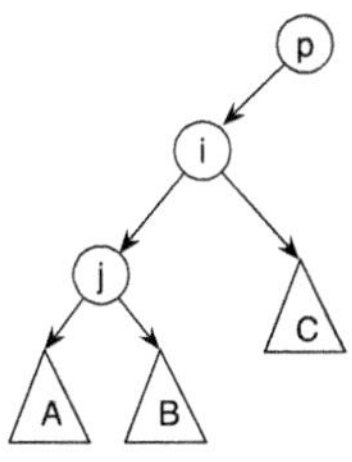

(a) Initial tree

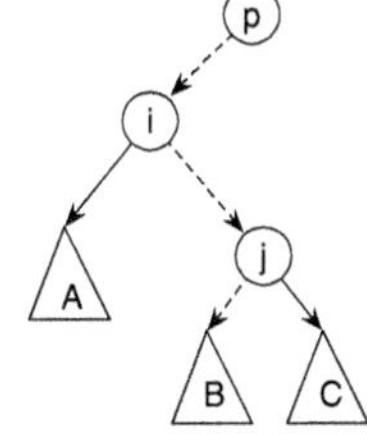

(b) Result of a classical right rotation

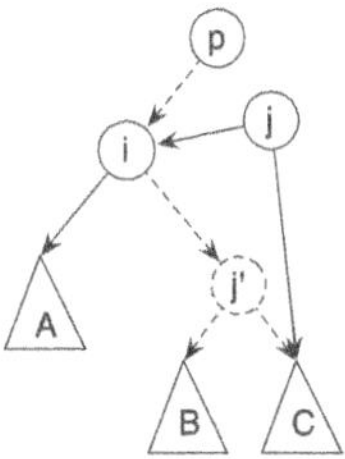

(c) Result of the new right rotation

Figure 2. The classical rotation modifies node j in the tree and forces a concurrent traversal at this node to backtrack; the new rotation left j unmodified, adds j' and postpones the physical deletion of j

probability of the node being in the set is much higher for nodes near the root and the root is guaranteed to be in the read set.

Illustration To briefly illustrate the effect of tightly coupling update operations on the step complexity of classical transactional balanced trees we have counted the maximal number of reads necessary to complete typical insert/remove/contains operations. Note that this number includes the reads executed by the transaction each time it aborts in addition to the read set size of the transaction obtained at commit time.

Update	0%	10%	20%	30%	40%	50%
AVL tree	29	415	711	1008	1981	2081
Oracle red-black tree	31	573	965	1108	1484	1545
Speculation-friendly tree	29	75	123	120	144	180

Table 1. Maximum number of transactional reads per operation on three 2^{12}-sized balanced search trees as the update ratio increases

We evaluated the aforementioned red-black tree, an AVL tree, and our speculation-friendly tree on a 48-core machine using the same transactional memory (TM) algorithm[2]. The expectation of the tree sizes is fixed to 2^{12} during the experiments by performing an insert and a remove with the same probability. Table 1 depicts the maximum number of transactional reads per operation observed among 48 concurrent threads as we increase the update ratio, i.e., the proportion of insert/remove operations over contains operations.

For all three trees, the transactional read complexity of an operation increases with the update ratio due to the additional aborted efforts induced by the contention. Althought the red-black and the AVL trees objective is to keep the complexity of pessimistic accesses $O(\log_2 n)$ (proportional to 12 in this case), where n is the tree size, the read complexity of optimistic accesses grows significantly (14× more at 10% update than at 0%, where there are no aborts) as the contention increases. As described in the sequel, the speculation-friendly tree succeeds in limiting the step complexity raise (2.6× more at 10% update) of data structure accesses when compared against the transactional versions of state-of-the-art tree algorithms. An optimization further reducing the number of transactional reads between 2 (for 10% updates) and 18 (for 50% updates) is presented in Section 3.3.

3. The Speculation-Friendly Binary Search Tree

We introduce the speculation-friendly binary search tree by describing its implementation of an associative array abstraction, mapping a key to a value. In short, the tree speeds up the access transactions by decoupling two conflict-prone operations: the node deletion and the tree rotation. Although these two techniques have been used for decades in the context of data management [12, 25], our algorithm novelty lies in applying their combination to reduce transaction aborts. We first depict, in Algorithm 1, the pseudocode that looks like sequential code encapsulated within transactions before presenting, in Algorithm 2, more complex optimizations.

3.1 Decoupling the tree rotation

The motivation for rotation decoupling stems from two separate observations: (i) a rotation is tied to the modification that triggers it, hence the process modifying the tree is also responsible for ensuring that its modification does not break the balance invariant and (ii) a rotation affects different parts of the tree, hence an isolated conflict can abort the rotation performed at multiple nodes. In response to these two issues we introduce a dedicated rotator thread to complete the modifying transactions faster and we distribute the rotation in multiple (node-)local transactions. Note that our rotating thread is similar to the collector thread proposed by Dijkstra et al. [12] to garbage collect stale nodes.

This decoupling allows the read set of the insert/delete operations to only contain the path from the root to the node(s) being modified and the write set to only contain the nodes that need to be modified in order to ensure the abstraction modification (i.e., the nodes at the bottom of the search path), thus reducing conflicts significantly. Let us consider a specific example. If rotations are performed within the insert/delete operations then each rotation increases the read and write set sizes. Take an insert operation that triggers a right rotation such as the one depicted in Figures 2(a)-2(b). Before the rotation the read set for the nodes p,j,i is $\{p.\ell, j.r\}$, where ℓ and r represent the left and right pointers, and the write set is $\emptyset$. Now with the rotation the read set becomes $\{p.\ell, i.r, j.\ell, j.r\}$ and the write set becomes $\{p.\ell, i.r, j.\ell\}$ as denoted in the figure by dashed arrows. Due to $p.\ell$ being modified, any concurrent transaction that traverses any part of this section of the tree (including all nodes i, j, and subtrees A, B, C, D) will have a read/write conflict with this transaction. In the worst case an insert/delete operation triggers rotations all the way up to the root resulting in conflicts with all concurrent transactions.

Rotation As previously described, rotations are not required to ensure the atomicity of the insert/delete/contains operations so it is not necessary to perform rotations in the same transaction as the insert or delete. Instead we dedicate a separate thread that continuously checks for unbalances and rotates accordingly within its own node-local transactions.

More specifically, neither do the insert/delete operations comprise any rotation, nor do the rotations execute on a large block of

[2] TinySTM-CTL, i.e., with lazy acquirement [14].

Algorithm 1 A Portable Speculation-Friendly Binary Search Tree

```
1:  State of node n:
2:     node a record with fields:
3:        k ∈ ℕ, the node key
4:        v ∈ ℕ, the node value
5:        ℓ, r ∈ ℕ, left/right child pointers, initially ⊥
6:        left-h, right-h ∈ ℕ, local height of left/right
7:           child, initially 0
8:        local-h ∈ ℕ, expected local height, initially 1
9:        del ∈ {true, false}, indicate whether
10:          logically deleted, initially false

11: State of process p:
12:    root, shared pointer to root

13: find(k)_p:
14:    next ← root
15:    while true do
16:       curr ← next
17:       val ← curr.k
18:       if val = k then break
19:       if val > k then next ← read(curr.r)
20:       else next ← read(curr.ℓ)
21:       if next = ⊥ then break
22:    return curr

23: contains(k)_p:
24:    transaction {
25:       result ← true
26:       curr ← find(k)
27:       if curr.k ≠ k then result ← false
28:       else if read(curr.del) then result ← false
29:    } // current transaction tries to commit
30:    return result

31: insert(k, v)_p:
32:    transaction {
33:       result ← true
34:       curr ← find(k)
35:       if curr.k = k then
36:          if read(curr.del) then write(curr.del, false)
37:          else result ← false
38:       else // allocate a new node
39:          new.k ← k
40:          new.v ← v
41:          if curr.k > k then write(curr.r, new)
42:          else write(curr.ℓ, new)
43:    } // current transaction tries to commit
44:    return result

45: right_rotate(parent, left-child)_p:
46:    transaction {
47:       if left-child then n ← read(parent.ℓ)
48:       else n ← read(parent.r)
49:       if n = ⊥ then return false
50:       ℓ ← read(n.ℓ)
51:       if ℓ = ⊥ then return false
52:       ℓr ← read(ℓ.r)
53:       write(n.ℓ, ℓr)
54:       write(ℓ.r, n)
55:       if left-child then write(parent.ℓ, ℓ)
56:       else write(parent.r, ℓ)
57:       update-balance-values()
58:    } // current transaction tries to commit
59:    return true

60: delete(k)_p:
61:    transaction {
62:       result ← true
63:       curr ← find(k)
64:       if curr.k ≠ k then
65:          result ← false
66:       else
67:          if read(curr.del) then result ← false
68:          else write(curr.del, true)
69:    } // current transaction tries to commit
70:    return result

71: remove(parent, left-child)_p:
72:    transaction {
73:       if left-child then
74:          n ← read(parent.ℓ)
75:       else
76:          n ← read(parent.r)
77:       if n = ⊥ or ¬read(n.del) then return false
78:       if (child ← read(n.ℓ)) ≠ ⊥ then
79:          if (child ← read(n.r)) ≠ ⊥ then return false
80:       if left-child then
81:          write(parent.ℓ, child)
82:       else
83:          write(parent.r, child)
84:       update-balance-values()
85:    } // current transaction tries to commit
86:    return true
```

nodes. Hence, local rotations that occur near the root can still cause a large amount of conflicts, but rotations performed further down the tree are less subject to conflict. If local rotations are performed in a single transaction block then even the rotations that occur further down the tree will be part of a likely conflicting transaction, so instead each local rotation is performed as a single transaction. Keeping the insert/delete/contains and rotate/remove operations as small as possible allows more operations to execute at the same time without conflicts, increasing concurrency.

Performing local rotations rather than global ones has other benefits. If rotations are performed as blocks then, due to concurrent insert/delete operations, not all of the rotations may still be valid once the transaction commits. Each concurrent insert/delete operation might require a certain set of rotations to balance the tree, but because the operations are happening concurrently the appropriate rotations to balance the tree are constantly changing and since each operation only has a partial view of the tree it might not know what the appropriate rotations are. With local rotations, each time a rotation is performed it uses the most up-to-date local information avoiding repeating rotations at the same location.

The actual code for the rotation is straightforward. Each rotation is performed just as it would be performed in a sequential binary tree (see Figure 2(a)-2(b)), but within a transaction.

Deciding when to perform a rotation is done based on local balance information omitted from the pseudocode. This technique was introduced in [5] and works as follows. *left-h* (resp. *right-h*) is a node-local variable to keep track of the estimated height of the left (resp. right) subtree. *local-h* (also a node-local variable) is always 1 larger than the maximum value of *left-h* and *right-h*. If the difference between *left-h* and *right-h* is greater than 1 then a rotation is triggered. After the rotation these values are updated as indicated by a dedicated function (line 57). Since these values are local to the node the estimated heights of the subtrees might not always be accurate. The propagate operation (described in the next paragraph) is used to update the estimated heights. Using the propagate operation and local rotations, the tree is guaranteed to be eventually perfectly balanced as in [5, 6].

Propagation The rotating thread executes continuously a depth-first traversal to propagate the balance information. Although it might propagate an outdated height information due to concurrency, the tree gets eventually balanced. The only requirement is that a node knows when it has an empty subtree (i.e., when *node.ℓ* is ⊥, *node.left-h* must be 0). This requirement is guaranteed since a new node is always added to the tree with *left-h* and *right-h* set to 0 and these values are updated when a node is removed or a rotation takes place. Each propagate operation is performed as a sequence of distributed transactions each acting on a single node. Such a transaction first travels to the left and right child nodes, checking their *local-h* values and using these values to update *left-h*, *right-h*, and *local-h* of the parent node. As no abstract transactions access these three values, they never conflict with propagate operations (unless the transactional memory used is inherently prone to false-sharing).

Limitations Unfortunately, spreading rotations and modifications into distinct transactions still does not allow insert/delete/contains operations that are being performed on separate keys to execute concurrently. Consider a delete operation that deletes a node at the root. In order to remove this node a successor is taken from the bottom of the tree so that it becomes the new root. This now creates a point of contention at the root and where the successor was removed. Every concurrent transaction that accesses the tree will have a read/write conflict with this transaction. Below we discuss how to address this issue.

3.2 Decoupling the node deletion

The speculation-friendly binary search tree exploits logical deletion to further reduce the amount of transaction conflicts. This two-phase deletion technique has been previously used for memory management like in [25], for example, to reduce locking in database indexes. Each node has a *deleted* flag, initialized to false when the node is inserted into the tree. First, the delete phase consists of removing the given key k from the abstraction—it logically deletes a node by setting a *deleted* flag to true (line 68). Second, the remove phase physically deletes the node from the tree to prevent it from growing too large. Each of these are performed as a separate transaction and the rotating thread is also responsible for garbage collecting nodes (cf. Section 3.4).

The deletion decoupling reduces conflicts by two means. First, it spreads out the two deletion phases in two separate transactions, hence reducing the size of the delete transaction. Second, deleting logically node i simply consists in setting the *deleted* flag to true (line 68), thus avoiding conflicts with concurrent abstract transactions that have traversed i.

Find The find operation is a helper function called implicitly by other functions within a transaction, thus it is never called explicitly by the application programmer. This operation looks for a given key k by parsing the tree similarly to a sequential code. At each node it goes right if the key of the node is larger than k (line 19), otherwise it goes left (line 20). Starting from the root it continues until it either finds a node with k (line 18) or until it reaches a leaf (line 21) returning the node (line 22). Notice that if it reaches a leaf, it has performed a transactional read on the child pointer of this leaf (lines 19–20), ensuring that some other concurrent transaction will not insert a node with key k.

Contains The contains operation first executes the find starting from the root, this returns a node (line 26). If the key of the node returned is equal to the key being searched for, then it performs a transactional read of the *deleted* flag (line 28). If the flag is false the operation returns true, otherwise it returns false. If the key of the returned node is not equal to the key being searched for then a node with the key being searched for is not in the tree and false is returned (lines 27 and 30).

Insertion The insert(k, v) operation uses the find procedure that returns a node (line 34). If a node is found with the same *key* as the one being searched for then the *deleted* flag is checked using a transactional read (line 36). If the flag is false then the tree already contains k and false is returned (lines 37 and 44). If the flag is true then the flag is updated to false (line 36) and true is returned. Otherwise if the *key* of the node returned is not equal to k then a new node is allocated and added as the appropriate child of the node returned by the find operation (lines 38-42). Notice that only in this final case does the operation modify the structure of the tree.

Logical deletion The delete uses also the find procedure in order to locate the node to be deleted (line 63). A transactional read is then performed on the *deleted* flag (line 67). If *deleted* is true then the operation returns false (lines 67 and 70), if *deleted* is false it is set to true (line 68) and the operation returns true. If the find procedure does not return a node with the same *key* as the one being searched for then false is returned (line 65 and 70). Notice that this operation never modifies the tree structure.

Consequently, the insert/delete/contains operations can only conflict with each other in two cases.

1. Two insert/delete/contains operations are being performed concurrently on some key k and a node with key k exists in the tree. Here (if at least one of the operations is an insert or delete) there will be a read/write conflict on the node's *deleted* flag. Note that there will be no conflict with any other concurrent operation that is being done on a different key.
2. An insert that is being performed for some key k where no node with key k exists in the tree. Here the insert operation will add a new node to the tree, and will have a read/write conflict with any operation that had read the pointer when it was $\perp$ (before it was changed to point to the new node).

Physical removal Removing a node that has no children is as simple as unlinking the node from its parent (lines 81–83). Removing a node that has 1 child is done by just unlinking it from its parent, then linking its parent to its child (also lines 81–83). Each of these removal procedures is a very small transaction, only performing a single transactional write. This transaction conflicts only with concurrent transactions that read the link from the parent before it is changed.

Upon removal of a node i with two children, the node in the tree with the immediately larger key than i's must be found at the bottom of the tree. This performs reads on all the way to the leaf and a write at the parent of i, creating a conflict with any operation that has traversed this node. Fortunately, in practice such removals are not necessary. In fact only nodes with no more than one child are removed from the tree (if the node has two children, the remove operation returns without doing anything, cf. line 79). It turns out that removing nodes with no more than one children is enough to keep the tree from growing so large that it affects performance.

The removal operation is performed by the maintenance thread. While it is traversing the tree performing rotation and propogate operations it also checks for logically deleted nodes to be removed.

Limitations The traversal phase of most functions is prone to false-conflicts, as it comprises read operations that do not actually need to return values from the same snapshot. Specifically, by the time a traversal transaction reaches a leaf, the value it read at the root likely no longer matters, thus a conflict with a concurrent root update could simply be ignored. Nevertheless, the standard TM interface forces all transactions to adopt the same strongest semantics prone to false-conflicts [16]. In the next paragraphs we discuss how to extend the basic TM interface to cope with such false-conflicts.

3.3 Optional improvements

In previous sections, we have described a speculation-friendly tree that fulfills the standard TM interface [22] for the sake of portability across a large body of research work on TM. Now, we propose to further reduce aborts related to the rotation and the find operation at the cost of an additional lightweight read operation, uread, that breaks this interface. This optimization is thus usable only in TM systems providing additional explicit calls and do not aim at replacing but complementing the previous algorithm to preserve its portability. This optimization complementing Algorithm 1 is depicted in Algorithm 2, it does not affect the existing contains/insert/delete operations besides speeding up their internal find operation. Here the left rotation is not the exact symmetry of the right rotation code. Please refer to the technical report [9] for a desciption of this subtlety.

Lightweight reads The key idea is to avoid validating superfluous read accesses when an operation traverses the tree structure. This idea has been exploited by elastic transactions that use a bounded buffer instead of a read set to validate only immediately preceding reads, thus implementing a form of hand-over-hand locking transaction for search structure [15]. We could have used different extensions to implement these optimizations. DSTM [21] proposes early release to force a transaction stop keeping track of a read set entry. Alternatively, the current distribution of TinySTM [14] comprises

Algorithm 2 Optimizations to the Speculation-Friendly Binary Search Tree

```
1:  State of node n:
2:    node the same record with an extra field:
3:      rem ∈ {true, false} indicate whether
4:        physically deleted, initially false

5:  remove(parent, left-child)_p:
6:    transaction {
7:      if read(parent.rem) then return false
8:      if left-child then
9:        n ← read(parent.ℓ)
10:     else
11:       n ← read(parent.r)
12:     if n = ⊥ or ¬read(n.deleted) then return false
13:     if (child ← read(n.ℓ)) ≠ ⊥ then
14:       if read(n.r) ≠ ⊥ then return false
15:     else
16:       child ← read(n.r)
17:     if left-child then
18:       write(parent.ℓ, child)
19:     else
20:       write(parent.r, child)
21:     write(n.ℓ, parent)
22:     write(n.r, parent)
23:     write(n.rem, true)
24:     update-balance-values()
25:   } // current transaction tries to commit
26:   return true

27: find(k)_p:
28:   curr ← root
29:   next ← root
30:   rem ← true
31:   while true do
32:     while true do
33:       parent ← curr
34:       curr ← next
35:       val ← curr.k
36:       if val = k then
37:         if ¬(rem ← read(curr.rem)) then break
38:       if val > k then next ← uread(curr.r)
39:       else next ← uread(curr.ℓ)
40:       if next = ⊥ then
41:         if ¬(rem ← read(curr.rem)) then
42:           if val > k then next ← read(curr.r)
43:           else next ← read(curr.ℓ)
44:           if next = ⊥ then break
45:         else
46:           if val ≤ k then next ← uread(curr.r)
47:           else next ← uread(curr.ℓ)
48:     if curr.k > parent.k then tmp ← read(parent.r)
49:     else tmp ← read(parent.ℓ)
50:     if curr = tmp then
51:       break
52:     else
53:       next ← curr
54:       curr ← parent
55:   return curr

56: right_rotate(parent, left-child)_p:
57:   transaction {
58:     if read(parent.rem) then
59:       return false
60:     if left-child then
61:       n ← read(parent.ℓ)
62:     else
63:       n ← read(parent.r)
64:     if n = ⊥ then
65:       return false
66:     ℓ ← read(n.ℓ)
67:     if ℓ = ⊥ then
68:       return false
69:     ℓr ← read(ℓ.r)
70:     r ← read(n.r)
71:     // allocate a new node
72:     new.k ← n.k
73:     new.ℓ ← ℓr
74:     new.r ← r
75:     write(ℓ.r, new)
76:     write(n.rem, true)
77:     if left-child then
78:       write(parent.ℓ, ℓ)
79:     else
80:       write(parent.r, ℓ)
81:     update-balance-values()
82:   } // current transaction tries to commit
83:   return true
```

unit loads that do not record anything in the read set. While we could have used any of these approaches to increase concurrency we have chosen the unit loads of TinySTM, hence the name uread. This uread returns the most recent value written to memory by a committed transaction by potentially spin-waiting on the location until it stops being concurrently modified.

A first interesting result, is that the read/write set sizes can be kept at a size of $O(k)$ instead of the $O(k \log n)$ obtained with the previous tree algorithm, where k is the number of nested contains/insert/delete operations nested in a transaction. The reasoning behind this is as follow: Upon success, a contains only needs to ensure that the node it found is still in the tree when the transaction commits, and can ignore the state of other nodes it had traversed. Upon failure, it only needs to ensure that the node i it is looking for is not in the tree when the transaction commits, this requires to check whether the pointer from the parent that would point to i is $\bot$ (i.e., this pointer should be in the read set of the transaction and its value is $\bot$). In a similar vein, insert and delete only need to validate the position in the tree where they aimed at inserting or deleting. Therefore, contains/insert/delete only increases the size of the read/write set by a constant instead of a logarithmic amount.

It is worth mentioning that ureads have a further advantage over normal reads other than making conflicts less likely: Classical reads are more expensive to perform than unit reads. This is because in addition to needing to store a list keeping track of the reads done so far, an opaque TM that uses invisible reads needs to perform validation of the read set with a worst case cost of $O(s^2)$, where s is the size of the read set, whereas a TM that uses visible reads performs a modification to shared memory for each read.

Rotation Rotations remain conflict-prone in Algorithm 1 as they incur a conflict when crossing the region of the tree traversed by a contains/insert/delete operation. If ureads are used in the contains/insert/delete operations then rotations will only conflict with these operations if they finish at one of the two nodes that are rotated by rotation operation (for example in Figure 2(a) this would be the node i or j). A rotation at the root will only conflict with a contains/insert/delete that finished at (or at the rotated child of) the root, any operations that travel further down the tree will not conflict.

Figure 2(c) displays the result of the new rotation that is slightly different than the previous one. Instead of modifying j directly, j is unlinked from its parent (effectively removing it from the tree, lines 78–80) and a new node j' is created (line 71), taking j's place in the tree (lines 78–80). During the rotation j has a removed flag that is set to true (line 76), letting concurrent operations know that j is no longer in the tree but its deallocation is postponed. Now consider a concurrent operation that is traversing the tree and is preempted on j during the rotation. If a normal rotation is performed the concurrent operation will either have to backtrack or the transaction would have to abort (as the node it is searching for might be in the subtree A). Using the new rotation, the preempted operation will still have a path to A.

Find, contains and delete The interesting point for the find operation is that the search continues until it finds a node with the *removed* flag set to false (line 37 and 41). Once the leaf or a node with the same key as the one being searched for is reached, a transactional read is performed on the *removed* flag to ensure that the node is not removed from the tree (by some other operation) at least until the transaction commits. If *removed* is true then the operation continues traversing the tree, otherwise the correct node has been found. Next, if the node is a leaf, a transactional read must be performed on the appropriate child pointer to ensure this node remains a leaf throughout the transaction (lines 42–43). If this read does not return $\bot$ then the operation continues traversing the tree. Otherwise the operation then leaves the nested while loop (lines 37 and 44), but the find operation does not return yet.

One additional transactional read must be performed to ensure safety. This is the read of the parent's pointer to the node about to be returned (lines 48–49). If this read does not return the same node as found previously, the find operation continues parsing the tree starting from the parent (lines 53–54). Otherwise the process leaves the while loop (line 51) and the node is returned (line 55).

The advantage of this updated find operation is that ureads are used to traverse the tree, it only uses transactional reads to ensure atomicity when it reaches what is suspected to be the last node it has to traverse. The original algorithm exclusively uses transactional reads to traverse the tree and because of this, modifications to the structure of the tree that occur along the traversed path cause conflicts, which do not occur in the updated algorithm. The contains/insert/delete operations themselves are identical in both algorithms.

Removal The remove operation requires some modification to ensure safety when using ureads during the traversal phase. Normally if a contains/insert/delete operation is preempted on a node that is removed then that operation will have to backtrack or abort the transaction. This can be avoided as follows. When a node is removed, its left and right child pointers are set to point to its previous parent (lines 21–22). This provides a preempted operation with a path back to the tree. The removed node also has its *removed* flag set to true (line 23) letting preempted operations know it is no longer in the tree (the node is left to be freed later by garbage collection).

3.4 Garbage collection

As explained previously, there is always a single rotator thread that continuously executes a recursive depth first traversal. It updates the local, left and right heights of each node and performs a rotation or removal if necessary. Nodes that are successfully removed are then added to a garbage collection list. Each application thread maintains a boolean indicating a pending operation and a counter indicating the number of completed operations. Before starting a traversal, the rotator thread sets a pointer to what is currently the end of the garbage collection list and copies all booleans and counters. After a traversal, if for every thread its counter has increased or if its boolean is false then the nodes up to the previously stored end pointer can be safely freed. Experimentally, we found that the size of the list was never larger than a small fraction of the size of the tree but theoretically we expect the total space required to remain linear in the tree size.

3.5 Correctness

THEOREM 1. *The* insert, contains *and* delete *operations of Algorithm 1 with optimizations from Algorithm 2 are linearizable.*

By lack of space, the proof of Theorem 1 has been deferred to the companion technical report [9]. In short, the key argument lies in showing that the tree remains routable at any time despite concurrent modifications.

4. Experimental Evaluation

We experimented our library by integrating it in (i) a micro-benchmark of the synchrobench suite to get a precise understanding of the performance causes and in (ii) the tree-based vacation reservation system of the STAMP suite and whose runs sometimes exceed half an hour. The machine used for our experiments is a four AMD Opteron 12-core Processor 6172 at 2.1 Ghz with 32 GB of RAM running Linux 2.6.32, thus comprising 48 cores in total.

4.1 Testbed choices

We evaluate our tree against well-engineered tree algorithms especially dedicated to transactional workloads. The red-black tree is a mature implementation developed and improved by expert programmers from Oracle Labs and others to show good performance of TM in numerous papers [7, 11, 13, 14, 19, 21, 34]. The observed

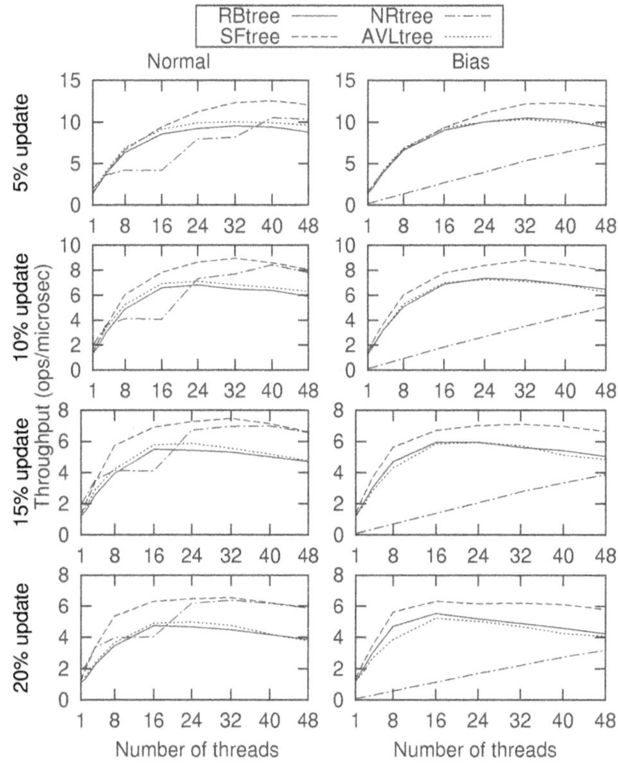

Figure 3. Comparing the AVL tree (AVLtree), the red-black tree (RBtree), the no-restructuring tree (NRtree) against the speculation-friendly tree (SFtree) on an integer set micro-benchmark with from 5% **(top)** to 20% updates **(bottom)** under normal **(left)** and biased **(right)** workloads

performance is generally scalable when contention is low, most of integer set benchmarks on which they are tested consider the ratio of attempted updates instead of effective updates. To avoid the misleading (attempted) update ratios that capture the number of calls to potentially updating operations, we consider the *effective* update ratios of synchrobench counting only modifications and ignoring the operations that fail (e.g., remove may fail in finding its parameter value thus failing in modifying the data structure).

The AVL tree we evaluate (as well as the aforementioned red-black tree) is part of STAMP [7]. As mentioned before one of the main refactoring of this red-black tree implementation is to avoid the use of sentinel nodes that would produce false-conflicts within transactions. This improvement could be considered a first-step towards obtaining a speculation-friendly binary search tree, however, the modification-restructuring, which remains tightly coupled, prevents scalability to high levels of parallelism.

To evaluate performance we ran the micro-benchmark and the vacation application with 1, 2, 4, 8, 16, 24, 32, 40, 48 application threads. For the micro-benchmark, we averaged the data over three runs of 10 seconds each. For the vacation application, we averaged the data over three runs as well but we used the recommended default settings and some runs exceeded half an hour because of the amount of transactions used. We carefully verified that the variance was sufficiently low for the result to be meaningful.

4.2 Biased workloads and the effect of restructuring

In this section, we evaluate the performance of our speculation-friendly tree on an integer set micro-benchmark providing remove,

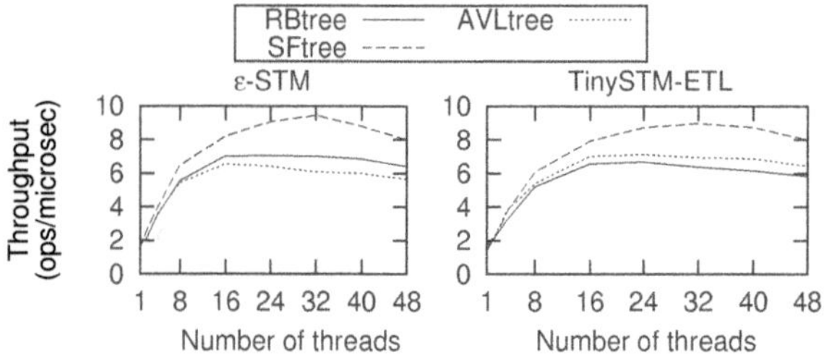

Figure 4. The speculation-friendly library running with **(left)** another TM library ($\mathcal{E}$-STM) and with **(right)** the previous TM library in a different configuration (TinySTM-ETL, i.e., with eager acquirement)

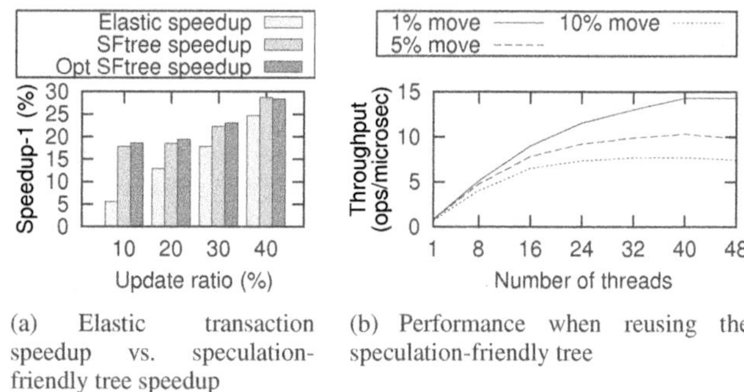

(a) Elastic transaction speedup vs. speculation-friendly tree speedup

(b) Performance when reusing the speculation-friendly tree

Figure 5. Elastic transaction comparison and reusability

insert, and contains operations, similarly to the benchmark used to evaluate state-of-the-art TM algorithms [10, 14, 15]. We implemented two set libraries that we added to the synchrobench distribution: our non-optimized speculation-friendly tree and a baseline tree that is similar but never rebalances the structure whatever modifications occur. Figure 3 depicts the performance obtained from four different binary search trees: the red-black tree (RBtree), our speculation-friendly tree without optimizations (SFtree), the no-restructuring tree (NRtree) and the AVL tree (AVLtree).

The performance is expressed as the number of operations executed per microsecond. The update ratio varies between 5% and 20%. As we obtained similar results with 2^{10}, 2^{12} and 2^{14} elements, we only report the results obtained from an initialized set of 2^{12} elements. The biased workload consists of inserting (resp. deleting) random values skewed towards high (resp. low) numbers in the value range: the values always taken from a range of 2^{14} are skewed with a fixed probability by incrementing (resp. decrementing) with an integer uniformly taken within [0..9].

On both the normal (uniformly distributed) and biased workloads, the speculation-friendly tree scales well up to 32/40 threads. The no-restructuring tree performance drops to a linear shape under the biased workload as expected: as it does not rebalance, the complexity increases with the length of the longest path from the root to a leaf that, in turn, increases with the number of performed updates. In contrast, the speculation-friendly tree can only be unbalanced during a transient period of time which is too short to affect the performance even under biased workloads.

The speculation-friendly tree improves both the red-black tree and the AVL tree performance by up to 1.5× and 1.6×, respectively. The speculation-friendly tree is less prone to contention than AVL and red-black trees, which both share similar performance penalties due to contention.

4.3 Portability to other TM algorithms

The speculation-friendly tree is an inherently efficient data structure that is portable to any TM systems. It fulfills the TM interface standardized in [22] and thus does not require the presence of explicit escape mechanisms like early release [21] or snap [8] to avoid extra TM bookkeeping (our uread optimization being optional). Nor does it require high-level conflict detection, like open nesting [2, 26, 27] or transactional boosting [19]. Such improvements rely on explicit calls or user-defined abstract locks, and are not supported by existing TM compilers [22] which limits their portability. To make sure that the obtained results are not biased by the underlying TM algorithm, we evaluated the trees on top of $\mathcal{E}$-STM [15], another TM library (on a 2^{16} sized tree where $\mathcal{E}$-STM proved efficient), and on top of a different TM design from the one used so far: with eager acquirement.

The obtained results, depicted in Figure 4 look similar to the ones obtained with TinySTM-CTL (Figure 3) in that the speculation-friendly tree executes faster than other trees for all TM settings. This suggests that the improvement of speculation-friendly tree is potentially independent from the TM system used. A more detailed comparison of the improvement obtained using elastic transactions on red-black trees against the improvement of replacing the red-black tree by the speculation-friendly tree is depicted in Figure 5(a). It shows that the elastic improvements (15% on average) is lower than the speculation-friendly tree one (22% on average, be it optimized or not).

4.4 Reusability for specific application needs

We illustrate the reusability of the speculation-friendly tree by composing remove and insert from the existing interface to obtain a new atomic and deadlock-free move operation. Reusability is appealing to simplify concurrent programming by making it modular: a programmer can reuse a library without having to understand its synchronization internals. While reusability of sequential programs is straightforward, concurrent programs can generally be reused only if the programmer understands how each element is protected. For example, reusing a library can lead to deadlocks if shared data are locked in a different order than what is recommended by the library. Additionally, a lock-striping library may not conflict with a concurrent program that locks locations independently even though they protect common locations, thus leading to inconsistencies.

Figure 5(b) indicates the performance on workloads comprising 90% of read-only operations (including contains and failed updates) and 10% move/insert/delete effective update operations (among which from 1% to 10% are move operations). The performance decreases as more move operations execute, because a move protects more elements in the data structure than a simple insert or delete operation and during a longer period of time.

4.5 The vacation travel reservation application

We experiment our optimized library tree with a travel reservation application from the STAMP suite [7], called vacation. This application is suitable for evaluating concurrent binary search tree as it represents a database with four tables implemented as tree-based directories (cars, rooms, flights, and customers) accessed concurrently by client transactions.

Figure 6 depicts the execution time of the STAMP vacation application building on the Oracle red-black tree library (by default), our optimized speculation-friendly tree, and the baseline no-restructuring tree. We added the speedup obtained with each of these tree libraries over the performance of bare sequential code of

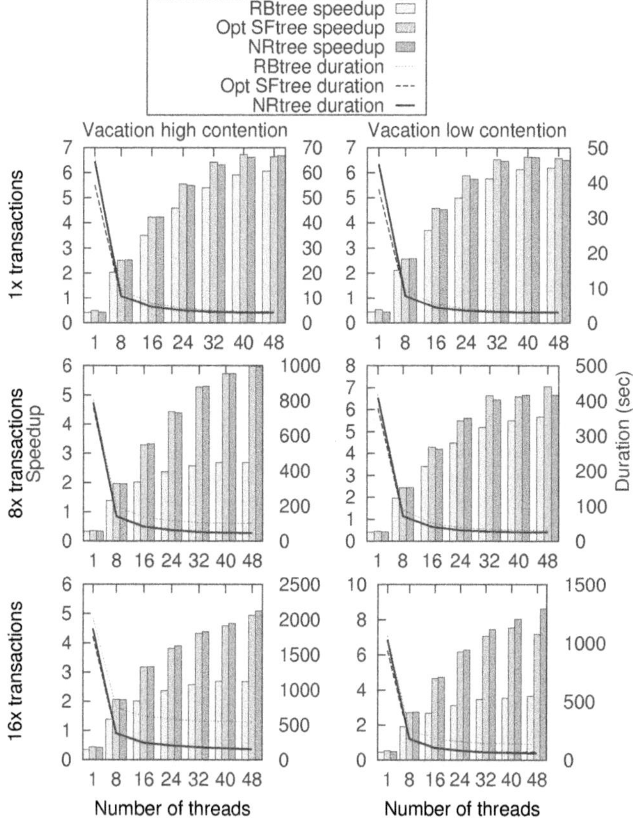

Figure 6. The speedup (over single-threaded sequential) and the corresponding duration of the vacation application built upon the red-black tree (RBtree), the optimized speculation-friendly tree (Opt SFtree) and the no-restructuring tree (NRtree) on **(left)** high contention and **(right)** low contention workloads, and with **(top)** the default number of transaction, **(middle)** 8× more transactions and **(bottom)** 16× more transactions

vacation without synchronization. (A concurrent tree library outperforms the sequential tree when its speedup exceeds 1.) The chosen workloads are the two default configurations ("low contention" and "high contention") taken from the STAMP release, with the default number of transactions, 8× more transactions than by default and 16× more, to increase the duration and the contention of the benchmark without using more threads than cores.

Vacation executes always faster on top of our speculation-friendly tree than on top of its built-in Oracle red-black tree. For example, the speculation-friendly tree improves performance by up to 1.3× with the default number of transactions and to 3.5× with 16× more transactions. The reason of this is twofold: (i) In contrast with the speculation-friendly tree, if an operation on the red-black tree traverses a location that is being deleted then this operation and the deletion conflict. (ii) Even though the Oracle red-black tree tolerates that the longest path from the root to a leaf can be twice as long as the shortest one, it triggers the rotation immediately after this threshold is reached. By contrast, our speculation-friendly tree keeps checking the unbalance to potentially rotate in the background. In particular, we observed on 8 threads in the high contention settings that the red-black tree vacation triggered around 130,000 rotations whereas the speculation-friendly vacation triggered only 50,000 rotations.

Finally, we observe that vacation presents similarly good performance on top of the no-restructuring tree library. In rare cases, the speculation-friendly tree outperforms the no-restructuring tree probably because the no-restructuring tree does not physically remove nodes from the tree, thus leading to a larger tree than the abstraction. Overall, their performance is comparable. With 16× the default number of transactions, the contention gets higher and rotations are more costly.

5. Related Work

Aside from the optimistic synchronization context, various relaxed balanced trees have been proposed. The idea of decoupling the update and the rebalancing was originally proposed by Guibas and Sedgewick [17] and was applied to AVL trees by Kessels [23], and Nurmi, Soisalon-Soininen and Wood [29], and to red-black trees by Nurmi and Soisalon-Soininen [28]. Manber and Ladner propose a lock-based tree whose rebalancing is the task of separate maintenance threads running with a low priority [24]. Bougé et al. [5] propose to lock a constant number of nodes within local rotations. The combination of local rotations executed by different threads self-stabilizes to a tree where no nodes are marked for removal. The main objective of these techniques is still to keep the tree depth low enough for the lock-based operations to be efficient. Such solutions do not apply to speculative operations due to aborts.

Ballard [3] proposes a relaxed red-black tree insertion well-suited for transactions. When an insertion unbalances the red-black tree it marks the inserted node rather than rebalancing the tree immediately. Another transaction encountering the marked node must rebalance the tree before restarting. The relaxed insertion was shown generally more efficient than the original insertion when run with DSTM [21] on 4 cores. Even though the solution limits the waste of effort per aborting rotation, it increases the number of restarts per rotation. By contrast, our local rotation does not require the rotating transaction to restart, hence benefiting both insertions and removals.

Bronson et al. [6] introduce an efficient object-oriented binary search tree. The algorithm uses underlying time-based TM principles to achieve good performance, however, its operations cannot be encapsulated within transactions. For example, a key optimization of this tree distinguishes whether a modification at some node i grows or shrinks the subtree rooted in i. A conflict involving a growth could be ignored as no descendant are removed and a `search` preempted at node i will safely resume in the resulting subtree. Such an optimization is not possible using TMs that track conflicts between read/write accesses to the shared memory. This implementation choice results in higher performance by avoiding the TM overhead, but limits reusability due to the lack of bookkeeping. For example, a programmer willing to implement a `size` operation would need to explicitly `clone` the data structure to disable the growth optimization. Therefore, the programmer of a concurrent application that builds upon this binary search tree library must be aware of the synchronization internals of this library (including the growth optimization) to reuse it.

Felber, Gramoli and Guerraoui [15] specify the elastic transactional model that ignores false conflicts but guarantees reusability. In the companion technical report, the red-black tree library from Oracle Labs was shown executing efficiently on top of an implementation of the elastic transaction model, $\mathscr{E}$-STM. The implementation idea consists of encapsulating the (i) operations that locate a position in the red-black tree (like `insert`, `contains`, `delete`) into an *elastic* transaction to increase concurrency and (ii) other operations, like `size`, into a regular transaction. This approach is orthogonal to ours as it aims at improving the performance of the underlying TM, independently from the data structure, by introducing relaxed transactions. Hence, although elastic transactions can cut themselves upon conflict detection, the resulting $\mathscr{E}$-STM, still suffers from congestion and wasted work when applied to non-speculation-friendly data structures. The results presented in Section 4.3 confirm that the elastic speedup is even higher when the tree is speculation-friendly.

6. Conclusion

Transaction-based data structures are becoming a bottleneck in multicore programming, playing the role of synchronization toolboxes a programmer can rely on to write a concurrent application easily. This work is the first to show that speculative executions require the design of new data structures. The underlying challenge is to decrease the inherent contention by relaxing the invariants of the structure while preserving the invariants of the abstraction.

In contrast with the traditional pessimistic synchronization, the optimistic synchronization allows the programmer to directly observe the impact of contention as part of the step complexity because conflicts potentially lead to subsequent speculative re-executions. We have illustrated, using a binary search tree, how one can exploit this information to design a speculation-friendly data structure. The next challenge is to adapt this technique to a large body of data structures to derive a speculation-friendly library.

Source Code

The code of the speculation-friendly binary search tree is available at http://lpd.epfl.ch/gramoli/php/synchrobench.php.

Acknowledgements

The research leading to these results has received funding from the European Union Seventh Framework Programme (FP7/2007-2013) under grant agreement number 238639, ITN project TransForm, and grant agreement number 248465, the S(o)OS project.

References

[1] G. Adelson-Velskii and E. M. Landis. An algorithm for the organization of information. In *Proc. of the USSR Academy of Sciences*, volume 146, pages 263–266, 1962.

[2] K. Agrawal, I.-T. A. Lee, and J. Sukha. Safe open-nested transactions through ownership. In *Proc. of the 14th ACM SIGPLAN Symp. on Principles and Practice of Parallel Programming*, 2009.

[3] L. Ballard. Conflict avoidance: Data structures in transactional memory, May 2006. Undergraduate thesis, Brown University.

[4] R. Bayer. Symmetric binary b-trees: Data structure and maintenance algorithms. *Acta Informatica 1*, 1(4):290–306, 1972.

[5] L. Bougé, J. Gabarro, X. Messeguer, and N. Schabanel. Height-relaxed AVL rebalancing: A unified, fine-grained approach to concurrent dictionaries, 1998. Research Report 1998-18, ENS Lyon.

[6] N. G. Bronson, J. Casper, H. Chafi, and K. Olukotun. A practical concurrent binary search tree. In *Proc. of the 15th ACM SIGPLAN Symp. on Principles and Practice of Parallel Programming*, 2010.

[7] C. Cao Minh, J. Chung, C. Kozyrakis, and K. Olukotun. STAMP: Stanford transactional applications for multi-processing. In *Proc. of The IEEE Int'l Symp. on Workload Characterization*, 2008.

[8] C. Cole and M. Herlihy. Snapshots and software transactional memory. *Sci. Comput. Program.*, 58(3):310–324, 2005.

[9] T. Crain, V. Gramoli, and M. Raynal. A speculation-friendly binary search tree. Technical Report PI-1984, IRISA, September 2011.

[10] L. Dalessandro, M. Spear, and M. L. Scott. NOrec: streamlining STM by abolishing ownership records. In *Proc. of the 15th ACM SIGPLAN Symp. on Principles and Practice of Parallel Programming*, 2010.

[11] D. Dice, O. Shalev, , and N. Shavit. Transactional locking II. In *Proc. of the 20th Int'l Symp. on Distributed Computing*, 2006.

[12] E. W. Dijkstra, L. Lamport, A. J. Martin, C. S. Scholten, and E. F. M. Steffens. On-the-fly garbage collection: an exercise in cooperation. *Commun. ACM*, 21(11):966–975, 1978.

[13] A. Dragojevic, P. Felber, V. Gramoli, and R. Guerraoui. Why STM can be more than a research toy. *Commun. ACM*, 54(4):70–77, 2011.

[14] P. Felber, C. Fetzer, and T. Riegel. Dynamic performance tuning of word-based software transactional memory. In *Proc. of the 13th ACM SIGPLAN Symp. on Principles and Practice of Parallel Programming*, 2008.

[15] P. Felber, V. Gramoli, and R. Guerraoui. Elastic transactions. In *Proc. of the 23rd Int'l Symp. on Distributed Computing*, 2009.

[16] V. Gramoli and R. Guerraoui. Democratizing transactional programming. In *Proc. of the ACM/IFIP/USENIX 12th Int'l Middleware Conference*, 2011.

[17] L. J. Guibas and R. Sedgewick. A dichromatic framework for balanced trees. In *Proc. of the 19th Annual Symp. on Foundations of Computer Science*, 1978.

[18] T. Harris, S. Marlow, S. Peyton-Jones, and M. Herlihy. Composable memory transactions. In *Proc. of the 10th ACM SIGPLAN Symp. on Principles and Practice of Parallel Programming*, 2005.

[19] M. Herlihy and E. Koskinen. Transactional boosting: A methodology for highly-concurrent transactional objects. In *Proc. of the 13th ACM SIGPLAN Symp. on Principles and Practice of Parallel Programming*, 2008.

[20] M. Herlihy and J. E. B. Moss. Transactional memory: Architectural support for lock-free data structures. In *Proc. of the 20th Annual Int'l Symp. on Computer Architecture*, 1993.

[21] M. Herlihy, V. Luchangco, M. Moir, and W. N. Scherer, III. Software transactional memory for dynamic-sized data structures. In *Proc. of the 22nd Annual ACM SIGACT-SIGOPS Symp. on Principles of Distributed Computing*, 2003.

[22] Intel Corporation. Intel transactional memory compiler and runtime application binary interface, May 2009.

[23] J. L. W. Kessels. On-the-fly optimization of data structures. *Comm. ACM*, 26:895–901, 1983.

[24] U. Manbar and R. E. Ladner. Concurrency control in a dynamic search structure. *ACM Trans. Database Syst.*, 9(3):439–455, 1984.

[25] C. Mohan. Commit-LSN: a novel and simple method for reducing locking and latching in transaction processing systems. In *Proc. of the 16th Int'l Conference on Very Large Data Bases*, 1990.

[26] J. E. B. Moss. Open nested transactions: Semantics and support. In *Workshop on Memory Performance Issues*, 2006.

[27] Y. Ni, V. Menon, A.-R. Abd-Tabatabai, A. L. Hosking, R. L. Hudson, J. E. B. Moss, B. Saha, and T. Shpeisman. Open nesting in software transactional memory. In *Proc. of the 12th ACM SIGPLAN Symp. on Principles and Practice of Parallel Programming*, 2007.

[28] O. Nurmi and E. Soisalon-Soininen. Uncoupling updating and rebalancing in chromatic binary search trees. In *Proc. of the 10th ACM Symp. on Principles of Database Systems*, 1991.

[29] O. Nurmi, E. Soisalon-Soininen, and D. Wood. Concurrency control in database structures with relaxed balance. In *Proc. of the 6th ACM Symp. on Principles of Database Systems*, 1987.

[30] V. Pankratius and A.-R. Adl-Tabatabai. A study of transactional memory vs. locks in practice. In *Proc. of the 23rd ACM Symp. on Parallelism in Algorithms and Architectures*, 2011.

[31] C. J. Rossbach, O. S. Hofmann, and E. Witchel. Is transactional programming actually easier? In *Proc. of the 15th ACM SIGPLAN Symp. on Principles and Practice of Parallel Programming*, 2010.

[32] N. Shavit. Data structures in the multicore age. *Commun. ACM*, 54 (3):76–84, 2011.

[33] N. Shavit and D. Touitou. Software transactional memory. In *Proc. of the 14th ACM Symp. on Principles of Distributed Computing*, 1995.

[34] R. M. Yoo, Y. Ni, A. Welc, B. Saha, A.-R. Adl-Tabatabai, and H.-H. S. Lee. Kicking the tires of software transactional memory: why the going gets tough. In *Proc. of the 20th ACM Symp. on Parallelism in Algorithms and Architectures*, 2008.

PARRAY: A Unifying Array Representation for Heterogeneous Parallelism

Yifeng Chen
HCST Key Lab, School of EECS, Peking University
Beijing 100871, P.R.China
cyf@pku.edu.cn

Xiang Cui Hong Mei
HCST Key Lab, School of EECS, Peking University
Beijing 100871, P.R.China
cuixiang08@sei.pku.edu.cn / meih@pku.edu.cn

Abstract

This paper introduces a programming interface called PARRAY (or Parallelizing ARRAYs) that supports system-level succinct programming for heterogeneous parallel systems like GPU clusters. The current practice of software development requires combining several low-level libraries like Pthread, OpenMP, CUDA and MPI. Achieving productivity and portability is hard with different numbers and models of GPUs. PARRAY extends mainstream C programming with novel array types of the following features: 1) the dimensions of an array type are nested in a tree structure, conceptually reflecting the memory hierarchy; 2) the definition of an array type may contain references to other array types, allowing sophisticated array types to be created for parallelization; 3) threads also form arrays that allow programming in a Single-Program-Multiple-Codeblock (SPMC) style to unify various sophisticated communication patterns. This leads to shorter, more portable and maintainable parallel codes, while the programmer still has control over performance-related features necessary for deep manual optimization. Although the source-to-source code generator only faithfully generates low-level library calls according to the type information, higher-level programming and automatic performance optimization are still possible through building libraries of subprograms on top of PARRAY. The case study on cluster FFT illustrates a simple 30-line code that 2x-outperforms Intel Cluster MKL on the Tianhe-1A system with 7168 Fermi GPUs and 14336 CPUs.

Categories and Subject Descriptors D.1.3 [*Programming Techniques*]: Concurrent Programming – Parallel programming; D.3.3 [*Programming Languages*]: Language Constructs and Features – Concurrent programming structures; D.3.4 [*Programming Languages*]: Processors – Code generation

General Terms Languages, Performance, Theory

Keywords Parallel Programming, Array Representation, Heterogeneous Parallelism, GPU Clusters

1. Introduction

Driven by the demand for higher performance and lower hardware and energy costs, emerging supercomputers are becoming more and more heterogeneous and massively parallel. Several GPU-accelerated systems are now ranked among the top 20 fastest supercomputers. Despite the rapid progress in hardware, programming for optimized performance is hard.

The existing programming models are designed for specific forms of parallelism: Pthread and OpenMP for multicore parallelism, CUDA and OpenCL for manycore parallelism, and MPI for clustering. A simple combination of these low-level interfaces does not provide enough support for software productivity and portability across different GPU clusters with varied numbers/models of GPUs on each node. A current common practice is to combine MPI and CUDA. However on a cluster of GPU-accelerated multicore nodes, the number of MPI processes cannot be the number of CPU cores (to use the CPU cores) and the number of GPUs (to use GPUs) at the same time. A seemingly obvious solution is to use the number of GPUs for MPI processes and use OpenMP to control CPU cores, but the complexity of programming with all MPI, CUDA and OpenMP will discourage most application developers.

Such difficulties have led to a variety of new ideas on programming languages (more detailed comparisons in Section 6). Language design is a tradeoff between abstraction and performance. For high-performance applications, the concern of performance is paramount. We hence ask ourselves a question:

how abstractly can we program heterogeneous parallel systems without introducing noticeable compromises in performance?

The design of PARRAY follows the approach of bottom-up abstraction. That means if a basic operation's algorithm or implementation is not unique (with considerable performance differences), the inclination is to provide more basic operations at a lower level. Our purpose is not to solve all the programmability issues but to provide a bottom level of abstraction on which performance-minded programmers can directly write succinct high-performance code and on which higher-level language features can be implemented without unnecessary performance overheads. This kind of "performance transparency" allows other software layers to be built on top of this layer, and the implementation will not be performance-wise penalized because of choosing PARRAY instead of using low-level libraries directly. A programmer can then choose the right programming level to work with.

A common means to achieve abstraction is to adopt a unifying communication mechanism, *e.g.* synchronous message passing in process algebra [14], distributed memory sharing or Partitioned Global Address Space (PGAS). However, heterogeneous parallel systems are often equipped with different kinds of hardware-based communication mechanisms such as sequentially-consistent shared memory for multicore parallelism, asynchronous message-passing or RDMA for clustering, inconsistent shared memory (with explicit but expensive consistency-enforcing synchronization) for many-

PPoPP'12 February 25-29 2012, New Orleans, Louisiana, USA.

core parallelism, as well as PCI data transfer between servers and their accelerators. These mechanisms exhibit significantly different bandwidth, latency and optimal communication granularity (*i.e.* the size of contiguous data segments).

Encoding all data-transfer operations of a source program into a unified communication pattern does not always yield efficient code. For example, programs with assumption of a global-address space (either Distributed Shared Memory or PGAS) tend to issue data-transfer commands when data are needed for computation, but a better strategy may instead use prefetching to better overlap communication and computation. Another challenge is to maximize communication granularity. Shared-memory programs tend to issue individual data-access commands in the actual code for computation, but communication channels such as PCI (between CPU and GPU) and Infiniband (among nodes) require granularity to reach a certain level to achieve peak bandwidths. The source-program information about granularity is easily lost with global-address accesses. Compile-time and runtime optimization alleviates the issues but it remains to be seen to what extent such lost source information is recoverable automatically.

In this paper, we take a different perspective and do not attempt to devise any unifying memory model. Instead we invent novel types that unify the representation of different communication mechanisms. It allows programmers to specify what needs to be done in a communicating operation, and the compiler will then generate the corresponding library calls. This is not restricted to generating hardware-based communication calls. If the required data transfer is one-sided and there exists a well optimized PGAS protocol, the compiler simply generates PGAS calls [17] instead.

How can we uniformly represent such a diverse variety of communication mechanisms?

The answer is to identify their common unifying mathematical structure. To get a glimpse of the intended representational unification, consider an example to partition a 4096x4096 row-major array in the main host memory (hmem) to two 2048x4096 blocks, each being copied to a GPU device memory via PCI. Experiments show that the overall bandwidth of two parallel PCI transfers is 1.6x of single PCI transfers. The two CPU multicore threads that control GPUs are therefore programmed to invoke `cudaMemcpy` simultaneously, followed by inter-thread synchronization. Interestingly similar communication patterns arise elsewhere *e.g.* in collective communication `MPI_Scatter` that scatters the two-block source array to two MPI processes. This is illustrated in the following figures.

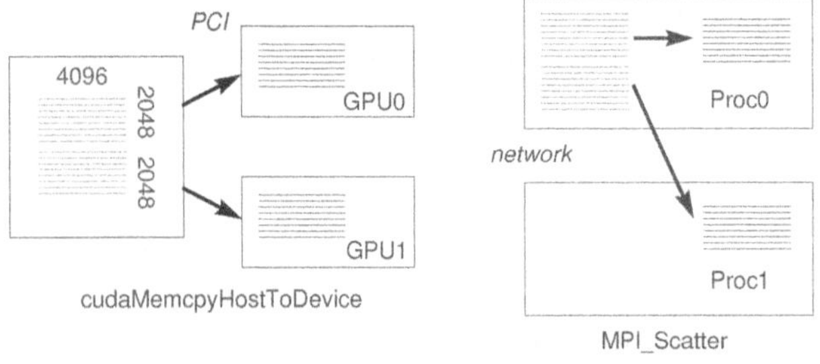

Although the two seemingly disparate communication patterns describe data transfers of different library calls (CUDA and MPI), via different media and to different memory devices, they do share the same logical pattern of data partition, distribution and correlation. Such similarities motivate us to unify them as one communication primitive and treat the data layouts of communication's origin and destination as typing parameters.

There have been a large body of research on arrays (*e.g.* HTA [11]), but the existing array notations are not expressive and flexible enough to reflect the complex memory hierarchy of heterogeneous parallel systems, control various system-level features, unify sophisticated communication patterns including dimensional transposition, noncontiguous transfer, uncommon internode connections etc., and convey enough source information to the compiler to generate performance-optimal code. The solution is to increase representational expressiveness.

PARRAY adopts a new array type system that allows the programmer to express additional information about parallelization that can guide the compiler to generate low-level library calls. The following features are claimed to be original contributions not seen in other array notations that we know about:

1. Dimension tree

   The dimensions of an array type are nested in a tree, conceptually reflecting the memory hierarchy. Unlike HTA's dimension layers that have default memory types, PARRAY's dimension tree is logical and independent of any specific system architecture. The memory-type information is specifiable for each sub-dimension. Such flexibility allows dimensions to form a hierarchy within individual memory devices.

2. Array-type references

   The definition of an array type may contain references to other array types' definitions. This allows sophisticated array types to be created for transposition, partition, distribution and distortion. Such types form an algebraic system with a complete set of algebraic properties (see Section 3).

3. Thread arrays

   Threads also form arrays. A thread array type indicates the kind of processor on which the threads are created, invoked and synchronized. The SPMD codes of different thread arrays are compacted in a nested-loop-like syntactical context (Single-Program Multiple-Codeblocks or SPMC) so that the order of commands in the nested context directly reflects that of the computing task. An array type may consist of a mixture of dimensions that refer to data and thread array types and represent the distribution of array elements over multiple memory devices. A communication pattern is represented as the pairing between such types.

PARRAY essentially organizes various array types in a unifying mathematical framework, but:

how do we know to what extent the basic framework's design is already expressive enough and unnecessary to be extended for future applications and architectural changes?

The answer derives from a theoretical analysis showing that any location-indexing expression (called *offset expression*) for array elements is representable with PARRAY types, as long as it just consists of integer (independent) expressions, multiplication, division and modulo operators, and additions and compositions between expressions. Such level of expressiveness is not seen in any existing array notations.

PARRAY is implemented as a preprocessing compiler that translates directives into C code and macros. As the array types already convey detailed information about the intended communication patterns, the code generation is straightforward and faithful in the sense that the compiler need not second-guess the programmer's intention, and hence little runtime optimization is required. The compiler does generate various conditional-compilation commands, which are usually optimized by the underlying C compiler without causing performance overheads. In a sense, the PARRAY's data-transfer command is like an extremely general MPI collective that invokes the actual communication libraries according to the type parameters. Little overhead-inducing code is generated before or after the invocations. Paradoxically, by not relying on runtime optimization, PARRAY can guarantee performance (for well-coded programs) and form a performance-transparent portable layer of abstraction.

Section 2 introduces PARRAY notation. Section 3 studies the mathematical foundation of PARRAY; Section 4 explains the rationale behind the implementation including the concept of SPMC; Section 5 investigates into a case study on large-scale FFT; Section 6 reviews previous works.

2. Parallelizing Array Types

This section introduces the PARRAY type notation on which the actual programming syntax is based.

2.1 Dimension Tree

Let us first look at a simple definition:

$$A \mathrel{\hat{=}} \texttt{pinned}\,\texttt{float}[[3][2]][4].$$

The type describes 3x2x4=24 floating-point elements in three dimensions, but it is also a two-dimensional array type with 6x4 floats and or a one-dimensional array type with 24 floats. The indicated memory type is "`pinned`" which denotes the main host memory allocated by CUDA for fast DMA with GPU.

Note that in the actual code generation, the size of a dimension can be any arbitrary integer expression of C.

As slightly simplified code generation, the compiler translates the *offset expression* (*i.e.* mapping from indices to element offsets) $A[[x][y]][z]$ into a C expression $x*8+y*4+z$, $A[x][y]$ into expression $x*4+y$, and $A[x]$ into the index x itself. Such offset expressions are used for row-major element accesses in program.

Let the *partial array type* A^0 denote the left subtree of A, *i.e.* a 2D type of size 3x2, and A^1 denote the right 1D subtree of size 4. The compiler will translate $A^0[x][y]$ into $x*8+y*4$ (instead of $x*2+y$)! The following figure illustrates the dimension tree (or *dimtree* in short).

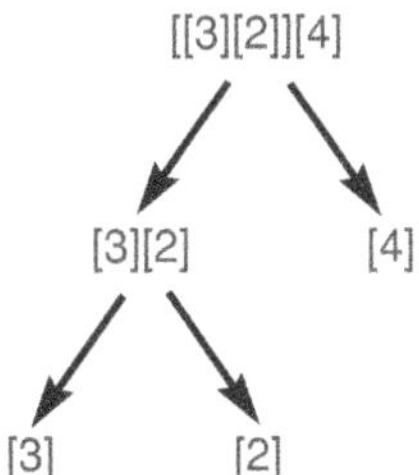

2.2 Type Reference

A dimtree may contain references to other array types. The following device-memory (or dmem) array type

$$B \mathrel{\hat{=}} \texttt{dmem}\,\texttt{float}[[\#A^{01}][\#A^{00}]][\#A^1]$$

contains references to A with the sub-dimensions of the left subtree transposed. Their offset expressions satisfy an equation:

$$B[[x][y]][z] = A[[y][x]][z].$$

Unlike the elements of A, those of type B are not contiguously laid out in memory: neither row-major as C convention nor column-major as Fortran. Many sophisticated array layout patterns correspond to the combined uses of dimtree and type references.

2.3 Data Transfer

To represent data transfer from an array of type *A* to an array of type *B*, we use the following notation:

$$B \leftleftarrows A.$$

The data transfer involves two real array objects in an actual program and describes the operation to copy every element of a type-*A* array at location $A[i]$ to an element of a type-*B* array at $B[i]$. In practice, as the source array is located in hmem and the target array in dmem, the compiler will generate:

```
cudaMemcpy(..., cudaMemcpyHostToDevice)
```

according to the memory types. Other low-level data transfers such as `memcpy` of C, message passing `MPI_Send`/`MPI_Recv`, collectives `MPI_Alltoall` and so on are generated if the memory types and the dimensions conform to other pairing patterns.

As the offset expressions $A[i]$ and $B[i]$ are not equal, the copying cannot be achieved in a single `cudaMemcpy`. A loop is hence needed to cudaMemcpy every 4 contiguous elements from the starting location $A^0[i]$ in the host memory to the starting location $B^0[i]$ in GPU's device memory as a partially contiguous transfer.

Whether the compiler generates one Memcpy command or a loop of Memcpys depends on the array type's contiguity, which the compiler will generate extra code to check.

2.4 Threads Arrays

The following type describes two (Pthread) CPU threads:

$$P \mathrel{\hat{=}} \texttt{pthd}[2].$$

Here `pthd` is called a *thread type*. No element type is required. Other possible thread types include `mpi` for MPI processes and `cuda` for GPU threads. For example, the type

$$M \mathrel{\hat{=}} \texttt{mpi}[2]$$

describes two MPI processes. A GPU thread array type is two-dimensional: the column dimension indicates the blocks in a grid, while the row dimension indicates the threads in every block. For example, the following array type

$$C \mathrel{\hat{=}} \texttt{cuda}[N/256][256]$$

describes N GPU threads of which every 256 threads form a CUDA block. Here N can be any C expression (possibly including runtime variables). The compiler will generate code that lexically includes the size expressions. CUDA thread-array dimensions may contain sub-dimensions just like CUDA's grids and blocks.

2.5 Distributed Array Types

If an array type has memory or thread type, its references to other array types only affect the offset expressions, but if that is absent, it becomes *mixed* or *distributed* and are often useful in collective data transfers. Consider an array type in ordinary `paged` memory:

$$H \mathrel{\hat{=}} \texttt{paged}\,\texttt{float}[2][[2048][4096]]$$

and another type half of its size in device memory $D \mathrel{\hat{=}} \texttt{dmem}\,\texttt{float2}\,\#H^1$. The mixed type

$$[\#P][\#D]$$

logically has the same number of elements as H but does not describe array stored in a single memory device. Instead it is distributed over the threads of P and stored in the GPU device memory associated with each CPU control thread.

2.6 PCI Scattering

The communication pattern characterized by the type pairing

$$[\#P][\#D] \leftleftarrows H$$

describes data copying from every element at location $H[i][j]$ in ordinary paged hmem to the element at location $D[j]$ in the dmem of the GPU that is associated with the control thread $P[i]$. The above communication pattern uses two parallel CPU threads to scatter hmem data to the dmem of two GPUs.

2.7 MPI Scattering

The following communication pattern, on the other hand, collectively scatters the source data to two MPI processes:

$$[\#M][\#H^1] \leftleftharpoons H.$$

In practice, a communication pattern may generate different code for synchronous, asynchronous, or one-sided communications.

The communication's mode is determined by the programmer. If that is one-sided, the compiler can generate PGAS code and take advantage of any available runtime optimization [17].

2.8 Other MPI Collectives

Other MPI collective communications such as Alltoall and Gather have similar a type representation. For example, the following communication pattern describes MPI's Alltoall collective:

$$[[\#H^0][\#M]][\#H^1] \leftleftharpoons [[\#M][\#H^0]][\#H^1]$$

where each element at location $H[j][k]$ on process $M[i]$ is copied to the location $H[i][k]$ on process $M[j]$. It effectively swaps the column dimension of H with the distributed "virtual" dimension M. The compiler detects this pattern and generates the `MPI_Alltoall` command based on the fact that the array type H is contiguous and conforms to the semantics of the MPI command.

Unsurprisingly, MPI gathering accords with the converse communication pattern of MPI scattering:

$$H \leftleftharpoons [\#M][\#H^1].$$

2.9 Non-MPI Collectives

Some PARRAY communication patterns do not correspond to any single standard MPI collective. Consider 2x2 four MPI processes:

$$M' \,\widehat{=}\, \texttt{mpi}[2][2]$$

The following pairing of types describes two separate groups of MPI processes performing Alltoall within each individual group:

$$[[\#M'^0][\#H^0][\#M'^1]]\,[\#H^1] \leftleftharpoons$$
$$[[\#M'^0][\#M'^1][\#H^0]]\,[\#H^1].$$

The pid row dimension M'^1 and the data column dimension H^0 are swapped by the communication.

What gives rise to non-MPI collectives includes not only non-standard inter-process connectivity but also discontiguity in process-to-process communication. In the large-scale 3D FFT algorithm [8] developed for turbulence simulation, a distributed array of size up to 14336^3 is transposed over the entire Tianhe-1A GPU cluster with 7168 nodes (see Section 5). The algorithmic optimization requires discontiguous data transfer between processes to adjust the displacements of elements during communication so that main-memory transposition can then be avoided. The data array of complex numbers (`float2`) on every node has the following type:

$$G \,\widehat{=}\, \texttt{pinned float2}\ [2][[7168][2]][14336].$$

The array type for 7168 MPI processes is defined:

$$L \,\widehat{=}\, \texttt{mpi}[7168].$$

The required discontiguous Alltoall communication pattern (with adjusted displacements) corresponds to the following pairing types:

$$[[\#G^{10}][\#G^{11}][\#L][\#G^0]]\,[\#G^2] \leftleftharpoons$$
$$[[\#L][\#G^0][\#G^{10}][\#G^{11}]]\,[\#G^2]. \qquad (1)$$

The types have two dimensions. Only the row dimensions are contiguous. The dimension L is swapped with G^{10} instead of G^0. That means the starting locations of communicated data are different from those of the standard Alltoall. The dimensions G^0 and G^{11} are also swapped during the communication between every pair of processes. As the communication granularity *i.e.* the size of G^2 already reaches 14x8KB, its performance should be very close to that of a standard Alltoall, despite the fact that no such displacement-adjusting collective exists[1].

The above examples have illustrated the advantage of adopting a unifying representational framework such that the communication library need not keep adding *ad hoc* collectives to suit originally unforeseen communication patterns that arise from new applications and emerging architectures.

Because all necessary information has been represented in the types, the generated code is as efficient as the underlying MPI implementation. It is also possible to skip the MPI layer and directly generate Infiniband's IB/verbs invocation with less overheads.

2.10 Detecting Contiguity

How does the compiler know a communication pattern corresponds to MPI's Alltoall collective or any other sub-routines? This is achieved by checking the memory/thread types of the dimensions and generating C boolean expressions that can check whether the concerned dimensions are *contiguous* in the sense that the offsets of such a dimension are linearly ordered in memory and located adjacently to each other. Usually contiguity-checking expressions are determined in compile-time and induce no performance overheads. Details of this question are beyond our agenda.

3. Theory

The theoretical foundation of this paper follows the style of *algebraic semantics* that can be traced back to Tarski's Boolean Algebra with Operators [18] and C.A.R. Hoare's Laws of Programming [15, 16]. Compared to operational semantics and denotational semantics, algebraic semantics focuses on organizing complicated structures into simple and succinct algebraic systems. Its power of abstraction is exactly what is needed in programming sophisticated heterogeneous parallel systems. Less theoretically minded readers may choose to skip this section. For now, the element types like `float` and memory/thread types like `pinned` are ignored.

3.1 Syntax

Let $e, e_0, e_1, \cdots$ denote index expressions in C (variables allowed), the symbols $U, U_0, U_1, \cdots$ denote array types, $S, S_0, \cdots$ be multi-dimensional types. Array types have the following simple syntax:

$$S ::= [U_0] \cdots [U_{n-1}]$$
$$U ::= e \mid \texttt{disp}\ e \mid S \mid U\#U \mid U^s \mid \texttt{func}(x)\ e.$$

where s is a path sequence of dimension indices to refer a sub-dimension deep in a dimension tree, and $(U^{s_1})^{s_2}$ is considered the same as $U^{s_1 s_2}$. A C expression e describes a 1D array type of size e. The displacement type ($\texttt{disp}\ e$) describes a dimension of size 1 with offset e. A dimension may have multiple (up to 10) sub-dimensions. The dimension size of a type reference $\#$ coincides with that of the LHS, while RHS refers to another type and describes the offset expression. A functional offset expression $\texttt{func}(x)\ e$ describes a dimension of size 1 with a C offset macro. Functional expressions, as user-defined offset mappings, further strengthen expressiveness but will not be considered in our theoretical analysis.

[1] This communication pattern is equivalent to a loop of asynchronous Alltoallv collectives followed by a global synchronization. Such implementation is possible owing to more recent MPI development [19].

3.2 Dimension Sizes

Let $\langle U \rangle$ denote the dimension-size expression. The size of a C expression without sub-dimensions is the expression itself, while that of a subtree is the multiplied sizes of its sub-dimensions:

DEF 1.
$$\begin{aligned} \langle e \rangle &\mathrel{\widehat{=}} e \\ \langle \mathtt{disp}\, e \rangle &\mathrel{\widehat{=}} 1 \\ \langle (U \,\#\, V)^s \rangle &\mathrel{\widehat{=}} \langle U^s \rangle \\ \langle ([U_0]\cdots[U_{n-1}])^{ks} \rangle &\mathrel{\widehat{=}} \langle U_k^s \rangle \\ \langle [U_0]\cdots[U_{n-1}] \rangle &\mathrel{\widehat{=}} \textstyle\prod_{k=0}^{n-1} \langle U_k \rangle. \end{aligned}$$

Note that, we adopt a convention simply to write $\langle U \rangle \,\#\, U$ as $\#\, U$. A partial dimension size of some sub-dimensions is defined:

$$\langle [U_0]\cdots[U_{n-1}] \rangle_k \mathrel{\widehat{=}} \langle [U_k]\cdots[U_{n-1}] \rangle.$$

3.3 Informal Rules

Every array-access expression can be decomposed into unary offset expressions called *offset functions*. For example:

$$\begin{aligned} A[[x][y]][z] &= A^{00}[x] + A^{01}[y] + A^{1}[z] \\ &= 8(x \,\mathtt{mod}\, 3) + 4(y \,\mathtt{mod}\, 2) + (z \,\mathtt{mod}\, 4). \end{aligned}$$

That means we only need the definition for every offset function. Another such example is $A^0[x] = 4(x \,\mathtt{mod}\, 6)$. The above semantic definition uses modulo operator. *In the actual implementation the programmer is required to ensure a safe range for every index expression, and the modulo operators are not always generated.*

Consider a type $E \mathrel{\widehat{=}} [2][2] \,\#\, A^0$. The array size is 2x2, but the offset function of E follows that of A^0. The offset function of E^0 is derivable top-down from that of A^0:

$$E^0[x] = A^0[2(x \,\mathtt{mod}\, 2)] = 8(x \,\mathtt{mod}\, 2). \qquad (2)$$

Then consider the previous example B^0. As its sub-dimensions B^{00} and B^{01} refer to A^{01} and A^{00} respectively, the offset of B^0 is computed bottom-up by decomposing the index into separate indices of its sub-dimensions:

$$\begin{aligned} B^0[x] &= A^{01}[x \,\mathtt{div}\, 3] + A^{00}[x] \qquad (3) \\ &= 4((x \,\mathtt{div}\, 3) \,\mathtt{mod}\, 2) + 8(x \,\mathtt{mod}\, 3). \end{aligned}$$

The above two cases are intuitive and common in practice. The general array representation, however, allows more sophisticated cases where a dimension itself does not refer to other types but both its parent dimension and some sub-dimensions contain type references. The adopted rule is to first compute top-down according to case (2), and then bottom-up according to case (3).

3.4 Formal Rules

We use $U\,|_h$ to denote the offset function of U where the parameter h represents the top-down propagation of offset mapping. The identity function is denoted as id.

LAW 1.
$$\begin{aligned} &(1)\ \ e\,|_h\,(x) = h(x \,\mathtt{mod}\, e) \\ &(2)\ \ (\mathtt{disp}\, e)\,|_h\,(x) = h(x+e) \\ &(3)\ \ S^{ks}\,|_h\,(x) = U_k^s\,|_{h'}\,(x) \\ &(4)\ \ S\,|_h\,(x) = \textstyle\sum_k S^k\,|_h\,(x \,\mathtt{div}\, \langle S \rangle_{k+1}) \\ &(5)\ \ (U \,\#\, V)^s\,|_h\,(x) = U^s\,|_{V|_{id}}\,(x) \end{aligned}$$

where $S = [U_0]\cdots[U_{n-1}]$ *and* $h'(x) \mathrel{\widehat{=}} h(x) * \langle S \rangle_{k+1}$.

A dimension e uses the top-down propagated offset gap with modulo of the dimension size. Displacement `disp` e does not assume modulo but shifts the index expression. The path sequence follows the dimension tree down by multiplying the offset parameter function h, which is overridden by the referred type V in $U \,\#\, V$.

The bottom-up propagation combines the offset functions of sub-dimensions according to (3). The offset expression $(U)[x]$ is defined as $U\,|_{id}\,(x)$.

For example $(1)[x] = 0$ and $(\mathtt{disp}\, e)[x] = x + e$. We introduce some special types that yield the basic offset operators:

$$\begin{aligned} CONST_e &\mathrel{\widehat{=}} 1 \,\#\, (\mathtt{disp}\, e) \\ MUL_e &\mathrel{\widehat{=}} [\mathtt{disp}\, 0][e]^0 \\ DIV_e &\mathrel{\widehat{=}} [\mathtt{disp}\, 0 \,\#\, \mathtt{disp}\, 0][e \,\#\, 1] \\ U + V &\mathrel{\widehat{=}} [U][\mathtt{disp}\, 0 \,\#\, V]. \end{aligned}$$

Basic integer operators are offset functions of the special types:

LAW 2.
$$\begin{aligned} &(1)\ \ (CONST_e)[x] = e \\ &(2)\ \ (MUL_e)[x] = x * e \\ &(3)\ \ (DIV_e)[x] = x \,\mathtt{div}\, e \\ &(4)\ \ (e)[x] = x \,\mathtt{mod}\, e \\ &(5)\ \ (U + V)[x] = U[x] + V[x] \\ &(6)\ \ (U \,\#\, V)[x] = (V)[(U)[x]]. \end{aligned}$$

The following completeness theorem is a direct result of the above laws. It illustrates the exceptional expressive power of PARRAY types. More thorough theoretical analysis about recursive references is not on the agenda of this paper.

THEOREM 1 (Completeness). *For any integer expression $f(x)$ formed of independent expressions e, integer multiplication $*$, integer division* `div`*, integer modulo operator* `mod`*, as well as functional addition $+$ and composition, there exists an array type U such that $(U)[x] = f(x)$.*

To illustrate how the the formal rules reflect the informal rules, we manually calculate a previous example:

$(A^{00})[x]$

$=$ definition

$([[3][2]][4])^{00}\,|_{id}\,(x)$

$=$ Law 1(3) and $h(x) \mathrel{\widehat{=}} id(x) * 4$

$([3][2])^0\,|_h\,(x)$

$=$ Law 1(3) and $h'(x) \mathrel{\widehat{=}} h(x) * 2$

$3\,|_{h'}\,(x)$

$=$ Law 1(1)

$8(x \,\mathtt{mod}\, 3)$.

3.5 Displacement and Index Range

Displacement is a type notation not mentioned in the previous section. It is useful to shift an offset function. In practice we often use $(n..m) \mathrel{\widehat{=}} (m - n + 1) \,\#\, (\mathtt{disp}\, n)$ to represent a dimension with a range of indices.

The case study in Section 5 partitions the 3D data in hmem into two-dimensional slices and use GPU to compute the FFT for every slice separately. The type for a slice in dmem is characterized as

$$Q \mathrel{\widehat{=}} \mathtt{dmem}\ \mathtt{float2}\ [N][N],$$

while one of the slices with displacement in hmem is typed as

$$F \mathrel{\widehat{=}} \mathtt{pinned}\ \mathtt{float2}\ [\mathtt{disp}\, i][N][N].$$

Then the type pairing $Q \Leftarrow F$ describes contiguous data transfer of size N^2 from hmem to dmem. The starting location of transfer in hmem is $(N^2 * i)$. We may also declare a smaller two-dimensional "window" in the middle of Q:

$$[4..(N-5) \,\#\, Q^0][4..(N-5) \,\#\, Q^1].$$

Such window types are useful in stencil computation. Cyclic displacement is also easily representable.

4. Implementation

This section describes how PARRAY is currently implemented and the rationale behind it.

4.1 Data Array Types

PARRAY is implemented as a C preprocessor that generates CUDA, MPI, and Pthread code and a basic library of sub-programs including the general `DataTransfer` command. The preprocessor is detached from the C compiler to maximize cross-platform compatibility and insensitivity to the constant upgrades of hardware and system-level software. That means only directive errors are caught by the preprocessor. C compilation errors are only detectable in the generated code. The following table compares PARRAY notation and the corresponding program syntax.

Notation	Program Syntax
A^{01}	`A_0_1`
$\langle A \rangle$	`$dim(A)$`
$A[5][2]$	`$A[5][2]$`
$A \mathrel{\hat{=}}$ `pinned float`$[[3][2]][4]$	`#parray {pinned float[[3][2]][4]} A`
$\leftleftarrows$	`DataTransfer`

The following example shows how an array `a` is declared, created, initialized, accessed and freed in the end:

```
#parray {pinned float[[3][2]][4]} A
float* a;
#create A(a)
printf("array access: %d\n", a[$A[5][2]$]);
#destroy A(a)
```

It first declares an array type `A` in pinned memory. The command `#create A(a)` then allocates the pinned memory to the pointer. Note that `#parray` only defines an array type. An actual array is a C pointer that allows multiple typing views as long as the array is a pointer of the element type.

Other memory types include `paged` memory that is managed by the operating system only reaching about 60% the bandwidth of pinned memory for data transfer with GPU device memory (which is denoted by the keyword `dmem`). The keyword `smem` stands for shared memory in GPU, `rmem` for GPU registers (allocated as direct array declaration in GPU kernels), and `mpimem` for MPI-allocated page-lock DMA-able buffer memory. Mellanox and Nvidia's GPU-Direct technology makes `pinned` and `mpimem` interoperable.

The following table lists the actual library calls for memory allocation. Thread types will be explained in Section 4.2.

	#create	#destroy	Library
paged	malloc	free	C/Pthread
pinned	cudaMallocHost	cudaFreeHost	CUDA
mpimem	MPI_Alloc_mem	MPI_Free_mem	MPI
dmem	cudaMalloc	cudaFree	CUDA
smem	__shared__		CUDA
rmem			CUDA

It is recommended that all index expressions and data transfers should use array notation (instead of native C notation) so that when an array type is modified, all corresponding expressions and library calls will be updated automatically by the compiler over the entire program. This following code declares a type `B` in dmem by referring to `A`'s dimensions and transfers data between their arrays:

```
#parray {dmem float[[#A_0_1][#A_0_0]][#A_1]} B
float* b;
#create B(b)
#insert DataTransfer(b, B, a, A){}
```

The sub-program `DataTransfer` automatically detects that the dimensions `A_1` and `B_1` are contiguous, and cudaMemcpy data from the main memory to GPU device memory in a loop of 6 segments, each with 4 floats.

The following table lists the library calls used between memory types. `hmem` refers to `paged`, `pinned` and `mpimem` all in the main memory but allocated for different purposes. Data transfer from or to GPU's shared memory `smem` or GPU's registers `rmem` is always performed element-by-element within a loop.

from\to	hmem	dmem	smem/rmem
hmem	memcpy	cudaMemcpy	
dmem	cudaMemcpy	cudaMemcpy	C loop
smem/rmem		C loop	C loop

4.2 Thread Array Types

SPMD is adopted by a wide range of parallel languages. The idea of SPMD programming is that one code is executed on multiple homogeneous parallel threads (or processes), though at any time different threads may be executing different commands of the code.

SPMD alone does not work for heterogeneous parallelism. For example, FFT on a GPU cluster starts multiple MPI process, each of which initiates several threads to control GPUs on that node, and each thread then launches thousands of GPU threads. Another example is GPU-cluster's Linpack code [9], which performs DGEMM on CPU and GPU threads at the same time.

In the existing explicitly parallel languages, the code segments for different processes are declared separately. The interaction between such code segments requires explicit matching synchronization command. The codeblocks of thread arrays, however, are statically nested in the same program context. The control flow may deviate from one thread array whose code is in an outer codeblock to another thread array whose code is in its immediate inner block and return after the execution of the inner block. The compiler will later extract the codeblocks and sequentially stack those from the same thread array to form a separate SPMD code in which matching synchronization and communication commands are automatically inserted. Thus SPMC (or *Single Program Multiple Codeblocks*) is like a compile-time RPC: the control flows travel across different thread arrays. The purpose is to imply the dynamic control flow as much as possible through the static structure of code and helps the programmer "visualize" the interactive pattern of the control flows among different thread arrays. Each thread array is a SPMD unit consisting of multiple homogeneous processes sharing the same code. A SPMC program may consist of multiple *thread arrays*, each as an array of homogenous threads sharing the same codeblock. The codeblocks of different thread arrays are nested in "one single program".

The following example declares and creates an array of 2 CPU threads and then triggers them to run.

```
#parray {pthd[2]} P
_pa_pthd* p;
#create P(p)
#detour P(p) {printf("thread id %d\n", $tid$);}
#destroy P(p)
```

The expression `$tid$` returns the thread id of the current running thread. The following table lists the actual library calls for creating and freeing thread arrays. The code inside a detour can access global variables as it is generated as a global C function or CUDA kernel in the global context.

	#create	#destroy	Library
pthd	pthread_create	pthread_join	Pthread
mpi	MPI_Comm_split	MPI_Intercomm_merge	MPI
cuda			CUDA

The synchronization between thread arrays is implemented with inserted synchronization commands. The following table lists the actual library calls for triggering and waiting.

synchronization		Library
pthd	sem_post / sem_wait	Pthread
mpi	MPI_Isend / MPI_Recv	MPI
cuda	kernal launch / cudaThreadSynchronize	CUDA

The following figure illustrates how the control flow takes a "detour" from the current thread *caller* to trigger all created *callee* threads to run the codeblock and return on completion. The boxes in the figure represent synchronization.

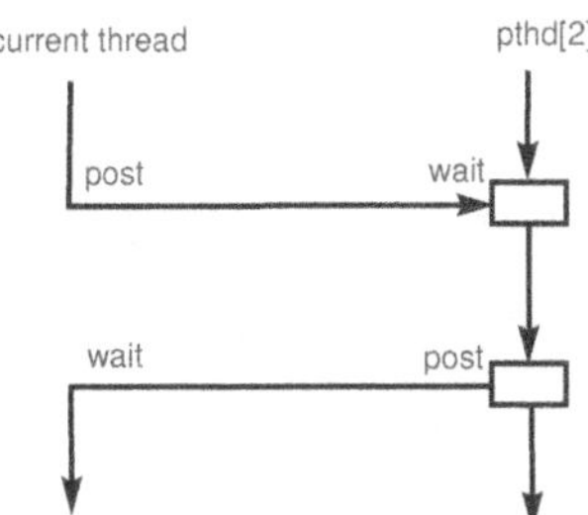

The callee codeblock will be extracted by the compiler separately. If in a program there are two detour commands to the same type of thread array, the callee codeblocks as well as the inserted synchronization commands will be *statically* piled up in the generated C function according to their syntactical order in the source program.

Traditional MIMD programming keeps the sequential code of each thread (or process) in the same syntactical context. Control-flow causality between two threads is achieved with matching synchronization commands executed on two sides. SPMC, however, aggregates the codes of both sides in one nested syntactical context. The synchronization is implicit in the nesting, and control flows can "travel" across different thread arrays. The syntactical order of SPMC codeblocks mainly reflects the natural order of the computating tasks. It is not only more succinct but arguably more natural than the usual way of isolating each individual thread's code in a separate function, which instead reflects how each type of processors works. Conceptually SPMC bears similarity to Remote Procedure Call (or RPC), though RPC typically identifies remote threads as sub-routines, while SPMC uses nested codeblocks.

If the caller and callee thread arrays are the same, then the callee codeblock is simply inserted. Two or more `detour` commands can be placed in a `#parallel` environment that will execute the codeblocks in parallel. This style of programming allows GPU and CPU to run codes in parallel.

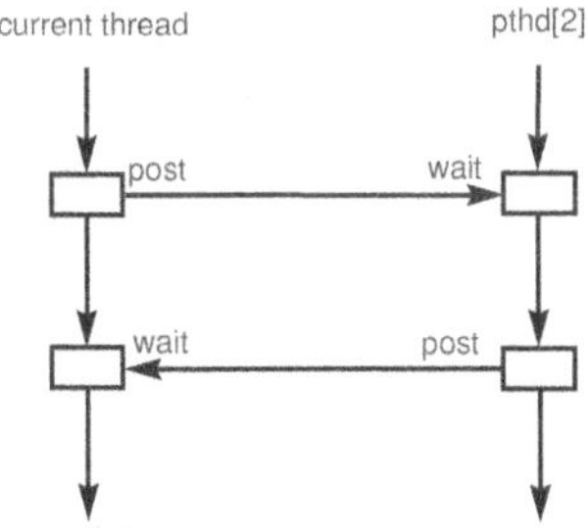

4.3 Sub-Programming

A sub-program is like a general C macro function in which array types as well as program codes can be passed as arguments, sometimes achieving surprising flexibility. The following simple code, despite its appearance, directly corresponds to a CUDA kernel that performs general copying within the device memory of a GPU.

```
#subprog GPUDataTransfer(t, T, s, S)
   #parray {cuda($elm(T)$* t,$elm(S)$* s)
                [$dim(S)$/256][256] } C
   #detour C(t,s){ t[$T[$tid$]$]=s[$S[$tid$]$]; }
#end
```

The arguments `T` and `S` are input types assumed to have an equal (possibly variable) size that is a multiple of 256. The expressions `$elm(T)$` and `$elm(S)$` extract the element types from the input types. The CUDA thread array `C` declares as many threads as the elements with every 256 threads forming a block. The overall thread id `$tid$` here combines CUDA block id and thread id. The inputs `t` and `s` are passed as actual arguments into the CUDA kernel. Every thread copies an element of array `s` at the location `$S[$tid$]$` to the location `$T[$tid$]$` of array `t`. A sub-program is invoked by the command `#insert`. For example the following code declares and creates two arrays of type `Q` in dmem and contiguously copies elements of array s to array t.

```
#parray {dmem float[N][N]} Q
float* s; #create Q(s)
float* t; #create Q(t)
#insert GPUDataTransfer(t,Q,s,Q)){}
```

This sub-program' effect is the same as

```
cudaMemcpy(,,,cudaMemcpyDeviceToDevice)
```

as both input types `T` and `S` of the sub-program are contiguous.

With different input types, the sub-program `GPUDataTransfer` may perform a different operation with entirely different generated kernel codes. For example, the following added code effectively performs an out-place array transposition with the row and column dimensions swapped.

```
#parray {dmem float[#Q_1][#Q_0]} R
float* u; #create R(u)
#insert GPUDataTransfer(u,R,s,Q)){}
```

Both data copying and transposition share the same PARRAY code. No existing array representation supports this kind of code reuse. PARRAY sub-programs are insensitive to the layout of the input and output arrays as long as the layout information is described correctly in the declared types. In comparison, a typical function SGEMM for matrix multiplication in the basic math library BLAS has a rather clumsy signature:

```
void sgemm(char transa, char transb,
           int m, int n, int k, ......);
```

where `transa` (or `transb`) is either `'n'` indicating the first array to be row-major or `'t'` being column-major. Other memory layouts are not representable with the BLAS signature. PARRAY's sub-programming mechanism is therefore more flexible than C functions. Like C macros, the price paid for such flexibility is to re-compile a sub-program on every insertion and generate code according to the type arguments.

In fact the general `DataTransfer` command is also a sub-program with the same signature as `GPUDataTransfer`. Its implementation is a series of compile-time conditionals that check the type arguments for structure, memory type and dimension contiguity . The conditional branches eventually lead to various specialized sub-programs like `GPUDataTransfer`.

`GPUDataTransfer` itself too is subject to more specialized optimization. For example, for GPU transposition from Q to R with contiguous column `R_0` and discontiguous `R_1`, shared memory can be used to coalesce both read and write. Other well-known optimization techniques from the CUDA SDK can further minimize bank conflict within shared memory and dmem.

5. Case Study: Large-Scale FFT

For *small-scale* FFTs whose data are held entirely on a GPU device, their computation benefits from the high device-memory bandwidth [1, 2, 12, 20, 23]. This conforms to an application scenario where the main data are located on dmem, and FFT is performed many times. Then the overheads of PCI transfers between hmem and dmem are overwhelmed by the computation time.

If the data size is too large for a GPU device or must be transferred from/to dmem every time that FFT is performed, then the PCI bandwidth becomes a bottleneck. The time to compute FFT on a GPU will likely be overwhelmed by data transfers via PCIs. This is the scenario for large-scale FFTs on a GPU cluster where all the data are moved around the entire cluster and between hmem and dmem on every node. Compared to a single node, a cluster will provide multiplied memory capacity and bandwidth. The performance bottleneck for a GPU cluster will likely be either the PCI between hmem and dmem or the network between nodes — whichever has the narrower bandwidth. The fact that GPUs can accelerate large-scale FFTs is surprising, as FFT is extremely bandwidth-intensive, but GPUs *do not* increase network bandwidth.

In our previous work [8], we proposed a new FFT algorithm called PKUFFT for GPU clusters. The original implementation uses CUDA, Pthread, MPI and even the low-level infiniband library IB/verbs for performance optimization. That implementation is unportable and specific to a 16-node cluster with dual infiniband cards and dual Tesla C1060 GPUs on each node. To port that code to Tianhe-1A, we first rewrite the code in PARRAY and then re-compile it on the target machine, drastically reducing its length (from 400 lines to 30 lines) while preserving the same depth of optimization. 3D PKUFFT has been deployed to support large-scale turbulence simulation.

Two factors have contributed to the acceleration of FFT with GPUs. Firstly dmem like a giant programmable cache is much larger than CPU cache and hence allows larger sub-tasks to be processed in whole and reduces repeated data transfers between memory and processors. Secondly one major operation of the algorithm requires transposing the entire array, which usually involves main-memory transposition within every node and Alltoall cluster communication. The main optimization of the algorithm [8] is to re-arrange and decompose the operation into small-scale GPU-accelerated transposition, large-scale Alltoall communication and middle-scale data-displacement adjustment that is performed during communications. Then the main-memory transposition is no longer needed! The price paid is to use a non-standard Alltoall with discontiguous process-to-process communications (see Section 2.9).

At source level, porting code from one platform to another platform is straightforward. For simplicity of presentation, the following code is fixed for N-cubic 3D FFTs and requires the GPU-Direct technology (which was not available originally) to use `pinned` memory as a communication buffer. Without GPU-Direct, the main data and `mpimem` communication buffer cannot share the same addresses. The variable `K` is the number of MPI processes.

```
#parray {mpi[K]} L
#detour L(){
 #parray {pinned float2 [N/K][[K][N/K]][N]} G
 #parray {pinned float2 [disp i][N][N]} F
 #parray {dmem float2 [N][N]} Q
 #parray {dmem float2 [#Q_1][#Q_0]} R
 #parray {[[#L][#G_0][#G_1_0][#G_1_1]][#G_2]} S
 #parray {[[#G_1_0][#G_1_1][#L][#G_0]][#G_2]} T
 float2* g; #create G(g)
 float2* gbuf; #create G(gbuf)
 float2* q; #create Q(q)
 float2* qbuf; #create Q(qbuf)
 cufftHandle plan2d;
 cufftPlan2d(&plan2d,N,N,CUFFT_C2C);
 for(int i=0; i<N/K; i++) {
  #insert DataTransfer(q,Q, g,F){}
  cufftExecC2C(plan2d,q,q,CUFFT_FORWARD);
  #insert DataTransfer(gbuf,F, q,Q){}
 }
 #insert DataTransfer(g,T, gbuf,S){}
 cufftHandle plan1d;
 cufftPlan1d(&plan1d,N,CUFFT_C2C,N);
 for(int i=0; i<N/K; i++) {
  #insert DataTransfer(q,Q, g,F){}
  #insert DataTransfer(qbuf,R, q,Q){}
  cufftExecC2C(plan1d,qbuf,qbuf,CUFFT_FORWARD);
  #insert DataTransfer(q,Q, qbuf,R){}
  #insert DataTransfer(gbuf,F, q,Q){}
 }
 #insert DataTransfer(g,S, gbuf,T){}
 cufftDestroy(plan2d);
 cufftDestroy(plan1d);
 #destroy G(g) #destroy G(gbuf)
 #destroy Q(q) #destroy Q(qbuf)
}
```

This code consists of a series of data-transfer operations that we already studied in previous sections. The main 3D complex data are stored in array `g` of type `G`. Another array `gbuf` acts as a buffer. The inner dimension `G_2` is contiguous; `G_1` is the middle dimension; the outer dimension is a combination of thread dimension `L` and `G_0`. Each MPI processes in `L` contains `N/K` pages of size `N*N`. In the first step, every page (with middle and inner dimensions) is transferred to the dmem array `q` for 2D FFT computation (by calling CUDA library) with results transferred back into `qbuf`. The following communication over the entire network is the non-standard discontiguous Alltoall communication pattern (1) that we studied in Section 2.9. The communication effectively swaps the outer and middle dimensions, so that the middle dimension is aggregated on each MPI process. Every 2D page of the middle and inner dimensions is transferred to dmem again. Before performing batched 1D FFT on the new middle dimension, we use GPU transposition (see Section 4.3) to swap the middle and inner dimensions to make the middle dimension contiguous. The original positions of the data are restored after FFT by GPU transposition and communication.

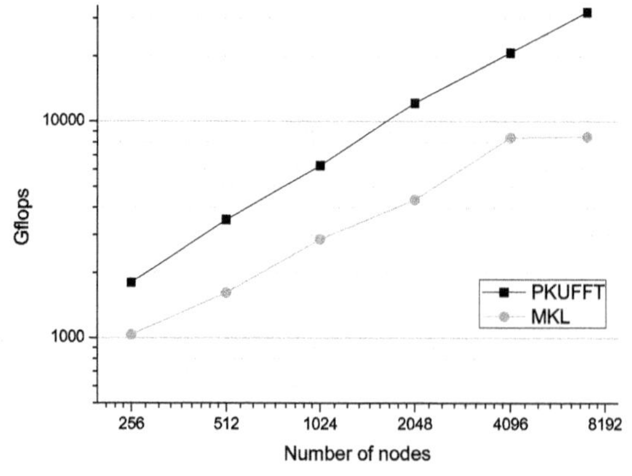

Figure 1. PKUFFT *vs.* Intel Cluster MKL on Tianhe-1A

The above FFT code is tested on Tianhe-1A using up to 7168 nodes, each with 24GB main memory, two 6-core Intel Processors and one Tesla Fermi 448-core GPU. The special customized network has 80Gb/s bandwidth for each node and a fat tree structure for switching. CUDA version is 3.0; CUFFT version is 3.1. For comparison, Intel Cluster MKL (or CMKL) 10.3.1.048 is used on the same cluster but does not use GPU. CMKL is already highly optimized because of the heavy communication load of very-large FFTs. The tests are performed for 3D FFT of different sizes for single-precision C2C forward (with returning communication that restores the data to their original positions). Double-precision FFTs perform at the half speed of single precision (on Fermi as well as data transfers). Figure 2 (tested for best supported array sizes) shows that on a large GPU cluster, the GPU-based algorithm significantly outperforms CMKL which does not use GPU. GPU-accelerated FFT also scales better than CPU-based FFT. The next figure illustrates the scalability in more details. Note that we do not swap the outer and inner dimensions directly, as that will affect the granularity of network communication.

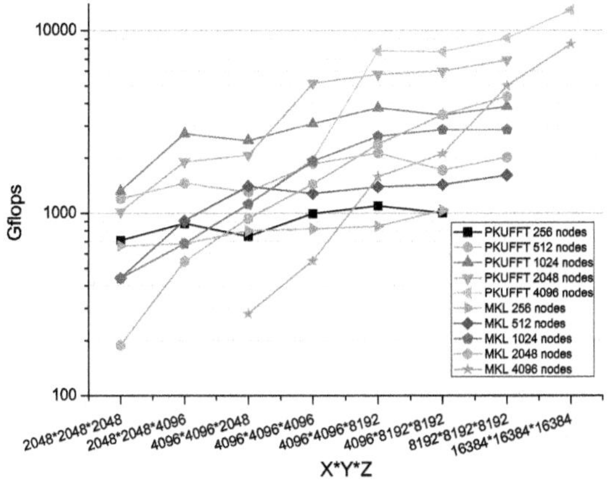

Figure 2. Detailed Comparisons of Scalability

Figure 3 places PKUFFT performance along with FFT benchmark results (data from HPCC web site until Sep 2011). The first performance of 17Tflops (double-precision) is from our PKUFFT test, and the second is obtained with Intel Cluster MKL 10.3.1.048.

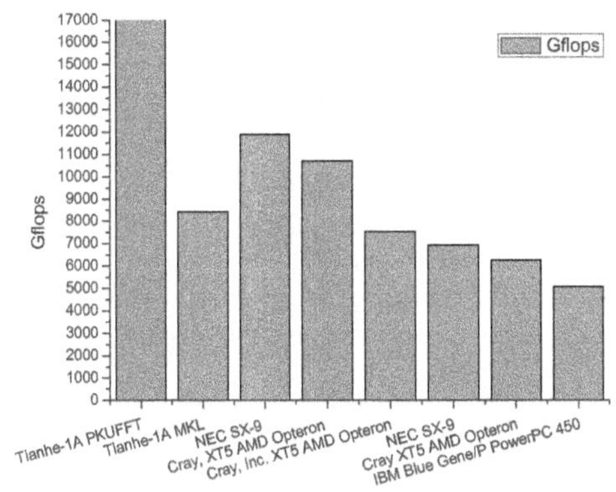

Figure 3. FFT Performance Results of Large Systems

Some FFT algorithms [22] adopt two-dimensional decomposition. This is no longer necessary using PARRAY. On a traditional CPU cluster, the number of MPI processes is usually the number of cores so that MPI utilizes multicore parallelism without the need for OpenMP. That leads to a large number of MPI processes exceeding FFT's dimension size. As we can program each node's internal (multicore and manycore) parallelism, there is no need for over-decomposition that reduces message sizes and performance.

We mainly develop R2C and C2R single-precision 3D FFTs, which are used for large direct numerical simulation of turbulent flows up to the scale of 14336 3D on Tianhe-1A. .

6. Literature Survey

In this section, we compare our design with other parallel programming interfaces in a table where, for example, "Global" and Local" denote addressing. The languages considered for comparisons include Chapel [5], Co-Array Fortran (CAF) [21], HMPP [10], Hierarchically Tiled Arrays (HTA) [11], Titanium [24], Stanford PPL [3, 4], UPC [25], X10 [7], ZPL [6], Global Arrays [17] etc.

These programming interfaces as well as some parallel functional languages [13] all support some kind of (array) domains. Common dimensional features include Block, Cyclicity, Replication (*i.e.* indices mapped to replicated value) etc. Such domains are special cases of PARRAY types. CAF also represents multiple cooperating instances of an SPMD program (known as images) through a new type of array dimension called a co-array. Titanium adds several features including multidimensional arrays supporting iterators, subarrays, and copying to Java. ZPL uses a series of array operators to express different access patterns including translation, broadcast, reduction, parallel prefix operations, and gathers/scatters. In UPC a shared array variable has elements distributed among program instances (or threads). X10 also supports multidimensional arrays that can be distributed among cluster nodes.

PARRAY does not directly offer numerical operations between arrays. An operation as simple as matrix multiplication may have different algorithms and implementations on a heterogeneous parallel system. PARRAY is intended to be a performance-transparent layer of abstraction. All effort to lift programming level and hide algorithmic decisions is left to library development of sub-programs.

Among the existing language designs, HTA is perhaps the closest. The claimed points of novelty 1) dimension tree, 2) type references, and 3) thread arrays are not supported by HTA. The improvement is mainly the fact that the array representation in PA RRAY is more expressive. The theory part shows a certain algebraic completeness of the representation. Hierarchical tiles arrays assume several default levels (for multicore/cluster parallelism). On the other hand, PARRAY's dimension trees are logical. We believe that hierarchical structure is so important that it should be general and not tied to a specific memory structure.

A large class of languages are PGAS languages. PGAS expects the programmer to think about locality but supports random accesses like shared memory regardless the underlying communication mechanism — essentially something between message passing and variable sharing. PARRAY is not based on any unifying memory model. Instead it is designed to support a variety of communication mechanisms. However, if there exists a well-optimized PGAS library such as Global Arrays, PARRAY can generate code to invoke that library. If the low-level libraries offer both two-sided and one-sided communications, the programmer can use commands `GetDataTransfer` and `PutDataTransfer` to generate one-sided code explicitly.

7. Conclusions and Future Work

Our array representation is proposed to unify three forms of parallelism: multicore, manycore and clustering. Other programming ideas often focus on two of them. An advantage of our array representation is its simplicity of semantics and implementation. The source-to-source translation and code generator reach only 2000 lines of C++ code. Basic forms of new data types are intuitive and easy to understand, though some sophisticated types may require

	Language	Library	Global	Local	Cluster	Multicore	Manycore	Dimtree/Type Reference
PARRAY	√			√	√	√	√	√
Chapel	√		√		√	√		
CAF	√		√		√			
HPF	√		√		√			
HMPP	√			√		√	√	
HTA		√	√		√	√	√	
MPI/PVM		√		√	√			
PPL		√			√			
Titanium	√		√			√	√	
UPC	√		√		√			
X10	√		√		√	√		
ZPL	√		√		√			

Figure 4. Comparisons among Parallel Programming Languages and Libraries

more mathematical intuition to handle the inherent complexity of some communication patterns (*e.g.* the non-standard Alltoall).

Our code generator has been tested on a wide range of other program examples such as matrix operations and stencil computation. In particular we have used FFT in direct numeral simulation of turbulent flows scalable up to 14336^3 single precision. This ongoing experiment (to be reported elsewhere) requires 12 arrays of this size and has reached 36Tflops on Tianhe-1A. Porting the original MPI code to PARRAY for Tianhe-1A took us only five days.

PARRAY only provides abstraction for regular data structures like arrays. Irregular data structures such as trees and graphs must be encoded as arrays to benefit from PARRAY's integrated code generation. The encoding is left to the user or any higher-level software layers/libraries. PARRAY's performance transparency makes sure that any higher-level layers implemented on top of PARRAY will not be performance-wise penalized because of using PARRAY instead of the low-level libraries of its generated code.

The most important thing for a new programming interface is to encourage user acceptance. Training courses have been carried out. Trainees especially those with background in computational sciences respond remarkably well to the new notation. Unlike computer engineers who are more used to language mechanisms like pointer arithmetic, application programmers (*e.g.* those from oil industry) seem to be more conformable with matrix notation and even find those advanced forms of array types intuitive. For example in stencil computation, a window within a two-dimensional array can be accessed either by moving the pointer to the starting address or using dimensional displacement. Programmers in CS background often prefer pointer arithmetic while many with science backgrounds prefer displacement type. The nature of this interesting difference is perhaps due to their different programming familiarity with C and Fortran, different earlier mathematical education or a combination of the two factors.

In future, PARRAY will support other accelerator devices such as FPGA and Intel MIC and lower-level communication libraries like IB/Verbs. We do not foresee obvious technological hurdles.

Acknowledgment

We are grateful to the anonymous referees for their comments that have helped improve the presentation of this paper. This work is supported by China HGJ Significant Project 2009ZX01036-001-002-4, National 973 Project 45210130-0442, NSFC Project 61170053 and BJNSF Project 4112027.

References

[1] *CUDA CUFFT Library, Version 2.3.* NVIDIA Corp., 2009.

[2] N. Akira and M. Satoshi. Auto-tuning 3D FFT library for cuda GPUs. In *SC'09*, pages 1–10. ACM, 2009.

[3] K. Brown and et al. A heterogeneous parallel framework for domain-specific languages. In *PACT'11*, 2011.

[4] H. Chafi and et al. A domain-specific approach to heterogeneous parallelism. In *PPoPP'11*, 2011.

[5] B. Chamberlain, D. Callahan, and H. P. Zima. Parallel programmability and the Chapel language. *IJHPCA*, 21(3):291–312, 2007.

[6] B. Chamberlain and et al. The high-level parallel language ZPL improves productivity and performance. In *IJHPCA'04*, 2004.

[7] P. Charles and et al. X10: An object-oriented approach to nonuniform cluster computing. In *OOPSLA'05*, 2005.

[8] Y. Chen, X. Cui, and H. Mei. Large-scale FFT on GPU clusters. In *ACM Inter. Conf. on Supercomputing (ICS'10)*, pages 50–59, 2010.

[9] M. Fatica. Accelerating linpack with CUDA on heterogenous clusters. *GPGPU'09*, June 2009.

[10] B. Francois. Incremental migration of C and Fortran applications to GPGPU using HMPP. Technical report, hipeac, 2010.

[11] B. Ganesh and et al. Programming for parallelism and locality with hierarchically tiled arrays. In *PPoPP'06*, pages 48–57, 2006.

[12] N. Govindaraju and et al. High performance discrete fourier transforms on graphics processors. *SC'08*, November 2008.

[13] G. Hains and L. M. R. Mullin. Parallel functional programming with arrays. *Comput. J.*, 36(3):238–245, 1993.

[14] C. A. R. Hoare. *Communicating Sequential Processes.* Prentice Hall, 1985.

[15] C. A. R. Hoare and et al. Laws of programming. *Communications of the ACM*, 30(8):672–686, 1987.

[16] C. A. R. Hoare and J. He. *Unifying Theories of Programming*. Prentice Hall, 1998.

[17] J. J. Nieplocha, R. J. Harrison, and R. J. Littlefield. Global arrays: A nonuniform memory access programming model for high-performance computers. *The Journal of Supercomputing*, 10(2), 1996.

[18] B. J'onsson and A. Tarski. Boolean algebras with operators, part I. *American Journal of Mathematics*, 73:891–939, 1951.

[19] K. Kandalla and et al. High-performance and scalable non-blocking All-to-All with collective offload on infiniband clusters: A study with parallel 3D FFT. In *ISC'11*, 2011.

[20] A. Nukada and et al. Bandwidth intensive 3-D FFT kernel for GPUs using cuda. In *SC'08*, pages 1–11, 2008.

[21] R. Numerich and J. Reid. Co-Array Fortran for parallel programming. *SIGPLAN Fortran Forum*, 17(2):1C31, 1998.

[22] D. Pekurovsky. http://www.sdsc.edu/us/resources/p3dfft.php.

[23] V. Volkov and B. Kazian. Fitting FFT onto the G80 architecture. *http://www.cs.berkeley.edu/*, May 2008.

[24] K. Yelick and et al. Titanium: A high-performance Java dialect. In *In ACM*, pages 10–11, 1998.

[25] Y. Zheng and et al. Extending Unified Parallel C for GPU computing. In *SIAM Conf on Parallel Processing for Scientific Computing*, 2010.

Internally Deterministic Parallel Algorithms Can Be Fast

Guy E. Blelloch[*] Jeremy T. Fineman[†] Phillip B. Gibbons[‡] Julian Shun[*]

[*]Carnegie Mellon University [†]Georgetown University [‡]Intel Labs, Pittsburgh

guyb@cs.cmu.edu jfineman@cs.georgetown.edu phillip.b.gibbons@intel.com jshun@cs.cmu.edu

Abstract

The virtues of deterministic parallelism have been argued for decades and many forms of deterministic parallelism have been described and analyzed. Here we are concerned with one of the strongest forms, requiring that for any input there is a *unique* dependence graph representing a trace of the computation annotated with every operation and value. This has been referred to as *internal determinism*, and implies a sequential semantics—*i.e.*, considering any sequential traversal of the dependence graph is sufficient for analyzing the correctness of the code. In addition to returning deterministic results, internal determinism has many advantages including ease of reasoning about the code, ease of verifying correctness, ease of debugging, ease of defining invariants, ease of defining good coverage for testing, and ease of formally, informally and experimentally reasoning about performance. On the other hand one needs to consider the possible downsides of determinism, which might include making algorithms (i) more complicated, unnatural or special purpose and/or (ii) slower or less scalable.

In this paper we study the effectiveness of this strong form of determinism through a broad set of benchmark problems. Our main contribution is to demonstrate that for this wide body of problems, there exist efficient internally deterministic algorithms, and moreover that these algorithms are natural to reason about and not complicated to code. We leverage an approach to determinism suggested by Steele (1990), which is to use nested parallelism with commutative operations. Our algorithms apply several diverse programming paradigms that fit within the model including (i) a strict functional style (no shared state among concurrent operations), (ii) an approach we refer to as *deterministic reservations*, and (iii) the use of commutative, linearizable operations on data structures. We describe algorithms for the benchmark problems that use these deterministic approaches and present performance results on a 32-core machine. Perhaps surprisingly, for all problems, our internally deterministic algorithms achieve good speedup and good performance even relative to prior nondeterministic solutions.

Categories and Subject Descriptors D.1 [*Concurrent Programming*]: Parallel programming

General Terms Algorithms, Experimentation, Performance

Keywords Parallel algorithms, deterministic parallelism, parallel programming, commutative operations, graph algorithms, geometry algorithms, sorting, string processing

PPoPP '12 February 25–29, 2012, New Orleans, Louisiana, USA.

1. Introduction

One of the key challenges of parallel programming is dealing with nondeterminism. For many computational problems, there is no inherent nondeterminism in the problem statement, and indeed a serial program would be deterministic—the nondeterminism arises solely due to the parallel program and/or due to the parallel machine and its runtime environment. The challenges of nondeterminism have been recognized and studied for decades [23, 24, 37, 42]. Steele's 1990 paper, for example, seeks "to prevent the behavior of the program from depending on any accidents of execution order that can arise from the indeterminacy" of asynchronous programs [42]. More recently, there has been a surge of advocacy for and research in determinism, seeking to remove sources of nondeterminism via specially-designed hardware mechanisms [19, 20, 28], runtime systems and compilers [3, 5, 36, 45], operating systems [4], and programming languages/frameworks [11].

While there seems to be a growing consensus that determinism is important, there is disagreement as to what degree of determinism is desired (worth paying for). Popular options include:

- *Data-race free* [2, 22], which eliminate a particularly problematic type of nondeterminism: the data race. Synchronization constructs such as locks or atomic transactions protect ordinary accesses to shared data, but nondeterminism among such constructs (*e.g.*, the order of lock acquires) can lead to considerable nondeterminism in the execution.
- *Determinate* (or *external determinism*), which requires that the program always produces the same output when run on the same input. Program executions for a given input may vary widely, as long as the program "converges" to the same output each time.
- *Internal determinism*, in which key aspects of intermediate steps of the program are also deterministic, as discussed in this paper.
- *Functional determinism*, where the absence of side-effects in purely functional languages make all components independent and safe to run in parallel.
- *Synchronous parallelism*, where parallelism proceeds in lock step (*e.g.*, SIMD-style) and each step has a deterministic outcome.

There are trade-offs among these options, with stronger forms of determinism often viewed as better for reasoning and debugging but worse for performance and perhaps programmability. Making the proper choice for an application requires understanding what the trade-offs are. In particular, is there a "sweet spot" for determinism, which provides a particularly useful combination of debuggability, performance, and programmability?

In this paper, we advocate a particular form of *internal determinism* as providing such a sweet spot for a class of nested-parallel (*i.e.*, nested fork-join) computations in which there is no inherent nondeterminism in the problem statement. An execution of a nested-parallel program defines a dependence DAG (directed acyclic graph) that represents every operation executed by the computation (the nodes) along with the control dependencies among them (the edges). These dependencies represent ordering within sequential code sequences, dependencies from a fork operation to its children, and dependencies from the end of such children to the join point of the forking parent. We refer to this DAG when annotated with the operations performed at each node (including arguments and return values, if any) as the *trace*. Informally, a program/algorithm is *internally deterministic* if for any input there is a *unique* trace. This definition depends on the level of abstraction of the operations in the trace. At the most primitive level the operations could represent individual machine instructions, but more generally, and as used in this paper, it is any abstraction level at which the implementation is hidden from the programmer. We note that internal determinism does not imply a fixed schedule since any schedule that is consistent with the DAG is valid.

Internal determinism has many benefits. In addition to leading to external determinism [37] it implies a sequential semantics—*i.e.*, considering any sequential traversal of the dependence DAG is sufficient for analyzing the correctness of the code. This in turn leads to many advantages including ease of reasoning about the code, ease of verifying correctness, ease of debugging, ease of defining invariants, ease of defining good coverage for testing, and ease of formally, informally and experimentally reasoning about performance [3–5, 11, 19, 20, 28, 36, 45]. Two primary concerns for internal determinism, however, are that it may restrict programmers to a style that (i) is complicated to program, unnatural, or too special-purpose and (ii) leads to slower, less scalable programs than less restrictive forms of determinism. Indeed, prior work advocating less restrictive forms of determinism has cited these concerns, particularly the latter concern [25].

This paper seeks to address these two concerns via a study of a set of benchmark problems. The problems are selected to cover a reasonably broad set of applications including problems involving sorting, graphs, geometry, graphics and string processing. Our main contribution is to demonstrate that *for this wide body of problems, there exist fast and scalable internally deterministic algorithms, and moreover that these algorithms are natural to reason about and not complicated to code.*

Our approach for implementing internal determinism for these benchmarks is to use nested parallel programs in which concurrent operations on shared state are required to commute [42, 44] in their semantics and be linearizable [27] in their implementation. Many of the algorithms we implement use standard algorithmic techniques based on nested data parallelism where the only shared state across concurrent operations is read-only (*e.g.*, divide-and-conquer, map, reduce, and scan) [6]. However, a key aspect to several of our algorithms is the use of non-trivial commutative operations on shared state. The notion of commutativity has a long history, dating back at least to its use in analyzing when database transactions can safely overlap in time [44]. A seminal paper by Steele [42] discusses commutativity in the context of deterministic nested-parallel programs, showing that when applied to reads and writes on memory locations, commutativity of concurrent operations is sufficient to guarantee determinism.

Although there has been significant work on commutativity, there has been little work on the efficacy or efficiency of using non-trivial commutativity in the design of deterministic parallel algorithms. Much of the prior work on commutativity focuses on enforcing commutativity assuming the program was already written within the paradigm (*e.g.*, using type systems [12]), automatically parallelizing sequential programs based on the commutativity of operations [39, 40, 43], or using commutativity to relax the constraints in transactional systems [26, 30], an approach that does not guarantee determinism. In contrast, this paper identifies useful applications of non-trivial commutativity that can be used in the design of internally deterministic algorithms.

We describe, for example, an approach we refer to as *deterministic reservations* for parallelizing certain greedy algorithms. In the approach the user implements a loop with potential loop carried dependencies by splitting each iteration into *reserve* and *commit* phases. The loop is then processed in rounds in which each round takes a prefix of the unprocessed iterates applying the reserve phase in parallel and then the commit phase in parallel. Some iterates can fail during the commit due to conflicts with earlier iterates and need to be retried in the next round, but as long as the operations commute within the reserve and commit phases and the prefix size is selected deterministically, the computation is internally deterministic (the same iterates always fail).

We describe algorithms for the benchmark problems using these approaches and present performance results for our Cilk++ [31] implementations on a 32-core machine. Perhaps surprisingly, for all problems, our internally deterministic algorithms achieve good speedup and good performance even relative to prior nondeterministic and externally deterministic solutions, implying that the performance penalty of internal determinism is quite low. We achieve speedups of up to 31.6 on 32 cores with 2-way hyperthreading (for sorting). Almost all our speedups are above 16. Compared to what we believe are quite good sequential implementations we range from being slightly faster on one core (sorting) to about a factor of 2 slower (spanning forest). All of our algorithms are quite concise (20-500 lines of code), and we believe they are "natural" to reason about (understandable, not complicated, not special purpose). The paper presents code for two of the algorithms as illustrative examples; code for all of the algorithms (as well as complete descriptions of the benchmarks) can be found at `www.cs.cmu.edu/~pbbs`. We believe that this combination of performance and understandability provides significant evidence that internal determinism is a sweet spot for a broad range of computational problems.

The paper is organized as follows. Section 2 defines key terms and our programming model. Section 3 presents useful commutative building blocks. Section 4 describes the benchmark problems studied. Section 5 presents our approaches and algorithms. Our experimental study is in Section 6, and conclusions in Section 7.

2. Programming Model

This paper focuses on achieving *internally deterministic* behavior in "nested-parallel" programs through "commutative" and "linearizable" operations. Each of these terms limits the programs permitted by the programming model, but as Section 5 exhibits, the model remains expressive. This section defines each of these terms.

Nested parallelism. Nested-parallel computations achieve parallelism through the nested instantiation of fork-join constructs, such as parallel loops, parallel map, parbegin/parend, parallel regions, and spawn/sync. More formally, nested parallel computations can be defined inductively in terms of the composition of sequential and parallel components. At the base case a *strand* is a sequential computation. A *task* is then a sequential composition of strands and parallel blocks, where a *parallel block* is a parallel composition of tasks starting with a fork and ending with a join. Figure 1 shows an example of a nested-parallel program using a syntax similar to Dijkstra's parbegin [21].

A nested parallel computation can be modeled (a posteriori) as a series-parallel ***control-flow DAG*** over the operations of the computation: the tasks in a parallel block are composed in parallel, and the operations within a strand as well as the strands and parallel blocks of a task are composed in series in the order they are

```
1. x := 0
2. in parallel do
3.     { r3 := AtomicAdd(x, 1)  }
4.     { r4 := AtomicAdd(x, 10)
5.       in parallel do
6.           { r6 := AtomicAdd(x, 100)  }
7.           { r7 := AtomicAdd(x, 1000)  }
       }
8. return x
```

Figure 1. A sample nested-parallel program. Here, the **in parallel** keyword means that the following two $\{\ldots\}$ blocks of code may execute in parallel. $\texttt{AtomicAdd}(x, v)$ atomically updates x to $x := x + v$ and returns the new value of x.

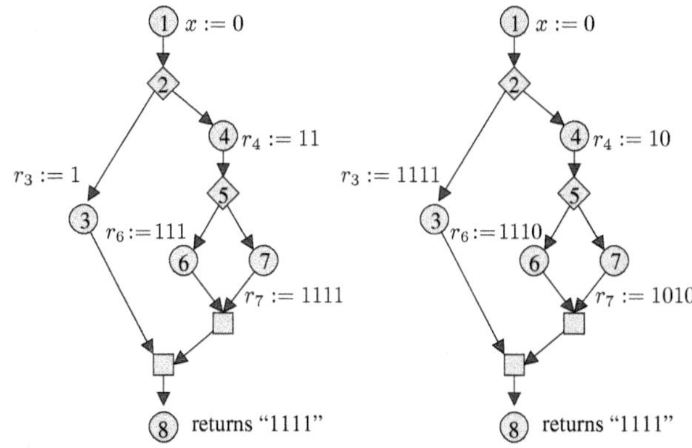

Figure 2. Two possible traces for the program in Figure 1. The diamonds, squares, and circles denote forks, joins, and data operations, respectively. Nodes are numbered by line number, as a short hand for operations such as $\texttt{AtomicAdd}(x, 1)$. The left trace corresponds to the interleaving/schedule $1, 2, 3, 4, 5, 6, 7, 8$, whereas the right trace corresponds to $1, 2, 4, 5, 7, 6, 3, 8$. Because the intermediate return values differ, the program is not internally deterministic. It is, however, externally deterministic as the output is always the same. If AtomicAdd did not return a value, however, then the program would be internally deterministic.

executed. We assume all operations take a state and return a value and a new state (any arguments are part of the operation). Nodes in the control-flow DAG are labeled by their associated operation (including arguments, but not return values or states). We say that an operation (node) u *precedes* v if there is a directed path from u to v in the DAG. If there is no directed path in either direction between u and v, then u and v are ***logically parallel***, meaning that they *may* be executed in parallel.

The support of nested parallelism dates back at least to Dijkstra's parbegin-parend construct. Many parallel languages support nested parallelism including NESL, Cilk, the Java fork-join framework, OpenMP, the TBB, and TPL. Although not appropriate for certain types of parallelism, *e.g.*, pipeline parallelism, nested parallelism has many theoretical and practical advantages over more unstructured forms of parallelism, including simple schedulers for dynamically allocating tasks to cores, compositional analysis of work and span, and good space and cache behavior (*e.g.*, [1, 6, 8, 10]).

Languages with nested parallelism rely on runtime schedulers to assign subcomputations to cores. Whereas these runtime schedulers are inherently nondeterministic to handle load balancing and changes in available resources, our goal is to guarantee that the program nevertheless behaves deterministically.

Internal determinism. We adopt a strong notion of determinism here, often called internal determinism [35]. Not only must the output of the program be deterministic, but all intermediate values returned from operations must also be deterministic. We note that this does not preclude the use of pseudorandom numbers, where one can use, for example, the approach of Leiserson *et al.* [33] to generate deterministic pseudorandom numbers in parallel from a single seed, which can be part of the input.

This paper defines determinism with respect to abstract operations and abstract state, not with respect to machine instructions and memory state. Nevertheless, the definition supplied here is general and applies to both cases. The difference hinges on the notion of "equivalence." Given a definition of equivalent operations, states, and values, we define internal determinism as follows.

For a (completed) computation its ***trace*** is the final state along with the control-flow DAG on which operation nodes are (further) annotated with the values returned (if any). Figure 2 shows two traces corresponding to executions of the program shown in Figure 1. Two control-flow DAGs are equivalent if they have the same graph structure and corresponding nodes are labeled with equivalent operations. Two traces are ***equivalent traces*** if they have equivalent final states, equivalent control-flow DAGs, and corresponding DAG nodes are annotated with equivalent return values.

Definition 1. *A program is* ***internally deterministic*** *if for any fixed input I, all possible executions with input I result in equivalent traces.*

Note that since the parallelism is dynamic, a nondeterministic program may result in dramatically different DAGs. Because all decisions in a computation are based only on the result of operations performed, however, if operations return equivalent results despite different schedulings, then the structure of the DAG is guaranteed to remain the same.

For primitive types like integers, it is clear what equivalence means. When working with objects and dynamic memory allocation, however, a formal definition of equivalent objects and states becomes more complicated, and not within the scope of this paper. Informally, when we say that states or values are equivalent, we mean semantically equivalent, *i.e.*, that no sequence of valid operations can distinguish between them (see, *e.g.*, [26]).

Commutativity. Internally deterministic programs are a subset of parallel programs, and thus programming methodologies that yield internal determinism restrict a program's behaviors. The methodology we adopt in this paper is to require all logically parallel accesses of shared objects to use operations that commute. The fact that this restriction yields internally deterministic programs is observed in many works, see for example [15, 40, 42] among others.

We adopt Steele's notation and definition of commutativity [42]. We use $f(S) \rightarrow S' \Rightarrow v$ to denote that when the operation f is executed (without any concurrent operations) starting from system (object) state S, the system transitions to state S' and f returns the value v. To simplify notation, operations not returning values are viewed as returning $v = \emptyset$.

Definition 2. *Two operations f and g* ***commute with respect to state*** *S if the order in which they are performed does not matter. That is, if*

$$f(S) \rightarrow S_f \Rightarrow v_f$$
$$g(S_f) \rightarrow S_{fg} \Rightarrow v_g$$

and

$$g(S) \rightarrow S'_g \Rightarrow v'_g$$
$$f(S'_g) \rightarrow S'_{gf} \Rightarrow v'_f$$

then f and g commute with respect to S if and only if $S_{fg} = S'_{gf}$, $v_f = v'_f$, and $v_g = v'_g$, where "$=$" here denotes equivalence. (Note that there is no requirement that $S_f = S'_g$.)

Moreover, we say that two operations ***commute*** if they commute with respect to *all* valid states S. It is possible to relax this definition (*e.g.*, [26, 44]), but we found this definition sufficient for our purposes.

Linearizability. Commutativity is not a sufficient condition for deterministic behavior, as commutativity alone does not guarantee that the implementation of the operations work correctly when their instructions are interleaved in time. To guarantee safety of concurrent execution of operations we use the standard definition of linearizability [27], which enforces atomicity of the operations. In our setting, operations are concurrent if and only if they are logically parallel. Thus, linearizability guarantees that there is a total order (or *history*), H, of the annotated operations in a trace T such that H is a legal sequential execution of those operations, starting from the initial state. That is, (i) H is a valid scheduling of T's control-flow DAG, and (ii) each annotated operation in T remains legal (including its return value) when executed atomically in the order of H. We note that linearizability is a property of the implementation and not the semantics of the operation (*e.g.*, two insertions into a dictionary might semantically commute, but an implementation might fail when interleaved). One way to guarantee linearizability is to use a lock around all commuting operations, but this is inefficient. In this paper we use only non-blocking techniques to achieve linearizability among commuting operations. We however do not guarantee that all commuting operations are linearizable, just that the logically parallel ones are.

Summary. The model we will use for internally deterministic behavior is summarized by the following theorem.

Theorem 1. *Let P be a nested-parallel program. If for all inputs, all logically parallel operations commute and are linearizable, then P is internally deterministic.*

Proof. (sketch) Consider any fixed input I and any fixed (completed) execution of P with input I. Let G (T) be the resulting control-flow DAG (trace, respectively), and let H be its linearizability history. We will show that T is equivalent to a canonical trace T^* obtained by executing P with input I using only a single core. Let G^* and H^* be the control-flow DAG and linearizability history for T^*. We show by induction on the length of H^* that (i) G and G^* are equivalent and (ii) H permuted to match the order in H^* of equivalent nodes is also a linearizability history for T, implying equivalent return values. We construct such a permutation, H', inductively, with $H' = H$ initially. Assume inductively that (i) the subgraph of G^* corresponding to the nodes in $H^*[1..i]$ has an equivalent subgraph in G, and (ii) H' is a linearizability history for T such that $H'[1..i]$ and $H^*[1..i]$ are equivalent ($[j..k]$ denotes subsequence). Consider $i+1$, and let σ^* be the $i+1$'st annotated node in H^*. It follows inductively that there is a node σ in T with equivalent parent(s) and an equivalent operation, say the jth node in H'. If $j = i+1$, we are done, so assume $j > i+1$. None of the nodes in $H'[i+1..j-1]$ can precede or be preceded by σ, so σ must commute with each such node. Thus, σ can be pairwise swapped up to position $i+1$ in H' while preserving a linearizability history, establishing both inductive invariants. The argument is readily extended to show the equivalence of the final states by augmenting each execution with operations that read the final state. The theorem follows. □

Our approach is similar to previous models for enforcing deterministic behavior [15, 42] except that in Steele [42] commutativity is defined in terms of memory operations and memory state, and in Cheng *et al.* [15] commutativity is defined with respect to critical sections and memory state. Here we define commutativity in terms of linearizable abstract operations and abstract state.

3. Commutative Building Blocks

Achieving deterministic programs through commutativity requires some level of (object or operation) abstraction. Relying solely on memory operations is doomed to fail for general purpose programming. For example requiring a fixed memory location for objects allocated in the heap would severely complicate programs and/or inhibit parallelism, possibly requiring all data to be preallocated. Instead, this section defines some useful higher-level operations that we use as commutative operations in many of our algorithms. They are all defined over abstract data types supporting a fixed set of operations. We also describe non-blocking linearizable implementations of each operation. These implementations do not commute at the level of single memory instructions and hence the abstraction is important.

Priority write. Our most basic data type is a memory cell that holds a value and supports a priority write and a read. The priority write on a cell x, denoted by $x.\texttt{pwrite}(v)$ updates x to be the maximum of the old value of x and a new value v. It does not return any value. $x.\texttt{read}()$ is just a standard read of the cell x returning its value. We often use priority write to select a deterministic winner among parallel choices, *e.g.*, claiming a next-step neighbor in breadth first search (Section 5.3).

Any two priority writes $x.\texttt{pwrite}(v_1)$ and $x.\texttt{pwrite}(v_2)$ commute, in accordance with Definition 2, because (i) there are no return values, and (ii) the final value of x is the maximum among its original value, v_1, and v_2, regardless of which order these operations execute. A priority write and a read do not commute since the priority write can change the value at the location. We implement non-blocking and linearizable priority writes using a compare and swap. With this implementation the machine primitives themselves do not commute.

Priority reserve. In our "deterministic reservation" approach described later in Section 5, multiple program loop iterates attempt to reserve the same object in parallel, and later the winner operates on the reserved object. For deterministic reservations we use a data type that supports three operations, a priority reserve ($x.\texttt{reserve}(p)$), a check ($x.\texttt{check}(p)$), and a check-and-release ($x.\texttt{checkR}(p)$), where p is a priority. As with a priority write, a higher priority value overwrites a lower priority and hence the highest priority will "reserve" the location. The one difference is that we require a unique priority tag $\perp$ to denote when the location is currently unreserved. The priority $\perp$ has the lowest priority, and it is invalid to make a `pwrite` call with $p = \perp$. As with `pwrite`, any number of `reserves` commute, and we implement a linearizable non-blocking version using compare and swap.

The $x.\texttt{checkR}(p)$ call requires $p \neq \perp$. If the current value at location x has priority p, then the reservation is released (*i.e.*, the value $\perp$ is written to x), and TRUE is returned to indicate that p was the highest priority reservation on x. If the current priority is not p, then the state does not change and FALSE is returned. Operations $x.\texttt{checkR}(p_1)$ and $x.\texttt{checkR}(p_2)$ commute if and only if $p_1 \neq p_2$. A `check` is the same as a `checkR` without the release and commutes in the same way. A priority reserve and either form of check do not commute.

Our algorithms ensure that for any given location, (i) priority reserves are not called logically in parallel with either form of check, and (ii) all logically parallel operations use distinct priorities. Thus, the commutativity and resulting internal determinism extend to those algorithms.

Dynamic map. The purpose of our dynamic map is to incrementally insert keyed elements and, once finished inserting, to return an array containing a pseudorandom permutation of these elements, omitting duplicates. A dynamic map supports two operations: M.`insert`(x), which inserts keyed element x into the map M without returning any value, and M.`elements`(), which returns an arbitrary, but deterministic, permutation of all the elements in the map M. The map removes duplicate keys on insert: if elements y and x have the same key and y is already in the map when M.`insert`(x) is called, one of the elements (chosen deterministically based on a user specified priority) is discarded.

We implement our dynamic map using a history-independent hash table [7]. In a history-independent data structure the final layout does not depend on the operation order. In particular, the key of each element is treated as a priority, and the hash table is equivalent to one in which all insertions were performed sequentially in a nonincreasing priority order using linear probing. Elements are inserted by first hashing the key and going to the corresponding hash location, then scanning consecutive hash-table slots until finding either an empty slot or a slot containing and equal- or lower-priority element. If empty, the new element is inserted and the operation completes. If the slot is occupied by an equal-priority element, either the new or old element is discarded (deterministically based on priority) and the operation completes. If the slot is occupied by a lower-priority element, the higher-priority element is put in that slot (using compare and swaps to provide linearizability), and the lower-priority element is evicted. The linear probe continues to find a slot for the lower-priority element. An `elements` call simply filters the underlying array (using the parallel filter operation discussed in Section 5), finding all the nonempty slots and placing them in order in a return array. Our implementation is non-blocking requiring no locks.

To see that two `inserts` commute, it is easy to show inductively that after each `insert`, the hash table is identical to one in which those elements present were inserted in priority order. This property implies that the ordering between two insertions does not matter. The M.`insert`(x) operation does not commute with M.`elements`() operation since for some states of S, x is not in M and will affect the result of `elements`.

Disjoint sets. Our spanning-forest algorithms rely on a structure for maintaining a collection of disjoint sets corresponding to connected components. Each set is associated with a unique element acting as the identifier for the set. A disjoint-set data type supports two operations: a find and a link. For an instance F, the F.`find`(x) operation returns the set identifier for the set containing x. The F.`link`(S, x) operation requires that S be a set identifier and the set containing x be disjoint from the set S. It logically unions the set S with the set containing x such that the identifier for the resulting unioned set is the identifier of the set containing x. Here, x and S denote references or pointers to elements in the sets.

We implement an instance F of the disjoint set data type as a collection of trees with parent pointers, where the root of each tree acts as a unique identifier for the set [17]. A F.`find`(x) operation simply follows parent pointers up the tree and returns the root. It may also perform path compression [17], which points nodes along the query-to-root path directly to the root, thereby accelerating future queries. A `link`(S, x) operation is implemented by pointing S to the root-node of the set containing x.

Two `find` operations commute with each other as they cause no semantic modifications—i.e. any changes to the pointer structure caused by path compression cannot be discerned by future operations on F. Two `link` operations commute with each other as long as they do not share the same first argument. That is to say, F.`link`(S_1, x_1) and F.`link`(S_2, x_2) commute as long as $S_1 \neq S_2$; having x_1 and x_2 be equal or from the same set is allowed, as is having x_1 in set S_2 or x_2 in set S_1. The `link`(S_1, x_1) and `find`(x_2) only commute if $x_1 = x_2$.

We now consider linearizability. Even with path compression, `find` operations are linearizable (and non-blocking) since there is only one possible update to each pointer (the *a priori* root of the tree). This requires no compare and swap or any other special memory operations. Logically parallel `link` operations with distinct first arguments, and no cycles among the linked sets, are also linearizable and non-blocking with no special memory operations since they only require updating a pointer which is not shared by any other logically parallel operation. In our implementation we do not guarantee that `finds` and `links` are linearizable. Hence, in our algorithms that use disjoint sets, `finds` are never logically parallel with `links`: they alternate phases of only `finds` and only `links`.

We note that we use an asymmetric `link` operation instead of the standard symmetric `union`. This is because `union` does not commute in our definition which requires two operations to commute for all start states. In a more relaxed definition of commutativity, `union` can be made to commute [30].

4. Benchmark Problems

For testing the utility of nested-parallel internally deterministic algorithms we use a set of *problem-based* benchmarks. These benchmarks are defined in terms of the problem they solve instead of any particular code or algorithm to solve the problem. We feel that this is important for our purposes since it might be that very different algorithmic approaches are suited for a deterministic algorithm vs. a nondeterministic algorithm. The benchmark suite is selected to cover a reasonable collection of fundamental problems. The focus, however, is on problems involving unstructured data since there is already very good coverage for such benchmarks for linear algebra and typically deterministic algorithms are much simpler for these problems. The problems are selected to be simple enough to allow reasonably concise implementations, but interesting enough to be non-trivial. For all problems we use a variety of different inputs and avoid just random inputs. Here we define the problems.

Comparison Sort: For a sequence S and comparison function $<$ defining a total order on elements of S, return the values of S sorted by $<$. Sorting is a fundamental problem and a subroutine in many algorithms. The benchmark code must work with any element type and comparison function.

Remove Duplicates: For a sequence of elements of type t, a hash function $h : t \rightarrow int$, and comparison function f, return a sequence in which any duplicates (equal valued elements) are removed. This is an example of a dictionary-style operation that can use hashing.

Breadth First Search: For a connected undirected graph G, and source vertex s, return a breadth-first-search (BFS) tree, rooted at s, of the vertices in G.

Spanning Forest: For an undirected graph $G = (V, E)$, return edges $F \subset E$, such that for each connected component $C_i = (V_i, E_i)$ in G, a spanning tree T_i ($|T_i| = |V_i| - 1$) of C_i is contained in F. Furthermore, $|F| = \sum_{C_i \subset G}(|V_i| - 1)$.

Minimum Spanning Forest: For an undirected graph $G = (V, E)$ with weights $w : E \rightarrow \Re$, return a spanning forest of minimum total weight.

Maximal Independent Set: For a connected undirected graph $G = (V, E)$, return $U \subset V$ such that no vertices in U are neighbors and all vertices in $V \setminus U$ have a neighbor in U. This is an important subroutine in many parallel algorithms because it can be used to identify a set of vertices that can be operated on deterministically in parallel (due to disjoint edge sets).

Triangle Ray Intersect: For a set of triangles T and rays R in three dimensions, return the first triangle each ray intersects, if any.

Problem	D&C	Reduce	Scan	Filter	DR	CL
Comparison Sort	yes		yes			
Remove Duplicates				yes		DM
Breadth First Search			yes	yes		PW
Spanning Forest				yes	yes	DS
Min Spanning Forest	sub			yes	yes	DS
Max Independent Set		yes		yes	yes	
Triangle Ray Intersect	yes		yes	yes		
Suffix Array	sub	yes	yes	yes		
Delaunay Triangulation	sub	yes	sub	yes	yes	
Delaunay Refine		yes		yes	yes	DM
N-body	yes	yes	yes			
K-Nearest Neighbors	sub			yes		

Table 1. Techniques used in our algorithms for each of the benchmarks. D&C indicates divide-and-conquer; Reduce, Scan and Filter are standard collection operations; DR indicates deterministic reservations; and CL indicates the use of a non-trivial commutative and linearizable operation other than reservations: dynamic map (DM), disjoint sets (DS), or priority write (PW). **sub** indicates that it is not used directly, but inside a subroutine, *e.g.*, inside a sort. See Section 5 for further details.

This is a common operation in graphics and is the most widely used special case of ray casting.

Suffix Array: For a string S of n characters return an equal length integer array A that specifies the sorted order of the suffixes of S. This is an important operation used in many applications in computational biology, compression, and string processing.

Delaunay Triangulation: For a set of n points in two dimensions, return a triangulation such that no point is contained in the circumcircle of any triangle in the triangulation [18]. Delaunay triangulations are likely the most widely used partitioning of space in two and three dimensions and used in many CAD applications.

Delaunay Refine: For a Delaunay Triangulation on a set of n points, and an angle α, add new points such that in the resulting Delaunay Triangulation, no triangle has an angle less than α.

N-body: For a set of n point sources in three dimensions, each point p with coordinate vector $\vec{p}$ and a mass m_p, return the force induced on each one by the others based on the Coulomb force $\vec{F}_p = \sum_{q \in P, q \neq p} m_q m_p (\vec{q} - \vec{p})/||\vec{q} - \vec{p}||^3$. The N-body problem is important in protein folding, astrophysics, and slight generalizations are now often used for solving PDEs.

K-Nearest Neighbors: For n points in two or three dimensions, and a parameter k, return for each point its k nearest neighbors (euclidean distance) among all the other points. The problem is fundamental in data analysis and computational geometry.

5. Internally Deterministic Parallel Algorithms

In this section we describe the approaches we used when designing our internally deterministic parallel algorithms and outline the resulting algorithms for each of the benchmarks. Many of the approaches used are standard, but we introduce what we believe to be a new approach for greedy algorithms based on deterministic reservations. This approach plays a key role in our implementation of five of the problems. We also make use of our commuting and linearizable implementations of various operations for five problems. Table 1 summarizes what approaches/techniques are used in which of our algorithms.

5.1 Nested Data Parallelism and Collection Operations

The most common technique throughout the benchmark implementations is the use of nested data parallelism. This technique is applied in a reasonably standard way, particularly in the use of fork-join and parallel loops (with arbitrary nesting) in conjunction with parallel operations on collections. For the operations on collections we developed our own library of operations on sequences. We make heavy use of divide and conquer. In the divide-and-conquer algorithms we almost always use parallelism within the divide step (to partition the input data), and/or the merge step (to join the results), typically using the collection operations in our sequence library.

The three collection operations `reduce`, `scan`, and `filter` are used throughout our algorithms. As is standard, `reduce` takes a sequence S and a binary associative function f and returns the "sum" of elements with respect to f, while `scan` (prefix sum) takes a sequence S and a function f and returns a sequence of equal length with each element containing the sum with respect to f of all preceding elements in S. Our implementations of `reduce` and `scan` are deterministic even if f is not associative—*e.g.*, with floating point addition. The `filter` operation takes a sequence S and a function f returning a boolean and returns a new sequence containing only the elements e for which $f(e)$ is true, in the same order as in S. Filter uses a scan in its implementation.

Reduce is used to calculate various "sums": *e.g.*, to calculate the bounding box (maximum and minimum in each coordinate) of a set of points. Filter is used in most of our algorithms. In the divide-and-conquer algorithms it is typically used to divide the input into parts based on some condition. In the other algorithms it is used to filter out elements that have completed or do not need to be considered. It plays a key role in deterministic reservations. Scan is used in a variety of ways. In the sorting algorithm it is used to determine offsets for the sample sort buckets, in the suffix array algorithm it is used to give distinct elements unique labels, and in the breadth first search algorithm it is used to determine the positions in the output array to place distinct neighbor arrays.

5.2 Deterministic Reservations

Several of our algorithms (maximal independent set, spanning forest, minimum spanning forest, Delaunay triangulation, and Delaunay refine) are based on a greedy sequential algorithm that processes elements (*e.g.*, vertices) in linear order. These can be implemented using speculative execution on a sequential loop that iterates over the elements in the greedy order.

Various studies have suggested both compiler [39, 40] and runtime techniques [25, 43] to automate the process of simulating in parallel the sequential execution of such a loop. These approaches rely on recognizing at compile and/or run time when operations in the loop iterates commute and allowing parallel execution when they do. Often the programmer can specify what operations commute. We are reasonably sure that the compiler-only techniques would not work for our benchmark problems because the conflicts are highly data dependent and any conservative estimates allowing for all possible conflicts would serialize the loop. The runtime techniques typically rely on approaches similar to software transactional memory: the implementation executes the iterations in parallel or out of order but only commits any updates after determining that there are no conflicts with earlier iterations. As with software transactions, the software approach is expensive, especially if required to maintain strict sequential order. In fact in practice the suggested approaches typically relax the total order constraint by requiring only a partial order [39], potentially leading to nondeterminism. A second problem with the software approach is that it makes it very hard for the algorithm designer to analyze efficiency—it is possible that subtle differences in the under-the-hood conflict resolution could radically change which iterates can run in parallel.

We present an approach, called *deterministic reservations*, that gives more control to the algorithm designer and fits strictly within

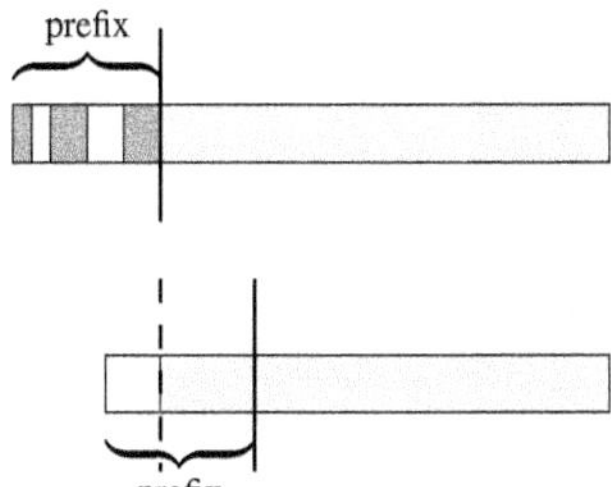

Figure 3. A generic example of deterministic reservations. Top and bottom depict the array of iterates during consecutive rounds. In each round, a prefix of some specified size is selected. All of these prefix iterates perform the reserve component. Then they all perform the commit component. The dark regions in the top array represent iterates that successfully commit. All uncommitted iterates (shown in white) are packed towards the right, as shown in the bottom array. The next round then begins by selecting a prefix of the same size on the bottom array.

the nested-parallel framework (needing neither special compiler nor runtime support). In this approach the algorithm designer controls exactly on what data the conflicts occur and these conflicts are deterministic for a given input. The generic greedy algorithm for deterministic reservations works as follows, illustrated in Figure 3. It is given a sequence of iterates (*e.g.*, the integers from 0 to $n-1$) and proceeds in rounds until no iterates remain. Each round takes any prefix of the remaining unprocessed iterates, and consists of two phases that are each parallel loops over the prefix, followed by some bookkeeping to update the sequence of remaining iterates. The first phase executes a *reserve* component on each iterate, using a priority reserve (`reserve`) with the iterate priority, in order to reserve access to data that might interfere (involve non-commuting or non-linearizable operations) with other iterates. The second phase executes a *commit* component on each iterate, using a `check` to see if the reservations succeeded, and if the required reservations succeed then the iterate is processed, otherwise it is not. Typically updates to shared state (at the abstraction level available to the programmer) are only made if successful. After running the commit phase, the processed iterates are removed. In our implementation the unprocessed iterates are kept in a contiguous array ordered by their priority. Selecting a prefix can therefore just use a prefix of the array, and removing processed iterates can be implemented with a `filter` over the boolean results of the second phase.

The specifics of the reserve and commit components depend on the application. The work done by the iterate can be split across the two components. We have found, however, that in the unstructured problems in the benchmarks just determining what data might interfere involves most of the work. Therefore the majority of the work ends up in the reserve component. In most cases all reservations are required to succeed, but we have encountered cases in which only a subset need to succeed (*e.g.*, our minimum spanning-forest code reserves both endpoints of an edge but only requires that one succeeds).

We note that the generic approach can select any prefix size including a single iterate or all the iterates. There is a trade off, however between the two extremes. If too many iterates are selected for the prefix, then many iterates can fail. This not only requires repeated effort for processing those iterates, but can also cause high-contention on the reservation slots. On the other hand if too few iterates are selected then there might be insufficient parallelism. Clearly the amount of contention depends on the specific algorithms and likely also on the input data.

As long as the prefix size is selected deterministically and all operations commute and are linearizable within the reserve phase and separately within the commit phase, a program will be internally deterministic. This means the algorithm designer only needs to analyze commutativity/linearizability within each phase. In our code we have implemented a function `speculative_for` that takes four arguments: a structure that implements the `reserve` and `commit` components (both taking an index as an argument), a start index, an end index, and a prefix size.

5.3 Algorithms

We now describe each of the algorithms we use to implement the benchmarks discussed in Section 4. In all cases we considered a variety of algorithms and selected the one we felt would perform the best. In many cases we arrived at the algorithm discussed after trying different algorithms. In all cases the algorithms are either motivated by or directly use results of many years of research on parallel algorithm design by many researchers. Due to limitations of space we only very briefly describe any algorithms that mostly use previous ideas.

Comparison Sort: We use a low-depth cache-efficient sample sort [9]. The algorithm (1) partitions the input into $\sqrt{n}$ blocks, (2) recursively sorts each block, (3) selects a global sample of size $\sqrt{n}\log n$ by sampling across the blocks, (4) sorts the sample, (5) buckets each of the blocks based on the sample, (6) transposes the keys so keys from different blocks going to the same bucket are adjacent, and (7) recursively sorts within the buckets. The transpose uses a cache-efficient block-transpose routine. When the input is small enough, quicksort is used. The algorithm is purely nested parallel. There is nesting of the parallelism (divide-and-conquer) in the overall structure, in the merge used for bucketing blocks, in the transpose, and in the quicksort.

Remove Duplicates: We use a parallel loop to concurrently `insert` the elements into the dynamic map described in section 3. This data structure already removes all duplicates internally and returns the distinct elements with a call to `elements` (which internally uses a `filter`). The ordering returned by the routine is deterministic but does not correspond to the input ordering in any natural way and different hash functions will give different orderings. We set the hash table size to be twice the size of the input.

Breadth First Search: We use a level-ordered traversal of the graph that guarantees the same BFS tree as the standard sequential queue-based algorithm [17]. In level-order traversal each vertex u adds each of its unvisited neighbors v to the next frontier and makes u the parent of v in the BFS tree. In standard parallel implementations of BFS [32, 39] each level is processed in parallel and nondeterminism arises because vertices at one level might share a vertex v at the next level. These vertices will attempt to add v to the next frontier concurrently. By using a compare-and-swap or similar operation, it is easy to ensure that a vertex is only added once. However, which vertex adds v depends on the schedule, resulting in internal nondeterminism in the BFS code and external nondeterminism in the resulting BFS tree.

We avoid this problem by using a priority write. The vertices in the frontier are prioritized by their position in the array and we process each level in two rounds. In the first round each vertex in the frontier writes its priority to all neighbors that have not been visited in previous rounds. In the second round each vertex v in the frontier reads from each neighbor u the priority. If the priority of u is v (v is the highest priority neighbor in the frontier), then we make v the parent of u and add u to the next frontier. The neighbors are added to the next frontier in the priority order of the current frontier. This uses a `scan` to open enough space for each neighbor list, and maintains the same ordering on every frontier as the sequential queue-based algorithm maintains.

```
struct STStep {
  int u;  int v;
  edge *E;  res *R;  disjointSet F;
  STStep(edge* _E, disjointSet _F, res* _R)
    : E(_E), R(_R), F(_F) {}

  bool reserve(int i) {
    u = F.find(E[i].u);
    v = F.find(E[i].v);
    if (u == v) return 0;
    if (u > v) swap(u,v);
    R[v].reserve(i);
    return 1;}

  bool commit(int i) {
    if (R[v].check(i)) { F.link(v, u); return 1;}
    else return 0;  }
};

void ST(res* R, edge* E, int m, int n, int psize) {
  disjointSet F(n);
  speculative_for(STStep(E, F, R), 0, m, psize);
}
```

Figure 4. C++ code for spanning forest using deterministic reservations (with its operations `reserve`, `check`, and `speculative_for`), where $\mathtt{m} = |E|$ and $\mathtt{n} = |V|$.

Spanning Forest: Sequentially a spanning forest can be generated by greedily processing the edges in an arbitrary order using a disjoint sets data structure. When an edge is processed if the two endpoints are in the same component (which can be checked with `find`) it is removed, otherwise the edge is added to the spanning forest and the components are joined (with `union`). This algorithm can be run in parallel using deterministic reservations prioritized by the edge ordering and will return the exact same spanning forest as the sequential algorithm. The idea is simply to reserve both endpoints of an edge and check that both reservations succeed in the commit component. Indeed this is how we implement Minimum Spanning Forest, after sorting the edges. However there is an optimization that can be made with spanning forests that involves only requiring one of the reservations to succeed. This increases the probability a commit will succeed and reduces the cost. This approach returns a different forest than the sequential version but is internally deterministic for a fixed schedule of prefix sizes.

The C++ code is given in Figure 4. For an iterate i corresponding to the edge $E[i]$ the reserve component does a `find` on each endpoint (as in the sequential algorithm) returning u and v (w.l.o.g., assume $u \leq v$). If $u = v$, the edge is within a component and can be dropped returning 0 (false)[1], otherwise the algorithm reserves v with the index i ($R[v]$`.reserve`(i)). The commit component for index i performs a $R[v]$`.check`(i) to see if its reservation succeeded. If it has, it links v to u and otherwise the commit fails. At the end of the algorithm the edges $E[i]$ in the spanning tree can be identified as those where $R[i] \neq \perp$. The only difference from the sequential algorithm is that after determining that an edge goes between components instead of doing the union immediately it reserves one of the two sides. It later comes back to check that the reservation succeeded and if so does the union (link).

We note that in a round the reservation guarantees that only one edge (the highest priority) will link a vertex v to another vertex. This is the condition required in Section 3 for commutativity of `link`. Also because the `link` and `find` are in different phases they are never logically parallel, as required. Finally we note that

[1] If false is returned by `reserve()` then the iterate is dropped without proceeding to the commit.

```
enum FlType {LIVE, IN, OUT};

struct MISStep {
  FlType flag; vertex *V;
  MISStep(char* _F, vertex* _V) : flag(_F), V(_V) {}

  bool reserve(int i) {
    int d = V[i].degree;
    flag = IN;
    for (int j = 0; j < d; j++) {
      int ngh = V[i].Neighbors[j];
      if (ngh < i) {
        if (Fl[ngh] == IN) { flag = OUT; return 1;}
        else if (Fl[ngh] == LIVE) flag = LIVE; } }
    return 1; }

  bool commit(int i) { return (Fl[i] = flag) != LIVE;}
};

void MIS(FlType* Fl, vertex* V, int n, int psize)
  speculative_for(MISStep(Fl, V), 0, n, psize);
}
```

Figure 5. C++ code for maximal independent set using deterministic reservations.

because we link higher to lower vertex numbers the algorithm will never create a cycle. In this algorithm our code sets `psize`, the size of the prefix, to be $.02|E|$ and we have observed that on our test graphs less than 10% of the reservations fail.

Minimum Spanning Forest: We use a parallel variant of Kruskal's algorithm. The idea of Kruskal's algorithm is to sort the edges and then add them one-by-one using disjoint sets as in the spanning forest code. We can therefore use deterministic reservations prioritized by the sorted order to insert the edges. Unlike the spanning forest described above, however, we need to reserve both endpoints of an edge to guarantee the edges are inserted in "sequential" order. However, during the commit component we only need that one of the two endpoint succeeds because to commute `link` only requires that one of the two arguments is unique. If v succeeds, for example, then we can use `link`(v, u). Note this is still internally deterministic because which endpoints succeed is deterministic. In our code we also make a further optimization: We sort only the smallest k edges ($k = \min(|E|, 4|V|/3)$ in our experiments) and run MSF on those, so that the remaining edges can be filtered out avoiding the need to sort them all. The sequential algorithm to which we compare our code does the same optimization.

Maximal Independent Set: Sequentially the maximal independent set can easily be calculated using the greedy method: loop over the vertices in an arbitrary order and for each vertex if no neighbors belong in the set add it to the set. There is a particularly simple way to implement this with deterministic reservations without even requiring an explicit `reserve`. The C++ code based on our interface is given in Figure 5 and an example of how the algorithm proceeds is shown in Figure 6. The `struct MISStep` defines the code for the reserve and commit components for each loop iteration. The array `V` stores for each of the `n` vertices its degree and a pointer to an array of neighbors. The array `Fl` keeps track of the status of each vertex—`LIVE` indicates it is still live, `IN` indicates it is done and in the set, and `OUT` indicates it is done and not in the set (a neighbor is in the set). The reserve phase for each iteration `i` loops over the neighbors of `V[i]` and sets a local variable `flag` as follows:

$$\mathtt{flag} = \begin{cases} \mathtt{OUT} & \text{any earlier neighbor is } \mathtt{IN} \\ \mathtt{LIVE} & \text{any earlier neighbor is } \mathtt{LIVE} \\ \mathtt{IN} & \text{otherwise} \end{cases}$$

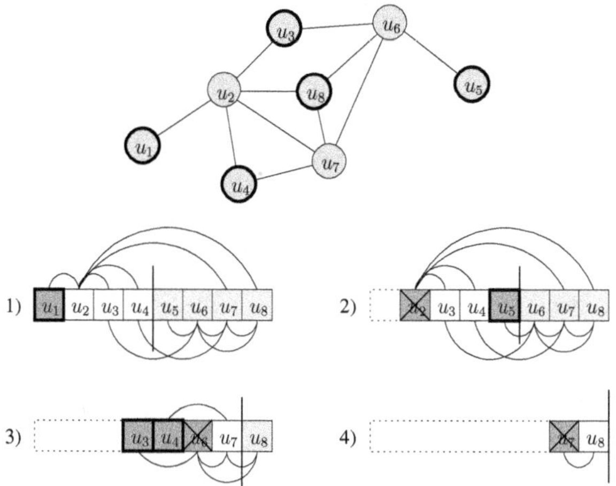

Figure 6. A sample graph and an execution of deterministic reservations for finding a maximal independent set. Here, the subscript of a node corresponds to its priority in the deterministic reservations. The prefix size is chosen to be 4. (1) shows the initial graph in priority order, and (2)-(4) show subsequent rounds of the algorithm. The vertical line indicates the end of the current prefix. Dark-gray nodes are those that become IN or OUT during that round: nodes with a thick border are IN and accepted into the MIS, and nodes with an "X" are OUT as they have a neighbor already in the MIS. For example, u_1 is the only node accepted into the MIS during the first round. Similarly, u_2 becomes OUT in the second round as it has a neighbor already in the MIS (namely, u_1). White nodes are those belonging to the current prefix that remain LIVE. For example, in the first round u_2, u_3, and u_4 all have a higher priority neighbor in the same prefix and remain live. Only nodes that survive the previous round (LIVE nodes) are displayed in the array and part of the current prefix, so u_5 is skipped in (3). Nodes in the MIS are also shown with thick border in the graph.

The second case corresponds to a conflict since for an earlier neighbor it is not yet known if it is IN or OUT. The commit phase for iteration `i` simply copies the local `flag` to `Fl[i]`. Since `Fl` is only read in the reserve phase and only written (to location `i`) in the commit phase, all operations commute.

Triangle Ray Intersect: We use a k-d tree with the surface area heuristic (SAH) [34] to store the triangles. Our algorithm is similar to the parallel algorithm discussed in [16] and makes use of divide-and-conquer and heavy use of `scan` and `filter`.

Suffix Array: We use a parallel variant of the algorithm of Karkkainen and Sanders [29]. It uses sorting and merging as subroutines, which involves nesting, but otherwise only makes use of `reduce`, `scan` and `filter`.

Delaunay Triangulation: We use a Boyer-Watson style incremental Delaunay algorithm with deterministic reservations. The points are used as the elements. To reduce contention, the prefix is always selected to be smaller than the current size of the mesh. The algorithm therefore starts out sequentially until enough points have been added. The reserve component of the code, for a point p, identifies all triangles that contain p in their circumcircle, often referred to as the hole for p. Adding p requires removing the hole and replacing it with other triangles. The reserve component therefore reserves all vertices around the exterior of the hole. The majority of the work required by a point p is in locating p in the mesh and then identifying the triangles in the hole. The commit component checks if all the reserved vertices of the mesh have succeeded, and if so, removes the hole and replaces it with triangles surrounding p and filling the hole. The reservations ensure that all modifications to the mesh commute since the triangles in the mesh only interact if they share a vertex. In fact, reserving the edges of the hole would be sufficient and reduce contention, but our mesh implementation has no data structures corresponding to edges on which to reserve. For efficiently locating a point p in the mesh we use the nearest neighbor structure described below.

Delaunay Refine: This algorithm uses the same routines for inserting points as the Delaunay triangulation. However, it does not need a point location structure but instead needs a structure to store the bad triangles. We use dynamic map for this purpose.

N-body: We use a parallel variant of the Callahan-Kosaraju algorithm [13]. This is a variant of Greengard and Rothkin's well-known FMM algorithm but allows more flexibility in the tree structure. The algorithm makes use of traditional nested parallelism with divide-and-conquer, as well as `reduce` and `scan`.

K-Nearest Neighbors: We use a quad- and oct-tree built over all input points for 2d and 3d inputs, respectively. As with the k-d tree used in triangle-ray intersection, the tree is built using only divide-and-conquer and nested parallelism. Once built, the tree is static and used only for queries of the points.

6. Experimental Results

We ran our experiments on a 32-core (with hyper-threading) Dell PowerEdge 910 with 4×2.26GHZ Intel 8-core X7560 Nehalem Processors, a 1066MHz bus, and 64GB of main memory. The parallel programs were compiled using the `cilk++` compiler (build 8503) with the `-O2` flag. The sequential programs were compiled using `g++` 4.4.1 with the `-O2` flag.

This section reports on the results for the benchmarks, as summarized in Table 2. We discuss six of the benchmarks in some detail, relating the performance to other published results. For each benchmark and given core count, the reported time for each input is the median time over three trials. We give only average timings over all inputs for the remaining benchmarks due to limited space.

For *Comparison Sort*, we used a variety of inputs all of length 10^7. This includes sequences of doubles in three distributions and two sequences of character strings. Both sequences of character strings are the same but in one the strings are allocated in order (*i.e.*, adjacent strings are likely to be on the same cache line) and in the other they are randomly permuted. We compare our internally deterministic sample sort to three other sorts: the standard template library (STL) sort, the parallel STL sort [41], and a simple divide-and-conquer quicksort that makes parallel recursive calls but partitions the keys sequentially. The results are summarized in Figure 7(a) and Table 3(a). Due to the cache-friendly nature of our algorithm, on average it is more efficient than any of the algorithms even on one core. However it is not quite as fast on the double-precision values since there the cache effects are less significant. As expected the quicksort with serial partitioning does not scale.

For *Remove Duplicates*, our inputs were all of length 10^7. We use both sequences of integers drawn from three distributions and sequences of integers corresponding to character strings. As shown in Figure 7(b) and Table 3(b), our parallel internally deterministic algorithm obtains good speedup (over 24x on 64 threads) and outperforms the serial version using 2 or more threads. On a single thread, it is only slightly slower than the serial version.

For *Breadth First Search (BFS)*, and all of the graph algorithms, we use three types of graphs: random graphs, grid graphs, and rMat graphs [14]. The rMat graphs have a power-law distribution of degrees. All edge counts are the number of undirected edges—we actually store twice as many since we store the edge in each direction. We compare our internally deterministic BFS to a serial version and a nondeterministic version (ndBFS). The results are summarized in Figure 7(c) and Table 3(c). Our nondeterministic

Application Algorithm	**1 thread**	**64 threads** (32h)	**Speedup**
Comparison Sort			
serialSort	3.581	–	–
*stlParallelSort	3.606	0.151	23.88
sampleSort	2.812	0.089	31.6
quickSort	3.043	0.68	4.475
Remove Duplicates			
serialHash	0.882	–	–
deterministicHash	1.034	0.042	24.62
Breadth First Search			
serialBFS	3.966	–	–
**ndBFS	5.4	0.28	19.29
deterministicBFS	7.136	0.314	22.73
**LS-PBFS†	4.357	0.332	13.12
Spanning Forest			
serialSF	2.653	–	–
deterministicSF	6.016	0.326	18.45
**Galois-ST$	12.39	1.136	10.91
Minimum Spanning Forest			
serialMSF	8.41	–	–
parallelKruskal	14.666	0.785	18.68
Maximal Independent Set			
serialMIS	0.501	–	–
**ndMIS	1.649	0.056	29.45
deterministicMIS	0.782	0.054	14.48
Triangle Ray Intersect			
kdTree	8.7	0.45	19.33
Suffix Array			
parallelKS	13.4	0.785	17.07
Delaunay Triangulation			
serialDelaunay	56.95	–	–
deterministicDelaunay	80.35	3.87	20.76
*Galois-Delaunay	114.116	39.36	2.9
Delaunay Refine			
deterministicRefine	103.5	6.314	16.39
**Galois-Refine‡	81.577	5.201	15.68
N-body			
parallelCK	122.733	5.633	21.79
K-Nearest Neighbors			
octTreeNeighbors	37.183	3.036	12.25

Table 2. Weighted average of running times (seconds) over various inputs on a 32-core machine with hyper-threading (32h). A "*" indicates an internally nondeterministic implementation and a "**" indicates an externally (and hence internally) nondeterministic implementation. All other implementations are internally deterministic. †LS-PDFS does not generate the BFS tree, while our programs do. $Galois-ST generates only a spanning tree, while our code generates the spanning forest. ‡Galois-Refine does not include the time for computing the triangle neighbors and initial bad triangles at the beginning while our code does (takes 10-15% of the overall time).

version is slightly faster than the deterministic version due to the fact that it avoids the second phase when processing each round. We have also compared times to published results. We ran the parallel breadth-first search algorithm from [32] on our graphs and our performance is very close to theirs (their algorithm is labeled LS-PBFS in our tables and figures). Our performance is 5 to 6 times faster than the times reported in [25] (both for 1 thread and 32 threads), but their code is written in Java instead of C++ and is on a Sun Niagara T2 processor which has a clock speed of 1.6Ghz instead of 2.26Ghz so it is hard to compare.

For *Minimum Spanning Forest (MSF)*, we compare our internally deterministic algorithm to an optimized version of Kruskal's serial algorithm (see Section 5). Our results are shown in Figure 7(d) and Table 3(d). Our code is about 1.7x slower on a single thread. We also compared our times to the parallel version of Boruvka's algorithm from the recent C++ release (2.1.0) of the Galois benchmark suite [38] (labeled as Galois-Boruvka in our table) on our inputs. Their code did not terminate in a reasonable amount of time on the random and rMat graphs; for the 2D-grid graph, our code is much faster and achieves much better speedup than their algorithm.

For *Maximum Independent Set (MIS)*, we compare our internally deterministic algorithm to the very simple and efficient serial algorithm and a nondeterministic version that uses locks (with compare-and-swap) before adding a vertex to the set. The results are summarized in Figure 7(e) and Table 3(e). As the experiments show, for this problem the deterministic algorithm is actually faster than the nondeterministic one. This is presumably because the deterministic version can avoid the reservation as discussed in Section 5 and therefore has little overhead compared to the serial algorithm. On one thread the nondeterministic algorithm is about a factor of 1.6x slower than the serial algorithm. We view this as quite good given the simplicity of the serial code. We note that MIS is about 5-10x faster than BFS on the same size graph.

For *Delaunay Triangulation*, we use two point distributions: points distributed at random and points distributed with the Kuzmin distribution. The latter has a very large scale difference between the largest and smallest resulting triangles. We compare our internally deterministic algorithm to a quite optimized serial version. Our results are shown in Figure 7(f) and Table 3(f). On one core it is a factor of about 1.4 slower, but it gets good speedup. We compared our code to the implementations in the Galois benchmark suite [38] (labeled as Galois-Delaunay and Galois-Refine in our tables and figures), and our triangulation code is faster and achieves better speedup on the same machine. We note, however, that on the Delaunay refinement problem we achieve almost the same run time as the Galois benchmarks (after subtracting the time for computing the initial processing of triangles from our times, which is about 10-15% of the overall time, since this is not part of the timing in the Galois code). Since the time for the refinement code is dominated by triangle insertion and the code for triangulation is dominated by point location, it would appear that the reason for our improved performance is due to our point location, and triangle insertion performs about equally well.

7. Conclusion

This paper has provided evidence that internally deterministic programs can remain efficient and indeed even rival the best nondeterministic approaches. In fact, in the case of MIS, using deterministic reservations revealed that some synchronization overheads could be removed, thereby improving performance.

Our approach uses nested parallelism with commuting and linearizable parallel operations. We have not addressed the issue of how to verify that operations commute or are linearizable, but the techniques we use are simple enough that it is quite easy to reason about the correctness. For example in deterministic reservations a user only needs to verify that the operations within the reserve component and separately within the commit component commute. It should also be feasible to adapt efficient techniques for runtime race detection [15] to check for parallel non-commuting operations.

It would also be interesting to conduct an empirical study supporting the programmability and debuggability claims for internal determinism. We have provided evidence that the programs in this paper have short code descriptions, but we have not studied how natural these programs are to develop in the first place.

(a) **Comparison Sort Algorithm**	10^7 random (1)	10^7 random (32h)	10^7 exponential (1)	10^7 exponential (32h)	10^7 almost sorted (1)	10^7 almost sorted (32h)	10^7 trigram (1)	10^7 trigram (32h)	10^7 trigram (permuted) (1)	10^7 trigram (permuted) (32h)
serialSort	1.42	–	1.1	–	0.283	–	4.31	–	5.5	–
*stlParallelSort	1.43	0.063	1.11	0.057	0.276	0.066	4.31	0.145	5.57	0.236
sampleSort	2.08	0.053	1.51	0.042	0.632	0.028	3.21	0.095	3.82	0.131
quickSort	1.58	0.187	1.06	0.172	0.357	0.066	3.35	0.527	4.78	1.31

(b) **Remove Duplicates Algorithm**	10^7 random (1)	10^7 random (32h)	10^7 random (values up to 10^5) (1)	10^7 random (values up to 10^5) (32h)	10^7 exponential (1)	10^7 exponential (32h)	10^7 trigram (1)	10^7 trigram (32h)	10^7 trigram (permuted) (1)	10^7 trigram (permuted) (32h)
serialHash	0.654	–	0.311	–	0.504	–	0.849	–	1.31	–
deterministicHash	0.895	0.037	0.419	0.019	0.658	0.026	0.997	0.046	1.45	0.052

(c) **BFS Algorithm**	random local graph $n = 10^7$ $m = 5 \times 10^7$ (1)	random local graph (32h)	rMat graph $n = 2^{24}$ $m = 5 \times 10^7$ (1)	rMat graph (32h)	3d grid $n = 10^7$ (1)	3d grid (32h)
serialBFS	4.14	–	4.86	–	2.9	–
**ndBFS	6.07	0.226	6.78	0.294	3.35	0.322
deterministicBFS	7.13	0.255	9.25	0.345	5.03	0.343
**LS-PBFS	4.644	0.345	5.404	0.426	3.023	0.225

(d) **MSF Algorithm**	random local graph $n = 10^7$ $m = 5 \times 10^7$ (1)	random local graph (32h)	rMat graph $n = 2^{24}$ $m = 5 \times 10^7$ (1)	rMat graph (32h)	2d grid $n = 10^7$ (1)	2d grid (32h)
serialMSF	8.47	–	11.2	–	5.56	–
parallelKruskal	14.3	0.78	19.7	1.08	10.0	0.49
*Galois-Boruvka[†]	–	–	–	–	35.128	7.159

(e) **MIS Algorithm**	random local graph $n = 10^7$ $m = 5 \times 10^7$ (1)	random local graph (32h)	rMat graph $n = 2^{24}$ $m = 5 \times 10^7$ (1)	rMat graph (32h)	2d grid $n = 10^7$ (1)	2d grid (32h)
serialMIS	0.447	–	0.669	–	0.388	–
**ndMIS	1.49	0.051	2.11	0.068	1.35	0.042
deterministicMIS	0.665	0.047	1.09	0.07	0.593	0.041

(f) **Delaunay Triangulation Algorithm**	2d in cube $n = 10^7$ (1)	2d in cube (32h)	2d kuzmin $n = 10^7$ (1)	2d kuzmin (32h)
serialDelaunay	55.1	–	58.8	–
deterministicDelaunay	76.7	3.5	84.0	4.24
*Galois-Delaunay	110.705	39.333	117.527	36.302

Table 3. Running times (seconds) of algorithms over various inputs on a 32-core machine (with hyper-threading). A "*" indicates an internally nondeterministic implementation and a "**" indicates an externally (and hence internally) nondeterministic implementation. [†]Galois-Boruvka did not terminate in a reasonable amount of time for the first two inputs.

Acknowledgments. This work is partially supported by the National Science Foundation under grant number CCF-1018188, and by Intel Labs Academic Research Office for the Parallel Algorithms for Non-Numeric Computing Program.

References

[1] U. Acar, G. E. Blelloch, and R. Blumofe. The data locality of work stealing. *Theory of Computing Systems*, 35(3), 2002. Springer.

[2] S. V. Adve and M. D. Hill. Weak ordering–a new definition. In *ACM ISCA*, 1990.

[3] T. Bergan, O. Anderson, J. Devietti, L. Ceze, and D. Grossman. CoreDet: A compiler and runtime system for deterministic multithreaded execution. In *ACM ASPLOS*, 2010.

[4] T. Bergan, N. Hunt, L. Ceze, and S. D. Gribble. Deterministic process groups in dOS. In *Usenix OSDI*, 2010.

[5] E. D. Berger, T. Yang, T. Liu, and G. Novark. Grace: Safe multithreaded programming for C/C++. In *ACM OOPSLA*, 2009.

[6] G. E. Blelloch. Programming parallel algorithms. *CACM*, 39(3), 1996.

[7] G. E. Blelloch and D. Golovin. Strongly history-independent hashing with applications. In *IEEE FOCS*, 2007.

[8] G. E. Blelloch and J. Greiner. A provable time and space efficient implementation of NESL. In *ACM ICFP*, 1996.

[9] G. E. Blelloch, P. B. Gibbons, and H. V. Simhadri. Low-depth cache oblivious algorithms. In *ACM SPAA*, 2010.

[10] R. D. Blumofe, C. F. Joerg, B. C. Kuszmaul, C. E. Leiserson, K. H. Randall, and Y. Zhou. Cilk: An efficient multithreaded runtime system. *J. Parallel and Distributed Computing*, 37(1), 1996. Elsevier.

[11] R. L. Bocchino, V. S. Adve, S. V. Adve, and M. Snir. Parallel programming must be deterministic by default. In *Usenix HotPar*, 2009.

[12] R. L. Bocchino, S. Heumann, N. Honarmand, S. V. Adve, V. S. Adve, A. Welc, and T. Shpeisman. Safe nondeterminism in a deterministic-by-default parallel language. In *ACM POPL*, 2011.

[13] P. B. Callahan and S. R. Kosaraju. A decomposition of multidimensional point sets with applications to k-nearest-neighbors and n-body potential fields. *J. ACM*, 42(1), 1995.

[14] D. Chakrabarti, Y. Zhan, and C. Faloutsos. R-MAT: A recursive model for graph mining. In *SIAM SDM*, 2004.

[15] G.-I. Cheng, M. Feng, C. E. Leiserson, K. H. Randall, and A. F. Stark. Detecting data races in Cilk programs that use locks. In *ACM SPAA*, 1998.

[16] B. Choi, R. Komuravelli, V. Lu, H. Sung, R. L. Bocchino, S. V. Adve, and J. C. Hart. Parallel SAH k-D tree construction. In *ACM High Performance Graphics*, 2010.

[17] T. H. Cormen, C. E. Leiserson, R. L. Rivest, and C. Stein. *Introduction to Algorithms, Second Edition.* MIT Press and McGraw-Hill, 2001.

[18] M. de Berg, O. Cheong, M. van Kreveld, and M. Overmars. *Computational Geometry: Algorithms and Applications.* Springer-Verlag, 2008.

[19] J. Devietti, B. Lucia, L. Ceze, and M. Oskin. DMP: Deterministic shared memory multiprocessing. In *ACM ASPLOS*, 2009.

[20] J. Devietti, J. Nelson, T. Bergan, L. Ceze, and D. Grossman. RCDC: A relaxed consistency deterministic computer. In *ACM ASPLOS*, 2011.

[21] E. W. Dijkstra. Cooperating sequential processes. Technical Report EWD 123, Dept. of Mathematics, Technological U., Eindhoven, 1965.

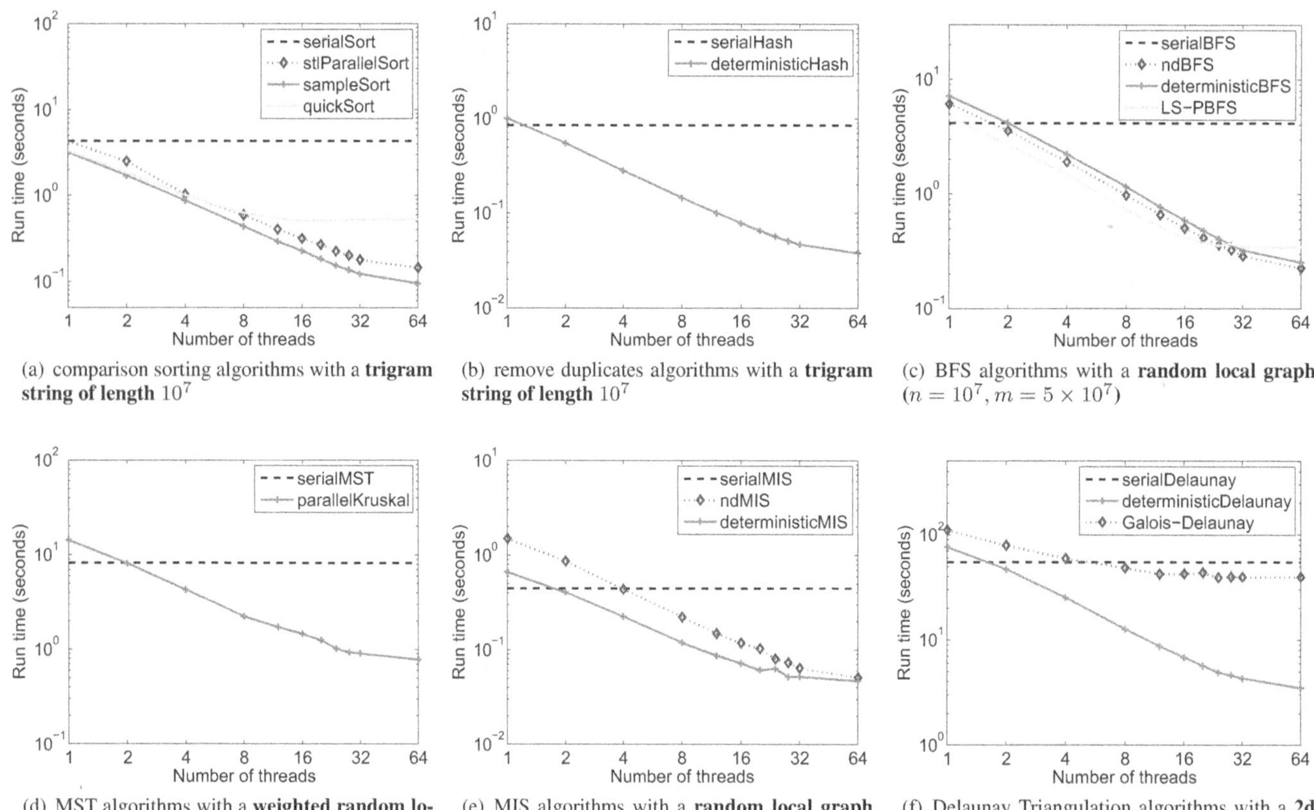

(a) comparison sorting algorithms with a **trigram string of length** 10^7

(b) remove duplicates algorithms with a **trigram string of length** 10^7

(c) BFS algorithms with a **random local graph** ($n = 10^7, m = 5 \times 10^7$)

(d) MST algorithms with a **weighted random local graph** ($n = 10^7, m = 5 \times 10^7$)

(e) MIS algorithms with a **random local graph** ($n = 10^7, m = 5 \times 10^7$)

(f) Delaunay Triangulation algorithms with a **2d in cube graph** ($n = 10^7$)

Figure 7. Log-log plots of running times on a 32-core machine (with hyper-threading). Our deterministic algorithms are shown in red.

[22] K. Gharachorloo, D. Lenoski, J. Laudon, P. Gibbons, A. Gupta, and J. Hennessy. Memory consistency and event ordering in scalable shared-memory multiprocessors. In *ACM ISCA*, 1990.

[23] P. B. Gibbons. A more practical PRAM model. In *ACM SPAA*, 1989.

[24] R. H. Halstead. Multilisp: A language for concurrent symbolic computation. *ACM TOPLAS*, 7(4), 1985.

[25] M. A. Hassaan, M. Burtscher, and K. Pingali. Ordered vs. unordered: A comparison of parallelism and work-efficiency in irregular algorithms. In *ACM PPoPP*, 2011.

[26] M. Herlihy and E. Koskinen. Transactional boosting: A methodology for highly-concurrent transactional objects. In *ACM PPoPP*, 2008.

[27] M. P. Herlihy and J. M. Wing. Linearizability: A correctness condition for concurrent objects. *ACM TOPLAS*, 12(3), 1990.

[28] D. Hower, P. Dudnik, M. Hill, and D. Wood. Calvin: Deterministic or not? Free will to choose. In *IEEE HPCA*, 2011.

[29] J. Karkkainen and P. Sanders. Simple linear work suffix array construction. In *EATCS ICALP*, 2003.

[30] M. Kulkarni, D. Nguyen, D. Prountzos, X. Sui, and K. Pingali. Exploiting the commutativity lattice. In *ACM PLDI*, 2011.

[31] C. E. Leiserson. The Cilk++ concurrency platform. *J. Supercomputing*, 51(3), 2010. Springer.

[32] C. E. Leiserson and T. B. Schardl. A work-efficient parallel breadth-first search algorithm (or how to cope with the nondeterminism of reducers). In *ACM SPAA*, 2010.

[33] C. E. Leiserson, T. B. Schardl, and J. Sukha. Deterministic parallel random-number generation for dynamic-multithreading platforms. In *ACM PPoPP*, 2012.

[34] J. D. MacDonald and K. S. Booth. Heuristics for ray tracing using space subdivision. *The Visual Computer*, 6(3), 1990. Springer.

[35] R. H. B. Netzer and B. P. Miller. What are race conditions? *ACM LOPLAS*, 1(1), 1992.

[36] M. Olszewski, J. Ansel, and S. Amarasinghe. Kendo: Efficient deterministic multithreading in software. In *ACM ASPLOS*, 2009.

[37] S. S. Patil. Closure properties of interconnections of determinate systems. In J. B. Dennis, editor, *Record of the Project MAC conference on concurrent systems and parallel computation*. ACM, 1970.

[38] K. Pingali, D. Nguyen, M. Kulkarni, M. Burtscher, M. A. Hassaan, R. Kaleem, T.-H. Lee, A. Lenharth, R. Manevich, M. Méndez-Lojo, D. Prountzos, and X. Sui. The tao of parallelism in algorithms. In *ACM PLDI*, 2011.

[39] P. Prabhu, S. Ghosh, Y. Zhang, N. P. Johnson, and D. I. August. Commutative set: A language extension for implicit parallel programming. In *ACM PLDI*, 2011.

[40] M. C. Rinard and P. C. Diniz. Commutativity analysis: A new analysis technique for parallelizing compilers. *ACM TOPLAS*, 19(6), 1997.

[41] J. Singler, P. Sanders, and F. Putze. MCSTL: The multi-core standard template library. In *Euro-Par*, 2007.

[42] G. L. Steele Jr. Making asynchronous parallelism safe for the world. In *ACM POPL*, 1990.

[43] J. G. Steffan, C. B. Colohan, A. Zhai, and T. C. Mowry. A scalable approach to thread-level speculation. In *ACM ISCA*, 2000.

[44] W. E. Weihl. Commutativity-based concurrency control for abstract data types. *IEEE Trans. Computers*, 37(12), 1988.

[45] J. Yu and S. Narayanasamy. A case for an interleaving constrained shared-memory multi-processor. In *ACM ISCA*, 2009.

Deterministic Parallel Random-Number Generation for Dynamic-Multithreading Platforms

Charles E. Leiserson Tao B. Schardl Jim Sukha

MIT Computer Science and Artificial Intelligence Laboratory

{cel, neboat, sukhaj}@mit.edu

Abstract

Existing concurrency platforms for dynamic multithreading do not provide repeatable parallel random-number generators. This paper proposes that a mechanism called ***pedigrees*** be built into the runtime system to enable efficient deterministic parallel random-number generation. Experiments with the open-source MIT Cilk runtime system show that the overhead for maintaining pedigrees is negligible. Specifically, on a suite of 10 benchmarks, the relative overhead of Cilk with pedigrees to the original Cilk has a geometric mean of less than 1%.

We persuaded Intel to modify its commercial C/C++ compiler, which provides the Cilk Plus concurrency platform, to include pedigrees, and we built a library implementation of a deterministic parallel random-number generator called DOTMIX that compresses the pedigree and then "RC6-mixes" the result. The statistical quality of DOTMIX is comparable to that of the popular Mersenne twister, but somewhat slower than a nondeterministic parallel version of this efficient and high-quality serial random-number generator. The cost of calling DOTMIX depends on the "spawn depth" of the invocation. For a naive Fibonacci calculation with $n = 40$ that calls DOTMIX in every node of the computation, this "price of determinism" is a factor of 2.65 in running time, but for more realistic applications with less intense use of random numbers — such as a maximal-independent-set algorithm, a practical sample-sort program, and a Monte Carlo discrete-hedging application from QuantLib — the observed "price" was less than 5%. Moreover, even if overheads were several times greater, applications using DOTMIX should be amply fast for debugging purposes, which is a major reason for desiring repeatability.

Categories and Subject Descriptors G.3 [*Mathematics of Computing*]: Random number generation; D.1.3 [*Software*]: Programming Techniques—Concurrent programming

General Terms Algorithms, Performance, Theory

Keywords Cilk, determinism, dynamic multithreading, nondeterminism, parallel computing, pedigree, random-number generator

This research was supported in part by the National Science Foundation under Grant CNS-1017058. Tao Benjamin Schardl was supported in part by an NSF Graduate Fellowship. Jim Sukha's current affiliation is Intel Corporation.

PPoPP'12, February 25–29, 2012, New Orleans, Louisiana, USA.
Copyright © 2012 ACM 978-1-4503-1160-1/12/02...$10.00

1. Introduction

Dynamic multithreading,[1] or ***dthreading***, which integrates a runtime scheduler into a concurrency platform, provides a threading model which allows developers to write many deterministic programs without resorting to nondeterministic means. Dthreading concurrency platforms — including MIT Cilk [20], Cilk++ [34], Cilk Plus [28], Fortress [1], Habenero [2, 12], Hood [6], Java Fork/Join Framework [30], OpenMP 3.0 [40], Task Parallel Library (TPL) [33], Threading Building Blocks (TBB) [42], and X10 [13] — offer a ***processor-oblivious*** model of computation, where linguistic extensions to the serial base language expose the logical parallelism within an application without reference to the number of processors on which the application runs. The platform's runtime system schedules and executes the computation on whatever set of ***worker*** threads is available at runtime, typically employing a "work-stealing" scheduler [5, 10, 23], where procedure frames are migrated from worker to worker. Although a dthreading concurrency platform is itself nondeterministic in the way that it schedules a computation, it encapsulates the nondeterminism, providing the developer with a programming abstraction in which deterministic applications can be programmed without concern for the nondeterminism of the underlying scheduler.

A major reason parallel programming is hard is because nondeterminism precludes the repeatability programmers rely on to debug their codes. For example, the popular ***pthreading*** model — as exemplified by POSIX threads [27], Windows API threads [24], and the threading model of the Java programming language [22] — is well known to produce programs replete with nondeterminism and which are thus difficult to debug. Lee [31] cites the nondeterminism of multithreaded programs as a key reason that programming large-scale parallel applications remains error prone and difficult. Bocchino *et al.* [7] argue persuasively that multithreaded programs should be deterministic by default. The growing popularity of dthreading concurrency platforms seems due in part to their ability to encapsulate nondeterminism and provide a more deterministic environment for parallel programming and debugging.

Nevertheless, dthreading concurrency platforms fail to encapsulate an important source of nondeterminism for applications that employ (pseudo)random number generators (RNG's). RNG's are useful for randomized algorithms [37], which provide efficient solutions to a host of combinatorial problem, and are essential for Monte Carlo simulations, which consume a large fraction of computing cycles [35] for applications such as option pricing, molecular modeling, quantitative risk analysis, and computer games.

Unfortunately, typical implementations of RNG's are either nondeterministic or exhibit high overheads when used in dthreaded code. To understand why, we first review conventional serial RNG's and consider how they are traditionally adapted for use in parallel

[1] Sometimes called ***task parallelism***.

programs. Then we examine the ramifications of this adaptation on dthreaded programs.

A serial RNG operates as a stream. The RNG begins in some initial state S_0. The ith request for a random number updates the state S_{i-1} to a new state S_i, and then it returns some function of S_i as the ith random number. One can construct a parallel RNG using a serial RNG, but at the cost of introducing nondeterminism. One way that a serial RNG can be used directly in a dthreaded application is as a global RNG where the stream's update function is protected by a lock. This strategy introduces nondeterminism, however, as well as contention on the lock that can adversely affect performance.

A more practical alternative that avoids lock contention is to use ***worker-local RNG's***, i.e., construct a parallel RNG by having each worker thread maintain its own serial RNG for generating random numbers. Unfortunately, this solution fails to eliminate nondeterminism because the underlying nondeterministic scheduler may execute a given call to the RNG on different workers during different runs of the program, even if the sequence of random numbers produced by each worker is deterministic.

Deterministic parallel random-number generators (DPRNG's) exist for pthreading platforms, but they are ineffective for dthreading platforms. For example, SPRNG [35] is an excellent DPRNG which creates independent RNG's via a parameterization process. For a few pthreads that are spawned at the start of a computation and which operate independently, SPRNG can produce the needed RNG for each pthread. For a dthreaded program, however, which may contain millions of ***strands*** — serial sequences of executed instructions containing no parallel control — each strand may need its own RNG, and SPRNG cannot cope.

Consider, for example, a program that uses SPRNG to generate a random number at each leaf of the computation of a parallel, exponential-time, recursive Fibonacci calculation `fib`. Every time `fib` spawns a recursive subcomputation, a new strand is created, and the program calls SPRNG to produce a new serial RNG stream from the existing serial RNG. The `fib` program is deterministic, since each strand receives the same sequence of random numbers in every execution. In an implementation of this program, however, we observed two significant problems:

- When computing `fib(21)`, the program using SPRNG was almost 50,000 times slower than a nondeterministic version that maintains worker-local Mersenne twister [36] RNG's from the GNU Scientific Library [21].
- SPRNG's default RNG only guarantees the independence of 2^{19} streams, and computing `fib(n)` for `n` $>$ 21 forfeits this guarantee.

Of course, SPRNG was never intended for this kind of use case where many streams are created with only a few random numbers generated from each stream. This example does show, however, the inadequacy of a naive solution to the problem of deterministic parallel random-number generation for dthreading platforms.

Contributions

In this paper, we investigate the problem of deterministic parallel random-number generation for dthreading platforms. In particular, this paper makes the following contributions:

- A runtime mechanism, called "pedigrees," for tracking the "lineage" of each strand in a dthreaded program, which introduces a negligible overhead across a suite of 10 MIT Cilk [20] benchmark applications.
- A general strategy for efficiently generating quality deterministic parallel random numbers based on compressing the strand's pedigree and "mixing" the result.
- A high-quality DPRNG library for Intel Cilk Plus, called DOTMIX, which is based on compressing the pedigree via a dot-product [17] and "RC6-mixing" [15, 43] the result, and whose statistical quality appears to rival that of the popular Mersenne twister [36].

Outline

The remainder of this paper is organized as follows. Section 2 defines pedigrees and describes how they can be incorporated into a dthreading platform. Section 3 presents the DOTMIX DPRNG, showing how pedigrees can be leveraged to implement DPRNG's. Section 4 describes other pedigree-based DPRNG schemes, focusing on one based on linear congruential generators [29]. Section 5 presents a programming interface for a DPRNG library. Section 6 presents performance results measuring the overhead of runtime support for pedigrees in MIT Cilk, as well as the overheads of DOTMIX in Cilk Plus on synthetic and realistic applications. Section 7 describes related work, and Section 8 offers some concluding remarks.

2. Pedigrees

A pedigree scheme uniquely identifies each strand of a dthreaded program in a scheduler-independent manner. This section introduces "spawn pedigrees," a simple pedigree scheme that can be easily maintained by a dthreading runtime system. We describe the changes that Intel implemented in their Cilk Plus concurrency platform to implement spawn pedigrees. Their runtime support provides an application programming interface (API) that allows user programmers to access the spawn pedigree of a strand, which can be used to implement a pedigree-based DPRNG scheme. We finish by describing an important optimization for parallel loops, called "flattening."

We shall focus on dialects of Cilk [20, 28, 34] to contextualize our discussion, since we used Cilk platforms to implement the spawn-pedigree scheme and study its empirical behavior. The runtime support for pedigrees that we describe can be adapted to other dthreading platforms, however, which we discuss in Section 8.

Background on dynamic multithreading

Let us first review the Cilk programming model, which provides the basic dthreading abstraction of ***fork-join parallelism*** in which dthreads are spawned off as parallel subroutines. Cilk extends C with two main keywords: `spawn` and `sync`.[2] A program's logical parallelism is exposed using the keyword `spawn`. In a function F, when a function invocation G is preceded by the keyword `spawn`, the function G is ***spawned***, and the scheduler may continue to execute the ***continuation*** of F — the statement after the `spawn` of G — in parallel with G, without waiting for G to return. The complement of `spawn` is the keyword `sync`, which acts as a local barrier and joins together the parallelism specified by `spawn`. The Cilk runtime system ensures that statements after `sync` are not executed until all functions spawned before the `sync` statement have completed and returned. Cilk's linguistic constructs allow a programmer to express the logical parallelism in a program in a processor-oblivious fashion.

Dthreading platforms enable a wide range of applications to execute deterministically by removing a major source of nondeterminism: load-balancing. Cilk's nondeterministic scheduler, for example, is implemented as a collection of ***worker*** pthreads that cooperate to load-balance the work of the computation. The Cilk run-

[2] The Cilk++ [34] and Cilk Plus [28] platforms use the keywords `cilk_spawn` and `cilk_sync`. They also include a `cilk_for` keyword for defining a parallel `for` loop, which can conceptually be rewritten to use `spawn` and `sync` statements.

time employs ***randomized work-stealing*** [5, 20], where a worker posts parallel work locally, rather than attempting to share it when the parallel work is spawned, and idle workers become ***thieves*** who look randomly among their peers for ***victims*** with excess work. When a thief finds a victim, it ***steals*** a function ***frame*** from the victim, and resumes execution of the frame by executing the continuation after a `spawn` statement. Cilk-style dynamic multithreading encapsulates the nondeterminacy of the scheduler, enabling application codes without determinacy races[3] [18] to produce deterministic results regardless of how they are scheduled.

Pedigree schemes

Pedigrees are deterministic labels for the executed instructions in a dthreaded program execution that partition the instructions into valid strands. For the remainder of this section, assume that the dthreaded program in question would be deterministic if each RNG call in the program always returned the same random number on every execution. For such computations, a pedigree scheme maintains two useful properties:

1. ***Schedule-independence***: For any instruction x, the value of the pedigree for x, denoted $J(x)$, does not depend on how the program is scheduled on multiple processors.
2. ***Strand-uniqueness***: All instructions with the same pedigree form a strand.

Together, Properties 1 and 2 guarantee that pedigrees identify strands of a dthreaded program in a deterministic fashion, regardless of scheduling. Therefore, one can generate a random number for each strand by simply hashing its pedigree.

The basic idea of a pedigree scheme is to name a given strand by the path from the root of the ***invocation tree*** — the tree of function (instances) where F is a ***parent*** of G, denoted $F = \texttt{parent}(G)$, if F spawns or calls G. Label each instruction of a function with a ***rank***, which is the number of calls, spawns, or syncs that precede it in the function. Then the pedigree of an instruction x can be encoded by giving its rank and a list of ancestor ranks, e.g., the instruction x might have rank 3 and be the 5th child of the 1st child of the 3rd child of the 2nd child of the root, and thus its pedigree would be $J(x) = \langle 2, 3, 1, 5, 3\rangle$. Such a scheme satisfies Property 1, because the invocation tree is the same no matter how the computation is scheduled. It satisfies Property 2, because two instructions with the same pedigree cannot have a spawn or sync between them.

Spawn pedigrees improve on this simple scheme by defining ranks using only spawns and syncs, omitting calls and treating called functions as being "inlined" in their parents. We can define spawn pedigrees operationally in terms of a serial execution of a dthreaded program. The runtime system conceptually maintains a stack of ***rank counters***, where each rank counter corresponds to an instance of a spawned function. Program execution begins with a single rank counter with value 0 on the stack for the root (`main`) function F_0. Three events cause the rank-counter stack to change:

1. On a spawn of a function G, push a new rank counter with value 0 for G onto the bottom of the stack.
2. On a return from the spawn of G, pop the rank counter (for G) from the bottom of the stack, and then increment the rank counter at the bottom of the stack.
3. On a `sync` statement inside a function F, increment the rank counter at the bottom of the stack.

For any instruction x, the pedigree $J(x)$ is simply the sequence of ranks on the stack when x executes. Figure 1 shows the Cilk code for a recursive Fibonacci calculation and the corresponding invocation tree for an execution of `fib(4)` with spawn pedigrees labeled on instructions. Intuitively, the counter at the bottom of the rank-counter stack tracks the rank of the currently executing instruction x with respect to the spawned ancestor function closest to x. Thus, the increment at the bottom of the stack occurs whenever resuming the continuation of a `spawn` or a `sync` statement. This operational definition of spawn pedigrees satisfies Property 2, because an increment occurs whenever any parallel control is reached and the values of the pedigrees are strictly increasing according to a lexicographic order. Because a spawn pedigree is dependent only on the invocation tree, spawn pedigrees satisfy Property 1.

Runtime support for spawn pedigrees

Supporting spawn pedigrees in parallel in a dthreaded program is simple but subtle. Let us first acquire some terminology. We extend the definition of "parent" to instructions, where for any instruction x, the ***parent*** of x, denoted $\texttt{parent}(x)$, is the function that executes x. For any nonroot function F, define the ***spawn parent*** of F, denoted $\texttt{spParent}(F)$, as $\texttt{parent}(F)$ if F was spawned, or $\texttt{spParent}(\texttt{parent}(F))$ if F was called. Intuitively, $\texttt{spParent}(F)$ is the closest proper ancestor of F that is a spawned function. Define the ***spawn parent*** of an instruction x similarly: $\texttt{spParent}(x) = \texttt{spParent}(\texttt{parent}(x))$. The ***rank*** of an instruction x, denoted $R(x)$, corresponds to the value in the bottom-most rank counter at the time x is executed in a serial execution, and each more-distant spawn parent in the ancestry of x directly maps to a rank counter higher in the stack.

The primary complication for maintaining spawn pedigrees during a parallel execution is that while one worker p is executing an instruction x in $F = \texttt{spParent}(x)$, another worker p' may steal a continuation in F and continue executing, conceptually modifying the rank counter for F. To eliminate this complication, when p spawns a function G from F, it saves $R(G)$ — the rank-counter value of F when G was spawned — into the frame of G, thereby guaranteeing that any query of the pedigree for x has access to the correct rank, even if p' has resumed execution of F and incremented its rank counter.

Figure 2 shows an API that allows a currently executing strand s to query its spawn pedigree. For any instruction x belonging to a strand s, this API allows s to walk up the chain of spawned functions along the x-to-root path in the invocation tree and access the appropriate rank value for x and each ancestor spawned function. The sequence of ranks discovered along this walk is precisely the reverse of the pedigree $J(x)$.

We persuaded Intel to modify its Cilk Plus [28] concurrency platform to include pedigrees. The Intel C/C++ compiler with Cilk Plus compiles the spawning of a function G as a call to a ***spawn-wrapper*** function $\widehat{G}$, which performs the necessary runtime manipulations to effect the spawn, one step of which is calling the function G. Thus, for any function G, we have $\texttt{spParent}(G) = \widehat{G}$, and for any instruction x, the pedigree $J(x)$ has a rank counter for each spawn-wrapper ancestor of x.

Implementing this API in Cilk Plus requires additional storage in spawn-wrapper frames and in the state of each worker thread. For every spawned function F, the spawn wrapper $\widehat{F}$ stores the following rank information in F's frame:

- $\widehat{F} \rightarrow \mathit{brank}$: a 64-bit[4] value that stores $R(F)$.
- $\widehat{F} \rightarrow \mathit{parent}$: the pointer to $\texttt{spParent}(\widehat{F})$.

In addition, every worker p maintains two values in worker-local storage for its currently executing instruction x:

- $p \rightarrow \mathit{current\text{-}frame}$: the pointer to $\texttt{spParent}(x)$.
- $p \rightarrow \mathit{rank}$: a 64-bit value storing $R(x)$.

As Figure 2 shows, to implement the API, the runtime system reads these fields to report a spawn pedigree. In terms of the operational

[3] Also called ***general races*** [39].

[4] A 64-bit counter never overflows in practice, since 2^{64} is a *big* number.

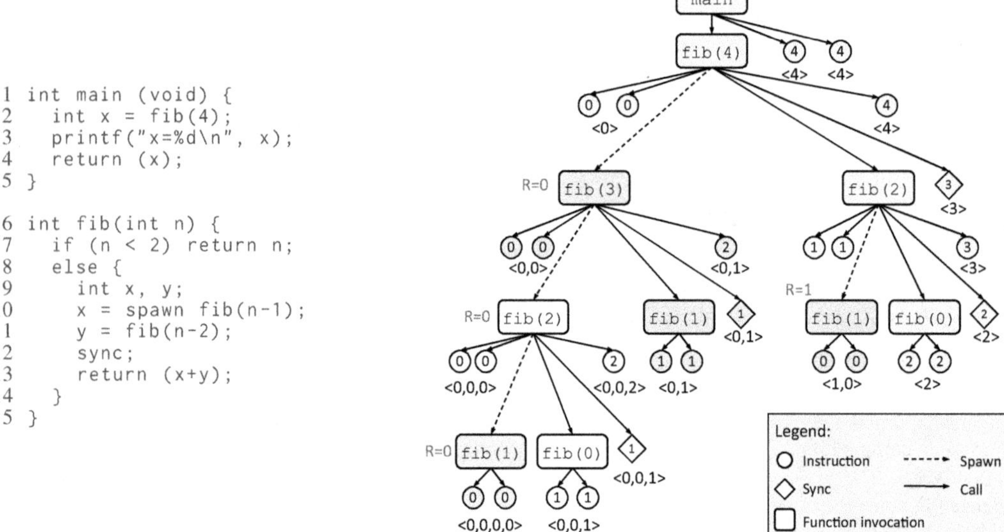

1 int main (void) {
2 int x = fib(4);
3 printf("x=%d\n", x);
4 return (x);
5 }
6 int fib(int n) {
7 if (n < 2) return n;
8 else {
9 int x, y;
10 x = spawn fib(n-1);
11 y = fib(n-2);
12 sync;
13 return (x+y);
14 }
15 }
main
fib(4)
fib(3)
fib(2)
fib(1)
fib(0)
R=0
R=1
Legend:
Instruction
Sync
Function invocation
Spawn
Call

Figure 1: Cilk code for a recursive Fibonacci calculation and the invocation tree for an execution of `fib(4)`. Pedigrees are labeled for each instruction. For example, sync instruction in `fib(4)` has pedigree $\langle 3 \rangle$. A left-to-right preorder traversal of the tree represents the serial execution order. For example, for the children of the node for `fib(4)`, the first two instructions with rank 0 correspond to lines 7 and 9 from Figure 1, the subtree rooted at node `fib(4)` between `fib(3)` and the sync node corresponds to the execution of the sync block (lines 10–12), and the last instruction with rank 4 corresponds to the return in line 13. Instructions and functions are labeled with their ranks. For example, `fib(3)` has a rank of 0.

Function	Description	Implementation
RANK()	Returns $R(x)$	Returns $p \rightarrow rank$.
SPPARENT()	Returns spParent(x)	Returns $p \rightarrow$ *current-frame*.
RANK($\widehat{F}$)	Returns $R(\widehat{F})$	Returns $\widehat{F} \rightarrow brank$.
SPPARENT($\widehat{F}$)	Returns spParent($\widehat{F}$)	Returns $\widehat{F} \rightarrow parent$.
STRANDBREAK()	Ends the currently-executing strand	$p \rightarrow rank$++.

Figure 2: An API for spawn pedigrees in Intel Cilk Plus. In these operations, x is the currently executing instruction for a worker, and $\widehat{F}$ is a spawn-wrapper function which is an ancestor of x in the computation tree. These operations allow the worker to walk up the computation tree to compute $J(x)$. A worker can also call STRANDBREAK() to end its currently executing strand.

definition of spawn pedigrees, the *rank* field in p holds the bottom-most rank counter on the stack for the instruction x that p is currently executing.

To maintain these fields, the runtime system requires additional storage to save and restore the current spawn-parent pointer and rank counter for each worker whenever it enters or leaves a nested spawned function. In particular, we allocate space for a rank and parent pointer in the stack frame of every ***Cilk function*** — function that can contain spawn and sync statements:

- $G \rightarrow rank$: a 64-bit value that stores $R(x)$ for some instruction x with spParent(x) $= G$.
- $G \rightarrow$ *sp-rep*: the pointer to spParent(G).

These fields are only used to save and restore the corresponding fields for a worker p. Whenever p is executing a Cilk function G which spawns a function F, it saves its fields into G before beginning execution of F. When a worker p' (which may or may not be p) resumes the continuation after the spawn statement, p' restores its values from G. Similarly, saving and restoring also occurs when a worker stalls at a sync statement. Figure 3 summarizes the runtime operations needed to maintain spawn pedigrees.

Although the implementation of spawn pedigrees in Cilk Plus required changes to the Intel compiler, ordinary C/C++ functions need not be recompiled for the pedigree scheme to work. The reason is that the code in Figure 3 does not perform any operations on entry or exit to called functions. Consequently, the scheme works even for programs that incorporate legacy and third-party C/C++ binaries.

(a) On a spawn of F from G:	(b) On stalling at a sync in G:
1 $G \rightarrow rank = p \rightarrow rank$ 2 $G \rightarrow$ *sp-rep* $=$ $p \rightarrow$ *current-frame* 3 $\widehat{F} \rightarrow brank = G \rightarrow rank$ 4 $\widehat{F} \rightarrow parent = G \rightarrow$ *sp-rep* 5 $p \rightarrow rank = 0$ 6 $p \rightarrow$ *current-frame* $= F$	1 $G \rightarrow rank = p \rightarrow rank$ **(c)** On resuming the continuation of a spawn or sync in G: 1 $p \rightarrow rank = G \rightarrow rank$++ 2 $p \rightarrow$ *current-frame* $=$ $G \rightarrow$ *sp-rep*

Figure 3: How a worker p maintains spawn pedigrees. **(a)** $\widehat{F}$ is a pointer to the spawn wrapper of the function F being spawned, and G is a pointer to the frame of the Cilk function that is spawning F. **(b)** G is the Cilk function that is attempting to execute a sync. The value $p \rightarrow$ *current-frame* need not be saved into $G \rightarrow$ *sp-rep*, because the first spawn in G will have saved this value already, and this value is fixed for G. **(c)** G is the Cilk function containing the continuation being resumed.

To implement DPRNG's, it is useful to extend the API in Figure 2 to include a STRANDBREAK function that allows the DPRNG to end a currently executing strand explicitly. In particular, if a user requests multiple random numbers from a DPRNG in a serial sequence of instructions, the DPRNG can let each call to get a random number terminate a strand in that sequence using this function, meaning that the DPRNG produces at most one random number per strand. Like a spawn or sync, when a worker p encounters a STRANDBREAK call, the next instruction after the STRANDBREAK that p executes is guaranteed to be part of a different strand, and thus have a different pedigree. The STRANDBREAK function is implemented by incrementing $p \rightarrow rank$.

Pedigree flattening for parallel loops

As an optimization, we can simplify spawn pedigrees for parallel loops. Intel Cilk Plus provides a parallel looping construct called `cilk_for`, which allows all the iterations of the loop to execute in parallel. The runtime system implements `cilk_for` using a balanced binary recursion tree implemented with spawn's and sync's, where each leaf performs a chunk of iterations serially. Rather than tracking ranks at every level of this recursion tree, the Cilk Plus pedigree scheme conceptually "cuts out the middle man" and ***flattens*** all the iterations of the `cilk_for` loop so that they share a single level of pedigree. The idea is simply to let the rank of an iteration be the loop index. Consequently, iterations in a `cilk_for` can be referenced within the `cilk_for` by a single value, rather than a path through the binary recursion tree. To ensure that spawn and sync statements within a loop iteration do not affect the pedigrees of other loop iterations, the body of each loop iteration is treated as a spawned function with respect to its pedigree. This change simplifies the pedigrees generated for `cilk_for` loops by reducing the effective spawn depth of strands within the `cilk_for` and as Section 6 shows, the cost of reading the pedigree as well.

3. A pedigree-based DPRNG

This section presents DOTMIX, a high-quality statistically random pedigree-based DPRNG. DOTMIX operates by hashing the pedigree and then "mixing" the result. We investigate theoretical principles behind the design of DOTMIX, which offer evidence that pedigree-based DPRNG can generate pseudorandom numbers of high quality for real applications. We also examine empirical test results using Dieharder [9], which suggest that DOTMIX generates high-quality random numbers in practice.

The* DOTMIX *DPRNG

At a high level, DOTMIX generates random numbers by first compressing the pedigree and then "mixing" the bits in the compressed pedigree. We assume that our computer has a word width of w bits, representing up to $m = 2^w$ integer values, and that each rank in the pedigree fits in a single word. Let $\mathbb{Z}_m$ denote the universe of (unsigned) w-bit integers over which calculations are performed, and let $2\mathbb{Z}_{m/2}+1$ denote the set of odd integers in $\mathbb{Z}_m$. We assume that the spawn depth $d(x)$ for any instruction x in a dthreaded program is bounded by $d(x) \leq D$.[5] A pedigree $J(x)$ for an instruction x at spawn depth $d(x)$ can then be represented by a length-D vector $J(x) = \langle j_1, j_2, \ldots, j_D \rangle \in \mathbb{Z}_m^D$. To ensure that instructions at different depths have distinct pedigrees, DOTMIX makes an additional assumption on pedigrees, namely, that the rank at depth $d(x)$ is nonzero. To satisfy this assumption, our library implementation of DOTMIX simply increments each rank in the spawn-pedigree scheme from Section 2.

For a given pedigree $J \in \mathbb{Z}_m^D$, the random number produced by DOTMIX is the hash $h(J)$, where $h(J)$ is the composition of

1. a ***compression function*** $c : \mathbb{Z}_m^D \rightarrow \mathbb{Z}_m$ that hashes each pedigree J into a single w-bit integer $c(J)$, and
2. a ***mixing function*** $\mu : \mathbb{Z}_m \rightarrow \mathbb{Z}_m$ that "mixes" the compressed pedigree value $c(J)$.

Let us consider each of these functions individually.

[5] A reasonable upper bound is $D = 100$.

The goal of a compression function c is to hash each pedigree J into a w-bit integer such that the probability of a ***collision*** — two distinct pedigrees hashing to the same integer — is small. To compress pedigrees, DOTMIX conceptually treats the pedigree as a vector and computes a dot product of the pedigree with a vector of random values [17]. More formally, DOTMIX uses a compression function c chosen uniformly at random from the following hash family.

DEFINITION 1. *Let $\Gamma = \langle \gamma_1, \gamma_2, \ldots, \gamma_D \rangle$ be a vector of odd integers chosen uniformly at random from $(2\mathbb{Z}_{m/2}+1)^D$. Define the compression function $c_\Gamma : \mathbb{Z}_m^D \rightarrow \mathbb{Z}_m$ by*

$$c_\Gamma(J) = \left(\sum_{k=1}^{D} \gamma_k \cdot j_k \right) \bmod m ,$$

where $J = \langle j_1, j_2, \ldots, j_D \rangle \in \mathbb{Z}_m^D$. The **DOTMIX** ***compression-function family*** *is the set*

$$C_{\text{DOTMIX}} = \left\{ c_\Gamma : \Gamma \in (2\mathbb{Z}_{m/2}+1)^D \right\} .$$

The next theorem proves that the probability is small that a randomly chosen compression function $c_\Gamma \in C_{\text{DOTMIX}}$ causes two distinct pedigrees to collide.

THEOREM 1. *Let $c_\Gamma \in C_{\text{DOTMIX}}$ be a randomly chosen compression function. Then for any two distinct pedigrees $J, J' \in \mathbb{Z}_m^D$, we have* $\Pr\{c_\Gamma(J) = c_\Gamma(J')\} \leq 2/m$.

PROOF. Let $J = \langle j_1, j_2, \ldots, j_D \rangle$ and $J' = \langle j'_1, j'_2, \ldots, j'_D \rangle$. Because $J \neq J'$, there must exist some index k in the range $1 \leq k \leq D$ such that $j_k \neq j'_k$. Without loss of generality, assume that $k = 1$. We therefore have (modulo m) that

$$c_\Gamma(J) - c_\Gamma(J') = \gamma_1 j_1 - \gamma_1 j'_1 + \sum_{k=2}^{D} \gamma_k \cdot j_k - \sum_{k=2}^{D} \gamma_k \cdot j'_k ,$$

and thus $c_\Gamma(J) - c_\Gamma(J') = 0$ implies that

$$j_1 - j'_1 = \left(\sum_{k=2}^{D} \gamma_k \cdot (j'_k - j_k) \right) \cdot \gamma_1^{-1} .$$

Consider fixed values for J, J', and $\gamma_2, \ldots, \gamma_k$, and let $y = j_1 - j'_1$, let $a = \left(\sum_{k=2}^{D} \gamma_k \cdot (j'_k - j_k) \right)$, and let $x = \gamma_1^{-1}$.

We now show that for any fixed choice of $a \in \mathbb{Z}_m$ and nonzero $y \in \mathbb{Z}_m$, there is at most one choice of $x \in 2\mathbb{Z}_{m/2}+1$ such that $y = ax$. For the sake of contradiction, suppose that there are two distinct values x_1 and x_2 such that $y = ax_1 = ax_2$. This supposition implies that $0 = ax_1 - ax_2 = a(x_1 - x_2)$, which is satisfied if $a = 0$ or if $x_1 - x_2 = 0$. Because we have $y \neq 0$, it follows that $a \neq 0$, and because $x_1 \neq x_2$, we must have $x_1 - x_2 \neq 0$, yielding a contradiction.

Therefore, there is at most one value of x satisfying $y = ax$. Because x is relatively prime to m, it has a unique inverse in $\mathbb{Z}_m$, and thus there is at most one choice of $x^{-1} = \gamma_1$ such that $y = ax$. Because γ_1 is a randomly chosen value from $2\mathbb{Z}_{m/2}+1$, the probability that $x = \gamma_1^{-1}$ satisfies $y = ax$ is $\leq 2/m$. □

This low probability of collision allows DOTMIX to generate many random numbers with a low probability that any pair collide. By Boole's Inequality [16, p. 1195], given n distinct pedigrees and using a random function from C_{DOTMIX}, the probability of a collision among any of their compressed pedigrees is at most $\binom{n}{2}(2/m) = n(n-1)/m$. Hence, with $m = 2^{64}$, the probability that hashing 4 million pedigrees results in a collision in their compressed values is less than one in a million.

Although the compression function effectively hashes a pedigree into a w-bit word with a small probability of collision, two similar pedigrees may yet have "similar" hash values, whereas we would like them to be statistically "dissimilar." In particular, for a given compression function c_Γ, two pedigrees that differ only in their kth rank differ in their compressions by a predictable multiple of γ_k. To reduce the statistical correlation in generated random values, DOTMIX "mixes" the bits of a compressed pedigree using a mixing function based on the RC6 block cipher [15, 43]. For any w-bit input z, where we assume that w is even, let $\phi(z)$ denote the function that swaps the high- and low-order $w/2$ bits of z, that is,

$$\phi(z) = \left\lfloor \frac{z}{\sqrt{m}} \right\rfloor + \sqrt{m}\,(z \bmod \sqrt{m}) \ ,$$

and let

$$f(z) = \phi(2z^2 + z) \bmod m \ .$$

DOTMIX uses the mixing function $\mu(z) = f^{(r)}(z)$, which applies r rounds of $f(z)$ to the compressed pedigree value z. Contini *et al.* [15] prove that $f(z)$ is a one-to-one function, and hence, for two distinct pedigrees J and J', the probability that $\mu(c(J)) = \mu(c(J'))$ is unchanged from Theorem 1.

To further randomize the generated random numbers, DOTMIX incorporates a random seed into the computation of the hash of a pedigree. The random number generated for a pedigree J is actually the value of a hash function $h(J, \sigma)$, where σ is a random seed. Such a random seed may be incorporated into the computation of $\mu(c_\Gamma(J))$ in several ways. For instance, we might XOR or otherwise combine the seed with the result of $\mu(c_\Gamma(J))$, computing, for example, $h(J, \sigma) = \sigma \oplus \mu(c_\Gamma(J))$. This scheme does not appear to be particularly good, because it lacks much statistical variation between the numbers generated by one seed versus another. A better scheme is to combine the seed with the compressed pedigree *before* mixing, for example, giving $h(J, \sigma) = \mu(\sigma \oplus c(J))$.

DOTMIX simply incorporates the seed as an additional term in the pedigree itself. DOTMIX is formally defined as follows.

DEFINITION 2. *For a given number r of mixing rounds, the* DOTMIX *DPRNG generates a random number by hashing the current pedigree $J = \langle j_1, j_2, \ldots, j_D \rangle$ with a random seed σ according to the function*

$$h_\Gamma(J, \sigma) = f^{(r)}(c_\Gamma(J, \sigma)) \ ,$$

where

$$c_\Gamma(J, \sigma) = (\sigma + c_\Gamma(J)) \bmod m$$

and c_Γ is a hash function chosen uniformly at random from the DOTMIX *compression-function family C_{DOTMIX}.*

The statistical quality of DOTMIX

Although DOTMIX is not a cryptographically secure RNG, it appears to generate high-quality random numbers as evinced by Dieharder [9], a collection of statistical tests designed to empirically test the quality of serial RNG's. Figure 4 summarizes the Dieharder test results DOTMIX and compares them to those of the Mersenne twister [36], whose implementation is provided in the GNU Scientific Library [21]. As Figure 4 shows, with 4 or more iterations of the mixing function, DOTMIX generates random numbers of comparable quality to Mersenne twister. In particular, Mersenne twister and DOTMIX with 2 or more mixing iterations fail the same three Dieharder tests (which we believe to be faulty). Because the Dieharder tests are based on P-values [26], it is not surprising to see statistical variation in the number of "Weak" and "Poor" results even from high-quality RNG's. Hence, for the results in Figure 4, one can consider an RNG to have effectively passed a Dieharder test if it did not explicitly fail it.

Test	r	*Passed*	*Weak*	*Poor*	*Failed*
Mersenne twister	–	34	2	1	3
DOTMIX (tree)	16	35	2	0	3
	8	32	3	1	4
	4	34	1	2	3
	2	32	2	2	4
	1	31	2	0	7
	0	8	1	3	28
DOTMIX (loop)	16	30	3	4	3
	8	34	2	1	3
	4	34	2	1	3
	2	31	2	3	4
	1	17	1	2	20
	0	4	2	0	34
LCGMIX (tree)	4	34	2	0	4
	0	9	2	1	28

Figure 4: A summary of the quality of DOTMIX on the Dieharder tests compared to the Mersenne twister. For the entries labeled "tree," DOTMIX generates 3^{20} random numbers in a parallel divide-and-conquer ternary tree fashion using spawns. For the entries labeled "loop," a `cilk_for` loop generates 3^{20} random numbers. The column labeled r indicates the number of mixing iterations. Each successive column counts the number of tests that produced the given status. The table also summarizes the Dieharder test results for LCGMIX.

When using Dieharder to measure the quality of a parallel RNG, we confronted the issue that Dieharder is really designed to measure the quality of serial RNG's. Since all numbers are generated by a serial RNG in a linear order, this order provides a natural measure of "distance" between adjacent random numbers, which Dieharder can use to look for correlations. When using an RNG for a parallel program, however, this notion of "distance" is more complicated, because calls to the RNG can execute in parallel. The results in Figure 4 use numbers generated in a serial execution of the (parallel) test program, which should maximize the correlation between adjacent random numbers due to similarities in the corresponding pedigrees. In principle, another execution order of the same program could generate random numbers in a different order and lead to different Dieharder test results.

In practice, DOTMIX uses $r = 4$ mixing iterations to generate empirically high-quality random numbers. The difference in performance per call to DOTMIX with $r = 0$ and with $r = 4$ is less than 4%, and thus DOTMIX can generate high-quality random numbers without sacrificing performance.

4. More pedigree-based DPRNG's

This section investigates several other pedigree-based schemes for DPRNG's. Principal among these schemes is LCGMIX, which uses a compression function based on linear congruential generators and the same mixing function as DOTMIX. We prove that the probability that LCGMIX's compression function generates a collision is small, although not quite as small as for DOTMIX. We examine Dieharder results which indicate that LCGMIX is statistically good. We also discuss alternative DPRNG schemes and their utility. These DPRNG's demonstrate that pedigrees can enable not only DOTMIX, but a host of other DPRNG implementations. We discuss a theoretical weakness with DOTMIX that would be remedied by a 4-independent compression scheme.

The LCGMIX *DPRNG*

LCGMIX is related to the "Lehmer tree" DPRNG scheme of [19]. LCGMIX uses a family of compression functions for pedigrees that generalize linear congruential generators (LCG's) [29, 32].

LCGMIX then "RC6-mixes" the compressed pedigree to generate a pseudorandom value using the same mixing function as DOTMIX.

The basic idea behind LCGMIX is to compress a pedigree by combining each successive rank using an LCG that operates modulo $m = 2^w$, where w is the computer-word width. LCGMIX uses only three random values $\alpha, \beta, \gamma \in \mathbb{Z}_m$, where α is odd, and avoids reading a value out of a table for each rank in the pedigree, as DOTMIX must do. Specifically, for an instruction x at depth d with pedigree $J(x) = \langle j_1, j_2, \ldots, j_d \rangle$, the LCGMIX compression function performs the following recursive calculation modulo

$$X_d = \begin{cases} \gamma & \text{if } d = 0, \\ \alpha \cdot (X_{d-1} + \beta \cdot j_d) & \text{if } d > 0. \end{cases}$$

The value X_d is the compressed pedigree. Thus, the LCGMIX compression function need only perform two multiplications and one addition per rank in the pedigree.

The family of compression functions used by LCGMIX can be defined as follows, where we use $\mathbb{Z}_m^*$ to denote the set of all pedigrees of arbitrary length.

DEFINITION 3. *Let $\alpha \in 2\mathbb{Z}_{m/2} + 1$, $\beta \in \mathbb{Z}_m$, and $\gamma \in \mathbb{Z}_m - \{0\}$ be integers chosen uniformly at random from their respective sets. Define $c_{\alpha,\beta,\gamma} : \mathbb{Z}_m^* \to \mathbb{Z}_m$ by*

$$c_{\alpha,\beta,\gamma}(J) = \left(\alpha^d \gamma + \beta \sum_{k=1}^{d} \alpha^{d-k} j_k \right) \bmod m \, ,$$

where $J = \langle j_1, j_2, \ldots, j_d \rangle \in \mathbb{Z}_m^d$. The **LCGMIX** ***compression-function family*** *is the set of functions*

$$C_{\text{LCGMIX}} = \left\{ c_{\alpha,\beta,\gamma} : \alpha \in 2\mathbb{Z}_{m/2} + 1, \beta \in \mathbb{Z}_m, \gamma \in \mathbb{Z}_m - \{0\} \right\} .$$

The next theorem shows that the probability a randomly chosen compression function $c_{\alpha,\beta,\gamma} \in C_{\text{LCGMIX}}$ hashes two distinct pedigrees to the same value is small, although not quite as small as for DOTMIX.

THEOREM 2. *Let $c_{\alpha,\beta,\gamma} \in C_{\text{LCGMIX}}$ be a randomly chosen compression function. Then for any two distinct pedigrees $J, J' \in \mathbb{Z}_m^*$ we have $\Pr\{c_{\alpha,\beta,\gamma}(J) = c_{\alpha,\beta,\gamma}(J')\} \leq 2d/m$, where d is the maximum number of terms in either pedigree.*

PROOF. Let $J = \langle j_1, j_2, \ldots, j_d \rangle$ and $J' = \langle j'_1, j'_2, \ldots, j'_{d'} \rangle$, where we assume without loss of generality that $d \geq d'$. The important observation is that the difference $c_{\alpha,\beta,\gamma}(J) - c_{\alpha,\beta,\gamma}(J')$ is a nonzero polynomial in α of degree at most d with coefficients in $\mathbb{Z}_m$. Thus, there are at most d roots to the equation $c_{\alpha,\beta,\gamma}(J) - c_{\alpha,\beta,\gamma}(J') = 0$, which are values for α that cause the two compressed pedigrees to collide. Since there are $m/2$ possible values for α, the probability of collision is $\leq 2d/m$. □

This pairwise collision probability implies a theoretical bound on how many random numbers LCGMIX can generate before one would expect a collision between any pair of numbers in the set. By Boole's Inequality [16, p. 1195], compressing n pedigrees with a random function from C_{LCGMIX} gives a collision probability between any pair of those n compressed pedigrees of at most $\binom{n}{2} 2d/m = n(n-1)d/m$. With $m = 2^{64}$ and making the reasonable assumption that $d \leq 100$, the probability that compressing 250,000 pedigrees results in a collision is less than one in a million. As can be seen, the 250,000 pedigrees for which the probability of a collision is less than one in a million is somewhat less than the 4 million for DOTMIX. Since our implementation of LCGMIX was only 3%-5% faster than our implementation of DOTMIX per function call, we favored DOTMIX for the Cilk Plus library.

We tested the quality of random numbers produced by LCGMIX using Dieharder, producing the results in Figure 4. The data suggest that as with DOTMIX, $r = 4$ mixing iterations in LCGMIX are sufficient to provide random numbers whose statistical quality is comparable to those produced by the Mersenne twister.

Other DPRNG's

We can define DPRNG's using families of compression functions that exhibit stronger theoretical properties or provide faster performance than either DOTMIX or LCGMIX.

One alternative is to use ***tabulation hashing*** [11] to compress pedigrees, giving compressed pedigree values that are 3-independent and have other strong theoretical properties [41]. This DPRNG is potentially useful for applications that require stronger properties from their random numbers. To implement this scheme, the compression function treats the pedigree as a bit vector whose 1 bits select entries in a table of random values to XOR together.

As another example which favors theoretical quality over performance, a DPRNG could be based on compressing the pedigree with a SHA-1 [38] hash, providing a cryptographically secure compression function that would not require any mixing to generate high-quality random numbers. Other cryptographically secure hash functions could be used as well. While cryptographically secure hash functions are typically slow, they would allow the DPRNG to provide pseudorandom numbers with very strong theoretical properties, which may be important for some applications.

On the other side of the performance-quality spectrum, a DPRNG could be based on compressing a pedigree using a faster hash function. One such function is the hash function used in UMAC [3], which performs half the multiplications of DOTMIX's compression function. The performance of the UMAC compression scheme and the quality of the DPRNG it engenders offers an interesting topic for future research.

4-independent compression of pedigrees

Although Theorem 1 shows that the probability is small that DOTMIX's compression function causes two pedigrees to collide, DOTMIX contains some theoretical weaknesses. Consider two distinct pedigrees J_1 and J_2 of length d, and suppose that DOTMIX maps J_1 and J_2 to the same value, or more formally, that DOTMIX chooses a compression function c_Γ such that $c_\Gamma(J_1) = c_\Gamma(J_2)$. Let $J + \langle j \rangle$ denote the pedigree that results from appending the rank j to the pedigree J. Because J_1 and J_2 both have length d, it follows that

$$\begin{aligned} c_\Gamma(J_1 + \langle j \rangle) &= c_\Gamma(J_1) + \gamma_{d+1} \cdot j \\ &= c_\Gamma(J_2) + \gamma_{d+1} \cdot j \\ &= c_\Gamma(J_2 + \langle j \rangle) \, . \end{aligned}$$

Thus, DOTMIX hashes the pedigrees $J_1 + \langle j \rangle$ and $J_2 + \langle j \rangle$ to the same value, regardless of the value of j. In other words, one collision in the compression of the pedigrees for two strands, however rare, may result in many ancillary collisions.

To address this theoretical weakness, a DPRNG scheme might provide the guarantee that if two pedigrees for two strands collide, then the probability remains small that any the pedigrees collide for any other pair of strands. A 4-independent hash function [46] would achieve this goal by guaranteeing that the probability is small that any sequence of 4 distinct pedigrees hash to any particular sequence of 4 values. Tabulation-based 4-independent hash functions for single words are known [45], but how to extend these techniques to hash pedigrees efficiently is an intriguing open problem.

5. A scoped DPRNG library interface

This section presents the programming interface for a DPRNG library that we implemented for Cilk Plus. This interface demonstrates how programmers can use a pedigree-based DPRNG library

```
1 template <typename T>
2 class DPRNG {
3   DPRNG();                        // Constructor
4   ~DPRNG();                       // Destructor
5   DPRNG_scope current_scope(); // Get current scope
6   void set(uint64_t seed, DPRNG_scope scope); // Init
7   uint64_t get();                 // Get random #
8 };
```

Figure 5: A C++ interface for a pedigree-based DPRNG suitable for use with Cilk Plus. The type T of the DPRNG object specifies a particular DPRNG library, such as DotMix, that implements this interface. In addition to accepting an argument for an initial seed, the initialization method for the DPRNG in line 6 also requires an lexical scope, restricting the scope where the DPRNG object can be used.

in applications. The interface uses the notion of "scoped" pedigrees, which allow DPRNG's to compose easily.

Scoped pedigrees solve the following problem. Suppose that a dthreaded program contains a parallel subcomputation that uses a DPRNG, and suppose that the program would like to run this subcomputation the same way twice. Using scoped pedigrees, the program can guarantee that both runs generate the exact same random numbers, even though corresponding RNG calls in the subcomputations have different pedigrees globally.

Programming interface

Figure 5 shows a C++ interface for a DPRNG suitable for use with Cilk Plus. It resembles the interface for an ordinary serial RNG, but it constrains when the DPRNG can be used to generate random numbers by defining a "scope" for each DPRNG instance. The `set` method in line 6 initializes the DPRNG object based on two quantities: an initial seed and a scope. The seed is the same as for an ordinary serial RNG. The ***scope*** represented by a pedigree J is the set of instructions whose pedigrees have J as a common prefix. Specifying a scope (represented by) J to the DPRNG object `rand` restricts the DPRNG to generate numbers only within that scope and to ignore the common prefix J when generating random numbers. By default, the programmer can pass in the global scope $\langle 0 \rangle$ to let the DPRNG object be usable anywhere in the program. The interface allows programmers to limit the scope of a DPRNG object by getting an explicit scope (line 5) and setting the scope of a DPRNG object (line 6).

Figure 6 demonstrates how restricting the scope of a DPRNG can be used to generate repeatable streams of random numbers within a single program. Inside `f`, the code in lines 3–4 limits the scope of `rand` so that it generates random numbers only within `f`. Because of this limited scope, the assertion in line 23 holds true. If the programmer sets `rand` with a global scope, then each call to `f` would generate a different value for `sum`, and the assertion would fail.

Intuitively, one can think of the scope as extension of the seed for a serial RNG. To generate exactly the same stream of random numbers in a dthreaded program, one must (1) use the same seed, (2) use the same scope, and (3) have exactly the same structure of spawned functions and RNG calls within the scope. Even if `f` from Figure 6 were modified to generate random numbers in parallel, the use of scoped pedigrees still guarantees that each iteration of the parallel loop in line 16 behaves identically.

Implementation

To implement the `get` method of a DPRNG, we use the API in Figure 2 to extract the current pedigree during the call to `get`, and then we hash the pedigree. The principal remaining difficulty in the DPRNG's implementation is in handling scopes.

Intuitively, a scope can be represented by a pedigree prefix that should be common to the pedigrees of all strands generating

```
1 uint64_t f(DPRNG<DotMix>* rand, uint64_t seed, int i) {
2   uint64_t sum = 0;
3   DPRNG_scope scope = rand->current_scope();
4   rand->set(seed, scope);
5   for (int j = 0; j < 15; ++j) {
6      uint64_t val = rand->get();
7      sum += val;
8   }
9   return sum;
10 }
11 int main(void) {
12   const int NSTREAMS = 10;
13   uint64_t sum[NSTREAMS];
14   uint64_t s1 = 0x42; uint64_t s2 = 31415;
15   // Generate NSTREAMS identical streams
16   cilk_for (int i = 0; i < NSTREAMS; ++i) {
17      DPRNG<DotMix>* rand = new DPRNG();
18      sum[i] = f(rand, s1, i);
19      sum[i] += f(rand, s2, i);
20      delete rand;
21   }
22   for (int i = 1; i < NSTREAMS; ++i)
23      assert(sum[i] == sum[0]);
24   return 0;
25 }
```

Figure 6: A program that generates `NSTREAMS` identical streams of random numbers. Inside function `f`, the code in lines 3–4 limits the scope of `rand` so that it can generate random numbers only within `f`.

random numbers within the scope. Let y be the instruction corresponding to a call to `current_scope()`, and let x be a call to `get()` within the scope $J(y)$. Let $J(x) = \langle j_1, j_2, \ldots, j_{d(x)} \rangle$ and $J(y) = \langle j'_1, j'_2, \ldots, j'_{d(y)} \rangle$. Since x belongs to the scope $J(y)$, it follows that $d(x) \geq d(y)$, and we have $j_{d(y)} \leq j'_{d(y)}$ and $j_k = j'_k$ for all $k < d(y)$. We now define the ***scoped pedigree*** of x with respect to scope $J(y)$ as

$$J_{J(y)}(x) = \langle j_{d(y)} - j'_{d(y)}, j_{d(y)+1}, \ldots, j_{d(x)} \rangle .$$

To compute a random number for $J(x)$ excluding the scope $J(y)$, we simply perform a DPRNG scheme on the scoped pedigree $J_{J(y)}(x)$. For example, DotMix computes $\mu(c_\Gamma(J_{J(y)}(x)))$. Furthermore, one can check for scoping errors by verifying that $J(y)$ is indeed the prefix of $J(x)$ via a direct comparison of all the pedigree terms.

Our implementation of scoped pedigrees fails to exploit one potential optimization. To hash a scoped pedigree $J_{J(y)}(x)$, our implementation first reads the entire pedigree $J(x)$, and then it removes the scope $J(y)$ from $J(x)$. In principle, however, an implementation need only read the scoped pedigree $J_{J(y)}(x)$ itself, rather than the entirety of $J(x)$. Unfortunately, in our implementation of pedigrees, extracting a scoped pedigree and verifying that the current pedigree $J(x)$ lies within a scope $J(y)$ seems to require reading all of $J(x)$. How this optimization might be exploited remains an open problem.

6. Performance results

This section reports on our experimental results investigating the overhead of maintaining pedigrees and the cost of the DotMix DPRNG. To study the overhead of tracking pedigrees, we modified the open-source MIT Cilk [20], whose compiler and runtime system were both accessible. We discovered that the overhead of tracking pedigrees is small, having a geometric mean of only 1% on all tested benchmarks. To measure the costs of DotMix, we implemented it as a library for a version of Cilk Plus that Intel engineers had augmented with pedigree support, and we compared its performance to a nondeterministic DPRNG implemented using worker-local Mersenne twister RNG's. Although the price of determinism from using DotMix was approximately a factor of 2–3 greater per

Application	*Default*	*Pedigree*	*Overhead*
fib	11.03	12.13	1.10
cholesky	2.75	2.92	1.06
fft	1.51	1.53	1.01
matmul	2.84	2.87	1.01
rectmul	6.20	6.21	1.00
strassen	5.23	5.24	1.00
queens	4.61	4.60	1.00
plu	7.32	7.35	1.00
heat	2.51	2.46	0.98
lu	7.88	7.25	0.92

Figure 7: Overhead of maintaining 64-bit rank pedigree values for the Cilk benchmarks as compared to the default of MIT Cilk 5.4.6. The experiments were run on an AMD Opteron 6168 system with a single 12-core CPU clocked at 1.9 GHz. All times are the minimum of 15 runs measured in seconds.

function call than Mersenne twister on a synthetic benchmark, this price was much smaller on more realistic codes such as a sample sort and Monte Carlo simulations. These empirical results suggest that pedigree-based DPRNG's are amply fast for debugging purposes and that their overheads should even be low enough for many production codes.

Pedigree overheads

To estimate the overhead of maintaining pedigrees, we ran a set of microbenchmarks for MIT Cilk with and without support for pedigrees. We modified MIT Cilk 5.4.6 to store the necessary 64-bit rank values and pointers in each frame for spawn pedigrees and to maintain spawn pedigrees at runtime. We then ran 10 MIT Cilk benchmark programs using both our modified version of MIT Cilk and the original MIT Cilk. In particular, we ran the following benchmarks:

- `fib`: Recursive exponential-time calculation of the 40th Fibonacci number.
- `cholesky`: A divide-and-conquer Cholesky factorization of a sparse 2000×2000 matrix with 10,000 nonzeros.
- `fft`: Fast Fourier transform on 2^{22} elements.
- `matmul`: Recursive matrix multiplication of 1000×1000 square matrices.
- `rectmul`: Rectangular matrix multiplication of 2048×2048 square matrices.
- `strassen`: Strassen's algorithm for matrix multiplication on 2048×2048 square matrices.
- `queens`: Backtracking search to count the number of solutions to the 24-queens puzzle.
- `plu`: LU-decomposition with partial pivoting on a 2048×2048 matrix.
- `heat`: Jacobi-type stencil computation on a 4096×1024 grid for 100 timesteps.
- `lu`: LU-decomposition on a 2048×2048 matrix.

The results from these benchmarks, as summarized in Figure 7, show that the slowdown due to spawn pedigrees is generally negligible, having a geometric mean of less than 1%. Although the overheads run as high as 10% for `fib`, they appear to be within measurement noise caused by the intricacies of modern-day processors. For example, two benchmarks actually run measurably faster despite the additional overhead. This benchmark suite gives us confidence that the overhead for maintaining spawn pedigrees should be close to negligible for most real applications.

DPRNG overheads

To estimate the cost of using DPRNG's, we persuaded Intel to modify its Cilk Plus concurrency platform to maintain pedigrees, and then we implemented the DOTMIX DPRNG.[6] We compared DOTMIX's performance, using $r = 4$ mixing iterations, to a nondeterministic parallel implementation of the Mersenne twister on synthetic benchmarks, as well as on more realistic applications. From these results, we estimate that the "price of determinism" for DOTMIX is about a factor of 2–3 in practice on synthetic benchmarks that generate large pedigrees, but it can be significantly less for more practical applications. For these experiments, we coded by hand an optimization that the compiler could but does not implement. To avoid incurring the overhead of multiple worker lookups on every call to generate a random number, within a strand, DOTMIX looks up the worker once and uses it for all calls to the API made by the strand.

We used Intel Cilk Plus to explore perform three different experiments. First, we used a synthetic benchmark to quantify how DOTMIX performance is affected by pedigree length. Next, we used the same benchmark to measure the performance benefits of flattening pedigrees for `cilk_for` loops. Finally, we benchmarked the performance of DOTMIX on realistic applications that require random numbers. All experiments described in the remainder of this section were run on an Intel Xeon X5650 system with two 6-core CPU's, each clocked at 2.67 GHz. The code was compiled using the Intel C++ compiler v12.1 with the `-O3` optimization flag and uses the Intel Cilk Plus runtime, which together provide support for pedigrees.

First, to understand how the performance of DOTMIX varies with pedigree length, we constructed a synthetic benchmark called CBT. This benchmark successively creates n/k complete binary trees, each with k leaves, which it walks in parallel by spawning two children recursively. The pedigree of each leaf has uniform length $L = 1 + \lg k$, and within each leaf, we call the RNG.

Figure 8 compares the performance of various RNG's on the CBT benchmark, fixing $n = 2^{20}$ random numbers but varying the pedigree length L. These results show that the overhead of DOTMIX of LCGMIX increases roughly linearly with pedigree length, but these pedigree-based DPRNG's are still within about a factor of two of using a Mersenne Twister RNG. From a linear regression on the data from Figure 8, we observed that the cost per additional term in the pedigree for both DOTMIX and LCGMIX was about 10 cycles, regardless of whether $r = 4$ or $r = 16$.[7]

Figure 9 breaks down the overheads of DOTMIX in the CBT benchmark further. To generate a random number, DOTMIX requires looking up the currently executing worker in Cilk (from thread-local storage),[8] reading the pedigree, and then generating a random number. The figure compares the overhead of DOTMIX with the overhead of simply spawning a binary tree with n leaves while performing no computation within each leaf. From this data, we can attribute at least 40% of the execution time of DOTMIX calls to the overhead of simply spawning the tree itself. Also, by measuring the cost of reading a pedigree, we observe that about 70–80% of the cost of an RNG call can be attributed to looking up the pedigree itself. These data suggest that the cost of reading the pedigree dominates the cost of the pedigree computation and mixing iterations, particularly for $r = 4$.

[6] The Intel C++ compiler v12.1 provides compiler and runtime support for maintaining pedigrees in Cilk.

[7] This linear model overestimates the runtime of this benchmark for $L < 4$ (not shown). For small trees, it is difficult to accurately measure and isolate the RNG performance from the cost of the recursion itself.

[8] Our implementation of a parallel RNG based on Mersenne Twister also requires a similar lookup from thread-local storage to find the worker-thread's local RNG.

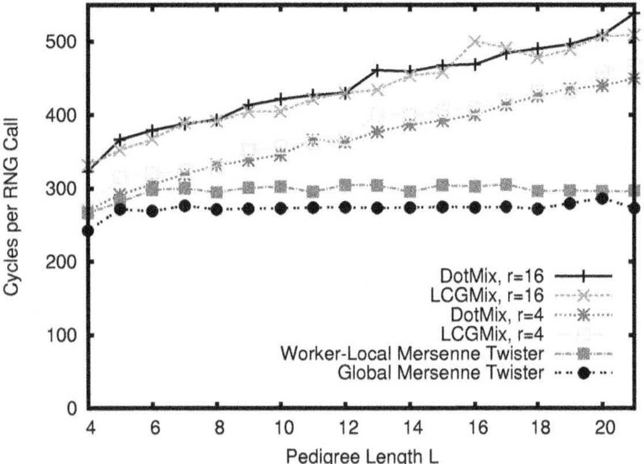

Figure 8: Overhead of various RNG's on the CBT benchmark when generating $n = 2^{20}$ random numbers. Each data point represents the minimum of 20 runs. The global Mersenne twister RNG from the GSL library [21] only works for serial code, while the worker-local Mersenne twister is a nondeterministic parallel implementation.

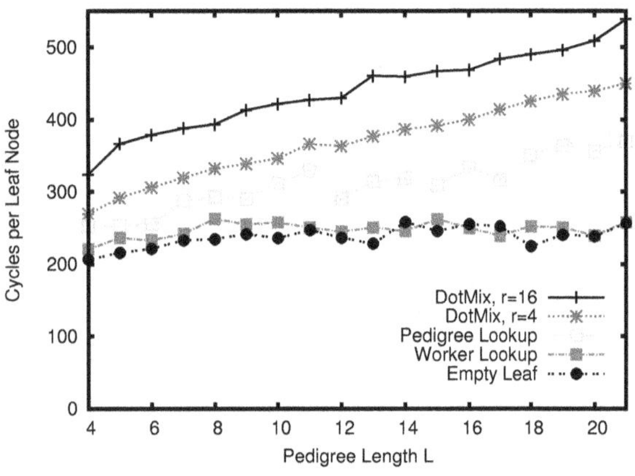

Figure 9: Breakdown of overheads of DOTMIX in the CBT benchmark, with $n = 2^{20}$. This experiment uses the same methodology as for Figure 8.

Pedigree flattening

To estimate the performance improvement of the pedigree-flattening optimization for `cilk_for` loops described in Section 2, we compared the cost performing n pedigree lookups for the CBT benchmark (Figure 9) to the cost of pedigree lookups in a `cilk_for` loop performing n pedigree lookups in parallel. Figure 10 shows that the `cilk_for` pedigree optimization substantially reduces the cost of pedigree lookups. This result is not surprising, since the pedigree lookup for recursive spawning in the CBT benchmark cost increases roughly linearly with $\lg n$, whereas the lookup cost remains nearly constant for using a `cilk_for` as $\lg n$ increases.

Application benchmarks

Figure 11 summarizes the performance results for the various RNG's on four application benchmarks:

- `pi`: A simple Monte-Carlo simulation that calculates the value of the transcendental number π using 256M samples.
- `maxIndSet`: A randomized algorithm for finding a maximum independent set in graphs with approximately 16M vertices, where nodes have an average degree of between 4 and 20.
- `sampleSort`: A randomized recursive samplesort algorithm on 64M elements, with the base case on 10,000 samples.

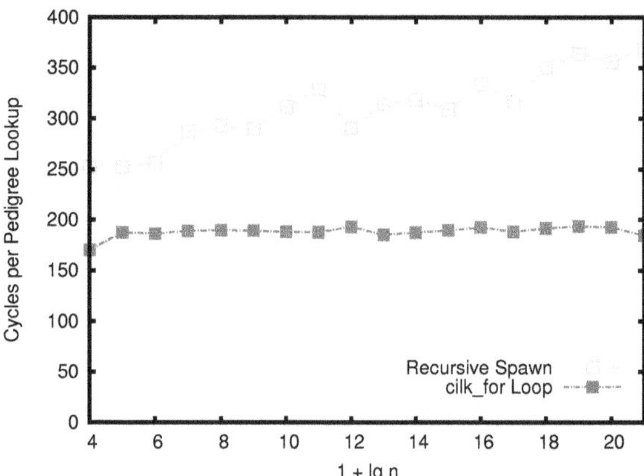

Figure 10: Comparison of pedigree lookups in a `cilk_for` loop with recursive spawns in a binary tree. The recursive spawning generates n leaves as in the CBT benchmark, with each pedigree lookup having $L = 1 + \lg n$ terms. The `cilk_for` loop uses a grain size of 1, and generates pedigrees of length 3.

Application	T_1(DotMix)/T_1(mt)	T_{12}(DotMix)/T_{12}(mt)
fib	2.65	2.42
pi	0.74	0.72
maxIndSet	0.99	0.98
sampleSort	0.99	0.99
DiscreteHedging	1.03	1.03

Figure 11: Overhead of DOTMIX as compared to a parallel version of the Mersenne twister (denoted by `mt` in the table) on four programs. All benchmarks use the same worker-local Mersenne twister RNG's as in Figure 8 except for `DiscreteHedging`, which uses QuantLib's existing Mersenne twister implementation.

- `DiscreteHedging`: A financial-model simulation using Monte Carlo methods.

We implemented the `pi` benchmark ourselves. The `maxIndSet` and `sampleSort` benchmarks were derived from the code described in [4]. The `DiscreteHedging` benchmark is derived from the QuantLib library for computation finance. More specifically, we modified QuantLib version 1.1 to parallelize this example as described in [25], and then supplemented QuantLib's existing RNG implementation of Mersenne Twister with DOTMIX and LCGMIX.

To estimate the per-function-call cost of DOTMIX, we also ran the same `fib` benchmark that was used for the experiment described in Figure 7, but modified so that the RNG is called once at every node of the computation. The results for `fib` in Figure 11 indicate that DOTMIX is about a factor of 2–3 slower than using Mersenne twister, suggesting that the price of determinism for parallel random-number generation in dthreaded programs is at most 2–3 per function call. The remaining applications, which perform significantly more computation per random number obtained, pay a relatively lesser price for determinism. The `pi` benchmark, which effectively consists of a single `cilk_for` loop, benefits significantly from the pedigree-flattening optimization, producing pedigrees of length only 4, and actually runs faster than the Mersenne-twister implementation.

7. Related work

The problem of generating random numbers deterministically in multithreaded programs has received significant attention. SPRNG [35] is a popular DPRNG for pthreading platforms that works by creating independent RNG's via a parameterization process. Other approaches to parallelizing RNG's exist, such as leapfrogging and splitting. Coddington [14] surveys these alternative schemes and their respective advantages and drawbacks. It may be possible to adapt some of these pthreading RNG schemes to create similar DPRNG's for dthreaded programs.

The concept of deterministically hashing interesting locations in a program execution is not new. The `maxIndSet` and `sampleSort` benchmarks we borrowed from [4] used an *ad hoc* hashing scheme to afford repeatability, a technique we have used technique ourselves in the past and which must have been reinvented numerous times before us. More interesting is the pedigree-like scheme due to Bond and McKinley [8] where they use an LCG strategy similar to LCGMIX to assign deterministic identifiers to calling contexts for the purposes of residual testing, anomaly-based bug detection, and security intrusion detection.

Recently, Salmon *et al.* [44] independently explored the idea of "counter-based" parallel RNG's, which generate random numbers via a independent transformations of the counter values. Counter-based RNG's use similar ideas to pedigree-based DPRNG's. Intuitively, the compressed pedigree values generated by DOTMIX and LCGMIX can be thought of as counter values, and the mixing function corresponds to a particular kind of transformation. Salmon *et al.* focus on generating high-quality random numbers, exploring several transformations based on both existing cryptographic standards and some new techniques, and show that these transformations lead to RNG's with good statistical properties. Counter-based RNG's do not directly lead to DPRNG's for a dthreaded programs, however, because it can be difficult to generate deterministic counter values. One can, however, apply these transformations to compressed pedigree values and automatically derive additional pedigree-based DPRNG's.

8. Concluding remarks

We conclude by discussing two enhancements for pedigrees and DPRNG's. We also consider how the notion of pedigrees might be extended to work on other concurrency platforms.

The first enhancement addresses the problem of multiple calls to a DPRNG within a strand. The mechanism described in Section 2 involves calling the STRANDBREAK function, which increments the rank whenever a call to the DPRNG is made, thereby ensuring that two successive calls have different pedigrees. An alternative idea is to have the DPRNG store for each worker p an ***event counter*** e_p that the DPRNG updates manually and uses as an additional pedigree term so that multiple calls to the DPRNG per strand generate different random numbers.

The DPRNG can maintain an event counter for each worker as follows. Suppose that the DPRNG stores for each worker p the last pedigree p read. When worker p calls the DPRNG to generate another random number, causing the DPRNG to read the pedigree, the DPRNG can check whether the current pedigree matches the last pedigree p read. If it matches, then p has called the DPRNG again from the same strand, and so the DPRNG updates e_p. If it does not match, then p must be calling the DPRNG from a new strand. Because each strand is executed by exactly one worker, the DPRNG can safely reset e_p to a default value in order to generate the next random number.

This event counter scheme improves the composability of DPRNG's in a program, because calls to one DPRNG do not affect calls to another DPRNG in the same program, as they do for the scheme from Section 2. In practice, however, event counters may hurt the performance of a DPRNG. From experiments with the `fib` benchmark, we found that an event-counter scheme runs approximately 20% slower per function call than the scheme from Section 2, and thus we favored the use of STRANDBREAK for our main results. Nevertheless, more efficient ways to implement an event-counter mechanism may exist, which would enhance composability.

Our second enhancement addresses the problem of "climbing the tree" to access all ranks in the pedigree for each call to the DPRNG, the cost of which is proportional to the spawn depth d. Some compression functions, including Definitions 1 and 3, can be computed ***incrementally***, and thus results can be "memoized" to avoid walking up the entire tree to compress the pedigree. In principle, one could memoize these results in a ***frame-data*** cache — a worker-local cache of intermediate results — and then, for some computations, generate random numbers in $O(1)$ time instead of $O(d)$ time. Preliminary experiments with using frame-data caches indicate, however, that in practice, the cost of memoizing the intermediate results in every stack frame outweighs the benefits from memoization, even in an example such as `fib`, where the spawn depth can be quite large. Hence, we opted not to use frame-data caches for DOTMIX. Nevertheless, it is an interesting open question whether another memoization technique, such as selective memoization specified by the programmer, might improve performance for some applications.

We now turn to the question of how to extend the pedigree ideas to "less structured" dthreading concurrency platforms. For some parallel-programming models with less structure than Cilk, it may not be important to worry about DPRNG's at all, because these models do not encapsulate the nondeterminism of the scheduler. Thus, a DPRNG would seem to offer little benefit over a nondeterministic parallel RNG. Nevertheless, some models that support more complex parallel control than the fork-join model of Cilk do admit the writing of deterministic programs, and for these models, the ideas of pedigrees can be adapted.

As an example, Intel Threading Building Blocks [42] supports software pipelining, in which each stage of the pipeline is a fork-join computation. For this control construct, one could maintain an outer-level pedigree to identify the stage in the pipeline and combine it with a pedigree for the interior fork-join computation within a stage.

Although Cilk programs produce instruction traces corresponding to fork-join graphs, the pedigree idea also seems to extend to general dags, at least in theory. One can define pedigrees on general dags as long as the children (successors) of a node are ordered. The rank of a node x indicates the birth order of x with respect to its siblings. Thus, a given pedigree (sequence of ranks) defines a unique path from the source of the task graph. The complication arises because in a general dag, multiple pedigrees (paths) may lead to the same node. Assuming there exists a deterministic procedure for choosing a particular path as the "canonical" pedigree, one can still base a DPRNG on canonical pedigrees. It remains an open question, however, as to how efficiently one can maintain canonical pedigrees in this more general case, which will depend on the particular parallel-programming model.

9. Acknowledgments

Thanks to Ron Rivest and Peter Shor of MIT for early discussions regarding strategies for implementing a DPRNG for dthreaded computations. Ron suggested using the RC6 mixing strategy. Thanks to Guy Blelloch of Carnegie Mellon for sharing his benchmark suite from which we borrowed the sample sort and maximal-independent-set benchmarks. Angelina Lee of MIT continually provided us with good feedback and generously shared her mastery of Cilk runtime systems. Loads of thanks to Kevin B. Smith and especially Barry Tannenbaum of Intel Corporation for implementing pedigrees in the Intel compiler and runtime system, respectively.

References

[1] E. Allen, D. Chase, J. Hallett, V. Luchangco, J.-W. Maessen, S. Ryu, G. L. S. Jr., and S. Tobin-Hochstadt. *The Fortress Language Specification Version 1.0*. Sun Microsystems, Inc., Mar. 2008.

[2] R. Barik, Z. Budimlic, V. Cavè, S. Chatterjee, Y. Guo, D. Peixotto, R. Raman, J. Shirako, S. Taşirlar, Y. Yan, Y. Zhao, and V. Sarkar. The Habanero multicore software research project. In *OOPSLA*, pp. 735–736. ACM, 2009.

[3] J. Black, S. Halevi, H. Krawczyk, T. Krovetz, and P. Rogaway. UMAC: Fast and secure message authentication. In *CRYPTO*, pp. 216–233. IACR, Springer-Verlag, 1999.

[4] G. E. Blelloch, J. T. Fineman, P. B. Gibbons, and J. Shun. Internally deterministic parallel algorithms can be fast. In *PPoPP*. ACM, 2012.

[5] R. D. Blumofe and C. E. Leiserson. Scheduling multithreaded computations by work stealing. *JACM*, 46(5):720–748, 1999.

[6] R. D. Blumofe and D. Papadopoulos. Hood: A user-level threads library for multiprogrammed multiprocessors. Technical Report, University of Texas at Austin, 1999.

[7] R. L. Bocchino, Jr., V. S. Adve, S. V. Adve, and M. Snir. Parallel programming must be deterministic by default. In *HOTPAR*. USENIX, 2009.

[8] M. D. Bond and K. S. McKinley. Probabilistic calling context. In *OOPSLA*, pp. 97–112. ACM, 2007.

[9] R. G. Brown. Dieharder: A random number test suite. Available from `http://www.phy.duke.edu/~rgb/General/dieharder.php`, Aug. 2011.

[10] F. W. Burton and M. R. Sleep. Executing functional programs on a virtual tree of processors. In *FPCA*, pp. 187–194. ACM, Oct. 1981.

[11] J. L. Carter and M. N. Wegman. Universal classes of hash functions. In *STOC*, pp. 106–112. ACM, 1977.

[12] V. Cavé, J. Zhao, J. Shirako, and V. Sarkar. Habenero-Java: the new adventures of old X10. In *PPPJ*. ACM, 2011.

[13] P. Charles, C. Grothoff, V. Saraswat, C. Donawa, A. Kielstra, K. Ebcioglu, C. von Praun, and V. Sarkar. X10: An object-oriented approach to non-uniform cluster computing. In *OOPSLA*, pp. 519–538. ACM, 2005.

[14] P. D. Coddington. Random number generators for parallel computers. Technical report, Northeast Parallel Architectures Center, Syracuse University, Syracuse, New York, 1997.

[15] S. Contini, R. L. Rivest, M. J. B. Robshaw, and Y. L. Yin. The security of the RC6 block cipher. Available from `http://people.csail.mit.edu/rivest/publications.html`, 1998.

[16] T. H. Cormen, C. E. Leiserson, R. L. Rivest, and C. Stein. *Introduction to Algorithms*. The MIT Press, third edition, 2009.

[17] M. Dietzfelbinger, J. Gil, Y. Matias, and N. Pippenger. Polynomial hash functions are reliable. In *ICALP*, pp. 235–246. Springer-Verlag, 1992.

[18] M. Feng and C. E. Leiserson. Efficient detection of determinacy races in Cilk programs. *Theory of Computing Systems*, 32(3):301–326, 1999.

[19] P. Frederickson, R. Hiromoto, T. L. Jordan, B. Smith, and T. Warnock. Pseudo-random trees in Monte Carlo. *Parallel Computing*, 1(2):175–180, 1984.

[20] M. Frigo, C. E. Leiserson, and K. H. Randall. The implementation of the Cilk-5 multithreaded language. In *PLDI*, pp. 212–223. ACM, 1998.

[21] M. Galassi, J. Davies, J. Theiler, B. Gough, G. Jungman, P. Alken, M. Booth, and F. Rossi. *GNU Scientific Library Reference Manual*, 1.14 edition, March 2010. Available from `http://www.gnu.org/software/gsl/`.

[22] J. Gosling, B. Joy, G. Steele, and G. Bracha. *The Java Language Specification*. Addison Wesley, second edition, 2000.

[23] R. H. Halstead, Jr. Implementation of Multilisp: Lisp on a multiprocessor. In *LFP*, pp. 9–17. ACM, 1984.

[24] J. M. Hart. *Windows System Programming*. Addison-Wesley, third edition, 2004.

[25] Y. He. Multicore-enabling discrete hedging in QuantLib. Available from `http://software.intel.com/en-us/articles/multicore-enabling-discrete-hedging-in-quantlib/`, Oct. 2009.

[26] W. Hines and D. Montgomery. *Probability and Statistics in Engineering and Management Science*. J. Wiley & Sons, third edition, 1990.

[27] Institute of Electrical and Electronic Engineers. Information technology — Portable Operating System Interface (POSIX) — Part 1: System application program interface (API) [C language]. IEEE Standard 1003.1, 1996 Edition.

[28] Intel Corporation. *Intel Cilk Plus Language Specification*, 2010. Document Number: 324396-001US. Available from `http://software.intel.com/sites/products/cilk-plus/cilk_plus_language_specification.pdf`.

[29] D. E. Knuth. *Seminumerical Algorithms*, volume 2 of *The Art of Computer Programming*. Addison-Wesley, third edition, 1998.

[30] D. Lea. A Java fork/join framework. In *JAVA*, pp. 36–43. ACM, 2000.

[31] E. A. Lee. The problem with threads. *Computer*, 39:33–42, 2006.

[32] D. H. Lehmer. Mathematical methods in large-scale computing units. In *Second Symposium on Large-Scale Digital Calculating Machinery*, volume XXVI of *Annals of the Computation Laboratory of Harvard University*, pp. 141–146, 1949.

[33] D. Leijen and J. Hall. Optimize managed code for multi-core machines. *MSDN Magazine*, 2007. Available from `http://msdn.microsoft.com/magazine/`.

[34] C. E. Leiserson. The Cilk++ concurrency platform. *J. Supercomputing*, 51(3):244–257, 2010.

[35] M. Mascagni and A. Srinivasan. Algorithm 806: SPRNG: A scalable library for pseudorandom number generation. *ACM TOMS*, 26(3):436–461, 2000.

[36] M. Matsumoto and T. Nishimura. Mersenne Twister: a 623-dimensionally equidistributed uniform pseudo-random number generator. *ACM TOMACS*, 8:3–30, 1998.

[37] R. Motwani and P. Raghavan. *Randomized Algorithms*. Cambridge University Press, Cambridge, England, June 1995.

[38] National Institute of Standards and Technology, Washington. *Secure Hash Standard (SHS)*, 2008. Federal Information Standards Publication 180-3. Available from `http://csrc.nist.gov/publications/fips/fips180-3/fips180-3_final.pdf`.

[39] R. H. B. Netzer and B. P. Miller. What are race conditions? *ACM LOPLAS*, 1(1):74–88, March 1992.

[40] OpenMP application program interface, version 3.0. Available from `http://www.openmp.org/mp-documents/spec30.pdf`, May 2008.

[41] M. Pătraşcu and M. Thorup. The power of simple tabulation hashing. In *STOC*, pp. 1–10. ACM, 2011.

[42] J. Reinders. *Intel Threading Building Blocks: Outfitting C++ for Multi-core Processor Parallelism*. O'Reilly Media, Inc., 2007.

[43] R. L. Rivest, M. Robshaw, R. Sidney, and Y. Yin. The RC6 block cipher. Available at `http://people.csail.mit.edu/rivest/publications.html`, 1998.

[44] J. K. Salmon, M. A. Moraes, R. O. Dror, and D. E. Shaw. Parallel random numbers: as easy as 1, 2, 3. In *SC*, pp. 16:1–16:12. ACM, 2011.

[45] M. Thorup and Y. Zhang. Tabulation based 4-universal hashing with applications to second moment estimation. In *SODA*, pp. 615–624. ACM/SIAM, 2004.

[46] M. N. Wegman and L. Carter. New hash functions and their use in authentication and set equality. *JCSS*, 22(3):265–279, 1981.

Scalable Parallel Minimum Spanning Forest Computation

Sadegh Nobari
National University of Singapore
snobari@nus.edu.sg

Thanh-Tung Cao
National University of Singapore
caothanh@nus.edu.sg

Panagiotis Karras
Rutgers University
karras@business.rutgers.edu

Stéphane Bressan
National University of Singapore
steph@nus.edu.sg

Abstract

The proliferation of data in graph form calls for the development of scalable graph algorithms that exploit parallel processing environments. One such problem is the computation of a graph's minimum spanning forest (MSF). Past research has proposed several parallel algorithms for this problem, yet none of them scales to large, high-density graphs. In this paper we propose a novel, scalable, parallel MSF algorithm for undirected weighted graphs. Our algorithm leverages Prim's algorithm in a parallel fashion, concurrently expanding several subsets of the computed MSF. Our effort focuses on minimizing the communication among different processors without constraining the local growth of a processor's computed subtree. In effect, we achieve a scalability that previous approaches lacked. We implement our algorithm in CUDA, running on a GPU and study its performance using real and synthetic, sparse as well as dense, structured and unstructured graph data. Our experimental study demonstrates that our algorithm outperforms the previous state-of-the-art GPU-based MSF algorithm, while being several order of magnitude faster than sequential CPU-based algorithms.

Categories and Subject Descriptors G.2.2 [*Discrete Mathematics*]: Graph Theory—Graph algorithms, Network problems; E.1 [*Data Structures*]: Graphs and networks

General Terms Algorithms, Experimentation, Performance

Keywords Parallel Graph Algorithms, Minimum Spanning Forest, GPU

1. Introduction

A spanning tree of a connected graph G is an acyclic subgraph of G that connects all vertices of G. The Minimum Spanning Tree (MST) problem calls to find a spanning tree of a weighted connected graph G having the minimum total weight [17]. In case the graph is not connected, i.e. consists of several connected components, the problem is generalized to finding the Minimum Spanning Forest (MSF), i.e. a subgraph containing an MST of each component.

MST computation finds applications in domains such as the optimization of message broadcasting in communication networks [10, 12, 22], biological data analysis [34], and image processing [27], while it forms a basis for clustering algorithms [32, 35]. For instance, assume a graph $G(V, E)$ where vertices stand for persons and weighted edges for the cost of communication among them, in which we wish to spread some news at the minimum cost in real time. We then need to efficiently compute an MST of G.

Past research has proposed several sequential MST algorithms, starting out with Borůvka's seminal work [9]. Highlights of this research are Kruskal's [18], Prim's [26], and the Reverse-Delete [20] algorithms. Other MST algorithms may have lower asymptotic complexity, but larger hidden constants [24]. While existing algorithms are reasonably efficient, modern applications call for algorithms that can scale well to very large and high-density graphs, including complete graphs, as in the case of computing the MST in Eucledian space, which finds applications in hierarchical clustering [23]. Parallel processing comes into play to achieve this objective. Thus, a large body of literature is devoted to parallel MST algorithms [14, 19]. Nevertheless, such works use specialized hardware that is not so readily available as low-cost and easily-programmable Graphics Processing Units (GPUs); GPUs are commonly installed on today's home computers, workstations, consoles, and gaming devices. Several pieces of work have exploited the GPU's ubiquity to suggest high-performance, general data processing algorithms therefor [15, 16, 21]. In a similar spirit, Vineet et al. have already offered a data parallel version of Borůvka's MST algorithm adopted for a GPU [31]. However, Borůvka's algorithm is ill-chosen if the objective is to solve the MST computation in a scalable manner for dense graphs[1], as its performance is known to deteriorate in comparison to Prim's algorithm as graph density grows [13]. To date, two parallel adaptations of Prim's algorithm have been proposed [8, 19]; however, out of these, [8] allows for limited parallelism, as it does not allow two growing subtrees to touch each other, while [19] necessitates costly inter-processor communication to merge subtrees when they do get in contact. Thus, there is still a need for a size-scalable and density-scalable GPU-based MST computation algorithm.

In this paper we respond to this need; we propose a novel Parallel MSF Algorithm (PMA) for undirected weighted graphs, which adapts Prim's algorithm while eschewing the drawbacks of [8] and

[1] By dense we refer to those graphs with a number of edges ten times larger than the number of vertices ($|E| > 10 \times |V|$).

PPoPP'12, February 25–29, 2012, New Orleans, Louisiana, USA.

[19]; in contrast to [8], it allows for full-scale flexible parallelism; still, unlike [19] it raises a much lower communication overhead. We implement PMA on the GPU[2] using the CUDA programming framework [2]. Our experimental study on both real and synthetic graphs verifies that our algorithm outperforms previous GPU-based MSF algorithms.

2. Related Work

The MSF problem was first formulated and solved by Borůvka [9]. Subsequently, three altervative algorithms were proposed, namely Kruskal's [18], Prim's [26] and the Reverse-Delete [20] algorithm. All these algorithms exploit two properties of the MSF [30]; the *cycle property*, which maintains that the heaviest edge in a cycle does not belong to the MSF; and the *cut property*, which maintains that, for every subset of the graph's vertex set, $C \subset V$, the lightest edge with one vertex in C and the other vertex in $V \setminus C$ belongs to the MSF.

The Reverse-Delete algorithm, based on the cycle property, iteratively removes the heaviest edge that does not break any graph component's connectivity. Likewise, Kruskal's algorithm iteratively adds the lightest edge that does not introduce a cycle. Prim's algorithm selects an arbitrary vertex and iteratively inserts the lightest edge from the current subtree to an unvisited vertex, based on the Cut property. Borůvka's algorithm differs from Prim's algorithm in starting from all vertices at once, and expanding all running subtrees at each iteration.

Several theoretical results highlight potential parallelism in MST computation, most of them do not lead to efficient practical algorithms as they incur large constant factors [7]. Thus, most practical parallel MST algorithms are merely parallelized versions of classical sequential algorithms, adapted for specific hardware architectures or programming models. As Borůvka's algorithm is naturally prone to parallelization, most of these works adapt that algorithm, sometimes in combination with Kruskal's or Prim's algorithm [7]. Chung and Condon [11] propose a parallel version of Borůvka's algorithm for asynchronous, distributed-memory machines. Borůvka's algorithm is divided into five steps and parallelize each step. Dehne and Götz [14] propose the Borůvka Mixed Merge (BMM) algorithm, which lets each processing unit find a local MST for its stored edges sequentially, and then prunes and merges the resulting partial MSTs at a single unit using a balanced D-ary tree.

The work that most related to ours, [8], stands between Prim's and Borůvka's algorithms. This MST-BC algorithm lets each processing unit run Prim's algorithm starting from different vertices simultaneously, marking the vertices in its own MST and coloring all neighbors of marked vertices. These local MSTs grow until a conflict occurs, i.e. one unit reaches a vertex marked or colored by another unit. Then, the conflicting unit starts building a new MST from another unvisited vertex. The algorithm terminates when all vertices are either colored or marked and merges the resulting local MSTs. MST-BC degenerates to Borůvka's algorithm for P processing units equal to the number of vertices n, and to Prim's algorithm for one only processing unit. The algorithm in [19] is a relaxed version of MST-BC for the transactional memory model, differing therefrom in the way it treats conflicts. When a conflict occurs, the two parties involved switch to a Merge state to resolve the conflict (see state transition diagram in Figure 1), with one unit appending the other's MST to its own, while the other starts building a new tree from another unvisited vertex; on a connected graph, this algorithm ends up having only one thread working on the final MST, hence reduces parallelism. Last, Vineet et al. [31] recently adapted Borůvka's algorithm for the GPU, using parallel primitives. This algorithm provides the current state of the art for GPU-based MSF computation in terms of efficiency; however, it cannot scale to large numbers of edges.

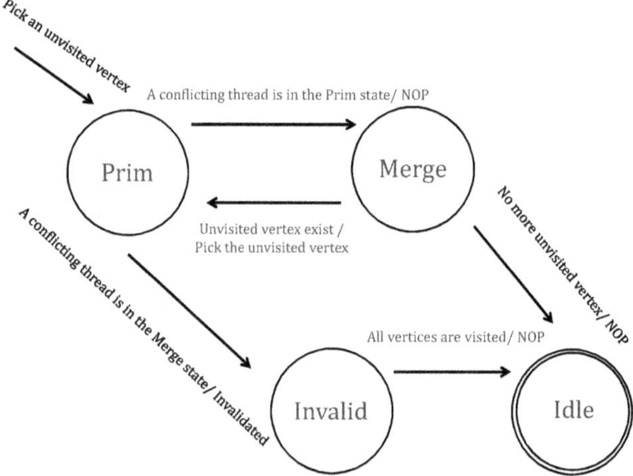

Figure 1. The state transition diagram of Kang and Bader's algorithm [19].

3. Motivation

We observe that most existing approaches to parallel MSF computation share a similar intuition: They build different trees in parallel, and, when conflicts occur (i.e. different trees run into each other), they merge the components and start over. However, this strategy is not equally efficient on all types of graphs; MST-BC [8] fares well with sparse graphs, its relaxation [19] manages well graphs with large diameter (thanks to a heuristic that may result in less conflicts), [14] does well only with sufficiently dense graphs, and [31], being an adaptation of Borůvka's algorithm, is challenged by high graph density; besides, the question of finding the MSF of a non-connected graph is mostly ignored. Most significantly, these approaches tend to be cautiously conservative when expanding their trees, as they have to be alert to potential conflicts, invoking too many redundant iterations that deteriorate their performance. Unfortunately, the attempt to alleviate this conservatism in [19], by merging the trees when a conflict occurs, ends up substituting that problem with another, as it raises the inter-processor communication cost and results into an unbalanced load as progressively fewer processors are left building fewer MSTs, forsaking the benefits of parallelism. Starting out from the next section, we present an alternative, elegant solution that eschews the conservatism of such methods, takes full advantage of parallelism, and keeps communication cost low.

4. Parallel MSF Algorithm

Algorithm 1 shows the overall design of our PMA algorithm, while Figure 2 depicts its state transition diagram. Given an undirected weighted graph $G = (V, E)$, PMA first performs a tailored version of Prim's algorithm, Partial Prim (PP), in parallel on P processors. Then it *unifies* each connected set of subtrees produced by PP into a single vertex and removes all self-loops. This process is repeated until no more edges are left. The union of the sets of edges returned by all PP executions is the desired MSF.

[2] Since each thread of PMA runs the same set of instructions on multiple data thus meeting the requirements of the Single Instruction Multiple Thread architecture of GPU. GPU allows running thousands of threads concurrently with low overhead.

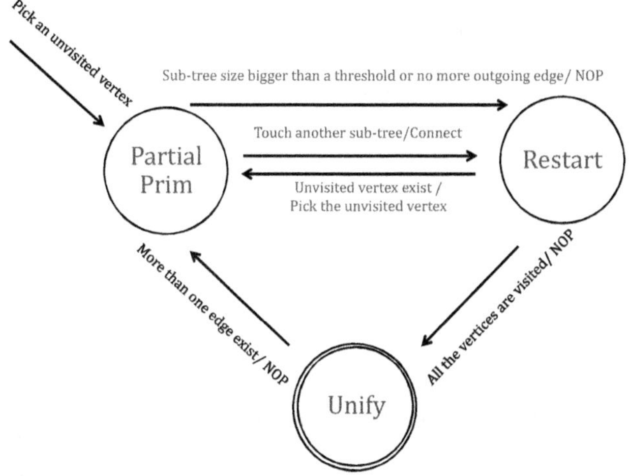

Figure 2. The state transition diagram of the PMA algorithm.

Algorithm 1: PMA algorithm

```
Input: G(V, E) : An undirected weighted graph; P :
       Number of processors;
Output: The MSF of graph G
while (|E| > 0) do
    Initialize the successor arrays ;
    Perform Partial Prim on P processors;
    Compact each connected component into a vertex;
```

4.1 Partial Prim

Algorithm 2 outlines our Partial Prim (PP) algorithm. PP finds an unvisited vertex s, and builds a tree from it as in Prim's algorithm, iteratively finding the lightest outgoing edge from the running subtree. Our implementation keeps the list of vertices in the current subtree in Q, and, at each iteration, goes through Q and finds the lightest outgoing edge to expand the subtree with. A vertex's $successor$ value represents the root of the subtree that contains it, or -1 if it is unvisited. During the parallel execution of PP, two different processors may try to visit the same vertex at the same time; thus, we use the atomic test-and-set instruction on the $successor$ array to avoid conflicts. Another conflict can occur when a processor p building a subtree rooted at s visits a vertex v that has already been visited; then p connects its subtree with that of v by setting $successor[s] = successor[v]$, stops building that tree, and picks another unvisited vertex to build a tree from. Section 4.3 proves the correctness of the algorithm in connection to this step.

4.2 Unification step

After the termination of PP on all processors, every vertex is visited and belongs to exactly one subtree. PMA then unifies all vertices in the same subtree into one vertex, by tracing the $successor$ array. In the resulting graph, it removes all self-loops and all redundant parallel edges, keeping only the lightest ones. After these operations, it is possible to be left with connected, non-island vertices (i.e., with non-eliminated edges); this is due to the fact that, after two subtrees mutually touch each other, both of them stop growing prematurely. Thus, even after a unification step, PMA (Algorithm 1) repeats its basic iteration, until all edges have been eliminated; only then is the MSF construction finished and the algorithm terminates.

Algorithm 2: Partial Prim algorithm

```
Input: G(V, E): An undirected weighted graph;
successor: The successor array, shared among all
processors;
γ: Maximum size that a sub-tree can grow (γ ≥ 2)
Output: A part of the MSF of G
while there is an unvisited vertex s do
    Atomic successor[s] = s if it is not set;
    if successor[s] was set by another processor then
        Continue;
    Q = {s} ;
    while |Q| < γ do
        Find the lightest edge e = (u, v) such that u ∈ Q
        and v ∉ Q;
        if no more edge e then
            Break;
        Include e in the global MSF;
        if successor[v] not set then
            Atomic successor[v] = s;
            Q = Q ⋃ {v};
        else
            successor[s] = successor[v];
            Break;
```

4.3 Proof of Correctness

The correctness of our PMA algorithm emanates from the *Cut property* of the Minimum Spanning Forest.

Lemma 1 (Soundness). *Each subtree constructed by each processor with the PP algorithm is a subset of the MSF of G.*

Proof. Under the assumption that edge weights are distinct, regardless of the vertex at which we start Prim's algorithm, we will build exactly the same MST in a connected component. The only difference between our PP algorithm and the standard Prim algorithm is that PP stops expanding the tree under certain conditions; thus, any constructed subtree is a subset of the MSF of G. □

Lemma 2 (Completeness). *The unification step in PP does not remove any edge belonging to the MSF of G.*

Proof. We can think of the unification step as repeatedly unifying two vertices at a time. We unify two vertices if and only if we have selected an edge between them in the MSF of G. It follows that any other parallel edges between these two vertices cannot be in the MSF of G, thus removing self-loop edges of the unified vertex is safe. After unifying all possible vertices, we only remove parallel edges that are not the lightest ones between two new vertices; these edges cannot be in the MSF of G either. □

Theorem 1. *PMA constructs the MSF of the input graph G.*

Proof. The proof follows from Lemma 1 and Lemma 2. □

Theorem 1 proves the correctness of our PMA algorithm. However, it is still unclear why there are no cycles in the resulting MSF while we allow subtrees to touch each other independently. The following property provides further intuition on this question.

Property 1 (Touch property). *If subtree T_1, constructed by PMA, touches subtree T_2 at edge e, then it stops growing. Subtree T_2 can continue to grow until it either reaches its desirable component size γ, touches another subtree T_3, or touches T_1. In the last case,* *assuming edge weights are distinct, the edge leading from T_2 to T_1 is the same edge e.*

Proof. Since e is chosen by PP, it is the lightest edge between T_1 and $V \setminus T_1$. In turn, when T_2 touches T_1, as it is also expanded by PP, it uses the lightest edge between T_2 and $V \setminus T_2$, say e'. Assume $e' \neq e$. Then the weight of e' should be lighter than that of e, since e' was chosen by PP for expanding T_2 while e was also available on its boundary. However, e had been also chosen by PP for expanding T_1 while e' was available on its boundary as well; thus, the weight of e should be lighter than that of e'. By reductio ad absurdum, and the distinct weight assumption, it follows that $e' = e$. □

4.4 Complexity Analysis

We now analyze the complexity of PMA. We start with estimating the number of iterations of the loop in Algorithm 1. We ignore vertices with degree 0, as they do not affect the MSF of G. With all processors running PP, each vertex is visited exactly once and is then compacted into a single vertex with at least one more vertex either in the same subtree or in another subtree. Thus, each iteration of the loop reduces the number of vertices by at least half, hence the loop runs at most $log_2(|V|)$ times. Besides, each edge in G is checked by at most two processors (each visiting one of the two end points of that edge), at most γ times. Thus, the total work of Algorithm 2 is $O(2\gamma|E|) = O(|E|)$ when γ is a small constant. Putting it all together, the total work of PMA is $O(|E|\ log_2(|V|))$. While having the same complexity as other parallel MSF algorithms, PMA allows each processor to grow its subtree without incurring costly merge and synchronization work. Thus, by increasing γ, we can increase the subtree size, and hence decrease the iterations of Algorithm 1 at the only cost of increasing the computation in line 7 of Algorithm 2.

5. Implementation

We now discuss some implementation details of PMA. We assume that the input graph is represented as an adjacency list. This data structure consists of a vertex list (an array of vertices that stores for each vertex, its index and a pointer to its adjacent vertices in the edge list) and an edge list (that stores for each edge, its weight and the index of the endpoint vertex of the edge). Our implementation assumes that the graph, adjacency list, fits into the GPU memory.

5.1 Graphic Processing Units

Although the GPUs are designed for graphics processing tasks, their performance, availability and ease of use render them an excellent platform for executing general-purpose algorithms. A modern GPU consists of several multiprocessors, each designed to execute hundreds of computing threads in parallel efficiently, with a zero-overhead thread switching capability and a small amount of high-performance on-chip shared memory. With a design of each multiprocessor similar to SIMD architecture, the GPU works best with fine-grain parallelism. To fully utilize the computing power of graphics hardware, it is desirable for a program to have a very high level of parallelism, in the order of tens of thousand of threads. At the same time, the communication between the GPU and the CPU memory, going through the slow PCI-Express bus, should be minimized. The main memory residing on the graphics card is shared among all processors. As such, the GPU can be treated as a shared memory architecture. To facilitate synchronization among different threads on the GPU, atomic operations such as the test-and-set instruction can be used.

We use the CUDA programming model [2] to program the GPUs. In order to exploit the advance features of GPU, we break our algorithm to different building blocks to leverage the parallel primitive algorithms, namely prefix sum, stream compaction, and sorting, as intermediate components of PMA. These primitives have been implemented and optimized for CUDA [3, 28, 29] by coalescing the memory accesses, using shared memory, avoiding bank conflicts, memory paddings and alignments and other GPU dedicated optimizations like unrolling loops. We use these parallel primitive algorithms in the PMA implementation to better utilize the graphics hardware.

In the following, we refer to a CUDA thread as a processor.

5.2 Partial Prim implementation

Each processor running Partial Prim needs to pick one unvisited vertex and grow a tree. When a growing tree is terminated, another unvisited vertex is picked. To reduce the conflict among P processors in picking vertices we divide the set of vertices into P partitions of equal size. Each processor only picks vertices in its own partition to start growing a tree. This operation is still done atomically since a processor growing its tree might visit a vertex in another's partition. The most important step in PP is to pick the lightest outgoing edge to grow from those in the list Q containing the vertices in a processor's current tree. We examine different ways for doing so.

Algorithm 3: MinPMA algorithm

Input: $G(V, E)$: An undirected weighted graph; Q : the list of vertices in the current sub-tree;
Output: The lightest edge $e(u, v)$ such that $u \in Q$ and $v \notin Q$

$minW = \infty$;
for *Each u in Q* **do**
  for *Each edge $e(u, v)$ of u* **do**
    if $successor[u] \neq successor[v]$ *and* $e.weight < minW$ **then**
      $minE = e$;
      $minW = e.weight$;
Return minE;

5.2.1 MinPMA algorithm

The first approach (Algorithm 3) is to go through the list of vertices in Q, and, for each vertex u, through its adjacent edges, and pick the lightest one with a destination $v \notin Q$. To check if a vertex v is in Q or not, we check whether $successor[v]$ is the same as the root of the current tree or not. By this approach, we have to go through the list of adjacent edges of each vertex in Q up to $|Q|$ times, thus its complexity is $O(\gamma|E|)$.

5.2.2 SortPMA algorithm

Our second approach (Algorithm 4) tries to alleviate the disadvantage of MinPMA. We first sort the list of adjacent edges of each vertex by increasing weight[3]. Then, whenever we look for the lightest edge going out from vertex u, we pick the first edge that does not have a destination in Q. By recording the previously chosen edges for each vertex u in Q, we only have to go through the list of adjacent edges of each vertex at most once. Thus, the cost of this step becomes $O(|E|)$, at the cost of sorting the edges, which takes $O(|E|\ log(|E|))$. The latter cost can render SortPMA more costly than MinPMA for small $|Q|$ or large $|E|$. Thus, for very sparse

[3] PMASort uses the parallel radix sort proposed in [28]. However, PMASort needs only adjacent edges of every vertex to be sorted in ascending order of their weights, not the whole edge list. Therefore, In order to have the edge list partially sorted, we first sort the whole edge list in ascending order by the weights then we sort the result in ascending order of the starting vertices.

Algorithm 4: SortPMA algorithm

Input: $G(V, E)$: An undirected weighted graph, with the list of adjacent edges of each vertex sorted by weight; $Last$: Last minimum outgoing edge found for each vertex. Q : the list of vertices in the current sub-tree;
Output: The lightest edge $e(u, v)$ such that $u \in Q$ and $v \notin Q$

$minW = \infty$;
for *Each* u *in* Q **do**
  for *Each edge* $e(u, v)$ *of* u *starting from* $Last[u]$ **do**
    if $successor[u] \neq successor[v]$ **then**
      if $e.weight < minW$ **then**
        $minE = e$;
        $minW = e.weight$;
      $Last[u] = e$;
      Break;
Return minE;

graphs, MinPMA fares better than SortPMA. On the other hand, for dense graphs, PP has a low level of parallelism, and, as a result, SortPMA becomes faster as most of the work is done in the sorting step, which runs efficiently on the whole edge list.

5.2.3 HybridPMA algorithm

As MinPMA is efficient for certain graphs and SortPMA for others, we combine the strengths of both in a hybrid approach, HybridPMA, where we use MinPMA for the first iteration and SortPMA for the rest. The rationale for this choice is that, in the later iterations, the graph gets a lot denser as multiple vertices get unified into one.

In order to pick the lightest outgoing edge, one can argue in favour of using a heap. We empirically observed that using heap for the purpose of finding the lightest outgoing edge in the list Q is much slower than the MinPMA algorithm. For instance, assume that the maximum subtree size (γ) is 10, then the MinPMA algorithm goes through the list of outgoing edges for each vertex at most 10 times. On the other hand, when we use heap, each time we find the lightest outgoing edge for a vertex, we need several rounds of min extraction to overlook the non-outgoing edges (i.e. edges that were visited). In addition, the overhead of creating multiple heaps for each vertex and the need of going through more heaps by a thread when its queue grows bigger, make using heap more costly than just going through all the edges and finding min, as in the MinPMA algorithm.

Algorithm 5: Unifying algorithm

Input: $G(V, E)$: An undirected weighted graph; $successor$: The successor array, shared among all processors;
Output: The simplified graph G with each connected component unified into one vertex

Find the root of the component for each vertex ;
Compute the new vertex indices ;
Update the starting and ending vertices of the edges ;
Remove self-loop edges ;
Return minE;

5.3 Unification implementation

The unification step is common to most parallel MSF algorithms. We opt to sacrifice the total work complexity a little, so as to achieve better parallelism and better utilize the GPU power. Our implementation is inspired from the merging algorithm of Vineet et al. [31]. The unification process with total work $O(|E|log(|V|))$ is explained in Algorithm 5. First, we use the distance doubling technique on the $successor$ array to find the root of the component for each vertex in the graph. We also have to remove cycles in the $successor$ array, created two subtrees touching each other at the same time, as in [31]. Having done that, we mark the root vertices as 1 and other vertices as 0, and perform a parallel prefix sum to compute the new vertex index for each connected component, and the total number of components. We then update the start and end vertex of all edges with the new component indices. Self-loop edges are removed. We then sort the edge list by start vertex so as to bring edges with the same starting point together. Thus, all edges that need to be removed are pushed to the end of the edge list, so we can easily remove them and compute the new number of edges. In case when the graph is dense, even if we can reduce the vertices by half, we still end up with almost the same number of edges, most of them being parallel edges between the same vertices (see Figure 3). In such a case, it is worth removing the parallel edges. To do that, we sort edges first by starting vertex, then by ending vertex, and finally by weight. Then we can easily identify the non-minimal parallel edges, and remove them using the stream compaction primitive.

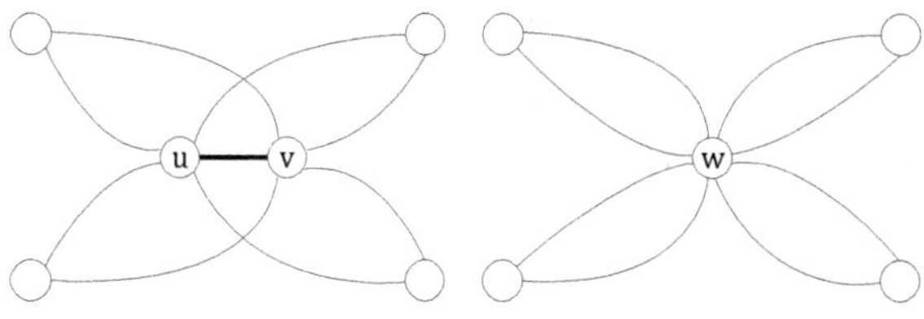

Figure 3. The graph (a) before and (b) after unifying u and v.

5.4 Implementation notes

We note that vertices of degree 0 contribute nothing in the MSF, so we should better remove them all before running the algorithm. We incorporate this logic in the Unification step too, removing any new vertices with no outgoing edge.

In MinPMA each time we find the minimum outgoing edge from a vertex u in Q to a vertex outside Q, we bring that edge to the top of the edge list of u. Next time when we need to scan the edge list of u, we first check its first edge; if it still goes out of Q, it is still the minimum outgoing edge.

6. Performance Evaluation

We now compare different implementations of PMA to Vineet et al's algorithm (Vineet) [31] and Bader and Cong's algorithm (BC) [7], the two state-of-the-art parallel algorithms tuned for GPU and CPU respectively. All runtimes are reported on an Intel Xeon 5420 $2.4Ghz$ workstation with $8GB$ of memory. The GPU algorithms are executed using CUDA Toolkit 3.1 running on the NVIDIA Tesla S1070 server with a single Tesla card. When measuring the execution time, for all algorithms, we exclude the time to copy the input graph to the GPU memory and the resulting MSF back to main memory (since this time is negligible[4] and independent of the algorithm). For the sequential algorithms, we use the Boost library [1].

[4] For instance, the time to copy the input graph to the GPU memory and the resulting MSF back to main memory for the New York graph(0.7 million edges) is 0.42 milliseconds and for the USA-West(15 million edges) graph is 6.45 milliseconds.

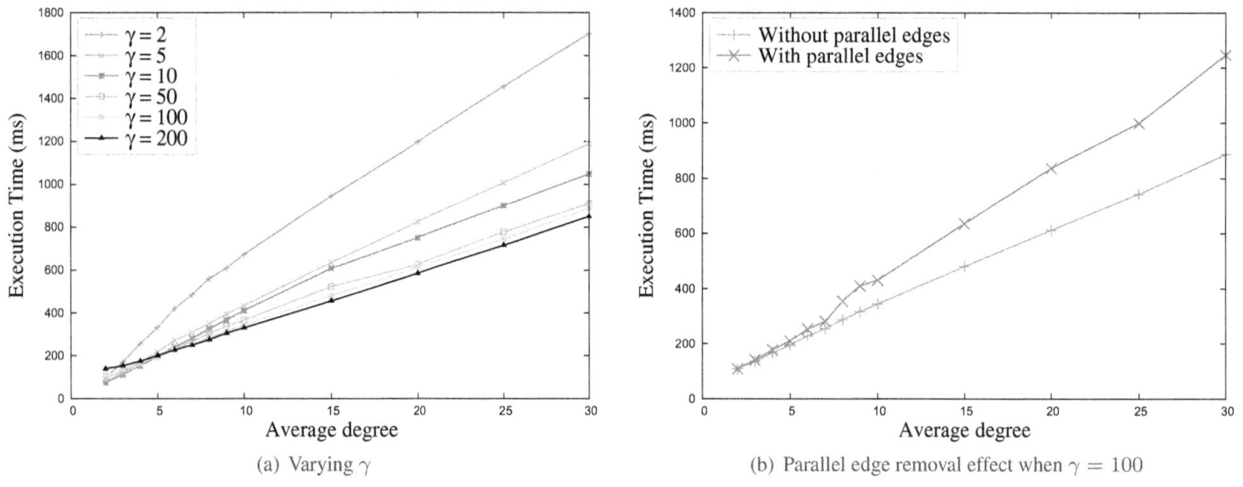

(a) Varying γ

(b) Parallel edge removal effect when $\gamma = 100$

Figure 4. Execution time of HybridPMA on Erdős-Rényi graphs, varying average degree.

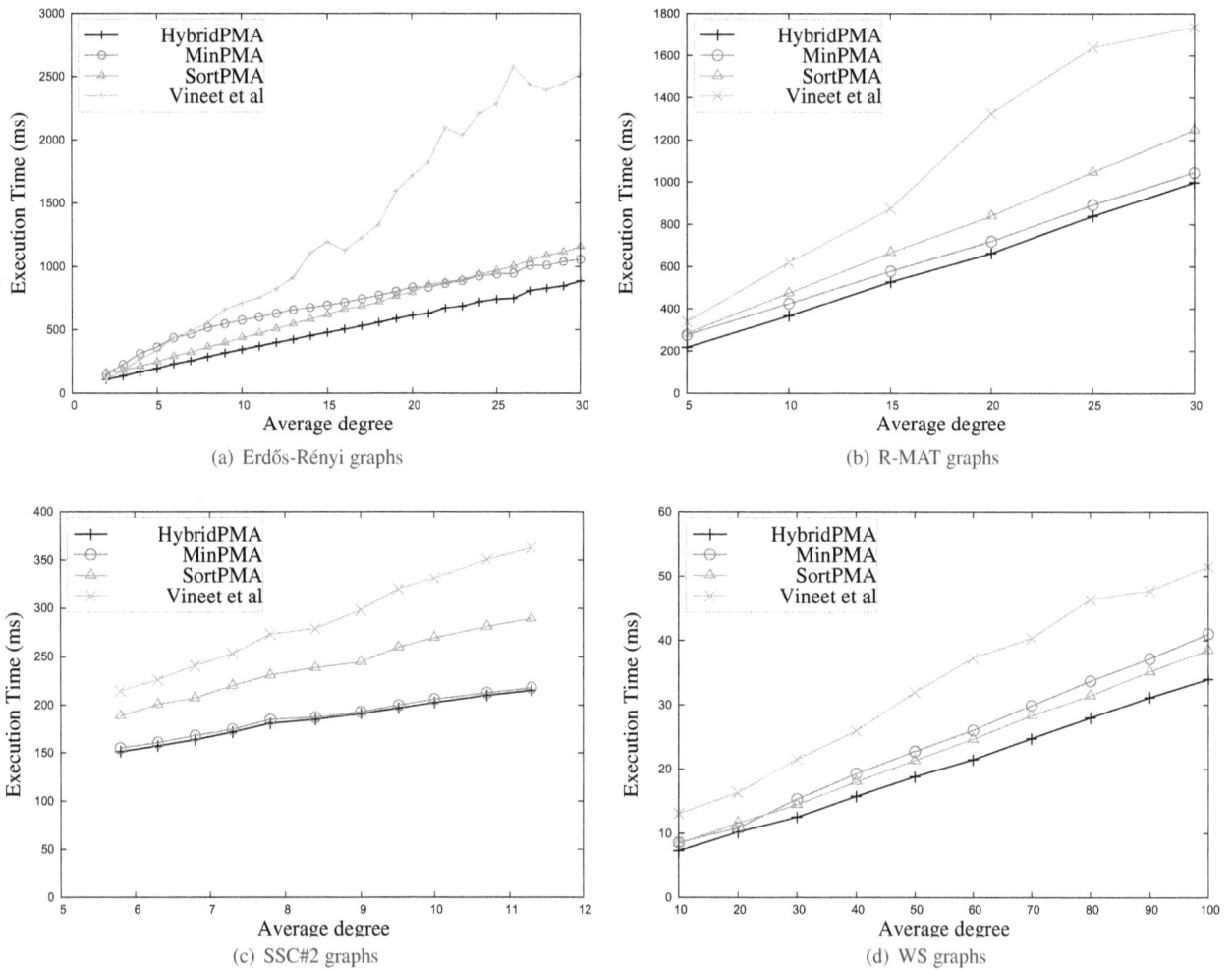

(a) Erdős-Rényi graphs

(b) R-MAT graphs

(c) SSC#2 graphs

(d) WS graphs

Figure 5. Experiments on varying average degree for four types of graph, $|V| = 1M$.

6.1 Datasets

We use both real and synthetic graphs. Our real data are the DIMACS USA road networks data [4] (also used in [31]) and large network data from the SNAP library [6]; for our synthetic data, we use the Georgia Tech graph generator suite [5] to generate the R-

Graph	Vertices	Edges	Execution Time (ms)						
			CPU			GPU	GPU		
			Prim	Kruskal	Boruvka	Vineet	MinPMA	SortPMA	HybridPMA
New York	264K	733K	183	216	541	29	18	27	18
San Francisco	321K	800K	207	255	477	30	19	27	19
Colorado	435K	1M	290	359	592	38	25	37	24
Florida	1.07M	2.7M	780	987	2139	79	51	81	50
Northwest USA	1.2M	2.8M	835	1111	1576	83	59	86	58
Northeast USA	1.52M	3.8M	1120	1571	2811	112	81	118	80
California	1.8M	4.6M	1451	2003	3246	137	103	144	102
Great Lakes	2.7M	6.8M	2076	3004	4832	193	158	213	157
USA-East	3.5M	8.7M	2752	3944	6964	242	195	267	193
USA-West	6.2M	15M	4852	7158	12052	430	346	469	343
USA-Central	14M	33.9M	- [1]	-	52306	-	912	1170	900
USA-Full	23.9M	57.7M	-	-	46890	-	1378	1909	1361
Arxiv Astro Physics	19K	7.9M	93	347	354	39	32	30	30
Penn Road network	1M	6.17M	1603	5522	3315	180	108	169	106
Amazon co-purchasing	410K	6.7M	1457	5923	24047	274	175	218	164
Google graph	876K	10.2M	2616	9730	59671	334	240	268	231
Internet topology	1.7M	22.2M	7000	24629	1408810	934	839	799	797
US Patents Citation	3.8M	33M	-	-	97175	2434	1482	1494	1221

Table 1. Runtime of different CPU and GPU algorithms on real-world networks.

MAT and SSCA#2 graphs and the techniques proposed in [25] to produce Erdős-Rényi (ER) and also Watts and Strogatz (WS) random graphs. WS model [33] generates random graphs with small-world properties in two steps. WS first draws a ring lattice, n vertices each connected to its k nearest neighbors. Then, in an ER fashion selects an edge, i.e. sampling the edges with probability p, from the so-called ring and rewires the edge.

6.2 Maximum subtree size (γ)

The maximum subtree size is the maximum number of vertices of the subtree that a thread is allowed to grow. This maximum allowed subtree size plays a crucial role in PMA. If $\gamma = 2$, PMA behaves like Vineet, while if $\gamma = |V|$, PMA degenerates to Prim's algorithm running sequentially. This is so because, to ensure that each processor has a fair chance to grow its subtree up to γ, we set the P (number of CUDA threads) to be $\frac{|V|}{\gamma}$.

Figure 7(a) shows the execution time of MinPMA and SortPMA with varying γ, processing the Florida road network, a very sparse graph with $|V| \approx 1M$ and $|E| \approx 2.7M$. Both implementations of PMA speed up as γ increases, reaching their peak performance with$\gamma = 8$. This is so because, as the subtree gets bigger, finding the lightest outgoing edge becomes more costly. We also note that MinPMA outperforms SortPMA for very sparse graphs.

Figure 7(b) examines the behavior of PMA on very dense graph, an R-MAT graph with 10K vertices and approximately 11M edges. For such a graph, the chance for two processors to conflict is very high. The performance of SortPMA peaks at $\gamma = 14$, and is unchanged after that, most likely because no processor can grow a subtree bigger than 14. On the other hand, due to the high cost of finding the minimum outgoing edge, the performance of MinPMA degrades as γ grows. MinPMA continues to slow down as γ grows because, as we increase γ, we decrease P. SortPMA is not much affected by this because sorting dominates the execution time. These results suggest that for sparse graphs, a small value of γ yields good performance, while for dense graphs, a bigger γ might be better.

To verify this trend, we run HybridPMA, on Erdős-Rényi Random graphs with varying average degree and $|V|$ fixed to $1M$ (Fig-

[1] Crashed, e.g. out of memory

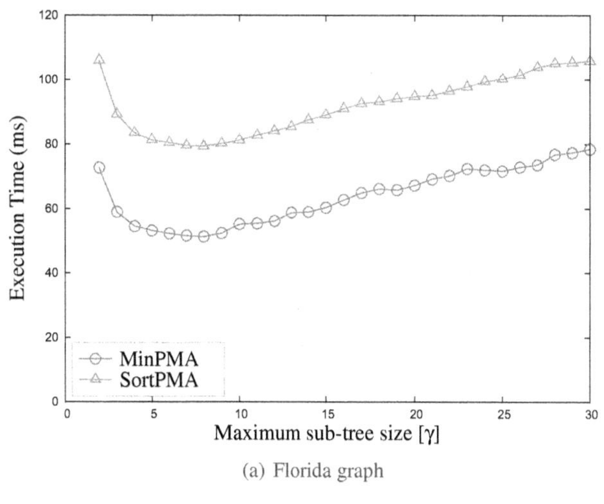

(a) Florida graph

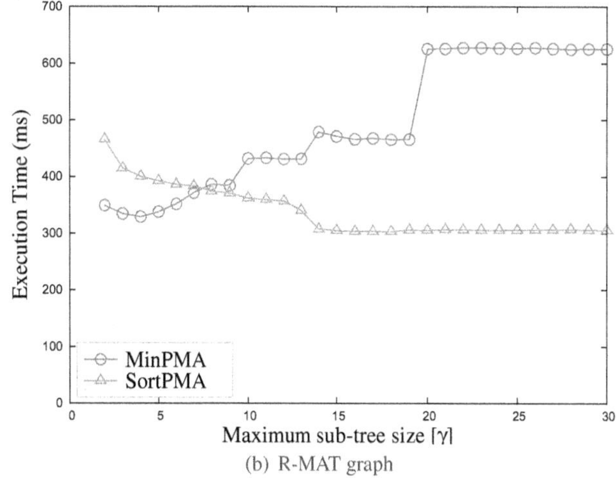

(b) R-MAT graph

Figure 7. Execution time of PMA with varying γ.

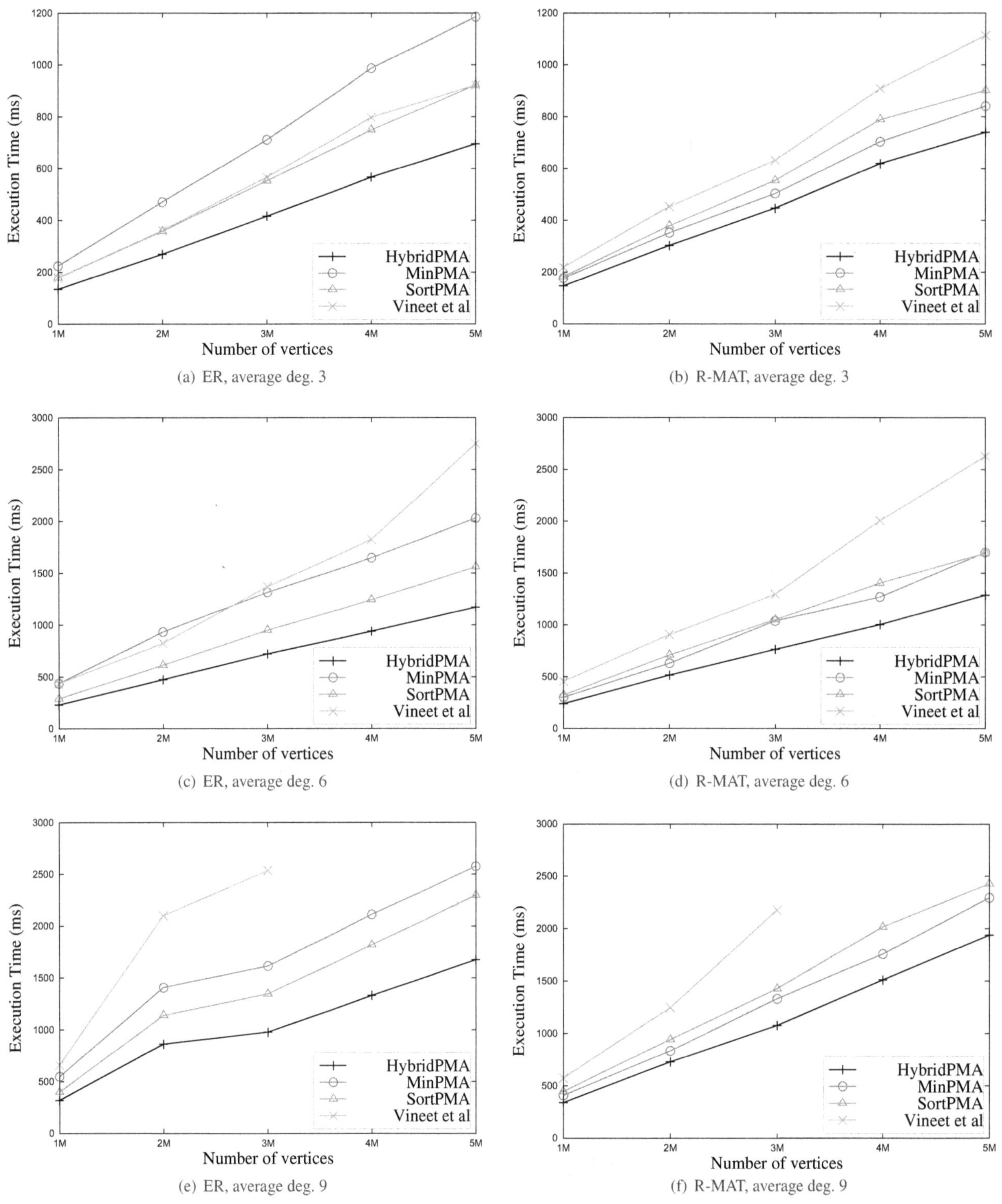

(a) ER, average deg. 3

(b) R-MAT, average deg. 3

(c) ER, average deg. 6

(d) R-MAT, average deg. 6

(e) ER, average deg. 9

(f) R-MAT, average deg. 9

Figure 6. Experiments on varying the number of vertices.

ure 4(a)). We observe that, for small average degree, a small γ of 5 or 6 gives the best performance, whereas for bigger average degree, a γ as big as 200 has an advantage.

However in the whole set of our experiments, we observe that very small γ like $\gamma = 2$ is always not efficient for any kind of graph. The reason is if $\gamma = 2$ we just find one edge for each vertex, while if we increase the γ we can find more edges (maximum $\gamma - 1$ for each Partial Prim). On the other hand, when we have a relatively large γ like $\gamma = 1000$ we need to pay the cost of iterating through the neighbors of γ vertices. Therefore both small (2) and (relatively) large (1000) γ do not yield good performance. We observe that the optimal maximum subtree size depends on the average degree of the graph and the graph structure, such as average shortest path length, average degree and the centralities.

6.3 Removing parallel edges

We also examine the effect of removing parallel edges to the performance of PMA. As discussed, after each unification step, we might end up with a lot of parallel edges. Figure 4(b) shows the execution time of HybridPMA with and without parallel edge removal. It is clear that removing parallel edges significantly improves the performance and, the denser the graph, the more significant is the performance boost. For the rest of the experiments, we always run PMA with parallel edge removal.

6.4 Reduction rate

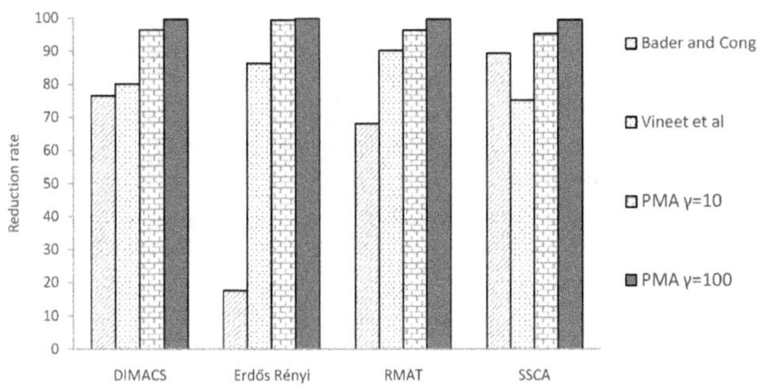

Figure 8. Reduction rate of different algorithms

The three compared parallel algorithms, namely BC, Vineet, and PMA, all have a similar workflow: first, some subsets of the MST are computed, then the connected components are unified into one vertex; if any edges remain the algorithm iterates. However, PMA is less conservative than Bader and Cong's algorithm, as it allows the subtrees it constructs to touch each other, and thus has much fewer components in the next iteration. To demonstrate this effect, Figure 8 shows our measurements of the *reduction rate*, i.e., the rate of vertices unified after the first iteration, with four different types of graphs: a DIMACS graph (Florida), an Erdős-Rényi graph ($|V| = 1M$, $|E| = 30M$), an R-MAT graph ($|V| = 1M$, $|E| = 10M$) and an SSCA graph ($|V| = 1M$, $|E| = 8M$). We have implemented Bader and Cong's algorithm in CUDA, using atomic operations instead of the coloring technique, thus allowing the subtrees to grow a little bit further. The number of processors used is very small to further reduce conflicts. Still, the observed reduction rate of Bader and Cong's algorithm is much lower than that of PMA, especially in dense graphs where the chance of conflict is high. Vineet also exhibits lower reduction rate than PMA, sometimes even lower than Bader and Cong's algorithm. In PMA, larger γ (100 vs 10) improves the rate. Since Bader and Cong's algorithm has very low reduction rate, especially when the number of processors is large, it becomes very inefficient on a massively multithreaded architecture like the GPUs. Thus, we do not include it in the rest of our evaluation.

6.5 Performance comparison

We now compare the performance of different PMA implementations to Vineet [31]. As the implementation of Vineet we obtained cannot handle disconnected graphs, in some cases we add extra edges to render the graphs connected. Table 1 shows the execution time on real world networks. These are mostly very sparse graphs and thus Vineet using Borůvka's algorithm is quite efficient. Nevertheless, in all cases, PMA is faster, up to 2 times for large graphs like the network of citations among US Patents. Besides, HybridPMA is faster than both MinPMA and SortPMA. Different sequential algorithms on CPU using Boost C++ library [1] are included for the sake of illustration. As GPU implementations are orders of magnitude faster than CPU implementations, we omit the CPU algorithms from the rest of our presentation.

Figure 5 shows the runtime on different types of synthetic graphs when we fix the number of vertices at 10^6 and vary the average degree (or number of edges). For all four type of graphs, PMA outperforms Vineet, and the speed up increases as the graphs get denser. This result reconfirms the advantage of using Prim's algorithm over Borůvka's algorithm.

In Figure 6, we measure runtime when we fix the average degree and vary the number of vertices in the graph. For Erdős-Rényi (ER) graphs, when the degree is small, Vineet performs quite close to PMA. However, as the average degree grows, the gap between them increases too, with PMA taking the lead. In addition, Vineet's implementation has a limitation on the maximum number of edges it can handle, so it cannot run some of the very big graphs. Varying the number of vertices in R-MAT graphs presents a similar trend, while now PMA is substantially faster even on very small average degree, as there are still many vertices with high degree in R-MAT graphs.

7. Conclusions

This paper proposed the first, to our knowledge, size- and density-scalable parallel algorithm for Minimum Spanning Forest computation. Our PMA algorithm, based on Prim's algorithm, avoids the conservatism and inter-processor communication cost of earlier approaches, while it is tailored for implementation on a GPU. The key to this achievement is that we allow different processors to grow their partial MSTs unimpeded, while conflicts are handled smoothly without raising extra communication demands. Our algorithm, implemented on a GPU, outperforms the previous state-of-the-art GPU-resident parallel MSF algorithm, which is built on Borůvka's algorithm.

A crucial underlying assumption for our algorithm is that edge weights are distinct. Still, our algorithm can be easily adapted to handle duplicate edge weights, by appending a unique number to the end of each edge weight; such appending does not affect the total weight of the MSF.

References

[1] Boost C++ graph library. http://www.boost.org.

[2] CUDA Zone: Toolkit & SDK. http://developer.nvidia.com/what-cuda.

[3] CUDPP. http://cudpp.googlecode.com.

[4] The Ninth DIMACS challenge on shortest paths. http://www.dis.uniroma1.it/~challenge9/.

[5] GTgraph - A suite of synthetic random graph generators. https://sdm.lbl.gov/ kamesh/software/GTgraph/.

[6] Stanford large network dataset collection. http://snap.stanford.edu/data.

[7] D. A. Bader and G. Cong. Fast shared-memory algorithms for computing the minimum spanning forest of sparse graphs. In *IPDPS*, 2004.

[8] D. A. Bader and G. Cong. Fast shared-memory algorithms for computing the minimum spanning forest of sparse graphs. *JPDC*, 66(11):1366–1378, 2006.

[9] O. Boruvka. O jistém problému minimálním (about a certain minimal problem). *Práce mor. prírodoved. spol. v Brne III*, pages 37–58, 1926.

[10] J. Carle and D. Simplot-Ryl. Energy-efficient area monitoring for sensor networks. *Computer*, 37(2):40–46, 2004.

[11] S. Chung and A. Condon. Parallel implementation of boruvka's minimum spanning tree algorithm. *Parallel Processing Symposium, International*, 0:302, 1996.

[12] J. Cong, L. He, C.-K. Koh, and P. H. Madden. Performance optimization of VLSI interconnect layout. 21(1-2):1–94, 1996.

[13] T. H. Cormen, C. Stein, R. L. Rivest, and C. E. Leiserson. Introduction to algorithms. MIT Press, third edition, 2009. ISBN 0070131511.

[14] F. Dehne and S. Götz. Practical parallel algorithms for minimum spanning trees. In *SRDS*, 1998.

[15] N. K. Govindaraju, B. Lloyd, W. Wang, M. Lin, and D. Manocha. Fast computation of database operations using graphics processors. In *SIGMOD*, 2004.

[16] N. K. Govindaraju, J. Gray, R. Kumar, and D. Manocha. GPUTeraSort: high performance graphics co-processor sorting for large database management. In *SIGMOD*, 2006.

[17] E. Horowitz and S. Sahni. Fundamentals of computer algorithms. *Potomac, Md., Computer Science Press*, 1978.

[18] J. Joseph B. Kruskal. On the shortest spanning subtree of a graph and the traveling salesman problem. *Proc. Amer. Math. Soc.*, 7:48–50, 1956.

[19] S. Kang and D. A. Bader. An efficient transactional memory algorithm for computing minimum spanning forest of sparse graphs. In *PPoPP*, 2009.

[20] J. Kleinberg and Éva Tardos. The minimum spanning tree problem. In *Algorithm Design*. Pearson/Addison-Wesley, Boston, 2006.

[21] E. S. Larsen and D. McAllister. Fast matrix multiplies using graphics hardware. In *Supercomputing*, 2001.

[22] X.-Y. Li, Y. Wang, and W.-Z. Song. Applications of k-local mst for topology control and broadcasting in wireless ad hoc networks. *IEEE TPDS*, 15(12):1057–1069, 2004.

[23] W. B. March, P. Ram, and A. G. Gray. Fast euclidean minimum spanning tree: algorithm, analysis, and applications. In *KDD*, 2010.

[24] B. M. E. Moret and H. D. Shapiro. An empirical assessment of algorithms for constructing a minimal spanning tree. *In DIMACS Monographs*, 1994.

[25] S. Nobari, X. Lu, P. Karras, and S. Bressan. Fast random graph generation. In *EDBT*, 2011.

[26] R. C. Prim. Shortest connection networks and some generalizations. *Bell System Technical Journal*, 36:1389–1401, 1957.

[27] P. W. Rafael C. Gonzalez. *Digital Image Processing*. Addison-Wesley, 1987.

[28] N. Satish, M. Harris, and M. Garland. Designing efficient sorting algorithms for manycore GPUs. In *IPDPS*, 2009.

[29] S. Sengupta, M. Harris, Y. Zhang, and J. D. Owens. Scan primitives for GPU computing. In *Graphics Hardware*, 2007.

[30] R. E. Tarjan. Data structures and network algorithms. *Society for Industrial and Applied Mathematics, Philadelphia*, 1983.

[31] V. Vineet, P. Harish, S. Patidar, and P. J. Narayanan. Fast minimum spanning tree for large graphs on the gpu. In *HPG*, 2009.

[32] X. Wang, X. Wang, and D. Mitchell Wilkes. A divide-and-conquer approach for minimum spanning tree-based clustering. *IEEE TKDE*, 21 (7):945–958, 2009.

[33] D. J. Watts and S. H. Strogatz. Collective dynamics of 'small-world' networks. *Nature*, (393):440–442, 1998.

[34] Y. Xu, V. Olman, and D. Xu. Clustering gene expression data using a graph-theoretic approach: an application of minimum spanning trees. *Bioinformatics*, 18(4):536–545(10), 2002.

[35] C. Zhong, D. Miao, and R. Wang. A graph-theoretical clustering method based on two rounds of minimum spanning trees. *Pattern Recogn.*, 43(3):752–766, 2010.

GKLEE: Concolic Verification and Test Generation for GPUs

Guodong Li *
Fujitsu Laboratories of America,
Sunnyvale, CA 94085, USA
gli@us.fujitsu.com

Peng Li   Geof Sawaya
Ganesh Gopalakrishnan
School of Computing,
University of Utah,
Salt Lake City, UT 84112, USA
{peterlee,sawaya,ganesh}@cs.utah.edu

Indradeep Ghosh
Sreeranga P. Rajan
Fujitsu Laboratories of America,
Sunnyvale, CA 94085, USA
{ighosh,sree.rajan}@us.fujitsu.com

Abstract

Programs written for GPUs often contain correctness errors such as races, deadlocks, or may compute the wrong result. Existing debugging tools often miss these errors because of their limited input-space and execution-space exploration. Existing tools based on conservative static analysis or conservative modeling of SIMD concurrency generate false alarms resulting in wasted bug-hunting. They also often do not target performance bugs (non-coalesced memory accesses, memory bank conflicts, and divergent warps). We provide a new framework called GKLEE that can analyze C++ GPU programs, locating the aforesaid correctness and performance bugs. For these programs, GKLEE can also automatically generate tests that provide high coverage. These tests serve as concrete witnesses for every reported bug. They can also be used for downstream debugging, for example to test the kernel on the actual hardware. We describe the architecture of GKLEE, its symbolic virtual machine model, and describe previously unknown bugs and performance issues that it detected on commercial SDK kernels. We describe GKLEE's test-case reduction heuristics, and the resulting scalability improvement for a given coverage target.

Categories and Subject Descriptors: D.2.4 [Software Engineering]: Software/Program Verification—*Validation*

General Terms: Reliability, Verification

Keywords: GPU, CUDA, Parallelism, Symbolic Execution, Formal Verification, Automatic Test Generation, Virtual Machine

1. Introduction

Multicore CPUs and GPUs are making inroads into virtually all aspects of computing, from portable information appliances to supercomputers. Unfortunately, programming multicore systems to achieve high performance often requires many intricate optimizations involving memory bandwidth and the CPU/GPU occupancy. A majority of these optimizations are still being carried out manually. Given the sheer complexity of these optimizations in the context of actual problems, designers routinely introduce correctness and performance bugs. Locating these bugs using today's commercial debuggers is always a 'hit-or-miss' affair: one has to be *lucky* in so many ways, including (i) picking the right test inputs, (ii) ability to observe of data corruption (and be able to reliably attribute it to races), (iii) whether the compiler optimization match programmer assumptions, and (iv) whether the platform masks bugs because of the specific thread/warp scheduling algorithms used. If the execution deadlocks, one has to manually reason out the root-cause.

Recent formal and semi-formal analysis based tools [1–3] have improved the situation in many ways. They, in effect, examine whole classes of inputs and executions, by resorting to symbolic analysis or static analysis methods. They also analyze abstract GPU models without making hardware-specific thread scheduling assumptions. These tools also have many drawbacks. The first problem with predominantly static analysis based approaches is *false alarms*. False alarms waste precious designer time and may dissuade them from using a tool. Another limitation of today's tools is that they do not help generate tests that achieve high code coverage. Such tests are important for unearthing compiler bugs or "unexpected" bugs that surface during hardware execution. Existing tools also do not cover one new data race category that we identify (we call it *warp-divergence race*). Compilation based approaches can, in many cases, eliminate the drudgery of GPU program optimization; however, their code transformation scripts are seldom separately formally verified.

We present a new tool framework called GKLEE for analyzing GPU programs with respect to important correctness and performance issues (the tool name coming from "GPU" and "KLEE [4]). GKLEE profits from KLEE's code base and philosophy of testing a given program using *concrete plus symbolic* ("concolic") execution. GKLEE is the first concolic verifier and test generator tailored for GPU programs. Concolic verifiers allow designers to declare certain input variables as 'symbolic' (the remaining inputs are concrete).

In GKLEE, the execution of a program expression containing symbolic variables results in constraints amongst the program variables, including constraints due to conditionals, and explicit constraints (`assume` statements) on symbolic inputs. Conditionals are resolved by KLEE's decision procedures ("SMT solvers [5]") that find solutions for symbolic program inputs. This approach helps concolic verifiers do something beyond bug-hunting: they can automatically enumerate test inputs in a *demand-driven* manner. That is, if there is a control/branch decision that can be affected by some input, a concolic verifier can automatically compute and record the input value in a test which is valuable for downstream debugging. Recent experience shows that formal methods often have the biggest impact when they can compute tests automatically, exposing software defects and vulnerability [6–8].

The architecture of GKLEE is shown in Figure 1. It employs a C/C++ front-end based on LLVM-GCC (with our customized

* Guodong Li started this project while a student of University of Utah.

PPoPP'12, February 25–29, 2012, New Orleans, Louisiana, USA.

extensions for CUDA syntax) to parse CUDA programs. It supports the execution of both CPU code and GPU code. GKLEE employs a new approach to model the symbolic state (recording the execution status of a kernel) with respect to the CUDA memory model.

Contributions: Our main contribution is a symbolic virtual machine (VM) to model the execution of GPU programs on open inputs. We detail the construction and operation of this virtual machine, showing exactly how it elegantly integrates error-detection and analysis, while not generating false alarms or missing execution paths when generating concrete tests. This approach also allows one to effect scalability/coverage tradeoffs. The following features are integrated into our symbolic VM approach:

- GPU programs can suffer from several classes of insidious data races. GKLEE finds such races (sometimes even in well-tested GPU kernels).
- GKLEE detects and reports occurrences of divergent thread warps (branches inside SIMD paths), as these can degrade performance. In addition, GKLEE guarantees to find deadlocks caused by divergent warps in which two threads may encounter different sequences of barrier (`__syncthreads()`) calls.
- GKLEE's symbolic virtual machine can systematically generate concrete tests while also taking into account any input constraints the programmer may have expressed through `assume` statements.
- While tests generated by GKLEE guarantee high coverage, it may lead to test explosion. GKLEE employs powerful heuristics for reducing the number of tests. We evaluate these heuristics on a variety of examples and identify those heuristics that result in high coverage while still only generating fewer tests.
- We can automatically run GKLEE-generated tests on the actual hardware; one such experiment alerted us to the need for a new error-check type, which we have added to GKLEE: *has a volatile declaration been possibly forgotten?* This can help eliminate silent data corruption caused by reads that may pick up stale write values.
- We target two classes of memory access inefficiencies, namely non-coalesced global memory accesses and shared memory accesses that result in bank conflicts, and show how GKLEE can spot these inefficiencies, also "understanding" platform rules (*i.e.*, compute capability 1.x or 2.x). Some kernels originally thought free of these errors are actually not so.
- GKLEE's VM incorporates the CUDA memory model within its concolic execution framework, while (i) accurately modeling the SIMD concurrency of GPUs, (ii) avoiding interleaving enumeration through an approach based on race checking, and (iii) scaling to large code sizes.
- GKLEE handles many C++/CUDA features including: struct, class, template, pointer, inheritance, CUDA's variable and function derivatives, and CUDA specific functions.
- GKLEE's analysis occurs on LLVM byte-codes (also targeted by Fortran and Clang). Byte-code level analysis can help cover pertinent compiler-induced bugs in addition to supporting future work on other binary formats.

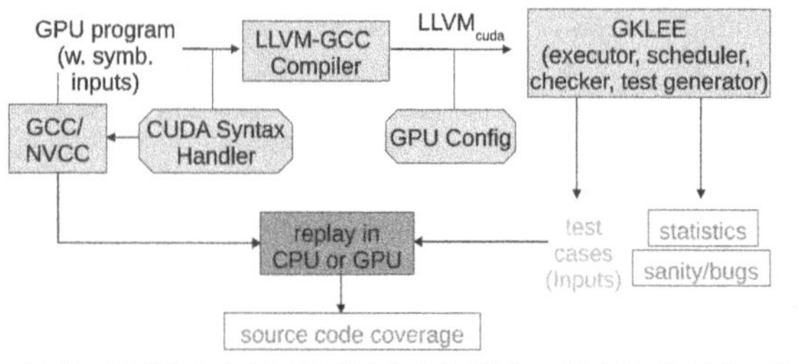

Figure 1. GKLEE's architecture.

Roadmap: § 2 explains the error-classes covered by GKLEE. § 3 presents GKLEE's concolic verification: state model, memory type inference, and concolic execution (§ 3.1) and error checking/analysis (§ 3.2). § 5 presents experimental results, covering issues pertaining to correctness checking/performance (§ 5.1) and test set generation/reduction (§ 5.2). § 6 presents related work and § 7 concludes.

2. Examples of our Analysis/Testing Goals

2.1 Basics of GPU Programs

GKLEE currently supports the CUDA [9] syntax (with OpenCL [10] to be addressed in future). A CUDA kernel is launched as an 1D or 2D *grid* of *thread blocks*. The total size of a 2D grid is `gridDim.x` × `gridDim.y`. Each block at location ⟨`blockIdx.x`, `blockIdx.y`⟩ has dimensions `blockDim.x`, `blockDim.y` and `blockDim.z`. Each block contains `blockDim.x` × `blockDim.y` × `blockDim.z` threads, with IDs ⟨`threadIdx.x`, `threadIdx.y`, `threadIdx.z`⟩. These threads can share information via *shared memory*, and synchronize via *barriers*. Threads belonging to distinct blocks must use the much slower *global memory* to communicate, and may not synchronize using barriers. The values of `gridDim` and `blockDim` determines the *configuration* of the system, *e.g.* the sizes of the grid and each block. For a thread, `blockIdx` and `threadIdx` give its block index in the grid and its thread index in the block respectively. For brevity, we use $gdim$ to denote $gridDim$, bid for $blockIdx$, $bdim$ for $blockDim$, and tid for $threadIdx$. The constraints $bid.* < gdim.*$ for $* \in \{x, y\}$ and $tid.* < bdim.*$ for $* \in \{x, y, z\}$ always hold. Groups of 32 (a "warp") consecutively numbered threads within a thread block are scheduled at a time in a Single Instruction Multiple Data (SIMD) fashion.

2.2 CUDA Error Classes and Test Generation

2.2.1 Deadlocks

Deadlocks occur when any two threads in a thread block fail to encounter the same *textually aligned* barriers [11], as in kernel `deadlock` below. Here, threads satisfying `tid.x + i > 0` invoke the barrier while the other threads do not:

```
__global__ void deadlock(int i) {
  if (tid.x + i > 0)
    { ...; __syncthreads(); }   }
```

Random test input generation does not guarantee path coverage especially when conditionals are deeply embedded, whereas GKLEE's *directed test generation* based on SMT-solving ensures coverage. While the basic techniques for such test generation have been well researched in the past, GKLEE's contributions in this area include addressing the CUDA semantics and memory model, and detecting non-textually aligned barriers, a simple example of which is below. Here, the threads encounter different barrier calls if they diverge on the condition $tid.x + i > 0$.

```
if (tid.x + i > 0) { ...; __syncthreads(); }
else { ...; __syncthreads(); }
```

2.2.2 Data Races

There are three broad classes of races: intra-warp races, inter-warp races, and device/CPU memory races. Intra-warp races can be further classified into intra-warp races without warp divergence, and intra-warp races with warp divergence.

Intra-warp Races Without Warp Divergence: Given that any two threads within a warp execute the same instruction, an intra-warp race (without involving warp divergence) has to be a write-write race. The following is an example of such a race which GKLEE can successfully report. In this example, writes to shared array `v[]` overlap; *e.g.*, thread 0 and 1 concurrently write four bytes beginning at `v[0]` (in a 32-bit system).

```
__global__ void race()
{  x = tid.x >> 2; v[x] = x + tid.x; }
```

Intra-warp Races With Warp Divergence: In a divergent warp, a conditional statement causes some of the threads to execute the *then* part while others execute the *else* part. But because of the SIMD nature, *both* parts are executed with respect to all the threads in *some unspecified order* (undefined in the standard). Thus, in example '`race`', depending on the hardware platform: (i) the even threads may read v first, and then the odd threads write v; or (ii) the odd threads may write v and then the even threads may read v:

```
__global__ void race()              {
  if (tid.x % 2) { ... = v ; }
  else { v = ... ; }                }
```

While on a given machine the results are predictable (either the `then` or the `else` happens first) an unpleasant surprise can result when this code is ported to a future machine where the `else` happens first (think of it as a "*porting race*"—race-like outcome that surfaces when the code is ported). The culprit is of course overlapped accesses across divergent-warp threads, but if v is a complicated array expression, this fact is virtually impossible to discern manually. GKLEE's novel contribution is to detect such overlaps exactly regardless of the complexity of the conditionals or the array accesses. (For simplicity, we do not illustrate a variant of this example where both accesses are updates to v.)

This example also covers another check done by GKLEE: it reports the number of occurrences of divergent warps over the whole program.

Inter-warp Races: Inter-warp races could be read-write, write-read, or write-write: we illustrate a read-write race below. Here there is the danger that thread 0 and thread $bdim.x - 1$ may access $v[0]$ simultaneously while these two threads also belong to different warps in a thread block.

```
__global__ void race() {
  v[tid.x] = v[(tid.x + 1) % bdim.x]; }
```

Testing may fail to reveal this bug because this bug is typically noticed only when the write by one thread occurs before the read by the other thread. However, the execution order of threads in a GPU is non-deterministic depending on the scheduling, and latencies of memory accesses. GKLEE guarantees to expose this type of race.

Global Memory Races: GKLEE also detects and reports races occurring on global device variables:

```
__device__ x;
__global__ void race()
{  ...conflicting accesses to x by two threads... }
```

2.2.3 Memory Access Inefficiencies

There are two kinds of memory access inefficiencies: bank conflicts and non-coalesced memory accesses. GKLEE reports their severity by reporting the absolute number and the percentage of accesses that suffer from this inefficiency, as described in § 5.1 in detail.

Shared Memory Bank Conflicts: Bank conflicts result when the threads in a half warp (for the CUDA compute capability 1.x model) or entire warp (for capability 1.2) access the same memory bank. GKLEE checks for conflicts by symbolically comparing whether two such accesses can fall into a memory bank.

Non-coalesced Device Memory Accesses: Non-coalesced memory accesses waste considerable bus bandwidth when fetching data from the device memory. Memory coalescing is achieved by following access rules specific to the GPU compute capability. GKLEE faithfully models all 1.x and 2.x compute capability coalescing rules, and can be run with the compute capability specified as a flag option (illustrates the flexibility to accommodate future such options from other manufacturers).

2.2.4 Test Generation

The ability to automatically generate high quality tests and verify kernels over all possible inputs is a unique feature of GKLEE. The `BitonicSort` (Figure 2) kernel taken from CUDA SDK 2.0 [9] sorts $values$'s elements in an ascending order. The steps taken in this kernel to improve performance (coalescing global memory accesses, minimizing bank conflicts, avoiding redundant barriers, and better address generation through bit operations) unfortunately end up obfuscating the code. Manual testing or random input-based testing does not ensure sufficient coverage. Instead, given a post-condition pertaining to the sortedness of the output array, GKLEE generates targeted tests that help exercise all conditional-guarded flows. Also, running this kernel under GKLEE by keeping all configuration parameters symbolic, we could learn (through GKLEE's error message) that this kernel works only if $bdim.x$ is a power of 2 (an undocumented fact).

Covering all control-flow branches can result in too many tests. GKLEE includes heuristics for test-case minimization, as detailed in § 4.

```
__shared__ unsigned shared[NUM];

inline void swap(unsigned& a, unsigned& b)
{  unsigned tmp = a; a = b; b = tmp; }

__global__ void BitonicKernel(unsigned* values) {
    unsigned int tid = tid.x;
    // Copy input to shared mem.
    shared[tid] = values[tid];
    __syncthreads();

    // Parallel bitonic sort.
    for (unsigned k = 2; k <= bdim.x; k *= 2)
      for (unsigned j = k / 2; j > 0; j /= 2) {
        unsigned ixj = tid ^ j;
        if (ixj > tid) {
          if ((tid & k) == 0)
            if (shared[tid] > shared[ixj])
              swap(shared[tid], shared[ixj]);
          else
            if (shared[tid] < shared[ixj])
              swap(shared[tid], shared[ixj]);
        }
        __syncthreads();
      }

    // Write result.
    values[tid] = shared[tid];
}
```

Figure 2. The Bitonic Sort Kernel

3. Algorithms for Analysis, Test Generation

Given a C++ program, the GKLEE VM (Figure 1) executes the following steps, in order, for each control-flow path pursued during execution (to a first approximation, one can think of a control-flow tree and imagine all the following steps occurring *for each tree path* and *for each barrier interval along the path*). Deadlock checking and test generation occur per path (spanning barrier intervals; the notion of barrier intervals is explained in § 3.2). GKLEE checks for barriers being textually aligned and applies a canonical schedule going from one textually aligned barrier to another one.

- Create the GPU memory objects as per state model; infer memory regions representing GPU memory dynamically (§ 3.1)
- Execute GPU kernel threads via the *canonical schedule* (§ 3.2)

- Fork new states upon non-determinism due to symbolic values, apply search heuristics and path reduction if needed (§ 2.2.4)
- In a state, at the end of the barrier interval or other synchronization points, perform checks for data races, warp divergence, bank conflicts, and non-coalesced memory accesses (§ 3.2)
- When execution path ends, report deadlocks and global memory races (if any), perform test-case selection, and write out a concrete test file (§ 4)

3.1 LLVM$_{cuda}$

The front-end compiles a C/C++ kernel program into LLVM bytecode with extensions for CUDA. Figure 3 shows an excerpt of its syntax. One main extension is that a variable is attached with its memory sort indicating which memory it refers to.

τ	$:=$	$\tau_{\_}, \tau_l, \tau_s, \tau_d, \tau_h$	memory sort
var	$:=$	$var_{cuda} \mid v : \tau$	variable
var_{cuda}	$:=$	$tid, bid, \ldots$	CUDA built-in
lab	$:=$	$l_1, l_2, \ldots$	label
e	$:=$	$var \mid n$	atomic expression
$instr$	$:=$	$br\ v\ lab1\ lab2$	conditional branch
	$\mid$	$br\ lab$	unconditional jump
	$\mid$	$\texttt{store}\ e\ v$	store
	$\mid$	$v = \texttt{load}\ v$	load
	$\mid$	$v = \texttt{binop}\ e\ e$	binary operation
	$\mid$	$v = \texttt{alloc}\ n\ \tau$	memory allocation
	$\mid$	$v = \texttt{getelptr}\ v\ e$	address calculation
	$\mid$	$\texttt{sync}$	synchronization barrier

Figure 3. Syntax of LLVM$_{cuda}$ (excerpt)

Figure 4 gives a small-step operational semantics of LLVM $_{cuda}$ using the following elements. A program is a map from labels to instructions; a value consists of one or more bytes (our model has byte-level accuracy); a memory or store maps variables to values, where each variable is assigned an integer address by the compiler. GKLEE models CUDA's memory hierarchy in a symbolic state as in Figure 5: each thread has its own local memory and stack (we combine them into a single local state in GKLEE); the threads in a block shares the shared memory; and all blocks share the device memory and the CPU memory. Each thread has a program counter (pc) recording the label of the current instruction.

Program	$:=$	$\mathbb{L} \subset lab \mapsto instr$
Value	$:=$	$\mathbb{V} \subset \texttt{byte}^+$
Memory, Store	$:=$	$M \subset var \mapsto \mathbb{V}$
Shared state	$:=$	$\mathbb{M} \subset (bid \mapsto M) \times M \times M$
Local state	$:=$	$\sigma \subset var \mapsto \mathbb{V}$
Data State	$:=$	$\Sigma \subset (tid \mapsto \sigma) \times \mathbb{M}$
Program counter	$:=$	$\mathbb{P} \subset tid \mapsto lab$
State	$:=$	$\Phi \subset \Sigma \times \mathbb{P}$

A state Φ consists of a data state Σ and a PC $\mathbb{P}$. Thread t's pc is given by $\mathbb{P}[t]$. Notations $\Sigma[v]$ and $\Sigma[v \mapsto k]$ indicate reading v's value from Σ and updating v's value in Σ to k respectively. Notation $\Sigma \vdash e$ evaluates e's value over Σ, *e.g.* $\Sigma \vdash e_1 = e_2$ is true if $\Sigma[e_1] = \Sigma[e_2]$. The semantics of an instruction is modeled by a state transition, *e.g.* the execution of an instruction br l' at thread t updates the t's pc to l' and keeps the data state unchanged. Rule 9 specifies the barrier's semantics: a thread can proceed to the next instruction only after all the threads in the same block have reached the barrier. As indicated by other rules, non-barrier instructions are executed without synchronizing with other threads (except for lock-step requirement for intra-warp threads).

Memory Typing. After a source program is compiled into LLVM bytecode, it is difficult to determine which memory is used when an

1. $$\frac{\mathbb{L}[l]{=}\texttt{br l}'}{(\Sigma,\mathbb{P}){\rightarrow}_t(\Sigma,\mathbb{P}[t{\mapsto}l'])}$$

2. $$\frac{\mathbb{L}[l]{=}\texttt{br v l}_1\ \texttt{l}_2 \quad \Sigma \vdash v}{(\Sigma,\mathbb{P}){\rightarrow}_t(\Sigma,\mathbb{P}[t{\mapsto}l_1])} \qquad \frac{\mathbb{L}[l]{=}\texttt{br v l}_1\ \texttt{l}_2 \quad \Sigma \vdash \neg v}{(\Sigma,\mathbb{P}){\rightarrow}_t(\Sigma,\mathbb{P}[t{\mapsto}l_2])}$$

3. $$\frac{\mathbb{L}[l]{=}(v{=}\texttt{alloc n}\ \tau)}{(\Sigma,\mathbb{P}){\rightarrow}_t(\Sigma[(v{:}\tau){\mapsto}0^n],\mathbb{P}[t{\mapsto}l{+}1])}$$

4. $$\frac{\mathbb{L}[l]{=}(v_2{=}\texttt{getelptr}\ v_1{:}\tau\ e)}{(\Sigma,\mathbb{P}){\rightarrow}_t(\Sigma[v_2{:}\tau{\mapsto}\Sigma[v_1]{+}\Sigma[e]],\mathbb{P}[t{\mapsto}l{+}1])}$$

5. $$\frac{\mathbb{L}[l]{=}(v{=}\texttt{binop}\ e_1{:}\tau\ e_2{:}\tau_{\_})}{(\Sigma,\mathbb{P}){\rightarrow}_t(\Sigma[v{:}\tau{\mapsto}\texttt{binop}(\Sigma[e_1],\Sigma[e_2])],\mathbb{P}[t{\mapsto}l{+}1])}$$

6. $$\frac{\mathbb{L}[l]{=}(v_2{=}\texttt{load}\ v_1{:}\tau) \quad \tau{\neq}\tau_{\_}}{(\Sigma,\mathbb{P}){\rightarrow}_t(\Sigma[v_2{:}\tau_{\_}{\mapsto}\Sigma[v_1]],\mathbb{P}[t{\mapsto}l{+}1])}$$

7. $$\frac{\mathbb{L}[l]{=}(\texttt{store}\ e\ v{:}\tau) \quad \tau{\neq}\tau_{\_}}{(\Sigma,\mathbb{P}){\rightarrow}_t(\Sigma[v{:}\tau{\mapsto}\Sigma[e]],\mathbb{P}[t{\mapsto}l{+}1])}$$

8. $$\frac{v{:}\tau_{\_} \quad ((v'{:}\tau'){\mapsto}k) \in \Sigma \quad \Sigma \vdash v' \underline{\leq} v \underline{\leq} v'{+}\texttt{sizeof}(k)}{v{:}\tau'}$$

9. $$\frac{\mathbb{L}[l]{=}\texttt{sync} \quad \forall t'{\in}\texttt{blk\_of}(t) : \mathbb{P}[t']{\in}\{l,l{+}1\}}{(\Sigma,\mathbb{P}){\rightarrow}_t(\Sigma,\mathbb{P}[t{\mapsto}l{+}1])}$$

Figure 4. Operational semantics of LLVM$_{cuda}$ (excerpt)

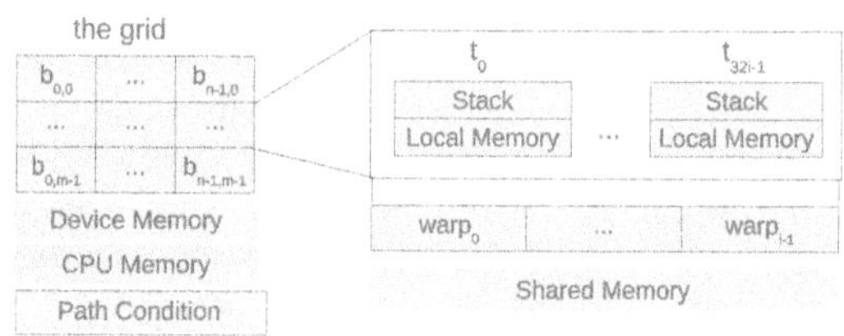

Figure 5. Components in a Symbolic State.

access is made because the address of this access may be calculated by multiple bytecode instructions. We employ a novel and simple GPU-specific memory sort inference method by computing for each (possibly symbolic) expression a sort τ which is either $\tau_{\_}$ (unknown), τ_l (local), τ_s (shared), τ_d (device), or τ_h (host), as per the rules (here we present the simplified version) in Figure 4. In our experience, these rules have been found to be sufficiently precise on all the kernels we have applied GKLEE to.

For example, Rule 4 models *getelptr* which refers to pointer dereferencing where v_2's type is obtained from v_1's type. Rule 6 indicates that a load instruction can be executed only if the address type is known; and the value loaded from memory has unknown type. Rule 8 says that a valid type is found for v if there exists a memory object associated with v' such that v's value falls within this object. Basically it searches the memory hierarchy to locate the target memory when the previous analysis fails to find v's type. If v represents a pointer which can refer to multiple objects (determined by SMT solving), then multiple states are generated, each of which needs to apply this rule. This often reveals memory type related bugs in the source kernel, *e.g.* mixing up the CPU and GPU memory. We plan to use Clang's ongoing support for LLVM+CUDA [12] to simplify such inference. More semantics rules (with sort inference) are available in [13].

State Model. In a symbolic state in GKLEE, each thread (in a block) has its own stack and local memory; each block has a shared memory; all blocks can access the device memory in the GPU and the main memory in the CPU. Figure 5 gives an example state for a GPU with grid size $n \times m$ and block size $32 \times i$. Each block consists of i of warps; each warp contains 32 threads. To support test generation, a state also contains a path condition recording the branching decisions made so far.

CUDA Built-in Variables. CUDA built-in variables include the block size, block id, thread id, and so on, The executor accesses these variables during the execution. GKLEE sets their values in respective memories before the execution. For example, the variable for the thread id, *tid*, is assigned *three* 32 bit words in the local memory of each thread. These words record the *tid*'s values in dimension x, y and z respectively.

tid : τ_l (96b)	...
{x : 32b, y : 32b, z : 32b}	...

3.2 Canonical Scheduling and Race Checking

We now focus on the interleavings of all the threads within a thread block *from one barrier call to another* (global memory accesses across thread blocks are discussed later). Naively interleaving these threads will result in an astronomical number of interleavings. GKLEE employs the following schedule generation approach:

- Pursue just one schedule, namely the canonical schedule shown in Figure 6 where each thread is fully executed within a barrier interval before moving on to another thread.
- During the execution of all the threads in the current barrier interval, build a read-set $\mathcal{R}$ and a write set $\mathcal{W}$, recording in them (respectively) all loads and stores (these will be in mixed symbolic/concrete form) encountered in the execution.
- After the check points (as shown in Figure 6), build all possible conflict pairs, where a pair $\langle r_1, w_1 \rangle$ or $\langle w_2, w_1 \rangle$ is any pair that could potentially race or other conflicts.
- Through SMT-solving, decide whether any of these conflicts are races. If none are races (do not overlap in terms of a memory address), then the canonical schedule is equivalent to any other schedule. Thus, we can carry on to the next barrier interval with the next-state calculated as per the canonical schedule.

Canonical scheduling is sound for safety properties (will neither result in omissions or false alarms). The caveats that go with this argument are that C/C++ has no standard shared memory consistency semantics to define safe compiler optimizations, and the CUDA programming guide [14] provides only an informal characterization of CUDA's weak execution semantics. Assume that the instructions within CUDA threads in a barrier interval can be reordered; then under no conflicts (DRF), reordering transformations are sound [15]. This result also stems from [16] where it is shown that race detectors for sequential consistency can detect the *earliest race* even under weak orderings. One can also infer this result directly from [17] where it is shown that under the absence of conflict edges, the *delay set* (set of required program orderings) can be empty. We further elaborate on the soundness of the canonical scheduling method (also considering SIMD execution) in [13].

Consider the following two schedules, we record the writes and reads on v_1 and v_2, and see whether these accesses overlap at the end point (the check is denoted by a "!"). A race occurs in schedule 2 if and only if it also occurs in schedule 1.

$$\text{Schedule 1}: \cdot \xrightarrow{\text{W } v_1}_{t_1} \cdot \xrightarrow{\text{W } v_2}_{t_1} \cdot \xrightarrow{\text{R } v_1}_{t_2} \cdot \rightarrow \cdots \rightarrow \cdot (!)$$
$$\text{Schedule 2}: \cdot \xrightarrow{\text{R } v_1}_{t_2} \cdot \xrightarrow{\text{W } v_2}_{t_1} \cdot \xrightarrow{\text{W } v_1}_{t_1} \cdot \rightarrow \cdots \rightarrow \cdot (!)$$

Intra-warp scheduling. A schedule is a sequence of state transitions made by the threads. The threads within a warp are executed in lock-step manner, and if they diverge on a condition, then one side (*e.g.* the "then" side) is executed first, with the threads in the other side blocked; and then the other side is executed (this is sound after checking for the absence of intra-warp races). (Note that GKLEE executes LLVM byte-codes, and is therefore able to capture the effect of compiler optimizations.)

In GKLEE, we schedule these threads in a lock-step manner, and provide an option to not execute the two sides sequentially. Now we show that these two scheduling methods are equivalent if no data race occurs. Specifically, the sequence (up to the next joint point)

$$\Phi_0 \xrightarrow{c}_{t_1} \Phi_1 \xrightarrow{c}_{t_2} \cdots \xrightarrow{c}_{t_n} \Phi_n \xrightarrow{\neg c}_{t_1} \cdots \xrightarrow{\neg c}_{t_n} \Phi_{2n}$$

can be shuffled into the following one provided that it is race-free. We use $\xrightarrow{c}_{t_i}$ to indicate that thread t_i makes the transition with condition c.

$$\Phi_0 \xrightarrow{c}_{t_1} \Phi_1 \xrightarrow{\neg c}_{t_1} \Phi'_2 \xrightarrow{c}_{t_2} \cdots \xrightarrow{c}_{t_n} \Phi'_{2n-1} \xrightarrow{\neg c}_{t_n} \Phi_{2n}$$

Since c exclusive-or ($\oplus$) $\neg c$ holds for a thread, the sequence is equivalent to the following one (where $\Phi''_n = \Phi_{2n}$) which GKLEE produces. This is the *canonical schedule for intra-warp* steps.

$$\Phi_0 \xrightarrow{c \oplus \neg c}_{t_1} \Phi''_1 \xrightarrow{c \oplus \neg c}_{t_2} \cdots \xrightarrow{c \oplus \neg c}_{t_n} \Phi''_n$$

Hence GKLEE's intra-warp scheduling is an equivalent model of the CUDA hardware's. It eases formal analysis and boosts the performance of GKLEE. Similarly, as in Figure 6 we can reduce a race-free schedule to a canonical one for inter-warps, multi-blocks, and barrier intervals (BIs). These transition relations are represented by $\rightarrow_w$, $\rightarrow_b$, and $\rightarrow_{bi}$ respectively.

$$\underbrace{\underbrace{\rightarrow_{t_0} \cdot \rightarrow_{t_1} \cdots \rightarrow_{t_{31}} \cdot}_{\rightarrow_{w_0} \cdot (!_1 : \text{intra\_warp})} \quad \underbrace{\rightarrow_{t_{32}} \cdot \rightarrow_{t_{33}} \cdots \rightarrow_{t_{63}} \cdot}_{\rightarrow_{w_1} \cdot (!_1 : \text{intra\_warp})} \quad \cdots}_{\rightarrow_{b_0} \cdot (!_2 : \text{inter\_warp})}$$

$$\underbrace{\rightarrow_{b_0} \cdot \rightarrow_{b_1} \cdots}_{\rightarrow_{bi_0} \cdot} \quad \cdots \quad \underbrace{\rightarrow_{b_0} \cdot \rightarrow_{b_1} \cdots}_{\rightarrow_{bi_m} \cdot (!_3 : \text{global\_mem})}$$

Figure 6. Canonical scheduling and conflict checking in GKLEE.

Conflict checking: Figure 6 indicates that GKLEE supports various conflict checking:

- Intra-warp race (denoted as $!_1$), checked at the end of a warp. Threads t_1 and t_2 incur such a WW race if they write different values to the same memory location in the same store instruction: $\exists l : \mathbb{L}[l] = \texttt{store}\ e\ v \ \wedge\ \mathbb{P}[t_1] = \mathbb{P}[t_2] = l$ and $\Sigma \vdash v_{t_1} = v_{t_2} \ \wedge\ e_{t_1} \neq e_{t_2}$ (GKLEE issues a warning if $e_{t_1} = e_{t_2}$). For a diverged warp, RW and WW races are also checked by considering whether the accesses in both sides can conflict (discussed in Section 2.2).
- Inter-warp race (denoted as $!_2$), checked at the end of a block for each BI. Thread t_1 and t_2 (in different warps) incur such a race if they access the same memory location, and one of them is a write, and different values are written if both accesses are writes. Formally, let $R\langle t, v, e \rangle$ and $W\langle t, v, e \rangle$ denote that thread t reads e from location v and writes e to v respectively. Then a RW race occurs if $\exists R\langle t_1, v_1, e_1 \rangle, W\langle t_2, v_2, e_2 \rangle : \Sigma \vdash v_1 = v_2$ (or the case of exchanging t_1 and t_2); a WW race occurs if $\exists W\langle t_1, v_1, e_1 \rangle, W\langle t_2, v, e_2 \rangle : \Sigma \vdash v_1 = v_2 \wedge e_1 \neq e_2$ (again GKLEE will prompt for investigation if $e_{t_1} = e_{t_2}$).
- Global race (denoted as $!_3$), checked at the end of the kernel execution. Similar to inter-warp race but on the device or CPU memory. Deadlocks are also checked at $!_3$.

Conflict checking is performed at the byte level to faithfully model the hardware. Suppose a thread reads n_1 bytes starting from address a_1, and another thread writes n_2 bytes starting from address a_2, then a overlap exists iff the following constraint holds.

```
__global__ void histogram64Kernel(unsigned *d_Result,
                                  unsigned *d_Data, int dataN){
  const int threadPos =
       ((threadIdx.x & (~63)) >> 0) |
       ((threadIdx.x &    15) << 2) |
       ((threadIdx.x &    48) >> 4);      ...
   __syncthreads();
   for(int pos = IMUL(blockIdx.x, blockDim.x) + threadIdx.x;
       pos < dataN; pos += IMUL(blockDim.x, gridDim.x))    {
     unsigned data4 = d_Data[pos]; // top 10 is symb. for t5,
     ...
     addData64(s_Hist, threadPos, (data4 >> 26) & 0x3FU);  }
  __syncthreads(); ...
}
inline void addData64(unsigned char *s_Hist, int threadPos,
                      unsigned int data)                   {
   // Race of T5 and T13 with threadPos of 20,52 resp.
   s_Hist[threadPos + IMUL(data, THREAD_N)]++; //<- Race!  }
```

Figure 7. Write-write race in Histogram64 (SDK 2.0)

$$(a_1 \leq a_2 \ \wedge \ a_2 < a_1 + n_1) \ \vee \ (a_2 \leq a_1 \ \wedge \ a_1 < a_2 + n_2)$$

Without abstracting pointers and arrays, GKLEE inherits KLEE's methods for handling them: suppose there are n arrays declared in a program. Then, when $*p$ is evaluated, for every array the concolic executor will check whether p can fall within the array, spawning a new state if so (works particularly well for CUDA, where pointers are usually used for indexing array elements).

Note that our method reports accurate results in contrast to static analysis methods such as [18] (where no decision procedures are applied) and [1] (which uses SMT solving but relies heavily on abstractions). The method in [2] uses run-time checking to rule out false alarms produced by its static analyzer; while GKLEE builds all the checks into its VM and produces no false alarms.

3.3 Power of Symbolic Analysis

We now present how GKLEE detected a WW race condition in `histogram64Kernel` (Figure 7), a CUDA SDK 2.0 kernel. Since the invocation of this kernel in `main` passes `d_Data` that can be quite large, a user of GKLEE (in this case, us) chose to keep only the first ten locations of this array symbolic, and the rest concrete at value 0. (This is the only manual step needed; without this, GKLEE's solver will be inundated, trying to enumerate every array location). GKLEE now determines that `addData64` can be called concurrently by two distinct threads. Drilling into this function, GKLEE generates constraints for `s_Hist[threadPos + IMUL(data, THREAD_N)]++` (not marked `atomic`) to race. The SMT solver picks two thread IDs 5 and 13; for this, `threadPos` assumes values 20 and 52, respectively. What flows into `data` is `data4 >> 26 & 0x3FU`, where `data4` obtains the value of `d_Data[pos]`. Since the top 10 elements of `d_Data[DATA_N]` are symbolic, thread 5 assigns a symbolic value denoted by `d_Data[5]` to `data4`, while thread 13 assigns the concrete value of 0 to `d_Data[13]`. The SMT solver now solves $20 + ((d\_Data[5] \gg 21)\&2016) = 52 + 0$ ($\gg 26$ changed to $\gg 21$ because `THREAD_N` is 32), resulting in `d_Data[5]` obtaining value `0x04040404` which causes a race! The user not only obtains an automatic race alert, but also the concrete input of `0x04040404` to set `d_Data[5]` to, in case they want to study this race through any other means.

4. Test Generation

During its symbolic execution, GKLEE's VM has the ability to *fork* two execution paths whenever it "encounters a non-deterministic situation;" *e.g.* when a conditional is evaluated and both choices are true, or when a symbolic pointer is accessed, and it may point to multiple memory objects. GKLEE organizes the resulting execution states as a tree. The initial state of the GPU kernel forms the root of this tree. It then searches the state space guided by various search reduction heuristics.

The essence of the VM executor: GKLEE can be regarded as a symbolic model checker (for GPU kernels) with the symbolic state modeling the hardware state and the transitions modeling non-determinism due to symbolic inputs.

With this view, it is natural that GKLEE supports facilities such as state caching and search heuristics (*e.g.* depth-first, weighted-random, bump-merging, *etc.*), all of which are inherited from KLEE. The checks discussed in Section 3 are essentially built-in global safety properties examined at each state. In the state space tree, a path from the root to a leaf represents a valid computation with a path condition recording all the branching decisions made by all the threads. At a leaf state, we can generate a test case by solving the satisfiability of this path condition. This ability makes GKLEE a powerful test generator.

Soundness and completeness of the test generator: Given a race free kernel with a set of symbolic inputs, GKLEE visits a path if and only if there exists a schedule where the decisions made by threads (recorded in the path condition) are feasible.

Note that the feasibility of a path condition is calculated by SMT solving, which is precise without any approximation. At the first glance, the completeness of test generation may be not be obvious since we consider only one (canonical) schedule, while another schedule may apply the branchings in a different order.

To clarify this, consider the following situation where thread t_0 (t_1) branches on conditions $c_{0,0}$ ($c_{1,0}$):

$$\begin{array}{cc} t_0 & t_1 \\ \text{if}\,(c_{0,0})\ldots; & \text{if}\,(c_{1,0})\ldots; \end{array}$$

If t_0 executes before t_1, then a depth-first search visits 4 paths with path conditions $c_{0,0} \wedge c_{1,0}$, $c_{0,0} \wedge \neg c_{1,0}$, ... If t_1 executes before t_0, then the 4 path conditions become $c_{1,0} \wedge c_{0,0}$, $c_{1,0} \wedge \neg c_{0,0}$ .... The commutativity of the $\wedge$ operator ensures, under the race-free constraint, the equivalence of these two path sets. Hence, it suffices to consider only one canonical schedule in test generation as in conflict checking (Section 3).

Example. Consider the Bitonic kernel running on one block with 4 threads. Suppose the input $values$ is of size 4 and has symbolic value v. Lines 1-4 copy the input to $shared$: $\forall i \in [0, 3]$: $shared[i] = v[i]$. For thread 0, since lines 7-8 involve no symbolic values, they are executed concretely. In the first iteration of the inner loop, we have $k = 2$, $j = 1$, and $ixj = 1$. The conditional branch at line 10 is evaluated to be true; so does that at line 11. Then the execution reaches the branch at line 12. GKLEE queries the constraint solver to determine that both branches are possible; it explores both paths and proceeds to the loop's next iteration. Finally the execution terminates with 28 paths (and test cases).

Coverage Directed State/Path Reduction. Given that a kernel is usually executed by a large number of threads, there is a real danger, especially with complex/large kernels, that multiple threads may end up covering some line/branch while no threads visit other lines/branches.[1] We have experimented with several heuristics that help GKLEE achieve *coverage directed* search reduction. Basically, we keep track of whether some feature (line or branch) is covered by all the threads at least once, or some thread at least once. These measurements help GKLEE avoid exploring states/paths that do not result in added coverage.

Another usage of these metrics is to perform *test case selection* which still explores the entire state space, but outputs only a subset of test cases (for downstream debugging use) after the entire execution is over, with no net loss of coverage. Details of these heuristics are discussed in § 5.2. To the best of our knowledge, coverage measures for SIMD programs have not been previously studied.

5. Experimental Results

As described in Section 1, a GPU kernel along with a CPU driver is compiled into LLVM bytecode, which is symbolically executed by GKLEE. Since GKLEE can handle GPU and CPU style code, we can mix the computation of CPU and GPU, *e.g.* execute multiple kernels in a sequence.

```
CPU code; GPU code; CPU code; GPU code; ...
```

Driver. The user may give as input a kernel file to test together with a driver representing the main (CPU side) program. To cater for the need of LLVM-GCC, we redefine some CUDA specific directives and functions, *e.g.* we use C attributes to interpret them, as illustrated by the following definition of __shared__.

```
#define __shared__
        __attribute((section ("__shared__")))

#define cutilSafeCall(f) f
void cudaMalloc(void** devPtr, size_t size) {
  *devPtr = malloc(size);
}
void cudaMemcpy(void* a, void* b, size_t size, ...)
{ memcpy(a,b,size); };
```

We show below an example driver for the Bitonic Sort kernel. The user specifies what input values should have symbolic values; and may place **assert** assertions anywhere in the code, which will be checked during execution. Particularly, the pre- and post- conditions are specified before and after the GPU code respectively. Function **__begin_GPU(NUM)** (a more general format is __begin_GPU(bdim.x,bdim.y,bdim.z,gdim.x,gdim.y,gdim.z)) specifies that the x dimension of the block size is NUM.

```
int main() {
  int values[NUM];
  gklee_make_symbolic(values, NUM, "input");

  int* dvalues;
  cutilSafeCall(cudaMalloc((void**)&dvalues,
                sizeof(int)*NUM));
  cutilSafeCall(cudaMemcpy(dvalues, values,
     sizeof(int)*NUM, cudaMemcpyHostToDevice));

  // <<<...>>>(BitonicKernel(dvalues))
  __begin_GPU(NUM);          // block size = <NUM>
  BitonicKernel(dvalues);
  __end_GPU();

  // the post-condition
  for (int i = 1; i < NUM; i++)
    assert(dvalues[i-1] <= dvalues[i]);

  cutilSafeCall(cudaFree(dvalues));
}
```

A concrete GPU configuration can be specified at the command line. For instance, option –blocksize=[4,2] indicates that each block is of size 4×2. These values can also be made symbolic so as to reveal configuration limitations.

5.1 Results I: Symbolic Identification of Issues

GKLEE supports (through command-line arguments) bank conflict detection for 1.x (memory coalescing checks cover 1.0 & 1.1, and 1.2 & 1.3), as well as 2.x device capabilities. Table 1 presents results from SDK 2.0 kernels while Table 2 presents those from SDK 4.0 (many of these are written for 2.x). These are widely publicized kernels. Our results are with respect to symbolic inputs. **Tables (1 and 2)**: (#T denoting the number of threads analyzed) asserts that, under valid configurations, (i) all barriers were found to be well synchronized; (ii) the functional correctness is verified (w.r.t the configurations); *but only the canonical schedule is considered for cases with races (marked with *)* (thus for cases with fatal races, we are unsure of the overall functional correctness); (iii) performance defects (to specific degrees) were found in many kernels; (iv) two races were observed (Histogram64 and RadixSort kernels); and (v) several alerts pertaining to the use of **volatile** declarations were reported. 'WW' denotes write-write races; they are marked *benign* (ben.) if the same value is written in our concrete execution trace. The computation is expected to be deterministic.

The race in Radix Sort was within function radixSortBlockKeysOnly() involving sMem1[0] = key.x for distinct key.x written by two threads. In **Histogram64**, we mark the race WW$^?$ as we are unsure whether **s_Hist[..]++** of Figure 7 executed by two threads *within one warp* is fatal (apparently, CUDA guarantees[2] a net increment by 1). It is poor coding practice anyhow (we notate correctness as 'Unknown').

One row result is presented for Bank Conflicts, Memory Coalescing, and Warp Divergence, this row averaging over barrier intervals. The 71% for Scan Best under Bank Conflict (compute capability 2.x) is obtained by: 14 BIs were analyzed, and out of it, 10 had bank conflicts, which is 71%. All other "z%" entries may be read similarly. This sort of a feedback enables a programmer to attempt various optimizations to improve performance. When a kernel's execution contains multiple paths (states), the average numbers for these paths are reported. Also, with GKLEE's help, we tried a variety of configurations (*e.g.* symbolic configurations) and discovered undocumented constraints on kernel configurations and inputs.

To show that the numbers reported by GKLEE track CUDA profiler reports, we employed GKLEE-generated concrete test cases and ran selected kernels on the Nvidia GTX 480 hardware. GKLEE includes a utility script, gklee-replay, that compiles the kernels using nvcc, executes them on the hardware and optionally invokes the NVIDIA command line profiler (which is the back end to their Compute Visual Profiler). We found GKLEE's findings to be in agreement with that discovered by the profiler. GKLEE's statistics can be used for early detection of these performance issues on symbolic inputs.

Volatile Checking Heuristic GKLEE employs a heuristic to help users check for potentially missed volatile qualifiers. Basically, GKLEE analyzes for data sharings between threads within one warp involving two *distinct* SIMD instructions. The gist of an example (taken from the CUDA SDK 2.0) when it was compiled for device capability of 2.x, was as follows: a sequence '**a;b**' occurred inside a warp where SIMD instruction '**a**' writes a value into addresses a_1 and a_2 on behalf of t_0 and t_1, respectively; and SIMD instruction '**b**' reads a_0 and a_1 in t_0 and t_1, respectively. Now t_1 was meant to see the value written into a_1, but it did not, as the value was held in a register and not written back (a volatile declaration was missing in the SDK 2.0 version of the example). An Nvidia expert confirmed our observation and has updated the example to now have the volatile declaration.

We now provide a few more details on this issue. The SDK 4.0 version of this example *has* the volatile declaration in place. We exposed this bug when we took a newer release of the **nvcc** compiler (released around SDK 4.0 and does volatile optimizations), compiled the SDK 2.0 version of this example (which omits the volatile), ran the program on our GTX 480 hardware, finding incor-

[1] We have extended GKLEE's symbolic VM to measure statement and branch coverage in terms of LLVM byte-code instructions.

[2] As confirmed through discussions with engineers at Nvidia.

rect results emerging. The solution in GKLEE is to flag for potentially missed volatiles in the aforesaid manner; in future, we hope to extend GKLEE to "understand" compiler optimizations and deal with this issue more thoroughly.

Table 3 compares the execution times of GKLEE and our functional correctness checking tool PUG [1]. This result shows the pros and cons of a full SMT based static analyzer (like PUG) or a testing based approach (like GKLEE) which is far more scalable. We performed experiments on a laptop with an Intel Core(TM)2 Duo 1.60GHz processor and 2GB memory. Here the GPU times in GKLEE count in sanity checking and test generation. Similar to GKLEE, PUG also sequentializes the threads and unrolls the loops when checking functional correctness. GKLEE outperforms PUG due partially to its various optimizations such as expression rewriting, value concretization, constraint independence, and so on. A more important factor is that GKLEE is a *concolic* tool which simplifies the expressions on-the-fly and puts much less burden to the SMT solver, in addition to generating concrete tests, which PUG does not. Both tools perform poorly on the "Bitonic Sort" kernel since the relation between this kernel's input elements are complicated, *e.g.* thus GKLEE needs to explore many paths. Section 2.2.4 presents GKLEE's reduction heuristics to ameliorate this.

As an added check, we tested GKLEE on the same 57 kernels used in [1]. GKLEE found the same 2 real bugs (one deadlock and one WR race). It also revealed that 4 of other kernels contain functional correctness bugs.

5.2 Results II: Testing and Coverage

We assess GKLEE with respect to newly proposed coverage measures and coverage directed execution pruning. In Table 4, we attempt to measure the source-code coverage by converting the given kernel into a sequential version (through Perl scripts) and applying the `gcov` tool (better means are part of future work). The point is that source-code coverage may be deceptively high, as shown ("`a/b`" means "statements/branches" covered; collectively, we call this a *target*). This is the reason we rely upon only byte-code measures, described in the sequel.

GKLEE first generated tests for the shown kernels covering all feasible paths, and subsequently performed *test case selection*. For example, it first generated the 28 execution paths of Bitonic Sort; then it trimmed back the paths to just 5 because these five tests covered all the statements and branches at the byte-code level.

Four byte-code based target coverage measures were assessed first: (i) avg. Cov^t measures the number of targets covered by threads across the whole program, averaged over the threads, (ii) max. Cov^t that measures the maximum by any thread, (iii) avg. CovBI^t computes Cov^t separately for each barrier interval and reports the overall average, and (iv) max. CovBI^t is similar to avg. CovBI^t except for taking a maximum value. From Table 4, we conclude that the maximum measures give an overly optimistic impression, so we set them aside. We choose avg. CovBI^t for our baseline because activities occurring within barrier intervals are closely related, and hence separately measuring target coverage within BIs tracks programmer intent better.

Armed with avg. CovBI^t and min #tests, we assess several benchmarks (Table 5) with 'No Reductions', and two test reduction schemes. Runs with 'No Reductions' and no *test case selection* applied show the total number of paths in the kernels, and the upper limits of target coverage (albeit at the expense of considerable testing time). Red_{TB} is a reduction heuristic where we separately keep track of the coverage contributions by different threads. We continue searching till each thread is given a chance to hit a test target. For instance, in one barrier interval, if one target is reachable by all the threads, we continue exploring all these threads; but if the same target is reachable again (say in a loop), we cut off the search through the loop. In contrast, Red_{BI} only looks for some thread reaching each target; once that thread has, subsequent thread explorations to that target are truncated (more aggressive reductions). While the coverage achieved is nearly the same (due to the largely SIMD nature of the computations), it is clear that Red_{TB} is a bit more thorough.

The overall conclusion is that to achieve high target coverage (virtually the same coverage as with 'No Reductions'), reduction heuristics are of paramount importance, as they help contain test explosion. Specifically, the number of paths explored with reductions is much lower than that done with 'No Reductions.' A powerful feature of GKLEE is therefore its ability to output these minimized high-quality tests for downstream debugging.
Additional sanity-checking: we generated purely random inputs (as a designer might do); in all cases, GKLEE's test generation and test reduction heuristics provided far superior coverage with far fewer tests.

6. Related Work

Traditional CUDA program debuggers [19–21] do not solve path constraints to home into relevant inputs that can trigger bugs. They examine bugs that occur only within platform executions.

Symbolic techniques for program analysis go back to works such as [22] with concolic versions proposed in [6, 8] and more recently in KLEE [4]. GKLEE's approach is based on [4] which has inspired many projects [7] similar to ours. Concolic-execution based solvers for special domains also exist. None of these methods incorporate ways to deal with SIMD concurrency in GPUs and look for GPU-specific correctness or performance issues.

Except for GKLEE, there are only few GPU-specific checkers reported in the past. Table 6 gives a comparison of these tools. An instrumentation based technique is reported [3] to find races and shared memory bank conflicts. This is an ad-hoc testing approach, where the program is instrumented with checking code, and only those executions occurring in a platform-specific manner are considered. A similar method [2] is used to find races with the help of a static analysis phase. Static analysis is performed first to locate possible candidates so as to reduce the runtime overheads caused by instrumented code. These runtime methods cannot accept symbolic inputs and verify function correctness on open inputs, not to mention test generation. Moreover GKLEE supports a rich set of C++ language features (including those considered specifically in tools such as [23]) which other tools do not handle. In [24], a static analysis based method for divergence analysis and code optimization is presented.

Aiken and Gay [18] proposed a type system to check global synchronization errors by applying a simple single-value analysis, which may produce false alarms by rejecting correct programs. GKLEE uses SMT solving to compare expressions and is more precise.

While the approach of PUG [1] is SMT-based, it is not very scalable as shown in Table 3. Recently, simple analysis for memory coalescing was added to it [25]. PUG is also a kernel-at-a-time analyzer while GKLEE can analyze whole GPU programs.

Even if we narrow down to race detection on concrete inputs, instrumentation based tools may suffer from performance or extensibility problems because it is hard to implement sophisticated execution controls and decision procedures on the source level, while GKLEE does everything over an optimized symbolic virtual machine. As pointed out by Boyer [3], although it is possible to run an instrumentation based tool on the GPU (thus parallelizing its execution), CUDA only supports useful features (*e.g.* display debugging information, or recording traces in a file) in emulation mode which disables parallelism in GPU. Note that GKLEE supports test case replaying on the GPU. It also supports kernel simulation on

Kernels	Loc	Race	Func. Corr.	#T	Bank Conflict (↓ perf.)		Coalesced Accesses (↑ perf.)			Warp Diverg. (↓ perf.)	Volatile Needed
					1.x	2.x	1.0 & 1.1	1.2 & 1.3	2.x		
Bitonic Sort	30		yes	4	0%	0%	100%	100%	100%	60%	no
Scalar Product	30		yes	64	0%	0%	11%	100%	100%	100%	yes
Matrix Mult	61		yes	64	0%	0%	100%	100%	100%	0%	no
Histogram64$^{tb.}$	69	WW$^?$	Unknown	32	66%	66%	100%	100%	100%	0%	yes
Reduction (7)	231		yes	16	0%	0%	100%	100%	100%	16∼83%	yes
Scan Best	78		yes	32	71%	71%	100%	100%	100%	71%	no
Scan Naive	28		yes	32	0%	0%	50%	100%	100%	85%	yes
Scan Workefficient	60		yes	32	83%	16%	0%	100%	0%	83%	no
Scan Large	196		yes	32	71%	71%	100%	100%	100%	71%	no
Radix Sort	750	WW	yes*	16	3%	0%	0%	100%	100%	5%	yes
Bisect Small	1,000	WW	–	16	38%	0%	97%	100%	100%	43%	yes
Bisect Large$^{tb.}$	1,400	ben.	–	16	15%	0%	99%	100%	100%	53%	yes

Table 1. SDK 2.0 Kernel results. "Reduction" contains 7 kernels with different implementations; we average the results. Results for "Histogram64," and "Bisect Large" are time-bounded (tb.) to 20 mins. Func. Corr. results about float values are skipped at –. We checked the integer version of "Radix Sort"; and CUDPP library calls involved in "Radix Sort" were not analyzed.

Kernels	Loc	Race	#T	Bank Conflict(↓ perf.)		Coalesced Accesses (↑ perf.)			Warp Diverg.	Volatile(N/M)
				1.x	2.x	1.0 & 1.1	1.2 & 1.3	2.x	(↓ perf.)	
Clock	38		64	0%	0%	0%	100%	100%	85%	no/no
Scalar Product	47		128	0%	0%	50%	100%	100%	36%	no/no
Histogram64$^{tb.}$	70		64	0%	33%	0%	0%	0%	0%	no/no
Scan Short	103		64	0%	0%	0%	100%	100%	0%	yes/no
Scan Large	226		64	0%	0%	0%	67%	67%	25%	yes/no
Transpose (8)	172		256	0∼50%	0∼100%	0∼100%	0∼100%	0∼100%	0%	no/no
Bisect Small	1,000	WW	16	38%	0%	97%	100%	100%	43%	yes/yes

Table 2. SDK 4.0 Kernel results. If volatiles needed (N) is 'yes' and missed (M) is 'no', the code annotation is correct. Examples with both 'yes' (missed volatiles) were found. Transpose contains 8 different implementations; we report the results as a range through "∼". Kernels having the same results as their SDK 2.0 versions, including Bitonic Sort, MatrixMult and Bisect Large, are not presented.

Kernels	#T = 4		#T = 16		#T = 64	#T = 256	#T = 1,024
	PUG	GKLEE	PUG	GKLEE	GKLEE	GKLEE	GKLEE
Simple Reduct.	2.8	$< 0.1(< 0.1)$	T.O	$< 0.1(< 0.1)$	$< 0.1(< 0.1)$	0.2(0.3)	2.3(2.9)
Matrix Transp.	1.9	$< 0.1(< 0.1)$	T.O	$< 0.1(0.3)$	$< 0.1(3.2)$	$< 0.1(63)$	0.9(T.O)
Bitonic Sort	3.7	0.9(1)	T.O	T.O	T.O	T.O	T.O
Scan Large	–	$< 0.1(< 0.1)$	–	$< 0.1(< 0.1)$	0.1(0.2)	1.6(3)	22(51)

Table 3. Execution times (in seconds) of GKLEE and PUG [1] on some kernels for functional correctness check. #T is the number of threads. Time is reported in the format of GPU time (entire time); T.O means > 5 minutes.

Kernels	src. code coverage	min #test	avg. Cov^t	max. Cov^t	avg. CovBI^t	max. CovBI^t	exec. time
Bitonic Sort	100%/100%	5	78%/76%	100%/94%	79%/66%	90%/76%	1s
Merge Sort	100%/100%	6	88%/70%	100%/85%	93%/86%	100%/100%	1.6s
Word Search	100%/100%	2	100%/81%	100%/85%	100%/97%	100%/100%	0.1s
Suffix Tree Match	100%/90%	7	55%/49%	98%/66%	55%/49%	98%/83%	31s
Histogram64$^{tb.}$	100%/100%	9	100%/75%	100%/75%	100%/100%	100%/100%	600s

Table 4. Cov^t and CovTB^t measure bytecode coverage w.r.t threads. min #test tests are obtained by performing test case selection after the execution. Result for "Histogram64" is limited to 600 s. No test reductions used in generating this table. Exec. time on typical workstation.

the CPU as the CUDA debugger does. Last but not least, GKLEE can look for compiler-related bugs due to omitted volatiles.

The KLEE-FP [26] tool extends KLEE to cross-check IEEE 754 floating-point programs and their SIMD-vectorized versions. Two floating-point expressions are equivalent if they can be normalized to the same form. This tool does not address the same class of correctness and performance bugs as GKLEE, neither does it produce concrete test cases. However, its floating-point package can help overcome GKLEE's current inability to handle float numbers. Recently KLEE-FP has been extended [27] [3]to handle OpenCL code, targeted in particular at crosschecking OpenCL code against an initial scalar sequential version, and on finding races in such code.

[3] This work and that in this paper were concurrent and independent.

Some Limitations of GKLEE. GKLEE cannot be used to analyze the functional correctness of CUDA applications that involve floating-point calculations (efficient SMT methods for floating-point arithmetic, when available, will help here). The concolic nature of GKLEE can help ameliorate this drawback by sometimes "concretizing" the floating numbers to integers. All other analyses done by GKLEE are unaffected by floating-point types, as typically variable addresses involve only unsigned integers.

7. Concluding Remarks

We presented GKLEE, the first symbolic virtual machine based correctness checker and test generator for GPU programs written in CUDA/C++. It checks several error categories, including one pre-

Kernels	No Reductions		Red_{TB}		Red_{BI}	
	#path	avg. $CovBI^t$	#path	avg.$CovBI^t$	#path	avg. $CovBI^t$
Bitonic Sort	28	79%/66%	5	79%/66%	5	79%/65%
Merge Sort	34	93%/86%	4	92%/84%	4	92%/84%
Word Search	8	100%/97%	2	100%/97%	2	94%/85%
Suffix Tree Match	31	55%/49%	6	55%/49%	6	55%/49%
Histogram64	13	100%/100%	5	100%/100%	5	100%/100%

Table 5. Reduction Heuristic Comparisons.

Comparison Categories	GKLEE	PUG [1]	GRace[2]	[3]
Methodology	Concolic Exec. in virtual machine	Symbolic Analysis	Static Analysis + Dyn. Check	Dynamic Check
Level of Analysis	LLVM Bytecode	Source Code	Source Code (Instrument.)	Source Code (Instrument.)
Bugs Targeted	Race (intra-/inter- warp, all memory), Warp Divergence, Deadlocks, Memory Coalesce, Bank Conflicts Compilation level bugs (e.g. Volatiles)	Shared Mem. Race, Deadlocks, Bank Conflict	Intra-/Inter- Warp Race	Shared Mem. race, Bank Conflict
False alarm elim.	SMT-solving, GPU replaying	Auto./Manual Refinement	Dynamic Execution	Dynamic Execution
Test Generation	Automatic, Hardware Execution, Coverage Measures, Test Reduction	Not supported	Not supported	Not supported

Table 6. Comparison of Formal Verifiers of GPU Programs

viously unidentified race type. We discussed logical errors and performance bottlenecks detected by GKLEE in real-world kernels. For many realistic kernels, finding these issues takes less than a minute on a modern workstation. We propose several novel code coverage measures and show that GKLEE's test generation and test reduction heuristics achieve high coverage. Several future directions are planned: (i) OpenCL [10] support, (ii) handling formats other than LLVM (*e.g.*, Nvidia's PTX) using frameworks such as Ocelot [28], (iii) scalability enhancement, including parameterized methods for SIMD programs, and (iv) using static performance analysis results of GKLEE to guide dynamic performance analysis on typical input data sets.

Acknowledgements: We thank the authors of [4] for releasing KLEE well designed and documented. The Utah authors were supporte by NSF awards CNS-1035658 and CCF-0935858.

References

[1] G. Li and G. Gopalakrishnan, "Scalable SMT-based verification of GPU kernel functions," in *SIGSOFT FSE*, 2010.

[2] M. Zheng, V. T. Ravi, F. Qin, and G. Agrawal, "GRace: A low-overhead mechanism for detecting data races in GPU programs," in *PPoPP*, 2011.

[3] M. Boyer, K. Skadron, and W. Weimer, "Automated dynamic analysis of CUDA programs," in *Third Workshop on Software Tools for Multi-Core Systems*, 2008.

[4] C. Cadar, D. Dunbar, and D. R. Engler, "KLEE: Unassisted and automatic generation of high-coverage tests for complex systems programs," in *OSDI, 8th USENIX Symposium*, 2008.

[5] "SMT-COMP. `http://www.smtcomp.org/2011`."

[6] P. Godefroid, N. Klarlund, and K. Sen, "DART: Directed automated random testing," in *PLDI*, 2005.

[7] "KLEE open projects," `http://klee.llvm.org/OpenProjects.html`.

[8] K. Sen, D. Marinov, and G. Agha, "CUTE: a concolic unit testing engine for C," in *10th ESEC/FSE*, 2005.

[9] "CUDA zone. `www.nvidia.com/object/cuda_home.html`."

[10] OpenCL. `http://www.khronos.org/opencl`.

[11] A. Kamil and K. A. Yelick, "Concurrency Analysis for Parallel Programs with Textually Aligned Barriers," in *LCPC*, 2005.

[12] "The LLVM compiler infrastructure. `http://www.llvm.org/`."

[13] "GKLEE Technical Report. `http://www.cs.utah.edu/fv/GKLEE`."

[14] "Cuda programming guide version 4.0. `http://developer.download.nvidia.com/compute/cuda/4_0/toolkit/docs/CUDA_C_Programming_Guide.pdf`."

[15] J. Sevcik, "Safe Optimisations for Shared-Memory Concurrent Programs," in *PLDI*, 2011.

[16] S. V. Adve, M. D. Hill, B. P. Miller, and R. H. Netzer, "Detecting data races on weak memory systems," in *ISCA*, 1991.

[17] D. Shasa and M. Snir, "Efficient and correct execution of parallel programs that share memory," *ACM TOPLAS*, vol. 10, no. 2, pp. 282–312, 1988.

[18] A. Aiken and D. Gay, "Barrier inference," in *POPL*, 1998.

[19] NVIDIA, "CUDA-GDB," Jan. 2009, an extension to the GDB debugger for debugging CUDA kernels in the hardware.

[20] Nvidia, "Parallel Nsight," Jul. 2010.

[21] Rogue Wave, "Totalview for CUDA," Jan. 2010.

[22] J. M. Cobleigh, L. A. Clarke, and L. J. Osterweil, "Flavers: A finite state verification technique for software systems," *IBM Systems Journal*, vol. 41, no. 1, 2002.

[23] S. K. Lahiri, S. Qadeer, and Z. Rakamaric, "Static and precise detection of concurrency errors in systems code using SMT solvers," in *21st Computer Aided Verification (CAV)*, 2009.

[24] B. Coutinho, D. Sampaio, F. M. Quintao Pereira, and W. Meira Jr., "Divergence analysis and optimizations," in *PACT*, 2011.

[25] J. Lv, G. Li, A. Humphrey, and G. Gopalakrishnan, "Performance degradation analysis of GPU kernels," in *EC2 Workshop*, 2011.

[26] P. Collingbourne, C. Cadar, and P. H. J. Kelly, "Symbolic crosschecking of floating-point and SIMD code," in *EuroSys*, 2011.

[27] P. Collingbourne, C. Cadar, and P. Kelly, "Symbolic testing of OpenCL code," in *Haifa Verification Conference (HVC)*, 2011.

[28] G. F. Diamos, A. R. Kerr, S. Yalamanchili, and N. Clark, "Ocelot: a dynamic optimization framework for bulk-synchronous applications in heterogeneous systems," in *PACT*, 2010.

Algorithm-based Fault Tolerance for Dense Matrix Factorizations

Peng Du   Aurelien Bouteiller   George Bosilca   Thomas Herault   Jack Dongarra

Innovative Computing Laboratory, University of Tennessee, Knoxville

{du,bouteill,bosilca,herault,dongarra}@eecs.utk.edu

Abstract

Dense matrix factorizations, such as LU, Cholesky and QR, are widely used for scientific applications that require solving systems of linear equations, eigenvalues and linear least squares problems. Such computations are normally carried out on supercomputers, whose ever-growing scale induces a fast decline of the Mean Time To Failure (MTTF). This paper proposes a new hybrid approach, based on Algorithm-Based Fault Tolerance (ABFT), to help matrix factorizations algorithms survive fail-stop failures. We consider extreme conditions, such as the absence of any reliable component and the possibility of loosing both data and checksum from a single failure. We will present a generic solution for protecting the right factor, where the updates are applied, of all above mentioned factorizations. For the left factor, where the panel has been applied, we propose a scalable checkpointing algorithm. This algorithm features high degree of checkpointing parallelism and cooperatively utilizes the checksum storage leftover from the right factor protection. The fault-tolerant algorithms derived from this hybrid solution is applicable to a wide range of dense matrix factorizations, with minor modifications. Theoretical analysis shows that the fault tolerance overhead sharply decreases with the scaling in the number of computing units and the problem size. Experimental results of LU and QR factorization on the Kraken (Cray XT5) supercomputer validate the theoretical evaluation and confirm negligible overhead, with- and without-errors.

Categories and Subject Descriptors G.4 [*Mathematical Software*]: Reliability and robustness

General Terms Algorithms

Keywords ABFT, Fault-tolerance, Fail-stop failure, LU, QR

1. Introduction

Today's high performance computers have paced into Petaflops realm, through the increase of system scale. The number of system components, such as CPU cores, memory, networking, and storage grow considerably. One of the most powerful Petaflop scale machines, Kraken [2], from National Institute for Computational Sciences and University of Tennessee, harnessed as many as 112,800 cores to reach its peak performance of 1.17 Petaflops to rank No.11 on the November 2011 Top500 list. With the increase of system scale and chip density, the reliability and availability of such systems has declined. It has been shown that, under specific circumstances, adding computing units might hamper applications completion time, as a larger node count implies a higher probability of reliability issues. This directly translates into a lower efficiency of the machine, which equates to a lower scientific throughput [24]. It is estimated that the MTTF of High Performance Computing (HPC) systems might drop to about one hour in the near future [7]. Without a drastic change at the algorithmic level, such a failure rate will certainly prevent capability applications from progressing.

Exploring techniques for creating a software ecosystem and programming environment capable of delivering computation at extreme scale, that are both resilient and efficient, will eliminate a major obstacle to scientific productivity on tomorrow's HPC platforms. In this work we advocate that in extreme scale environments, successful approaches to fault tolerance (e.g. those which exhibit acceptable recovery times and memory requirements) must go beyond traditional systems-oriented techniques and leverage intimate knowledge of dominant application algorithms, in order to create a middleware that is far more adapted and responsive to the application's performance and error characteristics.

While many types of failures can strike a distributed system [16], the focus of this paper is on the most common representation: the fail-stop model. In this model, a failure is defined as a process that *completely* and *definitely* stops responding, triggering the loss of a critical part of the global application state. To be more realistic, we assume a failure could occur at any moment and can affect any parts of the application's data. We introduce a new generic hybrid approach based on algorithm-based fault tolerance (ABFT) that can be applied to several ubiquitous one-sided dense linear factorizations. Using one of these factorizations, namely LU with partial pivoting, which is significantly more challenging due to pivoting, we theoretically prove that this scheme successfully applies to the three well known one-sided factorizations, Cholesky, LU and QR. To validate these claims, we implement and evaluate this generic ABFT scheme with both the LU and QR factorizations. A significant contribution of this work is to protect the part of the matrix below the diagonal (referred to as "the left factor" in the rest of the text) during the factorization, which was hitherto never achieved.

The rest of the paper is organized as follows: Section 2 presents background and prior work in the domain; Section 3 reviews the features of full factorizations. Section 4 discusses the protection of the right factor using the ABFT method. Section 5 reviews the idea of vertical checkpointing and proposes the new checkpointing method to protect the left factor. Section 6 evaluates the performance and overhead of the proposed algorithm using the example of LU and QR, and section 7 concludes the work.

PPoPP'12, February 25–29, 2012, New Orleans, Louisiana, USA.

2. Algorithm Based Fault Tolerance Background

The most well-known fault-tolerance technique for parallel applications, checkpoint-restart (C/R), encompasses two categories, the system and application level. At the system level, message passing middleware deals with faults automatically, without intervention from the application developer or user ([5, 6]). At the application level, the application state is dumped to a reliable storage when the application code mandates it. Even though C/R bears the disadvantage of high overhead while writing data to stable storage, it is widely used nowadays by high end systems [1]. To reduce the overhead of C/R, diskless checkpointing [21, 23] has been introduced to store checksum in memory rather than stable storage. While diskless checkpointing has shown promising performance in some applications (for instance, FFT in [14]), it exhibits large overheads for applications modifying substantial memory regions between checkpoints [23], as is the case with factorizations.

In contrast, Algorithm Based Fault Tolerance (ABFT) is based on adapting the algorithm so that the application dataset can be recovered at any moment, without involving costly checkpoints. ABFT was first introduced to deal with silent error in systolic arrays [19]. Unlike other methods that treat the recovery data and computing data separately, ABFT approaches are based on the idea of maintaining consistency of the recovery data, by applying appropriate mathematical operations on both the original and recovery data. Typically, for linear algebra operations, the input matrix is extended with supplementary columns and/or rows containing checksums. This initial encoding happens only once; the matrix algorithms are designed to work on the encoded checksum along with matrix data, similar mathematical operations are applied to both the data and the checksum so that the checksum relationship is kept invariant during the course of the algorithm. Should some data be damaged by failures, it is then possible to recover the application by inverting the checksum operation to recreate missing data. The overhead of ABFT is usually low, since no periodical global checkpoint or rollback-recovery is involved during computation and the computation complexity of the checksum operations scales similarly to the related matrix operation. ABFT and diskless checkpointing have been combined to apply to basic matrix operations like matrix-matrix multiplication [4, 8–10] and have been implemented on algorithms similar to those of ScaLAPACK [3], which is widely used for dense matrix operations on parallel distributed memory systems.

Recently, ABFT has been applied to the High Performance Linpack (HPL) [12] and to the Cholesky factorization [18]. Both Cholesky and HPL have the same factorization structure, where only half of the factorization result is required, and the update to the trailing matrix is based on the fact that the left factor result is a triangular matrix. This approach however does not necessarily apply to other factorizations, like QR where the left factor matrix is full, nor when the application requires both the left and right factorization results. Also, LU with partial pivoting, when applied to the lower triangular L, potentially changes the checksum relation and renders basic checkpointing approaches useless.

The generic ABFT framework for matrix factorizations we introduce in this work can be applied not only to Cholesky and HPL, but also to LU and QR. The right factor is protected by a traditional ABFT checksum, while the left factor is protected by a novel vertical checkpointing scheme, making the resulting approach an hybrid between ABFT and algorithm driven checkpointing. Indeed, this checkpointing algorithm harnesses some of the properties of the factorization algorithm to exchange limited amount of rollback with the ability to overlap the checkpointing of several panel operations running in parallel. Other contributions of this work include correctness proofs and overhead characterization for the ABFT approach on the most popular 2D-block cyclic distribution (as opposed to the 1D distributions used in previous works). These proofs consider the effect of failures during critical phases of the algorithm, and demonstrate that recovery is possible without suffering from error propagation

3. Full Factorizations of Matrix

In this work, we consider the case of factorizations where the lower triangular part of the factorization result matters, as is the case in QR and LU with pivoting. For example, the left factor Q is required when using QR to solve the least square problem, and so is L when solving $A^k x = b$ with the "LU factorization outside the loop" method [17]. In the remaining of this section, we recall the main algorithm of the most complex case of one-sided factorization, block LU with pivoting. Additionally, we highlight challenges specific to this type of algorithms, when compared to algorithms studied in previous works.

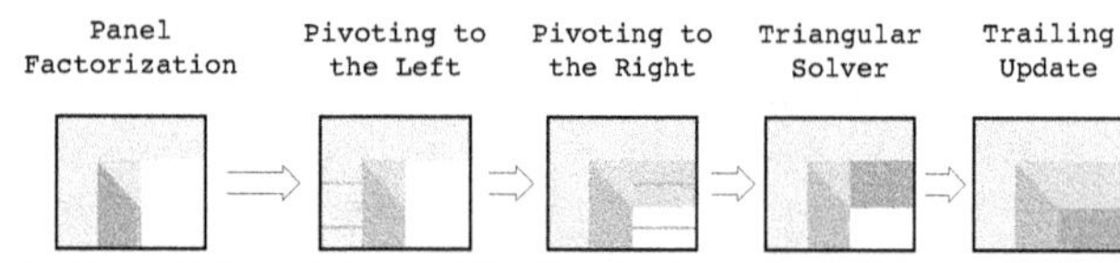

Figure 1. Steps applied to the input matrix in an iteration of the LU factorization; Green: Just finished; Red & Orange: being processed; Gray: Finished in previous iterations

Figure 1 presents the diagram of the basic operations applied to the input matrix to perform the factorization. The block LU factorization algorithm can be seen as a recursive process. At each iteration, the panel factorization is applied on a block column. This panel operation factorizes the upper square (selecting adequate pivots and applying internal row swapping as necessary to ensure numerical stability), and scales the lower polygon accordingly. The output of this panel is used to apply row swapping to the result of previous iterations, on the left, and to the trailing matrix on the right. The triangular solver is applied to the right of the factored block to scale it accordingly, and then the trailing matrix is updated by applying a matrix-matrix multiply update. Then the trailing matrix is used as the target for the next iteration of the recursive algorithm, until the trailing matrix is empty. Technically, each of these basic steps is usually performed by applying a parallel Basic Linear Algebra Subroutine (PBLAS).

The structure of the other one-sided factorizations, Cholesky and QR, are similar with minor differences. In the case of Cholesky, the trailing matrix update involves only the upper triangle, as the lower left factor is not critical. For QR, the computation of pivots and the swapping are not necessary as the QR algorithm is more stable. Moreover, there are a significant number of applications, like iterative refinement and algorithms for eigenvalue problems, where the entire factorization result, including the lower part, is needed. Therefore, a scalable and efficient protection scheme for the lower left triangular part of the factorization result is required.

4. Protection of the Right Factor Matrix with ABFT

In this section, we detail the ABFT approach that is used to protect the upper triangle from failures, while considering the intricacies of typical block cyclic distributions and failure detection delays.

4.1 Checksum Relationship

ABFT approaches are based upon the principle of keeping an invariant bijective relationship between protective supplementary blocks and the original data through the execution of the algorithm, by the application of numerical updates to the checksum. In order to use ABFT for matrix factorization, an initial checksum is generated before the actual computation starts. In future references we use G to refer to the generator matrix, and A to the original input matrix. The checksum C for A is produced by

$$C = GA \text{ or } C = AG \tag{1}$$

When G is all-1 vector, the checksum is simply the sum of all data items from a certain row or column. Referred to as the *checksum relationship*, (1) can be used at any step of the computation for checking data integrity (by detecting mismatching checksum and data) and recovery (inverting the relation builds the difference between the original and the degraded dataset). With the type of failures we consider (Fail-Stop), data cannot be corrupted, so we will use this relationship to implement the recovery mechanism only. This relationship has been shown separately for Cholesky [18], and HPL [12], both sharing the property of updating the trailing matrix with a lower triangular matrix. However, in this work we consider the general case of matrix factorization algorithms, including those where the full matrix is used for trailing matrix updates (as is the case for QR and LU with partial pivoting). In this context, the invariant property has not been demonstrated; we will now demonstrate that it holds for full matrix based updates algorithms as well.

4.2 Checksum Invariant with Full Matrix Update

In [22], ZU is used to represent a matrix factorization (optionally with pairwise pivoting for LU), where Z is the left matrix (lower triangular in the case of Cholesky or full for LU and QR) and U is an upper triangular matrix. The factorization is then regarded as the process of applying a series of matrices Z_i to A from the left until $Z_i Z_{i-1} \cdots Z_0 A$ becomes upper triangular.

Theorem 4.1. *Checksum relationship established before ZU factorization is maintained during and after factorization.*

Proof. Suppose data matrix $A \in \mathbb{R}^{n\times n}$ is to be factored as $A = ZU$, where Z *and* $U \in \mathbb{R}^{n\times n}$ and U is an upper triangular matrix. A is checkpointed using generator matrix $G \in \mathbb{R}^{n\times nc}$, where nc is the width of checksum. To factor A into upper triangular form, a series of transformation matrices Z_i is applied to A (with partial pivoting in LU).

Case 1: No Pivoting

$$U = Z_n Z_{n-1} \dots Z_1 A \tag{2}$$

Now the same operation is applied to $A_c = [A,\ AG]$

$$\begin{aligned} U_c &= Z_n Z_{n-1} \dots Z_1 [A,\ AG] \\ &= [Z_n Z_{n-1} \dots Z_1 A,\ Z_n Z_{n-1} \dots Z_1 AG] \\ &= [U,\ UG] \end{aligned} \tag{3}$$

For any $k \le n$, using U^k to represent the result of U at step k,

$$\begin{aligned} U_c^k &= Z_k Z_{k-1} \dots Z_1 [A,\ AG] \\ &= [Z_k Z_{k-1} \dots Z_1 A,\ Z_k Z_{k-1} \dots Z_1 AG] \\ &= \left[U^k,\ U^k G\right] \end{aligned} \tag{4}$$

Case 2: With partial pivoting:

$$\begin{aligned} U_c^k &= Z_k P_k Z_{k-1} P_{k-1} \dots Z_1 P_1 [A,\ AG] \\ &= [Z_k P_k Z_{k-1} P_{k-1} \dots Z_1 P_1 A, \\ &\qquad Z_k P_k Z_{k-1} P_{k-1} \dots Z_1 P_1 AG] \\ &= \left[U^k,\ U^k G\right] \end{aligned} \tag{5}$$

Therefore the checksum relationship holds for LU with partial pivoting, Cholesky and QR factorizations. □

4.3 Checksum Invariant in Block Algorithms

Theorem 4.1 shows the mathematical checksum relationship in matrix factorizations. However, in real-world, HPC factorizations are performed in block algorithms, and execution is carried out in a recursive way. Linear algebra packages, like ScaLAPACK, consist of several function components for each factorization. For instance, LU has a panel factorization, a triangular solver and a matrix-matrix multiplication. We need to ensure that the checksum relationship also holds for block algorithms, both at the end of each iteration, and after the factorization is completed.

Theorem 4.2. *For ZU factorization in block algorithm, checksum at the end of each iteration only covers the upper triangular part of data that has already been factored and are still being factored in the trailing matrix.*

Proof. Input Matrix A is split into blocks of data of size $nb \times nb$ (A_{ij}, Z_{ij}, U_{ij}), and the following stands:

$$\begin{bmatrix} A_{11} & A_{12} & A_{13} \\ A_{21} & A_{22} & A_{23} \end{bmatrix} = \begin{bmatrix} Z_{11} & Z_{12} \\ Z_{21} & Z_{22} \end{bmatrix} \begin{bmatrix} U_{11} & U_{12} & U_{13} \\ 0 & U_{22} & U_{23} \end{bmatrix}, \tag{6}$$

where $A_{13} = A_{11} + A_{12}$, and $A_{23} = A_{21} + A_{22}$.

Since $A_{13} = Z_{11}U_{13} + Z_{12}U_{23}$, and $A_{23} = Z_{21}U_{13} + Z_{22}U_{23}$, and using the relation

$$\begin{cases} A_{11} &= Z_{11}U_{11} \\ A_{12} &= Z_{11}U_{12} + Z_{12}U_{22} \\ A_{21} &= Z_{21}U_{11} \\ A_{22} &= Z_{21}U_{12} + Z_{22}U_{22} \end{cases}$$

in (6), we have the following system of equations:

$$\begin{cases} Z_{21}(U_{11} + U_{12} - U_{13}) = Z_{22}(U_{23} - U_{22}) \\ Z_{11}(U_{11} + U_{12} - U_{13}) = Z_{12}(U_{23} - U_{22}) \end{cases}$$

This can be written as:

$$\begin{bmatrix} Z_{11} & Z_{12} \\ Z_{21} & Z_{22} \end{bmatrix} \begin{bmatrix} U_{11} + U_{12} - U_{13} \\ -(U_{23} - U_{22}) \end{bmatrix} = 0$$

For LU, Cholesky and QR, $\begin{bmatrix} Z_{11} & Z_{12} \\ Z_{21} & Z_{22} \end{bmatrix}$ is always nonsingular, so $\begin{bmatrix} U_{11} + U_{12} - U_{13} \\ U_{23} - U_{22} \end{bmatrix} = 0$, and $\begin{cases} U_{11} + U_{12} &= U_{13} \\ U_{23} &= U_{22} \end{cases}$.

This shows that after ZU factorization, checksum blocks cover the upper triangular matrix U only, even for the diagonal blocks. At the end of each iteration, for example the first iteration in (6), Z_{11}, U_{11}, Z_{21} and U_{12} are completed, and U_{13} is already $U_{11} + U_{12}$. The trailing matrix A_{22} is updated with

$$A_{22}{}' = A_{22} - Z_{21}U_{12} = Z_{22}U_{22}.$$

and A_{23} is updated to

$$\begin{aligned} A_{23}{}' &= A_{23} - Z_{21}U_{13} \\ &= A_{21} + A_{22} - Z_{21}(U_{11} + U_{12}) \\ &= Z_{21}U_{11} + A_{22} - Z_{21}U_{11} - Z_{21}U_{12} \\ &= A_{22} - Z_{21}U_{12} = Z_{22}U_{22} \end{aligned}$$

Therefore, at the end of each iteration, data blocks that have already been and are still being factored remain covered by checksum blocks. □

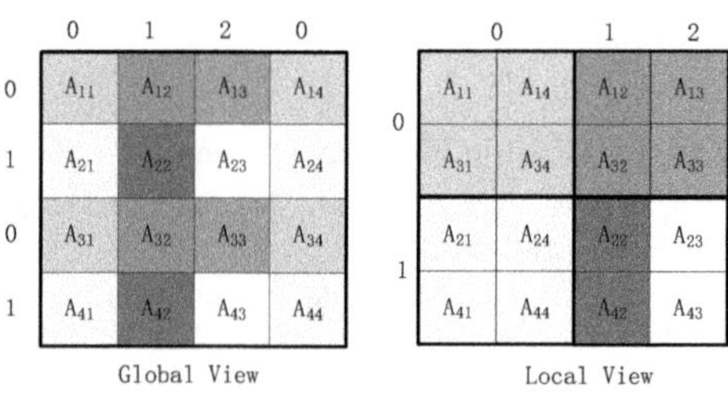

Figure 2. Example of a 2D block-cyclic data distribution

4.4 Issues with Two-Dimensional Block-cyclic Distribution

It has been well established that data layout plays an important role in the performance of parallel matrix operations on distributed memory systems [11, 20]. In 2D block-cyclic distributions, data is divided into equally sized blocks, and all computing units are organized into a virtual two-dimension grid P by Q. Each data block is distributed to computing units in round robin following the two dimensions of the virtual grid. Figure 2 is an example of a $P = 2, Q = 3$ grid applied to a global matrix of 4×4 blocks. The same color represents the same process while numbering in A_{ij} indicates the location in the global matrix. This layout helps with load balancing and reduces data communication frequency, because in each step of the algorithm, many computing units can be engaged in computations concurrently, and communications pertaining to blocks positioned on the same unit can be grouped. Thanks to these advantages, many prominent software libraries (like ScaLAPACK [13]) assume a 2D block-cyclic distribution.

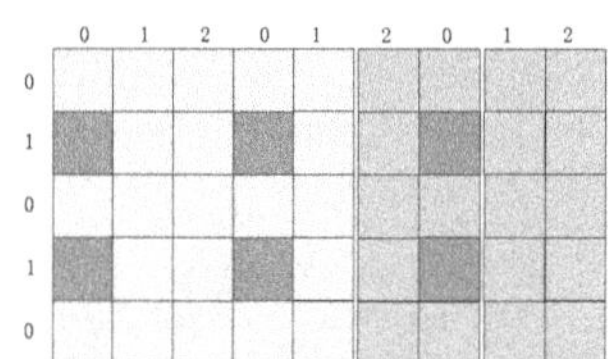

Figure 3. Holes in a checksum protected matrix caused by a single failure and the naive checksum duplication protection scheme (3x2 process grid)

However, with a 2D block-cyclic data distribution, the failure of a single process, usually a computing node which keeps several non-contiguous blocks of the matrix, results in holes scattered across the whole matrix. Figure 3 is an example of a 5×5 blocks matrix (on the left) with a 2×3 process grid. Red blocks represent holes caused by the failure of the single process (1, 0). In the general case, these holes can impact both checksum and matrix data at the same time.

4.5 Checksum Protection Against Failure

Our algorithm works under the assumption that any process can fail and therefore the data, including the checksum, can be lost. Rather than forcing checksum and data on different processes and assuming only one would be lost, as in [12], we put checksum and data together in the process grid and design the checksum protection algorithm accordingly.

4.5.1 Minimum Checksum Amount for Block Cyclic Distributions

Theoretically, the sum-based checksum C_k of a series of N blocks $A_i, 1 \leq i \leq N$, where N is the total number of blocks in one row/column of the matrix, is computed by:

$$C_k = \sum_{k=1}^{N} A_k \tag{7}$$

With the 2D block-cyclic distribution, a single failure punches multiple holes in the global matrix. With more than one hole per row/column, C_k in (7) is not sufficient to recover all lost data. A slightly more sophisticated checksum scheme is required.

Theorem 4.3. *Using sum-based checkpointing, for N data items distributed in block-cyclic onto Q processes, the size of the checksum to recover from the loss of one process is $\lceil \frac{N}{Q} \rceil$*

Proof. With 2D block-cyclic, each process gets $\lceil \frac{N}{Q} \rceil$ items. At the failure of one process, all data items in the group held by the process are lost. Take data item a_i, $1 \leq i \leq \lceil \frac{N}{Q} \rceil$, from group k, $1 \leq k \leq Q$. To be able to recover a_i, any data item in group k cannot be used, so at least one item from another group is required to create the checksum, and this generates one additional checksum item. Therefore for all items in group k, $\lceil \frac{N}{Q} \rceil$ checksum items are generated so that any item in group k can be recovered. □

Applying this theorem, we have the following checksum algorithm: Suppose Q processes are in a process column or row, and let each process have K blocks of data of size $nb \times nb$. Without loss of generality, let K be the largest number of blocks owned by any of the Q processes. From Theorem 4.3, the size of the checksum in this row is K blocks.

Let C_i be the ith checksum item, and A_i^j, be the ith data item on process j, $1 \leq i \leq \lceil \frac{N}{Q} \rceil$, $1 \leq j \leq Q$:

$$C_k = \sum_{k=1}^{Q} A_k^k \tag{8}$$

Under (8), we have the following corollary:

Corollary 4.4. *The ith block of checksum is calculated using the ith block of data of each process having at least i blocks.*

4.5.2 Checksum Duplicates

Since ABFT checksum is stored by regular processors, it has to be considered as fragile as the matrix data. From Theorem 4.3 and using the same N and Q, the total number of checksum blocks is $K = \lceil \frac{N}{Q} \rceil$. These checksum blocks can be appended to the bottom or to the right of the global data matrix accordingly, and since checksum is stored on computing processes, these K checksum blocks are distributed over $\min(K, Q)$ processes (see Figure 3). If a failure strikes any of these processes, like (1, 0) in this example, some checksum is lost and cannot be recovered. Therefore, checksum itself needs protection; in our work, duplication is used to protect checksum from failure.

A straightforward way of performing duplication is to make a copy of the entire checksum block, as illustrated by the two rightmost columns in Figure 3. While simple to implement, this method suffers from two major defects. First, if the checksum width K is a multiple of Q (or P for column checksum), the duplicate of a checksum block is located on the same processors, defeating the purpose of duplication. This can be solved at the cost of introducing an extra empty column in the process grid to resolve the mapping conflict. More importantly, to maintain the checksum invariant property, it is required to apply the trailing matrix update on the checksum (and its duplicates) as well. From corollary 4.4, once all the ith block columns on each process have finished the panel factorization (in Q step), the ith checksum block column is no longer active in any further computation (except pivoting) and should be excluded from the computing scope to reduce the ABFT overhead. This is problematic, as splitting the PBLAS calls to avoid excluded columns has a significant impact on the trailing matrix update efficiency.

4.5.3 Reverse Neighboring Checksum Storage

With the observation of how checksum is maintained during factorization, we propose the following reverse neighboring checksum duplication method that allows for applying the update in a single PBLAS call without incurring extraneous computation.

Algorithm 1 Checksum Management

On a $P \times Q$ grid, matrix is $M \times N$, block size is $NB \times NB$
C_k represents the kth checksum block column
A_k represents the kth data block column
Before factorization:
Generate the initial checksum:
$C_k = \sum_{j=(k-1)\times Q+1}^{(k-1)\times Q+Q} A_j, k = 1, \cdots, \left\lceil \frac{N}{NB\times Q} \right\rceil$
For each of C_k, make a copy of the whole block column and put right next to its original block column
Checksum C_k and its copy are put in the kth position starting from the far right end
Begin factorization
Host algorithm starts with an initial scope of M rows and $N + \left\lceil \frac{N}{Q} \right\rceil$ columns
For each Q panel factorizations, the scope decreases M rows and $2 \times NB$ columns
End factorization

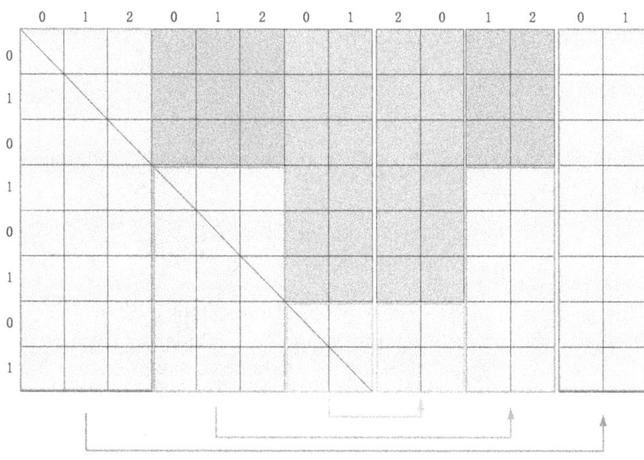

Figure 4. Reverse neighboring checksum storage, with two checksum duplicates per Q-wide groups

Figure 4 is an example of the reverse neighboring checksum method on a 2×3 grid. The data matrix has 8×8 blocks and therefore the size of checksum is 8×3 blocks with an extra 8×3 blocks copy. The arrows indicate where checksum blocks are stored on the right of the data matrix, according to the reverse storage scheme. For example, in the LU factorization, the first 3 block columns produce the checksum in the last two block columns (hence making 2 duplicate copies of the checksum). Because copies are stored in consecutive columns of the process grid, for any 2D grid with $Q > 1$, the checksum duplicates are guaranteed to be stored on different processors. The triangular solve (TRSM) and trailing matrix update (GEMM) are applied to the whole checksum area until the first three columns are factored. In following factorization steps, the two last block columns of checksum are excluded from the TRSM and GEMM scope. Since TRSM and GEMM claim most of the computation in the LU factorization, this shrinking scope greatly reduces the overhead of the ABFT mechanism. One can note that only the upper part of the checksum is useful, we will explain in the next section how this extra storage can be used to protect the lower triangular part of the matrix.

4.6 Delayed Recovery and Error Propagation

In this work, we assume that a failure can strike at any moment during the life span of factorization operations or even the recovery process. Theorem 4.2 proves that at the moment where the failure happens, the checksum invariant property is satisfied, meaning that the recovery can proceed successfully. However, in large scale systems, which are asynchronous by nature, the time interval between the failure and the moment when it is detected by other processes is unknown, leading to delayed recoveries, with opportunities for error propagation.

The ZU factorization is composed of several sub-algorithms that are called on different parts of the matrix. Matrix multiplication, which is used for trailing matrix updates and claims more than 95% of the execution time, has been shown to be ABFT compatible [4] , that is to compute the correct result even with delayed recovery. One feature that has the potential to curb this compatibility is pivoting, in LU, especially when a failure occurs between the panel factorization and the row swapping updates, there is a potential for destruction of rows in otherwise unaffected blocks.

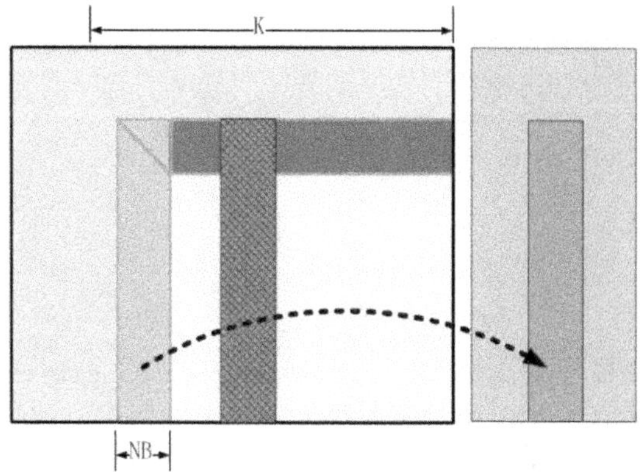

Figure 5. Ghost pivoting Issue
Gray: Result in previous steps
Light Green: Panel factorization result in current step
Deep Green: The checksum that protects the light green
Blue: TRSM zone Yellow: GEMM zone
Red: one of the columns affected by pivoting

Figure 5 shows an example of such a case. Suppose the current panel contributes to the ith column of checksum. When panel factorization finishes, the ith column becomes intermediate data which does not cover any column of matrix. If a failure at this instant causes holes in the current panel area, then lost data can be recovered right away. Pivoting for this panel factorization has only been applied within the light green area. Panel factorization is repeated to continue on the rest of the factorization. However, if failure causes holes in other columns that also contribute to the ith column of checksum, these holes cannot be recovered until the end of the trailing matrix update. To make it worse, after the panel factorization, pivoting starts to be applied outside the panel area and can move rows in holes into healthy area or vice versa, extending the recovery area to the whole column, as shown in red in Figure 5 including triangular solving area. To recover from this case, in addition to matrix multiplication, the triangular solver is also required to be protected by ABFT.

Theorem 4.5. *Failure in the right-hand sides of triangular solver can recover from fail-stop failure using ABFT.*

Proof. Suppose A is the upper or lower triangular matrix produced by LU factorization (non-blocked in ScaLAPACK LU), B is the right-hand side, and the triangular solver solves the equation $Ax = B$.

Supplement B with checksum generated by $B_c = B * G_r$ to extended form $\hat{B} = [B,\ B_c]$, where G_r is the generator matrix. Solve the extended triangular equation:

$$\begin{aligned} Ax_c &= B_c = [B,\ B_c] \\ \therefore\ x_c &= A^{-1} \times [B,\ B_c] \\ &= [A^{-1}B,\ A^{-1}B_c] \\ &= [x,\ A^{-1}BG_r] \\ &= [x,\ xG_r] \end{aligned}$$

Therefore data in the right-hand sides of the triangular solver is protected by ABFT. □

With this theorem, if failure occurs during triangular solving, lost data can be recovered when the triangular solver completes. Since matrix multiplication is also ABFT compatible, the whole red region in Figure 5 can be recovered after the entire trailing matrix update is done, leaving the opportunity for failure detection and recovery to be delayed at a convenient moment in the algorithm.

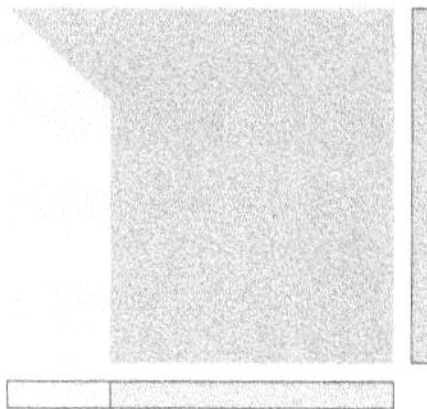

Figure 6. Separation of lower and upper areas protected by checksum (green) and checkpoint (yellow) during the course of the factorization algorithm

5. Protection of the Left Factor Matrix with Q-parallel Checkpoint

It has been proven in Theorem 4.2 that the checksum only covers the upper triangular part of the matrix until the current panel, and the trailing matrix is subject to future updates. This is depicted in Figure 6, where the green checksum on the right of the matrix protects exclusively the green part of the matrix. Another mechanism must be added for the protection of the left factor (the yellow area).

5.1 Impracticability of ABFT for Left Factor Protection

The most straightforward idea, when considering the need of protecting the lower triangle of the matrix, is to use an approach similar to the one described above, but column-wise. Unfortunately, such an approach is difficult, if not impossible in some cases, as proved in the remaining of this Section.

5.1.1 Pivoting and Vertical Checksum Validity

In LU, partial pivoting prevents the left factor from being protected through ABFT. The most immediate reason is as follow: The PBLAS kernel used to compute the panel factorization (see Figure 1) performs simultaneously the search for the best pivot in the column and the scaling of the column with that particular pivot. If applied directly on the matrix and the checksum blocks, similarly to what the trailing update approach does, checksum elements are at risk of being selected as pivots, which results in exchanging checksum rows into the matrix. This difficulty could be circumvented by introducing a new PBLAS kernel that does not search for pivots in the checksum.

Unfortunately, legitimate pivoting would still break the checksum invariant property, due to row swapping. In LU, for matrix A,

$$\begin{aligned} A &= \begin{pmatrix} A_{11} & A_{12} \\ A_{21} & A_{22} \end{pmatrix} = \begin{pmatrix} L_{11} & 0 \\ L_{21} & L_{22} \end{pmatrix} \begin{pmatrix} U_{11} & U_{12} \\ 0 & U_{22} \end{pmatrix} \\ &= \begin{pmatrix} L_{11}U_{11} & L_{11}U_{12} \\ L_{21}U_{11} & L_{21}U_{12} + L_{22}U_{22} \end{pmatrix} \end{aligned} \tag{9}$$

Panel factorization is:

$$\begin{pmatrix} A_{11} \\ A_{21} \end{pmatrix} = \begin{pmatrix} L_{11}U_{11} \\ L_{21}U_{11} \end{pmatrix} = \begin{pmatrix} L_{11} \\ L_{21} \end{pmatrix} U_{11} \tag{10}$$

To protect L_{11} and L_{21}, imagine that we maintain a separate checksum, stored at the bottom of the matrix, as shown in the yellow bottom rectangle of Figure 6, that we plan on updating by scaling it accordingly to the panel operation. In this vertical checksum, each P tall group of blocks in the 2D block cyclic distribution is protected by a particular checksum block. Suppose rows i_1 and i_2 reside on blocks k_{i_1} and k_{j_1} of two processes. It is not unusual that $k_{i_1} \neq k_{j_1}$. By Corollary 4.4, block k_{i_1} and k_{j_1} contribute to column-wise checksum block k_{i_1} and k_{j_1} respectively in the column that local blocks k_{i_1} and k_{j_1} belong to. This relationship is expressed as

$$\begin{aligned} row\ i_1 &\mapsto checksum\ block\ k_{i_1} \\ row\ j_1 &\mapsto checksum\ block\ k_{j_1} \end{aligned}$$

$\mapsto$ reads 'contributes to'. After the swapping, the relationship should be updated to

$$\begin{aligned} row\ i_1 &\mapsto checksum\ block\ k_{j_1} \\ row\ j_1 &\mapsto checksum\ block\ k_{i_1} \end{aligned}$$

This requires a re-generation of checksum blocks k_{i_1} and k_{j_1} in order to maintain the checkpoint validity. Considering there are nb potential pivoting operations per panel, hence a maximum of $nb+1$ checksum blocks to discard, this operation has the potential to be as expensive as computing a complete vertical checkpoint.

5.1.2 QR Factorization

Although QR has no pivoting, it still cannot benefit from ABFT to cover Q, as we prove below.

Theorem 5.1. *Q in Householder QR factorization cannot be protected by performing factorization along with the vertical checksum.*

Proof. Append a $m \times n$ nonsingular matrix A with checksum GA of size $c \times n$ along the column direction to get matrix $A_c = \begin{bmatrix} A \\ GA \end{bmatrix}$. G is $c \times m$ generator matrix. Suppose A has a QR factorization Q_0R_0.

Perform QR factorization to A_c:

$$\begin{bmatrix} A \\ GA \end{bmatrix} = Q_cR_c = \begin{bmatrix} Q_{c11} & Q_{c12} \\ Q_{c21} & Q_{c22} \end{bmatrix} \begin{bmatrix} R_{c11} \\ \varnothing \end{bmatrix}$$

Q_{c11} is $m \times m$ and Q_{c21} is $c \times m$. R_c is $m \times n$ and $\varnothing$ represents $c \times n$ zero matrix. $R_c \neq 0$ and is full rank. Because R_c is upper triangular with nonzero diagonal elements and therefore nonsingular.

$$Q_c Q_c^T = \begin{bmatrix} Q_{c11} & Q_{c12} \\ Q_{c21} & Q_{c22} \end{bmatrix} \begin{bmatrix} Q_{c11}^T & Q_{c21}^T \\ Q_{c12}^T & Q_{c22}^T \end{bmatrix} = I$$

Therefore

$$Q_{c11} Q_{c11}^T + Q_{c12} Q_{c12}^T = I. \tag{11}$$

Since $A = Q_{c11} R_{c11}$ and R_{c11} is nonsingular, then $Q_{c11} \neq 0$ and nonsingular.

Assume $Q_{c12} = 0$:

$Q_{c11} Q_{c21}^T + Q_{c12} Q_{c22}^T = 0$, therefore $Q_{c11} Q_{c21}^T = 0$. We have shown that Q_{c11} is nonsingular, so $Q_{c21}^T = 0$ and this conflicts with $GA = Q_{c21} R_{c11} \neq 0$, so the assumption $Q_{c12} = 0$ does not hold. From Equation 11, $Q_{c11} Q_{c11}^T \neq I$. This means even though $A = Q_{c11} R_{c11}$, $Q_{c11} R_{c11}$ is not a QR factorization of A. □

5.2 Panel Checkpointing

Given that the ZU factorization cannot protect Z by applying ABFT in the same way as for U, separate efforts are needed. For the rest of this paper, we use the term "checksum" to refer to the ABFT checksum, generated before the factorization, that is maintained by the application of numerical updates during the course of the algorithm, in contrast to "checkpointing" for the operation that creates a new protection block during the course of the factorization. LU factorization with partial pivoting being the most complex problem, it is used here for the discussion. The method proposed in this section can be applied to the QR and Cholesky factorizations with minimal efforts nonetheless.

In a ZU block factorization using 2D cyclic distribution, once a panel of Z is generated, it is stored into the lower triangular region of the original matrix. For example, in LU, vectors of L, except the diagonal ones, are stored in L. These lower triangular parts from the panel factorization are final results, and are not subject to further updates during the course of the algorithm, except for partial pivoting row swapping in LU. Therefore only one vertical checkpointing *"should be"* necessary to maintain each panel's safety, as is discussed in [12]. We will show how this idea, while mathematically trivial, needs to be refined to support partial pivoting. We will then propose a novel checkpointing scheme, leveraging properties of the block algorithm to checkpoint Z in parallel, that demonstrates a much lower overhead when compared to this basic approach.

5.3 Postponed Left Pivoting

Although once a panel is factored, it is not changed until the end of the computation, row swaps incurred by pivoting are still to be applied to the left factor as the algorithm progresses in the trailing matrix, as illustrated in Figure 1. The second step (pivoting to the left) swaps two rows to the left of the current panel. The same reasoning as presented in section 5.1.1 holds, meaning that the application of pivoting row swaps to the left factor has the potential to invalidate checkpoint blocks. Since pivoting to the left is carried out in every step of LU, this causes significant checkpoint maintenance overhead.

Unlike pivoting to the right, which happens during updates and inside the panel operation, whose result are reused in following steps of the algorithm, pivoting to the left can be postponed. The factored L is stored in the lower triangular part of the matrix without further usage during the algorithm. As a consequence, we delay the application of all left pivoting to the end of the computation, in order to avoid expensive checkpoint management. We keep track of all pivoting that should have been applied to the left factor, and when the algorithm has completed, all row swaps are applied just in time before returning the end-result of the routine.

5.4 Q-Parallel Checkpointing of Z

The vertical checkpointing of the panel result requires a set of reduction operations immediately after each panel factorization. Panel factorization is on the critical path and has lower parallelism, compared to other routines of the factorization (such as trailing matrix update). The panel factorization works only on a single block column of the matrix, hence benefits from only a P degree of parallelism, in a $P \times Q$ process grid. Checkpointing worsens this situation, because it applies to the same block column, and is bound to the same low level of exploitable parallelism. Furthermore, the checkpointing cannot be overlapped with the computation of the trailing matrix update: all processes who do not appear on the same column of the process grid are waiting in the matrix-matrix multiply PBLAS, stalled because they require the panel column to enter the call in order for the result of the panel to be broadcasted. If the algorithm enters the checkpointing routine before going into the trailing update routine, the entire update is delayed. If the algorithm enters the trailing update before starting the checkpointing, the checksum is damaged in a way that prevents recovering that panel, leaving it vulnerable to failures.

Our proposition is then twofold: we protect the content of the blocks before the panel, which then enables starting immediately the trailing update without jeopardizing the safety of the panel result. Then, we wait until sufficient checkpointing is pending to benefit from the maximal parallelism allowed by the process grid.

5.4.1 Enabling Trailing Matrix Update Before Checkpointing

The major problem with enabling the trailing matrix update to proceed while the checkpointing of the panel is not finished is that the ABFT protection of the update modifies the checksum in a way that disables protection for the panel blocks. To circumvent this limitation, in a $P \times Q$ grid, processes are grouped by section of width Q, that are called a *panel scope*. When the panel operation starts applying to a new section, the processes of this panel scope make a local copy of the impending column and the associated checksum, called a *snapshot*. This operation involves no communication, and features the maximum $P \times Q$ parallelism. The memory overhead is limited, as it requires only the space for at most two extra columns to be available at all time, one for saving the state before the application of the panel to the target column, and one for the checksum column associated to these Q columns. The algorithm then proceeds as usual, without waiting for checkpoints before entering the next Q trailing updates. Because of the availability of this extra protection column, the original checksum can be modified to protect the trailing matrix without threatening the recovery of the panel scope, which can rollback to that previous dataset should a failure occur.

5.4.2 Q-Parallel Checkpointing

When a panel scope is completed, the $P \times Q$ group of processes undergo checkpointing simultaneously. Effectively, P simultaneous checkpointing reductions are taking place along the block rows, involving the Q processes of that row to generate a new protection block. This scheme enables the maximum parallelism for the checkpoint operation, hence decreasing its global impact on the failure free overhead. Another strong benefit is that it scales with the process grid perfectly, whereas regular checkpointing suffers from scaling with the square root of the number of processes (as it involves only one dimension of the process grid).

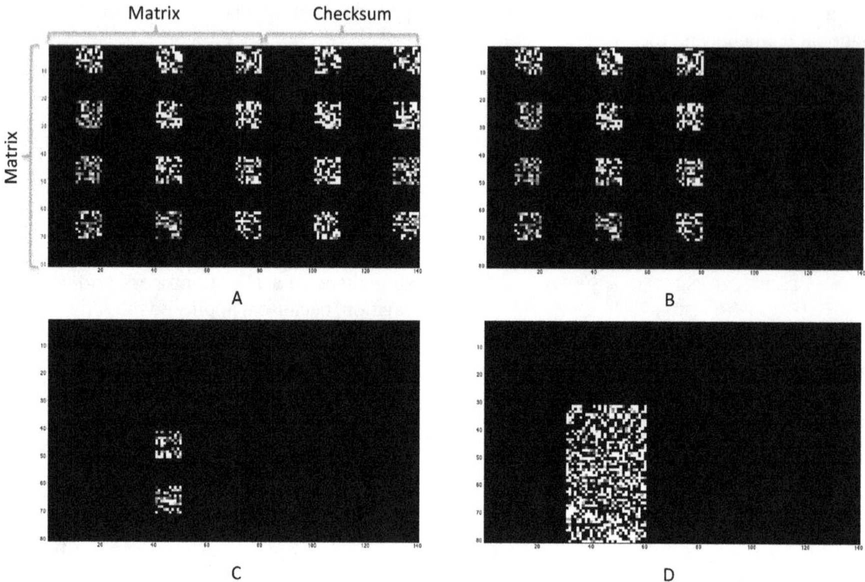

Figure 7. Recovery example
(matrix size 800×800, grid size 2×3, failure of process (0,1), failure step:41,
A: Failure occurs B: Checksum recovered
C: Data recovered using ABFT checksum and checkpointing output D: Three panels restored using snapshots

5.4.3 Optimized Checkpoint Storage

According to Corollary 4.4, starting from the first block column on the left, every Q block columns contribute to one block column of checksum, which means that once the factorization is done for these Q block columns, the corresponding checksum block column becomes useless (it does not protect the trailing matrix anymore, it has never protected the left factor, see Theorem 4.2). Therefore, this checksum storage space is available for storing the resultant checkpoint block generated to protect the panel result. Following the same policy as the checksum storage, discussed in Section 4.5.2, the checkpoint data is stored in reverse order from the right of the checksum (see Figure 4). As this part of the checksum is excluded from the trailing matrix update, the checkpoint blocks are not modified by the continued operation of the algorithm.

5.4.4 Recovery

The hybrid checkpointing approach requires a special recovery algorithm. Two cases are considered. First, when failure strikes during the trailing update, immediately after a panel scope checkpointing. For this case, the recovery is not attempted until the current step of the trailing update is done. When the recovery time comes, the checksum/checkpointing on the right of the matrix matches the matrix data as if the initial ABFT checksum had just been performed. Therefore any lost data blocks can be recovered by the simple reverse application of the ABFT checksum relationship.

The second case is when a failure occurs during the Q panel factorization, before the checkpointing for this panel scope can successfully finish. In this situation, all processes revert the panel scope columns to the snapshot copy. Holes in the snapshot data are recreated by using the snapshot copy of the checksum, applying the usual ABFT recovery. The algorithm is resumed in the panel scope, so that panel and updates are applied again within the scope of the Q wide section; updates outside the panel scope are discarded, until the pre-failure iteration has been reached. Outside the panel scope, regular recovery mechanisms are deployed (ABFT checksum inversion for the trailing matrix, checkpoint recovery for the left factor). When the re-factorization of panels finishes, the entire matrix, including the checksum, is recovered back to the correct state. The computation then resumes from the next panel factorization, after the failing step.

Figure 7 shows an example of the recovery when the process (1,0) in a 2×3 grid failed. It presents the difference between the correct matrix dataset and the current dataset during various steps of failure recovery as a "temperature map", brighter colors meaning large differences and black insignificant differences. The matrix size is 80×80 and $NB = 10$, therefore the checksum size is 80×60. Failure occurs after the panel factorization starting at (41,41) is completed, within the $Q = 3$ panel scope. First, using a fault tolerant MPI infrastructures, like FT-MPI [15], the failed process (0,1) is replaced and reintegrates the process grid with a blank dataset, showing as evenly distributed erroneous blocks (A). Then the recovery process starts by mending the checksum using duplicates (B). The next step recovers the data which is outside the current panel scope (31:80,31:60), using the corresponding checksum for the right factor, and the checkpoints for the left factor (C). At this moment, all the erroneous blocks are repaired, except those in the panel scope (41:80, 41:50). Snapshots are applied to the three columns of the panel scope (31:80,31:60). Since these do not match the state of the matrix before the failure, but a previous state, this area appears as very different (D). Panel factorization is re-launched in the panel scope, in the area (31:80,31:60), with the trailing update limited within this area. This re-factorization continues until it finishes panel (41:80,41:50) and by that time the whole matrix is recovered to the correct state (not presented, all black). The LU factorization can then proceed normally.

6. Evaluation

In this section, we evaluate the performance of the proposed fault tolerant algorithm based on ABFT and reverse neighboring checkpointing. For a fault tolerant algorithm, the most important consid-

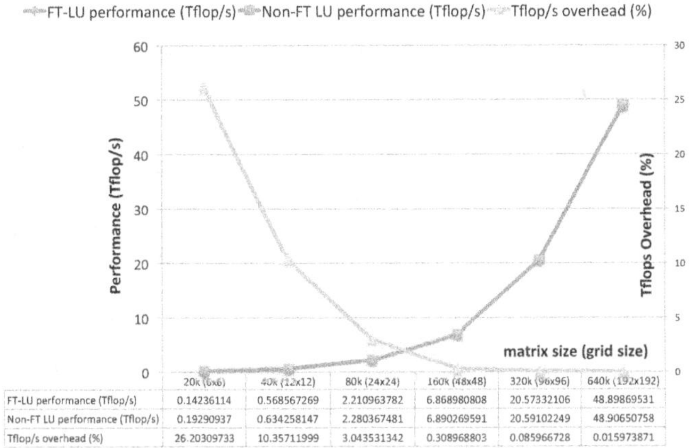

	20k (6x6)	40k (12x12)	80k (24x24)	160k (48x48)	320k (96x96)	640k (192x192)
FT-LU performance (Tflop/s)	0.14236114	0.568567269	2.210963782	6.868980808	20.57332106	48.89869531
Non-FT LU performance (Tflop/s)	0.19290937	0.634258147	2.280367481	6.890269591	20.59102249	48.90650758
Tflop/s overhead (%)	26.20309733	10.35711999	3.043531342	0.308968803	0.085966728	0.015973871

Figure 8. Weak scalability of FT-LU: performance and overhead on Kraken, compared to non fault tolerant LU

FT overhead (Tflop/s)	0.051	0.066	0.070	0.021	0.018	0.008
FT overhead (%)	26.203	10.357	3.044	0.309	0.086	0.016

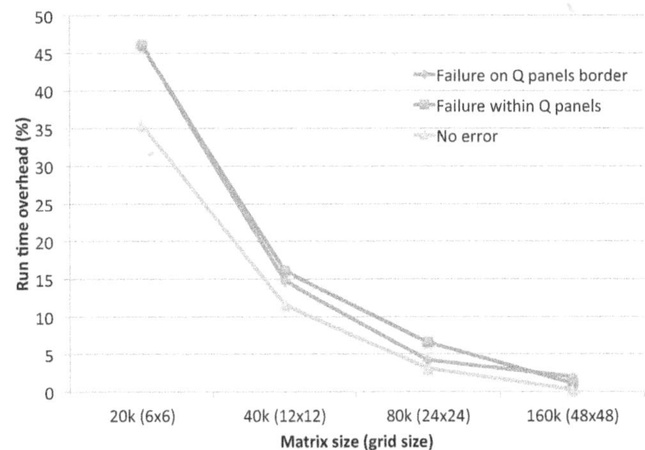

Figure 9. Weak scalability of FT-LU: run time overhead on Kraken when failures strike at different steps

eration is the overhead added to failure free execution rate, due to various fault tolerance mechanisms such as checksum generation, checkpointing and extra flops. An efficient and scalable algorithm will incur a minimal overhead over the original algorithm while enabling scalable reconstruction of lost dataset in case of failure.

We use the NSF Kraken supercomputer, hosted at the National Institute for Computational Science (NICS, Oak Ridge, TN) as our testing platform. This machine features 112,896 2.6GHz AMD Opteron cores, 12 cores per node, with the Seastar interconnect. At the software level, to serve as a comparison base, we use the non fault tolerant ScaLAPACK LU and QR in double precision with block size $NB = 100$. The fault tolerance functions are implemented and inserted as drop-in replacements for ScaLAPACK routines.

In this section, we first evaluate the storage overhead in the form of extra memory usage, then show experimental result on Kraken to assess the computational overhead.

6.1 Storage Overhead

Checksum takes extra storage (memory), but on large scale systems, memory usage is usually maximized for computing tasks. Therefore, it is preferable to have a small ratio of checksum size over matrix size, in order to minimize the impact on the memory available to the application itself. For the sake of simplicity, and because of the small impact in term of memory usage, neither the pivoting vector nor the column shift are considered in this evaluation.

Different protection algorithms require different amounts of memory. In the following, we consider the duplication algorithm presented in Section 4.5.2 for computing the upper memory bound. The storage of the checksum includes the row-wise and column-wise checksums and a small portion at the bottom-right corner.

For an input matrix of size $M \times N$ on a $P \times Q$ process grid, the memory used for checksum (including duplicates) is $M \times \frac{N}{Q} \times 2$. The ratio R_{mem} of checksum memory over the memory of the input matrix, equals to $\frac{2}{Q}$, becomes negligible with the increase in the number of processes used for the computation.

6.2 Overhead without Failures

Figure 8 evaluates the completion time overhead and performance, using the LU factorization routine PDGETRF. The performance of both the original and fault tolerant version are presented, in Tflop/s (the two curves overlap due to the little performance difference). This experiment is carried out to test the weak scalability, where both the matrix and grid dimension doubles. The result outlines that as the problem size and grid size increases, the overhead drops quickly and eventually becomes negligible. At the matrix size of $640,000 \times 640,000$, on $36,864$ (192×192) cores, both versions achieved over 48Tflop/s, with an overhead of 0.016% for the ABFT algorithm. As a side experiment, we implemented the naive vertical checkpointing method discussed in section 5.2, and as expected the measured overhead quickly exceeds 100%.

As the left factor is touched only once during the computation, the approach of checkpointing the result of a panel synchronously can, *a-priori*, look sound when compared to system based checkpoint, where the entire dataset is checkpointed periodically. However, as the checkpointing of a particular panel suffers from its inability to exploit the full parallelism of the platform, it is subject to a derivative of Amdahl's law, its parallel efficiency is bound by P, while the overall computation enjoys a $P \times Q$ parallel efficiency: its importance is bound to grow when the number of computing resources increases. As a consequence, in the experiments, the time to compute the naive checkpoint dominates the computation time. On the other hand, the hybrid checkpointing approach exchanges the risk of a Q-step rollback with the opportunity to benefit from a $P \times Q$ parallel efficiency for the panel checkpointing. Because of this improved parallel efficiency, the hybrid checkpointing approach benefits from a competitive level of performance, that follows the same trend as the original non fault tolerant algorithm.

6.3 Recovery Cost

In addition to the "curb" overhead of fault tolerance functions, the recovery from failure adds extra overhead to the host algorithm. There are two cases for the recovery. The first one is when failure occurs right after the reverse neighboring checkpointing of Q panels. At this moment the matrix is well protected by the checksum and therefore the lost data can be recovered directly from the checksum. We refer to this case as "failure on Q panels border". The second case is when the failure occurs during the reverse neighboring checkpointing and therefore local snapshots have to be used along with re-factorization to recover the lost data and restore the matrix state. This is referred to as the "failure within Q panels".

Figure 9 shows the overhead from these two cases for the LU factorization, along with the no-error overhead as a reference. In the "border" case, the failure is simulated to strike when the 96th panel (which is a multiple of grid columns, $6, 12, \cdots, 48$) has

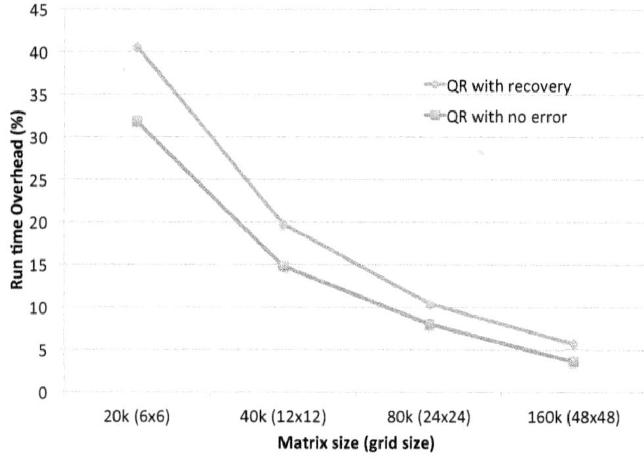

Figure 10. Weak scalability of FT-QR: run time overhead on Kraken when failures strike

just finished. In the "non-border" case, failure occurs during the $(Q+2)^{th}$ panel factorization. For example, when $Q = 12$, the failure is injected when the trailing update for the step with panel (1301,1301) finishes. From the result in Figure 9, the recovery procedure in both cases adds a small overhead that also decreases when scaled to large problem size and process grid. For largest setups, only 2-3 percent of the execution time is spent recovering from a failure.

6.4 Extension to Other factorization

The algorithm proposed in this work can be applied to a wide range of dense matrix factorizations other than LU. As a demonstration we have extended the fault tolerance functions to the ScaLAPACK QR factorization in double precision. Since QR uses a block algorithm similar to LU (and also similar to Cholesky), the integration of fault tolerance functions is mostly straightforward. Figure 10 shows the performance of QR with and without recovery. The overhead drops as the problem and grid size increase, although it remains higher than that of LU for the same problem size. This is expected: as the QR algorithm has a higher complexity than LU ($\frac{4}{3}N^3$ v.s. $\frac{2}{3}N^3$), the ABFT approach incurs more extra computation when updating checksums. Similar to the LU result, recovery adds an extra 2% overhead. At size 160,000 a failure incurs about 5.7% penalty to be recovered. This overhead becomes lower, the larger the problem or processor grid size considered.

7. Conclusion

In this paper, by assuming a failure model in which fail-stop failures can occur anytime on any process during a parallel execution, a general scheme of ABFT algorithms for protecting one-sided matrix factorizations is proposed. This scheme can be applied to a wide range of dense matrix factorizations, including Cholesky, LU and QR. A significant property of the proposed algorithms is that both the left and right factorization results are protected. ABFT is used to protect the right factor with checksum generated before, and carried along during the factorizations. A highly scalable checkpointing method is proposed to protect the left factor. This method cooperatively reutilizes the memory space originally designed to store the ABFT checksum, and has minimal overhead by strategically coalescing checkpoints of many iterations. Large scale experimental results validate the design of the proposed fault tolerance method by highlighting scalable performance and decreasing overhead for both LU and QR. In the future this work will be extended to support multiple simultaneous failures.

References

[1] Fault tolerance for extreme-scale computing workshop report, 2009.

[2] http://www.top500.org/, 2011.

[3] L. Blackford, A. Cleary, J. Choi, E. D'Azevedo, J. Demmel, I. Dhillon, J. Dongarra, S. Hammarling, G. Henry, A. Petitet, et al. *ScaLAPACK users' guide*. Society for Industrial Mathematics, 1997.

[4] G. Bosilca, R. Delmas, J. Dongarra, and J. Langou. Algorithm-based fault tolerance applied to high performance computing. *Journal of Parallel and Distributed Computing*, 69(4):410–416, 2009.

[5] A. Bouteiller, G. Bosilca, and J. Dongarra. Redesigning the message logging model for high performance. *Concurrency and Computation: Practice and Experience*, 22(16):2196–2211, 2010.

[6] G. Burns, R. Daoud, and J. Vaigl. LAM: An open cluster environment for MPI. In *Proceedings of SC'94*, volume 94, pages 379–386, 1994.

[7] F. Cappello. Fault tolerance in petascale/exascale systems: Current knowledge, challenges and research opportunities. *International Journal of High Performance Computing Applications*, 23(3):212, 2009.

[8] Z. Chen and J. Dongarra. Algorithm-based checkpoint-free fault tolerance for parallel matrix computations on volatile resources. In *IPDPS'06*, pages 10–pp. IEEE, 2006.

[9] Z. Chen and J. Dongarra. *Scalable techniques for fault tolerant high performance computing*. PhD thesis, University of Tennessee, Knoxville, TN, 2006.

[10] Z. Chen and J. Dongarra. Algorithm-based fault tolerance for fail-stop failures. *IEEE TPDS*, 19(12):1628–1641, 2008.

[11] J. Choi, J. Demmel, I. Dhillon, J. Dongarra, S. Ostrouchov, A. Petitet, K. Stanley, D. Walker, and R. Whaley. ScaLAPACK: a portable linear algebra library for distributed memory computers–design issues and performance. *Computer Physics Comm.*, 97(1-2):1–15, 1996.

[12] T. Davies, C. Karlsson, H. Liu, C. Ding, , and Z. Chen. High Performance Linpack Benchmark: A Fault Tolerant Implementation without Checkpointing. In *Proceedings of the 25th ACM International Conference on Supercomputing (ICS 2011)*. ACM.

[13] J. Dongarra, L. Blackford, J. Choi, A. Cleary, E. D'Azevedo, J. Demmel, I. Dhillon, S. Hammarling, G. Henry, A. Petitet, et al. ScaLAPACK user's guide. *Society for Industrial and Applied Mathematics, Philadelphia, PA*, 1997.

[14] E. Elnozahy, D. Johnson, and W. Zwaenepoel. The performance of consistent checkpointing. In *Reliable Distributed Systems, 1992. Proceedings., 11th Symposium on*, pages 39–47. IEEE, 1991.

[15] G. Fagg and J. Dongarra. FT-MPI: Fault tolerant MPI, supporting dynamic applications in a dynamic world. *EuroPVM/MPI*, 2000.

[16] G. Gibson. Failure tolerance in petascale computers. In *Journal of Physics: Conference Series*, volume 78, page 012022, 2007.

[17] G. Golub and C. Van Loan. *Matrix computations*. Johns Hopkins Univ Pr, 1996.

[18] D. Hakkarinen and Z. Chen. Algorithmic Cholesky factorization fault recovery. In *Parallel & Distributed Processing (IPDPS), 2010 IEEE International Symposium on*, pages 1–10. IEEE, 2010.

[19] K. Huang and J. Abraham. Algorithm-based fault tolerance for matrix operations. *Computers, IEEE Transactions on*, 100(6):518–528, 1984.

[20] V. Kumar, A. Grama, A. Gupta, and G. Karypis. *Introduction to parallel computing: design and analysis of algorithms*, volume 400. Benjamin/Cummings, 1994.

[21] C. Lu. *Scalable diskless checkpointing for large parallel systems*. PhD thesis, Citeseer, 2005.

[22] F. Luk and H. Park. An analysis of algorithm-based fault tolerance techniques* 1. *Journal of Parallel and Distributed Computing*, 5(2):172–184, 1988.

[23] J. Plank, K. Li, and M. Puening. Diskless checkpointing. *Parallel and Distributed Systems, IEEE Transactions on*, 9(10):972–986, 1998.

[24] F. Streitz, J. Glosli, M. Patel, B. Chan, R. Yates, B. Supinski, J. Sexton, and J. Gunnels. Simulating solidification in metals at high pressure: The drive to petascale computing. In *Journal of Physics: Conference Series*, volume 46, page 254. IOP Publishing, 2006.

Efficient Deadlock Avoidance for Streaming Computation with Filtering

Jeremy D. Buhler   Kunal Agrawal   Peng Li   Roger D. Chamberlain
Department of Computer Science and Engineering, Washington University in St. Louis
{jbuhler,kunal,pengli,roger}@wustl.edu

Abstract

Parallel streaming computations have been studied extensively, and many languages, libraries, and systems have been designed to support this model of computation. In particular, we consider acyclic streaming computations in which individual nodes can choose to *filter*, or discard, some of their inputs in a data-dependent manner. In these applications, if the channels between nodes have finite buffers, the computation can *deadlock*. One method of deadlock avoidance is to augment the data streams between nodes with occasional *dummy messages*; however, for general DAG topologies, no polynomial time algorithm is known to compute the intervals at which dummy messages must be sent to avoid deadlock.

In this paper, we show that deadlock avoidance for streaming computations with filtering can be performed efficiently for a large class of DAG topologies. We first present a new method where each dummy message is tagged with a destination, so as to reduce the number of dummy messages sent over the network. We then give efficient algorithms for dummy interval computation in series-parallel DAGs. We finally generalize our results to a larger graph family, which we call the *CS4 DAGs*, in which every undirected Cycle is Single-Source and Single-Sink (CS^4). Our results show that, for a large set of application topologies that are both intuitively useful and formalizable, the streaming model with filtering can be implemented safely with reasonable overhead.

Categories and Subject Descriptors C.2.4 [*Computer-Communication Networks*]: Distributed Systems—Distributed applications; D.1.3 [*Programming Techniques*]: Concurrent Programming—Distributed programming; F.1.2 [*Computation by Abstract Devices*]: Modes of Computation—Parallelism and concurrency

General Terms Algorithms, Design, Theory

Keywords Deadlock Avoidance, Graph Theory, Streaming Computation

1. Introduction

Streaming is an effective paradigm for parallelizing complex computations on large datasets across multiple computing resources. Examples of application domains that use the streaming paradigm include media [7], signal processing [15], computational science [12], data mining [6], and others [16]. Languages that explicitly support streaming semantics include Brook [1], Cg [13], StreamIt [17], and X [5]. A streaming application is typically implemented as a network of *compute nodes* connected by unidirectional communication *channels*. Abstractly, the streaming application is a directed dataflow multigraph, with the node at the tail of each edge (channel) able to transmit data, in the form of one or more discrete *messages*, to the node at its head. When a node *fires*, it may consume messages from some subset of its input channels and produce messages on some subset ot its output channels. In this paper, we consider only directed acyclic multigraphs.

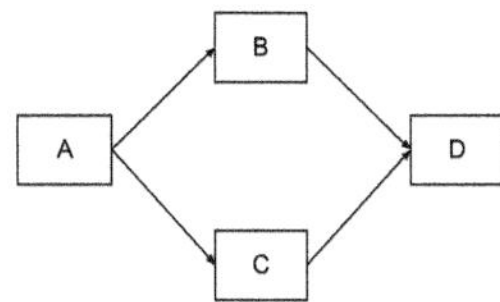

Figure 1: A simple split/join streaming topology.

Many streaming languages and libraries support the synchronous dataflow (SDF) [9] model, where, for a given input message stream, the number of messages consumed and produced by each node on each channel incident on it is known at compile time. However, the assumptions of SDF are not an intuitively good fit for all streaming applications. In particular, the node's decision on whether to send an output message in response to an input, and which subset of output channels to send messages on, may naturally be data-dependent. We say that nodes that can make such decisions at run-time exhibit *filtering* behavior.

Consider, for example, the simple split/join topology shown in Figure 1. In a streaming application, the split node A might analyze an input and decide to send it to some subset of its children for further processing. For example, an object recognition system might receive a video frame and, based on some initial segmentation and analysis in the split node, might forward that frame to one or more dedicated modules that recognize particular types of object. Each recognizer in turn might or might not trigger a "success" message to the join node D. Finally, any information collected at D might be sent downstream to be merged with other analyses that were performed in parallel on the same frame. Two applications of this type are considered in [11].

This work addresses the challenge of safely realizing streaming applications when nodes are permitted to filter. For most streaming languages, the programmer is allowed to assume infinite buffer capacity on channels that connect compute nodes. In practice, however, the compiler allocates finite channel buffers. With finite buffers, a filtering application can deadlock, even if it has no directed cycles (which is not true for SDF DAGs).

Table 1: Mercury BLAST performance

Dummy Interval	16	128
Dummy Msgs	8.51e+10	5.59e+10
Avg. Time (s)	639.8	421.0

One viable strategy for preemptively avoiding deadlocks in the presence of filtering is to send occasional *dummy messages* in addition to the regular stream of messages generated by the computation. Application nodes send dummy messages at pre-defined intervals, computed at compile time for the whole application, that are chosen to minimize the total number of dummies sent. We previously described this basic strategy and gave algorithms for computing the intervals for dummy transmission in [10].

Keeping the number of dummy messages added to a computation low, as we attempt to do, is beneficial for application performance. For example, we adopted dummy-based deadlock avoidance in Mercury BLAST [3], a streaming FPGA-based application for biological sequence comparison that exhibited deadlocks in practice. Using fewer dummy messages when possible by increasing the interval between them substantially reduced the performance impact of deadlock avoidance on Mercury BLAST, as shown in Table 1. While not every application may see such a dramatic impact, it is important to limit dummy message frequency when, as in Mercury BLAST, doing so frees up bandwidth and on a heavily loaded communication channel.

Unfortunately, the intervals at which nodes in an application must emit dummy messages to avoid deadlock while minimizing dummy message traffic are challenging to compute. In particular, our fastest algorithms for computing a safe set of such intevrals in [10] run in worst-case time exponential in the size of the application's topology, raising the question of whether a deadlock-free filtering can be implemented efficiently as part of compiling a streaming application.

In this work, we show that for a large class of intuitive and useful DAG topologies, deadlock avoidance in the presence of filtering *can* be guaranteed efficiently. Our contributions are:

1. We present a new deadlock avoidance strategy, the *Destination-Tagged Propagation Algorithm*, in which every dummy message is tagged with a specific destination and does not propagate past this destination. This strategy improves on the Propagation Algorithm of [10] by reducing the total number of dummies sent and the associated computation and communication overhead.
2. We provide small polynomial-time algorithms to compute dummy message schedules that guarantee deadlock freedom when the application topology is a series-parallel DAG, or SP-DAG [18]. Our results cover two specific runtime deadlock avoidance strategies: the Destination-Tagged Propagation Algorithm above, and an alternate, Non-Propagation Algorithm described in [10].
3. We extend our results to a larger family of topologies, which we call the CS4 DAGs, that permit limited communication between parallel branches of a computation. We precisely characterize the structure of CS4 DAGs and use this structure to extend our efficient deadlock avoidance algorithms to them. The CS4 DAGs represent an abstraction that balances expressibility with efficiency of deadlock avoidance.

Related Work

SDF was generalized to Dynamic Data Flow (DDF) by Lee [8] and Buck [2]. In a DDF graph, firing of nodes can be determined through the use of of an explicit boolean-valued [8] or integer-

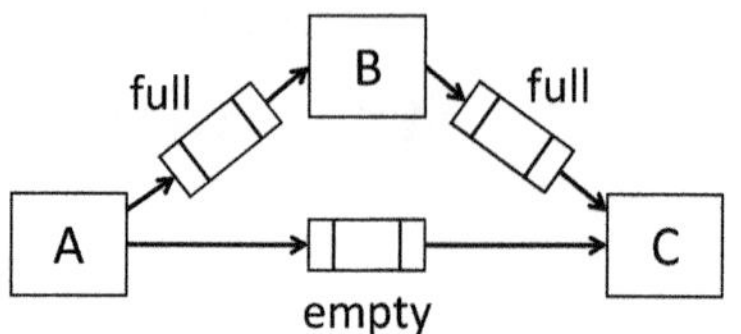

Figure 2: A deadlock condition in a streaming application.

valued [2] control input. In our streaming computation model, this control information is encapsulated within the node and is therefore unavailable to the compiler and/or scheduler. Here, synchronization between multiple streams into each node is supported via the use of a non-negative sequence number associated with each data item.

StreamIt [17] is a streaming language and compilation toolkit that supports slightly generalized SDF semantics. Applications in StreamIt are constructed from three topology primitives: pipeline, split-join, and feedback. While these three primitives generate hierarchical application topologies that facilitate compiler analysis, they limit the kinds of streaming topologies that StreamIt can support well [16]. In this paper, we will discuss broader classes of DAG topologies than those that StreamIt supports. Moreover, unlike StreamIt's split/join structures, which have special, language-defined semantics such as round-robin or broadcast, split and join nodes in this work can perform arbitrary computation and filtering just like any other node.

2. Background

In this section, we review our formal model for streaming applications with filtering, the conditions for deadlock in the model, and the dummy-message approach to deadlock avoidance. We first formulated and investigated these formalisms in [10]. We also briefly review the definition of SP-DAGs, a well-known class of graph that we will use extensively later on.

2.1 Model of Streaming Applications with Filtering

A streaming application is a DAG of computation nodes connected by reliable, one-way communication channels, each of which has a finite channel buffer. We assume that channel buffer sizes are fixed *a priori*. Input messages arrive at a unique first node of the application and are labeled with monotonically increasing sequence numbers. All channels are assumed to deliver messages in FIFO order. A node always consumes all messages with sequence number $= i$ together and may then produce messages with sequence number i on any subset of its input channels.

A node does not necessarily need messages with sequence number i on all its input channels, but it must be sure that no message with sequence number i will arrive on a channels after it has already consumed other messages with sequence number i. Therefore, a node can only accept input with sequence number i when, for each of its input channels, the head of the channel buffer contains a message with sequence number $\geq i$. If an input of sequence number i to a node does not result in an output on a given channel, we say that the node *filters* the input i on that channel.

In the presence of finite buffers between nodes, filtering behavior can lead to deadlock, as illustrated in Figure 2. If the buffer from A to C is empty because A filters its output to C and the buffers from A to B and B to C are full, the application is deadlocked. A must wait for B to consume an input before it can proceed; B must wait for C to consume an input; and C must wait until it sees an input from A.

Any cycle of G can be decomposed into a sequence of nodes, where alternating nodes have two incoming and two outgoing directed paths on C. As Figure 2 illustrates, a deadlock arises in a DAG G through the creation of a *blocking cycle*. Roughly, a deadlock can occur whenever each of these nodes has a directed path with completely full buffers on one side, and an oppositely directed path with completely empty buffers (due to filtering) on the other side. Therefore, any undirected cycle has a potential to become a blocking cycle and cause a deadlock.

We verified the precise conditions under which deadlock can occur in this model in [10].

2.2 Deadlock Avoidance Through Dummy Messages

Our strategy to avoid deadlock is to have nodes periodically send *dummy messages* – content-free messages whose sequence number is that of some input that was filtered by the node. The idea of dummy messages originates in the parallel discrete-event simulation (PDES) literature [14], which used null messages for deadlock avoidance in conservative PDES algorithms. A dummy message prevents a blocking cycle from forming by ensuring that the "empty" side of a potentially blocking cycle cannot remain empty (i.e., free of message traffic) while the "full" side fills completely. To meet this goal, dummy messages are sent at fixed intervals calculated from the buffer sizes of channels in the application's network.

The choice of dummy message intervals can be made in multiple ways, each corresponding to a different runtime strategy for sending dummies. Consider a DAG with node u and a potentially blocking cycle C, such that u has two outgoing edges. In order to prevent C from becoming a blocking cycle, we want to ensure that at runtime, one of the two directed paths out of u cannot become full of blocked messages while the other path remains empty.

We described two runtime strategies for sending dummy messages in [10]. In one strategy, which we call the "Propagation Algorithm", only nodes with two outgoing edges on some undirected cycle (like node u) send dummy messages, which may not be filtered but must be propagated on *all* output channels of any node they reach. In a second strategy, the "Non-Propagation Algorithm," *every* node may send dummy messages, but the dummies are never propagated beyond the channel on which they are emitted. In this case, not only u but all nodes on cycle C work together to prevent C from becoming a blocking cycle.

In the Propagation Algorithm, we compute dummy intervals at compile time as follows. Consider an edge e leaving a node u with at least two outgoing edges. Let F be the set of edges leaving at u, and let $\mathcal{C}$ be the set of undirected simple cycles that contain both e and another edge from $F - \{e\}$. For a cycle $C \in \mathcal{C}$, let e' be other edegs out of u on cycle C, and let $L(C, e)$ be the total buffer size of the maximal directed path on C starting from u via e'. The dummy interval $[e]$ for e is then given by

$$[e] = \min_{C \in \mathcal{C}} L(C, e).$$

Intuitively, $[e]$ is chosen short enough to ensure that for every potentially blocking cycle C involving e and another edge e' out of u, u sends a dummy along e often enough that the path along e' cannot become full while the path along e remains empty.

We use Figure 3 as a dataflow graph to illustrate the dummy interval calculation for the Propagation Algorithm. Let $[ab]_p$ be edge ab's dummy interval, and let $L(abef)$ be the path $abef$'s total buffer size. We show the calculation process for some edges rather than all of them for illustrative purpose. Let cycles $C_1 = abdc$, $C_2 = abefdc$, and $C_3 = bdfe$, respectively. Then the algorithm dictates

$[ac]_p = \min(L(C_1, ac), L(C_2, ac)) = 7;$
$[bd]_p = L(C_3, bd) = 6.$

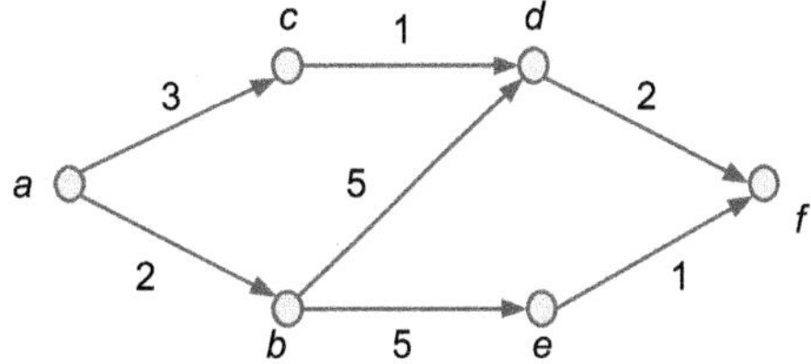

Figure 3: A DAG with three undirected cycles

The intervals $[cd]_p$, $[df]_p$, and $[ef]_p$ are ∞, since no dummy message need be generated on these channels.

Given a calculated interval I_p, during runtime, a node sends a dummy message to the channel if the current sequence number $CSN \geq I_p + LDS$, where LDS is the sequence number of last dummy message sent to this channel. For example, on channel bd, if a dummy message is sent with $LDS = 10$, after the node b computes on sequence number 16, it sends a dummy message to bd regardless of filtering. If b never receives a token with sequence number 16, which is filtered by a, b then sends a dummy message after it computes on a next higher sequence number.

In the Propagation Algorithm, every node on a directed path out of a dummy-emitting source receives a dummy message as often as the source sends one on its first edge. In contrast, the Non-Propagation Algorithm does not forward messages beyond a single edge, so the edges in a path must collaborate to ensure that the end of the path receives a dummy often enough to prevent deadlock. Consider an edge e leaving node u. Let $\mathcal{C}'$ be the set of undirected simple cycles containing e, and for each cycle $C \in \mathcal{C}'$, let $L(C, e)$ be as above. Let $h(C, e)$ be the number of edges in the maximal directed path out of u on C that begins with e. Then the dummy interval for e is then given by

$$[e] = \min_{C \in \mathcal{C}'} L(C, e)/h(C, e).$$

In effect, we divide the dummy interval needed to prevent deadlock on each cycle C evenly among the edges on the path starting with e, so that the end of this path receives a dummy at least as often as it did in the Propagation Algorithm.

We still use Figure 3 to explain the calculation. Let and $[ab]_n$ be edge ab's dummy intervals for the Non-Propagation Algorithm, and let $h(abef)$ be the number of hops on path $abef$. For the Non-Propagation Algorithm, we have

$[ac]_n = \min(\lceil L(C_1, ac)/h(acd) \rceil, \lceil L(C_2, ac)/h(acdf) \rceil) = 3;$
$[bd]_n = \min(\lceil L(C_1, bd)/h(abd) \rceil, \lceil L(C_3, bd)/h(bdf) \rceil) = 2;$
$[cd]_n = \min(\lceil L(C_1, cd)/h(acd) \rceil, \lceil L(C_2, cd)/h(acdf) \rceil) = 3.$

The runtime node behavior in the Non-Propagation Algorithm is also different from that in the Propagation Algorithm. Given a calculated interval I_n, a node sends a dummy message to the channel if the current output is filtered and the current sequence number $CSN = I_n + LTN$, where LTN is the sequence number of last token, whichever a data token or a dummy message, sent to this channel. For example, if a token with sequence number 10 is sent to bd, and b filters sequence numbers 11 and 12. After filtering 12, b should send a dummy message to bd with sequence number 12. However, if b does not filter 12, no dummy message is needed and b simply updates bd's LTN to 12.

The above methods apply to general DAGs, but a direct implementation of them to compute dummy intervals requires worst-case time exponential in the size of the DAG (since a DAG may have exponentially many undirected simple cycles). It is currently unknown whether polynomial-time algorithms exist for dummy interval computation on general DAGs.

2.3 SP-DAGs

Series-parallel (SP) DAGs, which were defined by Valdes et al. [18], intuitively describe a large class of natural streaming topologies that can be built up recursively via pipelining and parallel splits and joins.

DEFINITION 1 (**Series-parallel DAG**). *A series-parallel DAG (SP-DAG) is a connected, directed acyclic multigraph with two distinguished terminals, a source and a sink. The set of all SP-DAGs is defined recursively as follows:*

Base*: a source and sink connected by any non-zero multiplicity of edges is an SP-DAG.*

Ind. 1 *(Serial composition, Sc): if H_1 and H_2 are SP-DAGs, connecting them by merging the sink of H_1 and the source of H_2 yields an SP-DAG $Sc(H_1, H_2)$.*

Ind. 2 *(Parallel composition, Pc): if H_1 and H_2 are SP-DAGs, connecting them by merging the sources of H_1 and H_2, and the sinks of H_1 and H_2, yields an SP-DAG $Pc(H_1, H_2)$.*

For example, in Figure 1, each of the four edges AB, BD, AC, and CD is a base-case SP-DAG; we have $ABD = Sc(AB, BD)$, $ACD = Sc(AC, CD)$, and $ABCD = Pc(ABD, ACD)$. We sometimes refer to subgraphs H_1 and H_2 in the composition operations as *components* of the composed graph.

3. Destination-Tagged Dummy Messages

In the Propagation Algorithm, whenever any node receives a dummy message, it propagates it along all its outgoing edges. Therefore, if a node u generates a dummy message on edge (u, v), it is received by all the successors of v in the DAG, even if it is no longer useful. These extra propagation steps incur needless communication overhead in the DAG.

To avoid unnecessary overhead, we devise a new method, the *Destination-Tagged Propagation Algorithm*. As before, only source nodes can generate dummy messages, but these messages are now tagged with a destination node d. When a node receives a dummy message with destination d, it does not necessarily forward it along all its outbound edges; rather, it forwards the message only along edges that can reach d. (Node d itself need not propagate the message at all.) Under this scheme,unlike the previous algorithm, a message need never propagate to successors of its destination node.

Because each source can generate dummy messages for multiple destinations, each edge can have more than one dummy interval associated with it. Formally, we represent the *dummy message schedule* of an edge e as a set $[e] = \{p_1, p_2, ..., p_k\}$, where each $p_i = (\tau_i, d_i)$ is a *dummy interval-destination pair*. τ_i represents an interval at which a dummy message must be sent, while d_i represents its destination node. In addition, each dummy message pair p_i has a counter c_i associated with it, and the maximum value of the counter is c_i. A source node uses the dummy message schedule and the counters to decide when to send dummy messages along e. In Sections 4 and 6, we show how to efficiently compute the dummy message schedules for SP-DAGs and CS4 DAGs respectively, and also how nodes must behave at run-time in order to correctly propagate tagged dummy messages.

4. Efficient Deadlock Avoidance for SP-DAGs

We now show that restricting filtering application topologies to SP-DAGs permits efficient implementations of both the Destination-Tagged Propagation Algorithm and the Non-Propagation Algorithm for deadlock avoidance. We first briefly cover the properties of SP-DAGs that allow us to efficiently calculate dummy schedules for these topologies. We then describe how to compute dummy schedules for both avoidance algorithms in small polynomial time. We also specify the runtime behavior required of nodes in each algorithm. Finally, we argue that this behavior, in conjunction with its companion method for determining dummy intervals, guarantees deadlock freedom for SP-DAGs.

4.1 SP-DAG preliminaries

The next few lemmas elucidate the undirected cycle structure of SP-DAGs, which we will exploit later to build efficient deadlock avoidance algorithms. In particular, we use the property, verified in Lemma 4.4, that every undirected cycle on an SP-DAG has a single source and a single sink. We also use the hierarchical decomposition structure of SP-DAGs to efficiently compute dummy message schedules.

OBSERVATION 1. *In an SP-DAG, every node has an immediate postdominator (follows trivially from single-sink property).*

LEMMA 4.1. *In an SP-DAG G, let Z be a node with at least two outgoing edges. Let W be the immediate postdominator of Z. Then for any directed path P from Z to W, Z dominates all nodes of P other than W.*

Proof. By induction on the structure of G.

Base: in an SP-DAG with a single multi-edge, P is a single edge from Z to W. Z trivially dominates itself.

Ind.: Otherwise, G is either $Sc(H_1, H_2)$ or $Pc(H_1, H_2)$ for SP-DAGs H_1, H_2. If Z is the source of G, then Z trivially dominates all of G, since SP-DAGs have a single source. Z can not be the sink of G since the sink has no outgoing edges.

Now Z lies either in $H_1 - H_2$ or in $H_2 - H_1$, or $G = Sc(H_1, H_2)$ and Z is the sink of H_1 and the source of H_2. If Z is in $H_1 - H_2$, then H_1's sink always postdominates Z, so W, the immediate postdominator of Z, is a node in H_1. Applying the IH to subgraph H_1, the Lemma holds for Z and W. Analogous reasoning holds if Z is in $H_2 - H_1$. Finally, if Z is the source of H_2 and the sink of H_1, then W is in H_2 and Z dominates all of H_2. □

LEMMA 4.2. *Let $G = Pc(H_1, H_2)$ be an SP-DAG, where X is its source and Y is its sink. Let Z be a node of $H_1 - \{X, Y\}$ that has at least two outgoing edges e and e' in G. Let C be an undirected simple cycle that contains both e and e'. Then C contains no edge edge $e'' \in H_2$.*

Proof. Suppose not. WLOG, let the counterexample simple cycle C leave Z via edge $e = Z \to U$ and return via edge $e' = Z \to V$. Since C passes through an edge in H_2, it must also pass through both X and Y, since those are the only two nodes that connect H_1 and H_2. So there must be two vertex-disjoint undirected paths in H_1: P_1 goes from Z to U to Y, and P_2 (entirely in H_1) goes from Z to V to X.

Let W be the immediate postdominator of Z, which lies in H_1. We claim that both paths P_1 and P_2 must pass through W.

Suppose path P_1 does not pass through W. Now U is a predecessor of W, while Y is not, so there is some first edge in P_1 that connects a predecessor A of W to a non-predecessor B. We have two cases.

1. If the edge is oriented $A \to B$, then there is a directed path from Z to A to B to Y that bypasses W, which contradicts W's postdomination of Z.
2. If the edge is oriented $B \to A$, then B is not a successor of W, since G is acyclic. There is then a directed path from X to B to A that bypasses Z, which contracts Z's domination of A by Lemma 4.1.

Conclude that P_1 must indeed pass through W.

Suppose P_2 doesn't pass through W. Now V is a successor of Z, while X is not; hence, there is some first edge on path P_2 that connects a successor A of Z to a non-successor B. This edge must be oriented $B \to A$, else B would be a successor of Z.

Now A cannot be a predecessor of W; otherwise, there would be a directed path from X to B to A that bypasses Z, contradicting Z's dominance of A by Lemma 4.1. Hence, A is a successor of W. The subpath of P_2 from V to A therefore contains some first edge connecting a predecessor C of W to a successor D of W. This edge must be oriented $C \to D$, since G is acyclic. But then there is a directed path from Z to C to D to Y that bypasses W, which contradicts W's postdomination of Z. Conclude that P_2 must indeed pass through W.

Since P_1 and P_2 both contain W, they are not vertex disjoint, leading us to a contradiction. □

LEMMA 4.3. *For an SP-DAG $G = Pc(H_1, H_2)$, any undirected simple cycle C in G that has edges in both H_1 and H_2 consists of a pair of directed paths P_1 through H_1 and P_2 through H_2 that connect the source X of G to its sink Y.*

Proof. We know from Lemma 4.2 that undirected simple cycles in G that traverse edges of both H_1 and H_2 do not pass through two outgoing edges of any node other than X. Moreover, each such cycle passes through two incoming edges of node Y, since Y does not have any outgoing edges.

Let P_1 be the directed path on C that exits X in (WLOG) H_1. If this path were to terminate at some node Z prior to Y, then the portion of cycle following P_1 would traverse two adjacent incoming edges of Z. But if the cycle leaves Z via an edge that points into Z and eventually reaches Y via an edge that points into Y, it must at some point "change direction" by passing through two outgoing edges of a node Q other than X, which is impossible by Lemma 4.2.

Conclude that C must be fully directed from X to Y in both components. □

LEMMA 4.4. *Each undirected simple cycle in an SP-DAG G has a single source and a single sink.*

Proof. By induction on the structure of G.

Base: Trivially true for a single multi-edge.

Ind.: If $G = Sc(H_1, H_2)$, then the property holds for H_1 and H_2, and their serial composition creates no new cycles. Hence the property holds for every cycle of G.

If $G = Pc(H_1, H_2)$, then every new cycle created by their parallel composition connects the common source X of G to its common sink Y by directed paths passing through H_1 and H_2, respectively. All such cycles therefore have one source X and one sink Y. □

LEMMA 4.5. *If X is the source for two components with sinks Y and Z, and these components share a common edge, then either Y is a successor of Z in G or vice versa.*

(Proof omitted due to space limitations.)

4.2 Destination-Tagged Propagation Algorithm

We now present the Destination-Tagged Propagation Algorithm as applied to SP-DAGs. We will describe both the compile-time algorithm used to compute dummy schedules for each edge, and the runtime behavior of nodes. The calculation of dummy schedules at compile time requires $O(|G|^2)$ time.

In our approach, the source node of each component H of an SP-DAG is responsible for preventing deadlock on undirected cycles of H that cross more than one of its sub-components. Since a node can be a source for multiple distinct components, it may need to send dummy messages that target multiple sinks. Therefore, an edge e from source u has a dummy message schedule $[e] = \{p_1, p_2, ..., p_k\}$, where in each pair $p_i = (\tau_i, d_i)$, d_i is a sink of some component for which u is the source. τ_i is the interval at which a dummy message must be sent to sink d_i. We keep this list of pairs sorted by τ_i. In addition, for each edge, we have at most one pair for a particular destination.

Computing Dummy Message Schedules

At compile time, we compute the dummy message schedule for each edge using a recursive decomposition of the SP-DAG as follows:

1. We first recursively decompose G according to the construction rules for SP-DAGs, using e.g. the linear-time recognition algorithm of Valdes, Tarjan, and Lawler [18]. The decomposition results in a tree T whose leaves are single (multi-)edge graphs and whose internal nodes are labeled with the composition operators *Sc* or *Pc*, such that applying the composition operations in post-order results in graph G. The size of this tree is $O(|G|)$.
2. For every component H of G, we compute $L(H)$, which is the length of a shortest directed path (with buffer lengths as edge weights) from the source of H to its sink. This calculation can be done bottom-up on the tree T in $O(|G|)$ time.
3. We then compute schedules for all edges in total time $O(|G|^2)$ as follows.

The schedule computation algorithm performs a post-order traversal of G's component decomposition tree T. For each component H of G, we have three possibilities.

Case 1: Say H is a leaf of T corresponding to a multi-edge $X \to Y$. Let e be one edge of this multi-edge, and let τ be the minimum buffer size over all edges other than e between X and Y. Set $[e] = \{(\tau, Y)\}$. If $X \to Y$ is only a single edge, then $[e] = \emptyset$.

Case 2: Say $H = Sc(H_1, H_2)$. Since H_1 and H_2 are joined by a single articulation point, their composition creates no new simple cycles. The schedules for edges in H_1 and H_2 do not change.

Case 3: Say $H = Pc(H_1, H_2)$, where X is H's source and Y is H's sink. Now we add new pairs for each edge e out of X in H_1 as follows:

$$[e] \leftarrow [e] \cup \{(L(H_2), Y)\}.$$

Similarly, for each edge e' out of X in H_2, we set a new interval

$$[e'] \leftarrow [e'] \cup \{(L(H_1), Y)\}.$$

Finally, to eliminate unneeded dummy messages, we postprocess the schedule of each edge e as follows.

- If $[e]$ has more than one pair with the same destination, we retain only the pair with the smallest interval τ_i.
- If $[e]$ contains two pairs $p_a = (\tau_a, d_a)$ and $p_b = (\tau_b, d_b)$, such that d_b succeeds d_a and $\tau_b \leq \tau_a$, then we remove p_a.

This postprocessing requires only $O(|G|)$ time per edge. We now prove that this calculation preserves the invariants we require.

LEMMA 4.6. *In any edge's dummy schedule $[e]$, there is at most one dummy interval per destination, and the dummy messages are sorted by increasing τ.*

Proof. The first step of postprocessing ensures that there is at most one dummy message per destination on an edge. In addition, since the dummy intervals are calculated in post-order, if pair $p_i = (\tau_i, d_i)$ comes before pair $p_j = (\tau_j, d_j)$ in the original calculation, then d_j is a successor of d_i. Therefore, after step 2 of postprocessing, the schedule is sorted by increasing τ_i. □

Runtime Node Behavior

We now describe how the schedules of each edge are used at runtime to decide when to send dummy messages. We assume that the pairs of each edge's schedule $[e]$ are ordered by increasing τ. To track the time between successive dummy messages to each destination, edge e maintains a counter c_i for each pair p_i. The value of counter c_i ranges from 0 to τ_i.

Each time node X processes an incoming message, it acts as follows:

- If the message is a dummy (or a real message that is also marked as dummy), and X is not its destination, then X schedules a dummy message on all its outgoing edges and zeros out all counters on these edges.
- If the message is not a dummy, or is a dummy message with destination X, then X increments all counters on all outgoing edges, starting with the largest τ_i (end of the list). If a counter c_i on edge e reaches its maximum value, then X schedules a dummy message with destination d_i along e and zeroes out all counters c_j on e with $j \leq i$.

In all cases, if X has scheduled a dummy message on an edge e, and is also sending a real message on edge e, then it merges the dummy message with the real message and sends them as a single message.

Proof of Freedom from Deadlock

We now argue that the Destination-Tagged Propagation Algorithm ensures freedom from deadlock for SP-DAGs. As noted in Section 2.1, deadlock can arise in a DAG G only through the creation of a blocking cycle. Since SP-DAGs have exactly one source and one sink on each cycle, a blocking cycle consists of one path from the source to the sink with full buffers and another path from the source to the sink with empty buffers.

We claim that, because of the design of our dummy message scheme above, no sequence of messages sent on G can ever give rise to a blocking cycle, no matter how nodes choose to filter the non-dummy messages. The following sequence of results proves this claim.

LEMMA 4.7. *Let H be a component of G with source X and sink Y. If X propagates an incoming dummy message, then that message will reach Y.*

Proof. A dummy message arriving at X was generated by the source of some super-component H' of H with sink Z. By the properties of SP-DAGs, Z must be either Y or a successor of Y. In either case, all paths from X to Z lead through Y, so Y will eventually receive the dummy message. □

LEMMA 4.8. *If an edge's schedule includes pairs $p_i = (\tau_i, d_i)$ and $p_j = (\tau_j, d_j)$, and $\tau_i < \tau_j$, then d_j is a successor of d_i.*

Proof. Step 1 of postprocessing ensures that $d_i \neq d_j$. By Lemma 4.5, one of these nodes is a successor of the other. If d_i were a successor of d_j, then step 2 of postprocessing would have removed p_j. □

LEMMA 4.9. *Suppose that, for edge e out of node X, pair $(\tau_i, d_i) \in [e]$. For each τ_i messages that X receives, it sends at least one dummy message along e that will reach d_i.*

Proof. Consider a span of τ_i consecutive messages received by X. Before these messages arrive, counter c_i on e has some value $< \tau_i$. One of two cases will occur:

1. If one of the messages is a dummy that does not target X, then by Lemma 4.7, the dummy will reach d_i.
2. If all the messages either are non-dummies or target X, then either counter c_i will increase until it reaches τ_i, triggering a dummy message to d_i, or some other counter c_j, $j > i$, will reach τ_j, triggering a dummy message to d_j. By Lemma 4.8, we know that d_j is a successor of d_i, and so this message will pass through d_i.

□

LEMMA 4.10. *Consider a parallel component $H = Pc(H_1, H_2)$ with source X and sink Y. Let $L(H_1)$ be the length of a shortest path from X to Y through H_1. Consider any edge $e \in H_2$ that starts at X. In any time period during which X receives $L(H_1)$ messages, it sends (or forwards) at least one dummy message on e with destination either Y or a successor of Y.*

Proof. When the schedule-setting algorithm first processes H, it adds the pair $(L(H_1), Y)$ to $[e]$. Postprocessing will remove this pair only if X is also scheduled to send a more frequent dummy message to Y or to one of its successors. Hence, Lemma 4.9 guarantees that X will send at least one dummy message along e that reaches Y for each $L(H_1)$ messages it receives. □

THEOREM 4.11. *If dummy messages are sent as described in Section 4.2, using the interval-destination pairs computed as described in Section 4.2, then deadlock cannot occur in G.*

Proof. Suppose a deadlock does occur in G. Then there must be a blocking cycle C in G. Since G is an SP-DAG, C lies in some smallest parallel component H and consists of two directed paths s_1 and s_2 joining H's source X to its sink Y.

Suppose WLOG that s_1 is full and s_2 is empty. We can decompose H into parallel sub-components H_1 and H_2 such that $s_1 \subseteq H_1$ and $s_2 \subseteq H_2$. By construction, the total length of all edges' buffers along path s_1 is $\geq L(H_1)$, while that along s_2 is $\geq L(H_2)$.

Now consider the first edge e on path s_2, which leaves source X. This edge lies in component H_2. For s_1 to fill, X must have received and passed on at least $L(H_1)$ messages. But then Lemma 4.10 guarantees that X has sent a dummy message along e within its last $L(H_1)$ received messages. This dummy will eventually propagate to Y, where it will allow Y to consume at least one of the buffered messages from s_1. Since s_1 remains full, we conclude that the dummy must still be somewhere on path s_2, and so s_2 cannot be empty. This contradicts our assumption that cycle C is blocking. □

4.3 The Non-Propagation Algorithm on SP-DAGs

We now show how to efficiently calculate dummy intervals for the Non-Propagation Algorithm when the graph topology is restricted to be an SP-DAG. The approach is broadly similar to that for the Destination-Tagged Propagation Algorithm, except that the schedule $[e]$ for an edge e now consists of only a single pair whose destination is the node at the end of the edge. For this section, we therefore adopt the convention that $[e]$ is a single number, the dummy interval for e. In addition, all nodes, not just sources, may generate dummy messages on their outgoing edges.

Dummy interval calculation

Our algorithm for dummy interval computation is as follows.

1. Decompose the graph into a tree of components.
2. Compute $L(H)$ for each component H, where $L(H)$ is the shortest path from H's source to H's sink, with buffer lengths as edge weights.

3. Compute $h(H)$ for each component H, where $h(H)$ is the longest path (in terms of the number of hops) from the source of H to its sink.
   - For a single multi-edge, $h(H) = 1$.
   - If $H = Sc(H_1, H_2)$, $h(H) = h(H_1) + h(H_2)$.
   - If $H = Pc(H_1, H_2)$, $h(H) = \max(h(H_1), h(H_2))$.
4. Compute $h(H, e)$ for each edge $e \in H$, where $h(H)$ is the longest path (in terms of the number of hops) from the source of H to its sink that passes through e. For a single multi-edge, $h(H, e) = 1$. For a series composition, for all $e \in H_1$, $h(H, e) = h(H_1, e) + h(H_2)$. Similarly for $e \in H_2$, $h(H, e) = h(H_2, e) + h(H_1)$. For parallel composition, if $e \in H_2$, $h(H, e) = h(H_1, e)$. Similarly for $e \in H_2$. All these computations can be done in $O(|G|^2)$ time.
5. Compute the dummy interval $[e]$ for each edge e in a bottom-up fashion.

The first four steps in the above procedure are straightforward. For the fifth step, we visit the components of T in post-order. When considering component H, we update $[e]$ for all the edges in H considering only cycles internal to H.

Case 1: If H is a multi-edge from $X \to Y$, let e be an edge from X to Y. If we consider only cycles internal to H, $L(H, e)$ is the minimum buffer size over all edges other than e between X and Y, and $h(H, e) = 1$. Therefore, the calculation in this case is identical to the that for the Dummy-Tagged Propagation Algorithm.

Case 2: If $H = Sc(H_1, H_2)$, serial composition introduces no new simple cycles through e, so $[e]$ is unchanged.

Case 3: If $H = Pc(H_1, H_2)$, suppose WLOG that e is in H_1. Let X be the source of H, and let Y be its sink. Every new cycle created by the parallel composition consists of two confluent paths from X to Y, one in each of H_1 and H_2. Let C be the newly created cycle that traverses a longest (in hop count) directed path in H_1 that includes e and returns via a shortest (in buffer length) path in H_2. Then the ratio $L(C, e)/h(C, e)$ for C is minimum among all new cycles created by the composition. Since, $L(C, e) = L(H_2)$ and $h(C, e) = h(H_1, e)$, we have $[e] = \min([e], L(H_2)/h(H_1, e))$. The symmetric computation applies if e is in H_2.

Each case above takes constant time per edge in the component H, or $O(|G|)$ time per component. Conclude that the entire tree traversal is $O(|G|^2)$.

Runtime node behavior and correctness

We previously described the runtime behavior of nodes for the Non-Propagation Algorithm in a general graph in [10]. Briefly, a node sends a dummy message along an edge e if it filters $[e]$ continuous messages on edge e. This behavior applies unchanged to SP-DAGs. The dummy intervals $[e]$ of the previous section minimize a ratio between the length of a component-dependent shortest path and the number of hops in an edge-dependent longest path, as for the computation we previously gave for general graphs. Correctness for SP-DAGs therefore follows by the proof given for the algorithm on general graphs [10].

5. CS4 DAGs: a Larger Set of Simple Streaming Topologies

We have shown how to efficiently prevent deadlock in SP-DAGs, a large, practically useful class of DAG topologies that can be constructed with simple composition operations. A natural question at this point is, do there exist "natural" topologies that are not SP-DAGs? Might these topologies also have efficient algorithms for deadlock avoidance?

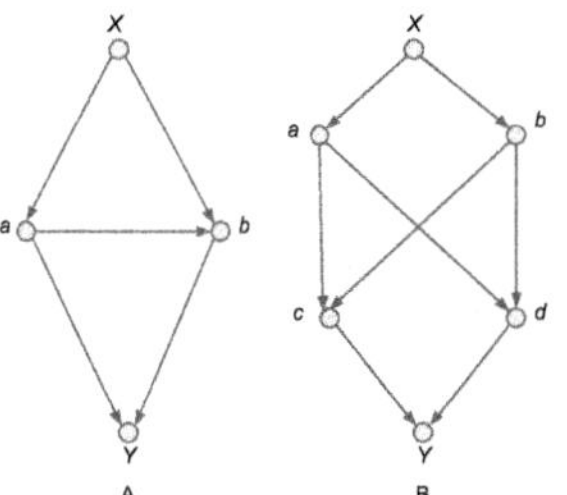

Figure 4: two simple non-SP-DAGs.

Figure 4 shows two simple two-terminal DAGs that are not SP-DAGs. The topology on the left augments a trivial split/join with a one-way communication channel linking its two sides; it is perhaps the simplest DAG that is not series-parallel. The topology on the right adds slightly more complexity, creating a "butterfly" structure like that commonly used to decompose large FFT computations. A key feature distinguishing the two graphs is that, in the left-hand example, every undirected simple cycle has only one source and one sink. This property is true for SP-DAGs, and we exploited it implicitly in the algorithms of the previous section. On the other hand, the butterfly graph contains a cycle *a-c-b-d* with two sources and two sinks.

In this section, we characterize the set of all DAGs whose undirected cycles each contain one source and one sink. The next section shows that all such DAGs are amenable to efficient deadlock avoidance using generalizations of our algorithms from Sections 4.2 and 4.3.

DEFINITION 2. *Let G be a DAG with a single source and sink. We say that G is "CS4" if every undirected simple* **C***ycle in G has a* **S***ingle* **S***ource and a* **S***ingle* **S***ink (for short, CS^4).*

A streaming application with the butterfly topology of Figure 4B is neither an SP-DAG nor even a CS4 DAG. However, it can be transformed to topologies with these properties by removing and redirecting certain graph edges. To transform this topology to a CS4 DAG without adding or removing nodes, we remove edge *ad* and add a directed edge from *c* to *d*. All messages passed from *a* to *d* directly in the original topology would then be routed via node *c*. However, if we are limited to using only SP-DAGs, besides removing *ad* and adding *cd*, we would also need to remove edge *bd* and route messages from *b* to *d* via node *c*, as Figure 5 shows. Hence, we can realize the original topology as a CS4 DAG with fewer changes than are needed to realize it as an SP-DAG.

A practical consequence of the difference between the CS4 and SP-DAG realizations of Figure 4B is that the CS4 DAG requires removing fewer edges, and hence less forwarding of messages that were delivered directly in the original topology. Moreover, the total number of messages sent is greater for the SP-DAG than for the CS4 DAG. As our experiments illustrate, reducing the total number of messages sent by a given node can significantly improve its real-world performance.

We can formally characterize CS4 graphs by the absence of a forbidden graph minor as follows.

LEMMA 5.1. *G is CS4 only if no subgraph of G is homeomorphic to K_4, the complete graph on 4 vertices.*

Proof. Suppose G has a subgraph H homeomorphic to K_4. H has 4 "corner" vertices and 6 connections (which may in general be paths rather than single edges) connecting them in the pattern of K_4. There are therefore 12 incidences of connections on corner vertices in H. WLOG, suppose that at least 6 of these are incoming. Now we have two cases.

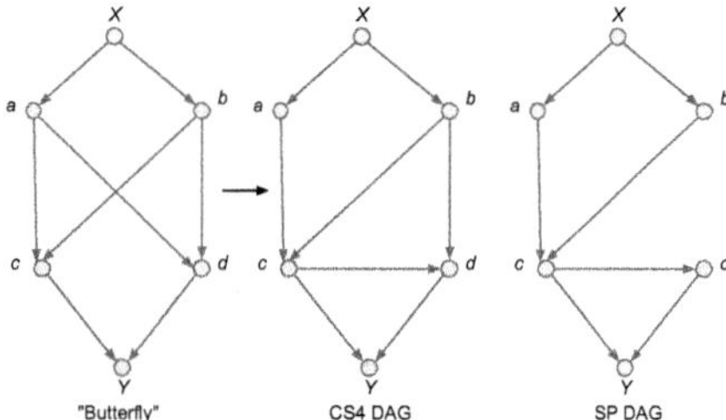

Figure 5: transforming butterfly to CS4 DAG and SP-DAG.

1. Two vertices X and Y of H have exactly two incoming edges apiece.
2. One vertex has 3 incoming edges.

Consider case 1. If the (unique) shared connection between X and Y is oriented identically w/r to X and Y (either into both or out of both), then it is possible to find a cycle through X and Y with two sinks. Now consider the case when the connection $X - Y$ is directed out of one vertex and into the other. Suppose WLOG that connection $x - y$ is directed out of X and into Y. Let W and Z be the other two corner vertices of H.

Exactly one of the connections $Y - W$ and $Y - Z$ must be directed out of Y. Suppose WLOG that $Y - Z$ is directed out of Y. Because each of X and Y have exactly two incoming edges, we know the following: (1) $X - Z$ must be directed into X; (2) $W - X$ must be directed into X; (3) $W - Y$ must be directed into Y. Now $Y - Z$ must be directed into Z; otherwise, there must be a sink on this connection, and the cycle $XWYZ$ would contain two sinks. It follows that $X - Z$ is directed out of Z; otherwise, X and Z would constitute the forbidden case (1).

Now we established above that $Y - Z$ may not contain a sink. Similarly, $X - Z$ may not contain a sink because of cycle XWZ, and $X - Y$ may not contain a sink because of cycle XWY. Hence, cycle XYZ must be a directed cycle, which is forbidden because G is a DAG.

Consider case 2 above, where one corner vertex v of H has three incoming edges. Then no other corner vertex of H can have two incoming edges without creating a cycle with two sinks. Since H has at least six incoming edges on its corner vertices, it follows that the other three corner vertices of H each have exactly one incoming, and hence two outgoing, edges. Repeat the argument of Case (1) for any two of these vertices, swapping "in" and "out".

Conclude that there is no way to direct the edges of H so as to ensure that all its cycles have one source and one sink. □

Now absence of K_4 is a characteristic property of *undirected* series-parallel graphs [4]. Hence, we may expect that CS4 DAGs have an undirected series-parallel structure. However, this does not imply that a CS4 DAG is an SP-DAG; our simple four-node graph above provides a counterexample. Fortunately, as we now show, it turns out that just a small amount of extra complexity is needed to capture all CS4 DAGs.

DEFINITION 3. *A 2-path cycle is a DAG consisting of a single source X, a single sink Y, and two directed paths connecting X to Y that are disjoint except at their endpoints.*

DEFINITION 4. *Let C be a cycle. A chord graph H is a DAG with a single source and sink that connects two vertices of C, such that H's source and sink lie on C.*

DEFINITION 5. *Let C be a 2-path cycle with paths P_1 and P_2. A cross-link is a chord graph that connects a vertex of P_1 to a vertex of P_2, where neither endpoint of the connection is C's source or sink. A down-link is a chord graph that is not a cross-link.*

DEFINITION 6. *An* SP-ladder *G is a DAG consisting of a 2-path cycle with paths P_1 and P_2, called the outer cycle of G, and one or more chord graphs $H_1 \dots H_k$, such that:*

- *Each H_i is an SP-DAG;*
- *At least one H_i is a cross-link;*
- *If G contains two chord graphs with endpoints (u_1, v_1) and (u_2, v_2), then these chord graphs do not cross; that is, in tracing the outer cycle around G, we never encounter both u_2 and v_2 between u_1 and v_1.*

Intuitively, we call G an SP-ladder because it can be viewed as a 2-path cycle "decorated" with non-cross-link chord graphs, plus one or more cross-links connecting the paths, none of which cross each other. The cross-links are similar to the rungs of a ladder. Examples of simple and complex SP-ladders are given in Figure 6.

DEFINITION 7. *Say that a cycle C of SP-ladder G traverses a chord graph H if C passes through a node of H other than its source or sink but is not confined to H.*

LEMMA 5.2. *If an undirected simple cycle C in G traverses a chord graph H, then C contains a directed path in H from its source u to its sink v.*

Proof. C reaches an internal vertex of H from outside, so it must consist of a simple path P in H that connects u to v, plus a path to return from v to u outside H. We claim that path P is directed. Suppose not; P enters and leaves H through edges directed out of its source and into its sink, so P must contain an internal source at some node Z. But Lemma 4.2 showed that there is no simple path connecting the source and sink of H that contains an internal source. □

LEMMA 5.3. *Suppose that C traverses $k \geq 0$ cross-links of G. Then there is a cycle C' in G with at least as many sources/sinks as C that does not traverse any cross-link of G.*

Proof. By induction on k.

Base: Trivially true if $k = 0$; set $C' = C$.

Ind.: Suppose that C traverses k cross-links of G. Order these links as $H_1 \dots H_k$ in topologically increasing order of their endpoints (which is possible, because they cannot cross). Let $u_i < v_i$ be the endpoints of H_i in G.

We claim that either C does not pass through any strict predecessor of u_1 or v_1, or that it does not pass through any strict successor of u_k or v_k. Since C traverses H_1, it contains a directed path from u_1 to v_1. Starting from v_1, C must return by some undirected path P to u_1. Now if the first edge on this path touches a predecessor of v_1, then C must return to u_1 without touching any successor w of u_1 or v_1; indeed, to reach w without passing through u_1 or v_1 itself, the path would have to traverse a chord graph that crosses H_1, which cannot exist. If, on the other hand, P's first edge touches a successor of v_1, then C must return to u_1 without touching any predecessor w of u_1 or v_1, for the same reason.

Suppose that C does not touch a predecessor of u_1 or v_1. Construct C' from C by removing the path through H_1 and replacing it with the path on G's outer cycle that connects u_1 and v_1, passing through G's source X. C' does not contain the source that lies at endpoint u_1 of H_1 in C, but it does contain a new source at X. Removing H_1 cannot eliminate any other source or sink of C, so C' has as many sources/sinks as C.

If instead C does not touch a successor of u_k or v_k, construct C' from C by removing the path through H_k and replacing it with the path on G's outer cycle that directly connects u_k and v_k, passing through G's sink Y. C' does not contain the sink that lies at endpoint v_k of H_k in C, but it does contain a new sink at Y. Removing H_k cannot eliminate any other source or sink of C, so C' has as many sources/sinks as C.

By the IH, there is a cycle C'' in G with at least as many sources/sinks as C' that does not pass through any cross-link of G. □

COROLLARY 5.4. *Every SP-ladder is CS4.*

Proof. Let C be any cycle in an SP-ladder G. If C traverses $k > 0$ cross-links of G, Lemma 5.3 guarantees that there is a cycle C' that does not traverse any cross-links of G with at least as many sources/sinks as C. Now either C' is confined to some chord graph H of G, or C' lies in the graph G' obtained by removing all cross-links from G. H and G' are both SP-DAGs, which are CS4 by Lemma 4.4. Hence, C' has only one source and one sink. Conclude that C has only one source and one sink, and so G is CS4. □

LEMMA 5.5. *Let G be a DAG with a single source and sink that is CS4. Then G is a serial composition of one or more graphs $G_1 \ldots G_k$, s.t. each G_i is either an SP-DAG or an SP-ladder.*

Proof. Divide G into subgraphs $G_1 \ldots G_k$ at its articulation points, so that G is the serial composition of $G_1 \ldots G_k$. If every G_i is an SP-DAG, we are done. Otherwise, let G^* be a component of G that is not an SP-DAG. Now G^* has no internal articulation points, so it is composed of a 2-path outer cycle cut by one or more chord graphs.

Let H_1, H_2 be two chord graphs in G^*, with endpoints u_1/v_1 and u_2/v_2. If these subgraphs cross, then there exist paths P_1 connecting u_1 and v_1 in H_1 and P_2 connecting u_2 and v_2 in H_2. Moreover, G^*'s outer cycle contains u_1, v_1, u_2, and v_2 in some alternating order. Hence, the union of P_1, P_2, and this cycle is homeomorphic to K_4, and so G^* (and hence G) cannot be CS4. Conclude that no two chord graphs of G^* cross.

Now suppose that some chord graph H is not an SP-DAG. Let H^* be a smallest subgraph of H that is not an SP-DAG. H^* cannot be a serial composition of multiple subgraphs, so it is a 2-path outer cycle with one or more chord graphs, all of which are SP-DAGs. If H^* had no cross-link, we could decompose it as an SP-DAG via repeated parallel compositions to extract all of its chord graphs. Hence, some chord graph J of H^* is a cross-link.

Let u, v be the endpoints of J, and let x, Y be its source and sink. The outer cycle of H^* connects these vertices in the order $x - u - y - v$. Moreover, there is a path from u to v bypassing X and Y (through the cross-link) and a path from X to Y bypassing u and v (from X outwards to the source of H, then via the outer cycle of G^* to the sink of H, and finally inwards to y). The union of these two paths and the outer cycle of H^* is therefore homeomorphic to K_4 , and so H^* (and hence G) cannot be CS4. Conclude that H^*, and therefore H, cannot exist, and so every chord graph of G^* is indeed an SP-DAG.

Finally, if no chord graph of G^* is a cross-link, G^* can be decomposed via repeated parallel compositions to expose all its chord graphs and so is an SP-DAG. Otherwise, it is an SP-ladder. Conclude that every component of G is either an SP-DAG or an SP-ladder. □

THEOREM 5.6. *The set of single-source, single-sink CS4 DAGs is exactly the family of graphs of which each one is a serial composition of one or more graphs $G_1 \ldots G_k$, s.t. each G_i is either an SP-DAG or an SP-ladder.*

Proof. Lemma 5.5 shows that every single-source, single-sink CS4 DAG is in the claimed family. Conversely, Lemma 5.1 and Corollary 5.4 show that SP-DAGs and SP-ladders respectively are CS4. Serial composition of such graphs cannot introduce new cycles, so all such compositions remain CS4. □

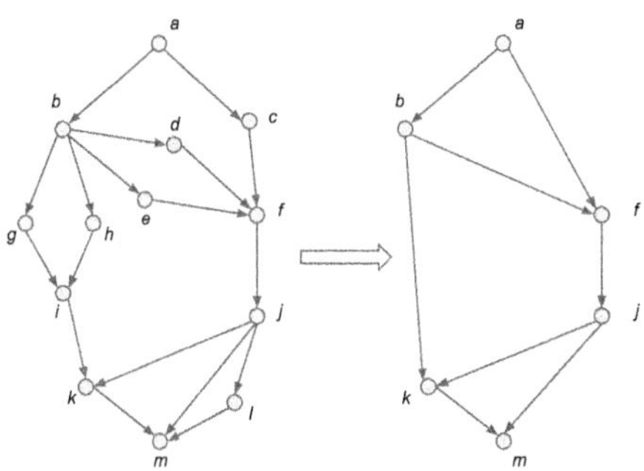

Figure 6: decomposition of an SP-ladder graph.

6. Efficient Deadlock Avoidance for CS4 DAGs

We now present algorithms to compute optimal dummy message schedules for deadlock avoidance on CS4 graphs. Since a CS4 graph is serial composition of SP-DAGs and SP-ladders, edges on different SP-DAGs and SP-ladders cannot be on the same simple cycle. Hence, we can first decompose a CS4 graph into SP-DAGs and SP-ladders, then compute schedules for edges in each of these subgraphs separately. We have already described algorithms for SP-DAGs, so here we focus on SP-ladders.

An SP-ladder can be decomposed into its constituent SP-DAGs as shown in Figure 6, where each edge represents an SP-DAG directed the same way as the edge. This simplified representation of an SP-ladder has two paths from the source X to the sink Y. For convenience, we assume the two paths go from top to the bottom and distinguish them as the "left path" and the "right path". We call the vertices that connect these paths to cross-links *corner vertices* and mark them from top to bottom, with the vertices on the left labeled $u_0, u_1, u_2, \ldots, u_{k+1}$ and the vertices on the right path from top to bottom labeled $v_0, v_1, v_2, \ldots, v_{k+1}$. The source $X = u_0 = v_0$ and the sink $Y = u_{k+1} = v_{k+1}$. All other nodes are called *internal nodes*. This graph has k cross-links, which are numbered from top to bottom as K_1 through K_k, and the SP-DAGs on the outer cycle are numbered S_0 through S_k on the left and D_0 through D_k on the right. Note that in some cases, $u_i = u_{i+1}$, in which case S_k is a graph with a single node. Figure 7 illustrates the general decomposition and this special case.

DEFINITION 8. *We say that an undirected simple cycle is* external *if it traverses at least two of the constituent SP-DAGs.*

The following facts about external cycles can be derived using structural properties of SP-ladders.

FACT 6.1. *Any external cycle with source $X = u_0 = v_0$ has a path through S_0 and another path through D_0. Any external cycle with source u_i ($i \neq 0$) has one path going through S_i and another path going through K_i. Similarly for source v_i ($i \neq 0$). All external cycles have corner nodes as sources and sinks.*

FACT 6.2. *Consider any external cycle C with source u_i. There are three possibilities:*

- *The sink of this cycle is u_k, where $i < k < m$ and K_k goes from right to left. In this case, one path on the cycle crosses K_j, goes through all v_j where $i \leq j \leq k$, and then traverses K_j. The other path traverses S_i, goes through all u_j where $i < j < k$.*

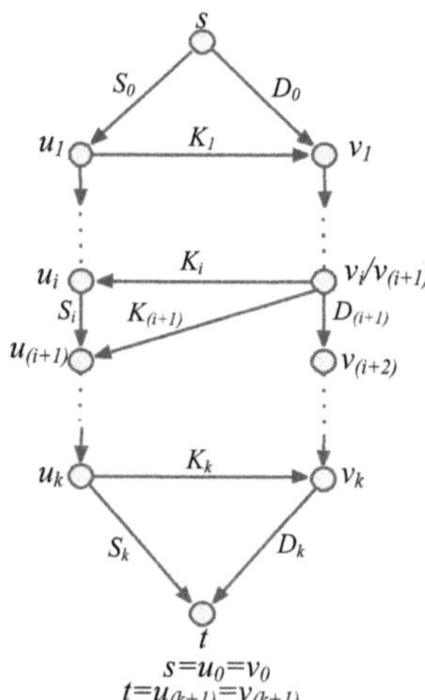

Figure 7: general structure of a decomposed SP-ladder graph, including an example of cross-links sharing an endpoint.

- *The sink of the cycle is v_k, where $i < k < m$ and K_k goes from left to right. In this case, one path on the cycle crosses K_i and passes through all v_j where $i \leq j < k$. The other path traverses S_i, goes through all u_j where $i \leq j \leq k$ and then crosses K_k.*
- *The sink of the cycle is $Y = u_m = v_m$, the sink of the ladder. One path on the cycle crosses K_i and passes through all v_j where $i \leq j$. The other path traverses S_i, goes through all u_j where $i \leq j$.*

We call the sinks defined in Fact 6.2 the *potential sinks* of u_i. We can similarly define potential sinks for an internal source v_i.

6.1 Destination-Tagged Propagation Algorithm

We now give an efficient version of the Destination-Tagged Propagation Algorithm specialized for SP-ladders. Again, only sources send dummy messages. An SP-ladder has two types of cycle sources: *internal sources* and *corner sources*. The algorithms for internal nodes are similar to those described in Section 4. We will concentrate on describing the algorithms for the corner sources. We will describe all the algorithms for some u_i, where u_i is a corner node on the left path of the ladder. Analogous algorithms can be derived for nodes on the right path.

The corner sources have two kinds of edges: edges on cross links K_i, and edges on down-links (S_i or D_i). An edge going out of a corner source u_i has three types of dummy interval-destination pairs:

1. $[e]_i$ consists of pairs for messages that stay within the chord for which u_i is a source (S_i for down-link, and K_i for cross-link). These are kept sorted by increasing τ as in the case of SP-DAGs.
2. $[e]_X$ consists of pairs for nodes v_k where $k > i$, i.e. corner nodes on the opposite side of the ladder from u_i
3. $[e]_W$ consists of pairs for nodes u_i where $k > i$, i.e. corner nodes on the same side of the ladder as u_i

The second and third lists are stored separately by increasing k. The schedule $[e] = [e]_i \cup [e]_X \cup [e]_W$.

Computing Dummy Message Schedules

We calculate the dummy message schedules for edges as follows:

1. Decompose the SP-ladder into the component SP-DAGs, identifying the u_i's, v_i's, S_i's, D_i's and K_i's. In addition, mark each edge as either belonging to a cross-link or a down-link. This can be done in $O(|G|)$ time.
2. Compute $[e]_i$, schedules for all edges due to cycles internal to each chord graph , using the algorithm of Section 4.2.
3. For all $H \in \bigcup_{0 \leq i \leq k} S_i \cup D_i \cup K_i$, compute $L(H)$, which is the length of a shortest path from H's source to its sink (in terms of buffer sizes). Again, this is done as shown in Section 4.2.
4. Starting at the bottom of the SP-ladder, for each u_i, and for each potential sink t of u_i, compute $L_s(u_i, t)$, which is defined as the shortest directed path starting at u_i, going through S_i and ending at t. Similarly, define $L_k(u_i, t)$ as the shortest directed path starting at u_i, going through K_i and ending at t. If u_i is not the source of K_i, then just set $L_k(u_i, t) = 0$. Define and compute $L_d(v_i, t)$ and $L_k(v_i, t)$ in a similar manner.
5. Using these L values, update the set of dummy intervals pairs for all edges that start at internal sources and at source X. No other sets change.

For step 1 above, we decompose an SP-ladder into its constituent SP-DAGs in $O(|G|)$ time as follows: Identify an outer cycle C for G with left and right sides, using DFS in linear time. For each vertex u on the left side of C, determine (via DFS) whether any directed path leaving u encounters the right side of C at some vertex v before it encounters the left side again. If so, the nodes and edges on all such paths from u to v form a cross link. Repeat for the right side of C to identify cross-links directed from right to left. Now that we have identified all u_i's and v_i's, we can easily compute S_i's, D_i's and K_i's.

For step 4 above, we compute $L_s(u_i, t)$ and $L_k(u_i, t)$, where t is a potential sink u_k or v_k of u_i. We consider u_i's in decreasing order of i. In order to compute $[e]_X$ and $[e]_W$ in sorted order, for a particular u_i, we consider t in increasing order of k.

$$
\begin{aligned}
L_s(u_i, u_i) &= 0 \\
L_s(u_i, t) &= L(S_i) + \\
&\quad \begin{cases} L(K_{i+1}) & \text{if } v_{i+1} = t, \\ L_s(u_{i+1}, t) & \text{otherwise} \end{cases} \\
L_k(u_i, t) &= \begin{cases} L(K_i) + L_d(v_i, t) & \text{if } u_i \text{ is } K_i\text{'s source} \\ 0 & \text{otherwise} \end{cases}
\end{aligned}
$$

Say $t = v_k$, that is, t is on the opposite side of the ladder as u_i. For each edge e that starts at u_i, if e is a cross-link edge, then set $[e]_X \leftarrow [e] \cup (L_s(u_i, t), t)$, and if e is a down-link edge, set $[e]_X \leftarrow [e] \cup (L_k(u_i, t), t)$. On the other hand, if $t = u_k$, that is, on the same side of the ladder as u_i, then the same updates happen to $[e]_W$. Since we compute t in increasing order of k, these lists are sorted by increasing k The calculations for v_i are analogous.

Now we do some postprocessing to remove some superfluous pairs of dummy messages. For the internal dummy pairs, we do the same processing as SP-DAGs. For the external dummy messages, we do the following for the node u_i.

- If any edge e has an internal pair $p_a = (\tau_a, d_a)$ and an external pair $p_b = (\tau_b, d_b)$, where $\tau_a \geq \tau_b$, then p_a is removed.
- If a particular edge e has more than one interval with the same destination, we keep only the one with the smallest τ.

6.2 Runtime Node Behavior

The behavior of all nodes except the corner source remains the same as in the corresponding algorithm for SP-DAGs. As mentioned above, a corner source u_i has 3 lists of dummy message pairs, $[e]_i$, $[e]_X$ and $[e]_W$, where $[e]_i$ is sorted by increasing τ and

$[e]_X$ and $[e]_W$ are sorted by increasing k, where destination is a corner sink v_k or u_k respectively. Each dummy pair $p_a = (\tau_a, d_a)$ has counter c_a associated with it, and the maximum value of the counter is τ_a. One other difference from SP-dags is that in some cases, a dummy message can have more than one destination. If that is the case, the dummy message carries the list of destinations with it. There are two cases in the runtime behavior of a corner source u_i

Case 1: u_i receives a non-dummy message. For each outgoing edge e, increment the counters for in $[e]_i$, $[e]_X$ and $[e]_W$ starting from the end (decreasing τ for $[e]_i$ and decreasing k for $[e]_X$ and $[e]_W$). If a pair $p_a = (\tau_a, d_a)$ reaches its maximum value, then a dummy message with destination d_a is scheduled along that edge, and the counter for p_a is zeroed out. If d_a is an internal destination, then it behaves in the same way as the SP-dag algorithm. If $d_a = u_k$ $(k > i)$ or $d_a = v_k$ $(k \geq i)$, a corner node, all the counters in $[e]_W$ are zeroed out. In addition, the following occurs.

- If e is in a cross-link, then counters for pairs in $[e]_X$,to all v_j, $j \leq k$, are zeroed out.
- If the e is in a down-link, then counters for pairs in $[e]_W$, to all u_j, $j \leq k$, are zeroed out.

Case 2: u_i receives a dummy message, or a real message also marked as a dummy. If u_i is the only destination, then no action need be taken. Otherwise, destination(s) are always another corner node. Consider a destination $d_a = u_k$ $(k > i)$ or v_k $(k \geq i)$.

- Say d_a is some u_k, or v_k, $k > i$, [1] then the message is scheduled on all the down-link edges, and the counter for the pairs going to this destination are zeroed out. For a down-link edge e, all the counters in $[e]_i$ (for all the internal dummy messages) on these down-links are zeroed out. All the counters on $[e]_W$ with destination $u_j, j \leq k$ are zeroed out. All the counters (on down-links and cross-links) that are not zeroed out are incremented.
- If d_a is some v_k, $k = i$, [2] then the message is scheduled on along all the cross-link edges and all the counters in $[e]_i$ are zeroed out. All the other counters are incremented.

If u_i wants to send multiple dummy messages on the same edge, then they are merged and a list of destinations is created. In this formulation, assuming all buffer sizes are non-zero, there are at most 2 destinations for each dummy message. In both cases, if the node wants to send both a real message and a dummy message along the same edge, then the real message is also marked as dummy, and a total of one message is sent.

6.3 Proof of Correctness

SP-ladders have the CS4 property that each undirected cycle has at most one source and one sink. Therefore, in order for a deadlock to occur one path from the source to the sink must be full and another path must be empty. Here, we show that this can not occur when using the above algorithm for dummy schedules and node behavior.

The following lemma shows why the node can safely zero out the counters as described in the previous subsection.

LEMMA 6.3. *The following claims are true.*

1. *If a corner source u_i forwards a dummy message along an edge of a chord graph, it will go through all the nodes within that chord.*
2. *If a corner source u_i sends or forwards a dummy message along a down-link to some sink u_k or v_k, where $k \geq i$, this message will go through all the sinks u_j, $i \leq j \leq k$.*
3. *If a corner source u_i sends or forwards a dummy message along a cross link K_i intended for v_k or u_k, where $k \geq i$, it reaches all the nodes v_j, $i \leq j \leq k$.*

Proof. From the For claim 1, if a source forwards a dummy message, it is an external dummy message, and therefore its sink must be a corner node, and it must traverse the entire chord graph on which it is forwarded. In addition, when a corner source gets a dummy message not intended for itself, it forwards it along all its edges. Therefore, it must go through all the nodes of the chord graph before it reaches the sink.

Claims 2 and 3 are true due to Lemma 6.2. □

The following lemmas are analogous to Lemmas 4.9 and 4.10 for SP-dags.

LEMMA 6.4. *Suppose that, for edge e out of node X, pair $(\tau_i, d_i) \in [e]$. For each τ_i messages that X receives, it sends at least one dummy message along e that will reach d_i.*

Proof. Consider a span of τ_i consecutive messges received by X. Before these messages arrive, c_i has some value $< \tau_i$. For each incoming message, one of the following will occur.

1. The counter will be incremented until it reaches τ_i, triggering a dummy message to d_i.
2. The counter will be zeroed out because some other dummy message is sent or forwarded. From node behavior and Lemma 6.3, the counter is zeroed out only if the dummy message sent or forwarded will pass through d_i.

□

LEMMA 6.5. *Suppose that an external cycle in G starts at u_i and ends at t. Every time u_i receives $L_S(u_i, t)$ messages, it sends at least one dummy message with destination t along all its cross-link edges. Every time u receives $L_K(u_i, t)$ messages, it sends at least one dummy message along all its down-link edges.*

Proof. Using the above procedure for setting intervals, to start with, every cross-link edge will have a dummy interval with $p_a = (L_K(u_i, t), t)$ set. If the dummy interval was later removed, it is because another dummy pair p_b causes a dummy message with the same or higher frequency to be sent, and this dummy message will traverse all the paths that a dummy message due to p_b would take.

Therefore, by Lemma 6.4 implies the proof. □

Using the above lemmas, we can prove the correctness theorem.

THEOREM 6.6. *If dummy messages are sent as described in Section 4.2, using the interval-destination pairs computed by the above procedure, then deadlock cannot occur in G.*

Proof. Suppose a deadlock does occur in G. Then there must be a blocking cycle C in G. WLOG, say that the blocking cycle starts at u_i and ends at some sink t, and one path from u_i to t goes through K_i and another one goes through S_i. Say that the path s_1 through K_i is full and the path s_2 through S_i is empty.

We know that $length(s_1) \geq L_K(u_i, t)$. If we consider the first edge of path s_2, it leaves u_i through its cross-link. From Lemma 6.5, u_i sends a dummy message along this edge every time it gets $L_K(u_i, t)$ messages. Since this message is propagated all the way to t, s_2 cannot be completely empty, which contradicts our assumption that cycle C is blocking. □

[1] If there are two cross-links out of u_i, then we use the larger index i to make this decision.

[2] If there are two cross-links from i, we forward along the one that is equal.

6.4 Non-Propagation Algorithm

Computing the dummy intervals for the Non-Propagation Algorithm takes longer than for the Destination-Tagged Propagation Algorithm on SP-ladders. Here we give an $O(|G|^3)$ algorithm.

Again, we decompose into constituent SP-DAGs. As in the Non-Propagation Algorithm for SP-DAGs, for each constituent SP-DAG H, we precompute $h(H)$ as the length of the longest path (in terms of the number of hops) from H's source to its sink. In addition, for each edge e in H, compute $h(H, e)$ as the longest path from H's source to its sink that passes through e. In addition, we compute the initial estimate of the dummy intervals considering only the cycles internal to the constituent SP-DAGs.

Now consider every source u_i in the SP-ladder. We can enumerate all the potential sinks t for that source using Lemma 6.2. As we defined $L_s(u_i, t)$ and $L_K(u_i, t)$ we define $h_s(u_i, t)$ is the length of the longest directed path (in terms of hop count) from u_i to t that goes along S_i and $h_k(u_i, t)$ as the length of the longest directed path from u_i to t that goes along K_i.

Now consider an edge e in some constituent SP-DAG H along the path from u_i to t. We can update the dummy interval for e as follows: If e lies along some path from u_i to t that goes across K_i, then $[e] = L_s(u_i, t)/(h_k(u_i, t) - h(H) + h(H, e))$. If on the other hand, e lies along some path from u_i to t that goes across S_i, then $[e] = L_k(u_i, t)/(h_s(u_i, t) - h(H) + h(H, e))$. We can do the analogous procedure for each potential source v_i.

Running time: There are $O(|G|^2)$ source-sink pairs. For a given pair u_i and t, we can calculate $L_s(u_i, t)$, $L_k(u_i, t)$, $h_s(u_i, t)$ and $h_k(u_i, t)$ using L and h values of the constituent SP-DAGs in $O(|G|)$ time. We can also update all dummy intervals for edges on some path from u_i to t in $O(|G|)$ time. Therefore, the overall algorithm takes $O(|G|^3)$ time.

7. Conclusions

In this work, we have explored the practicality of a flexible, general model of streaming computation that permits computation nodes to arbitrarily filter their inputs. We have shown that, if the allowed streaming topologies are restricted to the CS4 DAGs (or, more stringently, to the SP-DAGs), then we can efficiently compute dummy message intervals for all edges. In addition, we have extended one of their dummy message-based algorithms to reduce the amount of propagation, thereby potentially reducing overheads. Hence, if the streaming application programmer agrees to use such topologies, the compiler and runtime system can guarantee safe execution of the resulting applications, in a way that is non-intrusive to application code and that scales even to large and complex applications.

Our work raises several directions for future research. One open question is whether one devise alternate dummy-based deadlock avoidance algorithms can further reduce the number of dummy sent; alternatively, can one derive lower bounds for the number of messages that *must* be sent by any algorithm to avoid deadlock? A second question is whether one can efficiently and systematically translate arbitrary DAGs to equivalent CS4 topologies by adding a small number of nodes and edges. Finally, we plan to augment an existing language for streaming computation, such as the X language [5], to support the filtering model.

Acknowledgments

We sincerely thank the anonymous reviewers for their devoted time and insightful comments, without which we could not have brought the paper to the final shape.

References

[1] I. Buck, T. Foley, D. Horn, J. Sugerman, K. Fatahalian, M. Houston, and P. Hanrahan. Brook for GPUs: Stream computing on graphics hardware. *ACM Trans. Graphics*, 23(3):777–786, 2004.

[2] J. T. Buck. Static scheduling and code generation from dynamic dataflow graphs with integer-valued control streams. In *Asilomar Conf. on Signals, Systems, and Computers*, pages 508–513, Nov. 1994.

[3] J. Buhler, J. M. Lancaster, A. C. Jacob, and R. D. Chamberlain. Mercury BLASTN: Faster DNA sequence comparison using a streaming hardware architecture. In *Proc. Reconfigurable Systems Summer Institute*, Urbana, IL, July 2007.

[4] R. J. Duffin. Topology of series-parallel networks. *Journal of Mathematical Analysis and Applications*, 10:303–318, 1965.

[5] M. A. Franklin, E. J. Tyson, J. H. Buckley, P. Crowley, and J. Maschmeyer. Auto-pipe and the X language: A pipeline design tool and description language. In *IEEE Int'l Parallel and Distributed Processing Symp.*, Apr. 2006.

[6] M. M. Gaber, A. Zaslavsky, and S. Krishnaswamy. Mining data streams: a review. *SIGMOD Rec.*, 34(2):18–26, 2005.

[7] B. Khailany, W. Dally, S. Rixner, U. Kapasi, P. Mattson, J. Namkoong, J. Owens, B. Towles, and A. Chang. Imagine: Media processing with streams. *IEEE Micro*, pages 35–46, March/April 2001.

[8] E. A. Lee. Consistency in dataflow graphs. *IEEE Trans. on Parallel and Distributed Systems*, 2(2):223–235, Apr. 1991.

[9] E. A. Lee and D. G. Messerschmitt. Synchronous data flow. *Proceedings of the IEEE*, 75(9):1235–1245, Sept. 1987.

[10] P. Li, K. Agrawal, J. Buhler, and R. D. Chamberlain. Deadlock avoidance for streaming computations with filtering. In *ACM Symp. on Parallelism in Algorithms and Architectures*, 2010.

[11] P. Li, K. Agrawal, J. Buhler, R. D. Chamberlain, and J. M. Lancaster. Deadlock-avoidance for streaming applications with split-join structure: Two case studies. In *IEEE Int'l Conf. on Application-specific Systems, Architectures and Processors*, pages 333–336, July 2010.

[12] Y. Liu, N. Vijayakumar, and B. Plale. Stream processing in data-driven computational science. In *IEEE/ACM Int'l Conf. on Grid Computing*, pages 160–167, 2006.

[13] W. R. Mark, R. S. Glanville, K. Akeley, and M. J. Kilgard. Cg: a system for programming graphics hardware in a C-like language. *ACM Trans. on Graphics*, 22(3):896–907, July 2003.

[14] J. Misra. Distributed discrete-event simulation. *ACM Comput. Surv.*, 18(1):39–65, 1986.

[15] J. W. Romein, P. C. Broekema, E. van Meijeren, K. van der Schaaf, and W. H. Zwart. Astronomical real-time streaming signal processing on a Blue Gene/L supercomputer. In *ACM Symp. on Parallelism in Algorithms and Architectures*, pages 59–66, 2006.

[16] W. Thies and S. Amarasinghe. An empirical characterization of stream programs and its implications for language and compiler design. In *Int'l Conf. on Parallel Architectures and Compilation Techniques*, pages 365–376, 2010.

[17] W. Thies, M. Karczmarek, and S. Amarasinghe. StreamIt: A language for streaming applications. In *Int'l Conf. on Compiler Construction*, pages 179–196, 2002.

[18] J. Valdes, R. E. Tarjan, and E. L. Lawler. The recognition of series parallel digraphs. In *ACM Symposium on Theory of Computing*, 1979.

Lock Cohorting: A General Technique for Designing NUMA Locks

David Dice, Virendra J. Marathe
Oracle Labs
dave.dice@oracle.com, virendra.marathe@oracle.com

Nir Shavit
MIT and Tel-Aviv University
shanir@csail.mit.edu

Abstract

Multicore machines are quickly shifting to NUMA and CC-NUMA architectures, making scalable NUMA-aware locking algorithms, ones that take into account the machines' non-uniform memory and caching hierarchy, ever more important. This paper presents *lock cohorting*, a general new technique for designing NUMA-aware locks that is as simple as it is powerful.

Lock cohorting allows one to transform any spin-lock algorithm, with minimal non-intrusive changes, into scalable NUMA-aware spin-locks. Our new cohorting technique allows us to easily create NUMA-aware versions of the TATAS-Backoff, CLH, MCS, and ticket locks, to name a few. Moreover, it allows us to derive a CLH-based cohort abortable lock, the first NUMA-aware queue lock to support abortability.

We empirically compared the performance of cohort locks with prior NUMA-aware and classic NUMA-oblivious locks on a synthetic micro-benchmark, a real world key-value store application memcached, as well as the libc memory allocator. Our results demonstrate that cohort locks perform as well or better than known locks when the load is low and significantly out-perform them as the load increases.

Categories and Subject Descriptors D.1.3 [*Programming Techniques*]: Concurrent Programming

General Terms Algorithms, Design, Performance

Keywords NUMA, hierarchical locks, spin locks

1. Introduction

In coming years, as multicore machines grow in size, one can expect an accelerated shift towards distributed non-uniform memory-access (NUMA) and cache-coherent NUMA (CC-NUMA) architectures.[1] Such architectures, examples of which include Intel's multi-socket Nehalem-based systems and Oracle's 4-socket 256-way Niagara-based systems, consist of collections of computing cores with fast local memory (e.g. caches shared by cores on a single multicore chip), communicating with each other via a slower inter-chip communication medium. Access by a core to the local memory, and in particular to a shared local cache, can be several times faster than access to the remote memory or cache lines resident on another chip [12].

[1] We use the term NUMA broadly, noting that it includes Non-Uniform Communication Architecture (NUCA) machines as well.

PPoPP'12, February 25–29, 2012, New Orleans, Louisiana, USA.

Dice [5], and Radović and Hagersten [12] were the first to identify the benefits of designing locks that improve locality of reference on CC-NUMA architectures by developing NUMA-aware locks: general-purpose mutual-exclusion locks that encourage threads with high mutual cache locality to acquire the lock consecutively, thus reducing the overall level of cache coherence misses when executing instructions in the critical section. Specifically, these designs attempt to minimize *lock migration*. We say a lock L *migrates* if two threads running on a different NUMA clusters (nodes) acquire L one after the other.

Radović and Hagersten introduced the *hierarchical backoff lock* (HBO): a *test-and-test-and-set* lock augmented with a new *backoff scheme* to reduce cross-interconnect contention on the lock variable. Their hierarchical backoff mechanism allows the backoff delay to be tuned dynamically, so that when a thread notices that another thread from its own local cluster owns the lock, it can reduce its delay and increase its chances of acquiring the lock next. This algorithm's simplicity makes it quite practical. However, because the locks are test-and-test-and-set locks, they incur invalidation traffic on every modification of the shared global lock variable, which is especially costly on NUMA machines. The issue of fairness that arises because threads backoff with different delays can be addressed, but requires more tuning parameters, which invariably makes the lock's performance highly unreliable.

Luchangco et al. [15] overcame these drawbacks by introducing HCLH, a hierarchical version of the CLH queue-lock [4]. The HCLH algorithm collects requests on each cluster into a local CLH-style queue, and then has the thread at the head of the queue integrate each cluster's queue into a single global queue. This avoids the overhead of spinning on a shared location and eliminates fairness and starvation issues. The algorithm's drawback is that it forms the local queues of waiting threads by having each thread perform an atomic *register-to-memory-swap* (SWAP) operation[2] on the shared head of the local queue, which becomes a contention bottleneck, implying that the thread merging the local queue into the global one must either wait for a long period (10s of microseconds) or globally merge an unacceptably short local queue.

More recently, Dice et al. [7] showed that one could overcome the synchronization overhead of HCLH locks by collecting local queues using the flat-combining technique of Hendler et al. [8], and then splicing them into the global queue. The resulting NUMA-aware FC-MCS lock outperforms previous locks by at least a factor of 2, but uses significantly more memory and is relatively complicated.

In summary, the HBO lock has the benefit of being simple, but is unfair, and requires significant application and platform dependent tuning. Both HCLH and FC-MCS are fair and deliver much better performance, but are rather complex, and it is therefore questionable if they will be of general practical use.

[2] On some architectures the SWAP operation is emulated using a *compare-and-swap* instruction loop.

This paper presents *lock cohorting*, a new general technique for turning practically any kind of spin-lock or spin-then-block lock into a NUMA-aware lock that allows sequences of threads – local to a given node/cluster – to execute consecutively with little overhead and requiring very little tuning beyond the locks used to create the cohort lock.

Apart from providing a new set of high performance NUMA-aware locks, the important benefit of lock cohorting is that it is a general transformation, not simply another NUMA-aware locking algorithm. This provides an important software engineering advantage: programmers do not have to adopt new and unfamiliar locks into their system. Instead, they can apply the lock cohorting transformation to their existing locks. This will hopefully allow them to enhance the performance of their locks (by improving locality of reference, enabled by the NUMA-awareness property of cohort locks), while preserving many of the original properties of whatever locks their application uses.

1.1 Lock Cohorting in a Nutshell

Say we have a spin-lock of type G that is *thread-oblivious*, that is, allows the acquiring thread to differ from the releasing thread, and another spin-lock of type S that has the *cohort detection property*: a thread releasing the lock can detect if it has a non-empty cohort of threads concurrently attempting to acquire the lock.

We convert a collection of locks S and G into a single NUMA-aware lock by having a single thread-oblivious global lock G and by associating each NUMA cluster i with a distinct local lock S_i that has the cohort detection property. We say a cohort lock is locked if and only if its global lock G is locked. Locks S and G can be of different types. For example, S could be an MCS queue-lock [10] and G a simple *test-and-test-and-set backoff lock* [3] (BO) as depicted in Figure 1. To access the critical section a thread must hold both the local lock S_i of its cluster, and the global lock G. However, the trick is that given the special properties of S and G, once some thread in a cluster acquires G, ownership of the cohort lock can be passed in a deadlock-free manner from one thread in cluster to the next using the local lock S_i, without releasing the global lock. To maintain fairness, the global lock G is at some point released by some thread in the cohort (not necessarily the one that acquired it), allowing a cohort of threads from another cluster S_j to take ownership of the lock.

In more detail, each thread attempting to enter the lock's critical section first acquires its local lock S_i, and based on the state of the local lock, decides if it can immediately enter the critical section or must compete for G. A thread T leaving the critical section first checks if it has a non-empty cohort (some local thread is waiting on S_i). If so, it will release S_i without releasing G, having set the state of S_i to indicate that this is a local release. On the other hand, if its local cohort is empty, T will release G and then release S_i, setting S_i's state to indicate that the global lock has been released. This indicates to the next local thread that acquires S_i that it must re-acquire G before it can enter the critical section. The cohort detection property is therefore necessary in order to prevent a deadlock situation in which a thread leaves the local lock, without releasing the global lock, when there is no subsequent thread in the cohort, so the global lock may never be released.

The cohort lock's overall fairness is easily controlled by deciding when a cluster gives up the global lock. A simple cluster-local policy is to give up the local lock after an allowed number consecutive local accesses. We note that a cohort lock constructed from unfair underlying locks will itself be unfair, but if the underlying locks are fair then the fairness of a cohort lock is determined by the policy that decides when a cohort releases the global lock. If a cohort retains ownership of the global lock for extended periods then throughput may be improved but at a cost in fairness.

The benefit of the lock cohorting approach is that sequences of local threads accessing the lock are formed at a very low cost. Once a thread in a cluster has acquired the global lock, control of the global lock is subsequently passed among contending threads within the cluster – the cohort – with the efficiency of a local lock. In other words, the common path to entering the critical section is the same as a local version of the lock of type S with fairness, as we said, easily controlled by limiting the number of consecutive local lock transfers allowed. This contrasts sharply with the complex coordination mechanisms that create such sequences in the previous top performing HCLH and FC-MCS locks, and the platform-dependent, load-dependent, and application-dependent performance tuning required for the HBO lock.

1.2 Cohort Lock Designs and Performance

It is easy to find efficient locks that are thread-oblivious: the BO or ticket locks have this property, and since the global lock is not expected to be highly contended, they can easily serve as the global locks. With respect to the cohort detection property, there are locks such as the MCS queue lock of Mellor-Crummey and Scott [10] that provide cohort detection by design: each spinning thread's record in the queue has a pointer installed by its successor. There are however locks, for example, BO locks, that require us to introduce an explicit *cohort detection mechanism* to allow releasing threads to determine if other cohort threads are attempting to acquire the lock.

More work is needed when the lock algorithms are required to be abortable. In an abortable lock, simply detecting that there is a successor is not enough to allow a thread to release the local lock but not the global lock. One must make sure there is a viable successor, that is, one that will not abort after the thread releases the local lock, as this might leave the global lock deadlocked. As we show, one can convert the BO lock (which is abortable by design) and the abortable CLH lock [14] into abortable (NUMA-aware) cohort locks, which to our knowledge, are the first set of NUMA-aware abortable queue-locks.

We tested our new lock cohorting transformation on an Oracle SPARC Enterprise T5440^{TM} Server, a 256-way 4-socket multicore machine. Our tests show several variations of cohort NUMA-aware locks that outperform all prior algorithms, and in some situations are over 60% more scalable than FC-MCS, the most scalable NUMA-aware lock in the literature. Furthermore, unlike FC-MCS, we found that cohort lock designs are simple to implement and require significantly lower space than FC-MCS. Our novel abortable NUMA-aware lock, the first of its kind, outperforms the HBO lock (abortable by definition) and the abortable CLH lock [14] by about a factor of 6. Our experiments with memcached [2] demonstrate that in some configuration settings cohort locks can improve the application's performance by over 25%, without degrading performance on all other configurations. Finally, our libc allocator experiments demonstrate how cohort locks can directly benefit multithreaded programs and significantly boost their cluster-level reference locality both for accesses by the allocator to allocation metadata and for accesses by the application to allocated memory blocks. In experiments conducted on a memory allocator stress test benchmark [6], cohort locks allow the benchmark to scale up to nearly a factor of 6X, while all other reported locks provided a scalability gain restricted to about 50%.

We describe our construction in detail in Section 2, both our general approach and seven specific example lock transformations. We provide an experimental evaluation in Section 4.

2. The Lock Cohorting Transformation

In this section, we describe our new lock cohorting transformation in detail. Assume that the system is organized into clusters (nodes)

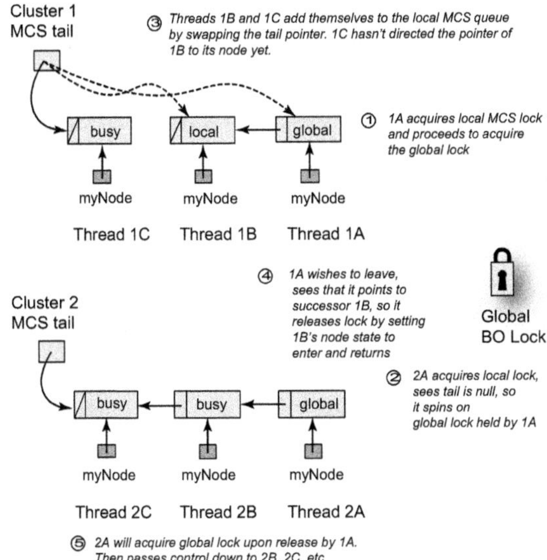

Figure 1. A NUMA-aware C-BO-MCS lock for two clusters. A thread spins if its node state is *busy*, and can enter the critical section if the state is *local release*. A thread attempts to take the global lock if it sees the state set to *global release* or if it is added as the first in the queue (setting a null *tail* pointer to its own record).

of computing cores, each of which has a large cache that is shared among the cores local to that cluster, so that inter-cluster communication is significantly more expensive than intra-cluster communication. We use the term *cluster* to capture the collection of cores, and to make clear that they could be cores on a single multicore chip, or cores on a collection of multicore chips (nodes) that have proximity to the same memory or caching structure; it all depends on the size of the NUMA machine at hand. We will also assume that each cluster has a unique *cluster id* known to all threads running on the cluster.

2.1 Designing a Cohort Lock

We describe lock cohorting in the context of spin-locks, although it could be as easily applied to blocking-locks. We assume the standard model of shared memory based on execution histories [9].

A *lock* is an object providing mutual exclusion with *lock* and *unlock* methods, implemented in shared memory, and having the usual safety and liveness properties (see [9]). At a minimum we will require that the locks considered here will provide mutual exclusion and be deadlock-free. In addition, we define the following properties:

Definition A lock x is *thread-oblivious*, if in a given execution history, for a *lock* method call of x by a given thread, it allows the matching *unlock* method call (the next *unlock* of x that follows in the execution history) to be executed by a different thread.

Definition A lock x provides *cohort detection* if one can add a new predicate method *alone?* to x so that in any execution history, if there is no other thread concurrently executing a lock method on x, *alone?* will return true.

Note that we follow the custom of not using linearizability as a correctness condition when defining our lock implementations. In particular, our definition of *alone?* refers to the behavior of concurrent lock method calls and says *if* rather than *iff* so as to allow false-positives: there might be a thread executing the lock operation and *alone?* (not noticing it) could still return true. False-positives are a performance concern but do not affect correctness. False-negatives, however, could result in loss of progress. This weaker definition is intended to allow for very relaxed and efficient implementations of *alone?*.

We construct a NUMA-aware cohort lock by having each cluster i on the NUMA machine have a local instance S_i of a lock that has the cohort detection property, and have an additional shared thread-oblivious global lock G. Locks $S_i, i \in \{1 \dots n\}$ (where n is the number of clusters in the NUMA system), and G can be of different types, for example, the S_i could be slight modifications of MCS queue-locks [10] and G a simple *test-and-test-and-set backoff lock* [3] (BO) as depicted in Figure 1.

The *lock* method of a thread in cluster i in a cohort lock operates as follows. The state of the lock S_i is modified so that it has a different detectable state indicating if it has a *local release* or a *global release*.

1. Call *lock* on S_i. If upon acquiring the lock the lock method detects that the state is:
   - A *local release*: proceed to enter the critical section.
   - A *global release*: proceed to call the *lock* method of the global lock G. Once G is acquired, enter the critical section.

We define a special *may-pass-local* predicate on the local lock S_i and the global lock G. The *may-pass-local* predicate indicates if the lock state is such that the global lock should be released. This predicate could, for example, be based on how long the global lock has been continuously held on one cluster or on a count of the number of times the local lock was acquired in succession in a *local release* state. It defines a tradeoff between fairness and performance, as typically the shorter successive access time *may-pass-local* grants to a given cohort, the more it loses the benefit of locality of reference in accessing the critical section.

Given this added *may-pass-local* predicate, the *unlock* method of a thread in cluster i in a cohort lock operates as follows.

1. Call the *alone?* method and *may-pass-local* on S_i.
   - If both return false: call the *unlock* method of S_i, setting the release state to *local release*. The next owner of S_i can directly enter the critical section.
   - Otherwise: call the *unlock* method of the global lock G. Once G is released, call the *unlock* method of S_i, setting the release state to *global release*.

As can be seen, the state of the lock upon release indicates to the next local thread that acquires S_i if it must acquire G or not, and allows a chain of local lock acquisitions without the need to access the global lock. The immediate benefit is that sequences of local threads accessing the lock are formed at a very low cost: once a thread in a cluster has acquired the global lock, ownership is passed among the cluster's threads with the efficiency of a local lock. This reduces overall cross-cluster communication and increases intra-cluster locality of reference when accessing data within the critical section.

3. Cohort Lock Designs

Though most locks can be used in the cohort locking transformation, we briefly explain six specific constructions here: The first four are non-abortable (do not support timeouts [13]) locks and the last two are abortable (timeout capable) locks. Of the non-abortable locks, we first present a simple *test-and-test-and-set backoff lock* [3] (which we will refer to as the BO lock) based cohort lock that employs a BO lock globally and local BO locks per NUMA cluster. We refer to this lock as the C-BO-BO lock. The second lock is a similar combination of ticket locks [10], which we call the C-TKT-TKT lock. The third is a combination of a global BO lock, and local MCS locks [10] per NUMA cluster. The last non-abortable lock contains MCS locks both globally and locally. For the abortable locks, we first present an abortable variant of the C-BO-BO lock, which we call the A-C-BO-BO lock, and then we present an abortable cohort lock comprising of an abortable global BO lock and abortable local CLH locks [14], which we call the A-C-BO-CLH lock.

3.1 The C-BO-BO Lock

In the C-BO-BO lock, the local and global locks are both simple BO locks. The BO lock is trivially thread-oblivious. However, we need to augment the local BO lock to enable cohort detection by exposing the *alone?* method. Specifically, to implement the *alone?* method we need to add an indicator to the local BO lock that a successor exists.

To that end we add to the lock a new *successor-exists* boolean field. This field is initially false, and is set to true by a thread immediately before it attempts to CAS the test-and-test-and-set lock state. Once a thread succeeds in the CAS and acquires the local lock, it writes false to the *successor-exists* field, effectively resetting it. The *alone?* method will check the *successor-exists* field, and if it is true, a successor must exist since it was set after the reset by the local lock winner. *Alone?* returns the logical complement of *successor-exists*.

The lock releaser uses the *alone?* method to determine if it can correctly release the local lock in *local release* state. If it does so, the following lock owner of the local lock implicitly inherits ownership of the global BO lock. Otherwise, the local lock is in the *global release* state, in which case, the new local lock owner must acquire the global lock as well. Notice that it is possible that another successor thread executing *lock* exists even if the field is false, simply because the post-acquisition reset of *successor-exists* by the local lock winner could have overwritten the successor's setting of the *successor-exists* field. This type of incorrect-false result observed in *successor-exists* is allowed – it will at worst cause an unnecessary release of the global lock, but not affect correctness of the algorithm.

However, incorrect-false conditions can result in greater contention at the global lock, which we would like to avoid. To that end, a thread that spins on the local lock also checks the *successor-exists* flag, and sets it back to true if it observes that the flag has been reset (by the current lock owner). This is likely to lead to extra contention on the cache line containing the flag, but most of this contention does not lie in the critical path of the lock acquisition operation. Furthermore, intra-cluster write-sharing typically enjoys low latency, mitigating any ill-effects of contention on cache lines that might be modified by threads on the same cluster. These observations are confirmed in our empirical evaluation.

3.2 The C-TKT-TKT Lock

The C-TKT-TKT lock has the ticket lock [10] as both the local lock, as well as the global lock. A traditional ticket lock consists of two counters: *request* and *grant*. A thread intending to acquire the lock first atomically increments the *request* counter and then spins, waiting for the *grant* counter to contain the incremented *request* value. The lock releaser subsequently releases the lock by incrementing the *grant* counter.

The ticket lock is trivially thread-oblivious; a thread can increment the *request* and another thread can correspondingly increment the *grant* counter. Cohort detection is also easy in the ticket lock; all the thread needs to do is determine if the *request* and *grant* counters match, and if not, it means that there are more requesters waiting to acquire the lock.

In C-TKT-TKT, a thread first acquires the local ticket lock, and then the global ticket lock. To release the C-TKT-TKT lock, the owner first determines if it has any cohorts that may be waiting to acquire the lock. The *alone?* method is a simple check to see if the *request* and *grant* counters are the same. If not, it means that there are additional requests posted by waiting cohort threads. In that case, the owner informs the next cohort in line that it has inherited the global lock by setting a special *top-granted* field that residees in the local ticket lock. [3] It then releases the local ticket lock by incrementing the *grant* counter. If the *request* and *grant* counters are the same, the owner releases the global ticket lock and then the local ticket lock (without setting the *top-granted* field).

3.3 The C-BO-MCS Lock

The design of the C-BO-MCS lock, depicted in Figure 1, is also straightforward. The BO lock is a simple test-and-test-and-set lock with backoff, and is therefore thread-oblivious by definition: any thread can release a lock taken by another.

We remind the reader that an MCS lock consists of a list of records, one per thread, ordered by their arrival at the lock's *tail* variable. Each thread adds its record to the lock by performing a swap on a shared *tail*. It then installs a *successor* pointer from the record of its predecessor to its record in the lock. The predecessor, upon releasing the lock, will follow the successor pointer and notify the thread of the lock release by writing to a special *state* field in the successor's record.

The MCS lock can be easily adapted to be the local cohort detecting lock as follows. We implement the *alone?* method by simply checking if a thread's record has a non-null successor pointer. The release state is augmented so that instead of simple *busy* and *released* states, the *state* field encodes *busy*, *release local* or *release global*. Each thread will initialize its record state to busy unless it encounters a null tail pointer, indicating it has no predecessor, in which case it is in the *release global* state and will access the global lock.

With these modifications, the global BO lock and local modified MCS locks can be plugged into the cohort lock protocol to deliver a NUMA-aware lock.

3.4 The C-MCS-MCS Lock

The C-MCS-MCS lock comprises a global MCS lock and local MCS locks. The cohort detection mechanism of the local MCS locks is the same as in C-BO-MCS. So the implementation of the local MCS lock remains the same. However, the thread-obliviousness aspect is somewhat more interesting.

A key property of MCS is what is called *local spinning* [10], where a thread spin-waits on its MCS queue node, and is informed by its predecessor thread that is has become the lock owner. Thereafter, the thread can enter the critical section, and release the lock by transferring lock ownership to its queue node's successor. The thread can subsequently do whatever it wants with its MCS queue node; it usually deallocates it. In order to make the global MCS lock thread-oblivious, the thread that enqueues its MCS queue node in the global MCS lock's queue cannot always get its node back immediately after it releases the C-MCS-MCS lock – the node has to be preserved in the MCS queue so as to let another cohort thread release the lock. We enable this feature by using thread-local pools of MCS queue nodes. A thread that posts a request node in the global MCS lock must get a free node from its local pool. On releasing

[3] The *top-granted* flag is reset by the thread that observed it set and took possession of the the local ticket lock.

the global lock, the lock releaser can return the node to the original thread's pool. This circulation of MCS queue nodes can be done very efficiently and does not impact performance of the lock [13].

With this extra modification we achieve a thread-oblivious MCS lock, which can be combined with the local MCS locks that are enabled with cohort detection to deliver the NUMA-aware C-MCS-MCS lock.

3.5 The C-TKT-MCS Lock

The C-TKT-MCS lock combines local MCS queue locks with a global ticket lock. We believe this lock combines the best of C-TKT-TKT and C-MCS-MCS: First, because the global lock is a ticket lock, it does not contain the complexity of circulating queue nodes between threads as in C-MCS-MCS. Second, since the local locks are MCS locks instead of ticket locks, the C-TKT-MCS lock retains their local-spinning property. As we shall see in Section 4, having local MCS locks indeed helps C-TKT-MCS to scale better than C-TKT-TKT.

3.6 Abortable Cohort Locks

The property of *abortability* [13] in a mutual exclusion lock enables threads to abandon their attempt of acquiring the lock while they are waiting to acquire the lock. Abortability poses an interesting difficulty in cohort lock construction. Even if the *alone?* method, which indicates that a cohort thread is waiting to acquire the lock, returns false (which means that there exists a cohort thread waiting to acquire the lock), all the waiting cohort threads may subsequently abort their attempts to acquire the lock. This case, if not handled correctly, can easily lead to a deadlock, where the global lock is in the acquired state, and the local lock has been handed off to a cohort thread that no longer exists, and may not appear in the future either.

Thus, we must strengthen the requirements of the lock cohorting transformation with respect to the *cohort detection* property: if *alone?* returns false, then some thread concurrently executing the local *lock* method will not abort before completing the local *lock* method call. Notice that a thread that completed acquiring the local lock with the *release local* lock state cannot be aborted since by definition it is in the critical section.

3.6.1 The A-C-BO-BO Lock

The A-C-BO-BO lock is very similar to the C-BO-BO lock that we described earlier, with the difference that aborting threads also reset the *successor-exists* field in the local lock to inform the local lock releaser that a waiting thread has aborted. Each spinning thread reads this field while spinning, and sets it in case it was recently reset by an aborting thread. Like the C-BO-BO lock, in A-C-BO-BO, the local lock releaser checks to see if the *successor-exists* flag was set (which indicates that there exist threads in the local cluster that are spinning to acquire the lock). If the *successor-exists* flag was set, the releaser can release the local BO lock by writing *release local* into the BO lock. [4]

However, at this point the releaser must double-check the *successor-exists* field to determine if it was cleared during the time the releaser released the local BO lock. If so, the releaser conservatively assumes that there may be no other waiting cohort, and atomically changes the local BO lock's state to *global release*, and then releases the global BO lock.

[4] Note that the BO lock can also be in 3 states: *release global* (which is the default state, indicating that the lock is free to be acquired, but the acquirer must thereafter acquire the global BO lock to execute the critical section), *busy* (indicating that the lock is acquired by some thread), and *release local* (indicating that the next acquirer of the lock implicitly inherits ownership of the global BO lock).

3.6.2 The A-C-BO-CLH Lock

The A-C-BO-CLH lock has a BO lock as its global lock (which is trivially abortable), and an abortable variant of the CLH lock [14] (A-CLH) as its local lock. Like the MCS lock, the A-CLH lock also consists of a list of records, one per thread, ordered by the arrival of the threads at the lock's tail. To acquire the A-C-BO-CLH lock, a thread first must acquire its local A-CLH lock, and then explicitly or implicitly acquire the global BO lock.

Because we build on the A-CLH lock, we will first briefly review it as presented by Scott [14]. The A-CLH lock leverages the property of "implicit" CLH queue predecessors, where a thread that enqueues its node in the CLH queue spins on its predecessor node to determine if it has become the lock owner. An aborting thread marks its CLH queue node as aborted by simply making its predecessor explicit in the node (i.e. by writing the address of the predecessor node to the prev field of the thread's CLH queue node). The successor thread that is spinning on the aborted thread's node immediately notices the change and starts spinning on the new predecessor found in the aborted node's prev field. The successor also returns the aborted CLH node to the corresponding thread's local pool.

The local lock in our A-C-BO-CLH builds on the A-CLH lock. For local lock handoffs, much like the A-CLH lock, the A-C-BO-CLH leverages the A-CLH queue structure in its cohort detection scheme. A thread can identify the existence of cohorts by checking the A-CLH lock's tail pointer. If the pointer does not point to the thread's node, it means that a subsequent request to acquire the lock was posted by another thread. However, now that threads can abort their lock acquisition attempts, this simple check is not sufficient to identify any "active" cohorts, because the ones that enqueued their nodes may have aborted, or will abort.

In order to address this problem, we introduce a new *successor-aborted* flag in the A-CLH queue node. We colocate the *successor-aborted* flag with the prev field of each node so as to ensure that both are read and modified atomically. Each thread sets this flag to false, and its node's prev field to *busy*, before enqueueing the node in the CLH queue. An aborting thread atomically (with a CAS) sets its node's predecessor's *successor-aborted* flag to true to inform its predecessor that it has aborted (the thread subsequently updates its node's prev field to make the predecessor explicitly visible to the successor).

While releasing the lock, a thread first checks its node's *successor-aborted* flag to determine if the successor may have aborted. If not, the thread can release the local lock by atomically (using a CAS instruction) setting its node's prev field to the *release local* state (just like the release in C-BO-MCS). This use of a CAS coupled with the colocation of prev and *successor-aborted* fields ensures that the successor thread cannot abort at the same time. The successor can then determine that it has become the lock owner. If the successor did abort (indicated by the *successor-aborted* flag), the thread releases the global BO lock, and then sets its node's state to *release global*.

Our use of a CAS instruction to do local lock handoffs seems quite heavy-handed. And we conjecture that indeed it would be counter-productive if the CAS induced cache coherence traffic between NUMA clusters. However, since the CAS targets memory that is likely to already be resident in cache of the local cluster in writable state, the cost of local transactions is quite low – equivalent to a store instruction hitting the L2 cache on the system we used for our empirical evaluation.

3.7 Bounding Local Lock Handoff Rates

All the locks described above are deeply unfair, and with even modest amounts of contention can easily lead to thread starvation. To address this problem, we add a *may-pass-local* method that increments a simple counter of the number of times threads in a cohort have consecutively acquired the lock in a *release local* state. If the counter crosses a threshold (64) in our experiments, the lock releaser releases the global lock, and then releases the local lock, transitioning it to the *release global* state. This simple solution appears to work very effectively for all our algorithms.

4. Empirical Evaluation

We evaluated cohort locks, comparing them with the traditional, as well as the more recent NUMA-aware locks, on multiple levels: First we conducted several experiments on microbenchmarks that stress test these locks in several ways. This gives us a good insight into the performance characteristics of the locks. Second, we integrated these locks in memcached, a popular key-value data store application, to study their impact on real world workload settings. Third, we modified the libc memory allocator to study the effects of cohort locks on allocation intensive multi-threaded applications; we present results of experiments on a microbenchmark [6].

Our microbenchmark evaluation clearly demonstrates that cohort locks outperform all prior locks by at least 60%. Additionally, the abortable cohort locks scale vastly better (by a factor of 6) than the state-of-the-art abortable locks. Furthermore, cohort locks improved the performance of memcached by about 20% for write-heavy workloads. Finally, our libc allocator experiments demonstrate that simply replacing the lock used by the default Solaris allocator with a cohort lock can significantly boost cluster-level reference locality for accesses by the allocator to allocation metatdata and for accesses by the application to allocated blocks, resulting in improved performance for multi-threaded application that make heavy use of memory allocation services.

In our evaluation we compare the performance of our non-abortable and abortable cohort locks with existing state-of-the-art locks in the respective categories. Specifically, for our microbenchmark study, we present throughput results for our C-BO-BO, C-TKT-TKT, C-BO-MCS, C-TKT-MCS and C-MCS-MCS cohort locks. We compare these with MCS [10] (as a base line NUMA-oblivious lock), and other NUMA-aware locks, namely, HBO [12], HCLH [15], and FC-MCS [7]. We also evaluated our abortable cohort locks (namely, A-C-BO-BO and A-C-BO-CLH) by comparing them with an abortable version of HBO, and the abortable CLH lock [14].

Memcached uses pthread locks for synchronization. To test our locks with memcached, we decided to adhere to the policy of not changing the memcached sources or its binary. This choice is facilitated by the fact that the pthread library is dynamically linked to the application. So we can easily use a Solaris LD_PRELOAD *interpose* library that installs any kind of lock we want under the pthread library API. The scalability results for memcached are reported in Section 4.2. For the libc allocator experiments, we used the same interpose library to inject our locks into the allocator.

We implemented all of the above algorithms in C and compiled them with the GCC 4.4.1 at optimization level -O3 in 32-bit mode. The experiments were conducted on an Oracle T5440 series machine which consists of 4 Niagara T2+ SPARC chips, each chip containing 8 cores, and each core containing 2 pipelines with 4 hardware thread contexts per pipeline, for a total of 256 hardware thread contexts, running at a 1.4 GHz clock frequency. Each chip has a 4MB L2 cache, and each core has a shared 8KB L1 data cache. For all the NUMA-aware locks, a Niagara T2+ chip is the NUMA clustering unit, so in all we had 4 NUMA clusters.

Memcached was evaluated using a standard client application called *memaslap*, which is a part of a larger suite of memcached applications called *libmemcached*. Results reported were averaged over 3 test runs.

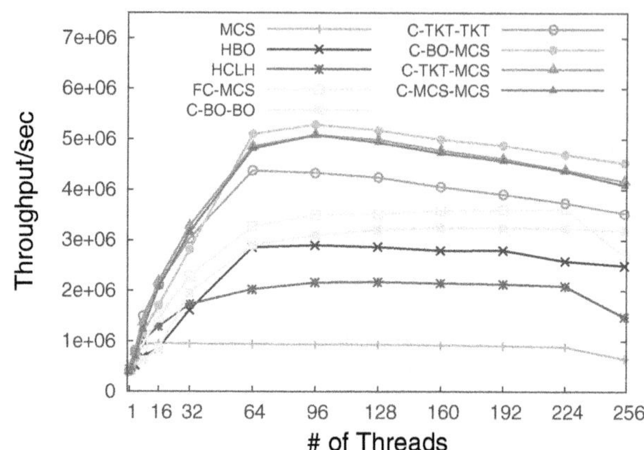

Figure 2. The graph shows the average throughput in terms of number of critical and non-critical section pairs executed per second. The critical section accesses two distinct cache blocks (increments 4 integer counters on each block), and the non-critical section is an idle spin loop of up to 4 microseconds.

4.1 Microbenchmark Evaluation

4.1.1 Scalability

We constructed what we consider to be a reasonable representative microbenchmark, LBench, to measure the scalability of various lock algorithms. LBench launches a specified number of identical threads. Each thread loops as follows: acquire a central shared lock, access shared variables in the critical section, release the lock, and then execute a non-critical work phase of about 4 microseconds. The critical section reads and writes shared variables residing on two distinct cache lines. At the end of a 60 second measurement period the program reports the aggregate number of iterations completed by all threads as well as statistics related to the distribution of iterations completed by individual threads, which reflects gross long-term fairness. Finally, the benchmark can be configured to tally and report lock migrations.

Figure 2 depicts the performance of the non-abortable locks on LBench. (We conducted other experiments varying the critical section length, non-critical section length, and number of cache lines accessed within the critical section, but observed similar results to those reported). As a baseline to compare against, we measured the throughput of the MCS lock, which is a classic scalable queue lock. This lock performed the worst because it does not leverage reference locality, which is critical for good performance on NUMA architectures. The HCLH, HBO and FC-MCS locks perform as expected – with FC-MCS generally performing the best among the three. HBO's performance, which is better than HCLH in this workload, is highly sensitive to the underlying workload, and is generally very unstable (as we will see in Section 4.2).

Our C-BO-BO lock scales very well, approaching the performance of FC-MCS. Because it is based on the BO lock, C-BO-BO is sensitive to backoff parameters – different workloads might require different backoff parameters for the best possible performance. However, this sensitivity is related only to the parameters associated with local backoff locks, unlike HBO, where the backoff parameters need to be tuned for both the local and remote backoffs. Under C-BO-BO we expect that the global lock will remain lightly contended; and in fact, in our implementation, threads contending at the global BO lock continuously spin on it and never backoff, much like the "bare bones" test-and-test-and-set lock. Our C-TKT-TKT lock scales even better (generally 30-40% better than the prior state-of-the-art NUMA-aware lock, FC-MCS). C-BO-MCS scales

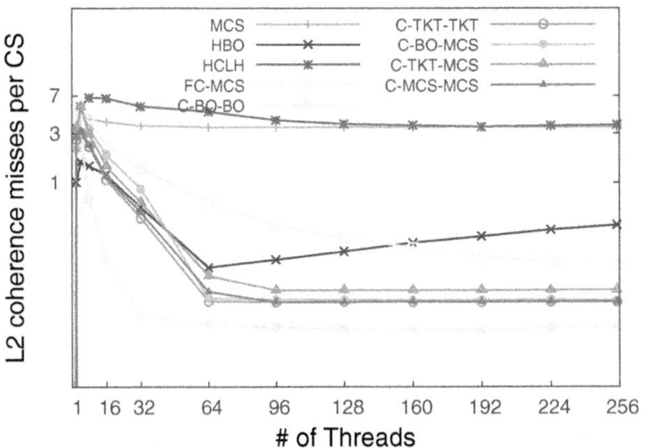

Figure 3. The graph shows the average number of L2 cache coherence misses per critical section for the experiment in Figure 2 (lower is better). The Y-axis is in log scale.

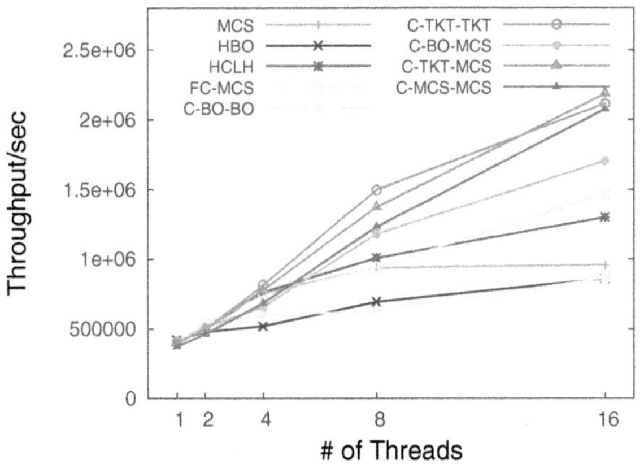

Figure 4. A closer look at the throughput results of Figure 2 for low contention levels (1 to 16 threads).

the best with scalability 60% better than FC-MCS, whereas C-TKT-MCS and C-MCS-MCS trail slightly behind C-BO-MCS.

In all the tests reported in this paper, the allowable maximum number of consecutive local lock handoffs for cohort locks was limited to a constant (64). As described in Section 3.7, this bound is necessary to avoid the deep unfairness that the basic cohort locks can possibly generate in an application. We conducted microbenchmark tests (not reported in this paper) on cohort lock versions without the local handoff limits and found that generally the deeply unfair versions out-scale the fair versions by about 10% during high contention loads. However, in our tests we found that, for LBench, the unfair versions typically led to local lock handoffs in the order of hundreds of thousands before the lock was acquired by a remote thread/cohort. Thus, we believe that the cost of 10% is small to avoid the potential problem of gross long-term unfairness and starvation.

4.1.2 Locality of Reference

Figure 3 provides the key explanation for the observed scalability results. Recall that each chip (a NUMA cluster) on our experimental machine has an L2 cache shared by all cores on that chip. Furthermore, the latency to access a cache block in the local L2 cache is much lower than the latency to access a cache block on a remote L2 cache (on our test machine, remote L2 access is approximately 4 times slower than local L2 access during light loads). The latter also involves bus transactions that can adversely affect the latency during high loads, further compounding the cost of remote L2 accesses. That is, remote L2 accesses always incur latency costs even if the interconnect is otherwise idle, but they can also induce interconnect channel contention if the system is under heavy load. Figure 3 reports the L2 coherence miss rates collected during the scalability experiment. These are the local L2 misses that were fulfilled by a remote L2, which represents the local to remote lock handoff events and related data movement.

MCS has a high L2 coherence miss rate because it is the fairest among all the locks, and does not prioritize local lock acquisition requests over remote requests. Interestingly, HCLH also has a high miss rate, which clearly explains its performance in Figure 2. We can attribute the high miss rate in HCLH to its complexity [7] and high rates of accesses to shared lock metadata, which translates to lower rate of batching of requests coming from the same NUMA cluster. HBO shows a very good miss rate until the number of threads is substantially high (64), after which, the miss rate deteriorates considerably. In our experiments with HBO, we observed that its backoff parameters are highly sensitive to the underlying workload; the HBO lock results discussed here are for a version whose backoff parameters were tuned for this microbenchmark (we will show later that these same backoff parameters hurt the performance of memcached). The L2 miss rate in FC-MCS degrades gradually, but consistently, with increasing thread count.

All our cohort locks have significantly lower (by a factor of two or greater – note that the Y-axis is in log scale) L2 miss rates than all other reported locks. This is because the cohort locks consistently provide long sequences of successive accesses to the lock from the same NUMA cluster (cohort), which accelerates the critical section performance by reducing inter-core coherence transfers for data accessed within and by the critical section. There are two reasons for longer cohort sequences (or, more generally, *batches*) in cohort locks, compared to prior NUMA-aware locks, such as FC-MCS. First, the simplicity of cohort locks streamlines the instruction sequence of batching requests in the cohort, which makes the batching more efficient. Second, and more importantly, a cohort batch can dynamically "grow" during its execution without the interference by threads from other cohorts. As an example, consider a cohort of 3 threads $T1$, $T2$, and $T3$ (ordered in that order in a local MCS queue M in a C-BO-MCS lock). Let $T1$ be the owner of the global BO lock. So $T1$ can enter its critical section, and handoff the BO lock (and the local MCS lock) to $T2$ on exit. The BO lock will eventually be forwarded to $T3$. However, note that in the meantime, $T1$ can return and post another request after $T3$'s request in M. If $T3$ holds the lock during this time, it ends up handing it off to $T1$ after it is done executing its critical section. This dynamic growth aspect of our cohort locks can significantly boost local handoff rates when there is sufficient cluster-local contention. This dynamic batch growth aspect in cohort locks contrasts with the more "static" approach of other NUMA-aware locks, which in turn gives more power to cohort locks to enhance the locality of reference of the critical section. In our experiments, we have observed that the batching rate in all the locks is inversely proportional to the lock migration rate and observed coherence traffic reported in Figure 3, and that the batching rate in cohort locks increases more quickly with contention compared to other locks.

4.1.3 Low Contention Performance

We believe that for a highly scalable lock to be practical, it must also perform efficiently at low or zero contention levels. At face value, the hierarchical nature of cohort locks appears to suggest that they will be expensive at low contention levels. That is because each thread must acquire both the local and the global locks, which become a part of the critical path in low contention or contention free scenarios. To understand this cost we took a closer look at

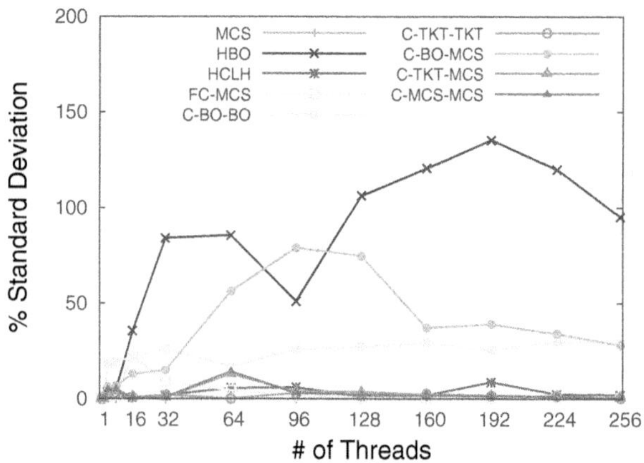

Figure 5. The graph shows the standard deviation in percentage points of per-thread throughput from the average throughput reported in Figure 2 (the lower the standard deviation, the more fair the lock is in practice).

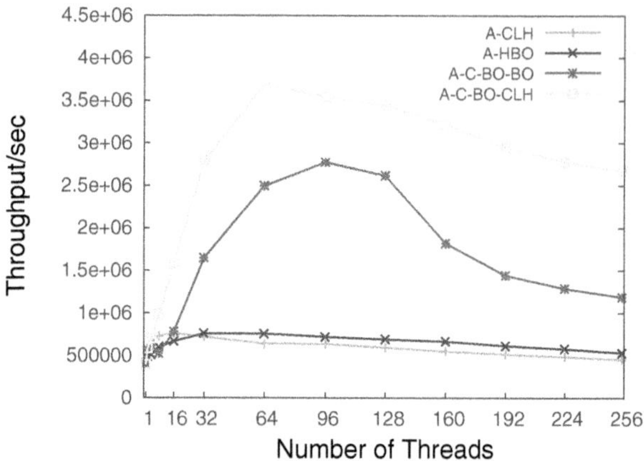

Figure 6. Abortable lock average throughput in terms of number of critical and non-critical sections executed per second. The critical section accesses two distinct cache blocks (increments 4 integers counters on each block), and the non-critical section is an idle spin loop of up to 4 micro seconds.

the scalability results reported in Figure 2 with an eye toward performance at low contention levels. Figure 4 zooms into that part of Figure 2. Interestingly, we observed that the performance of all the cohort locks was competitive with all other locks that do not need to acquire locks at multiple levels in the hierarchy (viz. MCS, HBO, and FC-MCS). On further reflection, we note that the extra cost of multi-level lock acquisitions in cohort locks withers away as background noise in the presence of non-trivial work in the critical and non-critical sections. In principle, one can devise contrived scenarios (for example, where the critical and non-critical sections are empty) to show that cohort locks might perform worse than other locks at low contention levels. However, we believe that such scenarios are most likely unrealistic or far too rare to be of any consequence. Even if one comes up with such a scenario, we can add the same "bypass the local lock" optimization that was employed in FC-MCS to minimize the flat combining overhead at low thread counts.

4.1.4 Fairness

Given that cohort locks are inherently unfair (which is the key "feature" that all NUMA-aware locks harness and leverage to enhance locality of reference for better performance), we were interested in quantifying that unfairness. To that end, we report more data from the experiment reported in Figure 2 on the standard deviation of per-thread throughput from the average throughput of all the threads. The results are shown in Figure 5. These results give us a sense of how far each thread progressed during its one minute of execution in a test run.

We found HBO to be the least fair lock, where some threads executed only a handful of critical sections, while others completed millions of critical sections. The next most unfair lock, to our surprise, was C-BO-MCS. (Recall that the cohort locks contain a constant limit of 64 local handoffs after which a lock releaser must release the global and local locks.) On further reflection, the reason for this unfairness is clear – the global BO lock in C-BO-MCS is unfair. After a thread releases the global BO lock, causing the cache block of the BO lock to be invalidated from other caches, and go to modified state in the releaser's cache, it immediately releases the local lock, which is also quickly detected by the next thread waiting to acquire the local lock. This next local thread, identifying that it must acquire the global BO lock, almost instantly attempts to do so, and usually succeeds because the BO lock's cache block is in its (and the last releaser's) L1 or L2 cache. Hence the obvious unfairness arises from unfairness in cache coherence arbitration.

We also observe that the standard deviation for C-TKT-MCS and C-MCS-MCS are low, because their global locks (ticket and MCS) are comparatively fair.

C-BO-BO is fairer than C-BO-MCS because the interval between a lock releaser releasing the global lock and the next local lock acquirer attempting to acquire the global BO lock is inflated because the acquirer must first acquire the local BO lock. The extended interval increases the window in which a remote thread/cohort can acquire the global BO lock.

All other locks, MCS, HCLH, FC-MCS, and C-TKT-TKT are also fair, as expected, with the standard deviation well under 5% (the deviation of FC-MCS spikes to about 20% at 16 threads, but is reasonably low at other concurrency levels).

4.1.5 Abortable Lock Performance

Our abortable lock experiments in Figure 6 make an equally compelling case for cohort locks. Our cohort locks (A-C-BO-BO and A-C-BO-CLH) outperform the best prior abortable lock (A-CLH) and an abortable variant of HBO (called A-HBO in Figure 6, where a thread aborts its lock acquisition by simply returning a failure flag from the lock acquire operation) by up to a factor of 6. Since lock handoff is a "local" operation in A-C-BO-CLH involving just the lock releaser (that uses a CAS to release the lock) and the lock acquirer (just like a CLH lock), A-C-BO-CLH scales significantly better than A-C-BO-BO, where threads incur significant contention with other threads on the same NUMA cluster to acquire the local BO lock. (For these and other unreported experiments, the abort rate was lower than 1%, which we believe is a reasonable rate.)

4.2 Memcached

Memcached [2] is a popular open-source, high-performance, distributed in-memory key-value data store that is typically used as a caching layer for databases in high-performance applications. Memcached has several high profile users including Facebook, LiveJournal, Wikipedia, Flickr, Youtube, Twitter, etc.

In memcached, the key-value pairs are stored in a huge hash table, and all server threads access this table concurrently. Access to the entire table is mediated through a single lock (called the cache_lock). The cache_lock is known to be a contention bottleneck [11], which we believe makes it a good candidate for the evaluation of cohort locks. Among other things, the memcached API contains two fundamental operations on key-value pairs: get (that returns the value for a give key) and set (that updates the value of

#	pthread locks	Fib-BO	MCS	HBO	HBO (tuned)	FC-MCS	C-BO-BO	C-TKT-TKT	C-BO-MCS	C-TKT-MCS	C-MCS-MCS
1	1.00	0.89	0.99	0.83	1.01	0.83	0.99	0.82	0.81	0.77	0.95
4	3.06	3.17	3.15	1.58	3.37	2.70	3.11	3.09	3.09	3.05	2.99
8	4.37	4.48	4.47	1.96	4.43	4.25	3.48	4.46	4.45	4.49	4.45
16	4.55	4.59	4.60	2.55	4.58	4.47	2.56	4.56	4.60	4.58	4.53
32	4.47	4.57	4.53	3.05	4.53	4.18	3.03	4.54	4.57	4.56	4.55
64	4.40	4.54	4.45	3.37	4.51	4.26	2.98	4.52	4.49	4.51	4.44
96	4.39	4.50	4.46	3.37	4.52	4.32	2.97	4.48	4.50	4.52	4.46
128	4.39	4.49	4.47	3.39	4.52	4.28	2.98	4.46	4.49	4.53	4.46
(a) 90% gets and 10% sets											
1	1.00	1.04	1.15	0.97	0.93	0.95	1.14	1.00	0.92	1.12	1.11
4	2.84	3.21	3.30	1.45	3.23	2.73	2.98	3.10	3.19	2.98	3.16
8	3.55	4.63	4.51	1.73	4.75	4.00	2.46	4.53	4.51	4.47	4.32
16	3.56	4.95	4.93	2.17	5.18	4.51	2.59	5.08	5.05	5.03	4.97
32	3.42	4.93	4.77	2.57	5.10	3.92	2.79	4.99	5.04	4.95	4.94
64	3.29	4.81	4.45	2.86	5.08	3.93	2.67	4.88	4.88	4.79	4.74
96	3.32	4.80	4.47	2.84	5.07	3.94	2.69	4.84	4.86	4.78	4.71
128	3.32	4.81	4.24	2.84	5.09	3.90	2.68	4.87	4.85	4.71	4.68
(b) 50% gets and 50% sets											
1	1.00	1.05	1.03	1.02	1.22	1.00	1.03	0.97	1.05	1.06	1.13
4	2.62	3.03	2.74	1.43	2.95	2.44	2.82	2.65	2.66	2.57	2.60
8	2.74	3.80	3.62	1.76	4.23	3.21	2.27	3.80	3.80	3.74	3.61
16	2.77	4.08	3.92	1.99	4.76	3.62	2.50	4.54	4.52	4.48	4.30
32	2.67	4.08	3.94	2.27	4.86	3.31	2.53	4.81	4.70	4.70	4.50
64	2.59	3.89	3.62	2.49	4.63	3.34	2.44	4.47	4.41	4.40	4.23
96	2.62	3.92	3.65	2.49	4.64	3.35	2.45	4.44	4.40	4.38	4.23
128	2.59	3.94	3.51	2.49	4.67	3.33	2.44	4.46	4.47	4.30	4.20
(c) 10% gets and 90% sets											

Table 1. Scalability results (in terms of speedup over single thread runs that use pthread locks) for memcached for (a) read-heavy (90% get operations, and 10% set operations), (b) mixed (50% get operations, and 50% set operations), and (c) write-heavy (10% get operations, and 90% set operations) configurations.

the given key). These are the most frequently used API calls by memcached client applications.

To generate load for the memcached server, we use memaslap, a load generation and benchmarking tool for memcached. memaslap is a part of the standard client library (called libmemcached) for memcached [1]. memaslap generates a memcached workload consisting of a configurable mixture of get and set requests. We experimented with a wide range of get-set mixture ratio, ranging from configurations with 90% gets and 10% sets (representing read-heavy workloads) to configurations with 10% gets and 90% sets (representing write-heavy workloads). The read-heavy workloads are the norm for memcached applications. The write-heavy workloads, however uncommon, do exist. Examples of write-heavy workloads include servers that continuously collect huge amounts of sensor network data, or servers that constantly update statistical information on a large collection of items. These applications at times can exhibit bi-modal behavior, alternating between write-heavy and read-heavy phases, collecting and processing large amounts of data respectively.

As discussed earlier, we used an interpose library to inject our locks under the pthreads API used by memcached. For our experiments, we ran an instance of memcached on the T5440 server, and an instance of memaslap on another 128-way Niagara II machine. We varied the thread count for memcached from 1 to 128 (the maximum number of threads permitted by memcached). We ran the memaslap client with 32 threads for all tests so as to keep the load generation high and constant. For each test, the memaslap clients were executed for one minute, after which the throughput, in terms of operations per second, was reported. Table 1 shows the relative performance of memcached while it was configured to use the different locks. The figure contains 3 tables for three different get-set proportions, each representing read-heavy, mixed, and write-heavy loads respectively. Each entry in each table is normalized to the performance of pthread locks at 1 thread.

The first column in all the tables represents the number of memcached threads used in the test. The second column reports the performance of pthread locks. The remaining columns report the performance of memcached when used with MCS, a test-and-test-and-set lock with Fibonnaci backoff (Fib-BO), the HBO lock (representing prior NUMA-aware locks), a tuned version of HBO (we had to add this version because the default version did not scale well), and all the non-abortable cohort locks discussed in Section 3. Note that the fine tuning for the HBO lock was done on the local and remote backoff parameters. The version that we first used in the experiments (column titled HBO) had the backoff parameters tuned for our microbenchmark experiments. As is clear from all three tables, these did not work well on memcached. This clearly demonstrates the instability of HBO's performance.

For read-heavy loads (Table 1 (a)), the performance of all the locks except HBO and C-BO-BO is identical, with all locks enabling over 5X scaling. For loads with moderately high set ratios (Table 1 (b)), we observe that all the spin locks except HBO and C-BO-BO significantly outperform pthread locks, and are generally competitive with each other. For write-heavy loads (Table 1 (c)), the NUMA-aware locks clearly out-scale the NUMA-oblivious locks by at least 20%. The untuned HBO and C-BO-BO locks scale poorly in all configurations. It appears that C-BO-BO suffers because of contention on the local BO locks, whereas HBO suffers with contention on the central lock. FC-MCS performs better than HBO and C-BO-BO, but worse than all other spinlocks.

4.3 malloc

Memory allocation and deallocation is a common operation appearing frequently in all kinds of applications. A vast number of C/C++ programs use libc's malloc and free functions for managing their dynamic memory requirements. These functions are thread-safe, but on Solaris the default allocator relies on synchronization via a single lock to guarantee thread safety. For memory intensive multi-threaded applications that use libc's malloc and free functions, this lock can quickly become a contention bottleneck. Consequently, we found it to be an attractive evaluation tool for cohort locks. We modified libc's malloc.c file to use pthread locks, and injected our locks in the code via the interpose library discussed previously.

We used the mmicro benchmark [6] to test various lock algorithms via the interpose library. In the benchmark, each thread repeatedly allocates a block of memory (size 64 bytes), initializes it

thrds	pthread locks	fib-BO	MCS	HBO	HBO (tuned)	FC-MCS	C-BO-BO	C-TKT-TKT	C-BO-MCS	C-TKT-MCS	C-MCS-MCS
1	198	211	197	206	206	190	197	195	191	191	183
2	197	237	224	204	231	231	223	220	214	218	208
4	125	258	271	206	300	288	253	326	252	307	249
8	145	294	307	230	382	322	320	486	326	456	432
16	151	318	307	244	420	327	483	592	513	576	564
32	149	323	307	248	291	329	783	839	941	827	814
64	149	302	303	259	151	328	883	1011	1183	1001	952
128	146	225	290	263	73	321	932	884	1120	863	822
255	142	139	277	257	38	264	926	695	961	682	651

Table 2. Scalability results of the malloc experiment (in terms of malloc-free pairs executed per millisecond.

(by writing to the first 4 words of it), and subsequently frees it. Each test runs for 10 seconds and reports the aggregate number of malloc-free pairs completed in that interval. We add an artificial delay after each of the calls to malloc and free functions. This delay is a configurable parameter; we injected a delay of about 4 microseconds, which enables some concurrency between the thread executing the critical sections (malloc or free), and the threads waiting in the delay loop. The results of the tests appear in Table 2, showing that cohort locks outperform all the other locks. While the other locks scale the benchmark's throughput by up to a factor of 2X, the scalability with cohort locks ranges between a factor of 5X and 6X.

There are two reasons for this impressive scalability of cohort locks: First, they tend to effectively batch requests coming from the same NUMA cluster, thus improving the lock handoff latency. The second reason has to do with the recycling of memory blocks deallocated by threads: The libc allocator maintains a single *splay tree* of free nodes of various sizes (it also maintains lists of small – 40 bytes or less – memory blocks used for small size requests). Since mmicro requests 64 byte blocks, all the requests go to the splay tree. A newly inserted node always goes to the root of the tree, and as a result, the most recently deallocated memory blocks tend to be reallocated more often (allocation is done by returning the first matching block in the splay tree). Thus a small number of tree nodes (and their respective memory blocks) are continuously circulated between threads. The tree node cache lines are updated on every delete (malloc) and insert (free). Additionally, the allocated memory blocks are also updated by the benchmark. All these writes play a crucial role in the performance of the underlying locks used by the allocator. Because all the cohort locks create large batches of consecutive requests coming from the same NUMA cluster, they manage to recycle blocks in the same cluster for extended periods. In contrast, for all other locks, a block of memory migrates more frequently between NUMA clusters, thus leading to greater coherence traffic, and the resulting performance degradation.

While highly scalable allocators exist and have been described at length in the literature, selection of such allocators often entails making tradeoffs such as footprint against scalability. In part because of such concerns the default on Solaris remains the simple single-lock allocator. By employing cohort locks under the default libc allocator we can improve the scalability of applications but without forcing the user or developer to confront the issues and decisions related to alternative allocators.

FC-MCS does not show any significant improvements over prior locks. The performance of HBO continues to be unstable: The first HBO column in Table 2 shows the libc allocator's performance with the backoff parameters picked from our earlier microbenchmark experiments, while the second HBO column, titled: HBO (tuned), uses the parameters tuned for good performance on memcached. In this case, the tuned version of HBO scales better than the untuned version up to modest levels of contention. However, the performance dramatically deteriorates with higher contention. In contrast, cohort locks are vastly more stable across a broad swath of workloads. This property of "parameter parsimony" makes cohort locks a significantly more attractive choice for deployment in real world applications.

5. Conclusion

The growing size of multicore machines is likely to shift the design space in the NUMA and CC-NUMA direction, requiring a significant rehash of existing concurrent algorithms and synchronization mechanisms. This paper tackles the most basic of the multicore synchronization algorithms, the lock, presenting a simple new lock design approach – *lock cohorting* – fit for NUMA machines. The wide range of cohort locks we presented in the paper, along with their empirical evaluation, demonstrates that lock cohorting is not only a simple approach to NUMA-aware lock construction, but also a powerful one that delivers locks that out-scale prior locks by significant margins, while remaining competitive at low contention levels.

References

[1] libmemcached. *www.libmemcached.org*.

[2] memcached – a distributed memory object caching system. *www.memcached.org*.

[3] A. Agarwal and M. Cherian. Adaptive backoff synchronization techniques. *SIGARCH Comput. Archit. News*, 17:396–406, April 1989.

[4] T. Craig. Building FIFO and priority-queueing spin locks from atomic swap. Technical Report TR 93-02-02, University of Washington, Dept of Computer Science, February 1993.

[5] D. Dice. *US Patent # 07318128: Wakeup affinity and locality.*

[6] D. Dice and A. Garthwaite. Mostly Lock Free Malloc. In *Proceedings of the 3rd International Symposium on Memory Management*, pages 163–174, 2002.

[7] D. Dice, V. Marathe, and N. Shavit. Flat Combining NUMA Locks. In *Proceedings of the 23rd ACM Symposium on Parallelism in Algorithms and Architectures*, 2011.

[8] D. Hendler, I. Incze, N. Shavit, and M. Tzafrir. Flat Combining and the Synchronization-Parallelism Tradeoff. In *Proceedings of the 22nd ACM Symposium on Parallelism in Algorithms and Architectures*, pages 355–364, 2010.

[9] M. Herlihy and N. Shavit. *The Art of Multiprocessor Programming*. Morgan Kaufmann, 2007.

[10] J. Mellor-Crummey and M. Scott. Algorithms for scalable synchronization on shared-memory multiprocessors. *ACM Trans. Computer Systems*, 9(1):21–65, 1991.

[11] M. Pohlack and S. Diestelhorst. From Lightweight Hardware Transactional Memory to LightWeight Lock Elision. In *Proceedings of the 6th ACM SIGPLAN Workshop on Transactional Computing*, 2011.

[12] Z. Radović and E. Hagersten. Hierarchical Backoff Locks for Nonuniform Communication Architectures. In *HPCA-9*, pages 241–252, Anaheim, California, USA, Feb. 2003.

[13] M. Scott and W. Scherer. Scalable queue-based spin locks with timeout. In *Proc. 8th ACM SIGPLAN Symposium on Principles and Practices of Parallel Programming*, pages 44–52, 2001.

[14] M. L. Scott. Non-blocking timeout in scalable queue-based spin locks. In *Proceedings of the twenty-first annual symposium on Principles of distributed computing*, PODC '02, pages 31–40, New York, NY, USA, 2002. ACM.

[15] Victor Luchangco and Dan Nussbaum and Nir Shavit. A Hierarchical CLH Queue Lock. In *Proceedings of the 12th International Euro-Par Conference*, pages 801–810, 2006.

Revisiting the Combining Synchronization Technique

Panagiota Fatourou
Department of Computer Science
University of Crete & FORTH ICS
faturu@csd.uoc.gr

Nikolaos D. Kallimanis
Department of Computer Science
University of Ioannina
nkallima@cs.uoi.gr

Abstract

Fine-grain thread synchronization has been proved, in several cases, to be outperformed by efficient implementations of the combining technique where a single thread, called the *combiner*, holding a coarse-grain lock, serves, in addition to its own synchronization request, active requests announced by other threads while they are waiting by performing some form of spinning. Efficient implementations of this technique significantly reduce the cost of synchronization, so in many cases they exhibit much better performance than the most efficient finely synchronized algorithms.

In this paper, we revisit the combining technique with the goal to discover where its real performance power resides and whether or how ensuring some desired properties (e.g., fairness in serving requests) would impact performance. We do so by presenting two new implementations of this technique; the first (CC-Synch) addresses systems that support coherent caches, whereas the second (DSM-Synch) works better in cacheless NUMA machines. In comparison to previous such implementations, the new implementations (1) provide bounds on the number of remote memory references (RMRs) that they perform, (2) support a stronger notion of fairness, and (3) use simpler and less basic primitives than previous approaches. In all our experiments, the new implementations outperform by far all previous state-of-the-art combining-based and fine-grain synchronization algorithms. Our experimental analysis sheds light to the questions we aimed to answer.

Several modern multi-core systems organize the cores into clusters and provide fast communication within the same cluster and much slower communication across clusters. We present an hierarchical version of CC-Synch, called H-Synch which exploits the hierarchical communication nature of such systems to achieve better performance. Experiments show that H-Synch significantly outperforms previous state-of-the-art hierarchical approaches.

We provide new implementations of common shared data structures (like stacks and queues) based on CC-Synch, DSM-Synch and H-Synch. Our experiments show that these implementations outperform by far all previous (fine-grain or combined-based) implementations of shared stacks and queues.

Categories and Subject Descriptors D.1.3 [*Programming Techniques*]: Concurrent Programming—Distributed programming, Parallel programming

PPoPP'12, February 25–29, 2012, New Orleans, Louisiana, USA.

General Terms Algorithms, Experimentation, Theory, Performance

Keywords Synchronization techniques, combining, hierarchical algorithms, blocking algorithms, concurrent data structures

1. Introduction

The last decade, the computer industry has made a significant turn towards developing multicore systems which nowadays, are used in any computing device. In such machines, increased performance can be achieved by exploiting parallelism; thus, harnessing the difficulty of concurrent programming is currently very important.

Several applications that are to be parallelized contain parts whose parallelization requires significant synchronization and coordination. Amdhal's law [1] implies that failing in parallelizing these parts may result in a significant limitation on the speed-up that could be achieved. However, these parts usually contain accesses to shared data and thus, parallelizing them requires the design of low-overhead synchronization mechanisms; without efficient such mechanisms the synchronization cost may overshadow any performance gain that could result from the parallelization of these parts.

Synchronization requests (e.g., accesses to the same shared data) must be executed in mutual exclusion; so, their execution often becomes a hot spot in a concurrent environment. Due to mutual exclusion, the best time that can be achieved to execute a number of such requests by any number of threads is no less than the time required by a single thread to execute them sequentially sidestepping the synchronization protocol. Therefore, ideally, the elapsed time to execute the same number of synchronization requests should be the same regardless of the number of threads that issue them. Apparently, this ideal behaviour is highly scalable and therefore very desirable. In practice, however, the contention effects may have a drastic impact in performance.

The *combining* synchronization technique [7, 12, 23] has recently gained ground since it has been experimentally proved that efficient implementations of this technique outperform all other synchronization mechanisms in several cases. In this technique, a list is employed to store the synchronization requests of active threads. After announcing its request by placing a node in the list, a thread tries to acquire a global lock. The thread that manages to acquire the lock, called the *combiner*, serves, in addition to its own synchronization request, active requests announced by other threads. In the meantime, each active thread that does not hold the lock, busy waits until either its request has been fulfilled by the combiner thread or the global lock has been released.

The combining technique has been employed for the design of common concurrent data structures like queues and stacks. Interthread communication is heavily based on accessing such concurrent data structures and therefore their efficient implementation is of major importance for achieving good performance and scalability. The combining-based implementations of such data structures have experimentally been proved [7, 12] to outperform all previous state-of-the-art implementations of such structures which mainly employ some kind of fine-grain thread synchronization and take into consideration the data structure's access pattern.

In this paper, we revisit the combining technique aiming at discovering where its real performance power resides, understanding the performance implications of using different primitives when implementing it, and investigating whether and how ensuring some desired properties (e.g., fairness in serving requests) would impact performance. We do so by presenting two new implementations of this technique. The first, called CC-Synch, is suitable for *cache coherent* (CC) shared memory systems where accesses to shared objects are performed via cached copies of them; an access to a shared object is a *remote memory reference* (RMR) if the cached copy of this object is invalid, so the access causes a cache miss[1]. The vast majority of modern parallel architectures follow the CC shared memory model. The second implementation, called DSM-Synch, is better suited for the *distributed shared memory* (DSM) model, where a part of the shared memory is associated with each processor; so, each shared object is allocated (and resides) in the part of the shared memory that is associated to a specific processor. Processors do not have access to local caches, so a thread p performs a *remote memory reference* (RMR) if it accesses a shared object residing in the shared memory part of some processor other than that where p is being executed. Since an RMR is significantly more costly than a local memory reference [20], it is highly desirable to design algorithms that perform as few RMRs as possible; CC-Synch and DSM-Synch perform a bounded number of RMRs.

CC-Synch and DSM-Synch use a single FIFO queue to do both (1) implement the lock and (2) store the active synchronization requests. Therefore, the synchronization needed for implementing the list of active requests comes for free. Specifically, each newly activated thread adds a node to the tail of the queue to announce its request and participate to the implementation of the lock. Thus, each active thread is assigned one of the nodes of the queue. The active thread q that owns the first node of the queue becomes the combiner and undertakes the responsibility of applying some (or all) of the requests listed in the queue. Each active thread whose record is not first in the queue performs local spinning.

The experimental analysis (Section 3) reveals that the use of a highly-efficient queue-like lock which, in addition to its low synchronization overhead, provides the implementation of the list of announced requests for free, significantly reduces the synchronization required to implement the combining technique. Moreover, the new implementations are simpler to program than previous combining-based synchronization approaches. These result in a performance benefit in comparison to all previous combining-based synchronization approaches and in many cases to all fine-grain methods. Additionally, the new implementations exhibit several nice properties, not ensured by previous combining implementations [12, 23]. First, they provide stronger fairness guarantees in serving the requests. Second, they provide bounds on the number of remote memory references that are executed. Specifically, in CC-Synch, the combiner thread performs $O(h+t)$ RMRs, where h is an upper bound on the number of synchronization requests that the combiner may serve, and t is the size of the shared data that should be accessed in order to execute these h requests; we remark that h is a parameter that can be determined by the user and it can be chosen to be constant. The combiner in DSM-Synch performs $O(dh)$ RMRs, where d is the average number of RMRs required to serve a single request. In both algorithms, all threads, other than the combiner, perform local spinning and cause only a constant number of RMRs. Thus, the amortized number of performed RMRs is $O(d)$. Moreover, no thread may ever starve. Finally, the new implementations do not employ any form of backoff and they need minimal tuning to achieve the best performance.

CC-Synch uses a `Swap` object in addition to read-write (r/w) registers; a `Swap` object O supports in addition to `read`, the operation `Swap`(O, v) which (atomically) writes in O the value v and returns the previous value of O. DSM-Synch uses an object that supports `CAS` and `Swap` in addition to r/w registers; a `CAS`(O, u, v) (atomically) checks if the current value of O is u and if this is so, it changes the value of O to v and returns `TRUE`, otherwise the value of O remains unchanged and `FALSE` is returned. CC-Synch and DSM-Synch use just one primitive stronger than r/w registers and in CC-Synch this is a `Swap` object which is weaker than `CAS`. In CC-Synch, each thread maintains a single record to insert in the list, and therefore the total space overhead of CC-Synch is $O(n)$, where n is the number of threads; this is no more than that of previous combining-based synchronization approaches. The total space overhead for DSM-Synch is also $O(n)$.

We experimentally compare CC-Synch and DSM-Synch with several state-of-the-art synchronization approaches, like P-Sim [7], flat-combining [12], CLH spin locks [5, 18], and a simple lock free technique. The experiments (Figures 1 – 10) show that CC-Synch outperforms all these approaches in most cases. DSM-Synch outperforms all algorithms other than CC-Synch. DSM-Synch has the advantage over CC-Synch that it is designed to be efficient even in machines that support the DSM model; so, it can be executed efficiently by general scope applications which should run on different, not-necessarily predetermined architectures.

The experimental analysis reveals that the number of cache misses incurred per request is smaller in the new implementations than in previous techniques and the same is true for the cycles invested in memory stalls. Based on our experiments, we conclude that the technique of repeatedly performing CAS until it succeeds, even if it comes together with an appropriately-tuned back-off scheme, causes more cache misses and more branch mispredictions than employing Swap or other non-comparison primitives. Experiments also show that the average number of requests served by a combiner in CC-Synch and DSM-Synch is larger than in other algorithms, so the synchronization overhead paid to serve an amount of requests in these implementations is closer to the ideal than in previous approaches. So, the achieved combining degree has a significant impact on the performance of combining implementations.

We used CC-Synch and DSM-Synch to implement shared stacks and queues (Section 4). The stack implementation (CC-Stack) based on CC-Synch, outperforms all state-of-the-art shared stack implementations like the wait-free[2] stack implementation, called SimStack, presented in [7], the linked stack implementation based on flat-combining [12] where elimination has also been applied [13], and the stack implementation based on CLH spin locks [5, 18]. The stack implementation (DSM-Stack) based on DSM-Synch, outperforms all implementations other than CC-Stack. We also use CC-Synch and DSM-Synch to get two highly efficient shared queue implementations, called CC-Queue and DSM-Queue. More specifically, these implementations are derived by simply replacing the ordinary locks in the two-locks queue implementation presented by Michael and Scott in [21] with two instances of either CC-Synch or DSM-Synch. These implementations were experimentally compared to the wait-free queue implementation presented in [7] (called SimQueue), the two-locks

[1] Once the cache miss is served and as long as the data item is not updated by threads that are being executed on other processors, future accesses to the data item by threads that are being executed on this processor are local.

[2] An implementation is *wait-free*, if each thread completes the execution of an operation in a finite number of steps independently of the speeds or failures of other threads; wait-freedom is the strongest progress guarantee.

implementation [21], and the queue implementation based on flat-combining presented in [12]. CC-Queue performs up to 2.5 times faster than the queue implementation of [12] and outperforms SimQueue by a factor of up to 1.5.

For modern multi-core systems that organize the cores into clusters and provide fast communication (via shared caches) to the threads running in the same cluster and much slower communication across clusters, we present an hierarchical version of CC-Synch, called H-Synch, which exploits the hierarchical communication nature of such systems to achieve better performance. Experiments show that in such systems, H-Synch significantly outperforms CC-Synch and DSM-Synch as well as the state-of-the-art flat-combining NUMA locks recently presented by Dice *et. al* in [6]. We used H-Synch to design highly efficient implementations of stacks and queues for such machines. These implementations outperform by far, in such machines, CC-Stack, DSM-Stack, CC-Queue, and DSM-Queue, respectively, as well as all other concurrent stack and queue implementations with which these implementations have been compared.

CC-Synch and DSM-Synch are linearizable [15]. *Linearizability* is a well-accepted consistency condition for implementations of shared objects. It states that in any execution α of the implementation, each operation *op* on the simulated shared object executed in α appears to take effect, instantaneously, at some point, called the *linearization point* of *op*, in its execution interval.

Many hardware manufactures have been influenced by the universality result [14], and they have equipped their machines with the strongest atomic primitives (like CAS and LL/SC). As shown in [7], machines that additionally support Fetch&Add instructions, can have important performance advantages, while it is additionally possible to ensure wait-freedom. Our experiments show that machines that support Swap objects have significant performance benefits as well. Fortunately, Swap instructions are already supported by a large variety of machine architectures (x86, sparc, etc.).

We note that CC-Synch, similarly to Sim [7] and flat-combining [12], cannot be trivially applied in an efficient way for designing data structures such as search trees, where m lookups can be executed in parallel performing just a logarithmic number of shared memory accesses each. In such cases, it is expected that CC-Synch will perform well, only if several instances of it are employed. However, it is an interesting open problem to find efficient ways to synchronize these instances. We remark that using the combining technique to implement even simpler data structures, like shared linked lists, is also not obvious if several instances of the combining implementation should be employed to achieve good speed-up.

1.1 Related Work

Software combining was first realized in combining trees [8, 29]. To reduce the synchronization overhead of combining trees, a lot of research work has focused on designing adaptive versions of them [10, 20] (e.g., for implementing barriers) or decentralized algorithms for dynamically changing tree size [25, 26]. For some of these techniques [10, 20], it is not clear how they can be used to design general concurrent data structures, others [25] satisfy weaker consistency conditions than linearizability, and for others, experiments [12] have shown that their synchronization overhead is still high.

Oyama, Taura, and Yonezawa [23] present an implementation of the combining technique which we will call OyamaAlg. In OyamaAlg the lock is implemented using a CAS object O and the list of announced requests is implemented as a stack, so requests are served in a LIFO order. The CAS object is also used to maintain a pointer to the topmost element of the stack. To discover whether it is the combiner, a thread performs just a single CAS on O; however, to append its node in the stack, it repeatedly performs CAS until one of them is successful. So, the thread may starve. Before leaving the system, the combiner serves all other requests that have arrived in the system during the course of its execution, so the combiner may also starve. Finally, OyamaAlg has significant performance overheads for the following reasons. First, threads need to succeed on a CAS in order to have their requests announced; this causes a lot of contention and leads to a significant performance degradation. Second, the number of RMRs performed by a thread can be unbounded since threads may starve.

Flat-combining is another implementation of the combining technique presented by Hendler *et. al* in [12]. There are two main differences between flat-combining and OyamaAlg. In flat-combining, the list of announced requests usually contains one record for each thread independently of whether the thread has a currently active request; this reduces the number of insertions in the list. However, it increases the work of the combiner which should now traverse a longer list than necessary. To avoid this extra overhead, the combiner cleans up the list periodically keeping in it only the nodes of those threads that have recently initiated a request. Second, the CAS object O is not used to manipulate the head of the list as in OyamaAlg. This results in less overhead since the combiner does not interfere with threads that are trying to insert their records in the list. The combiner may choose to return without serving all the active requests in the list (so it does not starve), but this comes with a performance penalty since it makes it necessary to have each active thread checking regularly whether the coarse-grain lock has been released by the combiner and if yes, trying to become a combiner itself. In flat-combining, requests that have been inserted in the list later than other requests, may be served first. Moreover, flat-combining experiences some performance overheads. The cost paid by the combiner is larger than necessary if it traverses a list containing requests of currently non-active threads. Additionally, threads may perform an unbounded number of RMRs when trying to insert their nodes in the list.

Fatourou and Kallimanis have presented in [7] efficient universal constructions that implement the combining technique in a wait-free manner; a *universal* construction can be used to simulate any concurrent object. The first universal construction presented in [7], called Sim, performs a constant number of memory accesses, but it is only of theoretical interest since it uses unrealistically large objects. A practical version of Sim, called P-Sim, is also presented in [7]. P-Sim exhibits good performance in practice; it outperforms flat-combining (and other state-of-the-art synchronization techniques) in many cases. Efficient concurrent stack and queue implementations, based on P-Sim, are also presented and experimentally analyzed in [7]; in addition to being wait-free, these implementations significantly outperformed all previous state-of-the-art implementations of shared stacks and queues.

P-Sim does not easily cope with shared objects whose state size is large since it needs to copy locally the part of the state that it should be changed and then write back any updates. In contrast, the algorithms presented in this paper efficiently handle any shared object since the unique thread that applies the updates can do so directly on the shared data structure. More significantly, our experiments show that CC-Synch and DSM-Synch exhibit performance advantages over P-Sim. It is worth pointing out however that P-Sim has the benefit over CC-Synch and DSM-Synch that it ensures wait-freedom and therefore it is highly fault-tolerant.

Dice, Marathe and Shavit [6] have recently presented an hierarchical spin-lock implementation, called flat-combining NUMA lock; this hierarchical lock is based on flat-combining and exploits the cache hierarchies in order to provide good performance. As it is shown in [6], this lock greatly outperforms the previous (hierarchical and non-hierarchical) spin locks presented in [5, 17, 18, 20, 24]. Experiments show that H-Synch exhibits significant performance

Algorithm 1 Pseudocode for CC-Synch algorithm.

```
struct Node {
    Request req;
    RetVal ret;
    boolean wait;
    boolean completed;
    Node *next;
};
shared Node *Tail;
// Tail initially points to a dummy node
// with value ⟨⊥, ⊥,FALSE, FALSE, null⟩

// The following variable is private to each thread p_i; it is a pointer to a
// struct of type Node with initial value ⟨⊥, ⊥,FALSE, FALSE, null⟩
private Node *node_i;

RetVal CC-Synch(Request req) {      // Pseudocode for thread p_i
    Node *nextNode, *curNode, *tmpNode, *tmpNodeNext;
    int counter = 0;
1. nextNode = node_i;               // p_i uses a (possibly recycled) node
2. nextNode→next = null;
3. nextNode→wait = TRUE;
4. nextNode→completed = FALSE;
5. curNode = Swap(Tail, nextNode); // curNode is assigned to p_i
6. curNode→req = req;               // p_i announces its request
7. curNode→next = nextNode;
8. node_i = curNode;                // reuse this node next time
9. while (curNode→wait == TRUE)     // p_i spins until it is unlocked
       nop;
10. if (curNode→completed==TRUE)// if p_i's req is already applied
11.     return curNode → ret;       // p_i returns its return value
12. tmpNode = curNode;              // p_i is the combiner
13. while (tmpNode → next ≠ null AND counter < h) {
14.     counter = counter + 1;
15.     tmpNodeNext=tmpNode→next;
16.     apply tmpNode→req to object's state
          and store the return value to tmpNode→ret;
17.     tmpNode→completed = TRUE;// tmpNode's req is applied
18.     tmpNode→wait = FALSE;       // unlock the spinning thread
19.     tmpNode = tmpNodeNext;      // and proceed to next node
    }
20. tmpNode→wait = FALSE;           // unlock next node's owner
21. return curNode→ret;
}
```

advantages over flat-combining NUMA locks [6]. We believe that this is due to the fact that H-Synch (1) is simpler, (2) employs combining to serve the thread requests in each cluster (whereas this is not the case in the hierarchical lock presented in [6]), and (3) is based on CC-Synch which performs better than flat-combining.

CC-Synch implements a combining-friendly version of CLH [5, 18] queue lock; in contrast to CLH where the maintained queue is implicit, the queue maintained by CC-Synch is explicit so that the combiner can traverse it. DSM-Synch implements a combining-friendly version of MCS [20] queue lock.

2. Implementations of the Combining Technique

In this section, we present CC-Synch (Algorithm 1), H-Synch, and DSM-Synch (Algorithm 2).

2.1 CC-Synch

CC-Synch (Algorithm 1) maintains a list which contains one node for each thread that has initiated an active request; the list also contains a dummy node which is always the last node of the list. Each thread first announces its request by recording it in the last node of the list (i.e., in the dummy node of the list) and by inserting a new node as the last node of the list (which will comprise the new dummy node). At each point in time, we say that a node of the list *is assigned* to a thread p_i, if p_i has written the request recorded in the node; in CC-Synch, p_i is assigned the previous node to the node that it inserts in the list.

The thread that is assigned the head node of the list plays the role of the combiner, so it is the only thread that is allowed to access the shared data. The combiner starts by serving its own request. Other threads that have announced requests perform spinning on the $wait$ field of their assigned node. The combiner does not give up the lock when it completes the execution of its request; it rather continues accessing the next nodes of the list, it serves the requests announced in them, and sets their $wait$ field to FALSE in order to stop the threads that have been assigned these nodes from spinning. It also changes their $completed$ field to TRUE to identify that their requests have been completed. The combiner returns when it serves either all requests in the list or a pre-specified number h of such requests. In the later case, the combiner identifies the thread which owns the next to the last node that the combiner helps, as the new combiner; this is done by changing the $wait$ field of this node to FALSE while leaving its $completed$ field equal to FALSE.

We now give a more detailed description of CC-Synch. Pointer $Tail$ is a Swap object which initially points to a dummy node. Whenever thread p_i wants to announce a request req, it executes Swap on $Tail$ (line 5) in order to read the pointer to the dummy node pointed to by $Tail$ and update $Tail$ to point to its node (i.e., to the node pointed to by p_i's local variable $node_i$). Once this has been performed, p_i has been assigned the node that was previously pointed to by $Tail$, so it announces its request by recording req in the req field of this node (line 6) and then it sets the $next$ field of this node to point to the new dummy node (line 7). Next, p_i starts spinning on the $wait$ field of its assigned node until this field becomes FALSE. When p_i reads FALSE in $wait$, either its request has been executed by a combiner or p_i's record is the first in the list and therefore it owns the lock. In the former case, p_i simply returns (line 11), whereas in the later, p_i becomes the combiner.

Notice that the list could grow forever while the combiner thread p traverses it since a thread may add a node at the end of the list more than once after its request has been served by p. In order to prevent p from traversing a continuously growing list, an upper bound h (line 13) on the number of requests that p may serve is employed; once p serves h requests, it identifies the thread that has been assigned the next node of the list as the new combiner, and returns. Our experiments show that the choice of h does not significantly impact the performance of the algorithm. Specifically, setting h to a value equal to cn, where $c > 0$ is a small constant, is a good choice in terms of performance.

One criticism of CC-Synch could be that when a thread p executes Swap, it splits the list in two parts. If p is swapped out before executing line 7, all other threads can continue to add requests to the end of the list, but no thread can go over the list to execute the requests. However, several operating systems allow a thread to give a hint to the scheduler that it will soon execute a critical section [9] so that the scheduler avoids swapping out this thread. For instance, Solaris provides schedctl_start to announce that a thread will soon access the critical section, and schedctl_stop for informing the scheduler that the thread has finished executing the critical section. By using this technique, swapping out the combining thread can usually be avoided. We remark that schedctl_* is just a macro which executes a few assembly instructions with negligible performance cost.

Linearizability. CC-Synch is linearizable. Let req_i be any request initiated by thread p_i in an execution of CC-Synch. Let nd_i be the node of the list that is assigned to p_i for req_i. Thread p_i completes the execution of CC-Synch for req_i either on line 11 or on line 21. Assume first, that p_i returns on line 11. In this case, a combiner thread p_j has served req_i before the execution of line 11 by p_i. Therefore, p_j has executed line 17 for nd_i at some iteration $l > 1$ of its while loop (lines $13 - 19$). Request req_i is linearized just before the execution of this instance of line 17 by p_j. Assume now that p_i returns on line 21. Then, p_i serves its request on its own when it executes line 16 at the first iteration of its while loop (lines $13 - 19$). In this case, req_i is linearized just before the execution of line 17 of the first iteration of p_i's while loop. Obviously, in both cases the linearization point of req_i is within its execution interval. Consistency is guaranteed since all requests are served sequentially. Due to lack of space, the complete proof of correctness will be provided in the full version of the paper.

RMR Complexity and Space Overhead. By the pseudocode (Algorithm 1), it follows that each thread returns either on line 11 or on line 21. If p_i returns on line 11, it obviously executes a constant number of RMRs. Assume now that p_i returns on line 21. By the pseudocode (line 13), p_i executes at most h iterations of the while loop (lines $14-19$). Lines $15-19$ contribute just a constant number of RMRs, and line 14 is executed on a local variable. Thus, p_i executes $O(h+t)$ RMRs, where t is the size of the shared memory data that they should be accessed in order to serve these h requests; we have assumed that the cache size of p_i's processor is greater than t. Notice that the amortized time complexity is $O(d)$, where d is the average number of RMRs required to serve a single request. We remark that in most cases, d equals a small constant. The space overhead of CC-Synch is $O(n)$, since each thread allocates one struct of type $Node$.

Required memory barriers. When implementing CC-Synch, memory barriers may need to be inserted in the code to ensure its correct execution. In architectures that implement either the TSO (Total Store Order) or the PO (Process Order) consistency model, we need to insert just one store memory barrier. These memory consistency models are very common and they are used in many contemporary multiprocessors, among which those that we used for our experiments. The first model is implemented on SPARC machines of version v8 and newer [28], while the second is implemented on AMD64 [22] and on Intel64 [4] architectures. SPARC processors support weaker consistency memory models as well, but they are rarely used and the TSO model is the default option for Solaris [19]. Both of these consistency models do not reorder two read operations, and the same holds for two store operations [19]. However, a read can be reordered with an older store only in case that the read and the store instructions access different memory locations [19]. Thus, for the correct execution of lines $6-7$ and lines $17-18$, no store barrier is needed. Similarly, no load barrier is needed just before line 10. A store memory barrier is inserted just before the return instruction of line 21. In cases where a weaker memory model is considered, additional memory barriers may have to be inserted; this is not the case in the architectures we employed for our experiments.

2.2 H-Synch

We now discuss how we can modify CC-Synch to get H-Synch. We consider a system of m processors which are partitioned into C clusters; each cluster consists of m/C processors. In such a system, communication among the processors of the same cluster is performed much faster than among processors residing in different clusters. A characteristic example of such a system is Niagara 2 in which we have executed some of the experiments in Section 3.

In H-Synch, the threads use C instances of CC-Synch one per cluster. Each instance of CC-Synch is used, as described in Section 2.1, to identify at each point in time, the combiner thread of each cluster and the list of announced requests of the threads that are executed at processors of the cluster. In addition to the C instances of CC-Synch, a queue lock L [5, 18] is used; L is accessed only by the combiner threads of the clusters. The CLH lock [5, 18] is a good choice for implementing L in systems where the intra-cluster communication is achieved with a cache coherent (CC) protocol, whereas the MCS lock [20] is expected to be a better choice in other systems.

Whenever a thread q has a newly activated request, it calls H-Synch. If q does not become the combiner of its cluster, it waits until its request has been served by a combiner of the cluster. Otherwise, before q starts serving requests, it executes an `acquire` operation on L in order to ensure that it is the only combiner (among those of the different clusters) that has access to the shared data. A combiner q serves only requests initiated by threads that are running on its local cluster. By doing so, intra-cluster communication is kept low. After finishing its work as a combiner, q releases L, so that a combiner of some other cluster can acquire L and have access to the shared data. In cases that the communication between clusters is performed through a more complex interconnection network (for instance, one that has an hierarchical structure), H-Synch can be easily modified to exploit the characteristics of the communication hierarchy by using more levels of queue locks (one queue lock per communication level). H-Synch ensures that requests initiated by threads of the same cluster are served in FIFO order and that the combiners acquire the global lock in FIFO order but, apparently, it does not globally ensure the FIFO property.

2.3 DSM-Synch

CC-Synch performs an unbounded number of RMRs in the DSM model. Here, we present DSM-Synch (Algorithm 2) which performs $O(hd)$ RMRs in this model. It maintains a list of announced requests which is updated in a manner similar to that of CC-Synch (and which also implements the lock). In contrast to CC-Synch, the list does not contain any dummy node and it is initially empty. Each thread p maintains two list nodes; p announces each request it wants to perform in one of these nodes, it inserts this node at the end of the list using `Swap`, and if its record is not the first in the list, it performs spinning on the $wait$ field of its node. If p's node is the first in the list, p becomes the combiner and serves up to h requests from those recorded in the list in FIFO order. A thread that wants to append a node updates the $next$ field of the previous node to point to the inserted node. The combiner serves requests recorded in list nodes up to the second last element of the list (see condition of the if statement of line 19). It does so to avoid accessing a node whose next field has not yet been updated although this node is not the last node in the list any more. Thus, a combiner will execute lines $22 - 25$ only if its node is the only node in the list. This ensures that a combiner performs a bounded number of RMRs.

We explain now why it is not enough to have each thread p_i using just one node. Let's assume that p_i has a single node that it reuses each time it initiates a new request. Let q be a combiner that serves p_i's request. Assume that there is a thread p_j whose assigned node is the next node of p_i's node in the list. Assume also that p_j's node is the last node in the list. After serving p_i's request, q sees that less than two nodes are left in the list and stops the execution of its while loop (lines $19-20$). Suppose that q stalls before executing line 26 of the pseudocode (pointer $tmpNode$ points to the node assigned to p_i). Assume now that p_i wants to immediately apply a new operation. Thus, p_i initializes its node again and inserts it at the end of the list by executing a `Swap` instruction on $Tail$. Then, q continues by executing line 26 of the pseudocode and makes an invalid memory reference.

Correctness & Memory Barriers. Using similar arguments as in CC-Synch, we can prove that DSM-Synch is linearizable. Specifically, consider a request req_i initiated by thread p_i, and assume that req_i is recorded in list node nd_i. As in CC-Synch, if

Algorithm 2 Pseudocode for DSM-Synch algorithm.

```
struct Node {
    Request req;
    RetVal ret;
    boolean wait;
    boolean completed;
    Node *next;
};
shared Node *Tail = null;

// the following variables are private to each thread p_i
private Node MyNodes_i[0..1] = {⟨⊥, ⊥, FALSE, FALSE, null ⟩};
private int toggle_i = 0;

RetVal DSM-Synch(Request req) {     // pseudocode for thread p_i
    Node *tmpNode, *myNode, *myPredNode;
    int counter = 0;

1.  toggle_i = 1 - toggle_i;                  // p_i toggles its toggle variable
2.  myNode=&MyNodes_i[toggle_i]; // p_i chooses to use one of its nodes
3.  myNode→wait = TRUE;
4.  myNode→completed = FALSE;
5.  myNode→next = null;
6.  myNode→req = req;                          // p_i announces its request
7.  myPredNode = swap(Tail, myNode); // p_i inserts myNode in the list
8.  if (myPredNode ≠ null) {              // if a node already exists in the list
9.      myPredNode→next = myNode;   // fix next of previous node
10.     while(myNode→wait == TRUE)  // p_i spins until it is unlocked
            nop;
11.     if(myNode→completed == TRUE) // if p_i's req is already applied
12.         return myNode→ret;              p_i returns its return value
    }
13. tmpNode = myNode;
14. while(TRUE) {                              // p_i is the combiner
15.     counter++;
16.     apply tmpNode→req to object's state
          and store the return value to tmpNode→ret;
17.     tmpNode→completed = TRUE;  // tmpNode's req is applied
18.     tmpNode→wait = FALSE;         // unlock the spinning thread
19.     if (tmpNode→next == null or
            tmpNode→next→next == null or counter ≥ h)
20.         break;     // p_i helped h threads or fewer than 2 nodes are in list
21.     tmpNode = tmpNode→next;        // proceed to the next node
    }
22. if (tmpNode→next == null) {      // p_i's req is the single record in list
23.     if(CAS(Tail, tmpNode, null)==TRUE)  // try to set Tail to null
24.         return myNode→ret;
25.     while (tmpNode→next == null)// some thread is appending a node
            nop;                              // wait until it finishes its operation
    }
26. tmpNode→next→wait = FALSE;   // unlock next node's owner
27. tmpNode→next = null;
28. return myNode→ret;
}
```

p_i returns on line 12, req_i is linearized just before the execution of line 18 for nd_i by the combiner; if p_i returns on line 28, req_i is linearized just before the execution of line 18 at the first iteration of the while loop executed by p_i. As in CC-Synch, when implementing DSM-Synch, a store memory barrier is inserted in the code just before line 28 where the algorithm returns.

RMR Complexity and Space Overhead. DSM-Synch performs $O(hd)$ RMRs when it executes the while loop of line 14. The only extra piece of code that may cause DSM-Synch to perform more RMRs is that of lines $22-25$. However, as explained above a thread p executes these lines only when the node it inserts is the single node in the list. So, if these lines are executed, p's local variable called $tmpNode$ is equal to $myNode$, and therefore spinning on $tmpNode \rightarrow next$ on line 25 is local. The space overhead of DSM-Synch is $O(n)$.

3. Performance evaluation

We evaluated CC-Synch and DSM-Synch in two different multiprocessor machine architectures. The first is a 32-core machine consisting of four AMD Opteron 6134 processors (Magny Cours). Each processor consists of 2 dies and each die contains 4 processing cores. Communication among the cores of the same die is achieved with a fast L3 cache. Dies communicate with HyperTransport links which create a complex topology that resembles a hypercube [3]. The second machine is a 128-way Sun consisting of 2 UltraSPARC-T2 processors (Niagara 2). Each processor consists of 8 processing cores, each of which is able to handle 8 threads. Communication among the cores of the same processor is achieved with a fast L2 cache. All experiments on the Magny Cours machine were performed using the gcc 4.3.4 compiler, while experiments on the Niagara 2 machine were performed using gcc 4.5.1. In order to avoid bottlenecks in memory allocation, the Hoard memory allocator [2] was used. The operating system running on the Magny Cours machine was Linux with kernel 2.6.18, while the operating system running on the Niagara 2 machine was Solaris 10.

Thread binding is employed for the following reason. Assume that the number of threads is smaller than the number of cores and suppose that two threads are running. The scheduler may decide to run them either on different processors (chips) or within the same chip. In the first case the communication cost is an order of magnitude more than in the second. Thus, if thread binding is not used, a significant uncertainty factor is introduced which may lead to an unreliable experiment. We observed that this was a usual phenomenon. So, on the Magny Cours machine, the i-th thread was bound to the i-th core of the machine; we first exploited multi-core, then multi-chip and then multi-socket configuration. On the Niagara 2 machine, we follow a slightly different scheduling similar to that used in [6] in order to better explore the performance properties of hierarchical algorithms. More specifically, we split threads into two groups, one for each socket.

In order to evaluate CC-Synch and DSM-Synch, we compare their performance with that of state-of-the-art synchronization techniques. Specifically, they are compared with P-Sim (the wait-free universal construction presented in [7]), flat-combining [11, 12], the CLH spin-lock [5, 18][3], OyamaAlg [23], and a simple lock-free implementation. The lock-free implementation was implemented using a `CAS` object. Specifically, whenever a thread wants to apply a `Fetch&Multiply`, it repeatedly executes `CAS` until it succeeds; a backoff scheme is employed to increase the scalability of this implementation. Since the Niagara 2 machine does not support `Fetch&Add` which is employed by P-Sim and is necessary, as shown in [7], for its good performance, no experiment was performed for P-Sim on the Niagara 2 machine. We also evaluated a variation of CC-Synch (called CAS-Synch), in which `Swap` is simulated with a `CAS` object in a lock-free manner. This allows us to explore the performance advantages of `Swap` over `CAS`.

On the Niagara 2 machine, H-Synch and the hierarchical NUMA lock (called FC-MCS below) recently presented in [6] were also evaluated. On the Magny Cours machine, experiments show no performance benefit when using any of the hierarchical techniques. This is rational to the fact that the machine consists of many but very small clusters of cores. Thus, we have not included any performance measurements for the hierarchical algorithms on the Magny Cours machine. All algorithms were carefully optimized and for those that use backoff schemes, we performed a large number of experiments in order to choose the best backoff parameters. We used the flat-combining implementation

[3] As expected for cache-coherent NUMA architectures, we experimentally saw that MCS [20] spin locks have slightly worse performance than CLH locks in both machines, so we present experimental results for CLH locks.

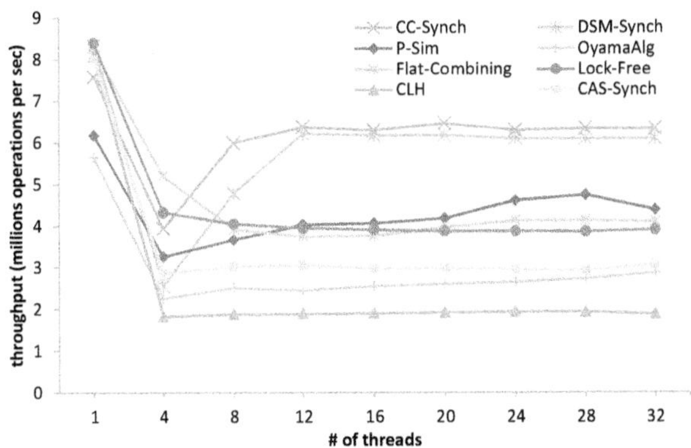

Figure 1: Average throughput of each implementation on the Magny Cours machine while simulating a `Fetch&Multiply` object.

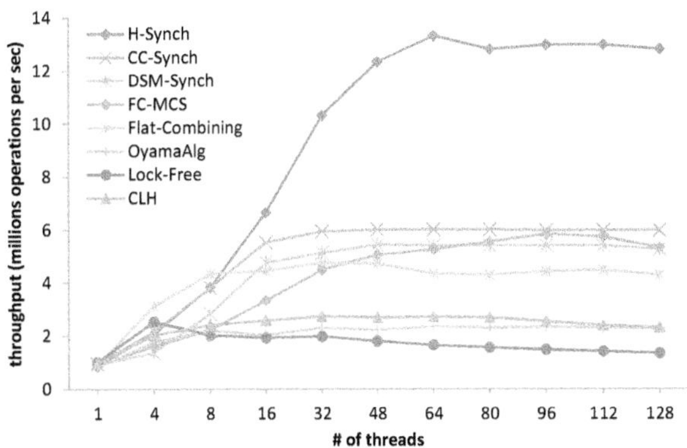

Figure 2: Average throughput of each implementation on the Niagara 2 machine while simulating a `Fetch&Multiply` object.

that was provided by its inventors [11, 12] and we choose its parameters very carefully in order to achieve the best performance. We further optimized the code of flat-combining to run faster than its original version [11, 12] on the Magny Cours machine. We used the latest version of P-Sim code (version 0.8) [7, 16]. The source code of our implementations is provided at `http://code.google.com/p/sim-universal-construction/`.

The first experiment we performed is a synthetic benchmark (Figures 1, 2), where a simple `Fetch&Multiply` object is simulated. We measure the average throughput (`Fetch&Multiply` per second) that each synchronization technique achieves when it executes 10^7 `Fetch&Multiply` operations (i.e., always the same amount of work), for different values of n; each thread executes $10^7/n$ `Fetch&Multiply`. Specifically, the horizontal axis of Figures 1, 2 represents the number of threads n, while the vertical axis displays the throughput (in millions of operations per second) that each synchronization technique has performed. For each value of n, the experiment has been performed 10 times and averages have been calculated. A random number of dummy loop iterations (up to 64) have been inserted between the execution of two `Fetch&Multiply` by the same thread; specifically, in each iteration a volatile counter is increased. In this way, we simulate a random work load large enough to avoid unrealistically low cache miss ratios and long runs (but not too big to reduce contention). Figure 6 studies the performance behavior of our algorithms for different values of the random work.

In the experiments performed on the Magny Cours machine (Figure 1), CC-Synch outperforms all other synchronization techniques. Specifically, CC-Synch achieves up to 1.54 higher throughput than flat-combining and outperforms P-Sim by a factor of up to 1.52. The lock free implementation of `Fetch&Multiply` is slightly slower than P-Sim and flat-combining. Also, CC-Synch is up to 2.7 times faster than OyamaAlg [23]. DSM-Synch performs also very well; its performance is close to that of CC-Synch, despite the fact that it is designed for machines following the DSM model. Figure 1 also shows that simulating **Swap** using **CAS** (in a lock-free way) induces a serious performance penalty; specifically, CAS-Synch is two times slower than CC-Synch.

Similarly to the experiments performed on the Magny Cours machine, CC-Synch outperforms all algorithms other than H-Synch on the Niagara 2 machine (Figure 2). More specifically, CC-Synch outperforms flat-combining by a factor of up to 1.4. It is noticeable that even CC-Synch itself (not its hierarchical version) outperforms FC-MCS [6] by a factor of up to 1.65, despite the fact that FC-MCS exploits the hierarchical characteristics of communication in the machine. The relatively small performance gap between flat-combing and FC-MCS may seem surprising at first; however, this result is rational to the fact that FC-MCS causes more cache misses when accessing the shared data. Specifically, in FC-MCS, combining is not used in applying the requests, so each request may be applied by a different thread; thus, each time a thread accesses the shared data cache misses may occur. This is avoided when combining is employed in serving the requests, as done by the other studied combining-based synchronization techniques. DSM-Synch exposes almost the same performance to CC-Synch on the Niagara 2 machine. H-Synch which is the hierarchical version of CC-Synch outperforms FC-MCS by a factor of up to 2.65 and flat-combining itself by a factor of up to 3.0. CC-Synch is up to 2.55 times faster than OyamaAlg [23], while H-Synch is more than 6 times faster. The performance of CAS-Synch is not illustrated in Figure 2 since CAS-Synch results in very poor performance on the Niagara 2 machine.

As shown in Figure 1, on the Magny Cours machine, all algorithms perform faster in case $n = 1$ than for larger values of n. On the contrary, Figure 2 shows that, on the Niagara 2 machine, the performance of all algorithms is always better for larger values of n. This is due to the fact that the Magny Cours machine implements atomic instructions (**CAS**, **Swap**, etc.) in the private L1 cache which is very fast; in contrast, a Niagara 2 processor implements atomic instructions in the shared L2 cache which is slower (Niagara 2 processor is optimized for contented workloads, i.e. in case of $n > 1$).

In Figure 3, we study the performance of each implementation on the Niagara 2 machine for $n > 128$, i.e., when n is larger than the number of threads that the machine is able to handle simultaneously; thus, the machine is oversubscribed. We do not include any measurement from FC-MCS and CLH locks since in this experiment they do not achieve good performance. As illustrated in Figure 3, H-Synch, CC-Synch, and DSM-Synch achieve better performance than any other synchronization technique for any value of n.

Figures 4 - 5 aim at investigating the reasons for the good performance of CC-Synch and DSM-Synch. More specifically, from Figure 5, it follows that on the Magny Cours machine, P-Sim and flat-combining execute slightly more (up to 10% more) atomic instructions than CC-Synch and OyamaAlg [23]. The experiments showed that to achieve the best performance for the lock-free algorithm, the back-off should not be too high. By appropriately choosing the back-off to get the best performance, it turned out that the average number of CAS performed by each instance of the algorithm is two which is bigger than the average number of atomic instructions executed by each instance of CC-Synch and DSM-Synch. Thus, the lock-free algorithm has a performance disadvantage compared to these algorithms.

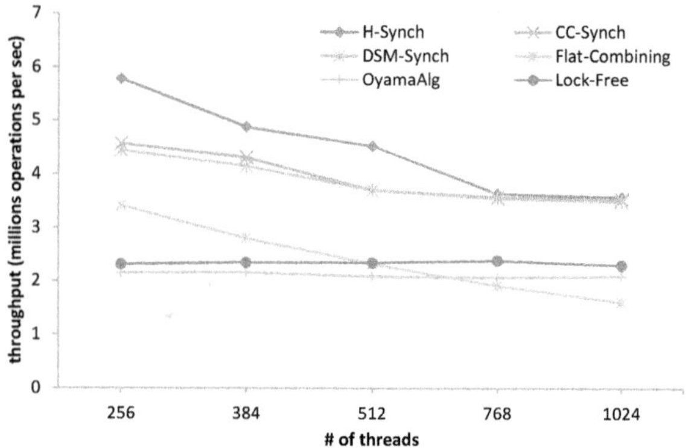

Figure 3: Average throughput of each implementation for $n > 128$ on the Niagara 2 (oversubscribing) machine while simulating a `Fetch&Multiply` object.

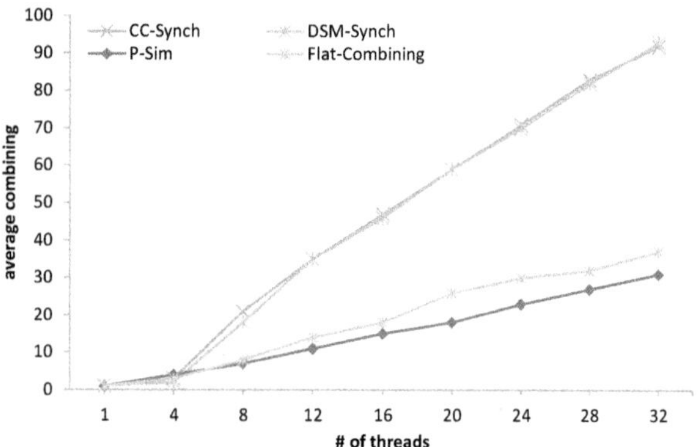

Figure 4: Average degree of combining of each implementation while simulating a `Fetch&Multiply` object.

Figure 4 displays the average degree of combining, i.e., the average number of requests that are executed by a combiner. It shows that CC-Synch and DSM-Synch achieve better degree of combining which is almost 3 times more than that of P-Sim and flat-combining[4]. Our efforts to increase the average degree of combining for flat-combining by carefully tuning its parameters (i.e., by increasing the combining rounds or by changing the polling level), revealed that when the combining degree was increased the average throughput was decreased. On the contrary, P-Sim operates in a way that it can help as much threads as the system's point contention (i.e., as the maximum number of threads that can be simultaneously active at any point in time which might be equal to n).

In the experiment of Figure 6, we studied the behavior of the competing algorithms for different amounts of random work. This experiment was executed on the Magny Cours machine; the number of threads was fixed to 32. Figure 6 shows that for a wide range of values for random work ($64 - 2048$), most algorithms have a small difference in the exhibited throughput. This shows that the communication cost is the dominant factor, whereas the time invested to execute the local random work does not play any significant role. An exception is the lock-free algorithm, which, in case the random work is equal to zero, has unrealistically high performance. This is due to the fact that, in this case, a thread could uninterruptedly execute thousands of `Fetch&Multiply` before some other thread starts its execution. This phenomenon (called long runs) has been also discussed in [7, 21] as an unrealistic workload. Figure 6 shows that by slightly increasing the random work, the performance of the lock-free algorithm rapidly decreases. The same phenomenon, although in a smaller scale, was also noticed for flat-combining. Similarly to the lock-free implementation, flat-combining has high throughput for very small amounts of random work, although its performance vastly decreases when the random work is slightly increased. In cases that the number of iterations is 2048 or more, the time needed to execute this loop becomes the dominant performance factor, i.e., executing the loop becomes more expensive than executing the algorithm for applying a FetchAndMultiply instruction. Thus, the performance of all algorithms starts to decrease and the performance gap between them becomes insignificant. We remark that the scale of the horizontal axis of Figure 6 is logarithmic.

[4] In Figure 4, we have not included results for OyamaAlg since the variance of the combining degree in this algorithm was too high to get a realistic view. This is due to the fact that a combiner thread in this algorithm may be enforced to help an unbounded number of operations.

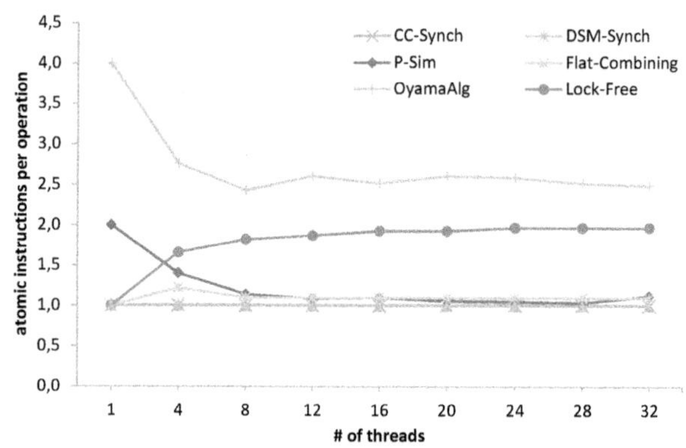

Figure 5: Average number of atomic instructions (`CAS`, `Swap`, `Fetch&Add`) that each implementation executes while simulating a `Fetch&Multiply` object.

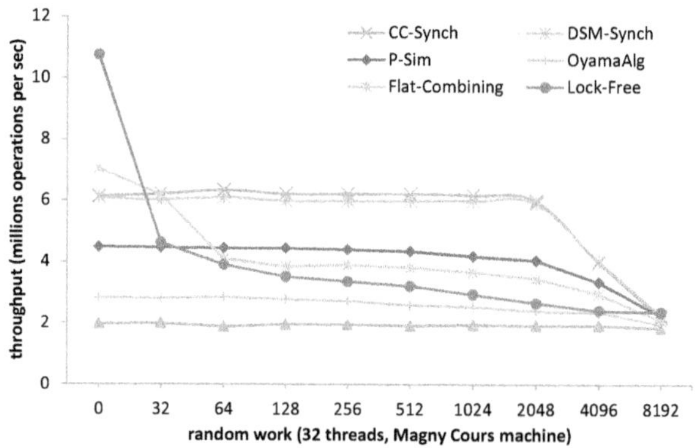

Figure 6: Average throughput of CC-Queue and DSM-Queue on the Magny Cours machine, with different values of random work, $n = 32$.

Algorithm	cache misses	cpu cycles spent in memory stalls
CC-Synch	4.1	2747
Sim	4.9	6328
flat-combining	5.8	6501

Table 1: Cache misses and memory stalls per operation, $n = 16$.

Table 1 shows some measurements from performance counters. We observed that the extra cache misses incurred by P-Sim and flat-combining was caused due to the number of failed `CAS` instructions; this number becomes worse if these algorithms are not properly tuned. Since failed `CAS` instructions cause cache misses and branch mispredictions, we conclude that a combining technique that avoids them has a serious performance advantage.

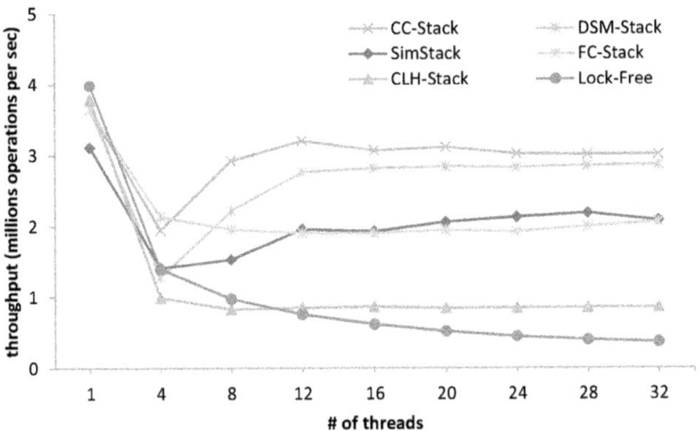

Figure 7: Average throughput of the CC-Stack and DSM-Stack on the Magny Cours machine.

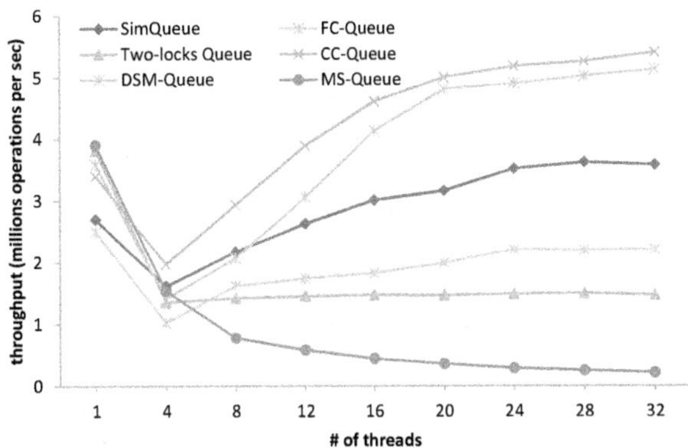

Figure 9: Average throughput of the CC-Queue and DSM-Queue on the Magny Cours machine.

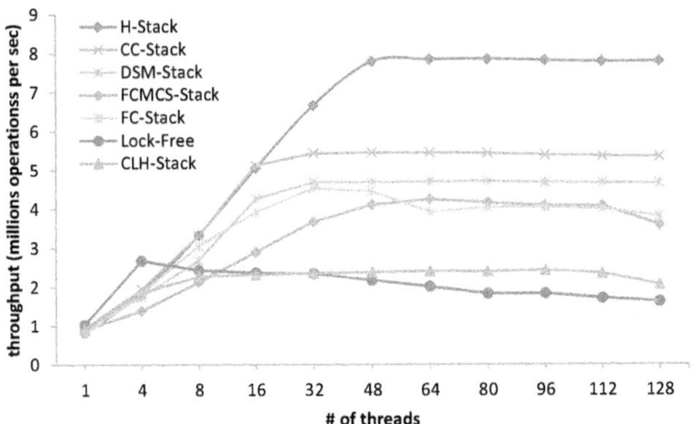

Figure 8: Average throughput of H-Stack, CC-Stack and DSM-Stack on the Niagara 2 machine.

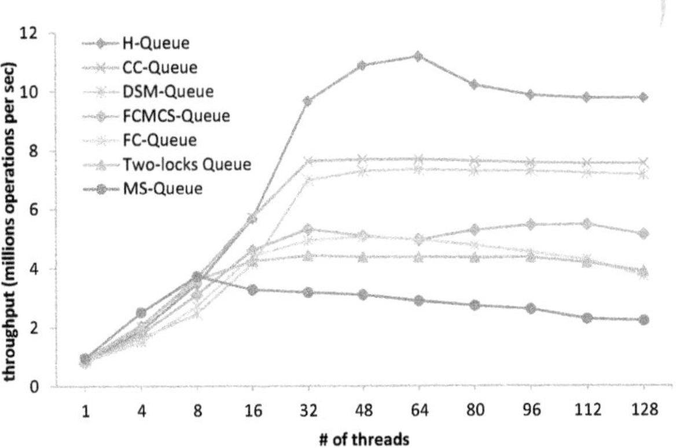

Figure 10: Average throughput of H-Queue, CC-Queue and DSM-Queue on the Niagara 2 machine.

4. Highly Efficient Data Structures

We further investigate the performance of CC-Synch, DSM-Synch, and H-Synch by implementing common concurrent data structures (i.e., shared stacks and queues). We compare the performance of these implementations with state-of-the-art shared stack and queue implementations. Specifically, the shared stack implementation based on CC-Synch, called CC-Stack, was evaluated against SimStack [7], the lock-free stack implementation presented by Treiber in [27], a stack implementation based on CLH spin locks [5, 18], and a linked stack implementation based on flat-combining [11, 12] (called FC-Stack). Both CC-Stack and FC-Stack eliminate pairs of push and pop whenever possible; the performance of elimination [13] has been studied in [7] and [12] where experiments show that elimination is outperformed by SimStack and FC-Stack. We also implemented a shared stack based on H-Synch and FC-MCS [6] and evaluated their performance on the Niagara 2 machine.

The experiment we perform is similar to that performed by Michael and Scott for queues in [21]. We measure the average throughput (operations per second) that each algorithm achieves (every thread executes $10^7/n$ pairs of ENQUEUE and DEQUEUE operations) for different values of n. Again, the experiments have been performed several times and averages have been taken; we have simulated a random workload by executing a random number of iterations (up to 64) of a dummy loop after each operation.

As it is shown in Figure 7, on the Magny Cours machine, CC-Stack performs up to 1.68 times faster than FC-Stack, and up to 1.59 times faster than SimStack. The stack implementation based on the CLH spin lock had much lower performance. The stack implementation based on DSM-Synch, called DSM-Stack, performs slightly worse than CC-Synch but it is much better than all other algorithms. On the Niagara 2 machine, the shared stack based on CC-Synch performs 1.4 times faster than FC-Stack (Figure 8). The stack implementation based on DSM-Synch performs worse than CC-Stack but it is again better than all other algorithms. It is noticeable that the stack implementations based on CC-Synch and DSM-Synch outperform by a factor of up to 1.49 the shared stack based on FC-MCS of [6]. The stack implementation based on H-Synch significantly outperforms all other implementations, being up to 2.0 times faster than FC-Stack and up to 2.1 times faster than the stack based on FC-MCS [6].

We also implement and experimentally analyze shared queues based on CC-Synch, DSM-Synch, and H-Synch (called CC-Queue, DSM-Queue, and H-Queue, respectively). Specifically, the two-locks queue implementation presented in [21] is enhanced by replacing the ordinary locks with instances of CC-Synch, DSM-Synch, and H-Synch, respectively. These implementations are compared (Figures 9-10) with SimQueue [7], the lock free queue implementation and the two-locks implementation presented in [21], and the queue implementation based on flat-combining [11, 12] (called FC-Queue). On the Niagara 2 machine, we additionally implemented and evaluated a two-locks queue variant using FC-MCS [6]. The queue experiment was similar to that for stacks.

As illustrated in Figure 9, on the Magny Cours machine, SimQueue exhibits better performance than any algorithm other than CC-Queue and DSM-Queue, as expected based on results in [7]. CC-Queue performs up to 2.53 times faster than FC-Queue (Figure 9) and 2.1 times faster than SimQueue. DSM-Queue performs slightly worse than CC-Queue but better than all other algorithms. On the Niagara 2 machine (Figure 10), FC-Queue performs better than all algorithms other than CC-Queue, DSM-Queue, and H-Queue (recall that SimQueue has not been implemented in this machine since `Fetch&Add` instructions are not included in its instruction set). CC-Queue performs up to 1.8 times faster than FC-Queue and up to 1.55 times faster than the queue based on [6]. The queue implementation based on H-Synch greatly outperforms all other candidates by being up to 2.25 times faster than the queue implementation based on FC-MCS [6]. It is also noticeable that the performance gap between FC-Queue and the two-locks queue is smaller on the Niagara 2 machine. This is due to the fact that the CLH locks perform very well in this machine and the parallel use of two different locks (one for enqueues and one for dequeues) gives a performance boost in the two-locks algorithm. Again, DSM-Queue performs slightly worse than CC-Queue but better than all other algorithms except from H-Queue on the Niagara 2 machine.

Acknowledgments

We would like to thank Dimitris Nikolopoulos for arranging the provision of access to some of the multi-core machines of the CS Dept. of Virginia Tech where we ran our experiments. Many thanks also to Michael Scott for providing access to the Rochester's Niagara 2 machine. We would like to especially thank Victor Luchangco and Faith Ellen for several fruitful discussions and for their valuable feedback on the paper. Thanks also to Nir Shavit for several interesting discussions on a preliminary version of this paper and to the anonymous reviewers for their interesting comments on the submitted version of the paper.

Nikolaos Kallimanis is supported by a PhD scholarship from the Empirikion Foundation, Athens, Greece. The work of Panagiota Fatourou was supported by the European Commission under the 6th and 7th Framework Programs through the TransForm (FP7-MC-ITN-238639), Hi-PEAC2 (FP7-ICT-217068), and ENCORE (FP7-ICT-248647) projects.

References

[1] G. Amdahl. Validity of the single processor approach to achieving large-scale computing capabilities. In *AFIPS Conference Proceedings*, page 483485, 1967.

[2] E. D. Berger, K. S. McKinley, R. D. Blumofe, and P. R. Wilson. Hoard: A scalable memory allocator for multithreaded applications. In *Proceedings of the 9th International Conference on Architectural Support for Programming Languages and Operating Systems*, pages 117–128, 2000.

[3] P. Conway, N. Kalyanasundharam, G. Donley, K. Lepak, and B. Hughes. Blade Computing with the AMD Opteron Processor (Magny-Cours). *Hot chips 21*, August 2009.

[4] I. Corporation. *Intel(R) 64 and IA-32 Architectures Software Developer's Manual Volume 3A: System Programming Guide, Part1*, January 2011.

[5] T. S. Craig. Building FIFO and priority-queueing spin locks from atomic swap. Technical Report TR 93-02-02, Department of Computer Science, University of Washington, February 1993.

[6] D. Dice, V. J. Marathe, and N. Shavit. Flat-Combining NUMA Locks. In *Proceedings of the 23nd Annual ACM Symposium on Parallel Algorithms and Architectures*, pages 65 – 74, 2011.

[7] P. Fatourou and N. D. Kallimanis. A highly-efficient wait-free universal construction. In *Proceedings of the 23nd Annual ACM Symposium on Parallel Algorithms and Architectures*, pages 325 – 334, 2011.

[8] J. R. Goodman, M. Vernon, and P. J. Woest. Efficient synchronization primitives for large-scale cache-coherent multiprocessors. In *Proceedings of the Third International Conference on Architectural Support for Programming Languages and Operating Systems (ASPLOS)*, pages 64–75, April 1989.

[9] A. Gupta, A. Tucker, and S. Urushibara. The impact of operating system scheduling policies and synchronization methods of performance of parallel applications. *SIGMETRICS Perform. Eval. Rev.*, 19:120–132, April 1991.

[10] R. Gupta and C. R. Hill. A scalable implementation of barrier synchronization using an adaptive combining tree. In *Proceedings of the Third International Conference on Architectural Support for Programming Languages and Operating Systems (ASPLOS III)*, pages 54–63, 1989.

[11] D. Hendler, I. Incze, N. Shavit, and M. Tzafrir. The code for Flat-Combining. http://github.com/mit-carbon/flat-combining.

[12] D. Hendler, I. Incze, N. Shavit, and M. Tzafrir. Flat combining and the synchronization-parallelism tradeoff. In *Proceedings of the 22nd Annual ACM Symposium on Parallel Algorithms and Architectures*, pages 355–364, 2010.

[13] D. Hendler, N. Shavit, and L. Yerushalmi. A scalable lock-free stack algorithm. In *Proceedings of the 16th ACM Symposium on Parallel Algorithms and Architectures*, pages 206–215, 2004.

[14] M. Herlihy. Wait-free synchronization. *ACM Transactions on Programming Languages and Systems (TOPLAS)*, 13:124–149, jan 1991.

[15] M. P. Herlihy and J. M. Wing. Linearizability: A correctness condition for concurrent objects. *ACM Transactions on Programming Languages and Systems (TOPLAS)*, 12:463–492, 1990.

[16] N. D. Kallimanis and P. Fatourou. The code for sim universal construction. http://code.google.com/p/sim-universal-construction/.

[17] V. Luchangco, D. Nussbaum, and N. Shavit. A Hierarchical CLH Queue Lock. In *Proceedings of the 12th International Euro-Par Conference*, pages 801–810, 2006.

[18] P. S. Magnusson, A. Landin, and E. Hagersten. Queue locks on cache coherent multiprocessors. In *Proceedings of the 8th International Parallel Processing Symposium*, pages 165–171, 1994.

[19] P. E. McKenney. *Memory Barriers: a Hardware View for Software Hackers*, June 2010.

[20] J. M. Mellor-Crummey and M. L. Scott. Algorithms for scalable synchronization on shared-memory multiprocessors. *ACM Transactions on Computer Systems*, 9(1):21–65, 1991.

[21] M. M. Michael and M. L. Scott. Simple, fast, and practical non-blocking and blocking concurrent queue algorithms. In *Proceedings of the 15th ACM Symposium on Principles of Distributed Computing*, pages 267–275, 1996.

[22] A. Micro Devices. *AMD64 Architecture Programmer's Manual Volume 2: System Programming*, June 2010.

[23] Y. Oyama, K. Taura, and A. Yonezawa. Executing parallel programs with synchronization bottlenecks efficiently. In *Proceedings of International Workshop on Parallel and Distributed Computing for Symbolic and Irregular Applications (PDSIA '99)*, pages 182 – 204, 1999.

[24] Z. Radovic and E. Hagersten. Hierarchical backoff locks for nonuniform communication architectures. In *Proceedings of the 9th IEEE International Symposium on High-Performance Computer Architecture*, pages 241–252, 2003.

[25] N. Shavit and A. Zemach. Diffracting trees. *ACM Transactions on Computer Systems*, 14(4):385–428, 1996.

[26] N. Shavit and A. Zemach. Combining funnels: A dynamic approach to software combining. *Journal of Parallel and Distributed Computing*, 60(11):1355–1387, 2000.

[27] R. K. Treiber. Systems programming: Coping with parallelism. Technical Report RJ 5118, IBM Almaden Research Center, April 1986.

[28] D. L. Weaver and T. Germond. *The SPARC Architecture Manual, Version 9*, 1994.

[29] P.-C. Yew, N.-F. Tzeng, and D. H. Lawrie. Distributing hot-spot addressing in large-scale multiprocessors. *IEEE Trans. Computers*, 36(4):388–395, 1987.

A Work-Stealing Scheduler for X10's Task Parallelism with Suspension

Olivier Tardieu
IBM T.J. Watson Research Center, Yorktown Heights, NY, USA
tardieu@us.ibm.com

Haichuan Wang
University of Illinois at Urbana-Champaign, Urbana, IL, USA
hwang154@illinois.edu

Haibo Lin
IBM Research - China, Beijing, China
linhb@cn.ibm.com

Abstract

The X10 programming language is intended to ease the programming of scalable concurrent and distributed applications. X10 augments a familiar imperative object-oriented programming model with constructs to support light-weight asynchronous tasks as well as execution across multiple address spaces. A crucial aspect of X10's runtime system is the scheduling of concurrent tasks. Work-stealing schedulers have been shown to efficiently load balance fine-grain divide-and-conquer task-parallel program on SMPs and multicores. But X10 is not limited to shared-memory fork-join parallelism. X10 permits tasks to suspend and synchronize by means of conditional atomic blocks and remote task invocations.

In this paper, we demonstrate that work-stealing scheduling principles are applicable to a rich programming language such as X10, achieving performance at scale without compromising expressivity, ease of use, or portability. We design and implement a portable work-stealing execution engine for X10. While this engine is biased toward the efficient execution of fork-join parallelism in shared memory, it handles the full X10 language, especially conditional atomic blocks and distribution.

We show that this engine improves the run time of a series of benchmark programs by several orders of magnitude when used in combination with the C++ backend compiler and runtime for X10. It achieves scaling comparable to state-of-the art work-stealing scheduler implementations—the Cilk++ compiler and the Java fork/join framework—despite the dramatic increase in generality.

Categories and Subject Descriptors D.1.3 [*Concurrent Programming*]: Parallel programming; D.3.3 [*Language Constructs and Features*]: Concurrent programming structures; D.3.4 [*Processors*]: Code generation, Run-time environments

General Terms Languages, Performance

Keywords Scheduling, Task Parallelism, Work-Stealing, X10

1. Introduction

The X10 programming language [5, 6, 22] is intended to ease the programming of scalable concurrent and distributed applications, targeting modern multicore and clustered architectures. X10 augments a familiar imperative object-oriented programming model with constructs to support light-weight asynchronous tasks as well as execution across multiple address spaces. It is a strongly-typed and class-based language much like Java or Scala [19]. It supports two levels of concurrency. The first level corresponds to concurrency within a single shared-memory process, which is represented by an X10 place. The second level supports parallelism across places, i.e., across processes that do not share memory. In each place, X10 encourages programmers to decompose computations into loosely-synchronized light-weight asynchronous tasks—asyncs—with the promise that theses tasks will run in parallel on parallel hardware. Fulfilling this promise however is hard. How can the runtime system efficiently allocate tasks to parallel execution units? What if the tasks are too small or too many? What about ordering dependencies?

Work-stealing schedulers [4] have emerged as the approach of choice to tackle these issues. A work-stealing scheduler uses a pool of worker threads to run a task-parallel program. Each worker maintains a queue of pending jobs[1] and pushes new jobs to its own queue. When a worker completes a job, it pops a pending job from its own queue, or, if empty, attempts to steal a job from another worker's queue. Work-stealing queues are double-ended: workers push and pop from the bottom of the queue, but steal from the top. Work-stealing schedulers typically perform well because they minimize contention among workers.

Work-stealing schedulers have acquired their reputation in the context of several programming models (Cilk [9], Java fork/join [16], Habanero [20], PFunc [14], Intel Threading Building Blocks [21], Microsoft Task Parallel Library [17]). In order to make work-stealing effective, these models are very constrained, and programmers have to renounce a lot of the power and flexibility of modern programming languages. For instance, parallel scopes in Cilk do not extend beyond procedure boundaries: a procedure cannot return if it has outstanding children. Cilk also adopts a weak exception semantics. Habanero's work-stealing scheduler only handles async-finish task graphs. Library-based frameworks offer less flexible scheduling policies and lack compiler support to statically rule out unsupported task dependencies. Java fork/join tasks may only use synchronization classes that are advertised to cooperate with fork-join scheduling. These restrictions are deemed necessary to make work-stealing effective and its implementation tractable.

In contrast, X10 permits arbitrary task synchronizations, adopts a determinate exception semantics, and makes no connection between task and method boundaries. While it is unrealistic to expect work-stealing to be as effective on arbitrary programs, we would like Cilk-like performance for Cilk-like codes and, at the same time, full language support with limited and predictable overhead.

[1] The scheduler may divide each source-level task into multiple jobs.

PPoPP'12, February 25–29, 2012, New Orleans, Louisiana, USA.

This work tackles these challenges. We design and implement an efficient portable work-stealing execution engine for the full X10 language. Its contributions are:

- *Dynamic load balancing at each place.* The engine supports multi-place programs and balances the computation in each place, automatically mapping tasks to worker threads. We do not consider load balancing across places, that is, task migration from place to place.
- *Full language support.* The engine is designed to handle task suspension by means of compiler-generated continuations, exceptions, asynchronous initialization, etc.
- *Portability.* Because X10 is intended to be available on a wide variety of platforms ranging from Systems-on-a-Chip to supercomputers, portability is a prime concern. The engine combines a compiler plugin and a runtime library. The compiler plugin implements an X10-source-to-X10-source program transformation that generates code artifacts (frame classes and continuation methods) required by the runtime scheduler. The runtime library written in X10 implements the work-stealing scheduler. Thanks to this X10-centric approach, we can plug this engine into both the C++ and Java backend compilers and runtimes for X10 and use any C++ compiler or JDK supported by X10.
- *Performance (C++ backend).* We develop a series of optimizations to obtain a scalable scheduler with low overhead. Some of these optimizations—lazy frame initialization and migration—require extending the backend compilers for X10. We extend the C++ backend compiler accordingly.

We evaluate performance on a series of shared-memory fork-join benchmarks translated from Cilk (Problem-Based Benchmark Suite [2]) and Java fork/join.

We discuss related work in Section 2. We give a brief introduction to X10 in Section 3. Sections 4 to 6 describe the architecture of our work-stealing scheduler and its implementation. We report on our experimental evaluation in Section 7 and conclude in Section 8.

2. Related Work

Work-stealing runtimes are increasingly popular to handle the scheduling of dynamic task parallelism.

Languages and libraries. These runtimes are often directly exposed to the programmer as libraries. Java's fork/join framework [16], Intel's Threading Building Blocks [21], and Microsoft's Task Parallel Library [17] follow this approach. The XWS library for X10 [7] implements a work-stealing scheduler dedicated to graph algorithms. Tasks correspond to vertices; programs submit vertices to the scheduler; the scheduler dynamically partition vertices across processing units to balance the load using a work-stealing policy.

Other work-stealing runtimes hide inside implementations of new language constructs and require matching compiler support to transparently map constructs to runtime routines. The Cilk-5 runtime [9] and the Habanero runtime [11] belong this category. Thanks to its built-in constructs for fine-grain concurrency, X10 is an ideal candidate for the latter approach, which we adopt here.

Shared beliefs. These many runtimes share common principles. A work-stealing scheduler uses a pool of threads (OS threads or VM threads) called workers. Each worker maintains a double-ended queue—a deque—of pending things to do. A worker primarily operates on its own deque, pushing content to the deque when a task is spawned and going back to the deque every time it finishes its current task. The deque is also the mechanism by which work is made available to other workers: if a worker empties its own deque, it then attempts to steal work from the deque of another worker. Usually, workers push and pop work from the bottom of their deque, but steal from the top, further reducing contention.

Work-stealing deques. X10's standard library provides a `Deque` class that is essentially a replica of the deque of Java's fork/join framework [15, 16]. Our engine is implemented using this deque.

Scheduling policies. Work-stealing algorithms first differ in what they push to the deque when a task is spawned. Under the work-first policy promoted by Cilk, the worker pushes the continuation of the parent task to the deque, executing the spawned task first. Under the help-first policy typical of library-based schedulers, the worker pushes the spawned task to its deque, while continuing the execution of the parent task. Previous research has looked into the pros and cons of these scheduling policies and how to combine them [4, 7, 11, 12, 18]. In this work, we implement a pure work-first scheduling policy. Our goal is to enlarge the class of languages and programs amenable to work-stealing rather than improving performance for a specific subclass. With work, our scheduler could be made more flexible using the recipes developed for Habanero.

Fork-join schedulers. Library-based schedulers are primarily targeted at fork-join parallelism. Fork-join tasks may only suspend to wait for subtasks to complete. As a consequence, when a task suspends, a fork-join scheduler can safely assign to the same worker a subtask of the suspended task, without bothering with context switches or continuations. The state of the suspended parent task simply remains on the thread stack underneath the state of the subtask. Obviously the parent task cannot be returned to until after the subtasks have completed. But this is just fine for fork-join tasks.

The standard X10 runtime, a.k.a XRX, has to support arbitrary suspension. It therefore adopts an hybrid approach: when a task suspends on a finish construct (waiting for subtasks) the worker starts running subtasks, but if a task suspends on a when construct (conditional atomic block) the scheduler suspends the worker thread and allocates or wakes another thread in its pool to compensate for the decrease in parallelism.

Among others, Java's fork/join framework goes beyond pure fork-join tasks. It ships with a few compatible synchronization classes. PFunc permits synchronization barriers as long as the number of tasks involved is less than the number of workers. By nature, these frameworks cannot handle arbitrary synchronization patterns without reverting to a one-to-one mapping from tasks to threads.

Scheduling with continuations. In contrast, compilers such as the Cilk compiler, the Habanero compiler, and our augmented X10 compiler can synthesize code artifacts that makes it possible for a runtime to queue a continuation for later execution without sacrificing a thread. As a consequence, our runtime uses a fixed number of threads (intended to match the number of available cores) and a unified approach, where continuations are used to implement both finish and when. Incidentally, this means our runtime makes it possible to run X10 programs on computer systems without support for dynamic thread creation, such as IBM's BlueGene/P, whereas XRX can only run async-finish programs on such architectures.

The drawback of this approach is known: compiler-generated continuations have overheads (code size, run time). Carefully engineered fork-join schedulers are capable of lower overhead. But Cilk has already established that aggressive compiler and runtime optimizations can make the approach successful. In this work, we cannot be as aggressive in our optimizations as the Cilk++ compiler as we intend to interface with a wide variety of backend compilers and runtimes for X10. We do however take advantage of C++-backend-only features and we suspect that a deeper integration with the C++ compiler itself would enable further reduction of our overhead.

Beyond shared-memory fork-join parallelism. Our compiler plugin is inspired by the work on compiler support for work-first work-stealing in the Habanero project [20]. Habanero handles a larger class of task graphs than Cilk—async-finish graphs—by permitting arbitrary nesting of finish and async constructs. Various scheduling policies have been proposed to handle several classes of task graphs with more flexible synchronization constructs, e.g., synchronization variables [3] or futures [24]. Our work takes compiler support much further by also permitting conditional atomic blocks and distributed code. Thanks to the former, we can handle any kind of synchronization: cyclic barriers, futures, FIFOs, etc.

We handle distributed programs but only provide dynamic mapping from tasks to workers in each place. X10 requires programs to specify the place of each task. The X10 runtime is not permitted to migrate tasks across places. It is however possible for an application or library to interface with the runtime so as to dynamically choose where to spawn tasks in an attempt to balance the load across places [23]. These two levels of load balancing could be combined.

3. The X10 Language

This section briefly describes the context for the X10 project and introduces the key programming language concepts that will be discussed in later sections of the paper. This work is done in the context of the most recent revision of the X10 language: X10 2.2.

The genesis of the X10 project was the DARPA High Productivity Computing Systems (HPCS) program. As such, X10 is intended to be a programming language that achieves "Performance and Productivity at Scale." The primary hardware platforms being targeted by the language are clusters of multicore processors linked together into a large scale system via a high-performance network. Therefore, supporting both concurrency and distribution are first class concerns of the X10 language design and implementation.

X10 is a familiar strongly-typed, imperative, class-based, object-oriented programming language much like Java or Scala. Like functional languages, X10 supports first-class functions and encourages using immutable state. X10 emphasizes statically-checked guarantees by means of a rich type system with generics, constraints (i.e., dependent types), structs, and type definitions.

A computation in X10 consists of one or more asynchronous activities (light-weight tasks). A new activity is created by the statement `async S`. To synchronize activities, X10 provides the statement `finish S`. An activity that executes a finish statement will not execute the statement after the finish until all activities spawned within the finish's body have terminated.

Every activity executes in a single `Place` (address space). While executing in this place, it may freely access any object that also resides in the place. It may manipulate remote references (`GlobalRefs`) to objects that reside in other places, but is not able to actually access the state of any remote object. Therefore computations must sometimes "shift" from one place to another to access the data they need. When this happens, the compiler and runtime system collaborate to ensure that the necessary data and control information are communicated from one place to another. The fundamental X10 construct for "place-shifting" is `at (p) S`. An at statement shifts execution of the current activity from the current place to place p and executes S at the remote place. For instance, the program below prints one message from each place.

```
class HelloWorld {
  public static def main(Array[String]) {
    finish for(p in Place.places())
      async at(p) Console.OUT.println("Hello from place " + p);
  }
}
```

The set of available places (`Place.places()`) and the mapping from places to nodes in a cluster is decided by the user at launch time.

X10 includes an unconditional atomic block construct `atomic S` and a conditional atomic block construct `when (E) S`. An atomic block is executed by an activity as if in a single step during which all other concurrent activities in the same place are suspended. Execution of `when (E) S` suspends until a state is reached in which the condition E is true. In this state, the statement S is executed atomically.

X10 defines a "rooted" exception model in which a finish acts as a collection point for any exceptions thrown by activities that are executing under the control of the finish. Only after all such activities have terminated (normally or abnormally) does the finish propagate exceptions to its enclosing environment by collecting them into a single `MultipleException` object.

A great deal more information on X10 can be found online at `http://x10-lang.org`. In particular, the language specification [22], programmer's guide [5], and a collection of tutorials and sample programs are available.

4. A Scheduler for Single-place Async-Finish X10

We organize the discussion of our work-stealing scheduler into three sections. We start with an unoptimized scheduler for single-place async-finish programs in the current section, discuss optimizations in the next, and add full language support in Section 6. An async-finish program only uses async and finish to spawn and synchronize tasks (as opposed to at and when).

4.1 Principles

Using a simplified divide-and-conquer Fibonacci example method, we first explain informally how our scheduler works. In the second half if this section, we take a closer look at the required compiler and runtime support and show snippets of the generated code and runtime code.

```
static def fib(n:Int):void {
  if (n<=1) return;
  finish {
    async fib(n-2);
    fib(n-1);
  }
}
```

For simplicity, this method does not return anything (see Section 6.4 for the real thing).

Frames and cactus stacks. We decompose each method into a series of scopes and associate a *frame* with each scope. This example method has four scopes for (1) the method itself, (2) the finish construct, (3) the finish body, (4) the async construct. The work-stealing scheduler builds the *cactus stack* of the running program by chaining these frames into trees, such as:

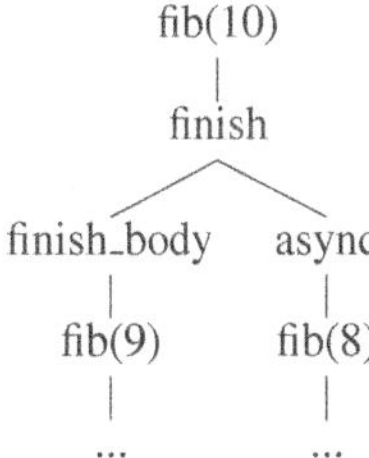

Observe the finish frame has two children. When the execution enters the method the "fib(n)" frame is pushed to the top of the stack. Assuming n is greater than 1, it then reaches the finish construct. The corresponding frame is pushed to the stack shortly followed by the finish_body frame. It now reaches the async construct. An async frame however is not pushed to the top of the stack but to the top of the topmost finish on the stack *next* to any other child frame the finish frame might already have.

This cactus stack captures the current state of the execution and is shared and maintained by all the worker threads collaborating to execute the program. Each worker owns one top of the stack, i.e., one leaf of the tree. For instance, the worker running the finish_body frame will eventually push frame "fib(n-1)" on top of it; the worker handling the async frame will push frame "fib(n-2)" on top of it. This may be the same worker at a different point in time or a distinct worker.

The frames are regular X10 objects, that is, instances of X10 classes. They are created by means of constructor invocations. They are linked together just like object graphs are usually constructed. Each frame object is an instance of a subclass of the root `Frame` class. The `Frame` class has an `up` field of type `Frame` which holds a reference to the parent frame in the cactus stack. This reference is `null` for the root stack frame.

The cactus stack is intended to fully encapsulate the state of the execution. Each frame class has a field for each local variable declared in the corresponding scope. In addition, a method frame has a field for each parameter of the method. Most frames also have a `pc` field of integer type, which encodes the next position in the frame, that is, the index of the instruction in sequence after the one currently processed.

In summary, the state of the execution is encoded as an explicit cactus stack. The cactus stack preserves the caller-callee relationship, keeps track of return addresses (saved pc), and store the values of the variables.

In the remainder of this paper, when ambiguous, we use the term *cactus stack* to refer to this data structure and the term *thread stack* to refer to the pthread- or VM-level stack of a worker thread.

Deques and continuations. Our scheduler implements a work-first policy. Each worker maintains a deque of pending continuations. A continuation is simply a frame with valid pc, which specifies the point of reentry.

When a worker is about to enter an async it pushes the continuation of the async onto its deque. Concretely, it saves the index of the statement in sequence after the async in the current frame's pc field and pushes a reference to that frame onto its deque. In the previous example, just before entering the async scope, the worker stores the index of the "fib(n-1)" method invocation in the finish_body frame and pushes it onto the deque.

The worker then processes the async. When done with the async, it attempts to pop the continuation from the deque. If successful, the continuation has not been stolen and the execution continues. Another worker however might have stolen the continuation in the meantime and taken charge of its execution. In that case, the victim is left with nothing to do and in turn becomes a thief.

In summary, the leaves of the cactus stack are dynamically split into two sets. Some leaves correspond to frames that workers are currently processing (one per worker). The other leaves constitute the elements of the worker deques, that is, the pending continuations (not currently processed by any worker).

Scheduling. The first worker gets to execute the application main method. Other workers are idle. An idle worker attempts to steal a continuation from a random worker again and again until it finds something to run.

When a worker pops a completed frame to find a finish frame below, it checks how many child frames still point back to this finish frame. If none, it means all the tasks governed by this finish have completed, therefore the worker pops the finish frame and continues with its parent frame. Otherwise, the worker just abandons the current computation. This worker or another will eventually consider the finish frame again when another branch of the finish subtree gets completed.

4.2 Implementation

We implement this scheduling policy by rewriting an X10 program with finish and async constructs into a new X10 program that only uses a few long-lived asyncs. Each one of these asyncs is a worker of our work-stealing scheduler. They all run the same top-level loop, alternating between finding a continuation to run, and running this continuation. As part of their executions, these worker asyncs build the cactus stack of the program and operate the deques.

We run the transformed program using the standard X10 runtime. It maps each worker async to its own runtime thread for the duration of the execution.

Of course there is no point in implementing a standalone program rewriting engine from scratch given the existing compiler infrastructure for X10—parser, type checker, Abstract Syntax Tree (AST) representation and traversal facilities, pretty-printer, etc. We implement a typed-AST-to-typed-AST transformation in the style of many intermediate passes of the X10 compiler and add a new `-WORK_STEALING` option to the X10 compiler that enables the transformation.

Moreover, part of the code we need to generate is independent of the particulars of one specific X10 program. We therefore write it once and for all as a runtime library.

4.2.1 Runtime Support

We add a package to the X10 runtime named `x10.compiler.ws`. This package contains a series of frame classes and a `Worker` class.

The frame classes all inherit from a root `Frame` class and are intended to declare and/or implement the mechanisms by which frame objects can be managed by the scheduler to compose cactus stacks and encode continuations. The `Frame` class declares a field `up` of type `Frame` intended to hold a reference to the frame above the current frame object in the stack. In addition to the `Frame` class, we declare the `FinishFrame`, `AsyncFrame`, and `RegularFrame` classes. `FinishFrames` are the only frames with potentially multiple children in the cactus stack. They maintain a count of these children. `RegularFrames` may be pushed to the deques. The parent frames of `AsyncFrames` are `FinishFrames`.

The `Worker` class implements the worker of the work-stealing scheduler. Each worker alternate between the idle state—looking for a continuation to steal—and the running state—executing application code. Moreover, static methods of the `Worker` class handle the creation and destruction of the pool of workers.

Each worker more or less runs this loop:

```
var k:Frame;
while ((k = findContinuation()) != null) {
  try {
    while (k != null) {
      k._run(k.pc);
      k = k.up;
      if (k != null && k instanceof FinishFrame) {
          val f = k as FinishFrame;
          f.decreaseChildrenCount();
          if (f.hasOustandingChildren()) break;
      }
  } catch (Stolen) {}
}
```

When an idle worker finds a continuation k, it invokes k, that is, resumes the execution of the stolen frame at the saved pc. If the frame's execution completes, the worker pops the frame from the cactus stack and proceeds with the parent frame. If the parent frame is a finish frame, the execution continues up the stack only if the finish frame has no outstanding children.

The findContinuation method implements the usual infinite loop: pseudo-random selection of a victim, attempt to steal from the victim's deque, break if successful, continue if not.

The pop method invocation in async frames may either succeed or throw the STOLEN exception (unique instance of the Stolen exception type). In the latter, the computation of the worker is cancelled and the worker returns to idle state.

4.2.2 Compiler Support

The compiler generates the representation of the frames of the cactus stack and instruments the source code to (1) operate on the cactus stack and (2) push and pop continuations to the deques.

Our compiler pass divides methods into scopes and synthesizes a frame class for each scope. It identifies the local variables and method parameters in the program and add fields to frames accordingly. It indexes the statements in each scope. It splits methods by generating one helper method in each frame, which implements the code fragment of the corresponding scope. It synthesizes a replacement method for the original method, which constructs an instance of the method frame class and invokes the generated helper method of that frame.

The compiler also instruments the code of the helpers methods as the following:

- It replaces accesses to local variables and method parameters with field accesses.
- Before each method call, it saves the pc of the next instruction in the current frame. The method call itself is rewritten into an invocation of the corresponding replacement method.
- It replaces each nested scope of the method in the same way. First, the pc of the next instruction is saved in the current frame. Then, a frame object for the scope is constructed. Finally, the helper method of the new frame is invoked.
- It inserts push-to-the-deque commands just before entering async scopes, pop-from-the-deque commands just before leaving async scopes.
- It adds to each helper method a top-level switch statement, which permits entering the method in the middle so as to resume its execution at a chosen instruction index.

Finally, the compiler generates the main method of the transformed program. This method initializes the worker pool then invokes the transformed application main method. Once the application main method completes, it destructs the worker pool and exits.

To illustrate these tasks, here is a skeleton of the code we generate for the example fib method. For brevity, we only show the pc-related code in the `_fib_finish_body` class.

```
class _fib extends RegularFrame {
  val n:Int;
  def this(up:Frame, n:Int) {super(up); this.n=n;}
  def _run(pc:Int) {
    if (this.n<=1) return;
    val _frame1 = new _fib_finish(this);
    _frame1._run(0);
  }
}
class _fib_finish extends FinishFrame {
  def this(up:Frame) {super(up);}
  def _run(pc:Int) {
    val _frame1 = new _fib_finish_body(this);
    _frame1._run(0);
  }
}
class _fib_finish_body extends RegularFrame {
  def this(up:Frame) {super(up);}
  def _run(pc:Int) {
    switch(pc) {
    case 0:
      this.pc = 1;
      deque().push(this);
      val _frame1 = new _fib_async(this.up);
      _frame1._run(0);
    case 1:
      this.pc = 2;
      _fib(this, this.up.up.n-2);
    }
  }
}
class _fib_async extends AsyncFrame {
  def this(up:FinishFrame) {super(up);}
  def _run(pc:Int) {
    _fib(this, this.up.up.n-1);
    deque().pop();
  }
}
static def _fib(up:Frame, n:Int):void {
  new _fib(up, n)._run(0);
}
```

There are four generated classes corresponding to the four identified scopes, four _run methods corresponding to the fragment of code in each scope, plus a _fib method to replace the original fib method.

We now review the main additional tasks undertaken by the compiler not illustrated by our naive example.

Class hierarchy. A replacement method always takes the callee's frame as its first parameter. The rest of its signature is the same as the original method. Therefore visibility, overriding, and overloading are not affected by the transformation. We rewrite the signatures of abstract and interface method in the same manner.

Instance methods. The frames classes obtained from a method of class C are generated inside class C. Occurrences of *this* inside instance methods are replaced by qualified C.*this* expressions.

Control-flow constructs. We handle loops and conditionals by dividing the code into more scopes. For example, we create a frame class for each branch of an `if` statement. When a worker encounters a `return`, `break`, or `continue` statement, it starts popping and discarding stack frames until it finds the target frame for the construct.

Return values. The frame of a non-void method has a field intended to hold the returned value. Upon return, the caller obtains the value from the callee's frame just before discarding the reference to that frame.

5. An Optimized Scheduler

The scheduler of the previous section would not perform very well. In particular, it would not scale beyond a few workers and it would have high sequential overhead. In other word, transformed sequential code would be much slower than the original. While some of the overhead is unavoidable, many reasons for this poor performance can be addressed.

In this section, we discuss performance improvements. These improvements are compatible with the extended language support we discuss in the next section. More precisely, the extensions of the next section are engineered to be compatible with these optimization and to only marginally affect their effectiveness on single-place async-finish programs.

The main issues we are trying to address are:

- The scheduler constantly allocates, constructs, and collects frame objects.
- The generated methods are too many and too tiny. Too much time is spent transferring from callers to callees and back.
- Large chunks of code are sequential but the compiler transforms them anyway.
- Steals are infrequent. Most of time a task and all of its subtasks get processed by the same worker one after the other. We should be taking advantage of this.

5.1 Selective Transformation

Before applying our program transformation, we build the call graph of the target program. A method m is transformed by our compiler pass iff m or any method reachable from m contains a concurrency construct (async, at, when). Otherwise, it is left unchanged.

We say a local variable is *ephemeral* if no task may be spawned while it is alive, that is, if there is no async, at, or when construct between a definition and a use of the variable. There is no need to store ephemeral variable values in the cactus stack. Our compiler pass leave them alone. For now, we work around the lack of live variable analysis in the X10 tool chain by manually annotating variables `@x10.compiler.Ephemeral`.

5.2 Lazy Frame Initialization

X10 local variables and fields have different initialization semantics. A local variable can only be read after it has been definitely initialized. A field on the other hand is initialized to the default value of its type if not explicitly initialized in a constructor. Therefore, by substituting fields for local variables, we incur the overhead of field initialization to no avail since this default value will never be accessed. To eliminate this overhead, we annotate the fields of the frame classes `@x10.compiler.Uninitialized` and teach the C++ backend compiler not to zero annotated fields.

5.3 Inlining

We systematically inline frame constructors at call sites. In order to avoid a method call to lookup the current deque for push and pop operations, we add a worker parameter to every generated method and use that reference to access the deque. The push and pop codes themselves are inlined. We also inline helper methods (i.e., _run methods) into transformed methods (e.g., _fib method). Moreover, we eliminate the switch statements from the transformed methods since the helper methods are always invoked with pc equals 0.

Ultimately, we end up with two copies of each source method in the transformed program. The first copy, traditionally named *fast clone* is the transformed method itself. Thanks to inlining, each transformed method ends up having the same structure as the corresponding source method. The second copy of the code—the *slow clone*—consists of the collection of helper methods in frame classes. The slow clone is seldom used, that is, by thieves to resume the execution of an existing call stack. Workers spend most of their time running fast clones, so the small size of slow clone methods does not hurt performance.

5.4 Finish Out-degree

By construction, the worker who creates a finish frame must process all of the non-stolen subtasks of this finish before returning to the finish frame. For simplicity, in the previous section, we suggested keeping track of how many frames are pointing to a finish frame. But this is an overkill. Instead, we count how many subtasks of the finish have been stolen so far and not yet completed, adding one to that count if one or more of the non-stolen subtasks has not completed yet. In other words, we aggregate all the non-stolen subtasks as one for counting purposes.

While this might seem like a minor change, the performance implications are profound. Indeed, this count is shared across workers. Therefore, it must be updated atomically. Thanks to this change, these atomic operations are only required from thieves and victims. In particular, if a single worker executes a finish body in its entirety, then no counting ever takes place.

5.5 Speculative Stack Allocation

Most often, a frame will be constructed and discarded by the same worker without ever being seen by another worker. Therefore, we speculatively allocate frames on the thread stack. A thief is responsible for copying the stolen continuation frame as well as all the frames on top of it from the victim's stack to the heap (except of course for those frames that have already been copied to the heap by a prior thief).[2]

Thieves and victims must synchronize to ensure the integrity of the copy. A thief grabs a lock (tryLock) on the victim's deque before attempting to steal. If the lock is acquired and the steal is successful, it keeps the lock while copying the frames. This prevents another thief from interfering with the copy. The victim when it fails to pop the stolen continuation acquires and releases the lock, hence ensuring that the copy is complete before trashing its stack.

While making the copy, the thief inserts a pointer in each source finish frame to the destination finish frame. This pointer is used by the victim to decrement the count of remaining tasks under the finish after it discovers that the continuation has been stolen.

Heap allocated frames objects are explicitly deallocated when popped from the cactus stack (using C++ free).

In the end, although we replaced locals by fields the data remains on the thread stack. We incur hardly any memory management cost for frames.

5.6 Miscellaneous Field Optimizations

In order to avoid the need for traversing the stack to identify the finish frame which to attach an async frame, we add a finish frame field to each `RegularFrame`. We only add a `pc` field to frames with multiple points of reentry.

Discussion. Our choice of creating many small frame objects at first might seem a fatal mistake. However, thanks to these careful optimizations, we alleviate most of the overhead while retaining the benefit of a straightforward code generation. Even path expressions such as "this.up.up.n" in the Fibonacci example could be eliminated from the fast clones by a trivial constant propagation.

Several of the optimizations we implement deviate from X10's official semantics, thus requiring changes in the C++ backend compiler for X10. While uninitialized fields or stack-allocated objects have no place in the Java specification, such things could be achieved in Jikes RVM [1] with essentially the same benefits, thanks to its stack-walking API [8].

6. A Scheduler for the Full X10 Language

In this section, we augment the scheduler of the previous section to account for the X10's conditional atomic blocks, remote tasks, exceptions, and asynchronous variable initialization. We also discuss the current limitations of our implementation.

6.1 Suspension

The execution of `when (E) S` suspends until a state is reached in which the condition E is true. In this state, the statement S is executed atomically. Moreover, changes to E outside of atomic sections might not trigger the execution of S.

In order to cope with when constructs, our scheduler maintains in each place a queue of suspended continuations. Concretely, when a worker encounters a when statement whose condition evaluates to false, it saves the index of the when statement in the pc field of the current frame and pushes this frame to the extra queue. It then aborts its computation and switches to the idle state in which it will look for something else to run in the usual way. Dually, when a worker exits an atomic block, it grabs a lock on the extra queue and

[2] To be exact, a thief always copies the stolen frames up to the first finish frame, then only copies those frame that are not on the heap yet.

moves its entire content to its own deque, which will eventually lead to the re-evaluation of the condition of each suspended task.

Speculative stack allocation. In an async-finish program, a worker only aborts its computation if it finds the continuation it is about to execute has been stolen from it. By construction, this means all the frames on the thread stack have already been copied to the heap by one or several thieves. It is therefore ok for the victim to discard the content of its thread stack by means of the STOLEN exception.

In contrast, when a worker aborts because of a false condition in a when statement, its deque may be full of pending continuations and its thread stack filled with frames essential to continued execution of the program. Hence, we need to take extra care to make the scheme for when constructs work with speculative stack allocation.

We add an extra deque per worker. Both the old and the new deques contain continuations. But while the continuations of the old deque may point to stack-allocated frames, continuations of the new deque can only refer to heap-allocated frames. Before a worker aborts because of a false when condition, it "steals" all of the tasks from its normal deque and pushes them to its extra deque using the exact same protocol thieves use to steal tasks. Then it can safely abort since there remain no pointer to its thread stack.

We update the findContinuation algorithm accordingly. When a worker is idle it first processes the continuations of its extra deque if any before trying to steal from others. When worker A decides to steal from worker B it first accesses the extra deque of B then if empty its normal deque. Of course, if it acquires a continuation from the extra deque, it does not need to migrate frames to the heap since the stolen frames are already there.

6.2 Distribution

The execution of `at (p) S` suspends the execution of the caller while S is executed at place p.

When a worker encounters `at (p) S`, it instantiates a special at frame. Then it migrates the content of its normal deque to its extra deque in the manner of the previous section and sends the at frame to place p.[3] Finally it aborts. At this point, the parent frame of the at frame only exists as a remote reference in the up field of the at frame at place p.

We augment findContinuation so that idle workers not only try to steal from collocated workers but also listen for incoming continuations from other places.

When a worker at place p picks up the at frame, it starts executing S. When done with S, it sends back the reference to the parent of the at frame to the place of origin. There a worker can pick up the frame and continue its execution.

Remote finish. One problem with that scheme is that asyncs spawned by S at place p may need to update finish subtask counts at the place of origin. In order to avoid a stream of costly increment and decrement messages between the two places, we create a proxy finish object in place p in the manner of the standard X10 runtime, which effectively coalesce these messages into much fewer remote updates.

Async at. While `async at (p) S` is truly the combination of an async and an at construct, the pattern deserves a dedicated implementation. Our scheduler simply creates a frame for S and sends it to place p.

We treat this frame S as a stolen continuation. Indeed there are now two workers at least—one local, one remote—working concurrently in the finish scope containing this async. Therefore, the worker who encountered the async statement in the first place aborts and immediately resumes the continuation of the async, which happens to be the first thing on its deque. In other words it stops executing the fast clone of the code and starts executing the slow clone of the same code. This ensures that the actions of the local and remote workers will be properly synchronized.

6.3 Exceptions

Exceptions require ubiquitous changes (Frame classes, Worker class, codegen). Basically, we add to the state of each worker an exception field. When an exception is thrown by the user code, it gets stored in this field. While the field value is not null, the worker keeps popping frames from the cactus stack until in reaches either a try-catch frame, an async frame, or a finish frame. If the exception is caught by the try-catch frame, the field is cleared. Exceptions are accumulated in a list field of the finish frame. When an exception reaches a finish frame it is added to the list. If it reaches an async frame it is added to the list of the parent finish frame of the async frame. In both cases, the exception field of the worker is cleared.

When a finish frame has no outstanding children, the exceptions of the list are combined into a MultipleException object which is loaded in the worker exception field.

Unfortunately, the scheduler itself makes use of the STOLEN exception. This exception must not be affected by the scheme we just described. Moreover, the STOLEN exception should not trigger the execution of finally blocks. After our work-stealing compiler pass, we schedule an additional compiler pass to rewrite all try-catch-finally blocks in the generated code to "ignore" this exception.

6.4 Asynchronous Initialization

The X10 compiler extends a Java-like definite assignment analysis to permit initializing final variables (X10's *vals*) from asynchronous tasks. For instance, here is how to actually compute Fibonacci numbers using this feature:

```
static def fib(n:Int):Int {
  if (n<=1) return 1;
  val u1:Int; val u2:Int;
  finish {
    async u2 = fib(n-2); // async init of u2
    u1 = fib(n-1);
  }
  return u1 + u2;
}
```

Thanks to this language feature, asynchronous tasks can "return" values without going through expensive heap-allocated objects. Moreover, the compiler guarantees race freedom.

Asynchronous initialization makes it possible for a worker to write into an inner frame of the cactus stack, possibly shared among multiple workers. This is not a concern per se as the compiler guarantees that reads happen after writes and that writes are unique. But this becomes an issue in the context of speculative stack allocation of frames. In short, a worker may write to a stale frame that has been migrated to the heap by a thief. We could of course prevent this but only by means of costly synchronization that would hinder performance irrespective of steals.

Instead, we let a worker update stack frames (not knowing whether these have been stolen or not), but migrate the values to the replacement frames when the worker finally recognizes it has been mugged. Because of the definite assignment analysis, the compiler knows statically which task is initializing which final variables. We can therefore generate as part of our code transformation a method in each async frame to propagate the right set of values. If the continuation of the async frame is stolen, the worker invokes this method before aborting. For instance, in the Fibonacci example, if the continuation of the async is stolen we know statically that u2's value must be propagated.

[3] For lack of space, we cannot discuss here the detail of the serialization operations.

6.5 Current Limitations

While our scheduler is designed from the ground up to support the full X10 language, its current implementations is not 100% complete yet and suffers a few temporary limitations, primarily:

- Closure literals and constructor bodies must be sequential. Concurrent instances may be replaced by anonymous classes and factory methods.
- X10's call graph construction is buggy. As a result, our compiler pass may incorrectly assume a method is sequential and fail to process it. This can be worked around by annotating missed methods with `@x10.compiler.WS`.
- Clocks are a form of distributed cyclic barriers with the convenience of a dedicated syntax. Our scheduler supports cyclic barriers but cannot handle the clock syntax yet.

7. Experimental Results

In this section, we evaluate the performance of our scheduler by comparing against the Cilk++ runtime and the Java fork/join framework when applied to single-place async-finish programs. While these runtimes have some support for limited forms of synchronization beyond fork-join, they are incapable of the equivalent of handling X10's when and at constructs.

Our compiler and runtime extensions are distributed as part of the X10 distribution [25] under the Eclipse license. Benchmark codes are available upon request.

7.1 Benchmarks

We consider two sets of benchmarks. The first one is composed with three micro benchmarks, including *Fibonacci*, *Integrate*, and *QuickSort*. These benchmarks have small to absurdly small tasks, making it possible to measure overheads at their worst. *Fibonacci* computes Fibonacci numbers as seen in Section 6.4. *Integrate* was suggested by Doug Lea. It computes the numerical integration of a polynomial function of degree 3 using Gaussian quadrature. *QuickSort* is a parallel quick sort implementation of a randomly generated data set. To be fair, we use the same random input generator across all implementations. We implement these three benchmarks in X10, Cilk++, and Java using the fork/join framework.

The second set of benchmarks is derived from the Problem-Based Benchmark Suite [2], which is a collection of 19 fine-grain task-parallel graph algorithms implemented in Cilk++. We translated 6 of them (randomly selected) to X10. We have no Java fork/join implementation of these benchmarks.

7.2 Porting Methodology

Our X10, Cilk++, and Java fork/join micro benchmark implementations follow the style of the respective programming paradigms. Neither implementation tries to aggregate tasks either statically or dynamically. Our goal with these benchmarks is to measure the overhead of each runtime. If we were to for instance dynamically bound the number of spawned tasks, then all of the compared runtimes would have close to zero overhead and close to perfect scaling, which is not very interesting.

Our translation of the PBBS benchmarks preserves the original algorithms as much as possible: we want to spawn the same tasks, with the same granularity and the same dependencies. Here is a list of the non-trivial changes to the code:

- PBBS codes make ubiquitous use of type-unsafe idioms: unchecked arrays, pointer arithmetic, and function pointers. We replace pointer arithmetics with explicit offsets. We disable array bound checks via the `-NO_CHECKS` option of the X10 compiler. We replace function pointers with closures. We mitigate the higher cost of closure invocation in X10 by hoisting interface lookups out of critical loops.[4]
- PBBS codes are memory-intensive. We turn off the garbage collector of the X10 runtime and preserve the free calls of the original code. Otherwise, execution time would be dominated by GC pauses.
- PBBS codes use compare-and-swap instructions on array cells. We extend the X10 standard library to support these.
- X10 structs are immutable. PBBS codes use mutable C++ structs. We replace them with classes.
- PBBS codes use the *cilk_for* construct. The Cilk runtime converts a cilk_for loop into an efficient divide-and-conquer recursive traversal over the loop iterations. We extend our code transformation to generate helper methods to do the same.

7.3 Evaluation Environment and Methodology

We measure performance on a 16-way x86_64 blade with four AMD Quad-Core Opteron 8347 HE at 1.9GHz, 24GB of RAM, and running RHELS 5.6.

Cilk++ configuration. We use Intel's cilk++ SDK preview (build 8503) [13]. We compile with `-O2 -finline-functions` optimizations, which is what the C++ backend compiler for X10 is invoked with.

Java fork/join configuration. We use the Java fork/join library from the Concurrency jsr-166 interest site [15] atop an Oracle(Sun) Java SE build 1.6.0_22-b04 32bit VM.

X10 configuration. Our experiments are based on the X10 open-source distribution at revision 22646 [25]. Our C++ compiler is g++ (GCC) 4.4.4 (Red Hat 4.4.4-13). We compile the X10 runtime with flags `-DOPTIMIZE=true -DNO_CHECKS=true -DDISABLE_GC=true`. We compile the benchmarks with options `-WORK_STEALING -O -NO_CHECKS`. We link the generated code with the thread-caching malloc memory allocator of the google performance tools [10].

Methodology. We measure the run time of the benchmarks using 1 to 16 workers. We also measure the sequential performance of selected benchmarks by removing all concurrency related constructs in these codes.

All the performance data for X10 and Cilk++ were collected from the average of 10 runs. We do 5 warm-up iterations for Java fork/join benchmarks and report the average of the next 10 runs.

7.4 Micro Benchmark

Figure 1 shows the speedups for each micro benchmark when increasing the number of workers. Execution time is normalized to 1 for 1 worker. We can see X10's work-stealing scheduler scales nearly as well as Cilk++ and better than Java fork/join. Integrate has the largest spread. Cilk++ speedup is 15.8, X10 is 13.9 and Java fork/join only 9.0.

Figure 2 shows the run times for all benchmarks and all implementations with 16 workers. X10 is faster. We also ran the X10 codes using the unmodified X10 tool chain and 16 runtime threads. Compared to X10 with work-stealing, Fib(40) is 700x slower, Integrate(1536) is 300x slower, and QuickSort(10M) is 60x slower.

In Figure 3 we compare sequential overheads, that is, the execution time of the sequential version of each program with the execution time of the parallel version running with a single worker. X10 achieves the best result with overheads ranging from 7x to 28%.

[4] Function types in X10 are interface types. Invoking a closure literal requires a lookup of the function type in the interface table of the closure litteral, which has non-trivial cost.

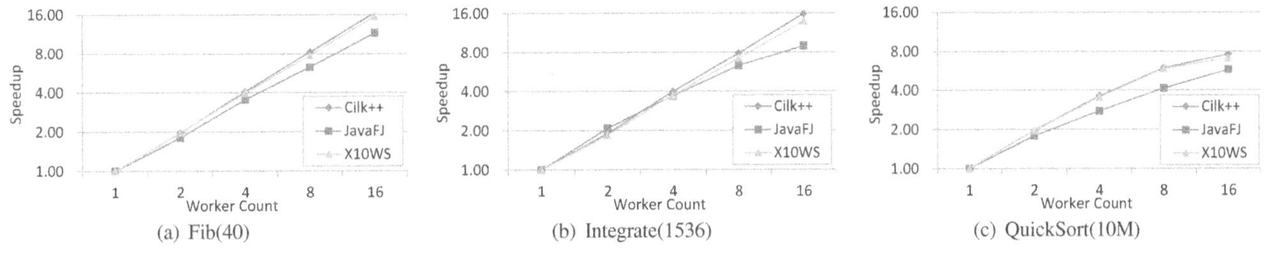

(a) Fib(40) (b) Integrate(1536) (c) QuickSort(10M)

Figure 1. Micro Benchmark Speedups

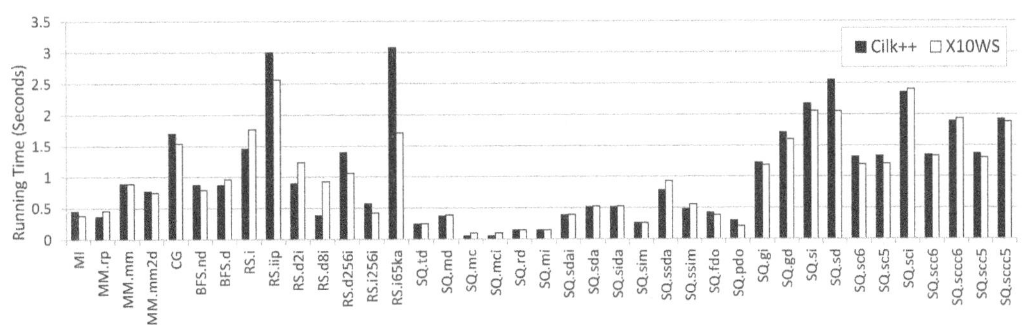

Figure 4. PBBS Running Time(s) (16 workers)

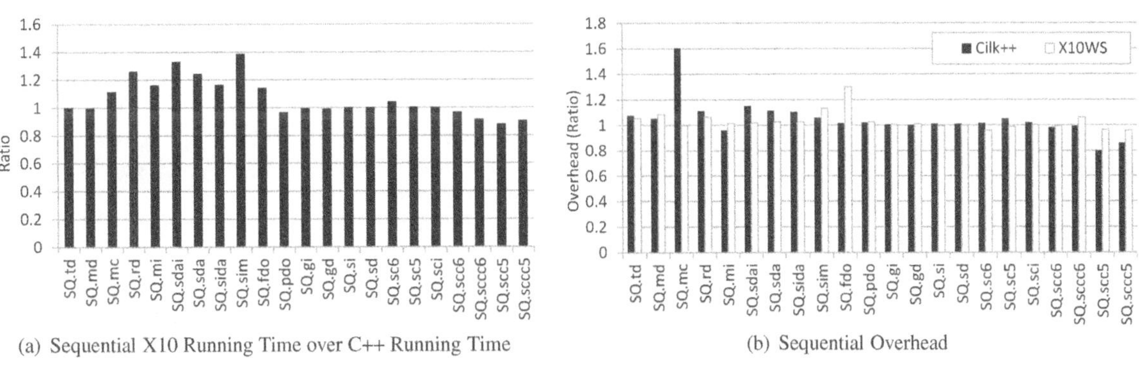

(a) Sequential X10 Running Time over C++ Running Time (b) Sequential Overhead

Figure 5. PBBS Overhead Analysis

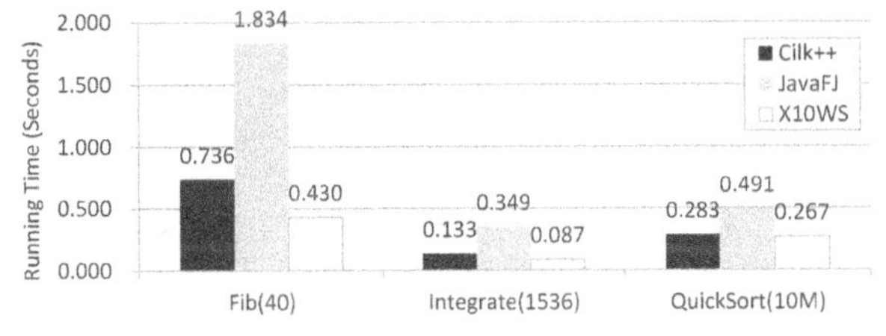

Figure 2. Micro Benchmark Running Time (16 workers)

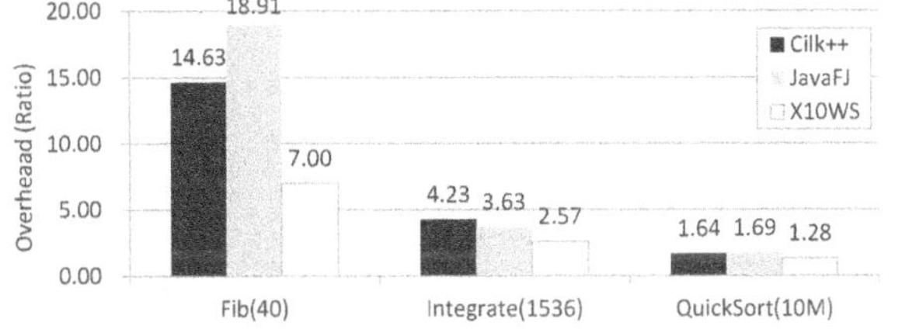

Figure 3. Micro Benchmark Sequential Overhead

If we disable exception support in the work-stealing transformation, we measure performance improvements never exceeding 10%. The cost of correct exception handling is therefore marginal.

7.5 PBBS Benchmark

We translated 6 of the 19 PBBS codes to X10. Most contain a series of measurements. In short, the Sequence tests (SQ) are unit tests. They measure the performance of building blocks used to construct the graph algorithms in the MaxIndSet (MI), MaxMatching (MM), ColorGraph (CG), BreadthFirstSearch (BFS), and RadixSort (RS) programs.

Figure 4 shows the execution time for every benchmark using 16 workers. Overall, X10 and Cilk++ performance are comparable and often very close. Neither runtime wins the comparison.

To better understand these results we plot a series of ratio in Figure 5 for the unit tests:

- The execution time of the sequential X10 code over the execution time of the sequential C++ code.

- The execution time of the single-worker Cilk++ test run over the execution time of the sequential C++ code.
- The execution time of the single-worker X10 test run over the execution of the sequential X10 code.

These numbers clearly identify two orthogonal contributing factors to the difference in performance between Cilk++ and our scheduler.

First, Figure 5(a), the raw sequential performance of the C++ code and the X10 code are not always the same due to the different nature of the languages and compilers. X10 is up to 40% slower than C++. X10 classes are slower than C++ mutable structs, closures are slower than function pointers, etc.

Second, in Figure 5(b), the X10 work-stealing code transformation overhead is often negligible, but in a few cases it slows down the code by up to 30%. Cilk++ is the same, with an overhead often but not always negligible. But affected benchmarks are different.

Overall, the relative sequential performance of the two languages matters more than the work-stealing code transformations.

8. Conclusion

We design and implement a portable work-stealing scheduler for the full X10 language.

We demonstrate it is possible to dramatically increase the coverage of work-stealing policies beyond single-place (shared-memory) async-finish (fork-join) programs while matching the performance of dedicated schedulers on this important class of programs. In particular, our scheduler handles task suspension in its full generality, hence data-dependent synchronization and remote task invocation.

To achieve performance we implement a series of low-level optimizations, which require support from the backend compilers. We implemented such support in the C++ backend compiler for X10. In the future, we plan to do the same with the Java backend compiler for X10 by taking advantage of non-standard capabilities of Jikes RVM.

Acknowledgments

This material is based upon work supported by the Defense Advanced Research Projects Agency under its Agreement No. HR0011-07-9-0002.

References

[1] B. Alpern, C. R. Attanasio, J. J. Barton, M. G. Burke, P. Cheng, J.-D. Choi, A. Cocchi, S. J. Fink, D. Grove, M. Hind, S. F. Hummel, D. Lieber, V. Litvinov, M. F. Mergen, T. Ngo, J. R. Russell, V. Sarkar, M. J. Serrano, J. C. Shepherd, S. E. Smith, V. C. Sreedhar, H. Srinivasan, and J. Whaley. The jalapeño virtual machine. *IBM Syst. J.*, pages 211–238, 2000.

[2] G. E. Blelloch. The problem-based benchmark suite. `http://www.cs.cmu.edu/~guyb/PBBS.html`.

[3] G. E. Blelloch, P. B. Gibbons, G. J. Narlikar, and Y. Matias. Space-efficient scheduling of parallelism with synchronization variables. In *Proceedings of the ninth annual ACM symposium on Parallel algorithms and architectures*, SPAA'97, pages 12–23, Newport, RI, USA, 1997.

[4] R. D. Blumofe and C. E. Leiserson. Scheduling multithreaded computations by work stealing. *J. ACM*, 46:720–748, 1999.

[5] J. Brezin, S. J. Fink, B. Bloom, and C. Swart. An introduction to programming with X10. `http://dist.codehaus.org/x10/documentation/guide/pguide.pdf`.

[6] P. Charles, C. Grothoff, V. Saraswat, C. Donawa, A. Kielstra, K. Ebcioglu, C. von Praun, and V. Sarkar. X10: an object-oriented approach to non-uniform cluster computing. In *Proceedings of the 20th annual ACM SIGPLAN conference on Object-oriented programming, systems, languages, and applications*, OOPSLA'05, pages 519–538, San Diego, CA, USA, 2005.

[7] G. Cong, S. Kodali, S. Krishnamoorthy, D. Lea, V. Saraswat, and T. Wen. Solving large, irregular graph problems using adaptive work-stealing. In *Processings of the 37th International Conference on Parallel Processing*, ICPP'08, pages 536–545, Portland, OR, USA, 2008.

[8] S. J. Fink and F. Qian. Design, implementation and evaluation of adaptive recompilation with on-stack replacement. In *Proceedings of the international symposium on Code generation and optimization: feedback-directed and runtime optimization*, CGO'03, pages 241–252, San Francisco, CA, USA, 2003.

[9] M. Frigo, C. E. Leiserson, and K. H. Randall. The implementation of the cilk-5 multithreaded language. In *Proceedings of the ACM SIGPLAN conference on Programming language design and implementation*, PLDI'98, pages 212–223, Montreal, QC, Canada, 1998.

[10] S. Ghemawat and P. Menage. TCMalloc : Thread-caching malloc. `http://google-perftools.googlecode.com/svn/trunk/doc/tcmalloc.html`.

[11] Y. Guo, R. Barik, R. Raman, and V. Sarkar. Work-first and help-first scheduling policies for async-finish task parallelism. In *Processings of the 23th IEEE International Parallel & Distributed Processing Symposium*, IPDPS'09, pages 1–12, Rome, Italy, 2009.

[12] Y. Guo, J. Zhao, V. Cave, and V. Sarkar. SLAW: A scalable locality-aware adaptive work-stealing scheduler. In *IEEE International Symposium on Parallel and Distributed Processing*, IPDPS'10, pages 1–12, Atlanta, GA, USA, 2010.

[13] Intel. Intel cilk++ sdk. `http://software.intel.com/en-us/articles/download-intel-cilk-sdk/`.

[14] P. Kambadur, A. Gupta, A. Ghoting, H. Avron, and A. Lumsdaine. PFunc: Modern task parallelism for modern high performance computing. In *Proceedings of the ACM/IEEE conference on Supercomputing*, SC'09, Portland, OR, USA, 2009.

[15] D. Lea. Concurrency jsr-166 interest site. `http://g.oswego.edu/dl/concurrency-interest/`.

[16] D. Lea. A java fork/join framework. In *Proceedings of the ACM conference on Java Grande*, JAVA'00, pages 36–43, San Francisco, CA, USA, 2000.

[17] D. Leijen, W. Schulte, and S. Burckhardt. The design of a task parallel library. In *Proceeding of the 24th ACM SIGPLAN conference on Object oriented programming systems languages and applications*, OOPSLA'09, pages 227–242, Orlando, FL, USA, 2009.

[18] E. Mohr, D. A. Kranz, and R. H. Halstead, Jr. Lazy task creation: a technique for increasing the granularity of parallel programs. In *Proceedings of the 1990 ACM conference on LISP and functional programming*, LFP'90, pages 185–197, Nice, France, 1990.

[19] M. Odersky and al. An overview of the Scala programming language. Technical Report IC/2004/64, EPFL Lausanne, Switzerland, 2004.

[20] R. Raman. Compiler support for work-stealing parallel runtime systems. Master's thesis, Rice University, Houston, Texas, 2009.

[21] J. Reinders. *Intel threading building blocks*. O'Reilly & Associates, Inc., Sebastopol, CA, USA, first edition, 2007. ISBN 9780596514808.

[22] V. Saraswat, B. Bloom, I. Peshansky, O. Tardieu, and D. Grove. X10 language specification. `http://dist.codehaus.org/x10/documentation/languagespec/x10-latest.pdf`.

[23] V. A. Saraswat, P. Kambadur, S. Kodali, D. Grove, and S. Krishnamoorthy. Lifeline-based global load balancing. In *Proceedings of the 16th ACM SIGPLAN symposium on Principles and practice of parallel programming*, PPoPP'11, pages 201–212, San Antonio, TX, USA, 2011.

[24] D. Spoonhower, G. E. Blelloch, P. B. Gibbons, and R. Harper. Beyond nested parallelism: tight bounds on work-stealing overheads for parallel futures. In *Proceedings of the twenty-first annual ACM symposium on Parallelism in algorithms and architectures*, SPAA'09, pages 91–100, Calgary, AB, Canada, 2009.

[25] The X10 team. The X10 distribution. `http://sourceforge.net/projects/x10/`.

Automatic Communication Optimizations Through Memory Reuse Strategies

Muthu Baskaran Nicolas Vasilache Benoit Meister Richard Lethin

Reservoir Labs Inc.
632 Broadway, New York, NY, USA
{baskaran,vasilache,meister,lethin}@reservoir.com

Abstract

Modern parallel architectures are emerging with sophisticated hardware consisting of hierarchically placed parallel processors and memories. The properties of memories in a system vary wildly, not only quantitatively (size, latency, bandwidth, number of banks) but also qualitatively (scratchpad, cache). Along with the emergence of such architectures comes the need for effectively utilizing the parallel processors and properly managing data movement across memories to improve memory bandwidth and hide data transfer latency. In this paper, we describe some of the high-level optimizations that are targeted at the improvement of memory performance in the R-Stream compiler, a high-level source-to-source automatic parallelizing compiler. We direct our focus in this paper on optimizing communications (data transfers) by improving memory reuse at various levels of an explicit memory hierarchy. This general concept is well-suited to the hardware properties of GPGPUs, which is the architecture that we concentrate on for this paper. We apply our techniques and obtain performance improvement on various stencil kernels including an important iterative stencil kernel in seismic processing applications where the performance is comparable to that of the state-of-the-art implementation of the kernel by a CUDA expert.

Categories and Subject Descriptors D.3.4 [*Programming Languages*]: Processors—Code generation, Compilers, Optimization

General Terms Algorithms, Performance

Keywords Data reuse, Memory reuse, Data transfer optimization

1. Introduction

The tension between parallelism and locality of memory references is an important topic for high-performance application optimization. More parallelism allows more concurrent execution of the parallel portions of a program. Increasing locality directly translates into communication reduction between memories and processing elements. Increasing parallelism may decrease locality and vice-versa. This presents a huge challenge to achieve good performance in modern multi-node and multi-socket architectures. One such example is the complexity in achieving good performance on GPGPUs. In a first approximation, simple translation from C to CUDA yields functional correctness. However performance is likely to be low. This is because only accesses to contiguous elements in memory result in efficient memory transactions. As soon as memory accesses are not contiguous, it is recommended to use explicit memory transfers into shared memory. Additionally, if temporal reuse can be exhibited, it is often recommended to use explicit communications into shared memory. On top of this, private memory exhibits the lowest access latencies but is not accessible by neighboring threads. The goal of the R-Stream compiler is to help solve all these complex implementation trade-offs in a generalized framework. R-Stream provides an automatic source-to-source mapping pathway from a high-level textbook-style code expressed in ANSI C to a target-specific source.

In this paper, we focus our attention on a specific capability of R-Stream , namely, optimizing communications by improving memory reuse at various levels of an explicit memory hierarchy. We pick GPGPUs as our target architecture, as these memory performance improvement techniques can be well-illustrated with the hardware properties of GPGPUs. We apply our techniques and show performance improvement on various stencil kernels and an important iterative stencil kernel in seismic processing applications, namely, the Discretized Wave Equation (DWE) kernel used in Reverse Time Migration algorithm of seismic computing. The performance of our optimized DWE kernel is within 23% of previously published hand-tuned results by an expert programmer [1].

PPoPP'12, February 25–29, 2012, New Orleans, Louisiana, USA.
ACM 978-1-4503-1160-1/12/02.

2. Details of Communication Optimizations

Our emphasis in this work is on the memory reuse optimizations in GPUs that particularly focus on managing on-chip memories such as the shared memory and registers. For clearer explanation of the concepts behind the optimizations, we run through the optimizations over the DWE kernel. The DWE is a 3D 8th order stencil (eight input elements in each dimension, not counting the center stencil point). We start our discussion from the following CUDA code excerpt that is automatically generated by R-Stream after applying a 2D tiling (with tile sizes of 8×32) and a 2D thread and thread block distribution on the DWE kernel.

```
float __shared__ U2_1[16][40];
for (i = 0; i <= 255; i++) {
      int ix = 32 * blockIdx.x + threadIdx.x;
      int iy = 8 * blockIdx.y + threadIdx.y;
      /* No register reuse */
      float U2_1_5 = U2_3[i][4 + iy][4 + ix];
      float U2_1_4 = U2_3[1+i][4 + iy][4 + ix];
      float U2_1_1 = U2_3[2+i][4 + iy][4 + ix];
```

```
        float U2_1_2 = U2_3[3+i][4 + iy][4 + ix];
        float U2_1_9 = U2_3[4+i][4 + iy][4 + ix];
        float U2_1_3 = U2_3[5+i][4 + iy][4 + ix];
        float U2_1_6 = U2_3[6+i][4 + iy][4 + ix];
        float U2_1_8 = U2_3[7+i][4 + iy][4 + ix];
        float U2_1_7 = U2_3[8+i][4 + iy][4 + ix];

        /* No shared memory optimization */
        #pragma unroll
        for (k = 0; k <= 1; k++){
         #pragma unroll
         for (j = 0; j <=(threadIdx.x+39 >>5); j++){
           U2_1[8 * k + threadIdx.y]
                   [32 * j + threadIdx.x] =
           U2_3[4 + i][8 * k + iy][32 * j + ix];
         }
        }
        ...
}
```

2.1 Register Reuse and Rotation

We define "register reuse/rotation" as the ability to move data into registers and reuse it and also to rotate data from one register to another for reusing it across various loop iterations. While there are various works in literature that target latency hiding in GPUs by moving data into registers and reusing the data, we are not aware of any prior work that automatically achieves the capability to rotate data from one register to another across loop iterations.

In the above code excerpt, data is moved into registers for each iteration of the i loop. However there is a clear reuse of data between different registers from one iteration of the loop to the next iteration. This is automatically exploited by R-Stream.

2.2 Shared Memory Optimization

Usual GPU optimizations involve moving data that is shared across various threads in a thread block into shared memory and reusing the data. Our "shared memory optimization" is not limited to storing and reusing shared data, but also, moving and reusing data from registers to shared memory and vice versa to reduce the number of global memory accesses and reduce communication latency and improve memory bandwidth.

The optimized code resulting from these optimizations from R-Stream looks like:

```
float __shared__ U2_1[16][40];
for(i = 0; i <= 255; i++) {
...
        int ix = 32 * blockIdx.x + threadIdx.x;
        int iy = 8 * blockIdx.y + threadIdx.y;
        /* Register reuse optimization */
        if (i == 0) {
           U2_1_5 = U2_3[0][4 + iy][4 + ix];
           U2_1_4 = U2_3[1][4 + iy][4 + ix];
           U2_1_1 = U2_3[2][4 + iy][4 + ix];
           U2_1_2 = U2_3[3][4 + iy][4 + ix];
           U2_1_9 = U2_3[4][4 + iy][4 + ix];
           U2_1_3 = U2_3[5][4 + iy][4 + ix];
           U2_1_6 = U2_3[6][4 + iy][4 + ix];
           U2_1_8 = U2_3[7][4 + iy][4 + ix];
           U2_1_7 = U2_3[8][4 + iy][4 + ix];
        }
        if (i >= 1) {
           U2_1_5 = U2_1_4;
           U2_1_4 = U2_1_1;
           U2_1_1 = U2_1_2;
           U2_1_2 = U2_1_9;
           U2_1_9 = U2_1_3;
           U2_1_3 = U2_1_6;
           U2_1_6 = U2_1_8;
           U2_1_8 = U2_1_7;
           U2_1_7 = U2_3[8 + i][4 + iy][4 + ix];
        }
        ...
        /* Shared memory opt - Filling from reg. */
        U2_1[threadIdx.y + 4]
             [threadIdx.x + 4] = U2_1_9;
         ...
}
```

2.3 Brief Discussion on the Method

In general, R-Stream compiler tries to move data to faster memories as much as possible and reuse data from faster memories to perform computation. The basic idea behind the determination of the feasibility of these optimizations is described below.

The first step is to find pairs of data transfers such that (1) they are executed within the same processing element (at the memory accessible level), (2) both involve reads from the same global memory location, and (3) both involve writes to a faster on-chip memory. The next step is to check if the value read from the first global memory read is "live" in a faster memory (and is not possibly flushed/overwritten) till the point of execution of the second global memory read. If it is the case, then replace the second global memory read with a read from the faster memory.

3. Performance Evaluation

We present our experimental results on two different GPU chips, namely, (1) GTX 285 (Tesla GPU) and (2) GTX 480 (Fermi GPU). We evaluate our techniques on three different types of stencils - (a) DWE kernel, (b) out-of-place Jacobi stencil (a 3-D 7 points stencil), and (c) finite-difference (FD) stencil used in acoustic modeling. The volume of the stencils evaluated is $256\times256\times256$. Table 1 presents the results of the stencil kernels. There are two baselines for comparison: (1) a "base" mapping, which uses good tile sizes and good thread and block distribution but none of the optimizations discussed in the paper, and (2) a hand-optimized "expert" version (only for DWE kernel) following the guidelines of [1]. It can be observed that the remaining speedup between the best DWE code generated automatically by our compiler and the hand-tuned DWE code is of 23% on Tesla and 10.2% on Fermi.

Version	DWE		Jacobi		FD	
	Tesla	Fermi	Tesla	Fermi	Tesla	Fermi
Base	12.91	7.79	6.6	2.5	6.04	4.7
R-Stream	5.99	4.68	4.10	2.21	4.74	3.50
Expert	4.58	4.20	-	-	-	-

Table 1. Execution time of 3D stencil kernels (in ms) on Tesla and Fermi GPUs

4. Conclusion

In this paper, we emphasized the importance of developing techniques to improve memory performance and developed communication or data transfer optimizations through various memory reuse strategies. We applied our techniques and showed performance improvement on various stencil kernels.

References

[1] Paulius Micikevicius. 3D Finite Difference Computation on GPUs using CUDA. In *Second Workshop on General-Purpose Computation on Graphics Processing Units, GPGPU-2*, March 2009.

FlexBFS: A Parallelism-aware Implementation of Breadth-First Search on GPU

Gu Liu, Hong An, Wenting Han, Xiaoqiang Li, Tao sun, Wei Zhou, Xuechao Wei, Xulong Tang

School of Computer Science & Technology, University of Science and Technology of China

gliu@mail.ustc.edu.cn, {han,wthan}@ustc.edu.cn, {lixq520,suntaos,greatzv,xcwei,tangxl}@mail.ustc.edu.cn

Abstract

In this paper, we present FlexBFS, a parallelism-aware implementation for breadth-first search on GPU. Our implementation can adjust the computation resources according to the feedback of available parallelism dynamically. We also optimized our program in three ways: (1)a simplified two-level queue management,(2)a combined kernel strategy and (3)a high-degree vertices specialization approach. Our experimental results show that it can achieve 3$\sim$20 times speedup against the fastest serial version, and can outperform the TBB based multi-threading CPU version and the previous most effective GPU version on all types of input graphs.

Categories and Subject Descriptors D.1.3 [*Concurrent Programming*]: Distributed programming, Parallel programming; D.3.3 [*Language Constructs and Features*]: Frameworks, Patterns

General Terms Algorithms, Performance

Keywords Graph algorithms, Breadth-first Search, CUDA, GPGPU

1. Introduction

Graphics processing unit (GPU) has recently become a popular parallel platform for general computing but it still can't dominate this field because many irregular applications exist. These irregular programs are usually involved with pointer-based data structures like graphs and trees, and share some common features in run-time characteristics which are critical to GPU architecture. One example of these irregular applications is the Breadth-first search (BFS). Several published works[1–3] have tried to implement BFS effectively on GPU, but the performance optimization is still a big problem. One of the challenges is to make the thread configuration adapt to the parallelism patterns of input graphs. Traditional BFS implementations on GPU used fixed thread configuration, which requires knowledge of parallelism pattern of the input graph prior to the kernel launching. Unfortunately, the parallelism patterns are usually in great variety and hard to predict, which contributes to one of the reasons for the low efficiency of BFS implementation on GPU.

In this paper, we will present a parallelism-aware GPU implementation with corresponding optimization techniques.

PPoPP'12, February 25–29, 2012, New Orleans, Louisiana, USA.
ACM 978-1-4503-1160-1/12/02.

Contributions:(1)We analyzed and profiled the available parallelism within BFS of different types of input graphs. The knowledge of various parallelism patterns can be used to yield a parallelism-feedback implementation for BFS.(2)We implement FlexBFS to effectively process working sets with different parallelism patterns for breadth-first search on GPU. (3)We introduced three optimization approaches. Our solution gained up to 20x speedup against the fastest serial version, and outperformed TBB based multi-threading CPU version and the previous most effective GPU version on all kinds of input graphs.

2. FlexBFS: Our GPU Implementation

2.1 Baseline

The available parallelism within BFS can be represented by the size of the frontier, in which the active nodes can be explored in parallel. By profiling the available parallelism of our benchmark graphs, we found they have a wide range of parallelism variation space, and the parallelism pattern within a single graph could be rather complex. In our baseline implementation, we used a global counter to record the size of the new frontier. At the end of the kernel, this counter is feedback to the host to assign adequate threads for the next kernel iteration. Since extra work generated by the redundant threads is cut off, GPU resource utilization is much higher than the fixed thread configuration.

Unfortunately, the baseline version of FlexBFS still surfers performance degradation which comes from the following three reasons. First, the non-coalesced memory accesses to the global frontier queue; second, the kernel launch overhead of separate kernel function call for each level; third, the imbalanced workload in those irregular graphs with skewed structure.

2.2 Optimizing Techniques

Two-level queue management In our baseline implementation, store operations into the next frontier queue will causes non-coalesced memory accesses. As a result, we present a two-level queue structure. A fast block-level queue is built in the shared memory within each multiprocessor, while the grid-level queue is still in the global memory. Each thread within a warp first stores the neighbor id into the block-level queue, then copy back into the grid-level queue in a regular way. It is noticeable that each thread access global memory at consecutive addresses, which meets the condition of coalescing memory operation.

Combined kernel strategy In the absence of support to global thread synchronization in CUDA, we have to launch one kernel instance for each level, which will bring huge kernel-launch overhead. Thus, we use an inter-block synchronization technique[4] to implement a combined kernel strategy, which lower down the launch overhead while the thread configuration still maintain flexible.We first evaluate the new frontier size. If it is within a certain

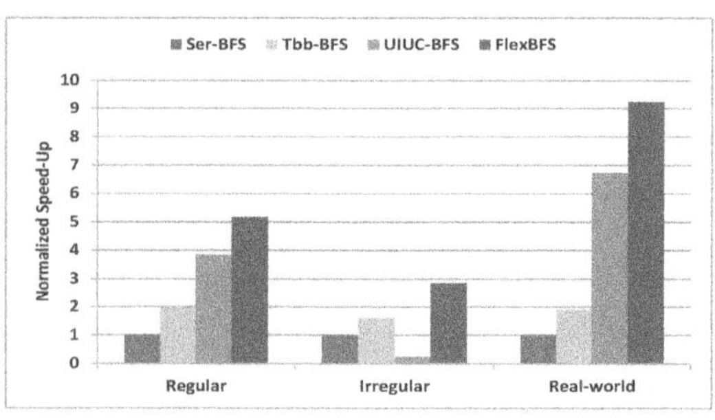

Figure 1. Comparison of average performances obtained by different BFS implementation.

range, there is no need to launch a new kernel instance. If the new frontier size is out of this threshold, a new thread configuration then will be set up for the next kernel invoking.

High-degree vertices specialization Load imbalance is a severe problem in BFS algorithm when input graph is irregular. To avoid this problem we present the high-degree vertices specialization approach. We process those high-degree vertices separately using a special queue. We first check the degree of each active node; if the degree is larger than a threshold, this node is inserted into a special queue instead of exploring neighborhood. After other low-degree vertices are finished, nodes in special queue are processed using all available threads.

3. Experimental Setup

Our experiments were conducted on an NVIDIA Tesla C2050 GPU with an Intel quad core Xeon E5506 CPU. To cover all types of graph instances, we choose three kinds of graphs as our input working set. They are classified as regular, irregular and real-word graphs. The regular graph is generated based on grid graph. The irregular graphs are built on the bases of regular ones. We add 0.1% high-degree vertices into the original grid graph, which causes extremely load imbalance. We also used a set of real-world graphs. They are traffic route nets in different parts of USA from DIMACS challenge website.

4. Experimental Results

To evaluate the performance of our FlexBFS, we compare it with the serial version and TBB version running on CPU and UIUC-BFS [3] running on GPU. The optimal TBB performance is obtained using 4 threads on our CPU platform.

Figure 1 illustrates the performance of the four BFS implementations on 3 sets of input graphs. Generally speaking, our solution outperforms the other ones. The FLexBFS obtains an average speedup of 5 times faster than serial CPU version and 2.5 times against TBB version. Our method is also 1.5 times faster than UIUC-BFS, the previous most effective GPU implementation, because of the parallelism-aware scheme and other optimization methods. It is noticeable that the performance of UIUC-BFS is particulary poor when processing irregular graphs, even worse than CPU versions. L.Luo et. al. mentioned in their paper that they had to convert the irregular graphs into near-regular graphs by splitting the big-degree nodes before applying their BFS implementation. Without this pretreatment process, their version suffers seriously from imbalanced work. In Section 2.2, we introduced three optimization methods to improve performance. We combine these techniques with the baseline implementation into three configurations summarized in Table1. Figure 2 illustrates the effectiveness of our proposed optimization methods. In most cases, the baseline FlexBFS is well

Name	Description
Fixed	Basic GPU BFS implementation using a fixed thread configuration
Baseline	baseline FlexBFS implementation using flexible thread configuration
Config1	Baseline + Combined kernel strategy
Config2	Config1 + Two-level queue management
Config3	Config2 + High-degree vertices specialization

Table 1. Optimization configurations of FlexBFS

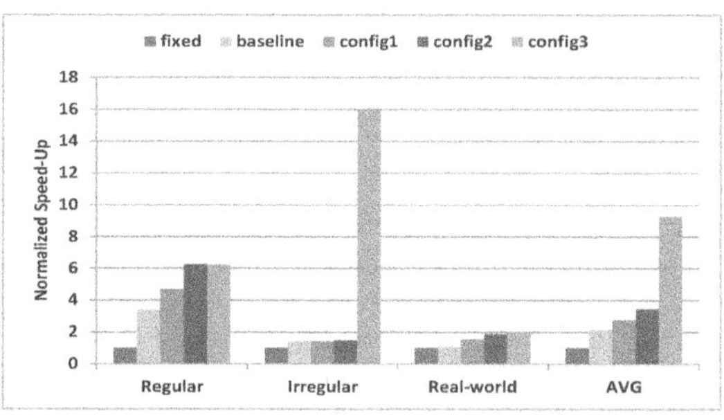

Figure 2. performance of BFS under a set of configurations using different optimization methods.

performed than the fixed configuration, which demonstrates that unexplored parallelism does exist in the fixed-thread BFS implementation. Config1 shows that the combined kernel strategy can shorten the overall execution time by up to 30%. Config2 improves the performance of regular graphs by reducing the random accesses overhead to a great extend. The rightmost bars of each column in figure 2 display the impact of the high-degree vertices specialization, from which the irregular graphs can benefit most.

5. Conclusions

We have presented a parallelism-aware implementation for breadth-first search algorithm on GPU. Our solution can deploy proper thread resources according to the dynamic profile of parallelism in BFS. We have analyzed the main reasons of performance degradation in BFS, and proposed several optimizing approaches for these problem. The experimental results show that our solution achieves up to 20x speedup over the fastest serial BFS program, and outperforms TBB version and previous GPU implementations on all three types of graphs.

Acknowledgments

This work is supported financially by the National Basic Research Program of China under contract 2011CB302501,the National Natural Science Foundation of China grants 60970023, the National Science & Technology Major Projects 2009ZX01036-001-002 and 2011ZX01028-001-002-3.

References

[1] P. Harish and P. J. Narayanan. Accelerating large graph algorithms on the gpu using cuda. In HiPC'07.

[2] S. Hong, S. K. Kim, T. Oguntebi, and K. Olukotun. Accelerating cuda graph algorithms at maximum warp. In PPoPP'11.

[3] L. Luo, M. Wong, and W. mei Hwu. An effective gpu implementation of breadth-first search. In 47th DAC 2010.

[4] S. Xiao and W. chun Feng. Inter-block gpu communication via fast barrier synchronization. In IPDPS 2010.

Programming Parallel Embedded and Consumer Applications in OpenMP Superscalar

Michael Andersch
TU Berlin
Einsteinufer 17
10587 Berlin
andersch@cs.tu-berlin.de

Chi Ching Chi
TU Berlin
Einsteinufer 17
10587 Berlin
cchi@cs.tu-berlin.de

Ben Juurlink
TU Berlin
Einsteinufer 17
10587 Berlin
juurlink@cs.tu-berlin.de

Abstract

In this paper, we evaluate the performance and usability of the parallel programming model OpenMP Superscalar (OmpSs), apply it to 10 different benchmarks and compare its performance with corresponding POSIX threads implementations.

Categories and Subject Descriptors D.1.3 [*Software*]: Programming Techniques—Concurrent Programming

General Terms Algorithms, Design, Measurement, Performance

Keywords OpenMP Superscalar, OmpSs, Embedded, Consumer

1. Introduction

OpenMP Superscalar (OmpSs) is a novel task-based parallel programming model which extends the OpenMP programming model with the StarSs [3] task directives. In OmpSs, programs are parallelized by annotating functions as tasks using the `omp task input output inout` pragmas. When these functions are called, they are added to a task graph instead of directly being executed. The task dependencies are resolved at runtime, using the input/output specification of the function arguments. Once all input dependencies of a task are resolved, it is ready to be executed.

In the past, OmpSs has mainly been used to parallelize HPC applications [2]. In this paper we will investigate and summarize the usability and performance of OmpSs for embedded and consumer applications.

This paper is organized as follows: Section 2 discusses our methodology. In Section 3 we investigate the expressiveness of OmpSs using pipelining in H.264 as a case study. In Section 4 the performance results of the ten benchmarks are presented. Finally, in Section 5, conclusions are drawn.

2. Methodology

Evaluating parallel programming models is different from evaluating processor architectures. Parallel programming models not only target good performance, but also must offer the right abstraction to the programmer. Therefore, it is necessary to investigate both the usability and performance of a parallel programming model to evaluate its overall quality.

The usability of a programming model is a subjective measure that differs from programmer to programmer. To provide the programmer with the necessary information to be able to form his/her own opinion about the usability, we conducted studies on numerous qualitative aspects, such as general expressiveness or the toolchain, of programming in OmpSs, of which we show H.264 pipeline parallelization as an example.

To evaluate the performance of OmpSs, we have created a benchmark suite to evaluate parallel programming models. The suite contains 10 C/C++ benchmarks (shown in the first column of Table 1) that cover a wide range of embedded and consumer application domains. The benchmarks are classified as kernels, workloads, or applications, based on their code size and parallelization complexity. For each benchmark a sequential, Pthreads, and OmpSs implementation have been developed. For comparability the Pthreads and OmpSs variants exploit the same parallelism.

To provide meaningful results not only for contemporary, but also for future multi-core systems, it is necessary to extend the benchmarking process beyond the core counts of what current off-the-shelve CMPs can offer. To achieve this, we use a 4-socket cc-NUMA machine with 32 cores in total for the performance evaluation.

3. Case Study: Parallelizing H.264 Decoding in OmpSs

The H.264 decoder pipeline in our design consists of 5 pipeline stages. In the read stage the bitstream is read from the disk and parsed into separated frames. In the parse stage the headers of the frame are parsed and a Picture Info entry in the Picture Info Buffer is allocated. The entropy decode (ED) stage performs a lossless decompression by extracting the syntax elements for each macroblock in the frame. The macroblock reconstruction stage allocates a picture in the Decoded Picture Buffer and reconstructs the picture using the syntax elements and motion vectors. The output stage reorders and outputs the decoded pictures either to an output file or the display.

In contrast to other task-based programming models, such as Cilk++ and OpenMP, pipeline parallelism can be easily expressed in OmpSs, because in OmpSs tasks can be spawned before their dependencies have been resolved [4, 5]. Listing 1 presents slightly simplified code of the pipelined main decoder loop using OmpSs pragmas. A task is created for each pipeline stage in each loop iteration. For correct pipelining of the tasks, it is required that all tasks in iteration *i* are executed in-order. To accomplish this, each task in the same iteration is linked to the previous task in the same iteration via one or more input and output/inout pairs. Additionally, task *T* of iteration *i* must be completed before the instance of the same task *T* in iteration *i+1* is started. To accomplish this, each task has a context structure parameter that is annoted as inout, e.g., ReadContext *rc, NalContext *nc, EntropyContext *ec, etc.

PPoPP'12, February 25–29, 2012, New Orleans, Louisiana, USA.
ACM 978-1-4503-1160-1/12/02.

```
EncFrame frm[N]; Slice slice[N];
H264Mb *ed_bufs[N]; Picture pic[N];
int k=0;
while(!EOF){
#pragma omp task inout(*rc) output(*frm)
  read_frame_task(rc, &frm[k%N]);
#pragma omp task inout(*nc,*frm) output(*s)
  parse_header_task(nc,&slice[k%N], &frm[k%N]);
#pragma omp task inout(*nc,*frm) output(*s)
  entropy_decode_task(ec,&slice[k%N], &frm[k%N],
    ed_bufs[k%N]);
#pragma omp task inout(*rc) input(*s,*mbs) output(*pic)
  reconstruct_task (rc,&slice[k%N],ed_bufs[k%N],
    &pic[k%N]);
#pragma omp task inout(*oc) input(*pic)
  output_task(oc,&pic[k%N]);
  k++;
#pragma omp taskwait on (*rc)
}
```

Listing 1. Pipelining the main decoder loop using OmpSs pragmas

Three additional important observations regarding the pipelining implementation can be made. First, the `taskwait on` pragma ensures that the read task has been performed before evaluating the while loop condition. This is necessary to prevent tasks from being added after the EOF has been reached.

Second, more importantly, some inputs and outputs of each task are read from/written to an entry of a circular buffer of size N. This eliminates the WAR and WAW hazards that would have occurred if the same entry is used in each iteration, which would eliminate all the parallelism. OmpSs does not support automatic renaming and, therefore, this manual renaming method is required.

Third, the Picture Info Buffer (PIB) and Decoded Picture Buffer (DPB) structures are not passed in any argument and, thus, are not considered for dependence checking. The dependencies to these buffer entries are purposely hidden from the OmpSs task specifications, because we cannot predict which buffers entries will be available at the time the task is spawned. This can only be determined when the task is executed.

To fetch and release the buffer entries in a thread-safe way, `omp critical` pragmas are used in the task bodies around the fetch and release statements to protect accesses to the PIB and DPB.

4. Quantitative Evaluation

In Table 1 the speedups of the OmpSs variants over the Pthreads variants are shown for each benchmark and core count. Overall, five benchmarks are faster with OmpSs and four with Pthreads. The largest gains are observed for the c-ray, rgbcmy, and ray-rot benchmarks. The largest loss is observed for h264dec.

In the rgbcmy benchmark multiple iterations are performed to stabilize the execution time, with a task/thread barrier separating each iteration. The absolute time for one iteration, however, is short with less than 20ms on 16 cores. For this benchmark, the OmpSs variant is able to scale better at higher core counts because it employs a polling task barrier instead of the more expensive blocking thread barrier.

In the ray-rot benchmark the output of the c-ray kernel is the input of the rotate kernel. For this benchmark OmpSs performs better than Pthreads, because the runtime scheduler places dependent tasks on the same core. Scheduling tasks that have an input output relation back-to-back on the same core improves cache locality. Interestingly, due to this locality advantage, the speedups for the combined ray-rot workload exceed the product of the speedups of the individual c-ray and the rotate kernel.

The largest performance difference between Pthreads and OmpSs occurs for the h264dec benchmark. Increasing the task granularity

Benchmark	1	8	16	24	32	Mean
c-ray	1.03	1.11	1.12	1.11	1.14	1.10
rotate	1.06	1.04	1.09	1.02	0.86	1.01
rgbcmy	1.02	0.98	1.14	1.40	1.53	1.19
md5	1.00	1.02	1.10	1.14	1.05	1.06
kmeans	0.91	0.87	1.30	0.95	0.88	0.97
ray-rot	1.02	1.10	1.65	1.46	1.20	1.27
rot-cc	1.00	1.06	1.17	1.14	1.04	1.08
streamcluster	0.93	0.84	0.91	0.99	0.99	0.93
bodytrack	0.98	0.99	1.05	0.97	1.00	1.00
h264dec	0.94	1.07	0.87	0.57	0.42	0.73
Mean	0.99	1.00	1.12	1.05	0.97	1.02

Table 1. Speedup factors and geometric means of OmpSs implementations over Pthreads implementations for each benchmark and core count.

is necessary to improve the overall performance of OmpSs. Grouping the tasks, however, reduces the parallelism, which in turn limits the performance at higher core counts. In the Pthreads version of h264dec the synchronization is highly optimized using a line decoding strategy [1] and, therefore, grouping of tasks is not necessary.

Over the entire benchmark suite, OmpSs performs 2% better than Pthreads. At 1 and 8 cores the performance is very close, while at 16 and 24 cores OmpSs is slightly faster. At 32 cores OmpSs is slightly slower mainly due to the lower performance in the h264dec benchmark. Thus, we argue that performance wise OmpSs can compete with manual threaded solutions for the embedded and consumer benchmarks considered in this paper.

To be a true alternative for manual threading, however, OmpSs processes must be able to dynamically share resources with other processes. Currently, OmpSs programs use a static number of cores controlled by an environmental variable. Furthermore, because the runtime implements core communication/synchronization, e.g. task barriers, in a polling fashion for performance reasons, all used cores are always fully loaded even if there is insufficient work. This reduces overall system responsiveness and power efficiency when too many cores are used.

5. Conclusions

Our studies have shown that OmpSs is, while not yet production-ready, a viable alternative to established parallel programming models such as Pthreads. The expressiveness is sufficiently powerful to program common parallelism patterns such as pipelining and the performance is comparable to Pthreads implementations.

References

[1] C. C. Chi and B. Juurlink. A QHD-Capable Parallel H.264 Decoder. In *Proc. 25th Int. Conf. on Supercomputing*, 2011.

[2] A. Duran, X. Teruel, R. Ferrer, X. Martorell, and E. Ayguadé. Barcelona OpenMP Tasks Suite: A Set of Benchmarks Targeting the Exploitation of Task Parallelism in OpenMP. In *Proc. Int. Conf. on Parallel Processing*, 2009.

[3] J. M. Perez, R. M. Badia, and J. Labarta. A Flexible and Portable Programming Model for SMP and Multi-cores. Technical report, BSC-UPC, 2007.

[4] A. Pop and A. Cohen. A Stream-Computing Extension to OpenMP. In *Proc. 6th Int. Conf. on High Performance and Embedded Architectures and Compilers*, 2011.

[5] H. Vandierendonck, P. Pratikakis, and D. Nikolopoulos. Parallel Programming of General-Purpose Programs Using Task-Based Programming Models. In *Proc. 3rd USENIX Workshop on Hot Topics in Parallelism*, 2011.

An Overview of Medusa: Simplified Graph Processing on GPUs

Jianlong Zhong
Nanyang Technological University
jzhong2@ntu.edu.sg

Bingsheng He
Nanyang Technological University
bshe@ntu.edu.sg

Abstract

Graphs are the de facto data structures for many applications, and efficient graph processing is a must for the application performance. GPUs have an order of magnitude higher computational power and memory bandwidth compared to CPUs and have been adopted to accelerate several common graph algorithms. However, it is difficult to write correct and efficient GPU programs and even more difficult for graph processing due to the irregularities of graph structures. To address those difficulties, we propose a programming framework named Medusa to simplify graph processing on GPUs. Medusa offers a small set of APIs, based on which developers can define their application logics by writing sequential code without awareness of GPU architectures. The Medusa runtime system automatically executes the developer defined APIs in parallel on the GPU, with a series of graph-centric optimizations. This poster gives an overview of Medusa, and presents some preliminary results.

Categories and Subject Descriptors D.1.3 [*Programming Techniques*]: Concurrent Programming-Parallel programming; D.2.13 [*Software Engineering*]: Reusable Software-Reusable libraries; I.3.1 [*Computer Graphics*]: Hardware Architecture-Graphics processors

General Terms Algorithms, Performance

Keywords GPGPU, GPU Programming, Graph Processing, Runtime Framework

1. Introduction

Graphs are de facto data structures in various applications such as social networks modeling and web link analysis. Graph processing algorithms have been the fundamental tools (e.g., visualization [7] and exploration [1]) in various fields. Developers usually apply a series of operations on the graph edges and vertices to obtain the final result. The operations can be BFS, PageRank, shortest path and even their customized variants. For example, developers may apply different application logics when traversing each edge/vertex in the BFS process. The efficiency of graph processing is a must for high performance of the entire system. On the other hand, writing a graph algorithm from scratch is inefficient and time consuming, which loses the opportunities of sharing the same operation patterns, optimization techniques and common software components among different algorithms. A programming framework with programmability on supporting common graph processing applications and with high efficiency can greatly improve productivity.

Recently, graphics processors (GPUs) have been used as an accelerator for various graph processing applications [3, 5]. The GPU has evolved into a powerful many-core processor for general-purpose computation. New-generation GPUs can have over an order of magnitude higher memory bandwidth and higher computation power (in terms of GFLOPS) than CPUs. While existing GPU-based graph processing implementations have significant performance improvement over their CPU-based counterparts, they are limited to specific graph operations. We usually need to implement and optimize GPU programs with little reuse or even from scratch for different graph processing tasks.

Writing a correct and efficient GPU program is challenging, especially for graph applications. First, the GPU is a many-core processor with massive thread parallelism. To fully exploit the GPU computation power, algorithms should be designed with sufficient fine grained parallelism. Second, the GPU has a memory hierarchy that is different from the CPU. Since graph applications usually involve irregular accesses to the graph data, careful designs on the data layout and memory accesses are the key factor to the efficiency of GPU acceleration. Finally, developers have to explicitly manage the GPU programming details. Device management programming such as PCI-e data transfer should be carefully examined for efficiency. All these factors make programming the GPU for graph processing a difficult task.

We propose a software framework named Medusa to simplify programming graph algorithms on the GPU. The merits of Medusa are easing the pain and increasing productivity of adopting GPUs in graph computation tasks. Medusa offers a sequential programming interface and encapsulates the GPU programming complexities into a runtime system. Like existing GPU programming frameworks such as Mars [4], Medusa provides a small set of APIs for developers to implement their applications. The APIs are defined at the granularity of edges and vertices for fine-grained parallelism. Medusa automatically executes developer-defined APIs in parallel on a single GPU or multiple GPUs, and hides the complexity of parallel programming and GPU programming details.

This poster gives an overview of Medusa design and its optimizations, and presents our preliminary results. We demonstrate that Medusa achieves our goal of simplifying graph processing on the GPU, with high programmability and efficiency.

2. Overview

Medusa runs on one or multiple GPUs within the same machine, as illustrated in Figure 1. We develop a graph-centric programming interfaces named "EMV (Edge-Message-Vertex)". It provides the APIs on graph edges and vertices, which only require sequential C programming. Based on the EMV model, developers implement their algorithms using the EMV APIs. On supporting data flows among graph vertices, we develop an efficient message

PPoPP'12, February 25–29, 2012, New Orleans, Louisiana, USA.
ACM 978-1-4503-1160-1/12/02.

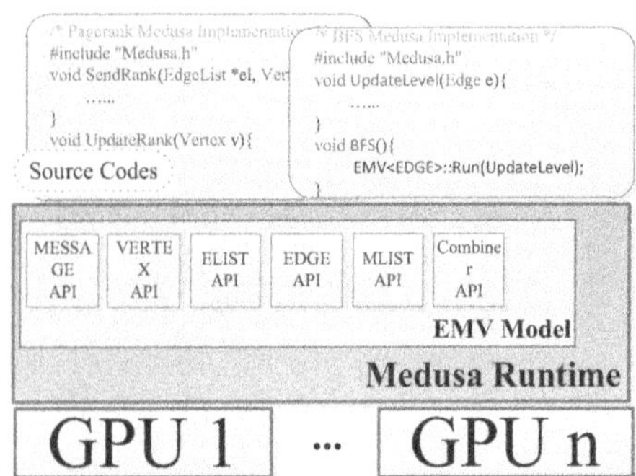

Figure 1. An overview of Medusa.

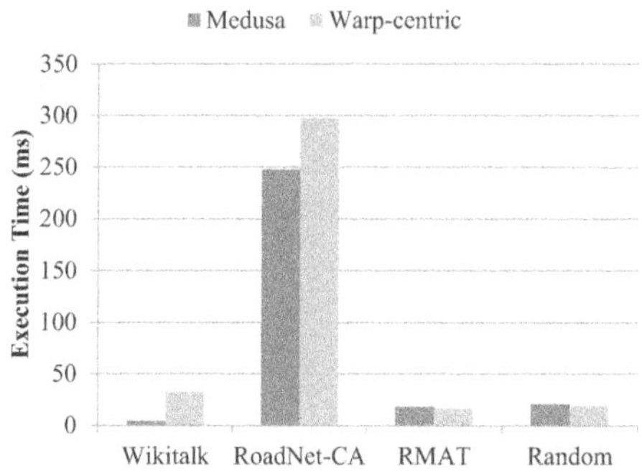

Figure 2. Performance comparison on BFS implementation between Medusa and the warp-centric approach [5].

passing mechanism that supports multiple GPUs. Medusa supports message passing between any pair of vertices. EMV supports two variants of APIs for individual and collective operations on graph edges/vertices and intermediate messages. The individual APIs take individual edge, message or vertex as input. The collective APIs works on groups of edges (grouped by head or tail vertex) or messages (grouped by destination vertex). Data exchange among vertices are realized by messages passing.

Medusa runtime is designed to meet the performance goal and to hide the underlying hardware details. We further develop a series of memory optimizations to improve the runtime efficiency. We briefly describe them here, and refer readers to our technical report [8] for more details.

- To reduce the uncoalesed memory access caused the irregular access patterns of graph algorithms, we study performance of different graph layouts on GPU and propose a novel layout to speed up iterative access of each individual edge in an edge group.
- Supporting message passing is a challenging task and we developed a graph-aware buffer scheme for message passing between adjacent vertices. Our message passing approach notably outperforms previous approaches such as hash table and pre-indexing [4].

Additionally, the Medusa runtime is extended to execute on multiple GPUs and this extension is transparent to developers. This further reduces the complexity of GPU programming. Medusa programs written for one GPU can run on multiple GPUs without modification.

We deliver Medusa with static libraries and source code templates. The current implementation is based on NVIDIA CUDA, and it is our future work for the implementations on OpenCL. The developer defined APIs are implemented as functors and passed to the system provided functions. This design overcomes the programming constrains of CUDA while offers both good encapsulation and simplicity. Tedious GPU related functions such as data transfer and multi-GPU coordination are implemented within the runtime. We expose the necessary configuration settings via simple C/C++ interfaces.

3. Preliminary Results

Our preliminary results examine the efficiency of Medusa in comparison with existing state-of-the-art GPU implementations. We conduct experiments on the Amazon EC2 Cluster GPU instance, which is equipped with two Nvidia Tesla M2050 GPUs. We choose both synthetic graphs (Random and RMAT) and real-world graphs (WikiTalk and RoadNet-CA) as our experimental data sets. We use the GTgraph graph generator [2] to generate the RMAT and Random graph. Wikitalk and Patent are downloaded from the Stanford Large Network Dataset Collection [6].

Figure 2 shows the performance comparison of the BFS algorithm between the warp centric method [5] and Medusa on a single GPU. Medusa achieves similar or even better performance than the warp-centric method. Moreover, Medusa greatly simplifies implementation of GPU programs for graph processing, with much fewer lines of source code written by developers.

4. Conclusion and Future Work

Massive parallelism architectures like GPUs have imposed great challenges in writing correct and efficient parallel graph processing programs. We propose a programming framework named Medusa, to address the efficiency and programmability issues of GPU-based graph processing. Medusa embraces an optimized runtime system to hide the programming complexity of implementing parallel graph computation tasks for the GPUs. Our preliminary results demonstrate the effectiveness of our optimizations and the efficiency of the framework. We are currently extending Medusa to utilizing both both GPUs and CPUs for heterogeneous execution as well as GPUs in a cluster. Beyond that, we are also interested in extending Medusa to handle dynamic graphs.

Acknowledgement

This work is supported by an NVIDIA Academic Partnership (2010-2011) and an AcRF Tier-1 grant in Singapore. The authors would like to thank Gao Cong for his constructive comments in the project.

References

[1] V. Agarwal, F. Petrini, D. Pasetto, and D. A. Bader. Scalable graph exploration on multicore processors. In *SC*, pages 1–11, 2010.

[2] GTGraph Generator. *http://www.cc.gatech.edu/ kamesh/GTgraph/.*

[3] P. Harish and P. J. Narayanan. Accelerating large graph algorithms on the GPU using CUDA. In *HiPC*, pages 197–208, 2007.

[4] B. He, W. Fang, Q. Luo, N. K. Govindaraju, and T. Wang. Mars: a MapReduce framework on graphics processors. In *PACT*, pages 260–269, 2008.

[5] S. Hong, S. K. Kim, T. Oguntebi, and K. Olukotun. Accelerating CUDA graph algorithms at maximum warp. In *PPoPP*, pages 267–276, 2011.

[6] Stanford Large Network Dataset Collections. *http://snap.stanford.edu/data/index.html.*

[7] J. Zhong and B. He. Gviewer: Gpu-accelerated graph visualization and mining. In *SocInfo*, pages 304–307, 2011.

[8] J. Zhong, B. He, and G. Cong. Medusa: A unified framework for graph computation and visualization on graphics processors. Technical Report NTU-PDCC, Feb 2011. URL `http://pdcc.ntu.edu.sg/`.

Optimizing Remote Accesses for Offloaded Kernels: Application to High-Level Synthesis for FPGA

Christophe Alias   Alain Darte   Alexandru Plesco
Compsys, LIP, UMR 5668 CNRS, INRIA, ENS-Lyon, UCB-Lyon
firstname.lastname@ens-lyon.fr

Abstract

In the context of the high-level synthesis (HLS) of regular kernels offloaded to FPGA and communicating with an external DDR memory, we show how to automatically generate adequate communicating processes for optimizing the transfer of remote data. This requires a generalized form of communication coalescing where data can be transferred from the external memory even when this memory is not fully up-to-date. Experiments with Altera HLS tools demonstrate that this automatization, based on advanced polyhedral code analysis and code generation techniques, can be used to efficiently map C kernels to FPGA, by generating, entirely at C level, all the necessary glue (the communication processes), which is compiled with the same HLS tool as for the computation kernel.

Categories and Subject Descriptors B.5.2 [*Register-Transfer-Level Implementation*]: Design Aids—Automatic Synthesis; D.3.4 [*Programming Languages*]: Processors—Compilers, Optimization

General Terms Design, Experimentation, Performance, Theory

Keywords Polyhedral optimizations, communication coalescing, pipelined processes, DDR memory, FPGA, HLS

1. Introduction

Most HLS tools for C-like languages [9], e.g., Catapult-C, C2H, Gaut, Impulse-C, Pico-Express, Spark, Ugh, use state-of-the-art back-end compilation techniques and are thus able to derive an optimized internal structure. However, integrating the automatically-generated hardware accelerators within the complete design, with optimized communications, synchronizations, and local buffers, remains a hard task, reserved to expert designers. In addition to the VHDL glue that has to be added, the input program must often be rewritten. For HLS tools to be viable, this tricky and error-prone step should be automated too. This paper shows how the handmade restructuring of [2], developed on top of Altera C2H HLS tool, can be *fully automated*, entirely at source level (i.e., in C).

We focus on the optimization of hardware accelerators that work on a large set of data to be transferred from a DDR memory at the highest possible rate, and possibly temporarily stored locally. For such a memory, making sure that successive requests access the same row (such accesses are pipelined an order of magnitude faster) is a direct way of improving the performances: if not, the hardware accelerator, even if its computational part is highly-optimized, keeps stalling and runs at the rate of the (unoptimized) DDR accesses. Our technique relies on loop tiling to increase the granularity of computations and communications. In each strip of tiles, transfers from/to the DDR are performed in a pipelined double-buffering fashion thanks to the introduction of communication processes in addition to the initial computation process. The accesses within each process are pipelined thanks to fine-grain software pipelining while the execution of the different processes is orchestrated thanks to coarse-grain software pipelining. Data reuse within a strip is fully exploited to avoid remote accesses when data are already available locally in the accelerator. To reduce the size of local storage, loads from the DDR (resp. stores to the DDR) are done as late (resp. soon) as possible. This requires a generalized form of communication coalescing, where loads are performed even when the external memory may not be up-to-date. Local memories are automatically generated, using allocations with modulo [1, 10, 12], to store the communicated data and exploit data & memory reuse.

2. Generalized Communication Coalescing

Our method can be applied to offload a kernel on which loop tiling [16] and polyhedral code transformations can be applied, i.e., a set of `for` nested loops, manipulating arrays and scalar variables, where loop bounds, `if` conditions, and access functions, are affine expressions of surrounding loop counters and structure parameters. This model can be extended through approximations when access functions or `if` conditions are not fully analyzable.

Example The code of Fig. 1 computes, in array c, the product of two polynomials of degree N, stored in arrays p and q. The offloaded kernel is the second set of loops. If commutativity and associativity are not exploited, loops are not permutable. A possible tiling is specified from the transformation $\theta : (i,j) \mapsto (N-j, i)$ (i.e., loop interchange + reversal of the outer loop), see Fig. 1. In each horizontal tile strip, tiles are pipelined so that the transfers of a tile overlap with the computations of the previous tile. Communications are optimized resulting in maximal inter-tile (resp. intra-tile) reuse for q (resp. p) and some intra- and inter-tile reuse for c (for adjacent tiles). For example, the elements of c that are loaded (resp. stored) before (resp. after) each tile are shown in grey (resp. black).

```
for (i=0; i<=2*N; i++) {
  c[i] = 0;
}

for (i=0; i<=N; i++) {
  for (j=0; j<=N; j++) {
    c[i+j] += p[i]*q[j];
  }
}
```

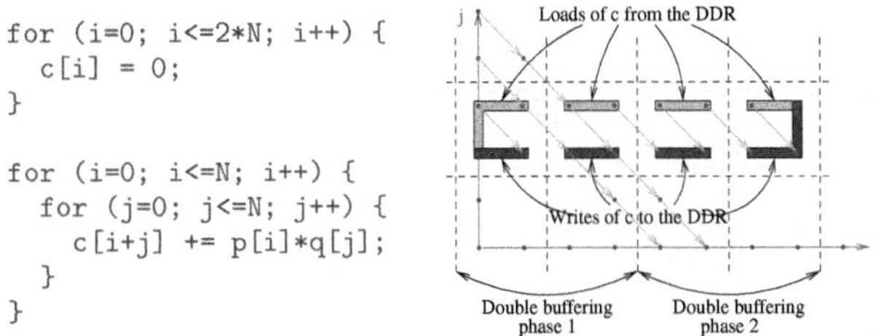

Figure 1. Product of polynomials example

PPoPP'12, February 25–29, 2012, New Orleans, Louisiana, USA.
ACM 978-1-4503-1160-1/12/02.

In the tiled code, iterations are identified by a 4d vector (I, J, ii, jj) where $(ii, jj) = \theta(i, j)$, $I = \lfloor ii/b \rfloor$, $J = \lfloor jj/b \rfloor$, and b is the tile size. The counters I and J iterate over the tiles, ii and jj within a tile. For a tile strip indexed by I, a fixed b, our technique derives, thanks to parametric linear programming, the set Load(J) of array elements $c(m)$ loaded before the tile (I, J). With $b = 10$, we get Load$(J) = \{m \mid \max(0, N-10I-9) \leq m \leq N-10I\}$ if $J = 0$ and $\{m \mid \max(1, 10J) \leq m + 10I - N \leq \min(N, 10J + 9)\}$ otherwise, which corresponds to the sets of loads depicted in Fig. 1.

We now give the main principles of our method to select the array regions to be loaded from and stored to the external DDR memory. This step impacts the amount of communications, the lifetimes of array elements in the local memory, and the size of this memory. Details are provided in the companion reports [3, 4].

To perform data transfers, the naive solution is to access the DDR for each remote data access. No local memory is needed but the latency to the DDR is paid for each access, roughly 400 ns on our platform. However, if data accesses are reorganized by blocks on the same row, thanks to loop tiling, and fully pipelined, the accelerator can work at full rate, receiving 32 bits every 10 ns. This can be done thanks to *communication coalescing* – a standard technique used in compilers of parallel languages and scratch-pad memory optimizations [5–8, 13–15] – which amounts to hoist transfers out of a tile and regroup the same accesses to eliminate redundancy. The form of communication coalescing we develop is more general as it exploits, *at the granularity of individual array elements*, not only intra-tile reuse but also inter-tile reuse, even if data dependences exist between tiles, while minimizing the lifetimes of array elements in the local memory. Usually, the approach is to load, just before executing a tile, all the data read in the tile, then to store to the DDR all data written in the tile, without exploiting inter-tile data reuse. The other solution is to first load all data needed in a tile strip, to execute all tiles in the strip, and finally to store to the DDR all data produced by the strip, in other words, to hoist communications outside the innermost tile loop. This exploits data reuse but requires a large local memory to store all needed data. Also, computations cannot start before all data have arrived. Another important difference is that our technique performs loads from the external memory *during the execution of the tile strip*, and before actual stores, thus even when the external memory is not fully up-to-date. This may cause memory consistency problems that need to be addressed. We solve this issue by generating *exact* communication sets when possible, in a way similar to exact data-flow analysis [11], and by defining valid approximations otherwise.

Our strategy consists in scheduling a load request just before a first read (unless previously written) and a store request just after a last write. Data are loaded/stored in a strip *only once* and, between the first and last accesses, they are kept and used (read and written) in local memory, exploiting data reuse. As a bonus, this method handles naturally the case where dependences exist between tiles: as data involved in inter-tile dependences are kept in local memory, the sequential execution of tiles guarantees the program correctness. Another consequence is that, unlike previous approaches where the resulting lifetimes of array elements are identical (either between the first and last tile, or just within a tile), memory allocation based on bounding box as in [5, 14, 15] is not enough: to exploit different lifetimes, modular mappings [1, 10, 12] are more suitable. For the previous example, a memory of only $3b$ elements is used to store the elements of array c, and even only $2b$ if the first tile of a strip does not overlap with the second tile.

3. Implementation and Experimental Results

We implemented all necessary program analysis, generation of communicating sets, and code generation for the different communicating processes, making an extensive use of the parametric linear programming tool PIP (`www.piplib.org`). Our prototype generates, from the C code of a small kernel to be optimized, a C code that implements a double-bufferized version of it. This code can be simulated using linux processes, FIFOs, and shared memories. Its different processes are then synthesized and integrated automatically using C2H and Altera SOPC builder. Before, we currently still need to do a few modifications by hand, such as inserting some adequate pragmas for C2H, linearizing array addresses with the right base addresses, instantiating memories in the SOPC builder, changing some arrays into non-aliasing pointers. All these changes are systematic, but not integrated yet in our code generator.

For the 3 kernels analyzed in [2], we retrieve the performances of the versions optimized by hand. They can run 6x or more faster than the direct implementations (the maximal speed-up is 8, if, in the initial code, successive DDR accesses are in different rows). Note that these speed-ups are obtained not because computations are parallelized (tiles are run sequentially) but because DDR requests are reorganized, fully pipelined, overlapped with computations, and because data reuse is exploited. These first experimental results show that our method is effective and promising compared to handmade design. To our knowledge, this is the first time, in the context of HLS, that such accelerators are automatically generated.

References

[1] C. Alias, F. Baray, and A. Darte. Bee+Cl@k: An implementation of lattice-based array contraction in the source-to-source translator Rose. In *ACM Conference LCTES'07*, San Diego, USA, June 2007.

[2] C. Alias, A. Darte, and A. Plesco. Optimizing DDR-SDRAM communications at C-level for automatically-generated hardware accelerators. In *IEEE Int. Conference ASAP'10*, pages 329–332, July 2010.

[3] C. Alias, A. Darte, and A. Plesco. Program analysis and source-level communication optimizations for HLS. TR 7648, Inria, June 2011.

[4] C. Alias, A. Darte, and A. Plesco. Kernel offloading with optimized remote accesses. TR 7697, Inria, July 2011.

[5] M. M. Baskaran, U. Bondhugula, S. Krishnamoorthy, J. Ramanujam, A. Rountev, and P. Sadayappan. Automatic data movement and computation mapping for multi-level parallel architectures with explicitly managed memories. In *ACM Symp. PPoPP'08*, pages 1–10, 2008.

[6] D. Chavarría-Miranda and J. Mellor-Crummey. Effective communication coalescing for data-parallel applications. In *ACM Symposium PPoPP'05*, pages 14–25, Chicago, IL, USA, 2005.

[7] W.-Y. Chen, C. Iancu, and K. Yelick. Communication optimizations for fine-grained UPC applications. In *IEEE Int. Conf. on Parallel Arch. and Compilation Techniques (PACT'05)*, pages 267–278, 2005.

[8] J. Cong, H. Huang, C. Liu, and Y. Zou. A reuse-aware prefetching scheme for scratchpad memory. In DAC'11, pages 960–965, 2011.

[9] P. Coussy and A. Morawiec. *High-Level Synthesis: From Algorithm to Digital Circuit*. Springer, 2008.

[10] A. Darte, R. Schreiber, and G. Villard. Lattice-based memory allocation. *IEEE Transactions on Computers*, 54(10):1242–1257, Oct. 2005.

[11] P. Feautrier. Dataflow analysis of array and scalar references. *International Journal of Parallel Programming*, 20(1):23–53, Feb. 1991.

[12] E. D. Greef, F. Catthoor, and H. D. Man. Memory size reduction through storage order optimization for embedded parallel multimedia applications. *Parallel Computing*, 23:1811–1837, 1997.

[13] I. Issenin, E. Borckmeyer, M. Miranda, and N. Dutt. DRDU: A data reuse analysis technique for efficient scratch-pad memory management. *ACM TODAES*, 12(2), Apr. 2007. Article 15.

[14] A. Leung, N. Vasilache, B. Meister, M. M. Baskaran, D. Wohlford, C. Bastoul, and R. Lethin. A mapping path for multi-GPGPU accelerated computers from a portable high level programming abstraction. In *ACM Workshop GPGPU'10*, pages 51–61, Mar. 2010.

[15] M. Kandemir and A. Choudhary. Compiler-directed scratch pad memory hierarchy design and management. In *DAC'02*, pp. 628–633, 2002.

[16] J. Xue. *Loop Tiling for Parallelism*. Kluwer Academic, 2000.

Using GPU's to Accelerate Stencil-based Computation Kernels for the Development of Large Scale Scientific Applications on Heterogeneous Systems

Jian Tao
Center for Computation & Technology, Louisiana State University, Baton Rouge, Louisiana, USA
jtao@cct.lsu.edu

Marek Blazewicz
Applications Department, Poznań Supercomputing and Networking Center, Poznań, Poland
marqs@man.poznan.pl

Steven R. Brandt
Center for Computation & Technology, Louisiana State University, Baton Rouge, Louisiana, USA
sbrandt@cct.lsu.edu

Categories and Subject Descriptors D.1.3 [*Concurrent Programming*]: Parallel programming; D.3.3 [*Language Constructs and Features*]: Frameworks

General Terms Algorithms, Design, Languages

Keywords GPGPU Programming, Computational Framework, HPC, Stencil Computation

Abstract

We present CaCUDA - a GPGPU kernel abstraction and a parallel programming framework for developing highly efficient large scale scientific applications using stencil computations on hybrid CPU/GPU architectures. CaCUDA is built upon the Cactus computational toolkit, an open source problem solving environment designed for scientists and engineers. Due to the flexibility and extensibility of the Cactus toolkit, the addition of a GPGPU programming framework required no changes to the Cactus infrastructure, guaranteeing that existing features and modules will continue to work without modification. CaCUDA was tested and benchmarked using a 3D CFD code based on a finite difference discretization of Navier-Stokes equations.

1. Introduction

Heterogeneous systems are becoming more common in the field of High Performance Computing (HPC). Three out of five of the fastest computers in the world use GPGPUs to achieve their performance[5], and more than 34 of the top 500 systems are GPU-based. However, even using tools like CUDA and OpenCL it is a non-trivial task to obtain optimal performance on the GPU, and it is even more difficult to achieve sustained performance at scale on hybrid supercomputers. The CaCUDA programming framework leverages the highly scalable Cactus framework [3], making use of its component infrastructure and parallel programming abstractions to design and implement a tool for creating stencil-based computation kernels. By using automatic code generation from a set of highly optimized code templates, CaCUDA frees scientific application developers not only from lower level programming issues such as parameter parsing and I/O, but more importantly, from the parallelization and optimization details of GPGPU programming. Our design assigns one GPU to one MPI process and is able to benefit from the Cactus grid abstractions without requiring any changes to the distributed grid structure, grid geometry, and inter-process communication. CaCUDA extends Cactus by adding a code generation system that automates the management of storage on the GPU, synchronization among threads, communication between CPU and GPU, and optimization on GPU. Everything except the kernel stencil computation itself can be handled in the CaCUDA programming framework automatically via a kernel descriptor and a code generator.

2. Cactus Computational Framework

Cactus [3] is a problem-solving platform that was designed and implemented by an international team of computational scientists led by Seidel, Suen et al., to free numerical relativists from lower level parallel programming as well as hardware concerns [4]. After years of development, Cactus has evolved into a generic, open-source framework for developing large scale parallel scientific applications based on structured meshes. Currently, there are at least 30 worldwide research groups using Cactus. The name *Cactus* is also a metaphor for its design. A Cactus application consists of a core piece of infrastructure called the *flesh* and user modules called the *thorns*. The flesh provides a framework for defining and parsing parameters, for scheduling work, interoperation between C, C++, F77, and F90, as well as interaction with other thorns. Thorns are described using a domain specific language (DSL) called the *Cactus Configuration Language (CCL)* [1]. The information in the CCL files includes the name of the implementation, the definition of functions and parameters, the schedule of the routines, and whether they require synchronization after execution, etc.

3. CaCUDA Programming Framework

In order to facilitate programming in the CaCUDA environment, we defined the term *Kernel Abstraction*, which consists of three major components: *Kernel Descriptor*, *Computation Templates*, and *Code Generator*. The definition of a kernel may be divided into three separate tasks:

- *Declaring the Kernel:* The *cacuda.ccl* configuration file is used to describe the data dependencies, namely the *grid functions* and *parameters* required by the kernel and stencil. This decla-

PPoPP'12, February 25–29, 2012, New Orleans, Louisiana, USA.
ACM 978-1-4503-1160-1/12/02.

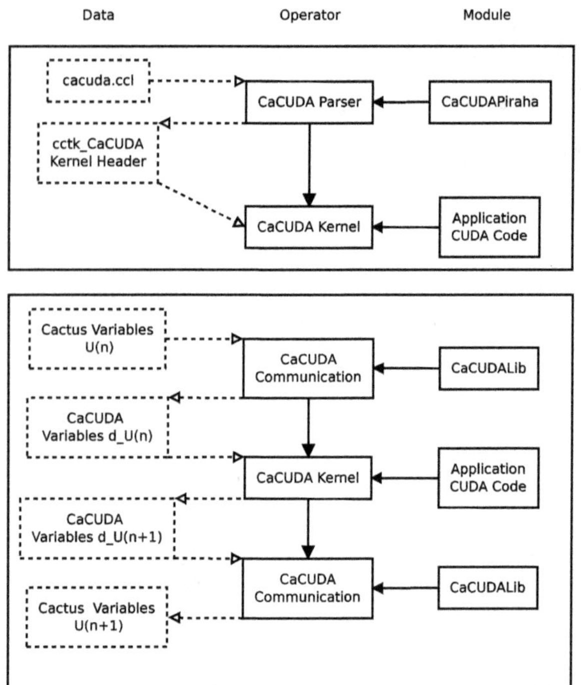

Figure 1. The workflow of a CaCUDA-based application: The upper box shows the generation of the CaCUDA kernel headers at the code compilation stage, while the lower box shows how the variables are evolved to the next time step.

ration file is then used to generate a kernel frame (macros) that performs automatic data fetching, caching and synchronization with the host.

- *Writing the Kernel:* Using kernel-specific auto-generated macros the programmer writes a set of stencil equations for one grid point only, accessing neighboring grid points by specifying the relative index in each direction. The code must be written to avoid *read-after-write* and *write-after-read* hazards, and thus requires some basic knowledge of parallel programming.
- *Scheduling the Kernel:* Insertion of the newly generated kernel into the Cactus schedule tree.

The CaCUDA kernel abstraction makes it easy to write and execute GPGPU kernels, and makes it possible to optimize the kernel without changing the kernel code itself. The whole optimization process is handled by swapping the templates or adjusting the kernel parameters. Furthermore, our system is not limited to the GPGPU architecture. The templates could be easily adapted to run as sequential CPU or parallel OpenMP code. The CaCUDA kernel code can be integrated in a straightforward manner within existing thorns (modules) without touching the flesh (core infrastructure). The workflow of the CaCUDA compilation process as well as the kernel execution is shown in Figure 1.

4. Sample Application

In this work we've focused on a simple test case in Computational Fluid Dynamics (CFD), namely lid-driven cavity with computations performed in single precision. Additional details regarding the testing of the application can be found in our previous work [2]. We adopted the computational patterns proven to be most efficient in stencil computations. These patterns were further generalized to fit wider variety of numerical problems. Our test application achieved

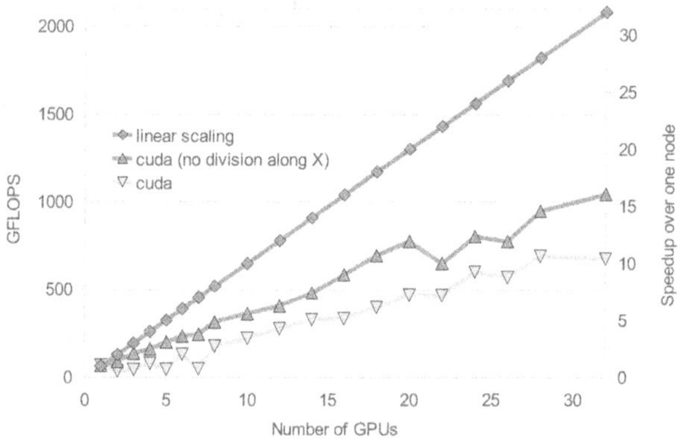

Figure 2. The graph presents the weak scaling test and shows the performance (in GFLOPS) and the speedup over a single GPU. The domain size on each GPU is 192^3. Two cases were considered: with and without domain decomposition along the X direction.

70GFLOPS on single NVIDIA Fermi GPU. However, due to communication overhead, the performance of computations conducted on 2 nodes is comparable to this on single node. The weak scaling test is shown in Figure 2.

5. Conclusions

We presented our work to design and implement a GPGPU kernel abstraction, which is suitable for developing highly efficient large scale scientific applications using stencil computations on hybrid CPU/GPU systems. By leveraging the MPI-based data parallelism implemented in Cactus, we have developed a tool which enables both MPI and GPU acceleration. The lid-driven cavity problem was implemented and benchmarked with CaCUDA, and the results presented. Our current efforts are focused on minimizing the costs of the data exchange between GPU and CPU and optimizing the boundary exchange.

6. Acknowledgments

This work was performed using the computational resources of LSU/LONI and was supported by the Center for Computation and Technology at LSU. This work was also supported by the UCoMS project under award number MNiSW(Polish Ministry of Science and Higher Education) Nr 469 1 N - USA/2009 in close collaboration with U.S. research institutions involved in the U.S. Department of Energy (DOE) funded grant under award number DE-FG02-04ER46136 and the Board of Regents, State of Louisiana, under contract no. DOE/LEQSF(2004-07).

References

[1] G. Allen, T. Goodale, F. Löffler, D. Rideout, E. Schnetter, and E. L. Seidel. Component Specification in the Cactus Framework: The Cactus Configuration Language. In *Grid2010: Proceedings of the 11th IEEE/ACM International Conference on Grid Computing*, 2010. (arXiv:1009.1341).

[2] M. Blazewicz, S. R. Brandt, P. Diener, D. M. Koppelman, K. Kurowski, F. Lffler, E. Schnetter, and J. Tao. A massive data parallel computational framework on petascale/exascale hybrid computer systems, submitted. In *International Conference on Parallel Computing*, Ghent, Belgium, 2011.

[3] Cactus. URL http://www.cactuscode.org/.

[4] E. Seidel and W.-M. Suen. Numerical relativity as a tool for computational astrophysics. *J. Comp. Appl. Math.*, 109:493, 1999.

[5] Top 500. URL http://www.top500.org/. Top 500 Supercomputer Sites.

Mechanizing the Expert Dense Linear Algebra Developer

Bryan Marker,
Robert van de Geijn, Don Batory
Dept. of Computer Science
The Univ. of Texas at Austin
Austin, TX, USA
{bamarker, rvdg,
batory}@cs.utexas.edu

Andy Terrel
Texas Advanced Computing Center
Austin, TX, USA
aterrel@tacc.utexas.edu

Jack Poulson
Institute for Computational Engineering
and Sciences
The Univ. of Texas at Austin
Austin, TX, USA
poulson@cs.utexas.edu

Abstract

The efforts of an expert to parallelize and optimize a dense linear algebra algorithm for distributed-memory targets are largely mechanical and repetitive. We demonstrate that these efforts can be encoded and automatically applied to obviate the manual implementation of many algorithms in high-performance code.

Categories and Subject Descriptors D.1.2 [*Automatic Programming*]
; D.1.3 [*Concurrent Programming*]
; G.4 [*Mathematical Software*]: Efficiency

General Terms Design,Performance

Keywords high-performance numerical algorithms, software for distributed-memory computing, dense linear algebra, program generation, MDE, libraries of the future

1. Introduction

Parallelizing and optimizing *dense linear algebra (DLA)* algorithms for distributed-memory machines has historically been done by domain experts who are very familiar with both linear algebra and the oddities of a target class of machines. When a DLA expert has no experience with a new architecture and wants to implement an algorithm, (s)he must live with an existing library, learn a lot about that architecture, or find an experienced developer. This is inefficient and unnecessary because the work of an expert is mechanical and systematic, and therefore automatable.

Expert-tuned, high-performance parallel code for distributed-memory architectures can be automatically produced by a tool via an approach we call *Design by Transformations (DxT)* [3], pronounced "dext". We demonstrated DxT on a handful of prototypical examples, simple and complex, in a broad class of dense linear algebra operations (e.g., the commonly used matrix operations in the BLAS and operations supported by libraries like LAPACK and `libflame` [5]). As our examples were targeted to a distributed-memory architecture, we believe DxT can be extended to target other architectures (such as multi-core processors, GPGPUs, and many-core processors).

PPoPP'12, February 25–29, 2012, New Orleans, Louisiana, USA.
ACM 978-1-4503-1160-1/12/02.

We expect the insights from this work to have a profound impact on the FLAME project [6], which encompasses a formalism for deriving DLA algorithms, notation for expressing these as algorithms, and APIs for implementation in code. Two library instantiations exist to support a variety of parallel architectures: the `libflame` library that targets sequential, multicore, and (multi-) GPU architectures, and Elemental [2], which targets distributed memory architectures. DxT would allow us instead to support a single encoding of algorithms and knowledge, with libraries like `libflame` and Elemental being the products (outputs) of applying DxT.

2. Mechanizing Expert Transformations

When an expert parallelizes a DLA algorithm for a distributed-memory target, (s)he typically focuses on the loop body. For each of the operations or functions in that loop body, (s)he chooses an implementation code. In distributed-memory programs, matrix data is distributed among processors. In Elemental, for example, the default distribution views processes as a 2-dimension grid and stores the data in a 2-dimensional, block-cyclic distribution with a block-size of one. To parallelize each operation in the loop body, an expert redistributes the data from the default distribution in some way that enables the computation to proceed in parallel, and then redistributes the result back to the default distribution. There are often multiple implementation choices that perform each loop body operation correctly, but they get varying performance depending on the machine architecture, problem size, etc. An expert chooses implementation codes based on a rough idea of the runtime cost of redistributing data and the runtime cost of computation. Redistributing data in Elemental requires an expensive collective communication operation, so an expert optimizes programs by reducing the amount of data redistribution. Once parallel implementations are chosen for loop body operations, an expert can see how data is redistributed and can remove redundant communication.

Step by step, an expert implements a DLA algorithm in high-performance code by transforming the algorithm with implementation choices of sub-operations, using a rough estimate of runtime costs, and transforming with optimizations that decrease the estimated runtime cost of communication. DxT attempts to mechanize this strategy by encoding the transformations performed by an expert instead of the resulting code. Then, those transformations can be applied automatically using a tool, as described below, instead of being re-applied by rote across many algorithms in the domain.

We view software as a stack of layers. Each layer provides details about an operation's implementation, so the transformations we encode break through these layers to expose implementation details that can be optimized (we encode transformations for many implementation choices, not just one). The optimizing transforma-

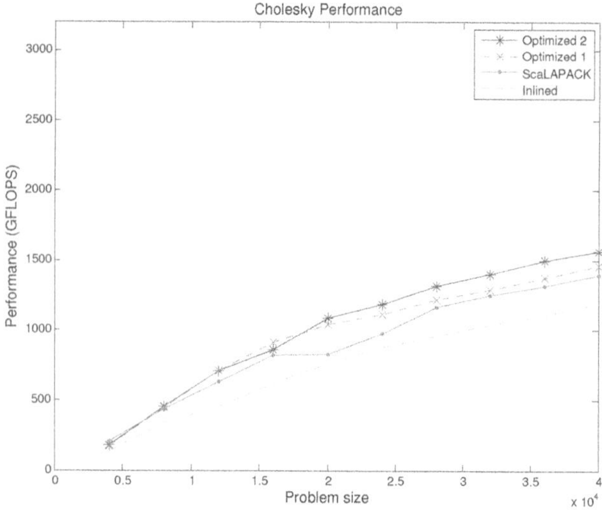

Figure 1. Automatically generated Cholesky Variant 3 implementations tested on 240 cores (and ScaLAPACK results for comparison). Peak performance, 3200 GFLOPS, is at the top of the graph.

tions are viewed as encoding equivalent sets of functionality. An expert's optimizing transformation replaces one piece of code with a functionally-equivalent piece of code that is better-performing. For DxT we encode many such equivalences.

When an expert applies transformations to generate parallel, optimized code, (s)he uses a rough estimate of operation costs to make choices on which transformation is best to use. We use rough estimates of operation costs in terms of the number of floating-point operations performed and the speed of the machine, and of the cost of collective communication operations in terms of the amount of data being moved and the network latency and bandwidth. For DxT we encode these cost estimates for each operation and they guide the choice of implementing and optimizing transformations to use [4]. The next section demonstrates the efficacy of this approach.

3. A Prototype for Automatic Program Generation

We developed a prototype to test DxT. Algorithms are represented as data-flow, directed, acyclic graphs (DAGs). Transformations are encoded as graph rewrites similar to the those performed by compilers on DAGs. The prototype has multiple implementing transformations for BLAS and LAPACK operations, and has dozens of optimizing transformations that replace patterns of collective communication with equivalent, but faster, implementations.

Our prototype takes as input the algorithm being implemented, encoded as a DAG, and iteratively applies transformations. At each step, the prototype applies any transformation that can be applied to any graph it has developed. Thus, all possible implementation codes from the input algorithm are generated. A cost estimate is attached to each graph, as described above, and is used to select the parallelized, optimized code that is least costly.

We tested the prototype, its transformations, and its cost estimates on two Cholesky factorizations variants, three matrix-multiplication (Gemm) variants, a triangular solve with multiple right-hand sides (TRSM) variant, and a significantly more complicated variant of a two-sided triangular solve [1]. The Cholesky factorization algorithm is prototypical in DLA codes. Its implementation and optimizations require an expert to perform many transformations that are common throughout the domain. For both variants of Cholesky that were tested, the system generated hundreds of implementations. The "best" versions were chosen using the above-described cost estimates, and these versions were the same as those hand-generated and optimized by the expert developer of Elemental. In Figure 1, we show performance of one of those variants on 240 cores. Here, the "Inlined" results come from simply implementing that algorithm directly in code, without applying any optimizations. The "Optimized 1" line shows performance with some simple optimizations applied by the system, removing redundant communication. The "Optimized 2" line shows performance for the expert-generated code, which the prototype also generated and calculated as "best" using its cost estimates. This version results from some additional optimizations being performed on the "Optimized 1" version; they have to do with memory access patterns and cache-reuse. ScaLAPCK results are shown for comparison.

Similar results can be seen for the other operations tested. The prototype generated and chose as "best" the same code developed by an expert. For the two-sided triangular side, the generated implementation was slightly better than the version written by the expert as the prototype applied an optimization the expert forgot (which has since been incorporated into Elemental).

4. Conclusion

We demonstrated for a handful of prototypical algorithms how the implementing and optimizing transformations an expert performs can be mechanized. Instead of requiring an expert to re-apply the transformations by hand for many algorithms in a domain, a tool can do this task automatically. We see DxT as a sustainable approach to library development as architectures continue to change, requiring code to be re-developed.

Acknowledgments. Marker was sponsored by a fellowship from Sandia National Laboratories and an NSF Graduate Research Fellowship under grant DGE-1110007. Poulson was sponsored by a fellowship from the Institute of Computational Engineering and Sciences. Batory is supported by the NSF's Science of Design Project CCF 0724979. This research was also partially sponsored by NSF grants OCI-0850750 and CCF-0917167 as well as by a grant from Microsoft.

Any opinions, findings and conclusions or recommendations expressed in this material are those of the author(s) and do not necessarily reflect the views of the National Science Foundation (NSF).

References

[1] J. Poulson et al. Parallel algorithms for reducing the generalized hermitian-definite eigenvalue problem. *ACM Transactions on Mathematical Software*. submitted.

[2] J. Poulson et al. Elemental: A new framework for distributed memory dense matrix computations. FLAME Working Note #44 TR-2010-20, The University of Texas at Austin, Department of Computer Sciences, 2010. Submitted to ACM TOMS.

[3] T. Riche et al. Software architecture design by transformation. Computer Science report TR-11-19, Univ. of Texas at Austin, 2011.

[4] P. G. Selinger et al. Access Path Selection in a Relational Database Management Syst em. In *ACM SIGMOD*, 1979.

[5] F. G. Van Zee. `libflame`*: The Complete Reference*. `www.lulu.com`, 2009.

[6] F. G. Van Zee et al. Introducing: The libflame library for dense matrix computations. *IEEE Computation in Science & Engineering*, 11(6): 56–62, 2009.

The Boat Hull Model: Adapting the Roofline Model to Enable Performance Prediction for Parallel Computing

Cedric Nugteren Henk Corporaal

Eindhoven University of Technology, The Netherlands

{c.nugteren, h.corporaal}@tue.nl http://parse.ele.tue.nl

Abstract

Multi-core and many-core were already major trends for the past six years, and are expected to continue for the next decades. With these trends of parallel computing, it becomes increasingly difficult to decide on which architecture to run a given application.

In this work, we use an algorithm classification to predict performance *prior* to algorithm implementation. For this purpose, we modify the *roofline model* to include class information. In this way, we enable architectural choice through performance prediction prior to the development of architecture specific code. The new model, the *boat hull model*, is demonstrated using a GPU as a target architecture. We show for 6 example algorithms that performance is predicted accurately without requiring code to be available.

Categories and Subject Descriptors C.1.4 [*Processor Architectures*]: Parallel Architectures; C.4 [*Performance of Systems*]: Modeling Techniques

General Terms Performance

Keywords Parallel computing, performance prediction, many-core accelerators, the roofline model

1. Introduction

For the past five decades, single-core performance has shown an exponential growth, enabling technology to become pervasive and ubiquitous in our society. The exponential growth of single-core performance has ended in 2004, making place for a parallel and heterogeneous computing era. Trends such as multi-core and many-core are expected to continue for the next decades. Although many-core architectures such as the Graphics Processing Unit (GPU) might be suitable for one type of application, other applications might prefer multi-core processors. This creates a heterogeneous computing environment, with both types of processors in one system or even on a single chip.

With current and future processors, it becomes increasingly difficult to decide on which processor to run an application or algorithm. Existing performance prediction techniques such as mathematical models or simulators require code to be available and optimized for a target processor. However, programming such processors has become increasingly challenging and time consuming [1]. Therefore, a performance prediction method which does not require code to be available is desirable.

In this work, we present the *boat hull model*. We modify the *roofline model* [3] such that it generates multiple inverse rooflines. Each of these inverse rooflines is specific for an algorithm class. Available algorithm classes are defined using an algorithm classification, of which more details are found in [2].

2. Background: the roofline model

The roofline model was introduced as an easy to understand performance model capable of identifying performance bottlenecks [3]. This model gives a rough performance estimate based on the assumption that performance is limited by either peak memory bandwidth or by peak ALU throughput. The roofline model is processor specific: for each processor there is a specific instance of the model.

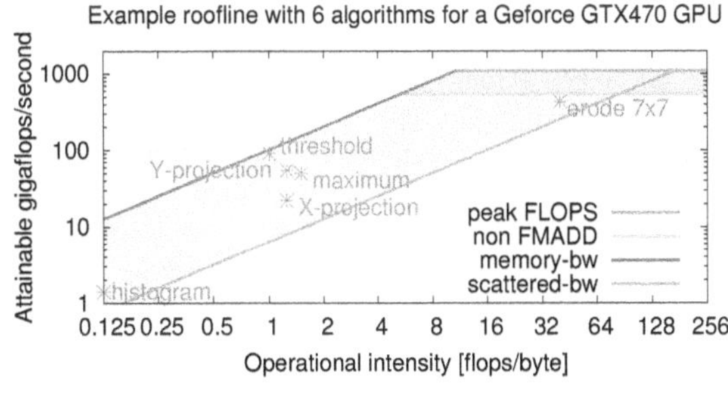

Figure 1. Applying the roofline model to 6 example algorithms.

We map 6 algorithms onto the roofline model, of which the results are shown in figure 1 for a GeForce GTX470 GPU. The location of each algorithm is based on two aspects: 1) the performance of a CUDA implementation executed on the GPU, and 2), the operational intensity in ALU operations per off-chip load/store.

Two obstacles for using this model to predict performance are observed: 1) the execution time is not directly visible, and 2), the range of the predicted performance is very wide. For example, as shown in figure 1, the performance of the `X-projection` algorithm is a factor 7 beneath the memory bandwidth roof.

3. The boat hull model

Selecting which processor architecture is best suited for a given application can be done using architecture models or hardware simulators. These methods do however require the presence of optimized target architecture code, which is often not available when making an architectural choice. The roofline model does give an indication of the expected performance without requiring code, but falls short when an application's compute or data-access patterns

PPoPP'12, February 25–29, 2012, New Orleans, Louisiana, USA.
ACM 978-1-4503-1160-1/12/02.

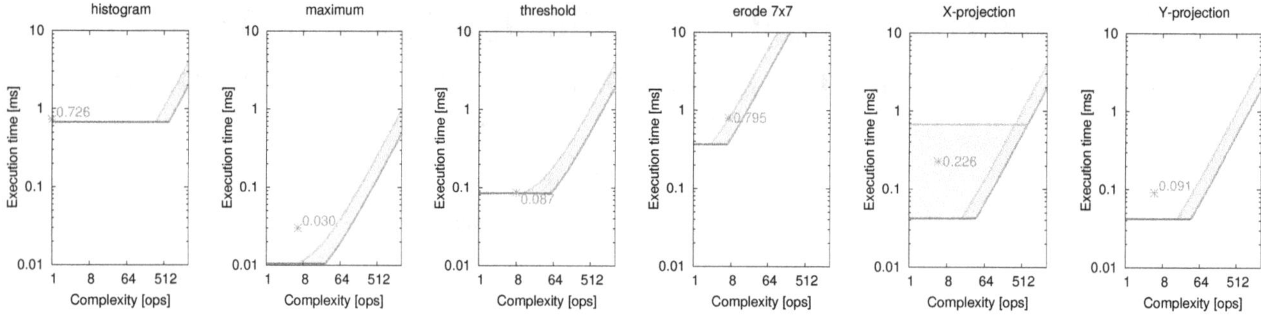

Figure 2. Applying the boat hull model to 6 example algorithms for the GeForce GTX470 architecture. Red star symbols show the measured performance, while the lines show the predicted performance. The legend is as shown in figure 1.

are non-ideal. To enable performance prediction prior to algorithm implementation, we introduce a modified version of the roofline model based on an algorithm classification presented in [2].

The modified model, referred to as the *boat hull model*, makes the following changes to the roofline model:

- For each algorithm class, we fine-tune the original model to match the properties of such a class. Because the amount of off-chip data accesses is inherent to a class-architecture combination, the metric on the horizontal axis of the model can be changed from 'operations per byte' into 'complexity': the number of operations given for a class' operator $f()$ (see [2]).
- The metric on the vertical axis of the model is changed from 'flops per second' into 'execution time'. This creates an inverse view of the roofline model, resembling a boat's hull.

We have developed a tool based on the boat hull model which requires as inputs processor parameters and an algorithm class, and outputs a visual model. The required processor parameters are high level and are similar to those required for the original roofline model, e.g. peak ALU performance and peak memory bandwidth. The tool currently supports both CPUs and GPUs. For each algorithm class, a set of parameters is pre-defined, limiting the original roofline model's roofs and ceilings. For example, on a GPU, a convolution type of operation might perform a certain number of scattered memory accesses based on its neighbourhood size. These scattered accesses will limit the maximum achievable bandwidth, which is taken into account in the class parameters.

4. Example application

To illustrate the use of this work, we present 6 example image processing algorithms from a computer vision application. They are targeted for GPU acceleration using a GeForce GTX470 and are classified as shown in table 1. The classification is according to the algorithm classification's grammar and vocabulary, which is explained in [2].

primitive	classification
histogram	1024x1024|element → 256|shared
maximum	262144|element → 1|shared
threshold	1024x1024|element → 1024x1024|element
erode 7x7	1024x1024|neighb(7x7) → 1024x1024|element
X-projection	1024x1024|tile(1x1024) → 1024|element
Y-projection	1024x1024|tile(1024x1) → 1024|element

Table 1. Classification of 6 example image processing algorithms.

For each algorithm we generate a boat hull model based on the corresponding algorithm class. The results are shown in figure 2, in which the measured performance is marked with a red star symbol. From the results, we observe that the performance of the algorithms `histogram`, `threshold` and `erode` are accurately predicted. The `maximum` primitive shows a higher execution time compared to the predicted time, which is caused by its small problem size, making the algorithm less suitable for GPU acceleration. Similarly, both the `X-projection` and `Y-projection` algorithms suffer from additional overheads for small problem sizes. Because memory accesses might be scattered for algorithms such as `X-projection`, a wider prediction range is given.

We compare the boat hull model (figure 2) with the roofline model (figure 1). Both figures show the performance of the 6 example algorithms. The roofline model appears not suitable for performance prediction, while the boat hull model predicts performance with a small error in most cases. Comparing to performance models and architecture simulators, we observe that the boat hull model has the following advantages: 1) it is straightforward to understand, 2) it requires little architectural information, and 3), most importantly, it requires no code implementation nor mapping for the target architecture to be available.

5. Summary

In this work we presented a processor and algorithm class specific visual model to predict an application's performance. This model is based on the roofline model, which is adapted to include algorithm class information. With the new *boat hull model*, we are able to predict performance without requiring code to be available. Programmers are not required to port and optimize code for the target processors, which enables rapid processor selection early in the design process.

We have given an overview of the concepts and ideas behind the boat hull model. We have also demonstrated the use of the model for an example application, for which we showed the predicted and measured performance.

References

[1] S. W. Keckler, W. J. Dally, B. Khailany, M. Garland, and D. Glasco. GPUs and the Future of Parallel Computing. *IEEE Micro*, 31:7–17, September 2011.

[2] C. Nugteren and H. Corporaal. A Modular and Parameterisable Classification of Algorithms. Technical Report No. ESR-2011-02, Eindhoven University of Technology, 2011.

[3] S. Williams, A. Waterman, and D. Patterson. Roofline: an Insightful Visual Performance Model for Multicore Architectures. *Communications of the ACM*, 52:65–76, April 2009.

Speculative Parallelization on GPGPUs

Min Feng Rajiv Gupta Laxími N. Bhuyan
University of California, Riverside
{mfeng, gupta, bhuyan}@cs.ucr.edu

Abstract

This paper overviews the first speculative parallelization technique for GPUs that can exploit parallelism in loops even in the presence of dynamic irregularities that may give rise to cross-iteration dependences. The execution of a speculatively parallelized loop consists of five phases: scheduling, computation, misspeculation check, result committing, and misspeculation recovery. We perform misspeculation check on the GPU to minimize its cost. We optimize the procedures of result committing and misspeculation recovery to reduce the result copying and recovery overhead. Finally, the scheduling policies are designed according to the types of cross-iteration dependences to reduce the misspeculation rate. Our preliminary evaluation was conducted on an nVidia Tesla C1060 hosted in an Intel(R) Xeon(R) E5540 machine. We use three benchmarks of which two contain irregular memory accesses and one contain irregular control flows that can give rise to cross-iteration dependences. Our implementation achieves 3.6x-13.8x speedups for loops in these benchmarks.

Categories and Subject Descriptors D.3.4 [*Programming Languages*]: Processors – compilers

General Terms Performance

1. Introduction

Dynamic irregularities have been widely studied for high performance computing on General-Purpose Graphics Processing Units (GPGPUs or GPUs for short) [3–5]. Existing works have focused on optimizing the performance in the presence of such irregularities. However, in this work, we consider a new class of dynamic irregularities in loops that may cause cross-iteration dependences at runtime. Thus, presence of such dynamic irregularities prevents existing techniques from parallelizing the loops for GPUs. In particular, we have identified two types of dynamic irregularities that may dynamically cause cross-iteration dependences to arise. Next we illustrate them using examples.

Dynamic irregular memory accesses refer to memory accesses whose memory access patterns are unknown at compile time. They may result in infrequent cross-iteration dependences at runtime. Figure 1(a) shows an example, where each iteration of the loop reads $A[P[i]]$ and writes to $A[Q[i]]$. The memory access patterns of $A[P[i]]$ and $A[Q[i]]$ are determined by the runtime values of the elements in arrays P and Q. It is possible that an element in

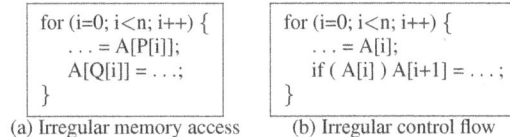

```
for (i=0; i<n; i++) {
    . . . = A[P[i]];
    A[Q[i]] = . . .;
}
```
(a) Irregular memory access

```
for (i=0; i<n; i++) {
    . . . = A[i];
    if ( A[i] ) A[i+1] = . . . ;
}
```
(b) Irregular control flow

Figure 1. Examples of dynamic irregularities that cause cross-iteration dependences.

array A is read in one iteration and written in another at runtime, which results in a dynamic cross-iteration dependence. Since the memory access patterns are unknown at compile time, it is not possible to identify the dynamic dependences at that time. Therefore, the loop cannot be parallelized by any existing GPU compiler.

Irregular control flows are introduced by conditional statements, which may cause execution of paths that may give rise to cross-iteration dependences at runtime, as illustrated in Figure 1(b), where each iteration of the loop usually only reads $A[i]$. In the loop, there is a conditional branch that guards a write to $A[i+1]$, which is to be read in the next iteration. The outcome of branch condition is determined by the runtime value of $A[i]$. If the condition is true in the current iteration, a cross-iteration dependence occurs between the current iteration and the next iteration. Since the value of $A[i]$ is unknown at compile time, there is no way to know at compile time in which iteration the branch condition will be true. Therefore, like the previous example, this loop cannot be parallelized by any existing GPU compiler.

In this paper, we propose a speculative execution framework for GPU computing. It is used to parallelize loops that may contain cross-iteration dependences caused by dynamic irregularities. The execution of a speculative parallel loop consists of five phases: scheduling, computation, misspeculation check, result committing, and misspeculation recovery. For efficiency, we develop a scheduling policy that is optimized for different types of cross-iteration dependences to reduce the misspeculation rate. We reduce the runtime overhead by performing misspeculation check on the GPU and utilizing its massive number of stream processors. We optimize the result committing procedure to reduce the size of data transferred between the CPU and GPU. Recovery is performed on the CPU for as few iterations as possible to minimize its runtime overhead.

Our preliminary evaluation was conducted on an nVidia Tesla C1060 hosted in a Intel(R) Xeon(R) E5540 machine. We used three benchmarks, where two benchmarks have loops with irregular memory accesses and one have loops with irregular control flows. Our implementation achieves 3.6x-13.8x speedup for the parallelized loops in these benchmarks.

2. Overview

Figure 2 gives the overview of executing a speculative parallel loop using GPUs. The procedure consists of five phases: *scheduling*, *computation*, *misspeculation check*, *result committing*, and *mis-*

PPoPP'12, February 25–29, 2012, New Orleans, Louisiana, USA.
ACM 978-1-4503-1160-1/12/02.

Benchmark	Description	Function	LOC	Irregularities	% of time	Speedup
ocean	Boussinesq fluid layer solver	ftrvmt	150	irregular memory accesses	45%	3.62
trfd	two-electron integral transformation	intgrl	37	irregular memory accesses	6%	5.43
mdg	water molecule simulator	interf	208	irregular control flows	94%	13.76

Table 1. Benchmark summary. From left to right: benchmark name, name of the function where the loop is located, lines of code in the function, type of irregularities that cause cross-iteration dependences, percentage of total execution time taken by the loop, and speedup of the loop.

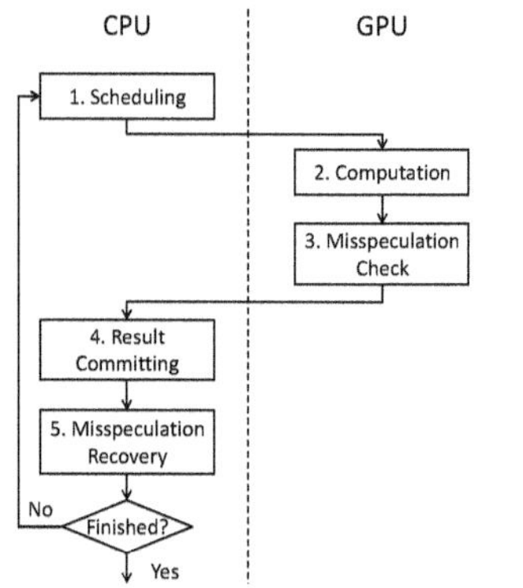

Figure 2. Execution framework of a speculative parallel loop with GPUs.

speculation recovery, among which *computation* and *misspeculation check* are performed on the GPU. The five phases are repeated until the entire loop is finished. We briefly describe the five phases as follows.

Scheduling. Upon entering a speculatively parallelized loop, the CPU needs to determine the proper number of iterations that will be executed on the GPU in the next phase. Assigning large number of iterations to the GPU may cause excessive misspeculations while assigning small number of iterations may limit performance while leaving the GPU under-utilized. Our scheduling policy adaptively adjusts the size of each assignment to minimize the misspeculation rate while keeping each assignment large enough to make full use of the massive parallel architecture on GPUs.

Computation. After scheduling, the GPU executes the iterations in parallel by speculating on the absence of cross-iteration dependence. To enable speculative execution, we need to track the irregular memory accesses and control flows during the computation.

Misspeculation check. Misspeculation check consists of two steps: detection and localization. Misspeculation detection is used to determine whether the iterations have been executed correctly. If misspeculation is detected, the misspeculation localization step is used to identify the iterations that were executed incorrectly. In addition, for speculative execution on GPUs, we need to identify the correct part of the results, which must be copied back to the CPU memory. To make misspeculation checks efficient, they are performed in parallel on the GPU. Since there is data parallelism in misspeculation checks, executing them on the GPU can lead to better performance.

Result committing. After misspeculation checks, we need to copy the results from the GPU memory to the CPU memory. For better performance, our runtime only copies the correct results using the information obtained through misspeculation check.

Misspeculation recovery. We need to re-execute the iterations where misspeculation occurs. We should re-execute on the CPU as few iterations as possible to minimize the recovery overhead. Executing more iterations on the GPU will get us better performance. Therefore, our runtime only re-execute on the CPU the misspeculated iterations on which other misspeculated iterations depend. Other misspeculated iterations will be executed on the GPU in the next assignment.

3. Preliminary Evaluation

This section presents our preliminary evaluation of the proposed speculative parallelization framework. We have developed a prototype implementation of our framework, whose core components consist of: a source-to-source translator and a runtime library. The source-to-source translator is based on OpenMPC [3], which is an OpenMP-to-CUDA compiler. The runtime library implements the core steps of our technique, i.e. scheduling, misspeculation check, result committing, and misspeculation recovery. We used an nVidia Tesla C1060 as the experimental platform. The device is connected to a host system consisting of Intel(R) Xeon(R) E5540 processors. The machine has CUDA 3.0 installed.

We evaluated our speculative parallelization framework on three benchmarks shown in Table 1. These benchmarks were obtained from the test benchmark suites for PIPS [1] and LLVM [2]. We selected them because they contain dynamic irregularities that may cause cross-iteration dependences at runtime. These benchmarks cannot be parallelized without speculation because all of them may have dynamic cross-iteration dependences due to irregularities.

The rightmost column of Table 1 shows the speedups of the speculative parallel loops in the three benchmarks. The baseline is the execution time of the sequential loops on the host system. Numbers higher than 1 indicate speedup. Overall, the speedups are between 3.62x and 13.76x, with 7.6x on average. *The speedups demonstrate the effectiveness of our framework for employing GPUs on irregular loops that may contain cross-iteration dependences.*

Acknowledgments

This research is supported by NSF grants CCF-0963996 and CCF-0905509 to UC Riverside.

References

[1] F. Irigoin, P. Jouvelot, and R. Triolet. Semantical interprocedural parallelization: An overview of the PIPS project. In *ICS*, 1991.

[2] C. Lattner and V. Adve. LLVM: A compilation framework for lifelong program analysis & transformation. In *CGO*, 2004.

[3] S. Lee, S.-J. Min, and R. Eigenmann. OpenMP to GPGPU: a compiler framework for automatic translation and optimization. In *PPoPP*, pages 101–110, 2009.

[4] Y. Yang, P. Xiang, J. Kong, and H. Zhou. A GPGPU compiler for memory optimization and parallelism management. In *PLDI*, pages 86–97, 2010.

[5] E. Z. Zhang, Y. Jiang, Z. Guo, K. Tian, and X. Shen. On-the-fly elimination of dynamic irregularities for GPU computing. In *ASPLOS*, pages 369–380, 2011.

Adapting the Polyhedral Model as a Framework for Efficient Speculative Parallelization

Alexandra Jimborean Philippe Clauss Benoît Pradelle
Luis Mastrangelo Vincent Loechner

CAMUS group, INRIA & LSIIT & University of Strasbourg
Strasbourg
France
first_name.last_name@inria.fr

Abstract

In this paper, we present a Thread-Level Speculation (TLS) framework whose main feature is to be able to speculatively parallelize a sequential loop nest in various ways, by re-scheduling its iterations. The transformation to be applied is selected at runtime with the goal of minimizing the number of rollbacks and maximizing performance. We perform code transformations by applying the polyhedral model that we adapted for speculative and runtime code parallelization. For this purpose, we designed a parallel code pattern which is patched by our runtime system according to the profiling information collected on some execution samples. Adaptability is ensured by considering chunks of code of various sizes, that are launched successively, each of which being parallelized in a different manner, or run sequentially, depending on the currently observed behavior for accessing memory.

We show on several benchmarks that our framework yields good performance on codes which could not be handled efficiently by previously proposed TLS systems.

Categories and Subject Descriptors D.3.4 [*Programming Languages*]: Processors – *Run-time environments, Optimization*

General Terms Performance

Keywords Speculative parallelization, dynamic system, polyhedral model, dynamic code transformations

1. Overview

With the advent of multicore processors, automatically parallelizing sequential code became increasingly important. Particularly, it is a challenging task to parallelize code at runtime, if the information available at compile time is not sufficient. Runtime parallelization techniques are usually based on thread-level speculation (TLS) [2–4], where straightforward parallelization transformations are optimistically applied on the original sequential code. In most TLS proposals, modest performance gains were obtained, since parallelization is attempted on unmodified code generated by the compiler: when considering loop nests, the unique strategy usually applied is to cut the outermost loop into contiguous chunks and to run these chunks separately in simultaneous threads, which yields numerous rollbacks in case of a dependence carried by the outermost loop. To be more efficient, TLS systems must handle more complex code transformations that can be profitably selected at runtime, depending on the current execution context. To our knowledge, no attempt on applying various parallelizing transformations using the TLS systems have been reported yet.

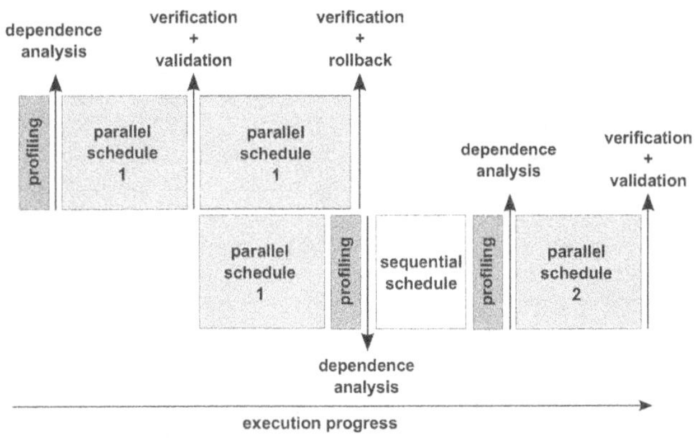

Figure 1. Illustration of the chunking mechanism

We propose performing advanced loop transformations provided by the polyhedral model [1] such as tiling, skewing, loop interchange, etc., by speculating on the linearity of the loop bounds and of the memory accesses. Not only that transforming code shows benefits in boosting performance, but also it exhibits parallelism in codes that cannot be otherwise parallelized in the original form. Additionally, our framework allows several parallel schedules, during one execution of the loop. We define a loop chunk as a set of consecutive iterations of the outermost loop and apply one parallel schedule per chunk.

Our goal is to parallelize the loop by chunks, by applying a suitable polyhedral transformation. We start by launching a profiling chunk dedicated to capturing the behaviour of the loop, based on which it can be decided whether a polyhedral transformation can be applied for parallelizing the loop. If the dependence analysis validates such a transformation, the corresponding code is generated and a new parallel chunk is launched. During the execution of the speculative parallel code, the speculation is verified and the chunk is validated, or a rollback is performed if a dependence violation occurs. In this case, the code is re-executed in a smaller chunk that completes its execution before the misprediction point, and another

PPoPP'12, February 25–29, 2012, New Orleans, Louisiana, USA.
ACM 978-1-4503-1160-1/12/02.

instrumentation chunk is launched which overcomes the rollback point and characterizes the new behavior of the loop. If the code cannot be parallelized, a sequential chunk is executed, followed again by an instrumented chunk. At some point, the loop might exhibit a new behavior allowing parallelism, provided that another polyhedral transformation is performed. On the other hand, if a parallel chunk is validated, execution continues with another parallel chunk of a larger size. This process is described in figure 1.

2. Implementation details

The framework consists of two parts: a *static* part, implemented in the LLVM compiler, designed to prepare the loops for instrumentation and parallelization, and a *dynamic* part, in the form of a runtime system whose role is to generate the parallel code and to guide the execution.

Static component: Loops are marked for speculative parallelization in the source code using a dedicated pragma. At compile time, these loops are automatically identified and three versions are generated: original, instrumented and a parallel code pattern, together with a mechanism for switching between the versions. Additionally, support for chunking the outermost loop is included.

The instrumented version contains instrumentation instructions which track the memory accesses performed inside the loop. The goal is to compute linear functions of the surrounding loop indices, used for performing the dependence analysis.

Instead of statically generating several parallel code versions, we build a generic code pattern from which these versions can be generated at runtime, by patching predefined code areas. The advantage is that the code size is significantly reduced and more parallel code versions can be build dynamically, guided by the results of the instrumentation. Also, patching a parallel code pattern is considerably faster than fully dynamic code generation. The limitation of the pattern is that it can only support a subset of the possible polyhedral transformations, which preserve the loop structure and do not reorder the statements.

In the parallel code pattern, the original loop is transformed into a *for*-loop with affine bounds and the original loop conditions are inserted as guarding code. Additionally, initialization code is inserted to assign the correct starting values for the variables at the beginning of each thread, using the linear functions obtained from instrumentation and a new polyhedral schedule. Correctness of the code is ensured by the verification code, which, for each memory access, compares the speculations against the actual values, at each iteration. The loop bounds, the initialization and the verification code, all use the linear functions computed during the profiling phase. Since they are not known at compile time, the coefficients are statically inserted as global variables, whose values will be assigned at runtime. Different values of these coefficients represent different schedules and will generate distinct parallel code versions.

A set of polyhedral transformations is proposed statically and is encoded in the binary file as matrices. Their computation follows a static dependence analysis, which ensures that the dependences which can be statically identified will not invalidate the schedules, minimizing the number of rollbacks.

Dynamic component: The runtime system collaborates tightly with the static component. During the instrumentation phase, it retrieves the memory locations being accessed and computes interpolating linear functions of the surrounding loop indices. Instrumentation is performed on loop samples, to limit the overhead, consequently the computed linear functions speculatively characterize the behavior of the loop. Instrumentation is followed by a dependence analysis which evaluates whether any of the proposed polyhedral transformations can be efficiently applied. If successful, the runtime system assigns values to the coefficients of the linear functions in the code pattern.

To limit the synchronization overhead, the validation system makes use of one flag per thread, which is set when a misprediction occurs. Each thread polls its own flag. As soon as a thread detects that a speculation is invalidated, it sets the flags of all threads. A misspeculation is followed by a rollback which restores the memory to a correct state. For this purpose, the runtime system creates a copy of the memory area that will be modified by the next parallel chunk, since it can be predicted using the interpolating linear functions. When a rollback is performed, the memory is overwritten with the content of the copy, and the rollbacked iterations are re-executed.

Results: We carried out experiments on synthetic benchmarks aimed to emphasize different characteristics of the framework. The "linked list" processes list elements allocated following either regular or irregular memory patterns. The "banded matrix" accesses elements of a matrix through indirect references whose linearity is discovered by our framework which then applies a parallelizing polyhedral transformation. The "cherry cake" performs different computations depending on properties of the elements of a linked list. It shows our system handling successively different parallel schedules. The "NO to overhead" evaluates the overhead of the instrumentation when no parallelization is possible.

Measurements were obtained by executing the benchmarks on 24 cores of two AMD Opteron 12 core-processors running Linux 2.6.35. Super-linear speed-up is obtained on the "banded matrix" thanks to the polyhdral transformation and loop tiling. Additionally, the memory accessing behavior remains unchanged and no rollbacks occur. In contrast, on the "linked list" and on the "cherry cake" examples, a number of rollbacks are performed, but their overhead is amorthized by polyhedral transformations and parallelization.

Benchmark	Sequential exec. time (s)	Spec. par. exec. time (s)	Speed-Up
linked list	26.65	3.78	7.04
banded matrix	219	8.4	26.07
cherry cake	516.23	57.15	9.03
NO to overhead	173.33	173.34	1

3. Conclusion

We propose a TLS system, using the polyhedral model at runtime, thus adapting to the current context, on chunks of the targeted loop nests, to perform speculative parallelization. The chunking strategy allows us to identify partial parallelism in loops and to apply the most suitable polyhedral transformation for each chunk.

References

[1] U. Bondhugula, A. Hartono, J. Ramanujam, and P. Sadayappan. A practical automatic polyhedral parallelizer and locality optimizer. In *PLDI '08*, pages 101–113, 2008.

[2] W. Liu, J. Tuck, L. Ceze, W. Ahn, K. Strauss, J. Renau, and J. Torrellas. POSH: a TLS compiler that exploits program structure. In *Procs of the eleventh ACM SIGPLAN symposium on Principles and practice of parallel programming*, PPoPP '06, pages 158–167, New York, USA.

[3] E. Raman, N. Va hharajani, R. Rangan, and D. I. August. Spice: speculative parallel iteration chunk execution. In *Procs of the 6th annual IEEE/ACM international symposium on Code generation and optimization*, CGO '08, pages 175–184, New York, USA, 2008. ACM.

[4] L. Rauchwerger and D. Padua. The LRPD test: speculative run-time parallelization of loops with privatization and reduction parallelization. In *Procs of the ACM SIGPLAN 1995 conference on Programming language design and implementation*, PLDI '95, pages 218–232, 1995.

An Overview of CMPI: Network Performance Aware MPI in the Cloud

Yifan Gong
Nanyang Technological University
gyf382@gmail.com

Bingsheng He
Nanyang Technological University
BSHE@ntu.edu.sg

Jianlong Zhong
Nanyang Technological University
jzhong2@e.ntu.edu.sg

Abstract

Cloud computing enables users to perform distributed computing tasks on many virtual machines, without owning a physical cluster. Recently, various distributed computing tasks such as scientific applications are being moved from supercomputers and private clusters to public clouds. Message passing interface (MPI) is a key and common component in distributed computing tasks. The virtualized computing environment of the public cloud hides the network topology information from the users, and existing topology-aware optimizations for MPI are no longer feasible in the cloud environment. We propose a network performance aware MPI library named CMPI. CMPI embraces a new model for capturing the network performance among different virtual machines in the cloud. Based on the network performance model, we develop novel network performance aware algorithms for communication operations. This poster gives an overview of CMPI design, and presents some preliminary results on collective operations such as broadcast. We demonstrate the effectiveness of our network performance aware optimizations on Amazon EC2.

Categories and Subject Descriptors D.1.3 [*Programming Techniques*]: Concurrent Programming-Parallel programming; D.2.13 [*Software Engineering*]: Reusable Software-Reusable libraries

General Terms Algorithms, Performance, Measurement

Keywords MPI, Collective Communication Operations, Cloud Computing, Scientific Computing

1. Introduction

Cloud computing has emerged as a popular computing paradigm for distributed computing applications, including scientific computing [5] and data analytic [3]. Many HPC applications have been deployed to public clouds such as Amazon EC2[1], with considerable performance. Since message passing interface (MPI) is a common and key component in distributed computing applications, improving MPI performance in the cloud is important.

Network topology aware algorithms have been applied to optimize the performance of communication operations in MPI [4, 7, 9, 10]. The network topology information is particularly important for the optimizations of MPI, especially for collective communication operations. For collective communication operations, most of the studies [4, 7, 9, 10] adopt tree-based algorithms, because the network topology is often tree-structured. The essential idea of those algorithms is to obtain the topology information with hardware or software mechanisms, and then to map the processes involved in the collective operation to the underlying topology. For example, Kandalla et al. [10] studied the tree-structured Infiniband network, and proposed to group the processes for intra-machine, intra-switch and inter-switch into multiple levels and to develop gather and scatter operations according to the hierarchy.

The topology aware algorithms are no longer feasible in the cloud environment, since the topology information is not available due to the virtualization and system management issues. First, virtualization hides the network topology from users. Virtualization offers a uniform interface to users, without exposing the real configurations of the underlying hardware. Second, cloud environments do not offer administrator privileges on the hardware and software under the virtualization layer, which is usually required when getting the network topology information. Third, due to the cloud system dynamics such as virtual machine consolidation and dynamic network flow scheduling [1], the static topology information is not sufficient for representing the network performance. All these factors make the existing topology aware algorithm unfeasible in such a public virtualized environment, and new algorithms should be invented for the awareness of network performance for optimizations.

Instead of relying on network topology knowledge, we develop network performance aware optimizations for MPI communications. The network performance characteristics between two virtual machines are explicitly captured by the latency and the bandwidth obtained from calibration or runtime measurements. Given a message size, the network performance can be estimated with the latency and the bandwidth. Thus, we are able to exploit the network performance awareness for optimizations. For example, in a broadcast operation, we should let the machines with high network performance communicate as much as possible, and minimize the communication between machines with relatively low network performance. That boils down to our proposed MPI library named CMPI (Cloud-MPI).

This poster gives an overview of CMPI design and its optimizations, and presents our preliminary results. We demonstrate that network performance aware optimizations significantly improve the network performance of the broadcast operation.

2. Overview

Figure 1 illustrates the architectural overview of the CMPI. CMPI is an intermediate layer between distributed computing application-

[1] Detailed case studies on Amazon EC2 can be found at http://aws.amazon.com/solutions/case-studies/#hpc.

PPoPP'12, February 25–29, 2012, New Orleans, Louisiana, USA.
ACM 978-1-4503-1160-1/12/02.

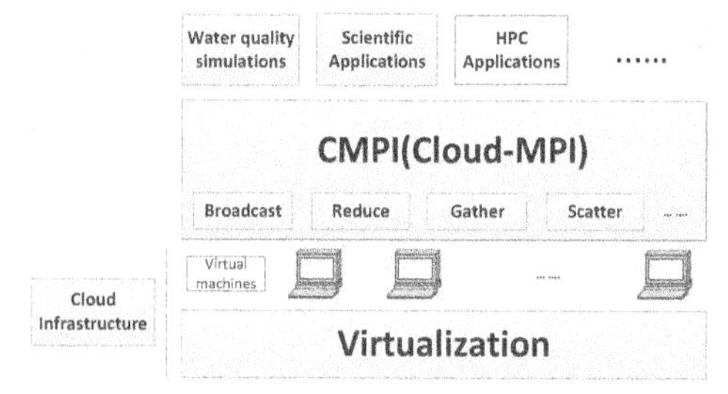

Figure 1. An overview of CMPI

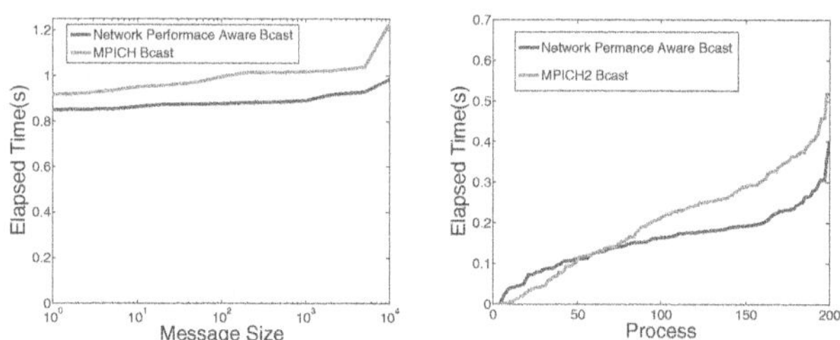

Figure 2. Results for broadcast: (a) Performance comparison with different message size. (b) Individual process elapsed time (Message Size=10K bytes).

s and cloud infrastructure. CMPI is designed to run on the public cloud environment, where network topology knowledge is unavailable or difficult to obtain. It is initiated by our Singapore funded project on water quality simulations in the cloud. The traditionally MPI-based applications are able to run on CMPI with little modification. If network topology knowledge is available, traditional MPI algorithms are adopted. Thus, CMPI is complementary to existing MPI implementation.

CMPI embraces network performance aware optimizations in communication operations. Take collective communication operations as an example. Our design adopts the tree-based algorithm, which is widely used in MPI [8]. We specifically consider two categories of operations: (a) broadcast and reduce: the message size is constant for the entire operation; (b) gather and scatter: the message size increases as the communications are close to the root process. We construct the tree communication pattern with the consideration on the network performance among virtual machine pairs. More details of the algorithm design can be found in our technical report [2].

3. Experimental Results

We implement CMPI by realizing network performance aware optimizations in MPICH2 [6]. We evaluate the performance of CMPI in comparison with MPICH2. The major metric in our study is the completion time of the collective operation. We are also interested in studying the elapsed time of the MPI program execution on each virtual machine to have a detailed profile on the performance. Each experiment was performed over one thousand times, and the average of the measurements is reported.

Due to the space constraint, we present the result for broadcast, and refer readers to our technical report [2] for more details.

We conduct the experiment on Amazon EC2, with the following setting: 64 small instances and 200 processes. Figure 2 (a) show the performance comparison of broadcast with different message sizes. Our network performance aware algorithm significantly outperforms its counterpart in MPICH2. The improvement is relatively larger for larger message sizes. The average improvement is 17.2% on broadcast.

Figure 2(b) shows the elapsed time of individual processes for the MPI program executions for broadcast. In this figure, the network performance aware algorithm has much more balanced distribution on the process execution time than MPICH2. The balanced process time distribution indicates the effectiveness of our algorithm on scheduling the links with similar performance and maximizing the impact of network latency overlaps.

4. Conclusion and Future Work

As more and more distributed computing tasks are moved from private clusters to public clouds, researchers should carefully examine the system design and implementation in the public cloud environment. We propose CMPI, a MPI implementation that is aware of network performance in the cloud. Our experiments on Amazon EC2 demonstrate the effectiveness of network performance aware optimizations. As for future work, we will implement a full-fledge MPI library, and investigate the monetary cost behavior of CMPI, following the previous study [11].

Acknowledgement

This work is supported by the funding from National Research Foundation through the Environment and Water Industry Programme Office (EWI) on project 1002-IRIS-09, a startup grant and an Inter-disciplinary Strategic Competitive Fund of Nanyang Technological University. The experiment on Amazon EC2 is supported by an Amazon AWS Research Grant (2010-2011).

References

[1] M. Al-Fares, S. Radhakrishnan, B. Raghavan, N. Huang, and A. Vahdat. Hedera: dynamic flow scheduling for data center networks. In *NSDI*, 2010.

[2] Y. Gong, B. He, and J. Zhong. Network performance aware mpi collective communication operations in the cloud. Technical Report NTU-PDCC, Dec 2011. URL `http://pdcc.ntu.edu.sg/`.

[3] B. He, M. Yang, Z. Guo, R. Chen, B. Su, W. Lin, and L. Zhou. Comet: batched stream processing for data intensive distributed computing. In *SoCC*, pages 63–74, 2010.

[4] T. Kielmann, R. F. H. Hofman, H. E. Bal, A. Plaat, and R. A. F. Bhoedjang. Magpie: Mpi's collective communication operations for clustered wide area systems. In *PPoPP*, 1999.

[5] J. Li, M. Humphrey, D. A. Agarwal, K. R. Jackson, C. van Ingen, and Y. Ryu. escience in the cloud: A modis satellite data reprojection and reduction pipeline in the windows azure platform. In *IPDPS*, 2010.

[6] MPICH2. *http://www.mcs.anl.gov/research/projects/mpich2/*.

[7] I. F. W. G. E. L. N. Karonis, B. de Supinski and J. Bresnahan. Exploiting hierarchy in parallel computer networks to optimize collective operation performance. In *IPDPS*, 2000.

[8] J. Pješivac-Grbović, T. Angskun, G. Bosilca, G. E. Fagg, E. Gabriel, and J. J. Dongarra. Performance analysis of mpi collective operations. *Cluster Computing*, 10, 2007.

[9] S. Sistare, R. vandeVaart, and E. Loh. Optimization of mpi collectives on clusters of large-scale smps. In *SC*, 1999.

[10] H. Subramoni, K. Kandalla, J. Vienne, S. Sur, B. Barth, K. Tomko, R. McLay, K. Schulz, and D. K. Panda. Design and evaluation of network topology-/speed-aware broadcast algorithms for infiniband clusters. In *IEEE Cluster*, 2011.

[11] H. Wang, Q. Jing, R. Chen, B. He, Z. Qian, and L. Zhou. Distributed systems meet economics: pricing in the cloud. In *HotCloud*, pages 1–6, 2010.

OpenCL as a Unified Programming Model for Heterogeneous CPU/GPU Clusters *

Jungwon Kim Sangmin Seo Jun Lee Jeongho Nah Gangwon Jo Jaejin Lee

Center for Manycore Programming
School of Computer Science and Engineering
Seoul National University, Seoul 151-744, Korea
{jungwon, sangmin, jun, jeongho, gangwon}@aces.snu.ac.kr, jlee@cse.snu.ac.kr
http://aces.snu.ac.kr

Abstract

In this paper, we propose an OpenCL framework for heterogeneous CPU/GPU clusters, and show that the framework achieves both high performance and ease of programming. The framework provides an illusion of a single system for the user. It allows the application to utilize multiple heterogeneous compute devices, such as multicore CPUs and GPUs, in a remote node as if they were in a local node. No communication API, such as the MPI library, is required in the application source. We implement the OpenCL framework and evaluate its performance on a heterogeneous CPU/GPU cluster that consists of one host node and nine compute nodes using eleven OpenCL benchmark applications.

Categories and Subject Descriptors D.1.3 [*PROGRAMMING TECHNIQUES*]: Concurrent Programming; D.3.4 [*PROGRAMMING LANGUAGES*]: Processors – Code generation, Compilers, Optimization, Run-time environments

General Terms Algorithm, Design, Experimentation, Languages, Measurement, Performance

Keywords OpenCL, Clusters, Heterogeneous computing, Programming models

1. Introduction

Open Computing Language (OpenCL)[3] is a unified programming model for different types of computational units in a single heterogeneous computing system. OpenCL provides a common hardware abstraction layer across different computational units. Programmers can write OpenCL applications once and run them on any OpenCL-compliant hardware.

However, one of the limitations of current OpenCL is that it is restricted to a programming model for a single heterogeneous parallel system. Thus, application developers for the heterogeneous CPU/GPU clusters are being forced to turn to an unattractive mix of programming models, such as MPI-OpenCL. This makes the application more complex, hard to maintain, and less portable.

In this paper, we propose an OpenCL framework and show that it can be a unified programming model for heterogeneous CPU/GPU clusters. The user can launch a kernel to a compute device or manipulate a memory object in a remote node using only OpenCL API functions. This enables OpenCL applications written for a single heterogeneous system to run on the cluster without any modification. That is, with our OpenCL framework, an OpenCL application becomes portable not only between heterogeneous computing devices in a single system, but also between those in the entire cluster environment.

2. The OpenCL Framework

2.1 Organization of Our Runtime

The target cluster architecture consists of a single host node and multiple compute nodes. The nodes are connected by an interconnection network. The host node executes the host program in an OpenCL application. Each compute node consists of multiple multicore CPUs and multiple GPUs. A set of CPU cores or a single GPU becomes an OpenCL compute device.

Our OpenCL runtime for the host node runs two threads: *host thread* and *command scheduler*. When a user launches an OpenCL application in the host node, the host thread in the host node executes the host program in the application. The command scheduler schedules the enqueued commands across compute devices in the cluster. When the command scheduler dequeues a command from a command-queue, the command scheduler *issues* the command by sending a *command message* to the target compute node that contains the target compute device associated with the command-queue.

The runtime for a compute node runs a *command handler*. The command handler receives command messages from the host node. It creates a command object from the message and enqueues the command object to the *ready-queue* of the target device.

The runtime for a compute node runs a *device thread* for each compute device in the node. If a CPU device exists in the compute node, each core in the CPU device runs a *CU thread* to emulate PEs. The CU thread emulates PEs using a kernel transformation technique, called work-item coalescing[5]. The device thread dequeues a command from its ready-queue and executes the command. When the target device is a GPU device, the device thread launches the kernel using GPU vendor-specific API functions, such as CUDA. Our source-to-source translator generates the CUDA code for a

* This work was supported in part by grant 2009-0081569 (Creative Research Initiatives: Center for Manycore Programming) from the National Research Foundation of Korea. This work was also supported in part by the Ministry of Education, Science and Technology of Korea under the BK21 Project. ICT at Seoul National University provided research facilities for this study.

PPoPP'12, February 25–29, 2012, New Orleans, Louisiana, USA.
ACM 978-1-4503-1160-1/12/02.

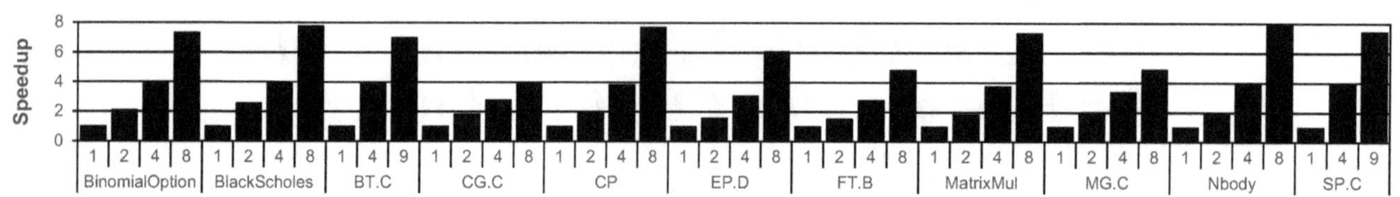

Figure 1. Speedup of the CPU cluster over a single CPU node.

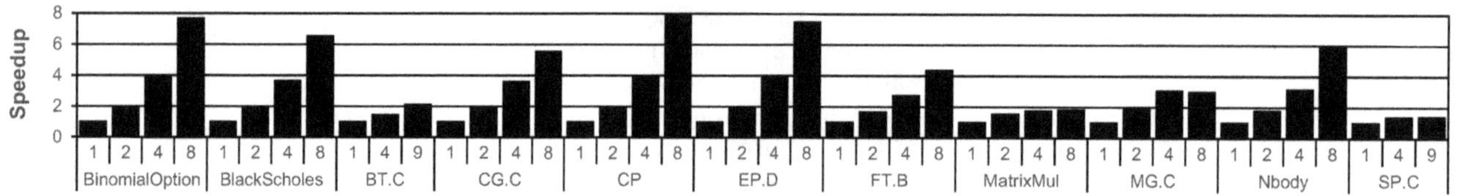

Figure 2. Speedup of the GPU cluster over a single GPU node.

GPU device and C code for a CPU device from an OpenCL kernel code, respectively.

When the compute device completes executing the command, the command handler sends a completion message to the host node. When the command scheduler in the host node receives the completion message, it resolves the dependence between commands.

2.2 Memory Management

An OpenCL buffer object can be shared between multiple compute devices. To efficiently handle buffer sharing, our OpenCL runtime maintains a *device list* for each buffer. The device list contains compute devices that have the same latest copy of the buffer in their global memory. It is empty when the buffer is created. When the command that accesses the buffer completes, the host command scheduler updates the device list of the buffer.

When the host command scheduler issues a command, it checks the device list of each buffer that is accessed by the command. If the target compute device is not in the device list, the runtime copies the buffer contents from a device in the device list to the target compute device.

To minimize the memory copying overhead, the runtime selects a source device in the device list that incurs the minimum copying overhead. As the source of copying, our runtime prefers a device that has a latest copy of the buffer and resides in the same node as that of the target device. If there are multiple such devices, a CPU device is preferred. When all of the potential source devices reside in other nodes that the target, a CPU device is also preferred to a GPU device.

3. Evaluation

We have implemented the OpenCL runtime and source-to-source translators. The GPU part of our runtime is implemented with CUDA Toolkit 4.0[6]. We have implemented our source-to-source translators by modifying clang that is a C front-end for the LLVM[4] compiler infrastructure

We evaluate our OpenCL framework using a heterogeneous CPU/GPU cluster system that consists of one host node and nine compute nodes. The nodes are connected by a Mellanox InfiniBand QDR switch. Each compute node consists of two Intel Xeon X5660 hexa-core CPUs and four NVIDIA GTX 480 GPUs.

We use eleven OpenCL applications from various sources: AMD[1], SNU NPB[7], NVIDIA[6], Parboil[8], and PARSEC[2]. Each application is translated to an OpenCL program manually. All applications are portable across CPU and GPU devices.

Figure 1 shows the speedup (over a single node) of each application with our OpenCL framework when we use only CPU devices in the target cluster. X-axis represents the number of compute nodes used. Similarly, Figure 2 shows the speedup (over a single node) when we use only GPU devices in the target cluster.

All of the applications scale well when we use only CPU devices. When we use only GPU devices in the cluster, all applications but MatrixMul, MG and SP scale well. Since the communication overhead due to data movement dominates the performance of MatrixMul and SP, they do not scale well. The speedup of MG at eight compute nodes is smaller than that at four compute nodes because its kernel index space is not large enough to fully utilize all the GPU devices and the communication overhead increases when the number of nodes is large.

4. Conclusions

We introduce the design and implementation of an OpenCL framework that provides an illusion of a single system for the programmer. It allows an OpenCL application to utilize compute devices in a remote compute node as if they were in the host node. No communication API, such as the MPI library, is required in the application source. The experimental results with eleven OpenCL benchmark applications on a heterogeneous CPU/GPU cluster indicate that our approach provides ease of programming and high performance.

References

[1] *AMD Accelerated Parallel Processing (APP) SDK With OpenCL 1.1 Support.* AMD, 2011. `http://developer.amd.com/sdks/AMDAPPSDK/Pages/default.aspx`.

[2] C. Bienia, S. Kumar, J. P. Singh, and K. Li. The PARSEC benchmark suite: characterization and architectural implications. In *Proceedings of the 17th international conference on Parallel architectures and compilation techniques*, PACT '08, pages 72–81, 2008.

[3] *The OpenCL Specification Version 1.1.* Khronos OpenCL Working Group, 2010. `http://www.khronos.org/opencl`.

[4] C. Lattner and V. Adve. LLVM: A Compilation Framework for Lifelong Program Analysis & Transformation. In *Proceedings of the international symposium on Code generation and optimization: feedback-directed and runtime optimization*, CGO '04, pages 75–86, 2004.

[5] J. Lee, J. Kim, S. Seo, S. Kim, J. Park, H. Kim, T. T. Dao, Y. Cho, S. J. Seo, S. H. Lee, S. M. Cho, H. J. Song, S.-B. Suh, and J.-D. Choi. An OpenCL framework for heterogeneous multicores with local memory. In *Proceedings of the 19th international conference on Parallel architectures and compilation techniques*, PACT '10, pages 193–204, 2010.

[6] NVIDIA. NVIDIA CUDA Toolkit 4.0. `http://developer.nvidia.com/cuda-toolkit-40`.

[7] S. Seo, G. Jo, and J. Lee. Performance Characterization of the NAS Parallel Benchmarks in OpenCL. In *Proceedings of the 2011 IEEE International Symposium on Workload Characterization*, IISWC '11, 2011.

[8] The IMPACT Research Group. Parboil Benchmark suite. `http://impact.crhc.illinois.edu/parboil.php`.

BDDT: Block-level Dynamic Dependence Analysis for Deterministic Task-Based Parallelism

George Tzenakis† Angelos Papatriantafyllou† John Kesapides† Polyvios Pratikakis†
Hans Vandierendonck†‡ Dimitrios S. Nikolopoulos†

†Institute of Computer Science, FORTH
‡Department of Computer Science, Ghent University
{tzenakis,angelpap,kesapid,hvdieren,dsn}@ics.forth.gr

Categories and Subject Descriptors D [/]: 3

General Terms Performance

1. Introduction

Task-parallel programming models [1, 4, 6] offer a more abstract, more structured way for expressing parallelism compared to threads. In these systems the programmer describes the parts of the program that can be computed in parallel, and does not have to manually create and manage the threads of execution. Such models still require the programmer to manually find and enforce any ordering or memory dependencies among tasks, and also maintain the inherent nondeterminism found in threads, which makes them hard to test and debug, as some executions might not be easy to reproduce. Implicitly parallel models [2, 5, 7, 8] further extend task-parallel models with automatic inference of dependencies; the programmer annotates the program [2, 3, 5, 8]; the system then discovers parallelization and manage dependencies transparently.

Dynamic dependence analysis can discover more parallelism than is possible to describe statically in the program, as it only synchronizes tasks that *actually* access the same resources. To benefit program performance, a dependence analysis must (i) be accurate, so that it does not discover false dependencies; and (ii) have low overhead, so that it does not nullify the benefit of discovering extra parallelism. Existing systems require the programmer to restrict task footprints into either whole and isolated program objects, one-dimensional array ranges, or static compile-time regions. This may cause false dependencies in programs where tasks have partially overlapping or unstructured (irregular) memory footprints, or disallow tasks that operate on a multidimensional tile of a large array. To solve these issues, existing systems use copies, such as marshalling all the relevant row parts of a multidimensional array tile into a buffer, and unmarshalling the result back into the array after the task is done. These techniques incur high overhead, and are cumbersome and error-prone for the programmer to use.

This poster abstract presents a task-parallel runtime system that dynamically discovers and resolves dependencies deterministically among parallel tasks, producing executions equivalent to a sequential execution. Lifting the above restrictions of existing systems, BDDT allows the programmer to specify detailed task footprints on any, potentially non-contiguous, memory address range or multidimensional array tile. We use a block-based dependence analysis with arbitrary granularity, making it easier to apply to existing C programs without having to restructure object or array allocation, introduce buffers and marshalling, or change the granularity of task arguments.

Overall, we make the following contributions:

- We present a novel technique for block-based, dynamic task dependence analysis that allows task arguments spanning arbitrary –potentially non-contiguous– memory ranges, argument overlapping across tasks, and dependence tracking at any granularity. The analysis is tunable, and facilitates balancing accuracy and performance. It is also deterministic, in that it always preserves the sequential program order for all read-after-write memory accesses.
- We have implemented this dependence analysis in BDDT, a runtime system for scheduling parallel tasks. Our implementation is adaptive, the programmer can enable or disable the dependence analysis for each task argument independently to minimize overhead when the analysis is not necessary.
- We have evaluated the performance of our runtime system on a representative set of benchmarks; BDDT performs better than SMPSs (an existing state-of-the-art task runtime that implements dynamic dependence analysis), and is able to handle tasks with one order of magnitude finer granularity than SMPSs (Figure 1(a)). In several benchmarks, dynamic dependence analysis in BDDT discovers additional parallelism, producing speedups of up to 3.6× compared to OpenMP (Figure 1(b)).

2. Dataflow Execution Engine Design

BDDT uses a dataflow execution engine based on block-level dependence analysis for identifying parallel tasks. We assume a programming language where tasks are annotated –through language keywords or directives– with data access attributes, corresponding to three access patterns: read (IN), write (OUT) and read/write (INOUT). The language runtime system detects dependencies between tasks, by comparing the access properties of arguments of different tasks that overlap in memory. BDDT splits arguments into virtual memory blocks of configurable size and analyzes dependencies between blocks. Similarly to whole-object dependence analysis used in tools such as SMPSs and SvS, block-based analysis detects true or anti-dependencies between blocks by comparing block starting addresses and checking their access attributes.

Block-based analysis can detect dependencies between tasks that whole object analysis does not; partially overalapping argu-

PPoPP'12, February 25–29, 2012, New Orleans, Louisiana, USA.
ACM 978-1-4503-1160-1/12/02.

ments are dependencies if a task writes on the overlapping part. Moreover, it supports tasks with non-contiguous arguments in memory, such as a tile of a multidimensional array. BDDT allows the programmer to adjust block granularity to be coarse enough to amortize overhead, yet fine enough to avoid false positives.

Each task in the program goes through four stages: task *issue* performs dependence analysis; task *scheduling* releases a task for execution when all its dependencies are resolved and inserts the task in a worker's queue; task *execution* executes it; task *release* resolves pending dependencies on the executed task, potentially releasing new tasks. Dynamic dependence analysis causes overheads in the issue and release stages. We design the data structures used in the dependence analysis specifically to minimize these overheads.

To efficiently and transparently maintain and retrieve task-argument metadata, we design a custom memory allocator that allows for fast lookup of metadata while still hiding metadata management in the runtime system. The memory allocator forces allocation in such a way that the location of metadata is efficiently deduced from the memory address.

The dependence analysis on blocks is similar to dependence tracking on whole objects, although a task argument may consist of multiple blocks. We have designed a mechanism that allows multiple blocks to share the same metadata information to reduce overhead. Critical dependence tracking operations operate on one metadata element instead of multiple, which greatly reduces the overhead of dependence tracking. We extend this mechanism to track strided arguments—usually multidimensional array tiles: are tracked on each block individually, the runtime system registers a single metadata element for the whole sparse region.

To detect dependencies between tasks, we consider that each block is assigned a new metadata element as new tasks write to it. In principle, each new writing task (i.e., a task that has an output or input/output annotation) creates a new metadata element for the block. All subsequent reading tasks use the same metadata. This divides the task graph into groups of tasks that may execute concurrently and each such group is tracked using a different metadata element. This design allows for an efficient characterization of concurrency while limiting the complexity of the data structures.

3. Implementation

The BDDT block-level runtime system consists of a custom block-based memory allocator; metadata structures for dependence analysis; and a task scheduler.

BDDT Memory Allocator BDDT requires that all memory that constitutes shared state between parallel tasks is allocated through the custom memory allocator. The allocator partitions the virtual address space in *slabs* containing fixed size blocks and services memory allocation requests from such slabs. Data blocks are allocated at the beginning of the slab and the corresponding metadata indices are allocated at the end. By using slabs of fixed size and alignment, we can calculate the address of a block's metadata through very simple and efficient integer arithmetic on the block address, which also increases locality on metadata.

Dependence Analysis The dependence analysis assigns a new version to each block as tasks write new data to it. To do this, BDDT maintains a chain of metadata elements accessed through a metadata array (indexed by the block index stored in the slab), which holds the metadata for each data block. Each metadata element corresponds to a version of the data block, created when a task writes to it. The metadata element includes pointers to the dependent tasks that wait on the corresponding version of the data block, used to resolve task dependencies. Every task element points to metadata elements for all task arguments, an atomic join counter that tracks unresolved dependencies, a function that is the task code, and the actual data, which can be strided array tiles.

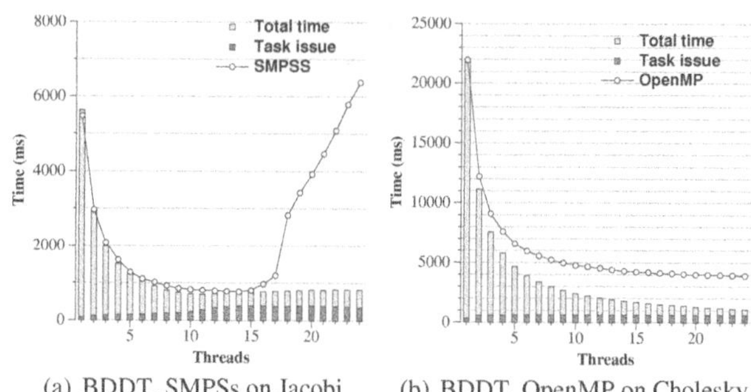

(a) BDDT, SMPSs on Jacobi (b) BDDT, OpenMP on Cholesky

BDDT performs dependence analysis on a per-block basis, depending on the access mode (IN, OUT, INOUT). In each case, the runtime system registers a metadata element for a block when it is first touched. For strided arguments, the runtime system registers a single metadata element for all blocks of the argument, as a single metadata array entry.

Task Scheduling BDDT is based on a master-worker program model. The master is responsible for task issue and dependence analysis, issuing ready tasks to the workers in round-robin order. The workers concurrently perform task scheduling, execution and release. BDDT schedules a task for execution whenever all its dependencies are satisfied. Each worker thread has its own concurrent queue of ready tasks. Upon task completion, the worker walks through the stacks of all of its metadata elements, decrements the join counters of tasks registered with the metadata elements, and releases for execution those tasks with no pending dependencies. Empty workers steal ready tasks from other workers.

4. Conclusions

BDDT is a runtime system that performs dynamic dependence analysis to schedule parallel tasks with memory footprints that span arbitrary memory ranges, producing deterministic execution. BDDT implements efficient and highly concurrent task instantiation, dependence analysis and scheduling techniques. In a set of benchmarks BDDT has similar or better performance than OpenMP, outperforming it by up to a factor of 3.8× at best. BDDT has lower overhead and a more efficient runtime implementation than SMPSs.

References

[1] E. Ayguadé, N. Copty, A. Duran, J. Hoeflinger, Y. Lin, F. Massaioli, X. Teruel, P. Unnikrishnan, and G. Zhang. The Design of OpenMP Tasks. *IEEE TPDS*, 20(3):404–418, 2009.

[2] M. J. Best, S. Mottishaw, C. Mustard, M. Roth, A. Fedorova, and A. Brownsword. Synchronization via Scheduling: Techniques for Efficiently Managing Shared State. In *PLDI*, 2011.

[3] R. Bocchino, V. S. Adve, D. Dig, S. V. Adve, S. Heumann, R. Komuravelli, J. Overbey, P. Simmons, H. Sung, and M. Vakilian. A Type and Effect System for Deterministic Parallel Java. In *OOPSLA*, 2009.

[4] K. Fatahalian, D. R. Horn, T. J. Knight, L. Leem, M. Houston, J. Y. Park, M. Erez, M. Ren, A. Aiken, W. J. Dally, and P. Hanrahan. Sequoia: Programming the Memory Hierarchy. In *SC*, 2006.

[5] J. C. Jenista, Y. H. Eom, and B. Demsky. OoOJava: Software Out-of-Order Execution. In *PPoPP*, 2011.

[6] C. E. Leiserson. The Cilk++ Concurrency Platform. *The Journal of Supercomputing*, 51(3):244–257, 2010.

[7] J. M. Pérez, P. Bellens, R. M. Badia, and J. Labarta. CellSs: Making it Easier to Program the Cell Broadband Engine Processor. *IBM Journal of Research and Development*, 51(5):593–604, 2007.

[8] J. Planas, R. M. Badia, E. Ayguadé, and J. Labarta. Hierarchical Task-Based Programming With StarSs. *International Journal of High Perfomance Computing Applications*, 23(3):284–299, 2009.

Portable Parallel Performance from Sequential, Productive, Embedded Domain-Specific Languages

Shoaib Kamil Derrick Coetzee Scott Beamer Henry Cook Ekaterina Gonina
Jonathan Harper† Jeffrey Morlan Armando Fox

UC Berkeley and †Mississippi State University

{skamil,dcoetzee,sbeamer,hcook,egonina,jmorlan,fox}@cs.berkeley.edu, jwh376@msstate.edu

Abstract

Domain-expert *productivity programmers* desire scalable application performance, but usually must rely on *efficiency programmers* who are experts in explicit parallel programming to achieve it. Since such programmers are rare, to maximize reuse of their work we propose encapsulating their strategies in mini-compilers for domain-specific embedded languages (DSELs) glued together by a common high-level host language familiar to productivity programmers. The nontrivial applications that use these DSELs perform up to 98% of peak attainable performance, and comparable to or better than existing hand-coded implementations. Our approach is unique in that each mini-compiler not only performs conventional compiler transformations and optimizations, but includes imperative procedural code that captures an efficiency expert's strategy for mapping a narrow domain onto a specific type of hardware. The result is source- and performance-portability for productivity programmers and parallel performance that rivals that of hand-coded efficiency-language implementations of the same applications. We describe a framework that supports our methodology and five implemented DSELs supporting common computation kernels.

Our results demonstrate that for several interesting classes of problems, efficiency-level parallel performance can be achieved by packaging efficiency programmers' expertise in a reusable framework that is easy to use for both productivity programmers and efficiency programmers.

Categories and Subject Descriptors D.3.3 [*Programming Languages*]: Frameworks; D.1.3 [*Programming Techniques*]: Parallel programming

General Terms Design, Languages, Performance

Keywords Asp, SEJITS, Python, Domain-Specific Languages

1. Introduction

Domain-expert *productivity programmers* must choose between writing high-level code or working with low-level *efficiency programmers* who understand details of hardware in order to obtain good parallel performance. Instead, we propose that these expert efficiency programmers encapsulate their knowledge of how to make computations in a particular domain fast and parallel into compilers for domain-specific embedded languages (DSELs[1]). These DSELs are coordinated and embedded into a high-level programming language such as Python that can be used by productivity programmers to write their own programmers, but obtain the performance benefits of low-level machine-aware code.

We have created a framework called Asp that helps efficiency programmers write DSEL compilers (which we call *specializers*) by abstracting away many common tasks, including code generation, code caching, and just-in-time compilation. Using this framework, we have built five DSELs in disparate areas such as stencil computations, statistical machine learning, and linear algebra; each of these DSEL compilers are being used in nontrivial applications that achieve performance portability across platforms and obtain peak performance that rivals low-level hand-coded performance for the domain.

```
class Laplacian3D(StencilKernel):
  def kernel(self, in_grid, out_grid):
    # the following lines are translated into
    # parallel C++ loops by the compiler & run
    for x in out_grid.interior_points():
      for y in in_grid.neighbors(x, 1):
        out_grid[x] = out_grid[x] + (1/6)*in_grid[y]
```

Figure 1. Python source code for 3D divergence kernel using the stencil DSEL. The user may specify grid connectivity or use defaults provided by the specializer (not shown).

2. Asp Infrastructure & Walkthrough

The Asp infrastructure provides a number of capabilities for building a DSEL compiler, which can be used as building blocks by the DSEL developer. Specializers are typically used by subclassing a particular class and providing a few functions, which follow documented restrictions based on the specializer's capabilities. On instantiation, the function definitions are introspected and a Python parse tree is generated from them by the Asp framework. At execution time, this tree is then transformed into a DSEL-specific intermediate form, which encapsulates the semantics of the expressed computation— we call this the semantic model (SM). Further tree transformation phases occur, optionally depending on aspects of the input to the specialized function. At the end of these phases, the domain-specific code has been turned into low-level optimized code that is automatically compiled, linked, and run, using

[1] Following Hudak's [3] terminology, we use the acronym DSEL for Domain-Specific Embedded Languages to distinguish them from standalone or "external" DSLs.

PPoPP'12, February 25–29, 2012, New Orleans, Louisiana, USA.
ACM 978-1-4503-1160-1/12/02.

Framework Feature	Used by Specializers	Provided by
Parse Python source to AST	Stencil, BSP, KDT	Asp/Python
Generic lowering translations (e.g. arithmetic expressions)	Stencil, BSP, KDT	Asp
Interrogate available hardware/software	Stencil, GMM	Asp
Generic optimizations	Stencil, BSP	Asp
C++ AST	Stencil, BSP, KDT	Asp
Instantiate templates	GMM, KDT, Akx	Asp
Compile/Invoke C++ with Caching	All except KDT	Asp/CodePy
Tree visitor and translation	Stencil, BSP, KDT	Asp
Tree grammar definition and checking	Stencil	Asp
Fallback to Python version	All	Asp
Auto-tuning & Timing Support	Stencil, GMM, Akx	Asp

Specializer	Application	Logic	Tmpl.	Targets	Performance Remarks
Stencil (structured grid)	Bilateral image filtering	656	0	C++/OpenMP, Cilk+	91% of achievable peak based on roofline model [6]
Gaussian mixture model (GMM) training	Speech diarization	800	3600	CUDA, Cilk+	CPU & GPU versions fast enough to replace original C++/pthreads code
Graph algorithms with KDT/CombBLAS	Graph500 benchmark	325	0	C++/MPI	99% of performance of handcoding in C++
Graph algorithms in BSP style	Social Network Analytics	250	280	C++	56–120% of performance of native C++ Boost version
Matrix powers ($\mathbf{A}^k\mathbf{x}$)	Conjugate gradient solver	200	2000	C/pthreads	2-4 times faster than SciPy

Figure 2. *Top:* Features of the Asp framework and which specializers use them. *Bottom:* For each specializer we report the LOC of logic, LOC of templates, target languages, and a summary of the performance of the Python+SEJITS application compared to the original efficiency-language implementations. Specializer logic is Python code that manipulates intermediate representations in preparation for code generation and templates are static efficiency-language "boilerplate" files into which generated code is interpolated. Our framework itself comprises 2094 LOC.

the CodePy (`http://mathema.tician.de/software/codepy`) library. Optionally, many versions can be generated in order to enable auto-tuning.

An overview of the different features of the Asp framework is shown in Figure 2 (top), as well as which specializers use which capabilities. The next section gives more details about the different DSELs we have implemented.

3. Implemented DSELs & Performance Results

We have implemented five specializers using the Asp framework. The first is a DSEL for stencil computations, which operate on a multidimensional grid and update each point with a function of a subset of its neighbors. We have also implemented two DSELs for graph computations: one using the Knowledge Discovery Toolbox framework (KDT, `kdt.sourceforge.net`) which casts graph algorithms as linear algebra[1]; and one for bulk-synchronous-style graph algorithms similar to Pregel [4]. We have also built auto-tuned libraries as specializers for training Gaussian Mixture Models [2] and for communication-avoiding $A^k x$, a building block in communication-avoiding Krylov subspace methods for solvers [5].

The five specializers, applications, and performance results are summarized in Figure 2 (bottom). Overall, the combination of auto-tuning and just-in-time compilation allows the creation of DSELs that enable non-expert programmers to write Python code that runs as fast or faster than existing low-level libraries or hand-tuned code in the domain in question.

4. Conclusion

With our Asp infrastructure for building DSEL compilers, DSEL developers can leverage the library to perform many common tasks. Our infrastructure is publicly available (`http://github.com/shoaibkamil/asp`), and a number of DSELs are under development. Ultimately, as the number of DSELs increases, parallelism and high performance will be even more accessible to domain scientists for use in their computations while still programming in high-level languages.

Acknowledgments

This work was performed at the UC Berkeley Parallel Computing Laboratory (Par Lab), supported by DARPA (contract #FA8750-10-1-0191) and by the Universal Parallel Computing Research Centers (UPCRC) awards from Microsoft Corp. (Award #024263) and Intel Corp. (Award #024894), with matching funds from the UC Discovery Grant (#DIG07-10227) and additional support from Par Lab affiliates National Instruments, NEC, Nokia, NVIDIA, Oracle, and Samsung.

References

[1] A. Buluç and J. R. Gilbert. The combinatorial BLAS: Design, implementation, and applications. Technical Report UCSB-CS-2010-18, University of California, Santa Barbara, 2010.

[2] H. Cook, E. Gonina, S. Kamil, G. Friedland, and D. P. A. Fox. Cuda-level performance with python-level productivity for gaussian mixture model applications. In *3rd USENIX conference on Hot topics in parallelism (HotPar'11)*, Berkeley, CA, USA, 2011.

[3] P. Hudak. Building domain-specific embedded languages. *ACM Comput. Surv.*, 28:196, December 1996. ISSN 0360-0300. doi: http://doi.acm.org/10.1145/242224.242477.

[4] G. Malewicz, M. Austern, A. Bik, J. Dehnert, I. Horn, N. Leiser, and G. Czajkowski. Pregel: A system for large-scale graph processing. *SIGMOD*, Jun 2010.

[5] M. Mohiyuddin, M. Hoemmen, J. Demmel, and K. Yelick. Minimizing communication in sparse matrix solvers. In *Supercomputing 2009*, Portland, OR, Nov 2009.

[6] S. Williams, A. Waterman, and D. A. Patterson. Roofline: an insightful visual performance model for multicore architectures. *Commun. ACM*, pages 65–76, 2009.

Communication-Centric Optimizations by Dynamically Detecting Collective Operations

Torsten Hoefler

Department of Computer Science
University of Illinois at Urbana-Champaign
htor@illinois.edu

Timo Schneider

Department of Computer Science
Chemnitz University of Technology
timos@cs.tu-chemnitz.de

Abstract

The steady increase of parallelism in high-performance computing platforms implies that communication will be most important in large-scale applications. In this work, we tackle the problem of transparent optimization of large-scale communication patterns using online compilation techniques. We utilize the Group Operation Assembly Language (GOAL), an abstract parallel dataflow definition language, to specify our transformations in a device-independent manner. We develop fast schemes that analyze dataflow and synchronization semantics in GOAL and detect if parts of the (or the whole) communication pattern express a known collective communication operation. The detection of collective operations allows us to replace the detected patterns with highly optimized algorithms or low-level hardware calls and thus improve performance significantly. Benchmark results suggest that our technique can lead to a performance improvement of orders of magnitude compared with various optimized algorithms written in Co-Array Fortran. Detecting collective operations also improves the programmability of parallel languages in that the user does not have to understand the detailed semantics of high-level communication operations in order to generate efficient and scalable code.

Categories and Subject Descriptors D. Software [*D.1. PROGRAMMING TECHNIQUES*]: D.1.3 Concurrent Programming, Parallel Programming

General Terms Performance, Languages

Keywords Collective Communication, Parallel Compiler Optimization, Parallel Dataflow

1. Introduction

Most of today's large-scale parallel codes are implemented in a message-passing programming model using the Message Passing Interface (MPI) standard. MPI offers a large set of predefined communication patterns as *collective operations*. However, parallel programmers sometimes use suboptimal point-to-point algorithms to implement collective semantics. One reason may be that the programmer found a particuler point-to-point algorithm to be faster than the collective implementation on a particuler machine. In addition, other programming paradigms, such as PGAS languages [5, 7] or declarative parallel languages provide a conceptually simpler interface and rely on the compiler or the underlying communication layer for optimizations.

In this work, we describe a detection scheme that can recognize arbitrary collective semantics in parallel codes. This scheme can be used to "search and replace" suboptimal implementations of collective operations during runtime. We use a parallel dataflow analysis to identify the collective semantics and outline automatic transformation schemes to dynamically optimize such detected operations. We utilize GOAL [3] as an intermediate representation (IR) for basic communication operations such as send and receive and the data dependencies between those operations. We show a detailed examples how such IR representations can be extracted from a PGAS code.

1.1 Related Work

Previous works that attempted to detect collective operations performed the detection *post-mortem* by analyzing traces of the program run. Knüpfer et al. proposed a scheme to detect alltoall, scatter, gather, and broadcast by analyzing point-to-point patterns in message traces [4]. Kranzlmüller et al. investigate the detection of repetitive communication patterns in [6]. Like Knüpfer, they only look at single point-to-point operations in MPI traces such that forwarding of data through proxy processes cannot be detected in this scheme.

In this work, we propose a scheme that is guaranteed to detect all collective operations on the full process set in a communication schedule.

2. An Example Transformation

To demonstrate the applicability to PGAS languages we use an example from the MG code—the multigrid kernel from the NAS benchmark suite that was ported to Co-Array Fortran (CAF) [2]:

```
! omitted initializations for brevity
if (this_image().eq.iimage) then
 ibuf(1:n) = ii(1:n)
  call sync_all()
else
  call sync_all()
  ii(1:n) = ibuf(1:n)[iimage]
endif
 call sync_all()
```

The compilation of the pCFG, similarly as described in [1], would be used to track the dataflow from one image to another. A dataflow analysis identifies the buffer `ibuf(1:n)` on process `iimage` as source and the buffers `ii(1:n)` on all images as destinations of the flow. The compiler can now simply insert send and

PPoPP'12, February 25–29, 2012, New Orleans, Louisiana, USA.
ACM 978-1-4503-1160-1/12/02.

receive statements at the synchronization points (`sync_all()`). This would then result in the following GOAL code:

```
! omitted initializations for brevity
if (this_image().eq.iimage) then
 ibuf(1:n) = ii(1:n)
endif
call GOAL_Create(g)
if (this_image().eq.iimage) then
  call GOAL_Send(g, ibuf, n*8, iimage, ierr)
else
  call GOAL_Recv(g,ii,n*8,GOAL_ANY_SOURCE,ierr)
endif
call GOAL_Compile(g, sched)
```

The serial compiler transformation to emit the communication schedule is outside the scope of this work. We now discuss how to recognize the logical broadcast and replace the messaging schedule in the GOAL compile step accordingly. The CAF NAS codes include numerous occurrences of logical broadcast and allreduce calls similar to the one demonstrated above because the presented code is a natural way to express data movement in PGAS languages.

2.1 Dataflow Analysis

The `GOAL_Compile()` step above is executed during runtime and allows for dynamic optimizations, similar to the well-known commit phase in MPI Datatypes. A dataflow analysis computes the flows from all *original sends* to all *final receives*. An original send is a send operation that specifies local memory that has not been received from another process and a final receive is a receive that specifies user memory as destination.

In the following, we assume that the transformed example CAF code is running with six processes. The compile call is collective across all images (processes) and collects the complete global communication graph. The left part of Figure 1 shows the global communication graph for the linear broadcast as collected in compile. Each arrow represents a send from the source buffer to the destination buffer. The source buffer and process for each final destination is encoded as a tuple and a simple pattern matching on this tuple determines that the pattern (or a subset) is a known collective operation. In this case, all processes receive data from a single buffer at rank `iimage`, i.e., `iimage` is source of a broadcast operation. Our scheme detects all collective operations defined in MPI.

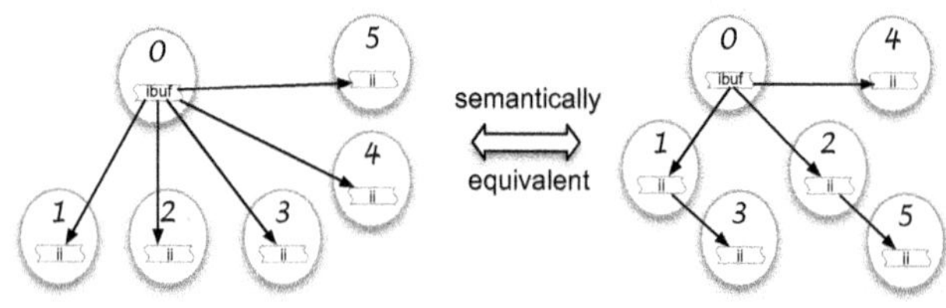

Figure 1. Example Schedules.

2.2 Schedule Transformation

The right part of Figure 1 shows a semantically equivalent communication graph in a tree shape. This graph was automatically transformed after the broadcast operation was detected by removing all communication edges of the broadcast and inserting a well-known binomial tree algorithm into the schedule.

2.3 Experimental Evaluation

We now compare the performance of the broadcast as shown in the CAF example code with an optimized implementation on a Cray XK6 system. We used the Cray 4.0.30 Programming Environment and the communicated data size was a single double value. Figure 2

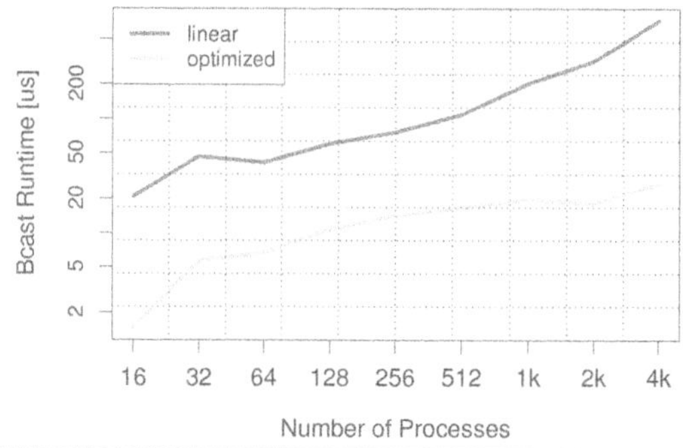

Figure 2. Naive vs. Optimized Performance in Cray XK6.

compares the performance of both implementations. The optimized implementation is up to a factor of 26 faster than the simple CAF implementation.

3. Discussion and Conclusion

We demonstrated novel dataflow techniques for the automatic and transparent detection and transformations of collective operations. These techniques can be used to detect arbitrary collective operations by pattern matching data-movement from source to destination buffers in arbitrary communication topologies. The techniques can easily extended to define semantic equivalence of other communication patterns and enable automatic transformations on the communication graph. For example, detecting collective operations on subsets of processes is a harder problem and left for future work.

Acknowledgments

This work was supported by the DOE Office of Science, Advanced Scientific Computing Research, under award number DE-FC02-10ER26011, program manager Sonia Sachs.

References

[1] G. Bronevetsky. Communication-sensitive static dataflow for parallel message passing applications. In *Proc. of the 7th IEEE/ACM Intl. Symp. on Code Generation and Optimization*, CGO '09, pages 1–12, 2009.

[2] C. Coarfa, Y. Dotsenko, J. Mellor-Crummey, F. Cantonnet, T. El-Ghazawi, A. Mohanti, Y. Yao, and D. Chavarría-Miranda. An evaluation of global address space languages: co-array fortran and unified parallel c. In *Proc. of the tenth ACM SIGPLAN Symp. on Princ. and Practice of Par. Progr.*, PPoPP '05, pages 36–47. ACM, 2005.

[3] T. Hoefler, C. Siebert, and A. Lumsdaine. Group Operation Assembly Language - A Flexible Way to Express Collective Communication. In *38th Intl. Conf. on Par. Proc., ICPP'09*, 2009.

[4] A. Knüpfer, D. Kranzlmüller, and W. E. Nagel. Detection of Collective MPI Operation Patterns. In *Proc. of EuroPVM/MPI'04*, volume 3241 of *LNCS*, pages 259–267. 2004.

[5] R. W. Numrich and J. Reid. Co-array fortran for parallel programming. *SIGPLAN Fortran Forum*, 17:1–31, August 1998. ISSN 1061-7264.

[6] R. Preissl, T. Köckerbauer, M. Schulz, D. Kranzlmüller, B. R. d. Supinski, and D. J. Quinlan. Detecting Patterns in MPI Communication Traces. In *Proc. of the 37th Intl. Conf. on Par. Proc., ICPP'08*, pages 230–237, 2008.

[7] UPC Consortium. UPC Language Specifications, v1.2. Technical report, Lawrence Berkeley National Laboratory, 2005. LBNL-59208.

LHlf: Lock-free Linear Hashing (poster paper)

Donghui Zhang
Microsoft Jim Gray Systems Lab
634 W Main St, 4th floor, Madison, WI 53703
dozhan@microsoft.com

Per-Åke Larson
Microsoft Research
One Microsoft Way, Redmond, WA 98052
palarson@microsoft.com

Abstract

LHlf is a new hash table designed to allow very high levels of concurrency. The table is lock free and grows and shrinks automatically according to the number of items in the table. Insertions, lookups and deletions are never blocked. LHlf is based on linear hashing but adopts recursive split-ordering of the items within a bucket to be able to split and merge lists in a lock free manner. LHlf is as fast as the best previous lock-free design and in addition it offers stable performance, uses less space, and supports both expansions and contractions.

Categories and Subject Descriptors E.1 [**Data Structures**]: distributed Data Structures.

General Terms Algorithms, Performance, Design.

Keywords lock-free; hash table; linear hashing; split-order.

1. Introduction

LHlf (Linear Hashing, lock-free) is a new lock-free hash table design. LHlf automatically grows and shrinks the table according to the load; previous lock-free designs have only supported expansion. LHlf is space efficient; in a quiescent state, its representation in memory is essentially the same as that of a sequential hash table. Finally, LHlf's performance is stable because the work of resizing the table is spread over threads and over time.

LHlf is based on linear hashing (LH) which was originally designed for hash files by Litwin [5] and adapted for main-memory hash tables by Larson [4]. LHlf implements dynamic arrays using segments of exponentially increasing size as proposed by Griswold and Townsend [1].

LH gradually expands a hash table by splitting buckets. During a split, on average, half of the items in the bucket are relocated to a new bucket. We adopt an idea by Shalev and Shavit [8] and order the items in a bucket in recursive-split order. This allows a bucket to be split in a lock-free manner; all that is required is to identify the split point and cut the linked list in two.

Table 1: Feature comparison of four hash table designs.

	Fixed size, lock free	LH with locks	RSO [8]	LHlf
Efficient in time	Not always	May block	X	X
Expandable		X	X	X
Contractible		X		X
Scales to a large number of threads	X		X	X
Efficient in space	Not always	X		X
Stable performance	X	X		X

PPoPP'12, February 25–29, 2012, New Orleans, Louisiana, USA.
ACM 978-1-4503-1160-1/12/02.

Table 1 summarizes six desired features of a hash table and compares four hash table designs. A fixed-size hash table is very efficient when correctly sized but if it is undersized, performance suffers; if it is oversized, space is wasted. LH with locking does not scale to a very large number of threads. Shalev's and Shavit's design (RSO) [8] does not support table contraction, requires extra space for dummy nodes, and its performance is not stable. Only LHlf has all six desired features.

2. Main Ideas

Figure 1 shows an example of an LHlf hash table. The table is essentially a variable-size array of pointers, which is implemented by a two level structure: a small directory and a set of array segments. Each segment is an array of bucket pointers where a bucket pointer is the head of a single linked list of data nodes.

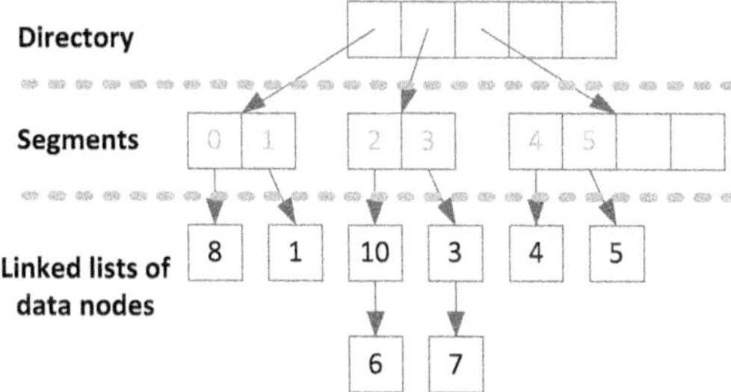

Figure 1. An example of an LHlf with six buckets.

2.1 Dynamic Array Implementation

The original version of linear hashing used array segments of fixed size. This has the drawback that for a very large table the directory also becomes very large. We want to use a small, fixed size directory for LHlf that fits entirely in an L1 cache. We adopted the solution proposed by Griswold and Townsend [1] of using segments of exponentially increasing size. In Figure 1, the second segment is 1X larger than the first segment; the third segment is 2X larger; the fourth segment will be 4X larger; and so on. We modified this idea slightly by allowing the table to have an upper size limit on a single segment.

2.2 Parallel Splitting and Merging

The original version of linear hashing expands or contracts the table by splitting or merging one bucket at a time, which means that the table cannot expand fast enough under very high insertion rates.

To avoid this limitation LHlf performs expansions and contractions in larger steps (multiple buckets at a time) and allows multiple threads to split (or merge) different buckets concurrently. When a thread detects that the table needs to be expanded, all it does is increment the table size by a fixed amount, set the table state to Splitting and the new buckets to Uninitialized. Any thread that hits an Uninitialized bucket first performs a bucket split. Similarly, any thread can contribute by splitting a bucket, allowing the splitting of a group of buckets to proceed in parallel.

2.3 Recursive-Split-Ordered Lists

The original version of linear hashing did not impose any ordering of the items on a list so splitting a bucket required a complete scan of its linked list. LHlf keeps the lists sorted in recursive-split order [8], that is, in increasing order of the reverse-bit values of the hash keys. This ordering makes it possible to split a bucket by cutting the list into two pieces and connecting the tail piece to the new bucket.

2.4 Atomic Operations Required

LHlf relies only on 64-bit and 128-bit atomic load, store and compare-and-swap (CAS) instructions to achieve consistency. Our actual implementation uses the machine-independent interlocked-compare-exchange family of functions available on Windows, such as *InterlockedCompareExchange128*, which are compiled into the appropriate assembly instruction.

2.5 Hazard Pointers

LHlf adopts Michael's hazard pointer scheme [7] to protect from memory access violations. Each thread uses up to five hazard pointers, two protecting segments and three protecting nodes. Note that other memory management schemes are possible, e.g. the Repeat Offender Problem and its solutions [3].

2.6 State Transitions and Helping

Like other lock free data structures, threads in LHlf help each other. LHlf breaks an operation into smaller atomic steps and carefully tracks what steps have been completed. Any thread can attempt the next atomic step. If it succeeds, it records that the step has been completed by atomically changing the state of the target object of the operation.

LHlf has state machines for four types of objects: hash table, segment, bucket, and node. Every state machine has a Normal state. When the data structure is quiescent, it looks just like a normal hash table in main memory. When the data structure is being updated, the threads do not immediately follow pointers that are not Normal; instead, they first help to fix up the state of the data structure to make the pointer Normal again.

3. Performance Evaluation

We experimentally evaluated four different hash table designs.

LHlf: lock-free linear hashing.

RSO: the dynamic lock-free hash table [8] that stores RSO values in every node and uses dummy nodes.

Fixed[8M]: a fixed-size lock-free hash table [2][6] with 8*1024*1024 buckets.

LH_lock: lock-based linear hashing using 1M spinlocks to protect buckets and one spinlock to protect expansions and contractions.

The experimental data consists of 480M distinct string keys with average length 12 bytes. 30M records were first loaded into the hash table and then a mixed workload (90% search, 6% insertions, and 4% deletions) was run for one second and the total number of operations counted. The experiments were performed on an HP ProLiant DL980 machine with eight Intel Xeon X7560 @ 2.27GHz Nehalem processors with a total of 64 cores and 128 hardware threads.

Figure 2 plots the throughput as the number of threads increases from 1 to 128. Average bucket size was 4 records. LH_Lock has the best performance when the number of threads is small but it does not scale to a large number of threads due to lock contention. Among the lock-free versions Fixed[8M] has the best performance, because it does not have to check for and handle concurrent table expansions and contractions, but the others are close.

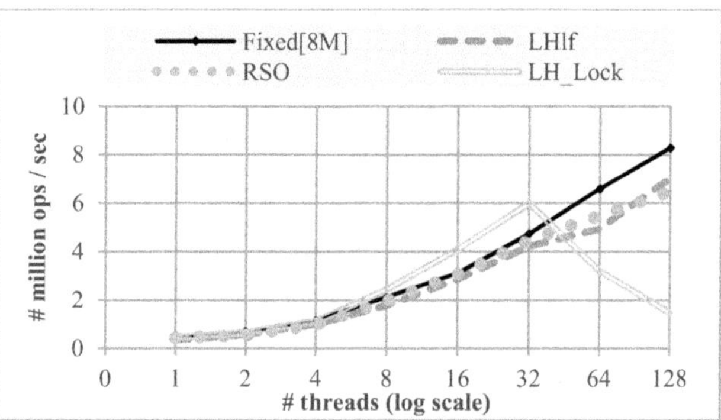

Figure 2: Varying #threads.

Figure 3 compares the performance when varying the number of pre-inserted records. Here the number of threads is 128, and the dynamic hash schemes expand the table when the average bucket size exceeds 4. The performance of Fixed[8M] drops as the number of records increases because the average chain length increases. The performance of RSO fluctuates significantly and in a cyclic manner with the length of each cycle doubling. The reason for this phenomenon is that, right after each directory doubling, half of the newly added buckets are uninitialized and accessing one of these buckets leads to an expensive bucket split. LHlf has much more stable performance because expansions are smooth and gradual.

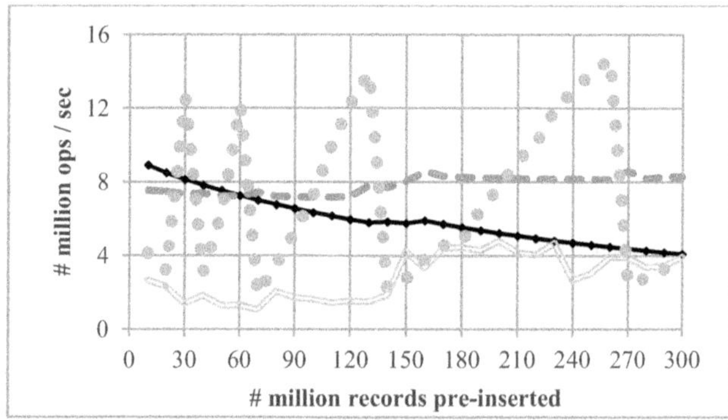

Figure 3: Varying amount of pre-insertions.

References

[1] Griswold, W. G. and Townsend, G. M. 1993. The Design and Implementation of Dynamic Hashing for Sets and Tables in Icon". *Software - Practice and Experience*, 23(4):351-67.

[2] Harris, T. L. 2001. A Pragmatic Implementation of Non-Blocking Linked-Lists. *DISC '01*: 300-314.

[3] Herlihy, M., Luchangco, V., and Moir, M. 2002. The Repeat Offender Problem: A Mechanism for Supporting Dynamic-Sized, Lock-Free Data Structures. *DISC '02*: 339-353.

[4] Larson, P.-Å. 1988. Dynamic Hash Tables, *CACM* 31(4): 446–457.

[5] Litwin, W. 1980. Linear Hashing: A New Tool for File and Table Addressing, *VLDB '80*: 212–223.

[6] Michael, M. M. 2002. High Performance Dynamic Lock-free Hash Tables and List-based Sets. *SPAA '02*: 73-82.

[7] Michael, M. M. 2004. Hazard Pointers: Safe Memory Reclamation for Lock-Free Objects. *IEEE TPDS* 15(6): 491-504.

[8] Shalev, O. and Shavit, N. 2006. Split-ordered Lists: Lock-free Extensible Hash Tables. *JACM* 53(3): 379-405.

Wait-Free Linked-Lists *

Shahar Timnat Anastasia Braginsky Alex Kogan Erez Petrank
Dept. of Computer Science, Technion
{stimnat, anastas, sakogan, erez}@cs.technion.ac.il

Abstract

The linked-list data structure is fundamental and ubiquitous. Lock-free versions of the linked-list are well known. However, the existence of a practical wait-free linked-list has been open. In this work we designed such a linked-list. To achieve better performance, we have also extended this design using the fast-path-slow-path methodology. The resulting implementation achieves performance which is competitive with that of Harris's lock-free list, while still guaranteeing non-starvation via wait-freedom. We have also developed a proof for the correctness and the wait-freedom of our design.

Categories and Subject Descriptors D.1.3 [*Programming Techniques*]: Concurrent Programming

General Terms Algorithms, Design, Performance

1. Introduction

A linked-list is one of the most commonly used data structures. The linked-list seems a good candidate for parallelization, as list modifications to different parts of the list may be executed independently and concurrently. Indeed parallel linked-lists with various progress properties abundant in literature. Most notably, lock-free linked-lists are well known. A lock-free data structure ensures that when several threads are concurrently accessing the data structure, at least one of them makes progress within a bounded number of steps. While this property ensures general system progress, it does not prevent starvation of a particular thread, or even of all the threads but one. Wait-free data structures ensure that each thread makes progress within a bounded number of steps, regardless of other threads' concurrent execution. However, practical concurrent data structures that ensure wait-freedom are notoriously hard to design. It was only recently that wait-free designs for the simple stack and queue data structures appeared in the literature [1, 6]. The stack and the queue have limited parallelism, as they have a limited number of contention points (e.g., the head of the stack, and the head and the tail of the queue). An interesting question that arises is whether it is possible to design an efficient wait-free algorithm for any highly parallel data structure. To the best of our knowledge, there is no wait-free linked-list algorithm available in the literature except for use of universal constructions, which are inefficient and impractical. We are not aware of any practical wait-free design for any more complex data structure as well.

The main contribution of this work is a practical, linearizable, fast and wait-free linked-list. Our construction builds on the lock-free linked-list of Harris [3], and extends it using a helping mechanism to become wait-free. The main technical difficulty is making sure that helping threads perform each operation correctly, apply each operation exactly once, and return a consistent result (of success or failure) according to whether each of the threads completed the operation successfully. Next, we extended our design using the fast-path-slow-path methodology of Kogan and Petrank [7], in order to achieve performance which is almost equivalent to that of the lock-free linked-list of Harris.

Our wait-free linked-list design follows the traditional practice, in which concurrent linked-list data structures realize a sorted list, where each key may only appear once [2, 3, 5, 8, 9]. An attempt to INSERT a new node with a key that already exists results in a failure.

We have implemented the wait-free linked-list and compared its efficiency with the implementation of Harris' lock-free linked-list. The naive algorithm has a substantial overhead, performing worse by a factor of three when compared to Harris' lock-free algorithm. However, the application of the fast-path-slow-path extension reduces the overhead significantly, bringing it to about 2-5%. This seems to be a reasonable overhead to be paid in practice for obtaining a non-starvation guarantee. In this brief announcement we present only a general description of our algorithm, and of the main challenges we encountered.

1.1 Background and Related Work

The first lock-free linked-list was presented by Valois [9]. A simpler and more efficient lock-free algorithm was designed by Harris [3], Michael [8] added a hazard-pointers mechanism to allow lock-free memory management for this algorithm. Fomitchev and Rupert achieved better theoretical complexity in [2]. Herlihy and Shavit implemented a variation of Harris's algorithm [5], and we used this implementation both for comparison and as the basis for the Java code that we developed. Recently, wait-free queues were presented in [1, 6]. A different approach for building concurrent lock-free or wait-free data structures, is the use of universal constructions [4, 5]. However, universal constructions (at least for the linked-list) are inefficient and non-scalable.

In these proceedings, Kogan and Petrank [7] present a technique called fast-path-slow-path, which makes wait-free algorithms almost as efficient as their lock-free counterparts. This technique combines a slower wait-free implementation of a data structure with a faster lock-free implementation, in order to achieve both the faster lock-free performance (or nearly so), and the stronger non-starvation guarantee of the wait-free implementation. We use the fast-path-slow-path methodology in this work to achieve an efficient and wait-free linked-list. The higher complexity of the

* This work was supported by the Israeli Science Foundation grant No. 283/10.

PPoPP'12, February 25–29, 2012, New Orleans, Louisiana, USA.
ACM 978-1-4503-1160-1/12/02.

linked-list (compared to the queue) and its higher potential parallelism, makes the application of the fast-path-slow-path methodology more involved than the application of this method for the queue as presented in [7].

2. The Algorithm: an Overview

The wait-free linked-list supports three operations: INSERT, DELETE, and CONTAINS. All of them run in a wait-free manner. The algorithm builds on Harris's lock-free linked-list [3], and uses an enhanced helping mechanism to make it wait-free. Similarly to Harris's linked-list, our list contains sentinel head and tail nodes, and the *next* pointer in each node can be marked using a special *mark bit*, to signify that the entry in the node is logically deleted.

To achieve wait-freedom, a helping mechanism is used. The helping mechanism employs a special *state* array, with an entry for each thread. When a thread wishes to perform an operation on the list, it first chooses a phase number, higher than all phase numbers previously selected, and posts an operation-descriptor in its *state* array entry. The operation descriptor describes the operation it wishes to perform and also contains the phase number. Next, the thread goes through all the *state* array, and helps perform operations with smaller or equal phase numbers. This ensures wait-freedom: a delayed operation eventually receives help from all threads and soon completes.

Designing a concurrent algorithm in the presence of helping threads is a lot more difficult than designing the lock-free counterpart, because the wait-free version with all the helping threads must deal with many more potential races. One major difficulty with helping threads occurs when several threads are attempting a similar operation (such as DELETE 6) concurrently and several more threads are helping them to apply it. At the end, we must apply this operation only once (correctly) and properly report success or failure to each of the threads that initiated the operation (even though the operation might have been applied by a helping thread who later stopped responding). While in the lock-free list, each thread knows whether or not it succeeded because it is the one who performs the CAS that causes the (logical) deletion, the same is not true for the wait-free linked-list. To deal with this added complexity, we employed a designated additional *success* bit in each node's *next* pointer, on which the concurrent DELETE operations compete to determine which of them completed *successfully*. The idea is that when several DELETE operations of the same key are executed concurrently, the actual deletion of the node is done using the help mechanism, but once the node is already deleted, only the threads that initiated the operation (and not the helping threads) compete on setting the additional *success* bit, to determine which of them owns this deletion. This settles the owner of the success in a wait-free manner.

To use this mechanism, we partitioned the DELETE operation into two distinct steps, and provided help for each of them independently. The first step in the DELETE operation is a *search_delete* step, in which the physical node, nominated for deletion, is selected (with help). Next, an *execute_delete* step is executed (with help), in which this selected node is logically deleted by marking its *next* pointer. This delicate partition ensures that for a single DELETE operation, all helping threads might only try to delete the same specific node, selected in the *search_delete state*. The thread that initiate the DELETE operation will compete on the *success* bit of this particular node. We believe that this technique for determining success of a thread in executing an operation in the presence of helping threads can be useful in future constructions of wait-free algorithms.

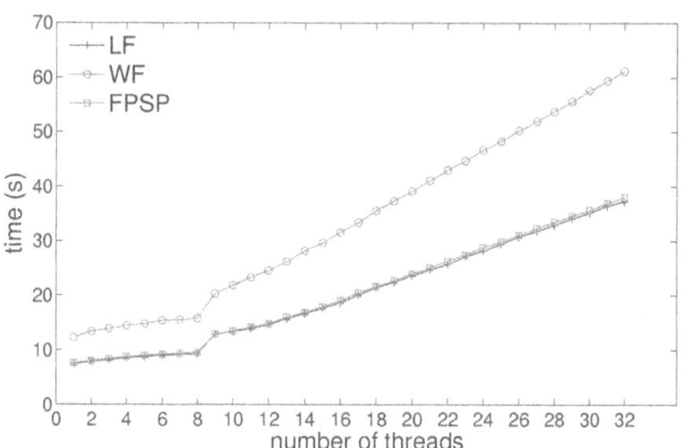

3. Performance

We compared both our basic wait-free linked-list implementation and the fast-path-slow-path version of it against the lock-free linked-list of Harris. The implementations we used were written in Java. The lock-free Java implementation we compared against is by Herlihy and Shavit [5] and available on the Internet. All the tests were run on SUN's Java SE Runtime, version 1.6.0. We ran the measurements on an IBM x3400 system featuring 2 Intel(R) Xeon(R) E5310 1.60GHz quad core processors (overall 8 cores) with a memory of 16GB and an L2 cache of 8MB per processor. In this brief announcement we only report a single micro-benchmark. In this benchmark each thread did one million operations, out of which 50% were insertions, and 50% were deletions. The keys were randomly and uniformly chosen in the range $[1, 1024]$. Each test was run with the number of threads ranging from 1 to 32. Each test was repeated 20 times, and the average of the runs is reported. The standard deviation remained below 2% in most measurements, once peaking above 5% and reaching 6.2%. It turns out that the fast-path-slow-path results nearly matches those of the lock-free algorithm.

Acknowledgments

We thank Maurice Herlihy for his enlightening comments.

References

[1] Panagiota Fatourou and Nikolaos D. Kallimanis. A highly-efficient wait-free universal construction. In *SPAA*, pages 325–334, 2011.

[2] Mikhail Fomitchev and Eric Ruppert. Lock-free linked lists and skip lists. In *PODC'04*, pages 50–59, New York, NY, USA, 2004. ACM.

[3] Timothy L. Harris. A pragmatic implementation of non-blocking linked-lists. In *DISC '01*, London, UK, 2001. Springer-Verlag.

[4] Maurice Herlihy. A methodology for implementing highly concurrent objects. *ACM Trans. Program. Lang. Syst.*, 15(5):745–770, 1993.

[5] Maurice Herlihy and Nir Shavit. *The Art of Multiprocessor Programming*. Morgan Kaufmann, 2008.

[6] Alex Kogan and Erez Petrank. Wait-free queues with multiple enqueuers and dequeuers. In *PPOPP*, pages 223–234, 2011.

[7] Alex Kogan and Erez Petrank. A methodology for creating fast wait-free data structures. In *PPOPP*, 2012.

[8] Maged M. Michael. High performance dynamic lock-free hash tables and list-based sets. In *SPAA '02*, pages 73–82, New York, NY, USA, 2002. ACM.

[9] John D. Valois. Lock-free linked lists using compare-and-swap. In *PODC '95*, pages 214–222, New York, NY, USA, 1995. ACM.

Scalable Parallel Debugging with Statistical Assertions

Minh Ngoc Dinh, David Abramson, Chao Jin
Monash University, Clayton, 3800, Victoria, Australia
{ngoc.minh.dinh,david.abramson,chao.jin}@monash.edu

Andrew Gontarek, Bob Moench, Luiz DeRose
Cray Inc, Saint Paul, MN 55101-2987, United States
{andrewg,rwm,ldr}@cray.com

Abstract

Traditional debuggers are of limited value for modern scientific codes that manipulate large complex data structures. This paper discusses a novel debug-time assertion, called a "Statistical Assertion", that allows a user to reason about large data structures, and the primitives are parallelised to provide an efficient solution. We present the design and implementation of statistical assertions, and illustrate the debugging technique with a molecular dynamics simulation. We evaluate the performance of the tool on a 12,000 cores Cray XE6.

Categories and Subject Descriptors **D.2.5** [Testing and Debugging:] Distributed debugging; Code inspections and walk-throughs

General Terms Performance, Verification.

Keywords parallel debugging, statistic, assertion

1. Introduction

Our earlier work has demonstrated that ad hoc debug-time assertions can assist in parallel debugging tasks because it is not necessary to examine every value in a large data structure [1]. More importantly, a parallel computer can be used to execute the assertion logic, making it efficient when used on large data structures and machines. This research introduces a new type of ad hoc debug-time assertion called a *Statistical Assertion.* Such assertions allow users to reason about derived metrics rather than the raw data. The essence of this approach is to (1) diminish the substantial amount of raw data to manageable "blocks"; (2) alleviate the complexity in managing the data decomposition across a large number of processors; and (3) leverage parallelism to make the system fast enough for real time debugging.

2. Statistical Assertions

A *statistical assertion* is defined as a user-defined predicate consisting of two *data models* in the form of either statistical primitives (e.g. mean or standard deviation values) or data models (e.g. histograms or density functions). Statistical assertions allow the user to compare data pattern information between two data structures, instead of comparing the exact values like the assertions used in our previous works [1, 2]. Our debugging framework addresses two significant issues. First, it needs to support a wide range of useful statistics, and it is desirable to compute these in parallel in order to provide real time debugging of large datasets. Second, the framework has to allow users to create arbitrary user-defined data models.

PPoPP'12, February 25–29, 2012, New Orleans, Louisiana, USA.
ACM 978-1-4503-1160-1/12/02.

2.1 Split-phase Statistical Operation

The parallel computation of basic statistics such as average, max, min is relatively straight forward; however, more complex statistics require special handling. The overall computation can be broken into two processes to make the parallel part explicit.

Parallel: calculate a set of primary statistics from the input dataset. This phase is embarrassingly parallel as it does not involving any inter-process communication; and

Aggregation: assemble a collection of primary statistics to form a full statistical model.

2.2 User-defined Abstract Data Model

As discussed earlier, users need to create arbitrary data models. In order to create accurate distributions, we need to perform quite a few computations, and it is desirable to parallelize this operation as well. The split-phase scheme presented above can be used to create distributions in parallel.

3. Implementation

3.1 User-defined Statistic Function

Users can create their own statistical reduction function using C programming language. The code is compiled and linked into the debugger binary in runtime. To make it easier for a user to write statistical functions, we have defined an API that standardises the interface. Furthermore, to enforce the split-phase statistic framework discussed in section 2.1, a general template is provided in which a few compulsory functions are expected.

```
func my_func(data)
    define my_func_server(data)=server_result
    define my_func_client(collection)=client_result
end
```

3.2 User-defined Data Models

To help users create abstract data models, we introduce a new debugger built-in function, called *randset*, that defines random variates. Currently, Guard supports various typical distribution models including Gaussian, Poisson, and Maxwell-Boltzmann.

```
randset(<distribution_name>,<dataset_size>,...)
```

3.3 Architectural Details

Guard employs a client/server model, where the debugger is divided into a single front-end client and multiple servers (Figure 2). The details of how this architecture is useful for processing ad hoc debug-time assertions is discussed fully in our previous works [1, 3]. More importantly, an assertion in Guard is compiled into a low-level graph description upon creation [3], and is executed by a special interpreter as illustrated in Figure 1.

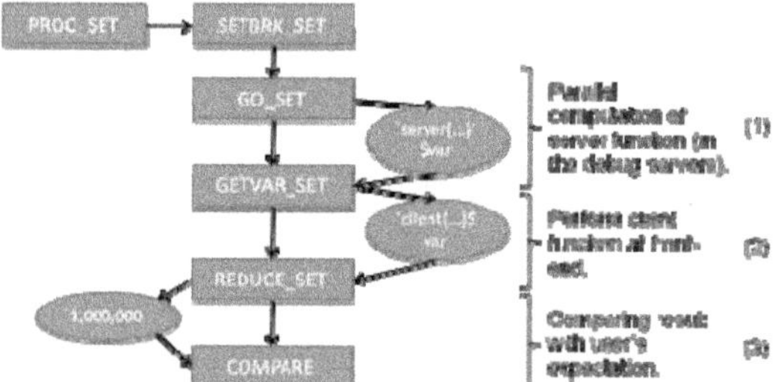

Figure 1 - Abstract execution of statistical assertion

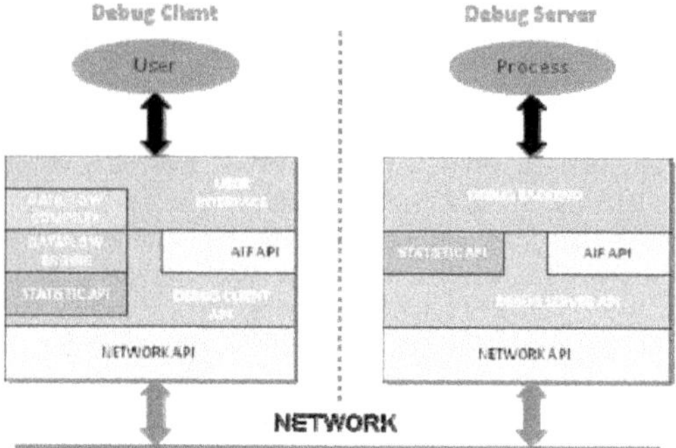

Figure 2 - Guard layered architecture with Statistic API

4. Case Study: Molecular dynamics

We used a parallel molecular dynamics code written in C using MPI and replicated a set of program bugs presented in Frenkel et. al. [4] to illustrate the expressive power and potential of statistical assertions for finding errors.

4.1 Monitoring Particles' Speeds

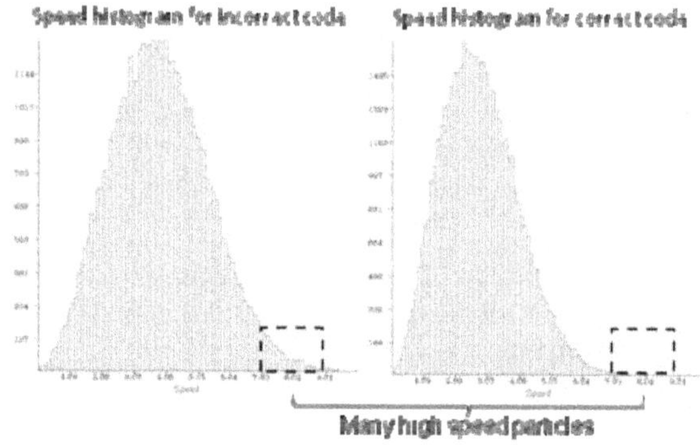

Figure 3 – Speed histogram comparison

In any given fluid, the speed varies a great deal, from very slow particles to very fast ones. However, this scalar value spreads according to Maxwell-Boltzmann distribution [4]. Therefore, monitoring particles' speeds can help detecting anomalies in a simulation. This is done with the *histogram assertion* below:

create $model=randset(maxwell, 49152, 6, 2)
set reduce histogram(100,0.0,10.0)
assert $a::speed_array@pmd.c:28~$model<0.02

4.2 Energy Conservation

The law of *energy conservation* states that the total amount of energy in an isolated system remains constant. Therefore, a drift of this quantity may signal programming errors. To detect this we trigger a *standard deviation assertion* after each simulation cycle to ensure this quantity does not alter significantly.

assert stdev($a::totEnergy@pmd.c:28) < 0.1#

5. Performance Evaluation

We evaluate the performance on a Cray XE6 system, with 17,472 cores. To demonstrate that the approach is applicable to large-scale scientific codes, we use data structure sizes in a real molecular dynamics simulation with a 209x10^6 atoms [5].

5.1 Strong Scaling Experiment

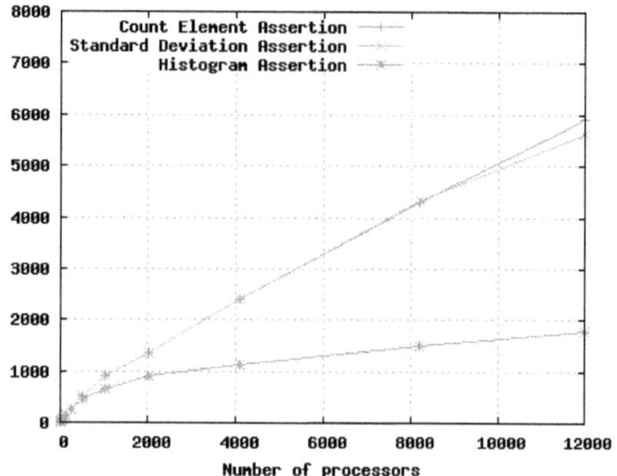

Figure 4 - Assertions speedup against #processors

5.2 Weak Scaling Experiment

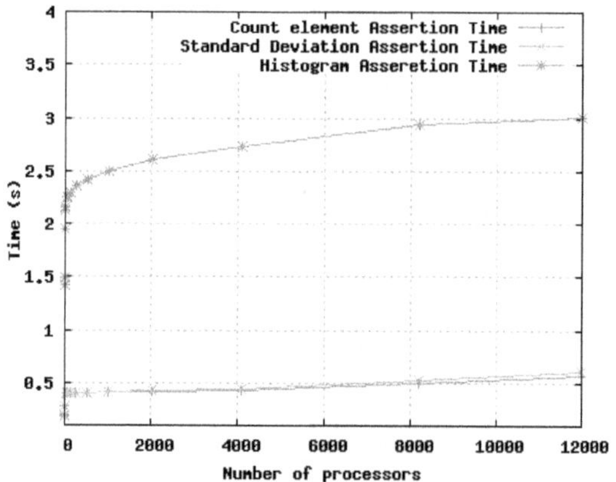

Figure 5 - Weak scaling assertion evaluation time

References

[1] M. N. Dinh, D. Abramson, D. Kurniawan, C. Jin, B. Moench, and L. DeRose, "Assertion based parallel debugging", in *CCGrid*, Newport Beach, 2011.

[2] D. Abramson, M. N. Dinh, D. Kurniawan, B. Moench, and L. DeRose, "Data Centric Highly Parallel Debugging", in *HPDC*, Chicago, 2010.

[3] G. R. Watson, "The Design and Implementation of a Parallel Relative Debugger", in *Faculty of Information Technology*. vol. PhD Thesis Melbourne: Monash University, 2000, p. 197.

[4] D. Frenkel and B. Smit, *Understanding Molecular Simulations: From Algorithms to Applications*, 2 ed. Elsevier Science & Technology, 2002.

[5] P. S. Branicio, R. K. Kalia, A. Nakano, and P. Vashishta, "Shock-Induced Structural Phase Transition, Plasticity, and Brittle Cracks in Aluminum Nitride Ceramic", *PHYSICAL REVIEW LETTERS*, vol. 96, issue 6, 2005.

Verification of Software Barriers

Alexander Malkis Anindya Banerjee
IMDEA Software Institute
{alexander.malkis,anindya.banerjee}@imdea.org

Abstract

This paper describes frontiers in verification of the software barrier synchronization primitive. So far most software barrier algorithms have not been mechanically verified. We show preliminary results in automatically proving the correctness of the major software barriers.

Categories and Subject Descriptors D.2.4 [*Software engineering*]: Software/program verification—Correctness proofs; Formal methods; Assertion checkers

General Terms verification, algorithms, reliability, theory

Keywords software, barrier, verification, invariant, safety, verifier, counting, central, dissemination, tournament, static, combining, implementation, client

1. Introduction

The software barrier is a standard concurrency primitive. It enables threads to synchronize in the following manner: if a thread calls the barrier function, the barrier function starts waiting until all other threads also call the barrier function. After all other threads have called the barrier function, the waiting stops, and all the threads are allowed to proceed with the instruction following the call to the barrier function.

The *barrier property* we would like to verify is: if one thread passes the barrier, all the other threads have already arrived at it. The paper is devoted to proving just this fact for the major barrier algorithms [1]. We present an overview of the results; the details and the related work are deferred to the full paper version.

2. The simplest central barrier

A trivial implementation of the barrier involves a counter. The counter is initially the number of (participating) threads and gets decreased when a thread enters the barrier. Only when the counter is zero, all the threads are allowed to proceed. Each thread executes thus the following code:

A: cnt−−; B: **while**(cnt≠0); C:

We want to show that when one thread arrives at location C, all the others are no more at location A. To show that, we need the ability to express that at any time point in an execution of the program, the value of cnt is at least the number of threads at location A, i.e., cnt$\geq|\{t\in Tid|pc_t=$A$\}|$. As of year 2011, no usable automatic theorem prover can reason about such formulas.

To overcome this restriction, we syntactically convert the multithreaded program into a nondeterministic one working on sets A, B, and C, where A (resp. B or C) is the set of threads whose current control flow location is A (resp. B or C). The problematic formula now turns into a benign cnt $\geq|A|$, which lies in the QFBAPA logic.

We have verified the central barrier in the verification system Jahob.

3. Tree-based barriers

We will verify the static and combining tree barriers in Jahob.

Static tree barrier. In the static tree barrier threads operate on a single tree, in which each thread is statically associated with a distinct tree node, e.g.:

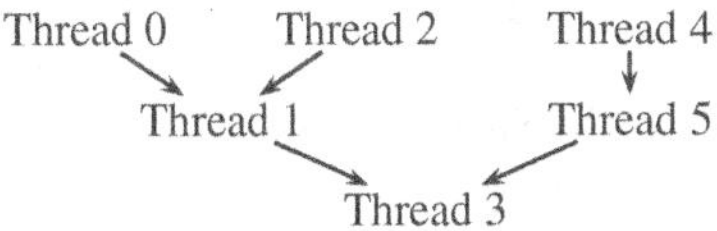

A thread proceeds in two phases: synchronization and wake-up. A thread (say, number 1) starts in the synchronization phase by waiting until its children (0 and 2) have synchronized, then telling the parent (3) that the whole subtree (0,1, and 2) rooted at the thread has synchronized, and then waiting for the wake-up command from the parent (3). In the wake-up phase, once the parent (3) wakes up the thread (1), the thread wakes up its children (0 and 2) and proceeds with the instructions following the barrier call. The root (3) does not wait for a wake-up at the end of its synchronization phase; the static barrier algorithm guarantees that the root starts waking up only if all the threads have started computation.

The threads convey signals via toggling boolean variables in the tree nodes. The crucial part of the inductive invariant that is needed to verify the barrier property speaks about the parent-descendant relation as follows. If a node m (say, 0) is a descendant of a node n (say, 3) and n has received signals from all its children (1 and 5) in the synchronization phase, then m has already sent a signal to its parent (1). This property is encodable in the WS2S logic.

Combining tree barrier. In the combining tree barrier each thread is initially associated with a distinct leaf of a common tree, e.g.:

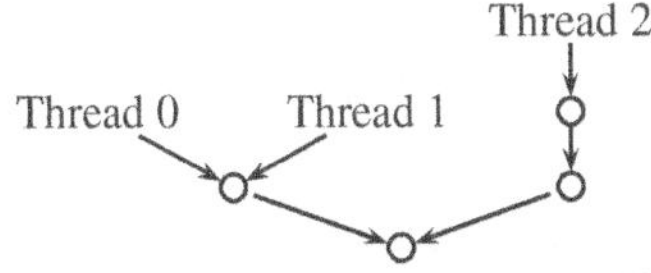

In the synchronization phase, threads start walking towards the root of the tree from their leaves such that each thread eventually begins waiting at a distinct node and such that exactly one thread reaches the root. In the wake-up phase, the thread pointing to the

PPoPP'12, February 25–29, 2012, New Orleans, Louisiana, USA.
ACM 978-1-4503-1160-1/12/02.

root initiates a wake-up process in which every thread stops waiting and walks towards a leaf of the tree.

Each node of the tree contains a field cnt that stores the number of threads that still have to arrive at the node; e.g., the common parent k of the leaves of threads 0 and 1 starts with $k \rightarrow \mathsf{cnt} = 2$. When some thread arrives at k first, it decrements $k \rightarrow \mathsf{cnt}$ to 1 and starts waiting for the wake-up. The next thread that arrives at k diminishes $k \rightarrow \mathsf{cnt}$ to 0, and, noticing the fact that no more threads are going to arrive at k, proceeds to the parent of k. Notice that in our picture, thread 2 decrements the counters of the nodes between the initial leaf of thread 2 and the root (excluding both) from 1 to 0 without waiting.

The crucial part of the inductive invariant for the synchronization phase is $J = (\forall\, m \in \mathrm{Node}\colon m \rightarrow \mathsf{cnt} \geq S_1 + S_2 + S_3)$, where
$S_1 = |\{t \in \mathrm{Thread} \mid n_t = m \wedge t \text{ is about to decrement } m \rightarrow \mathsf{cnt}\}|$,
$S_2 = |\{\overline{m} \in \mathrm{Node} \mid \overline{m} \rightarrow \mathsf{parent} = m \wedge \overline{m} \rightarrow \mathsf{cnt} > 0\}|$,
$S_3 = |\{t \in \mathrm{Thread} \mid n_t \rightarrow \mathsf{parent} = m \wedge t \text{ is about to go to } m\}|$,
where n_t is the pointer into the tree of the thread t.

It is possible to encode J into WS2S for finitely many threads and bounded degree of the tree nodes.

4. Array-based barriers

Now we will verify the dissemination and tournament barriers in the verifier Boogie.

Dissemination barrier. In the dissemination barrier, a thread executes $L = \lceil \log_2 n \rceil$ synchronization rounds. In round i, thread number t sends a signal to thread number $(t + 2^i) \bmod n$ (where $\bmod n$ gives the smallest nonnegative remainder after division by n) and starts waiting for a signal from thread $(t - 2^i) \bmod n$. It turns out that after L rounds, each thread x has received a signal from every other thread y, either directly or transitively, i.e., some thread z has received a signal (directly or transitively) from y and sent its signal to x.

The threads send signals and wait for them as follows.

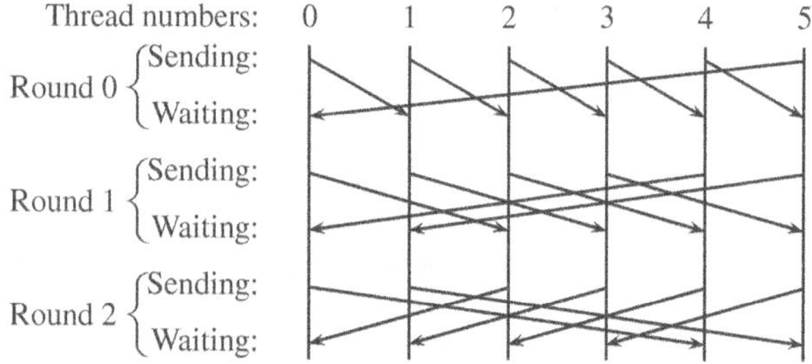

Signals are stored in an array A: ((thread number)×(round number))→bool. A crucial property that we had to prove automatically is that if a thread t has received a signal in round l, then all the threads which are less than $t - 2^l$ (including the wrapped ones) by a certain amount have already started. Such a property is a universally quantified property over the two-dimensional array. This property was approximated by a property in the AUFLIA logic and handed over to the SMT theorem prover Z3.

Tournament barrier. A computation of the tournament barrier is akin to a chess tournament: in each round, threads are partitioned into couples, in each couple one of the threads wins and proceeds to the next round, the other thread loses and starts waiting until the winner comes back and wakes the thread up. If the number of threads is not a power of two, threads without opponents skip certain rounds. The difference to the real tournament is that the winner and the loser, as well as the couplings, are statically determined by the bits of the thread identifiers (a nonnegative integer represented by a bitstring). For example, six threads will synchronize as follows:

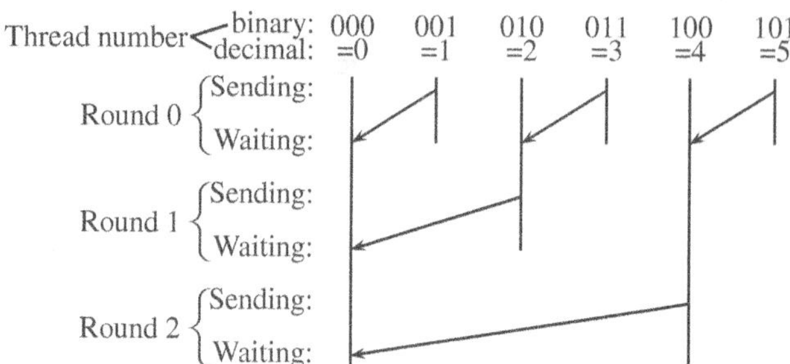

After the champion (here: 000) has arrived at the last round, it will wake up every thread that has lost to the champion directly during the synchronization phase (here: 100, 010 and 001). Once a thread is awake, it will wake up all the threads that have lost to it directly.

The signals are stored in an array A: ((thread identifier)×(round number))→bool. The crucial property we needed to prove automatically is that if $A[t, l]$ is set and some thread $\hat{t}$ loses to t transitively till and including round l, then $\hat{t}$ is waiting for the wake-up.

5. Central barrier coded in C

We will verify a C implementation of a central barrier in VCC:

```
shared int cnt = num_threads;   shared bool sense = false;
local bool local_sense = false; // needed for wake−up and reinitialization.
void barrier() {
  local_sense ^= true; // toggling, which means: no wake−up yet.
  if(cnt−−>1) // assume atomic fetch−and−decrement.
    while(sense!=local_sense); // wait for the wake−up.
  else{/*Reinit and wake−up*/ cnt=num_threads; sense=local_sense; }}
```

The necessary inductive invariant is similar to that of Section 2. Currently, VCC cannot reason about cardinalities of set comprehensions, so we get rid of cardinalities. Instead, the code is augmented with an auxiliary bijection between thread identifiers and local states (a local state is a valuation of the program counter and local_sense) such that the threads that have not yet fetched-and-decremented have identifiers below cnt. Namely, just before a thread decrements cnt we swap the thread's current identifier with the thread number cnt−1 by updating the aforementioned bijection.

6. A central barrier with a client

If the number of threads is small, as in the following example, and if the implementation of a barrier uses only relatively few states, as the barrier from .NET 4.0, exhaustive search may succeed. The example is a simplification of a client from the MSDN library:

```
int x = 0; Barrier barrier = new Barrier(3);
barrier.AddParticipants(2); barrier.RemoveParticipant();
Action action =  () => { Interlocked.Increment(ref x); // atomic x++
  barrier.SignalAndWait(); Interlocked.Increment(ref x);
  barrier.SignalAndWait(); Interlocked.Increment(ref x);
  barrier.SignalAndWait(); Interlocked.Increment(ref x);
  barrier.SignalAndWait(); assert(x==16); };
Parallel.Invoke(action, action, action, action); barrier.Dispose();
```

Here, four threads increment a variable x four times, calling the barrier function after incrementing. The Spin tool has used automata encoding and partial order reduction to prove no use-after-disposal and that the value of x is 16 at the end of each thread.

Acknowledgments

We thank Ernie Cohen, Viktor Kuncak, Rustan Leino, Michał Moskal, and Thomas Wies for help on Boogie, Jahob, and VCC.

References

[1] M. Herlihy and N. Shavit. *The art of multiprocessor programming*. Morgan Kaufmann, 2008.

Collective Algorithms for Sub-communicators

Anshul Mittal Thomas George
Yogish Sabharwal
IBM Research India, New Delhi, India
{mittal.anshul,thomasgeorge,ysabharwal}@in.ibm.com

Nikhil Jain
University of Illinois,
Urbana Champaign, USA
nikhil@illinois.edu

Sameer Kumar
IBM T.J.Watson Research Center,
Yorktown Heights, USA
sameerk@us.ibm.com

Abstract

Collective communication over a group of processors is an integral and time consuming component in many HPC applications. Many modern day supercomputers are based on torus interconnects. On such systems, for an irregular communicator comprising of a subset of processors, the algorithms developed so far are not contention free in general and hence non-optimal.

In this paper, we present a novel contention-free algorithm to perform collective operations over a subset of processors in a torus network. We also extend previous work on regular communicators to handle special cases of irregular communicators that occur frequently in parallel scientific applications. For the generic case where multiple node disjoint sub-communicators communicate simultaneously in a loosely synchronous fashion, we propose a novel cooperative approach to route the data for individual sub-communicators without contention. Empirical results demonstrate that our algorithms outperform the optimized MPI collective implementation on IBM's Blue Gene/P supercomputer for large data sizes and random node distributions.

Categories and Subject Descriptors D.m [*Software*]: Miscellaneous

General Terms Performance, Algorithms

Keywords Collectives, Torus, Sub-communicators

1. Introduction

MPI collective routines that perform one-to-many, many-to-one, and many-to-many communications among the processors are amongst the most important and time consuming components in most high performance computing applications. The performance of these MPI collectives is critical for improved scalability and efficiency of parallel scientific applications. With limited bandwith on most systems, for collectives on large messages, avoiding network contention is critical.

Many modern day supercomputers are based on interconnection networks with a k-ary n-cube topology, for example, the Blue Gene/P and Cray XT machines have a 3D torus topology. Applications on such architectures involve collective operations, not only on the entire processor partition (MPI_COMM_WORLD or the *full-communicator* in MPI) but also on sub partitions (i.e., sub-communicators in MPI). For example, in molecular dynamics, each processor communicates with other processors that contain atoms that interact with the atoms in the original processor, resulting in an arbitrary subset of processors forming a sub-communicator.

Optimizing MPI collectives has been a key topic of interest in high performance computing due to its importance in scaling parallel applications. Most of the existing algorithms are either generic algorithms which work well for most network topologies and a wide range of message sizes, or are specifically tailored for a particular class of collectives on a given network topology and typically large message sizes. The later outperform the generic algorithms for the specific target topologies and message sizes. For example, Van de Geijn et.al [3] proposed an algorithm for large message broadcast that has been shown to outperform the binomial algorithm. Optimization for 3D torus networks has been presented in [1] and [2]. However, most of these algorihms have focused on the cases involving *full-communicator*.

Our Contributions. In this paper, we propose algorithms for Broadcast, Reduce, and Allreduce based on the construction of novel edge disjoint spanning trees for a random sub-communicator. We make the following key contributions.

- We propose algorithms to construct contention free spanning trees for performing collective operations over a random sub-communicator on a 3D torus network. An SPI implementation of our approach shows an improvement of $2-4\times$ for Broadcast and Allreduce operations over an optimized MPI implementation available on Blue Gene/P.
- We extend earlier work by in [1] to handle special communicators such as the master/slave scenario where a single processor is excluded from the communicator, and the case where the communicator comprises of a random set of complete parallel 2D planes. An empirical evaluation of our approach demonstrates a speedup of $1.7-5.8\times$ using an SPI implementation.
- We also explore scenarios where multiple node disjoint irregular sub-communicators exist and communicate simultaneously. For such scenarios, with a moderate number of random sub-communicators we obtain a speedup in the range $1.6-2.6\times$.

2. Algorithm

The key new idea in our approach is to decouple the construction of edge-disjoint spanning trees from the collective operation which allows us to handle any arbitrary communicator and/or root. Our approach thus essentially consists of two steps. The first step is the construction of the edge-disjoint spanning trees. This is a one time operation that is extremely fast and is performed during the call to create the sub-communicator. The construction is based on two algorithms - the first one is a novel algorithm that we propose for constructing edge-disjoint spanning trees for arbitrary sub-communicators while the other one is a multi-color algorithm proposed by Faraj et at. [1], which we extend to handle special cases of irregular communicators. The second step is the actual collective operation performed over the spanning tree.

Construction of edge-disjoint spanning tree for an arbitrary sub-communicator in 2-D torus is done by carefully choosing a lin-

PPoPP'12, February 25–29, 2012, New Orleans, Louisiana, USA.
ACM 978-1-4503-1160-1/12/02.

earized (snake like) ordering of nodes which are part of the sub-communicator. The choice of communicating neighbors in this snake pattern ensures that no two communicating nodes use any common link for data transfer. The spanning tree for 3-D torus is obtained by a generalization of the 2-D case.

3. Common Sub-communicators

In this section, we demonstrate the use of the algorithms mentioned in Section 2, on a few commonly occurring scenarios that involve collective communication on sub-communicators. The different scenarios are classified on the basis of the number and kind of simultaneous sub-communicators.

Random communicator: In such cases, our algorithm can be directly used to achieve a single link throughput performance for the collective.

Single communicator with one node missing: Our solution for this scenario is based on extending the algorithm by Faraj et.al. [1]. In the first step, we follow the multi-color rectangular approach to create three edge disjoint trees for the collective operation using links only in the X+, Y+ and Z+ direction. However, we start the tree construction using a *pseudo root* that is at least one hop away from the missing node in every dimension. The missing node is bypassed during the tree construction. In the second step, the directions of the links is adjusted according to the user specified root.

Random subset of parallel planes: Without loss of generality, let us assume that the missing planes are along the Z- axis. Since each of the 2D planes do not have any missing nodes, we first perform phases 1 and 2 of the collective operation where the data is transferred along the X and Y dimensions respectively, as described in [1]. In phase 3, the data is transferred along the Z dimension, with the missing planes in Z dimension being bypassed to transfer the data to the nodes in next 2D plane in the sub-communicator. Phase 4 remains the same as before. In this case, we can obtain maximum throughput for both Broadcast and Allreduce.

Contiguous sub-communicator groups: In this case, all the sub-communicators can be readily mapped onto contiguous nodes on the processor space such that there are no overlapping paths.

Overlapping sub-communicator groups: For overlapping sub-communicators, we propose a novel approach where multiple sub-communicators co-operate to achieve an optimal performance for the collective operations.

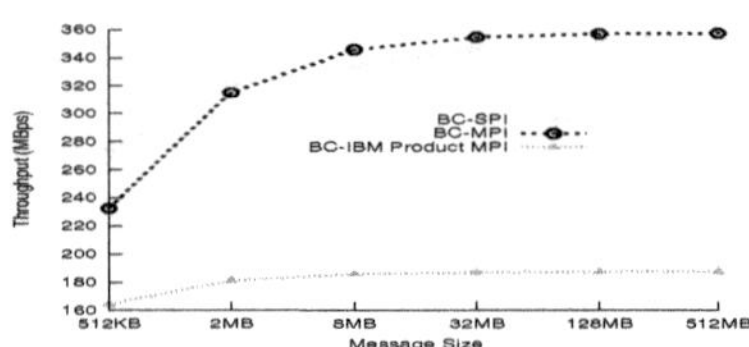

Figure 1. Broadcast on sparse random sub-communicator

4. Results

Hardware: All the experiments were performed on Blue Gene/P which is IBM's massively parallel supercomputer. Each node in BGP supports 850 MBps bidirectional links to each of its nearest neighbors for a total of 5.1GB/s bidirectional bandwidth per node.

Implementation Specifics: We present two versions of our algorithms; (i) an optimized version which uses a lower level API (SPI) and (ii) an MPI version by modifying the MPI stack. We refer to our Broadcast implementation using SPI as *BC-SPI* and the MPI stack implementation as *BC-MPI*. Similarly, we refer to our Allreduce implementations as *AR-SPI* and *AR-MPI* respectively. We compare our results against the IBM's product MPI referred to as *BC-IBM Product MPI* and *AR-IBM Product MPI* for Broadcast and Allreduce, respectively.

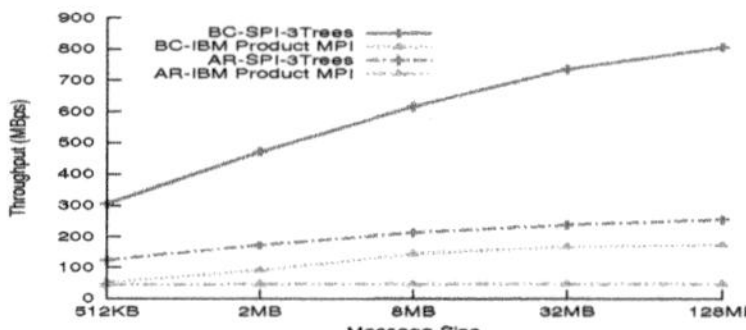

Figure 2. One node missing sub-communicator

We present the performance results of our Broadcast implementation for increasing message sizes in the range 512KB-512MB for a sparse (31/1024 nodes) random sub-communicator in Figure 1. Similar results were obtained for Allreduce. Figure 2 shows the plot of throughput vs. message size for Broadcast and Allreduce on sub-communictor with one missing node.

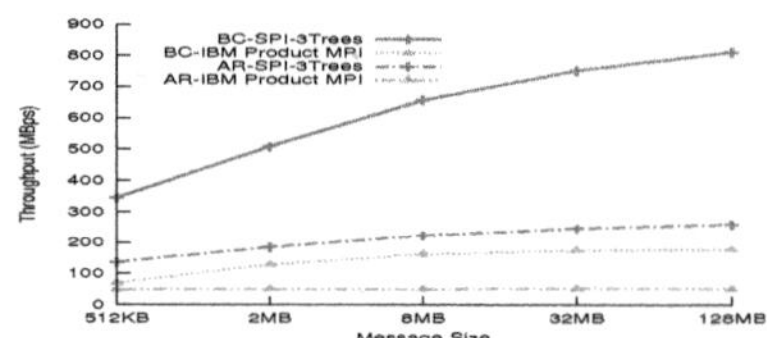

Figure 3. Missing plane sub-communicator.

In Figure 3, we show the plot of throughput vs. message size for Broadcast and Allreduce operations for sub-communicator with missing planes.

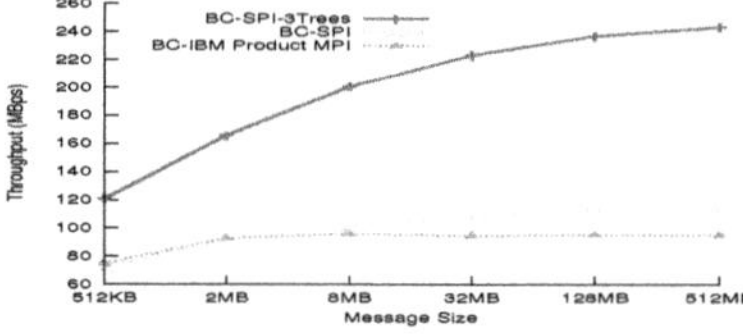

Figure 4. Broacast with mutiple random sub-communicators.

Figures 4 and 5 show the performance of our algorithms for the case when multiple random sub-communicators perform Broadcast and Allreduce respectively.

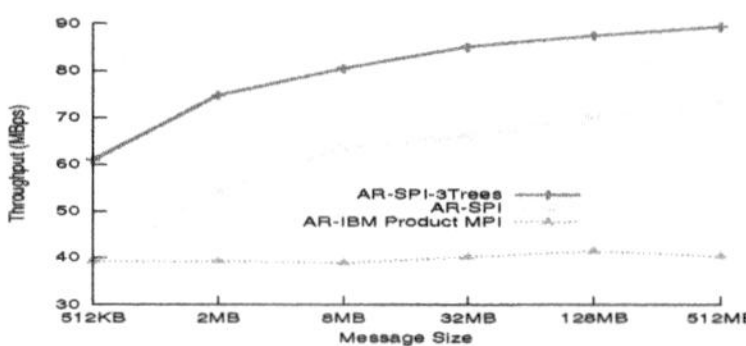

Figure 5. Allreduce with multiple random sub-communicators.

References

[1] A. Faraj, S. Kumar, B. Smith, A. Mamidala, J. Gunnels, and P. Heidelberger. MPI collective communications on the Blue Gene/P supercomputer: algorithms and optimizations". In *ICS*, pages 489–490, 2009.

[2] N. Jain and Y. Sabharwal. Optimal bucket algorithms for large MPI collectives on torus interconnects. In *ICS*, pages 27–36, 2010.

[3] M. Shroff and R. A. V. D. Geijn. Collmark: Mpi collective communication benchmark. Technical report, 2000.

Synchronization Views for Event-loop Actors

Joeri De Koster
Vrije Universiteit Brussel
jdekoste@vub.ac.be

Stefan Marr
Vrije Universiteit Brussel
smarr@vub.ac.be

Theo D'Hondt
Vrije Universiteit Brussel
tjdhondt@vub.ac.be

Abstract

The actor model has already proven itself as an interesting concurrency model that avoids issues such as deadlocks and race conditions by construction, and thus facilitates concurrent programming. The tradeoff is that it sacrifices expressiveness and efficiency especially with respect to data parallelism. However, many standard solutions to computationally expensive problems employ data parallel algorithms for better performance on parallel systems.

We identified three problems that inhibit the use of data-parallel algorithms within the actor model. Firstly, one of the main properties of the actor model, the fact that no data is shared, is one of the most severe performance bottlenecks. Especially the fact that shared state can not be read truly in parallel. Secondly, the actor model on its own does not provide a mechanism to specify extra synchronization conditions on batches of messages which leads to event-level data-races. And lastly, programmers are forced to write code in a continuation-passing style (CPS) to handle typical request-response situations. However, CPS breaks the sequential flow of the code and is often hard to understand, which increases complexity and lowers maintainability.

We proposes *synchronization views* to solve these three issues without compromising the semantic properties of the actor model. Thus, the resulting concurrency model maintains deadlock-freedom, avoids low-level race conditions, and keeps the semantics of macro-step execution.

Categories and Subject Descriptors D.1.3 [*Concurrent Programming*]; D.3.3 [*Language Constructs and Features*]: Concurrent programming structures

General Terms Design, Languages

Keywords Actor Model, Synchronization, Data Parallelism

1. Introduction

Because of the multicore evolution, parallel programming is no longer only useful for high performance computing (HPC) applications but is also useful in the desktop and embedded world. In contrast to HPC, where speedup is generally gained by splitting up a single problem and processing the input data in parallel, we assume that desktop applications are generally more task driven. That means, desktop, or more general user-centric applications have in general less parts that are data parallel but possible parallelism comes from distinctly different activities that need to be done in the problem domain.

Thus, the starting hypothesis of our research is that such application benefit more from a language model that provides good abstractions for expressing task driven parallelism in a safe way. The actor model [1, 2] is such a model. This model has mainly been used in a distributed setting (Erlang [3], SALSA [4], AmbientTalk [5]) where the architectural benefits of its concurrency model are more important than the speed gained by running multiple actors in parallel.

However, user-centric applications often have to deal with certain subproblems that are inherently data parallel. Examples are large data-intensive spread-sheets or search operations where the use of data parallel approaches could reduce the latency towards the user. Thus, task-driven parallelism should not be the only method of parallelism provided by a programming language, otherwise the application can not fully exploit the available parallelism of such data driven problems.

The goal of this paper is to argue for a computational model that combines a safe task-based parallelism model with the ability to use a restricted number of data-driven optimizations.

From that perspective, the actor model is a good starting point. It is free of low-level data races and in its original inception deadlock-free by construction. Those two properties are delivered by the actor model because it adheres to three fundamental rules:

- Actors do not share mutable state
- Actors communicate only asynchronously
- Actors are scheduled *fairly*, i. e., no actor is permanently starved

We however believe that it is the first two rules that place the largest restriction on the expressiveness of the actor model. A consequence of the first rule is that data-parallel algorithms that read from and write to a shared resource are impossible to express efficiently within an actor program. A consequence of the second rule is that communication with a remote shared resource[1] requires most of the time the use of some request-response idiom which is expressed in most languages using *continuation-passing style* (CPS) and results in less maintainable code (cf. Sec. 2).

Our solution is an extension of the actor model so that it, in addition to expressing task parallelism, also becomes useful for expressing data parallelism within an application. This extension has been crafted in such a way that the extended model keeps the same guarantees, such as race condition-freedom, deadlock-freedom and macro-step semantics, as the original model. We introduce synchronization views as a way of synchronizing access to a remote resource and demonstrate that this extension is useful when implementing data-parallel algorithms.

[1] A resource is remote for an actor if that resource is located in the memory space of another actor. Having different remote actors does not necessarily imply distribution.

PPoPP'12, February 25–29, 2012, New Orleans, Louisiana, USA.
ACM 978-1-4503-1160-1/12/02.

2. The problem: Accessing non-local shared state

The main problem of the actor model is that share state is traditionally represented by an additional independent actor which encapsulates that shared state or resource. However, this leads to the following three problems:

No parallel reads. State which is conceptually shared can never be read truly in parallel because all accesses to that state are sequentialized by the event queue of the encapsulating actor.

No synchronization conditions. The traditional actor model does not allow to specify extra synchronization conditions on different events since the order in which events from different senders are handled is nondeterministic. There are some solutions for this problem but as explained later in this section they often only solve part of the problem.

Continuation-passing style enforced. Using a distinct actor to represent conceptually shared state implies that this resource can not be accessed directly from any other actor since all communication happens asynchronously within the actor model. Thus, the programmer needs to explicitly handle a request-response situation, which usually forces the programmer to employ CPS.

3. Views as a synchronization mechanism

Most of the identified problems stem from the fact that an actor cannot have synchronous access on the state or part of the state of another remote actor. Our *view* abstraction solves that issue. Views are a synchronization mechanism that allows one actor to have synchronous access to multiple objects or parts of objects owned by other remote actors. There are two kinds of views, a shared and an exclusive view which mimic multiple reader, single writer access as a synchronization strategy. We added three new primitives to access shared state from within our language:

```
<far-reference>.whenExclusive(<closure>)
<far-reference>.whenShared(<closure>)
whenSharedAndExclusive(<far-reference>+,
                       <far-reference>+,
                       <closure>)
```

The only restriction imposed on the usage of these primitives is that the `far-reference` they access has to be a reference to a remote shallow object. This can be either an object with no scope such as an isolate [5] or a shallow primitive datatype such as an array. This restriction is imposed to guarantee race-condition freeness.

In the listing below, we give an example where sending an `increase` message to the actor will schedule an event that increases the counter in the cell when that cell becomes available for exclusive access. We can access the cell synchronously from within the closure we provided to the `whenExclusive` primitive. The body of that closure is executed in a separate turn if and only if the cell object becomes available for exclusive access. This means that the `get` and `set` method of the cell are executed atomically, which would not have been possible without using views or changing the implementation of the cell object. If we want to read the same value multiple times or read different values synchronously, we can do so for the duration of that turn. We no longer have to employ CPS or futures to read and/or write values from and to a shared resource.

Currently, only multiple reader, single writer access is provided as a synchronization strategy. We also prioritize writers to prevent their starvation. We chose this locking strategy to limit the expressiveness of our primitives in favor of more concise abstractions.

```
cell: isolate({
    c: 0;
    get()@reader:
        c;
    set(n):
        c := n});

act: actor({
    increase(cell):
        cell.whenExclusive(
            lambda(c):
                c.set(c.get() + 1));
```

View requests on a shared object are scheduled by a view-scheduler. These view-schedulers exist on a per-object basis and are created when the first view on that object is requested. This prevents our abstraction to have any overhead on the system when it is not used. Requested views are put in a queue and when the resource associated with that view-scheduler becomes available the next request is handled.

4. Conclusion

The engineering benefits of semantically coarse-grained synchronization mechanisms in general [6] and the restrictions of the actor model [7] have been recognized by others. In particular the notion of *view*-like constructs has been proposed before.

The main contribution of our view-abstractions is to address the inefficient and often confusing (CPS) access to shared state in the actor paradigm by allowing controlled synchronous access on shared state. The advantages of this system over the traditional event-loop model are threefold. Firstly we avoid the continuation passing style of programming when accessing shared state. Secondly we allow the programmer to introduce extra synchronization constraints on groups of messages and lastly we are able to model true parallel reads.

Acknowledgments

Joeri De Koster and Stefan Marr are supported by doctoral scholarships granted by the Institute for the Promotion of Innovation through Science and Technology in Flanders (IWT-Vlaanderen), Belgium.

References

[1] G. Agha. Actors: a model of concurrent computation in distributed systems. AITR-844, 1985.

[2] C. Hewitt, P. Bishop, and R. Steiger. A universal modular actor formalism for artificial intelligence. In Proceedings of the 3rd international joint conference on Artificial intelligence, pages 235245. Morgan Kaufmann Publishers Inc., 1973.

[3] J. Armstrong, R. Virding, C. Wikstrom, and M. Williams. Concurrent programming in erlang. 1996.

[4] C. Varela and G. Agha. Programming dynamically reconfigurable open systems with salsa. ACM SIGPLAN Notices, 36(12):2034, 2001.

[5] T. Van Cutsem, S. Mostinckx, E. Boix, J. Dedecker, and W. De Meuter. Ambienttalk: Object-oriented event-driven programming in mobile ad hoc networks. In Chilean Society of Computer Science, 2007. SCCC07. XXVI International Conference of the, pages 312. Ieee, 2007.

[6] B. Demsky and P. Lam. Views: Object-inspired concurrency control. In Proceedings of the 32nd ACM/IEEE International Conference on Software Engineering-Volume 1, pages 395404. ACM, 2010.

[7] R. Karmani, A. Shali, and G. Agha. Actor frameworks for the JVM platform: A comparative analysis. In Proceedings of the 7th International Conference on Principles and Practice of Programming in Java, pages 1120. ACM, 2009.

CPHASH: A Cache-Partitioned Hash Table

Zviad Metreveli
Dropbox / MIT CSAIL

Nickolai Zeldovich
MIT CSAIL

M. Frans Kaashoek
MIT CSAIL

Abstract

CPHASH is a concurrent hash table for multicore processors. CPHASH partitions its table across the caches of cores and uses message passing to transfer lookups/inserts to a partition. CPHASH's message passing avoids the need for locks, pipelines batches of asynchronous messages, and packs multiple messages into a single cache line transfer. Experiments on a 80-core machine with 2 hardware threads per core show that CPHASH has $\sim 1.6\times$ higher throughput than a hash table implemented using fine-grained locks. An analysis shows that CPHASH wins because it experiences fewer cache misses and its cache misses are less expensive, because of less contention for the on-chip interconnect and DRAM. CPSERVER, a key/value cache server using CPHASH, achieves $\sim 5\%$ higher throughput than a key/value cache server that uses a hash table with fine-grained locks, but both achieve better throughput and scalability than MEMCACHED. The throughput of CPHASH and CPSERVER also scale near-linearly with the number of cores.

Categories and Subject Descriptors D.1.3 [*Programming techniques*]: Concurrent programming—Parallel programming

General Terms Design, Performance

1. Introduction

Hash tables are heavily used data structures in servers. This paper focuses on fixed-size hash tables that support eviction of its elements using a Least Recently Used (LRU) list. Such hash tables are a good way to implement a key/value cache. A popular distributed application that uses a key/value cache is MEMCACHED. MEMCACHED is an in-memory cache for Web applications that store data, page rendering results, and other information that can be cached and is expensive to recalculate. As the number of cores in server machines increases, it is important to understand how to design hash tables that can perform and scale well on multi-core machines.

This paper explores designing and implementing a scalable hash table by minimizing cache movement. In a multi-core processor, each core has its own cache and perhaps a few caches shared by adjacent cores. The cache-coherence protocol transfers cache lines between caches to ensure memory coherence. Fetching lines from memory or from other cores' caches is expensive, varying from one order to two order of magnitude in latency, compared to an L1 fetch. If several cores in turn acquire a lock that protects a data item, and then update the data item, the cache hardware may send several hardware messages to move the lock, the data item, and to invalidate cached copies. If the computation on a data item is small, it may be less expensive to send a software message to a core which is responsible for the data item, and to perform the computation at the responsible core. This approach will result in cache-line transfers from the source core to the destination core to transfer the software message, but no cache-line transfers for the lock, the data, and potentially fewer hardware invalidation messages.

To understand when this message-passing approach might be beneficial in the context of multicore machines, this paper introduces a new hash table, which we call CPHASH. Instead of having each core access any part of a hash table, CPHASH partitions the hash table into partitions and assign a partition to the L1/L2 cache of a particular core. CPHASH uses message passing to pass the lookup/insert operation to the core that is assigned the partition needed for that particular operation, instead of running the lookup/insert operation locally and fetching the hash table entry and the lock that protects that entry. CPHASH uses an asynchronous message passing protocol, allowing CPHASH to batch messages. Batching increases parallelism: when a server is busy, a client can continue computing and add messages to a batch. Furthermore, batching allows packing multiple messages in a single cache line, which reduce the number of cache lines transferred.

To evaluate CPHASH we implemented it on a 80-core Intel machine with 2 hardware threads per core. The implementation uses 80 hardware threads that serve hash-table operations and 80 hardware threads that issue operations. For comparison, we also implemented an optimized hash table with fine-grained locking, which we call LOCKHASH. LOCKHASH uses 160 hardware threads that perform hash-table operations on a 4,096-way partitioned hash tables to avoid lock contention. The 80 CPHASH server threads achieve $1.6\times$ higher throughput than the 160 LOCKHASH hardware threads. The better performance is because CPHASH experiences 1.5 fewer L3 caches misses per operation and the 3.1 L3 misses that CPHASH experiences are less expensive. This is because CPHASH has no locks and has better locality, which reduce the contention for the interconnect and DRAM. CPHASH's design also allows it to scale near-linearly to more cores than LOCKHASH.

The follow sections summarize the design and provide one key performance result. For the interested reader, our technical report [1] provides more detail on CPHASH, as well as a detailed breakdown of its performance.

2. CPHASH Design

CPHASH splits a hash table into several independent parts, which we call *partitions*. CPHASH uses a simple hash function to assign each possible key to a partition. Each partition has a designated server thread that is responsible for all operations on keys that belong to it. CPHASH pins each server thread to its hardware thread. Applications use CPHASH by having client threads send operations to server threads using message passing (via shared memory). Server threads return results to the client threads also using message passing.

2.1 Partitions

Every partition in CPHASH is a separate hash table. Each partition consists of a bucket array, where each bucket is a linked list of hash table elements. Each partition also has an LRU linked list that holds hash table elements in the least recently used order. CPHASH uses the LRU list to determine which elements to evict from a partition when there is not enough space left to insert new elements.

PPoPP'12, February 25–29, 2012, New Orleans, Louisiana, USA.
ACM 978-1-4503-1160-1/12/02.

Each hash table element consists of two parts: a header, which fits in a single cache line and is typically stored in the server thread's cache, and the value, which fits in zero or more cache lines following the header, and is directly accessed by client threads, thereby loading it into client thread caches. The header consists of the *key*, the *reference count*, the *size* of the value (in bytes), and doubly-linked-list pointers for the bucket and for the LRU list to allow eviction.

The ideal size for a partition is such that a partition can fit in the L1/L2 cache of a core, with some overflow into its shared L3 cache. On our test machine with 80 cores, hash table sizes up to about $80 \times 256\text{KB} + 8 \times 30\text{MB} = 260\text{MB}$ see the best performance improvement, at which point CPHASH starts being limited by DRAM performance.

2.2 Server Threads

CPHASH server threads support two types of operations: `Lookup` and `Insert`. In the case of a `Lookup`, the message contains the requested `key`. If a key/value pair with the given `key` is found in the partition, then the server thread updates the head of the partition's LRU list and return the *pointer* to the value to the client thread; otherwise, the server returns a null pointer.

Performing an `Insert` operation is slightly more complicated, because memory must be allocated for the value, and the value must be copied into the allocated memory. It is convenient to allocate memory in the server thread, since each server is responsible for a single partition, and can use a standard memory allocator. However, copying the actual data is performed in the client thread, to avoid polluting the cache of the server core.

CPHASH uses reference counting to keep track of outstanding pointers to hash table elements. To drop a reference, clients send a message to the corresponding server core.

2.3 Message passing

CPHASH implements message passing between the client and server threads using pre-allocated circular buffers in shared memory. For each client and server pair there are two circular rings of buffers—one for each direction of communication—along with pointers to the first pending and last pending buffer in the ring. Each buffer can hold several messages. Message senders locate the next available buffer, and append as many messages to it as possible up before advancing the last pending pointer. Receivers poll for pending buffers, and process all messages in a buffer before moving on.

Buffers are a multiple of the cache line size, and each cache line can hold several messages. This allows a single cache line transfer to transmit many messages, thus enabling an amortized message passing cost of less than one cache miss per message. Pending indexes are cache-aligned to avoid false sharing. A ring of buffers allows asynchronous message passing, so that the sender can perform other tasks while waiting for the response.

3. Performance Evaluation

In this section we discuss the performance results that we achieved using CPHASH, and compare it to the performance achieved by LOCKHASH. To evaluate hash table performance, we created a simple benchmark that generates random queries and performs them on the hash table. A single query can be either a LOOKUP or an INSERT operation. The INSERT operation consists of inserting key/value pairs such that the key is a random 64-bit number and the value is the same as the key (8 bytes).

We use an 80-core Intel machine for our evaluation. This machine has eight sockets, each containing a 10-core Intel E7-8870 processor. All processors are clocked at 2.4 GHz, have a 256 KB L2 cache per core, and a 30 MB L3 cache shared by all 10 cores in a single socket. Each of the cores supports two hardware threads (Hyperthreading in Intel terminology). Each socket has two DRAM controllers, and each controller is connected to two 8 GB DDR3 1333 MHz DIMMs, for a total of 256 GB of DRAM.

To evaluate the overall performance of CPHASH relative to its locking counterpart, LOCKHASH, we measure the throughput of both hash tables over a range of working set sizes. Clients issue a mix of 30% INSERT and 70% LOOKUP queries. The maximum hash table size is equal to the entire working set, which means no eviction takes place. We run 10^9 queries for each configuration, and report the throughput achieved during that run.

For CPHASH, we use 80 client threads, 80 partitions, and 80 server threads. The client and server threads run on the first and second hardware threads of each of the 80 cores, respectively. This allows server threads to use the L2 cache space of each core, since client threads have a relatively small working set size. Each client maintains a pipeline of 1,000 outstanding requests across all servers; similar throughput is observed for batch sizes between 512 and 8,192. Larger batch sizes overflow queues between client and server threads, and smaller batch sizes lead to client threads waiting for server replies.

Figure 1 shows the results of this experiment. For small working set sizes, LOCKHASH performs poorly because the number of distinct keys is less than the number of partitions (4,096), leading to lock contention. In the middle of the working set range (256 KB–128 MB), CPHASH consistently out-performs LOCKHASH by a factor of 1.6× to 2×. With working sizes of 256 MB or greater, the size of the hash table exceeds the aggregate capacity of all CPU caches, and the performance of CPHASH starts to degrade as the CPUs are forced to incur slower DRAM access costs. At large working sets, such as 4 GB to the right of the graph, the performance of both CPHASH and LOCKHASH converges and is limited by DRAM.

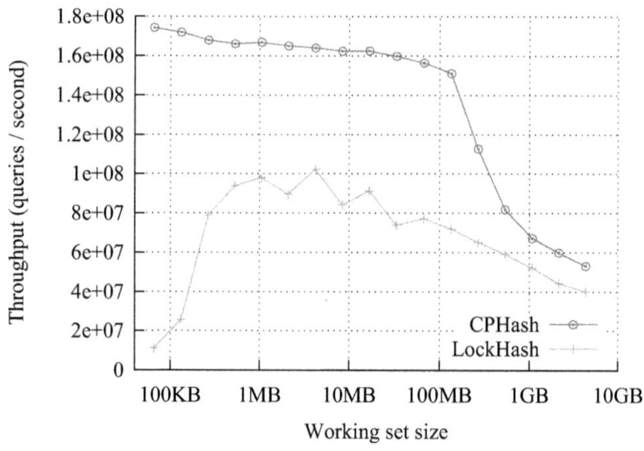

Figure 1. Throughput of CPHASH and LOCKHASH over a range of working set sizes.

Acknowledgments

We thank Robert Morris for helping us improve the ideas in this paper. This work was partially supported by Quanta Computer and by NSF award 915164.

References

[1] Z. Metreveli, N. Zeldovich, and M. F. Kaashoek. CPHash: A cache-partitioned hash table. Technical Report MIT-CSAIL-TR-2011-051, MIT Computer Science and Artificial Intelligence Laboratory, Cambridge, MA, November 2011.

RACECAR: A Heuristic for Automatic Function Specialization on Multi-core Heterogeneous Systems

John R. Wernsing, Dr. Greg Stitt

Department of Electrical & Computer Engineering
University of Florida
Gainesville, FL
wernsing@ufl.edu, gstitt@ece.ufl.edu

Abstract

High-performance computing systems increasingly combine multi-core processors and heterogeneous resources such as graphics-processing units and field-programmable gate arrays. However, significant application design complexity for such systems has often led to untapped performance potential. Application designers targeting such systems currently must determine how to parallelize computation, create device-specialized implementations for each heterogeneous resource, and determine how to partition work for each resource. In this paper, we present the RACECAR heuristic to automate the optimization of applications for multi-core heterogeneous systems by automatically exploring implementation alternatives that include different algorithms, parallelization strategies, and work distributions. Experimental results show RACECAR-specialized implementations achieve speedups up to 117x and average 11x compared to a single CPU thread when parallelizing computation across multiple cores, graphics-processing units, and field-programmable gate arrays.

Categories and Subject Descriptors D.2.2 [**Software Engineering**]: Design Tools and Techniques – computer-aided software engineering (CASE)

General Terms Algorithms, Design, Measurement, Performance

Keywords elastic computing; heterogeneous; optimization; RACECAR; speedup

1. Introduction

Over the past decade, computing architectures have started on a clear trend towards increased parallelism with multi-core processors. More recently, this trend has focused on increased heterogeneity, with devices such as graphics-processing units (GPUs) and field-programmable gate arrays (FPGAs) commonly being used to improve application performance for various scientific computing domains [1][3][5].

Although multi-core heterogeneous systems have significant high-performance computing potential, the increased application-design complexity commonly prevents designers from reaching this potential. In extreme cases, such as for FPGAs, this complexity has prevented designers without low-level device expertise from even using the devices [4]. Such complexity is primarily caused by three challenges: 1) creating parallel implementations to exploit multiple cores or devices, 2) creating device-specialized implementations, often requiring different algorithms, optimizations, and programming languages, and 3) partitioning and load balancing work across numerous resources.

Although in the ideal case, compilers would automatically solve these challenges by optimizing a given function to utilize all of a system's resources, decades of studies have been unable to achieve this goal. Compilers are effective at optimizing code for an individual resource, but generally do not consider optimizations across multiple, heterogeneous resources. Even for compilers/tools that do consider multiple resources, these tools cannot transform code to use different algorithms to more effectively exploit the features of a heterogeneous device [6].

We claim that the current inability of compilers and operating systems to effectively optimize applications for multi-core heterogeneous systems is caused by a fundamental problem: *no single implementation of a function is optimal across all different devices, resource amounts, and input parameters*. For example, a sorting function running on a microprocessor would likely use a quick-sort algorithm, whereas on an FPGA, a bitonic-sort algorithm would be more efficient. Furthermore, implementation efficiency extends beyond just algorithmic choices and also requires considering the input parameters, numbers of devices/cores, work partitioning, etc.

To address these issues, we introduce the RACECAR heuristic for automatic function specialization on multi-core, heterogeneous systems. Function specialization is traditionally a compiler optimization that creates more efficient custom (i.e., specialized) implementations of a function for known function invocations. For multi-core, heterogeneous systems, we extend function specialization to explore algorithmic and implementation alternatives, different parallelization strategies, and different work partitionings, which we refer to as *multi-core, heterogeneous function specialization (MHFS)*.

Given a knowledge base of implementation alternatives and parallelization strategies, RACECAR operates by first analysing the performance of each implementation. Based on the implementation performances, RACECAR then determines which implementations to select in different conditions and how to efficiently partition work to utilize parallel resources. By recursively applying this analysis, RACECAR considers nested levels of work partitioning resulting in implementations that utilize up to all of the resources on a system. As the results demonstrate, RACECAR-specialized implementations can utilize multiple microprocessors, GPUs, and FPGAs effectively and achieve speedups up to 117x compared to a single CPU thread.

We envision several usage scenarios for RACECAR. First, compilers could use the heuristic for multi-core heterogeneous

PPoPP'12, February 25–29, 2012, New Orleans, Louisiana, USA.
ACM 978-1-4503-1160-1/12/02.

systems, or even for individual devices where specialization using different algorithms for different input parameters would be beneficial. Furthermore, runtime optimizations tools (e.g. [6]) could use the heuristic to make dynamic optimization decisions. The knowledge base required by the heuristic could be realized in function libraries by including multiple implementations provided by device/system vendors, domain experts, or open-source efforts.

2. Experimental Results

To assess RACECAR, we selected eleven functions and created a total of thirty-three alternate heterogeneous implementations of those functions to use as an input for the heuristic. We evaluated RACECAR on four diverse systems, three of which are heterogeneous. The first system, referred to as Gamma, consists of a 2.8 GHz quad-core Intel Xeon W3520 CPU, an Altera Stratix-III L340 FPGA, and two Nvidia GTX-295 GPUs. The second system, referred to as Marvel, consists of eight dual-core 2.4 GHz AMD Opteron 880 CPUs. The third system, referred to as Novo-G, is a node of the Novo-G supercomputer [2] and consists of a quad-core Intel Xeon E5520 CPU and four Altera Stratix-III E260 FPGAs. The fourth system, referred to as Delta, consists of a 3.2 GHz Intel Xeon CPU and a Xilinx Virtex IV LX100 FPGA.

Figure 1 illustrates the speedup achieved by the RACECAR-specialized implementations for the eleven functions. All speedup numbers are relative to the same function executing on a single-thread on the same system. *2DConv* is a two-dimensional discrete convolution function. *CConv* is a discrete circular convolution function. *Conv* is a discrete convolution function. *FW* performs the Floyd-Warshall algorithm. *Inner* is an inner-product function. *Mean* applies a mean filter to an image. *MM* is a matrix multiply function. *Optical* performs an optical flow algorithm on a series of images. *Prewitt* applies the Prewitt edge filter to an image. *SAD* performs a sum-of-absolute differences image retrieval algorithm. *Sort* is a sorting function.

As illustrated in Figure 1, all functions achieved speedup relative to their single-threaded versions. The large amount of variance between different functions is mostly due to the varying efficiency of the implementations provided as an input to RACECAR. For the *Conv* and *SAD* functions, we provided FPGA and GPU implementations which were extremely efficient on the supporting systems. While ideally we would have included heterogeneous implementations for all functions, the lengthy process of creating the implementations limited the analysis. The large amount of variance between different systems is due to the different processing resources available on each system. Only the Gamma system includes a GPU and only the Delta, Marvel, and Novo-G systems include FPGAs. However, the Novo-G system includes four FPGAs, while the Gamma system only includes one, and the Delta system's FPGA is on a relatively slow bus.

3. Conclusions

In this paper, we introduce the RACECAR heuristic to create specialized function implementations for multi-core, heterogeneous systems. From a set of provided implementations, the heuristic evaluates different implementation alternatives and builds data structures that may inform compilers and runtime optimization tools of how to efficiently execute the function for any invocation.

We evaluated the performance of RACECAR-specialized implementations on four diverse systems with various combinations of microprocessors, GPUs, and FPGAs, using a set of eleven functions and thirty-three implementations. For these experiments, RACECAR achieved speedups up to 117x with an average speedup of 11x compared to a single CPU thread.

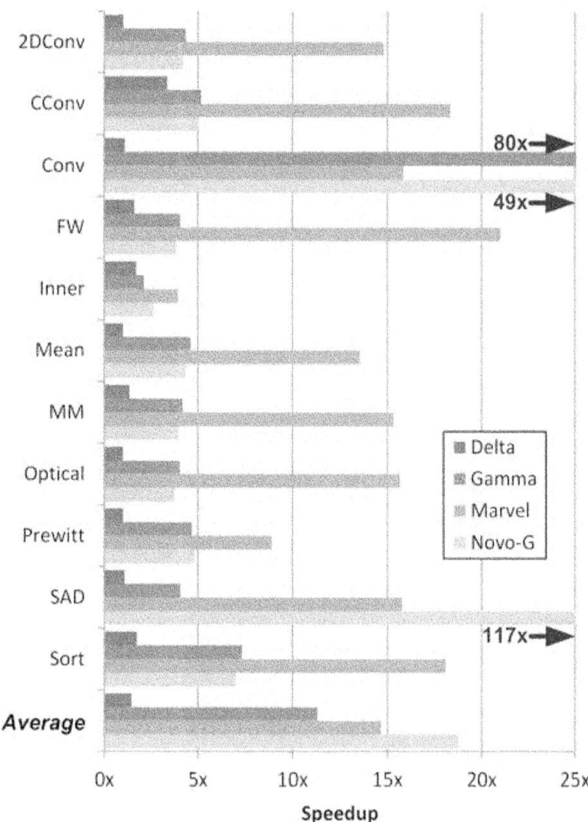

Figure 1. Speedup of RACECAR-specialized implementations for eleven functions relative to single-threaded implementations.

Acknowledgments

This work was supported by the National Science Foundation, grant CNS-0914474.

References

[1] A. DeHon, "The density advantage of configurable computing," *Computer*, vol. 33, no. 4, pp. 41–49, 2000.

[2] A. George, H. Lam, and G. Stitt. "Novo-g: at the forefront of scalable reconfigurable supercomputing". *IEEE Computing in Science and Engineering Magazine* (Jan/Feb 2011), pp. 82–86, 2011.

[3] Z. Guo, W. Najjar, F. Vahid, and K. Vissers, "A quantitative analysis of the speedup factors of FPGAs over processors," in *FPGA '04: Proceedings of the 2004 ACM/SIGDA 12th International Symposium on Field Programmable Gate Arrays*, pp. 162–170, 2004.

[4] B. Nelson, M. Wirthlin, B. Hutchings, P. Athanas, and S. Bohner. "Design productivity for configurable computing," in *ERSA '08: Proceedings of the International Conference on Engineering of Reconfigurable Systems and Algorithms*, pp. 57–66, 2008.

[5] P. Trancoso and M. Charalambous, "Exploring graphics processor performance for general purpose applications," in *Proceedings of the 8th Euromicro Conference on Digital System Design*, pp. 306–313, 2005.

[6] J. R. Wernsing and G. Stitt, "Elastic computing: a framework for transparent, portable, and adaptive multi-core heterogeneous computing," in *LCTES '10: Proceedings of the ACM SIGPLAN/SIGBED 2010 Conference on Languages, Compilers, and Tools for Embedded Systems*, pp. 115–124, 2010.

A Lock-Free, Array-Based Priority Queue *

Yujie Liu and Michael Spear
Lehigh University
{yul510, spear}@cse.lehigh.edu

Categories and Subject Descriptors D.1.3 [*Programming Techniques*]: Concurrent Programming—Parallel Programming

General Terms Algorithms, Design, Performance

Keywords Lock-Free, Linearizability, Randomization, Heap, Priority Queue, Synchronization, Mound

1. Introduction

Priority queues are useful in scheduling, discrete event simulation, networking (e.g., routing and real-time bandwidth management), graph algorithms (e.g., Dijkstra's algorithm), and artificial intelligence (e.g., A^* search). In these and other applications, not only is it crucial for priority queues to have low latency, but they must also offer good scalability and guarantee progress. Furthermore, the `insert` and `extractMin` operations are expected to have no worse than $O(log(N))$ complexity. In practice, this has focused implementation on heaps [1, Ch. 6] [4] and skip lists [6].

This paper introduces a new lock-free, linearizable [3] priority queue, called the mound. A mound is a tree of sorted lists. Mounds employ randomization when choosing a starting leaf for an `insert`, which avoids the need for insertions to contend for a mound-wide counter, but introduces the possibility that a mound will have "empty" nodes in non-leaf positions. The use of sorted lists avoids the need to swap a leaf into the root position during `extractMin`. Combined with the use of randomization, this ensures disjoint-access parallelism. Asymptotically, `extractMin` is $O(log(N))$. The sorted list also obviates the use of swapping to propagate a new value to its final destination in the mound `insert` operation. Instead, `insert` uses a binary search along a path in the tree to identify an insertion point, and then uses a single writing operation to insert a value. The `insert` complexity is $O(log(log(N)))$. Our lock-free mound employs a software `DCAS` [2] to implement multiword atomic operations.

2. The Mound Algorithm

We focus on the operations needed to implement a lock-free priority queue with a mound, namely `extractMin` and `insert`. We permit the mound to store arbitrary non-unique, totally-ordered values. We reserve $\top$ as the return value of an `extractMin` on an empty mound.

As is common when building lock-free algorithms, we require that every shared memory location be read via a single atomic `READ` operation, which stores its result in a local variable. All updates of shared memory are performed using `CAS`, `DCAS`, or `DCSS` [2]. Furthermore, every mutable shared location is augmented with a counter (c). The counter is incremented on every update, and is read atomically as part of the `READ` operation.

A mound is a rooted tree of sorted lists. The notation $\texttt{val}(n)$ denotes the value of the first element in the list stored at node n (namely $n.list$). If $n.list$ is empty, $\texttt{val}(n)$ returns $\top$.

In a traditional min-heap, the heap invariant only holds at the boundaries of functions, ensuring that the value of each node is no greater than the value of any child. This property is also the correctness property for a mound when there are no in-progress operations. When an operation is between its invocation and response, we employ a $dirty$ field to express this "mound property": for every node c and its parent p, $(\neg p.dirty) \Rightarrow \texttt{val}(p) \leq \texttt{val}(c)$.

When inserting a value v into the mound, the only requirement is that there exist some node c such that $\texttt{val}(c) \geq v$ and if c is not the root, for the parent p of c, $\texttt{val}(p) \leq v$. When such a node is identified, v can be inserted as the new head of c's list. Inserting v as the head of c's list clearly cannot violate the mound property: decreasing $\texttt{val}(c)$ to v does not violate the mound property between p and c, since $v \geq \texttt{val}(p)$. Furthermore, for every child c' of c, it already holds that $\texttt{val}(c') \geq \texttt{val}(c)$. Since $v \leq \texttt{val}(c)$, setting $\texttt{val}(c)$ to v does not violate the mound property between c and its children.

The $\texttt{insert}(v)$ method operates as follows: it selects a random leaf l and compares v to $\texttt{val}(l)$. If $v \leq \texttt{val}(l)$, then either the parent of l has a `val()` less than v, in which case the insertion can occur at l, or else there must exist some ancestor c such that inserting v at $c.list$ preserves the mound property. A binary search is employed to find this ancestor. Note that the binary search is along an ancestor chain of logarithmic depth, and thus the search introduces $O(log(log(N))$ overhead. The leaf is ignored if $\texttt{val}(l) < v$, since the mound property guarantees that every ancestor a of l must have a $\texttt{val}(a) < v$, and another leaf is randomly selected. If too many unsuitable leaves are selected (bounded by *THRESHOLD*), the mound is expanded by one level. After expansion, every leaf l is guaranteed to be available ($\texttt{val}(l) = \top > v$), and thus any random leaf is a suitable starting point for the binary search.

`extractMin` is similar to its analog in traditional heaps. When the minimum value is extracted from the root, we return (and remove) the first element of the root's list as the result, or $\top$ if the list is empty. This behavior is equivalent to the traditional heap behavior of moving some leaf node's value into the root. At this point, the mound property may not be preserved between the root and its children, so the root's $dirty$ field is set true.

`moundify` restores the mound property throughout the tree. When `moundify` is called on a node n, it first ensures the children

* This research was sponsored in part by National Science Foundation Grant CNS-1016828

PPoPP'12, February 25–29, 2012, New Orleans, Louisiana, USA.
ACM 978-1-4503-1160-1/12/02.

Listing 1 The Lock-free Mound Algorithm

```
type LNode
  T         value    ▷ value stored in this list node
  LNode*    next     ▷ next element in list

type CMNode
  LNode*    list     ▷ sorted list of values stored at this node
  boolean   dirty    ▷ true if mound property does not hold
  int       c        ▷ counter – incremented on every update

global variables
  tree_{i∈[1,N]} ← ⟨nil, false, 0⟩   : CMNode   ▷ array of mound nodes
  depth ← 1                          : ℕ        ▷ depth of the mound tree

func val(N : CMNode) : T
if N.list = nil return ⊤ else return N.list.value

proc insert(v : T)
while true
   c ← findInsertPoint(v)
   C ← READ(tree_c)
   if val(C) ≥ v
      C' ← ⟨new LNode(v, C.list), C.dirty, C.c + 1⟩
      if c = 1
         if CAS(tree_c, C, C') return
      else
         P ← READ(tree_{c/2})
         if val(P) ≤ v
            if DCSS(tree_c, C, C', tree_{c/2}, P) return
      delete(C'.list)

func findInsertPoint(v : ℕ) : ℕ
while true
   d ← READ(depth)
   for attempts ← 1 ... THRESHOLD
      leaf ← randLeaf(d)
      if val(leaf) ≥ v return binarySearch(leaf, 1, v)
   CAS(depth, d, d + 1)

func randLeaf(d : ℕ) : ℕ
return random i ∈ [2^{d-1}, 2^d − 1]

func extractMin() : T
while true
   R ← READ(tree_1)
   if R.dirty
      moundify(1)
      continue
   if R.list = nil return ⊤
   if CAS(tree_1, R, ⟨R.list.next, true, R.c + 1⟩)
      retval ← R.list.value
      delete(R.list)
      moundify(1)
      return retval

proc moundify(n : ℕ)
while true
   N ← READ(tree_n)
   d ← READ(depth)
   if ¬N.dirty return
   if n ∈ [2^{d-1}, 2^d − 1] return
   L ← READ(tree_{2n})
   R ← READ(tree_{2n+1})
   if L.dirty
      moundify(2n)
      continue
   if R.dirty
      moundify(2n + 1)
      continue
   if val(L) ≤ val(R) and val(L) < val(N)
      if DCAS(tree_n, N, ⟨L.list, false, N.c + 1⟩,
      tree_{2n}, L, ⟨N.list, true, L.c + 1⟩)
         moundify(2n)
         return
   elif val(R) < val(L) and val(R) < val(N)
      if DCAS(tree_n, N, ⟨R.list, false, N.c + 1⟩,
      tree_{2n+1}, R, ⟨N.list, true, R.c + 1⟩)
         moundify(2n + 1)
         return
   else ▷ Solve problem locally
      if CAS(tree_n, N, ⟨N.list, false, N.c + 1⟩) return
```

of n have $dirty$ set to false, by recursively invoking `moundify` on any $dirty$ children. `moundify` then inspects the `val()` of n and each child, and determines which is smallest. If n has the smallest value, or if n is a leaf, then the mound property already holds, and the operation completes. Otherwise, swapping n with the child having the smallest `val()` restores the mound property at n. However, the child involved in the swap now may not satisfy the mound property with its children, and thus its $dirty$ field is set true. Thus just as in a traditional heap, $O(log(N))$ calls suffice to restore the mound property.

3. Discussion

In a companion technical report, we present sequential and a fine-grained locking based mound algorithms [5]. In our evaluation, we found mound performance to exceed that of the lock-based Hunt priority queue, and to rival that of skiplist-based priority queues.

We also identified nontraditional uses for mounds. The first, probabilistic `extractMin`, is also available in a heap: since any $CMNode$ that is not dirty is, itself, the root of a mound, `extractMin` can be executed on any such node to select a random element from the priority queue. By selecting with some probability shallow, nonempty, non-root $CMNodes$, `extractMin` can lower contention by probabilistically guaranteeing the result to be close to the minimum value. Secondly, it is possible to execute an `extractMany`, which returns several elements from the mound. In the common case, most $CMNodes$ in the mound will be expected to hold lists with a modest number of elements. Rather than remove a single element, `extractMany` returns the entire list from a node, by setting the $list$ pointer to **nil** and $dirty$ to true, and then calling `moundify`. This technique can be used to implement lock-free prioritized work stealing.

References

[1] T. Cormen, C. Leiserson, R. Rivest, and C. Stein. *Introduction to Algorithms, 2nd edition.* MIT Press and McGraw-Hill Book Company, 2001.

[2] T. Harris, K. Fraser, and I. Pratt. A Practical Multi-word Compare-and-Swap Operation. In *Proceedings of the 16th International Conference on Distributed Computing*, Toulouse, France, Oct. 2002.

[3] M. P. Herlihy and J. M. Wing. Linearizability: a Correctness Condition for Concurrent Objects. *ACM Transactions on Programming Languages and Systems*, 12(3):463–492, 1990.

[4] G. Hunt, M. Michael, S. Parthasarathy, and M. Scott. An Efficient Algorithm for Concurrent Priority Queue Heaps. *Information Processing Letters*, 60:151–157, Nov. 1996.

[5] Y. Liu and M. Spear. A Lock-Free, Array-Based Priority Queue. Technical Report LU-CSE-11-004, Lehigh University, 2011.

[6] I. Lotan and N. Shavit. Skiplist-Based Concurrent Priority Queues. In *Proceedings of the 14th International Parallel and Distributed Processing Symposium*, Cancun, Mexico, May 2000.

An Infrastructure for Dynamic Optimization of Parallel Programs

Albert Noll
ETH Zurich
anoll@inf.ethz.ch

Thomas R. Gross
ETH Zurich
trg@inf.ethz.ch

Abstract

Object-oriented programming languages like Java provide only low-level constructs (e.g., starting a thread) to describe concurrency. High-level abstractions (e.g., thread pools) are merely provided as a library. As a result, a compiler is not aware of the high-level semantics of a parallel library and therefore misses important optimization opportunities. This paper presents a simple source language extension based on which a compiler can perform new optimizations that are particularly effective for parallel code.

Categories and Subject Descriptors D.1.3 [*Concurrent Programming*]: Parallel Programming

General Terms Performance, Languages

Keywords Parallel programming, performance, JIT compilation

1. Introduction

Modern object-oriented programming languages such as Java or C# are executed in a Virtual Machine (VM) that includes just-in-time (JIT) compilers and extensive libraries. These languages facilitate wide-spread portability and modularity. Unfortunately, these languages support parallelism only at a low-level of abstraction (e.g., starting, joining, or synchronizing threads) and high-level parallel constructs (e.g., thread pools) are merely provided as a library. Since the JIT compiler is not aware of the parallel library semantics, the JIT compiler misses important optimization opportunities (e.g., [3, 4]). Furthermore, using the parallel libraries requires the instantiation of new objects. Using objects to implement parallelism introduces overheads from object creation and garbage collecting these objects.

One parameter that has significant impact on the performance of a parallel program is, e.g., the parallel task size. The parallel task size determines the amount of work that must be processed by a parallel task. Consider the parallel program that is given in Figure 1. The code in Figure 1 contains a loop that creates a new parallel task object in every loop iteration. The parallel task is described as an anonymous inner class (line 4 – line 8). The minimum parallel task size is given by the variable `minTaskSize`, and the actual parallel task size is parametrized by a factor `x`.

In general, there is a tradeoff between the parallel task size and the number of parallel tasks. If the number of parallel task objects

PPoPP'12, February 25–29, 2012, New Orleans, Louisiana, USA.
ACM 978-1-4503-1160-1/12/02.

```
1  int minTaskSize = ...
2  int pts = minTaskSize * x;
3  for (int i = 0; i < work/pts; i++) {
4    Task t = new Runnable() {
5      public void run() {
6          execute(pts);
7      }
8    };
9    pool.execute(t);
10 }
```

Figure 1. Implementation of a simple parallel program using a parallel library.

that are created in the loop is too small (e.g., smaller than the number of available cores), the application is unbalanced and free resources remain unused. If, however, the number of parallel task objects is too large, the overhead from parallel task object creation and scheduling dominates the execution time of the program.

Finding the optimal parallel task size is a non-trivial problem, since the execution time of each parallel task can be different. Furthermore, the execution time of a parallel task depends on the underlying hardware, as well as the communication and synchronization between the individual parallel task objects. As shown in Figure 1, the parallel task size is determined by application code and cannot be changed by the VM or the JIT compiler if the chosen parallel task size results in suboptimal performance. The rest of the paper discusses the design of a concurrency-aware Java VM (JVM) that enables the JIT compiler to perform task size optimizations at runtime.

2. Parallel Task Size Optimizations for Java

This section discusses the design of a Java runtime environment that allows the JIT compiler to set the parallel task size at runtime. To allow the JIT compiler to change the parallel task size at runtime, the JIT compiler must know the concurrency structure of the application, i.e., which code regions can be executed in parallel. Identifying the concurrency structure of an application that uses parallel libraries is extremely difficult for a JIT compiler, because the notions of a parallel task and/or of a thread pool are not known to the JVM/JIT compiler. As can be seen in Figure 1 a parallel execution requires (1) the creation of new parallel task objects, (2) the creation of a thread pool, and (3) passing the parallel task objects to the thread pool for execution. None of these operations is defined in the Java Virtual Machine Specification and these operations are therefore not known to the JVM.

To make the concurrency structure visible to the JVM and the JIT compiler, we introduce *concurrent calls* in the source language that map to *concurrent regions* in the intermediate representation

```
void foo(int x) {
  concurrentCall(x+1);
  concurrentCall(x+2);
  sync();
}
@Concurrent
void concurrentCall(int x) {
  System.out.print(x);
}
```

Figure 2. Concurrent call example.

of the JIT compiler. A concurrent call is a method call that can be executed in parallel with the instructions that follow the concurrent call instruction in the caller. Furthermore, to guarantee the visibility of updates to shared memory that can be performed in a concurrent call, a synchronization method `sync()` is added to the type `Object`. Calling `sync()` suspends the execution of the calling thread until all concurrent calls (including recursive concurrent calls) have finished execution.

Figure 2 shows an example that contains two concurrent calls and one call to `sync()`. The thread that executes function `foo()` is called parent thread, and the thread that executes `concurrentCall` is called child thread. The code that is contained in a concurrent call must fulfill two requirements. First, a concurrent call must be *serializable*, i.e., the correctness of the program must not depend on whether a concurrent call is executed by a separate child thread or by the parent thread. Second, a concurrent call is executed *asynchronously* with the caller. Consequently, if `foo()` is called with the parameter $x = 1$ the output of the program can either be "2 1", or "1 2". Since there is no call to `sync()` between the two concurrent calls, and the execution of concurrent calls is asynchronous, the order in which concurrent calls are executed is undefined.

The serializability of a concurrent call allows the JVM to decide lazily (at runtime) if a concurrent call is compiled to sequential or parallel code. Furthermore, if the taken decision turns out to be unlucky (e.g., a concurrent call performs better if compiled to sequential code) the decision can be revoked by recompilation. The serializability property in conjunction with the asynchronicity property allows the JIT compiler to reorder concurrent/sequential method calls. The reordering increases the effectiveness of concurrent region merging, an optimization that allows the JIT compiler to set the parallel task size at runtime.

2.1 Concurrent Regions

A concurrent call is mapped to a concurrent region in the intermediate representation (IR) if the JIT compiler. This IR is referred to as a concurrency-aware IR (CIR). Figure 3 shows the CIR of function `foo()` in Figure 2.

```
1 t1 = x + 1;
2 cStart
3   call concurrentCall(t1);
4 cEnd
5 t2 = x + 2
6 cStart
7   call concurrentCall(t2);
8 cEnd
9 cSync
```

Figure 3. Concurrency-ware intermediate representation (CIR) of the code example given in Figure 1.

The `cStart` CIR node marks the beginning of a concurrent region. All instructions that follow `cStart` up to `cEnd` are part of the same concurrent region. `cEnd` represents the end of a concurrent region. All instructions that are contained in a concurrent region are executed by the same thread (either by the parent or by the child thread). The call to `sync()` in the source language is represented by the `cSync` CIR node.

2.2 Concurrent Region Merging Optimization

Concurrent region merging is an optimization that collapses multiple small concurrent regions into a concurrent region of a larger size. Concurrent region merging is particularly effective if the application contains a large number of short running parallel tasks. For example, if the execution time of the two concurrent calls in Figure 2 is too small, the overhead from scheduling the concurrent calls to child threads has a negative impact on the performance. To increase the parallel task size, the JIT compiler can merge the two concurrent regions that are illustrated in Figure 3 and thereby (1) increase the parallel task size and (2) decrease the scheduling overhead. Figure 4 shows the CIR of method `foo()` after concurrent region merging.

```
1 t1 = x + 1;
2 t2 = x + 2;
3 cStart
4   call concurrentCall(t1);
5 (cEnd)
6 (cStart)
7   call concurrentCall(t2);
8 cEnd
9 cSync
```

Figure 4. CIR of method `foo()` after concurrent region merging.

In Figure 4 the JIT compiler reorders the concurrent region (line 6 - line 8 in Figure 3) with the statement in line 5. This is a legal code transformation, because $t2$ is not used in the concurrent region that is defined in line 2 - line 4 and x is a local variable that does not escape method `foo()`. After the reordering, the JIT compiler can remove the two CIR nodes that are defined in line 5 and line 6 of Figure 4. As a result, both calls to `concurrentCall` are contained a single concurrent region and are therefore executed by the same thread.

3. Performance Evaluation

We implemented a prototype of the concurrency-aware IR and the concurrent region merging optimization in the Jikes RVM [1]. We use the NAS Parallel Benchmark Suite [2] to evaluate the effectiveness of concurrent region merging. The evaluation shows that using concurrent calls in combination with concurrent region merging results in a performance gain of up to 15% compared to a standard Java version.

References

[1] B. Alpern, C. R. Attanasio, J. J. Barton, M. G. Burke, P. Cheng, J.-D. Choi, A. Cocchi, S. J. Fink, D. Grove, M. Hind, S. F. Hummel, D. Lieber, V. Litvinov, M. F. Mergen, T. Ngo, J. R. Russell, V. Sarkar, M. J. Serrano, J. C. Shepherd, S. E. Smith, V. C. Sreedhar, H. Srinivasan, and J. Whaley. The Jalapeno virtual machine. *IBM Syst. J.*, 39 (1), 2000.

[2] M. A. Frumkin, M. Schultz, H. Jin, and J. Yan. Performance and scalability of the NAS parallel benchmarks in Java. In *IPDPS '03*, page 139.1. IEEE.

[3] A. Noll and T. R. Gross. Pervasive parallelism for managed runtimes. HotPar'11. USENIX Association.

[4] J. Zhao, J. Shirako, V. K. Nandivada, and V. Sarkar. Reducing task creation and termination overhead in explicitly parallel programs. In *PACT '10*. ACM.

Automatic Datatype Generation and Optimization

Fredrik Kjolstad[1]
Computer Science and Artificial Intelligence Laboratory
Massachusetts Institute of Technology
fred@csail.mit.edu

Torsten Hoefler Marc Snir
Department of Computer Science
University of Illinois at Urbana-Champaign
{htor,snir}@illinois.edu

Abstract

Many high performance applications spend considerable time packing noncontiguous data into contiguous communication buffers. MPI Datatypes provide an alternative by describing noncontiguous data layouts. This allows sophisticated hardware to retrieve data directly from application data structures. However, packing codes in real-world applications are often complex and specifying equivalent datatypes is difficult, time-consuming, and error prone. We present an algorithm that automates the transformation. We have implemented the algorithm in a tool that transforms packing code to MPI Datatypes, and evaluated it by transforming 90 packing codes from the NAS Parallel Benchmarks. The transformation allows easy porting of applications to new machines that benefit from datatypes, thus improving programmer productivity.

Categories and Subject Descriptors D.1.3 [*Programming Techniques*]: Concurrent Programming, Parallel programming

General Terms Performance, Design

Keywords MPI, Datatypes, Compiler Technique, Refactoring

1. Introduction

Data movement is the most expensive operation in modern high performance systems. It is therefore essential that we move data as few times as possible. MPI Datatypes are objects that describe arbitrary data layouts. Examples include strided and indexed data. Datatypes let us perform operations such as send, receive, put and write on non-contiguous data with a single call to the runtime.

If the programmer does not use datatypes when he sends non-contiguous data then he must either send it as multiple messages or first copy it to a contiguous buffer. Since it is expensive to send small messages, programmers typically opt for the copy. Such copy code is called packing code, because it packs data into a contiguous buffer. Datatypes allow the programmer to specify non-contiguous sends in one operation, *without* first performing a copy pass.

Traditional MPI systems pack data specified by datatypes into contiguous buffers, thereby forfeiting the performance gains from the removal of application packing code. However, modern network hardware such as InfiniBand provide support for transferring non-contiguous data (scatter/gather). In fact, communication performance improvements of 4.8x have been demonstrated, provided datatypes are specified [5]. Given this performance improvement

[1] The author did his work while he was at the University of Illinois.

PPoPP'12, February 25–29, 2012, New Orleans, Louisiana, USA.
ACM 978-1-4503-1160-1/12/02.

```
double buffer[N * 3];
for(int i=0; i < N; i++) {
  buffer[3*i]   = grid[i][0][0];
  buffer[3*i+1] = grid[i][0][1];
  buffer[3*i+2] = grid[i][0][2];
}
MPI_Send(buffer, N * 3, MPI_DOUBLE, left, tag, comm);
```

```
MPI_Datatype vec_t;
MPI_Type_vector(N, 3, N * 3, MPI_DOUBLE, &vec_t);
MPI_Type_commit(&vec_t);
MPI_Send(&grid[0][0][0], 1, vec_t, left, tag, comm);
```

Figure 1. Border exchange communication kernel before and after transformation from packing code to MPI Datatypes.

potential it is no surprise that emerging systems provide increasingly rich datatype support.

We present a novel algorithm that transforms packing code to optimized datatypes. The algorithm converts packing code to an internal datatype representation that is optimized through a number of passes before it is used to rewrite the application. The presentation assumes C and MPI, but the techniques generalize to other environments. For evaluation purposes, we implemented the algorithm as an Eclipse CDT refactoring tool. We then used the tool to transform 90 packing codes from the NAS Parallel Benchmarks [2]. Although we chose to implement the transformation in a refactoring tool, it is equally applicable in a compiler setting. For a detailed description of the algorithm including each optimization step, a full evaluation, discussion and two case studies we refer the reader to the accompanying technical report [3]. The tool, experimental data and additional case studies have been made available online [1].

1.1 Motivating Example

Figure 1 shows a very simple 2D left border exchange example before and after it has been transformed from packing code to MPI Datatype code. The example is similar to one of the packing codes in the NAS LU benchmark. The grid array stores three values for each cell of a two dimensional domain. Both kernels send the left border of the grid, which consist of noncontiguous strided data. The first kernel packs the column into a contiguous buffer. The second kernel uses a vector datatype.

1.2 Related Work

Several research groups have investigated techniques for *datatype generation*. These are exemplified by Tansey & Tilevich's tool for generating datatypes for C++ classes [6]. Our approach differs as it transforms packing code to datatypes. Other researchers have explored techniques to improve *datatype performance*. In one strand, researchers optimize runtime datatype parsing and packing code generation [4]. In a second strand, researchers have explored hardware and software support for non-contiguous transfers, achieving large communication speedups such as 4.8x [5]. Our approach statically optimize datatypes to reduce their runtime cost.

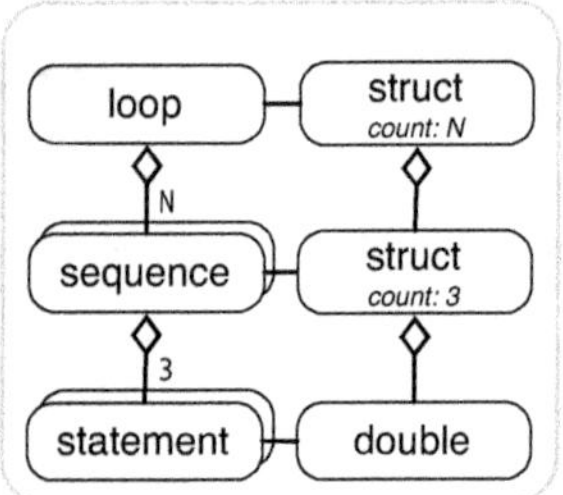

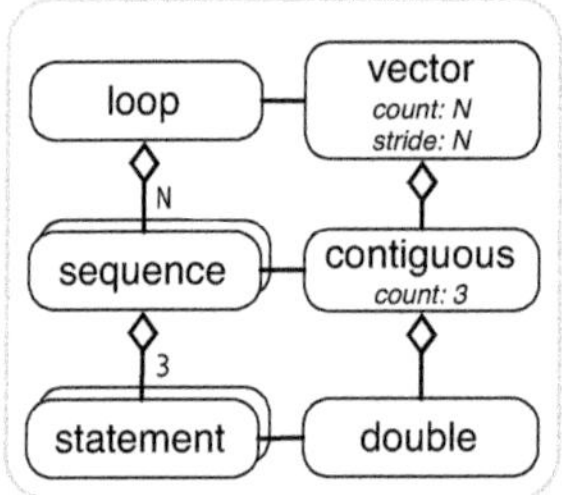

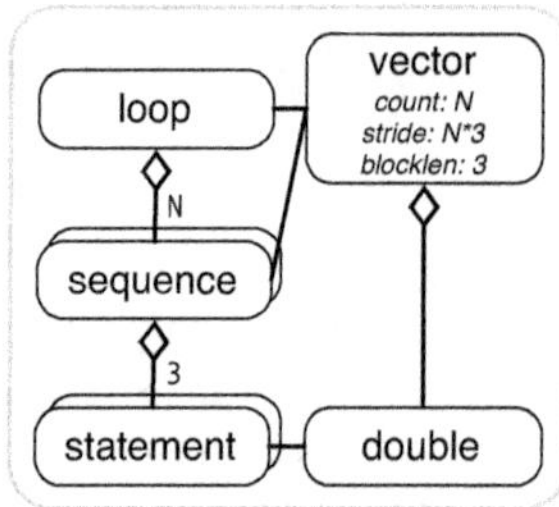

Figure 2. Equivalent Datatype IRs for the figure 1 example: initial IR (left), after specialization (center) and after compression (right).

2. Efficient Datatype Generation

Our algorithm for datatype generation and optimization is centered on an intermediate representation we call the Datatype IR. The Datatype IR captures the important (hierarchical) constructs of the packing code—packing statements, loops and sequences—and links them to equivalent datatypes. Figure 2 contains three Datatype IR examples. Our algorithm supports a number of datatypes. Some of these, listed in order of strictly decreasing generality, are struct, hindexed, hvector, vector and contiguous (see [3] for details). Note that most packing codes can be represented by different equivalent datatypes. For example, the three Datatype IRs in figure 2 are equivalent. We say a datatype representation is more efficient if it is expressed in terms of more specific datatypes, as these require fewer arguments in their construction. That is, a contiguous type can be expressed using fewer arguments than an indexed type. Our goal is therefore not merely to find a datatype that is equivalent to a packing construct, but to find one that is efficient. We achieve this by optimizing the datatype representation.

The Datatype IR can be constructed from any imperative language with packing code, such as C/C++/Fortran with MPI, or UPC. Two preconditions must hold before Datatype IR can be constructed in the current version: (1) the packing code block must only contain nested loops, assignments and if statements, and (2) the code block must write to consecutive locations in the packing buffer. Datatype IR construction requires identifying packing statements and then summarize loop nests containing packing statements, and sequences of packing statements and loops. Every packing statement, packing sequence and packing loop becomes part of a packing group. Once packing groups are summarized, a struct datatype is created to represent each composite group (loops and sequences) and a primitive datatype is set to represent each packing statement. Since struct datatypes can represent any data layout, the initial structs are equivalent to the packing code. The left box in figure 2 shows the initial IR for the example from figure 1.

Once the Datatype IR has been constructed our algorithm performs a number of optimization passes. These fall into two categories: specialization and compression. We currently support four specialization and three compression optimizations. Note that the Datatype IR allows optimization passes to be cleanly expressed in a language-independent manner. The optimizations are summarized below and detailed descriptions, as well as suggestions for additional optimizations, are provided in the technical report [3].

The specialization optimizations passes form a chain that successively specialize datatypes as much as possible. Let $\rightarrow$ denote a specialization pass, then the four specialization optimizations are struct $\rightarrow$ hindexed $\rightarrow$ hvector $\rightarrow$ vector $\rightarrow$ contiguous. That is, each optimization specializes one datatype to the next, provided specialization preconditions are met. Thus, depending on the access pattern of a given packing group, the specialization chain may be aborted at any point. For example, in the center IR in figure 2 the sequence was specialized to a contiguous type, while the loop could only be specialized to a vector. The distribution of the datatypes that replace the 90 packing codes in the NAS Parallel Benchmarks are given in the technical report [3].

Next, three compression optimization passes are performed to clean up the IR and hence the resulting datatype code. These are: (1) compress contiguous into parent block length, (2) merge struct and hindexed types, and (3) compress contiguous into send count. For example, the right IR in figure 1 depicts the center IR after compression optimizations have been applied.

The final step is to emit the datatypes as code. Note that in a compiler setting the target language can be different from the source language. For example, the source language could be UPC while the target language could be C with MPI. Hence it is possible to convert packing code to datatypes and emit these, even if the source language does not support datatypes. In a refactoring tool or a source to source compiler for C with MPI, datatype emit involves three stages. First, the datatype construction code is emitted (optionally with lazy initialization code). For hvector, vector and contiguous types it is sufficient to emit the datatype definition and constructor, as shown in figure 1. For struct and hindexed types we must also emit code that packs the indices. Second, the packing code consumer (e.g. a send call) must be identified and rewritten to use the new datatype. Third, a dead code elimination pass must be run to remove unused packing code.

3. Conclusions

Transfers of noncontiguous data are prevalent in many parallel codes; efficient scatter-gather capabilities that optimize such transfers and reduce the memory traffic generated by such transfers will be essential in future HPC architectures. We expect that future high performance network interfaces and memory controllers will have enhanced scatter-gather capabilities. This will enable direct transfer of noncontiguous data from memory to the network interface or to the CPU. Datatypes provide a means of communication between the executing code and a smart scatter-gather engine. The transformations we outlined will facilitate this communication—as part of a compiler, a refactoring tool or a run-time capability.

References

[1] Automatic datatype generation tool download. URL `http://people.csail.mit.edu/fred/datatypes`. Last Accessed 12/17/2011.

[2] D. Bailey, T. Harris, W. Saphir, R. Wijngaart, A. Woo, and M. Yarrow. The NAS parallel benchmarks 2.0. Technical report, NASA, 1995.

[3] F. Kjolstad, T. Hoefler, and M. Snir. A transformation to convert packing code to compact datatypes for efficient zero-copy data transfer. Technical report, University of Illinois at Urbana-Champaign, 2011.

[4] R. Ross, N. Miller, and W. Gropp. Implementing fast and reusable datatype processing. In *EuroPVM/MPI*, 2003.

[5] G. Santhanaraman, J. Wu, and D. K. Panda. Zero-copy MPI derived datatype communication over InfiniBand. In *EuroPVM/MPI*, 2004.

[6] W. Tansey and E. Tilevich. Efficient automated marshaling of C++ data structures for MPI applications. In *IPDPS*, 2008.

NDetermin: Inferring Nondeterministic Sequential Specifications for Parallelism Correctness

Jacob Burnim   Tayfun Elmas   George Necula   Koushik Sen

Department of Electrical Engineering and Computer Sciences, University of California, Berkeley

{jburnim,elmas,necula,ksen}@cs.berkeley.edu

Abstract

Nondeterministic Sequential (NDSeq) specifications have been proposed as a means for separating the testing, debugging, and verifying of a program's parallelism correctness and its sequential functional correctness. In this work, we present a technique that, given a few representative executions of a parallel program, combines dynamic data flow analysis and Minimum-Cost Boolean Satisfiability (MinCostSAT) solving for automatically inferring a likely NDSeq specification for the parallel program. For a number of Java benchmarks, our tool NDETERMIN infers equivalent or stronger NDSeq specifications than those previously written manually.

Categories and Subject Descriptors D.2.4 [*Software Engineering*]: Software/Program Verification; D.2.5 [*Software Engineering*]: Testing and Debugging; F.3.1 [*Logics and Meanings of Programs*]: Specifying and Verifying and Reasoning about Programs

General Terms Algorithms, Reliability, Verification

1. Nondeterministic Sequential Specifications

As multicore and manycore processors become increasingly common, more and more programmers must write parallel software. But writing such parallel software can be difficult and error prone. In addition to reasoning about the often-sequential functional correctness of each component of a program in isolation, a programmer must simultaneously consider whether multiple components running in parallel, their threads interleaving nondeterministically, can harmfully interfere with one another.

In an earlier paper [2] we proposed nondeterministic sequential (NDSeq) specifications as a means for decomposing the reasoning about a program's parallelism correctness and its functional correctness. To explain the problem addressed by NDSeq specifications, consider the simple parallel program in Figure 1(a). The program consists of a parallel for-loop, written as `coforeach`—each iteration of this loop attempts to perform a computation (Line 6) on shared variable `x`, which is initially 0. Each iteration uses an atomic compare-and-swap (`CAS`) operation to update shared variable `x`. If multiple iterations try to concurrently update `x`, some of these `CAS`'s will fail and those parallel loop iterations will recompute their updates to `x` and try again.

PPoPP'12, February 25–29, 2012, New Orleans, Louisiana, USA.
ACM 978-1-4503-1160-1/12/02.

```
1: coforeach (i in 1,...,N) {
2:   bool done = false;
3:   while (!done) {
4:
5:     int prev = x;
6:     int curr = i * prev + i;
7:     if (CAS(x,prev,curr)) {
8:       done = true;
9: } } }
```

(a) Parallel program

```
1: nd-foreach(i in 1,...,N) {
2:   bool done = false;
3:   while (!done) {
4:     if (*) {
5:       int prev = x;
6:       int curr = i * prev + i;
7:       if (CAS(x,prev,curr)) {
8:         done = true;
9: } } } }
```

(b) NDSeq specification

Figure 1. Example program to perform the reduction in line 6 for the integers $\{1,\ldots,N\}$, in some arbitrary order.

A natural approach to specifying parallelism correctness would be to specify that the program in Figure 1(a) must produce the same final value for `x` as a version of the program with all parallelism removed—i.e., the entire code is executed by a single thread. However, in this case we do not get a sequential program equivalent to the parallel program. For example, the parallel program in Figure 1(a) is free to execute the computations at line 6 in any *nondeterministic* order. Thus, for the same input value of `x`, different thread schedules can produce different values for `x` at the end of the execution. On the other hand, executing the loop sequentially from `1` to `N` will always produce the same, deterministic final value for `x`. Suppose that such extra nondeterministic behaviors due to thread interleavings are intended; the challenge here is how to express these nondeterministic behaviors in a sequential specification.

We addressed this challenge in [2] by introducing a specification mechanism that the programmer can use to declare the intended, algorithmic notions of nondeterminism in the form of a sequential program. Such a *nondeterministic sequential specification* (NDSeq) for our example program is shown in Figure 1(b). This specification is intentionally very close to the actual parallel program, but its semantics is sequential with two nondeterministic aspects. First, the `nd-foreach` keyword in line 1 specifies that the loop iterations can run in any permutation of the set 1, ..., N. This part of the specification captures the *intended* (or *algorithmic*) nondeterminism in the behavior of the program, caused in the parallel program by running threads with arbitrary schedules. Any *additional* nondeterminism is an error, due to unintended interference between interleaved parallel threads, such as data races or atomicity violations. Second, the `if(*)` keyword in line 4 specifies that the iteration body may be skipped nondeterministically, at least from a partial correctness point of view; this is acceptable, since the loop in this program fragment is already prepared to deal with the case when the effects of an iteration are ignored following a failed CAS statement. In summary, all the final values of `x` output by the parallel program in Figure 1(a) can be produced by a feasible execution of the NDSeq specification in Figure 1(b). Then, we say that the parallel program obeys its NDSeq specification, and, the functional correctness of a parallel program can be tested, debugged, and verified *sequentially* on the NDSeq specification, without any need to reason about the uncontrolled interleaving of parallel threads.

2. Inferring NDSeq Specifications

The key difficulty with the manual approach is that writing such specifications, and especially the placement of the **if(*)** constructs, can be can be a time-consuming and challenging process, especially to a programmer unfamiliar with such specifications. If a programmer places too few **if(*)** constructs, she may not be able to specify some intended nondeterministic behaviors in the parallel code. However, if she places too many **if(*)** constructs, or if she place them in the wrong places, the specification might allow too much nondeterminism, which will likely violate the intended functionality of the code.

Therefore, we believe that automatically inferring NDSeq specifications can save programmer time and effort in applying NDSeq specifications. In particular, we believe that using an inferred specification as a starting point is much simpler than writing the whole specification from scratch. More generally, such inferred specifications can aid in understanding and documenting a program's parallel behavior.

In [2], we proposed a sound runtime technique that, using conflict-serializability check, checks a given representative interleaved execution trace of a structured-parallel program, whether there exists an equivalent, feasible execution of the NDSeq specification. Our contribution in this work is to give an algorithm, running on a set of input execution traces, for inferring a *minimal* nondeterministic sequential specification such that the checking approach described in [2] on the input traces succeeds. Choosing a minimal specification—i.e., with a minimal number of **if(*)**, is a heuristic that makes it more likely that the inferred specification matches the intended behavior of the program.

Our key idea is to reformulate the runtime checking algorithm in [2] as a constraint solving and optimization problem, in particular a Minimum Cost Boolean Satisfiability (MinCostSAT) problem. In order to infer an NDSeq specification, we observe a set of representative parallel execution traces for which the standard conflict serializability check gives conflict cycles indicating possible violations of the NDSeq specification. Similarly to the algorithm in [2], we utilize a dynamic dependence analysis with a program's specified nondeterminism in our MinCostSAT formulation. The constructed MinCostSAT formula contains variables corresponding to possible placement of **if(*)**s in the program. If this formula is satisfiable, then the solution gives us a minimal set of statements $\mathcal{S}$ in the program such that the input traces are all serializable—i.e., conflict cycles involving these statements in the input traces can be soundly ignored—with respect to the NDSeq specification obtained by enclosing each statement in $\mathcal{S}$ with **if(*)**. The minimal such solution for our example in Figure 1(a) places a single **if(*)** that encloses lines 5-8. Thus, our algorithm produces the correct NDSeq specification given in Figure 1(b). We refer the reader to our technical report [1] for the further details of our MinCostSAT formulation.

3. Results

We implemented our technique in a prototype tool for Java, called NDETERMIN, and applied NDETERMIN to the set of Java benchmarks for which we had previously and manually written NDSeq specifications [2]. We compared the quality and accuracy of our automatically-inferred **if(*)**s to the manually-written NDSeq specifications.

Our experimental results are summarized in Table 1. The second-to-last column of Table 1 reports the number of **if(*)** constructs in the inferred NDSeq specification for each benchmark. We manually confirmed that each of the inferred **if(*)** annotation was correct. For many of the benchmarks, NDETERMIN correctly inferred that no **if(*)** constructs are necessary.

Benchmark		# Parallel Constructs	# `if(*)`'s in manual specification	Inferred NDSeq Specification	
				# `if(*)`'s	Correct?
JGF	`sor`	1	0	0	yes
	`matmult`	1	0	0	yes
	`series`	1	0	0	yes
	`crypt`	2	0	0	yes
	`moldyn`	4	0	0	yes
	`lufact`	1	0	0	yes
	`raytracer`	1	0	–	–
	`raytracer (fixed)`	1	0	0	yes
	`montecarlo`	1	0	0	yes
PJ	`pi3`	1	0	0	yes
	`keysearch3`	2	0	0	yes
	`mandelbrot`	1	0	0	yes
	`phylogeny`	2	3	–	–
	`phylogeny (fixed)`	2	3	1	yes
`(non-blocking) stack`		1	2	2	yes
`(non-blocking) queue`		1	2	2	yes
`meshrefine`		1	2	2	yes

Table 1. Experimental results. All **if(*)** annotations inferred by our tool were verified manually to be correct.

For benchmarks `stack`, `queue`, and `meshrefine`, we note that NDETERMIN finds specifications slightly smaller than the manual ones. Further, for benchmark `phylogeny` (fixed), while the previous manual NDSeq specification included three **if(*)** constructs, NDETERMIN correctly infers that only one of these three is actually necessary. The extra **if(*)**'s appear to have been manually added to address some possible parallel conflicts that, in fact, can never be involved in a non-serializable execution. Finally, our inference algorithm can detect parallel behaviors that *no* possible NDSeq specification would allow, which often contain parallelism bugs. In fact, as indicated by "–" in Table 1, NDETERMIN correctly refuses to infer NDSeq specifications for the buggy versions of `raytracer` and `phylogeny` (containing atomicity errors due to insufficient synchronization), since no solution to the MinCostSAT instance exists; NDETERMIN does infer correct NDSeq specifications for the correct (`fixed`) versions of these benchmarks. (For a more elaborate discussion of our experimental results, see our technical report [1].)

These experimental results provide promising preliminary evidence for our claim that NDETERMIN can automatically infer **if(*)** necessary for the NDSeq specification of parallel correctness for real parallel Java programs. We believe adding nondeterministic **if(*)** constructs is the most difficult piece of writing a NDSeq specification, and thus our inference technique can make using NDSeq specifications much easier. Further, such specification inference may allow for fully-automated testing and verification to use NDSeq specifications to separately address parallel and functional correctness.

Acknowledgments

This research supported in part by Microsoft (Award #024263) and Intel (Award #024894) funding and by matching funding by U.C. Discovery (Award #DIG07-10227), by NSF Grants CCF-101781, CCF-0747390, CCF-1018729, and CCF-1018730, and by a DoD NDSEG Graduate Fellowship. The last author is supported in part by a Sloan Foundation Fellowship. Additional support comes from Oracle (formerly Sun Microsystems), from a gift from Intel, and from Par Lab affiliates National Instruments, NEC, Nokia, NVIDIA, and Samsung.

References

[1] J. Burnim, T. Elmas, G. Necula, and K. Sen. NDetermin: Inferring nondeterministic sequential specifications for parallelism correctness. Technical Report UCB/EECS-2011-143, EECS Department, University of California, Berkeley, Dec 2011.

[2] J. Burnim, T. Elmas, G. Necula, and K. Sen. NDSeq: Runtime checking for nondeterministic sequential specifications of parallel correctness. In *Programming Language Design and Implementation (PLDI)*, 2011.

Concurrent Breakpoints

Chang-Seo Park
EECS Department, UC Berkeley, USA
parkcs@cs.berkeley.edu

Koushik Sen
EECS Department, UC Berkeley, USA
ksen@cs.berkeley.edu

Abstract
In program debugging, reproducibility of bugs is a key requirement. Unfortunately, bugs in concurrent programs are notoriously difficult to reproduce because bugs due to concurrency happen under very specific thread schedules and the likelihood of taking such corner-case schedules during regular testing is very low. We propose concurrent breakpoints, a light-weight and programmatic way to make a concurrency bug reproducible. We describe a mechanism that helps to hit a concurrent breakpoint in a concurrent execution with high probability. We have implemented concurrent breakpoints as a light-weight library for Java and C/C++ programs. We have used the implementation to deterministically reproduce several known non-deterministic bugs in real-world concurrent Java and C/C++ programs with almost 100% probability.

Categories and Subject Descriptors D.2.5 [*Software Engineering*]: Testing and Debugging

General Terms Languages, Reliability

1. Motivation
A key requirement in program debugging is reproducibility. Developers require that a bug can be reproduced deterministically so that they can confirm the bug and run the buggy execution repeatedly with the aid of a debugger and find the cause of the bug. For sequential programs, a bug can be reproduced deterministically by replaying the program with the recorded inputs and other sources of non-determinism. Bugs in sequential programs can be reported easily to a bug database because a user only needs to report the input on which the sequential program exhibits the bug.

Unfortunately, bugs in concurrent programs happen under very specific thread schedules and are often not reproducible during regular testing. Such non-deterministic bugs in concurrent programs are called *Heisenbugs*. One could argue that Heisenbugs could be made reproducible if the thread schedule is recorded along with program inputs during a program execution. Recording and replaying a thread schedule poses several problems: 1) It requires to observe the exact thread schedule either through program instrumentation or by using some specialized hardware. Instrumentation often incurs huge overhead and specialized hardware are often not readily available. 2) Replaying a thread schedule requires a special runtime which could again incur huge overhead.

Nevertheless, we need some information about the thread schedule along with the program inputs to reproduce a Heisenbug. We would like the information about thread schedules to be portable so that we do not need a special runtime to reproduce the bug. In this paper, we propose a simple light-weight technique called *concurrent breakpoints*, to specify enough information about a Heisenbug so that it can be reproduced with very high probability without requiring a special runtime or a full recording of the thread schedule.

PPoPP'12, February 25–29, 2012, New Orleans, Louisiana, USA
ACM 978-1-4503-1160-1/12/02.

Our technique for reproducibility is based on the observation that Heisenbugs can often be attributed to a *small* set of program states, called *conflict states*. A program execution is said to be in a conflict state if there exists two threads that are either 1) trying to access the same memory location and at least one of the accesses is a write (i.e. a data race), or 2) they are trying to operate on the same synchronization object (e.g. contending to acquire the same lock). Depending on how a conflict state is resolved, i.e. which thread is allowed to execute first, a concurrent program execution could end up in different states. Such difference in program states often lead to Heisenbugs. Therefore, in order to reproduce a Heisenbug, one should be able to reach those small set of conflict states and control the program execution from those states.

2. Concurrent Breakpoints
In this paper, we propose *concurrent breakpoints*, a light-weight and programmatic tool that facilitates reproducibility of Heisenbugs in concurrent programs. A concurrent breakpoint is an object that defines a set of program states and a scheduling decision that the program needs to take if a state in the set is reached. Typically, the states described by a concurrent breakpoint would be a set of conflict states.

Formally, a *concurrent breakpoint* is a tuple (ℓ_1, ℓ_2, ϕ), where ℓ_1 and ℓ_2 are program locations and ϕ is a predicate over the program state. A program execution is said to have triggered a concurrent breakpoint (ℓ_1, ℓ_2, ϕ) if the following conditions are met:

- the program reaches a state that satisfies the predicate: $\exists t_1, t_2 \in Threads.(t_1.pc = \ell_1) \wedge (t_2.pc = \ell_2) \wedge (t_1 \neq t_2) \wedge \phi$, and
- from the above state, the program executes the next instruction of thread t_1 before the next instruction of thread t_2.

That is, we say that a concurrent breakpoint (ℓ_1, ℓ_2, ϕ) is triggered if the program reaches some program state and takes an action from the state. The state is such that it satisfies the predicate ϕ and there exists two threads t_1 and t_2 such that t_1 and t_2 are at program locations ℓ_1 and ℓ_2 in the state, respectively. The action at the state executes the thread t_1 before the thread t_2.

Note that in our definition, a concurrent breakpoint involves two threads. The definition can be easily extended to involve more than two threads. For example, a concurrent breakpoint $(\ell_1, \ell_2, \ell_3, \phi)$ involves three threads.

Example. We can trigger a feasible data race in a program, i.e. reach a state in which two threads are about to access the same memory location and at least one of them is a write, using a concurrent breakpoint as follows. Consider the program in Figure 1. The concurrent breakpoint $(2, 5, t_1.\texttt{p1} == t_2.\texttt{p2})$ represents the state where two threads are at lines 2 and 5, respectively, and are about to access the same memory location denoted by the field `x` of the object referenced by both `p1` and `p2` and at least one of the accesses is a write. (If v is a local variable of thread t, then we denote the variable using $t.v$.) Such a racy state described by the concurrent breakpoint could be reached if `foo` and `bar` are executed in parallel by different threads on the same `Point` object. The concurrent breakpoint also specifies that if the racy state is ever reached, then the thread reaching line number 2 must execute its next instruction before the thread reaching line number 5 executes its next instruction. This forces the program to resolve the

```
1: void foo (Point p1) {
     // (new ConflictBreakpoint("bp1",p1)).
          breakHere(false,Global.TIMEOUT);
2:   p1.x = 10;
3: }
4: void bar (Point p2) {
     // (new ConflictBreakpoint("bp1",p2)).
          breakHere(true,Global.TIMEOUT);
5:   t = p2.x;
6: }
```

Figure 1. Example with data race

data race in a particular order. The commented out code represents the concurrent breakpoint in terms of library function calls. Interested readers are referred to our technical report [4] for full details of the library and its implementation.

Concurrent breakpoints could represent all conflict states, i.e. they could represent data races and lock contentions. Concurrent breakpoints could represent other buggy states, such as a deadlock state or a state where an atomicity violation or a missed notification happens. We argue in [4] that the necessary information about a buggy schedule could be represented using a small set of concurrent breakpoints: if a program execution could be forced to reach all the concurrent breakpoints in the set, then the execution hits the Heisenbug.

Given a concurrent breakpoint (ℓ_1, ℓ_2, ϕ), it is very unlikely that two threads will reach statements labelled ℓ_1 and ℓ_2, respectively, at the same time in a concurrent execution, even though each thread could reach the statements independent of the other threads several times during the execution. Therefore, a concurrent breakpoint could be difficult to hit during a normal concurrent execution.

We describe a mechanism called BTRIGGER that tries to force a program execution to a concurrent breakpoint. We rewrite the predicate for a concurrent breakpoint as: $\exists t_1, t_2 \in \mathit{Threads}.\ (t_1 \neq t_2) \wedge \phi_{t_1} \wedge \phi_{t_2} \wedge \phi_{t_1 t_2}$, where ϕ_{t_1} only refers to local variables of thread t_1, ϕ_{t_2} only refers to local variables of thread t_2, and $\phi_{t_1 t_2}$ refers to local variables of both t_1 and t_2. BTRIGGER works as follows. During the execution of a program, whenever a thread reaches a state satisfying the predicate ϕ_{t_i} where $i \in \{1, 2\}$, we postpone the execution of the thread for T time units and keep the thread in a set $\texttt{Postponed}_{t_i}$ for the postponed period. We continue the execution of the other threads. If another thread, say t, reaches a state satisfying the predicate ϕ_{t_j} where $j \in \{1, 2\}$ then we do the following. If there is a postponed thread, say t', in the set $\texttt{Postponed}_{t_i}$ where $i \neq j$ and local states of the two threads t and t' satisfy the predicate $\phi_{t_1 t_2}$, then we report that the concurrent breakpoint has been reached. Otherwise, we postpone the execution of the thread t by T time units and keep the thread in the set $\texttt{Postponed}_{t_j}$ for the postponed period. If the concurrent breakpoint is reached, we also order the execution of threads t and t' according to the order given by the concurrent breakpoint. Note that we do not postpone the execution of a thread indefinitely because this could result in a deadlock if all threads reach either ℓ_1 or ℓ_2 and none of the breakpoint predicates are satisfied by any pair of postponed threads.

BTRIGGER ensures that if a thread reaches a state satisfying the concurrent breakpoint partially (i.e. reaches a state satisfying the predicate ϕ_{t_1} or ϕ_{t_2}), it is paused for a reasonable amount of time, giving a chance to other threads to catch up and create a state that completely satisfies the concurrent breakpoint. This simple mechanism significantly increases the likelihood of hitting a concurrent breakpoint.

Our idea about concurrent breakpoints is motivated by recent testing techniques for concurrent programs, such as CalFuzzer [3], CTrigger [5], and PCT [1]. IMUnit [2], which is also closely related to this work, proposes a novel language to specify and execute schedules for multithreaded tests based on temporal logic and instrumentation of code.

Benchmark	Runtime (seconds)			Breakpoint type	Prob.[2]
	Normal	w/ ctr	OVH[1]		
cache4j	1.992	2.089	4.9	race	1.00
		2.051	3.0	atomicity	1.00
hedc	1.780	3.835	115.4	race	1.00
log4j 1.2.13	0.190	0.208	9	deadlock	1.00
	0.135	-	-	missed-notify	1.00
logging	0.140	0.140	0	deadlock	1.00
lucene	0.136	0.159	17	deadlock	1.00
moldyn	1.098	1.204	9.7	race	1.00
montecarlo	1.841	2.162	17.4	race	1.00
raytracer	1.097	1.274	16.1	race	1.00
stringbuffer	0.131	0.159	21	atomicity	1.00
swing	0.902	12.003	1230	deadlock	0.99
syncList	0.134	0.142	6	atomicity	1.00
	0.131	0.134	2	deadlock	1.00

Table 1. Experimental results for Java programs ([1]Overhead(%). [2]Empirical probability of triggering bug.)

3. Results

We have implemented concurrent breakpoints and BTRIGGER as a light-weight library (containing a few hundreds of lines code) for Java and C/C++ programs. We have used the implementation to reproduce several known Heisenbugs in real-world Java and C/C++ programs involving 1.6M lines of code. The breakpoints are inserted as extra code in the program under test using bug reports produced by CalFuzzer [3] and actual bug reports in bug databases. We ran each program with the breakpoints 100 times to measure the empirical probability of hitting the breakpoint. In our experiments, concurrent breakpoints made these non-deterministic bugs almost 100% reproducible.

Table 1 summarizes the results for our experiments on Java programs. For most of the benchmarks, the overhead of running the program with the concurrent breakpoint library was within 40% of the normal runtime. However, in some cases where we increased the waiting time to achieve a higher probability of hitting the breakpoint, the overhead became as large as 13x. Interested readers are referred to our technical report [4] for more detail on the results, including the results for C/C++ programs, and the methodology for inserting concurrent breakpoints.

4. Conclusion

Traditionally, programmers have used various ad-hoc tricks, such as inserting sleep statements and spawning a huge number of threads, to make a Heisenbug reproducible. These tricks are often found in various bug reports that are filed in open bug databases. We proposed a more scientific and programmatic technique to make a Heisenbug reproducible.

Acknowledgements

Research supported by Microsoft (Award #024263) and Intel (Award #024894) funding and by matching funding by U.C. Discovery (Award #DIG07-10227), by NSF Grants CCF-101781, CCF-0747390, CCF-1018729, and CCF-1018730, and by a DoD NDSEG Graduate Fellowship. The last author is supported in part by a Sloan Foundation Fellowship. Additional support comes from Par Lab affiliates National Instruments, Nokia, NVIDIA, Oracle, and Samsung.

References

[1] S. Burckhardt, P. Kothari, M. Musuvathi, and S. Nagarakatte. A randomized scheduler with probabilistic guarantees of finding bugs. In *ASPLOS '10*, pages 167–178, New York, NY, USA, 2010. ACM.

[2] V. Jagannath, M. Gligoric, D. Jin, Q. Luo, G. Rosu, and D. Marinov. Improved multithreaded unit testing. In *ESEC/FSE '11*, pages 223–233, New York, NY, USA, 2011. ACM.

[3] P. Joshi, M. Naik, C.-S. Park, and K. Sen. CalFuzzer: An extensible active testing framework for concurrent programs. In *CAV '09*, pages 675–681, Berlin, Heidelberg, 2009. Springer-Verlag.

[4] C.-S. Park and K. Sen. Concurrent breakpoints. Technical Report UCB/EECS-2011-159, EECS Department, UC Berkeley, Dec 2011.

[5] S. Park, S. Lu, and Y. Zhou. CTrigger: exposing atomicity violation bugs from their hiding places. In *ASPLOS*, pages 25–36. ACM, 2009.

Establishing a Miniapp as a Programmability Proxy

Andrew I. Stone
Colorado State University
stonea@cs.colostate.edu

John M. Dennis
National Center for Atmospheric Research
dennis@ucar.edu

Michelle Mills Strout
Colorado State University
mstrout@cs.colostate.edu

Abstract

Miniapps serve as test beds for prototyping and evaluating new algorithms, data structures, and programming models before incorporating such changes into larger applications. For the miniapp to accurately predict how a prototyped change would affect a larger application it is necessary that the miniapp be shown to serve as a proxy for that larger application. Although many benchmarks claim to proxy the performance for a set of large applications, little work has explored what criteria must be met for a benchmark to serve as a proxy for examining programmability. In this poster we describe criteria that can be used to establish that a miniapp serves as a performance and programmability proxy.

Categories and Subject Descriptors D.2.8 [*Metrics*]: Software Science

General Terms Languages, Measurement, Performance

Keywords Programmability Proxy, miniapp, benchmark, POP, conjugate gradient, parallel programming

1. Introduction

Miniapps are applications on the order of 1000 lines of code, that include a simple build system, and accurately model the performance of a larger application. In [4], Heroux et al. suggest that miniapps can be used to compare programming models and improve compilers. We contribute to the miniapp concept by introducing criteria for evaluating how well miniapps serve as a programmability proxy of a larger application.

A true measure of how well a miniapp acts as a programmability proxy is whether application developers would use results from the miniapp to evaluate possible changes in the full application. We believe three requirements must be fulfilled for application developers to find miniapps useful; these are that a miniapp include important code, is representative of the application, and is designed to allow for incremental change.

We use these criteria to evaluate a miniapp of the Conjugate Gradient solver for a large and heavily-used climate simulation code called the Parallel Ocean Program (POP). This miniapp is called CGPOP [5].

PPoPP'12, February 25–29, 2012, New Orleans, Louisiana, USA.
ACM 978-1-4503-1160-1/12/02.

2. Performance and Programmability Proxies

In [4] Heroux et al. introduce the concept of a miniapp. They state that a miniapp should on the order of 1000 SLOC and include a simple build process to enable easy porting. These size and simplicity requirements enable researchers to benchmark in immature environments. In this section we describe what criteria must be met for a miniapp to be considered a *performance proxy* and introduce additional requirements that must be met to show that a miniapp is a *programmability proxy*.

To be considered a *performance proxy*, a miniapp should accurately model the performance bottleneck of the full application at the range of cores that the full application typically targets. Also, the miniapp should be able to scale the problem size in a way that matches the performance of the full application when such scaling occurs. Once the baseline version of the miniapp has been shown to be performance proxy for the full app, modified versions of the miniapp can be compared to the baseline miniapp instead of the full application.

To be considered a *programmability proxy*, a miniapp should include the code from the full application that has the largest impact on performance (*code importance*), should enable incremental improvement to the full application (*incremental*), and should include a representative cross section of the implementation details (such as data distribution) that permeate the full application (*representative*). The programmability requirements for a miniapp are designed so that programmability conclusions made about the miniapp apply to the full application.

The *code importance* requirement often ensures that the code from the full application that is in the miniapp is code that is either often modified or dominates execution time. Often, the performance bottleneck in an application will require the most maintenance in the form of performance porting and debugging.

The *incremental* requirement aids in the realistic evolution of the full application. To be incremental, a miniapp should define a clean interface between the full application and itself to enable plugging in different versions of the miniapp while not negatively impacting performance due to any overhead introduced by the interface.

The *representative* requirement specifies that implementation details that affect the entire application should be included within the miniapp. This requirement suggests that simplifications to cross cutting data structures for details such as discretizations should not be done for a miniapp. The trade-off between this criterium and providing a small, modular miniapp for reintegration into the full application must be carefully managed.

3. The CGPOP Miniapp

The Parallel Ocean Program (POP) was developed at Los Alamos National Laboratory and is an important multi-agency code used for global ocean modeling and is a component within the Community Earth System Model (CESM) [1]. POP has been actively developed on for over 18 years, and is nearly 71,000 lines of Fortran 90 and MPI code. Due to its continued use, maintenance of the application in terms of porting it to new architectures is an ongoing issue. Several characteristics of POP and other earth system models present challenges to introducing changes in the application.

The POP application developers would like to experiment with new algorithms, data-structures, and programming models to improve performance and programmability given that new machines, with ever increasing numbers of cores, are being developed. However, experimentation is difficult to do within the context of the full application. The motivation for creating a miniapp for the POP developer team is that it will enable them to ensure that performance portability of the most critical portion of the application is maintained while also testing new algorithms, data-structures, and programming models.

The performance bottleneck in POP is a conjugate gradient (CG) computation. Conjugate gradient is a frequent target for benchmark and miniapp development. Examples include NPB CG [3] and HPCCG [4]. The main performance bottleneck in CG is the sparse matrix vector multiplies, which is a kernel that has also received significant attention in terms of performance [2, 6]. Although NAS CG has been referred to as a miniapp [4], based on the criteria we set forth it is not a miniapp relevant to POP because it is not a performance or programmability proxy for POP. Given that NAS CG does not fulfill the proxy requirements of a miniapp a new miniapp that models the Parallel Ocean Program has been developed. This miniapp is CGPOP. Whereas NAS does not fulfill the proxy requirements CGPOP does by design:

3.0.1 CGPOP Includes Important Code

The conjugate gradient solver within POP is the performance bottleneck when the application is executed on more than a thousand of cores. In a scientific application, the performance bottleneck code is often the most critical, and it consumes most of the developers' programming and maintenance time.

3.0.2 CGPOP is Incremental

We consider a miniapp to be incremental if a different version of the miniapp can be incorporated back into the full application. Incrementality would be threatened if reintegrating an implementation of the CGPOP miniapp back into the full POP application required conducting changes outside of the Conjugate Gradient solver routine that it is meant to model. We do not believe this to be a concern for CGPOP miniapp due to the fact that the difference between the base and studied CGPOP implementations predominantly lie in the construction of communication metadata and a subroutine (`UpdateHalo`) that performs the communication. Because communication metadata is solely used by the `UpdateHalo` routine and the fact that this routine is exclusively used by the conjugate-gradient algorithm, changes to this metadata or the `UpdateHalo` routine will not invasively impact any code outside of them when reintegrated into POP.

3.0.3 CGPOP is Representative

For the POP application, the most important implementation details are the discretization of the earth's surface including the exclusion of land, the domain decomposition for parallelization, the interaction between communication and computation, and the metadata generated to represent the communication schedule.

The discretization and the domain decomposition are used throughout the POP application and as such these important implementation details are part of the input for the CGPOP miniapp. Code within CGPOP uses the same domain decomposition as in the full POP application.

The interaction between communication and computation and the communication metadata are representative implementation details in POP that have been encapsulated within CGPOP. Thus programmability impacts for those implementation details are isolated within CGPOP. This makes it easier to reintegrate such changes back into the full application while making CGPOP a more representative programmability proxy.

4. Conclusions

Miniapps that serve as performance and programmability proxies can be used to evaluate the hypothetical impact a changes would have in a larger application. In this poster we discuss what criteria must be fulfilled for an application to be a performance and programmabiliy proxy. We then use these criteria to evaluate whether the CGPOP miniapp is a proxy for the Parallel Ocean Program (POP).

Acknowledgements

This work was supported by Department of Energy Early Career Award #DE-SC3956. This work was financially supported through National Science Foundation Cooperative Grant NSF01 which funds the National Center for Atmospheric Research (NCAR), and through the grant: #OCI-0749206.

References

[1] Community Earth System Model. http://www.cesm.ucar.edu/.

[2] K. Asanovic, R. Bodik, B. C. Catanzaro, J. J. Gebis, P. Husbands, K. Keutzer, D. A. Patterson, W. L. Plishker, J. Shalf, S. W. Williams, and K. A. Yelick. The landscape of parallel computing research: A view from Berkeley. Technical Report UCB/EECS-2006-183, EECS Department, University of California, Berkeley, Dec 2006.

[3] D. H. Bailey, E. Barszcz, J. T. Barton, D. S. Browning, R. L. Carter, R. A. Fatoohi, P. O. Frederickson, T. A. Lasinski, H. D. Simon, V. Venkatakrishnan, and S. K. Weeratunga. The NAS parallel benchmarks. Technical report, The International Journal of Supercomputer Applications, 1991.

[4] M. A. Heroux, D. W. Doerfler, P. S. Crozier, J. M. Willenbring, H. C. Edwards, A. Williams, M. Rajan, E. R. Keiter, H. K. Thornquist, and R. W. Numrich. Improving performance via mini-applications. Technical Report SAND2009-5574, Sandia National Laboratories, 2009.

[5] A. I. Stone, J. M. Dennis, and M. M. Strout. Evaluating coarray fortran with the CGPOP miniapp. In *Proceedings of the Fifth Conference on Partitioned Global Address Space Programming Models (PGAS)*, October 15, 2011.

[6] S. Williams, L. Oliker, R. Vuduc, J. Shalf, K. Yelick, and J. Demmel. Optimization of sparse matrix-vector multiplication on emerging multicore platforms. In *Proceedings of the 2007 ACM/IEEE conference on Supercomputing*, SC '07, pages 38:1–38:12, New York, NY, USA, 2007. ACM.

OpenMP-style Parallelism in Data-Centered Multicore Computing with R

Lei Jiang
Louisiana State University
Baton Rouge, LA, USA
ljiang@cct.lsu.edu

Pragneshkumar B. Patel
University of Tennessee
Knoxville, TN, USA
pragnesh@utk.edu

George Ostrouchov
Oak Ridge National Laboratory
Oak Ridge, TN, USA
ostrouchovg@ornl.gov

Ferdinand Jamitzky
Leibniz Supercomputing Centre
Garching, Germany
ferdinand.jamitzky@lrz.de

Abstract

R[1] is a domain specific language widely used for data analysis by the statistics community as well as by researchers in finance, biology, social sciences, and many other disciplines. As R programs are linked to input data, the exponential growth of available data makes high-performance computing with R imperative. To ease the process of writing parallel programs in R, code transformation from a sequential program to a parallel version would bring much convenience to R users. In this paper, we present our work in semi-automatic parallelization of R codes with user-added OpenMP-style pragmas. While such pragmas are used at the frontend, we take advantage of multiple parallel backends with different R packages. We provide flexibility for importing parallelism with plug-in components, impose built-in MapReduce for data processing, and also maintain code reusability. We illustrate the advantage of the on-the-fly mechanisms which can lead to significant applications in data-centered parallel computing.

Categories and Subject Descriptors D.1.3 [*Programming Techniques*]: Concurrent Programming-Parallel Programming

General Terms Languages, Performance, Design

Keywords parallelization, domain specific language, automatic code generation, data-centered applications, MapReduce

1. Introduction

As R is arguably the most popular programming environment used in data analytics, mining, and statistical computing, R's performance in handling large-scale data and its parallelism become imperative. R is a functional language and contains interfaces to other general-purpose programming languages. As of August 2011, there are more than 3,000 R packages and among these more than 20 are dedicated to parallel computing. There is some overlap in functionality between many of these and between them they cover some aspects of shared memory, cluster and GPU computing.

OpenMP is a popular specification for parallel programming that is primarily intended for shared memory multiprocessing. Several compilers implement the OpenMP API for C/C++/Fortran programming languages. While many R functions are written in C/C++/Fortran and potentially can access OpenMP parallelism of the compilers, this is not possible in general R code because it is an interpreted language; the interpreter must come along to every R thread. In this paper, we consider the OpenMP API separately from its compiler implementations. We use the API to specify parallelism in R code at the frontend but implement it with a mix of available parallel R packages. This brings a major parallel programming standard to R. Based on user-added pragmas, we make the necessary R code transformation with the following properties:

- **Flexible Plug-In to Parallel Backends**: Any supported R parallel backend can be loaded to transform the code on demand.
- **Data Processing with Built-In MapReduce Mechanism**: The R data frame or variable declared in pragma, associated with a combination function, leads to a multithreaded MapReduce-style execution of the R function after code transformation.
- **Code Reusability**: All the pragmas appear as comments in the code, so the sequential execution is never affected.

2. Related Work

Data-intensive computing continues to grow in modern sciences. The broad range of applications in statistics, machine learning and data mining result in a set of special-purpose languages and tools such as OptiML [1]. Such a domain-specific approach implements data-parallel operations at a higher level than a general-purpose programming language and users call such APIs with built-in parallelism. In R, *pnmath* [6] provides an OpenMP wrapper framework for some vector math functions that are written in C. Recent work [3, 5] in imposing parallelism through user-added pragmas illustrates the blending between advanced parallelism and lower-level code, but many are dedicated to one specific type of parallelism. We take advantage of multiple R parallel backends, Rcpp [4]

[1] The R Project for Statistical Computing: http://www.r-project.org/

PPoPP'12, February 25–29, 2012, New Orleans, Louisiana, USA.
ACM 978-1-4503-1160-1/12/02.

(as an interface between R and C++) and MapReduce [2] functionality in R to develop a general framework that can automatically generate parallel R codes based on OpenMP-style pragmas.

3. OpenMP-specified Parallelism in R

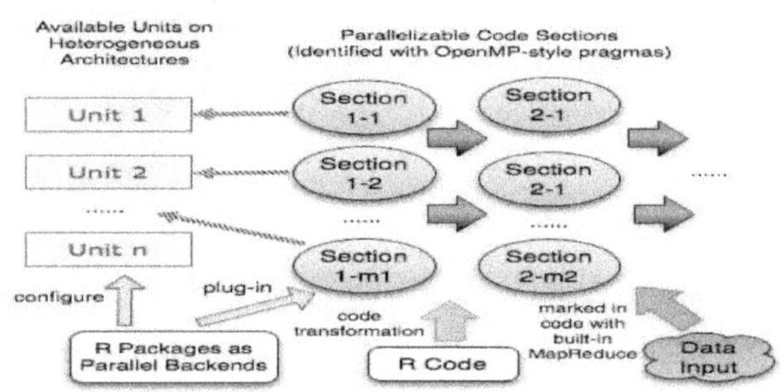

Figure 1. Imposing parallelism with plug-in components for heterogeneous architectures

Parallelizing R programs differs from that of a general-purpose language. R is a mix of interpreted and compiled components, it is single-threaded, and common parallel standards are not directly available in R. However, there are different levels of parallelism for R: in the spirit of the domain-specific approach taken by [1], a set of common functions, such as probability density functions, is implemented with OpenMP in *pnmath* and can scale very well up to 1,024 cores; multiprocessing, represented by R packages *multicore* and *foreach*, is widely used for its generality in handling R functions and types of system calls at process level; and R's interoperability allows linking external libraries for high-performance computing(e.g. BLAS and ATLAS). Figure 1 shows our proposed parallelism at a higher level: a piece of R code can be partitioned to sections with dependency (by data or as a workflow), and then other R packages provide support as parallel backends on heterogeneous hardware architectures.

We implement some OpenMP parallel specifications with existing parallel R components. Our R code translator function takes an R function with embedded OpenMP-style pragma comments and produces an R function that runs in parallel. Its parallel implementation is executed with a specified existing backend such as *foreach* and *multicore*. Because the implementation is with an existing backend, its performance is comparable to the usual performance of the given backend.

We illustrate this by inserting a Map-Reduce pragma comment in the example given for the function *find.matches* of package *Hmisc*[2], given in its documentation:

```
x <- matrix(runif(50000), ncol=2)
y <- matrix(runif(100000), ncol=2)
##pragma mpr parallel partition data(x:matrow)
w <- find.matches(x, y ,maxmatch=5, tol=c(.02, .03))
```

Fig. 2 shows its performance using a strong scaling test with up to 128 cores (on an SGI Altix UV 1000 system, 2.0GHz per core, 4 TB global shared memory and 8 GPUs in a single system image). The data-centered task is to find close row matches of two matrices. Detailed pragma specification and available parallel constructs will be provided with the alpha release of our package *ROpenMP*.

[1] R+GPU: http://brainarray.mbni.med.umich.edu/brainarray/rgpgpu/

[2] Hmisc: http://cran.r-project.org/package=Hmisc

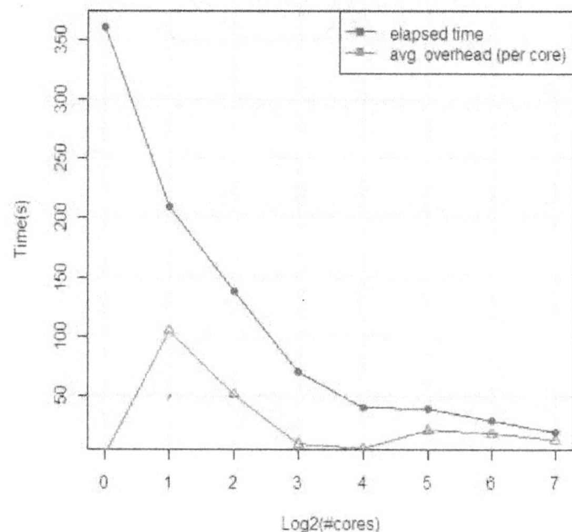

Figure 2. The result of strong scaling from sequential execution to a 128-core parallel run

4. Conclusion and Current Work In Progress

We introduce OpenMP-style parallelization to R via package *ROpenMP*. This is performed through a semi-automatic R code transformation into parallel R code based on existing parallel R packages. A given OpenMP pragma can be accompanied with several backends. Currently implemented backends include *multicore* and *foreach* for plug-in. Current work in progress includes exporting user-defined R code sections to C/C++ for multi-threaded execution. In data-centered computing, it is easy to identify time-consuming code sections and add pragmas which enable on-demand parallelization with a supported backend designated. While the quickly growing R community is developing R as a general computing environment for data, the link to heterogeneous parallel architectures can be continuously established, along with hybrid parallel programming by integrating multiple backends.

Acknowledgments

This research is based in part on work created during the Google Summer of Code 2011 program with the first author as student developer and the remaining three authors as mentors. P. Patel and G. Ostrouchov were supported in part by the National Science Foundation (NSF) under Grant No. (0906324).

References

[1] H. Chafi et al., A domain-specific approach to heterogeneous parallelism. *Proc. of PPoPP'2011*, Feb 2011.

[2] J. Dean and S. Ghemawat, MapReduce: simplified data processing on large clusters. *Proc. of OSDI'2004*.

[3] G. Dotzler, R. Veldema and M. Klemm, JCudaMP: OpenMP/Java on CUDA. *Proc. of the 3rd Int. Workshop on Multicore Software Engineering (IWMSE'2010)*, May 2010.

[4] D. Eddelbuettel and R. Francois, Rcpp: seamless R and C++ integration. *Journal of Statistical Software*, vol. 40, iss. 8, 2011.

[5] M. Feng, R. Gupta and Y. Hu, SpiceC: scalable parallelism via implicit copying and explicit commit. *Proc. of PPoPP'2011*, Feb 2011.

[6] M. Schmidberger et al., State of the art in parallel computing with R. *Journal of Statistical Software*, vol. 31, iss.1, 2009.

Performance Analysis of Parallel Constraint-Based Local Search

Yves Caniou
JFLI, CNRS / NII, Japan
yves.caniou@ens-lyon.fr

Daniel Diaz
University of Paris 1-Sorbonne, France
daniel.diaz@univ-paris1.fr

Florian Richoux
JFLI, CNRS / University of Tokyo, Japan
richoux@jfli.itc.u-tokyo.ac.jp

Philippe Codognet
JFLI, CNRS / UPMC / University of Tokyo, Japan
codognet@jfli.itc.u-tokyo.ac.jp

Salvador Abreu
Universidade de Évora and CENTRIA FCT/UNL, Portugal
spa@di.uevora.pt

Abstract

We present a parallel implementation of a constraint-based local search algorithm and investigate its performance results for hard combinatorial optimization problems on two different platforms up to several hundreds of cores. On a variety of classical CSPs benchmarks, speedups are very good for a few tens of cores, and good up to a hundred cores. More challenging problems derived from real-life applications (Costas array) shows even better speedups, nearly optimal up to 256 cores.

Categories and Subject Descriptors G [*1.6*]: Constrained optimization; G [*2.1*]: Combinatorial algorithms; F [2.2]: Sorting and searching; D [*1.3*]: Parallel programming

General Terms Experimentation, Performance, Algorithms

Keywords combinatorial optimization, meta-heuristics, parallelism, implementation, Constraints, local search

1. Introduction

During the last decade, the family of Local Search methods and Metaheuristics has been quite successful in solving large real-life combinatorial problems [8–10]. Solving Constraint Satisfaction Problems (CSP) by Local Search is a way to tackle CSPs instances far beyond the reach of classical propagation-based solvers [3, 9, 11]. An effcient and generic domain-independent Local Search method named "Adaptive Search" was proposed in [3, 4]. It takes advantage of the structure of the problem to guide the search and can be applied to a large class of constraints (*e.g.*, linear and non-linear arithmetic constraints, symbolic constraints). Moreover, it intrinsically copes with over-constrained problems.

Parallel implementation of local search metaheuristics has been studied since the early 90's, when multiprocessor machines started to become widely available, see [12]. With the increasing availability of PC clusters in the early 2000's, this domain became active again [1, 5]. Apart from domain-decomposition methods and population-based method (such as genetic algorithms), [12] distinguishes between single-walk and multiple-walk methods for Local Search. Single-walk methods consist in using parallelism inside a single search process, *e.g.*, for parallelizing the exploration of the neighborhood. Multiple-walk methods consist in developing several concurrent explorations of the search space starting from different initial configurations, either independently or cooperatively with some communication between concurrent processes. Sophisticated cooperative strategies for multiple-walk methods can be devised but requires shared-memory or emulation of central memory in distributed clusters, impacting thus on performances. A key point is that independent multiple-walk methods are the most easy to implement on parallel computers without shared memory and can lead in theory to linear speed-up if solutions are uniformly distributed in the search space and if the method is able to diversify correctly [12].

We thus developed an independent multiple-walks of the Adaptive Search constraint solver (i.e. launching in parallel several search engines starting from different initial configurations and performing the computation in a purely independent manner) and benchmarked it with classical CSP benchmarks from the CSPLIB [7] and with a very difficult combinatorial problem, the Costas Array Problem (CAP). Historically, Costas arrays have been developed in the 1960's to compute a set of sonar and radar frequencies avoiding noise. The problem is to find an $n \times n$ grid containing n marks such that there is exactly one mark per row and per column and the $n(n-1)/2$ vectors between the marks are all different. It is convenient to formalize the CAP as a permutation problem on $\{1, 2, \ldots, n\}$ together with a set of constraints on 2D distance vectors. Although there are constructive methods to produce Costas arrays of order up to 27, it remains unknown if there exist any Costas arrays of size 32 or 33. Indeed, the solution density of Costas arrays is very low, *e.g.*, among the 27! permutations, there are only 204 Costas arrays. A very complete survey on Costas arrays can be found in [6]. Obviously, the search space for finding a Costas array of size n grows exponentially with n and it is thus a very good benchmark for search and combinatorial optimization methods.

2. Parallel Performance Analysis

We performed our experiments on two different platforms:

PPoPP'12, February 25–29, 2012, New Orleans, Louisiana, USA.
ACM 978-1-4503-1160-1/12/02.

- the Hitachi HA8000 supercomputer of the University of Tokyo with a total number of 15232 cores. This machine is composed of 952 nodes, each of which is composed of 4 AMD Opteron 8356 (Quad core, 2.3 GHz) with 32 GB of memory. Users can only have a maximum of 64 nodes (1,024 cores) in normal service and we used up to 256 cores in our experiments.
- the GRID'5000 infrastructure, the French national Grid for the research, which contains a maximum of 5934 cores deployed on 9 sites distributed in France. We used two subsets of the computing resources of the Sophia-Antipolis node: Suno, composed of 45 Dell PowerEdge R410 with 8 cores each, thus a total of 360 cores, and Helios, composed of 56 Sun Fire X4100 with 4 cores each, thus a total of 224 cores.

We first reported in [2] the performance of classical CSP problems from CSPLIB: `all-interval` (prob007), `perfect-square` (prob009), `magic-square`: (prob019). Table 1 shows that speedups are more or less equivalent on the HA8000 machine and on the GRID'5000 platform. They are good but tend to level after 128 cores, except for `perfect-square` on GRID'5000.

Platform	Problem	Time	Speedup on k cores			
		1 core	32	64	128	256
HA8000	MS 400	6282	20.6	31.7	41.3	54.1
	Perfect 5	42.7	29.5	44.6	49.1	57.0
	A-I 700	638	14.8	17.8	23.4	27.7
Suno	MS 400	5362	22.8	32.6	41.3	52.8
	Perfect 5	106	23	46.1	70.7	106
	A-I 700	662	15.8	19.9	23.9	28.3
Helios	MS 400	6565	20.6	31	44	-
	Perfect 5	139.7	24.5	46.6	77.2	-
	A-I 700	865.8	14.9	23.5	27.3	-

Table 1. Speedups on HA8000, Suno and Helios

Platform	Problem	Time on	Speedup on k cores		
		32 cores	64	128	256
HA8000	CAP21	160.4	1.96	4.16	10.0
	CAP22	501.2	2.01	3.90	8.24
Suno	CAP21	171	3.32	4.90	9.94
	CAP22	731	1.92	3.66	7.09
Helios	CAP21	153	1.51	4.17	-
	CAP22	1218	2.34	5.53	-

Table 2. Speedups on HA8000, Suno and Helios for large instances of CAP

For big instances of Costas arrays, speedups w.r.t. 1 core are nearly linear, *e.g.*, 107 for 128 cores and 218 for 256 cores for $n = 21$ on Suno. For $n = 22$, as sequential computation takes many hours, we limited our experiments to executions on 32 cores and above, see Table 2. We can observe that on all platforms, execution times are halved when the number of cores is doubled, thus achieving ideal speedup. This is graphically depicted in Figure 1 on a log-log scale. As a final result, we note that we can now solve $n = 22$ in about one minute on average with 256 cores on HA8000.

3. Conclusion and Future Work

We presented performances of a parallel implementation of a constraint-based local search algorithm, the "Adaptive Search" method in a multiple independent-walk manner. Each process is an independent search engine and there is no communication between the simultaneous computations except for completion. Performance evaluation on a variety of constraint satisfaction problems over two

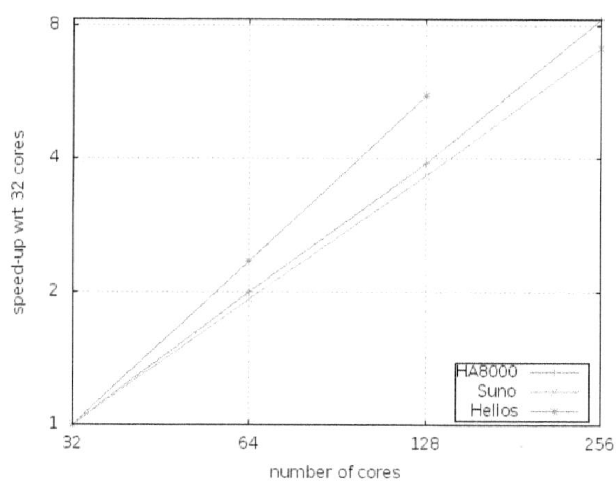

Figure 1. Speedups for CAP 22 w.r.t. 32 cores

different parallel architectures (a supercomputer and a Grid platform) shows that the method is achieving good but not optimal speedups for classical benchmarks and presents linear speedups for the Costas Array Problem, a hard combinatorial problem.

Current work focuses on more complex parallel methods with inter-processes communication, i.e., in the dependent multiple-walk scheme, in order to further improve performance. The communication mechanism is being designed with the goals of (1) minimizing data transfers as much as possible, as we aim at massively parallel machines with no hierarchical memory, (2) re-using some common computations and/or recording previous interesting crossroads in the resolution, from which a restart can be operated.

References

[1] E. Alba. Special issue on new advances on parallel meta-heuristics for complex problems. *Journal of Heuristics*, 10(3):239–380, 2004.

[2] Y. Caniou, P. Codognet, D. Diaz, and S. Abreu. Experiments in parallel constraint-based local search. In *EvoCOP11, 11th European Conference on Evolutionary Computation in Combinatorial Optimisation*, LNCS 6622, pages 96–107. Springer Verlag, 2011.

[3] P. Codognet and D. Diaz. Yet another local search method for constraint solving. In *proceedings of SAGA'01*, pages 73–90. Springer Verlag, 2001.

[4] P. Codognet and D. Diaz. An efficient library for solving CSP with local search. In T. Ibaraki, editor, *MIC'03, 5th International Conference on Metaheuristics*, 2003.

[5] T. Crainic and M. Toulouse. Special issue on parallel meta-heuristics. *Journal of Heuristics*, 8(3):247–388, 2002.

[6] K. Drakakis. A review of costas arrays. *Journal of Applied Mathematics*, 2006:1–32, 2006.

[7] I. P. Gent and T. Walsh. CSPLIB: A benchmark library for constraints. In *proceedings of CP'99*, pages 480–481. Springer Verlag, 1999.

[8] T. Gonzalez, editor. *Handbook of Approximation Algorithms and Metaheuristics*. Chapman and Hall / CRC, 2007.

[9] P. V. Hentenryck and L. Michel. *Constraint-Based Local Search*. The MIT Press, 2005.

[10] T. Ibaraki, K. Nonobe, and M. Yagiura, editors. *Metaheuristics: Progress as Real Problem Solvers*. Springer Verlag, 2005.

[11] S. Kadioglu and M. Sellmann. Dialectic search. In *CP'09, Int. Conf. on Principles and Practice of Constraint Programming*. Springer Verlag, 2009.

[12] M. Verhoeven and E. Aarts. Parallel local search. *Journal of Heuristics*, 1(1):43–65, 1995.

Author Index

Abramson, David 311
Abreu, Salvador 337
Agrawal, Kunal 235
Alias, Christophe 285
An, Hong 279
Andersch, Michael 281
Baghsorkhi, Sara S. 23
Bagwell, Phil 151
Ballard, Grey 35
Banerjee, Anindya 313
Baskaran, Muthu 277
Batory, Don 289
Beamer, Scott 303
Bhuyan, Laxmi N. 293
Binder, Walter 97
Blazewicz, Marek 287
Blelloch, Guy E. 181
Bonetta, Daniele 97
Bosilca, George 225
Bouteiller, Aurelien 225
Braginsky, Anastasia 309
Brandt, Steven R. 287
Bressan, Stéphane 205
Bronson, Nathan G. 151
Buhler, Jeremy D. 235
Burnim, Jacob 329
Burtscher, Martin 107
Caniou, Yves 337
Cao, Thanh-Tung 205
Chamberlain, Roger D. 235
Chen, Yifeng 171
Chi, Chi Ching 281
Clauss, Philippe 295
Codognet, Philippe 337
Coetzee, Derrick 303
Cook, Henry 303
Corporaal, Henk 291
Crain, Tyler 161
Cui, Xiang 171
Darte, Alain 285
Dasgupta, Aniruddha 11
De Koster, Joeri 317
Delahaye, Matthieu 23
Demmel, James 35
Demsky, Brian 85
Dennis, John M. 333
DeRose, Luiz 311
D'Hondt, Theo 317
Diaz, Daniel 337
Dice, David 247
Dinh, Minh Ngoc 311
Dong, Qunfeng 129
Dongarra, Jack 225
Du, Peng 225
Eigenmann, Rudolf 75
Elmas, Tayfun 329
Eom, Yong hun 85
Fatourou, Panagiota 257
Feng, Min 293
Fineman, Jeremy T. 181
Fox, Armando 303
Garland, Michael 117
Gelado, Isaac 23
George, Thomas 315
Ghosh, Indradeep 215
Gibbons, Phillip B. 181
Goh, Rick Siow Mong 1
Gong, Yifan 297
Gonina, Ekaterina 303
Gontarek, Andrew 311
Gopalakrishnan, Ganesh 215
Gramoli, Vincent 161
Grimshaw, Andrew 117
Gropp, William 45
Gross, Thomas R. 325
Gupta, Rajiv 293
Hack, Sebastian 65
Hagiescu, Andrei 1
Han, Hwansoo 55
Han, Wenting 279
Harper, Jonathan 303
He, Bingsheng 283, 297
Herault, Thomas 225
Hoefler, Torsten 305, 327
Huynh, Huynh Phung 1
Hwu, Wen-mei W. 23
Jain, Nikhil 315
Jamitzky, Ferdinand 335
Jenista, James C. 85
Jiang, Lei 335
Jimborean, Alexandra 295
Jin, Chao 311
Jo, Gangwon 299
Jubair, Fahed 75
Juurlink, Ben 281
Kaashoek, M. Frans 319
Kallimanis, Nikolaos D. 257
Kamil, Shoaib 303
Karras, Panagiotis 205
Kesapides, John 301
Kim, Hyesoon 11
Kim, Jungwon 299
Kim, Seonggun 55
Kjolstad, Fredrik 327
Knight, Nicholas 35
Kogan, Alex 141, 309
Kumar, Sameer 315
Kwon, Okwan 75
Larson, Per-Åke 307
Lee, Jaejin 299
Lee, Jun 299
Leiserson, Charles E. 193
Leißa, Roland 65
Lethin, Richard 277
Li, Guodong 215
Li, Peng 215, 235
Li, Xiaoqiang 279
Lin, Haibo 267
Liu, Gu 279
Liu, Yujie 323

Loechner, Vincent 295
Malkis, Alexander 313
Marathe, Virendra J. 247
Marker, Bryan 289
Marr, Stefan 317
Mastrangelo, Luis 295
Mei, Hong 171
Meister, Benoit 277
Méndez-Lojo, Mario 107
Merrill, Duane 117
Metreveli, Zviad 319
Midkiff, Samuel 75
Mittal, Anshul 315
Moench, Bob 311
Morlan, Jeffrey 303
Nah, Jeongho 299
Necula, George 329
Nikolopoulos, Dimitrios S. 301
Nobari, Sadegh 205
Noll, Albert 325
Nugteren, Cedric 291
Odersky, Martin 151
Ostrouchov, George 335
Papatriantafyllou, Angelos 301
Park, Chang-Seo 331
Patel, Pragneshkumar B. 335
Pautasso, Cesare 97
Peng, Kunyang 129
Peternier, Achille 97
Petrank, Erez 141, 309
Pingali, Keshav 107
Plesco, Alexandru 285
Poulson, Jack 289
Pradelle, Benoît 295
Pratikakis, Polyvios 301
Prokopec, Aleksandar 151
Rajan, Sreeranga P. 215
Raynal, Michel 161
Richoux, Florian 337
Sabharwal, Yogish 315
Sack, Paul 45
Sawaya, Geof 215
Schardl, Tao B. 193
Schneider, Timo 305
Sen, Koushik 329, 331
Seo, Sangmin 299
Shavit, Nir 247
Shun, Julian 181
Sim, Jaewoong 11
Snir, Marc 327
Spear, Michael 323
Stitt, Greg 321
Stone, Andrew I. 333
Strout, Michelle Mills 333
Sukha, Jim 193
Sun, Tao 279
Tang, Xulong 279
Tao, Jian 287
Tardieu, Olivier 267
Terrel, Andy 289
Tian, Xin 129
Timnat, Shahar 309
Tzenakis, George 301
van de Geijn, Robert 289
Vandierendonck, Hans 301
Vasilache, Nicolas 277
Vuduc, Richard 11
Wald, Ingo 65
Wang, Haichuan 267
Wang, Lin 129
Wei, Xuechao 279
Wernsing, John R. 321
Wong, Weng-Fai 1
Xu, Zhonghu 129
Yang, Ming 129
Yang, Stephen 85
Zeldovich, Nickolai 319
Zhang, Donghui 307
Zhong, Jianlong 283, 297
Zhou, Wei 279
Zu, Yuan 129

www.ingramcontent.com/pod-product-compliance
Lightning Source LLC
Chambersburg PA
CBHW080910220326
41598CB00034B/5533